History of the Polish Reformation
and Nine Related Documents

Stanislas Lubieniecki, 1664

Stanislas Lubieniecki

History of the
Polish Reformation
and Nine Related Documents

Translated and interpreted by

George Huntston Williams

FORTRESS PRESS   MINNEAPOLIS

Harvard Theological Studies 37

Editors

Helmut Koester
John B. Carman
David D. Hall
Jon D. Levenson
Francis Schüssler Fiorenza
Ronald F. Thiemann

History of the Polish Reformation
by Stanislas Lubieniecki
and Nine Related Documents
Translated and Interpreted by George Huntston Williams
Harvard Theological Studies 37

Typesetting and design: Chiron, Inc. and Graphic Sciences Corporation
Jacket design and plates layout: Linda Crittenden Graphic Design
Index: E. Virginia Hobbs

Library of Congress Cataloging-in-Publication data

Lubieniecki, Stanislas, 1623–1675.
　　[Historia Reformationis Polonicae. English.]
　　History of the Polish Reformation : and nine related documents /
Stanislas Lubieniecki : translated and interpreted by George
Huntston Williams.
　　　　p. cm.—(Harvard theological studies; no. 37)
　　Includes bibliographical references and index.
　　ISBN 0-8006-7085-X (alk. paper) :
　　1. Reformation—Poland—Early works to 1800.
　　2. Antitrinitarianism—Poland—History of doctrines—16th century—Early
works to 1800.　3. Poland—Church history.　I. Williams, George Huntston,
1914-　.　II. Title.　III. Series: Harvard theological studies
　　BR420.P7L813 1994
　　274.38′06—dc20　　　　　　　　　　　　　　　　　　　92-22680
　　　　　　　　　　　　　　　　　　　　　　　　　　　　　　　　CIP

The paper used in this publication meets the minimum requirements of American National Standard for Information Services–Permanence of Paper for
Printed Library Materials, ANSI Z329, 48–1984.　　　　　　　　　　∞

Manufactured in the U.S.A.　　　　　　　　　　　　　　　　AF 1-7085
99　　98　　97　　96　　95　　1　　2　　3　　4　　5　　6　　7　　8　　9　　10

Dedicated
to the memory of, apprised
of the intention
in their lifetime,

JOHN THOMAS MCNEILL
(1885–1974)
of Nova Scotia,
ecumenical Presbyterian minister,
professor of Church History
at the Divinity School of the University of Chicago
and at the Union Theological Seminary in New York

and

ROLAND HERBERT BAINTON
(1894–1984)
of Ikeston in Derbyshire,
of Yale Divinity School,
Congregationalist minister, serving in the Quaker Unit
of the American Red Cross in World War I,
historian and biographer of the classical Protestant Reformation
and multilingual expositor of the Left Wing of the Reformation

and,

in collegial and appreciative salutation,
Professor dr hab. LECH SZCZUCKI
of the Polish Academy of Sciences
who, amidst his indefatigable editing and writing, sustains,
in steadfast, generous, resourceful, exemplary ways
the solidarity of the scholarly community
in time and space

Contents

Preface

The *Historia Reformationis Polonicae* by Stanislas Lubieniecki is a major account of Protestantism in the Polish-Lithuanian Commonwealth, c. 1546 to c. 1638, with some uniquely preserved data on Unitarianism in Transylvania, on a number of emigrant Italian radicals, and on certain other nonconformist Protestants, some of whom migrated or fled from German and Swiss lands into the Eastern marches of Latin Christendom amid the throes of the Reformation and the Counter-Reform. With such coverage, the *Historia* ranks as the first history of European Unitarianism, a movement that, for all Lubieniecki's conviction that the Polish Brethren adhered to the perfectly restored Dominical truth as once for all delivered to the saints, as also to their valid apostolic practice recovered, was in its chief marks and principal thrusts an interconnected, international movement distinctive to the Age of Reformation; that is, it was theologically the most radical sector of the Radical Reformation. Only one ecclesial community shaped in that age still survives in its sixteenth-century seats in Romania and Hungary.

The *Historia* is, however, primarily a confessional account of the emergence of the Polish Brethren of the Minor Reformed synod that became separate, beginning in 1563, from that of the Major Reformed synod ("Major" not initially in reference to numbers but rather to its continued adherence to international Calvinism in its protective adoption in 1569 of the II Helvetic Confession of 1566). The *Historia* is palpably a partisan account that deals most completely with developments in Little Poland (*Polonia Minor*—Cracow/Lublin) but warrants its full title given by the Author in his touching on developments in Great Poland (Gniezno/Pozmań), in Royal and in Ducal Prussia (Danzig/Königsberg), and in the Grand Duchy of Lithuania (Vilna/Brest Litovsk).

The amply annotated American edition of the *Historia* confirms the privileged status of the account by Lubieniecki as of singular importance in being the first printed narrative of a European-wide movement in return to the Greek and Hebrew sources. This movement, initiated by Martin Luther within the Holy Roman Empire, for our Author reached its purest and most cogent expression in his "providentially guided" world of the upper, and particularly the middle and lower, *szlachta* (the titularly undifferentiated aristocratic classes) within the electively royal Polish-Lithuanian Commonwealth—the largest state of Europe at the opening of the sixteenth century. For Lubieniecki the Polish Reformation was the culmination of the whole Reformation movement, a claim and historiographical point of view all the more poignant for the plight of the Author and his co-believers, the Polish Brethren and Sisters, who were in exile from their fatherland when the *Historia* was written and posthumously published (1685).

For Lubieniecki the purest formulation and implementation of apostolic creed, polity, morality, and social ethic was a christocentric Baptist synodal Unitarianism. His *Historia,* despite its titular implication of covering the whole range of reformatory change in Poland from evangelical/humanist Catholic, through Lutheran and Reformed, to Anabaptist and Spiritualist, is mostly a narrative account of a *biblical* Antitrinitarianism distinctive to the Age of the Reformation; and it in fact, however fugitively at many points, deals with figures and events in Italia, Helvetia, Germania, Neerlandia, Hungaria, as well as Polonia and even here and there touches upon accessions to the movement from Orthodox Slavonia (Byelorussia, Ruthenia, Moldavia). Thus it is all the more noteworthy that Lubieniecki's *Historia* of Polonia, where the Hussite reformation of the preceding century had left major deposits, pays little attention to the Czech (Moravian) Brethren whether in Bohemia/Moravia or in Great Poland itself, where the refugee Czechs just might have constituted c. 1555 the well rooted synodal stock out of which, with the accession of fresh reformatory and humanist energies from Wittenberg, Zurich, and Geneva, a national Reformed Church in Poland might have sprung.

The *Historia* is also a major source for Reformed ecclesiastical and the general social history of Poland, containing in transcription a number of unique documents. Left unfinished (1675), it was posthumously edited by an exiled Polish Brother, Benedict Wiszowaty, in Amsterdam in 1685, a year after he had edited, also posthumously, the first Unitarian biobibliography by Christopher Sand, Jr., *Bibliotheca Antitrinitariorum* (Amsterdam, 1684; henceforth *BAnt*)[2], into which Wiszowaty had already incorporated a chapter from the *Historia,* as one among seven historiographical documents added as an appendix to the work of Sand. Wiszowaty thus intermeshed two works in such a way as to perpetuate a distinctive perspective and, as it were, tradition in the confessional interpretation of the Antitrinitarian legacy of Eastern Europe, all the more compelling because Lubieniecki had himself either drawn upon more than one of these documents or had shared sources common to them and which must therefore be adduced in assessing some of his accounts in the *Historia.*

Embedded therefore in parentheses in the English text of the *Historia* are cross references to some five parallel *BAnt* documents, which are printed in the Appendix of Related Documents (RD). While they could be taken note of as simply RD 1 or 2, etc., they are more specifically cited by the paragraphs numbered within them continuously through all five. For example, *BAnt no. 47, p. 6,* within the *Historia,* refers to the first paragraph of the fifth Related Document, the *Brief Narrative* of Andrew Wiszowaty, preserved by his son, Benedict Wiszowaty, in his posthumous edition of Sand's *BAnt.* The remaining four Related Documents, not so integral to the text of the *Historia,* are not drawn attention to within the text of the *Historia,* only in its annotation and in my Introduction.

The unique status of the *Historia* as an invaluable resource and perspective to be integrated into Polish historiography was recognized by the Lutheran professor of divinity in Warsaw, Edmund Bursche, who was able to publish two of the three books of the *Historia* in substantially annotated, clear, idiomatic Polish in 1938. In that same year, the American Unitarian historian, Earl Morse Wilbur, translated the whole text in preparation for his two-volume *History of Unitarianism* (1945/1952). Afterwards he offered for publication his sparsely annotated typescript, taxingly faithful to the convoluted Baroque Latin syntax, as a major

Unitarian historiographical document in its own right and as a theologically and morally serene narrative of confident and consistent perspective. His translation lies at the base of the American edition of the *Historia.*

The text of the *Historia* in three books is, to be sure, at times thin, turgid, turbid, elliptical, or obscure and it has at moments in my editing seemed too fragile a trellis for such a heavy bower of commentary. For example, in Book 2 Lubieniecki deals with the Second Person of the Trinity and the Lord's Supper and recounts how a large part of the Reformed Church, destined to be designated the Minor Church of the Polish Brethren, successively laid aside all but one of the four received ancient creeds (*Apostolicum, Nicaenum, Athanasium, Te Deum Laudamus;* Introduction IIIA) and, moving by stages amply documented by the Author, came to an understanding of Jesus Christ within the formulation of the Apostles' Creed (deemed wholly scriptural in language and without any philosophical—"scholastic," "papal"—terminology) as the fully human, Virgin-born Son of God the Father ordained by the Creator to discharge on earth and in heaven the threefold office of High Priest, Prophet, and King. But then when Lubieniecki comes to deal with the emergence of believers' Baptism on the model of Jesus at Jordan and to trace the growing perception of the Holy Spirit as Gift rather than as divine Third Person, he goes back over some of the same synods and other events of Book 2 as he tracks the third trajectory in the devolution of the received dogma of the Trinity. Or, by way of another example of the thematic sometimes prevailing over the chronological, our Author programatically obtrudes upon the opening of this second book on the emergence of the Reformed Church, the visit of Laelius Socinus in Cracow in 1551, chronologically obscuring the degree to which the later schism within the Reformed Church in Poland was driven by indigenous theological tensions. My annotation, following closely the narrative and the embedded documents therein, seeks to clarify by cross reference the sometimes overlapping and sometimes chronologically transposed sequences of events.

I have thus persisted in the line of Edmund Bursche (nn. 35, 72, 83) in choosing to enhance by quite elaborate annotation this richly laden text, shaped as it was in exile, a sometimes quite personal and vivid story rescued from oblivion by Benedict Wiszowaty. Readers in any case can leave at will my annotative byways and scholarly trails into the Reformation countryside and return as they please to the even thoroughfare in Polish Reformation history laid out by Lubieniecki with his distinctive, organizing perspective.

The whole work is extended with the help of three Maps, one showing the realms of the three Eastern Central European royal crowns during the period when an elected Catholic prince, Stephen Báthory (Batory), ruled largely Protestantized Transylvania from Alba Julia and concurrently from Cracow the multiconfessional, multiethnic Polish–Lithuanian Commonwealth, as of 1576; and when King Maximilian I ruled Bohemia from Prague, 1562–76, and over truncated Hungary, 1564–76, from Pressburg (Emperor Maximilian II as of 1564).

Visualization of some of the *Historia*'s complex scenes and familiarization with groupings of persons and events, amid the weltering plethora of personal and clan names, place names, and offices is accomplished in the album of sixty-four Plates and commentary. The album of annotated pictures, illustrative of the

Historia and in some instances fetching images from beyond its scope, bring the American edition in line with the expansive title of the Author: publicist, irenicist, savant, historian, minister, diplomat.

The album and commentary features some events and persons unheeded or taken for granted by Lubieniecki, while some Plates provide pictorial concentration on figures central to his narrative but of whom there are no portraits, only suggestive artifacts. The pictures and integrated commentary indeed can afford a secondary, and, as it were, scenic route through the same period and areas covered by the *Historia* and in the general background of the life and times of the Historian himself.

Many persons and institutions are part of the story of this edition. They should know that for the final editor of this edition of the *Historia* and the Related Documents it is an immense satisfaction to see in serried typographical ranks the names of the many people who, over a score of years, some in general supportiveness, others in specific acts of encouragement or substantive contribution, furthered this edition. I wish to recognize and to thank Professor James Luther Adams, Professor Antonio Alatorre (Mexico City), Alexander Altmann, Doamna Elisabeta Bajenaru (Bucharest), Dr. and Mrs. William Baker (Edinburgh), Professor Thomas Banchoff, Professor Stanislaw Baranczak, Dr. John Baker-Batzel, Miss Claudia Bisaccia, the Reverend Dr. Richard Boeke, Mr. T. Corby Brennan, the Reverend Charles Phelps Bush, Dr. B. Butkevičiene (Vilnius), Father Robert Byerly, S.J., Mr. Patrick Callahan, Mrs. Doris Carlin, Mrs. Bożena Zbrożek-Chołodzińska, Professor A. C. Cheyne (Edinburgh), Mrs. Stase Cibas, Dr. Juliusz Chrościcki (Warsaw), Miss Tibby Cole, Dr. Loring Conant, the Reverend Peter Conley, Mrs. Ann Ciecimirska Crawford, Mr. Gregory Crawford, Miss Elizabeth Curtis, Mr. Marius L. Cybulski, Mr. Paul Depta, Miss Julie Duncan, Miss Janice Erdman, Professor William Estep, Bishop Józef Ferencz (Budapest), Professor Samuel Fiszman, Principal Duncan Forrester (Edinburgh), Mrs. Doris Freitag, Dean Ulrich Gäbler (Amsterdam), Professor Samuel Leo Garrett, Dean Timothy George, Ms. Joie Gelband, Dr. Jurges Gimbutas, Dana McLean Greeley, Professor Leonard Gross, Dr. Maria Grossmann, Dr. Walter Grossman, Dr. Patricia Gruntel, Miss Anne Hallward (Montreal), Professor Mason Hammond, Dr. Patricia Hanen, Mr. Mark W. Harris, Rev. Dr. Andrew Harsányi, Madame Madeleine Heusch (Brussels), the Reverend Harry Hoehler, Miss Linda Holmes, Rev. Henry Horn, Rev. Dr. Duncan Howlett, Dr. James and Mrs. Susan Jackson, Mr. Darek Jarmola, Mrs. Eva Jonaš, Mr. Matthew W. Kay, Mrs. Ann Kelly, Dr. Juan Kessler (Costa Rica), Professor Jan Kiwiet, Mr. Detlev Koepke, Mr. Aleksander Kowalski (Cracow), Miss Christine Kraus, Mrs. Liliana Krysiak, Prof. Ludwik Krzyzanowski, Professor Alex Kurczaba, Professor Danièle Letocha (Ottawa), Professor Carter Lindberg, Professor Albert Bates Lord, Dean J. P. Mackey (Edinburgh), Professor Wallace MacCaffrey, Lt. Cdr. James McRae (Perth), Mr. Georg Michel (Bonn), Dr. Patrick Michel, Miss Louise Milne, Mrs. Norman Milne (Perth), the Reverend Prior Cyril, O.A.R. (Dr. Enrico Molnár; Costa Rica), Mr. Daniel Moody, Dr. Susan M. Hardman Moore (Edinburgh), Miss Suzanna Nagy, Dr. Halina Nelken, Elizabeth Wilbur Nelson, Mr. Newell Nelson, Professor Georges Nivat (Paris), Professor Dr. Zbigniew Ogonowski (Warsaw), Bruce Oparowski, Mrs. Leah Orent, Professor John S. Oyer, Mrs. Joanna Parker, Mr. Zbigniew Pasek (Cracow), the Reverend Professor Calvin Pater (Toronto), Dr. Rodney Petersen

(Geneva), Dr. Jan Pirożynski (Cracow), Dr. Assunta Pisani, Miss Brenda Pitts, Mrs. Anne Platinger Pauw, Ms. Wioleta Polińska, Dr. Douglas H. Powell, Professor Dr. Horst Priem (Munich), Mrs. Oksana Procyk, Mr. Eugene Lawrence Rogan, Mr. Dan Rae, Dr. Roman Rybicki (Warsaw), Dr. Hedwig Schleiffer, Professor Robert V. Schnucker, Mrs. Marion Schoon, the Reverend William Schulz, the Reverend Alan Seaburg, Professor André Seguenny (Strassbourg), Professor Michael Shank, Douglas H. Shantz (Vancouver), Mr. Thomas Sikora, Mrs. Grazyna Slanda, Mrs. Mary Sullivan Smith, Miss Charity Snyder, Mr. Joe Springer, Mr. Rick Stafford, Mr. Jósef Staša, the Very Reverend Krister Stendahl (Stockholm), Professor Zeph Stewart, Dr. Bohdan Struminskyi, Professor Dr. Jerzy Strzetelski (Cracow), Professor Frank Sysyn, Dr. Margaret Studier, Mr. Luis M. Szekely, Dr. John Tedeschi, Professor John Townsend, the Rev. Jerome Vereb, Professor Derk Visser, Mr. Athanasius Vlahos, Mrs. Jarmila Vogel, Professor Wacław Jan Urban (Cracow), the Reverend cogen Frank Weiskel, H. Bartlett Wells, Esq., the Reverend Dr. Frank Whaling (Edinburgh), the Reverend Dr. Rhys Williams, the Reverend Dr. Thomas D. Wintle, Dr. David F. Wright (Edinburgh), Miss Kathryn Woody, the Reverend Professor Jarold Knox Zeman (Wolfville, Nova Scotia).

As the original edition of the *Historia* carried at the outset by way of introduction the *Vita* of the Author by his son(s), published in translation elsewhere in the same Harvard series, *The Polish Brethren, 1601–1685* (1980), so now in the substantial Introduction to the English edition of the *Historia,* we turn first to an account of the Author.

Description of the Frontispiece

The Engraving of Stanislas Lubieniecki (1664) by Lambert Visscher of Amsterdam from a painting by Matthew Schietz of Hamburg is found in Lubieniecki's *Theatrum Cometicum* (Pl. 63). The copy in the Bibliothèque Nationale is colored. It would appear that about thirty of the copies were thus tinted. The original painting, done in Lubieniecki's forty-first year, is in the rectory of the University of Amsterdam. Lubieniecki sat for the painting in the very year he started writing his *Historia Reformationis Polonicae.*

Beneath the portrait is the poetic tribute of Clément Gauld, doctor of Sacred Theology in the Academy of the French Oratorians in Angers, addressed to Lubieniecki: "Stanislas of Lubieniec: May zeal for God be your glory!"

> *Stanislaus de Lubienietz: Zelus Dei sit tibi laus tua*
> Tu censes proavos sanguine nobilies.
> Gentis quique, suae lucida sydera.
> Immortale decus quod tibi construunt!
>
> Virtui poteris tu superaddere
> Horum si pietas te teneat suum
> Zelus sique Dei sit tibi laus tua.
>
> You value your forebears as noble of blood.
> Indeed brilliant stars of their race were they:
> A deathless honor on you they bestow.
>
> This virtue of theirs you shall yet increase
> If their piety keep you in firm embrace!
> *May for you zeal for God your glory be.*

In the Hamburg/Amsterdam portrait of 1664, Lubieniecki, elegantly attired with fine buttons, with skullcap, and notably long hair draped over a falling band (collar), holds his right hand over his heart in sign of faith and of zeal for God. The gathering of ribbons might be some kind of royal, diplomatic, or even academic distinction. The uncommonly ample, rounded band in the height of French fashion is worn with a dignity, self-possession, and high purposefulness that inhibits any impression of his being a court dandy and confirms rather the sense of his being an adroit gentleman of cosmopolitan society, although with a suggestion of insecurity in his intense, averted gaze. Although an ordained minister of the Polish Brethren in exile, he appears here, self-conscious of his noble race and God-ordained mission among the courts of the nations, as an agent of destiny, while his "swarthy countenance has a masculine and resolute expression overall giving the impression more of a Dutch than of a Polish nobleman" (Janusz Tazbir). The hand, noticeably fine and small relative to the face, may contribute to the immediate impression of a person coiled tight within, on the alert to respond with decisive energy and pre-cogitated formulations.

Lubieniencki, ordained polymath and fugitive international courtier of *dernier cri* fashion, will within three years of the portrait have written his memorial in Latin on the urgency and the appropriateness of the election of Louis XIV as King of the Holy Roman Empire. Lubieniecki presumably had his eyes fixed on the Edict of Nantes (1598), as offering much more than the more recent Treaty of Westphalia (1648), as a model for the toleration in the Polish-Lithuanian Commonwealth of the Reformed churches, including his own beloved Minor Reformed Church suppressed by Polish royal decree in 1660. It is not the least of the ironies in the confidence to the end of Lubieniecki in Providence that Louis XIV would revoke Henry IV's edict protective of the Huguenots in the very year of the posthumous publication of the *Historia Reformationis Polonicae,* 1685.

The only other readily accessible portrait of a nobiliary Polish Unitarian pastor, Peter Moskorzowski, may be adduced for comparison (The Polish Brethren, Pl. I). Moskorzowski served the same congregation of Czarków as Lubieniecki, and in his portrait Moskorzowski wears the same falling band that for gentlemen and ministers had, first in France and the Netherlands, come to replace the laced shoulder collar that in its turn, c. 1635, had begun replacing the ruff.

In any event, Matthias Scheitz, Lambert Visscher, and Clément Gauld have together successfully conveyed the intensity, alertness, collectedness, anguish, and zeal of *Baro Stanislaus de Lubieniec, pastor in exilio Fratrum Polonorum.*

List of Abbreviations

Italic type in text of the *History* indicates material that Lubieniecki is quoting (see p. 437 n. 163). The original pagination of the *HRP* and RD 1–5, as preserved in facsimile editions, is indicated by numbers in brackets and by italicized page numbers.

ADB	*Allgemeine Deutsche Biographie.* 56 vols.; Berlin, 1875–1912.
AS	Maria Sapaylĺo, ed., *Akta synodów Różnowierczych w Polsci.* 3 vols.: 1 (1550–59); Warsaw University Press, 1966. 2 (1560–70); Warsaw University Press, 1972. 3 (1571–1632); Jagiellonian University Press, 1983.
BAnt	*Bibliotheca Antitrinitariorum* by Christopher Sand, Jr., supplemented and edited by Benedict Wiszowaty. Amsterdam, 1684. Facsimile ed., edited by Lech Szczucki (BPR no. 6; Warsaw: Państwowe Wydawnictwo Naukowe, 1972). With index of proper names.
BAnt.[2]	*Bibliotheca Antitrinitariorum,* second projected edition from a ms. from B. Wiszowaty in Leiden. Annotated copy, not yet published in *OiRwP.*
BFP	*Bibliotheca Fratrum Polonorum.* 10 vols., Amsterdam, 1665–92.
BPR	Bibliotheka Pisarzy Reformacjynych series, published by Państwowe Wydawnictwo Naukowe in Warsaw.
Briefwechsel	Theodor Wotschke, *Der Briefwechsel der Schweizer mit den Polen. Archiv für Reformationsgeschichte* Texte und Untersuchungen, Erganzungsband 3; Leipzig, 1908.
EK	*Encyklopedia Katolicka.* In progress, 3 vols. to date: Lublin: KUL, 1973, 1976, 1979.
Historia	Stanislas Lubieniecki's unfinished manuscript of the *Historia Reformationis Polonicae.* 1675.
HRP	*Historia Reformationis Polonicae* by Stanislas Lubieniecki, edited by Benedict Wiszowaty. Amsterdam, 1685. Facsimile edition edited by Henryk Barycz (BPR no. 9; Warsaw: Państwowe Wydawnictwo Naukowe, 1971).
History	Stanislas Budziński, *History.* Largely surviving in *Historia,* denoted by italic type.
OiRwP	*Odrodzenie i Reformacja w Polsce.* Warsaw, 1956–.
PEK	*Podręczna Encyklopedya Kościelna.* 44 vols.; Warsaw, 1904–15.
Pl.	Plates in this volume
pp.	Page numbers in the facsimile ed. of *HRP.*

Polish Brethren	*The Polish Brethren: Documentation of the History and Thought of Unitarianism in the Polish-Lithuanian Commonwealth and in the Diaspora, 1601–1685.* Edited, translated, and interpreted by George Huntston Williams. 2 vols. Philadelphia: Fortress Press, 1984.
Poloneutychia	Andrew Lubieniecki the Elder, *Poloneutychia,* edited by A. Batowski. Lwów, 1843.
PSB	*Polski Słownik Biograficzny.* In progress, 29 vols. to date; Cracow, 1935–.
RD	Related Document in this volume.
RWP	*Reformacja w Polsce.* 12 vols.; Warsaw, 1921–55; superseded by *OiRwP.*

List of Plates and Maps

INTRODUCTION

I. Stanislas Lubieniecki, 1623 – 1675,
Author of the *Historia*

A good deal is known about Stanislas Lubieniecki, even apart from the filial *Vita* that introduced the Latin text (Amsterdam, 1685), much of it still in manuscript and unedited archives.[1] Lubieniecki was born in Raków, 23 August 1623, the son of Catherine Filipowska[2] and Christopher Lubieniecki, Jr. (II)[3] (c. 1598 – 1648), whose rich library the son knew as a youth and part of which he inherited.[4] His father may have studied in Raków. In any case, after studying abroad for three years in Altdorf (the university town of the Imperial City of Augsburg), Leiden, and France, the father became minister successively in Raków, Lublin (Pl. 33), and Piaski (Pl. 57). Personal memories of all of these places, along with the other reminiscences handed down from his parents, are richly interwoven by the Author in his *Historia*.

Our Author first studied in the Academy in Raków, in part under his father who was also scholarch there (Pl. 59). After the enforced closing of the Racovian community in 1638, he removed with many of the exiles in the company of his father to Kisielin in Volhynia, to study, 1638 – 41, in the school there, which was greatly enlarged by the accession of the Racovians. Then, he studied in Toruń, 1644 – 46, where he acquired German in the gymnasium and observed the preliminaries of the Colloquium Charitativum (at n. 68) of 1644. To this representatives of the Polish Brethren had been invited, though they were eventually excluded from the postponed gathering of Catholics, Lutherans, Czech Brethren, and Calvinists (Pl. 61); and Lubieniecki wrote it up in perhaps his earliest extant piece.[5]

A major spokesman of the Polish Brethren in Toruń was Jonas Schlichting (Szlichtyng; 1592 – 1661), who had published in Latin a commentary on the Apostles' Creed thickly bestrewn with supportive scriptural passages under the title, *Confession of Christian Faith published in the name of the Polish Churches that profess One God and His Only-Begotten Son Jesus Christ with the Holy Spirit* (Wrócmirowa, 1642). Originally commissioned and authorized by the synod of Kisielin, this systematic statement of faith was to have been submitted as authoritative for the Minor [Reformed] Church of the Polish Brethren by its representatives in Toruń.[6] In due course Lubieniecki would compose an idealized charitable colloquium among representatives of the major confessions: a

Byzantine-rite Cyril, Catholic Adrian, Lutheran Martin, Calvinist John, and Polish Brother Faustus (under which fictitious name—in allusion to Faustus Socinus—Lubieniecki bespoke *his own* views and preserved the positions and recollections of the Minor Church, never itself wholly Socinian), all hosted graciously by a hospitable lord of the manor, George. In the *Historia* Lubieniecki refers to this work as in progress or contemplated, namely, his *Compendium Veritatis Primaevae*.[7] Although Schlichting's *Confessio* would be burned by the hangman in Warsaw in 1647, Lubieniecki, in the person of Faustus in the *Compendium*, said of it: "I recall now, when that *libellus* of Schlichting was published, that it made a tremendous impression on the Roman Catholic bishops. And while they not long ago were gathered in Cracow for the obsequies of Queen Cecilia Renata of Hapsburg [d. 24 March 1644], they read and studied this *libellus* and asked the judgment of the scholars of the University. But they came at the time to no other conclusion than that the *libellus* was true but insufficient and might be tolerated but for its having been written by a heretic."[8] Lubieniecki would later (1665) write Schlichting's *vita* attached to the works in the nine-volume collected works of the Polish Brethren, the *Bibliotheca Fratrum Polonorum*, published under the direction of Andrew and Benedict Wiszowaty, father and son (Amsterdam, 1665–92, the first two volumes, the *Opera* of Socinus).[9]

With a scholarship for study abroad granted him by the Minor Reformed Church synod of Dążwa in Volhynia, Stanislas Lubieniecki with a Ruthenian companion, Stephen Niemirycz (c. 1630–1684), left by ship from Elbing, 13 August 1646, for Amsterdam, whence they proceeded to France. They studied law at the university of Orleans, then at the Huguenot academy in Saumur, then at the Catholic academy in Angers, where he won a life-long friend on its faculty (cf. frontispiece). At this point Niemirycz left by way of Amsterdam for Volhynia.

Lubieniecki stayed on, living in Paris with Edmond Mercier (successively a Catholic priest, a Calvinist, and then an Arminian), whose home had become the meeting place of liberal Protestants, and who brought Lubieniecki into contact with the savant and freethinker Giles Ménage. In this circle he became acquainted with the library of Jacques Auguste de Thou and with the historical collections of Pierre and Jacques Dupuy. On 26 May 1649 Lubieniecki was back in Amsterdam and on 4 June inscribed himself at the University of Leiden, which had already become a major academic center for Polish Brethren abroad, and he lived in the home of Daniel Heinsius, Hellenist, legist, and historian.[10] Our Author, after his return to the Commonwealth, March, 1651, resident at the castle of Kodeń, south of Brest Litovsk, set forth his versified impressions on the grand tour and specifically of the similarities and differences between the French and the Spaniards.[11]

For about two years Lubieniecki spent his days in Czerniechów within the palatinate of Kiev, on the estate of Stephen Niemirycz. On 22 January 1652 he married Sophia Brzeska, daughter of Paul Brzeski, a sometime Calvinist who was by then, however, the patron of the congregation of the Minor Church in

Pielień near Sanok. From occasional remarks in the *Historia* about ministers' choices of wives, it is possible to infer that his own marriage may not have turned out to be a wholly happy one. The Lubieniecki would bring into the world altogether seven sons (two dying in their infancy) and two daughters.

It is quite possible that Stanislas Lubieniecki, by reason of his close association with Niemirycz and dwelling for some time among Ruthenian families of the Byzantine rite, felt some sympathy with the Orthodox (represented in his *Compendium* by ''Cyril''). Some Ruthenian boyars in the eastern palatinates of the Commonwealth had come over from Orthodoxy to the Minor Church, others among them were resisting the Uniates of the Union at Brest Litovsk of the Orthodox under the Papacy (1595/96; Pl. 52). Possibly our Author sympathized with George Niemirycz, brother of Stephen, in his vision of an autonomous Duchy of the Ukraine under the Polish King, analogous to the Grand Duchy of Lithuania. Stephen held out hopes to this end in the Treaty of the Union of Hadiach (Hadziacz) of 23 April 1659.[12]

The synod of Czarków authorized the installation of Lubieniecki as minister coadjutor to John Ciachowski in Siedliska (Pl. 57) near Lublin (Pl. 33); and in 1654 he was ordained fulltime pastor in Czarków, on the Vistula (near Sandomierz), under the patronage of Jerome Gratus Moskorzowski, whom he had met in Amsterdam.

After the foray of the Swedes at the outset of the Swedish-Polish War (*Potop*, the Flood; 1655 – 60), the Lubieniecki escaped Czarków with other ''Arians'' to Gorlice in the Piedmont in September 1655; and in October a synod decided that a delegation from the Minor Church, to be headed by Lubieniecki as plenipotentiary, should be sent to invading King Charles X Gustavus, then in Cracow. On 25 October 1655 Lubieniecki had his audience with the Swedish king, which he reported in his *Diariusz*.[13]

Lubieniecki then returned to his family and associates, but when several of the manor houses of their protectors fell prey to pogroms in some cases instigated by priests among the peasants, he lost most of the library inherited from his father (d. 1648). The families fled to Cracow proper, settling in adjacent Kazimierz (Pls. 11 – 12), under the protection of the occupying Swedes, notably of General Paul Würtz. It was either Lubieniecki or Schlichting who, in a welcoming speech of 29 March 1657 (*Polish Brethren*, Doc. XXV), commended the refugees of the Minor Church to the protection of Calvinist Prince George II Rakóczy of Transylvania. The Prince had joined the Swedes possibly in the hope of being himself elected King of Poland in replacement of John II Casimir Vasa (Pl. 60).[14] After the capitulation of Cracow to the resurgent forces of John Casimir, 1 September 1657, Lubieniecki, Schlichting, and Christian Stegmann accompanied the Swedish forces to Wolgast, where on 7 October they had an audience with Charles X Gustavus and his entourage. Behind this flight of Lubieniecki was the unexpected resistance to the Swedish siege at Częstochowa in 1655 and then the vows of the rallying King John Casimir in the Latin-rite cathedral in Lwów, 6 April 1656, where he declared Mary Queen of Poland and promised to help the peasants and to rout the heretics. And in this mood of impending victory over the invaders the Diet of Warsaw in June 1658 would issue a fateful decree (*Polish Brethren*, Doc. XXVII) restoring to force the statute of *De hereticis* of 1424 against the invading Hussites, now applied to the Polish Brethren/Socinians/Unitarians as at once "Arians and Anabaptists," who were wholly removed from the licit *dissidentes de religione* of the Confederation of Warsaw of 1573 (Pls. 35, 36 and Section III D), even though John Casimir had himself confirmed its provision and related articles in his earlier coronation oath. By this decree, renewed twice, the membership and the noble leadership of the partly pacifistic Minor Reformed Church was singled out to bear the full punishment for treasonable collaboration with the Swedish enemy, although many Catholic, Czech Brethren, Lutheran, Calvinist, and Orthodox nobles had also in desperation become similarly compliant in the Cossack-Swedish-Polish wars (1648–60). By these three mandates (1658–60) the Polish Brethren were obliged to convert to Calvinism or Catholicism or to go into exile on pain of capital punishment on any attempted return to the fatherland.

Acting intermittently as plenipotentiary of the Minor Church accredited to the Swedish king, having received from him a salary in the amount of fifty talers monthly, Lubieniecki moved about incessantly: in Stettin, Stralsund, Wolgast (these three in Hither Pomerania under Swedish rule), and in Elbing, Soboty, Oliwa in Royal Prussia. He eventually had his wife and family join him in Stettin. One or two of his sons (Pl. 63), later artists in Holland, were born in Hither Pomerania.

From Stettin Lubieniecki addressed to King Charles Gustavus several appeals for amnesty for Unitarians in the process of being exiled under the mandate, also for the royal exercise of broader discretionary powers protective of all Protestants before the final signing of the instruments of the peace treaty at Oliwa, and for special indemnification of losses in lives and properties (Lubieniecki had lost two brothers) because Unitarians were suffering disproportionately for the machinations, particularly of the Jesuits, that had made of them the scapegoat for the many disaffections and defections in all sectors of the Polish-Lithuanian nobility during the Flood.

His first memorandum was the Stockholm manuscript of 10 May 1658, "*Vindiciae pro nostra patria libertate*," in which Lubieniecki unctuously compared the Swedish invader to several historic military shapers of conquered societies, from Julius Caesar to Gustavus Adolphus, and likened his ferocious armada that crossed the Baltic Sea to the redemptive passage of Moses through the Red Sea. He defended Unitarians from the charge of the Polish mandate of exile for being Arians and Anabaptists, arguing that they were simply universal or "catholic Christians" who postponed believers' baptism to the age of proper personal accountability and testimony. Pastor Lubieniecki, functioning religiously in exile primarily as apologist and *paterfamilias*, remained in this sense baptist to the end,[15] which meant the solemn blessing of his infant children "by the ritual laying on of hands,—quite privately within our own four walls,—for—according to God's word and the ancient usage of the Church we permit only catechumens to be baptized (immersed), that is, such as have been instructed in the Christian faith." As for the charge of their being Arians, Lubieniecki as a consistent Unitarian could truly say that the Unitarian/Socinian exiles were not adherents of the view of ancient Arius himself and hence of the subordination of the preexistent Logos/Son within the Godhead, created before the world and the instrument of its creation. But within the preferred nomenclature in territories of the Augsburg Confession Lubieniecki would soon be pressed to defend his coreligionists from the view of Photinus, bishop of Sirmium, a kind of Arian condemned by the Council of Constantinople in 361. For Lutherans, Photinianism included both an aberrant doctrine of God *and* Christian mortalism, which was indeed the special teaching of Faustus Socinus, namely, that the soul dies with the body and that only the souls of worthy believers in Christ are to be summoned to reanimate their gloriously resurrected bodies to stand with Him at the Last Judgment of the quick and the (righteous) dead (*Polish Brethren*, Doc. III). Lubieniecki does not appear to have relished being drawn into discussing this aspect of the Socinian legacy, which, in any case, entered into the theological heritage of the Polish Brethren only after (c. 1601) members of the Minor Church (1563) had been embraced by the Confederation of Warsaw (1573) among the licit dissidents. However his own personal views may have been modified in exile, Lubieniecki could not but have been aware of the degree to which the distinctive eschatology of Socinus did put quite a distance between his followers and other Christians (except for the Anabaptists) and even from incipient Deists, who for their part retained a belief in *natural* immortality.

Another manuscript defense of Unitarians still fleeing from the Commonwealth was that of Uppsala, 24 April 1659, "*Memoriale in causa fratrum unitariorum.*" In it Lubieniecki argued further that Unitarians had not acted much differently from other Christians in comparably parlous sectors of the vast theatre of war and that the exclusion of them from their historic, constitutional place among the recognized *dissidentes de religione Christiana* on the ground that they were merely *dissidentes in particulari*, was to risk the eventual civil status of the Swedish king's own dissenting coreligionists in the Commonwealth. This diminishing phrase, *dissidentes in particulari*, was the argument in a certain Lutheran appeal to the same king, on which manuscript Lubieniecki has left his own spirited marginalia. During this period Lubieniecki wrote his lost *De Deo, Christo et Spiritu Sancto ex ipsis scripturae sanctae verbis* and he also composed for the Swedes, the royal Polish high commissioners, and the envoys of the other powers gathered at Oliwa for the treaty that was to end the war, *The Legal Claims for the Freedom of the Religion of Unitarians in Poland*, c. 1660.[16] This is a prolix yet spirited defense of the constitutional and moral rights of the Minor Church in Poland. It is probably a first draft of what he had envisaged as Part II of his *Historia*.[17]

After the death of Charles Gustavus in 1660 and the unsatisfactory provisions on religious toleration (despite our Author's strenuous personal efforts) in the Treaty of Oliwa and therewith the expiration of his royal Swedish pension, Lubieniecki, with the help of a passport obtained from General Würtz, left Swedish Hither Pomerania and arrived 28 November 1660 in Copenhagen to seek the protection of King Frederick III for himself and his coreligionists, while still sending memoranda to the Swedish forlornly appealing for their even belated insistence on full religious toleration in the land they had almost conquered but had been forced to quit.

In a MS "*Memoriale*" (28 May 1661) addressed to Andrew Gyldenkloo, the Swedish royal counselor, Lubieniecki repeated some of the historical argumentation of *Legal Claims*, based upon classical, scriptural, and patristic loci and especially on the Confederation of Warsaw of 1573 and related articles (Section III D). He conceded that God could indeed gather all believers in one Church but had willed freedom of conscience for each believer's own personal affirmation of faith. He castigated the Polish Vice-Chancellor at the time of the election (1632) of Ladislas IV (Pl. 60; cf. *Legal Claims*, but also Introduction, n. 67) for his peremptory, unconstitutional exclusion from the political franchise of Polish Unitarian noblemen as though never of the company of those recognized as the royal electorate by the Confederation of Warsaw; for they were, he argued, equally professors of the Christian religion though dissenting from the Roman Catholic Church. Noting the constitutional uniqueness of the Commonwealth in marked contrast to the Empire wracked and bled by thirty years of war, Lubieniecki made another appeal through the Swedish courtier to his fellow Poles, entreating them to be mindful of the "bond of blood" that still united Catholic, Lutheran, and Reformed families in a common history and destiny, warning them against the civil disaggregation that might follow from the retrenchment of religious toleration and a failure to reconfirm it in its former plenitude.[18]

The Danish capital was the base for Lubieniecki, 1661–62, while his family remained installed in Stettin. He was on the go, reconnoitering places of settlement for his fellow denominational refugees, appealing repeatedly to the Swedes and the Poles to reconsider their fatal failure to require by the peace treaty the restitution of plenary toleration in his fatherland, earning a livelihood by the dispatch of newsletters to subscribing princely patrons, and engaging on every occasion in theological colloquy and disputation.

In Copenhagen Lubieniecki had altogether three disputations with Jerome Mühlmann, S.J., in the royal court, 12, 15, 22 February 1661. Mühlmann, chaplain to the Austrian ambassador, was himself a convert in Leipzig from Lutheranism to Catholicism and a redoubtable adversary, who argued against the adequacy of *Scriptura* without *traditio*. The first disputation was an encounter between the two men, which was overheard with fascination in the next chamber by Frederick the Wise, who had once held the bishopric of Bremen and who was theologically trained. The king arranged for two more disputations for the general courtly public. Lubieniecki argued against the Nicene formulary and for the sufficiency of Scripture alone, along with the Apostles' Creed, in the formulation of a saving doctrine of God and Christ without any reference to patristic tradition and conciliar canon. Lubieniecki preserved his record of the first encounter in the still only manuscript "*Brevis et fidelis relatio.*"[19] A year later, his disputations with Lutheran divines in February 1662 concentrated on the contested evidence for the Nicene dogma in Scripture alone. He debated Erik Grave (Gravius), later bishop of Aarhus, Daniel Pfeiff, pastor of the German congregation in Copenhagen and university professor of theology, and Christopher Parsberg, tutor to the crown prince. The filial *Vita* (n. 69) concentrates on an episode in which Lubieniecki seemed to have worsted his Lutheran opponents on two New Testament passages deemed by them and by the tradition as supportive of the received Triadology and Christology, and in the textual argumentation he appears to have shamed them. But from other sources it is known that Lubieniecki was also himself overturned on another text. Prov 30:4 ("What is his name, and what is his son's name?") had been adduced by Grave supportive of the eternity of the Son within the Godhead. Lubieniecki argued that it was an intrusion into the verse contrived by St. Athanasius himself and that it had, in fact, been dropped from the Danish version of the Bible (1647) authorized by severely orthodox Archbishop Hans Svane (for whom Lubieniecki had once answered questions as to his faith, on his first arrival in Copenhagen, *Vita*, n. 64). Amid astonishment and incredulity, it was the king himself who looked up the place. After ascertaining that it was indeed missing but by a printer's error, as the surviving marginalia made evident, Frederick thereupon declared Lubieniecki defeated in his textual cunning and presumption.

In reflection on these interconfessional disputations under, for the most part, benign royal patronage, Lubieniecki no doubt thought back to the failed Charitable Colloquy of Toruń "fifteen years before." And, driven by his conviction that peace should be ecclesiastical as well as political and that ecumenical peace might indeed be achieved through mutual recognition of diverse Christians on the basis solely of Scripture and the *Apostolicum*, he presented this thought to Frederick III the Wise in May 1661 in a manuscript "*Veritatis Primaevae prodromus*," intended to foster Christian harmony through the concerted marginalization of the *partialia dogmata*, on which believers might irenically differ, as these particular and divisive doctrines were in any case shaped by Greek philosophy, the councils, and the schools of medieval theology. The full title of the extant manuscript purported to present what its Author conceived to be "a forerunner" of the primitive truth to be recovered in colloquy and commentary on the faith of the early Christians and of the worthies before and after the Assumption of Christ (*Dei* in the title), and the faith of the apostles, martyrs, and the other worthies "who lived around the time of the Council of Nicaea and also during the ensuing decline of the Church and its eventual reformation." The work had evidently grown out of an impetus from the synod at the Minor Church held in his home church of Czarków in 1654. Lubieniecki was evidently unaware of a much earlier irenic work of a pastor of the Major Church, Bartholomew Bythner (1559–1629). This sometime senior of the presbyteral district of Zator and Oświęcim, responding to the intra-Protestant initiative of the Elector Palatine in Heidelberg, Frederick IV, had published his *Fraterna et modesta ad omnes per universam Europam reformatas ecclesias exhortatio* (Frankfurt am Main, 1618), in which he had said: "We heartily ask ourselves to get rid of the party labels of Lutheran, Calvinist, Socinian, along with all contentions, that we may be brethren together.''[20] The pan-Protestant appeal had thus included the Socinian Church, in contrast to the Catholic-Protestant Charitable Colloquy of Toruń, which had in the end excluded Lubieniecki's Minor Church (1645, below Section III D), while at that very moment the Lutheran gymnasium preceptor, Henry Nicolai, similarly argued for the reunion of the Catholics, Lutherans, Calvinists, and Socinians on the basis of Scripture and the Apostles' Creed, *Irenicum, sive de differentiis religionum conciliandum* (Danzig, 1645).

Running parallel with the manuscript "*Veritatis primaevae prodromus*" was Lubieniecki's subsequent, related, and unfinished *Veritatis primaevae compendium* of 535 pages (Pl. 63; Copenhagen, 1982). One or the other of these two was embryonically present as still only an *opusculum* when Lubieniecki referred to it thus in the *Historia* (p. 7). The already mentioned (above at n. 9) collections of successive colloquies in the palace of the irenic and procedurally impeccable lay host, George, resonates with the grave arguments and gracious but spirited exchange that Lubieniecki could himself no doubt recall from Toruń (1645), from the conversations in the court of Stephen Niemirycz in Czerniechów (1652–54) in Byzantine-rite territory, and from the disputations in the palace in Copenhagen itself. For his *Compendium* is notable for the verisimilitude of the dialogue among the Orthodox, the Roman Catholic, the Lutheran, the Reformed, and the Socinian participants, presided over by one whose name, George, connotated husbandmen of the ecclesiastical orchard and who in these colloquies prunes and grafts with such skill that all fruits of faith are allowed to ripen in refined debate and who as engaged moderator may indeed reflect the specific traits of Frederick the Wise himself.

Lubieniecki considered for places of refuge and settlement for the various companies of Unitarian nobles, burghers, merchants, and artisans exiled from the Commonwealth, among others: Friedrichstadt in Schleswig, Mannheim under the Reformed Elector of the Rhine Palatinate, the Hanse City of Lübeck, and Neundorf, an estate in Anhalt (Brandenburg) that had been given by the Elector to his boon companion Stephen Niemirycz, the former Kievan palatine, with an annual pension for Stephen in the rank artillery general and as the Elector's envoy to the Polish King.

Especially worthy among these places was Friedrichstadt, founded as a city of refuge in 1619 by the duke of Schleswig under the Danish crown. It had a flourishing Remonstrant (Arminian) congregation from Holland when Lubieniecki arrived there in March 1662. Presently seventeen Polish Brethren, among them the Racovian theologian John Crell (*Polish Brethren*, Pl. C), inscribed themselves as members, with the tacit understanding that they would hold also their own Unitarian services "after the Polish custom" in the house that Lubieniecki purchased. But in June 1663, the benign founder's son, Duke Christian Albrecht of Holstein-Gottorp, obliged the Unitarians to clear out (*Vita*, n. 73).

Lubieniecki considered returning to Swedish-controlled or protected towns, but after exploring several possibilities, decided on the Free Hanse City of Hamburg, where he settled in May 1662 (Pl. 63A), fetching his family from Stettin. Altona, down the Elbe where he would be part of the time, was a free port under Holstein (Denmark), surrounded by the archbishopric of Bremen under Swedish rule. He acquired houses in each of the rival towns, dwelling with his family in one town or the other from 1663 till his death. Of his seven sons, two may be here mentioned: Theodore (Bogdan) became, despite his father's pacifism, an officer (1671), later one of the rectors of the academy of fine arts in Berlin, and Christopher, a painter in Amsterdam (Pl. 63). One or both would draw up the *Vita* that introduced their father's posthumously published *Historia* (1685).

Lubieniecki lived in Hamburg and Altona off his fees from investing at very high interest the monies of Stephen Niemirycz in Neundorf, from boarding and educating the two sons and the nephew of this exiled former palatine of Kiev, and from retainer fees for supplying several courts with intelligence. It was in Hamburg, 1 September 1664, that Lubieniecki began his *Historia* (n. 31).

Lubieniecki got caught up in the confederational rebellion in Poland (1665–66), led by George Lubomirski (1616–67), Field Hetman and Grand Marshal of the Crown, who opposed the attempt of childless King John Casimir to press for the election of his successor while still ruling. Lubomirski opposed the election of a Frenchman, as the Queen desired, and parleyed with the imperial court in Vienna, while supporting the restoration of full religious toleration in the Commonwealth. In appreciation of Lubomirski, Lubieniecki anonymously published in quarto *Moriens Polonia suos et exteros alloquitur* (Danzig, 1665).[21]

In solidly Lutheran Hanseatic Hamburg Lubieniecki claimed the status of minister resident for both the Danish and the Polish king. The Lutheran clergy resented his presence all the more for his being engaged in theological discussion and in the circulation of Socinian books. Most watchful among the clergy was the Hebraist Esdra Edzard, who repeatedly challenged his diplomatic immunity on the ground that Lubieniecki was only a privy correspondent and he eventually succeeded in getting the city senate to expel him (1668). And Lubieniecki reluctantly took up habitation in Altona, but after five years would think it safe to resettle in Hamburg in what turned out to be the year of his death. And all during his local exile, he frequented the Hanseatic city because it was more propitious for gathering and writing up material for his subscribed newsletters and for their dispatch.

A phenomenon observed by Lubieniecki in the night sky over Hamburg, 28 January 1664 (Pl. 63), had turned him in his extensive irenic, diplomatic, and scientific correspondence to the question of comets. The response from his "senate of philosophers" constitutes an integral part of his enormous publishing enterprise, *Theatrum Cometicum* (Amsterdam, 1666–68). The "bouquets" of learned letters present the overview, reinforced by his own observations, researches, and lucubrations, that comets fix the attention of man on ultimate things and provide occasion for deep reflection on theodicy and morality but are not determinant of events and are not always baleful signs. In this work one may glimpse Lubieniecki's vision of cosmology, the role of revelation and reason, the social order, and salvation (Pl. 62).

Lubieniecki composed his *Theatrum Cometicum* in three distinct parts, Part I, *Communciationes de cometiis*, containing the correspondence of savants between 1664 and 1665 concerning the two comets of those years (Amsterdam, 1667), dedicated to Frederick III; Part II, *Historia [415] cometarum* from the Deluge till 1665 (Amsterdam, 1666), dedicated to George William and John Frederick, dukes of Brunswick and Lüneburg; and Part III, *De significatione cometarum*, with judgments of distinguished men collected by the Author (Amsterdam, 1668), dedicated to Philip William of Neuburg and Philip Christian August of Sulzbach, counts palatine of the Rhine and dukes of Bavaria. The many letters and related documents have significance for the biography of Lubieniecki, whose picture appears as the first of many plates.[22]

With the family of Lubieniecki under pressure to leave Hamburg, and, while he was in Copenhagen to present a copy of *Theatrum Cometicum* to Frederick III (April, 1668) and to appeal for intervention on his behalf, his wife on her own moved over to Altona, where the family had already acquired a church burial place and where they could be under direct royal Danish protection.

The unreliable printer, who caused him much anguish with misprints and extra charges, obliged Lubieniecki to spend several months in Amsterdam in 1668 cajoling him. And despite the outlay of energy on what was perhaps an ill-advised project, the small sale of the expensive work never covered its costs. Presently, Lubieniecki joined the three parts of *Theatrum Cometicum* in one huge volume, along with an unrelated panegyric, *Strena lugubris et orbi Christiani ineunte anno Christi 1670 exhibita*, or a Monument to Bogusław Radziwiłł (1620–69), governor of East Prussia, and dedicated the set (Pl. 63) to Marquis Frederick William, Elector of Brandenburg (Hamburg, 1670).

Lubieniecki kept up appeals for money owed him by subscribers of his newsletter in Sweden, writing importunely about this and religious toleration to such friends in Stockholm as Daniel Heinsius, now Dutch ambassador there, and Peter Grotius, the son of the Remonstrant jurisconsult. In his expression of concern and offer of strategies for the embassy chapels, he may have done more harm than good for the refugee Huguenots in Sweden.

In 1674, "after some years, on the advice of his friends, who believed that by now his [Lutheran clerical] enemies had recovered from their rage" (vaguely, as to date, *Vita*, by n. 84), Lubieniecki returned from Altona to resettle in Hamburg. All three of his surviving sons, Theodore, Paul, and Christopher, were evidently already established elsewhere—at the time respectively about twenty, seventeen, and fifteen—hence the imprecision. Soon after the confident resettlement, Lubieniecki, his wife, and their two daughters were overcome with food poisoning (ergot or mercury), almost certainly accidental.[23] The two daughters, Catherine Salomea and Griselda Constance, died first, and their father rallied to compose funeral hymns for them, but relapsing himself, died in May 1675. He was buried in a sarcophagus in the Hauptkirche in Altona, Holy Trinity (which would be torn down in 1740). Although he is remembered in the *Vita* as having died on 18 May, the church register kept on a regular basis records his death as of 11 May. He left unfinished both the *Veritatis primaevae compendium* and the *Historia.* Widowed Catherine Lubieniecka, who had indeed "been barely snatched from the jaws of the same death," went to Amsterdam to live with her son Christopher, a painter who joined the Remonstrant church, and who, along with martial Theodore, also a painter, preserved the family papers, and either one or the two together (Paul ended up in Venice) wrote the *Vita.*

II. Character of the *Historia*

The core of Lubieniecki's *Historia* is the half-century of development from the first organization of the Reformed Church in Little Poland by the Hebraist-theologian Francis Stancaro in Pińczów in 1550 through the various schisms, 1559 – 80, to the consolidation of a partially Socinianized Minor Reformed Church by the time of the death of the Sienese Reformer, Faustus Socinus (Pls. 47, 48, RD 8) in 1604. Lubieniecki still had, however, much to tell beyond this date, although most of his narrative does not extend beyond 1638, when the intellectual center of Raków was shut down by the highest authorities, King and Diet.

Lubieniecki seldom used the term "Unitarian" of his own church, mostly in the final chapters (cf. Bk. 1, n. 22), although he used the term frequently in several of his other writings in exile. He never called his own Church "Socinian" in the text of the *Historia.* The term "Socinian" came into general use only long after the death of Faustus Socinus in reference to the community in exile and especially to the movement of thought represented by his collected works in the *Bibliotheca Fratrum Polonorum* (above, at. n. 11). "Unitarian" was initially the distinctive designation of the comparably radical schismatic Reformed Church in Transylvania, where, however, it was, demographically, for a while in the last third of the sixteenth century, the Church of the majority of Magyars in that large principality. During the first two thirds of the seventeenth century, Magyar Unitarians with conservative Reformed Magyars and Lutheran Saxons constituted a "Protestant" state under a succession of comprehensive Catholic, then Calvinist princes. Under one of the latter in 1638 at the synod and diet of Dées the radically Reformed Church, making certain concessions, became officially the "Unitarian" Church (Pl. 64). Lubieniecki, not mentioning Dées, included in his *Historia* nevertheless some earlier developments in Transylvania, whither in 1578 Socinus, as christologically innovative *and* conservative, had been invited from Cracow to debate with Francis Dávid (cf. Pl. 40), superintendent of the radically Reformed Church (not yet called Unitarian) of Kolozsvár (Pl. 41). There he unwittingly compassed the leader's imprisonment (for "innovation") and death in 1579. Even though in 1660 bands of Socinianized Polish Brethren found refuge in Kolozsvár, because of the fateful entry of Socinus into the earlier affairs of the Davidians, and for other reasons, the Unitarians of Transylvania could never call themselves Socinian. But Lubieniecki, from his perspective in exile in Amsterdam and Hamburg, sought to embrace the Transylvanian Unitarians in a retrospective harmonizing account of Antitrinitarianism in the eastern realms.

Lubieniecki has told his story as an Evangelical Rationalist that is, as a kind of "Protestant" neoscholastic in applying the canons of reason, not as a Catholic scholastic to Scripture, Tradition, and magisterial Authority, but to the Bible alone, and within the Bible, primarily to the New Testament as decisive—the permanent legacy of Socinus, who, fully as much as the Evangelical Anabaptists, held to the superiority of the New over the Old Testament. As such, Lubieniecki has left us in the *Historia* a witness to a widespread sixteenth-century drive toward the simplification of doctrine through the scrutiny of Scripture as alone revelatory and as alone authoritative in theology and toward the further clarification and systematization of the divine intent therein, by God-given *reason*, all for the sake of emphasizing common-sense ethical probity and evangelical virtue and forthrightness. In the course of the *Historia* one can sense the degree to which the Reformation in the eastern marches of Latin Christendom, distant from its magisterial and genial centers in Wittenberg and Zurich, Strassburg and Geneva, then Heidelberg and Leiden, was received primarily as antiprelatical, as institutional and moral reform, as antischolastic evangelical rationalism, and as antimonastic personal and congregational self-discipline and yet also as the restoration and renewal of primitive polity and theology. The Minor Church in Little Poland purported to have embodied these most consistently of all the churches of the Reformation era. The minor Reformed churches of Poland, Lithuania, Moravia, and Transylvania all remained synodal-presbyterian in polity.

A. Lubieniecki's Intentions and Oversights

Lubieniecki intended to write the history of the Polish Reformation in the fullest sense of both Reformation and Poland. By the latter he meant more than Little and Great Poland (respectively, the Poland of Cracow and Lublin and the Poland of the old capitals, Gniezno and Poznań). He meant more than even the lands of the Commonwealth directly under the Polish royal Crown, for he was interested in developments in Ducal Prussia, in the Grand Duchy of Lithuania, the courtly, manorial, and synodal language of which had become Polish, even among ethnic Lithuanians in Samogitia (roughly modern Lithuania) and in the abutting Grand Ducal palatinates of Vilna and Troki (where Lithuanian but predominantly Byelorussian were spoken among the common people). By "Reformation" and "Reformed" Lubieniecki could be no clearer than his predecessors and contemporaries.

In the Latin-rite third of the Commonwealth reform and even reformation in the sixteenth century were susceptible to a range of meanings. Some bishops and many princes, lords, and publicists espoused aspects of a reformation in church and society without always sensing the degree to which some of them were departing from Catholic norms that would become clear to them only as the decrees of the Council of Trent were promulgated in the Commonwealth in 1564 but actually accepted only in 1577—the last Catholic state to conform. Thus for more than three quarters of the century of the Reformation the land now thought of as the most tenaciously Catholic was confessionally and ritually remarkably pluralistic.[24] Concurrently, the chief activists of the Counter-Reform, the Jesuits, entered the Commonwealth, first in the see of Stanislas Cardinal Hosius of Varmia. Lubieniecki did not take heed of the Catholic Reform in the spirit of the Jesuits, except as his Church had to deal with them as antagonists.

In no country in Europe were Christians faced with so many plausible options for reformation (and restoration) in church and society as in the Polish-Lithuanian Commonwealth, not even in multi-ethnic Transylvania.

Up to 1577, besides onsets to reformation within the old order in the spirit of Erasmus and an evangelical humanist Catholicism, there were several distinctive kinds of reformation within the Commonwealth, of which Lubieniecki was himself only partially cognizant, because of his overriding conviction that his own Church represented the climax of the reformatory energies of his age. But to understand his narrative these variants must be kept clearly in mind. They can only be called retrospectively "Protestant," for in the sixteenth century the term had special resonance in the context of the Holy Roman Empire. There the designation first arose among the "protesting" princes and envoys from the imperial cities at the diet of Worms of 1529 who expressly excluded the Swiss Reformed and all Anabaptists from their privileged Protestant confederation, the latter as disrupting the proper interpenetration of church and society by their repudiation of infant baptism and by their adherence to voluntarist congregations, and both Anabaptists and Zwinglians, as alike "Sacramentarians," because they considered the sacrament of the altar "only an act of commemoration." The main body of persons, movements, and churches chronicled by Lubieniecki belonged in the end to the Swiss Reformed tradition, notably of Zurich and Basel, of Geneva and Lausanne: that is, Reformed in the specialized sense of being Calvinian/Bullingerian rather than Lutheran. In Poland they were often imprecisely called "Lutherans" by their Catholic opponents, though also "Evangelicals," which was often their own name for themselves (and has remained the designation for the Polish Calvinists to the present). Most numerous in Little Poland, the Reformed in some districts came near to being the predominant group wherever they were protected by the manorial lords, although in the walled or unwalled towns they seldom gained enough of a following to have more than a single congregation.

Before the several schisms in the Reformed Churches in Little and Great Poland and in the Grand Duchy, there was another model of, and onset to, reformation, namely, "the First Reformation"[25] of John Hus. That late medieval reformation under the slogan of communion in both kinds (*sub utraque specie*) had, by the opening of the sixteenth century, divided in Bohemia into several schisms and parties; and one of these, the Czech Brethren or the Unitas Fratrum (later to be called the Moravian Brethren), had lost their "unity" to the extent of falling into a Major (urban) and a Minor (rural) Party. Driven from Bohemia proper into the more tolerant margraviate of Moravia and into Slovakia under the Hungarian crown, the Czech Brethren (Pl. 4) had, by way of Silesia (then under the Bohemian royal crown) by 1548 also entered Ducal Prussia until they were at length permitted to settle down in Great Poland where several Polish lords, like the Górkas and the Leszczyńskis (Pl. 19), espoused this sectarian but authentically Slavic kind of reformed Christianity. There was a phase in the history of the Polish Reformation when, indeed, the transplanted Unitas Fratrum with its still celibate bishops, its highly disciplined synodal and congregational polity, and its vernacular Scripture and hymnody, might have become the root and stock out of which a Polish reformed Church could have grown up. The only other land of Christendom with a comparable native tradition of ecclesiastical biblical reform was England where the Wycliffites, linked indeed to the Hussites, survived as Lollards into the era of the Reformation. Yet the refugee Czech Brethren in Great Poland, even as the Lollards in England, were not destined to become the basis of a reformed national or regional church of Poland in the age of Luther, Calvin, and Cranmer. Lubieniecki himself scarcely even hints at the degree to which the Czech Brethren both in Great Poland and in Moravia presented an unusually attractive and authentically Slavic mode of reformation that for a season was quite attractive to some Polish lords in both Great and Little Poland. Lubieniecki only mentions once and in passing John Amos Komenský (Comenius, 1572–1670, Pl. 16), the most renowned Slavic Protestant of his age, whose principal seat was Leszno in Great Poland.

A third model of reformation was that of princely and urban Protestantism, that is, the Lutheranism of the Augsburg Confession (1530). The Commonwealth had the distinction of being the first state of Christendom to have within it a princely Protestant establishment, Ducal Prussia, whose sometime Grand Master of the Teutonic Order became a vassal of the Polish King in Cracow, 1525, while such Germanized Hanseatic cities along the Baltic as Danzig and Elbing, Riga and Dorpat, all under or soon to be under the Polish Crown, followed the example of many comparably free cities within the Empire and became magisterially Protestant (Lutheran), including Toruń (Thorn) in Royal Prussia. Although Duke Albert Hohenzollern in Königsberg (Pl. 7) provided a princely model and the aforementioned long Germanized cities provided another, nothing comparable developed among lords and burghers of Polish speech. Only a few Lutherans ("Protestants" in the imperial sense) figure in the *Historia*.

Nor does Lubieniecki take cognizance of the reformatory ferment among the lords, priests, and monks of the Byzantine-rite two thirds of the Commonwealth. Yet the whole world of Orthodoxy was in agitation and yearning in the period covered by Lubieniecki: late medieval radical currents within Kievan and Muscovite Orthodoxy, sometimes characterized as Judaizing, penetrated as far west in the Commonwealth as Vilna and Lublin (see further section III A). Also unnoticed by Lubieniecki was the Union at Brest Litovsk in 1595 (Pl. 52) when a large portion of the bishops, princes, and lords of the Byzantine rite joined with Rome to constitute the large Uniate Church in the Ukraine, to the present day very much a force in the diaspora. Nor were the currents induced within the Orthodoxy that resisted the Union (Pl. 53) heeded by Lubieniecki, although these new energies account for some aspects of Protestant-Orthodox relations in Ruthenia, to which he does allude.

Lubieniecki was likewise unclear about the succession of schisms within the (Helvetic) Reformed Churches of Little Poland and in several of the palatinates of the Grand Duchy, even though he was primarily the historian of this tradition. Lubieniecki was quite partisan in his characterization of the Italian Hebraist-theologian Francis Stancaro, who was the first organizer of the Reformed Church of Little Poland in 1550, but he failed to mention specifically Stancaro's schism of 1559/61 – 70, centered in Dubiecko in Ruthenia, with its large school (Pl. 17). He did not make clear the temporary schism of the Ditheists (Farnovians), who only reluctantly gave up their belief in the preexistence of Christ before the incarnation and for a while constituted a separate synod, with its own liturgy, distinct from the proto-Unitarians.

Lubieniecki was, of course, preeminently concerned with recounting the schism of the Major (Calvinist) and the Minor (Unitarian) Church, beginning in 1563, irreversible by 1565. The Minor, his church, immersionist Unitarian and adorant of Christ the Ascended Lord, becomes in the *Historia* the center of his focus. Having dealt gently with John Łaski (1499 – 1560), as though the chief Polish reformer of international repute (Pl. 20) were truly a father and founder (however disgruntled) of the Minor Church, Lubieniecki never becomes entirely hostile to the ongoing and retrenching Major Church, which he occasionally calls Calvinist. At the same time he is clearly sympathetic with the several efforts of his own Minor Church to make a common cause with the Calvinists after the whole confessional climate had changed in the middle of the completion of their Reformed schism as the storm clouds built up in the Jesuit-led and royally sanctioned Counter-Reform, 1564. In pique he averted his attention from the Consensus of Sandomierz of 1570 (Pl. 34, section III D) of the federated Czech Brethren, the Lutherans, and the Major Church, who had expressly excluded his own Minor Church from the common Protestant front against the Counter-Reform. Reticent about the mode of baptism, Lubieniecki, who was himself baptized as a catechumen by immersion in Raków, presumably by his ministerial father, never lets the reader of his narrative sense the extent of still another kind of reformed church in the Commonwealth, a generically Anabaptist movement that penetrated areas of Polish speech from at least three centers of diffusion: from the Hutterites (Pls. 29, 30) and other groupings, like the Marpeckians, in Moravia; from the Mennonites in Royal Prussia; and from the typical German Anabaptists, some of them Sabbatarian, moving in from Silesia. As Lubieniecki shared the common revulsion of the Polish Brethren for the polygamous and martial Anabaptist theocrats of Münster (1535), he never makes clear the extent to which the Polish Brethren, especially from c. 1565 to 1580, were, in fact, the Polish-speaking analogues to the German, Dutch, and

Italian Anabaptists but with their distinctive practice of immersion. Immersion must have come into general usage in the confluence of a number of factors in the Commonwealth: immersion among the neighboring Ruthenian Orthodox; the contested insistence on the rebaptism of Ruthenians converting to Catholicism along the Byzantine-rite border (cutting through the Commonwealth; see Map); the example of the Czech Brethren who, while retaining pedobaptism for their own progeny, insisted until 1535 on the rebaptism of converts from among Catholics and Utraquists; the paradigm of baptism in the Gospels and the Acts, notably that of Jesus at the hands of John the Baptist and the conversion of the Ethiopian eunuch; the sacramental implication of the Protestant principle of salvation by (explicit) faith alone on the hearing of the word (*fides ex auditu*, Rom 10:17); and finally the recommendation of Michael Servetus and several learned Polish followers of Servetus.

So convinced was Lubieniecki that the Polish Brethren of the Minor Reformed Church represented the climax of Luther's (not Hus's) Reformation that he often refers to his people as "the confessors of the Truth," "Catholics," or simply "Christians." By their Calvinist opponents of the Major Church or Catholics they were more often called "Neobaptizers," "Anabaptists," "Samosatenians,"and "Arians."

Because Lubieniecki himself followed Faustus Socinus on most points, although not on baptism, he does not make clear the extent to which the Minor Church underwent a major transformation with respect to the two sacraments and church discipline under the Sienese lay theologian in the direction of a distinctive variant of Evangelical Rationalism (scriptural scholasticism) in a process that brought about a further differentiation among the Minor Church in the Grand Duchy, that in Little Poland, and that, with its own synod, in the new eastern Crown palatinates (after 1569), notably in Ruthenia and Volhynia. Under the tutelage of Socinus the main body of the Minor Church of the Poles remained adorant of Christ, reserved as to the use of the sword even in public office and nonaggressive war, while not wholly following Socinus in his disparagement of believers' baptism. But the "Lithuanian" Minor Church under the ongoing direction from Simon Budny (d. 1593; Pl. 15), translator of the Bible into Polish (Pl. 54), more responsive to the expectations of lordly and princely patrons, for the most part upheld the use of the sword for Reformed Christians, preserved the social order in baptism, and, like the Transylvanian Unitarians, eschewed the invocation and adoration of Christ, whom they did not envisage seated as Ascended Lord at the right hand of the Almighty but rather as the eschatological judge at the Second Advent. After the excommunication of Budny and, in effect, the whole Minor Church of Lithuania by Socinus, Lubieniecki had little to recount about the Lithuanian brethren, the baptist Unitarians principally of palatinates Vilna and Novogrodek, who disappear from his purview.

In the end, of course, it was the Catholic mode of reformation that prevailed, and the Catholic Church would become the bearer of Polish and of Lithuanian national identities after the final tripartition of the Commonwealth in the eighteenth century. Lubieniecki, a minister and a publicist for the one dissenting group forced in 1660 to conform either to Catholicism or Calvinism or to leave the Commonwealth, could hardly be expected to observe on his own in the midst of Counter-Reform that the bishops, the religious, and the Catholic lay patrons finally prevailed in Poland because by temperament, conviction, and policy they were more disposed to invective rather than to inquisition, to polemic rather than to heretical pyres, to hospitable and even festive colloquy rather than to coercion, to tolerance rather than to the total control of conscience. Catholics indeed prevailed in part because by their own counsel, prelatical, publicistic, and nobiliary, the Commonwealth was by and large "a state without stakes."[26]

B. The MS *Historia* (Hamburg, 1675) and the Posthumous Publication of it as *Historia Reformationis Polonicae* (Amsterdam, 1685)

The unfinished MS *Historia* left by Lubieniecki to posterity (1675) and the printed *Historia Reformationis Polonicae* (1685) are not quite identical. The *Historia Reformationis Polonicae* comes down as an account in three books posthumously edited by Benedict Wiszowaty (d. after 1704), the son of a major Socinian thinker, Andrew Wiszowaty (d. 1678). Both father and son had been exiled from their homeland in 1660, and settled in Amsterdam since 1666.

Andrew Wiszowaty (1608–78) had, with Joachim Stegmann, Jr., provided a long preface for a new edition of the Racovian Catechism ("Irenopolis" = Amsterdam, "after 1659" = 1665), substantially revised by several synodally authorized theologians since the first Latin edition (Raków, 1609), and in the preface he pled for freedom of religious teaching, liberty of conscience, and magnanimous mutual toleration. Andrew Wiszowaty, whose life appears in *Polish Brethren* (Doc. 1) and whose own *Brief Narrative* is included here as RD 5, initiated the publication of the *Bibliotheca Fratrum Polonorum*. His son carried out the work.

Benedict Wiszowaty had already edited posthumously the indispensable *Bibliotheca Antitrinitariorum* (BAnt; "Freistadt" = Amsterdam, 1684), assembled by the East Prussian proof-reader and classicist Christopher Sand (Sandius), Jr. (1644–80). Sand's father had distinguished himself in the state affairs of Brandenburg-Prussia, openly espoused *ancient* Arianism, and for this had to retire to his study for a score of years, outliving his son. The son, educated in Königsberg and then Oxford, was drawn to Platonism and Neoplatonism, becoming on the side a private scholar of Christian antiquity. A friend of many in the Socinian circle, especially of the Wiszowatys, and also an acquaintance of Baruch Spinoza (d. 1677), he adhered to no church but spiritedly defended ancient Arianism in his *Nucleus historiae ecclesiasticae* (Amsterdam, 1668;

revised with an *Appendix*, 1678),[27] a small excerpt from which constitutes RD 1. Sand found in some forms of Arianism the kernel of apostolic and patristic piety. Seeking to vindicate the ancient Arians, he traced the subordinationist Triadology and Christology as it survived through the centuries and he found the occasion to express himself strongly against the Christology of Faustus Socinus as an unprecedented, idiosyncratic *novum* (cf. at n. 42), to be excised from the body of teachings of his Polish friends, whose writings and rationalist, tolerant stance he otherwise found congenial, hence, too, the breadth of his *BAnt*, his inclusive Library of Sixteenth and Seventeenth-Century Antitrinitarians, ranging from Wolfgang Capito (d. 1541) of Germania, Juan de Valdés (d. 1541) of Hispania, and Bernadino Ochino (d. 1564) of Italia all the way in temporal and geographical coverage to István Pal (d. 1672) of Transylvania, to our own Stanisław Lubieniecki (d. 1675), once of Polonia, to Nathaniel Stuckey (d. 1678) of Anglia, and to Willem Davidz Redoch (d. 1680), Mennonite *oudeste* of Frisia.

Benedict Wiszowaty in editing *BAnt* included Sand himself among the writers, and amplified his section of Anonymous Authors. In the preparation of the MS Wiszowaty inserted about seventy additional authors with their works, more than doubling the information beyond that of the deceased biobibliographer (Szczucki, *Praefatio* to the facsimile edition, p. ix). To *BAnt* Wiszowaty attached an appendix of seven documents. One of these was the *Testamentum* (RD 3) of George Schomann (d. c. 1592), evidently in the first instance preserved by Lubieniecki's own father and then removed from the *Historia* (Bk. 3, chap. 6) as being a self-contained autobiographical synopsis of Schomann's life and times. Another document included among the seven in *BAnt* was Lubieniecki's own MS in defense of the civil liberties of Unitarians in Poland, *Legal Claims* (above at n. 18).

When Wiszowaty came to edit the *Historia* after *BAnt*, he saw fit to leave out Schomann's *Testamentum*. In working on the MS *Historia* and having to decipher it at several points, he may have improvised the chapter headings or at least the final wording. He may well have made substantial emendations and even cuts and he added a few clarificatory footnotes (preserved in the translation at the bottom of the page and thus distinguishable from my endnotes).

As an introduction to the *Historia* Wiszowaty placed the *Vita* of the Author by one or two of his sons and he added two epistolary accounts of the flight of the Brethren from Poland in 1660 in order thereby to give the printed work a more finished character and to enhance its value in making friends for the cause that both he and Lubieniecki so zealously espoused, convinced that their Church now largely in diaspora was the witness to the recovered saving truth as revealed by Jesus Christ and confirmed and clarified by his disciples and apostles.

Wiszowaty did all his editing of *BAnt* and then the *HRP* in Andreaswalde (Kosinowo; Pl. 64) in Electoral (East) Prussia, where he served as minister to the exiled Brethren (c. 1684–c. 1704). From there he sent to his Amsterdam printer his *corrigenda* and *addenda* for *HRP* (incorporated along with the additional *corrigenda* of the facsimile edition; still more of my own are in the translation). In Andreaswalde Wiszowaty also prepared for publication a fair copy, still in MS, of an augmented second edition of *BAnt* (consulted by me and cited throughout as *BAnt²*, on which see further in the preface to all the Related Documents). Wiszowaty composed not long after *BAnt*, his own modest History c. 1689 (still in MS) of the Primitive Church and of the faithful (Unitarian) witnesses to the saving truth throughout the ages, closing with a single skimpy chapter on the sixteenth century and his own age, *"Medulla historiae ecclesiasticae."*[28] As Lech Sczucki explains, Wiszowaty intended to lay down, over against the *Nucleus* of his Neoplatonist Arian friend Sand, of whom he had become the posthumous editor, how there was a Unitarian tradition from the Ebionites and the Nazarenes and others of the sub-Apostolic age. This tradition, with the *Apostolicum*, according to Wiszowaty, upheld the utter preeminence of God the Father and yet the uniqueness of his fully human, Virgin-conceived Son, whose pure message is the saving truth, all ideas of a preexistent Christ or of a premundane personal Logos being regarded as obtrusions on the saving articles of faith. For Wiszowaty the history of the Church was that ''of a minority, one defeated, persecuted and suffering, but one which nevertheless, dauntlessly convinced of the justice of its cause, passes on to succeeding generations the torch of divine truth'' (Szczucki). As both Wiszowaty and Lubieniecki were baptist Unitarians who had long since sloughed off any even scriptural interpretations of Christ as premundane, we see in the *Historia*, Bk. 1, chaps. 2 and 3, on witnesses to the truth between the Apostolic age and the opening of Luther's Reformation (chap. 4), a compact version of what Wiszowaty developed more fully in his *Medulla*; and indeed, as the two Poles began their Histories at only a score of years apart (1664 and 1684), it is possible that they conferred on their projects and even on the editing of *BAnt*. It is of interest that when editing Lubieniecki's *Legal Claims* for inclusion in *BAnt* (1684), Wiszowaty acknowledges in the epilogue of his MS ''*Medulla*'' (accessible in print through Szczucki) that he had annotated a section of the document, on religious liberty and loyalty to plighted troth even to enemies, with a list of the patristic authorities that featured in his own ''*Medulla*, like those in *Legal Claims*.''

As Socinians did not share with proto-Deists a belief in *natural* immortality, there is a poignancy in their historiographical care for the testimonies from the *mortal* cloud of witnesses to the revealed saving truth, whose salvation was faintly eschatological—testimonies to their fealty to God, under the sign of Christ, the uniquely resurrected Son of man, their Lord.

There is a utility in sometimes referring to Lubieniecki's original unfinished work as simply the *Historia* and to its edited form with its seventeenth-century editorial notes and captions and its three supplementary documents as *Historia Reformationis Polonicae* (*HRP*). Moreover, there is also a reference in the annotation to the History (unitalicized) of the sometime Franciscan Stanislas Budziński (c. 1530 – c. 1595), the very first account in Poland of the Reformation, of which he was eyewitness, a chronicle in Polish now lost but extensively excerpted and paraphrased by Lubieniecki in the *Historia*.

C. The Genesis and Reliability of the *Historia*

Lubieniecki began writing his *Historia* in Hamburg, 1 September 1664.[29] He had accessible only a part of MS History in Polish (c. 1593) by the Budnyite pedobaptist, nonadorant, Unitarian scribe Stanislas Budziński (see below, at n. 37), the excommunicated antagonist of Faustus Socinus.

The *Historia*, as already briefly characterized, records the rise of and then primarily the minor schism within the Reformed Church in Little Poland and Polish-colonized Volhynia and, though partisan and almost loftily indifferent to the development within the major branch of the schism, is the most comprehensive account of the early Reformed churches in the Commonwealth, stronger, fuller, and more coherent than *Systema/Slavonia Reformata* (1652; see more fully at n. 43) of Czech Reformed Andrew Węgierski, who dealt with all of Latinate reformed Slavdom. For the Czech Brethren in Great Poland and Latinate Slavonia in general, Węgierski had been preceded by: the Czech elder, Simon Theophilus Turnowski (cf. at n. 65), *Mirror of Christian Piety in Poland* (Polish: Vilna, 1594); the Leipzig polymath, Joachim Camerarius, in his *Historica narratio de Fratrum orthodoxorum* [Protestant] *ecclesiis in Bohemia, Moravia, et Polonia* (Heidelberg, 1605); and the Polish nobiliary Calvinist, John Łasicki (d. c. 1599), of whom only the eighth book of his comprehensive account was printed, posthumously, *Historia de origine et rebus gestis Fratrum Bohemorum* (Leszno, 1649).

The *Historia* (1675/85), as already noted, has something on the Reformed churches in Hungary-Transylvania, which for their part produced comparable printed Histories only a generation later, none in this same period by Unitarians: Francis Páriz Pápai (Hermannstadt, 1684), George Haner (Frankfurt, 1695), and Friedrich Adolf Lampe (Utrecht, 1728). The comparable Unitarian *Historia*, a collective chronicle, by Stephen Uzoni and others (Kolozsvár, 1775; Pl. 64), remains unpublished in three variant MSS.[30]

Lubieniecki was no doubt under an informal commission of the exiled Polish Brethren to prepare a history of their movement for the sake of commending themselves to liberal Protestants like the Remonstrants, Collegiants, urbanized Mennonites, English and Huguenot refugees in the Netherlands and elsewhere among whom they had established contact. And they and he were surely conscious that synods in the fatherland had more than once called for just such a *Historia*. For example, synods in Raków, 1624–25, had commissioned the son of his patron at Siedliska, namely, Andrew Christian Moskorzowski (Moskorzewski; d. c. 1650), to write a history (cf. above, in ¶ after n. 14, while his friend Joachim Stegmann, Jr. had been similarly encouraged to assemble the Acts of the Synods, RD 5, no. 1). When Lubieniecki assumed the synodal assignment as his own, starting to write the *Historia* in 1664 in Hamburg, he evidently visited Amsterdam and was encouraged there in the enterprise by the Wiszowaty circle.

With reference to the composition and reliability of the *Historia*, there have been several interpretations, notably by its first translator Edmund Bursche

(1938), Janusz Tazbir (1961), [31] E. K. Jordt-Jørgensen (1968),[32] and Henryk Barycz (1971, 1981).[33]

While all scholars recognize the immense value of *HRP*, Lech Szczucki (1979) in another connection characterized the *Historia* as ''a middling opus; part apologetic, part hagiographical, part sectarian.''[34] Barycz fully recognized its infelicities and mingling of narrative, analysis, and crude source material embedded in the text without adequate clarification, the Author's unembarrassed invention of plausible speeches in the manner of classical and Renaissance historians, and his partisan assessment of several figures who, so long as they were breaking from Rome, were lauded, but insofar as they could not go along with the final radicalization of theology, were denigrated. Tazbir conceded that the text was quite uneven with some valuable documents slapped into the narrative without adequate identification of persons and places and that it was at times ''quite partisan and chaotic with respect to composition.''

It was in Amsterdam presumably that Lubieniecki had at his disposal part of the subsequently lost MS History in Polish by Stanislas Budziński (c. 1530 – after 1595, Pl. 1), entitled in Latin ''The Ecclesiastical History of those things that in matters of religion took place in Poland and the neighboring lands from the beginning of the Reformation to the year 1593.''[35] A part of this MS had already been destroyed by an unnamed enemy of the Polish Brethren. Though Erasmus Otwinowski who reports this died as nonagenarian in 1614,[36] it is clear that his work referring to the loss came much earlier and that none of the exiles of 1660 in the Netherlands could have had anything but the salvaged Part One, which from references to it in the *Historia* and from the writings of others who made use of it (but much less extensively than Lubieniecki) is known to have contained at least 42 chapters.

Budziński, a pedobaptist, nonadorant Unitarian who was repelled by the social radicalism of the early Racovian phase (1569 – 72) in the history of the Brethren that had the marks of Germanic Anabaptism and evangelical Spiritualism, was an eyewitness to many of the events. He preserved precious records in his narrative. As an assiduous collector of documents, he laid down for Lubieniecki a conceptualization of the development of the Reformation movement, particularly in Little Poland and to some extent among nonadorant Unitarians in Transylvania with whom he was allied, a pattern of progression, emphasis, and marginalization that undoubtedly influenced not only the *Historia*, but also all subsequent historiography necessarily based upon it.

I have pulled together the little that we know about the life and thought of Budziński elsewhere.[37] The most important legacy of Budziński, only touched upon in my article, is what was copied or paraphrased by Lubieniecki in the *Historia*. Accordingly, I have introduced italics where Budziński's narrative or documents presumably lie at the base of the *Historia* without obtruding on the synthetic achievement of Lubieniecki.[38]

One cannot avoid the impression that Lubieniecki, as a believer of conviction and as an historian, experienced some difficulty in threading his way through Budziński's History, his other sources, and his own family recollections. Sorting out the data was all the more arduous for him because of the figure and the legacy of Faustus Socinus and the reverberations in the sources of the Italian's conflicts with Francis Dávid in Transylvania, 1578/79. Moreover, even after 1580 there was the residue of the more socially radical thought and practice of the Polish Brethren, of whom Socinus had become nevertheless the chief theological spokesman. Budziński himself opposed Socinus in his adoration of Christ and in his "sectarian" restraints on nobiliary and civic exercise of the office of the sword.

Because on these issues Budziński himself had been excommunicated from the Minor Church, 1576–88, an exclusion which Socinus promoted when he assumed leadership in 1580, Budziński in the lost Part Two of his History probably recounted a story of the Brethren quite different from that current in the Lubieniecki family and on their side! At the same time, Budziński was in warm relation with the Unitarians of Transylvania, some of whom were angered at the role precisely of Socinus among them in (unintentionally) bringing about the imprisonment and death of Francis Dávid (1579). As with the Transylvanian Unitarians, so with most of the Lithuanian Unitarians, of whom Simon Budny was the theological spokesman, Budziński was in solid agreement; and with Budny he collaborated on a common historiographical project. At the same time, on baptism, Budziński and Socinus agreed in general with the Budnyites and perhaps the majority of the Transylvanian leaders of their time, as distinguished from their parishioners, that it was not an important rite.[39]

Lubieniecki was discreetly against Socinus in holding to believers' immersion. Because, nevertheless, Lubieniecki was presumably a nominal Socinian on the adoration of Christ (without, to be sure, ever mentioning the uniquely Socinian notion of the pre-Ascension ascension of Christ)[40]; because also he was Socinian in the compromise on the office of magistrate and the use of the sword, accommodative to the status of the patrons who remained loyal to the Minor Church; because he was nevertheless not so exclusive and indeed sectarian as was Socinus himself, nor so restrictive in his understanding of the scope of God's redemption and was hence ecumenical and more tolerant than Socinus; and finally, because like Socinus and unlike Budziński and many of the Transylvanian Unitarians, Lubieniecki was indeed averse to the idea of an earthly millennium to be ushered in by Christ—the Author of the *Historia* was in fact obliged to sift his sources and even suppress or quickly pass by incompatible data and uncongenial happenings proffered by Budziński. Probably in the end he felt that he had exhausted the first work of Polish Reformation historiography. He might not have been desolate to learn that Budziński's History did not survive intact. In any case, his synthesizing *Historia* is in stance believers' baptist, Christocentric Unitarian, neither Budzinian (that is, on magistracy and the millennium in the orbit of the Transylvanian Unitarians), nor yet in some of the most distinctive ways Socinian. For all these reasons Socinus himself, whose name was given to the movement and whose concepts sometimes scholars retroject into the period before his advent in Poland and Transylvania, is not especially prominent in the *Historia* (hence the inclusion of RD 8, the first *Vita* of Socinus).

Another historian who drew upon Budziński's History was Andrew Węgierski (1600–49), a Reformed minister of the tradition of the colonizing refugee Czech Brethren who had settled in Great Poland. That he had access to Budziński's MS History attests to the surviving links between the two branches of the Reformed Church in Poland. Węgierski was first pastor in Opole in Silesia, then rector of the academy in Leszno (where John Amos Comenius, d. 1670, published his most important work *Didactica Magna*, 1657), ending up as elder of the Calvinist churches in the district of Lublin. Węgierski's history embraced the story of the Czech Brethren and that of many of the Slavic peoples, and was published posthumously as *Systema historico-chronologicum ecclesiarum slavonicarum* under the ascribed name of Adrianus Regenvolscius (Utrecht, 1652). It is in this form that Lubieniecki quoted Węgierski here and there, although the version most accessible today is the second edition undertaken by the Polish Brethren themselves with a substantial appendix of new material under the proper name of the author and titled *Libri quattuor Slavoniae Reformatae* (Amsterdam, 1679).[41]

The other histories on which Lubieniecki drew will be further identified in the annotation. Suffice it here to say that his expository style was shaped in part by the masters of ancient and Renaissance historiography, well represented in his father's library; by the Polish chroniclers, some of whom were ''Protestant'' or sympathized with the Reformation; and by contemporaneous historians of France and Germany, both Catholic and Protestant. Lubieniecki was often quite discriminating in his efforts to get at the exactitudes possible amid contradictory evidence in his sources. He was more unconsciously tendentious than willfully so. He was in fact often limited by lacunae in the material that survived in the diaspora. He was moreover held back from giving a balanced and smooth exposition by the exigencies of his own life and his travels and by his involvement in his other works proceeding *pari passu* with it, for example, the three-volume *Theatrum Cometicum* (1666–68).

Without his lost original MS we can never know for sure, but it would appear that Lubieniecki did not revise his text very much. He never refers to a previous or to an anticipated mention of a topic by more than an occasional *supra* or *infra*. There is some repetition. The whole structure of the work in three books was partly undergirded by the theological conviction that it was necessary to trace separately the devolution of the doctrine of the Trinity in terms first of the Son and then of the Holy Spirit, while presenting a chronologically overlapping, separate account of the emergence of the practice of believers' immersion, yet fighting off at every opportunity the common charge of anabaptism (in the sense of polygamous, chiliastic, theocratic, bellicose Münster), although Lubieniecki mentions quite a few converts, particularly from Germany, who submitted to immersion after the manner of the Polish Brethren. As an historian of the Reformation who knew the main ecclesiastical histories of the Age of the

Fathers, including notably, of course, that of Eusebius of Caesarea, Lubieniecki retained in his account of the consolidation of the final theological position of Polish Unitarianism an unusually large amount of primary documents of synodal debate, credal formulation, and correspondence on theology and church discipline, even some letters of Calvin or parts thereof uniquely preserved by him.

Lubieniecki held to a theology of salvation history grounded in the Jewish Christian Hegesippus, parts of whose Memoirs are preserved by Eusebius of Caesarea, and according to which the history of salvation could be divided into grand periods, one being presumably that from Adam through Abraham, another from Abraham through Moses (neither of these developed by Lubieniecki), that of the Jewish Church extending from Joshua to the birth of Christ, and that from the birth of Christ to the rise of Luther in Saxony in 1517. Each such period was the story of the restoration by God of his truth for his people who thereupon lived under its benign effects for only 110 or 111 years. After the lapse of the first thirty years of progressive restoration of divine and saving truth, according to Lubieniecki that truth would then be suddenly reproclaimed in a memorable manner. For example, thirty years after his birth Jesus himself formulated the saving truth in the Sermon on the Mount. For the period of which Lubieniecki was primarily the chronicler and interpreter, thirty years after Luther's Ninety-five Theses, 1517, God proclaimed his abiding, corrective truth for the age in the incipient Minor Church in Poland in 1546 or 1547 through the (inspired) questioning in the library in Cracow of Andrew Trzecieski of separate prayers directed to Father, Son, and Holy Spirit—a questioning pursued memorably by a Dutch visitor with the enigmatic name of Spiritus (cf. RD 1). And also in 1546 in far off Italy through his (inspired) departure from a fraternity of seekers in Vicenza, Laelius Socinus undertook the trek that would bring him twice to Poland (cf. RD 5 no. 50) and in a way prepare for the arrival there later of his nephew Faustus. Indeed our Author skewed his account of the beginnings of synodal Reformed Protestantism in Poland by opening Book 2 with the arrival of Laelius Socinus in Cracow in 1551 as a formative event, having elsewhere obscured the role of another Italian, Francis Stancaro, whom he detested. Stancaro in fact organized the first synod, in Pińczów in 1550 (Pl. 17). Lubieniecki's largely undocumented surmise that Laelius Socinus, Pl. 13, was the seminal source of christological radicality in both Poland and Transylvania is compellingly borne out by Antonio Rotondò, 1986. Although Lubieniecki did not expressly say so, not completing his *Historia* beyond c. 1638/58, the close of the new 111 years of glorious restoration of the saving truth in universal history in precisely Little Poland came, alas, with the royal decree of banishment in 1658 of the Polish Brethren, exactly 111 years after Luther's proclamation of the Gospel, this the onset of still one more Fall of the covenantal Church of the people of God. Since Lubieniecki thus entertained both a progressive and regressive view of Church history, he, the authority also on the history of comets as possible omens, could descry the hand of God in both nurture and rebuke, sometimes in rather small and even trivial episodes woven into his *Historia*.

From his *Vita*, however, and his strenuous publicistic endeavors, it is evident that until well launched into his *Historia*, Lubieniecki had not given up the hope that the fateful royal decree of 1658 might be reversed.

Lubieniecki, visionary Sarmatian royalist, could probably be integrated into any history of the idea of Poland as the Rampart of Christendom (*antemurale* against the tyranny of the East). It is noteworthy, in any case, that although he respectfully refers to the Sultan as *Imperator Turcicus*, he never, despite his principal earning profession as diplomatic intelligencer, refers to the Tsar as other than the Grand Duke of Muscovy, and though an ecclesiastical historian, he intimates no awareness of a Patriarch of Moscow.

Lubieniecki had some sense (never clearly articulated) that may have derived in part from Dr. George Biandrata (d. 1588; Pl. 18), who had a powerful and abiding influence in Little Poland, Lithuania, and Transylvania, namely, that in the Eastern lands of Latin Christendom, on the borders with Orthodoxy and Islam, God was enabling an international congeries of apostolic lay churches to take shape under benign kings, princes, and lesser lords and educated pastors, these latter to be devoted (preferably) wholly to things of the spirit and to instruction in the devout and moral life. Thus, despite his Polonocentric theodicy, as a polylingual cosmopolitan divine and lesser aristocrat, long engaged in amateur diplomacy, Lubieniecki included within his purview the Unitarians of Transylvania, who, in the person of Francis Dávid himself, seem to have held to a comparable restorationist and eschatological view that placed Reformed and expectant Transylvania at the center of Christ's prospective millennial realm.

Although Lubieniecki glosses, trims, passes over in silence, or exaggerates at points in his narrative, he was basically too good an historian not to weigh the evidence of the documentation before him so that his theology of history serves more to undergird and sustain him in his hard task as chronicler than to distort the factual evidence. But the position of his wider family in Polish society during the hopeful decades and his own position at many a court and colloquy clearly operated to induce him to minimize or pass by the radical social ferment in a tumultuous phase of the history (1569–72) of the Church he chronicled (hence my compensatory inclusion of an excerpt from the Author's uncle on the ferment and factionalism and a catechesis closing off that episode, RD 6 and 7).

III. More on the Churches and Peoples of the *Historia* and Its Rendering in English

Lubieniecki, after getting over his surprise that his narrative needed to be put into a world language other than his Baroque Latin, could be irritated by my edition of his *Historia* as a document of his age and that also of the age of Budziński, since, despite his evident haste in composition and its incompleteness, our Author considered his *Historia* to be a major record and interpretation of God's fulfillment of the Reformation and hence his Restoration of pure apostolic Christianity or, simply, the revealed *Veritas* under the new Augustus, Sigismund II, the last of the Lithuanian Jagiellonian dynasty to rule Poland.

Lubieniecki interpreted his native land as the world theatre of the mighty acts of God for the clarification of the simple terms of salvation for all Christendom. Any ambitious editing, apart from the clarification of names obscured in the meantime, and the correction of a few infelicities in the posthumous transmission of his Latin manuscript into print by Wiszowaty, could appear to Lubieniecki therefore as a trespass on his legacy. And even some users of his printed Latin text might find my subdivision of the chapters in English meddlesome.

But the fact is that Lubieniecki's valuable text has been quoted and plundered for data without much sustained attention paid to his overall vision of the history of Christianity, its fall and renewal in Saxony, its partial purification in Switzerland, and its "complete restoration" in Little Poland, and with some important reservations hinted at by Lubieniecki himself, in Transylvania. His *Historia* has thus seldom been grasped as a whole, even by those who read the Latin easily or who have used the Polish version of the first two books. But the text of Stanislas Lubieniecki, built on the Polish text of Stanislas Budziński and stimulated by the appearance of a Unitas/Reformed version of Slavonic religious history by Andrew Węgierski, emerged from his pen with such a freight of primary sources while being itself a witness to the faith of the Polish Brethren in the age of the banishment from the Commonwealth that it finally deserves to be seen not only as a composite of documents and a quarry of data, but also as an historiographical composition in its own right, an *apologia* for the Minor Church in the providence of God, regathered amid the exigencies of dispersion.[42] As already remarked, Lubieniecki intended a second tome to supply the constitutional context of the rise and fall of his Church.[43]

Lubieniecki, having grafted his scions into the winestock of Budziński, constructed also the trellis on which in due course my own leafy annotation flourishes intended to supplement and sustain by further documentation his compact planting. But the flowers, the grapes, the wine are his. The fragrance and both the sweet and the bitter taste of another age become ours in savoring his *Historia*, thanks to his sedulous effort to cultivate the roots of his own faith and that of his people of the same faith. It is poignant that despite all their ardor for the aristocratic democracy of "the Sarmatians," the royal Commonwealth of constitutionally guaranteed confessional liberty, the Polish Brethren had to flee from their vineyard in 1660, not however, without leaving upon the Polish soil and evidently in the national character and social culture something of their spirit and legacy of reasoned dissent.

Many of the Protestant architectural monuments and mounds in the territory of the old Commonwealth are locally, and sometimes even in the earlier scholarly literature, identified as "Arian" even when many of the sites are in fact Calvinist. And this frequent misidentification seems to attest at once to the ancient hatred of, and to the progressive admiration for, this exiled or underground component in the Polish national psyche, in which dissent has still an honorable resonance along with prudent conformity and courageous solidarity.

Lubieniecki, like his contemporaries who were driven out or obliged to renounce their distinctive tenets, disallowed as invalid the two charges of "Arianism" and "Anabaptism" and remained to the end half-puzzled over the reasons why the Brethren should have been proscribed, and hoped (despite a countervailing pessimistic cyclical theology of history) to the last that a new King would beckon their return to the Fatherland.

A. The Minor Church and the Ancient Symbols of Faith: The Apostolic Doctrine of the Oneness of God and the Redemptive Mission of His Son as Mediator

The proto-Unitarians of the Italian diaspora, of the Commonwealth, of Transylvania, and elsewhere, are today in the scholarly literature commonly called Antitrinitarians. The term will not have come into *general* pan-European usage until somewhere—and it was in Transylvania—the proto-Unitarians accepted the term Unitarian for themselves, namely, at the synod and diet of Dées in 1638 which in turn presupposed the acceptance by the orthodox Reformed of the term Trinitarian in their conservation of the ancient formularies. "Trinitarian," which could in the sixteenth century have designated a medieval Augustinian order, was for a brief period used also to designate precisely those later identified as Unitarian, for example, in the mandate against them by Maximilian II for his Hungarian lands in 1570 (Pl. 42). It is quite possible that the first to have used the term "Trinitarian" for the followers of the Nicene formulation was Michael Servetus (d. 1553; Pl. 25) himself and then, as though himself still Nicene, by the Unitarianizing Prince Nicholas Radziwiłł the Black of Vilna (Pl. 14) in a hortatory letter to Calvin in 1561. And the very first use of the term "Antitrinitarian" in English may have been in the *Relation* of the Elizabethan envoy to Poland (1598; RD 9, at n. 33). Given, however, the late emergence or clarification of these terms, Trinitarian (in the sense of orthodoxy as to the Trinity), Antitrinitarian, and Unitarian, the scholarly nomenclature for parties and churches in the sixteenth-century ferment is always fraught with the hazard of anachronism, the more so since many of those included approvingly, for example, by Sand and Wiszowaty as Antitrinitarians in the seventeenth century, were in their original intentions only striving to make the received Triadology more plausible in the Age of Renaissance and Reformation. For example, Michael Servetus was an Antitrinitarian only in the sense of proposing another Triadology in which Jesus Christ was almost physically engendered by the breath of the Almighty by way of the ear and lungs of the Virgin. And many of the proto-Unitarians in their first phases were unembarrassed to think of themselves as Tritheists and then Ditheists (RD 5, n. 20).

Indeed the latter, called sometimes in the Latin *Bideitae* in the Commonwealth, withdrew from the main body of Antitrinitarian Reformed to constitute a congeries of well disciplined congregations in the southeast of Little Poland from Nowy Sącz to Lusławice under the leadership of Stanislas Farnowski (d. c. 1615), an ordained Calvinist minister who undertook further philological and biblical study in the universities of Marburg and Heidelberg and the

Carolinum in Zurich to return to a renewed career as theologian and apologist for the Ditheist/Binitarian or Farnovian Reformed Church that survived into the early seventeenth century. Such was the range of theological conviction and schism among those in the Commonwealth who separated from the Major Church which upheld the Nicene formulary as loyal Calvinists (*Calviniani/Kalwini*) that the generic term for all the groupings to their left might well have been Anti-Nicenes (who in varying tempos of transition also thought of themselves as faithful to the Ante-Nicene as well as Apostolic testimony before Constantine imposed his will).

These two terms, "anti" and "ante" might indeed be used retrospectively among today's scholars seeking to clarify the range of theology and churchmanship in the eastern realms well into the opening of the century of Lubieniecki.

Although the term Antitrinitarian, scarcely used by proponents of theological reconception in the sixteenth century, has established itself in the scholarly literature, it is not amiss to encourage the occasional use of "Anti-Nicenes" as a complementary generic collective term, especially for the Commonwealth, where the designation Polish Brethren is mute as to theological positions, and in any case imprecise as to geographical and ecclesiastical scope.

Clearly from the rich documentation provided by Budziński and Lubieniecki, the Polish Brethren struggled harder than any other "sectarian" regional movement in the Reformation Era with the four ancient symbols of the Church, including the exclusively Western *Athanasium*. At the beginning even Luther and then Calvin openly acknowledged a preference among these symbols for the Apostles' Creed, while the Polish Brethren for their part retained to the end precisely the *Apostolicum*. Moreover, during the controversies within the Reformed Church that attended the devolution among the radical party of the dogma of the Trinity in adhesion to the *Apostolicum* as limpidly unphilosophical, as biblical, and as apostolic, the proto-Unitarians resolutely and in most cases validly disavowed as theirs the specific position of Arius himself ("there was [within the Godhead] when [before creation] he [the Son] was not") and that of many of several different schools of Arianism in the fourth century.

There was, of course, no acknowledgment, among those conscientiously and diligently engaged in unraveling the received dogmas of Christology and the Trinity that precisely the philosophical terms anciently and currently employed in their defense and to which the proto-Unitarians took exception, constituted a monumental humanistic achievement in pointing from within the scriptural experience to something profound about the abiding intra-deical reality that creates, sustains, forgives, and renews; that breaks through by grace the ordinary supportive or oppressive enclosures in evolving communities and larger societies; that is at once transcendent and immanent, above the created order and yet inextricably engaged and manifest in law and mercy, in justice and grace, in Christ prophetic, in Christ crucified, in Christ exalted, in Word and sacrament: a transcending immanence to which human beings have responded in wisdom and childlikeness, in awe and humility, in liturgy and good works.

So much were the theological radicals offspring of the great Reformers that, with them, they disparaged any demonstrations of an alleged *praeparatio Evangelii* among the heathen, while their classical Protestant adversaries were restrained and even hobbled in their attempts to defend the received dogmas concerning the divine plenitude and action by also seeking to confine themselves wholly to scriptural terms.

Almost the longest document embedded in Lubieniecki's *Historia (234–38)* is John Sommer's *De Papano Trino* (Kolozsvár, 1571), a spirited demonstration of the falsity of the dogma of the Trinity as allegedly imposed by the Pope. Its falsity is presumed precisely for the reason that the philosophical formulas used in its defense were repetitive of, or analogous to, phrasings about the divine reality, about "that which is" in Greek philosophy and notably in Plotinus, and that they were therefore palpably spurious because not scriptural, that is, not revealed. Biblical Unitarians were thus closing themselves off to a fundamental conception of many ancient Apologists that the eternal Word had as the *Logos spermatikos* working in the minds of the Greeks prepared the way for the fuller understanding of the special revelation in the Old Testament and the Christ event. Their distaste for the philosophical terminology that they ascribed to papal (scholastic) interference with the simplicities of the apostolic truth persisted even though the Brethren in *Polonia* were initially drawn to Irenaeus, even to Hilary of Poitiers on some special points; and it was their party that rendered from the Greek of Justin Martyr into Polish the *Dialogue with Trypho the Jew*—the first vernacular version anywhere (Nieśwież, 1564).

When Origen dealt with the Trinity in Περὶ Ἀρχῶν (*De principiis*), he set forth a Triadology in terms indeed related to those of Plotinus, for both had been pupils of Ammonius Saccas (d. 242), the reputed founder of Neoplatonism; but his Triadology was programmatically against any anthropomorphism of the three divine *Principia*. In the decisively formative period of Christian theology, that is, during the patristic and conciliar formulation of Triadology and Christology, Greek Orthodox theologians, retrieving and adapting a distinction in Aristotle, distinguished between apophatic (negative/reticent/later even mystical) theology and kataphatic (positivistic/explicit/even anthropomorphic) theology. These two modalities of theology were kept closely in touch with each other philosophically, devotionally, liturgically, and iconographically. In any case, the Byzantine Church all along the rite boundary through the eastern realms, having once gone through the First Iconoclastic Controversy (726–80), the seventh ecumenical council, on the veneration of icons, Nicaea II (787), and the Second Iconoclastic Controversy (814–43), each episode with only echoes in the Latin West, remained reserved about imaging the divine and the saintly and had habituated the societies of Eastern Christendom to represent the Godhead only through representations of the Second Person in the two Natures (Council of Chalcedon, 451), as Infant in Mary's arms, as Teacher, as the Crucified or, in the cupolas of their their basilicas, as the Ascended Lord, the Christos Pantocrator, Christ the Omnipotent, ruler and final Judge. Of the other persons of the Godhead there could be only the sparest and rarest of merely symbolic visualizations. This iconographic reticence was quite different from what obtained in

Latin Christendom in the throes of the Reformation, with their surviving Gothic anthropomorphic visualizations, common to most parties, of three divine Personages enthroned in heaven (Pl. 18)—even among those who were deliberately iconoclastic.

Repelled by late medieval iconography of the Trinity, the theological radicals could not accord any status to the view that the patristic and conciliar formulation of the triadic and yet triune character of the divine (as neither radically dualist nor incoherently multifarious) had been dogmatically forged to commend the received Christocentric redemptive monotheism of the Judaic tradition to the sophisticated Hellenistic mind. Nor were they aware of the degree to which the Fathers themselves eschewed any iconic visualization of the Three Hypostases of the Trinity, any visualization of the Three as anthropomorphic figures except for the exalted Christ. The early Church had inherited from Judaism the idea of a preexistent (created) Messiah. But for Hellenistic Christians, Jesus as that Christ was the unique visualization (embodiment) of the Godhead (John 1:18; 14:9, etc.), which remained otherwise invisible and for a long time beyond the scope and daring of Christian iconography. Indeed Byzantine Christianity, even after the definitive legitimation of holy pictures by Nicaea II in 787, remained reserved about iconographic representation of the Trinity (only symbolically in the three angelic visitors to Abraham and Sarah under the oaks of Mamre).

Protestant theological radicals, especially those on the Byzantine-rite and Muslim frontiers, found the late medieval iconographic representations of the Triune Persons as royal or prelatical personages intolerable. They soon began to question liturgical address and the practice of addressing the persons of the Trinity in separate prayers (RD 1). The questioners were no longer aware that in Christian antiquity these potencies in the divine had been conceptualized as *Principia/Archai*, among which were the filial principle as offspring, issuing from the First as eternally engendered, and the Third "proceeding" (but not emanating) from the First as the spiritual Principle, the *Creator Spiritus*, by whose will the world's foundations first were laid, yet visiting every pious mind. Apophatically the Fathers had pointed to the eternal pulsation of the triadic divine force, understood as uniquely embodied in Christ, against any fundamental separation into a cosmic good and cosmic evil. Triadology had emerged as a conciliar transcription of what the Fathers embraced as a coherent, stabilizing, and teleological understanding of the divine reality.

The initial debate within the eastern Protestant churches was christological rather than trinitarian in both Transylvania and the Commonwealth.

Among the first crucial figures in the debate in Lubieniecki's *Historia* were Lutheran Andreas Osiander (d. 1552; Pl. 7), a creative professor in Königsberg, and Reformed Francis Stancaro (d. 1574), who was patristically and scholastically more nearly "correct." They were the most spirited in coming to grips, as antagonists, with a problem that had come to center for them in the new Protestant formulations about justification and the mediatorial role of Christ, and whether this was accomplished in his human nature only (Stancaro) or in both natures (Osiander). The crucial text was 1 Tim 2:5: "For there is one mediator between God and man, the man Jesus Christ." Each theologian was in turn pilloried by Lutheran or fellow Reformed divines from Königsberg to Kolozsvár, and Stancaro is almost vilified in the *Historia*, even though in the end the proto-Unitarians came to offer exactly what Stancaro defended: Jesus Christ suffered solely in his human nature as the unique Son of God. What they put aside was the triune Godhead that (quite arrogantly) he had sought to uphold in patristic and scholastic terms.

The proto-Unitarians, whose history is chronicled by Lubieniecki, spurred on in part by the initial issue of Christ the Mediator, in their synodal disputation, far-ranging correspondence, and extensive local publication, relinquished—here more gradually and equivocally, there more swiftly and confidently—the two great conciliar formulations of patristic antiquity: that of "the three Persons in the one *substantia/essentia*, Greek: *ousia*" of the Councils of Nicaea and Constantinople I (325, 381) and that of the hypostatic union in Christ, "the one *persona/hypostasis* Greek: *prosopon* in (or: out of) two natures" of the Council of Chalcedon (451 and its further refinements to Nicaea II in 787). In going so far, the proto-Unitarians in their synodal churches separated themelves theologically from all other Christian bodies in the Reformation Age, whether territorial or separatist, even from most Anabaptists and Spiritualizers, although in common with the various separatists/dissenters most of their congregations were indeed "gathered churches" in contrast to "given churches" (both kinds, to be sure, usually under nobiliary patronage, section B).

In antiquity Triadology was conciliarly defined in the scriptural and liturgical life of the community of faith before Christology in the narrower sense. Christology could for the nonce be called "messianicity" or even "messianology," in order to restore to prominence "sacramental anointedness," covenantal kingship, and the prophetic and priestly offices of the Messiah. And thus to prescind for the moment from all Chalcedonian connotations of the One *Hypostasis/Prosopon* in two Natures, it could then be proposed that triadological speculation and controversy in the third and fourth century set forth the uniqueness of the religious experience of the Hebraic/Jewish people in terms sufficiently clear to commend to the Hellenistic mind, with its indisposition to conceive of God in motion or as suffering, the great ideas of creation and a decisive *historic* redemption, and then that the "messianological" speculation and conciliar controversy and definition from the fifth to the eighth century safeguarded the Hebraic sense of uniqueness in time, in history, and in the personhood of Jesus as Saviour and thereby prevented any "acute Hellenization" of the primordially Hebraic particularities: the Red Sea, stone tablets, uniquely incarnate anointed Word, the Jordan, the upper room, crucifixion, and the speaking in tongues.

In Christian "messianology," alongside the philosophically crafted conciliar formulations, another lesser formulary developed out of scriptural typology in reference to the succesion of divine unctions of the Hebrew prophets, priests, and kings, climaxing in the *triplex munus Christi*. The notion of the threefold office of Jesus Christ as Prophet, Priest, and King was put forward, among others, by Eusebius of Caesarea. Although only one prophet in ancient Israel is scripturally recorded as having, in fact, been anointed, Elisha by Elijah (1 Kgs 19:16), the priests and kings were covenantally consecrated. The prophetically anointed king was preeminently *mashiach*, the Lord's anointed. In the *triplex munus Christi* Jesus was perceived typologically as having discharged all three offices, even though there is, of course, no one passage in the New Testament where he is compactly called the final prophet/teacher, the high priest of redemption in the tabernacle of the Most High, and the King of the universe and eschatological judge of the human race. In the course of the Western Middle Ages the *triplex munus Christi* was lost to view in the perennial conflict between *sacerdotium* and *regnum*, between the two swords and the two powers (Gelasius I), between the sacerdotal authority of the Pope and the temporal power of the Emperor and the kings. Erasmus, editor of the collected works of several Church Fathers, first revived the patristic triad of Christ's offices. And several reformers (including Laelius Socinus in his *Confessio* of 1555), under the impact of the Hebrew and Greek text of the Bible, proffered several variants and emphases, until at length the threefold office was standardized in nomenclature and sequence as that of *propheta, sacerdos, rex.*

Although the *triplex munus Christi* came in time to be associated especially with John Calvin,—and indeed it developed its modern career first within the Reformed tradition—the formulary was fundamental and quite probably prior in John Łaski (Pl. 20), who appears to have derived it directly from his teacher Erasmus (cf. Pl. 2), when he was a student resident with him in Basel (1524 – 25). In any case, Łaski emphasized the *triplex munus* in his career of reformer of East Frisia, then as superintendent of the Strangers' Church in London, through to the close of his career as reformer in Poland (1556 – 60). The *Confessio* of the still undivided Reformed synod of Little Poland in Pińczów of 10 August 1559 records the effort of the Polish Reformed to combine the Chalcedonian plenitude of the person of Christ, the role of Christ as the only Mediator (in the Reformation thrust directed against the intercessary role of Mary and the saints), and Łaski's own personal attachment to the threefold office of Christ scripturally anchored by typology (*Historia*, Bk. 2, n. 446). And the Minor (Reformed) Church, never expressly disclaiming Łaski, retained in prominence his *triplex munus Christi* as modified in their first *Catechesis* of 1574 (RD 7) and in the Racovian Catechism of 1605.

The retention of the scriptural, patristic, Erasmian, Calvinian, but also Łaskian christological formulary, even when reworked by Faustus Socinus with his teaching about a pre-Ascension of Jesus as ordained and uniquely commisioned *teacher*, with Socinus's distinctive emphasis on Christ as *high priest* in the heavenly Tabernacle and there the Mediator of the New Covenant in his redemptive blood (Heb 9:11 – 12, 15), and with his adorant view of the ascended Christ as vice-gerent of the Father and governor of the world and of the Church from heaven, kept the ongoing disputation of Socinians and Unitarians with the diverse defenders of the received dogma of the Trinity and Christology well within the canon of Scripture and almost without recourse on either side in the sixteenth century to natural theology and hence under the same canopy of theological discourse as other Protestants.

Indeed, the classical Protestant Reformers themselves and their Polish and Hungarian associates, unlike some Catholic controversialists, sought to defend the received conciliar Triadology and Christology wholly in scriptural terms as best they could against the radical scripturalists on their margins. Calvinist superintendent Peter Méliusz in Debrecen (Pl. 40), for example, could resort to such a neologism as *Jehovalitas* for the divine *substantia* common to the three Persons.

In its Greek form this would never have occurred to the patristic users of the Septuagint. Most of the Fathers, at least, scrupulously avoided any preincarnational anthropomorphism, as though the eternal Speaker in the Psalms spoke with the very voice and through the countenance of the Logos eventually incarnate in Bethlehem, who taught in parables in Galilee and cried seven last words from the cross in Jerusalem. The Reformed Church had, for its part, on principle cut itself off from some important supporting scriptural passages from the Apocrypha, for example, Ecclesiasticus and the Wisdom of Solomon that had perhaps influenced even Paul himself in his affirmation of Christ as the descended Wisdom-Word and that had served the conciliar Fathers in their appeal to the witness of the Septuagint (fuller than the Hebrew Bible) in their emergent Logos-Christology, then in their Wisdom-Word Triadology, and finally in their Two-Natures Christology.

In the threatened unraveling of the dogmatic tapestry of the ancient conciliar looms into component warp yarn and weft, the defenders of the old patterns and the detractors could alike get entangled in all the loosened threads, while the most earnest and theologically adroit Catholics, preeminently concerned with the overall shredding in the Protestant revolt of the seamless robe of Christ's body, in effect their papal Church, took little note of the subtle innovations in formulary by the Lutherans and the Reformed, especially in their new emphasis on Christ the Mediator. Catholic controversialists seemed satisfied that on Triadology and Christology, at least, the normative classical Protestants remained, as they professed to be, credally Catholic. Yet the whole of the patristic synthesis was perhaps imperiled unwittingly almost as much by the Protestant defenders as by the theologically radical Protestant assailants, joined as they were together in their common anti-scholastic, anti-philosophical stance, all Protestant parties alike struggling under the same parole and order of the day: *sola scriptura* and *ad fontes*. In their eventually panicked repossession of the conciliar dogmas in the process of being stripped down by the theological radicals to primitive Jewish Christian *theologoumena*, the classical Protestant divines, for example, Calvin in the face of Servetus, or in Transylvania, Méliusz in the face of Dávid, were no more willing than their theologically radical antagonists to accord a place to natural theology (unlike the Catholic theologians from the Apologists through Aquinas) and hence to the immemorial philosophical undergirding of the great conciliar formularies of faith.

In the face of the immense threat to all Christendom in the religio-political

challenge in Ottoman expansion, the determined affirmation of the Transylvanians, God is One (Pl. 45), functioned differently from the *ancient* Hebraic
commandment, "Thou shalt have no other gods before me." In the once
henotheistic context the ancient Yahwists could not yet deny the marginal but
tempting vitalities of the gods of the nations. In contrast, the Unitarians on the
Muslim frontier were now saying something quite different, though it might
sound the same, namely, that God is without a consubstantial Son or creator
Spirit, and is thus not unlike Allah and quite like "the one eternal God for aye
the same" of contemporaraneous Judaism. And neither the classical Protestant
divines nor the theological radicals were aware in the sixteenth century of the
degree to which there were analogies to the Trinity even in the Jewish Cabala
and in the Muslim doctrines of the ontological reality of the divine attributes and
of the historic, revelatory inlibration of the uncreated Koran.[44]

In the textually erudite effort of the academy in Kolozsvár to return *ad fontes*
(the project, a critical Protestant Latin edition of the Bible), the Unitarian leadership found sanction for the restoration of a primitive Jewish Christian Church as
preserved in the earliest strata of the New Testament and accordingly they
observed a very simple Lord's Supper, mindful of the eschatological petition in
Aramaic surviving in 1 Cor 16:22: *Maranatha*. They appealed to God as the
Lord of history to have Jesus come again. With the Jews and the Muslims, many
Unitarians awaited the imminent advent of the Messiah for the Final Assize.
Lithuanian Unitarians and most of those in Transylvania became nonadorants of
Jesus (as not being in heaven but kept hidden by God the Father in some secret
place after a but brief, confirmatory ascension, Mark 16:19; Acts 1:9) while they
eagerly awaited his return as the judicial Messiah on the earthly throne of judg-
ment and glory.

Some Polish, more Lithuanian, and almost all Transylvanian Unitarians were,
moreover, in varying degrees of conviction millennialists. And nowhere in the
eastern realms from Novgorod through Lublin and Spisz (Szepes, Zips) to
Kolozsvár, where various Christian groupings professed to be Judaizers or more
commonly were pilloried by other Christians for Judaizing, did millennialism,
adhesion to Jewish disciplines, and the observance of the Sabbath enroll so
many radically reforming Christians as in Transylvania. Indeed, by the seventeenth century Sabbatarianism, claiming some sanction from the final positions
of Francis Dávid himself, spread beyond the Unitarian Church into that of the
Calvinists even into Hapsburg Hungary as a socially revolutionary movement of
considerable surge.

Although Lubieniecki occasionally uses the term "Judaizing"—always
disparagingly—he evades, when he comes to it in the *Historia* (Book 3, chap.
11), any clarification of the three months of disputation between Socinus and
Dávid in the parsonage the latter's in Kolozsvár, 1578–79, over the adoration
of Christ and invocation of him in prayer. Dávid had been charged with "innovation," beyond the terms of the earlier interconfessional settlement, by arguing
for the theological impropriety of prayers addressed other than to God the
Father. Lubieniecki dismisses the episode as "a tempest in a teapot," although,

it resulted in the imprisonment and death of the nonadorant Dávid. The debate marked the onset of an irreparable schism within the congeries of hitherto closely interconnected antitrinitarian Reformed synodal churches in the eastern realms, notably into the (1) the Hungarian-speaking Transylvanian Unitarians who came to look back to Dávid, worsted by adorant Socinus, as their martyr bishop; (2) the Polish-speaking Lithuanian Brethren who, under the leadership of Simon Budny, the translator of the Bible into Polish, were similarly non-adorant, and finally; (3) the partly Socinianized Polish Brethren, who continued to construe the New Testament as largely superseding the Old, who for the most part continued catechumenal baptism by immersion despite the programmatic minimilization of the ordinance by Socinus himself, yet who were nevertheless reinforced in their ongoing Christ-centered piety by Socinus's own eucharistic and adorational theology. Lubieniecki could not have been ignorant of the prevailing grouping among the Lithuanian Brethren who retained the Old Testament in full force and, regarding the Bible as revealing the one covenant in two dispensations, upheld their baptism as the counterpart of circumcision, and found biblical sanctions for their perpetuation of feudal arrangements, while as nonadorant Unitarians they could not countenance Socinus's hermeneutical legerdemain in defense of the adoration of Christ. Although his pages allow us no glimpse of the Budnyite lords and princes of Lithuania, Lubieniecki, who remained a catechumenal immersionist but may well have ceased to be an adorationist, could not but have known that Budny, a correspondent of John Foxe of the English Book of Martyrs, who was in close touch also with the radical biblical leadership among the Transylvanian Unitarians, was excommunicated by the Polish Brethren on the initiative of Socinus on the very issue of adorantism and several interlinked society-related ethical issues (for instance, the office of the sword) and also that for the same reasons Budziński, too, was excommunicated from the main body of the Polish Brethren.

Although adorant Socinus visualized the Ascended Christ as ceaselessly watchful vicegerent of God the Father in the throne room of heaven and as sustainer and quickener of his Church beneath, in word and at the eucharistic sacrament, the surviving iconography of the Polish Brethren centers in the crucifixion, while for Lubieniecki himself only the anthropomorphism of God the Father survives in his own notable iconography (Pl. 63).

The Socinianized Polish Brethren in Little Poland and increasingly in the Ukrainian palatinates, differentiating themselves from the Polish-speaking Unitarian Brethren within the retrenched boundaries of the Grand Duchy and also from the anti-Socinus Transylvanian Unitarians, sought reunion or merger with other evangelical bodies in and beyond the Commonwealth in a succession of overtures. In their retention of the Apostles' Creed linked with their catechumenal immersion, the Polish Brethren stood apart from the two other main groupings into which the congeries of antitrinitarian Reformed synods in the three eastern royal realms had divided. Their own faith and practice had been especially shaped in reference to the divine epiphany at the immersion of Jesus in the Jordan (Matt 3:17 – 17) when the Spirit of God descended like a dove (construed by the Polish Brethren as the divine gift of grace with the patristic sanction of Hilary of Poitiers) and when the voice of the heavenly Father was heard saying: "This is my beloved Son, in whom I am well pleased." Considering themselves, among the three main regional groupings of theological radicals, as the most conscientious and consequent restorationists of the primitive dogma of the saving truth and of the canons of apostolic practices, the Polish Brethren, confident that they were in line with the main Ante-Nicene tradition before the affirmations of the Primitive Church were "corrupted by philosophical formulations" in its entanglement with the imperial state apparatus, on many more occasions than Lubieniecki reports, extended repeated overtures for reunion to the Calvinist Major Church in Poland and for federation: with the Lithuanian-Polish Ditheists (RD 5, n. 20), with the anabaptist Hutterite communitarians in Moravia, with the Mennonites in the delta of the Vistula (and much later in exile in Holland), and with the Remonstrants (Arminians) in Holland. Yet their christocentric Unitarianism enframed in the *triplex munus Christi*, their practice of trine immersion, their classical, patristic, as well as scriptural learning, their critique in the light of the revelation of Christ of feudal institutions, all mitigated against the success of most of their initiatives. In their principal places of exile after 1660, East Prussia, Transylvania, and Holland, they rapidly lost ecclesial substance and discipline; and their movement was dissipated in dismembered philosophical and religio-political tracts and scriptural commentaries.

The *Historia* documents incidentally what appears to have been a structural instability in the Reformed Churches precisely in relation to the received dogma of the Holy Trinity, as distinguished from the lesser strain in the same period within both Anglicanism and Lutheranism. Although primarily recounting the history of the antitrinitarian Brethren in Little Poland, Lubieniecki directly or indirectly touches upon the cleavage into the equivalent of his Major and Minor *Reformed* Churches in Lithuania, in Ruthenia, Transylvania, and on a smaller scale and disproportionately in the Rhine Palatinate (Reformed, 1559–76), in several Swiss Reformed cantons, especially among refugee Italian converts there, and in the Netherlands, although here the split between the strict Calvinists and the Remonstrants of 1618 originated in the issue of predestination rather than in Triadology. He seldom glances in the direction of Bohemia-Moravia or of Upper Hungary (Slovakia).[45] Of the Polonian chroniclers of the Polish Brethren, only Wiszowaty survived until the time of the comparable Reformed schism in England and New England.

The proponents of the radical Reformations chronicled or alluded to by Lubieniecki, especially within the converging tradition of the Minor Church in Poland that had nurtured him, all yearned to recover the apostolic and the Ante-Nicene tradition in polity and discipline, no less than in theology. How the spokesman of these reforms in the interstices of several regions and societies within the three eastern royal realms—Slavic, Hungarian, and colonialist Germanic—variously dealt with the creeds, canons and liturgical legacy of the ancient Church under the impact of the Reformation belongs in its way to general Church history and is surely all the more integral to the record of the

Christian heritage in time and place by reason of the moral earnestness and the biblical and patristic scholarship that the exponents marshaled in their endeavor to return *ad fontes* all along the Byzantine-rite frontier of Latin Christendom amid reformatory and nationalistic convulsion. In their recurrent and eventually *characterizing* concern to uphold mutual confessional respect and religious toleration amid disparate convictions about the truth strongly sustained, these exponents of several radicalizations of the Reformation impulses also pioneered in shaping new modalities of relationship among churches, the state, and society in a congealment of a tradition of their own still to be more fully vindicated (Section III D).

B. The Minor Churches of Poland and Transylvania and the Radical Reformation

In the editing of the *Historia* I have had occasion to test further on eastern European terrain some of the principles that governed my conceptualization of an interconnected pan-European Radical Reformation. Notably involved was the validity and applicability of the term Evangelical Rationalist, which I introduced in 1958 as one of the three thrusts of the Radical Reformation, along with Anabaptism and Spiritualism.[46]

Under Evangelical Rationalism, among others, I then included Servetians, the Italian *eretici* of various convictions who became dissatisfied with Luther and then with the major Swiss divines, the Socinians, and the Transylvanian Unitarians. Without much use of the term itself, these with their kinsfolk appeared in various sections of my *The Radical Reformation*. While working on the English edition of *HRP*, I was also substantially revising and enlarging what became *La Reforma Radical*, translated by Antonio Alatorre.[47] My term Evangelical Rationalist may still be useful in referring to certain distinctive formulations and embodiments of the Radical Reformation in Romance lands, particularly in Italy, especially if it is fully acknowledged that there were concurrently also distinctive manifestations of Italian Anabaptism and that in lands remaining nominally Catholic Nicodemism, pilloried by Calvin, is best understood as a reformed faith expressed by holding out rather than resorting to flight, and that Nicodemism and other forms of spiritual accommodation were often the Romance counterparts of Germanic Spiritualism of various emphases.[48]

At the same time I became more certain that several forms of the radical Reformed faith and practice in the Polish-Lithuanian Commonwealth were the Slavic counterparts of Germanic (Swiss, German, Netherlandish, English) Evangelical Anabaptism that, however, became explicitly Unitarian—even while often retaining the Apostles' Creed—while Germanic Anabaptism usually remained, at least nominally or conventionally, trinitarian, usually in formulations that even then were scriptural and apostolic rather than expressly Nicene.

Under Peter of Goniądz (Gonesius; Pl. 26), originally of Podlachia (d. 1573), Gregory Paul (Pl. 26), originally of Great Poland (d.c. 1591), and Martin

Czechowic (Pl. 27), originally of Cujavia (Kujawy) (d. 163), immersionists and pacifists, each for a while a Tritheist or a Ditheist rather than strictly a Unitarian (although the last two became that gradually), their movement chronicled by Lubieniecki was up to 1580 and beyond in part Anabaptist, non-violent, and in part sectarian-egalitarian in its radical societary thrusts.[49] The Evangelical Rationalist component, stemming partly from the Italian refugees in Poland or Transylvania and partly from the experience of an Italian sojourn by some of these Poles (like Gonesius, notably in Padua), prevailed only after the consolidation of Socinus's authority (1580) in Poland. In Transylvania, too, it was the preeminence there of resident aliens, like John Sommer (d. 1572; Pl. 38), Jacob Palaeologus (d. 1585; Pl. 28), and George Biandrata (d. 1588; Pl. 18) that imparted to the proto-Unitarian Church its Evangelical Rationalist thrust. This observation should not obscure the fact that the radically reformed Francis Dávid (d. 1579; Pl. 40), an alumnus of Wittenberg, had returned so far *ad fontes* that he sought to reach back to the beliefs and practices of the primordial Jewish Christian community and not merely to the primitive or apostolic Church of the whole New Testament. Nor may this observation about an Evangelical Rationalist interlude anachronistically obscure the degree to which specifically under the impact of Biandrata in 1580, and then the Unitarian Church in Transylvania as a whole, as of the synod and diet of Dées in 1638, prudently retreated from the most radical positions of Dávid, Matthias Vehe-Glirius (d. 1590; Pl. 44), and Palaeologus.

To make the confessional position of the pre-Socinian Minor Church in Poland clearer than has Lubieniecki, I have included in the appendix (RD 7) George Schomann's Christocentric immersionist Unitarian *Catechesis* of 1574, the forerunner of the much better known series of Racovian Catechisms of 1605 and beyond. The Brethren came to be baptized by immersion usually in the name of the Father, the Son, and the Holy Spirit in appeal to apostolic usage and according to the formulary of Matt 28:19, although there were some early immersions in the name of Christ alone with several sanctioning scriptural loci. Although there were also many recorded rebaptisms, some noted by Lubieniecki, notably of Germans joining the Polish Brethren on profession of apostolic faith, the Minor Church as a whole thought of itself rather as believers' baptist, immersing their offspring as catechumens in ponds and streams. By 1684 (in a note on Lubieniecki) Benedict Wiszowaty observes: "[T]he Unitarian Brethren, do not *require* those who were baptized in infancy to repeat the baptism" (*Polish Brethren*, 560). Because of the legacy of Socinus on baptism as a superseded rite of the apostolic age, a view which he tried to obtrude upon I Racovian Catechism (in Polish, 1605), and because the Brethren may well have been instinctively and also prudentially reticent about the details of what may have been even nocturnal immersion, the inattentive reader of the *Historia* might not come away from its often prolix pages with the proper impression, namely, that the Polish Brethren were for the most part immersionist Unitarians, strongly moralistic and puritan, yet tolerantly (in the end) embracing in the fold, like the Unitas Fratrum, fully pacifistic members and "conscientious participants'' in ''government'' and in defense on the local level and on the borders of the Commonwealth.

It is enlightening to observe that the role of Socinus within the ascetically and socially sectarianized Minor ''Church'' in Little Poland as of c. 1580 was comparable to that about a century earlier in Bohemia of Brother Lukas of Prague, c. 1490. The sometime Florentine courtier and scion of Sienese jurisconsults, a lay theologian, master of four of the ancient biblical languages (that is, including Syriac), rather swiftly moved the Polish Brethren to accommodate to the civil responsibilities of the lesser *szlachta* who continued to adhere to apostolic Unitarianism, even if this reorganization involved the excommunication, instigated by Socinus, of persons and groupings both to the left and the right. In Bohemia Brother Lukas, educated as an Utraquist, converted to the cause of the Unity of the Czech Brethren, soon became part of their ruling council of elders, and, espousing the Major Party of townsmen (n. 27), prepared to accommodate it to new circumstances. He reshaped it by 1494 with the condemnation of the pacifistic founders (notably Peter Chelčický) and thereby swiftly marginalized the rural, ascetic, and pacifistic Minor Party (Amosites) and through his infusion of intellectual energy and discipline created the churchly Czech Brethren, increasingly Calvinizing, many of whose leaders rose to civilian and cultural prominence even more in Great Poland than in Moravia. To round off the comparison it needs to be noted that the Socinianized Minor Church in Poland retained through the lifetime of the Sienese remolder of it and in many sectors to the end a more reasoned defense of even nobiliary pacifism than the Czech Brethren in Great Poland, although both groupings were dispositionally irenic and ecumenical as well as mission-minded.

In the annotation of the *Historia* I have largely eschewed my own typological terms for divergent sixteenth-century radicalities that stemmed in part, at least, from the common impulse in Luther's great paroles: *sola scriptura* and *sola fides* with modification of his third, *sola gratia*. But I have been attentive to the degree to which all three main thrusts of the Radical Reformation within the Holy Roman Empire reappeared by a generation's remove within the jurisdictionally comparably variegated and decentralized Commonwealth and within its ethnically and confessionally even much more diverse and variegated society, for which a general retrospective account of our Author's great uncle, Andrew Lubieniecki, in a famous passage on religious ferment in the Commonwealth in his *Poloneutychia* (Raków, 1616), is the best witness (RD 6).

Yet it has become also clear from my own research over the score of years since *The Radical Reformation* (1962) that one of my marks for the churches and sects of the Radical Reformation, namely their purported stress generally on the New Testament Covenant/Dispensation over the Old in contrast to the vision of the classical/magisterial Reformation of the one covenant in two dispensations with pedobaptism roughly the Christian counterpart of circumcision (Henry Bullinger, 1535), does not hold up completely for the Transylvanian Unitarians, even in the sixteenth century. Under the radicalizing impulse to return to the norms of primitive Christianity, many in Transylvania, including their leader Francis Dávid, found themselves under the impact of several Christian Hebraists, like the Heidelberg alumnus and pastor Matthias Vehe-Glirius (d. 1596; Pl. 44), akin to the pristine Christian devotees of Christ, for instance, in the School of St. Matthew. They became upholders of the Law in espousing Jesus as the Messiah yet to come, to vindicate his own and who in the meantime had intended that no jot or tittle be removed from the old commandments. We noted above how some radical Davidians or radical Judaizers, appropriating the legacy of Dávid in the early seventeenth century as Sabbatarians, resorted to circumcision, and observed the dietary laws of Judaism. For them, and for the Davidians of the sixteenth century, theologically radical as they had become, the separation of church and state was not a determinative issue—the less so for the extraordinary degree of multiple confessional toleration-establishment that developed in multi-ethnic Transylvania (see further, Section III D).

In any case, Unitarians in Transylvania had for a season enjoyed almost a preferential ecclesial status under John II Sigismund, and then in the seventeenth century down almost to the present have intermittently regained the advantages and experienced the restrictions of what could best be called an interconfessional pluralistic establishment. Thus a second important mark of the Radical Reformation, as I had originally conceptualized and then generalized about it, has needed modification, especially in reference to Transylvania. There the disposition to radical separation of church/sect from the state/magistracy in the urge to return to the norms of pre-Constantinian or even more specifically apostolic Christianity and, in modern terms, to constitute voluntary self-governing confessional communities was inhibited by princely prerogative and the advantages of a territorial settlement, even though pluralistic, and also by the legalistic loyalism (obedience to those set in authority) of primordial Jewish Christianity itself as excavated from the oldest strata of the New Testament. While the Transylvanian Unitarians were indeed theologically and even ritually radical, in the sixteenth century their movement swept up in its train the whole parochial structure of village and town, from nobles to settled nomads (the Szeklers); and in their traditional view of the proper relation of the ''state'' and parliamentary ''nation'' to their partly territorial church they did not differ very much from the Erastians (Antidisciplinarians) of the Reformed Rhine Palatinate, from among whom two Unitarianizing refugees, scholarly Hebraists, Adam Neuser and Matthias Vehe-Glirius (Pls. 43, 44), came to them and also to the Poles.[50]

At the same time, the Minor Church of the Polish Brethren in the Commonwealth, particularly in Little Poland, Ruthenia, and Volhynia, had come very close to being, under the aforementioned Gonesius, Gregory Paul, Czechowic, George Schomann, and Simon Ronemberg, Polish-speaking Anabaptists, especially during the socially most radical phase when many of their number directly participated in the communitarian experiment in Raków, 1569 – 72. On the issues of magistracy and the sword even under the moderating leadership of Faustus Socinus, 1580 – 1604, they remained distinguishable from the Major Church of consistent Calvinists in the same territories and from the Budnyite Lithuanian Brethren.

My terms "magisterial"[51] and "radical" Reformers have, therefore, to be nuanced for the Transylvanian, the Polish, and the Lithuanian Minor Reformed Churches. Initially under the tutelage of the Saxons, then of the Swiss, then in Transylvania also of the Rhenish Palatiners, their several presbyteral polities were worked out in lands that had been in any case traditionally more tolerant of a diversity of rites, confessions, and polities than within the ancient bounds of the Holy Roman Empire. In these eastern lands of Latin Christendom the principle of *cuius regio, eius religio*, elaborated in the Peace of Augusburg of 1555, could not have been appropriately or acceptably extended (on nobiliary patronage and ecclesial irenicism, see additionally in Section III D).

In the Commonwealth there were no quasi-sovereign city states as in the Empire, unless they be Danzig, Elbing, Toruń, and Vilna. And in Poland proper there were no ecclesiastical states (except Varmia) as distinguished from episcopal land; while even the princes in the Grand Duchy, though owners of vast tracts of towns and villages and surrounded with retinues and private armies, did not have the same authority and tiered ranks among themselves as with the princes within the Empire (Section C). And although Transylvania, for its part, was indeed by 1541 a nearly sovereign principality, it was still a complex congeries of hereditary and ethnic jurisdictions, of greater and lesser lords, of federated Saxon cities under their own distinct law, of Szekler nomad-yeoman commune under elected chieftains, of Walachian shepherds and peasants under various feudatories and urban Saxon bailiffs, almost all in one way or another represented among the estates of the three nations (near n. 59) in the territorial diet. In Transylvania and Bohemia and Moravia the towns were much better represented among the estates than in the Commonwealth. Clearly the "church-state" relations in all eastern lands of the three venerable subimperial royal crowns of "St. Stanislas" (Cracow), of St. Wenceslas (Prague), and of St. Stephen (Budapest after 1541, in Trnava) differed not only from what obtained in the Empire but also in Scandinavia (whence came Poland's Vasa dynasty) and under the fearsome autocracy in Ottoman Hungary, to which some of the narrative of the *Historia* takes its reader.

Because of the distinctiveness of the state constitutions and the societies of Latin Christendom east of the Empire (or, in the case of the Kingdom of Bohemia, of a unique status within it), the actual ecclesial polities and even the political theologies demonstrably differed in the Commonwealth, in Bohemia-Moravia, Upper Hungary (Slovakia), and in Transylvania among the Protestant confessions, and therefore also among the proto-Unitarians, from what prevailed elsewhere in Latin Christendom in the sixteenth century from the kingdom of Sicily to Scandinavia, from Spain to Scotland. Although Lubieniecki himself was a royalist even after his exile from Poland, and even though Budziński, on whom he drew, was a strident and carping hater of all bishops and an ardent supporter of strong patrons among the lesser and the higher nobility and of King Sigismund II Augustus in particular, as always a prospective convert to the Reformation, the *Historia*, as it comes from both hands, still contains evidence of the socio-politically radical character of particularly the Minor Churches in

Little Poland and in Lithuania, traits and developments brought out further in the
annotation.

The feudal lords, whether small landowners, or, in the eastern palatinates of
the Commonwealth, magnates and princes, who sponsored the Reformation,
were, to be sure, in some sense magistrates as *panowie* (masters, lords) engaged
by feudal right in *panowanie* (rule), theoretically holding the right of life and
death over their servants and serfs. And thus the churches (edifices, congregations, and synods) under the patronage of even the most pacifistic among these
panowie, who were sometimes moved by the Gospel to free their serfs, were
still in some sense therefore "magisterial."[52] Although some Protestant lords in
converting church buildings on their estates into acceptable meeting houses simply eliminated more or less of the medieval furniture, many others, in constructing edifices for their new congregations (*zbory*), set forth in the new architecture
their sense of a gathered church (Pl. 57). The new edifices often looked like
diminutive synagogues, many of which were later taken over for Jewish use.
Since the peasants on the estates were seldom drawn or coerced to break with
traditional forms and the liturgical calendar of saints linked to seedtime and harvest, the Protestant system of patrons, whether Czech Brethren, Lutheran, Calvinist, or Unitarian, was therefore never in the Commonwealth a royal/princely
territorial church (with the sole exception of Lutheran Ducal Prussia) nor an
urban/patrician church, nor seldom even locally a comprehensive parish church
with peasants included, as was, pluralistically adapted, the case of the Unitarians
in Transylvania. In Poland the Minor Church was in effect a gathered church
under the patrons who were themselves members, commonly (lay) elders, as
with the Czech Brethren and some Moravian and Slovakian Anabaptists. They
were the noble *fratres* and plebeian *bracia* together constituting one fraternity in
Christ, the *Polish Brethren*. Clearly something new was appearing in the Commonwealth and to a lesser extent in Transylvania: the toleration of a plurality of
confessions, ideally the renunciation of the use of coercion whether by the
hierarchical Church or by the central state apparatus, and the increasing dependence of the life and discipline of the ecclesial communities from within the
synod or the congregations rather than from above. And hence in reference to
the *ancien régime* of Latin Christendom, socio-politically, psychologically, as
well as theologically, the minor churches and sects in Little and Great Poland, in
Lithuania and Ruthenia, in Bohemia and Moravia, in Transylvania and Ottoman
Hungary were indeed radical departures from the consolidations and retrench-
ments of the Reformation elsewhere in Latin Christendom and constituted
together the regionally distinctive polities of the Radical Reformation socially
more comprehensive and theologically more drastic than those within the
Empire, while among three postulated thrusts of Reformation radicality, the
Evangelical Rationalist tended to dominate.

The Evangelical Rationalist character of the faith of Stanislas Lubieniecki
himself is iconographically well represented in the frontispiece of his design for
the *Theatrum Cometicum* (Pl. 63), wherein the book of *Revelatio* and that of
Ratio are held in the hands of the Almighty, the Bible with its two clasps to

suggest the two covenants being held above Reason, that God-given instrument for sorting out his intentions in the written word, while the figure of Christ whether in heaven or on earth is virtually unrepresented: an icon of Socinianism on its way toward Deism. Even though admittedly the Transylvanian Unitarians under the impact of Renaissance Rationalists, of the philologists of the Three Languages, and in a quite specific way of the radically Reformed Christian Hebraists, like Matthias Vehe-Glirius, finally reduced their Evangel to the proclamation of Jesus as the fulfiller of the Law in every jot and tittle, they still understood Jesus as God's Messiah destined to come imminently in judgment and vindication of his own who had faithfully observed the Mosaic commandments and both the Dominical precepts and Evangelical counsels and kept to the simplest Judaic form as they thought back to what they considered the intention of Jesus' Passover Supper.

In other words the radicals on the eastern marches of Latin Christendom in the sixteenth century, from whom Lubieniecki preserves in his *Historia* a partly muffled witness, partook of all the main traits of the Radical Reformation elsewhere during that century, although in different admixtures of motifs: Spiritualist, Anabaptist, and Evangelical Rationalist. Further, except that the Evangelical Rationalist component was strengthened in each of the three regions after c. 1580 and that the Transylvanian Unitarians were largely content to participate in a (preferably) tolerant and in any case necessarily pluralistic state-church establishment (that would only much later include the Orthodox Walachians in their midst), the *Historia* of Lubieniecki with annotation affords a valuable record of the theologically and socio-politically radical outreach of Protestantism in general in the Slavic, Magyar, and German colonialist regions of Latin Christendom.

C. Some Non-Theological Observations on Class and Confessions in the *Historia*

A nobiliary Pole, ordained to the ministry, Lubieniecki, who styled himself only as *eques*, never as *minister*, was also a townsman, at home in the college towns of Raków and Kisielin, in Toruń and Lublin, before he became completely cosmopolitan as a religious refugee, sojourning in towns along the Baltic and the North Sea. In the Commonwealth the towns and royal boroughs were sometimes heavily populated with German artisans and merchants, largely responsible for the adoption of Magdeburg or Lübeck urban law and custom, from Cracow almost to Kiev, a major contribution of Germanic culture and institutions to the whole of Latin Christendom to the east of the Empire, from Riga and Dorpat on the Baltic to Klausenburg/Kolozsvár and Kronstadt/Braşov not far distant from the Black Sea. In the multi-lingual towns of Poland proper, one heard, not only Polish, but also German, Yiddish, Ruthenian, Armenian, Hungarian, and Tatar; in Great Poland also Czech; in the Vistula delta and the staple towns and ports, Low German, Dutch, and Scottish (more than English); in the Grand Duchy, besides most of the aforementioned languages, Low German,

Prussian, Lithuanian, Byelorussian, and Russian; and in the sixteenth century Italian was also spoken among artisans, architects, engineers, painters, tradesmen originally drawn to Cracow and environs in the suite of Queen Bona Sforza, second wife of Sigismund I the Old.

Lubieniecki, recording aspects of the Renaissance in Poland, gives his attention to its noble patrons. And although Protestantism in his land was primarily the cause of the lower and the middle *szlachta* in their manors and baronial halls and the diminutive *zbory* (now in the sense of new meeting houses) on their estates, he notes also its headway among artisans, burghers, and patricians, some of the latter among whom married or bought their way into landed estates and the nobiliary rank. Our Author gives us glimpses of the Reformation in the lesser courts and in the towns, even if the peasants, artisans, and grooms for their horses remain but shadowy or even vaguely threatening figures.

For burghers called in the narrative *dominus/pan* and their wives, such approximations as sir/lady, master/mistress, Mr./Mrs. seem not to fit well. In a few instances I have used lord/lady (lower case), as most of the patricians had acquired landed property outside their towns. I have retained Master (*dominus/pan*) only for a clergyman where the text has a title, as with Master Calvin. Among the several kinds of professional men of education, theologians, royal secretaries, teachers, printers, and men of medicine are the most prominent in the *Historia*. Several of the theologians are referred to in the text by their university title of doctor. The nomenclature for Reformed pastors and superintendents is not fixed and seldom employed in titles, while Lubieniecki seldom refers to bishops of the old order with much respect and most often, as was in any case general, as simply Andrew of Cracow, for example, although with the Primate, it might be John, Primate of Poland. As elsewhere in the period medicine was in the hands of three kinds of professionals: the university-trained physicians who were often more philosophical than practical (although by way of translations from the German into Latin of Theophrastus Paracelsus [Cracow, 1569] and by way of a number of immigrant Germans and several Padua-trained Italian physicians, the newer experimental medicine was being practiced in Poland); the apothecaries, who concocted and also dispensed the old and new medicaments; and the barber surgeons. The *Historia* mentions physicians by their university title, notably Dr. George Biandrata (Servetus never so entitled), and a couple of apothecaries, notably Simon Ronemberg of Cracow (cf. Pl. 12).

I have, however, retained uncapitalized ''lord'' for *dominus/pan* as titles of nonclerical members of the lower and the middle *szlachta*, represented in the dietines and the Chamber of Deputies, e.g. lord Jerome Filipowski (an ancestor of our Lubieniecki). For a member of the higher, senatorial *szlachta*, I have rendered the same *dominus/pan* in the upper case, for example Lord John Firley, Protestant spokesman and Marshal of the Crown; and when the personage is of the lands of the Byzantine-rite, often of vast possessions, or a magnate in the Grand Duchy and where *Dominus* may well cover *Princeps/Książę*, I have rendered it Prince, e.g. Reformed Prince Nicholas Radziwiłł the Black. Where Lubieniecki has *comes*, literally *hrabia/Graf*/Count, I likewise render it "prince" as more consonant with the usage of the sixteenth century.

As the men of the nobility in the three Eastern-Central European royal realms were not clearly differentiated from each other by title, the generic term appears frequently especially in my annotation: Polish *szlachta*, Bohemian *šlechta*, Hungarian *köznemesség*, which terms only at their lower economic reaches can be rendered as "gentry" or "squirearchy." A sense of fraternity prevailed among them, as lands did not devolve by right of primogeniture. Constitutionally and economically there were, of course, considerable differences, though some, as magnates, belonged to the senatorial order or upper house of a national diet. There were two houses in Poland: bishops and magnates in the Senate, knights and a very few burghers in the Chamber of Deputies; three chambers in Bohemia: magnates, knights, burghers (after the elimination of the ecclesiastical estate during the Hussite wars); three estates in Hapsburg Hungary: bishops, magnates, knights; and three nations in Transylvania (see further Section III D).

Although Lubieniecki himself was quite possibly more reserved about women in church and society than might have been another chronicler of his age, even in his text women were evidently more common in the cause of the Reformation than in many other lands; and while their names do not abound in the text, allusions to them are there. As editor I have wherever possible recovered their Christian names in brackets. The first extant Polish Protestant hymn was by Sophia Oleśnicka, 1556 (Pl. 57).

The word "clan" occurs many times in rendering Lubieniecki's text, so inordinately filled as it is with proud references to familial and clan affiliation. Along with the manorial families and the clans we also read frequently of a sworn confederation and a legitimate confederated resistance to central authority, akin to the swearing of religious and constitutional covenants in Scotland into the nineteenth century. But still, "laird" will not do for *pan*, nor covenant for *konfederacja* and *rakosz*.

In the Polish-Lithuanian Commonwealth the *pan* was of the *szlachta*, the nobiliary class with their intense sense of fraternal cohesion as almost a race apart from their peasants. Among the *panowie* (plural) in principle, as already observed no social differentiation was made in titles and decorum. Any titles in Poland other than those of royal and palatinate functionaries, military and civilian, were honorific and bestowed from abroad, for example, by the Holy See or the Empire. The nobiliary proportion of the population was higher than in any other part of Europe, in some parts of the Commonwealth, in Masovia, for example, embracing twenty percent of the inhabitants. At the lowest level was the landless gentry of heraldic families (*gołota*), who became retainers in the courts of the more powerful landowners. Higher was the knight with his own *dworek*, a manor sometimes no larger than today's commissar's *dacha*, with but a few servants and serfs, all working on the farm together, yet not to be translated as yeoman, probably better as squire. At the highest nobiliary level were the magnates, owners of sometimes hundreds of villages and several towns. In the Byzantine-rite territory of the Polish Crown and in the Grand Duchy of Lithuania, where the Jagiellonian (Lithuanian) King of Poland (or his son) was *ex officio* Grand Duke, there were indeed semi-autonomous princes, in wealth and ownership the equivalent of Polish magnates, but with *de jure* as well as *de facto* more constitutional authority and local martial autonomy than even the Polish magnates, more like the knezes and boyars of Muscovy, Moldavia, and Walachia. After the Union of Lublin in 1569 (Pl. 32) and the extinction of the Jagiellonian dynasty in 1572, the vast southeastern portions of the Duchy came directly under the Polish Crown; and thus from the last third of the sixteenth century to the end of the period covered in Lubieniecki's *Historia* there were also true princes (Ruthenian) as well as colonizing Polish magnates and lesser lords in the palatinates from Ruthenia through Volhynia to that of Kiev. In consequence of the economic, social and political differentiation within the Polish *szlachta*, the highest personages of the nobiliary class were often only residually felt to be embraced in the term *szlachta*. Hence when this term is meant to embrace only the middle and lower *szlachta*, it is by convention translated into English as the gentry. But this, too, is scarcely satisfactory, as this English term is no longer capable of invoking the degree to which the members of the middle and lower *szlachta* retained feudal rights over their servants and serfs. The gentry retained, for example, the right to beat and incarcerate them. Killing an underling in the excesses of estate discipline was under the customary law only manslaughter lightly or evasively punished, whereas the like deed of a serf or servant enraged by the conduct of his lord was construed as first degree murder, almost as lèse majesty, the capital punishment for it often carried out on the estate.

The Author of the *Historia*, of the middle *szlachta*, was at ease with courtiers and patricians wherever he sojourned, and appears to have been personally much less concerned with the serfs and other peasants than some of the early lay members of his Church. These early converts often drew conscientious, self-sacrificial inferences from the Sermon on the Mount, and from the other evangelical counsels respecting wealth and landownership. Lubieniecki scarcely alludes to this motif in his *Historia* nor commends them for their espousal of a social gospel.

The members, mostly middle and lower *szlachta*, of all three and then the four Protestant confessions, espoused the Reformation in the sixteenth century primarily to rid themselves of oversight by the episcopal peers of the Senate and from the jurisdiction of their ecclesiastical courts and chanceries, while their noncoercive religious tolerance of the old faith and parish arrangements for their own servants and serfs smacked often of indifference to the spiritual welfare and the temporal conditions of their underlings.[53] Many of the espousers of reformation in the several confessions were quite indisposed to mingle with the lesser breeds without their ''fraternal'' code as knights, without their own cosmopolitan education and humanistic orientation. Yet among the (roughly) four Protestant confessions, there were several remarkable instances of the application of the Dominical counsels to social arrangements, especially among the early Unitarians. It is, therefore, regrettable that Lubieniecki so wholly concentrates on the recovery of soteriological ''truth'' that he offers no sustained treatment of the new vision of, and experimentation with, a just society, as expounded, for example, by the great publicist Andrew Frycz Modrzewski (c. 1503 – 72; Pl. 22, RD 1), whom he indeed occasionally mentions but only as a sympathizer of the Minor Church, and as ending his days in their bosom.

Lubieniecki in death was removed by almost a century from the apogee of the socio-economic and constitutional struggle between the gentry and the magnates in the movement for the Execution of the laws which began in 1505 (when the Polish Diet became fully bicameral). James Cairns Miller, drawing upon his unpublished doctoral thesis on the Nobiliary Republic (1977), makes this protracted constitutional conflict the context of his rich and compact interpretation of ''The Origins of Polish Arianism'' (1985).[54] The Execution movement, demanding political, fiscal, military, and religious reforms, including the limitation of the power of ecclesiastical courts and church tithes and taxes, was directed by the gentry against both the royally appointed episcopal Senators with their own *cursus honorum* and the allurement of competitive emoluments and power at the royal court and of centrifugal ambitions of the Senatorial magnates not resident at the royal court. It is generally agreed that the program of Execution in purported support of the centralist royal power (though by many scholars interpreted negatively as the brake shoe on the chariot of royal absolutisism in Poland) put severe strain on emergent Protestantism in its most formative period of consolidation and then schism. The gentry Executionists, to be sure, hoped deperately in synod (1562) for order and unity of faith ''in one kingdom and under one King.'' And indeed the King, against his previous reserve and equivocation, supported the movement in that same year. As the monographic literature is much more extensive than can be indicated here, it may suffice to refer to my discussion in the foreward to Document IX as well as in the general annotation. Miller's article, interweaving much of my own writings on the Reformation in the three eastern realms, serve's well as a parallel and complementary account to my own Introduction here, especially for developments in Poland through 1572.

D. From Ritual to Confessional Toleration
in the Background of the *Historia*,
from the Ritual Peace of Kutná Hora of 1485
to the Colloquium Charitativum of Toruń of 1645

A major conviction sustaining Lubieniecki in the *Historia* was that commitment to the truth as revealed in Scripture and as clarified by reason was compatible with the policy of religious toleration by the state, and with irenic deportment in mutual respect as among members of different traditions and ecclesiastical obediences, and this by way of dialogue, disputation, colloquy, and correspondence. (In him all Reformation-era resonance of hope in some final ecumenical council, present in even some of the early Anabaptists within the Empire, is dissipated.) Although the conviction as to the civil importance of toleration and concern for mutual denominational respect sustains the Author in exile and informs his text, he does not illuminate his two precious principles adequately in the *Historia*. But the prominence of them in my annotation makes it appropriate here to set forth the general lines and notable moments in the cumulative implementation of the twofold theme under the three royal crowns, Bohemian, Polish, and Hungarian/Transylvanian.

Irenicists in the realm and age of Lubieniecki could look back to a series of interconnected, cumulative events in the evolution of the ideals and modalities of toleration and of dissent and confessional pluralism in the lands of the three crowns. This began with a precedent set at Kutná Hora (Kuttenberg) in 1485, when, after two generations of civil war the adherents of the two rites—Catholic and Utraquist, Germanic as well as Slavic adherents in each allegiance—were recognized and sustained for all Bohemia in accommodation and civil acknowledgment of ecclesiastical dualism and mutual respect, without either rite's gaining special advantages from the diet or organs of the state. Religious toleration in Poland and Transylvania owed much to this Bohemian precedent.

An important component of this Czech/Bohemian inter-ritual debate, colloquy, and treaty was university disputation. None of the heirs of John Hus ever forgot that he had engaged in disputations (*hádání, pře*), that his reformation rose out of the university milieu, and that he was condemned to death by an *ecumenical* council (Constance, 1415) in which university dons shared in the magisterium with the bishops and abbots. Nevertheless, there persisted among the ritually divided Bohemians the conviction that the final truth—as between Hussites and Romanists—was something that could be ascertained by disputation and dialogue. The heirs of Hus continued to adhere to modified conciliarism, but they also developed new and less coercive ways of colloquy. Structured disputations modeled on those of the university and which assumed that truth could be excogitated out of the common scriptural, philosophical, and canonical heritage, became integral to the interior life of the Utraquist Church and also to the Unity of Czech Brethren (Unitas Fratrum) that broke from its obedience. Moreover, the Utraquist Church, the majority church of Bohemia, hesitated a whole century before completing its break with Rome, which had never recognized the first and only Utraquist Archbishop of Prague (John Rokycana, 1395–1471). Thus there were two parties of the one Church in Bohemia. The moderate Utraquist King George of Poděbrady had regarded himself as the King of Both Peoples, the major party keeping to its privilege of communion for the laity in both kinds; and he occasionally summoned convocations of the clergy of both parties or, from another perspective, of the two churches. Under his elected Jagiellonian succesor, Ladislas II (1471–1516) and in his spirit, the Utraquists and the Romanists agreed to the Religious Peace (Truce) of Kutná Hora, 13 March 1485. Bohemia thereby set a model of colloquy between churches or their leadership on the basis of two presumed unities, the unity of the kingdom of Bohemia and the unity in Christ in the same Church, although under different disciplines and obediences. These convocations of clergy under two separate disciplines were enhanced in importance for the reason that in the Bohemian diet the ecclesiastical estate (*curia*) had been eliminated in the Utraquist thrust toward a lay-dominated political system.[55]

A Czech Catholic humanist, Bohuslav Hasištenjský, commenting scornfully on the rapid extension of the principle of theological discussion to all strata of society, remarked three years after the ritual Peace of 1485 that in Bohemia "everywhere people talk about faith. Young and old, men and women teach and explain the Scriptures in which they were not trained. Nor does any new sect, as soon as it appears, lack adherents."[56]

The heirs of the Hussites in the course of civil wars with each other and foreign allies had by then divided into the territorial and liturgically conservative Utraquists, who held St. Vitus Cathedral in Prague, and the pacifistic Unity of the Czech Brethren among small townsmen and peasants.

In the Bohemian diet of 1508, the socially conservative Utraquists holding the archiepiscopal see of Prague itself (under an administrator answerable to the diet shorn of its ecclesiastical estate), joined with the Romanists, territorially a minority, in the mandate of St. James that was intended to rid Bohemia of the sectarian (separatist) Unitas Fratrum. Most of these Czech Brethren were driven out of Bohemia proper but were welcomed as enterprising refugees in the quasi-autonomous margraviate of Moravia, whence they to this day derive their other name, Moravian Brethren. Full, constitutionally sanctioned *confessional* pluralism emerged first in Europe in the dietine of Moravia in 1528. The Moravians, unlike Bohemia proper, had for their part retained their ecclesiastical estate of bishops and abbots. The prelatical estate, the Utraquists among them, joined the lords temporal and the burgher estate and benignly resisted from the start the obliterative St. James mandate intended for all lands under the Bohemian crown. In the first article of the first message of the three Moravian estates in 1528 to the newly elected King Ferdinand of Hapsburg, the dietine urged that the king "might allow all and everyone of us to persevere unhindered in the faith of the Law of God [of the Scriptures] and of the Christian religion so that everyone might serve the Lord God in freedom and peace according to what one considers the right following of the Law and Teaching of the Lord."[57]

Both the communication of the Moravian dietine of 1528 to King Ferdinand of Bohemia (also of Hungary), calling for intra-Christian confessional toleration, and the earlier Peace of Kutná Hora would become a melded paradigm for constitutional developments beyond the bounds of the lands under the Bohemian crown, and first in Transylvania. This took place midway in the rule of Queen Isabelle Jagiellonka (Pls. 32, 39), widowed queen of the elected king of devastated Hungary, John Zápolya, Ferdinand's rival for the crown of Hungary—she regent for his heir in Transylvania. Isabelle had evidently become familiar with the provisions of Kutná Hora while she sojourned in temporary exile from her provisional capital of Alba Julia (Pl. 39) in Cracow and in a castle in the Bohemian Duchy of Silesia with her son (destined to be the only professed Unitarian sovereign in history).

The Polish queen regent for her Jagiellonian-Zápolyan heir to what was emerging as a separate throne in Alba Julia, in her Transylvanian diet(ine) faced a much broader challenge of religious toleration than that of the two plenary sacramental Latin rites as at Kutná Hora in 1485, and that of the two socio-ecclesial families of latter-day Hussites recognized by the Moravian dietine (1528). In Transylvania in 1557 she with her advisors (one a professor of the University of Cracow) had to reconceive constitutional religious toleration in the still broader context of a territory that had been an especially constituted frontier military district of the Apostolic Kingdom of Hungary, from which, for example, Jews had been expressly excluded, a region extensively colonized by various ethnic groups enlisted to populate the valleys and uplands devastated by the Tatar invasion. The three "nations" that constituted the estates of the Transylvanian (county) dietine, becoming under her regency the diet of the enlarged principality of Greater Transylvania, were (1) the Saxon burghers of the constitutionally seven boroughs (*Siebenbürgen*, the German name for the whole principality), (2) the communitarian *Szekly*, German: Szeklers, preserving nomadic folkways with elected nobiliary chieftains, and (3) Western Hungarians who had settled after the same Tatar devastation and others settling later as a consequence of the Ottoman incursions since the battle of Mohács of 1526. To these Hungarians under the princes of Transylvania, in contrast to those under Ferdinand, I refer in the annotation as Magyars, the Hungarians' name for themselves, for the sake of a useful distincion in English, since all Christians within the multiethnic tripartitioned realm of Hungaria could in one sense or another be regarded or regard themselves as "Hungarian." The Saxon nation, made up of the representatives of the quasi-sovereign, constitutionally tight urban league of German colonists dated from the thirteenth century.

Protestantism swept early through the three constitutional "nations" represented in the palatine (county) dietine. In the whole of Greater Transylvania only about half a dozen magnate families survived the reformatory tide. Roman Catholicism was prelatically decapitated. All the benefits of the see of Alba Julia, including the episcopal palace, were expropriated by the new ruler. Protestantism in Transylvania enrolled a much higher percentage of the population of all classes even than Hussitism had in Bohemia a century before. Like Hussite Utraquism, Transylvanian generic Protestantism was at the moment of Isabelle's edict of toleration about to fracture into roughly three groupings, partly along ethnic lines: Saxon Lutherans, Magyar-Szekler Calvinists, and Magyar-Szekler proto-Unitarians. But before the issues of the theological meaning of *communio sub utraque specie* (whether the regnant eucharistic theology be that of Wittenburg or of Zurich-Geneva-Heidelberg) and of Christology-Triadology were to be resolved by synodal schism, the Polish Queen regent Magyarized the idea of a "national" (ecumenical) council/synod to mean pan-Hungarian. Although the Byzantine-rite Walachian (Romanian) Orthodox shepherds, villagers, and monks were constitutionally unrepresented and culturally ignored—for she still thought in terms of Latin Christendom—nevertheless she construed differences in confession of faith to have the same constitutional standing as differences in ritual and thus laid the basis for a comprehensive religious toleration that was intended to safeguard the exercise of her own (very broad) Catholic faith and, by the eventual, overdue application of the principle, that of her Walachian subjects as well.

Specifically Isabelle hoped at the Pentecost Diet of Torda in 1557 for a stilling of controversies "when in the presence of devoted ministers of the Word of God, as well as other men of rank, genuine comparisons of doctrine may be made under God's guidance" and thereupon "dissension and difference of opinion in religion may be removed." She, her advisors, and the dietine conselors envisaged a procedural accession to the saving truth. In effect, hers was thus a comprehensive grant of dynamic religious toleration. The edict read in part as follows: "We have assented . . . to the supplication [of the diet] . . . that each person [be permitted to] maintain whatever religious faith he wishes, with old or new rituals [that is, Romanist, Augsburgian, Helvetic], while at the same time we leave it to their judgment to do as they please in the matter of their faith, just so long, however, as they bring no harm to bear on anyone else at all, lest the followers of a new religion be a source of irritation to the old profession of faith [Catholicism] or become in some way injurious to its followers."[58] The intent of "each person" within the constitutional context of the extensive franchise in the seven Saxon boroughs (see Map) and dependent villages, in the Magyar towns chartered somewhat like them, in the Szekler communes, and in the many nobiliary courts, had even in a generally late feudal military society extensive scope. The confidence that the Polish-Lithuanian queen lodged in diet and synodal discussion is notable; and the national synod proposed by Queen regent Isabelle, who was still thinking of a synod for all of Christian Hungaria, remained through the century the presumed ideal. By the end of the sixteenth century, however, there would be the three already mentioned ethno-confessional Protestant synodal federations of churches: Lutheran, Calvinist Reformed, and proto-Unitarian Reformed, and after these successive schisms Isabelle's ideal pan-Hungarian "national synod" could be only nominally a single Christian synod, and then more as a religious colloquy only of lords, deputies, and ministers, and for direct implementation only by those under Transylvanian princely rule. These Transylvanian territorial synods, synchronous with the diets, unlike the synods of the Czech Brethren in Moravia and in Great Poland and of the Reformed in Poland-Lithuania, convened, with a few emergency exceptions, only with the permission of the ruler.

Queen regent Isabelle's edict of confessional toleration was expanded a decade later by her son, unitarianizing John Sigismund (Pl. 39). His edict of 1568 in effect legitimated the schism within the Magyar-Szekler Reformed Church between those theologically loyal to the Swiss and the Rhenish Palatiners and the proto-Unitarians: "Our *royal* highness, together with the diet, . . . confirms that in every place the preachers shall preach and explain the gospel each according to his understanding of it, and if the congregation [worshiping usually in the inherited parish church] like it, well; if not, no one shall compel them, but they shall keep the teachers whose doctrines they approve." This far-reaching grant, the first in history based on New Testament sanctions, went

on to say that "None of the superintendents [of the three synods] or others shall
annoy or abuse preachers on account of their religion ... or allow any to be
punished by removal from his post on account of his teaching, for faith is a gift
of God [Eph 2:8] and this [faith] comes from hearing and hearing by the word of
God [Rom 10:17]."⁵⁹ In his Hungarian *royal* style (until 1570) John Sigismund,
like his Jagiellonian mother, thus expanded the precedent of ritual and confessional toleration (the truce of Kutná Hora and the letter of the Moravian dietine)
by *royal* intent for all Hungaria and effectually within Greater Transylvania over
which he held sway: namely, for any Moravian Brethren settled on his borders,
for Catholics, Lutherans, Calvinists, Biblical Unitarians, and the Walachian
Orthodox, soon to become the "Uniates" under the Calvinist superintendent
and the prince—but all without their being so denominated by the king.

Although John Sigismund had also been hailed as "son of Suleiman" as in
the protocol of several other rulers of buffer states and protectorates of the Ottoman Empire, his own extension of his Polish mother's edict of religious toleration went much further towards individual and congregational choice in faith
(confessional and ritual) than the toleration under the Sultan of non-Islamic
groups (millets), each under its own traditional hierarchs, although the Muslim
model could not have been absent from the mind of the king and the participants
in the Transylvanian diet of 1568.

Within multiconfessional Transylvania, the Ottoman protectorate, another
current gained notable momentum, irrigating there and elsewhere religious
toleration and irenicism. The source was 1 Corinthians 14, wherein Paul sorted
out the rules for prophetic glossolalia and the proper order for congregational
(or synodal) interpretation of the meaning of Scripture, sometimes including the
participation of the sisters in searching colloquy despite the Apostle's injunction
of silence on women in the same pericope. The first to use the pericope as the
basis of common prophecy (*prophetia communis*) or "prophecying" (the later
English Puritan term) were the Anabaptists who found in it what they called
their *Sitzerrecht*, and more learnedly the *lex sedentium*, the law or apostolic
canon that they construed as sanctioning their conviction and procedure
whereby those believers covenanted in faith by believers' baptism, after invoking the Holy Spirit in their gathered church, were vouchsafed insight into the
proper meaning for themselves of seemingly discordant passages of Scripture by
orderly, deferential, expectant colloquy sustained by the same Spirit that
inspired the original apostolic and prophetic authors. The generic term for all
seated together under the tutelage of the Spirit, the vernacular Bible open before
them, was derived from verses 29–30: "Let two or three prophets speak, and
let the others weigh what is said. If a revelation [clarification] is made to
another *sitting* (*sedenti*), let the first be silent."⁶⁰

It was an Italian engineer, James Aconcio of an aristocratic family of Trent,
who gave learned international status and circulation to this Anabaptist scriptural principle notably in both Transylvania and England. At the court of
Archduke Maximilian in Vienna, he had written two ironic dialogues in Italian
in which he sought to convert the Hapsburg Archduke to a simple, non-coercive

Christianity. In one of these, *Somma brevissima della dottrina christiana* he placed theological differences in the perspective of the Last Judgment. In his major work *Satanea stratagemata* (Basel, 1565), published in eight books and dedicated to Queen Elizabeth, he set forth his deep conviction that all doctrines necessary to salvation were present in Scripture, but that territorial or magisterial Protestantism, having proclaimed this in Wittenberg and Geneva, nevertheless through pride, vanity, and self-service of the new clergy, was repeating the mistakes of the displaced *sacerdotium* and *regnum*, Satan once again now tempting *ministerium* and *magistratus* to use the coercive power of princely states in the interconfessional controversies. Aconcio defended the freedom of engaged discussion on disputed points, confident that the saving truth would emerge in colloquy, and to this end he elevated to prominence the *communis prophetia* or the *lex sedentium*. He acknowledged the Anabaptists, to whom he often referred favorably and whose right to separation by reason of conscience he upheld, as also to those dissatisfied with the received formulation of the doctrine of the Trinity. This work could have been influential in Transylvania on its own; but John Sommer, lector in the academy of Kolozsvár, fluent in Greek and author of an elegaic saga of the Hungarian kings, reworked and stylistically improved the *Stratagemata* in five books, publishing the compact edition at the Transylvanian capital of Alba Julia, 1570.[61] It was thus from a regionally adapted edition of the work of Aconcio issuing from the princely press and the main academy of the principality that the Anabaptist *Sitzerrecht* became an integral part of the thought and procedures of the two Reformed synods and the diets of Transylvania, and at least reinforced the native disposition to religious toleration in the synods in Moravia, Poland, and Lithuania, amplifying the older signals of toleration and intrafaith irenicism from Kutná Hora and the mandate of the Moravian dietine.

An unusual latitude in the exercise of common prophecy, linked with the threefold office of Christ (above, Section III A) and specifically, the prophetic office of Christ, is strikingly illustrated in the reflections and literary colloquies of Jacob Palaeologus, the ex-Dominican of Greek-Genoese descent, who still in his habit attended the Catholic-Huguenot colloquy of Poissy, September 1561, who was present as an observer at the last session of Trent, and who was a supporter of Francis Dávid. Although he would end up as the vindictive antagonist of Faustus Socinus during the adorancy debate in Kolozsvár of 1578/79, nevertheless, something notably ecumenical in interconfessional colloquy resonates in his earlier intra-Christian and inter-faith dialogues (Pl. 28).

Palaeologus, an interfaith covenantal theorist of the ''three peoples,'' was never a communicating member of the Unitarian Churches in Cracovia, Transylvania, or Moravia. Yet he stood in relation to the Unitarian Church in Transylvania, the scene of his major activity, somewhat like Faustus Socinus in relation to the Polish Brethren. (Like Socinus he was indifferent to baptismal theology and like him made the eucharist central.) In a tract composed while briefly in Cracow, 1572, Palaeologus elaborated on the relationship of the three peoples of the Book and what was common to them. As a Unitarian, he attached importance to the fact that the Jews in the first instance understood that their own priests, prophets, and kings had been anointed and could some day therefore acknowledge that for Christians Jesus was the triply anointed Jew, as Priest, Prophet, and prospective King who made it possible for the Gentiles to enter into the heritage of Israel through the New Covenant. Having had religious parleys with Muslims in Istanbul and in the courts of his patron magnates in Transylvania, Palaeologus held in his *De tribus gentibus* that Muslims, too, were embraced in God's salvific intention, even without baptism, since they had largely descended from Christians and had thus, without baptism, entered "the republic of Israel" by the covenant of the faith of Abraham through Ishmael. While their Koran, he conceded, contained some absurdities, it retained, he argued, the essentials about the Virgin-born prophet of God as his intended Messiah who will judge alike Muslims, Christians, and Jews.

The interfaith ecumenicism among "the three peoples," theoretically possible for Palaeologus because of his nonadorant Unitarianism, was his theologically radical way of dealing with the presence of Muslims throughout the East living among or dominating Christians, but Palaeologus remained militarily and politically a vigilant anti-Ottoman and even a pro-Hapsburg politique, in contrast to most of his Transylvanian Unitarian associates.

Palaeologus also propounded intra-Christian colloquy on a broad scale. It was while he was briefly head of the academy in Kolozsvár that Palaeologus finished his *Catechesis Christiana*, 1 August 1574, which verbally reflects a real succession of colloquy over twelve days. The unitive Protestant principle of discussion was threefold: salvation by faith alone (Rom 3:28) and faith from the hearing of the word (Rom 10:17) to be clarified not only through preaching by the synodally ordained, but through discussion and listening to one another according to the *lex sedentium* (1 Cor 14), interpreted now as the coresponsibility of fellow discussants to seek to understand each other and proceed dialectically to the scripturally revealed truth.[62]

In the catechesis/colloquy of Kolozsvár, the figure of the benign discussant Pastor is at once an idealized Francis Dávid, the Unitarian superintendent, and Palaeologus himself. Samuel, in the colloquy, speaks as a Jew converted to (Unitarian) Christianity. Telephus is an Indian of the New World who joins the colloquy as a baptized convert from paganism, but he is also a surrogate for the ideal convert to (Unitarian) Christianity from Islam. Participating as major colloquists are a Hapsburg Papist, a Saxon Lutheran, and a Debrecen Calvinist. A Chorus of general observers is prominent. As a nonadorant Unitarian, the "Pastor" sees the whole history of salvation in terms of God's Elect People, who were given, after the expression of Abraham's faith and his circumcision, the whole Law and the promise of a Messiah.

Palaeologus, having incorporated the threefold office of the Messiah, undoubtedly thought of himself primarily as a prophet. It is his view in the colloquy that full salvation for the Jews involves the recognition of Jesus as their once rejected Messiah and the acknowledgment that he will come in imminent vindication of his own, both these Jews and faithful Gentiles. The acceptance of

Jesus as the eschatological Messiah does not dispense these Jews from the observance of the Law, nor does it require them to be baptized, although for the sake of general conformity Samuel has, in fact, received baptism. (There were no Jews in Transylvania at the time.) For Jewish converts the four Gospels are especially *their* part of the New Testament, whereas for pagans and Muslims the core of the New Testament is in the Acts of the Apostles and the Pauline Epistles. Converts in any area and generation are to be baptized, but the progeny of Christians, whether of old Christian lines or of the newly converted need not be baptized, as through their parents they already belong to the Elect People of God. The Pastor, in response to queries from several sides, nevertheless allows for the continuance of pedobaptism and the introduction of adult baptism, depending on the situation in the Transylvanian towns or villages, but in any case the rite was not regarded by the Palaeologian circle as of much importance.

To continue the ''internationally'' interconnected progression, in tandem of toleration and irenicism, we turn to an episode within Polish ''Protestantism.'' Going beyond the negotiated mutual toleration but also mutual exclusion of two rites of the same Catholic faith (creed) at Kutná Hora, also beyond the royal/parliamentary constitutional accord of toleration of personal belief and diverse religious assembly and synodal discipline and even of the ideals of interfaith colloquy (of 1574) at Alba Julia, there emerged at Sandomierz in Poland a mutual, fraternal, conciliar irenicism among three non-Catholic synods to form a federated synod.

The Bohemian model for ritual and then confessional pluralism was thus extended on Polish soil during the pan-Commonwealth interdenominational Federation and Consensus of Sandomierz (in Little Poland) in 1570. The first approaches had been made in Great Poland in 1567, and an accord was reached in Poznań in January 1570 between the Lutherans and the well organized Unity of the Czech (Moravian) Brethren. The next step was the joint synod and colloquium of the Lutherans and the Czech Brethren of Great Poland with the Reformed of Little Poland and Lithuania meeting in Sandomierz in April, 1570 (Pl. 34). The inititiative came from the Major Reformed, gravely shaken by the schism of the Minor Reformed Church (1563/65), which they considered with some reason in its different tendencies to be ''Tritheist, Ebionite, and Anabaptist.'' Lubieniecki concertedly avoids taking cognizance of this epochal event in his *Historia*.

Following a lead of the Hungarian orthodox Reformed at Debrecen (in the border land between Hapsburg Hungary and the Protestantized principality of Greater Transylvania), the Polish Reformed (the Major Church), who were likewise coping with Biblical (Budnyite) Unitarianism, adopted in 1569 the substantial and comprehensive Second Helvetic Confession (of 1566). They had thereby abandoned the whole Laskian conceptualization of the *Confessio* of Pińczów (1559) cast in terms of Christ's threefold office as Mediator and left this schema to the excluded Minor Church. The Czech Brethren at Sandomierz had long had their own *Confessio Bohemica* of 1535, which they had already reshaped under the influence of Luther and therein formally abandoned their earlier practice of the rebaptism of Catholics and Utraquists. This *Confessio*, complete with a preface by Luther, had been presented to three successive kings of Bohemia; and, rendered in Polish, it had been presented to Sigismund II Augustus in 1567. The Lutherans themselves had, of course, the Augsburg Confession of 1530 (while the Book of Concord excluding Melanchthonian and Calvinist positions still lay ahead, Dresden, 1580).

At a crucial moment in the interdenominational disputes in Sandomierz over the validity of each confession, the Czech Elder Theophilus Turnowski rose to say: "I have accepted the [II] Helvetic Confession [in Polish] as our own"—up to this point all cheered warmly at his apparent concession—"upon the condition only, that you will not expect the [Czech] Brethren to relinquish the Confession they already have, but that they will be free to adhere to that also, as they have ever done." The Czech Brother thereby set forth the principle by which the joint synod of Sandomierz would in its more limited way prove successful. Henceforth the colloquists worked on a clarificatory Consensus that presupposed the retention by each church (synod) of its own ritual, confession, and discipline, while agreeing to feel free to attend the divine services of the others and *in full communion* and to attend each others' synods and to arrange for periodic *joint synods* in the future.

The final *Consensus* was dramatically signed in Poznań by, among others, the bishop of the Czech Brethren in Poland, John Rokyta, upon his return from a royal mission and a missionizing encounter in the Kremlin with Tsar Ivan IV the Terrible (Pl. 19). The *Consensus* was celebrated in Poznań with the spontaneous chanting of the *Te Deum laudamus*, as the Lutheran and the Czech Brethren congregations processed from their respective meeting houses to embrace each other.[63]

The motif of mutually negotiated ritual toleration (Kutná Hora), that of constitutional confessional toleration (Alba Julia), and that of mutual ecclesiasal and fraternal irenicism (Sandomierz) were in the Polish-Lithuanian Commonwealth melded in a constitutional sequence of events (1572–74) of international resonance and for Poland of ongoing import into the present, roughly synchronous with Palaeologus's idealized interfaith colloquy of Kolozsvár, 1574.

When Sigismund Augustus (brother of Queen Isabelle of Alba Julia) died in 1572 without a male heir of the Jagiellonian dynasty, the kingship became again more than ceremonially elective. It was agreed that the Primate of Gniezno, as the celebrant at every royal unction in the cathedral of Cracow, serve for the interim as Interrex and convene a Convocation Diet to arrange for the election and to serve as sacred regent till the moment of the sacring of the King-elect. A Convocation Diet was convened near Warsaw in January 1573 under Interrex Jacob Uchański (Pl. 6). Confederations of armed nobles upholding their several rights were integral to the royal succession, even after the kingship had become dynastic in the house of the Lithuanian Jagiellonians. But the Confederation of Warsaw was notable. The Protestant parties of Czech Brethren, of Lutheran, Calvinist, and proto-Unitarian nobles, greater and lesser, secured among themselves in the Confederation of Warsaw the points agreed upon (*pacta conventa*) that affirmed constitutional religious liberty for all "dissenting in matters of religion (*dissidentes de religione*)." This was the epochal *Pax dissidentium* (Pls. 35 – 37).

Many Catholic and all Protestant lords present joined in the Confederation. One bishop, Andrew Zebrzydowski of Cracow (Pl. 5), was also a signatory. The wording in Latin was neutral as to religious allegiance. At least the Protestant signatories understood that Catholics and Protestants were alike mutually dissenting on religious affiliation, faith, and jurisdictional obedience; and both groupings were conscious of the Byzantine-rite palatinates of the the Commonwealth stretching beyond Kiev. Aware, too, and foremost, of the St. Bartholomew's Day massacre of the Huguenots of August 1572, all of the prospective electors feared religious civil war among their own nobiliary *fraternity*, their brotherhood of theoretical equals of the *szlachta*. They assembled to vote from horseback on the election field of Wola (outside Warsaw), yeoman-knights along with princely magnates, accompanied to the barrier by their liveried retainers. Many Poles of all Christian allegiances looked to Henry of Valois as a potential royal candidate, hoping to obtain greater advantages from him as conceivably willing to exculpate himself from the Parisian massacre by promising diverse concessions (the Henrician Articles).

After winning out over a field of seven candidates, including the Tsar, Henry was ceremonially notified of his electoral victory in Notre Dame by the Polish envoys to Paris, but had to be firmly reminded of his obligation to uphold the IV (Henrician) Articles. The envoys, among them three Protestant lords (with a young Andrew Lubieniecki, our Author's own great uncle, among them as a page), with their spirited, conditioning *Postulata Polonica*, succeeded in obtaining a promise from Henry to make through his royal brother indemnification to the Huguenot survivors of the Massacre, and to reaffirm the Huguenots in their continued right of worship and self-government and self-defense, notably in La Rochelle. Although in less than a year Henry left Cracow without even the formality of abdication (to become King Henry III of France), the Henrician Articles and the Warsaw provisions for the *Pax dissidentium* remained integral to the royal oath at liturgical unction of all elective Kings to the final tripartition of the Commonwealth in 1795.

Lubieniecki devoted his *Legal Claims (Vindiciae)* to upholding the *Pax dissidentium* in its plenary application. And it did continue to protect Mennonites, among others, to the end.

Stephen Báthory, a Catholic, elected Prince of the multiconfessional principality of Transylvania (1571 – 81), elected King of the Polish-Lithuanian Commonwealth (1575 – 86), swore by his coronation oath to uphold the *Pax dissidentium* in the presence of his Unitarian court councellor, Dr. George Biandrata, who had preceded him from Alba Julia as his chosen orator at the Election Diet. Stephen was to establish the two appellate tribunals of the realm (at Piotrków and Lublin), to charter as a university the Jesuit College in Vilna, and it was under him that the decrees of the Council of Trent were formally accepted (1577). King Stephen Batory (Polish spelling) was a notable upholder of the liberty of religious conscience, personal and corporate (Pl. 46).

It was on a punitive expedition against semi-autonomous Danzig in 1577, which had withheld its support of his election, at a stop in Brodnica, on the approaches to the Hanseatic city, that King Stephen was memorably asked by some priests in his retinue to take over one of the churches of Lutheran Danzig and order Mass to be celebrated there. To this clamorous demand, it is reported by the first Calvinist historian of Poland (Stanislas Sarnicki) and transcribed by the first historian of *Slavonica Reformata* (Andrew Węgierski) that King *Dobrze*—the king of Magyar speech and Latin eloquence who could only say "thank you," with varying intonations in Polish (*dobrze*)—responded at once: "I am King of peoples, not of their consciences . . . I am unwilling to rule consciences. I must uphold the oaths of my coronation."[64]

Another notable moment in the history of religious toleration and irenicism was likewise in Poland-Lithuania where the Union of Ferrara-Florence (1439) had been once embraced by the metropolitan of Kiev under the Grand Duke of Lithuania, but not by the metropolitan of Moscow under its Grand Duke, whose successor had, by 1547, assumed the style of Tsar. By this time, indeed, the old Union of Florence had so far gone from bad to worse in the Commonwealth that it had become Catholic usage to rebaptize converts (lay and clerical) from the Ruthenian rite (Pl. 22). In 1589 the Tsar and the Ecumenical Patriarch raised the metropolitan of Moscow to the dignity of Patriarch. By 1595, many among the Orthodox and the Catholic leadership within the multiconfessional Commonwealth, anxious about social cohesion in a period of expansionist wars between Cracow and Muscovy, looked for a *modus vivendi* for the adherents of the two quite disparate rites and countervailing ecclesiastical systems, Greek and Roman, in the same elective royal Republic. In effect, the Commonwealth had within its bounds the overlapping hierachies of two organizations of Christian life and liturgy once shaped within the ancient Roman Empire, long since displaced northward, Hapsburg Vienna and tsarist-patriarchal Moscow being the military and diplomatic seats of the two external powers. *Lay* lords of both Churches were electors of the King, as were the *Catholic* bishops, who were all *ex officiis* members of the Senate (the spiritual and temporal peers of the realm seated together).

The Union of the Churches in the Commonwealth of the two rites and the two obediences (Rome and Constantinople) was effectuated at Brest Litovsk in 1595/96 (Pl. 52). In their (re)submission to papal obedience the Orthodox, primarily the "Ruthenians" (Ukrainians) of the former Lithuanian palatinates annexed to Crown Poland (by the *constitutional* Union of Lublin in 1569), retained the Julian calendar and liturgical year, their clerical marriage, and their Liturgy (with certain explicit Westernizing interpretations of the Nicene Creed), and their sacramental practices.

The Union of Brest Litovsk was opposed by many Orthodox and also by many Protestants, who felt politically threatened by this sudden expansion of papal authority within the Commonwealth. The Confederation of Warsaw and successive coronation oaths to uphold the *Pax dissidentium* in adaptation of the

IV Henrician Articles had partly solved for the Commonwealth the constitutional problem of confessional fissures within Latinate Polish-Christendom, that is, as between Catholic and diverse Protestant rites and confessions. So now the *ecclesiastical* Union of Brest Litovsk provided for the toleration of two ancient rites under one Pope, a duality of partly interpenetrating holy bodies in the same political spaces under papal obedience different from anything that previous conciliar unions had foreseen or sought to implement, but analogous to the peace of Kutná Hora that likewise upheld the external jurisdiction of the Romanists, while the territorial Utraquists were administered by the Consistory of Prague, elective through the Bohemian diet. With the Union of Brest Litovsk, the nobiliary and burgher Latin-rite and the Byzantine-rite citizens (*obywateli*) of the Commonwealth and the subjects of these lords were joined in the same external (papal) obedience, while various Protestants lived by the *Pax dissidentium*. Yet a successful Union of Catholics of the two rites could have overwhemed the beneficiaries of this earlier Catholic-Protestant constitutional Peace. For the Union of the two rites under the Pope suddenly minoritized all Protestants in the Commonwealth with their manorial and relativley few town churches all enmeshed in a parish system of general papal obedience with all Poles henceforth, the Protestants included, coming to think of the Confederation of Warsaw formulary as now meaning those "dissenting *from* the royal, if not the established, religion, that is, from the Catholic Church of many new Counter-Reform orders and of two rites."

Those Old Slavonic bishops and nobles, supported by only a fraction of the powerful urban lay brotherhoods, in joining with fellow (nobiliary) citizens of the Latin rite by adhesion together in the same Counter-Reform-empowered external authority in Rome, had construed their rupture with the Ecumenical Patriarch in the Sultan's capital and the three other patriarchal sees under Islam as wholly warranted by canonical precedent (Florence) and politico-martial circumstances in that, in any case, the mothering see of their own Old Slavonic piety and polity, Kiev, remained well within the bounds of their Commonwealth (although the Uniate metropolitan of Kiev came to be primarily resident in or near Vilna).

However, because of the ultra-Catholic Latinate reserve and even hauteur, the Uniates (the derisive Orthodox term for the Greek Catholics) never came to full "parity of rites." In any event, the Union was promptly resisted by many Byzantine-rite nobles and urban craftsmen and merchants in their lay brotherhoods, who were commonly much more articulate in Orthodox concerns than married village priests close to the serfs and their celibate bishops (vladyks; Polish: *władyki*; Pls. 46, 52), recruited from the monasteries.

While the Union of Brest Litovsk was in preparation, the three federated Protestant bodies of Sandomierz met in alarm in Toruń in 1595 in the largest Protestant assembly ever gathered in Poland and made overtures to the holdout Orthodox magnates and brotherhoods. The assembled were moved by a precedent evoked in Toruń by Turnowski, the already mentioned president of the Czech Brethren, namely, that of the proto-Protestant Utraquist mission to the

Ecumenical Patriarch of Constantinople in 1451. The joint Protestant-Orthodox defensive talk and action against the Union of Brest Litovsk eventuated in the Confederation of Vilnius in 1599 (Pl. 53) with Orthodox, Czech Brethren, Lutheran, and Calvinist lords among the signatories, resolving to uphold the *Pax dissidentium* in defense of all non-Catholics and specifically of the holdout Orthodox lords, led by Prince Constantine Basil Ostrozhkyi (Ostrogski, Pl. 53), sponsor of the printing of the Old Slavonic Bible, 1581 (Pl. 54). The Union of Brest Litovsk, because of the Orthodox resistance, divided the Byzantine-rite Christians of the Commonwealth, the Ruthenians (that is, the Ukrainians, like Ostrozhkyi, under Crown Poland) and the Byelorussians (that is, the subjects of the Catholic Lithuanian princes and lords in the palatinates that were retained by the Grand Duchy after the cession of its lower palatinates by the Union of Lublin) among themelves into two external obediences, papal and Constantinopolitan. Some Catholics of each rite and alike from among the Ruthenians, Byelorussians, and also the Latinate Poles sought modification of the Union to recreate a Byzantine hierarchy throughout the Commonwealth in communion with *both* Rome and Constantinople.

But even more powerful forces pressed at the Convocation Diet of 1632 for the reestablishment of the Orthodox hierarchy and the abolition of the Uniates. In 1620 the visiting Patriarch of Antioch had already consecrated a metropolitan for Kiev and five suffragan bishops, all under the cover of darkness to avoid detection by the forces of the Union of Brest. Unable to function in their assigned sees for a dozen years, these six Orthodox bishops remained contenders for the Uniate sees at the Election Diet of 1632, when the Orthodox lords and prelates made their demands for full recogniton as the New Dissidents in their XIV Points, supported by some Protestant electors.[65] Ladislas IV Vasa (Pl. 60), in exchange for the electoral votes of the Orthodox lords and princes, promised the "Pacification of the Ruthenians," more accurately, the partial restoration of the Orthodox hierarchs and external obedience (to the Ecumenical Patriarch). The Pacification at the election was principally the work of the royal advisor of the King-elect, the Capuchin Valerian Magni (Pl. 50), who had worked out accommodation between Romanists and Utraquists in Bohemia, harking back to Kutná Hora. The Pacification provided for the outright return of two Uniate sees to the Orthodox. In the arrangements for peace between the adherents of one rite (Byzantine) with two obediences (Roman and Constantipolitan), the protocol of the the Pacification drew on the distant model of Kutná Hora, allowing the Ruthenian and Byelorussian parishes or brotherhoods *to choose* whether they wished to be under Uniate (papal) or Orthodox (Constantinopolitan) jurisdiction, with the consequence that basilicas and wooden churches over a vast area, all outwardly similar and inwardly resonating to a nearly identical Liturgy, were riven by disparate loyalties and driven by differentiating sacred energies. It was during the intense negotiations attending the elections of Ladislas that, as Lubieniecki observed (n. 20), the Vice Chancellor sought to exclude the Unitarian electors *dissidentes* from the franchise.

Another nexus of the toleration motif was in Raków itself, the "Sarmatian

Athens,'' as the Polish Brethren called their center. With its academy and two churches, Unitarian and Catholic, and renowned polyglot press, Raków remained until 1638 (Pl. 59) a model of what for a time could exist within the bounds of constitutional toleration as still another modality of interfaith irenicism in the Commonwealth. Moreover, in the period between the arrival of Socinus in Poland to the closing of Raków, that is, from 1579 to 1638, there were eighteen *published* disputations between spokesmen of the Minor Church and Catholics, in several instances involving Catholic disputants of the highest rank, like Father Peter Skarga, S.J. (Pl. 49), with George Schomann in the Cracow residence of the royal saltmaster of Wieliczka (Pl. 16), another time with the chancellor of George Cardinal Radziwiłł of Cracow, along with a canon of Poznań. Several Catholic disputants faced major figures of the Minor Church in their chapel in Lublin. Of the eighteen published disputations, several of them took place in this chapel in Lublin, others were in Great Poland and Lithuania. Seven were held in Catholic churches and in any case belong as much to the Catholic as to the Unitarian heritage. The last ditch colloquy in this ''series'' of brave Unitarians and forthcoming Catholic disputants was at Rożnów, 1660 (presented in *Polish Brethren*, Document XXXI).

The most notable and comprehensive episode of interfaith irenicism was the Colloquium Charitativum (Pl. 61) in Toruń (Thorn), of which the young Lubieniecki was himself an observer at the preparatory sessions (above, at n. 7). The Colloquium, at the call of King Ladislas, with the counsel again of Valerian Magni and with consent of the bishops of the province of Gniezno but without consultation with, or consent from, the Pope, opened in 1645 and lasted for three months. The conference from near the start excluded the messengers of the Minor Church as ''non-Christian,'' despite their acknowledging the Apostles' Creed. Protestants and Catholics assembled in three delegations in the town hall of the Lutheranized town of Toruń. Seventy-six theologians participated, representing the Catholics and the three Protestant groupings confederated at Sandomierz. Remarkably, the Czech Brethren and the Reformed sat there together as a single delegation, and were led by the Czech Brother, Amos Comenius (Pl. 16). The Colloquy at Toruń, hoping to set an example to a Europe in the last throes of the Thirty Years' War, took the Bible as authoritative and expanded the presumption of the Bohemian truce of 1485 so that now four rites and four obediences were construed as still within the one Church of Christ and furthermore the colloquists attested to their hope in Christ that by benevolent reasoning the parties might avoid bloodshed among themselves in the multi-confessional Commonwealth.[66]

Of all these episodes in the extraordinary succession of manifestations of civil religious toleration and inter-ritual peace or negotiated or synodally achieved inter-confessional irenicism in the three eastern realms, from Kutná Hora in Bohemia (1485) to Toruń in Great Poland (1645), Lubieniecki, as something of a partisan and a proselytizer for his own cause abroad, directed attention in the *Historia* only to the second edict of Alba Julia (1569) and the Confederation of Warsaw (1573). His own disputations in exile, however, his other writings, notably the *Legal Claims* and the *Compendium Primaevae Veritatis*, clearly draw on and extend the two related Central Eastern European motifs of constitutional religious toleration and ecclesial irenicism. In any case, these and related episodes constitute the immediate background of his narrative. Hence the fuller context and further details of these decisive moments of civil religious toleration and ecclesial irenicism, amid divergent social, political, and theological conviction and loyalty, are amplified at intervals in the annotation and in the picture commentary.

E. The Relation of the *History and Related Documents* (1989) to *The Polish Brethren, 1601–1685* (1980)

The original *Historia* and the *Historia Reformationis Polonicae* having been distinguished in Part IIB, it remains to distinguish and interrelate this *Historia* now supplemented with Nine Related Documents to the earlier volume in the same series, *The Polish Brethren* (1980).

Some users of *HRP*, not unlike Lubieniecki himself who could clearly be impatient with some of the patristic argumentation left in his sources, have shared the common impulse to move on from the pre-history of Socinianism in order to follow with empathy the wriggling of a rationalist Christianity from out of the sectarian chrysalis of Racovian restorationist apostolic primitivism. The first generations of readers of *HRP*, as of the permutations of the Racovian Catechism that developed under the tutelage of Socinus, saw in the *Historia* a bridge from the wranglings of the Reformation, its intolerances, mutual excommunications, and even inquisitions, across the abyss of confessional wars of the seventeenth century into the Age of Enlightenment with international Socinianism perceived as a forerunner of Deism. At the same time confessional historians, that is, scholars within the Unitarian tradition, whether of Hungary-Transylvania, of Remonstrant Holland, of England or New England, have sought to see in the several minor churches dealt with by Lubieniecki the roots and sap of their own religious growth.

When I came to divide up the Lubieniecki legacy, projecting two interrelated works for the Harvard Theological Studies (HTS) it was clear that the first work should be *The Polish Brethren*, a collection of documents illustrating the history and thought of Unitarianism in the Polish-Lithuanian Commonwealth and in the diaspora, 1601–85, among them the three documents Wiszowaty had added to the *Historia* to constitute *HRP*.

From near the beginning, I felt the considerable difference between the minor churches of eastern Europe in the *sixteenth* century and their transformations in the seventeenth.

The *Historia* is preponderantly a witness to a widespread sixteenth-century drive toward the simplification of doctrine through the scrutiny of Scripture and the clarification and systematization of its intent by reason for the sake of ethical probity and evangelical virtue. This was a process in which lay theologians, manorial lords, and other patrons were synodal discussants as well as protectors.

Hence my decision to round out this book with Nine Related Documents. These documents, together with those in *The Polish Brethren*, offer a complete annotated English version of Wiszowaty's addenda to Sand's *BAnt*.

Three of the seven documents of *BAnt*, primarily illustrative of the life and thought of the Polish Brethren in the seventeenth century, were included in *The Polish Brethren*. These were Benedict Wiszowaty's Life of Andrew Wiszowaty, Jr. (d. 1678; Doc. I), the Martyrdom of John Tyshkovych (d. 1611; Doc. X), and Stanislas Lubieniecki's *Legal Claims for the Freedom of the Religion of Unitarians in Poland* (c. 1660) (Doc. XXIX). For the same *Polish Brethren*, I took from *HRP* itself the three pieces on the seventeenth century printed with the *Historia*, namely the *Vita* (Doc. XXVIII) of Lubieniecki by his sons, and two letters (Doc. XXXIII, I–II), describing the exile of the Brethren in 1660, which Wiszowaty used to fill out the incomplete *Historia*. In thus "dismembering" the received text of *HRP*, I was carrying out my overall editorial intention of making the English edition of the *Historia* primarily a witness to the theologically and to some extent socio-politically Radical Reformation in the sixteenth century, since in any case the narrative draws heavily on the eyewitness of Chronicler Budziński, and since Lubieniecki has one whole chapter on sixteenth-century Transylvania and numerous other references to confessional developments from Livonia to Moldavia all along the Byzantine-rite frontier.

To enhance the English edition of the *Historia* (with its three editorially annexed pieces removed for *Polish Brethren*) as witness primarily to the sixteenth century, I have included among the Related Documents (RD) the remaining four *BAnt* documents, separated into five. I have added four other documents: an excerpt from the *Poloneutychia* (1616) of Lubieniecki's great uncle, Andrew Lubieniecki; the *Catechesis* (1574) of Schomann and Gregory Paul, the oldest Unitarian confession of faith and the forerunner of the Racovian Catechism (Raków, 1605); the Life of Faustus Socinus (d. 1604) by Samuel Przypkowski (d. 1670), but only that long portion of it dealing with his career in Poland, included here partly because Lubieniecki, though basically a Socinian, deals very little with Socinus in his *Historia*; and an English envoy's description of the Commonwealth (1598).

A word further about each of these last two documents. The swift diffusion of thought from east to west in a Europe perhaps less divided than the present one is attested dramatically by the fact that the *Vita* of Faustus Socinus, the theologically oriented scion of a great family of jurisconsults of Siena, who died in 1604, was written near Kiev in 1631, was published anonymously, possibly in Amsterdam, 1636, and was soon republished in English translation in London in 1653—within less than fifty years of the Italian's death near Cracow. It was in part to make tangible this mobility of thought and cosmopolitan vision of the Polish Brethren that I include the large portion of Samuel Przypkowski's *Life of Socinus* as it was translated by John Biddle, the Father of the English Unitarianism (RD 8).

To replace the *Vita* of Stanislas Lubieniecki already translated in *Polish*

Brethren, I have added *A Relation of the State of Polonia and the United Provinces of that Crowne Anno 1598*, a report drawn up by George Carew, an Elizabethan envoy to Brunswick, Sweden, and the Commonwealth.

Critically edited from a manuscript in the British Museum only as recently as 1963, it is even now not widely accessible.[67] A selection of a few pages surveying the religious and social setting of Poland a quarter of a century before the birth of Lubieniecki admirably places the *Historia* in a larger frame.

The Excerpt in sixteenth-century English can enable the reader of the *Historia* with its narrow confessional focus and Polonocentric aristocratic presuppositions to glimpse the broader religious horizons and the social institutions of the lands and to sense at the outset the ethos of the landowners, among whom the drama of the *Historia* unfolds. It is true that this Excerpt itself requires annotation to be fully understood.

That a contemporary *Relation* concerning the Commonwealth, in place of the *Vita* of Lubieniecki, can be understood fully in the Elizabethan original only with the aid of considerable annotation detracts, of course, from its role as an introduction to the American edition of the *Historia*, but it all the more enhances the reader's sense of the remoteness of the age about which Lubieniecki wrote and from which even Lubieniecki himself had largely emerged as retrospective chronicler and interpreter. The Excerpt from Carew can also be reread after the *Historia* in evocation (however disdainful the Anglican diplomat[68] may have been) of the age and of the tradition at the center of Lubieniecki's narrative, to which Carew refers only on the margins of his survey as made up of "Antitrinitaries," Anabaptists, and Ebionites. As already remarked (IIA), Carew's is perhaps the first English use of "Antitrinitarian."

Since I have stressed the sixteenth century in the annotation of the *Historia*, I have in many instances for the seventeenth century resorted to many cross references and leads to the annotation in *Polish Brethren*, notably in the final five chapters of Book 3 of the *Historia*, which already "function" as anticipated Docs. 16–20 among the 35 calendared documents in Polish Brethren.

To facilitate cross reference to *BAnt* documents, they have been broken up by me into a succession of consecutively numbered paragraphs. In anticipation of this, the Life of Andrew Wiszowaty (d. 1678) appearing in *Polish Brethren* (Doc. I), was also numbered in this sequence among the five *BAnt* documents that offer parallel accounts to events in the *Historia*. So close an editorial interconnection between two pulications, even though in the same series, may entangle readers in too many cross references but it testifies to the degree to which I have worked on the two as a comprehensive project, intending to make prominent the differences between the sixteenth and the seventeenth century in the Budziński-Lubieniecki-Wiszowaty legacy of narrative and documentation.

It was most unfortunate that the printer's oversight of an agreement between the publisher of *Polish Brethren* and myself resulted in throwing off four elaborate indices for the two consecutively paginated parts (volumes) by four pages for every reference in part/volume two. As long as the quirk in pagination is identified, the four indices are restored to full use.

The now two Earl Morse Wilbur-initiated and inspired publications of translation, annotation, illustration, and commentary in the Lubieniecki/Wiszowaty tradition of the first Polish diaspora together provide a substantial, accessible source and stimulus for further interpretation of an important minor current in European religio-political, cultural, and eventually even philosophical-scientific development.

F. Annotation and Illustration

In my rendering of proper and geographical names I have anglicized Christian names in the narrative and reverted to the native spelling in the notes, while for surnames, except for a few international and perhaps abidingly Latinized names, like Servetus, Socinus, and Grotius, I have consistently given the modernized native spelling, like Biandrata for Blandrata. Yet where there has been a convenient Latinization for certain Polish names, I have used the international Latin form in the notes, like Gonesius for Piotr of Goniądz, Cruciger for Krzyżak, Hosius for Hoziusz. And for the names of royal and princely personages the English form is regularly used in both the text and the notes.[69] In general I have supplied in the text the first or last name of Poles in brackets, where Lubieniecki may use only one or the other. For geographical names, I have used English forms, where possible, even in bibliographical references, but where the English might simply drop the diacritical marks, as with Rakow, in contrast to a respelling, Cracow, I give the modern national spelling, for example, modernized spelling Książ for sixteenth-century Xiąż or westernized (often in Germanized orthography) Xions. Although I have retained German place names for Silesia and the most northern parts of the Commonwealth as of the sixteenth and the seventeenth century, for example, Breslau, Danzig, Königsberg, where appropriate these are Polonized in bibliographical references to publications since 1945. Without intended prejudice, I have rendered the place names in ethnic Lithuania, Byelorussia, and the Ukraine in Polish when there is no well recognized English or international equivalent, like Brest Litovsk (Brześć Litewski; Lithuanian: Lietuvos Brasta), especially as so many of them were often mere villages of Protestant lords and occasionally of uncertain location on modern maps. For lands under the Bohemian Crown and the divided lands of the Crown of St. Stephen I have often used Saxon and Magyar names as of the sixteenth century, e.g., for Transylvania, which is no longer traceable in the administrative districts of the present Republic of Romania, Kolozsvár (Klausenburg/Cluj).

The notes themselves are of two ranks, those of Editor Wiszowaty, printed as footnotes to the main text, and the endnotes, my annotation that runs consecutively within each of Lubieniecki's three books. Many of my notes run into several paragraphs and although spared the clutter of actual sequential numbering within each note, cross-reference specificity can be enhanced, e.g. "see Bk. 2, n. 12, ¶4," which directs readers of n. 12 to ascertain the fourth paragraph on their own counting.

Through almost excessive cross referencing I have tried to avoid repetition, but in these interconnected tapestries of clarification and comment I have not squeezed out all surplusage, and indeed some minor inconsistency in spelling and emphasis survives the several revisions, even as I become myself more and more clear about certain figures and problems in the text. In the text brief Latin titles of books remain untranslated, only the Polish titles are translated. In the annotation the longer Polish and Hungarian titles are given in parentheses in English. The bibliographical entries in the notes are complete only at the first mention of a book or article. Thereafter, brief titles or *sigla* appear. Besides the List of Abbreviations for the most common abbreviations, the Index of Persons and Places enables the reader to find the notes where the full bibliographical information is given. In the first entry there is sometimes information on the history and significance of a given series of periodicals, encyclopedias, source collections, etc.

IV. The *Historia and Related Documents*: From Polish and Latin into English

When a work of scholarship appears under the names of three translators and interpreters, it is incumbent upon the final editor to relate his predecessors' toil to his own even at the risk of slowing down the general reader with details of an enterprise that will interest only a few, except that clues offered in such a section can perhaps help any user of Lubieniecki's narrative to understand the final contours of the English text, its extensive annotation, supplementary documents, and illustrations.

A. Work on the *Historia Reformationis Polonicae:* Edmund Bursche and Earl Morse Wilbur

The first translator of the *Historia* into a vernacular, the Rev. Professor Edmund Bursche, a Lutheran, was sustained by the conviction that Lubieniecki's text was an important interpretation of Polish religious history and more than an old archive to be ransacked for data. In an ecumenical spirit, Bursche intended that his translation of *HRP* be understood as a tercentenary tribute and act of expiation for the expulsion of the Brethren from Raków in 1638, expressing the hope that the accessibility of the translation might encourage readers in twentieth-century Poland to include the witness of the Brethren in the total history of the fatherland. Bursche did not live to complete the project. It appeared with introduction and notes as "Historia Reformacji Polskiej," Book 1, *Rocznik Teologiczny* 3 (1938) 180–281; Book 2, ibid., 4 (1939) 1–190. His manuscript translation of Book 3 perished in the Warsaw Uprising of 1944.[70] By way of Marek Wajsblum most of his annotation and readings of obscure passages have entered into the American edition.

The ranking historian of Unitarianism in his time and country, Earl Morse Wilbur (1866–1956), founder of the Pacific Unitarian School for the Ministry in Berkeley, California, and creator of its library of *Unitariana* at the time incomparable with anything like it in the Western hemisphere, finished his typescript translation of the *HRP* into English during the same years as Bursche published his Books 1 and 2 in Polish, namely, from 1938 to 1939. Wilbur originally never intended to publish his own translation. He had disciplined himself to set down a fairly literal translation to serve whenever he should wish to consult the *HRP* for the writing of his two-volume *History of Unitarianism: Socinianism and its Antecedents* (Cambridge: Harvard University Press, 1945) and *In Transylvania, England, and America* (ibid. 1952).[71]

But even before the completion of the second volume of his *History*, Dr. Wilbur was prevailed upon to change his mind. Harvard Divinity School alumnus, the Reverend Duncan Howlett, minister of the First Church, Unitarian, of Boston (1633), had become fascinated with the first volume and was chagrined that his own denomination had been so little responsive to Dr. Wilbur's scholarly effort. After paying a visit to the historian in Berkeley in 1948, Howlett as chairman of the commission on planning and review of his denomination was instrumental in having its General Conference, meeting in Portland, Oregon, August 1948, honor Dr. Wilbur with a denominational citation, which he had worded himself.[72] From this denominational acknowledgment ensued Dr. Wilbur's favorable response, 28 September 1949, to the proposal that Howlett seek a publisher for the Lubieniecki typescript and therewith the translator's promise to revise it somewhat for such publication. Dr. Wilbur subsequently presented Howlett with his own copy of the *HRP* (1685). Despite diligence, however, Howlett failed to secure a publisher, and had perhaps come to recognize that even Dr. Wilbur's penciled improvements here and there were not enough to get this ''basic document of Unitarian history,'' as Howlett wrote, published even by the denominational press in Boston; and, on moving to the Unitarian pulpit in Washington, D.C., he turned over to me as an appropriate stewart the Wilbur typescript, identical (even to the penciled improvements) with one that Wilbur himself, perhaps shortly before his death, had sent to Roland Bainton in Yale University and which was also turned over to me in due course.

B. Resumption of the Work: Marek Wajsblum

Although I was myself an instructor and assistant professor of Church history at the Pacific School of Religion till 1947, concurrently also at the successor to Wilbur's school, the Starr King School for the Ministry (which holds a portion of the Wilbur Library),[73] and came to know very well the Wilbur family, Dr. Wilbur himself never broached with me the possibility of my working on Lubieniecki.[74]

Dr. Wilbur's typescript came to me only by way of Dr. Howlett. I at first made an effort to have it worked on as the basis for the doctoral enterprise of my colleague Ralph Lazzaro, director of the study of classical languages at the Harvard Divinity School, then of my doctoral student, Harold H. O. J. Brown, who in the end, however, opted instead for a thesis on John Łaski (before the return of the reformer to Poland in 1556).

On the initiative of Professor Wiktor Weintraub of the Slavic Department of Harvard University, he and I obtained a grant for his friend Dr. Marek Wajsblum (1903–62), then in London, with the proposal that he work on *HRP* to make the translation less prolix and especially to bring it abreast of modern scholarship. In the end, after toiling over a wholly fresh translation, Wajsblum decided that what Wilbur had done could not be greatly improved; and he contented himself with rectifying a few infelicities. Dr. Wajsblum was a Jewish Polish patriot, a scholar at home in regional and national archives, and a cosmopolitan historian. His vision of the task before him in the prospective annotation of the *HRP* was perhaps best expressed by him in print in his review of the two writings of Father Aleksander Kossowski of the Catholic University of Lublin (KUL) on Protestantism in the Lublin district and in Volhynia. While appreciating the extensive local research and benign judgments of Professor Kossowski, he regretted that the Catholic scholar had not placed the movement in its pan-European setting nor sufficiently adduced the Western monographic literature and the internationally oriented, calendared source collections.[75] In an unsigned necrological notice, Wiktor Weintraub reviewed the scholarly career of Dr. Wajsblum, taking account of his work on the *Historia*, for which he intended to prepare an introductory discussion of Lubieniecki as historian.[76] Mrs. Wajsblum (whom my helper later visited in London) sent me a box of notes, some in Polish, some in English. They were not yet numbered nor attached to specifically designated places in the text.[77] Dr. Wajsblum had been in epistolary contact (1958–62) with Professor Henryk Barycz of Cracow and with the editorial board of the *Polski Słownik Biograficzny* (*PSB*) in progress.

The box of Wajsblum notes reposed for two years in the office of Mr. Lazzaro, when I decided that I was evidently the foreordained final editor of a project that had begun with Stanislas Budziński (d. probably in Cracow, after 1595),[78] of Stanislas Lubieniecki (d. in Hamburg, 1675),[79] of Benedict Wiszowaty (d. as pastor in Andreaswalde in Electoral Prussia, after 1704),[80] of Edmund Bursche (d. in the concentration camp Orianienburg-Sachsenhausen, 1940),[81] of Earl Morse Wilbur (d. in Berkeley, 1956),[82] of Marek Wajsblum (d. in London, 1962), and of Henryk Barycz.[83]

C. The Devolution of the Task:
The Facsimile Edition of *HRP* (Warsaw, 1971)

My work unfolded intermittently from when death stayed the hand of Dr. Wajsblum in 1962. I observed in the Harvard copy of *HRP* in the Widener Library stacks (Pl. 1) that it had been purchased in London, 23 May 1689, by none other than the Rev. Increase Mather, D.D., minister of the Second Church of Boston, president of Harvard (1685–1701), originator of the University's often controversial motto and seal, *Christo et Ecclesiae*. The earliest Puritans of the Massachusetts Bay Colony were familiar with the writings of John Łaski as superintendent of the Strangers' Church in London. An invitation was explored with John Amos Comenius of Leszno, while on a visit to London in 1641, to become president of Harvard College.[84] Harvard's first president was actually Henry Dunster (1640–54). Given the immersionist conviction of the (pres-byterian) Polish Minor Reformed Church, it is of interest that the first president of Harvard College, the Colony's foremost Hebraist, the Reverend Henry Dun-ster, a high Calvinist, in the end came to espouse believers' baptism as alone scriptural and that, after debating the issue in Latin at an especially convoked gathering in Boston, he was exiled by the ministry and the magistracy as a Bap-tist to the adjoining Separatist (pedobaptist) Congregational Plymouth Colony.

The last president/rector of Harvard in the seventeenth century, Dr. Increase Mather, an anti-Arminian, who negotiated the charter of the province of Mas-sachusetts and who contrived to save the original Puritan intent of the college charter against prospective Anglican (Episcopal) encroachments of the new royal governors, purchased in London his copy of the *Historia Reformationis Polonicae*, perhaps in the thought of acquiring an account of another Reformed Church subsisting ''likewise under a Catholic Monarch.'' There is no evidence that Mather discovered therein the Polish counterpart of the Arminian Church he abhorred! President Increase Mather bought also a copy of Lubieniecki's *Theatrum Cometicum*. He and his son Cotton Mather made references to usages in higher education in Poland, evidently instructed by *HRP*. And it was from a Polish professor in Franeker that Rector Mather evidently derived his seal for Harvard University, *Christo et Ecclesiae*. Cotton Mather, published the *Mag-nalia Christi Americana* (London, 1701), a regional ecclesiastical history of New England roughly comparable to the *Slavonia Reformata* (Utrecht, 1652) of the Polish Calvinist Czech Brother, Andrew Węgierski.

It was to secure the ''Non-Separating'' Congregational Reformed tradition represented by embattled Increase Mather in Boston, coincident with the last year of his rectorate at Harvard (1701), and with his approbation and that of his son, that Calvinist Congregationalist New England's second college was founded on local initiative in Connecticut, Yale University (the seat of Roland Bainton, one of the three to whom this volume is dedicated). There seem to have been several copies of the chief collected writings of the Polish Brethren, the nine-volume *Bibliotheca Fratrum Polonorum* in New England at the time of the Revolution, when on the military side Count Kazimierz Pułaski (d. 1779) and General Tadeusz Kościuszko (d. 1817) fought for the future of civil liberty in the New World after their own Commonwealth had undergone its First and Second Tripartition (1772 and 1793). Between these dismantling events, at the commencement exercises at Harvard, there had been in 1792 a lively public dis-cussion, comparing the new constitutions of the United States (1787), of limited monarchical France (1792), and that of electively monarchical Poland as reshaped by the Great Sejm of 3 May 1792, which gave voice to the towns in the Diet and suppressed the *liberum veto*.[85]

It is, in any case, fitting that the *Historia* and Related Documents be pub-lished in a learned series of New England's oldest institution of higher learning

(1636) and of its graduate school of ministerial training (1816) that were once decisively shaped by the Arminian, then the Unitarian tradition. The first in the Unitarian line in New England clearly to have read Lubieniecki's *Historia* (and probably the first to have read the Mather copy in the Harvard library) was William Ware (1797–1852), son of the Hollis Professor Henry Ware, Sr. This is evident in his denominational tract, *Antiquity and Revival of Unitarian Christianity* (Boston, 1831). Two years *before* the disestablishment of the Standing Order of Massachusetts (dominated by Unitarian Congregationalists), this scholarly ministerial alumnus of Harvard was surely the first in Antitrinitarian historiography to have gone so far as to assert "that during a period of fifty years, under the successive reigns of Constantine, Constantius, and Valens, Unitarianism was the established religion of the Roman Empire [!]." His acquaintance with the persons and events through the *Historia* (probably also Przypkowski's *Vita* of Socinus and perhaps also *BAnt*, with an appreciative evocation of the "opulent merchant" martyr Tyszkowic) enabled him to say of Poland "that it was within her borders that Christianity, after so long a corruption, first returned to nearly its original purity."[86] From the Divinity School, Earl Morse Wilbur was graduated in the S.T.B. class of 1890. I have myself served from 1947 to 1980 (eventually as Hollis Professor of Divinity, established in 1721) as general Church historian in the history department and on the faculty of theology of Harvard University.

The incumbent today in Yale University of the chair of Church history and Christian thought, Jaroslav Pelikan, of Lutheran affiliation, defines and vindicates in his History of Dogma the scriptural, patristic, scholastic, and reformatory Tradition as Catholic in its fourfold aspect of word, sacrament, worship, and confessional formulary. Although my Yale colleague has in mind in his compelling words *the* Tradition, from which my own ministerial forebears dissented and to which they declined to conform, nevertheless I join him in his admonition and exhortation recurrent or implied in his monumental five-volume *The Christian Tradition* (Chicago: University of Chicago Press, 1972, four volumes published as of 1989) and in others of his works, namely, the admonition at once "to avoid the dead faith of the living and to heed the living faith of the dead" and thus as Christians and fellow humanists to be ever concerned for "the inclusion of the dead in our circle of discourse."

With the help of many still living and with the energization from what seemed the bidding signals of the dead, some of whom died as martyrs to their convictions, I trust that I have acceptably discharged an assignment never sought but rather laid upon me, ever mindful of the gentle admonition of another Church historian, Nova Scotian Presbyterian John T. McNeill, my mentor at the Union Theological Seminary in New York, that however wideranging the Church historian's interests may be, he (or she) remains in his generation responsible for the ongoing denominational or regional tradition out of which he sprang. And, after working for a quarter of a century on the partly pulverized heritage of the reformatory biblical churches of the eastern realms, I am strongly disposed to hold that the testimony of these communities, places, and times belongs to the common store of Christian historiography and humanistic reflection.

At the invitation of Ludwik Chmaj and Lech Szczucki I had contributed my first essay in the field in 1958, and in August 1961, having finished a year as Fulbright lecturer at Strasbourg, I was a guest at the Polish Academy of Sciences (PAN) at the invitation of Adam Schaff and with a welcome from Dr. Leszek Kołakowski; and on the excursion from Warsaw to Cracow I stayed in the home of Dr. Tadeusz Przypkowski in Jędrzejów, who gave me copies of many of the photographs in his collection of *Sociniana*.

In 1964 with the help of Harvard candidate for the Ph.D. in History, Jean Martin, previously a classics major, I prepared the Wilbur/Wajsblum typescript for retyping and distributed bundles of notes from Dr. Wajsblum, where they best seemed to fit, into which I intercalated many more identifications and clarifications beyond the scope and range of his intentions. Subtopics within the chapters were introduced. The text was broken up into shorter sentences and paragraphs here and there improved especially in theological formulation and in the identification of scriptural allusions and patristic and scholastic citations. The whole was then retyped, or, in the case of the notes, typed for the first time, with extraordinary fidelity and perseverance by Mrs. Helen Aikenhead. The resultant third typescript from that of Wilbur (1938), with the expanded annotation, was made available to my seminar on Polish Reformation History at the Harvard Divinity School in the spring semester of 1971. At the time, the facsimile edition of *HRP* (n. 89) was not accessible, and the seminar had only the "Mather" copy and another from the bequest of librarian and Old Testament professor Ezra Abbot (d. 1884), in the Andover Harvard Library. Jean Martin had prepared an index (March 1971) of all proper names and topics that was made available to the seminar. Her work then and subsequently was rigorous, innovative, and substantial.

Thomas Collins wrote his seminar paper on Budziński and concluded that the MS History in Polish was intentionally allowed to disappear because it was theologically uncongenial to the leadership of the Polish Brethren in the Netherlands. Nelson Minnich, S.J., now professor of Church history in Catholic University of America, dealt in his paper with the Catholic orders as seen and interpreted by Lubieniecki. Both Collins and Minnich, particularly the latter, took an almost independent interest in going through the whole typescript against the Latin text and raising questions, making connections with the related documents in *BAnt*, identifying a number of the scriptural allusions in the text, challenging some of Wajsblum's or my notes, and in general contributing substantially to the coherence of the translation and the integration of the notes as of that stage. The Rev. Father John P. Forman traced the career of John Łaski in the English Public Records. Ronald Diener, whose doctoral dissertation was to be on the role of (the anti-Socinian) Johann Wigand (*Nebulae arianae*, Königsberg, 1575) in the achievement of the Magdeburg *Centuries*, left no trace in the annotation or translation of the text but he did persuade me to undertake a more confident and idiomatic translation.

I took this composite text of the seminar of 1971 with me in November of 1972 for my sabbatical year in Lublin and as of April in Cambridge, St. John's College, as Guggenheim Fellow and, while in Poland, as International Research and Exchange Fellow, assigned to the University there in the name of Marie Curie-Skłodowska (MCS). I had reasons for feeling at home in Lublin under the gracious welcome of sometime Rector Grzegorz Leopold Seidler, while being more directly sponsored by Professor Henryk Zins, and placed in the special care of Barbara and Leszek Kolek. Professor Stanislas Tworek was most supportive and generous. During my sojourn in Lublin I became also part of the life of the Catholic University (KUL), speaking there twice and also in the Church of the Holy Spirit. I shall remain indebted to many colleagues and friends there who took an interest in my project. I mention particularly the Rev. Prof. Mieczysław Krąpiec, O.P., who was rector at the time, Professor Jerzy Kłoczowski and all the members of his division on ecclesiastical history, and in other departments the very Rev. Prof. Marian Rechowicz, who possessed a rich personal library on Polish Protestantism, and the ecumenically spirited Rev. Professor Celestyn Stanislas Napiórkowski, O.F.M.

In the further acquisition of Polish I was helped by MCS Polonists Jerzy Borkowski and his colleague, Ewa Kosowska. Through her I entered into the language, literature, and feeling of the whole culture in which the *HRP* constitutes only a remote strand; and it is because of her encouragement, and her works that, despite many vicissitudes, this annotated translation of the *Historia* at long last appears in English. Pl. 34 on the Union of Sandomierz is specifically dedicated to her.

I acknowledge with appreciation the encouragement of a grant from the Lewis Solon Rosenstiel Foundation of the American Institute of Polish Culture.

In the meantime the editorial committee for the Biblioteka Pisarzy Reformacyjnych, no. 9, made up of Zbigniew Ogonowski, Lech Szczucki, and Janusz Tazbir, had published the facsimile edition of *HRP* with a preface by Henryk Barycz and an index of proper names by Maria Bohonos under the direction of Janusz Tazbir (Warsaw: PAN, 1971), to which were added two pages of supplementary *addenda* and *emendanda* identified in the course of the preparation of the facsimile edition. The Latin preface of Barycz, dated May 1969, noted that an English version with annotation and indices by Wilbur, Wajsblum, and myself was soon (*mox*) to be published![87]

Some related papers[88] were read at a succession of four notable international congresses devoted to Unitarianism in the sixteenth and seventeenth century: in Siklos in Hungary, May 1979, under Tibor Klaniczay and (the late) Robert Dán; in Warsaw, September 1979, under Zbigniew Ogonowski, Lech Szczucki, and Janusz Tazbir; in Kalamazoo, Michigan at the call of John C. Godbey of Meadville Theological School in Chicago, in May 1984; and in Hamburg, June 1985, at the call of Werner C. Erdt of Hamburg and of Wolfgang Deppert of Kiel; and outside this succession: at the international conference in Bloomington, Indiana, at the invitation of Samuel Fiszman in 1982, celebrating the 450th anniversary of the birth of Jan Kochanowski. I here express my great appreciation to the conveners and to the other participants, some of whom I have had the occasion in the Preface or will have in the notes to acknowledge. But I make particular mention here of Aldo Stella of Padua in attendance at two of these conferences and whose work on the Italians bulking large in Lubieniecki's text and in my annotation I especially appreciate; along with him Domenico Caccamo, and especially Antonio Rotondò, who dedicated his critical edition of the *Opere* of Laelius Socinus (1986) to me and my former student, Dr. John Tedeschi; Massimo Firpo, Balint Keserü, László Makkai, Paul Wrzecionko. Jeremy D. Bangs of Leiden and his father, Carl Bangs of Kansas City, attendants at one or another of these conferences, deserve special mention in having enabled me to use in strenuous circumstances the still to be published second edition by Wiszowaty of *BAnt²*. At the Sixteenth Century Studies Conference in Concordia Theological Seminary, St. Louis, October 1986, where the theme, at the call of Hans Hillerbrand, was "Radical Tendencies in the Reformation," it was Dr. David P. Daniel, who encouraged me with specifics for the drafting of my principal Map.

Dr. Marvin W. Anderson of Bethel College and Seminary in St. Paul, who is undertaking a study of "Pietro Martire Vermigli as a European Theologian," has kindly read sections of the annotated *Historia* in proof, for which close attention I am most grateful. Dr. Anderson is aware of several agendas consciously and subliminally operative in my editing of this cumulative composite of sources and commentary—some of these thrusts vibrating in unresolved cross-purpose. He has read the work for overall cohesion without himself being at all times comfortable with the theological (also ecclesiological) and other conceptual/typological lenses and methodological frames through which I have in the annotation extended the panorama of the *Historia* and in so doing sought to impose order on the sources, artifacts, and the monographic literature of the age and regions that Lubieniecki looked out on and back to through a narrower aperture in his mental fortification.

My colleague Wiktor Weintraub, doctoral alumnus of the Jagiellonian University, Alfred Jurzykowski Professor of Polish Literature at Harvard, was most encouraging from the start of my efforts in his fields. And as the posthumous editor of Wilbur's translation of the eminent Stanisław Kot's *Socinianism in Poland: The Social and Political Ideas* (Warsaw, 1932; Boston: Beacon Press, 1957), he kindly gave me a number of leads and otherwise steadfastly promoted my prolonged endeavor.[89]

In the final, redoubled work on completing the translation and on the annotation, almost my sole occupation after September 1979, a number of persons stand out as having made the edition possible. Kristine Alice Zakarison, a candidate then for a degree at Harvard Divinity School, typed the fourth typescript of the *Historia*. Hers was a daunting task that could not and probably would not have been tackled by any other person.

Near the end, Krzysztof Kowalski with a magister degree from the Jagiellonian University entered with tireless energy and attentive and cheering resourcefulness into my final sub-project: to help lighten—in two senses—the heavily annotated text with pictorial artifacts of the age. He also translated the threnody of John Kochanowski on the death of his young daughter Ursula.

To pull together this album of pictures provided with appropriate captions, acknowledgments, and supplementary commentary, the Rev. David Keyes, graduate of the Starr King School for the Ministry, and minister of the First (Unitarian) Church of Taunton, Massachusetts, volunteered to oversee the logistics of keeping the effort in order and on schedule. His quiet and hearty confidence in the outcome of the ambitious project has been a strong factor in its success. I am grateful to Douglas Henry, M.T.S., for his care and resourcefulness in reproducing the many pictures of disparate quality.

In her careful reading of the whole typescript as style-editor and knowing counselor, I am most grateful to Vicki Phillips, who constantly alerted me to any inconsistencies or unclarities. With her grasp on the intricacies of the publication schedule, she professionally discouraged my addenda but, herself concerned with the *dramatis personae*, allowed the most important new findings to nestle in their proper places to enhance the annotation before her departure to pursue a doctorate in biblical studies at Vanderbilt University.

The final work on the *Historia* gave way to a long commitment to deliver in November 1987 the Gunning Lectures on the centenary of their foundation in New College of the University of Edinburgh at the invitation of the Principal and the Dean of the Faculty of Theology. They were entitled "Sacred Energies: The Impact of the Reformation and the Counter-Reform in Eastern Central Europe." The map for that occasion appears among the maps of this edition, but the substance of the Lectures remains to be printed. Their preparation and delivery helped me personally in seeing my recent work in still a larger perspective.

In the meantime, a small grant from the funds of the Massachusetts Society for the Promotion of the Gospel (1811) enabled me to work in tandem on the Gunning Lectures and on the final arduous stages of the *Historia*. To Barbara June Bruce and Virginia Hobbs the reader is indebted for the comprehensive and analytical index, without which the *Historia* and its annotation would be a forest without trails or blazes.

Finally, in the editorial office I thank Joe Snowden, Th.D. in the New Testament field, who typeset the complicated text. Behind Vicki Phillips have stood the Editor and Managing Editor, respectively, of the Harvard Theological Review, Professor Helmut Köster and Ms. Pamela Chance, whose firm and professional commitment to, and oversight of, the project have been a source of assurance without which, during a particularly grave time in my personal life, I could have found it very hard to complete this work.

History of the Polish Reformation

GREETING TO THE READER[1]

This brief history of the Polish Reformation, though not brought to completion by its author, we have deemed not undeserving of publication, because it includes much that is hardly to be found elsewhere touching the beginning of the Reformation in Poland and the origins of Antitrinitarians.[2] It were surely to be desired that it might have received the author's final hand. But seeing that he was snatched away by untimely fate, we give you, reader, what we can, though we would say more, and more accurately, had material come to our hands. Yet that the *History* might not be issued quite incomplete, we have caused two letters to be added at the end, in which the misfortunes of the Antitrinitarians before they were banished from Poland, and their pitiable exile, are graphically portrayed.[3] And that you may not be ignorant who Lubieniecki was, here is a brief account of his life, prepared by one of his sons.[4] [1b]

of confessors of the truth carried on by Bishop Andrew Zebrydowski of Crawcow [*p. 55*]

5. Of the doctrines and death of Servetus, Valentine Gentile, John Sylvan, and Benardine Ochino, and something of Paul Alciati, Matthew Gribaldi, and Adam [Neuser], minister at Heidelberg [*p. 96*]

6. Of the beginnings of the pure Church of Christ, by the proposition of Servetus as to the preeminence of the Father, brought into Poland by Peter of Goniądz, defended by George Bilandrata and Francis Lismanino; the controversy of Francis Stancaro about the Mediator that intervened, and troubling and arousing them both [*p. 111*]

7. Of the preeminence of the Father affirmed by Gregory Paul, and of the Church of Catholic Christians formed and established after the schism made by Stanislas Sarnicki [*p. 131*]

8. Of the progress of the truth illustrated in Lithuania from 1558, in the Palatinate of Cracow from 1559, especially in the articles of the Son of God, the Holy Spirit, and baptism; also of the conference at Piotrków in 1562, and of other matters worthy of memory [*p. 144*]

9. History of the Prince Despot of Walachia, who stayed in Poland and embraced the Christian truth, was restored to his ancestral principate of Łaski, Lasocki, and Filipowski, but was assassinated by his subjects [*p. 153*]

BOOK III

1. In which are described the progress of the truth, the efforts of Sarnicki and Discordia for the sake of discord, in opposition to tthose of Lutomirski and Gregory and others for the sake of concord [*p. 158*]

2. In which are described the results of the discord: Lismanino's departure from Poland and his death; the persecution after the Edict of Parczów of 1564, and the strife of the Roman clergy against Erasmus Otwinowski; as well as against a Jew of Lublin and Semion, a member of the King's Court, for profaning the Most Holy Sacrament, as they call it; over and above also an account of the Italian Franco di Franco, and the Pole John Tyszkowic, martyrs of Christ [*p. 168*]

3. Of pedobaptism opposed, defeated, rejected [*p. 175*]

4. Of persecutions stirred up by Papists and Calvinists against the confessors of the truth in their impugning the doctrines of the Trinity and pedobaptism [*p. 193*]

5. Of the open schism of the Churches that arose after the colloquium held during the Diet of Piotrków in 1565 [*p. 201*]

6. Containing the Last Will and Testament of George Schomann, and the whole history of his life and death, as well as that of more acts of the Churches [*p. 207*, here RD3]

7. Containing the controversies about the Person and Deity of the Holy Spirit [*p. 208*]

8. Of efforts for harmony amid so many differences of opinion and controversies, especially of the synods held at Łańcut and Skrzynno in 1567 [*p. 214*]

9. Of the enmity of the Reformed against the lovers of the truth shown at the synod of Crawcow in 1568, which gave offense to Andrew Dudith, and so furnished him an incentive for inquiring into the truth; also a brief account of his life and death [*p. 221*]

10. Of the journey to Moravia undertaken by Filipowski and Schomann, and of the Moravian Brethren [*p. 227*]

11. Of the Trinitarian conflict that arose in Transylvania, and of the struggles undertaken by George Biandrata and Faustus Socinus in behalf of the invocation of Christ against Francis Dávid [*p. 228*]

12. Of the foundation of Raków, and of the Synod there that lasted for several years [1567–69]; of the conferences held by many godly men on matters of faith; of many and notable instances of divine providence watching over that place until its ruin, which took place in 1638 [*p. 239*]

13. Of the rise, progress, and end of the church at Lublin, as also of the churches at Gozdów and Zaporów [*p. 253*]

14. Of the same church of Lublin, removed first to Piaski, thence to Siedliska, and finally scattered together with the rest by the recent disaster of the Swedish war [*p. 269*]

15. Of the churches in the Piedmont, especially the very old and famous church at Luslowice in the Palatinate of Cracow; as also an account of the death of Faustus Socinus [*p. 273*]

16. Of the churches in the palatinates of Volhynia and Kiev [*p. 276*]

17. In this fragment are published [a letter of Samuel Przypkowski, 1663, about] some things pertaining to the history of subsequent times, in which especially is related how the Unitarians, after sundry persecutions, were expelled from Poland [printed in *Polish Brethren*, Document XXXIII–I]

18. Copy of a letter of the Unitarian Exiles [in 1661] to [John Nacranus] [printed in *Polish Brethren*, XXXIII–II]

History of the Polish Reformation

In Which Are Related the Rise and Progress of Both the Reformed and the Antitrinitarians[1] in Poland and in the Neighboring Provinces

Foreword

In human affairs, history is a pre-eminent subject and one of the highest utility, the record of every age agrees, and the consent of all wise men, confirmed by reason and experience, supports this. Therefore, no one can fail to see that I am undertaking a very great subject and a very difficult one, given the nature of religion. It is a thing most sacred, and in all respects and of all things the greatest. For since it is through religion that well-governed states (*res publicae*) endure, and since through it the minds and dispositions of men are moved, it is extremely hard to follow its history without a certain danger of a preconceived opinion on one side, or a prejudice on the other. But perhaps the consciousness of innate truthfullness and of subject matter related in good faith and well done can stand for a thousand witnesses and thereby be beyond cavil. Certainly, in handling this task I shall now try to show my industry and good faith, and to set forth everything faithfully and clearly with a view to the public good,[2] endeavoring by trustworthy proofs to satisfy my own conscience as well as the expectations, and concern for, others' salvation. And I hope indeed with the assistance of divine grace to add not a little to the diligence of the latter, and far more to the faith of the former.

BOOK ONE

In Which It Is Shown How God of His Boundless Wisdom and Goodness, from the Beginning of the Apostolic Truth, Dealt with Men in the Ages Following, and How by Certain Steps He Started the Reformation of the Church in Poland.

CHAPTER ONE

[2] The Primitive Faith in Jesus Christ Began at Once to Be Corrupted in the Next Century after the Death of the Apostles, Just As Did the Jewish Church Which Also Began at Once to Be Corrupted after the Death of Joshua and the Elders. The Periods of These Changes are Shown.

To trace the matter from the beginning: the whole Christian religion is summed up in the very brief confession that Jesus, being raised from the dead, is the Christ, the Son of God, and the heavenly King, and in following a life worthy of this most holy faith.[1] It has been both so witnessed by the clear teaching of Holy Scripture and approved by the common judgment of Christians,[2] that this alone has always been and will be the Catholic doctrine (*dogma*), the only one needed to obtain eternal salvation.

That such a simple confession of faith as this should soon after the passing of the Apostles have been corrupted by so many inventions and abuses would fairly cause one to wonder, had not the Holy Spirit so often forewarned that after the passing of the Apostles they would creep in. The Spirit forewarned that from the very elders (*seniores*) themselves and the rulers (*rectores*) of the Church perverse men were bound to arise, who would not spare the flock, tearing it like wolves, teaching strange doctrines, not approving the sound words of our Lord Jesus Christ and not assenting to the doctrine which is according to godliness. These are the false teachers, enemies of the cross of Christ.[3] And this [corruption] in fact ecclesiastical history has shown to have taken place, as we shall soon see. That the divine truth began to be corrupted so shortly after the death of the Apostles no one will wonder at who has recalled that quite the same thing happened in the Jewish Church since we have recorded [in the Old Testament] something similar to the testimony that Hegesippus, a trustworthy author close to the time of the Apostles, [3] has left on record in Eusebius [pupil] of Pamphilius. Eusebius was an excellent church historian, although much given to partisan zeal. [On what Hegesippus wrote] concerning the corruption of the Church which at once followed the passing of the Apostles, [see presently].[4] For thus we read in the history of Judges, 2:7[–12]:

> And the people served the Lord all the days of Joshua, and all the days of the elders that outlived Joshua, who had seen all the great works of the Lord that he did for Israel. And Joshua the son of Nun, the servant of the Lord, died, being a hundred and ten years old; and they buried him in the border of his inheritance in Timnath-heres in the mount of Ephraim, on the north side of the hill Gaash. And also all that generation were gathered unto their fathers, and there arose another generation after them, which knew not the Lord, nor yet the works which he had done for Israel. And the children of Israel did evil in the sight of the Lord and served Baalim; and they forsook the Lord God of their fathers, who brought them out of the land of Egypt, and followed other gods.

To these words, as I see it, are parallel those that Hegesippus has reported, that writer mentioned above, who according to Eusebius, "expounded the sound tradition of the Apostles' preaching in a very simple plan of history."[5] We may well regret that this work of a distinguished mind succumbed to the iniquity of time, and be glad to read some fragments preserved in Eusebius. For Hegesippus too, describing the death of Symeon and the son of Clopas, who was the last either of the Apostles or of men of the Apostolic Age and died as bishop of Jerusalem A. D. 111 at the age of one hundred and twenty, speaks to the same purpose, and directly:

> Up to this time the Church remained a virgin, pure and incorrupt, while those who endeavored to corrupt the sound rule of saving preaching, if there was any such then, lay hidden in some obscure darkness. But after the holy band of the Apostles came to their various allotted ends, and the generation passed away who had deserved to hear the divine wisdom with their own ears, then began a conspiracy of wicked error through the seduction of those who were delivering a strange doctrine. And, since none of the Apostles any longer survived, they now bodily undertook, in opposition to the preaching of the truth, to proclaim on the contrary, knowledge (*scientiam*) falsely so called [4] (*Historia ecclesiastica*).[6]

And why should one wonder that both the Jewish Church after the death of Joshua and the elders, and the Christian Church after the death of the Apostles and of the men of the Apostolic Age, at once began to be corrupted, when even in the lifetime of their leaders and teachers each of them not only hardly continued in pure obedience to their commandments and in the pure truth, but was also partly depraved. And each church had from the word of God a prediction of the future falling away (Exod 32:8; Deut 9:16, 31:27–29; Rom 16:17ff; Gal 3:1, 5:1ff; Phil 3:2ff; Acts 20:29, 30; and elsewhere). And this is a remarkable proof of the freedom, but also of the frailty, of human nature, both of which are indeed seen in a plain example from each church, clearly exhibited in the words of sacred and ecclesiastical history. Notable periodic revolutions are perceived in both dispensations. And although the accounts of the chronologists very often disagree, it was not foreign to my purpose here to touch upon them also.

For just as the Jewish Church began to be corrupted one hundred and eleven years after the birth of its leader, Joshua, so also did the Christian after the same lapse of time from the birth of the heavenly Joshua. And as the former, after being freed from its cruel Egyptian bondage, was led by Moses through the Red Sea which drowned the Egyptian hosts, and crossed over to the safe shore of salvation—so also the latter, after being freed from its most cruel bondage to Satan, was also led by our heavenly Moses through the red sea of blood shed on the cross, which drowned all the hosts of the spiritual Egypt but washed the faithful and ensured the crossing over to the safe shore of eternal salvation. And it remained in purity about seventy years [after A. D. 41 to 111],[7] so quickly did it forget the very great favors of God and the truth handed down by the living voice and attested by writings.

Again, just as there were 1517 years from the Israelites' crossing through the Red Sea and obtaining deliverance under their leader Moses to the birth of John, the forerunner of the heavenly Moses who was to bring the glad tidings of eternal salvation, so just as many years intervene until the reformation begun by Luther, and the full freedom obtained by the truth [in Poland]. Finally, just as the Church instituted by Christ,[8] after the period of 1517 years from the exodus of the Israelites to the forerunner of Christ had been fulfilled, obtained within five times [5] seven years full freedom by the blood of Christ, so also the restored Church, having fulfilled a like period up to the beginning of the Reformation, after thirty years,[9] namely about the year 1550, by the favor of God obtained complete reformation and freedom.[10]

And so we see the wonderful wisdom and justice of God, while we consider that these movements of the time are displayed to us by God in history itself. Yet we dare not rashly invade the secret sanctuary of his counsels, nor curiously explore those movements of the times which Christ testifies the Father has placed in his own power [Matt 24:36].

CHAPTER TWO

After the Time of the Apostles God Did Not Leave the Church without Witness and Instruction in the Truth.

Before I begin to speak of the reformation of the Church, I think that I should first point out that God, in accordance with his blameless justice and fatherly concern for the human race, graciously furnished all men with aids sufficient to obtain salvation. For to men endowed with sound reason and judgment he left and always recommended the canonical Scriptures, which the facts themselves teach and the consenting voice of all antiquity testifies to be the infallible rule of faith (for it is the most perfect, sufficient, and clear teacher of the saving truth) and to contain all things necessary to believe and to do with a view to salvation. Moreover, he next gave them witnesses of the primitive truth.[11] Or at least, when a prevailing adverse faction, with a mind thankless even to the point of perversity and tyranny, had shown itself undeserving of the divine favor, he gave them admonishers whose teaching was nearcr to the truth, although even they themselves were encompassed with errors. God did all this so that he might not leave them [the faithful] to fall headlong into vice and to heap errors upon errors, without evidence of his truth and grace. Here a very broad field of discussion opens to me in arranging these witnesses to the truth [6] by the established order of centuries,[12] although they were not free from errors, and hence must be received with discriminating and discreet judgment.

To wit, in the fourth century, when the power of Christians of the priestly (*sacer*) and the secular (*profanus*) order was weak and corrupted more and more both Christian truth and Christian piety,[13] I should place [among the conservers of the primitive truth] the Latin doctors of the Church and most of the Greek who asserted the preeminence (*praerogativa*) of the Father, whom they regarded as the author and cause of the Son, who was a true man exalted by God. They said that the Holy Spirit was a gift of God, but by no means God. And further they taught the freedom of the will and the predestination for all men, conditioned upon faith and obedience, and hence not on mere faith, but on faith joined with good works as necessary to salvation.

Here I should place the uncorrupted councils: those of Ancyra and Gangra,[14] the first of Toledo[15] that condemned the celibacy of the clergy,[16] and that of Elvira which condemned images,[17] as well as the third council of Carthage which decreed that only the Father should be invoked at the altar.[18] I should here place Augustine, who taught so many things that agreed with the truth, as that the bread of the Eucharist is a token (*signum*) of the body and of the blood (*passionis*) of the Lord in a figure; that the body of Christ is kept in the spaces of heaven; that the saints are to be adored only by our imitation of them; and that the one Mediator given by God, in a clear (*certa*) decree of predestination, had glory with the Father before the foundations of the world were laid.[19]

Also I should place here Epiphanius who broke in pieces an image of Christ which was then first seen hung up in a church, and thundered violently against the Mariolatry that was then beginning to be practiced.[20]

Here I should also place Aerius who opposed distinction (*delectum*) of foods and stood for the equality of priest (*presbyter*) and bishop.[21] I should here place also *Eustathius*, who held in check the errors of the Macedonians and of the Trinitarians.[22] I should place here Euphrantion,[23] Marcellus,[24] Photinus,[25] and others who oppose the dogma of the supreme divinity of Christ. I should also include here Vigilantius who objected to the veneration of saints and their relics and to the celibacy of the clergy as sprouting errors.[7] I should then also place here Arius himself and Donatus with their followers, who curbed the Homousian [Nicene Catholic] faction which was armed with the [imperial] sword.[8]

In the course of all the following centuries I should place not only individual teachers of, but also collectively witnesses to, the truth convened in councils and opposing both earlier errors and those later invented. Nor should I mention only the most prolific (*proletarios*) among them such as the Pelagii,[9] the Scoti,[10] the Samsons,[11] the Serlos,[12] the *Ratramni*,[13] the Berengars,[14] the Peters of Bruys,[15] and the Abelards,[16] the Henrys,[17] the Arnolds,[18] [7] the Waldenses,[19] to whom the Christian cause certainly owes much for their matchless steadfastness in religion. Concerning one of them, *Abelard*,[20] the celebrated Abbot Bernard recorded: "When he speaks of the Trinity, he savors of Arius; when of grace, he savors of Pelagius; when of the person of Christ, Nestorius" (*Epistula, 192*).[21] And Baronius notes three things in him: "That he made reason the judge of articles of faith, that he struck against the doctrine of the Trinity, and that he denied the death of Christ to be our satisfaction before God" (*Annales*, XI, year 1140).[22]

Then come such as Almaric,[23] Occam,[24] Alvaro,[25] Tauler,[26] Wycliffe,[27] Hus,[28] Wessel,[29] Platina,[30] Savonarola,[31] and countless others. For gold is gold in whosoever hands it is, even if not yet purified of the dross to be burnt off in repeated fire. But I should also include emperors themselves, namely such as Philip,[32] Leo,[33] Constantine,[34] Charlemagne,[35] Otto the Great,[36] and Louis the Pious,[37] who set about with great zeal to reform the vices of Catholics (*Pontifices*) and the corruption of the Church.

But this is for the present no part of our plan. At another time, with the good God's help, we shall bring forward the primitive truth,[38] not only from the sanctuary of Holy Scripture and the heart of sober reason, but also from the records of antiquity.[39]

That the primitive truth ceased to be pure soon after the time of the Apostles some gather not without reason from the words of the Apostle John [I, 2:18], where he speaks of the last hour as coming, although the account itself also clearly says that after the departure of the Apostles this truth disappeared forthwith, as it were.[40] And this is not only expressly taught by Hegesippus, but also confirmed by many others with trustworthy testimonies supporting the evident truth: [Callistus] Nicephorus, XLI, i;[41] [Michael] Neander, *Historia Ecclesiastica* (p. 522);[42] *Magdeburg Centuries*, Centuria II, i and iii, entitled *Inclinatio doctrinae* (although truth is there too often regarded as error, and error elsewhere as truth);[43] [John] Daillé, *De vero usu Patrum*, II, vi;[44] and others. Some men, accurate in making chronological calculations, such as [John] Funck and [John] Alsted,[45] allow the purity of the Gospel to have lasted a little longer: the former to A. D. 190, the latter to 194, thus both into the times of Pope Victor.

This also is much in favor of our purpose. For this Victor was the first who, for slight reason and with an anti-Christian audacity, ventured to smite with his anathema the dissenters, even the members of the churches of all Asia. And

among these was Theodotus of Byzantium,[65] [8] a man of great learning, who
steadfastly denied that Christ, being endued by God with divine power, had
existed before Mary (for many dared affirm this after the time of the Apostles),[66]
as did also Artemas[67] (or Artemon) [**cf. BAnt no. 47**][68] with great zeal about the
same time. He had no small number of followers when the Church split into
parties. And their protest is even inserted in the documents (*actis*) of Eusebius,
Historia Ecclesiastica V, xviii, although this was composed by their adversaries.[69] In it they had [evidently] boasted of the antiquity of their view so far as
to say and to affirm with great spirit that all their forefathers, even the Apostles
themselves, had thought and taught the same as they, and that this truth of their
preaching had been maintained down to the time of Victor. And these men
[despite their excommunication] were followed by others with devotion (*stre-
nue*), even to the point of having to give up their bishoprics. Among these were
Paul of Samosata at Antioch,[70] about the year 270, and Bishop Photinus of Sirmium,[71] about the year 350 [**cf. BAnt no. 47**]. They made not a few disciples,
who were oppressed by the ever growing opposite faction, especially after it had
been freed from the fear of persecution and had seized the sword of the civil
power.[72]

All these who assert the one God the Father, Creator of all things, and His
Son Jesus Christ by Him not only begotten, but also raised up and exalted,[73] are
supported by truth most clearly set forth and firmly defended by the whole text
of Holy Scripture, and even by the agreement of those who oppose and those
who support this Catholic truth, save that the former group wish more.[74] For
who, wishing to compose a work according to the Holy Scripture's infallible
rule of faith and salvation, would not naturally and freely believe that the one
God, the God of Israel, is the supreme Creator of all things by his mighty word
and will, and the kind Preserver and Ruler by the wise providence that is manifest in his fatherly care for men, especially the faithful? Again, who would not
believe and acknowledge that this God calls all men to repentance and saving
faith, since he had sent his only begotten Son, Jesus of Nazareth, to preach the
Gospel of salvation and confirm it by divine miracles as one whom, begotten by
the power of his Holy Spirit in the womb of a chaste virgin and taught by the
same marvelous power (*virtus*), God wished to be the most perfect interpreter of
his will, his messenger (*internuncium*), and mediator (*sequestrum*) with man?
Wished him to be, then, the Redeemer of the world after he had suffered a most
cruel death and at length been raised from the dead, the Lord and the heavenly
King, the High Priest, and the Judge of the quick [9] and the dead?[75]

Again, who would not congratulate himself and the human race that he [God
the Father through Christ] elects believers and, on account of the true faith
which works through love and is made alive by good works, justifies and pro-
nounces them righteous through his own righteousness imputed to them by that
faith, and then gives them the reward of eternal life?[76] Who, moreover, would
not believe and, greatly congratulating the race of mortals, would not confess
that the same most merciful Father gave the blood of his dearly beloved Son as a

pledge (*pignus*) and guarantee (*auctoramentum*) of the free remission of sins?[77] Who would not rejoice also that to those who have been cleansed by holy baptism (*lavacrum*) in the name of the Father, the Son, and the Holy Spirit,[78] and walk worthily of their confession,[79] he gave the death of Christ the Saviour, whom he also gave to the human race as an expiatory (*piacularis*) victim, expiating the sins of the people by a single sacrifice?[80] And who would not rejoice that to those who keep the memorial of both his broken body in the blessed broken bread and of his poured out blood in the wine poured out with due thanksgiving (*Eucharistia*), and who by a holy life bears witness to their communion with their head and his body, he gives it as a pledge of their future inheritance of his Holy Spirit, who is and proceeds from him as teacher (*Magistrum*) and comforter of the faithful?[81] Who would not exult for the joy conceived from this excellent knowledge: that all who with their Teacher (*doctore*) and leader tread the way of eternal blessedness and are members of the Holy Church subject to its one head, Christ, ought with a pure heart to serve the one God through Christ the only mediator?[82] Who if he reads either all the holy Bible or the commentaries of all who have ever written on religion (for which the lifetime of one man is not enough) does not acknowledge that with these few things necessary to salvation (and hence both very clearly stated and so many times inculcated in Scripture) the whole Christian religion is fulfilled, so far as concerns what is to be believed and done? And who, if he reads, does not acknowledge that this and no other is the kernel of Catholic truth, that, although it has lain hidden under the received husks of human commentators, yet has always remained in the Church? Finally, who dare deny that these, as genuine marks of the true Church, are enough for anyone's salvation unless one wishes to sew on to a comfortable and well-fitting garment tails (*caudas*)[83] that are not only unnecessary, but also unbecoming and inconvenient? It is clear enough that such things are inventions of later ages, not proofs of the primitive [10] simplicity, which had far less of speculation and ceremonies, but all the more of solid piety.

CHAPTER THREE

The Stages of the Corruption of the Church are Pointed Out.

Although a great many writings under the names of ancient teachers of the Church are even now being hawked without regard to their truth,[84] and despite the objections of the more judicious men, and also although many things have been either inserted into them or removed from them by force and by most wicked dishonesty, yet it is well enough established that the primitive doctrine of the belief about God was handed down until the Council of Nicaea in such wise that the prerogative (*praerogativa*) of the one God is left to the Father. The existence and divinity before all ages, or from the beginning of creation, were [to be sure, by some] ascribed to the Son. Thereby [indeed] the ancients paved the way for Arius, as everyone sees and many of the adversaries confess. But, the personality of the Holy Spirit was asserted by none of them, not even by the fathers of the Nicene Council themselves. After this again, the dogma of the Trinity being at last established, especially such as was introduced into the Christian world by the creed falsely ascribed to Athanasius[85] (according to the opinion of such great men as Camerarius,[86] Pelargus,[87] Vossius,[88] and others), other errors were brought forward. For soon came the fabrications as to the necessity of baptism and hence also of the Eucharist for infants,[89] about the invocation of the saints, the celibacy of the clergy, and the universal (*Oecumenica*) preeminence (*praestantia*) of the authority (*dignitatis*) of the Roman Pope. [This last did not accord with] the judgment of the most ancient and celebrated bishops and doctors of even the Roman Church such as Bishop Gregory the Great of Rome[90] and abbot Bernard of Clairvaux[91] (who are even recorded among the saints), thereafter Archbishop Eberhard of Salzburg,[92] and others. This preeminence at length resulted in un-Christian pride and tyranny, the mistress and most zealous protectress of countless errors and abuses. And finally impatient of the primitive simpleness, curiosity brought in more and different things. But occasion to discuss these other things also will be given in *Compendium Veritatis primaevae*.[93] Suffice it here for the present to have pointed out by what stages such great corruption of the Church was introduced. Now let us see by what stages God removed it from the Church.

[11] CHAPTER FOUR

The Stages of the Reformation Are Shown.

Because immediately after the Apostles, under the specious pretext of religion (which deceived men with the greater impunity, and therefore more easily and successfully), the ambition of the popes of Rome, especially after Victor above mentioned, began more and more to increase, to spread various errors and abuses throughout the Christian world under the color of Apostolic authority. And at length, usurping the supreme stage of divinity on earth, the Papacy arrogantly drew under its laws all things divine and human, and finally transformed the entire Christian religion into idolatry and superstition and a silly confidence in works of special merit, nay even supererogatory ones, as they are called. God began a reformation of the Church [**cf. BAnt no. 43**] by suppressing the former and correcting the latter. And indeed he made use here of the attack of the fiery [Martin] Luther,[94] but added to him Philip Melanchthon[95] and [Martin] Bucer,[96] whose discretion and moderation were of great assistance, while [Andrew Bodenstein von] Carlstadt[97] and [John] Bugenhagen[98] also labored vigorously.

And so Luther established men in the first grade of the truth, having proposed and ratified these laws: that Holy Scripture is the sole rule of faith; that traditions contrary to it are on no account to be received; that Christ is the sole head of the Church, and that the Pope who makes himself such is Antichrist; also that Christ is the sole Mediator,[99] and hence that the saints are not to be invoked nor images to be worshiped; that the sins of men are atoned for solely by Christ's sacrifice alone, and hence that in the holy Eucharist there is no sacrifice, nor is the bread that is used in it changed in substance or converted into the very body of Christ;[100] that ministers of the Word are permitted to assume the marriage bond; that the people are permitted to read Holy Scripture; that only two sacraments were instituted by Christ, namely baptism and the Eucharist; that there is no Purgatory; that good works are not of merit in the stricter sense.

And God, desiring in this difficult matter to recall men from an extreme to a moderate position, permitted Luther [12] to go to the other extreme in the matter of faith alone.[101] But [God did this] not with the intention that those coming to an extreme of this sort (when teaching that faith alone and through it the application of the meritorious satisfaction of Christ are sufficient) should also [fatuously] hold that good works are in no wise necessary for salvation for the man who has been justified or the man who has yet to be justified. For this is certainly most contrary to Holy Scripture, which throughout teaches and enforces nothing but zeal for good works and obedience to God's commands by those who desire to be saved. In fact, God intended by this teaching of Luther that all who love the right and heaven should take their stand as if midway in truth in order to serve a faith issuing in good works or a faith joined with works like a tree joined with its fruits, or the body with the soul. God intended a faith efficacious through charity and consisting in obedience to God's commands, so that through it God might impute his righteousness to us. But by what means? Why, by this: cognizant of his great beneficence that he wished through the blood of his only begotten Son freely to blot out our sins and to lead us to forsake them, we continually testify to our grateful mind for this offer, not only by recalling in memory the death of Christ in the solemn rite of the Eucharist, but also by living our whole life according to his precepts.

Alas, the arrogance of the servants (*ministri*) of the Church was indeed not in fact sufficiently restrained by Luther. Auricular confession and the rather lucrative authority to forgive sins were left to the ministers, and consequently a road to ambition and awesome power over the people and civil government (*magistrati*) itself.[102] Besides, the memorial of the Mass was also left. Then again there remained papist (*romanenses*) relics in eucharistic consubstantiation,[103] in the toleration of images, and in other things. Moreover, there had crept into [Lutheranism] harmful doctrines about separating good works from faith, or excluding them from the matter of justification,[104] and about other things.

Hence God sent [Ulrich] Zwingli,[105] [John] Oecolampadius,[106] [John] Calvin,[107] and Peter Martyr [Vermigli],[108] who removed much of the holy arrogance, threw the images out of the churches, abolished also the memorial of the Mass,[109] and other abuses neither few nor small. To good works indeed they gave some recognition,[110] yet saving the satisfaction of Christ. And at the same time the [Reformed] changed eucharistic consubstantiation and the real presence, enhanced by oral manducation, into a [purely] spiritual presence of the body and blood.[111] Some of them, however, not content with Zwingli's doctrine and inclined to novelty as well as concord, [13] invented a presence, sacramental, though in its own way real, concealed in the spiritual manducation. To this day they are fiercely fighting with Luther's followers, having led their forces out into the broadest field of the Sacrament. This was a word unknown to the Holy Spirit and, being a military term[112] rather than theological, is therefore liable to disputes and quarrels.

These stages of the Reformation are touched upon or indicated by Andrew Frycz Modrzewski[113] in his *Sylvae*, III, tract 1, viii. He writes as follows:

> Formerly there prevailed in the Church traffic in Masses, the fires of Purgatory, the trade in indulgences, the endless assistance of the saints (*patronorum*), and the various schemes for gaining the kingdom of heaven for a price. These things were overthrown by Luther, as all the world knows. Zwingli destroyed and overthrew the panoply of Masses.[114]

After God thus by sure degrees brought back to the marvelous light of heavenly truth men who had been thrust into a prison of gloomy idolatry and of various inventions, he plainly showed that there was not only to be no turning back. To be sure by perverse counsel the former [the Lutherans] did this in their doctrine of ubiquity,[115] and the latter [the Reformed] in their newly invented sacramental presence.[116] But he also plainly showed that those whose eyes had gradually become accustomed to the dimmer light had to make further progress and come into the full light of the truth. Outstanding by example are those shining here whom the crowd charges, now with the unfair names of "Ebionites,"[117] "Paulians,"[118] "Samosatenians,"[119] and "Socinians,"[120] now with the mutually contradictory ones of "Arians"[121] and "Photinians,"[122] although their [own] confession of the truth defines, acknowledges, and proclaims them as Christians.[123] Nor indeed do these believe and confess that any other than Jesus Christ, conceived of the Holy Spirit, born of the Virgin, raised up and glorified by God, is the Son of God, and Mediator, and Saviour, and Teacher, and Lord.[124] This pure and in fact only Catholic truth, both set forth in many passages in the plainest Holy Scriptures and confirmed by the consent of all Christians in all ages and places, which took its rise in Poland and in the provinces thereto adjacent,[125] is now to be expounded.

[14] CHAPTER FIVE

How the Reformation, after the Preparations Made under Sigismund I, Began in Poland from 1546 to 1550 Inclusively under King [Sigismund II] Augustus. His History at First Briefly Related.

[The military and political achievement of Sigismund II Augustus]

If we want to trace[126] the matter from the egg, as the saying is, the great and good God[127] vouchsafed a happy privilege to King Sigismund II, in name and fact Augustus, most laudable of princes. In his reign [1548–72], as the most illustrious both for the glory of his deeds in peace and war, and for the renown of his virtues, he accomplished a very great work among a noble people, and one that produces lofty souls, so that in this way Christ, once born under an Augustus in Judaea and by a happy omen reborn under an Augustus in Poland, might be perceived in the body [the noble laity] at least of the Church (*in corpore nempe Ecclesiae cerneretur*). For this great prince was feared by his enemies, admired by foreigners, honored by his neighbors, and revered by his subjects. For it was under his auspices that Nicholas Sieniawski, one of the magnates of the Royal Commonwealth, in 1552 set Alexander over *Moldavia*, Stephen having been driven out.[128]

Sigismund quieted the disorders in Danzig when the populace (*plebe*) rose against the patricians (*Patres*), and in the same year drew up regulations for them to live under their ancient laws.[129] In 1554 he warded off his kinsman, Duke Henry of Brunswick, from Prussia.[130] Then Sigismund managed and settled the affairs of this province with a vigorous hand, while through his commissioners, sent in 1566, he inflicted the supreme punishment upon John Funck, the celebrated historian, and others guilty of forming a conspiracy with Duke John Albert of Mecklenburg.[131]

In 1557, Sigismund restored to office William Fürstenberg, Master of the Teutonic Order in Livonia.[132] In 1559, he undertook to protect Livonia, [as an ally of the Royal Commonwealth] against the tyranny of Grand Duke, Ivan [IV, the Terrible] Vasilievich of Muscovy,[133] who had invaded this province in 1558. And then, in the following year, at Marienburg, he inflicted defeat upon the latter's army through Prince Alexander Połubiński.[134] He made Gotthard Kettler Duke of Courland in 1562.[135] In the same year, at the Diet of Piotrków, wisely undertaking the Execution of laws, he established [15] the legal basis of the Royal Commonwealth.[136]

In the following year [19 August 1562], at Nevel, with 1,500 spearmen under the command of Stanislas Leśniowolski,[137] castellan of Czersk, he [Sigismund] so badly routed 40,000 Muscovites that more than 8,000 of them fell.[138] A little later, with an army of 10,000 under the command of [Hetman] Gregory Chodkiewicz,[139] and of Nicholas Radziwiłł,[140] palatine of Vilna and Grand Hetman (*praefectus*) of the Lithuanian troops, Sigismund annihilated 20,000 Muscovites near Uła (Starowolski here puts it higher, 7,000 against 30,000, while yet others reckon the latter number as 25,000).[141] In 1565, through the command of Stanislas Cikowski and also of Philo Kmita,[142] and again in the following years 1566, 1567, and 1568, through the Cossacks, the King utterly defeated Muscovy at Vitebsk.[143] Meanwhile, through Prince Roman Sanguszko, he routed 8,000 Muscovites, and a little later carried off the palm of victory by recapturing Uła.[144] With [John] Sapieha, brave commander of 5,000 troops, he defended Wenden, and as Starowolski reports, overthrew at one stroke 24,000 Muscovites and Livonians.[145]

He [Sigismund] restrained the Tatars, who were accustomed to making frequent raids on the borders of Poland and sometimes into the interior and to living off their booty, through the fear alone of his royal power, especially after Albert Łaski,[146] palatine of Sieradz, had inflicted a great slaughter upon them in 1568 at Oczaków, where the Dnieper and the Bug empty into the Black Sea.[147]

By both his renown in war and in the arts of peace, and by the mere respect of his name, he [Sigismund] impelled Suleiman [the Magnificent], Sultan of the Turks, the conqueror of Hungary and terror of the world, to cultivate friendship with him throughout the whole time of the rule, which the tyrant held for almost twenty years during the King's life. Indeed, the year 1520 was the first in the life of [Sigismund] Augustus and in the rule of Suleiman.[148] This was true also in respect to the latter's son Selim, who in 1569 sent to him Ibrahim Pasha, by birth a Pole, to establish peace and friendship.[149] In that same year this new Solomon Sigismund [Augustus] reconciled John [Sigismund] Zápolya, the elected king of Hungary and son of his sister Isabella, with Emperor Maximillian II.[150] And in the year following [1570], Sigismund reconciled King John of Sweden, husband of his other sister, Catherine, with King Frederick II of Denmark.[151] And victorious throughout more than ten years, he forced the Muscovites to keep an unbroken peace.

Finally, it was Sigismund II in the same year [1569] when the God of peace was crowning the Augustan age with the olive and the laurel, [16] who brought to a wise and happy conclusion the very difficult negotiation of uniting Lithuania with his kingdom at the Diet of Lublin,[152] at which he also celebrated the capture of Uła[153] and a triumph over the Muscovites, so often defeated. He quieted the Commonwealth, disturbed by sundry quarrels, and ruled it with the highest reputation for piety, justice, and mercy, as well as for singular patience and discretion. In a word, in peace and in war, at home and abroad, he was renowned; and for such great merits he was easily forgiven his minor faults, from which he was not free.

[The first Polish reformers, 1540–45]

And so in the time of this most glorious and best of kings, it was the will of God that a beginning of reformation should be made in the Royal Commonwealth, in order that no one might hinder so great a work without showing disrespect for such a great King. And first indeed some preachers (*ecclesiastae*), namely John of Koźmin and Lawrence of Przasnysz, called Discordia, inveighed at the King's court against the errors and corruptions found in the Church.[154] But also in Cracow, after the great plague which in the year 1543[155] had devoured 20,000 in that city (having been foreshadowed by a swarm of locusts which is never seen without some mischief), some preachers (*concionatores*) did the same, though more secretly, as though with minds disciplined for humility and disposed to investigate the truth.

Meanwhile, in the year 1540, God had set the shining example of John of Łask (John à Lasco) especially to the clergy [**cf. BAnt no. 21**]. For this man of illustrious ancestry and great learning, although provost (*praepositus*) of Gniezno and Łęczyca, and bishop-elect of Veszprém [in Hungary], having imbibed elements of the truth from the teaching of Luther, Zwingli, and Calvin, left both the priesthood and the papacy and his native land in the year aforesaid; and, going to Holland (*Belgiam*) and thence to England, he took a wife. While active in promoting the truth abroad, he also exerted himself vigorously in trying to allay the eucharistic controversy. But as we are to say more hereafter of this very distinguished man, we now proceed with the matter in hand.[156]

[German influence for reform, 1522–48]

About this time the example of [Ducal] Prussia was taking effect [in Royal Prussia] the fatal difficulty had been overcome which had arisen under King Sigismund I in the year 1526, when John Schultz, a member of [the Danzig town] council, and thirteen others wished boldly to cleanse the papal temples.[157]

[Ducal] Prussia had begun the reformation [in 1525] in accordance with the teaching of Luther, and was more freely preaching the Augsburg Confession, which was publicly presented to the Emperor Charles V at the imperial diet in 1530. This example added courage to the no small number in the Royal Commonwealth who were embracing the Reformation.[158] [17] And the [influence was all] the greater because Duke Albert of Prussia, born of the sister of King Sigismund [I], following the example of many princes and estates of the Empire, also had subscribed the Augsburg Confession.[159] Moreover, for the sake of the Poles who were living there or going thither, he was at his own expense supporting a Polish preacher at Königsberg, John Seklucjan,[160] who by his own effort and at his own expense procured the publication there of the four Gospels in Polish, and published several booklets in the Polish tongue against the worship of the saints and other abuses.[161]

[Counterattack by the Polish episcopacy, 1539]

For terror had fallen on many in the Kingdom on account of the sad case of Catherine, wife of Melchior Weigel,[162] councilor (*consul*) of the city of Cracow. Stanislas Budziński[163] in the Polish manuscript of his "Commentary on Polish History," chap. 4, calls her "Zalaszowska." *For because she censured the corruptions of the Roman Church, especially with regard to the idolatrous adoration of the host, she was condemned to the stake by Bishop Peter Gamrat of Cracow,[164] went to the execution as if to her marriage, and joyfully suffered her cruel death in the year 1539.*[165] This was the very year in which we have the tradition that Faustus Socinus was born in Siena, that most illustrious man, whose father was Alexander and whose mother was Agnes Petrucci, his parents thus being of very high birth, blood relations of several Popes of Rome and of several princes of Italy.[166] I do not conceal the fact that I have found in the *Chronicle* of Luke Górnicki, prefect of Tykocin, that Catherine was suspected of Judaism, because she denied (I understand) the Son of God to have been eternally generated from the substance (*essentia*) of the Father.[167]

[Quality of the episcopacy]

This bishop [Gamrat] through the extraordinary favor of Queen Bona, mother of [Sigismund II] Augustus, obtained both the aforesaid bishopric [of Cracow 1538–40] for an annual rent (*annuo censu*) and the archbishopric of Gniezno [1540–45], the highest in the Royal Commonwealth with its primatial dignity. He was doing everything to gratify his desires, being commonly said to lead an epicurean life because he was stuffing his fat belly with the choicest feasts. Gamrat worked hard to cover up his wickedness by his zeal (which even today, alas! is a common failing). In his archbishopric he was succeeded by Nicholas Dzierzgowski [1546–59], and in his bishopric [of Cracow] by Samuel Maciejowski [1545–50]. Both of them, especially Dzierzgowski, bitterly opposed the purer truth which had begun to be introduced into Poland. Maciejowski, the better man in both ability and character, was more just toward dissenters and, as [Stanislas] Orzechowski testifies in his *Annales*, 3: "He would terrify men of the Lutheran faction by threats sooner than inflict punishment on them."[168] Wherefore some asserted that he encouraged the heresy [18] of Luther in his diocese. But Budziński says and proves by examples that *[H]e was a hypocrite and a secret adversary of the truth and of those who love it. The devout Cracovians, finding him [Maciejowski] either a rather moderate bishop or a more covert opponent, made more and more progress in inquiring into the truth.*

[Reform stirrings among the Cracow intellectuals, 1545–47]

There was living in the city at that time John Trzecieski the Elder, highly distinguished for his noble birth, as well as for his scholarship and knowledge of

Hebrew, Greek, and Latin, who also had a very well furnished library. He, together with his companion in studies, Bernard Wojewódka,[169] worthy citizen, alderman (praetor) and printer at Cracow, sowed seeds of the truth, which they had derived from the great Erasmus,[170] in the mind of the noted Francis Lismanino of Corfù.[171] Although he was overseer (ephor) of the convents of the order of St. Francis and St. Clare, confessor to Queen Bona, and parish priest (parosus) of Czchów, yet from his reading of the sermons (presented to him by Queen Bona) of the Italian Bernardine Ochino (a man of the highest reputation for learning, eloquence, and devoutness among his brethren in Rome, and an exile from Rome for his bold preaching),[172] Lismanino came to suspect the whole Roman religion.

Moreover, there quite often came thither [to Trzecieski's library] Jacob Przyłuski,[173] notary of the castle court of Cracow and a very distinguished jurist, whose statute book we possess written in Latin.[174] Andrew Frycz Modrzewski,[175] secretary to the King, also came—a man in all respects of the highest distinction, the splendid monuments of whose genius we posses even now. What he thought on matters of faith it is not difficult to see for those who read his works with understanding. And that the more, both because Przyłuski, held in great favor by Peter Kmita,[176] palatine of Cracow and Marshal of the Kingdom, succeeded in instilling the purer truth into him [Kmita] and his court, and opposed the celibacy of the clergy and other abuses and also because Frycz, though through his learning he might have arrived at high honors, lived in modest circumstances, content with knowledge of the truth.

[Decisive discussion of the Trinity in the home of
John Andrew Trzeciewski, Cracow 1546: The Netherlander Spiritus]

What I have related here, I find in Budziński's aforementioned History under the years 1545, 1546, and 1547; as also that something singular took place in the house of this Trzecieski in the year 1546. For (as Frycz himself relates in his *Sylvae*, I, Tract 2, p. 81)[177] [**cf. RD 1, BAnt nos. 64, 65**], Trzeciewski had invited for dinner Frycz, Przyłuski, Wojewódka, and a certain man devout and well versed in the Scriptures, by birth a Netherlander (*Belgam*), whose name was Spiritus.[178] [19] Before they sat down to dine, they gathered in their host's library, crammed with all sorts of books. And each one taking up one or another book, the Netherlander fell upon a certain book of Christian prayers. In the [exact] words of Frycz:

> When he found prayers, one to God the Father, another to God the Son, a third to God the Holy Spirit, he said addressing us: "Well, have you three Gods, good friends?" And when we replied: "We have one God, who in unity of essence has (*habeat*) three persons," he said: "But now, 'what has' and 'what is had' are different things. He that has the three is therefore different from the three that are had by him." "Why, Spiritus," we said, "you are playing the sophist. Our confession is simple: that God is one in

essence, threefold in persons.'' ''Is your God, then,'' said he, ''both three-fold and one?'' ''Assuredly,'' we said, ''but the one in one respect, while the other in another.'' Then said he: ''If then this threefold being is one (*trinus unus est*) why do you address *them* with different prayers? Why do you in these prayers ask from them the different blessings that they confer upon the human race?'' These matters were then discussed among us back and forth. As we believed this proposition to be of all things the most certain, and were forbidden by our religion to engage in debates about it, we turned the conversation to other matters.

Briefly relating the same event in chapter iv, Budziński adds:

> *The conversation was then turned into another channel. Meanwhile, however, the guests took note of this, and took home the question, that is, about the Trinity, which was about to spring up in Poland* [**cf. BAnt no. 65; RD 1**].

For Frycz also adds:

> But when I was afterwards pondering the subject more carefully I wondered to myself how it happened that though all the outward actions of the persons were thought to be undivided, yet we addressed them in different prayers, praying separately to the Father, separately to the Son, separately to the Holy Spirit, as though one asked something from Peter, Paul, Andrew, James, and Philip in different prayers, and then in one prayer begged aid from all the Apostles, whose essences are distinct as well as their persons. In the common books of prayers there are distinct prayers of this sort to three persons. In these, unless I am mistaken, the things also that are asked of them, are also regarded as distinct. [20] But I know not whether this is done in the new kind [of prayer book].

And he then goes on to discuss this at greater length.

[Reform stirrings among some prelates]

Moreover, these meetings and pious conversations used often to be attended by Jacob Uchański. He was then only canon of Cracow and referendary, or master of requests, but afterwards rose through various sees to the archbishopric of Gniezno, and thus to the dignity of Primate. These meetings were attended[179] as well by Adam Drzewicki and Andrew Zebrzydowski,[180] likewise canons of Cracow. The latter afterwards succeeded Maciejowski[181] as bishop of Cracow and, as we shall see, was a very bitter persecutor of the lovers of the truth, so that following Gamrat's example, he concealed a like wickedness by a zeal equally wicked. This also refers to Uchański. [Joachim] Bielski relates in his *Polish History* (V, pp. 599, 608),[182] that while serving as bishop of Chełm, he was suspected of heresy, as was also John Drohojowski,[183] bishop of Kujawy, and they were solemnly warned on this account by Pope Julius III of Rome.

Indeed, [Paul] Piasecki also, though himself a bishop, writes of him thus:

> Jacob Uchański, when he could not obtain Rome's confirmation for the bishopric of Włodzisław on account of his being suspected of heresy, got possession of that church in the office of preacher; and when for this he was visited with an anathema by the Supreme Roman Pontiff, he himself also showered curses upon the latter.[184]

Caspar Cichocki (canon and pastor of Sandomierz) relates also of Bishop [Michael] Pac of Kiev in his *Addresses from Osiek*[185] that he would rather have professed the Lutheran than the Catholic religion.[186] Certainly Frycz also, in the preface of his fourth *Sylva*,[187] addresses this same Uchański not only as Primate, but also as one bound to him by his benevolence of long standing, and as one fairer to other dissenters, and inclined to restore harmony.

Erasmus Otwinowski of the Gryph clan [was] a devout man and the ingenious author of the little book on *Christian Heroes*.[188] In [connection with] his life of Thomas Falconius [therein] (the priest and preacher at the cathedral church of Lublin, who was thrown into chains for acknowledging the truth, then when freed from them, composed a Harmony of the four Gospels in his native tongue, and remained steadfast in the faith he had acknowledged).[189] Otwinowski has recorded that this Drohojowski opposed the Roman Pontiff, and [Otwinowski says] especially that [21] the aforesaid Uchański wished to take away from the Roman Pontiff the right of confirming bishops. [Otwinowski says further] that when cited by the Inquisitors, [Uchański] boldly resisted, wrote against the bull of citation or the pernicious process (*dicacem dicam*) brought against him at Rome, and offered it to the judgment of the renascent Church, and that he almost brought the matter to the point where Poland would have been subject to its own patriarch (*Patriarchae*).[190]

As to Drzewicki,[191] he steadfastly befriended the truth to the very end. And together with Trzecieski and Wojewódka he also supplied Lismanino with the books of Luther, Zwingli, Calvin, and others, from which in addition material for preaching to the people was supplied to the friars (*monachis*) of the Franciscan family, namely, to a Francis of Lithuania, to Stanislas [of] Opoczno, to Albert Kozakowski, also of Lithuania, and to others, of whom some died as promoters of the truth, while others, to employ the words of Budziński, "returned to their vomit [Prov 26:11]" such as Opoczno and John Szółdra.[192]

To these [reformers] should be added John of Koźmin, a man of learning and integrity, who enjoyed great influence with King Sigismund II[193] and the esteem of all as a man wise, prudent, and modest. I rather ought to include Lawrence of Przasnysz, *alias* Discordia in name and in fact, the rival of John of Koźmin.[194] John caused not a few scandals and hence was displeasing in the King's eyes and ears. Consequently after John's death Lawrence could make no progress for the truth in the King's mind. Indeed, he neither wished to nor was he worthy of so holy an office.[195]

[The bishops and the King's secret marriage, 1547–50]

Progress of the truth in the King's mind was hindered by the industry, watchfulness, and cunning of the Roman bishops, who always besieged the King. They filled his ears, kept the insignia of the Royal Commonwealth and the heart of the King, kept guard over the laws, and published the royal edicts. Indeed, Maciejowski was at the same time both bishop of Cracow and chancellor of the Royal Commonwealth, although contrary to the ancient traditions (as had been also a little earlier Peter Tomicki and John Chojeński).[196] And the bishops—what just then greatly suited their circumstances and interests— approved and defended the marriage that the King had contracted with Barbara Radziwiłł, widow of Stanislas Gasztołd,[197] palatine of Troki, a woman of the most enviable beauty. For many even of those who had begun to favor the truth and the reformation would have this marriage [22] annulled as one contracted with a commoner (*privata*) and privately, without counsel of the Senate, while in contrast Maciejowski and after him the bishops Andrew Zebrzydowski of Chełm, John Drohojowski of Kujawy, Leonard [Słończewski] of Kamieniec,[198] and other bishops and higher prelates stood by it. [In the circumstances] it came to pass that the King altered his disposition toward the bishops from one of aversion to one of favor.

For the King, according to Orzechowski, defended this deed in the full Senate, so that he burst out in these words:

> "Life itself is not dearer to me than the Commonwealth. But though the Commonwealth stands safe for you if I keep faith, how will you have this faith unimpaired if at your command I break faith with my wife? You have no reason to expect me to be a faithful King to you if I am an unfaithful husband to my wife. Wherefore as you wish me to keep my sworn faith with you, so you ought not to wish that by force or fraud I should violate the oath of that faith which before God I have sworn to my wife, especially since it is plainly said by the Lord Jesus and so reads in Scripture." Then he read from the open book [Matt 16:26]: "What doth it profit a man if he gain the whole world but suffer the loss of his own soul?" "Wherefore [the King continued], since my marriage with my wife is lawful, I will lay down my life sooner than abandon my wife" (*Annales*, 2).[199]

And so those good men, promoters of the truth, committed a grave error by opposing the King so strongly in this matter, while those who hated the truth and opposed them won the King's favor by taking the opposite side. So here too the saying of Christ [Luke 16:8] proved true: "The children of darkness are wiser in their generation than the children of light."

[Early lay proponents of the Reformation]

Among these promoters of the truth, Conrad Krupka Przecławski deserves to be reckoned, a man of distinguished birth, who, while the papacy was still flourishing and the voice of the truth had scarcely been heard, first accepted and used communion in both kinds. And how strong an attack of persecution he bravely bore, we shall relate below.[200]

Here also John Filipowski[201] should be mentioned (a member of the King's Court, a man most noble both for his ancient and splendid descent and for his virtues), who, having acknowledged the purer truth, was successful in recommending it to many, and who used to inveigh strongly against the traffic in indulgences and Masses, and against both the application of another's faith in infant baptism and the communication of Christ's body in the Eucharist, both of which are iniquitous and dishonoring to Christ. And he was against the [23] tormenting of souls in the purgatorial fire through so many ages, and against other errors and abuses that were bringing gain to the popes, though no profit to the people, least of all with regard to their salvation. So Otwinowski relates in his biography.

He [Otwinowski] also writes that [Andrew] Trzecieski instilled the truth into Samuel of Pińczów, the above mentioned [John] of Koźmin, and Leonard [Słończewski], preachers to the King, then into Jacob of Iłża,[202] professor at the University of Cracow (who had to flee into Silesia and escaped the hands of his enemies), and into others. Stanislas Rapagelanus,[203] also of the Franciscan order, [fared] like Iłża: for professing the truth, he had to flee into Prussia, where he died at Königsberg in *1545*.[204] However, Leonard [Słończewski],[205] captivated by the allurements of the world and by the gift of a bishopric, buried in the earth the gifts with which God had entrusted him and his own talent of knowledge of divine things, and like Esau sold his birthright for a mere dish of worldly pleasures [Matt 25:24; Gen 25:34].

The singularly happy zeal of this Trzecieski shone in his promoting those religious colloquies and in spreading the truth (God always aiding devout efforts, despite the ill will of the world), especially in that he won over Lismanino to the purer teaching. For through his indulgence and care, some of the order of St. Francis,[206] more apt than others to acknowledge the truth, left their monastic cloisters and prepared the way for their superior. Such were Alexis,[207] who was later active at Raków, and Jerome,[208] who used to preach to the Italians at Cracow and to instil into them purer teaching and religion. This Lismanino and [Martin] Opoczno[209] formed an intimate friendship with the noble Stanislas Ivan [Karniński][210] who, owning Aleksandrowice, an estate two miles from the city [of Cracow], often came to the city, and from this intercourse gained knowledge of the truth. [As a consequence Karniński] used to have spirited discussions about communion in both kinds and about other subjects of religious controversy with his kinsman [Stanislas] Podlodowski,[211] canon of Cracow, with whom (as is the custom) he used to drink rather freely. Also Ivan sharply disputed with the monks associated with Opoczno, so that he brought both Lismanino and Opoczno under suspicion of heresy. And Opoczno indeed rather frequently found it necessary to leave the city and to go into hiding.

[Episcopal harassment of Lismanino][212]

When Bishop Maciejowski had drunk deeply and the wine [24] had excited his wicked zeal and then excused his impertinence, he would sometimes call on Lismanino under the pretext of friendship, though in fact what he desired was to discover heretical books in his possession. But Lismanino was forewarned by Przyłuski[213] and by Bojanowski.[214] The latter was prefect of the bishop's court, a sagacious and generous man, who used often to joke even in their hearing about the ambition and pride of the successors of St. Peter, since Peter had no court, and hence no marshal for it. Forewarned, Lismanino, then, looked out for himself studiously and took pains to display the works of Scotus, Thomas, and others of that sort in his library and closets. Indeed, Bojanowski, a jovial lackey who prepared the way for his lord, cast his eyes here and there in the library, and noticed that works of scholastics were scattered about, said laughing at the evil inquisitiveness of his lord: "It is Scotus here, not Paul, M.K. (I suppose he meant: 'Mościwy Książę,' i.e., Your Serene Highness), who guards the threshold of our host against the enemy."[215] Budziński, who was at that time one of Lismanino's household, records this as an eye- and ear-witness and he relates *that when the bishop arrived unexpectedly, he himself carried off and hid in an oven the works of Luther, Calvin, and the like, which Lismanino was engaged in reading and used to have at hand; and that though the bishop not only looked at but even searched in all the corners, yet the providence of God, which especially watches over the faithful (and gives occasion for reflection), foiled his devices.*[216]

This [providence] also was shown later, when Lismanino had gone to Venice, having been sent thither by Queen Bona to offer congratulations on July 30 to [Giovanni] del Monte, who in 1550 had just been made Supreme Pontiff.[217] Planning to have him for this reason thrown into prison, this same bishop [Maciejowski] caused him to be held suspect of heresy in the Roman Court, so that he might not again return to Poland. Meanwhile, Lismanino had already left Rome, and was returning to Poland. On the way he was met by [Andrew] Czarnkowski[218] (later bishop of Poznań), who had been sent from the [Royal] Court to Rome to offer [on the same occasion] congratulations. He, being friendly to Lismanino, reported this machination of the bishop and also his death which had intervened unexpectedly in 1550. Thus it appears everywhere that God of his marvelous wisdom confounds the vicious plans of the wicked and directs them to a good end.

[Lord Stanislas Ivan Karniński converts the Cracow cathedral preacher][219]

Of this [divine wisdom] we have shining and memorable [25] examples in this [Stanislas] Ivan [Karniński] himself (a man outstanding for his noble birth and his piety) as we are informed by a man also of well-known nobility and piety, dignity, and learning, Adam Gosławski[220] of the Oksza clan. For he was both a blood relation of Ivan and expert (as well as deeply interested) in such matters, and had the lease on the estate of that village of Aleksandrowice [belonging to Karniński].

As Ivan used frequently to come to the city, he was on intimate terms with the chief preacher of the cathedral and had convinced the honest man of the errors of the Papists, especially of their execrable idolatry. Not content with this, long and often Ivan tried to persuade him—reluctant as the preacher was, for the flesh is timid and clever in weaving the snares of excuses. Yet at length he began yielding to the claims of conscience and trusting to the providence of God. [Ivan insisted] that he could not attain eternal salvation unless by a public recantation he would declare the truth that he had come to acknowledge; unless he would strive to give better instruction to those whom he had led astray by his sermons or had confirmed in their errors; and finally, unless having bidden his hearers farewell, he would betake himself to Ivan's home, riding a horse which would be kept in readiness.

Accordingly, after delivering a sermon on a holy day before a very large crowd of people, when [the priest] knew that a faithful servant was already standing with the horse at the church door as agreed upon, he made a supplementary address to the people, bade them farewell, declared that he was soon going on a journey, thanked his hearers of every age and condition and of both sexes for all their acts of kindness and friendship, and at length confessed that he had taught them wrong, nay false, doctrines, and especially that he had not warned them against idolatry. Thereupon he solemnly urged them all, as they loved God's glory and their own salvation, to read the Holy Writ, and to worship the true, invisible, eternal God as it directed, rejecting the inventions of men. But the people were struck with amazement at his words, and urged him to stay with them. He bade them, however, a renewed farewell. And, again expressing his gratitude for all their kindness and his concern for true religion, he seriously reminded them of their duty. And at last leaving his pulpit and the sanctuary, without staying for any of his effects, he mounted the waiting horse, and came to Ivan.

Through constant companionship with this man he imbibed a fuller knowledge of the truth. Imbued with piety, he took strength and courage from the burning zeal of his fearless host and from his example in going every Sunday, Wednesday, and Friday into the city to [Reformed] worship, so that while at first [26] he used to go there with his patron, he at length went there alone and indeed stayed for some time.

[Bishop Maciejowski and lord Karniński contend
for the soul of the cathedral preacher, c. 1550][221]

This affair gave the bishop, of whom we have just spoken, occasion to pour out in revenge the resentment inwardly engendered by all his perverse zeal. He seized the priest in the absence of his patron, threw him into prison, and tried to bring him back to papacy by threatening him with the extreme penalty. While many of the princes (*procerum*) and nobles interceded for him in vain, Ivan, a man of invincible bravery, took the bold step of going to the bishop and addressing him. He mingled threats with pleas, and skillfully and felicitously using with the bishop the influence provided by descent, his former military prowess, the righteousness of his cause, and the state of the times, with so many of the magnates and of the priests (as we have said) abjuring popery in Poland, and Germany being aflame with religious war, Ivan, after many disputes, at last got this response from the bishop: If the man preferred heresy to Catholic truth and would rather adhere to Ivan than return to him, he would set him free, although the latter was a deserter not only from the Catholic Church, but also from holy orders, over whom he had full authority. But he would continue holding him if, as he had heard, the man was sorry for the crime and would return to the right way. Ivan accepted the condition, sure of the steadfastness of his convert (*proselyti*).

The man was brought from prison, overwhelmed with the most generous promises on the one hand and the most grievous threats on the other, and was placed before his judge and his patron. Then someone addressed him in the name of the bishop and offered him pardon for his crime, especially as he had heard that he was being brought to repentance and was sorry for the sins committed. On the other hand, the noble lord Ivan earnestly entreated him and gave him the choice of either adhering to his patron or returning to the bishop and the Church. The priest, being more perturbed by the authority of the bishop—and what is more, by the threats given in private—than enticed by promises, fell at the bishop's knees, confessed his error, begged and received pardon, and promised to abandon Ivan and his religion.

But, sorely stirred by indignation mingled with shame and sorrow, Ivan roundly rebuked him as a liar and deceiver, thanked the bishop for his just decision, and threw all the blame on the one who had twice been a deserter, heaping sarcasm on him. The bishop tried to calm him, as he found him panting. He [27] rejoiced with the crowd of bystanders, yet spoke to Ivan courteously, because he saw that he was angry, and invited him to dinner. But Ivan, sick at heart, rushed rather than withdrew from the bishop's palace, having with due courtesy thanked him for the offered hospitality.

When Ivan had taken his leave, a sumptuous and very abundant banquet was spread, flowing with wine stronger than that at prelatical dinners. But the priest, in the intervals of the applause, was likewise sick at heart when reflecting more upon what he had done, and as he came to himself and gave ear to his conscience, he began to be more and more stalked[222] by the terror of it.

Now Ivan, when on the road, told his servant to give him his gloves. The servant replied that he had handed them to him as [Ivan] was about to enter the bishop's chamber, and asserted that they had been left behind. Ivan bade him return to fetch them, and he did as he was bidden. The servant returned to the bishop's palace, tied his horse at the door, and went up to the place flowing with luxury to ask for his master's gloves. When the matter was reported to the bishop, and no one after careful search could find the gloves, the bishop ordered one of his chamber servants at once to buy the best pair of gloves in a shop.

Meantime the priest, left behind by the others in some bedroom alone, and with his mind full of anxious thoughts, saw Ivan's servant whom he knew, and noted that he had entered that palace. As he was not under guard, the priest rushed out and, seen by nobody, mounted the servant's horse and followed Ivan at full speed.

Meanwhile, a very fine pair of gloves was brought from the market place to the bishop's dining room, where he had full beakers of the noblest unmixed wine drained to the health of the noble Ivan in the presence of his servant, and after offering him one or two cups of wine, gave him also the gloves and bade him give his master his best greetings. The servant left the palace and, not finding his horse, returned to the bishop with the complaint that his horse, which had been seen by all, had been stolen at the bishop's own palace gate. He begged most earnestly that this one or another be forthwith presented to him, as he feared his master's severity. Here the bishop addressed his table companions: "Why, this is a greater loss than that of the gloves! What ill fortune ever brought this Master Ivan to me?" Then he gave orders to search for the stolen horse and, finally, moved by the servant's prayers and tears, said to his court servants standing by: "Let whoever [28] among you has a horse at hand give it to this servant, whose horse either may have run home or can be found; but if not found, I shall make good the loss."

So the servant was sent away with a new and fair gift. Meantime, a mile from the city, the priest caught up with Ivan, who at first thought he was seeing a ghost. At length, when the priest told him the whole story, he upbraided him, yet turned his indignation into joy and received him gladly. [Lord Ivan was gladdened] especially after [the runaway priest] told the matter from the beginning and related in what way the bishop had broken down his purpose when it was not yet fully settled, both by promising to restore him to his former dignities and to promote him to new ones, and by threatening him with the extreme penalty, yet being unwilling to fulfill the promised stipulation of a free release. Upon this Ivan, with his mind calmed, at once gave thought to protecting his convert. Meantime he was wondering what might be the reason for the long delay of his servant, when lo! the latter rushed up, mounted on a new horse and with a new and fine gift. So the devout man got back his runaway attendant and his horse, and received besides another horse and a new pair of gloves, as though in lieu of gratuity. After this the bishop himself, so often foiled, was very much enraged and was especially chagrined in that he knew that his ruses had been revealed to all by the priest.

[A divine thunderbolt arbitrates a dispute in favor of lord Karniński][223]

The same Ivan was being wronged, as it happened, by a powerful neighbor, Severin Boner,[224] castellan of Cracow, although the latter was an adherent of the same Evangelical[225] religion, nay, even patron of the Cracow church. No entreaties or persuasions, even of ministers of the divine word themselves, prevailed with him, but rather made him the bolder, so that he was preparing to inflict a still greater wrong upon his peaceable, or at least inoffensive, neighbor. And when arbitration had been agreed to, he came to the field which was the object of controversy surrounded by a great crowd of his friends and dependents. Then Ivan, moved by the injury and by strong feeling, raised his eyes to heaven and cried: ''O God who hatest all falsehood, wrong and iniquity, thou seest how much I am being wronged by this powerful neighbor. Show forth thy majesty and put forth the strength of thy might against the power of this unbridled and wilful man.'' Scarcely had he said this, when he saw Heaven settling his just complaints. For immediately, out of a clear sky, a thunderbolt discharged from the clouds, killed the horses nearest the castellan's coach, together with their driver.[226] [29] The castellan, struck with consternation, deprecated the wrong done to Ivan, restored his land to him, and henceforth held him in honor.

[Otwinowski and Budziński on several Evangelical leaders]

This same [Erasmus] Otwinowski [in his *Christian Heroes*] includes among the first promoters of the Reformation Simon Żak,[227] a man celebrated in Lithuania for his piety and his preaching of the purer truth; and Martin of Opoczno,[228] Master of Arts (different from the one mentioned above), a man highly distinguished and great in his own time for his learning and as the educator of many noble youths in the home of Peter Kmita, and most of all for being steadfast to the last in his devotion to the truth he had begun to hold. He counts among them also his true companion Martin Taurinus,[229] who in view of the state of the times prudently laid the truth before honest men in private and made many, though silent, disciples of Christ, who were a little later to speak out the truth openly. Among these he also numbers Nicholas of Kurów, whom he deservedly calls ''the Martyr'' (of whom we mean to speak a little later in due order),[230] and Felix Cruciger[231] of Szczebrzeszyn who, scorning and giving up rich parishes and church dignities that he had a right to expect, left the Church of Rome himself and then caused others to leave it also. Cruciger, strange to say, when brought into court by an ill-willed bishop on suspicion of heresy, and asked whether in his sermons he followed the lead of Calvin (of whom hitherto he had heard nothing), began to read him and to make progress in knowledge of the truth— a manifest proof that God often turns evil into good. Of this there is a similar instance in the sermons of Ochino given to Lismanino by the Queen, as we have seen above.[232]

In this list of outstanding men Otwinowski later places Martin Krowicki, whom he commends, along with the two aforementioned, for his exceptional piety and zeal for the glory of God. He briefly relates that this man enjoyed great favor with his master (the Kmita above mentioned) and with the world. Although a priest under the fierce papal tyranny, Krowicki led many to Christ.

He disproved the claim that an impure celibacy is superior to a chaste marriage.[233] At first according to the teaching of Luther, he defended the real presence of the body of Christ in the Eucharist and the use of images, but afterwards, the firm hand of God pressing him to go on in the knowledge of the truth, he taught all by his own example not to resist God. He wrote a little book on the spiritual cross [30] (which he was at the time first to bear), then also a powerful *Apologia* for his faith against Bishop Andrew Zebrzydowski of Cracow. He was treacherously captured by him, but soon set free. Although through a plot of the same bishop he had afterwards been assaulted in vain at Cracow, he continued most ardent in preaching sermons and quite often had on his tongue the words of Paul [1 Cor 9:16]: "Woe is me if I preach not the Gospel." He was generous to the poor, to whom he sometimes gave even his own undergarments, though his wife protested that he should not give anything. And he was constant even to the last. We shall treat all of them in chronological order.[234]

Treating jointly these three men who are among the foremost in their services toward the Church, Budziński says: *The aforesaid Nicholas of Kurów,[235] chaplain to Peter Zborowski[236] (whether still castellan of Wojnicz, or palatine of Cracow, I do not know), Felix [Cruciger], a man learned and pious, and [Martin] Krowicki, an eminent instrument of God, were chosen to preach. They taught against images as well as against the invocation of the saints as things not only unknown to the primitive truth, but also plainly contrary to it. And they separated many people from popery, and thus signally carried through the beginnings of the Reformation from 1546 to 1550, and, removing the Latin Mass, instituted the Polish one with less ceremonial.* Of Krowicki [the reconverted Catholic] Orzechowski has recorded the following (*Annales*, 3):

> After [Francis] Stancaro[237] had been driven from Pińczów, he was succeeded in that place by refugees through whose efforts this sect brought in by Stancaro, spreading more widely, crept into many honest families.[238] Of these the foremost was Martin Krowicki who had been for many years steward of the estates of the palatine, Peter Kmita. This priest, when in charge of the church at Wisznia [Sądowa] in the diocese of Przemyśl, at the very time that these things were going on in Cracow, married [13 December 1550] Magdalena, daughter of Stanislas Pobiedziński[239] at the home of Stanislas Orzechowski in the village of Żurowice. Driven out for this by Bishop John Dziaduski, he fled to Pińczów and, wanderer and exile that he was, having abandoned the religion that he had practised at the town of Wisznia in Red Ruthenia, he followed the party of Zwingli and taught the Sacramentarian heresy (*sectam Sacramentariam*) at Pińczów according to Stancaro's regulations.[240]

[Nicholas Oleśnicki supports Stancaro in reform at Pińczów, 1550]

Here it is appropriate that I mention the most valiant deed of Nicholas Oleśnicki of the Dębno clan, owner of Pińczów, a great souled man and really incomparable Christian hero (richly deserving eternal remembrance and praise). [31] For he, the first of the nobles, once the Roman superstition had been bravely attacked, met the counterattack of its defenders with outstanding bravery.[241] At about this time there had come to Poland Francis Stancaro,[242] an Italian by birth, a man deeply versed not only in Latin, but also in Hebrew and Greek. He took upon himself the reformation of the churches as set forth in printed books according to the rule of Zwingli.[243] He was thrown into prison in the fortified castle of Lipowiec by the aforementioned Bishop Samuel Maciejowski of Cracow. However, through the efforts of Stanislas Lasocki, sub-chamberlain or rather high chamberlain[244] of Łęczyca, Andrew Trzecieski[245] (son of the above-mentioned John), and Christopher Gliński,[246] in the extraordinary providence of God, Stancaro was freed and taken to a place of safety.

Oleśnicki, not fearing the bishop's anger or the spite of so many enemies, took Stancaro first into his own residence [**cf. BAnt no. 52**]. Then he turned the monks out of their cloister and threw the images out of the church, and even had them broken and burned up. So Oleśnicki dared to do this unusual thing, taking example from bishops whose ambition and avarice led them to uphold all the abuses, even the idolatrous ones, which though inveterate were nevertheless unknown to the primitive purity of the Church. And when he [Lord Oleśnicki] had baffled and outwitted [them in] their [ecclesiastical] court, since he was accompanied by a large group of the nobility, the King was induced to institute a serious lawsuit against him and ordered him to appear before his own tribunal. Orzechowski describes this case so accurately that the account deserves to be inserted by me here:

> When Stancaro had betaken himself to Pińczów, he began to establish the error of Zwingli, and to take pains to lead Oleśnicki away from the religion of his fathers and to persuade him to a foreign religion. According to these precepts he ordered that images be removed from the church, an outlandish (*peregrinam*) Lord's Supper be instituted in place of the usual one,[247] and the rites be abolished that the monks used to perform under the old religion in the church of his town. This church together with the adjoining monks' house, had been erected with great pains and richly endowed by the generosity of [Bishop] Zbigniew Oleśnicki[248] and Stancaro was making haste to profane it. But since his plan seemed dangerous to [Lord] Oleśnicki, in order that nothing be done unadvisedly, he called his friends and took them into counsel, in which after various judgments had been debated, the following judgment prevailed: the images, together with the rest of the utensils, should remain undisturbed in the church. The monks also should perform their rites according to the old rule, since none of these things could safely be changed. As the King was near at hand, the bishop also had not yet left Cracow. [32] And another time would be more fit for making these changes. For the present it was thought best to institute the Lord's Supper, but this should be done in private in the castle, not publicly in the church, which being in the town is adjacent to the castle. In accordance with this view they permitted Stancaro to appoint the manner of the new Supper and to teach the use of it.[249]

Thus far Orzechowski. Otwinowski adds that when pleading his cause before the King, although savagely bitten and wounded by the King's dog and bleeding, this invincible hero nevertheless stood firm and unmoved: an eminent omen that though not uninjured by biting dogs, he had to stand firm, invincible, and unmoved, God's grace assisting. For who can believe otherwise of so splendid a deed? In this excellent man and confessor of the truth which he had acknowledged there were certainly fulfilled the words of Christ [2 Cor 12:9]: "My strength is made perfect in weakness." For he must be said to have broken the ice, as the saying is, and to have prepared and opened for all other people the way that God was pointing out for approaching and entering the sanctuary of divine truth.

Thus then, as also before, not only the power of the ecclesiastical and temporal Senate, but also the King's Majesty saw and realized not only that truth cannot be conquered, but that she cannot but conquer. For she is peaceful, nay unharmed, but yet being furnished with those spiritual weapons which prevail with God. These the Apostle Paul (that matchless Christian hero, easily first among the leaders of Christ's people) celebrates and by his own example approves and commends [2 Cor 10:1 – 3]. These instructions and these alone are always and everywhere availing—"to the pulling down of strongholds with which we cast down imaginations, and every high thing that exalteth itself against the knowledge of God, and bringing into captivity every thought to the obedience of Christ," even as the Apostle there adds [2 Cor 4 – 6].[250]

But having seen this divine armor[251] in passing, let us return to the man [Lord Oleśnicki] who then, before King Augustus and his whole council, brought it forth, not more bravely than also fortunately. That his enemies were daunted by the man's great firmness and courage, both Otwinowski reports, quoting a trustworthy witness, and the incident itself testifies. For the man's remarkable strength of body as well as of mind is celebrated. Moreover, the very vigor of his prime of life and the preeminence of his family (ancient, illustrious, and of senatorial rank, which is also the same as that of the Sienieńskis, [33] and boasts of the notable ornament of Cardinal Zbigniew)[252] and what especially deserves consideration here, the consciousness of a good case, all imparted very great confidence and bravery to the young man born for whatever is noble. He therefore, withdrawing from the King's presence victorious and triumphant, not only did not desist from the work so well begun, but rather continued undauntedly in promoting it and in carrying it through to the desired end. And of this development we are presently to speak.

His courage was increased also by the disposition of the King, who was by nature gracious and merciful and therefore did not enforce the law of his great grandfather Jagiełło, passed against heretics in *1424*, seeing that it had been clearly abrogated by that King himself,[253] as we shall, please God, point out in the civil history.[254] Moreover, the King did not put into effect the edict passed in the case of Oleśnicki. (It was after this that the Decree of Parczów was issued in 1564.).[255] And thus Sigismund readily approved the inchoate beginnings of the [recovered] truth, both winking at them and assenting to them.

[Pińczów emerges as a center of the reform]

Therefore also Oleśnicki, having marshaled the greater courage to promote the truth of God, thus in 1550 founded a church consisting of those who confessed the purer doctrine, carrying off the palm from all the rest of the followers and patrons of the truth. And as to his other virtues, he added extraordinary liberality and hospitality. Thus he drew many men excelling in learning and virtue to his town of Pińczów and attracted their love. Such was Stancaro, whom nevertheless it would later seem expedient to send away to Königsberg, where he found a violent opponent in Andrew Osiander. The latter launched a new doctrine of justification in 1551, namely that the justice of man is the very essence of God.[256] The direct opposite of it was taught a little later, about 1559, by Flacius Illyricus, that original sin is the very essence of man.[257] Such were also John Łaski,[258] George Biandrata,[259] Francis Lismanino, Martin Krowicki, Peter Statorius,[260] George Schomann,[261] Gregory Paul,[262] [Samuel] Brelius,[263] [Andrew] Trzecieski,[264] and others, so that Pińczów was then celebrated as the Sarmatian Athens.[265]

[Religious publications in Polish]

And there the entire Holy Bible[266] was translated into the vernacular by these pious and learned men, and was printed at Brest in Lithuania at the expense of Nicholas Radziwiłł, Palatine of Vilna [**cf. BAnt no. 52**], a most noble prince and a most valiant champion of the reviving truth. For he had been appointed captain of this royal borough, [34] in which with his private means he set up a printing office and put it in charge of Wojewódka,[267] whom he summoned from Cracow. Thence also issued a book of psalms and hymns,[268] and other works of the same character, by reading which the people were being recalled from the superstitions of Rome to the true way of worshiping God.

[Increasing nobiliary support for the Reformation, 1550]

Indeed, in this praiseworthy and wholesome undertaking the people were led by many of the chief nobility and not a few of the magnates (*procerum*), especially in the palatinate of Cracow and in its districts of Proszów and Książ on the river Śreniawa, the terrritory well known as the ancestral seat of the Lubomirskis, Rupniowskis, Wiejskis, and other very distinguished families, so that the clergy called it the river of the Lutherans or the ''Luthers.'' All dissenters are commonly called by this name in Poland by the Roman and Greek Catholics.[269] Thus at this time the efforts of the bishops to suppress the truth, nay rather to molest those that confessed it, were for the most part futile. An excellent example of this is furnished by Valentine, pastor Krzczonów, of whom Paul Piasecki himself speaks as follows:

> Canon Stanislas Orzechowski[270] of Przemyśl took a wife [in 1550], and stubbornly persevered in keeping her. Not long before this, Valentine, pas-

tor (*sacerdos parochus*) of Krzczonów, for his having taken a wife, was
ordered to plead his cause before Bishop Samuel Maciejowski of Cracow.
Under the protection of Nicholas Oleśnicki of Pińczów, Nicholas Rey,[271]
and Remigian Chełmski,[272] he defended his error in public, so that the
bishop, fearing that his sentence would be treated with contempt, thought it
best to refrain from passing judgment.[273]

But the bishops also wasted their time in opposing the marriage of
Orzechowski, for the nobility were vehemently defending their rights against
episcopal arrogance. Yet after a decade Orzechowski left off attacking the
clergy, being won over by the allurements of the world. The [nuptial] example
of Orzechowski was followed in the same year, 1550, and indeed at the same
place, by Martin Krowicki, who took a wife, as we have heard Orzechowski
himself tell in the passage quoted above.[274] The same time saw the brothers
Białobreski,[275] two abbots, the one of Mogiła and the other of Jędrzejów, married after the custom of the ancient bishops. Soon, therefore, in the year 1551,
the celibacy of the clergy was confirmed by a new decree at a diet in
Piotrków.[276]

About that time these nobles caused the purer doctrine to be preached to
them within the walls of their own residences. Among these was Martin
Zborowski,[277] palatine of Kalisz, [35] in the King's town of Stobnica, which he
ruled with the title of captain (*praefecto*). Then there was Stanislas Lasocki,[278]
chamberlain of Łęczyca, a man highly esteemed for his rank, devotion and merits as owner of Pełsznica; and, nearly his equal, Jerome Filipowski, [owner of]
Krzcięcice,[279] a real pair of comrades. Stanislas Stadnicki [owner of]
Niedźwiedź,[280] and Nicholas Dłuski in Iwanowice,[281] like the preceding, caused
the purer doctrine to be preached to them within the walls of their own homes.
This same [reception of Reformed preachers] was undertaken in Great Poland
by Andrew Górka, castellan of Poznań and captain general (*starosta generalny*)
of Great Poland, a man of great power owing to his wealth, influence, and
exceptional gifts of mind;[282] by Stanislas and Jacob Ostroróg in the palatinate of
Kujawy;[283] by [Raphael] Leszczyński,[284] captain of Radziejów; by Christopher
Lasocki at Brzeziny;[285] and by others elsewhere.

At this Lasocki, as also at the Ostrorógs (as Bielski relates in his *Chronicle*,
V),[286] a little after the synod at Piotrków, Archbishop Nicholas Dzierzgowski of
Gniezno struck in vain with a spent thunderbolt as also did Bishop John Dzia-
duski of Przemyśl, at Stanislas Stadnicki; and Bishop Andrew Zebrzydowski of
Cracow, at Conrad Krupka.[287]

Indeed the seed of the truth scattered here and there grew up, though enemies
tried in vain to nip it in the bud, which God prevented, making the wide sowing
fruitful with the dew and rain of heaven's blessings, and confounding the
wicked designs of the enemies of the truth. And of this there was at the time a
signal instance in the case of the Orzechowski already mentioned, who by taking a wife in 1550 had stirred up a hornet's nest, as the saying is, and had roused

against himself the ill-will of all the bishops and of their partisans, as he himself relates in his *Annales*.[288]

[The *exemplum* of Stanislas Lasocki]

And when Barbara Radziwiłł was being crowned at Cracow according to ancient ceremony on 7 December 1550 (Bielski, *Chronicle*, V, states that this took place on 6 April),[289] Stanislas Lasocki, full of zeal for divine truth and therefore hated by the bishops and struck with an anathema (which at that time was not yet a mere spent thunderbolt), while standing among the leading men near the King and listening to, or rather looking at, the ceremony of the Mass, was ordered by the Marshal of the Kingdom, as the supreme governor of the Royal Court, to leave the church.

At first he refused to obey. In defense of his innocence, he adduced as the just cause the maintenance of propriety, namely, that it was not proper for a wellborn citizen and a man honorable and without reproach to yield [36] to any other than his Lord. But when the Marshal repeated the command upheld by royal authority, Lasocki, taking counsel of good discretion, withdrew. Meanwhile the bishops looked with fury on the Christian hero who was disapproving the ceremony as idolatrous. Nevertheless at length, unable to bear his presence, the bishops interrupted the celebration of the Mass.[290] This made clear enough in the eyes of the King and his Court that injustice had been conquered and that truth was the conqueror. So much the more when Lasocki afterwards in a large company of distinguished gentlemen excused his refusal to obey the command so unexpectedly given, on the ground of his being confident of his innocence. He did not so much clear his guilt, as, by his modest reproach, bring out into the open that of his unjust judge.

And this tribute deserves to be paid to the very high honor and singular worth of this man, whom no one of the time is said to have equaled in fervent zeal for the heavenly truth. He was tireless and invincible in promoting it and in confirming the [Reformed] Church by his efforts, in his exceptional love of piety, his constancy in offering prayers and in listening to and arranging religious discussions, his open-handed and far-seeing kindness to the ministers of God, his hatred of drunkenness, luxury, and all vices. Over against this was his devotion to the virtues, of which he was said to be a living example. Of this we shall also see clear proofs in what follows. So here also a magnanimous man is rightly to be placed among those who by their rugged strength aided the first reformers of the Polish churches and were wholly intent on confirming the Church of Christ, having undertaken suitable measures.

[Rising influence of Francis Lismanino]

Among these first reformers, but in holy orders, is to be placed Francis Lismanino. And among the measures for promoting the truth and founding the Church is to be reckoned the singular favor that he enjoyed with the King and his mother Bona [Sforza].[291] For after he safely returned from his journey to Italy in 1550 to Warsaw[292] where Queen Bona was living, and gave account of his mission to Rome, he a little later received a letter from the King, who was then at Cracow after the coronation of Queen [Barbara] had taken place. In the letter he commanded him to win for his Queen Consort the favor of his mother, Queen Bona. For the marriage of her son the King had been especially displeasing to her and exasperated her disposition, spiteful enough as it was by nature. Nor was it accidentally that somebody jeered at her: [37]

> Whoever, when you were being bathed in sacred waters, imposed the name
> Bona on you, imposed on us all.[293]

Having made three journeys to Cracow in January, February, and March 1551, he discharged this duty more to the satisfaction of the King than to that of Queen Bona. In the castle church [the cathedral of Cracow] amidst a large court attendance, he [Lismanino] publicly though imprudently, by the King's management, carried through his mission of reconciling the two queens, mother-in-law and daughter-in-law.[294] From that time on the King held him in high esteem, and in token of his grateful and gracious mind, he promised him the first episcopal dignity vacant, through Grand Chancellor [John] Ocieski,[295] who had been appointed in place of Bishop Maciejowski.

But here, at the turn of the year 1550 and 1551, as I reach its Easter celebration [29 March 1551] in my account of the acts of Lismanino, I stop. Having related the beginnings of the Reformation [in Poland] from 1545 to 1550 inclusive, and then having pointed out the preparations for founding the Church, I proceed to follow out in order the occurrences of the year 1551 and of the following years.[296]

[38]BOOK TWO

How the Reformation Was Advanced
from the Year 1551
to the Year 1562 Inclusively,
in which Gregory Paul at Cracow
Founded a Church of Catholic Christians

CHAPTER ONE

How the Seeds of Divine Truth
Were Brought from Italy
to Poland by Laelius Socinus in 1551.

God conferred upon our nation a very great distinction, and one deserving forever to be remembered with grateful mind, when by the coming of many learned
and godly men, not only from the neighboring land of Germany, but also from
more distant countries, especially Italy, he implanted in it books, a reputation for
education, and knowledge of the truth. From Italy, indeed, a factory of distinguished minds, where the engines of so many errors and superstitions were
forged, he fittingly sent us the arms of the heavenly truth cast there by himself.

From the manuscript History by Budziński and from the course of the Life of
Laelius Socinus,[1] I gather that *[A]bout the year 1546* [**cf. BAnt no. 49**], at
Vicenza[2] and in other cities in the territory of Venice, there were not a few who
took the pains to investigate the truth and to this end held religious meetings and
conferences. They discussed the main topics of the Christian faith, namely:
That *there is one God most high who both created all things by his powerful
word and effectual command, and sustains all by his wise and kind providence.*
That *his only begotten Son is Jesus of Nazareth, a true but not a mere* (simpli-
cem) *man, since he was begotten in a chaste virgin by the power* (virtute) *of the
Holy Spirit.* That *he, having been promised by God to the Patriarchs, was at the
time appointed to be sent to their posterity; he proclaimed to men the mystery of
the saving Gospel;* [39] *he showed the way of eternal life to be attained not by
indulging the flesh, but by living piously; according to the will of the Father he
devoted his life to procuring and confirming the remission of sins; and he was
raised by him from the dead and exalted.[3]* That *those who believe in Christ and
are obedient to him are justified by God.* That *pious men thus recover in the
second* (novissimo) *Adam the immortality lost in the first Adam.[4]* That *he alone
is head and lord of the people subject to him.* That *he, being appointed judge of
all the quick and the dead, will come to us at the last day; that in the meantime
he will recover and hold rule for a thousand years [Rev 20:4]; that at last he
will deliver the rule to God the Father and will be subject to him, so that God*

may be all in all [1 Cor 15:28].⁵ That, however, commonly accepted dogmas are opinions introduced by Greek philosophers. These are the dogmas of the Trinity, of the Christ of God who is himself God the Creator and the same God as the Father, of the Holy Spirit of God who is also God, of justification either through meritorious works or through faith alone in application of the merits of Christ to oneself, and others like these. These dogmas certainly constitute the principal part of the Christian religion and, when brought to the light, aroused the whole Christian world to awake and shake off the lethargy of its faults.

There was in this devout society in Vicenza a certain abbot named [Jerome] Buzzale,⁶ who when his secret meetings and studies had been divulged, with forty other men took flight, since they were living in immediate danger of their lives, and sought and found among Turks the safety which as a Christian he could not enjoy among Christians. They went to Thessalonica, all except three: Julius of Treviso,⁷ Francis of Rovigo,⁸ and Jacob of Chieri,⁹ of whom the former two were strangled at Venice,¹⁰ while the third died a natural death. And the abbot ended his life at Damascus. But those who did not betake themselves to the Turks, though protected by seasonable silence, were nevertheless not safe enough in their own country, and found shelter in Switzerland, Moravia, and at length in our Poland.¹¹

Among these was Laelius Socinus in Siena, a man highly renowned not only for his illustrious birth (being as we have seen related either by blood or marriage to Popes and many Italian princes),¹² but also for his learning and for the singular uprightness of his character. He therefore, both for fear of this danger [40] and because, having detected errors and loathing them, was eager to examine and to confess the truth, left his native land in 1547 and came first to Switzerland. He traveled thence through France, Britain, the Netherlands, and Germany and also visited Poland in 1551; and having sown the seed of piety in the hearts of Lismanino¹³ and others, he returned a little later to Moravia, and thence to Switzerland.¹⁴ But in Moravia Paruta,¹⁵ Gentile,¹⁶ Dario,¹⁷ and Alciati¹⁸ were actively and ably engaged in exploring the truth, as were also Francis Negri¹⁹ and Bernardine Ochino [**cf. BAnt no. 50**]. *Some of them departed this life in Poland, others elsewhere. Those who were living in Moravia used frequently to send theses on the Trinity and obscure passages of Holy Scripture²⁰ to the neighboring country of Poland. And these were seed-beds of the truth, as we shall see in due course.*

CHAPTER TWO

In What Way Lismanino Came to the Knowledge and Public Profession of the Truth, and with What Good Result.

Lismanino, having by his services won the especial favor of King Augustus ever since his mission of reconciliation (although Queen Barbara soon afterwards, i.e., 23 May [1551] had exchanged life for death, to the great grief of the King), did not misuse this favor which he was constantly experiencing in the years 1551, 1552, and 1553, as is commonly done, in order to satisfy his ambition or avarice. From this source the streams of all evils flow upon the human race. Instead Lismanino made use of the favor to recommend the truth to the King and to promote the truth that he harbored in his heart. Meanwhile Laelius [Socinus] had come to Poland in 1551, as we saw a little bit before.[21] And as he had not only come to Cracow, but had also become intimate with learned and upright men, that is, those who were devoted to the truth, he was most active in leading Lismanino [in Geneva] to throw off the cowl,[22] and then encouraged him to investigate the truth and to visit the splendidly reformed churches of Switzerland [**cf. BAnt no. 50**].

These seeds of the truth, sown in the field of a heart adapted to virtue, in due time bore rich [41] fruit. Moreover, the King quite often discussed with Lismanino, as the Queen Mother's principal adviser (for he was not only her secretary but also her confessor), a third marriage to be contracted with Catherine,[23] granddaughter of Charles V, daughter of Ferdinand I, who had been left a widow by Francis Gonzaga, Duke of Mantua.[24] And since as he was on this account associated with the King in constant intimacy, he talked with him on matters of religion, both of them being equally interested in religious topics. In this way it came to pass that the King opened to him the innermost secrets of his mind: That he was displeased with the corruption of the Church. On Wednesdays and Fridays after dinner Lismanino would bring Calvin's *Institutes* (than which no better book was then to be had) and would talk freely with the King on all topics of faith in detail, with no one else present. This lasted up to his marriage in Cracow in 1552 to Catherine of Austria.[25]

When a little before this, both were suffering from a sudden and serious illness, they had the same physicians to care for their health. These, on leaving the King, used by his command to go to Lismanino. After recovering from this illness, while conversing on the subject of religion, they decided that Lismanino, with the title of King's minister (we commonly say agent, *factor*), should at his expense furnish the royal library with books of every kind, as well as visit learned and godly men, survey the various churches and their customs, rites, and forms of government, and on his return report to the King concerning all these matters.

We have discovered a similar instance in the collection of the *Annals of Russia* (the more important parts of which, however, the vagaries of time have begrudged us) concerning Vladimir, the powerful Prince of Kiev.[26] For he, not yet being illuminated by the light of the Gospel (which finally took place about the year 988,[27] upon his marriage to the sister of Basil and Constantine, Emperors of the East),[28] and dwelling in the darkness of heathen wickedness, deeper than the proverbial darkness of the Cimmerians (who were neighbors to his dominions),[29] about the year 980 sent Ivan Smera Polevicius,[30] a learned physician and upright man to Constantinople to investigate the state of the Christian churches in Greece. From Alexandria this man wrote a letter[31] to the Prince informing him about the many worshipers of the truth and adherents of a religion freed from idolatry, who both opposed the commonly accepted errors and [42] corruption and also suffered much harsh treatment at the hands of the Greeks, in all respects similar to us. This letter also contained predictions of the ruin of the Greeks, given over to idolatry, hypocrisy, haughtiness, dissension, cruelty (which vents its rage upon human consciences on account of their celibacy and distinction of foods in the Roman custom), and to other vices; and [the letter speaks] about a new Slavonic people (*novissimae gentis Slavonicae*) that is, our Church,[32] joining with these confessors of the truth, while themselves being joined by the remnant of the Jewish people converted to the true Messiah of the God of Israel.[33]

[Lismanino in Western Europe, 1553 – 56][34]

Even [as Ivan Smera with Prince Vladimir] so Lismanino afterwards reported the whole matter [of the Reformed churches] to King [Sigismund], also by letter though contrary to the intentions of the King, who was looking for his return and oral presentation and not for a letter and a mute narration. [But to speak first of the travels of Lismanino.] He spent a half-year at Venice.[35] Afterwards he visited Padua.[36] Thence he went to Milan, where the monks drew him into suspicion of heresy and reported him to the governor of that celebrated city and fortress.[37] But, having disposed of the trifles and produced the letter of safe-conduct given him by the King, he was released, and passed into Switzerland. At Zurich he was glad to see for the first time a practice (*ratione*) of the Holy Eucharist which was very different from the false and utterly idolatrous papal worship of God, and which he had never seen before. He paid his respect to the learned men who were then in their prime in that great Swiss center: Rudolph Gualther,[38] Conrad Pellican,[39] Henry Bullinger,[40] Theodore Bibliander,[41] Leo Jud,[42] Conrad Gesner,[43] and others. He soon made his way to Bern, thence to Geneva, then to Lyons, and finally to Paris, in order to observe the religious customs and institutions of all these peoples, and at the same time to procure the furnishing of the library, and thus to carry out the King's mandate.

But a little later he neglected this, when, having returned to Geneva,[44] he took a wife, so as not to return to Poland wearing the horrid cowl. In this he was encouraged by Calvin and Laelius Socinus. The latter, shortly after he had sown the seeds of truth at Cracow, in the same year [1551] had returned to Geneva.[45] But he soon left Geneva, because he either could not endure, or else feared, Calvin's disposition,[46] and took up his abode at Zurich. [Lismanino took this step into marriage] despite the objections of Budziński, his attendant, who *put vividly before him the [*inevitable*] indignation of the King, who at his own expense had sent him abroad to examine and investigate everything, and was expecting some other outcome of all these efforts than the marriage of his envoy* [43]—*and he a monk. Moreover, he had committed himself by a promise to the King [who had not expected such a marriage], which is more likely to overturn what has been built up than to build up anything. In due course we shall also see that this in fact happened.*[47] *But he sang to deaf ears. For the monk [Lismanino], detesting celibacy, which both spirit and flesh justly condemn, and, making haste to a chaste though untimely marriage, put his decision into effect, took a wife, and remained in Geneva.*[48]

[King Sigismund Augustus grows cool toward reform: 1554–55][49]

But taking offense at his action, the King recoiled from his attempt to investigate religion, although it is conceivable that his mind remained averse to the errors of Rome which he had discovered (as Piasecki also points out and notes),[50] and that he no longer gave his inward and firm approval to them, because of the incandescent torch of great examples such as those which monks or other priests (even of great repute) had furnished in themselves.[51] This had certainly struck the minds of many, even of the princes of that age.

For not only had Germany, France, Italy produced such men as Luther, Melanchthon, Bugenhagen, Carlstadt, Zwingli, Oecolampadius, Calvin, [Peter] Martyr, Brenz,[52] Bucer, Bullinger, Marlorat,[53] Beza,[54] Ochino, Paul Vergerio,[55] and other famous names, but from the papacy itself and monastic cloisters, nay from sanctuaries of darkness, also our Poland produced many outstanding and wise men of this sort to carry forward the light of truth. Here in a single list I commend their names to distant posterity. They were these, namely: John Łaski, a most worthy leader; Aloisius, by birth an Italian, the King's preacher at Cracow;[56] John of Koźmin, the King's preacher; Stanislas Rapolionis/Rapagelanus; Simon Zak; Felix Cruciger; Stanislas Orzechowski; Martin Krowicki; Thomas Falconius; Stanislas Lutomirski; Valentine of Krzczonów; the great Andrew Dudith,[57] well known at the Council of Trent, ambassador at the courts of three emperors,[58] bishop of Knin, later of Csanád, and at length of Pécs [**cf. BAnt no. 60**].

And finally [there was] he too of whom I am speaking, Lismanino. Yet mindful of the promise he had given the King, and of the kindness received from him, in order to show his gratitude he rendered the King an account of his itinerary as well as of his activity, and two years after he had taken a wife sent him the books he had bought at the King's command and expense [44] and also the letters that the most famous men in Switzerland had written him. The originals of these, thirty years after the King's death, came into the hands of Budziński, so that to his diligence we owe the preservation of them.[59] I give here no copy of these, since they have long since seen the light.[60] But, as becomes a Christian man and a faithful writer, I warn lovers of the truth, in order that they may see how they ought to be on their guard in reading writings of celebrated authors, that the publishing of these copies of important letters has not been done in good faith by men unfriendly to the truth. Thus, in order that I may not conceal anything [I adduce a letter from Calvin].

[Calvin to Sigismund, 1555, restoring an omitted paragraph on Lismanino]

The letter that Calvin [at the suggestion of Lismanino] had addressed to King Augustus on 5 December 1554, sagaciously enough written against papal and episcopal (*pontificam*) arrogance, is extant among Calvin's letters (p. 139), but Lismanino's name at the beginning of the letter was unfairly omitted by the editor.[61] Yet I have not deemed it necessary to insert it here on this account, as it is very long.

But I insert a later and shorter one [of 24 December 1555] because the printed copy [of Geneva, 1575] omitted, you will see, all things concerning Lismanino:[62]

> *To the Most Serene King of Poland, my Most Gracious Lord:[63] Although I do not wonder nor doubt, Most Excellent King, that while your Majesty was holding the assembly of the estates of your Kingdom[64] you were distracted amid such a load of business by very great and manifold cares, so that no leisure remained for reading my exhortation, yet I trust that when more leisure was afforded, you took some of the unoccupied and free time, so that in the end my labor was not in vain.[65] For from the letter that your Majesty deigned to send,[66] I understand that my earnestness was appreciated, and that what I had written, trying briefly to show what is the true way of reforming the Church, and what is the most suitable way of proceeding, was not cast aside in disgust or contempt. Indeed, since your majesty declares that you have received it kindly and examined it gladly, and intend, when more leisure presents itself, to consider the several parts of it more carefully, I feel the more encouraged to undertake the office of writing. If, therefore, I now [45] venture again to exhort your Majesty, I do not think that I need trouble to ask your leave, and indeed no further excuse is necessary.*
>
> *I am of course not unaware nor unmindful of how far my humble and lowly condition is from the sublimity in which God has placed a great King. Your Majesty well knows, however, the meaning of the heavenly command in which all the kings of the earth are bidden to kiss the Son of God.[67] And since your Majesty is not ignorant that the outward ceremony of a kiss denotes the faithful allegiance which reverently embraces the sacred admonitions that issue from the mouth and the spirit of Christ, I deem any fear or hesitation[68] of slight account.*
>
> *Therefore, I, whom the Supreme King has appointed preacher of his*

*Gospel and minister of his Church, appeal to your majesty in his name,
since true religion has now begun in Poland to emerge from the baneful
darkness of the papacy, since many godly and wise men, rejecting wicked
superstitions, freely aspire to the pure worship of God, appeal to your
Majesty in God's name to perform this duty in preference to all others! And
assuredly, by how much the eternal glory of God surpasses the shadowy and
fleeting state of this world, even so does it become us, putting all other
things aside, to devote our chief attention to maintaining or affirming doctrinal piety.*

*That Poland hitherto was befouled and polluted by the corruptions of the
papacy and in its perverse worship of God went after the inventions of men,
that it finally sank under the filth of its errors and lost sight of the light of
heaven, was a sad and pitiable spectacle. But now that the Lord is beginning to set the whole world free from this common madness and stupor with
which it[69] had been smitten, all men, from the highest to the lowest, must
bestir themselves from their torpor. Should kings then delay whom God has
raised to such a height that from it they may give light to all nations? How
much, in fact, we ought now to value pure religion, by which a tribunal for
Christ is being set up among us, how much also the lawful worship of God,
in which the sign and living image of his presence shines forth, your
Majesty knows full well without my saying it. And, indeed, if the single
example of David is not enough to encourage us in this respect, our slug-
gishness is by no means to be excused. For although the patriarchs were
then worshiping God only under shadowy forms in an earthly sanctuary,
[46] yet we are told of the solemn oath that he swore that he would not give
sleep to his eyes nor slumber to his eyelids, nor would he enter the door of
his house, until he had found a place for the Lord, a habitation for the God
of Jacob.[70] If a pious concern for lawful worship did not suffer that king to
rest, but day and night he was both anxiously and continually eager to find
a place for the Ark of the Covenant, how much more ought now the worship
of a spiritual God enlist the zeal of a Christian king and to kindle all his
efforts and thoughts to discharge this honorable and noble duty, in order
that Christ may be honored! And also that David, though he was deprived
of the honor of erecting the temple, yet during the whole course of his life
ceased not to gather stones, timber, silver, and gold, that his successor
Solomon might be provided with all supplies, and at once without delay
proceed the more eagerly to the work.*

*Ought not a Christian king the more eagerly to muster all his powers to
repair the temple of God, and especially to strive that the neglected worship
of God no longer lie among shapeless ruins? But though obstacles are
never lacking to hinder this pious purpose, yet for your Majesty it is far
easier to offer a ready and eager compliance in order to maintain the faith
of Christ, than it was once for the pious kings Hezekiah and Josiah, to
whom it was difficult and hard. By what inducement ought a wise king to be
so aroused that he in his turn may put forth his hand not less vigorously?
Nor indeed should ear be given to those flatteries by which Satan, spreading
a deadly chill among wicked men, sinks the senses of many in slothful sleep.
Nay rather, shaking off all torpor from hands and feet, one must persevere
in this splendid work, and this especially when the time appears ripe for*

action, lest if the occasion offered by God be neglected, we have at last to stand in vain before a door that is closed.[71]

Indeed,[72] when that excellent man and faithful servant of Christ, Francis Lismanino, sought my advice, I did not hesitate to be the one to encourage him to withdraw promptly if there should be any to employ his services. At all events, I willingly endorsed his pious desire. Nor did I fear that his setting out might displease your Majesty as ill-timed, [47] since experience itself[73] shows his presence useful in many ways. But if it shall not yet seem advisable for him to be openly promoted by the King immediately upon his arrival, yet I must humbly pray and beseech your Majesty by the sacred name of Christ, to see at least that a way is opened somewhere else for one who is running a straight course. Meanwhile we shall pray with unceasing desire that the Lord, of his boundless power, may accomplish the work that he has happily begun, furnish your Majesty with a heroic spirit, and preserve you unharmed in your prosperous estate.

At Geneva, on the day before the Nativity of the Lord, wishing that as he was given supreme power by the Father, so may he be reverently received into your palace, in his own right be worshiped by all. 24 December 1555,

Your Majesty's most devoted,
John Calvin[74]

Calvin also wrote the King another letter [earlier], 9 February 1555,[75] as did also Henry Bullinger, on November 12 of the same year;[76] but we omit these, since they were published long since.

CHAPTER THREE

Of the Things That Followed the Action of Lismanino in Poland, and Were Otherwise Done in the Matter of Religion.

In the meantime, while Lismanino was abroad, the Polish [Reformed] churches grew remarkably, as the Gospel steadily gained greater power throughout the palatinate of Cracow, nay throughout all of Little and Great Poland and Lithuania; and the nobility stood upon their rights.[77] Thus the ministers of the word, who were also commonly called "parsons (*parochi*) of the Evangelicals," passed the time undisturbed, carrying on with great ardor and happy effort. But since no home had yet been provided for the truth in the city (*Metropoli*) of Cracow, it first found shelter at Wola, the estate of Justus Decius outside the city walls,[78] [48] whither the pious had learned Gregory Paul of Brzeziny had been called,[79] who conducted divine service there as well as at Chełm, the estate of the noble Remigian Chełmski, also near the city.[80]

Wherefore many of the burghers of Cracow, both men and women, used to gather and listen to sermons, even though the road thither was often rather bad, and also ill-disposed people, instigated by Bishop Andrew Zebrzydowski of Cracow, often attempted by abuse and molestations and obstacles to hamper them.[81] But a burning zeal for the glory of God and for their own salvation overcame all this, divine providence favoring and protecting their pious efforts, even as the royal Psalmist (84:5 – 7) once sang:

> Blessed is the man whose strength is in thee,
> In whose heart are the ways of them.
> Who passing through the valley of Baca make it a well;
> The rain also filleth the pools.
> They go from strength to strength,
> Every one of them in Zion appeareth before God.[82]

He [David] thereby signifies that the faithful worshipers of God, hastening to his beloved tabernacles, overcome pathless wastes, deserts, and every difficulty and obstacle, that they may come to the house of the Lord, who is kind to his own people and supplies them by his singular favor.

For so, in fact, it then fell out when Stanislas Lasocki and [Stanislas] Matthew Stadnicki, as well as John Boner,[83] grand governor of the castle of Cracow and castellan of Biecz, all of them illustrious men, brought ministers into their own halls to preach sermons. And Boner indeed set aside a place for holding religious meetings on his own grounds, adjoining the very walls of the city, outside the gate near St. Nicholas' church, and named from it.[84] And there Gregory [Paul] afterwards preached to a great concourse of people who gathered, as often happens, to hear something new.[85] And [Remigian] Chełmski gave them a burying ground on his own estate, to which the Papists in their wickedness gave the name of Dogs' Hill.[86] Indeed, they used to go for the same purpose even to Iwanowice, a village three miles distant from the city, where the noble [Nicholas] Dłuski, its owner, had been so bold as to order the images thrown out of the church.[87]

[Mrs. Jelieniowa confronts Bishop Zebrzydowski][88]

In this connection an exemplary incident occurred, deserving of mention. It relates to a certain worthy woman, wife of John Jeleń, a burgher of Cracow.[89] As she excelled not only in beauty but also in chastity, she did not follow in the steps of other women in that city who not infrequently [49] allow their marriage vows to be desecrated by the priests, to whom, under the cloak of religion, everything is open and supposed to be allowed. For when Andrew Zebrzydowski, bishop of that city, a man given to all manner of wantonness, had learned from his archdeacon, cast of the same mold, that this woman, very beautiful in person, was dwelling near his palace in the street commonly called Bracka (after the fraternity of the followers of Francis' fables),[90] he summoned her before himself on the charge that she went to Chełm or Iwanowice to listen to Lutheran sermons. We have already noted that in Poland all who dissent from the Romanists fall under this name. She went together with her husband, who ought to have been cited for this rather than his wife, if a matter of religion or of morality, rather than of lust, had been in question.

But when she had appeared before the bishop, she drew his eyes and heart (though in vain) to herself, "For he saw her, and desired her when seen."[91] But he did not obtain the object of his desire though, spreading the snares of his lust to take his prey, he thus addressed her, with the archdeacon and a large circle of courtiers standing by: *"Is it not you, O devotée of Luther, who although dwelling hard by the church dedicated to St. Francis, yet do not enter it, but go a mile or two out of the city to hear Lutheran sermons? I shall take from you your liking for Luther's sect. If you do not ply the distaff at home and do not frequent the church, I will have you taken soon to the castle of Lipowiec."[92]* This was the bishop's castle, near the city. To this proposal, full of pretence of religion, the woman, who had formerly been brought up at court and knew how to preserve her modesty in the midst of jests, pleasantly replied: *"Most Reverend Prince,[93] some good man—it was in fact the archdeacon standing next to the bishop—having nothing to do, wished to render your Most Reverend Highness an acceptable service by accusing me of Lutheranism, which is no concern of his. For as I do not watch to see where he is accustomed to go, so I doubt whether this informer was moved by piety when watching to see where I go. However, if I deserved imprisonment, I ought to suffer it not at Lipowiec which was built for priests alone, but in the castle of Promnik which was designed for women."*

The bishop felt the sting of what the woman [50] aimed at him and those like him, and as the hearers were rather making a game of it, he, looking at the archdeacon, said to them: *"You have been admitted to the show, my friends, but pray restrain your laughter."[94] And to him [the archdeacon, wistfully:] "Alas, good man, you tried your best in attending to it." Together with the archdeacon he fell silent. But the woman, quite self-possessed, steadfast and well-mannered, bowed obeisance and returned home,* while those who had seen the comedy called to mind the old saying: *"You surely carry off unusual glory and ample spoils."[95]*

We must not omit to mention here the observation of Budziński:[96] *[T]his bishop, while filled with bitter and malicious zeal, was nevertheless given to gluttony and destitute of true piety. For he [the bishop] regarded as a fable all belief in the resurrection and the whole religion of Christ, profanely reviling Christ the Saviour and quoting an irreverent saying about "the three impostors."* Whether there is any book about them, I do not know; but I do know that it is wrongly ascribed to Bernardine Ochino.[97] Budziński quotes as witness of these blasphemies Andrew Patrycy,[98] his old tutor, but afterwards secretary of this bishop:

For in the intimacy of their old friendship he related to him this and many things more: as also that once when traveling in a carriage with his master, they were taken out into a meadow, the latter said to him: "You see this meadow, Andrew. It is more fortunate than I. For the grass that lies mown by this scythe will grow again. But I, once mown by the scythe of death, shall not rise again." Also he was wont to say: "Believe even in a goat, if you like, provided you pay me your tithes."

[Such a] one likes, however, to conceal such a life and wicked nature by feigning zeal and by persecuting godly men.

[Growing tension between Bishop Zebrzydowski and
Reformed noblemen, 1551 – 52]

And so he [Zebrzydowski] first attacked Conrad Krupka-Przecławski, a nobleman, whom, for his different view of the faith and for [refusing] tithes, he ordered to appear before his ecclesiastical court. To this, before the Reformation was effected and a just liberty obtained for body and spirit, noblemen were customarily haled with risk of honor and life. As the yoke of episcopal jurisdiction was heavy upon the necks of the nobility, he appeared, but with a crowd of noblemen.[99]

In fact, his innocence was especially assisted by the bravery of Martin Zborowski, palatine of Kalisz, a man illustrious and very powerful, [51] and indeed almost reckless.[100] [This was] shown in the case of Prince [Demetrius] *Sanguszko* who, in the heart of Bohemia, was captured and killed for ravishing the princess [Halszka] of Ostróg.[101] *For he [Zborowski], as was his wont, indignant at the oppression of a weak man [Przecławski] by a strong one [Bishop Zebrzydowski] was at hand with a band of his servants and retainers in the hall which he had near the bishop's palace and the church dedicated to Francis. But the bishop, upon learning of this, ordered the palace to be closed, the gate bolted and fortified, some cannon kept in readiness, and only a small gate to be left open. The palatine therefore, wishing to call upon him, sent [word] to him, asking him to order the gate to be opened, for he would not enter the palace through a hole, in the manner of menials, [adding that] since he had not entered the Senate through a hole, as the bishop [had] the episcopate, but through the open gate of virtue, he therefore was worthy also to enter the bishop's palace through an open gate in order to visit the bishop with his friends.* Budziński relates [n]othing further was then done between them. But Otwinowski[102] states that the palatine [Zborowski] came thither as though unaware of what was going on, pointed out the unlawfulness of the bishop's jurisdiction, foretold that there would soon be a release from this bondage, and by reason of the respect due his authority restrained the further rage of the bishop. Thereupon the bishop launched the bolt of his anathema, spent though it was, against this nobleman with zeal for the truth.

Piasecki ought to be heard here, saying

> When Bishop Andrew Zebrzydowski of Cracow had condemned Krupka-Przecławski, accused of Luther's heresy, and for this branded him with the punishment of infamy, Catholic and heretical nobles alike so rose against this ecclesiastical power that at the Diet of Piotrków in 1552 they would not let any public business be transacted unless this sentence of the episcopal court with respect to the penalty of judicial infamy were first annulled. And from that time on the execution of all decrees of the ecclesiastical court against nobles was suspended pending compromise between the estates; although hitherto the royal chancery used to give the local royal captains orders of execution against an excommunicated person if he had not obtained absolution within a year, such as are wont to be given against those proscribed by the King or land justices [52] of the equestrian order.[103]

When the blow aimed at Krupka had been parried or repulsed, this same bishop turned his headstrong disposition in another direction. *When [Nicholas] Dłuski, the owner of Iwanowice, died [in 1551], his neighbors and friends gathered to pay their last respects to him. The bishop, hearing that this was being done in the neighborhood of the city, sent thither one of his servants to learn by what rite the services were performed and who was the leader conducting the whole funeral ceremony. The servant returned and related that a great crowd of nobles had attended the services, that the Mass had been celebrated in the Polish tongue, that only one candle had been lighted and no other rites observed, and that the conductor of the funeral ceremonies had been Andrew, son of John [Andrew] Trzecieski.[104] Upon this, the bishop blazed up with such anger that he abstained from food and kept threatening Trzecieski with the stake. But also in this case anger without power was vain.* Yet it did not fail of a certain success a little later in the case of a similar funeral ceremony, as will be told presently.

[Episcopal persecution of Jerome Filipowski, 1557]

With the increasing number of confessors of the truth and of their churches, and with the growing liberty of the nobles, who had divine service performed not only in their villages but also in the very city of Cracow under the eyes of the bishop, the indignation of the bishop grew daily. He was bursting with visceral rage because he saw all his wicked efforts frustrated. Yet he did not refrain from threats nor from other malicious schemes in order to show himself a sworn foe of piety. Jerome Filipowski, at the time already patronizing a numerous congregation at Krzczęcice, came to Cracow with his wife (whom he had married when she was widow of the eminent Niemsta).[105] Thereupon the bishop ordered an alarm to be rung for three days on the castle's greatest bell, which bears the name of Sigismund I,[106] as if to extinguish a general conflagration. Then he hurled the thunderbolts of his anathemas not only against the heretics but also against the populace, interdicting them from the ceremonies of the Mass in order, through their resentment, to stir up the ignorant and superstitious multitude to a riot liable to call forth persecution against Filipowski and other promoters of the truth.

But when even this way of open pursuit had not succeeded, Zebrzydowski tried another, and that a covert and specious one, namely, that of slander, well knowing that a lion's skin and a wolf's should be worn in turn. [53] A childbirth of Filipowski's wife afforded an opportunity for the slander. He shamelessly spread a report through the city that she had given birth to a horrible monster, a three-headed dragon equipped with several tails, although she had borne a male child named after his father.[107] This son afterwards pursued the blandishments of the world, by means of ancestral nobility and by his family kinship with the Koniecpolskis, with whom he shared the arms of the clan.[108] He was commonly known as a favorite of King Stephen (because he was made grand carver of the Kingdom throughout his reign, grand steward of the royal bedchamber, marshal of the court, captain of Stryj, Nur, Ostrzeszów and Ostrołęka), and discharged an embassy to the Emperor of the Turks when he had hardly passed his twenty-fifth year.[109]

But, as often happens, the deceit planned with as little foresight as shame became forthwith as plain as the fire in a Punic lamp,[110] and brought the priest with his company into contempt. And by his affair also the people, who on the one hand detested wicked deceit and had long been restless under the heavy yoke of the priests, and on the other were eager for change and hence ready to believe and accept anything new, were invited and spurred on to listen to "Lutheran" sermons. (Again I am willing to retain this popular designation for the followers of the truth.) [The people responded] all the more readily because it was seen that these sermons could be safely preached and listened to in the city [Cracow], whither the nobles used to bring in preachers from their villages.

Among these [nobles, Stanislas] Lasocki and Filipowski, two very intimate companions, were the special object of the ill-will of the bishop, who sought to injure them however he could. And the opportunity to cause trouble to the latter (which, together with a pretext, those who would do evil never fail to find) the bishop found when Filipowski with his friends was decently carrying the body of his wife (who had expired in this childbirth) out of the city for burial.[111] *For on that occasion, when a mob of students, whose unruliness and insolence are not inferior to their physical power, and of others keen on daring anything, being armed for a riot with swords, spears, and audacity, one [Wacław] Uhrowiecki,[112] staining the nobility of his family and the good fame of the university by his infamous wantonness, rushed out of the crowd in the middle of the market-place upon Filipowski as he led the funeral train, and slapped him in the face.*

But when his friends and servants would have avenged the insult and repelled by force not only the youth but also the whole crowd of rowdies, [54] Filipowski, mindful of Christian patience and of his love for his wife, himself bore the insult meekly, like a man with good aim spitting out a spark that might kindle a great blaze. And suitably and wisely he restrained his friends and retainers who were drawing their swords. Certainly this was the wisest course. For the priests and other ill-disposed persons were seeking the opportunity to accuse the confessors of the Evangelical truth of some incident, to charge that a vicious and wicked sort of man, dangerous to the public peace, was promoting sedition, not religion. And so Filipowski, by his admirable example demonstrated to all who in fact were enduring, and who were inflicting injury; and the provocation was to sedition. And in truth modesty then fared well, while savagery badly. For the former received praise, while the latter was publicly covered with censure. And the success of the Evangelicals increased as much as the credibility of the bishops and their reputation for uprightness decreased.

[The martyrdom of Nicholas of Kurów, 1550]

Since even here the bishop had failed to attain the hoped-for result of his malice, and both suspicion of his party and esteem for the opposite one had grown, he attacked men of humble station, whose uprightness and meek endurance of wrong alone was unable to protect them against his unbridled wickedness. A little while before, namely in 1550, the year in which he had been appointed bishop of Cracow in place of Samuel Maciejowski, Zebrzydowski gave a glaring example of wicked tyranny in the case of *Nicholas* of Kurów,[113] minister of the word of God, a man altogether devout and blameless. For he seized this man, confined him in prison at Bodzentyn, and starved him to death, which not even a Chrysippus would do,

> Nor the gentle nature of Thales,
> And the aged man nursed on sweet Hymettus,
> Who would not give his accuser a portion of the hemlock
> Taken among the cruel cups.[114]

Why, even Pliny, a worshiper of Nature rather than of God, would detest it and say: "A death by dreadful hunger, most averse to the earth's kindness, consumed us with its lingering wasting" (2.63).[115]

That devout and holy martyr of Jesus Christ, having nothing with him but the Holy Book and a little butter [55] while tormented by his fierce hunger, consumed the butter along with the book so that what he had devoured with mind and memory and had converted into strength and blood, he might also devour with his mouth and have buried with him in the earth. And he lay half dead in the presence of the bishop, who, not content with having ordered the torture, gazed on with [Marc] Antonian rather than Neronian ferocity.[116] Thus [Nicholas] died for his confession of the truth. But while the priests (not yet satisfied with his death) were looking at this corpse defiled with innocent blood, and still raging at one beyond death and barbarity, a certain woman took her petticoat and covered the nakedness and the blood of the victim. As of old the priests were surpassed by a Samaritan, a foreigner and a heretic to the Jews,[117] so here a woman surpassed men, a humble person surpassed those of eminent dignity, in showing mercy to the wretched.

CHAPTER FOUR

Of the Proscription of Lismanino in His Absence and the Further Persecution of Confessors of the Truth Carried on by Bishop Andrew Zebrzydowski of Cracow.

As wickedness is ever wont to rush headlong from bad to worse, so here also hearts harder than adamant could not be softened nor turned to humanity by the persecution of so many godly men, or even by the shedding of innocent blood. The case of Lismanino galled the malicious. So did letters of distinguished men like Conrad Gesner, Henry Bullinger, and John Calvin, which, sent to the King and written as well to the great men (*proceres*) of the Royal Commonwealth and the nobles who followed the Gospel truth, were much spoken about and passed from hand to hand.[118] Thus these things could not escape the notice of the malicious, who are wont to be more than sharp-sighted and keen-scented in tracing opportunities for persecution. In following them they are indeed so diligent and cunning that one may fairly wish that the words of the Saviour [Luke 16:18] might be more seriously taken to heart: 'Would that the sons of light were not less wise in their generation or order than the sons of this world,' namely, in knowing how to trace out, take, seize, follow up opportunities of doing good, and so [56] furnish aids to a better life.

At that time indeed both those of the light and those of the world competed in discretion and industry. For the confessors of the Evangelical truth were considering how to spread it; their oppressors, how to root it out by any means. The former then appointed a synod at Pińczów for 1 May 1555 and attended it in large numbers: this was the first synod of the Evangelicals in Poland[119] and was followed by one held at Koźminek in Great Poland in the month of August in the same year.[120] Here it was voted to ascertain the views of the Moravian Brethren (who are also commonly called Waldenses, Poor Men of Lyons, Albigenses, and Picards), with whom not a few of the Polish Brethren shared an understanding, being attracted by their singular zeal for church discipline and piety.[121]

[Waldenses]

In the middle of the twelfth century after the birth of Christ, these men (to say something of them on this occasion) began with great courage to thunder against the corruptions of the Roman Church, especially with regard to the tyranny of the Pope of Rome and hence of the whole clergy, the sale of indulgences, the trafficking in masses, the manifold idolatry, and all things connected with it.

They spread far and wide the teaching which is in accordance with piety. Their founder was Peter Waldo, a citizen of Lyons, a pious and wise man as his deeds show, who was inflamed with extraordinary zeal as a result of the unexpected and horrible case of the sudden death of one of a company of rich men who met to pass away the time.[122] This led him, together with his friends, to repent and to preach seriously repentance and uprightness of life along with contempt for riches and the world. About the year 1370, this teaching was revived in England by John Wycliffe, of whom the remarkable fact is related that he both translated the Bible into his native tongue, and wrote two hundred works against the Pope (as though with the zeal of a Waldo returning after a lapse of two hundred years).[123] Within thirty years, that is, at the beginning of the fifteenth century, their footsteps were bravely followed by John Hus and Jerome of Prague,[124] even unto their cruel deaths [1415, 1416], by which was sanctioned that more than wicked doctrine (for it surpasses even the wickedness of the heathen), "that faith need not be kept with heretics."[125]

[The Reformation in Germany][126]

Within a hundred years of this time (as Hus is said to have foretold),[127] Martin Luther of Eisleben, [57] a doctor of theology of the Augustinian order, took the occasion of traffic in indulgences (which, more than others, John Tetzel[128] of the Dominican order was carrying on in Germany by authority of Pope Leo X of Rome,[129] to the shame of the more devout, the indignation of the more noble, and the grief of the more virtuous), to rise up against this unbridled license, which was condemned even by the better clergy themselves (Polydorus, *De inventoribus rerum*, 8.4;[130] De Thou, *Historiae*, I;[131] Laurentius Surius, *Commentarius*);[132] and he opposed to it his [Ninety-five] theses published at Wittenberg. Therein indeed he performed the duty of a wise Christian by pointing out and proving the great corruptions of a thing, in itself false, and devised by the priests for their own advantage, namely, that the remission of sins, which are obtained [freely] by the blood of Christ, the redeemer for all who truly repent, is to be declared by the Church through the mouth of a bishop or pastor in virtue of the authority conferred by the whole Church upon them alone.[133] But when he touched the sore, he found the priests not at all well disposed towards him.

However, the better cause also found patrons, especially the Elector Frederick of Saxony, a magnanimous prince, who undertook to defend Luther and the cause he had taken up against the fury of the Papists.[134] And he was a little later joined by other princes and also by free cities of the Empire. And that the more, since as an outcome of the view of Luther, and also of the truth itself, the ambition and arrogance of the pontiffs and their immense annual incomes were held in restraint and the wealth, which was not only unsuitable but even harmful to them, was converted to the use of the princes and of the commonwealth (*respublica*).[135] But let us leave to others these things which have been carefully described, and let us return to our subject.

The shining examples of the princes and states of neighboring Germany, whose hearts glowed with noble-minded virtue, so that they earnestly joined together to do away with the corruptions in the faith and morals of the Church, inveterate though these were, mightily inflamed our people also. And that the more because, responding to good plans and efforts, propitious results more and more stirred up and attracted the better minds.

[The synod at Pińczów of 1 May 1555 sends for Lismanino]

From the synod at Pińczów, just now mentioned, a letter was sent by the noble patrons of the churches and the ministers of the word to Lismanino, who was then staying in Switzerland, [58] in which they unanimously called him [to serve the synod], whenever he should return to Poland.[136] They were, to be sure, opposed by Stanislas Sarnicki, pastor of the church at Niedźwiedź, a man of outstanding noble lineage, not only of acute mind, but also of haughty spirit, who was even then scheming (*grassor*) for leadership through destruction of the harmony of the churches. This was brought about a little later, namely in 1565 (as we shall see below[137]) by his instigation. Yet the influence of the majority prevailed, furnishing support to the more just cause.[138] And so this letter was sent to Lismanino through his secretary Budziński, who also bore letters from the King to Gesner, Calvin, and Bullinger in answer to theirs.[139]

But as at this time a book of prayers and hymns[140] was brought from Bohemia into Poland, malicious men, seizing this occasion, heaped upon the Evangelicals the odium of the hated name of Picards.[141] However, the virtue of the godly men, who were burning with zeal for spreading the purer truth, prevailed over this. Thus in this synod they took bold and, what is of prime importance, timely action for introducing a proper order into the churches, which by divine favor were increasing more and more.

[An episcopal attack on the synod at Pińczów, 1 May 1555]

This exceedingly vexed Bishop Zebrzydowski of Cracow. Therefore, to disturb this pious assembly, he sent his chancellor [Martin Rusiecki][142] to Pińczów with a considerable troop of cavalry which he maintained in every way resembling Herod more than Peter. But God defeated his wicked and audacious designs, and did not suffer that place (so famous for proofs of his singular providence and for its reputation for honorable business) to be profaned by the contrivances of the bishop, a man (as trustworthy rumor ran), wholly given over to the flesh and even impiety, who dwelt at a place of evil omen, although of good name. This was the village of Dobrawoda (which means "good water"), situated only a mile from Wiślica, from which Pińczów is four miles distant. Here a sometime predecessor of Zebrzydowski, Zawisza of Kurozwęka, in the year 1382 broke his neck and died while ascending a ladder to fornicate with a maid who slept above, as the records of the country's history bear witness.[143]

Forewarned of the designs of Bishop Zebrzydowski, Oleśnicki, the proprietor of Pińczów, used the greater care and foresight in foiling them. So when the bishop's chancellor had come [59] with his armed horsemen to the gate of the town in order to capture and to bring back one of the ministers of the word by his master's command, if an opportunity should be afforded, but if not, to deal with the nobles and induce them to break up the assembly, he was admitted with only three companions, and that only because he said he was bringing a royal order under seal.

Leaving the ministers of the word in the cloister from which Oleśnicki had lately turned out the monks, the congregated nobles negotiated alone with the bishop's chancellor in the church-yard. The matter was done thus. He showed them a royal order written by John Przerębksi, who lately as administrator *pro tempore* of the bishopric of Cracow had in vain haled the same Oleśnicki before the King's tribunal on the same charge, and was then already Vice-Chancellor of the Kingdom.[144] When the nobles had received this and seen by whom it was written, in order to secure their innocence against slander, they had the customary noble witnesses and a public crier (whom we call the Usher General of the Royal Commonwealth) present, and declared: That they received the royal seal with due reverence, but not the order itself, seeing that it was composed by bishops, without the King's knowledge; for they knew what was due to the King as their lord, and he knew what he ought to demand from them or not; that wrong was being done to them in that the bishops accused them of crime in holding meetings (*conventicula*); that this was certainly committed by those who meet secretly for the purpose of wicked plots and treason; that such were the bishops themselves who promise upon oath to reveal to the Roman Pope all, even the greatest, secrets of their princes, and had lately held such a conventiculum at Łowicz;[145] and that time would soon show whether it was not the bishops themselves who were plotting seditious and treacherous designs. With this reply the bishop's chancellor was dismissed. He excused himself modestly enough to the nobles, saying that he had presented the orders of his master to them as a delegate, and would take their reply back to him.

[Prior conflict between the episcopacy and the nobility: 1550 – 52]

But the bishops took diligent care by royal mandates and privileges both to oppress the liberty of the Evangelicals, however innocent and just, and to fix their tithes and other obligations, however oppressive, at least with respect to those who had withdrawn from their instruction and care. That stormy time witnessed such a document [as that delivered to Oleśnicki. This one the bishops] contrary to all loyalty had extorted from the King, unbeknownst to the lay Senators of the political order of the Royal Commonwealth and to the nobles [in general]. This was when he desired to have his second wife, Barbara Radziwiłłówna, crowned with the consent of the bishops and by them alone.[146] [60] A copy of this [document of 1550] was obtained by Nicholas Lutomirski, castellan of Zawichost, and exhibited by him to the nobility of the Cracow area assembled at the dietine in Proszowice.[147] And it showed them what serpents they were cherishing in their bosom, namely the bishops. Though reckoned

among the Senators of the Royal Commonwealth, the bishops were flying at the
throat of the common liberty and of the Commonwealth. And I also give a copy
of it here [from] Budziński, chap. xi:[148]

> *For a perpetual record of the matter: Whereas, all things human are vain
> and wholly useless unless they be held in their bounds by divine laws and
> the fear and observance of these, and are rendered firm especially by the
> soundness and unity of religion;*
>
> *Therefore we, Sigismund Augustus, by the grace of God King of Poland,
> wish it to be manifest and acknowledged by all and singular to whom it is or
> may be of concern that, inasmuch as we have learned from our counselors
> of both Estates that various heresies are sprouting here and there in our
> Realm, and that new doctrines and rites in religion are not only being
> brought in from elsewhere, but also that certain rash subjects of ours are
> openly professing and teaching the same;*
>
> *We, following the footsteps of our ancestors, whose chief care and
> endeavor it ever was to spread and to support the holy Christian faith, and
> to cut off all occasion of discord among our subjects, and of any distur-
> bance in the Commonwealth (which without doubt is wont to accompany
> dissensions in religion), and deeming that this properly belongs to the duty
> of Christian Kings and Princes, do by this writ of ours bear witness and
> promise that, in accordance with our duty toward the Christian religion and
> the Holy Church, we will with zeal and love profess first of all the truth of
> the doctrine of the Church, and the purity of the Christian, Catholic, and
> Apostolic faith which the Holy Roman Church professes, and which our
> fathers receiving from the beginning have constantly professed even to the
> present, and we will preserve it whole and inviolate by all our strength
> everywhere throughout our Realm and Dominions, but that we will fight and
> drive from our Realm enemies not only Gentiles (*Ethnicos),[149] *who pur-
> posely wish to be alien from the Christian name, but also the heretics who
> under the cover of the Christian name and by a false use of the Word of God
> wholly destroy and overthrow all Christian teaching, and prove themselves
> alien from that faith and religion [61] that was handed down by the Apostles
> and is professed by the one Roman and Universal Church to the present;*
>
> *And that we will never appoint to our Royal Council and Senate those
> who (to our knowledge) have been infected by any heresy, nor confer upon
> them any honors and offices; nay, if any are reported to us, we will cause
> (Almighty God helping) that the statutes of our Realm be enforced against
> them and executed with all diligence, so that they may ever remain inglori-
> ous, infamous, banished, and exiled from their native land, unless they show
> diligence to return to the bosom of Holy Mother Church and to be recon-
> ciled with her.*
>
> *Also we will protect and maintain and with all our strength will defend
> the persons of the clergy, and their rights, immunities, and privileges, public
> and private. Moreover, we command our officers and captains whosoever,
> not to be remiss or negligent in executing these laws and keeping them in
> force, on threat of our great and serious displeasure; otherwise, if any are*

*reported to us who will not perform both their duty and our command, we
will not suffer them to go unpunished.*

*And, the reverend Father in Christ, lord Nicholas Dzierzgowski,
archbishop of Gniezno, and his other bishops, as well as the rest of our
councilors advising us according to their duty, we have promised and given
our royal word that we will do all written above, and we will firmly observe
it under the oath of our royal faith made to our subjects by us at our coronation. In testimony whereof, by these present, etc.*

*Given at Cracow on the sixth Sunday after the Conception of the Blessed
Mary, in the year 1550, and of our reign the twenty-first.[150]*

This ordinance, injurious to the liberty of the nobles, nay destroying it, later
caused great disturbance in the Diet. For the bishops were by no means willing
to be deprived of this right, once it had been granted them; on the other hand,
the nobles kept striving to that end. The speech of the same [Nicholas] Lutomirski should be quoted, worthy of a wise Senator:

> It ought to be provided by a public law in the Diet that whoever ventures to
> accuse another of heresy be subject to the penalty that the law has decreed
> for evil-speaking and defamation; for it is no light [62] insult if one accuse
> any one of the crime of heresy, which is difficult of proof. A heretic is not
> one who will not comply with the wishes of the Pope of Rome, but one who
> stubbornly opposes the true teaching taken from the Word of God, and
> treats the divine commands with contempt, utters or follows new opinions
> plainly contrary to them (Decreta, *Part. 2, Case 24, Question 3, chap.
> Haereticus*)[151] and for the sake of some temporal advantage and especially
> of his own vain glory and advancement, as the canon law itself defines.[152]

And certainly at that time the nobles, noticing what mines the bishops were laying to overthrow the common liberty, boldly resisted their crooked undertakings
and attempts, so that the bishops found it necessary to abate something of their
arrogance.

[Attempted seduction of Martin Krowicki,
chaplain in the palace and in the
town of Pińczów, late summer, 1554][153]

*After the matter was managed at Pińczów in the way that we have said, the
bishop of Cracow grew in no wise better, nor did he abate anything of his rage
but, full of anger, he kept breathing out vengeance that very year, being vexed
by the modest, wise, and forthright reply of the nobles. An opportunity for
accomplishing his purpose, convenient for him and worthy of such villainy,
presented itself through a monk who, after the rest had been driven out, was living alone in the cloister together with Alexander Witrelin, minister of the
Word.[154] The bishop instructed the monk to invite to dinner this companion of
his and Martin Krowicki, also a minister of the Word, who was living in the castle, so that meanwhile servants sent by the bishop should seize Krowicki. For he*

aimed especially at the latter, since (as we have seen above) a little while before, being pastor of a church, he had used his primordial liberty to take a wife.[155] Having been expelled by the bishop [Dziaduski] of Przemyśl,[156] he had fled to Pińczów[157] and, burning with extraordinary zeal, attacked with word and pen the corruptions of the Roman Church and the craft of bishops.[158]

The [bishop's undertaking] succeeded. It was carried out as planned in the absence of the owner from the town. Had he been present, a man endowed with uncommon valor not only of mind but also of body, he would not have permitted such things to be attempted in his town. The plot contrived against honest men did not fall short of a certain success, since these measure another's cunning by their own integrity, forgetting that "the Greeks are to be feared even when bearing gifts."[159] *Krowicki* [63] *was seized and overpowed by a certain Mazowiecki,[160] a servant of the bishop, who arrived at dinner time with some assistants, then thrown face down into the bottom of a cart such as we are wont to use to haul crops to the barns, and, covered with straw, was held down by some barbarously cruel servants sitting upon him, and taken away with all speed. Thus driven over stones and roots of trees, he had his face sorely bruised, and could scarcely draw breath.*

But by the marvelous providence of God, the noble Balthasar Łukowski,[161] judge of the palatinate of Sandomierz, opportunely ran to his aid together with his own servant and one of Oleśnicki's, who was following them alone as they fled. Raising a shout in the forest, they so frightened Mazowiecki and his servants that, leaving their cart, they turned their backs on Łukowski and returned liberty and life to Krowicki, while a little later Oleśnicki himself came running up.

Thus the efforts of Bishop Zebrzydowski this time also came to naught, and cost him not a little in quiet, good reputation, and the value of the horses that were carried off.

[Zebrzdowski against Krowicki, in Cracow, 1555–56]

Yet with a mind bent on any cruelty, the bishop was anxious here to conceal the infamy of his wickedness and to win for himself fame for his zeal. For he again secured a new mandate from the King upon complaint of [the Rev.] Vice-Chancellor Przerębski, a man of the same stripe, by which it was ordered that all ministers of the Word be brought from the homes of the nobles to their bishops. And this he did especially to prepare a thrust at Jerome Filipowski, an inhabitant of his diocese, who was both one of the leading noblemen and one of the leading patrons of the rising Church. The bishop also aimed no light blow at the latter's warm friend Stanislas Lasocki, his faithful ally in promoting the work of Lord by his unwearied efforts and his uprightness of life, and at the same time at Krowicki. For when Krowicki was preaching the word of God in Lasocki's mansion at Cracow, the bishop wanted to attack the house by force and throw Krowicki into chains.[162]

The bishop's boldness grew, as his party was favored by John Ocieski, Grand

Chancellor of the Kingdom and captain of the city.[163] For this man, while endowed with splendid gifts of talents and genius, was nevertheless much devoted to the bishops. He sent two nobles, his second in command, Secygniewski, and [Peter] Kmita,[163] to Lasocki, severely admonishing the latter to refrain from gathering a congregation in the first city of the Royal Commonwealth, and to dismiss his minister. But they, seeing that Lasocki's spirit was undaunted, nay fearless, wondered at it, and withdrew not without shame. Thus also this [64] blow of the bishop was manfully parried by Lasocki.[164]

From these few instances one may see how fiercely the adversaries of the truth were then persecuting its confessors, and also how the latter resisted their wicked plots and daring attempts, since whenever God permitted the former to perpetrate savageries, he by his invincible hand yet always protected the latter, who were experienced in adversity. Despite so many hindrances, the churches of Christ increased in their former way, both in Great and Little Poland and in Lithuania.

[The Reformation spreads in Lithuania, 1553]

In Lithuania, Prince Nicholas Radziwiłł the Black, palatine of Vilna, held the leading place in promoting the truth after the fashion of that time. For when the Royal Court was held at Vilna, the chief city of Lithuania, in which he saw many burning with desire to learn the truth, he founded a church in the neighboring village of Łukiszki.[165] This act of the magnanimous prince not a little weakened the credit of the bishops with King and people, and impaired the influence of Vice-Chancellor Przerębski, who in the King's name used frequently to issue mandates to the nobles who loved the truth. So then the Court and the whole Polish Commonwealth saw many confessors and witnesses to the truth! These God sent to convert our nation to himself, as being furnished and endowed with singular gifts of liberty. And he desired that Christ's truth be reborn in it under King Augustus, even as Christ also, who is himself the very truth, was born under the emperor Augustus.[166]

[Lismanino and Łaski return to Poland, 1556–57]

Among the first restorers of the primitive truth we have put Lismanino. Before returning home, he urged and took all pains to the end that John Łaski should return to his fatherland at a most favorable time. In this way, [he hoped,] if he himself should happen to be driven from the country by the bishops, this great man, whose noble ancestry and illustrious relations,[167] as well as his extraordinary learning[168] and strict morals, secured influence for him, might leave incontestable proofs of the truth which he himself [Lismanino] had uttered by word of mouth, and in his stead establish as it were a firm pillar of it.

John Łaski had once been dean of the churches of Gniezno and Łęczyca and bishop-elect of Veszprém.[169] But, observing corruptions of the Roman Church and being able neither to remove nor to endure them, he betook himself to

Holland[170] and thence to England.[171] There he took a wife[172] and conferred with many learned men orally and in writing on matters of faith. [65] The return of Łaski was urged with all zeal by Stanislas Myszkowski,[173] captain of Marienburg, John Boner, the Ostrorógs, Albert Łaski, [174] his *nephew*, Lasocki, Filipowski, and other illustrious and noble men. Nor did the matter fail of accomplishment. Lismanino returned to Poland in 1556,[175] and Łaski at the beginning of 1557.[176]

Lismanino experienced the utmost hostility of the bishops towards himself, so that he was proscribed from the Kingdom by a royal mandate.[177] Nevertheless he remained in the Kingdom, and by advice of the brethren lay hidden for seven weeks at Iwanowice, at the home of the noble and pious Agnes Dłuska.[178] Meanwhile both the brethren and he himself took action with the Senators of the Royal Commonwealth in order that he might by the King's favor be set free from the proscription as innocent. And in fact the King, who was a kindhearted prince, and had not long since held Lismanino in deep affection, did not agree to his proscription. But it was the bishops who did it, who held in their hands the lesser seal of the Royal Commonwealth.[179] How the Senators were disposed towards Lismanino, was witnessed by the foremost of the lay Senators, Prince John Tarnowski, castellan and captain of Cracow and Grand Hetman of the armies of the Royal Commonwealth,[180] in his letter written to Lismanino in the month of July of the same year [1556], of which I here offer a copy:

Quite as your Lordship writes, I have received from you three letters already since your return here to Poland. The first indeed I answered as soon as it was delivered to me, by the hand of your Lordship's servant [Budziński] who had brought it to us. But as for my failure hitherto to reply to the second, I should like our Lordship to believe that this was for no other reason but that I was hoping that in the meantime I might be able to talk and confer with your Lordship in person about certain matters far better and more conveniently than by letter, when some opportunity should present itself for meeting you, either at the Diet of the Royal Commonwealth or somewhere else. I am indeed sorry that this did not happen. But now to the last one, which Master Lasocki[181] has brought to me on your behalf, I will here reply.

In this your Lordship sets forth for me the present state of your affairs, and also that the matter has fallen out contrary to your own and my surmise and all expectation, [66] insomuch that you are forced to suffer proscription from this Kingdom in accordance with a decree of his Royal Majesty. At this I most certainly grieve, as I ought, for your sake as a friend. But as a great many other things are now being done rashly and without consulting the Senators of the Royal Commonwealth, I do not wonder that even this too could have been done by the agency of some persons. For there is no doubt but that this was done, and this ill-will stirred up against your Lordship at the instance and by the agency of some of those who vaunt themselves as "spiritual" and have great reputation and influence with his Royal Majesty, and have his Royal Majesty's pen and seal in their power. Nor did it ever happen either by my vote or, as I believe, by that of other Senators of the Royal Commonwealth. And even in the very decree of proscription, of which your Lordship has sent me a copy, some things appear to have been written with greater vehemence and expression of hatred than can be thought even to have entered the mind of his Royal Majesty himself.

However, although your Lordship had indeed not even expected that this would be the case, nor had you besides merited that this be done, yet I do not doubt but that as a man of wide experience your Lordship long since had this in mind, so that you deem that you must with brave and patient spirit bear all these ills and adversities which you think may occur and fall out for the sake of promoting the glory of God, and has so determined with yourself. I, moreover, if only some relief or assistance can properly be furnished by my influence or even by my efforts, should be willing and glad to come to your assistance at once and to prove to you my goodwill which I have entertained for you now for not a few years, as your Lordship shall also learn more at length from the relation of Master Lasocki. Indeed, I have confided to him some things which he should make known to your Lordship in my name. Farewell [John Tarnowski].

The same testimony is borne by letters of Nicholas Lutomirski, then castellan of Czechów, dated 11 July [1556]; of Stanislas and Jacob Ostroróg, dated 9 August; of Stanislas Tarnowski,[182] castellan of Zawichost, dated 10 September; of Spytek Jordan,[183] palatine of Sandomierz, dated 12 September; and of Nicholas Myszkowski, castellan of Wojnicz, [67] dated 25 September.

[Letters of September 1556 to Sigismund from Senators Myszkowski, Boner, and Superintendent Cruciger]

I am glad to append copies of letters from certain Senators to the King,[184] written in this connection with much feeling, the utmost sincerity, and uncommon tact, which, so far as I know, have never been offered to the memory of posterity, as they deserve. Here then [is the letter of Nicholas] Myszkowski 25 September 1556:

> To his Sacred Royal Majesty, Most Clement Prince and Lord.
> Your Sacred Royal Majesty, Most Gracious Prince and Lord, I have received a letter and confession [of faith][185] from Doctor Lismanino, a man pious and learned, together with a copy of the mandate by which order of your Sacred Royal Majesty he has been proscribed from this Royal Commonwealth. In the letter this thing is of the greatest concern to me. In the first place, he complains of the slanderous accusation made to your Sacred Royal Majesty, his most Gracious Prince, and of the wrong done to him contrary to all law in this Royal Commonwealth, the praise of which he used to spread among the foreign nations for its justice, humanity, and other noble virtues. Hence he urges and begs me together with other Senators of the Royal Commonwealth, to address your Sacred Royal Majesty by letter in order that your Sacred Royal Majesty may vouchsafe to set him free from this proscription, which was obtained against him by his adversaries not legally but secretly.

And I am greatly amazed and grieved that your Sacred Royal Majesty
could have been led by misinformation to suffer this man, whom you so
highly esteemed while he was still in monastic life, and often commended
for his judgment as well as his wide experience, to be now proscribed from
this Royal Commonwealth as a "vagrant (*vago*)" and a "Sacramentarian."[186] I certainly cannot believe that your Sacred Royal Majesty
allowed himself to be led to this act for the reason that this man entered
another kind of life; especially as by this very deed of his he has shown us
all an uncommon proof of his virtue, in that he was unwilling under cover of
a pretended piety to deceive your Sacred Royal Majesty and many others.
Instead he wished rather to be to all a living example of a certain perfection
of life, even though this be with far less advantage to himself, or even praise
with the men [68] of this world who measure good faith by the extent of its
advantages.

Yet I do not suppose that it is this that has hitherto injured him in the
eyes of your Sacred Royal Majesty, but rather the slanderous representations of his adversaries. For it is manifest to all that Lismanino is not a
"vagrant," but a man having distinguished and intimate relations with
many princes, and especially with your Sacred Royal Majesty. Moreover,
he did not land with us here presumptuously like some vagrant, but had
been wished for, nay even duly called by many,[187] and also was sent by
those men of highest position in response to the request of our people, so
that they might have in him a man whose counsel they could employ in
cases of doubt. Surely it came about as though by divine providence that
our people chose for themselves this doctor who is most devoted to your
Sacred Royal Majesty. Furthermore, his having been accused before your
Sacred Royal Majesty as a Sacramentarian was a mere slander of his adversaries, as appears from his confession, in which he clearly enough expresses
his opinion as to the Lord's Supper. To this confession also the decree of
proscription is almost diametrically opposed.

Inasmuch, therefore, as your Sacred Royal Majesty, both from his own
confession of faith and also from the testimony of your counselors fully and
plainly enough acknowledges the innocence of this good man, I beg (if one
may beg in behalf of an innocent man) that now at length your Sacred Royal
Majesty, being now better informed by his counselors as to the faith, life,
and innocence of this man, may set aside the proscription published against
him and declare him to be free from it.

For the wrong was in this way done not only to him alone, but also to all
those very great men by whom he was sent hither to us. Among them,
moreover, it very often happens that our own men go to sojourn in order to
pursue their studies, or to see the country and its learned men. Hence we
ought to beware lest we gain ill repute with those foreign nations on account
of our unjust proceedings, which without doubt might easily take place on
account of this man who, as appears from the letters of those great men,
enjoys high esteem and influence [69] among them. I doubt not therefore
that your Sacred Royal Majesty will willingly do that which he judges more
useful to the honor of our Commonwealth, so that among other people, we
may not be charged with injustice. The Lord God bless your Sacred Royal

Majesty through his Son and preserve you to us as long and as happily as possible. To his grace I humbly commend myself. Given at Zator,[188] 15 September 1556,

Himself your Majesty's most obedient servant,

Nicholas Myszkowski of Mirów, castellan of Wojnicz, etc.

And John Boner, castellan of Biecz, wrote as follows:

To his Most Sacred and Serene Royal Majesty of Poland, etc., my Most Clement Lord and Master.

Your Sacred and Most Serene Royal Majesty, my Most Gracious Lord and Master, from my earliest years I have always striven with the utmost pains to honor and revere your Sacred Royal Majesty, and with great diligence respectfully to submit to your laws and edicts. And this I do the more readily now that I have reached riper age, judgment, and understanding. Being fully conscious of this, I shall the more freely undertake the office of intercessor with your Sacred Royal Majesty on behalf of the most learned and worthy man, Doctor Lismanino, led thereto chiefly by these reason: namely, that I may perform my duty towards your Majesty, and aid an innocent friend (if I can) in honorable ways, since a place for mercy to the innocent can never be wanting with your Sacred Royal Majesty.

Wherefore may your sacred Royal Majesty grant me this favor, if I beg from you with humble entreaty and sincere heart, that you revoke and annul the edict of proscription by a new edict, especially since this supplication [70] of mine in no wise contradicts your Majesty's former edict. I therefore trust that this intercession will in no way cause me injury, relying upon your Majesty's mercy, in which I take refuge as a suppliant as I briefly give reason for the cause I have undertaken.

For many years the closest intimacy and friendship has existed between Doctor Lismanino and me, and I can affirm that he has always regarded your Sacred Royal Majesty and all the leading men of this Kingdom with uncommon honor. When he returned to Poland, I received him into my own house in order to show him my old friendship and in performing this act of kindness I deem I did nothing unworthy an honorable man. But while he was enjoying my hospitality as a friend, there arose a rumor that a mandate had come from your Sacred Royal Majesty by which it appeared that Lismanino was proscribed from this Kingdom. This was indeed called a question by many, but any hope or occasion of doubt was removed by your Majesty's title, by whose authority the edict against Lismanino was said to have been issued. Now, however hard it would be for me to separate in this way from a rare friend, and however repugnant to Christian piety and laws, yet this grief gave way before your Majesty's command which, saving only my reverence for the Deity, I would never disobey on any occasion, not even were my life at stake.

The true reason why I am now writing to your Majesty is this: I have received a letter from this man in which he bitterly complains that he has been condemned without a hearing. And since a report of this has already reached foreign nations, he asks me to beg your Majesty of your royal mercy and justice to free him from proscription, since he desires and is ready, if need be, in the Kingdom and in your Majesty's presence to give proof of his innocence and faith (of which he has already published a confession), and to refute the calumnies of his ill-wishers. I therefore earnestly beg that your Majesty may not condemn this man unheard in this own cause, which will do your Majesty the highest honor, and will be very necessary to an innocent man. And I shall acknowledge sharing this kindness, as becomes the office of a true friend. Moreover I beseech your Majesty [71] to free a pious and religious man from the edict of proscription not for my prayers, but in accordance with your highest justice, kindness, native goodness, and mercy towards all men. And for this I hope and pray to the Great and Good God. May the Great and Good God preserve you in health and prosperity long to reign.

Given at Balice,[189] 16 September 1556.

Your Sacred Majesty's most devoted servant,
John Boner of Balice, castellan of Biecz, etc.

I am glad on this occasion also to add a copy of a letter to the King on the same subject, wisely written by a minister of the Word of God, Felix Cruciger of Szczebrzeszyn, and to exhibit an example of Christian fortitude defending a most worthy cause with intrepid spirit before the King.

Most Serene King and our Most Gracious Lord, some Pharisees,[190] moved of late by the father of lies, have been shamelessly attempting to overthrow us by grave calumnies before your Sacred Majesty. We are therefore driven in this letter to bear witness and to show our regard, reverence, and in short all zeal for true and scrupulous obedience toward your Sacred Majesty, our most Gracious Prince and Lord.

Furthermore, when we earnestly seek the causes of their enmity toward us, the sincerity of our Christian faith at once presents itself, which we, having rejected the impostures of Antichrist, are endeavoring to follow and to maintain. They, in contrast, are attempting to destroy our integrity with the thunderbolts of their rage. And when they see that this can in no wise be done, they do not blush at abusing your Sacred Majesty's mercy for the sake of their iniquity.

We therefore [72] do not hesitate to testify and affirm, Most Gracious King, and that in the sight of God most high, to whom all counsels are plain, that we are not in the least degree conscious of those crimes of which we are accused before your Sacred Majesty. Wherefore we beg of your Graciousness that you may think thus of our gathering,[191] and be persuaded that the prayers of them all tend to this: that they desire the welfare and safety of your Sacred Majesty and of your whole Kingdom. And when it shall seem fit to your Sacred Majesty, they will not only spend all their fortunes, but also most willingly give their lives and shed their blood.

Some years ago the Great and Good God by the rays of his Spirit enlightened our minds, sunk in deepest darkness, so that we realized the wiles and impostures by which the Chimaera of the Roman See has now for many centuries oppressed men's consciences, ensnared as it were in tightest bonds. While therefore the light of the Gospel was increasing in our hearts, we were unwilling to neglect the talent entrusted to us by our heavenly Father, having been, in any case, clearly taught by the disastrous indolence of the unprofitable (*piger*) servant.[192] Hence in prayers addressed to the Lord and in counsels taken among ourselves, we began to inquire whether in any way the most flourishing Royal Commonwealth of our Sacred Majesty could be set free from the deceits and tyranny of Antichrist, and the corrupt state of the Church be gradually restored. Nor indeed were we so carried away by rashness as to undertake this difficult task without the advice of learned men, but especially of that most illustrious man, Doctor Francis Lismanino, as we had no doubt that he was by no means a novice in this field (*palaestra*) and was very much devoted and dear to your Sacred Majesty. He presented himself to us as deserving to be the first of all called to this most sacred task. But far were we from ever wishing to employ his efforts and counsel save insofar as we were allowed by your Sacred Majesty's grace.

But lo! while we are preparing a letter to your Sacred Majesty in order to make our plans known to you, a crowd of Pharisees condemns a perfectly innocent man by a most severe proscription. This was surely an atrocious wrong, Most Gracious King, which not only affected a thoroughly upright worshiper of God, but also was so decreed by all opinions coming from the most distant parts of Germany.[193] [73] Moreover, we do not doubt that both from his confession of faith lately issued and from the letters and conversations of many of your own Sacred majesty's counselors, your Sacred Majesty learns that the charges brought by them against this innocent man are false and invented.

Wherefore we pray your Sacred Majesty (if one may entreat pardon for an innocent man) that you may be pleased of your mercy to remove and annul the edict of proscription, and declare the good man free from it. When this is done, foreign nations will in highest praises proclaim the mercy and justice of your Sacred Majesty, and we as most obedient subjects of your Sacred majesty will ourselves sincerely give unceasing thanks.

Moreover, although it is plain that the whole design of those men in this matter is that by means of this sort they may succeed in alienating our minds in turn from your Sacred Majesty. But this neither they themselves nor Satan, the father of discord, will ever accomplish. Yet we rely upon your Sacred Majesty being so just that he will not condemn us without the case being pleaded; so temperate in spirit that he will kindly hear us before he puts faith in the accusations of our adversaries. Therefore, Most Gracious King, we beseech your Sacred Majesty that if you entertain any sinister suspicion concerning us in consequence of their accusations, you may deign to remove and delete it entirely, and may be persuaded of our reverence for you being the same as that of your most faithful and loving subjects. May the King of kings enlighten the mind of your Sacred Royal Majesty with the light of the Holy Spirit to the knowledge of his holy truth, establish your throne in heavenly wisdom; confirm it in justice and equity; and long preserve you unharmed in your prosperous reign. Given at Secemin,[194] 15 September 1556.

The same your Sacred and Most Serene Majesty's most loyal and obedient subject,

Felix Cruciger of Szczebrzeszyn, Superintendent[195] of the renascent Church of Christ in Little Poland, in the name of all the ministers and nobles united in the faith of Jesus Christ.

[Controversy over the Eucharist, 1556]

[74] While upright and prominent men were thus taking the part of Lismanino with the King, who was kind by nature, the attempts of his enemies did not attain the wished for end. Upon the return of this man [Lismanino], there arose a heated controversy about the Sacrament of the body and blood of our Lord. For he had got a truer view of the Holy Eucharist, not only from books but also from his acquaintance with Calvin and other outstanding men who were then living among the Swiss, and was sharply attacking the detestable dogma of the Church of Rome about the bread consecrated by the priest being converted into God Himself the Creator or, to use their more than barbarous expression, the doctrine of *transsubstantiatio* and *transelementatio;*[196] and Lismanino was defending the view that the bread as well as the consecrated wine are nothing but *sacramenta* of the body and the blood of the Lord.[197]

To be sure, at that time the pious men occupied in reforming the Church retained the word *sacramenta*, although unknown to Scripture and to the earliest age, and more appropriate to a [military] camp than to the Church.[198] Yet since even she, under the heavenly leadership of Christ, the King of kings, spends her time on earth continually in warfare and in keeping guard against the enemy of our salvation, this word may still be retained, seeing that we too, when being baptized, are sworn in by the sacrament of Christ, bound by oath, given orders, recruited, and engaged for our whole life.[199] And that the more because to the ancients sacraments were nothing other than sacred signs or symbols. (See, among others,[200] Augustine, *Epistola* 23 *ad Bonifacium*,[201] also *Contra Maximinum*, liber 3, caput 22, distinctio 2, "De consecratione Christi Sacrificium;"[202] Chrysostom, *Homilia in Mattaeum* 83;[203] Theodoret, *Dialogus* I.)[204]

These pious men therefore acted wisely in taking into account the capacity of simple men, especially in those beginnings, when they retained a convenient word while abandoning its bad meaning, and continued the use of the thing while rejecting its abuse. They therefore said and affirmed that this papal dogma was not only unknown to canonical Scripture and to all antiquity, and was not established until the thirteenth century after Christ by Pope Innocent III of Rome,[205] but also [added] that its wording sounds barbarous and that, as the abuse was more and more increasing, it led to an idolatry worse than that of the heathen who laughed at deities born in the gardens of the Egyptians, and thought it a horrid thing for a god to be eaten.[206]

[The reformers argued further that] the Holy Eucharist, as even the word shows, [75] was instituted in order to give solemn thanks to God through Christ for his great benefit in the remission of sins, and to celebrate the memory of the broken body of Christ by the breaking of bread, and [the memory] of his shed blood by the pouring of wine. That the bread and wine are thus representative and commemorative signs and a figure of the body and blood of the Lord, this they declared in common with Scripture. For Scripture speaks in this fashion, as of many things, so also of the Paschal lamb as a type of Christ, calling him Pascha, or the passover. And [they did so] in agreement with all antiquity. Thus they vigorously inveighed against the errors commonly accepted.

But this teaching won them the serious ill-will of the bishops. For this is their chief workshop, in which they have forged not only such great riches and so many dignities, but also whole dominions, and under cover of religion have declared themselves creators of their own Creator, nay, more. (I shudder to relate such things.) [They declare themselves] fathers and makers of Christ, as does John Eusebius Nieremberg, a Jesuit, in the *Panegyrica narratio de tribus martyribus* (p. 521),[207] as if no creator (*nullus*) existed in heaven and earth. Hence they have exempted themselves from all law and government, and not content with this, have at last made themselves masters and rulers of all men. Therefore, desiring to render the heralds of the Gospel and the champions of the true view odious to the people subject to themselves, they called them Sacramentarians, as though they were enemies of the Sacrament. And by this artifice they brought not a little ill-will upon them among simple people (who are carried away by superstition and act more from feeling and impulse than from judgment), striving thus with all diligence to preserve their false dogmas and arrogantly usurped rights.

[Aloysius Lippomano, papal legate in Poland, 1555 – 58]

And that they might do this with the greater authority and success, they not only tried to bring over to their side the King, who (as we have said) was kind by nature, but also, on finding him disinclined to cruelty, they besought the aid of the Pope. Sending him a letter therefore, they prayed to him to send a legate *a latero* to Poland, and to manage his affairs and theirs in the same way as in the Empire, France, Spain, and in other Christian states. The author and promoter of this plan was a certain Francis Krasiński of the ecclesiastical estate, afterwards created bishop of Cracow.[208]

When this had become known to the nobility, they gave instructions to their land deputies (*nunciis terrestribus*) [76] who were to go to the general Diet of the Kingdom. We commonly call it the Assembly (*comitia*), not without reason, since the people (*populus*) have a prevailing power in this country).[209] [These deputies from the dietines were charged] with directions that they should consult about this matter and see that the Republic should suffer no harm. What was done in this Diet about the matter, we shall with the Good God's help say in a second volume.[210] The bold and stubborn arrogance of the Papists prevailed with the easy-going King, Senate, and Deputies, so that the nuncio of the Supreme Pontiff (or, as they like to say, Apostolic) was admitted to the Royal

Commonwealth and to the Royal Court in the way accepted in other Christian states.

[An anti-Semitic episode, 1556][211]

The first to act in this capacity with us was Aloysius Lippomano of Venice, a man (as his deeds prove) obstinate and crude.[212] This is the less to be wondered at since: "None is more severe than a lowly man when raised to high station."[213] For it was said that he was born of an unknown father.[214] As soon as the land deputies saw him in the Diet (*comitia*), they forthwith greeted him: "Hail, offspring of vipers!" Such indeed Lippomano proved himself to have been.

For seeing that their dogma of the Most Holy Sacrament, as they call it, was in great danger, he brought together at Łowicz [1556] a synod of prelates of every kind. In view of their situation they decided that, in order to strike fear into the people subject to them and horror into the dissenters,[215] a severe or rather a savage example should be made of a person from the lowest dregs of the populace, hence with the greater impunity. Since, however, they knew that all things bow to money, and that "Gold passes through go-betweens,"[216] being stronger also than iron to break the very rocks, and hence that there are few who can bear the attack of those fighting with silver spears,[217] they bribed and drew over to their party Borek,[218] captain of Sochaczew, a royal town near Łowicz. Then striking at the Jews, who both bore the burden of popular hatred and lacked defense of their innocence, they threw three from a crowd of them and a certain woman, Dorothy Łazięcka, into prison.[219]

The articles of accusation were these: That when Łazięcka, according to the usual custom, went to Holy Communion before the Paschal feast, she concealed the host in her mouth and sold it to the Jews; that they pierced it with needles; and that from this they collected a vial of blood of which they have need to heal the wound of circumcised infants. But when people, though [77] given to superstition, nevertheless called the matter in question as hard to believe, and asked to see the vial full of blood as proof of the charge, the bishops made a sport of the credulity of the simple people, replying that it had been hidden by the crafty Jews.

Budziński, who was an eye-witness, then serving Stanislas Myszkowski, the cupbearer to the King throughout his reign,[220] notes that *[W]hen the King was staying at Vilna and was just at his breakfast, Przerębski, Vice-Chancellor of the Kingdom, feigning grief in his countenance, brought this story to the King. Myszkowski, who stood high in the King's favor as a man not only highminded but also industrious, wise, and witty, smiled at it, suspecting the plot laid for the unfortunate people. But Przerębski, full of confidence,[221] said:*

> *Well, Myszkowski, do you listen with laughter to a matter that ought to be heard with great pain and utmost indignation? Is this not piety and reverence for a most holy thing? But why should I be amazed? It is not unusual for you to mock at God and holy things.*

To this the former, as he was a sensible man, replied:

> *To tell the truth, Przerębski, I am not in the least mocking at God, but at your slanders and tales and the silly stories that you are spreading and bringing to the ears of the King. In this you respect neither divine nor royal majesty and being keen on every deceit, you cast off not only the fear of God but also decency. God I fear and honor and know who he is and I am sure that, since he is a Spirit who can be reached by no senses, still less can he be pierced by needles or hands.*

The King showed himself neutral in this affair and acted as an unprejudiced judge, giving an open ear to each, but making no reply to either.

The next day the case grew hotter. Przerębski raised his hand with a threat. Thereupon, Myszkowski replied:

> *Przerębski, if you were not doing this in the sight of the King, I would cut off your threatening hand with my own, which is ever ready to defend my life and honor.*

Then the King, intervening with his authority in this heated quarrel, bade both hold their peace. Privately also he told Myszkowski to disregard the prelate, to take account also of the King's presence, and to avoid giving occasion for further strife. And he said that he saw through these plots and himself put no faith in such vain and silly tales.

In the meantime the Jews of Sochaczew,[78] relatives and friends of the prisoners, came to the King and through Myszkowski as their spokesman complained to him of the grave wrong. The King came to the aid of the wretched people, strictly commanded Captain Borek to release the prisoners, and sent a servant of the Court with these mandates.[222] But, by divine permission, sheer boldness, stopping at no wickedness, Borek carried off the plot as planned. For Przerębski with others of the same stripe dispatched orders by post horses to Borek in the name of the King that, in accordance with the intention of the Holy Spirit and of the apostolic legate (that is to say, of the one presiding over the synod at Łowicz), he should consign the Jews to the stake.

The sentence was passed against the Jews. When brought to the stake, they said publicly and freely:

> *We never have bought the host nor pierced it with needles, for we by no means believe that in the host there is the body of God. On the contrary, we know that there is no body or blood in God. And after the manner of our fathers we believe that the Messiah was not to be God himself, but his anointed (*unctum*) and ambassador (*legatum*). We also know for certain that there is no blood in flour. We bear witness to the end that we have no need of blood.*

Hearing this, the agents of the cruelty of Lippomano and of the Papists poured burning pitch into the mouths of the wretched creatures.[223]

*This in every way horrible crime was inserted in the Roman records and pub-
lished as a miracle,[224] with the King's name added in order to win belief for the
fiction. This writ, delivered by Myszkowski to the King, aroused his indignant
anger and alienated him from Lippomano. The King did not hesitate to say to
his face that he detested this monstrous crime, and was not in the least moved to
believe that there was blood in that host.*

*After this Lippomano wrote a letter to Prince Nicholas Radziwiłł, palatine of
Vilna, a man wise and high-minded, and fervent with rare zeal for restoring
God's truth. In this he tried to win him back to the Papacy by holding out the
hope of gaining the Pope's favor. But he found the noble prince unmoved to
take such a step, for he openly declared that he would not return from the
Church of God to the den of thieves and the dwelling of idolaters.[225]*

[Stanislas Myszkowski, attended by Budziński, delivers two letters
to the King, one by Łaski and one brought by him from
Melanchthon, written respectively December and October 1556]

*Meantime John Łaski, of whom we have spoken,[226] having returned to Poland,
wrote the King a letter[227] which he entrusted to his uncle Myszkowski[228] to put
into the King's hands. This was discovered by Przerębski and his associates,
and so they used every effort to intercept it. The King on the other hand [79]
sought an opportunity to read it through with Myszkowski. Yet for a considerable time this could not be accomplished because of many obstacles that were
interposed by Przerębski. It happened indeed that this letter was laid by the
King on a bench, whence it fell to the ground, was torn by the King's dog, and
was taken from the dog by Fabian, keeper of the King's bedchamber, who
picked up the pieces and gave them to Myszkowski. His attendant Budziński
skillfully pasted them together and copied them. A copy of this I duly give here
(Budziński, History, xvi):*

[Łaski to Sigismund]

*Your Sacred Royal Majesty, my Lord and Most Gracious Master, a
perpetual assurance of fidelity and reverence and of my obedience.*

*In accordance with my fidelity and reverence for you, Most
Serene King, I could not but inform you at the earliest opportunity of
my return to my native land. For although I have no doubt at all of
your forbearance with me, yet I have thought that I ought to counter
before your Majesty the rumors spread by some persons, since we
seem hardly ever safe from the slanders of malicious men, especially
those of the Pharisees of our times. They are certainly thus far
reproducing the nature of their ancestors, even if (as we say of a
wolf) they wish to seem to have changed their skins.[229]*

*And even as their ancestors were utterly unable to spare from
their lying slanders the Prophets and Apostles sent by the Lord, nay*

even the Lord Christ himself, so now also their offspring neither will
nor can spare anyone who merely seems in any way to wish to follow the teaching of the Lord Christ and his Apostles, otherwise they
would show themselves degenerate, unless, as their master,[230] they
did it perpetually.

And I have thought that first of all I ought to set before you, Most
Gracious King, the reason of my returning hither, lest some slander
arise hence contrived by them; furthermore indeed that I ought
humbly to implore your royal authority, as that of a Christian
Prince, against the insidious bites of the pharisaical sycophants of
this sort.

In the first place then, I doubt not [80] that you still remember
well, illustrious King, that I actually had my representative[231]
proceed to you, and he incidentally inquired through the illustrious
Prince, the lord palatine of Vilna,[232] whether you could bear with
my return hither, if indeed any lawful and Christian invitation (consistent with the will of God) happened to offer itself to me here. This
reply was then given me by you, namely, that you certainly did not
command my return to my native land, lest you might be called the
instigator of it. Yet neither did you go so far as to forbid it, as
though you were unwilling to bear with me here. But if I quite
wished to come, you advised me (for the sake of your kindness to
me) not to come before St. Bartholomew's day, for it was then
expected that a Diet would be held at which something definitive
was also to be decided about religion itself.[233] I should especially
take all pains by some public proof to clear myself of any suspicion
of my disagreement with the Augsburg Confession, particularly in
the matter of the Lord's Supper.[234]

Immediately upon the return of the messenger with this reply, a
good man, men prominent in this Kingdom, and they not the least
important, wrote letters to me, in which some wished me to return
hither, while others even urged me to do so. And the same was done
besides by a good many of my kinsfolk, some my blood relations,
some also related by marriage. But most of all my return hither was
urged by a great many men of the equestrian order, who also were
devoted to the Evangelical doctrine. Gathering in a synod with most
of the ministers of the Church, they all unanimously summoned me
to them in a letter sent through my very same messenger, and
pressed me by very many and strong reasons to yield to this call of
theirs.[235]

When therefore this messenger of mine (as I have said already)
had brought me this answer of your Majesty, together with so many
and strong demands of others, and finally also this call, I decided
that I ought to take account of all these things. [Thus nevertheless]
as a result I deemed that my services, which I was rendering to

others abroad, should not be refused to my own country, especially when I had received a call. Nevertheless I [held off], that thus I [236] *might in the meantime also submit to your Majesty's judgment.*

I therefore determined to return hither in order to accept the call, but not before this autumn, that I might comply with your Majesty's wish, [81] *even though I was at the time (especially in view of such a call) possessed by a quite incredible desire to see my native land again. From then on, so far as in me lay, I neglected nothing that I thought in any way affected the allaying of the controversy about the Lord's Supper. With princes (not a few nor the least among princes), to whom I undertook journeys (not without danger to my health, to say nothing of the expense involved), I tried whether any way could be found of arranging some conference on this subject to which all the most learned men from each side should be invited. To this the princes themselves, to whom I went, will bear me witness, if occasion requires.* [237]

And since to many the time seemed not yet ripe for this matter, and the affair was being long drawn out, I myself, as briefly as I could, wrote a purgatio *[Frankfurt, October 1556] in defense of our doctrine against all those who claim (although without warrant) that we disagree with the Augsburg Confession. And, when this was read and unanimously approved, first by Calvin and his friends, for they chanced at the time to have come to us at Frankfurt, then by all the churches of foreigners at Frankfurt,* [238] *a little later by the leading ministers of the churches in Hesse, and finally at Wittenberg by Master Philip Melanchthon, I put it to press, long ago.* [239] *And as it is still in press, [I offer] a manuscript copy of it—as it was now possible to have one made quickly— to Your Majesty [that it might be evident that I have desired to omit no possible disclosure concerning my observance] to your Majesty so far as in me lay.* [240]

But when all these matters were done as far as could be, and I again heard that the Diet of the Kingdom had now been deferred to the middle of September, even to the end of October, I delayed my journey so that I might come hither at the end of November, in order not to do anything contrary to your Majesty's wish, and I kept hoping that meanwhile either the Diet itself or at least the discussion of religion in it might be completed. [241] *So then I have now come hither, Most Gracious King, in obedience to my summons and relying upon your wisdom.* [242]

At once on my very arrival here, however, I learned that those who have invited me hither are (without any fault of their own) being brought under many, grave suspicions. And since these things also seem somewhat to concern me, as [82] *I have been invited by them, and may involve me also in the same suspicions through the slanders of those who would injure me, I must touch upon them at least briefly, and I must humbly beg your Royal Majesty (as becomes the office of a Christian prince) to give no ear at all to those tale-bearers who are wont to accuse others only in secret, and meanwhile scarcely suffer their own names to be known. Rather may you determine to follow the example of David, the most holy king, who declares that in his household such secret informers shall have no credit with him, rather they shall not even have any place in his house to dwell in.*[243]

So far as particularly concerns me, I have indeed, praise be to the Lord, always so behaved, wherever I have been in my ministry hitherto, that in every way I would sooner accuse than excuse myself before the Lord God. But in civil judgment before men, I have so good a conscience that I do not think that there is any one who can truly call in question my ministry and its faithfulness and worth. As to my loyalty and reverence for you, and also my zeal, I take no other for both witness and judge than you yourself, Most Serene King, and especially the Great and Good God who knows and sees all things.

Now, therefore, should I who while living abroad have always been anxious to defend your dignity, should I now, I say, when at length in my country, join myself to those who were endeavoring in my ministry to undermine your Majesty's dignity and authority (if it so please those pharisaical detractors).[244] *Be this as far as possible from me and all my friends! And indeed, by the grace of God, this is and ever shall be so far from me and from all those who have called me hither, that we not only do not even dream of such a thing, but can by no means even bear any one of this sort among us. In fact, we should even wish to be the first, not indeed to disgrace him with secret abuse, but (if the case should be also well established) openly to accuse him, whoever he might be.*

But perhaps those who accuse us would of themselves also judge and weigh us, [83] *and want to impute to others on account of their holiness (if it please God),* not *to themselves, what they would easily allow themselves to do for their admirable fidelity and observance to their creator the Pope even against your Majesty, in order to establish their own tyranny in every way. Of this we have indeed not a few examples and even instructions in writing. However, we have an excellent judgment of Christ the Lord against the underhanded denunciations of such men, namely: that those who hate the light and above all wish their designs to be concealed in the darkness of the night, are evil-doers, in fact both thieves and robbers.*[245]

Let all our underhanded detractors, then, have this reputation for themselves, as they do not come forth into the light. And let them have it indeed not from us, who in these words of ours are saying nothing, but from Christ the Lord himself whose judgment this is,

*and cannot be gainsaid. To this judgment, having a good con-
science, we appeal. And we beg you, invincible King, to have it set
before your eyes, to the glory of Christ the Lord, if our accusers
seem in any wise to have good conscience in trying to disgrace us.
But if they only wish to show their fidelity (as they ought) to both
your Majesty and to the whole Kingdom (as they never fail to boast),
let them do it openly and in the light of day, and come themselves
and bring forward their incriminations, not to say slanders. For,
especially in the light of the word of God, no one's evil deeds can be
so cloaked that they do not the more betray themselves the more one
wishes them to be concealed by hypocrisy.*

*I indeed, as well as all those who have called me hither, having
besides (thanks be to God!) the best conscience as to our fidelity and
reverence for your Majesty, neither shun nor fear any light at all,
but frankly desire both to be accused and to reply to all who would
lawfully accuse us on any account. If our adversaries henceforth
refuse this, and meanwhile do not cease gnawing with their clandes-
tine detractions at all that we do, we appeal to the eternal and
immutable censure of Christ the Lord. And we doubt not that it [the
censure] will be approved both by your Royal Majesty and by pious
men everywhere. [For this censure] tears away from them every
mask of hypocrisy, however fair otherwise, and clearly proves them
to be nothing else but* φαῦλα πράσσοντες *(mischief-makers),*[246] *that
is, laborers of iniquity, [84] and thieves and robbers.*

*But there is also another thing, most powerful King, that I have
thought should not be here passed over in silence. Namely, about
Aloysius Lippomano. [He is] truly unworthy indeed, as he himself
confesses, yet by far the most worthy and the most appropriate
legate from the Apostolic See of Rome.*[247] *The Pope in his letter to
the most illustrious Prince, the Lord Palatine of Vilna, etc. writes
quite predictably that I am a heretic.*[248] *For that prince, most illustrious for his notable piety and virtue, amply rebuffed the man's
impudence in his most admirable reply,*[249] *so that Lippomano's
hypocrisy and a certain hypocritical civility are only too well known
to the whole Christian world, so that whoever is praised by him may
deservedly be suspected by all good men, while one who is traduced
may be deemed a very good and upright man! [But] even if [that
prince rebuffed Lippomano in his hypocritical civility], yet even I
could not myself be quite silent in this case in repelling a too bare-
faced slander and accusation.*

*To be sure, he deals cleverly, not to say cunningly and deceit-
fully, in that while citing no heresy, he pretends, though, that I am a
heretic, so that of course he does not have to prove anything. But
yet is free, of course, to fabricate whatever he wants (at least if*

pressed), or like a wasp can leave his sting and flee. Forsooth, a fine accuser and judge in one!

But if he lays to my charge also the crime of those on whose account he taunts the Lord Palatine of Vilna, then—even as not all those things can apply to me (insignificant as I am)—I shall readily allow that those that in any wise can fit me, do indeed apply to me. Nay [250] indeed, I could wish that they might all apply to me, provided also that his preposterous use of words (in which the good man seems greatly to delight) may be either abandoned or amended. For even if I acknowledge all these things, insofar indeed as we regard the matter itself, though not the man's twisted words, yet I certainly have no fear for myself in the judgment of God on account of them all. Indeed, I feel that I should fear much more, if I did not acknowledge these things.

But let Lippomano beware lest, while fancying himself (upon his Pope's authority) the accuser and likewise the judge of heretics, he himself being sunk in heresies (together with his Pope and all his school), [85] he be handed over (in God's judgment) to the eternal torments of Gehenna. For the point of issue there will be not about approving the primacy of the Pope, and about masks and puppets, and again about all the tricks of the Antichristian priesthood itself, and of all its creatures, but the point will be about all the dignity and authority of the only-begotten Son of God and our Lord Jesus Christ. This, whether we consider the person of Christ or even his universal office (functionem universam), his Church being violated and trampled underfoot by the Popes and their flock.

These matters indeed will be much more weighty before that judge, before whose judgment-seat both the Popes themselves and all their legates, and even all their patrons and hangers-on will sometime have to stand. Then let Lippomano with his fellows see to it that they come off free there. Nay, do you also see to it, Most Gracious King, that you do not bind yourself in any way to such men by your association, approval, or patronage.

I doubt not but that many and diverse things are reported to you which also affect your mind in various ways. I doubt not but that you are offended by many things that seem to threaten you, to whichever side you incline. But in all these both many and diverse matters it behooves you to remember the heavenly oracle uttered by God the Father himself, "HEAR YE HIM, HEAR YE HIM," [251] so that in whatever forms you ever [think that you] hear the sound of the voice of Christ the Lord (which you ought at the same time also to hear above all others), you may determine that they should be ignored, however many and diverse, nay even plausible, they may be, so that you may hear Christ the Lord (according to the heavenly *oracle of God the Father). For he alone is true of speech, and is indeed the very truth, while every man is a liar, without any exception[252] either of any Pope or of any of his creatures whatsoever.*

But as to those things in us that may have offended you hitherto, you ought, most excellent King, not so much to consider us, who have not ceased to be men, and freely confess (always with voluntary accusation of ourselves) that we are still slaves of the sin which is in us, as rather the admirable providence of the divine design in this respect by which he (even if he has of his free mercy in Christ the Lord adopted us as his beloved sons) has nevertheless wished the terrible [86] remnants of our past sins to stand out.

And this he does so that to the glory of his divine name he may restrain the pride of that infernal viper towards the infirmity of us, sinners hitherto, by the continual and earnest accusation of ourselves before the throne of his grace and the humble and constant supplication for his assistance and divine grace through Christ. This he does so that by the acknowledgment of our past sins he may keep us in our condition and duty, to wit, lest we either be too well pleased with ourselves on account of the grace bestowed upon us and be puffed up in our minds or, as we are wont, scorn others before ourselves. But also that we, all alike acknowledging our past inner infirmity and wretchedness, may indeed not revile one another and magnify one another's failings to the dishonor of the whole cause, but that we also all alike instead humble ourselves beneath the mighty hand of God, always practicing our faith by the constant reminders of the word of God, with mutual exhortations and reproofs in Christian gentleness and modesty, adding also the consolations and the promises.

Wherefore, while some of us are offended in one way, others in another, Most Serene King, we certainly ought not exaggerate one another's faults and failings, as if we were without them ourselves, likewise not to seize upon them to the prejudice of the whole cause. For this is a design of Satan, who is always trying to bring everything to the disturbance and confusion of religion. But we ought rather to follow the design of the Great Good God, so as to regard others' faults, failings, and mistakes (to which we ourselves also are sometimes subject) as our own faults, our failings, and our mistakes.

And just as we desire that our own faults, failings, and mistakes be not exaggerated in a hostile spirit to our disgrace and reproach, but instead be lovingly corrected and amended to our repentance, so also without any doubt ought we in charity to do the same in the case of others, unless we see that the things by which we are offended are either skillfully excused, or even stubbornly defended to the dishonor of God himself. Thus indeed these faults ought seriously to be assailed in defense of the glory of God, as it is evident in fine that they are being stubbornly and tyrannically defended and supported contrary to the laws of God. So then we, too, [87] desire that our faults, failings, and mistakes be corrected, amended, reproved, nay even punished (if indeed we have deserved it), provided they are clearly pointed out to us according to the word of God. And of course we desire that this be done not only by your Royal Majesty, my most Gracious Lord, but also in general by whoever might in truth convict us according to the word of God and to the glory of God of the things by which they are offended. But if it might also be obtained from the Papists by your Majesty that they should not stubbornly and tyrannically defend those things that are manifestly at war with the teaching and honor of Christ the Lord, as they themselves cannot deny, we should forthwith have an end of all controversy with them. Nor would there be many mediators needed with regard to this matter.

And concerning the dangers which you would have to fear in case you incline to either side, much could be said on this head which it would take too long to recount. One thing only will I say: If on account of the instauratio *of religion,[253] which they [254] call a* novatio,[255] *dangers are to be feared, what* novationes, *pray, will they cite to us in Judaea, Egypt, Syria, Assyria, Armenia, and all Asia Minor, all of which broad kingdoms we [now] see subjected to the horrible tyranny of the Turks? Unless they interpret it as a* novatio *the fact that, though these [peoples] had for a long time refused, at last however they began to submit to the Roman Papism and to follow its teaching. For once they had done that, then and only then they really began to fall![256]*

If, then, such a novatio *has been so fatal to all those realms, how (I ask) will it not be fatal to your Majesty and this whole Kingdom to retain and defend here this ''novatio'' (God forbid) which has evidently been fatal to so many and such great kingdoms and empires?[257]*

They, on the contrary, cite the examples of the present disorders in Germany and of the ruin of Hungary, which they would, of course, charge to our novationes.[258] *But in truth they do this unjustly. For all this ought to be charged not so much to the true religion[259] which was beginning to be established there, as to the public carelessness and negligence in restoring (*restituenda) *the true religion (the light of the Gospel already shining so bright), and in abolishing the marks and remains of Antichristian impiety. And I fear, Most Gracious King, that the same or worse things [88] threaten your Majesty and all this Kingdom, if you either reject the light of the Gospel teaching that has also arisen here, or even are remiss in wishing to embrace it.*

If we seek counsel against dangers, let us seek it with Him who alone can both admit and restrain and prevent them. He indeed long ago gave us most wholesome counsel on this matter through his Prophet Samuel, adding his clear, undoubted promise of our liberation, if we hear him. Israel was publicly giving signs of its repentance, after suffering numerous defeats at the hands of the Philistines, on account of the foolish worship of the Ark, which the Philistines had then restored with some propitiatory offerings of gold, from their own store, added. Here therefore Samuel by the mouth of the Lord first counts those offerings of the Philistines, which were hung on the Ark of Lord, as strange gods, and reckons them among idols. Then to Israel, so long afflicted, he says concerning their deliverance from the Philistines: If ye do return unto the Lord God with all your heart, PUT AWAY the foreign gods FROM AMONG YOU, and prepare your heart unto the Lord, and serve Him only. And then at last he will deliver us out of the hands of the Philistines.[260]

According to this counsel, then, proceeding from the Spirit of God himself, if you also, Most Serene King, fear for yourself and your Kingdom, you must first return not with a half, but with your whole heart. And as proof that you are doing this truly and without hypocrisy, do what you see that the Prophet here directs, for so you will show that you are truly and sincerely doing what you ought to do. But if you do not do it, you will certainly not be able to say before the eyes of God that you return to God WITH YOUR WHOLE HEART,[261] *according to the Prophet's writing.*

Do therefore, most excellent King, with your leading men, what the Lord has commanded. Put away the foreign gods from your Kingdom, but especially the guardian god of the papal kingdom which anyway our ancestors, that is, the Prophets and Apostles, never knew: I mean the tonsured god MAYZIM in which alone resides all the strength and protection of the Antichristian impiety,[262] *and serve God alone in the* restitutio *of the true and perfect worship of God. Then and only then [89] the Lord will indubitably deliver both you and your Kingdom from all the Philistines of this world.*

But if you do not do this, beware, lest from the source whence you may be promising yourself deliverance you instead bring ruin upon yourself and your Kingdom. There is no counsel against the Lord. And, outside of Christ alone, it is a wretched thing to seek refuge from the judgment of God. For who is there who hideth himself from his wrath? To him therefore determine that you must hasten, and certainly WITH YOUR WHOLE HEART, if you are to be set free from the Philistines of our age who are threatening us on every hand.

We continually pray, indeed, that the Lord may be with you and direct and prosper all your counsels and all your doings by his Holy

Spirit. But you also have to do your part, lest our prayers for you be found vain and wanting in the sight of the Lord our God. We therefore also humbly pray you, Most Gracious King, that you will now at length once for all, in the fear of God, with your whole heart put your mind to these things which you know that the Lord your God demands from you in your exalted royal calling.

You see what the times are, what the customs, what the dispositions of men. All these things surely and justly ought to remind you of your royal duty. Ignorance, however it may excuse our ancestors, I certainly think that you cannot now, especially at this present time, plead before the judgment-seat of God. That the light has again returned to the world, as though having recovered the right to return home and resume lost privileges, according to the prediction of Christ the Lord himself, you yourself in your own heart surely cannot deny, having been particularly reminded of it so many times and even by so many men of God. This light besides has now so shone forth (thanks to the Lord our God) that it can in no wise, by any force or power of the world, be longer shut out. It will therefore behoove you to beware, lest you ever be found before the judgment-seat of Christ, that under pretence of ignorance you have loved darkness rather than the light.[263] And that this indeed is the sole cause of all our condemnation, Christ the Lord himself testifies by his own divine mouth.

Here you will, of your Royal Graciousness, pardon our liberty which proceeds from my deepest loyalty to and respect for you. For if I had not at heart your royal dignity as well as also the salvation of your soul, if moreover my loyalty [90] *and respect for you did not demand it from me, I could easily indeed still be elsewhere, as by divine favor I have been until now, and besides I could also keep silent here. But since, instead, I reverently acknowledge the supreme power of God in this Kingdom and venerate the image thereof with the highest respect, and in all submission duly wish well to you, as the Father of our Fatherland ordained by the Lord,[264] I cannot indeed but admonish you according to my poor ability (as it behooves me) about the things that I know pertain to your royal office, and to your salvation as well. Others may flatter you as they please, speak pleasant words as they please. Let me choose rather to speak with you as from the mouth of the Lord. I also humbly pray the Lord that whatever makes for your lawful royal dignity, together with your eternal salvation, He may deign to impress and engrave upon your heart through his Holy Spirit, as the Teacher (*Doctorem*) of all truth. Amen.[265]*

I am being long, I see. But my loyalty and respect for you, which somehow crowds all these things upon me, knows no end. But I am drawing to a close. I commend myself in all submission and

Christian obedience to your royal Grace, my most Gracious Lord, and with myself also those who have called me back hither to my native land.

I also humbly pray that you may be most firmly persuaded about us that we are all much more willing to suffer the loss of all our property, and even of our lives, than that we should ever suffer to be in anything wanting in our fidelity, submission, and Christian reverence for you. Christian, I say. That is, reverence that is rendered neither in hope of this world's rewards nor in fear of transitory punishments, but for God himself who commands it to us, and for our own consciences. For this alone is indeed the true loyalty and submission and reverence in subjects toward lords, which is not shaken by storms of fortune nor weakened by any dangers. And what is not so, can be neither true, nor indeed lasting, but, bending to every wind of fortune it looks not so much to you and your dignity [91] as to your wealth and the honors that all expect from you.

Philip Melanchthon, greatly devoted to your Majesty,[266] *when I was lately with him at Wittenberg and had much familiar conversation with him, also concerning your Majesty, gave me this letter to your Majesty which I here enclose with mine, and asked to be most courteously remembered to your Majesty. I myself should wish also to see your Majesty's face, so long desired, if only I were permitted by your Majesty. But here too I wish to venture nothing without your Majesty's will and command. I shall therefore wait to be informed of your Majesty's mind.*

May the Great and Good God preserve your Majesty and keep from you all those who do not so much love God's and your own glory and dignity, as pursue and seek their own power, their own profit, and their own honors with you. May He govern and direct all your counsels to the glory and continual increase of His adorable name, of His Church here under you (sub te), and to your own welfare and that of all your Kingdom. Amen.

Balice, 2 December A.D. 1556.

    Your Sacred Royal Majesty's most devoted
    John Łaski[267]

At the same time Philip Melanchthon, a man outstanding not less for the goodness of his character than for the excellence of his talents, sent the King a letter on the same subject, of which I here deem it worthy to add a copy:[268]

[Melanchthon to Sigismund]

Illustrious King and Most Gracious Lord,
    There is no doubt that the society of the human race, so far as it

is preserved, is preserved by God, and that by the wisdom of God, monarchies and other governments have been established with a view to the service that they render to the human race. Thus the realm of the Turks is a desolation of the world and only a horrible punishment, not a government. With regard to such great concerns as these, God's counsel must be considered, and for serviceable governments [92] thanks ought to be given to God.

The Kingdom of Poland has been of especial service indeed to the rest of Europe for five hundred years now, for it has been our bulwark against the Tatars,[269] and has waged no wars against us. The other kingdoms of Germany and France have neglected their duty toward the general welfare, while fighting each other for the possession of Italy.[270] Since, therefore, peculiar gratitude is due to the Kingdom of Poland, deserving so well of all Europe, I pray God to preserve your Kingdom and your Majesty.

I also wish, since serviceable kingdoms are the work of God, and the knowledge of God should be especially apparent in them, that in our Kingdom too God may be rightly acknowledged and worshiped. Nor can it indeed be denied that in the churches there are great abuses, which God has commanded to be reformed by the wisdom of kings, saying: "And now, ye kings, understand."[271] Wherefore, in undertaking this office, your Royal Majesty is acting piously. No sacrifice could be more pleasing to God than that some kings, setting up a consultation of pious and learned men, should undertake to make clear the truth, to destroy idols, and to establish pious harmony.

We have read the writings of Hosius[272] and certain others who undertake by their wiles to extinguish the rising light of truth, and establish idols. But it becomes your Royal Majesty's wisdom to inquire into the sources. What we profess, is shown by the Confessio,[273] in which we have briefly included the sum of the doctrine of the Church. Wherefore I am sending a copy, and offer myself also to the judgment of the true Church. And I pray the Son of God, our Lord Jesus Christ, the guardian of his Church, to preserve your royal Majesty unharmed, and to govern your counsels.

Given in Wittenberg 18 October 1556.

Your Royal Majesty's most humble servant,
Philip Melanchthon.[274]

To the Illustrious and Most Serene King and Lord,
Lord Sigismund Augustus, King of Poland and Grand
Duke of Lithuania, etc., my most Gracious Lord.

[93] The patrons of notorious errors regarded Łaski with the same disapproval as they did Lismanino.[275] It was recorded by John Utenhove,[276] Łaski's attendant, in a letter to Calvin from Cracow of 19 February 1557,[277] that the bishops, meeting at the palace of the archbishop of Gniezno together with the papal legate Lippomano, discussed secret plans for driving Łaski out of the country. The above mentioned Bishop Zebrzydowski of Cracow, although knowing the man's great learning and piety, called Łaski the executioner of his class and his party (*carnificem sui ordinis suaeque partis*). They approached the King asking that he would grant them this [banishment] as a thing necessary to his own safety and to the quiet of the Royal Commonwealth. The King, however, refused them so unfair and even unjust a thing, and at length enjoined silence on them. Yet afterwards he was disturbed by slanders spread concerning a wicked plot of Łaski against the King, but being better informed by a friend of Łaski, maintained his former kindness to him. Meantime the ill-wishers no more changed their nature than a leopard his black-spotted skin.

[Nobiliary opposition to episcopal jurisdiction; Diet of
Warsaw, 6 December 1556 to 14 January 1557]

Hence at the Diet of Warsaw, which Budziński (*History, 19*) calls the first,[278] the subject of religion caused no small disturbance of feelings. The Romanist prelates endeavored with all their might to suppress the growing truth and to strengthen their jurisdiction over the Evangelical ministers who dwelt in the towns and villages of the nobles. But being unable to accomplish anything by force, as the number of the lovers of Evangelical truth was daily increasing, they turned to artful debates and fought, using the influence of the entire ecclesiastical estate [and] of the magnates (*procerum Politicorum*), as well as that of all antiquity. Hence the Evangelicals valiantly defended themselves for a fortnight. So this matter was vigorously thrashed out on both sides orally and in writing. Let it suffice to have related this in brief.

Seeing that their efforts were futile, the prelates turned to various wiles, used threats and flattery, and at last agreed that the Evangelical magnates and nobles might support in their own homes and at their own expense ministers of the word of God who had been confirmed by the bishops, but that they were to leave untouched the ancient tithes and parishes. Moreover, the ministers were to interpret Holy Scripture according to these four *doctores* of the Roman Church: Augustine, Jerome, Chrysostom, and Ambrose.[279] The matter seemed tolerably [94] satisfactory to some of the land deputies. Wherefore many were stuck fast in this bird-lime while the prelates sang sweetly, and others were caught by the error and superstition and blandishment of the age, being unable to distinguish "between true coin and false,"[280] and to see how far apart are the doctrines of the *doctores* who lived when the pure truth was more and more changing, as the fourth century drew to a close, not only from the judgment of Christ and his Apostles, but also from that of the Ante-Nicene and even Nicene Fathers of the Church.

Yet there were not lacking those who perceived that a work was going on that was full of dangerous risk, and that they would ere long be burned up[281] by fires concealed under deceptive embers. These [perceptive Senators and Deputies] were from Great Poland and the palatinate of Cracow, among whom was prominent Stanislas Lasocki, who judged prudently about this matter, being mindful of the ancient saying, "I fear the Greeks, even, when they bear gifts."[282] But though the Papists were superior in number and power, yet nothing could be settled against the will of the Evangelicals.

Meanwhile the Papists, having strewn the King's highway with coals scattered among the embers, were closely watching the steps and even the slightest motions of the Evangelicals, while the latter were on guard on every hand. Nicholas Rey intervened,[283] a man highly distinguished by birth, intelligence, eloquence, and virtue, and [he] proposed to send someone to the prelates, asking them to state their intentions more clearly: whether these interpretations of the four most celebrated *doctores* were to be made in accordance with the judgment of the Roman Church or with that of simple and plain Holy Scripture. This counsel pleased all, and so all asked that its author should carry it into effect. Nor did he decline. But when in the name of the Chamber of the Deputies he proposed the question to the bishops in the Senate Chamber, he received the reply that the judgment of the Roman Church was to be heeded in this.

This, being unacceptable to all the Evangelicals, was received with the brief laconic response: "We do not consent." Not a few of the Papists agreed with them, being unwilling to place either themselves or their posterity, if these should happen to go over to the camp of the Evangelicals, under the yoke of papal servitude. They knew indeed that the Evangelicals force no one to adopt their religion, while the bishops on the other hand employ all manner of threats and cruelty to this end. So they naturally perceived that in the one case they and their posterity would be safe, while in the other everything would be unsafe [95] and rightly to be feared.

A quarrel then arose between [Nicholas] Kossobudzki,[284] a deputy of Masovia, and Stanislas Szafraniec,[285] a deputy from the palatinate of Cracow. The former angrily charged the latter in plain words with being a plunderer of churches. But it was settled by the intervention of the rest, and Kossobudzki asked pardon for his misconduct. Hence all unanimously and with one voice resolved to go up to the Senate Chamber and tell the King and the Senate that they would not submit to prelatical tyranny; that the prelates should be warned not to inflict injury or disgrace upon any of the Evangelical ministers, or cause them trouble, or lay snares against them; that, on the contrary, they should allow them to enjoy public peace, if they loved their own. And [they resolved further] that they should be mindful not only of the Spirit of Christ (who urges nothing more than modesty and humility, nay rather especially recommends and enjoins love as a token of the disciples of Christ, the fulfillment of the law, and "the bond of perfectness''[286]), but also of the primitive Church which to the most cruel persecutions of the Gentiles opposed nothing but invincible patience, and grew by admonishing, not by threatening, by teaching, not by hurting, by suffering, and not by doing wrong. As it was said, so it was done. This wholesome counsel pleased the King and the Senate. Hence a law was made that the bishops should leave the ministers of the Evangelicals equal liberty and undisturbed quiet, if they wished their own to be preserved.[287] This did much at that time to promote public peace and welfare. Nor in fact can anything be found more suitable or more effective for its preservation, to say nothing of this proposition as standing on firm footing: such holy tyranny is opposed not only to the instruction of Christ and the Apostles, but also directly to the practice of the early Church.

While the enemies of Lismanino and Łaski were greatly displeased at their return, neither they nor others like them ceased to spread the purer truth. The prelates of Cracow reviled Krowicki in a published writing, calling him apostate and heretical.[288] He, on the other hand, quite aware of the secrets of the Papists, answered the bishop with an *apologia* pointing out the errors of the Roman Church and the wiles and tyranny of the Papists, with the title: *A Defense of the Primitive Teaching of Christ against the new and false Roman Teaching, which Andrew, Bishop of Cracow, defends by arms, not by Holy Scripture*.[289] [96] This book, written in the vernacular tongue, is even yet being passed from hand to hand among people, and not without notable profit. For it sets forth and points out to view the secrets and idolatrous rites of the priests. But the truth stirred up a hornet's nest, the priests pursuing in their minds nothing but persecution of confessors of the truth, for which occasion was offered by the cruelty with which the Genevans had treated Servetus,[290] and by the books of Calvin[291] and Beza[292] asserting that heretics must be punished by death.

CHAPTER FIVE

Of the Doctrines and Death of Servetus, Valentine Gentile, John Sylvan, and Bernardine Ochino, and Something of Paul Alciati and Matthew Gribaldi and Adam [Neuser], Minister at Heidelberg.

Since we have mentioned Servetus just now and are a little later to mention him again,[293] it will not have been foreign to our purpose on this occasion to say something of his doctrines and death, as well as of those of Valentine Gentile, and then of John Sylvan,[294] and of Bernardine Ochino, Paul Alciati, and Matthew Gribaldi,[295] and Adam [Neuser],[296] minister at Heidelberg. It may prove, moreover, that we here say something either unknown to others or overlooked by them.

[Michael Servetus, 1511 – 53]

Michael Servetus, called *Reves,*[297] a Spaniard in race and Aragonese by birth, was a man endowed with rare talents, who gave his attention especially to medicine, but also to other literary studies, and to improve his mind also crossed over into Africa, as the crossing from Spain to Africa is easy.[298] Like a bee that everywhere gathers anything that will be of use to it, he sucked honey even out of the very thistles of the Koran, which violently attacks the dogmas of the Triune (*Trinuno*) God and of Jesus Christ, God most high, eternally begotten from the substance (*essentia*) of the Father, as well as idolatry and Mariolatry. Yet he ascribes to Christ no common honor as the Word and Ambassador of God, a great Prophet, the light of all races in this world and in that to come, and a man endowed with divine power.

[97] It also could not escape him, as he was a man excellently versed in secular and sacred writings, that all the Ante-Nicene and even the Nicene, nay [also] the Constantinopolitan Fathers, that is, altogether all Christians for about four centuries, held, as the unalterable foundation of Catholic truth, this: ''I believe in One God the Father Almighty, Creator of heaven and earth, and in his only-begotten Son, Jesus Christ our Lord,'' that the Latin *doctores* of the Church, especially Justin[300] and Hilary,[301] taught that the Father was the author of the Son, while the Greek *doctores* taught that he was the cause of the Son, and that all the Church prayers were directed to the one God through Christ as Mediator. Hence he did not conceal his opinion about One God the Father and his Son Jesus Christ, whom, raised from the dead, the Father made Lord and appointed God and Judge of the living and the dead, as being consistent not only with the divine Scriptures, but also with all antiquity and as truly Catholic. And on this subject he conferred both in person and in writing with learned and pious men, of whom that age, so golden, had produced a great many to reform gradually the countless corruptions of the Christian world.

Indeed, by this zeal in investigating and spreading the truth, he incurred the enmity of evilly disposed men who everywhere oppose all righteousness, especially after his seven books *De Trinitatis erroribus* had been published in Germany in 1531.[302] So, having endured much in France and in Germany, he intended to go to Venice. But on the way he was intercepted by Calvin and, as we shall soon say, came to the sad end of his life at Geneva: a man certainly deserving of a longer life and of a better end, so far as we are concerned. For if you regard the judgment and permission of God, he lived long enough, because well enough, and made the best and most glorious end of his living.[303]

He was planning to explain the whole Old Testament with commentaries, had he not been burned at Geneva as he was passing through.[304] He was

> going to publish many discourses ... if I am not mistaken, under these titles: "On the true understanding of the Scriptures;" "On the beginning of the departure from the apostolic doctrine;" "On the power of the truth;" "On the true knowledge of the one God;" "On the error of the Triad;" "On the true Holy Spirit;" "On the exaltation of the man Jesus;" "On the nature and ministry of Angels;" "On zeal and knowledge;" "On the efficacy [98] of faith;" "On the power of love;" "On body, soul and spirit;" "On the born and reborn;" "On calling and election;" "On fore-knowledge and predestination;" "On human works and ceremonies;" "On baptism of water and of Spirit;" "On the Lord's Supper;" "On sin and satisfaction;" "On justification;" "On the fear and the love of God;" "On the true Church;" "On the Head and members;" "On the death of the saints;" "On the resurrection of the dead and transformation of the living;" "On the Day of Judgment;" "On the blessedness of the elect;" etc. [See] Alphonse Lyncurius,[305] in the *preface* to the five books of the *Declaratio Jesu Christi Filii Dei*.[306]

I pass by without notice what has been observed about the doctrines of Servetus by ill-wishers, whose judgment of an adversary is never sound. Nay more, for the sake of brevity I also omit extracts from his books, which I have at hand.[307] Suffice it to add these few things which fairness requires. His three [christological] propositions[308] were these:

(1) *He is Jesus the Christ*, that is, this Jesus of Nazareth, a real (*verus*) man, conceived of the Holy Spirit, born of a Virgin, is the Christ of God, or the Messiah promised to the [Old Testament] Fathers.

(2) *He is the Son of God*, that is, this man, substantially begotten by God as from the very substance of God, to wit by the Holy spirit, is a real and natural and proper Son of God, whereas we are adoptive sons, so that the body of Christ really has participation in the substance of God.[309]

(3) *He is God*, not the one and supreme who alone is God the Father, but substantially, since Deity is in him bodily, the God of us all, exalted by God his Father.[310]

And of some of these things, indeed, we do not approve, especially with regard to the literally understood and essential generation within the Divine (*in divinis*), as well as of certain other doctrines of his. Yet we do not on this account condemn the man who with pious zeal and invincible courage succeeded in struggling out of bondage to the prelates.[311] Nor do we think that anyone should be condemned to the stake for these or like opinions, as was done by Calvin. As for this I shall add an accurate narrative, but shall prefix to it a discourse of Servetus himself, as a swan song which he uttered before his horrible death.

[99] *A Discourse of [''\]Michael Servetus of Aragon[''] on the true knowledge of God and his Son before he was burned at Geneva*[312]
[actually a Binitarian/Ditheist argumentation,
perhaps by Matthew Gribaldi]

Those who hold to three substantial persons or hypostases in the Divine Being (*Divinis*), thrust upon us three Gods equal in *natura*.[313] For they offer us three distinct and different substantial beings (*res*), and each of these beings (*rerum*), or as they call them, Hypostases, they regard as God. For since these Persons or Hypostases, though different in fact and in number, are declared each to be God, it necessarily follows that there are as many predicates as subjects, and that the number of Gods is multiplied to correspond to the number of Persons. And though they tell us in words that there is only one God, yet in effect and in very deed they present three Gods to our understanding. For there is no understanding so keen and sound as not to see that three are offered to it to worship. Moreover, in what way one is to understand that these three, of which each is God, are numerically one God, no one has ever been able to tell or teach. There remains, therefore, both in spirit and in understanding this insoluble perplexity and inexplicable confusion that three are one and one is three. For however the whole understanding may tend and be directed toward one God, and may offer itself one God to be worshiped in spirit, and may with all its force bind itself to unity, yet three distinct objects at once offer themselves and appear before the mind's eye, each of which it recognizes as God. And so seeing in effect three equal and distinct Gods shown, the mind succumbs in confusion between the one and the three. This is the outcome of the Grecian Triad or *triplicitas*).

But if drawing aside this veil, we test the whole matter with the word of the Sacrosanct Scripture as though with a touchstone, and inquire into the true knowledge of God according to the utterances of God himself, without doubt all confusion and perplexity will cease, and our understanding will not be forced to accept anything in itself incompatible.

In the first place, then, it should be known that God is an appellative name denoting all power, dominion, and superiority, and it properly applies to Him [100] who is over all, who is first of all, King of kings, and Lord of lords, from whom all things are and depend, who is the sole Father and Creator of all. But less properly taken, it can also apply to creatures, so that whoever has power and superiority over any one conferred upon him by God's dispensation, the same can be called that man's god. Thus Moses is called ''a god to Pharaoh'' (Exod 7:1), and Cyrus ''the god of Israel'' [cf. Isa 45:3]. And if merely for the sake of example one may add profane writings to sacred, Augustus Caesar is called the god of Virgil,[314] and Lentulus the god of Cicero,[315] because he caused his reinstatement. And in this way Scripture calls those gods whom the Supreme and Eternal God has distinguished and elevated above others by any favor, power, and privilege. Thus the Psalmist (82:6): ''I have said, Ye are gods; and all of you are children of the Most High.'' And Exodus 22:28: ''The master of the house shall bring him unto the gods,"[316] and "The cause of both parties shall come before the god."[317] Yet these are gods not by nature, but by grace and the gift of the supreme God. And so they are never called by the name of deity which applies to the only supreme God. For among the Hebrews such gods and lords, for whom these names of deity are properly reserved, are called "Elohim" or "Adonai." Nor are they ever designated by a proper or singular name, such as "Jehovah," although the Lord. . . . [Here there is a gap in the autograph from which I have taken this.][318] And hence Paul everywhere at the beginning of his epistles [e.g., Rom 1:7] says beforehand the following: "Grace and peace from God our Father and our Lord Jesus Christ."

However to make three Gods, equal in nature, is supreme blasphemy and execrable wickedness. For all things ought to be traced back to one, namely, to him who is the author of all things and of his own will created all things, as he alone is of himself God by nature. But the others, as many as are not of themselves gods, receive and acknowledge the nature of their deity from the one God the Father, and are called gods from God. For the supreme and Prime (*Princeps*) God can sanctify his creatures and fill them with divinity. On the contrary, we can in no way make three gods equal by nature. Otherwise we ought of necessity also to make three authors of things or *Pantocratores*, and three Fathers. [101] For the plain name of God is due to the Father alone, who is God of himself, and who founded all things. He alone is plainly and absolutely called God.

Now then, from what has been said, it can easily be concluded in what way our Lord Jesus Christ is called the very Son of God, or even God. For the *ratio* of his deity is derived from God the Father, and he is called very God of very God, the God indeed of all creatures, but not the God of the Father who subjected all things to him [cf. 1 Cor 15:28]. Nay rather, it is the Father himself who alone of himself is God by nature, so that he is also Lord and God of the Son, as the Son says: "I go unto the Father, who is greater than I" (John 14:28); "I go unto my Father and your Father, to my God and your God" (John 2:17); "My God, why hast thou forsaken me?" (Matt 28:46); "I will write upon him the name of my God, and the name of the city of my God" (Rev 3:12). Nor does the interpretation of those who say that the Son spoke this as a man, not as God, fit here. To them the answer is that even as the nature of deity that is in the Son suits a man (for the Son is a man deified or filled with divinity), so the supremacy of the Father is not annulled as regards the Son himself. For although the Son was by the Father made Lord and God to us, and our head, yet the Father is both Lord and God and head of the Son himself (1 Cor 15:3). And the Son is subject to the Father (1 Cor 15:28). And he is steward and administrator of his Father's house (Heb 3:8).[319]

And so the Son as our God and our head acknowledged the deity and supremacy of the Father with regard to himself. Hence the Prophet, clearly explaining this two-fold *ratio* of the deity of the Father and of the Son, spoke to the Son:

> "Thou art fairer than the children of men; grace is poured into thy lips; therefore God hath blessed thee for ever. . . . Thy throne, O

God, is for ever and ever; the scepter of righteousness is the scepter
of thy kingdom. Thou lovest righteousness, and hatest wickedness;
therefore God, thy God, hath anointed thee with the oil of gladness
above thy fellows'' (Ps 45:2, 6 – 7).

Behold how David in spirit calls the Son God, and the Father God of the
Son. For ''thy throne, O God'' and ''God hath anointed thee'' are in the
vocative case, and refer to the Son. When he afterwards adds ''thy God,''
he is speaking of God the Father, [102] who anointed and sanctified the Son.
Likewise Wisdom, which represents the Son of God, thus cries aloud: ''And
I took root in a people that was glorified, even in the portion of the Lord's
own inheritance'' (Wis 24:12).[320]

Thus I now think it is clearer than daylight to any one who will adhere to
the Scriptures that the Son is God from the Father, and is appointed for all
as God by the Father, and he recognized the deity and superiority of the
Father in respect of himself. To be sure, among the Greeks and Latins this
distinction of divine names is not found, and all are called by the one common name of God.[321] One then is by nature God of himself, eternal, most
high, supreme, immortal, invisible, incomprehensible, dwelling in light
inaccessible, who founded all, governs all, from whom all things are and
depend. He is the God of gods, the King of kings, and Lord of lords, Jehovah the Father, whom alone Scripture simply and absolutely calls God and
Father—the universal Father of all men indeed, but properly and uniquely of
our Lord Jesus Christ, as Paul also clearly explains, saying:

''For though there be those who are called gods, whether in heaven
or on earth, as there be gods many and lords many; yet to us there is
one God the Father, of whom are all things and we in him, and one
Lord Jesus Christ through whom are all things and we through him''
(1 Cor 8:5 – 6).

Whence it plainly comes to pass that even creatures are honored by this
name of deity, yet by the grace and allowance of the one supreme God, who
is God of Gods, Chief and ''Father of all, above all, through all, and in all''
(Eph 4:6), to whom as the only supreme and natural God of himself all others are referred, and to whom they are subject and obedient.

And this plurality of inferior gods introduces no confusion and does not
prejudice the divine unity, since every creature praises God the Creator and
regards and longs for him alone as the most high and supreme God, wor-
ships and adores him alone, to whom all Scripture bears witness that there is
no other God but him: ''Hear, O Israel: The Lord thy God is one God''
(Deut 6:4); and, ''the lord God, great, mighty, and terrible, who regardeth
not [103] nor taketh reward'' (Deut 10:17); and, ''the God of Gods hath
spoken'' (Ps 50:1); and, ''Howbeit at that time when ye knew not God, ye
were in bondage to them that by nature are no gods; but now that ye have
come to know God, how turn ye back again to the weak and beggarly rudiments?'' (Gal 4:8 – 9); ''Which in his own times he shall show, the blessed
and only potentate, the King of kings, and Lord of lords; who only hath
immortality, dwelling in light unapproachable, whom no man hath seen or
can see'' (1 Tim 6:15 – 16); ''to serve a true and living God, and to wait for
his Son from heaven, whom he raised from the dead, even Jesus'' (1 Thess
1:9 – 10); ''unto the King eternal, immortal, invisible, the only wise God, be

honor and glory, forever and ever. Amen'' (1 Tim 1:17); ''one God, and one mediator between God and man, the man Christ Jesus; who gave himself a ransom for all'' (1 Tim 2:5 – 6); ''I give thee charge in the sight of God, who quickeneth all things, and of Jesus Christ, who witnessed before Pontius Pilate a good confession'' (1 Tim 6:13); ''For the grace of God that bringeth salvation hath appeared to all men, teaching us that denying ungodliness and wordly lusts, we should live soberly, and godly, and righteously in the present world; looking for the blessed hope, even the bright appearing in glory of the great God, and our Saviour Jesus Christ; who gave himself for us, that he might redeem us from all iniquity,'' etc. (Titus 2:11 – 14).

See therefore how the Scriptures are wont always to distinguish between God and the Son of God. And if you look closely, you will see that Scripture always, three or four passages excepted, simply and absolutely calls God the Father, and Jesus his Christ and Son. Yet the divinity of the Son differs from that of other gods. Wherefore God the Father deified and sanctified other gods to a degree, as adoptive sons, and thus Moses and Cyrus were particular gods to Pharaoh and Israel; but God sanctified Christ without measure as his own blessed Son, and filled him entirely with his Holy Spirit and with all divinity, of whose fullness we all received.

Nor is it anything against what has been said that the Son was made equal to the Father in deity, power, and glory, [104] since all deity, glory, and equality of the Son is from God the Father, and is recognized by the Son as the gift of the Father, when he says: ''All power is given to me in heaven and on earth'' (Matt 28:18). And Peter: ''that God hath made Lord and Christ this Jesus whom ye crucified'' (Acts 2:36). And Paul: ''Wherefore God hath exalted him with supreme honor, and given him a name above every name, that in the name of Jesus every knee should bow, of those in heaven, on earth, and under the earth'' (Phil 2:9 – 10); ''And let all the angels of God worship him'' (Heb 1:6),''Who raised up Christ from the dead, and made him sit at his own right hand in the heavenly places, above all principality and piety and might and dominion, and every name that is named not only in this world but in that which is to come; and hath put all things under his feet, and gave him to be the head over all things to the Church itself, which is his body, the fulness of him that filleth all in all'' (Eph 1:20 – 23);[322] ''to which of the angels said he at any time, Thou art my Son, this day have I begotten thee? . . . Thy throne is forever and ever: a scepter of righteousness is the scepter of thy kingdom. . . . Sit thou on my right and until I make thine enemies thy footstool'' [323] (Heb 1:5, 8, 13). And John: ''Worthy is the lamb that was slain, to receive power, and riches, and wisdom, and strength, and honor, and glory, and blessing'' (Rev 5:12). And so Paul declares that this deity of the Son and his equality with the most high God the Father is to be understood not with respect to the Father himself, but with respect to creatures: ''For he hath put all things under his feet. But when he saith that all things are put under him, it is manifest that this is said excepting him that did put all things under him. And when all things shall be subdued unto him, then shall the Son also himself be subject unto him that put all things under him, that God may be all in all'' (1 Cor 15:27 – 28).

But although the Son acknowledged that by the gift of the Father he had been made equal to the Father in power and glory and might, yet he was not willing to misuse that gift of equality and turn it into tyranny and robbery, as Paul says: "He humbled himself, becoming obedient even unto death, even the death of the cross. Wherefore God hath raised him up to the most sublime height, and hath put under him all things in heaven and on earth and under the earth" (Phil 2:8–10). He set him forth to be adored by all creatures as God and Lord.

In short, the omnipotent Father conferred upon his dearly beloved Son as much strength, power, grace, blessing, [105] glory, and Deity as he could possibly confer. And in his equality and his throne he provided as much honor for the Son as he wished to be shown to himself. Henceforth he who does not acknowledge the Son, also denies the Father.[324] "For there is no name under heaven given to men in which one must hope for salvation" (Acts 4:12), but in the name of the Son of God, our Lord Jesus Christ, who is our very Lord and God, as Thomas (John 20:28), Paul, and John in very truth confessed. To whom, therefore, together with God the Father, the Most Great and merciful God, be praise, honor, and glory forever and ever. Amen.[325]

Servetus's execution was indeed an atrocious deed, and one in the judgment of all fair-minded people directly opposed to the kind and humble spirit of Christ, though consistent with that of the Boanerges who both wished, following the examples of Elijah, to call down fire from heaven to destroy some inhospitable Samaritans[326] (except that they wished to destroy guilty men, while Calvin destroyed a guiltless one).

The senate of Geneva was openly and even strongly urged to perpetrate this deed by the ministers of Basel, Bern, Schaffhausen, and Zurich. Calvin in a letter written to Sulzer[327] boasts that it was at his instigation that Servetus was thrown into prison by a syndic of Geneva, and also exhorts him, saying: "In this case I am determined that he at all events shall not escape the end that we desire."[328] Calvin writes to Farel:[329]

The messenger has returned from the Swiss.[330] With one accord they declare that Servetus has now revived wicked errors with which Satan formerly troubled the Church, and is a monster not to be endured. Those at Basel are prudent; those at Zurich fiercest of all, for they both set forth seriously the wickedness of his impious deeds and urge our senate to use severity. Those of Schaffhausen assent to the letter of the Bernese which is also enclosed and add the letter of their council as well, by which our people are not a little encouraged.[331]

Farel also not only considers that Servetus should be put to death, but also confirms Calvin (who, as he says, desired the cruelty of the punishment be mitigated)[332] in using severe measures against Servetus, and even declares that all heretics should be exterminated[333] (Calvin, *Epistolae* 115 and 116,[334] [106] see Beza, *Vita Calvini* and *Epistola* to Dudith).

Thus Grotius, great in name and in fact,[337] justly says somewhere: "The spirit of Antichrist has appeared not only on the Tiber, but also on the Lake of Geneva."[338] And as for Calvin, who not only carried out that wicked deed but also defended it in a published book,* nay furnished all magistrates with arms against heretics, and as for Beza likewise, who defended the same things in a publication** (both of whom, while reckoned among the heretics by the Roman Church and her crowd, thus offer those enraged against them weapons against themselves), and as for all who either do or approve such things, that word of Christ should be spoken to them which was uttered to the Sons of Thunder: "Ye know not what Spirit ye are of. The Son of man is not come to destroy men's souls, but to save them" (cf. Luke 9:55f.). And also the one uttered at another time: "Whosoever shall break one of these least commandments, and shall teach men so, he shall be called the least in the kingdom of heaven" (Matt 5:19). And they have broken the commandment about loving one's neighbor, which is next and similar to the first one,[341] and have taught men so.

I indeed am glad to leave the judgment to God, yet if the choice were given to me, I should rather be in the place of Oecolampadius and Zwingli than of Calvin and Beza, far more learned though they were.[342] Meanwhile I recollect what the truth commands about loving one's neighbor, and even one's enemy,[343] about convincing and not constraining,[344] shunning and not slaying heretics.[345] Calvin of course pleased himself in that deed and plucked the dead lion's beard when calling Servetus a "Spanish dog" (*Commentary on Acts*, XX).[346] But Francis Lismanino, of whom I spoke at length a little while back, in his copy of Calvin's *Commentaries* (which I possess),[347] opposite these words of Calvin "that Spanish dog Servetus," noted in his own hand on the margin: "made a dog by you!" And he adds this couplet:

> Why do you call me a dog, O Calvin? Your fire, alas,
> Makes me called not dog (*canis*), but pitiable ashes (*cinis*).[348]

Chamier in *Panstraticae Catholicae* (II, i *On the Trinity*, v) was not ashamed to speak thus:

> As long as Servetus lived among Papists, he lived in safety; but afterwards, when he came to Geneva, he experienced the force of truth [107] in Calvin and holy severity in the magistracy.[349]

Yet he [a moderate] fatuously credited the Papists with having snatched moderation from his own party. Also a little before (iv)[350] he bestows similar (that is, exceptional) praise on Calvin, where he says that "Calvin gave the public authority a reason for severely castigating Valentine."

---

*Entitled: *Defense of the orthodox creed about the Holy Trinity against the prodigious errors of Michael Servetus, a Spaniard; in which it is shown that the heretics should be punished by the law of the sword*.[339]

**Entitled: *That heretics should be punished by the public authority*. Both this and Calvin's work published by Robert Etienne in 1554.[340]

[The martyrdom of Valentine Gentile, 1566][351]

This was Valentine [Gentile] from Cosenza in Campania, who in 1558 was imprisoned at Geneva, on account of a difference in religion, and then forced to recant (greatly in opposition to Evangelical liberty) and banished. [Chamier says that he] was treated more kindly by the Papists at Lyons in France. For he[352] was put to death by the Evangelicals at Bern in 1566.

This Valentine [Gentile] and Paul Alciati of Piedmont,[353] since they were unable to live at Geneva on account of Calvin's bitter hatred, came in *1562* to Poland and conferred with pious men who were seriously devoted to inquiring into the truth. But Valentine was pursued by the power of his adversaries, whom Calvin's letters and friends had procured for him both in Lyons, where he was staying through Alciati's generosity, and in Poland. He returned to the Swiss and indeed betook himself to the bailiff of the town of Gex (see Beza, *Vita Calvini*)[354] who some years before had had him thrown into prison for a differing view in religion, but had set him free upon Alciati's petition. And to the bailiff Valentine had inscribed his brief *Confession*[355] together with *In Symbolum Athanasii notationes*[356] wishing thus to show his grateful mind.

But the bailiff was not so grateful for this, since he had fallen under suspicion of heresy with his lords, the Bernese. So when Valentine returned, in order to free himself from suspicion and ill-will, Wurstenberger again threw him in prison and informed the Bernese of what he had done. These men ordered that he be brought to them as if for examination. This done, seeing the perseverance of Valentine, they put the old man to death.

I[357] *remember reading this opinion of his "That God had the power of creating because he wished to do so, and so he begot the* Λόγος *before all worlds, and generated the Spirit."*[358] *But at the synod of Pińczów, 4 November 1562, he gave out this confession "That God in the breadth of eternity created a certain most excellent Spirit which afterwards in the fulness of time was incarnated."*[359] This was the opinion of the Ante-Nicene fathers, especially of Justin and Lactantius, on whom Arius afterwards [108] erected his dogmas.[360] Budziński in his manuscript *History*, 27, was of the opinion:

> That these opinions are erroneous and deserve to be refuted from Scripture, which teaches no more about Christ than that he was fore-known (praecognitum)[361] and predestinated before all ages, and in the last times was manifested as begotten of a Virgin by the power of the Holy Spirit, but that they are in no wise to be defended by sword or fire.

Although not on all points agreeing with us, Budziński

> abominates this death of Valentine, punished with a dreadful punishment, with papal tyranny. That which Cain had before used on Abel, Calvin used on Servetus. (See his chapter 35.)

[The martyrdom of John Sylvan c. 1571]

The burning alive of John Sylvan, superintendent at Heidelberg,[362] was cruelly perpetrated a little while afterwards, namely about 1571, although he was a man of upright life, famed for his great learning, and distinguished for his services to Frederick, the elector palatine, for whom in tender years he had cared with fatherly interest, and to whom, when appointed his tutor, he had taught humane letters. Thus the elector shrank from the charge of an ungrateful mind and would have saved him from danger and set him free, had not the spirit of Geneva, despite the fairness and good-will of the judge, brought up that venerable [scriptural verse]: "If thou let this man go, thou wilt not be Caesar's friend."[363] For Maximilian II, on evidence of intercepted letters, was accusing the elector's ministers of Arianism to his face. They were Adam [Neuser], whom God had marvelously freed from prison at Heidelberg, and this Sylvan.[364]

[Italian Protestant refugees: Gribaldi, Alciati, and Ochino]

The spirit of Calvin, Beza, and their like, contrary to the gentle and humble spirit of Christ, had also prepared a like punishment for Matthew Gribaldi, a celebrated jurist from Padua, owner of the village of Farges, had not his death anticipated it, as Beza acknowledges in his *Calvini Vita*. He had indeed with difficulty gotten free from prison at Bern.[365] He was, to be sure, the host and patron and also follower of Valentine [Gentile], as appears from a certain writing[366] in which he says that he reverently understands that there are three eternal spirits (*spiritus*), not confused but distinct in rank and number; that God the Son and the Holy Spirit are thus subordinate to one supreme God and Father, the author of all things; that every kind of deity, both of the Son and of the Holy Spirit, and of all other heavenly spirits, is properly traced back to the one and only God the Father, without beginning and God of himself, as the only source and head of all being (*essentia*) and divinity.

[109] These words of his literally agree with the letter of Holy Writ, excepting the existence of the Son before the world.[367] And yet what great passions were aroused by this in minds inflamed by perverted zeal! For they also fiercely pursued Alciati, intending nothing better for him than for his companion Valentine [Gentile]. Of Alciati I have read that in letters to Gregory Paul, from Austerlitz in 1564 and 1565, he argued against the view that Christ existed before he was born of Mary,[368] and fiercely opposed the common doctrine of the Trinity. Indeed it is written there[369] that regardless of prudence in the very critical and difficult beginning of the Reformation in Poland, he had sought to interest Paul in Mohammedanism but this was stopped by Calvin and his like, inflamed with deadly hate against him and other lovers of the truth.

To Calvin and Beza, who boldly commit and teach things unfair, unjust, even injurious to the members of their flock, to Chamier and others who agree with them I reply. Apart from [adducing those usual] passages out of Holy Scripture, to which should fairly be added that of John, when he had cast off the spirit of

Elijah,[370] and being moved by the spirit of God, recommended and urged love above all to the apostles: "Whosoever hateth his brother is a murderer; and ye know that no murderer hath eternal life abiding in him" (I John 3:15), I reply [to Calvin *et al.*] with a few sayings of ancient doctors of the Church. Thus Jerome on Psalm 7:

> He that saith he believeth in Christ ought also himself to walk even as he walked. For he came not to kill, but to be killed. He gave no strikes on the cheek, but received them. He did not crucify, but was crucified. He slew not others, but suffered himself. He that is killed imitates Christ, but he that kills is Antichrist. For God willeth not the death [of a sinner], but that he should live and change his life for the better.[371]

Also:

> The spiritual man never takes vengeance on the carnal, but forgives him.[372]

Also:

> I have learned to avoid a heretic, according to the Apostle's precept, but not to give him over to fire.[373]

Augustine, *Contra Cresconium Grammatium*, 3:

> Yet it is not acceptable to any good men in the Catholic Church, if any one (though he be a heretic) is violently put to death.[374]

I should be tedious if I cited here all the passages that I have collected on this subject from Justin, Tertullian, Athanasius, Hilary, and other doctors of the Church, who severely censure such tyranny of Gentiles and Jews.

We ought also to say something here of Bernardine Ochino, for he was contemporary both with [110] Servetus, Valentine, and Gribaldi, and their equal in pious zeal and steadfastness. He was a Sienese by birth, a monk by calling, and chaplain and confessor to the Pope of Rome. For the boldness of speech with which he was moved, in the very ears of the Supreme Pontiff and of all the Curia of Rome, to rebuke the Antichristian pride and tyranny of the Pope, as though in the spirit of the Lutherans, and to spend a carefully appointed hour upon these charges, without any objections being made to them,[375] he was forced, on completion [of the confrontation], to leave Italy, and afterwards to abandon both Zurich and Basel when persecution arose on account of the truth. Hence Beza says of him (*Epistola* 81):[376]

> Ochino seems to have been more eager to question particular doctrines, after the manner of the Academicians, than to settle anything.

And this he did in his *Dialogi* which were afterwards translated into various languages, and by Castellio into Latin. He wrote . . . .[377] Peter Perna[378] asserts in a certain letter that when this aged man, seventy-six years old, being suspected of Arianism, was expelled by those of Zurich, he recommended him to Martin Czechowic[379] who was then in 1563[380] teaching at Vilna. But[381] I find that he came from Venice to Moravia and Poland, and that he returned to Moravia, because virulent letters of Calvin followed him to Poland also. And King Augustus [was] induced by the persuasions of Sarnicki's patrons [to act].³⁸² The influence [of these patrons] was now great in the Senate and with the King. [These Calvinists] were much offended by the sharp opposition to the errors concerning the Trinity and to infant baptism, and had given our brethren the odious names of Tritheists, Arians, and Anabaptists.³⁸³ [The King thereupon] had in 1564 at the Diet of Parczów by a severe law condemned to banishment all [foreigners] who bore these hated names.³⁸⁴ Some nobles indeed attempted to keep Ochino, he being an old man, infirm, pious, and modest, and to obtain from the King a permission for him to remain in the Kingdom under the right of hospitality.

But for all their persuasions, Ochino replied that obedience must be rendered to the magistracy, and again, that he would obey the magistracy even though he would have to die in the fields or among wolves in the forests. When about to leave, the plague held him for some time at Pińczów; and when he was smitten by it, [Jerome] Filipowski, neither fearing nor scorning it, received him into his own home,³⁸⁵ took care of him, and attended to him. For this extraordinary kindness he thanked him thus: "Brother Filipowski, thank God that he has deemed you worthy to be good to Ochino in such misfortune." Having lost two sons and a daughter by the plague,³⁸⁶ [111] he bade the brethren his last farewell until the day of the coming of the Lord and the gathering of all the faithful from every quarter, took up his journey to Moravia, and within three weeks died at Slavkov.³⁸⁷

Chapter Six

Of the Beginnings [1556–62] of the Pure Church of Christ, by the Proposition of Servetus As to the Preeminence of the Father,³⁸⁸ Brought into Poland by Peter of Goniądz, Defended by George Biandrata and Francis Lismanino; the Controversy of Francis Stancaro about the Mediator that Intervened, and Troubling and Arousing Them Both.³⁸⁹

In these times took place the return of Peter of Goniądz [Gonesius] to his native land.³⁹⁰ He was a Pole by nation, a native of Podlasie, who while traveling in foreign lands to pursue his studies, heard those at Geneva and Wittenberg teaching about matters of faith. From them he imbibed the doctrines of the purer truth, and returned home a passionate opponent of the corruptions in the Church and of the depraved life of priests, by whom he had been sent abroad to improve his mind by liberal studies. And as beginnings are apt to be impetuous, both his initial fervor and his acquaintance with the *Anabaptistae* living in Moravia[391] carried this good man also to the borders of superstition. He brought home the view of Servetus as to the preeminence of the Father, and made no secret of it.

[Gonesius as Servetian pacifist at the synod of Secemin, 1556]

Indeed he came to the synod at Secemin which was held at the beginning of 1556 (immediately following the synod at Pińczów) [**cf. BAnt nos. 1, 2, 7, 53**] and delivered this wise speech:[392]

> Beloved brethren and friends in Christ, I greatly congratulate myself that having survived the difficulties of long travels and endured the inconveniences of tedious journeys on my return to my dear native land, I have been brought at once to this venerable assembly of the faithful. Wherefore I render due thanks to God our most merciful Father, my guardian abroad as well as yours at home, and exceedingly rejoice that you have come hither in such large numbers in the midst of sworn enemies of the truth whose multitude is numberless, and each one a Hannibal in his hatred of you.[393]
>
> [112] You know, I think, that several years ago I was sent by the priests of Vilna to improve my mind in foreign parts by liberal arts. But while I was, like Saul, preparing the means of a bloodless, or perhaps even a bloody, persecution of the faithful (as is the habit of the priests to sew a lion's skin on that of a fox), the Lord Jesus struck me by the heavenly voice of truth and called me to him.[394] And without dishonoring myself by a base, ungrateful mind, I left my earthly patrons and devoted my faith and effort to Christ the heavenly King, my Redeemer.
>
> Believe me indeed (far be it from me that I should boast) that I have examined and wondered whatever Wittenberg and all Germany, whatever Geneva and all Switzerland, teach of the purer truth, and that I have not overlooked any of the things that either sect (I use this equivocal word without ill-will) either professes or tries to establish by weight of reasons.[395] Likewise I am not unaware either of what was taught by the Apostles endowed with the gifts of the Holy Spirit, nor after them by the men of the Apostolic Age, nor of what after their death was introduced by the very celebrated Church Fathers, things unheard of, unseen, unknown to its primitive simplicity. Neither am I ignorant by what degrees error grew in the Church of Christ, so that I am altogether sure that the certain truth cannot safely be looked for, save in the Holy and Canonical Scriptures.
>
> Quite rightly did the early Fathers, when wishing to portray the perfection of Holy Scripture, say both that an elephant swims and a lamb walks in this plain and deep stream,[396] meaning thereby that it instructs the wise and the simple. But would that they had well and usefully attested by deed what

they so wittily and cleverly said. However, the Christian Church, following the example of the Jewish by a clear instance of human weakness, which soon scorns pure simplicity and delights in variety, did not long adhere to its original integrity. Well known in this respect are the divine oracles of the spirit of prophecy, speaking especially through Paul the Apostle.[397] Well known also the records of history, the testimonies of the more wise and upright men,[398] especially of Hegesippus who wrote soon after the time of the Apostles.

An unimportant man I am. Perhaps in no respect am I better known throughout my native land than for the wooden sword (*ligneus ensis*)[399] with which the unwarlike [113] custom of the Moravian [Hutterite] brethren girded me unarmed. Neither my condition or the narrow limit of time—for you consider how to spend it with due economy on so many weighty matters—permits me at present to tarry longer on these things.[400] Indeed, even the subject itself does not care for, certainly does not require, proofs from abroad when it rejoices in so many genuine ones at home. Nay, it bids me abridge what I must say and what in this sacred meeting (*coetu*) is not to be passed over in silence, short of the crime of faithless sloth; and it calls me to the ancient Church.

Alas, how quickly she scorned the simplicity of the fishermen, which at present a great many prate of in words, but scorn in deed. So by the arts of Satan, her crafty foe, she has experienced many and great disturbances. These have at length broken out into bitter quarrels, stupid thunders of anathemas, and fierce and cruel persecutions, which are all directly contrary to the meek and lowly spirit of Christ. All these might have been provided against, had not so many unnecessary or even injurious things been admitted by the Church. Such things as were not only not commanded in the word of God, but were even at variance with the light of the things commanded in it. Or even if they had been admitted once, they had been removed from her!

And here of course the prudent and wise counsel of Gregory justly should be appealed to, of the very celebrated Doctor of the Latin Church,[401] bishop of the city of Rome, who well deserved to be called both saint and Great: "Let the things that have been introduced by the new order be removed in the very order in which they were brought in, and peace unimpaired in the Lord will endure for us" (*Epistola* 31, 7).[402] This statement he opposed to the presumption, novel at the time (at the beginning of the seventh century), of the Bishop of Constantinopole when he, John, began to call himself "Ecumenical" [Patriarch]; and this he again asserted against Cyriac himself, successor to John's see and ambition, who was the first to presume to implement that Antichristian term.[403] But carnal power prevailed, and these things were not only received but also established by the use of many centuries, and more and more led the Church away from her early integrity.

The point of faith about the divinity of the Son of God has now long been the subject of bigger controversies, though still, when he is called the Son of God, that very fact offers testimony to the truth. It is a matter of the greatest moment to ascertain in what order corruptions regarding both beliefs and practices were introduced into the Church. But now, dismissing these things, [114] something must be said on that point of faith alone which until now has proved to be the source of controversies, through inability of refusal to progress in the knowledge of it. For as to the faith in one God the Father, there was no doubt in the Church during four centuries. But the deity of the Son was bitterly discussed soon after the death of the Apostles, and even while they survived, and alas set the Christian world in conflict! Irenaeus, the most eminent of the early Fathers, plainly says:* ''All heresies whatsoever say that there is one God; but they alter him by their bad thinking.''[404] While the very learned Tertullian says:** ''We have found no teaching so twisted among so many contrarieties as that which has aroused controversy about God the creator of all things.''

No one has dared conjecture another God. There was hesitation more readily about the Son than about the Father. But why say so much? Faith in Jesus Christ, the Son of God, the Redeemer of the world, is the only and immovable foundation of all the faith and hope of Christians. And herein agreed the divine Scriptures, and not only the words of all antiquity but also those of all Christians, however seriously differing for the present. These words of the Church from which the whole Church had her beginnings, these words of the Apostles, these words ''of the disciples of their Lord, who after the Lord was received up, through the spirit both continued perfect and called on the God who made heaven and earth, who was proclaimed by the prophets, as well as his Son Jesus whom God anointed,''*** as Irenaeus again expressly says,[406] a writer whom I shall prefer before all the recent ones.

Nevertheless, whoever is pleased to examine the special nature of this general teaching, that is: *how* the Son of God *was* in the beginning and before Abraham, *is* from heaven, *came* forth (*prodierit*) from the Father (since the Scripture clearly says all this) and then, *how* it can be said, saving the proposition handed down in sacred Scriptures, that ''God is one'' and then that ''God the Father is one,'' and indeed that ''God over all, blessed forever''[407]—whoever examines this, I say, must above all be free from passion and preconceived opinion and must adhere to the express word of God alone as the most sure and unshaken foundation. For it deserves to be believed that in this very important [115] matter, on which his eternal salvation turns, such a man wishes to act prudently and with due consideration.

I,[408] to be sure, as behooves an intelligent man, do not conceal *that* to me, as Christ himself his Ambassador (*Legato*) [cf. Luke 14:3, *legationem*] teaches, the only true God, greater than the Son (seeing that the one is Father and the other is Son [cf. John 14:28]) is the one God, the God of Israel, the author of all things; *that* from him Christ received everything and is indeed his Son, also God; *that*, especially, as I also believe, the Λόγος who was in the beginning, descended upon the Virgin, and was changed into flesh; and *that* the Word was thus made flesh and was God, yet truly and properly died, always having shown honor to the Father, was by him raised up again and glorified, and thus delivered to him all that he had received [cf.

**Adversus haereses*, I, 9.161.
***De praescriptione haereticorum*, 34.[405]
****Adversus haereses*, 3, 12,

1 Cor 15:28]. But I believe that a Trinity of persons, consubstantiality, communication of *idiomata*, and other things brought into the Church from the schools, are inventions of the human brain, and hence deserve to be rejected in order to arrive at Holy Scripture alone as the most certain rule (*norma*) of faith. In a word: I adhere to the Apostles' Creed, into which I was baptized as were you all, and to it alone. Of course I firmly believe that I have no need of the Nicene and the Athanasian Creed.

Nevertheless I submit all my views to your judgment, and myself to your examination. And I humbly pray that God the Father of lights, the Father of mercy, the Father of our Lord Jesus Christ, may through the Holy Spirit take part in your sacred synod and in your pious efforts.

[Results of the speech]

Many things, of which most at the time had never heard, led their minds in different directions, according as men do not live at one in taste, wish, and interest. Indeed these things led not a few to search more carefully after the pure truth, as events soon showed. Among these was Gregory Paul, of whom we have spoken above, and who was present at the examination of Peter of Goniądz held at this synod [cf. **BAnt no. 1**].[409] In fact, a letter from this synod was written to Melanchthon, in which his advice was requested as to explaining the articles of faith about God and Christ. This letter was given to Peter of Goniądz to take to Wittenberg; and he was recommended to Melanchthon by the synod, although it gives this account of him: "He [Gonesius] believed that the Logos is less than the Father in divinity; that the divine nature was changed into a human one, [116] and that God actually died."[410]

These things in this exasperated age would be condemned out of hand as blasphemous ravings of the Arian, Eutychian,[411] and Patripassian[412] heresies. And no fair man will wonder that these two latter (which indeed deserve to be rejected as foreign to the truth) were uttered by Peter of Goniądz when he was endeavoring to escape from the bonds of error and giving a sign of inquiry into the pure truth. But the first one [as the Arian heresy] we have learned from the mouth of Christ, who plainly declares [John 14:28] that his "Father is greater" than he (insofar, that is, as the one is Father and the other is Son), while according to the view of our adversaries, the former from eternity begot the Son from his own substance and the latter is co-eternal and consubstantial with the Father. This [Arian view] was also acknowledged for four centuries by the ancient Church, especially by the Fathers of the Greek Church, but also by Hilary [of Poitiers] among the Latins, as Maldonado himself bears witness.[413] And thus the opinion of Peter of Goniądz caused no light disturbance among those who then held to the commonly received errors. Hence he was sent to Melanchthon that he might be brought back to the right way. Yet this opinion did not stop here, but made further progress, as we shall say a little later. Peter of Goniądz found the churches situated at the second stage of the purer truth. For, having now abandoned the doctrine of the Saxons about consubstantiation, they had embraced the view of the Swiss as to the Sacrament. This matter was very sharply discussed until the year 1558.[414]

And here, in connection with Servetus and Peter of Goniądz, we must mention Francis Dávid, although to be dealt with further at a later time. For as Josias Simler says: "Moreover there is Francis Dávid, whom I will briefly characterize as an enlightened Servetus; and what he is in Transylvania, that Peter of Goniądz is in Poland" (preface to the *Libri [adversus veteres et novos] Antitrinitarios*).[415]

[More on Stancaro, 1550–54][416]

But that we return to our narrative and bring it down to these times, the history of which we are following: Stancaro, of whom we have spoken above,[417] had from the year *1550*[418] applied himself with great zeal to reforming the churches; and to this end, at the request of *Starosta (Comes)*[419] Jacob Ostroróg, he had composed some books.[420] Because persecution had been stirred up in the diocese of Cracow (of which we see no slight proofs in the violent death of Martin of Kurzów[421] and in the persecution of Valentine, pastor of Krzczonów,[422] of Nicholas Oleśnicki, and of Conrad Krupka [Przecławski]), Stancaro was, along with Felix Cruciger and other godly men, forced to find other quiet places. He removed to Great Poland [117] and remained safe under the protection of Ostroróg.[423] Dismissed by him in 1553, Stancaro returned [from Great Poland] to Little Poland with the same Cruciger, and devoted himself for a time to reforming churches from idolatry, enjoying the favor of Stanislas Stadnicki, Jerome Filipowski, Nicholas Oleśnicki, and other noble and generous patrons. But when in the next year [1554] Stancaro had stirred up a controversy about the Mediator, he incurred the enmity[424] of many not only in Poland but also in Germany,[425] so that he seems on this account to have withdrawn into Transylvania.[426]

[Stancaro's view of Christ the Mediator][427]

He certainly declared that the Son, since he is believed to be one and the same God with the Father, is not Mediator with respect to his divine nature, but only with respect to his human nature, lest he should be Mediator of himself, since a mediator, as Scripture [Gal 3:20] teaches, "is not a mediator of one, but God is one."[428] But even here those who held to the received errors found a way of escape, asserting that the Son, being God, with a human nature and a divine joined personally, as they say,[429] is a mediator also to himself. And so the view of Stancaro was condemned by many at the synod held at Słomniki in 1554,[430] and again at that in Sandomierz in 1559, though approved and defended by not a few.[431] Certainly in the synod held at Pińczów in November 1558 it was sharply discussed [**cf. BAnt nos. 2, 3.1, 21**].[432] So that when we reckon what was done before at the first synod [of Pińczów] held in 1555, as we have noted,[433] and also what took place a little later, and then thereafter in the course of time, as we shall be taking note, it may be fairly said that this town was chosen by

God for building a nest for the pure truth. To its confessors everywhere, accordingly, the name "Pinczovians" was also applied, as may be seen in the *Sylvae* of Andrew Frycz [Modrzewski].[434] But at the time they [the contenders] came off on equal terms: each returning home with his own opinion, Stancaro [for his part] returning to Dubiecko to his patron Stanislas Stadnicki.[435] For Stancaro, as he was not only a great linguist but also a man of great learning, argued his view from the Scriptures and the ancient writers, with reason certainly supporting it. And so neither John Łaski (who finally died at Pińczów at the beginning [8 January] of 1560), no less famous—as that age held—for his great learning, piety, and zeal for the truth [**cf. BAnt no. 21**], than for his birth and the ecclesiastical [118] honor received or preordained (so long as he was under the papacy), nor Lismanino, nor Peter of Goniądz, nor Krowicki, nor Biandrata, nor others living in Pińczów or coming thither, ever stirred him [Stancaro] from his opinion [**cf. BAnt no. 2**].[436]

[The swell of radical theological reform]

Yet this view [of Stancaro], like that of Servetus concerning the preeminence of the Father, soon aroused pious and learned men to discuss this subject of the Mediator. And so it was well said by Andrew Lubieniecki the Elder in his manuscript on the synods[437] that this synod held at Pińczów in [November] 1558[438] "made a large beginning toward demolishing the dogma of the Trinity [**cf. BAnt no. 2**]."[439]

All the more [was this so] as in the following month of the same year [December 1558][440] the view of Peter of Goniądz about the preeminence of the Father was repeated at the ninth synod held in Brest in Lithuania,[441] this, together with a book of his *Contra paedobaptismum* [**cf. BAnt nos. 3, 7, 53**].[442] (Infant baptism had been first opposed by Matthew Albin,[443] minister at Iwanowice near Cracow.) The view of Peter was defended by Jerome Piekarski,[444] who openly confessed that he rejected other doctrines also that had crept in from the papacy. Among these [were] those of the Trinity, of the two natures in Christ, of the communication of *idiomata*. And [Piekarski also confessed] that he could not go against his conscience, although others, vainly, forbade this [appeal] under pain of excommunication.

[Amidst the challenge of Stancaro, Biandrata wins Lismanino, 1558–61]

And certainly from what followed in this synod at Pińczów [date?][445] no one can help seeing that the door was opened to discussion of the commonly accepted dogmas. For in this very year [1558] when Biandrata had come to Pińczów, driven from Geneva by Calvin's ill-will [**cf. BAnt nos. 2, 8, 21–2, 52**], he had many discussions on this subject at Pińczów with Lismanino.[446] And, seeing that the opponents of Stancaro had not sufficiently answered the latter, he [Biandrata] accomplished so much that Lismanino too began having doubts about the doctrine of the Trinity. Henceforth Lismanino fell under suspicion of Arianism among those ministers who held more stoutly to rooted errors, and he was accused before the church of Cracow which Gregory Paul was guiding (*regebat*) in Boner's garden.

From now on (*Hinc*),[447] Lismanino gave more and more thought to Biandrata's view, and at length [**cf. BAnt nos. 5, 10**] boldly defended it in a letter written to Ivan Karniński, of which Ivan made a copy for Gregory.[448] In the church he declared the preeminence of the Father. I am glad to give here a copy of this letter.[449]

[Lismanino's letter on the Trinity to Lord Karniński, 10 September 1561]

[119] From (*A*) God the Father from (*ex*) whom are all things through (*per*) Christ the Lord through whom are all things [1 Cor 8:6; cf. Col 1:11], consubstantial and co-eternal with the Father and with the Holy Spirit, I sincerely pray for grace and peace to your gracious Lordship.

Did I not see at what Satan is aiming, I should be mightily amazed at what lord Doctor Biandrata has reported. We are being accused by Stancaro of Arianism, and are being forbidden by our brethren to expose him publicly as a liar. It is, my Lord Ivan, the ignorance and ambition of certain men that is disturbing the Church, and not Lismanino, whose purpose is to show that Christ was Mediator before the incarnation of the Word.[450] Let the whole of judgment turn on this: we labor in vain to promote the truth unless it be demonstrated from Holy Scripture and approved authors.[451] To this end a *Confessio*[452] has been published about the Mediator and very many letters have been sent by the German, Swiss, and Savoyard churches [in response thereto]. By these they [the supporters of Lismanino] accomplish nothing, since the nobles are deceived by Stancaro. Is Lismanino committing a sin when proving the same thing by reasons drawn from the Holy Scriptures and from the most learned interpretations of them? If what I am saying seems strange and monstrous to our brethren, let them blame themselves who are touching holy things with unclean hands, as they say.[453] When they have read the theologians of the early Church, men as learned as they are holy, Ignatius the disciple of the most blessed John the Evangelist, Justin, Origen, Irenaeus, Tertullian, Hilary, Basil, Gregory of Nazianzus, Ambrose, also Erasmus of Rotterdam—all of these I have had to peruse after we had made no progress with Stancaro either by writings of our [Reformed] Church on the Mediator or by the replies of so many learned men[454]—when, I say, those who dare charge me with saying monstrous things have read all these with discretion, then they will change their minds and then they will deal with me happily and candidly.

An Arian, my Lord Ivan, is one who does not confess that the Son is consubstantial and coeternal with the Father, and not one who is setting men free from Sabellianism, that they may not be compelled to declare that the Father and the Holy Spirit were incarnate and suffered.[455] In words, Stancaro distinguishes the Father from the Son but, in fact, he so confuses them as wholly to destroy the generation of the Son and the procession [of the Holy Spirit].[456]

But of all this George Negri[457] also will discourse more fully with your gracious Lordship when he is permitted to confer with you in person. Meantime, in order to have means to defend myself, if anyone [120] should dare charge that I am saying monstrous things, may your gracious Lordship yourself carefully read what follows and show the same to theirs.

St. Basil, *Contra Eunomium haereticum*, I.134:[458] But we, in accordance with the nature of causes with regard to things that are self-existent, say that the Father is placed before the Son, yet neither [according to the difference] of nature nor of time.[459]

Again:

Wherefore it follows that "greater" is here understood as relating to cause. For since the Son's origin is from the Father, the Father is greater insofar as he is cause and source. Wherefore the Lord said: "My Father is greater than I,"[460] so that he be understood to be greater by the fact that he is Father. Moreover, what else does the name of father express? Does it not mean that he who is produced from himself is cause and origin? And in any case, according to your [Eunomius] wisdom it does not say "greater by substance" or "lesser by substance." And so both according to them and according to the truth itself, these words by no means signify "superiority in the given substance." Indeed it is plain that he [Eunomius] himself here denies that the Father is *more* than the Son in size, since he declares that one ought not to conceive any quantity in God. Therefore, no other kind of greater is left, except the one that we have spoken of, which is in relation to cause and origin.[461]

Again St. Basil, against the same heretic Eunomius, II.338, where he proves that the Holy Spirit is God:

For what need is there, if the Holy Spirit is third in rank and station, that it be also third by nature[?][462]

Again:

The doctrine of piety indeed teaches us that in rank it is next after the Son. For as the Son is next in order after the Father, since he is of the Father, so also in dignity, since the Father himself is the origin and cause that he be. And since approach and access to God even the Father are through him, he is no longer second in nature.[463] For the Godhead in both is one.

The same St. Basil in his *Sermo de Sancta Trinitate* said:

Moreover, I do not care how much you say, running hither and thither, whether because you do not accurately attend to what we are saying, or besiege us in order to misinterpret us, not seeking any benefit from us, but laying traps for our words. He [Eunomius] preaches two Gods, he proclaims the worship of many. [121] There are not two Gods, nor are there two Fathers. He who introduces two origins, also preaches two Gods. Such is the heretic Marcion and any one else who is like him in impiety. And again, he who says that the Begotten is of another essence than that of him who begets Him (*genitore*), says there are two Gods, introducing the error of plurality of Gods because of the unlikeness (*dissimilitudem*) of essence.[464]

Again:

Where one origin (*principium*) is taught, and one derived from the origin itself, and one archetype and one image of that, there the doctrine of the unity is not vitiated.[465]

Gregory of Nazianzus, *De Theologia [Oratio]* IV.262:

But in fact is it not evident that this "greater" must have reference to the cause, but "equality" to the nature.[466]

My Lord Ivan, if you have understood these two lines of St. Nazianzen, you yourself will know and you will be able to teach others in what way the Father is greater than the Son, and in what way the Son is equal to the Father. Hence you will also understand that the Son as God intercedes [cf. text at n. 450] with the Father, because without this clear distinction it will be impossible to persuade him [Stancaro], as we have hitherto learned.

For it is altogether necessary that the Father be in some way greater than the Son *before* his incarnation, not in nature or essence. For they are of the same nature and essence. Hence he is called consubstantial with the Father. Not in power for, as St. Basil says, "to say that in power Christ falls short of the power of God is exceedingly silly, and proper to men who do not hear the voice of the Lord saying: 'The Father and I are one,'[467] and taking 'one' as meaning equality in power (*virtutis*), as we shall prove from the very words of the Gospel," etc. Nor is the Father greater than the Son in might (*potestate*) or honor, for the Father has subjected all things to the Son, and wishes that the Son be honored even as the Father is honored.

Nor is the Father greater than the Son only as God the Father is greater than the Son as man (*filio homine*). For, as Nazianzen says, "[I]t is true indeed that the Father is evidently greater than Christ, so far as he is understood as a man, but that is not important. For what news is it that God is greater than man?"[468]

In what way, then, is he greater, if not in essence, if not in power, if not in might, if not in honor; for we have shown that in these respects the Son is equal to the Father? For, my Lord Ivan, the Father is greater than the Son, even apart from the same view of the divine Basil and Nazianzen. [122] Erasmus writes in his *Apologia* to Jacob Sturm [correctly: Jacques Lefèvre]: "Because the Father is the origin of the Son, the Father is for this reason greater as cause and origin. Wherefore also the Lord said: 'My Father is greater than I,' for the reason that he is Father. And what else does the word 'father' mean than the cause and origin of him that was begotten of him?" Thus far Erasmus.[469]

I say and repeat that unless it is quite clearly shown in what way the Son is equal to the Father, and [also] in what way the Father is greater than the Son [even] before he became man, our misled brethren will never give up Stancarism.[470]

To this end serve many very learned views of the early writers who teach both that the Father commanded the Son, and the Son obeyed and ministered to the Father before the incarnation.

Hilary, *De Trinitate*, 4, unless I am mistaken, [said]:

"Let there be Light" [Gen 1:3]. The words are the Father's commanding the Son what he wished to be done.[471]

The same:

He was not yet born as a man. In any case one who is sent carries out the orders of him who sent him, obeys, and submits to him.[472]

Ignatius, the disciple of St. John the Evangelist:

The Lord was really crucified by impious men and this because he who was born of woman is the Son of God, and he who was crucified is "the firstborn of creation"[473] and God the Word, and who made all things by command of the Father, which the Apostle confirms, saying: "one God the Father, of whom are all things, and one Lord Jesus Christ through whom are all things."[474] Again: "For there is one God, and one Mediator between God and men, the man Christ Jesus,"[475] who is "the image of the invisible God." . . . (And a little later:) "It is not he himself who is God over all, but his Son."[476]

Hilary, *De Trinitate*, IV, after showing that God the Father said [Gen 1:6] "Let there be a firmament," and that God the Son made the firmament [cf. Col 1:16], adds:

But we see, I say, that surely the God commanding and the God making is treated of.[477]

The same, in the same book p. 55 of the last edition:

"And God saw that they were good [Gen 1:4]." The Father was pleased by his own work. He rejoices at what had been done by himself, in accordance with his command.[478]

In book 5.75:

He [Moses] proves [this] to you clearly, he proves by the whole volume of the Law, ordained through angels, which he received by the hand of the Mediator.[479] Inquire whether the one who gave the law [123] be one God, since it was assuredly the Mediator who gave it.[480]

Justin Martyr the Philosopher, in his *Dialogue with Trypho the Jew*, says:[481]

I will try by explaining the Scriptures to prove what I say: that there is and is said to be another God and Lord [besides] the Creator [of all things], that he is called an Angel or messenger who announces to men whatever the Creator of all things, [above whom there is no other God], wishes to announce to them.[482]

Again:

"Let us [Justin goes on] return to the Scriptures. I will take pains to persuade you [Trypho] that he who is said to have appeared to Abraham, Jacob, and Moses,[483] and in Scripture is called God, is yet distinct form the Creator—numerically, I mean, not in will (*sententia*), for it is certain that he has never done anything except what the Creator of the world himself—above whom there is no other God—judged should be done and said.''[484]

Again:

It should by all means be admitted that some other than he who is understood to be the Creator of all things is called Lord by the Holy Spirit, not only through Moses, but also through David.[485]

Again:

You do not even now understand, my friends, that one of the three (meaning the three who sought out by Abraham) is the God and Lord who ministers to him in the heavens.[486]

Again, Trypho speaks:

Proceed to give a reason how this God, who appeared to Abraham as minister to God the Creator of all things, was born of a virgin as a man subject to like passions with other men.[487]

Again:

Brethren, Moses also wrote this, that he who is said to have appeared to the Patriarchs is called God and Angel and Lord, in order that from this you may acknowledge that he ministers to the Father of all things, as you have now admitted.[488]

Again:

And now indeed the Scripture relates that an angel of the Lord appeared to Moses, and presently made it known that he was Lord and God, and revealed him as the very one of whom we often read as ministering to the God who is above the world, above whom there is no other.[489]

My Lord Ivan, my letter would run out to an unreasonable length if I should compile all the opinions of the ancients leading to the same end. And anyone who is not content with these will not be persuaded even though I copied a thousand others. These amount to this, that all may know that the confession about the Mediator with respect to both natures contains nothing absurd, if we say that the Son as God interceded with God the Father, or God as Son interceded with God as Father.

[124] But Stancaro, because confusing the divine persons, and out of three beings (*rebus*) numerically making one being numerically, not only destroys the mediation—without which there is no salvation[490]—but also destroys the generation of the Son and the *emissio* of the Holy Spirit, as St. Athanasius has left in his writing against the followers of Sabellius:[491]

Let us accept an undivided coexistence and let us understand that these mutually coexisting with each other, even though they are really three, have one form, which indeed begins with the Father, but is resplendent in the Son, and also appears and demonstrates itself in the Holy Spirit.[492]

Again:

Since then Deity is so indivisible, learn reverently from the sacred writers to understand one form in the three, not to compose one being out of the three.[493]

Again:

Since however all things are done by GOD the Father through Christ in the Holy Spirit, I behold an undivided working of Father and Son and Holy Spirit, not however enfolding them all in one: the From Whom, the Through Whom, the In Whom—[494]

That is, the Father, the Son, and the Holy Spirit. I strive to make a unity out of the Trinity,[495] but those who make it as does Stancaro cannot understand how in such a unity the Son intercedes and mediates with the Father.

My Lord Ivan, consider these words of St. Athanasius and you will be delivered from many fantasies. If one can understand that the same thing cannot be one and more than one in the same way, but can be in different ways, one will understand also that we here at Pińczów are not teaching things unheard of and monstrous. Indeed those who teach otherwise fall into the view of the heretic Sabellius, who knew no real distinction between Father, Son, and Holy Spirit, and was saying that they were only names of the one God, such as Creator, almighty, good, merciful. This means from three beings numerically to make one being (*rem*) numerically, and hence he was compelled to say that Father, Son, and Holy Spirit are one person.[496] But where one person, or one being numerically, is understood, there cease both begetting (*generatio*) (since nothing begets itself) and sending (*emissio*) forth, or as they now say, breathing (*spiratio*) and procession (*processio*) of the Holy Spirit. We here at Pińczów freely confess and believe in one God the Father, from whom are all things, unbegotten, without beginning, from whom are not only all creatures, but also the divinity and the goodness of the Son and of the Holy Spirit, as Nazianzen teaches in his *Apologeticus*.[497]

[125] We also confess and believe in our Lord Jesus Christ the Son of God, who is the Word incarnate, God-man, God of God, Light of Light, very God of very God, consubstantial with the Father, coeternal and coequal in essence or nature, in virtue, in glory, in power, and in honor. We believe also in the Holy Spirit, very God, from eternity ineffably proceeding from the Father and from the Son, or as the Greek Fathers say, through the Son,[498] consubstantial, coeternal, and coequal with the Father and the Son, as has been said above, in essence, virtue, majesty, glory, power, and honor. We acknowledge three persons of the same essence, and confess with St. Basil: "Whatever good things from the divine virtue reach through to us, working all things in all men, are the working of grace, even as the Apostle said: 'For all these worketh the one and the same Spirit, dividing to each one severally, even as he will.'"[499]

But inquiring whether also the supply of good things helps [?un]worthy men, as something that takes its beginning from the Holy Spirit alone, again we are led and taught by Scripture to believe that the only-begotten God is the author and cause of the supplying of those good things which the Holy

Spirit works in us. For we are taught by Holy Scripture that by him all things were made and in him all things consist [Col 1:15 – 17].

Since therefore we are brought around to this thought, let us again proceed, led by divinely inspired assistance. Although by that power (*potentiam*) indeed all things are brought into being from what is not, lest these things come forth from that which is inoriginate (*absque initio*), still there is a certain power, unbegotten (*ingenita* [in the sense of unbegun]) and without beginning (*sine principio*) present (*assistens*) that is the cause of that cause through (*per*) which all things are made.[500]

These are the things, my Lord Ivan, brother dearly beloved, which have seemed to me deserving of your reading, that you too may learn sound doctrine and may teach others who are astray not from wilful ignorance nor from perverse disposition. All of this however I submit to the examination and judgment of the Churches that have the word of God for their rule. If there is anything that you do not understand, Master George Negri will explain it. If you do understand and approve it all, communicate it to the brethren, [126] and especially to my son, Master Jacob Sylvius.[501] Farewell in the Lord Jesus.

Pińczów, 10 September 1561.[502]

[Biandrata defends simplicity in doctrinal formulations,
synod of Cracow, 1561]

After this letter of Lismanino was read and discussed at [the synod of] Włodzisław, 23 September 1561,[503] a few from the patrons and ministers gathered at a synod in Cracow, appointed for 10 December 1561, which was the twentieth in number.[504] At this meeting a letter from Calvin was read in which he said that he had given Martin Czechowic, minister to Prince [Nicholas] Radziwiłł, palatine of Vilna, a letter for this patron, to whom he had laid bare the heresies of Biandrata [**cf. BAnt nos. 5, 21 – 22**].[505]

For the latter, when staying at Geneva, had a sharp discussion with Calvin on the subject of religion, and pointed out errors in his books akin to those of the Papists and injurious to the Church. Among others, [he used] this very strong argument, from which the former could not by any proper reply escape: "Whoever calls on the God set forth in Deuteronomy 6[:4], who in the view of the Trinitarians is [at once] Father, Son, and Holy Spirit, ought to call on him through a Mediator. But Father, Son, and Holy Spirit have at the same instant (*simul*) no mediator. Therefore they are not invoked together at the same moment (*simul*)."[506] He persisted, Calvin bore it impatiently, grew angry, threatened him. Biandrata recalled the case of Servetus, with whose impieties Calvin taunted him. He foresaw danger, hastily fled, and left Geneva. Not content with this, Calvin, unable otherwise to pursue him, severely accused Biandrata to the patrons and brethren in letters sent to Poland, and so did everything to ruin him.[507] Biandrata took it as his task, with all the power and influence of his talents and eloquence, to further the cause of the reformation he had begun. But these letters of Calvin had found credit in the minds of many.

For Peter Martyr also was as vehemently defending the current errors, as attacking their opponents, and among them Biandrata. Thus from Zurich, on 11 June 1558, he wrote to a certain minister at Geneva[508] that George the Physician (meaning Biandrata himself) had been with him, having left Geneva because of the troubles he had started, and that he seemed to introduce a kind of monarchy into the Deity, nor did he admit that Father and Son were of the same essence, which results in a plurality of Gods [monarchical Tritheism]; that Gribaldi hearing this, asserted it in explicit words; that he [Biandrata] had with him John Paul of Piedmont (to wit Alciati) whom he had advised to subscribe to the formula established in the Italian Church at Geneva, and when he would not assent, he was persuaded, following Bullinger's suggestion, to leave before being forced by the city government [127] to do so.

[The triadological views of Lismanino and Biandrata at the synod of Cracow, 10 December 1561][509]

In this synod at Cracow the [above quoted] letter of Lismanino to Ivan was [again] given close examination and diverse judgments of it were expressed. Indeed, thanks to the efforts of Sarnicki and others, not a few deemed it a mistake (*vitium*) in Lismanino and Biandrata that they should raise the question as to the preeminence of the Father. Biandrata therefore defended the better cause in the following manner:

> Brethren, whoever with a clear mind's eye looks at and thoroughly examines the ancient stratagems of Satan, the crafty architect of a thousand tricks, sees that in forming plots against the soundness of the Church and the salvation of men, he has also forced into the discussion matters of no importance, while keeping the important matters in the background. And surely not without reason did the spirit of prophecy, speaking through the mouth of the great Apostle to the Gentiles, long ago fear lest, as the serpent had once led Eve astray by his cleverness, so also the corrupted minds of the faithful might fall away from the simplicity that is in the teaching of Christ.[510]
>
> For this teaching contains within itself such admirable and heavenly wisdom as by its native simplicity to commend itself to all. The greatest minds here have room for exercise, if indeed they are led by zeal for true piety. And yet there is nothing that cannot profit even the most simple unto salvation. However, since the style of Scripture is clear, it is plain that we see in the Apostles' Creed certain phrases that are unusual in Scripture. And it seems that there are more of these in the Nicene, and the most in the Athanasian. Notwithstanding, I should not reject even these foreign elements from these creeds, were they explained in a natural way, in harmony with Scriptures. But to do this, there is need of much study, of extensive knowledge of the Holy Scriptures and of the ancient Church, of great patience and endurance.
>
> Of course, the article on the deity of the Son of God, our Lord and Saviour Jesus Christ, deserves careful examination. But this ought to be without bias. For if you here show any hatred or favor, you will not attain the desired end. I wish we could return to the original simplicity without

stirring up any feelings. But if the tenets of our faith are to be submitted to an examination (which, I confess, is indeed necessary in seeking and finding the truth), it is necessary only that we refrain from disputes which result in nothing good.[511]

Thus far Biandrata. To him Jerome Ossoliński,[512] a very noble man, greatly devoted to religious conversations [cf. **BAnt no. 5**], replied in the name of the rest:

> So [128] it is indeed, George Biandrata—he said—that errors and corruptions were introduced into the Church of God after the times of the Apostles. Yet watchful care must be taken lest pious doctrines and rites harmonious with piety be reckoned among them. Certainly, it would have been well had these controversies about the Son of God not been raised, and had all things been avoided that are not contained in the Word of God. For this is also my opinion entirely that Holy Scripture alone is infallible and the surest rule of faith from which no one should depart. Many things, though, might have been ignored and left untouched for the present.
>
> However, I see that now certain writings on the Holy Trinity have been spread abroad among the common people. What the outcome of these will be I cannot say. Yet I can hardly look for a happy one. Instances before our eyes teach this. I am bound to fear whether some book of this sort by Stancaro presented to [Anna Konarska Zborowska], the wife of the Palatine of Poznań, will accomplish any good in her woman's heart.[513] For we see that Lismanino himself, when it had been handed to him, would not read it, nay even persuaded others not to honor it with reading, and said that the whole controversy was of no importance.

To this Lismanino, who was there present, rejoined:

> It is true, Jerome Ossoliński, that I have dissuaded some from reading the book by Stancaro, for Stancaro's view about the Mediator does not exhaust the whole difficulty about that matter. For if we uphold a Triune God together with Stancaro, we need not be much concerned whether God the Son was Mediator in his human nature only, or also in his divine.[514] And so in this sense I have held that the controversy of Stancaro is of no importance, if the opinion about the Triune God is retained and insisted upon. That the words 'Trinity," "hypostases," "persons," "communication of *idiomata*," and many others invented by Peter Lombard and other scholastics are unknown to Scripture, is clear and is well known.
>
> For we see how both Luther and Calvin and other men very celebrated in the Church disliked these terms.[515] So if their judgment is to stand, and truth complaining that she is involved in these trifles is to be heard, all these terms would justly and deservedly have to be rejected, so that in this way the primitive simplicity [? of the Apostles' Creed] might return to us. But if this cannot be accomplished, especially at present, these terms must be endured for a time, yet on this condition: that no one be compelled to accept them. And unless a person is willing to do it this way, however repugnant to his conscience, let him be judged unworthy of the communion of the

Church. My epistle to the noble Lord Ivan bears on this point. In it [129] I have shown from the ancient Fathers that their view about the deity of the Son was not such as is now received.[516]

And in this place also let me freely and without any one's taking offense tell what I think and what the issue is: Let the ancient *doctores* of the Church leave me one God, and let them [**cf. BAnt nos. 5, 10**] make no distinction of persons in him. For when these, as primary intelligent substances (*substantiis primis intelligentibus*), are multiplied, the substances or, what is the same thing, the essences and the natures, must needs be multiplied. Let them in no way divide him, nor make any dispensation (*oeconomiam*) in him. Then I for my part will cause no one any trouble about the Mediator, of whatever sort he pleases.[517]

And so these speeches and more of this sort were made there on this subject. These were listened to with varying sentiments since they were indeed quite varied. But the more moderate spirits brought everything back to harmony. Stanislas Lasocki proposed this plan: that the ministers who had charged Lismanino and Biandrata with maintaining heresy, and who had impaired the high esteem in which the two were held, be called together and reasoned with. At length it was unanimously concluded that Biandrata should compose a confession of his faith and affirm his innocence [**cf. BAnt no. 5**].

From this synod letters on this matter were written to Calvin and Bullinger,[518] [a copy of] which on February 23 of the following year, 1562, Lismanino sent to Czechowic in order to see what he now thought about their doctrine and about "those two calumniators,"[519] as the words of the letter read, who had traduced them[520] throughout the world as "Arians."[521]

Indeed, in the very same year [of the synod of Cracow], 1561, that magnanimous and pious prince, Nicholas Radziwiłł the Black, palatine of Vilna, had sent this Czechowic to Geneva in concern for Biandrata. As the instruction given Czechowic by the prince himself testifies,[522] Biandrata had confessed three consubstantials, coeternals, coequals. And therefore he was unwilling to have him secretly slandered by letters from [Swiss] theologians, to the great scandal of the Church [in Poland], unless he be publicly convicted, if indeed the Church be otherwise well convinced as to his doctrine and character by John Łaski and Doctor Lismanino. The prince also asked that the Biandrata letter be sent to him in which—as it was stated by those from Zurich—the latter had asserted that the Son is plainly less than the Father. From this it is patent how much displeased the prince was at Calvin's unfriendly zeal against Biandrata, which he was not concealing.

[Biandrata's radically simplified *Confessio* at the synods of
Książ Wielki and Pińczów, March and April 1562]

After the synod at Cracow [130] had been dissolved, a synod was appointed to meet at Książ on March 10 of the next year, 1562, at which Biandrata presented a confession of his faith. This also I insert here:

I confess that I believe in one God the Father, on one Lord Jesus Christ his Son, and in one Holy Spirit, each one of whom is essentially God. I detest a plurality of Gods, since to us there is only one God, in *essentia* indivisible. I confess that there are three distinct *hypostases*; and the eternal divinity and generation of Christ; and the Holy Spirit, true and eternal God, proceeding from both.[523]

Regenvolscius [Węgierski], *Historia Ecclesiarum Slavonicarum*, 86,[524] says that by this "tinted *Confessio*" it was brought about that a testimonial on Biandrata's behalf from the whole synod of Pińczów, held on 25 January 1562, was given in letters written to the palatine of Vilna and to John Calvin.[525] But Budziński writes (chap. 21) that the confession was presented by Biandrata to the synod of Książ on 10 March 1562, and that it was soon discussed and the reconciliation effected at the synod of Pińczów in the following month [2 April 1562].[526] He says:

A little while after (this synod of Książ) a synod met at Pińczów, April 2, at which twenty-eight ministers and twelve noble patrons were present. The rather long confession of Biandrata (I have no copy aside from that given by Regenvolscius) was not rejected, and his apologia *was accepted. So the synod promised him to see to it that he should return to favor with Calvin through letters they were going to send. For his part he promised to consent to all that should be determined by Calvin and the Churches of God, provided Calvin should permit him to confess that He [Jesus] is Son of the most high and eternal God, and that Calvin himself speak simply of the one God without any interpretation, but that if Calvin should not like this, let him at least promise this: that he will abide by the simple word of God and the Apostles' Creed; and let him revoke his recently published epistle [against the suppliant] to the palatine of Vilna, prefixed to* In Acta Apostolorum [**cf. BAnt no. 6**].[527]

Thus far Budziński. But I find [only] a dedicatory epistle to King Christian of Denmark, prefixed to Calvin's *Commentarius in Acta* [*Apostolorum*]. However, in other manuscript commentaries [on the synods][528] I find that at the synod of Książ Biandrata's confession was approved by some, disapproved by others, and only read in private, though finally read publicly at the synod of Pińczów [2 April 1562].

[131] And as it was expressed in words of Scripture, it found opposition from few, and reconciliation with Calvin was promised to him [**cf. BAnt no. 6**]. At the same synod [of Pińczów] it was voted that the ministers should abstain from philospchical terms such as "Trinity," "essence," "generation," "the manner of proceeding," which are all foreign to the word of God; but that each should confine himself to the terms of the prophets, apostles, and the Apostles' Creed [**cf. BAnt nos. 6.1, 54**]. This was certainly a fair way of settling the quarrels arising at the time. But these decisions were disregarded by turbulent minds; and, when the power of the world entered in, they were rejected; indeed their opposite was accepted. Lismanino and Biandrata agreed in this: unless God (who in Holy Writ is called the Father of Jesus Christ) is stated to be the Most

High it is impossible to satisfy Stancaro, nay, neither will the honor due to the most high God remain, since Christ himself said to him: "My Father is greater than I."[529]

CHAPTER SEVEN

Of the Preeminence of the Father Affirmed by Gregory Paul, and of the Church of Catholic Christians Formed and Established after the Schism Made by Stanislas Sarnicki.[530]

After the synod of Pińczów [of 2 April 1562], a way of harmony having been established, all ought to have kept within the limits of modesty and charity. But it came to pass in quite another way, until a sad division ensued, as we shall see a little later.

[Sarnicki[531] attacks Gregory Paul: 1562][532]

Gregory,[533] the minister of the congregation at Cracow, rendering obedience to the canon of the Pińczów synod to abstain from scholastic terms in preaching, preached simply one God the Father, his Son Jesus Christ, and his Holy Spirit. On the other hand, Sarnicki, disregarding not only Christian charity but also the rule adopted at Pińczów, openly accused him and [cf. BAnt nos. 6.1, 11, 54] stirred up others against him, saying that he was tearing (*avellere*) the Son away from God.[534] Indeed, Sarnicki used rather often to come from Niedźwiedź into the city, especially because many were joining the new church, and because in the castle,[535] at the residence [132] of Boner who was governor of the castle,[536] as we call it, there was preaching attended by large numbers of people, partly in search of the new, partly glowing with love of the truth. Hence he was consumed with envy[537] that, though he himself was of noble birth, Gregory had been preferred to him in the direction of the church at the capital; and he contrived a higher degree of honor through the ruin of one whom he had taken as his rival. Yet at all events he had now already brought it about that [Stanislas] Aichler,[538] the city notary, and Valerian Pernus[539] wrote letters to Lismanino, upbraiding him for having, by his epistle to Ivan,[540] given Gregory occasion for a novel preaching on the preeminence of the Father as if indeed it were a new thing to ascribe to God, the author of all things, all things including even the Son himself.

Sarnicki, not content with his lot and aspiring to the ministry of the church at Cracow, since he could not attain it directly, proceeded by roundabout ways. He wished at least to be appointed to a teaching position, even to become tutor to the illustrious Myszkowski youths,[541] step-sons of Stanislas Cikowski,[542] so that being constantly at Cracow, he might be not so much a hearer as an observer and accuser of Gregory, and be chosen in his place, should Gregory be removed from it. But since he could in no wise attain his wish, he denounced Gregory to many as a preacher of a new and blasphemous doctrine of God, Christ, and the Holy Spirit. Then, pursuing a different design, he wrote to Gregory, asking him to suspend his exposition of the Gospel of Luke, and to explain the Creed to the people.[543] But Gregory, seeing through the plot, went on with the exposition of the Gospel that he had begun, addressed the people on God as God, on the Son of God as Son of God, on the Holy Spirit of God as the Holy Spirit of God, adhering strictly to the words of the text so far as he could. And thus he made a catholic confession of his faith, vindicated his innocence, bore testimony to the truth, refuted his slanderer, and covered him with shame. This he did with singular carefulness on 5 July 1562, in place of a sermon, in the presence of some elders and of Sarnicki himself [**cf. BAnt nos. 6.1, 11**]. These therefore asked Sarnicki how he liked Gregory's sermon, and whether he wished to engage him, or at least to confer with him on any points, and admonished him to show himself a man.

Sarnicki avoided a meeting and said that he would have to speak with him separately about the *essentia* of God. As if, to be sure, [133] ''the simple, I would not say the unwise [and unlearned who] are the major part of the believers,'' as Tertullian in *Adversus Praxeam*, 3 says,[544] needed to apply themselves to examining and investigating such scholastic trifles, of which not only the sacred pages but also the primitive Church knew nothing.

But Sarnicki, instead of having the private conference that he had led the elders to expect, went to [Gregory's master] Stanislas Myszkowski,[545] then captain of Marienburg, and to John Boner, castellan of Biecz and governor of the castle of Cracow [protector of the local congregation]. He laid new charges against Gregory, even accused him openly. Hence Boner, employing his senatorial authority,[546] undertook to settle the differences. He forthwith summoned them to Balice for July 14,[547] inviting them to a friendly conference. They held it in his presence, but not even then could Sarnicki find any just ground for indictment. Nevertheless he did not desist from accusing of heresy, and indeed from defaming here and there, the man whom he had chosen for his rival, and whose safety he could not believe was consistent with his own.

[The synod of Rogów, 20 July 1562: long exchanges between
Gregory Paul and Sarnicki]

Wherefore Stanislas Szafraniec,[548] a most illustrious and magnanimous man, judging that the matter admitted of no delay, invited them both to Rogów for

July 20,[549] for a friendly conference [**cf. BAnt no. 6.2**], both convenient and necessary for healing the threatening division. He also invited illustrious and noble men as well as ministers of the word from the neighborhood, so that this assembly in fact constituted a true synod.[550]

There were present of the equestrian order: Stanislas Lasocki, chamberlain of Łęczyca, with his inseparable friend Jerome Filipowski, Nicholas Rey,[551] and many others; of the ministers: Felix Cruciger, superintendent of the churches of Little Poland, minister to Szafraniec at Secemin, Stanislas Lutomirski, elder of the district (*tractus*) of Pińczów, a man of distinguished nobility, John Pustelnik, Jacob Sylvius.[552] When it came to the conference, Gregory [Paul] opened somewhat as follows:

> Patrons, brethren, and friends in Christ, to be honored with all observance of respect, I give my God thanks that you have come hither in such large numbers. This is a shining proof of your zeal and piety. This great ardor of Christian hearts, with which they burn day and night in spreading the pure truth, is the more to be praised, the more the opponents of the truth attempt to extinguish it. But God lives, his Christ the King of kings lives, who against all [134] threats and rage of his adversaries and even of princes themselves imparts invincible and unshaken strength to the minds of the faithful. He is the heavenly fire with which you burn, and because the Son of God himself, receiving it from the bosom of the Father, has brought it to the race of mortals and kindles it in the hearts that breathe out probity, it can be extinguished by no human power or craft. It is going well with us, not only because the fire of your zeal cannot be extinguished by men, but also because it glows perpetually, kindles hearts numbed by the deep sleep of errors and sins, and thus arouses them into wakefulness, once aroused rewarms them with warmth of piety, once rewarmed inflames them with ardor for spreading the truth.
>
> I say it is going well with us, because we are so secure abroad. Would that all were equally well ordered at home. But to tell the truth, the fact is that by the arts of Satan the strange fire of unholy zeal and violent discords is being brought into the Lord's sanctuary, is being kindled even upon the altar itself. How adverse this is to God, how ruinous to man, is taught by the sad example of the sons of Aaron.[553] And, to come to the point, as several times hitherto I have shown myself willing and compliant, when invited by some of you and by other patrons and brethren to hold a fraternal conference with Brother Stanislas Sarnicki on matters of faith, so too in the present instance I have been willing to do what is fitting. I know that I am being publicly and privately accused by Brother Sarnicki of innovation in doctrine, because I preach one God, the Father of our Lord Jesus Christ. But that this is the very thing that the Apostles preached, you yourselves know without my saying so. And indeed this teaching is, as it were, the very marrow of the primitive truth.
>
> It is no secret to you that immediately after the death of the Apostles grievous wolves were to break in and to fall upon the Lord's fold, not sparing the flock [Acts 29:29], nay, that false brethren [cf. Gal 2:4] were to come, and false teachers, setting forth things perverse and opposed to the

instruction of the Apostles. That this in fact happened, the records of the history of the Church bear witness. And not to mention other things, I must cite to you the testimony of Hegesippus, the earliest writer and the one nearest the Apostolic Age, as quoted by Eusebius, the famous author of the *Historia Ecclesiastica* (3,32),[554] speaking of the state of the Church after the death of Simeon Cleopas, whom many regard as the last of the apostles, and who was certainly at least of the Apostolic [135] Age, and died in the year 111 A.D. And this [passage] runs:

> Up to this time the Church remained a virgin, pure and incorrupt, while those who endeavored to corrupt the sound rule of saving preaching, if there were any such then, lay hidden in some obscure darkness. But after the holy band of the apostles came to their various allotted ends, and the generation passed away who had deserved to hear the divine wisdom with their own ears, then began a conspiracy of wicked error through the seduction of those who were delivering a strange doctrine. And, since none of the apostles any longer survived, they now boldly undertook, in opposition to the preaching of the truth, to proclaim on the contrary knowledge, falsely so called.[555]

That from now on errors were by degrees introduced into the Church of God is plain to all who intelligently read the records of the *Historia Ecclesiastica*. Yet things went well even in the ages most corrupt through both the power of the Roman emperors and the arrogance of the Popes, because the Apostles' Creed was always kept as the watchword of faith and the rule of truth and mark (*nota*) of Christianity, and has been preserved to this day, and on this alone holy baptism was instituted. That I have not departed from it by a hair's breadth any fair man can see. I am accused of Arianism and Servetianism, while I believe and confess one God and Jesus Christ his Son. But for this reason the apostles themselves would have to be accused of heresies, because unanimously and with one voice they preached the one God of Israel,[556] creator of heaven and earth, and Jesus of Nazareth,[557] the Messiah promised by him to the fathers, the King of the people of God and Saviour of the world, conceived by the Holy Spirit, born of the Virgin, resuscitated and exalted by God.[558] Indeed each of you sees that this is not heresy but the very truth, primitive and catholic.

I am not unaware that in subsequent times many dogmas were added to this, about three persons in the one *natura* of God,[559] and on the other hand about two natures in one person,[560] and countless others, of which the first age of the Church and apostolic artlessness knew not at all, and which thus also by us can be safely ignored. Yet to teach the preeminence of the Father, this is Arian, this is Servetian! But I, together with all lovers of the truth, have learned from Scripture [1 Thess 5.21] [136] "to test all things, to hold fast what is good." Whatever this man or that may have said contrary to Scripture, that I detest: but whatever he has asserted in agreement with it, that I receive. In this matter I follow the word and example of all Christian antiquity. Begone odious names as well as tyrannical deeds from Christian people (*gens*), also from our Poland! We are the people (*populus*) of God, we are Christ's own chattel, redeemed by his blood; we are the serfs (*man-*

cipia) of Christ, not of men.[561] We are Poles, therefore a people free in every respect, but called to full liberty in such wise that we mete it out in the obedience owed to laws human and divine.

We see the preeminence of the Father in Holy Scripture clearer than the light at midday, as he is most evidently proclaimed in so many words and letters as the God of Abraham, the God of Isaac, and the God of Jacob, the God of the Fathers, God and Father (that is, even so God as also the Father) of our Lord Jesus Christ, whom he anointed with the Holy Spirit, raised from the dead, and placed at his right hand [Heb 1:3 and passim].

And if we stop here and do not wish to proceed further, who would say that we act harshly or unfairly, unless he himself were acting harshly and unfairly? Yet we will grant something to the unsound curiosity which, not content with apostolic simplicity, seeks a variety of food, as they are wont to do who seek foreign things when weary of those at home. I say therefore and affirm, as the fact itself bears witness, that to all the Ante-Nicene Fathers, nay even to the Fathers of Nicaea themselves, and finally to those of Constantinople [381], and thus to the whole Christian world for four centuries, there was one God the Father Almighty, creator of things visible and invisible, also his Son Jesus Christ, God of God, light of light, whom the Nicene Fathers against Arius declared to be consubstantial with the Father.[562]

And albeit it does not escape my notice that after the Council of Nicaea one God, the Father, Son, and Holy Spirit began to be taught, yet in this place it is neither fitting nor expedient to conceal [several] facts. At first the word *homoousios* (consubstantial, coessential), then also the dogma itself, was displeasing to not a few of the Nicenes. All said that the Son was begotten before all ages, [but they] did not venture to make any pronouncement as to the Holy Spirit. Hilary, in his twelve books *De Trinitate*, nowhere said that the Holy Spirit [137] was either to be worshiped or prayed to as God. Athanasius was the *first* and *only* one (or with *very few*, as [Gregory] of Nazianzus testifies) to begin teaching the deity of the Holy Spirit about the year 365.[563] All the rest who professed the Christian teaching were divided into three parties, many of them (in the judgment of the same Nazianzen, writing at the end of the fourth century), having "a weak faith" about the Son, "even more about the Holy Spirit," but that "few on either side were sound and unshaken."[564]

Nevertheless it deserves justly to be said—especially by me, who am so often accused before you on this account—that in later times also the Fathers of the Church asserted the preeminence of the Father. It might perchance seem a small thing that one God the Father, the unbegotten (*ingenitum*) God, is declared and taught by Hilary to be the author not only of all things, but also of both the Deity of the Son and of the Son himself.[565] And the later Fathers of the Greek Church, beginning in the fifth century, taught that the Father is the cause and origin of the Son, and greater than the Son, so far as he is God. Let it be enough to name Chrysostom,[566] Cyril,[567] Damascene,[568] Theophylact,[569] as a few out of many. No wonder! Also Athanasius himself, also Nazianzen, and others before them, taught the same thing and confessed the Son deified.[570]

Although those who are acquainted with the ancient Church know these things, yet I stand ready to prove them to any one in the words of the Fathers.[571] But to be brief in what I am to say, this is my judgment and so I have determined: that we ought to go back to the first principles of the Christian religion and return by degrees to the truth of the first ages, even as it was by degrees departed from. And now, although I am prepared to hear what has been brought forward against me, and to add modesty and patience to my innocence, that it may be entire and complete, and to submit to your judgment, yet I doubt not but that you will here be mindful of the canon adopted at the synod of Pińczów[572] about giving up the scholastic terms of ''Trinity,'' ''essence,'' ''person,'' ''communication of *idiomata*,'' and many things of this sort, and about teaching truth and piety from the word of God. And surely, I humbly pray the Great and Good God, through the High Priest Jesus Christ reigning at his right hand [Heb 8:1], that he may bestow upon you the spirit of counsel and wisdom, of virtue and charity, and fill you with his gifts that you may rightly weigh matters of the greatest importance.

[138] As such things are wont to be received, both by different ears and different minds, so were they received even at that time. Some were irritated, some mollified, others delighted, all of them moved and they reached a judgment according to their several inclinations and sympathies. Sarnicki, together with his friends, did not fail to make some objection to these things, somewhat as follows:

All these things, though plausibly said, should be taken with a grain of salt, as the saying goes. And although all ought to be carefully noted and considered, yet many of them ought to be disapproved. Anyone who denies that the one God has revealed himself in Father, Son, and Holy Spirit, must be ignorant of the history of creation, the confusion of tongues,[573] the visions and missions of the prophets, the Trisagion of the angels,[574] the baptism both received and commanded by Christ,[575] the three witnesses in heaven,[576] and other things related in Holy Writ. He must also contradict not only the teaching of the holy Fathers individually, but also together in their councils, even the entire Holy and Catholic Church, vigorous and flourishing, from the beginning until now.[577] The things that have been now brought forward, were long ago formally condemned by the Holy orthodox Catholic Church in Ebion,[578] Cerinthus,[579] the Samosatene,[580] Arius, Photinus,[581] and other heretics of the sort.

To what purpose is it then to revive them from the dead and to call them back from hell (*orco*) now, when the thrice Great and Good God, taking pity on us all, has chosen that the Church be reformed through magnanimous men filled with the Holy Spirit and called to this office, of whom some are even now fiercely fighting on the stage of the Christian world against all heresies and corruptions? What audacity and rashness, to say nothing worse, when some man of obscure name opposes so many and such great Christian heroes, the blessed men! Really it annoys and wearies me to speak, and that so often of things that the Church has long since rejected and detested, as if any doubt could arise concerning the Catholic truth that was explained and established so many centuries ago.

What need is there of many words? The whole Church sings: "Glory be to the Father and to the Son and to the Holy Spirit, as it was in the beginning."[582] Yet because it has pleased you that I should appear now also in this place, behold, here I am, ready here and everywhere to fight against all heretical and impious doctrines. We know that it was predicted in the Holy Scriptures[583] [139] of the New Testament that heretics should come to rend the flock of the Lord as wolves. But this was in every truth fulfilled in Ebion, Cerinthus, Simon Magus,[584] the Monarchians,[585] Alogi,[586] and other men or rather monsters of the same stripe.

Whoever yields to please these heretics on only one person of Deity, on Christ as a mere (*nudo*) man who had his beginning from Mary and was a creature, may he perish with them! Or else may he keep the most holy and venerable doctrine of the Trinity, and with us and with the Catholic Church confess God the Father, God the Son, God the Holy Spirit as three *hypostases* in unity of *essentia*.

This Triune God I also now implore, that he may be with me and you all in this holy synod, to whom be the glory through our Lord Jesus Christ for ever and ever. Amen.[587]

This also, as is wont, was then received in different ways by different people. There were some who took one side, while others the other. However, Gregory replied to Sarnicki's speech somewhat as follows:

Whatever I have heard brought up against me, though unnamed, in defense of the dogma of the Trinity, can by no means be compared with what I have brought forward from both the Holy Scripture and the earliest Church. For to those who are ignorant of the Hebrew tongue, those things either seem to indicate a plurality of persons in the Divine (and were for the most part rejected by Calvin himself and others), or out of the mention of Father, Son, and Holy Spirit (which as most holy names we also confess, and hence also use in baptism[588]) seem to make three persons in one God. Both these things are in fact contrary to fairness and truth. It is as certain as can be that in the Scripture it is most clearly, expressly, and demonstrably taught that God is one and not threefold, one God the Father, and not Father, Son, and Holy Spirit. If this foundation be preserved, there will not be much difficulty about the rest. Now as regards the early Church, I have nothing in common with Ebion, Cerinthus, and other heretics. In other respects I approve nothing but what fits the rule of Holy Scripture. Yet whatever differs from it, that I disapprove. Among these things is the hymn *Gloria [Patri]* unknown not only to Scripture (which teaches that God and Christ, or God through Christ, is perpetually [140] to be glorified, adored, and worshiped), but also the earliest Church.[589] For it is evident from the *Historia Ecclesiastica* of Theodoret and Nicetas[590] that this hymn did not begin to be sung until the fourth century by Flavian of Antioch.[591] And so I do not hesitate to confess, together with plainest Scripture, that I believe in

God through Christ, that unto him who sitteth on the throne and unto the Lamb,[592] or to the only wise God,[593] through Jesus Christ, to the one God—I say—'through the one Mediator the Man Jesus Christ,'[594] I ascribe honor and glory, and for all the faithful pray grace and peace from God our Father and our Lord Jesus Christ. This I myself now here pray also for you who are here. I trust that I am abiding by the apostolic instruction which was the only one from the beginning, by the fisherman's simplicity, by the pristine integrity, by the Catholic truth. And I certainly hope that I shall soon prove it to you when we come into conference.

Hereupon it was ordered by the patrons that a conference be held between Gregory and Sarnicki. In this [conference], to tell much in a few words, Gregory, giving a reason for his faith, proved by words of the New Testament Scripture that the Christian faith differs from the Jewish in this: that the Jews believe in the one God of Israel, creator of all things, but Christians believe also in his Son Jesus Christ, the promised Messiah. For Christ himself says: "Ye believe in God, believe also in me" (John 14:1), and the Apostle Peter confirms the same [1 Pet 1:21]: "Through Christ ye believe in God, who raised him from the dead."[595] Therefore it is called a new song, in which honor and glory are ascribed 'to him who sitteth upon the throne, and to the Lamb,'[596] and much more of the same sort.

> To this Sarnicki objected:
> In these passages, by God the Trinity is meant; but by Christ, the human nature which was taken up, as they say, into hypostatic union.
> Gregory then retorted:
> In this way there will be a Quaternity in the divine,[597] that is, three persons mutually distinct from one another, and the man Christ. Besides, God taken absolutely and simply, or even with the emphatic particle, the God, means the Father, and hence he is very often so named. Witness Christ himself and the Apostle Peter, that he is the God of Israel, Creator and Lord of heaven and earth (John 8 [:41]; Matt 9 [:8]; Acts 3 – 5;[598] and in various passages elsewhere); and that Jesus of Nazareth [141] is represented as being distinct from him, as Son and Christ, or Messiah, that is, his Anointed. And so in all these passages, it is not the Trinity but God the Father that is obviously meant, sinced they are speaking of God, whose Son was Jesus.

By these and similar arguments Gregory powerfully refuted Sarnicki, so that unprejudiced and fair judges saw that the latter had lost his case. For the fact that they did not side with Sarnicki but tried to preserve harmony in the new Church is clearly obvious from the fact that it was then unanimously voted by all that the canon of the synod at Pińczów[599] must be observed: that Trinity and other scholastic terms that produce disputes should not be employed in preaching, but that the doctrine about God should be simply set forth as about God, and that about the Son of God as about the Son of God. Sarnicki on the other hand offered vain opposition and kept saying that the truth had then been betrayed, that canons opposed to it ought not to be obeyed, and that on the contrary it

ought to be defended not less against false brethren than against false teachers
and raging adversaries. But this was said by him to the end that he might find an
opening by which to leave the Church and bring the matter to an open quarrel.

Nevertheless all opposed him. Some felt that they ought by rights to go on in
the knowledge of divine truth and make progress in the matter of reformation,
returning to pristine simplicity and assenting to what is written. Some felt that
what is not plainly found in the Holy Scriptures can safely be passed by in
silence, that the greatest degree of harmony ought to be maintained and hence
much should be endured, and that truth and peace should be striven for together.
And all at length said that the canon of the synod of Pińczów should be
observed in order that harmony might be maintained [**cf. BAnt no. 6.2**].

[The disputation in Cracow of 5 August and the meeting in Balice of
12 August 1562: Sarnicki brings on a schism]

So Sarnicki bowed to the agreement and authority of all the rest and promised to
work for peace. And so you might say that this assembly was held not without
great profit. But matters fell out far otherwise; for Sarnicki, aspiring to leadership, drew over to his side some magnates not so much inclined to keeping
peace with the weaker party (*infirmiora pars*).[600] For once they had left Rogów,
Sarnicki persuaded Boner and [Stanislas] Myszkowski that Gregory ought to be
examined about his teaching heterodoxy.

They assented and invited Gregory to give reason for his faith at the city [of
Cracow] on August 5. Gregory complied with their wish. Ministers were summoned from neighboring places. Among them was [Stanislas] Wiśniowski,
minister of the church at Wieliczka.[601] [142] Sarnicki charged them with not
invoking Christ in prayers, while Wiśniowski flatly said the case was otherwise.
So the quarrel increased more and more. Hearing this, the elders of the church
at Cracow warned Sarnicki to be mindful of the peace and harmony of the
Church[602] and to keep in mind the canon of the Pińczów synod, not to provoke
disturbances and not to engage the patrons and brethren in quarrels with one
another. They requested him to confer with Gregory anew in their presence at
Boner's house at Balice.

This was done, so that a meeting was held on August 12, at Balice, attended
by several elders and ministers.[603] There, among other subjects, these words of
Paul [1 Tim 2:5] were examined: "For there is one God, and there is one Mediator between God and men, the man Christ Jesus." Now, Sarnicki explained the
words "one God" as meaning the Trinity.[604]

Gregory, on the other hand, held that it meant simply God, and pointed out
four things: (1) One God does not mean Triune under the way of speaking usual
in Scripture; (2) by "one God" is plainly indicated the Father, likewise according to the style of Scripture commonly used; (3) between this one God the
Father and men, a Mediator is appointed, since, as Scripture says, "a mediator is
not of one, but God is one" (Gal 3:20), and no one can be mediator of himself;

and (4) this Mediator of God and men is not God and man, but is expressly said to be man [1 Tim 2:5].[605]

But Sarnicki objected that Gregory was distorting Scripture, and that, at last, *he* perceived on what point the controversy hinged, and with what effort he must fight in behalf of the Trinity against Gregory who spoke simply of God, that is, in behalf of the Triune God against the confessor of one God.[606]

[The triadological struggle:[607] Pińczów, 18 August 1562]

From then on [the meeting in Balice of 12 August 1562, Sarnicki] traduced Gregory more and more, accused him to the patrons and brethren as heterodox and heretical, nay even defamed him. This pained all who loved peace and harmony very much [**cf. BAnt no. 6.2**]. So a larger synod was appointed at Pińczów for August 18,[608] as a remedy apt to put an end to such controversy by public authority (*publica auctoritate*). To this the elders (*Seniores*) invited Sarnicki.[609] He promised to be present, but afterwards, through hatred and fear of Gregory, he refused to attend and endeavored to crush the latter.

You might say that the great controversy between John of Constantinople and Gregory of Rome, in which the former aimed at a universal papacy, while the latter [143] opposed him as trying in anti-Christian pride to trample under foot the Church and the imperial majesty through the arrogance of a personal title, foreshadowed the one in the little (*parva*) church in which no small disturbance was stirred up by Sarnicki against Gregory.[610]

Those who had come together at the synod at Pińczów composed a confession of their faith.[611] Sarnicki carped at it, everywhere misinterpreted it, and seized the occasion for splitting the Church.

He drew over to his party [Paul] Gilowski,[612] who preached the word of God to Myszkowski at Spytkowice. This done, he set up another synod in opposition to that of Pińczów. He put this audacious plan into effect at the very capital of the Kingdom, taking advantage of the occasion of the funeral of Boner, which was solemnized there on *September 16*.[613] For this illustrious man, carried away by sudden death, was hastily committed to the earth, as his wife was hurrying on to a second marriage.[614] So when Boner's grounds passed in to other hands, the church [in his garden outside Cracow] also had to be transferred to another place [**cf. BAnt no. 54.1**]. Yet he himself, disgusted by the quarrels of Sarnicki, had three days before his death already ordered the benches removed from the place in which the religious meetings used to be held [**cf. BAnt no. 23**]. But Stanislas Cikowski, a man of distinguished ancestry worthy of being called a truly great-hearted hero, granted the church a place in his own house, which he had in Szpitalna street, in the neighborhood of the cathedral church.[615]

[Sarnicki's schism at Cracow, 16 October 1562[616]]

In the meantime Sarnicki, having drawn some over to his party, held a synod at the time of these obsequies, to which many magnates and nobles had flocked, but also some ministers of Sarnicki's flock, agitated by his letters. So then the first *Antisynodus Sarniciana* was seen in the young Polish [Reformed] Church. In this he put forth his own confession,[617] and had it subscribed by some, as the presence of Turnus[618] always urges. Gregory was indeed in the city, but he was excluded by Sarnicki and his faction, nay rather was adjudged heretical and deprived of his ministry, and Sarnicki was put in his place [**cf. BAnt no. 54.2**]. The latter, scattering his confession from house to house, ventured to parcel out (*distrahere*) copies of it in Gregory's own congregation. So he drew some to his side. In this dissension he had as confederate the notorious Lawrence Discordia [**cf. BAnt no. 54.2**]—that there might be an omen of discord in his very name—a man by no means of upright character, and hence in the synod [at Włodzisław in 1560] judged unworthy of the ministry.[619] [Jacob] Sylvius[620] and Gilowski sided with him, with all their might opposing Gregory, while he meantime, patiently bearing wrongs, [144] diligent in his office, upright in life, and innocent of crimes, presided over the congregation lawfully committed to his charge.

Seeing this, the elders and other ministers grieved deeply that a schism was being caused by Sarnicki and that the Church was being divided. And so again they called a new synod at Pińczów for 4 November [1562].[621] To this the elders of the church at Cracow earnestly begged Sarnicki to go for the sake of settling the quarrel. He stubbornly refused, saying: "What good would it do for me to go there? That I might, forsooth, stand like a pupil in school before those masters?" Thus the inflexible ambition of Sarnicki brought about a schism. Gregory, however, did not cease to make his congregation stronger and stronger. Therefore, if one may compare small things with great, you might say that a new Diotrephes had raised his head and horns in the Church.[622]

Chapter Eight

Of the Progress of the Truth Illustrated in Lithuania from 1558, in the Palatinate of Cracow from 1559, Especially in the Articles on the Son of God, the Holy Spirit, and Baptism; Also of the Conference at Piotrków in 1562, and of Other Matters Worthy of Memory.[623]

The view of Peter of Goniądz [Gonesius][624] about the prerogatives of the Father, which he both strongly defended by word of mouth and recommended by a striking example of piety, had, as we see, made no slight progress [despite his excommunication as an ''Arian'' in the synod of Pińczów 1556].

[The synod of the Lithuanian Brethren of Brest-Litovsk: December 1558]

After Peter of Goniądz came to the synod convened at Brest Lithuania on 15 December 1558, he there openly professed this view of his about God the Father in the same place, and also brought forth a *libellus* against infant baptism [**cf. BAnt nos. 3, 7, 53**], in which he held that this rite is not consistent either with Holy Scripture or with the first age of the Church, or with sound reason. When it was read in public, it gave offense. Almost all spoke in opposition to it. Jerome Piekarski[625] alone defended the view of Peter of Goniądz, and when silence was imposed upon him on pain of excommunication, he is said to have spoken as follows.[626]

[The speech of Piekarski in defense of Gonesius, Brest, 1558]

No one who has eyes to see fails to see in what profound sleep mortals were buried through diverse wiles of Satan, when the Christian world was covered by the thick darkness of error. [145] Even while the holy apostles of the Lord were still alive, the sworn enemy of human kind, who deserves to be called Satan because he is the adversary of God and man, attempted to assail the stronghold of our salvation, namely, the true birth from Mary of Jesus Christ, the Son of God and the son of man. But though his attempt was in vain, after their death he attacked the stronghold and tried to overthrow it. For unless the Son of God was really born and really suffered, what hope of salvation henceforth remains to us whom, enslaved to Satan, he redeemed by the precious price of his blood? It is no secret to anyone even moderately acquainted with history, in what quarrels about their profesion of Christ (whose teaching breathed concord more than anything) the irreconcilable enemy both in the Church and in public life thenceforth engaged the new people of Christ (*novellus populus Christi*) who had lately professed Christ's name, as he even yet engages them, attacking not only the truth, but also harmony and therefore all the piety of Christianity.

You know the wars of Constantine the Great and Licinius,[627] the mutual persecution of the Homoousians and the Arians,[628] unquestioned instances of both piety and corrupted truth. From this, it has gone on through the wiles of the same most crafty foe, to other points of faith which in their turn also will be discussed by armed and gory men, thirsting too much for blood. Thus indeed, as the old maxim has it, ''In heated argument we are likely to lose sight of the truth.''[629]

St. Hilary, bishop of Poitiers, a writer of the fourth century,[630] deploring not only the quarrels of the Arians but also those of his own party about words (meaning *ousia*, *homoousios*, *homoiousios*, and *homoios*), questions about innovations, quarrels about ambiguous expression and authorities, in a word deploring partisan zeal, did not hesitate as though the cause were lost, to break out in these words: ''When one begins to be anathema to another, hardly any one is Christ's any longer.'' Nay, he adds: ''It finally came to such a point that nothing remained holy and inviolable with us or with anyone before us."[631] And much more of the sort.

How from then[632] on the power and arrogance of the Roman Pontiff increased, and how many corruptions it introduced into the Church, you all know. It would be too long and tedious to follow them one by one. The mass alone—how many gesticulations, partly ridiculous and partly shameful, and idolatrous superstitions [146] did it add, after transubstantiation (a barbarous word, unknown to Scripture, nature, philosophy, the ancient Church)—had at the beginning of the thirteenth century been received into the number of the heads of faith, along with auricular confession.[633] Yet all these dogmas, though recent and directly contrary to the primitive simplicity, the Pope of Rome defends by his supreme and anti-Christian tyranny, and enjoins on the minds of men. No wonder that anti-Christian cruelty shows itself where—in the judgment of St. Gregory himself—anti-Christian pride appeared, when bishop John of Constantinople began to be called "Ecumenical Pope."[634] This anti-Christian title Bishop Boniface III of Rome obtained a little later from Phocas, a cruel parricide notorious for all his crimes.[635] And [Boniface] handed it down, to be furnished with all arrogance and cruelty, to his successors, who—as Bernard of Clairvaux[636] and others of their household bear witness—were thus like himself successors of Romulus and Constantine rather than of the Apostle Peter.

Who therefore would not wish to be as far as possible away from the time when the sad night of errors and vices enveloped everything? My brethren, we must withdraw far from those who like to snore deeply in their more than Cimmerian, nay Tatarian, darkness.[637] The resounding trumpet of the word of God has aroused us from our profound sleep. We must straightway awake, and such thick darkness must be driven far away by the light of truth.

But God forbid that once it has been put to flight from this closet or that, we should be willing to be plunged into it elsewhere.

Yet his happens, brethren, so long as we reject a part of the errors of the Papists, but retain another. It must be said that it is a case where we are dealing with a very grave matter, in which one is far less at liberty than in war to make the same mistake twice. You have heard what relics of papacy we are retaining in the matter of the Trinity and infant baptism, as Peter of Goniądz has pointed out to you. Indeed, the fact is certain that not only the Apostolic Age but also the early age of more than three centuries[638] following knew nothing of a Triune God, while all were professing the Catholic faith in one God the Father of our Lord Jesus Christ. But there were also more things of the same sort of which it knew nothing: the dogmas about the Son consubstantial (*homoousios*) with the Father, about the two natures in Christ, about the hypostatic (*personalis*) union [of these two natures], about the communication of idioms [the interchange of the two natures of Christ], about the operations of the Trinity within and without, and countless others.[639]

[147] Now, what shall I say of infant baptism? The water, of course, adheres to its [true] defenders when one comes to the command of Holy Scripture, or the mode of the thing, or the testimony of antiquity. Certainly the Fathers of the second century, Justin, Irenaeus, and others, deny the

baptism of infants. In the age of Tertullian, in Africa, which was said to be always bringing forth something new, the beginnings of this childish error experienced much opposition, even from Tertullian himself.[640] Nor do we read that any need of baptizing infants was imposed before the Council of Milevis, held also in Africa, in 418.[641] And it is known for certain that it was decreed in order that the holy eucharist might be administered to infants. This lamentable superstition, notwithstanding that the eucharist for infants was abolished by a decree of the Council of Trent in the West,[642] still holds the West in one hand, the East in the other.[643] For it is known that of old only catechumens were baptized in the Church, after having first confessed the Apostles' Creed, and this by the true method of baptism which is done by immersion. But those who are acquainted with the early ages know that also in the fourth, nay even in the fifth century, before the tyranny of the Bishop of Rome was established, children born to believing parents, even to bishops or educated by them, were baptized in adult life. Indeed, some came to the episcopate (witness just for instance St. Ambrose)[644] before they came to baptism, to say nothing of baptism having been put off by many to the last hour of life.

Why then, brethren, do you rise against me for these relics of popery which deservedly ought to be rejected? Why do you by such severe commands, armed by the thunder of an anathema, impose silence upon me, where most of all there is need of speech? Is this the liberty, charity, tolerance, worthy of the people of Christ? Shall I keep silence, when knowledge of the pure truth has imposed upon me the duty of speaking? [**cf. BAnt nos. 3, 7**]. Nay, but I earnestly urge and beseech you: reject all those things that have crept into the Church from the papacy, and cleanse the house of God from such dregs and filth. And it is my sincere prayer indeed that God the Father of our Lord Jesus Christ may fill you with his Holy Spirit, may instruct, guide, and strengthen you.

These points [of Jerome Piekarski in support of Peter of Goniądz] powerfully impressed the minds of all there present, and although they aroused ill-will in many, they yet stirred not a few [148] to diligence. And certainly many in those regions from now on openly spoke against the errors concerning the Trinity and infant baptism, as we shall see later.

But at the synod, assembled [in Pińczów] on 25 April 1559,[645] Łaski and Sarnicki being present, it was resolved that an examination of the ministers be ordered as to what opinion they held about God, and what about the unity of the Trinity and of the Persons in the Trinity.

[Peter Statorius[646] questions the invocation of the Holy
Spirit, the enunciation of Ditheism 1559–61]

Nevertheless, by the ancient nature of truth, it kept increasing among hindrances, and like a palm tree, the more it was repressed the more it flourished [**cf. BAnt no. 3.1**].[647] For on November 22 of the same year [1559], at the twelfth synod of Pińczów, there was a long and wordy dispute with Stancaro, with almost no result, since those who had not yet gotten free from the bonds of error concerning the Trinity were in no way able to convince Stancaro.[648] But there was brought thither a letter of [lord] Remigian Chełmski, a man of distinguished family, although in this instance he had not signed his name [**cf. BAnt nos. 3.1, 9**].[649] In it he called in question the invocation of the Holy Spirit, since the manner of praying implies nothing else than that all things, including the gifts of the Holy Spirit, are to be asked of God the Father through the Son as Mediator.[650] Not without, reason, I infer that this scruple was raised in Chełmski's conscience by Peter Statorius of Thionville.

The latter was a Frenchman by nationality, who had followed Lismanino from Geneva to Poland, and brought thither the books of Servetus. Having been advanced to the rectorship of the famous school at Pińczów succeeding *Gregory Orszak*,[651] he was on intimate terms with Chełmski.

Chełmski's letter, as was natural, stirred the minds of not a few. The reply[652] that was sent to Chełmski from the synod at Pińczów did not satisfy him, as Statorius reported at the nineteenth synod held at Pińczów on 30 January 1562 *(from a manuscript of John Stoiński, who was grandson of this Statorius)*:[653]

> He [Peter Statorius] was therefore directed to make a reply, as prompted by God. Statorius replied [30 January 1561], but in such a way that the meaning he had in mind on this subject was not apparent [**cf. BAnt no. 4**]. He only said that Biandrata had been spoken of by Calvin ''as one who was carrying the virus of Servetus's impiety.''[654] Meanwhile, he says that the view that he had put forth at the synod was well-received by all, though he was nevertheless asked whether he asserted a plurality of Gods when saying that the Father is alone unbegotten and believes the Son begotten. ''In fact, all of us [149]—the words are those of Statorius himself—that are living with Biandrata come, I know not how, under suspicion of heresy. But if they are heretics who believe in Father, Son, and Holy Spirit after the precept of Holy Scriptures, I willingly confess myself one of their number. The ill-will that the evil Demon had contrived for me on the issue of the Holy Spirit had not yet come, but I am at peace with my good conscience.''[655]

Budziński, chap. 30, adds the note that[656] *Statorius had not only spoken to Chełmski in the bonds of intimate friendship about not invoking the Holy Spirit, but he had also taught in the school at Pińczów that it was something idolatrous to invoke the Holy Spirit, since in all Scripture no trace appears of his deity, or of adoring, or invoking, or even believing in him* (eum). *Although this matter set some people wondering, yet it did not arouse such great disturbances as the teaching of the dogma of the Trinity.*

[? The speech of Statorius among the ministers]

And so a colloquy on this subject was arranged between some of the ministers and Statorius. But he, both with the learning and with the eloquence for which *he was distinguished, powerfully argued with them all from the Scriptures, pointing out that the Holy Spirit is not a third person of the Deity nor God, but a power (*virtutem*) and gift of God which God rouses in the hearts of the faithful, and gives a measure of to each of them even as he will. But to the Son he did not give it by measure, but anointed him with it above his fellows,*[657] *and of this fulness of the Son which God wished to dwell in him, each of the faithful has received some portion. Indeed this very thing is a proof that the Holy Spirit is not God the Creator of heaven and earth, since God cannot be measured, given, or divided into parts.*

And assuredly, as there is nothing that can more clearly disprove the dogma of the Trinity than the teaching about the Holy Spirit, whether you consult Holy Scripture or the early Church, so also many soon surrendered to the truth and contended for this truth more strongly than Statorius himself. Indeed, they argued that faith and saving knowledge, as Christ himself teaches, are directed to God and to Christ, no mention being made of the Holy Spirit*; so also that the Son ascended to his God and his Father,[658] *but not to the Holy Spirit. They argued that the Spirit is to be asked of God and to be proved [cf. 1 John 4.1]. Moreover, as to the third part of the Creed that is called the Apostles' Creed, [150] in which we profess that we also believe in the Holy Spirit, this in no wise proves that the Spirit is to be invoked.*

[Statorius continues now in direct discourse]

Indeed, the Most High God is believed in one way, his Son in another, his Holy Spirit in another again, as are also the Holy Catholic Church and the communion of the saints. And these things seem indeed to have been inserted in the Creed from the words of Paul: "I hear of thy love, and of the faith which thou hast toward the Lord Jesus and toward all the saints" (Philemon 5). Yet the case itself teaches clearly that faith is directed to the Lord in one way, to the saints in another. So in Exodus 14:31 it reads: "The people believed in God and in Moses his servant." For history itself teaches that the Israelites believed in God in one way and in Moses in another, just as God is different from all angels, men, and things. For to believe in God is "to believe that he is and that he is a rewarder of them that seek him,"[659] *to believe in his promises, revelations, and commands given through angels, prophets, and finally through Christ his Son, and to be obedient to his commands in hope of his promises. To believe in Jesus Christ is to believe that Jesus of Nazareth, conceived of the Holy Spirit, born of a virgin, is the one promised to the Fathers, the Messiah foretold by the prophets, the ambassador of God, the most perfect Teacher of the truth of the gospel, the Saviour of the world, the heavenly King that to him as giver of the*

---

*John 14:1; 17:3; compare 20:31 and 20:17.

commandments of God obedience must be rendered; that he will hereafter be sent by God to judge the quick and the dead. Again, to believe in the Holy Spirit is to believe that there is a Holy Spirit. This the disciples at Ephesus are said in Holy Scripture not to have known,[660] and yet they are called disciples, of course, because they believed not only in one God together with the Jews but also in Jesus Christ, together with John the Baptist and other believers. It is the Spirit, the breath, a power, a gift of God that is being poured out and communicated to the faithful, and is being divided into parts and is being asked for from God through Christ.

Finally, to believe in the Holy Catholic Church is to believe that the company (coetus) of the faithful or of Christians ought to be holy in life, Catholic in faith, namely: that which from the beginning has always and everywhere been received and understood by all[661] such as it has here been handed down.

But it is evident to everyone that there are different degrees of this faith: [151] namely, to believe in God as God and author of all; in Christ as Christ, the anointed, the Son of God; in the Holy Spirit as the Spirit of God, the breath, power, gift of God; in the saints as the saints of God; finally in the Church as the Church of God. And so the saints in the Church believe and confess, moved by the Holy Spirit, that "there is one God the Father, of whom are all things, and we unto him; and one Lord Jesus Christ, through whom are all things and we through him, although there be many that are called Gods, whether in heaven or on earth, as there are Gods many and Lords many."[662] But of the Holy Spirit in particular, according to the Scripture composed by its inspiration, [the same believe] that it was sent by the Father as another comforter and teacher in the place of Christ;[663] that the disciples received it when Christ breathed on them;[664] and that it also was given them by Christ who had received it from the Father,[665] and hence it is also called the Spirit of Jesus;[666] that it alone knows the things that are God's[667] since it is in God (not as a person distinct from him, but as his Spirit, his power);[668] that it arouses us to all good deeds and makes us able to perform them;[669] that it intercedes for us, that is, by moving us to prayer;[670] that the sin and most serious blasphemy against it, namely that its works are maliciously ascribed to an unclean spirit, is forgiven neither in this world nor in that to come;[671] that the Jews in their stubbornness fell into this sin;[672] that Ananias, wishing by a lie to deceive the apostles (who were endowed with the Holy Spirit), as devoid of it;[673] that every such man as is not furnished with this heavenly gift is in his deeds more foul than a brute;[674] that the Apostles, before Christ was glorified, did not have it when they wished to call down fire from heaven to avenge the offense of their having been denied hospitality,[675] or when they deserted Christ or even denied him as passionately as they afterwards boldly announced the name of the Lord Jesus before kings, judges of the earth, and magistrates, and declared the great works of God in the face of the hatred of the whole word;[676] that those who sing Veni Creator Spiritus[677] *lack it and do not even know it; that none of the Apostles or other men filled with the*

Holy Spirit prayed to it that it might come to them; that Cardinal Hugo in his Explicatio *on the Mass expressed the view about it that prayer is not directed to the Holy Spirit, since it is not God but a gift of God, hence prayer is not to be directed to the gift, but to him who bestows the gift.*[678]

It is related that these and many other things of the sort were then brought forward. [152]   But Statorius, as we shall see below, afterwards denied [? by his *confessio*] these things so finely and truly said.   That these religious controversies meantime aroused the ingenuity of many men in inquiring into the truth, the event (*eventus* [evidently the speech]) showed, as will likewise appear below [in Book III, chap. 3], when we see how sharply those of Kujawy, those of Brest, and other pious men dwelling in Lithuania opposed infant baptism.

[Sarnicki's divisive tactics, 1562]

While thus, as has been said, sharp controversies about the Son of God had arisen, and affairs were more and more being carried to a schism through the overbearing conduct of Sarnicki, it was Gregory, together with many who were desirous of harmony, who was endeavoring to provide a remedy for this dangerous disease and to supply it to the sick.[679]   Sarnicki with his friends, on the other hand, scorned all remedies for curing the disease, and was maneuvering so that when Gregory should be overthrown and crushed, he alone might survive.   He grasped a convenient opportunity for entering upon his holy tyranny at the Diet meeting at Piotrków in 1562.[680]   He drew aside ministers, who had come there in large numbers together with their patrons.   Then at last he managed everything after his heart's desire: he convened synods,[681] appointed a superintendent of the churches of Great Poland [**cf. BAnt nos. 6.2, 54.2**], [and] advanced to the ministry Discordia, that man of not very upright life, disregarding the resolution of the synod to which he himself had assented.[682]   However, an excuse for the schism was sought, and a conference was arranged there.[683]   The result of this was that besides John Niemojewski, the district judge of Inowrocław, Jerome Filipowski, John Kazanowski, and other nobles, also Stanislas Lutomirski (likewise of noble birth, but admitted to holy orders both under the papacy and in the Church of Christ), elder of the district of Pińczów, Martin Krowicki, Stanislas Paklepka, George Schomann, and others undertook along with Gregory to defend the better cause.[684]   And of Paklepka,[685] Otwinowski in his *Christian Heroes*[686] relates this as worthy of mention: that he was the first who laid bare the errors about the Trinity and infant baptism, and that this view of his was afterwards elucidated and confirmed by others.   However, he writes that Matthew Albin also, the minister at Iwanowice, although until his death he admittedly remained steadfast in his view about the Trinity, yet pointed out the error regarding infant baptism, and taught that no one ought to be baptized unless believing and repentant.[687]   But of baptism we shall treat more at length below.[688]

CHAPTER NINE

History[689] of the Prince Despot[690]
[Jacob Heraclides Basilicus][691]
of Walachia [Moldavia],[692]
Who Stayed in Poland[693]
and Embraced the Christian Truth,
Was Restored to His Ancestral Principate[694]
by [Albert] Łaski, Lasocki, and Filipowski,
but Was Assassinated by His Subjects.

Before we proceed further, we must here, faithfully as always, relate the history of Despot Jacob Heraclides Basilicus,[695] and that for many reasons. For he had both imbibed knowledge of the divine truth in Poland and promised to introduce it into Walachia, and also had been restored to his principate by Lasocki[696] and Filipowski[697] who are so often mentioned in our *Historia*, and more especially by Albert Łaski,[698] palatine of Sieradź. And on account of his name, the two former were accused by malicious men of treason to the King and the country (**cf. BAnt no. 55.1** and Bk. 3, at n. 454).[699]

Budziński, who had looked into these matters and knew as much about them as any one, relates (chap. 18) that *he came [to the Commonwealth] about 1556, before King Augustus made his campaign against Livonia.*[700] So this will have taken place before the first campaign, which was in 1557 against William Fürstenburg, master of the Swordbearers in Livonia.[701] The other campaign at all events, which was in 1559 against Grand Duke Ivan Basilides of Muscovy,[702] does not seem to fit this time. For the Despot first lived for some time in the palatinate of Cracow.[703] There, as has been said [above], he gained knowledge of the truth.[704] From here he proceeded to Vilna[705] with a letter from the Elector of Brandenburg in which he recommended him to the King.[706] There [in Cracovia] he formed an intimate friendship with Andrew Trzecieski,[707] John Łaski,[708] and others of the gentry, and even with the magnates.[709] Then also he offered his services to the King, having followed his camp into Livonia.[710] Thence he returned to Poland,[711] bearing a letter of recommendation to the emperor of the Turks.[712] At a somewhat later time he went to Ruthenia[713] and thence to Moldavia, where he stayed for some time and won the good will not only of Prince Alexander of Walachia[714] but also of the leading magnates. [154] He was asked to come inside a Greek [Orthodox] basilica (*templi*) by the magnates who bitterly hated Alexander's tyranny, and there he made with them a compact for seizing the reins of government after

Alexander's death, though he was unwilling to obtain power by murdering him.[715]

Alexander who, aware of his own tyranny, was wont to regard any popular and praiseworthy man as one who reproached him, appointed him to a spurious embassy to Prince Mircea of Moldavia.[716] Jacob was poisoned by the latter, through arrangement with Alexander; but at length having destroyed the effect of the poison by vomiting, he was restored to health.[717] He had various adventures in Hungary, and was at length called by leading magnates of Walachia to assume the principate.[718] Afterwards at Kamieniec in Podolia, through a plot of Alexander, an attempt was made on his life by an Armenian merchant. The latter, carelessly tasting the wrong decanter of wine, the one in which poison had been mixed, paid for the crime of treachery by [his own] sudden death.[719] From there Jacob escaped both the enmity of the King [of Poland], who had issued an edict against him[720] (as princes do who, burdened with anxious care for the security of their throne, are wont sometimes to load even the innocent with unjust suspicion), and the plots of Alexander in Polish territory by fleeing to [Upper] Hungary. He informed Stanislas Lasocki, chamberlain of Łęczyca, of all these things.[721] And Jacob, having been recommended through him [Lasocki] to John Łaski, and through him in turn to his brother's son, Albert Łaski,[722] who was residing in [Upper] Hungary,[723] was kindly treated by the latter.[724]

Furnished with counsel by Lasocki and Filipowski, he [the Despot] had proceeded to Albert Łaski in [Upper] Hungary. And he sent to the Emperor Ferdinand[725] for confirmation the document of the leading magnates of Walachia, calling him to the principate. He received it back by the hand of a Doctor [Sigismund] of Torda, confirmed by him [the Emperor] with an annual stipend granted him in Hungary.[726] Thereupon he brought Łaski around wholly to the plan of restoring[727] him to ["]his["] principate. After this he received news of the serious illness of the tyrant Alexander, and a new letter of invitation from the leading magnates.[728] So he began to muster his forces, and with these he moved towards Walachia.[729] Meanwhile Lasocki together with Filipowski had returned home from [Upper] Hungary,[730] having promised him their aid and service in all ways that were not contrary to God, the King, and their good reputation, and having also stipulated with him that, in order to avoid giving offense, he would not lead his army through the King's territory, especially in view of the state of affairs.[731]

But [155] when, having mustered an appropriate force [of their own], they reached Podolia[732] and learned that the Despot was leading his forces under the command of Łaski through the King's territory,[733] they naturally deplored this greatly, fearing lest they incur the King's displeasure, unfavorable suspicions, and accusations against not only themselves but also the Church,[734] as unfortunately often happens. They at once repaired to Nicholas Sieniawski,[735] palatine of Ruthenia and grand hetman of the Royal Commonwealth, and sought to clear their counsel from blame.[736] They said and declared openly that the

Despot had acted contrary to his given pledge, he at once sent word to the Despot demanding that he should remember his given pledge and turn back. He replied that he could not do so without great loss, and excused what he had done by other good reasons to be told them in person. These he stated the next day, when by leave of the palatine he met with them.[737] He accused of perfidy the leading noblemen of Ruthenia on whose word he was leading his army through the King's territory, and whom he now found opposed to his wishes.[738]

Seeing Lasocki and Filipowski overwhelmed with inmost pain,[739] he [the Despot] himself was also pained deeply. He considered going back, but decided that it was impossible. He therefore offered to give his services to the grand general of the Kingdom against the Tatars who had a little while before carried off a very great booty from the Kingdom,[740] or against the current Muscovite enemy, or else to the King in Livonia where the King already held several fortresses,[741] if only by their[742] influence he might be reconciled with Alexander, tyrant of Walachia, by repairing the damage.[743] Meanwhile, before the King's orders were brought,[744] Jacob requested provisions for his soldiers and offered to show his troops drawn up in battle array.[745] However, the general refused everything.[746] At this the Despot grew indignant and angry; and, if he had not had regard for Lasocki and Filipowski, his friends of the highest mark, he would have fought. And thus was the peril (*res*) overcome.[747] To this interpretation credence is given by a letter in the Despot's hand written to Lasocki[748] and preserved by the care of Budziński, a copy of which I rightly append:

Dearest Brother in Christ, highly esteemed Lord,

> *I have learned that there are some who are trying to slander your lordship and Filipowski, saying that you had brought me there with an army, as if wishing in the end to ruin the country. I beg you by the Son of God, pay no attention to this. For the same thing is befalling you as befell me through the agency of some Italian servants and one Frenchman, when I was being persecuted on account of the true use of the sacraments, while they were spreading the rumor that I had fallen away from the Christian faith and embraced [156] that of the Turkish. So now this is happening to your lordship. It was the Ruthenian nobles who called me.[749] But after that, having accepted bribes, they would, contrary to the ancient faith and virtue of the Poles, have betrayed me to the tyrant hateful to all Christendom.[750] For I have a letter from those who called me, while your lordship knew nothing of this matter.[751] And if I had not had regard for you and for your entreaties, I should not have withdrawn. On account of your loyalty, faith, singular virtue, and integrity (which are gifts of God), I have regarded your entreaties as equivalent to a command, and have withdrawn to my great loss.[752] For I preferred to suffer hurt and to expose myself to danger rather than go against your wish (who are holy men by the grace of God through Christ) anything that might offend your most serene King and all the distinguished nobles. Those faith-breakers [the Ruthenian lords] therefore can thank you, after God, because it is certain that I should have given them battle, and I doubt not that God would have punished them for their broken*

faith. I have not withdrawn from fear, and what manner of man I am by the
grace of God, many know who bore witness to me before their sacred
majesties Charles and Ferdinand.

Both your most illustrious King and the whole Royal Commonwealth can
now acknowledge your loyalty and uprightness. For what those wicked
faith-breakers could by no means have accomplished by their own power,
you have done by your entreaties through Jesus Christ. Nor is what they
say true, that your lordships were traitors, since you always said to me pub-
licly that you were ready to oblige me in word and deed in everything not
against God and your most serene King. This is the truth. They therefore
do wrong to you, good men, you who are anxious that everything be for the
upbuilding of the Church of the living God.[753] *This witness I wished for the*
present to bear against your slanderers, to relieve my own conscience.

The Despot, in his own hand.

And having dispatched this letter on account of the loyalty and friendship
established with Lasocki and Filipowski, he at once sent a copy dated at Kassa,
8 February 1561, under his own seal and that of Łaski.[754]

All these things seem to me clearly to indicate that the deeds of the Despot
ought to be assigned to 1557 and not 1559.[755] They also show that malicious
men[756] did great wrong to Lasocki and Filipowski in the preface to the *Collo-*
quium [157] *at Piotrków held in 1565*,[757] when they blabbered that if the Despot
were alive, they could be convicted of treason to their fatherland.

On November 18 of the same year [1561], Albert Łaski, having defeated and
routed the forces of Alexander in a memorable battle,[758] placed the Despot on
the throne of the principality.[759] That he was grateful to Łaski,[760] Abraham
Bakschay,[761] then Łaski's secretary, bears witness. So also does Budziński,
[saying] that *he did not keep the promise given Lasocki and Filipowski about*
reforming the churches of Walachia. Both [report] that the Despot was mur-
dered by his subjects, a treacherous and fickle people if ever there was one.[762]
The former [Bakschay] adds a note that this took place 5 November 1567.[763]

BOOK THREE

In Which an Account Is Given
of the Progress of the Truth, and then,
when the Division between
the Major or Calvinist
and the Minor or Catholic
Christian Church Had Been Made Permanent
at the Diet of Piotrków in 1565,
of the Organization and
Progress of Both Churches
down to the Destruction of Both,
which Took Place at Cracow in 1591,
and of the Change in Affairs that Began
from that Time On.

CHAPTER ONE

In Which Are Described the Progress of the Truth, the Efforts of Sarnicki and Discordia for the Sake of Discord, in Opposition to Those of Lutomirski and Gregory and Others for the Sake of Concord.

How the seed of the truth was brought over from Italy to Moravia we have told in the preceding book [Book I, chap. 1]. Among the pious Italians who had gone into exile were Dario[1] and Alciati.[2] The latter, having got from the former *Theses de Deo trino et uno*,[3] some twenty, gave them to his friend and fellow-countryman Prosper Provana,[4] who had bought, subject to mortgage, the estate of [Stanislas] Szafraniec at Rogów,[5] where we have said that a synod was held in 1562[6] [**cf. BAnt no. 6.2**].

Once, after reading these, he had left them on this table, Stanislas Budziński, the renowned historian of the Church, whose lead we are here following in many particulars, being Provana's chamberlain (*familiaris*) and the steward of his estate, *happened upon them, and having read them through, handed them over for reading to John Pustelnik,[7] minister of the word at that place. The latter soon made a copy of them for Stanislas Lutomirski, elder of the Pińczów district, who a little later became superintendent. Meanwhile Budziński forgot what he had done. Provana looked for the* Theses *and, not finding them, was upset. When he learned what Budziński had done,* [159] *he was displeased and grew angry. Lutomirski and Pustelnik shared the* Theses *with others, and thus began great controversies about the Trinity.*

Meantime Gregory Paul, as we have said, was at Cracow teaching the preeminence of the Father. Sarnicki, maddened by the gadfly of ambition, attacked Gregory, first in hidden ways and soon by open means, indicted at home and among the Swiss. He begged and pressed patrons to turn out ministers who favored Gregory's view, and to supplant them with others recommended by himself. Thus he disturbed the state of the Church more and more by his rash counsel. But to return to the history subsequent to the colloquium held at Piotrków in 1562.[8]

[The death of Felix Cruciger, 1563][9]

Felix Cruciger, superintendent of the Churches, having celebrated Easter, 1563, departed this life[10] when about to take leave of Secemin.[11] He blamed his hearers for neglecting their duty and for an ungrateful spirit. But also some quarrel had arisen between the wife of his patron, Stanislas Szafraniec, a woman of ungovernable temper, and his own wife, who was troubling him by her habits.[12] We see indeed that unsuitable marriages not infrequently fall to the lot even of pious men of probity in charge of divine worship. And so Cruciger, on the solemn day itself of Easter, before a great audience of hearers, said farewell to his patron, his wife, the villagers, and others who lived on their estate, and also to hearers and others from their neighborhood who had gathered there in large numbers. He thanked them for all the kindness they had shown him. He said that the cause of his leaving was not lack of food or other things, but their ungrateful spirit. He affirmed the truth of his teachings. By his swansong he drew tears and sobs from all, beginning with the patron. And thus ended his sermon. This done, he at once went home, lay down to rest, and bade his wife give him some food to refresh him. Soon he lost the power of speech and his life, that is, this poor one, and was transported to the happy one beyond.[13]

These things smote the hearts of all, especially his patron, who soon had the funeral for the saintly man fittingly performed. He himself presiding over it, thus addressed his dependents and serfs:

*There is none of you, countrymen (*cives*), who as he sees what has happened to this saintly man and to us all, does not reflect upon the circumstances of what has happened, and is not profoundly moved by it. All the churches have lost a saintly man, worthy to be compared to a prophet; [160] but ours of Little Poland, a faithful, watchful superintendent. Our Church has lost a pious, learned, wise, most excellent pastor. We have all lost a brother, a friend, a helper worthy of a very long life. Why should we wonder, indeed, that he, being subject equally with us to the laws of mortality, has been taken away from us by the power of death? We know both from Holy Writ and from daily and continual experience that all things human and men themselves are forever moving towards sunset and their end, nor is there anything in this vale of of tears so constant as inconstancy itself.*

But yet for this reason why not wonder that so great a man has suddenly been snatched away from us? Why not grieve? A thing surely unusual and almost unheard of has happened before our eyes. It is therefore right that this, being worthy of carefully examination, should admonish us all of our duty.

You yourselves heard the saintly man say to our face that he had prepared to leave us on account of the ungrateful spirit that he noticed in us. So why not grieve that so great and good a man has been taken from us, and that by our own fault? It ought to be said candidly and openly, though not without deserved shame and proper grief, that the fact is that you did not come together to hear the word of God often enough nor attentively enough. The care of your property and the love of riches have indeed made many of you neglectful of duty and irreverent worshipers of God. But at least in my opinion, to be in the church only in body, while one's mind is flitting about the fields, the gardens, the forests, the world, is no better than not to come to church at all. I should say that the latter stray from the entrance, the former from the way.

Nay, I should rather say that these [the idle attendants] are the more to be blamed, since they despise and refuse the gifts being offered to them. "O citizens, citizens," said someone, "money is first to be sought, but virtue after coins."[14] *But Christ, the Son of God, the very truth, I say, said far otherwise: "Seek ye first the kingdom of God and his righteousness, and all these things shall be added unto you."*[15]

And so in the exercise of a landlord's but also of a Christian's duty, I charge and exhort you that you diligently and seriously weigh what God has done in this place; that you acknowledge with grief that God, provoked by your fault, has bereft us of this saintly man, the guardian of our salvation, life, fortunes, peace, welfare, who day and night used to lift up pure hands to heaven for us all; [161] and that henceforth you be more diligent in your duty. For now at length you yourselves will see to it that we too perceive what is for our good, which, when we did have it, we lost.[16]

Thereupon the obsequies for this pious man were performed, and his memory is full of grace to all pious men. Then Sarnicki, as though a way were open for further carrying out his plans, set to work with Discordia and others of his crowd to contrive a synod. Soon he ordered it at Cracow for 14 May [1563],[17] drew some patrons to his part, and more and more followed up the schism for which he had been working.

[Stanislas Lutomirski attempts to forestall Sarnicki:
Two spirited letters of May 1563]

But Stanislas Lutomirski by reason of his official position[18] called together twenty-two ministers to quench the fire of a general schism.[19] He also invited the more distant patrons and ministers living in Lithuania and Podlasie to share in the task, and addressed a letter to them. A copy of this,[20] which the diligence of Budziński has preserved for us, I here add in Latin translation:

Illustrious, magnificent, notable, noble, honored, kind Masters and Brethren in the Son of God,

*This eagerness which you manifest in observing and maintaining, nay in promoting the glory of the living God, and of his eternal, only-begotten Son, equal and like (*similis*) unto him, as also of the Holy Spirit,*[21] *we heartily esteem, and in fraternal love we embrace and heartily greet you. That the*

Lord may stir this up in you and increase it more and more, we all with one mind and voice say Amen, Amen.

Not only are men of high repute unwilling to regard as a synod that gathering of certain persons which is being held at Cracow in these days,[22] but also brother Paul Gilowski himself,[23] with other brethren, has affirmed the same.[24] Even[25] the notice (decision)[26] ordering this synod openly says that the case is otherwise, although for all that, many Christian men who are charged with the care of the affairs of the Church were not invited by it to this synod.[27] [Indeed] we have no knowledge of synods at Piotrków and Cracow which, as we have learned, were held towards the end of the year now past.[28] [162] Nor indeed was there any one who, after the last synod held by us at Pińczów, 4 November 1562,[29] requested that another synod be called.

Now, however, we do beseech you, for the love of God, to take diligent care that a synod be called of all ministers in charge of Reformed Churches in both Little and Great Poland, in Lithuania, and in Ruthenia, and appoint for them the time and place of meeting, with the consent of the elders of the Church of the Son of God, if perchance any of them should gather there.[30] (Indeed we count on their due diligence in this respect.)[31] For such a synod must needs be called to preserve order in the Church of God, to admonish all of their duty, and to draw up synodal acts (canons).[32] We bid you likewise, since God of his infinite grace is calling many into his Church and is increasing the number of his people, that you consider a way by which business may be transacted in better order than hitherto.

But meantime we beseech you in the name of the living God that with genuine, steadfast, Christian judgment, according to the word of God you examine these lamentable, unnecessary, and most mischievous disorders— which, with God's good help, we shall on our part see do not recur— "judging not according to appearance, but with righteous judgment."[33] This too is very necessary—you have indeed the counsel of Scripture regarding this: "Thou shalt not follow the crowd to do evil, nor agree to the judgment of the many, to depart from the truth. If God is, his word is truth and wheat. But men and their teachings that wander from the command of the word of the eternal God are as chaff."[34] In Ezekiel 20:18f. we read: "Wait not in the precepts of your fathers, nor keep their judgments, nor pollute yourselves with their idols. I am the Lord your God; walk in my precepts, and keep my judgments, and do them."

We beg you therefore again and again, by the living God our eternal Father, and his only-begotten Son, and the Holy Spirit, be mindful that we shall all appear before the judgment-seat of God, and restrain the stubborn minds of men who obstinately hold to their own opinions, but do not show regard and obedience to the word of God,[35] as they should. [163] Do not place confidence in one party (parti*) while ignoring and refusing to hear the other. We are all but men.*

We indeed much regret that the gentlemen (viri Generosi*) and noblemen (* nobiles*) who last Friday[36] met at the house of the noble lord [Joachim] Lubomirski[37]—although we had requested them to do this urgently (* sollicite)—would not appoint four of their number who should hear and* *judge of the conferences that we have had with our brother ministers.*[38] *For you would have perceived the whole matter with little trouble and would have seen how unfairly our brethren are acting, as God will soon very clearly show you. But for the present we beg you not to give credence to anyone's evil tales about brother Gregory, minister of the congregation at Cracow, lawfully sent hither by the Church of God, nor hold him under suspicion.*[39] *For to this very day we cannot discover anything ill in his teaching or in him. At all events, by the grace of the merciful God, we have his word by which to form our judgment, and we are members of the Church of God. We add no more. When it shall please you, God helping us therein, we will give our testimony in very deed, not only in words. Meanwhile we commend ourselves to the good-will and Christian prayers of you all.*

Given at Cracow, 17 May A.D. 1563:[40]

> *Stanislas Lutomirski, Elder of the Pińczów district; Gregory Paul, Elder of the Cracow district; George of Cracow, Minister at Zielenice;*[41] *Albert Episcopius, Minister of Christ;*[42] *Stanislas Krystyński, Minister of Jesus Christ at Włodzisław;*[43] *Stanislas Wiśniowski, Minister of the congregation at Wieliczka;*[44] *John of Chęciny, Minister at Rogów;*[45] *Melchior Palipowski, Minister of the word of God at Łoniów;*[46] *Tiburtius Boryszowski, Minister at Siekluka;*[47] *Christopher Milvius, Minister of Christ at Góry;*[48] *Martin Castronius, Minister of Jesus Christ at Sobolów;*[49] *Peter Fedrych, Minister of the flock of Christ at Szczekociny;*[50] *John Siekierzyński, Minister of the Word of God in the congregation at Bobin;*[51] *[164] Jacob Sigismund [Megalius], Minister of the gospel at Pińczów;*[52] *Bartholomew Łuczycki, Minister of the Word of God at Dziekanowice;*[53] *Jacob, Minister at Wielogłowy;*[54] *George Schomann, Minister of the Word of God at Książ; Stanislas Farnowski,*[55] *Minister at Tarnowa; Martin of Kalisz;*[56] *George Niger, Minister of Christ in the congregation at Jedlińsko;*[57] *Stanislas Moicius, Minister of Christ at Kuczków;*[58] *Albert Dzieszowski, Minister of Christ at Kuropatniki;*[59] *Victor Marek, Minister of the Word of God at Chomranice.*[60]

> *To the Magnificent and Noble Lords and Brethren gathered in Cracow,*

> *Stanislas Lutomirski*

What this letter means, written by so many ministers of the word of God, and how it strikes at Sarnicki, no one can fail to see.

But soon another letter of the same Lutomirski, written [from Cracow, 20 May 1563] to the brethren at Vilna,[61] strikes far more clearly at this champion of discord and companion of Discordia. I here give it as I found it in Latin, among Budziński's papers:[62]

> *Honored men, distinguished for true piety and for your guardianship of the heavenly doctrine,*

> *Grace, mercy, peace, and health from God the Father,*[63] *from (ex) whom and by (a) whom are all things,*[64] *through Jesus Christ, through (per)*

whom[65] *are all things and we through him, Saviour and intercessor (*inter-
pellatorem*) of his Elect,*[66] *consubstantial Son, coeternal, and coequal with
him; in the Holy Spirit, coessential and likewise coeternal and coequal with
both, animating all things,*[67] *in whom we cry Abba, Father.*[68]

*In the name of Jacob Sylvius, Sarnicki, and Discordia a pseudo-synod
was called at Cracow for May 14,*[69] *in disregard of the order usual in the
Church of God, in scorn and contempt of the elders of both orders
(*ordines*)*[70] *and without their knowledge and advice, in disdain and to the
ruin of the discipline of the Church. The minutes of this synod were published, full of lies, which they, taking advantage of the kindness of certain
leading men who were evidently not familiar with the affairs of the Church,
[165] caused to be signed by illustrious men: the castellan of Cracow,*[71] *the
palatine of Lublin,*[72] *the castellan of Zawichost,*[73] *the captain of Marienburg,*[74] *Joachim Lubomirski,*[75] *Jost Ludwik Decjusz,*[76] *and four burghers of
Cracow, among whom are reckoned even some who follow the Papist (*pap-
isticam*) impiety.*[77] *To this pseudo-synod we neighboring ministers were not
invited. Indeed pains were taken that the design should by no means come
to our knowledge, for their intention was to condemn us together with sound
doctrine, and to remove the minister of Cracow*[78] *from his position, and
unfairly to substitute in his place Discordia, who is notorious for his
deeds.*[79]

*In order therefore that the Church of God may suffer no harm from the
ambition, evil counsels, and actions of these brethren, twenty-three of us
ministers hastened to Cracow, where I am writing you a brief account of
what has been done out of the brotherly love that I bear you, so that you
may know the truth, lest perchance, according to present habits, these good
brethren make false charges, as they are wont.*

*We spent three whole days, making generous concessions to their
obstinacy, etc. While they, having adjourned the synod, contrary to the
tenor of the acts published by them (which they issued so carefully composed that none heretofore were ever so exquisitely written), referred the
whole action of the synod to the leading noblemen who had not yet met,
refusing conference with us. But that the brethren may know what has here
been done, I am sending you here a brief record of all that we did by way of
protest, as well as of the reply made by us to the brethren who are now
unjustly hostile to us.*

These ministers,[80] *brethren swollen by ambition, took pains to have me
in their party,*[81] *and to achieve this used a craftiness unworthy of their ministry. But by the grace of God, their wishes were not realized as they had
hoped; indeed, this pseudo-synod, assembled by them with such care, dissolved into thin air. Nothing was done in it. For fearing for their cause, and
lest their tricks be brought out into the light by us, they secretly persuaded
the castellan of Cracow*[82] *and the palatine of Lublin*[83] *not to commence
synodical proceedings, etc., but to call a similar meeting in general for St.
Stanislas Day,*[84] *[166] and to set Discordia over the Cracow church. But it
was not right to treat with us in the absence of the captain of Marienburg
[and] castellan of Sandomierz,*[85] *and many others, etc. You judge, brethren,
whether such things are becoming in ministers.*

For their sake, we met at Cracow on the 13th of this month. Despite them we continue steadfast, lest in our absence they throw the blame on us. Pray for them and for us, and attend the coming synod, so that led by Emmanuel we may by unanimous consent, as we ought, put out the fire that imperils the Church of God and may gather in the brethren who are break- ing away from us.[86] For some are following the vapors[87] of the human brain, and not the commandment of the eternal word. And by their efforts and persuasion, Calvin, a man in other respects great, has been led, cer- tainly unjustly, to reproach our Gregory and the ministers of our churches.[88] Simler of Zurich has acted more modestly, for in his booklet, in which he replies to the abusive one of Stancaro, he writes: "For we have not, as some suppose, intended a quarrel about words, but about the things themselves; and if we agree about these, we do not allow the terms essentia *or* persona, *or others of the sort which the ancients used, to stand in the way of our harmony."[89]*

See to it then, brethren, that the coming synod at the end of September be well attended, by whomsoever it is finally called.[90] We will take care that the notice of it be not put off beyond the month of September. I wonder that we are never summoned by you. Certainly we shall count it no burden to labor in guarding and spreading the glory of God and of his only begotten, coeternal Son. May they be, whoever they are, at length, etc.

Given at Cracow, 20 May 1563,

Your lordships' brother and servant, Stanislas Lutomirski, minister of the word of God, secretary to the King, in his own hand. To reverend men, distinguished by their piety and heavenly teaching, Masters Nicho- las Wędrogowski of Vilna,[91] Thomas Falconus[92] and Martin Czechowic,[93] faithful ministers of the Church of Christ, greatly respected lords and brethren. To be shown to Paklepka[94] and Krowicki,[95] and to other pious brethren.

[167] From this any fair-minded person can now see that Sarnicki with his Discordia acted unjustly, not only with Gregory but also with the whole Church, which they miserably lacerated. And the brethren lamented deeply on this account, when they had learned this, from the letter of Lutomirski, whose honesty was then as little suspected as his influence was great, and from else- where. All of these, even if not favoring Gregory's views, were yet desirous of harmony.[96]

[The Brethren in Lithuania move against Sarnicki, 1563]

The patrons and ministers living in Lithuania were also indignant. And not to be found wanting in diligence, they gave attention to calling a synod as an effective and lawful means for quenching the fire of discord kindled by Sarnicki and Discordia, discussed plans for this, and at length, by leave of the Most Illustri- ous Prince Nicholas Radziwiłł, palatine of Vilna, called it for June of the same year, 1563, at Mordy,[97] a town in Podlasie[98] that belonged to him. For this praiseworthy undertaking there was no lack of pious men, and they met to the number of forty-two, although at an unusual, that is, difficult time, in which agricultural workers are unusually busy.[99] At this synod many sharply attacked the common (*vulgare*) doctrine of the Trinity.[100] Others, taking account of circumstances, and having regard to the consciences of the weaker brethren, put off the decision of the matter until the weak (*imbecilles*) should be gradually formed in their minds about the pure truth, and voted accordingly. The synod wrote out its opinion as follows, in a letter to the aforesaid prince, the palatine of Vilna:

> Even though we have not been able altogether to reject the word Trinity on account of some weaker brethren (*infirmiores*), yet have we for the most part purified it from the current abuse, so that now, as a word of man and not of God, it has with many won less credit than hitherto.[101]

And thus this synod too found a fitting and convenient way (*rationem*) of preserving harmony, namely [in mutual] tolerance and instruction according to the express word of God. But these things were in vain as against the unrestrained ambition of Sarnicki and the unbridled Discordia, God permitting that one who had wantonly opposed the truth, should in fact and in name be branded with the odium of discord.[102] And in this matter who is there who would not regard the omen as noteworthy?

[168]CHAPTER TWO

In Which Are Described the Results of the Discord; Lismanino's Departure from Poland and his Death; the Persecution after the Edict of Parczów of 1564, and the Strife of the Roman Clergy against Erasmus Otwinowski; As Well as against a Jew of Lublin and Semion, a Member of the King's Court, for Profaning the Most Holy Sacrament, as They Call It;

Over and above Also an Account of the Italian Franco Di Franco and of the Pole John Tyszkowic, Martyrs of Christ.

As in this way the fire of discord stirred up by Sarnicki and Discordia was not only not quenched, but just as if a small quantity of water had been poured into it by the synod's enjoining tolerance or silence, it even burned more fiercely and daily spread more widely, according to the nature of reaction (as the explorers of Nature say),[103] this [trinitarian] matter brought great pain to pious hearts. Hence some urged concord, others recommended tolerance, both counseled peace, yet others appealed to the authority of the canons passed in the synods.[104] But when by God's permission, who thus punishes ungratefulness, and through Satan's effort, the temporal power took its stand with Sarnicki and Discordia, no remedies availed to maintain the ecclesiastical commonwealth (*Respublica Ecclesiastica*).[105]

[Lismanino's efforts to heal the schism, 1563]

Yet Lismanino renewed his efforts to restore harmony and establish order, and sought suitable means for attaining this end. At last he proposed the authority of the four Doctors of the Church in the fourth century, Ambrose, Jerome, Augustine, and Chrysostom, as a means purportedly fit to reconcile the dissenting parties. Hence he patched together a compilation from their writings. I have not happened to see his writing, although it was published.[106]

As the writings of these Doctors are at hand, however, their views as to the Trinity are known, or at all events can be learned with little trouble. Further, as we have said elsewhere,[107] in their writings not a few things are contained that either oppose the received doctrines of the day, or even openly favor the truth. We shall here mention only three instances: In Ambrose, *De Trinitate*, 2, the Son "was made God."[108] In Augustine, *De Trinitate*, 7, 1, "God was born;"[109] [169] [in his] *In Joannis Tractatus*, 105;[110] *De agone christiano*, 20; *In Psalmum*, 37;[111] and elsewhere, especially *Retractationes*, 1, 24, "the man Jesus Christ was Mediator of God and men."[112] In Jerome, "the man Christ in his humiliation was given a name that he did not have before."[113] In Chrysostom, "the Father, as head (*principium*), is called greater than the Son."[114] Therefore, as these and all the other Doctores agree, faith is very safely placed in the divine Scriptures.[115]

Lismanino desired among other things to prove, on the authority of these Doctors, that it is just as if "the three" that are said in Scripture [1 John 5:7] "to bear witness" are called "united or one entity (*unum sive unus*)."[116] And it is indeed true that if you regard the agreement and harmony of the testimony, it may be said that "the three witnesses are one (*unus*)," as Holy Scripture [Gal 3:28] says of the harmony among believers: "Ye are all one (*unum*) in Christ Jesus." Yet it is safer, especially when controversy about the Trinity is rife, to say with Scripture that "the three that bear witness in heaven are (adverbially) one (*unum*)," than that they are "one being (*unus*)."[117] For the three heavenly witnesses are especially enumerated by St. John [1 John 5:7], while according to the opinion of the Trinitarians,[118] it would have to be called "one witness," not "three witnesses," just as not three Gods but one God is acknowledged by them. Not to mention that this passage is not found in the oldest and best Greek texts, the originals of the New Testament, or in the Syriac, Arabic, Ethiopic, Armenian, Latin, Slavonic versions, and hence was unknown to any of the ancients, not even to Hilary himself who was almost contemporary with

Ambrose and Jerome.[119] Indeed it was omitted by Chrysostom himself, by Augustine, as well as by other Doctors, Greek as well as Latin, not to mention Luther, Pomeranus,[120] those of Zurich, and others in recent times, as it suffices here merely to suggest. But this plan and effort of Lismanino was futile. The preaching of the truth against the dogma of the Trinity and the animosity of the patrons of this party [of the Trinity] increased impetuously.

And this [development] was the more notable for the reason that the theologians of the Roman Church, following in the steps of Augustine himself and of other early writers, would acknowledge that the doctrine of the Trinity is founded not in Holy Scriptures, but solely on the traditions and authority of the Church. Nay, indeed, they urged this against the followers of Luther and Calvin—who themselves try hard to use the authority of Holy Scripture alone to destroy the errors of the Papists and the corruption of the church—in order to annoy them,[121] saying that they had been unable to prove the doctrine of the Trinity against [170] the Tritheists (*Trideitae*). Thus do our [Calvinist] opponents unjustly call us who are least of all Tritheists, we being in fact worshipers of one God the Father, through Christ the only Mediator.[122] (And in Transylvania we are therefore called Unitarians.[123]) Hence they[124] could not resist us. Add thereto that Luther and Calvin seemed to the Catholics to have written with little respect to the Holy Trinity, as Calvin indeed, by his valid explanation of a great many passages of Holy Writ that are in controversy between us and our adversaries, [inadvertently] snatched these [crucial passages] away from his own followers.[125] The effort of Lismanino [in any case] failed of success.[126] But the death that befell him at Königsberg, where he went insane, was burdened (unfortunately) with suspicion and evil rumor.[127]

In the meantime, Prince John of Hungary and Transylvania,[128] born of John Zápolya (elected King of the Hungarians) [**cf. BAnt no. 57**] and of Isabella (daughter of King Sigismund I of Poland), had summoned [1563] to Transylvania George Biandrata,[129] who by distinguished services to him, had won considerable influence with him. Biandrata accepted the call the more gladly because Calvin had not ceased to persecute him, sending letters throughout Poland and Lithuania with the result that, due to the latter's evil zeal, he was not permitted to pass his life within these boundaries without danger, as we have related in previous chapters.[130]

[The Brest Bible, 1563]

When now some of the most active opponents of errors had scattered here and there, and some had been removed by death, God furnished all an opportune means of spreading the truth, when in the same year of 1563 a translation of the whole Bible,[131] which had not yet been seen in Poland, was published at Brest in Lithuania through the effort and at the cost of the never-to-be-forgotten hero Nicholas Radziwiłł, palatine of Vilna.[132] This [Bible] indeed did not escape suspicion and disparagement from adversaries, but it survived them and was held in deserved esteem, as it still is. For thus a way was opened to men to read, examine, and understand the Holy Scriptures, and to notice the corruptions of the Roman Church which she had long defended with armed tyranny.

This version was followed in 1572 by another, also of the whole Bible, by Simon Budny,[133] and in 1577 by another [**cf. BAnt nos. 44, 44.1**], of the New Testament, by Martin Czechowic, with no small success.[134] For in the former [the Budny Bible], in which the words of the Holy Scripture were faithfully translated in accordance with the meaning of the Hebrew text, truth-loving men saw the received errors as in a glass; and in the latter [that of Czechowic], to which notes were also added, hearts which burned with eagerness for the truth and with heavenly zeal, were greatly warmed.

[The Edicts of Parczów, August, 1563]

[171] That was a year, 1563. It carried off Stanislas Lasocki at Piotrków [**cf. BAnt no. 25**], a man distinguished not only by birth and office but also by his services to the Commonwealth, and especially to the [Minor] Church.[135] To his place succeeded Stanislas Cikowski of the Radwan clan,[136] nearly his equal in zeal, who joined his by no means dilatory effort with Filipowski in defending and spreading the truth of God. He was a man illustrious in birth and merit, and was therefore honored with the senatorial dignity of castellan of Biecz and the distinguished office of grand hetman of the Kingdom. (He was related by blood and marriage with the Komorowskis, Myszkowskis, Lanckorońskis, and many other illustrious families.) He was most illustrious, however, by far for his invincible and tireless zeal for true religion (*verae pietatis*). He disregarded the royal Parczovian edict,[137] since he had been taught by the word and example of the Apostles that we ought "to obey God rather than man,"[138] and was diligent in his office. Even the leading men of the Evangelical confession, fearing the danger of that decree of doubtful meaning, nay foreseeing that a blow as unexpectedly threatening all dissenters from the Roman Church, asked and obtained from the kind and compliant King an interpretation of it to the effect that the severity of the law was aimed only at foreigners.[139]

[Erasmus Otwinowski and Stanislas Paklepka in an iconoclastic episode in Lublin, 1564][140]

Certainly no pains or efforts were spared by either strangers or natives in opposing and destroying the errors of the Papists. A notable example of such zeal was shown in Erasmus Otwinowski of the Gryph clan,[141] a man highly distinguished for his piety and for his writings, deserving to be reckoned among the *Christian Heroes*,[142] of whom he sang in Polish verse along with his brother.

This George, having entered the monastic life in the cloister of Tyniec, left it shortly after and until his death lived with his brother in wonderful harmony and steadfastness.[143] George was a man not only pious, but also learned and clever, witness the considerable *Liber sententiarum ex Sacris Literis et antiquae*

Ecclesiae Doctoribus collectarum, compiled at the end of the last century, of which I own the autograph.[144]

With what zeal this Erasmus glowed for the glory of God, which had been stained by most foul idolatry, is shown by his pamphlet written in vernacular verse, entitled *A Dispute between a Baker and a Painter about their Gods*,[145] in which he both wittily and piously refuted the detestable idolatry of the Papists in their worship of what they call the most holy sacrament, and pointed out the shameful vanity of it, [172] yet granting the palm to the painter because his God, portrayed and pictured, lasts longer, while the baked one is more exposed to various chances.

Erasmus proved his intrepid spirit and burning zeal in a notable deed. He had just then been visiting Stanislas Paklepka, first minister of the church at Lublin. This church first met in his house (where a proud Jesuit church now stands),[146] then in the residence of the noble Lady (*matrona*) Ostrowska *née* Suchodolska (mother of Peter Ostrowski of the Gryph clan, a man highly distinguished by having been ambassador to Turkey and by his many services to the Commonwealth).[147] Afterwards, the church met elsewhere, as we shall relate in its proper place.[148] While engaged there in a devout conversation with some other devout men, and listening to the hymn for Corpus Christi day[149] being sung by those who were carrying the most holy sacrament, as they call it, to the cathedral church,[150] he was deeply impelled by the words of Paklepka, who at those [processional] words, "non est panis sed est deus," said: "Alas, where now are men who will not abide this idolatry!" He quickly arose, rushed from the house, and approaching the priest whom he intimately knew, said to him: "How many times have I warned you not to do this thing in which you sin against God, and you promised me that you would do it no more. And yet you are obstinate. Repeat the Lord's Prayer!" Handing to another the pyx with the host, the priest did as he was bidden. After he recited "Our Father who art in heaven," Otwinowski [broke in and] said that was enough, and reproached him, saying: "You said truly that God is in heaven. Then he is not in the bread, and not in your pyx." Thereupon he snatched it, threw it to the ground, and trod it under foot. All the followers of idolatry were astonished at the unwonted occurrence. Some were amazed and shocked at such unheard-of audacity, others were hot with anger and threatened vengeance, and judged that the foolhardy heretic ought to be heavily fined. But he passed through the crowd and sought shelter in the house of a nobleman, Peter Suchodolski of the Janina clan, an adherent of the purer religion.

Meantime the patrons of idolatry went to the magistrate, demanded punishment, and reported the case to the deputy palatine (*provinciae propraefectum*), Peter Suchodolski, uncle of the aforementioned [namesake, himself] a stout supporter of the Papist errors. He sent the governor (*praefectum*) of the castle, commonly called the burgrave,[151] to arrest Otwinowski. Accompanied by his retinue, he also tried the same thing himself, and he urged his brothers' son[152] to surrender the criminal. But the nephew bolted the doors of his house and refused to admit his uncle, [173] warned him to refrain from violence, and persuaded him to take milder measures.[153]   Finally Otwinowski, eluding all attempts of his enemies, escaped from the town.

Since Otwinowski was an inhabitant of the palatinate, owned estates there, and had very influential connections, and the nobility were fiercely defending their rights against the arrogance of the bishops whose jurisdiction was finally abolished by public laws in [the Diets of] 1562 and 1565,[154] he escaped any harm, save that he was ordered by royal command to appear and to render to the Diet an account of what he had done.

When this gathered [1564],[155] Nicholas Rej, a man highly distinguished by his birth, character, and public honors (for he was a member of the royal court, and also deputy to the Diet of the Kingdom representing the municipality of Cracow),[156] used his influence to settle his quarrel between the parties.[157]   And, since the man was good-natured and often used to season his talk with an abundance of jokes, we read that he then spoke on behalf of Otwinowski as follows:

> Otwinowski has offended God allegedly, and certainly a man, a priest. So he will satisfy the latter as the law prescribes, since he will beg his pardon and will repair the damage he has inflicted. This is quite right, and compensation is easily made, that is, if he pays the priest a penny (*obolum*) for the broken glass, and a farthing (*teruncium*) for the broken wafer of the host (for with this he can get a new glass and a handful of flour). God's injury must be left to Him to punish, for vengeance is his alone.[158]   And so time must be allowed for punishment. God will inflict this, if wrong has been done to him, either by sending down lightning, or by opening a gap in the earth, or in some other dreadful way. For if he severely punished the wrong done to Moses by Korah, Dathan, and Abiram by having the earth swallow them up alive together with their families and possessions,[159] so much the more will he now punish this man, if he has done him such injury as is thought. Besides, no law has been passed against such a crime.

In this way Rej saved Otwinowski from danger.[160]   But a vote was now passed that in future orderly behavior should be observed by all when sacred rites were being performed. And from now on this rite began to be celebrated accompanied by instruments of war. This was a matter that afterwards, when the times were exacerbated, often wrought injury even to the most temperate burghers of Cracow, and to others who were averse to this idolatry.[161]

[Two accidental and two other assaults in Lublin and Vilna upon the sacrament of the altar]

Also the same priest there at Lublin, a little later, when taking such a host to be administered to a sick man, in passing a tavern, with his hand struck a Jewish bystander from behind, saying: "Fall [174] on your knees, Jew!" Whereupon the latter, surprised by the unexpected act and suddenly turning round, by his motion knocked the host from the priest's hands. For this a fine, though light enough, since hardly exceeding a hundred pounds (*libra*), was imposed on the Jew.

And a little before, a memorable case like this happened at Vilna. There was then living at the court one Semion, a nobleman and courtier of the King, at a time when solemn parades (*cursitationes*) with idols, commonly called processions, were being made through the city at the beginning of the month of May.[162] As a priest was passing Semion's lodgings, his servant happened to be emptying a chamber pot (begging your pardon) from an upper window, and with its contents wet him and the idol that he was carrying. The crime (*facinus*) was treated by the priests as done in contempt of the Divine Majesty, and what had been an accident was made out to be a crime (*culpa*). Semion, accused before the King and sued, appeared before the King. Accusers presented themselves, reinforced by the number and influence of their patrons. There they accused Semion, exaggerating the deed and demanding severe punishment under the pretext that he had insulted and therefore seriously offended the Deity. Semion, accompanied by many friends and intimates of the court, complained of the wrong done to him, in that though he possessed lawful estates, he had been haled into court like a vagrant with no fixed abode or property. He deplored the rude injustice of his accusers who had not called upon him to punish the servant responsible for the deed, nor had they addressed him by word of mouth. He appealed to the witness of his life which he had always lived at the court honestly and without reproach. He contended that they had not proceeded according to the proper course of justice and equity. And they excused what they were doing, declaring that as far as possible they must avenge the wrong done to God, for it was his cause that was at stake, not theirs, but that they forgave him the private wrong.

Then again Semion, calling a herald according to custom, and noble witnesses, had the words of the priests inscribed in the records, to wit, that the priests forgave him the wrong done to them and wished only to punish that done to God; and, as to that done to God, he demanded that a cause of such moment ought to be postponed to be defended by the divine Patron (*Patronus*). This request was not denied him.

Having taken leave of the King, Semion arranged a banquet and invited his friends. After he had wined and dined them amply, he addressed them saying that he had an important matter to settle with the King; that he invited them to be present then and there with him; that he would not forfeit his bail, for he had something that would turn out to be for himself a comfort [175] and defense. Given that the priests who were accusing him had forgiven him his crime, meaning only to avenge the wrong done to God, he had had this entered in the records. [He said further] that the time [of trial] fixed upon was not yet at hand; that before it approached that the wooden God would ascend into heaven and hence would not appear at the trial;[163] nor would He leave to the priests the full power of Christ to prosecute the case, hence that they would not prosecute the case. Instead, He [Christ] would give them fresh trouble, justly and deservedly, on account of the wrong they had done Him.

Having heard this, they[164] did not appear on the day set. He did appear; and he publicly called on his accusers to witness that the alleged injured party [the image] had not appeared at the tribunal but had [presumably] ascended into heaven, nor was anyone present authorized to represent the opposite party. [He declared] that he was guilty of no crime and asked to be discharged. So this case too ended in a jest and a joke.[165]

Happy indeed were those times up to that point! In the same city of Vilna in 1611 Franco di Franco, an Italian, did not escape vengeance for his free speech alone with which on Corpus Christi day, as they call it, he admonished the followers of the idol of their duty; and he was put to a cruel and wicked death.[166] And also John Tyszkowic, an inhabitant of the town of Bielsk in Podlasie, was condemned on the false charge of throwing the idol to the ground and trampling it under foot, and he was put to a cruel death at Warsaw in the same year, of which we shall speak in the proper place.[167]

Chapter Three

Of Pedobaptism Opposed, Defeated, Rejected.

A childish error mocked the Christian world long enough and with impunity, though based on no divine authority whatsoever, and contrary to the original (*primaevae*) practice of several centuries.[168] For in Holy Writ we so often read the instruction of Christ, the most heavenly Teacher, and of the Apostles, about teaching men, bringing them to faith and religious obedience, and at length baptizing them, but never about baptizing infants or about infants baptized. This indeed began in the third century to be practiced by some in Africa,[169] which was always hatching monsters,[170] [176] though disapproved by others not only in Asia but also in Africa itself, so that even in the fourth century children of bishops (witness Gregory of Nazianzus)[171] and of other believers, and indeed those trained (witness Chrysostom)[172] and brought up by bishops in the Christian religion, called catechumens, for whom catechisms were composed, did not finally receive baptism until adult age, while some who had not yet been baptized either became famous for their miracles (as St. Martin),[173] or were elevated to the imperial majesty (as Constantine the Great,[174] his son Constantius,[175] Theodosius the Elder,[176] and Valentinian[177]), or are even said to have assumed the care of an episcopate (as Ambrose[178] and Nectarius[179]). Among these men, some purposely postponed baptism to the very end of their lives under the influence of a false belief, that they might by that washing at their last breath wash away, as it were, the stain of their sins. Then it is clear that Valentinian the Younger, though highly praised by Ambrose, died without baptism.[180] And whether the brothers Constantine the Younger and Constans[181] received it, is unknown. At length, in the eighteenth year of the fifth century, at the Council of Mileve[182] (so fitting was it that this infant be born, be nourished, and grow up in Africa[183]), by authority of Pope Innocent of Rome[184] and Bishop Augustine of Hippo,[185] the necessity of baptism was imposed upon infants, so that they might be able to partake of the holy Eucharist.[186] This practice, although the communion of infants was abolished by the authority of the Council of Trent, even now exercises a tyrannical power over a great many.[187]

[Controversy over pedobaptism][188]

There were not lacking men indeed who immediately after, in the earlier ages, opposed this commonly received error, as we have shown elsewhere.[189] But in our Poland the first whom we read of as having opposed it, was Matthew Albin, minister of the word of God at Iwanowice near Cracow, as we have related in the previous book.[190] Following him was the German, Peter Pulchranin,[191] rector of the school at Bychawa in the palatinate of Lublin, Stanislas Paklepka, pastor at Lublin, but especially Peter of Goniądz [**cf. BAnt nos. 3, 7, 53; 24, 26**] (who in 1562 wrote a letter against infant baptism to Lawrence Krzyszkowski, a nobleman and minister of the word of God among the Lithuanians),[192] and Jerome Piekarski,[193] all of whom we have mentioned above. There is a tradition that the Cujavians, whose palatinate borders on Prussia,[194] were the first to rise up against infant baptism under the leadership of Martin Czechowic, [177] who besides other doctrines had also imbibed this about the baptism of adults from Peter of Goniądz.[195]

The baptism of infants or rather the sprinkling (*rhantismus*), to employ the term used by religious writers for lawful aspersions (*aspersionibus legalibus*), since it shows a pretence of piety and compassion for the infants, has hitherto increased by daily practice, and brings the baptizers and the parents of the baptized no small gain. It happens to be fought for not only by the Papists but also the Calvinists not less fiercely than for their Triune God, while on the other hand those who are zealous for the purer truth defend their good cause bravely.

[Antipedobaptism in Vilna and in Brzeżny in Great Poland;
Lutomirski's letter from the synod of Brzeżiny, June 1565][196]

A disagreement on this matter arose at Vilna in Lithuania. There Simon ak of Proszowice,[197] elder of that church, had published a confession of his church in favor of infant baptism, printed there in 1559.[198] The disagreement was especially intense between the ministers Martin Czechowic[199] (more conspicuous than the rest) and Nicholas Wędrogowski.[200] The former attacked and the latter, together with Paul [of Wizna],[201] the superintendent of the Lithuanian churches, defended infant baptism.[202]

This led to the calling of a synod at Brzeziny in Kujawy (*Braesia Cujavorum*) on 10 June 1565.[203] In this thirty-two ministers and eighteen listeners took part. Here, indeed, the disagreement between Czechowic and Wędrogowski was assuaged, but the resolution of the question itself was put off to the synod to be held at Węgrów in Podlasie. Meanwhile a letter from this synod [at Brzeziny] to the congregation at Vilna was written by the hand of Stanislas Lutomirski, superintendent of the churches of Little Poland. This follows, as regard for truth and religion demands, that I give a copy here:

> Grace and peace eternal with increase of light, we invoke for you, beloved Brethren, with a sincere Christian heart.
>
> Let believers render due thanks to the heavenly Father who makes us daily more and more to see that believers, though dwelling far apart from one another, have one heart and one mind with one another, as has appeared, to the great comfort of us all, from your good will toward us, your brethren, in sending to us, from so great a distance and sparing no expense, two brethren from your midst, Wędrogowski and Andrew Cizner,[204] [178] and what is more, in declaring your confidence in us, to whom you have entrusted the composing of the differences that have arisen among you. May the same heavenly Father strengthen you and us by his Holy Spirit, that we may grow in true charity unto eternal life.
>
> To you in turn, dearly beloved brethren, we offer our hearts, sincere and full of ready good-will, none of us doubting that you will accept them, as you are wont, with the same kind feelings. Relying on this hope, we have willingly undertaken to compose the differences that have arisen among you, hurtful to the Church of God; and this to the glory of God and in the name of our Lord Jesus Christ, but not that we may lord it over you on this occasion of disagreement.
>
> And we therefore inform you that a reconciliation has been made between Brother Wędrogowski and Superintendent Paul on the one side, and on the other Martin Czechowic and other brethren who thought themselves wronged by Brother Wędrogowski. For the Holy Spirit showed us that there had been wrong on both sides, and that the Church of God had been gravely wounded and saddened by their thoughtless and rash deeds. And when these things were placed before their eyes, the Holy Spirit led them to acknowledge their fault and repent, and so they were led to restore harmony in our presence. There remains only this: that brothers Wędrogowski and Martin lay aside and dismiss the scandal they have caused in the place where it was committed, namely before your Church, and this without mentioning in ill-will the wrong suffered, nor the provocation of spirits, only publicly confessing their faults, so that they may preserve peace and charity together with zeal for the glory of God, according to God's holy will, and may before the brethren and sisters[205] with truly contrite hearts ask pardon for their faults.
>
> However, since we have learned that other brethren of your congregation, especially Katerla[206] and Karnicki,[207] had given this scandal great occasion, we therefore pray you for God's sake that they may comfort not only the brethren and sisters[208] there, but also us, with their humbled hearts and mutual supplication and reconciliation, so that God may be glorified, and thereby Satan, the enemy of concord and love, be put to shame. That you of your ready good-will will do this, we do not in the least doubt, so

that the sadness that has come of discord may bring the faithful so much the greater joy.

[179] Moreover, we beseech you for God's sake that henceforth your moderation (*modestia*) in all things may be known to all men,[209] and that nothing be done to treat the name of God with contempt, but that all be done in the spirit of gentleness and true charity.

Likewise we beseech you that the trouble that has resulted from the dispute arising about baptism may turn out for the mutual comfort of you and us. For as far as baptism is concerned, about which some question has arisen among you, let us by no means resist the Spirit of God, being taught by our own frequent experience according to the counsel of the Holy Spirit. Such moderation (*temperamentum*) has been found by us, whereby those who are at variance think themselves to be placed on an even level with each other, so that no one on either side is compelled to do anything against the protest of conscience, but all keep the peace unimpaired, refraining from the opprobrious names of Anabaptists or antagonists (*antagonistarum*), continuing constant in fervent prayers to God, waiting until the time appointed for the synod, where God of his mercy will show us the one way in which none of the faithful will offend, since a sheep is obedient to its shepherd, nay rather with the greater comfort leaps for joy only to hear the voice of its Shepherd in a matter of eternal salvation: according as we have found it, having been led forth from the gloomy prison and the bonds of the infinite errors of Antichrist.

But of this the brethren will report to you more fully. For to this end also they will have a synod convoked [at Węgrów] by the superintendent whom you have harmoniously chosen, and to whom you owe obedience in the Lord according to the word of God, and whom you are bound to assist.

So far the letter by Lutomirski for the synod of Brzeziny.[210]

[The synod of Węgrów in Palatinate Podlachia, December 1565; debate over baptism; Lutomirski's account of the synod]

This synod was appointed for December 25 at Węgrów,[211] which is a town in Podlasie (Podlachia), in order that more Lithuanian brethren, who defended infant baptism, might conveniently gather from the vicinity. Forty-seven ministers were in attendance, and fourteen leading men and nobles, besides the ordinary laity (*populus*). By unanimous consent Jerome Filipowski was appointed the moderator. Letters were sent to this synod from the most honorable lady Anna Radziwiłłowna Kiszka[212] (wife of the palatine of Vitebsk), and from other private parties, brethren and sisters; also from the churches and elders of the districts of Szydłowiec, Lublin, Brzeziny, and Chełm, and by the synod of the churches in the district of the [Carpathian] foothills.[213] All of them [180] admonished in their letters that they should be mindful of their duty toward God and not suffer anything to be introduced into the churches which the divine

Scriptures did not allow, but that they should take diligent care that all might hear that harmony and love were flourishing among them unto edification, not quarrels and divisions.

After much discussion on each side, some as vigorously attacking infant baptism as others defended it, the following decision was reached:[214]

> The decision of the holy synod at Węgrów on the article of true baptism, now passed, confirmed, and concluded, 30 December 1565:[215] To the glory of our Lord and his Son Jesus Christ and the comfort of all the faithful.
>
> The matter of baptism, that has been especially considered here at Węgrów was at first and also publicly brought up at the synod of Brzeziny—not to say anything here of the fact that this question had been already examined three years ago by brethren in Poland [1562: allusion obscure], and long before that in Lithuania [Brest, December 1558].[216] But since it could not there be brought to a conclusion, because some were saying that they had come thither unprepared, and others that they had received no mandate from the brethren without whose approval they were bound not to take any action. And since they requested that another synod be appointed without any delay for this purpose, all therefore yielded to their desire, with this stipulation: That henceforth no one should plead ignorance or offer any other excuse, but that each should prepare to defend his cause as well as possible, and should inform others who are interested to know of it and who wish to come hither and act on this matter. This was done at Brzeziny at the feast of Pentecost just past [10 June 1565].
>
> To this end a synod was called here at Węgrów for the present, that is, at the feast which commemorates the anniversary of the birth of the Son of God [25 December 1565],[217] the previous synod consenting thereto.
>
> At this previous synod [at Brzeziny] were present the superintendents: Brother Lutomirski, Nicholas Żytno,[218] Daniel Bieliński,[219] Gregory Paul, Stanislas Paklepka, Martin Krowicki, Bartholomew [Codecius] from Great Poland, [181] Paul [of Wizna] from Lithuania, and many other ministers and brethren.[220] The above named superintendents were urged by the duty imposed upon them by the said synod at Brzeziny, upon their return home to call synods, so that each of the hearers to whom they dispense the word of God might become settled on this subject, and that the churches might send to the synod at Węgrów whomever they wanted from their own midst to discuss this question.[221]
>
> To this end also this synod has met here at Węgrów, for the reason that the brethren living in Lithuania complained that they were always being called to Poland to attend synods, whereas the Polish brethren had never come for this purpose to Lithuania or to a neighboring province. Of this the most illustrious Lord palatine of Vilna,[222] of blessed memory, reminded us, and this deserved to be mentioned here, lest any one suppose that we have chosen this place for some other reason.[223]
>
> In this synod this order was observed. After prayers in the church each day the brethren met at the place appointed, where this question was proposed: Whether the baptism of infants was instituted according to a command of the word of God, or not? On the question each and all gave their

votes by rank, the superintendents and the ministers of the word of God as well as the rest of the brethren, each one weighing the matter according to the measure of the abilities vouchsafed to him by the Lord. Then speeches on the subject were made by some of the brethren, favoring one side or the other. This continued for the space of six days, and so that whole days indeed were devoted to this subject. None of the brethren left.

Some showed the instruction and command of God about baptism from the word of God and the Gospel history. Then they brought forward examples from the Acts and the Epistles of the Apostles, citing many passages on which they built their opinion and founded their faith, saying that only the divine Scriptures satisfied them. But since many have regard for human authority, inquiring what was done in past ages, they also showed by certain proofs for the sake of others that infants (*parvulos*) were not baptized in the early (*antiqua*) Church, deriving their assertion from the history of the Church and the writings of the early Fathers nearest the times of the Apostles. [182] Moreover, they proved this from service books (*Agenda*), that is, books according to which the Romans, Ruthenians,[224] Armenians,[225] Greeks,[226] and Wittenbergers administer baptism,[227] and by our own which we have used hitherto, or indeed still use. From all this it is obvious, to any one who will faithfully consider it, that this matter does not relate to infants. Others on the contrary, who did not like this, opposed them and expressed much disapproval, defending the baptism of infants and citing arguments of recent writers who have written extensively on this matter, of which the church at Vilna also sent a written copy that was read here.[228]

Thereupon this was the conclusion reached: That those who held that little ones (*parvulos*) should be baptized, held their opinion tenaciously (*mordicus*); but others, who hesitated at this point, and if not yet agreeing, were nevertheless unwilling to oppose it [infant baptism] obstinately (*contumaciter*), promised rather that they wished to learn what is true and right. Therefore, since in the true Church of God one cannot lord it over another in faith nor coerce anyone, each party held to its own opinion, as indeed the will of God then moved each. And so those who were then firmly convinced by their knowledge of the word of God are unwilling any longer to do anything that they see and feel is opposed to the word of God. Nay rather, they ought in future sincerely to teach what agrees with the pure word of God. Likewise they can also publish books on this subject, provided they publish nothing without the knowledge of the elders (*senioribus*) of the neighboring churches, and at the same time with such moderation (*moderatione*) as not to oppress or accuse anyone, except such a one who openly and deliberately undertakes to oppose this ordinance of the Son of God [believers' baptism]; and this in order that they may preserve the charity unimpaired, provided nothing be done contrary to the glory of God, or placing a burden upon conscience.[229]

The objection to this [compromise] was made by some that baptism is not suitable for infants: thus still less can anyone baptized in his infancy think that he has been validly baptized. They went on to prove this by reasons and examples. To be sure, few gave their assent to this [anabaptism], yet there were some who desired to be further instructed. But there were some who [183] brought forward the crime of Münster,[230] in order to cause revulsion from the newly introduced view (about baptising [only] catechumens) and thus to lead us to reject it upon consideration of that enormity. Then those at whom that suspicion was aimed called God and man to witness that, even as they had hitherto sincerely obeyed the magistracy (*Magistratui*) given by God, so in future, they would with God's help take greater pains to labor so far as in them lay (even to the very end) to bear witness to this not in words but in deed, calling upon God and beseeching him for their magistracy "not only because of the wrath, but also for conscience's sake," as the Apostle teaches (Rom 13:[5]).[231] But if anyone wishes to impute to them anything else, he shall render account for such slander before the judgement-seat of God.

And at the same time they reminded themselves of their duty that they should both do it themselves, and should likewise diligently instruct the hearers entrusted to them by God. Then also that they should shine by a conspicuous example of true regeneration and piety, in modesty, sincere love, and a notable spirit of mildness towards opponents. And they should pray God for their adversaries, lest the word of God be treated with disrespect.[232]

But as some have not given their consent, they have been admonished, lest a stumbling block be placed in their way, to remember how, since God has begun to set us free from the bonds of Antichrist,[233] many agreements have been made about treating matters of minor importance, namely, about images, the Mass, also for a long time about the Lord's Supper, then about the Mediator, and at last about knowledge of the one true God and his true and only Son, not to mention other things.[234]

[They have been admonished] how disputes and controversies have sprung up among them over separate topics; how not all have received the word of God, though some have made good progress, while others on the contrary have fallen short, and once they became deserters, no longer follow our camp (*castra nostra*), which indeed was not unusual even in the time of the Apostles. Nor finally did they themselves all put their faith even in the Son of God, nor did they all believe together. Then also they were admonished that no one should marvel at this, nor take it in bad part, that in these conferences (*colloquia*) discussions were sometimes held that to someone may seem intemperate and unjust, since in matters of this nature it can hardly happen otherwise. [184] Yet even there they begged one another's pardon and forgave any offense given, and separated in mutual charity.[235]

All these things, however, have been mentioned for memory's sake, according to the nature of the case. And as for the accuracy of this account we rely on the probity of competent witnesses for anyone who wishes to be sufficiently informed about it. For there were present at this transaction all the superintendents, as well as ministers and brethren, and it was in their sight and hearing that all this was done and this conclusion was reached, which was afterwards written out and read before them all.[236]

Moreover, we all beg and admonish you that if anything displeases anyone about us, or if anyone goes around disparaging our good reputation, let him not be quick to blame and condemn this decision, but rather lend us his other ear. And then when he has heard both sides, let him pass judgment according to the gift vouchsafed to him by God. We are ready, divine grace assisting us, to give anyone sufficient reason for these things according to the word of God, even as we ourselves have learned from it. To it alone we completely assent and desire always in all things to assent, giving God thanks that he is leading us out of this abominable Babylon and in him reposing our greatest joy and consolation. This we desire for all others, and remind them not to place their dependence on the vain things of this world, which they must needs soon leave behind and appear before that Lord who will stand in awe of none, even those of greatest authority, and to whom each one will have to render an account of all his deeds.[237]

Węgrów, 30 December 1565,

> Stanislas Lutomirski, Superintendent,
> in the name of the Synod[238]

[Exchange of letters on believers' baptism between the congregation of Vilna, opposed, to the congregation of Brest Litovsk, favoring it, February 1566]

Those who had been delegated to attend the synod [of Węgrów] from Vilna[239] returned after its conclusion to report how each side had discussed the matter in controversy, what had there been decided about it, and they declared that, with the exception of themselves and some few [other] ministers of Lithuania, the vote about abandoning baptism of infants and restoring that of catechumens (*catechumeni*) and believers (*credentes*) had been passed [185] unanimously. The congregation in Vilna (*Vilnenses*) did not agree with this [reported] action but instead wrote with a sharpened stylus to the congregation of Brześć (*Brestia*) [Litewski],[240] a letter of which it is right that I add a copy:

Beloved Brethren in Christ,

> We have all felt great pain, which others of the faithful must also have felt, at seeing such lamentable and hurtful discords in the Church of God, especially in these recent unfortunate times in which, as Christ, the Apostles, and the Prophets of the Lord clearly foretold,[241] many are appearing who were to strike fear into the hearts of the faithful—even as they are now doing—namely, and especially those who, quite untrue to their judgment, so strongly and determinedly rage against the baptism of children of unbelieving parents.[242] And such prophets are found among you and among us not a few. This abominable plague is being followed by other things as some not long ago learned to their great cost, which the clear testimonies of [sacred] writers teach. Therefore we, beloved brethren, wishing to discharge the duty incumbent upon Christians, urge you by that fraternal love in which we enfold you, and, diligently and constantly foreseeing what evil may follow, beseech you by God not to be carried away by idle winds of doctrine[243] proceeding from men who employ their leisure ill.
>
> It is certain that from this opinion [antipedobaptism] for some time now much ventilated in the Church of God, sedition in the *Res Publica*, and subversion in the Church are arising.[244] That this is the case, God made

plain not long ago. For we see how these wretched manikins (*homunciones*) are proceeding in their undertaking. They declared formerly that they would assent if they might baptize only adults (*adultas*) at the dictation of a good conscience.[245] At present, advancing from strength to strength, they have now called their own baptism in question, openly saying that they have not been baptized. But after they have attained their wish, they will judge that by such a baptism they were made free and truly spiritual (*spirituales*).[246] Thus they will extend their wiles further and further, so that these good *Spirituales*[247] will consign to eternal damnation and the pains of hell those who will fall away from their ranks or sin, denying them repentance.[248]

This liberty will encourage them to hold too high an opinion of themselves, and this ambitious opinion will lead them to tolerate no one above themselves, so that they all, in the words of the Apostle Paul, have their liberty as a cloak for their own desires.[249] Not to mention other evil deeds that have already flowed out of that foul stream, [186] and which even yet must flow thence if things turn out as they wish, and if those who are laying the foundations of this establishment, try to commend it and coat it by specious colors. But all this will the day of the Lord reveal.

Again and again we exhort and beg you, beloved brethren, flee far from this Anabaptist plague and admonish others, adhering to the simple instruction and Gospel of Christ which knows nothing of such fine spun fancies, but to all who draw near to the Lord promises grace and eternal life. We believe, beloved brethren, that you will take kindly and in good part this fraternal admonition of ours, and will remain constant to the end, praying the heavenly Father mercifully to preserve you with us from such restless men in honesty and in peace. With this we commend you to God.

Given in Vilna, 1566

The Ministers and Elders and Deacons
of the Church of Christ that gathers at Vilna

To this so harsh a letter the brethren of Brest[250] sent the following reply:

May God the Father of the Lord Jesus increase your faith, Amen.

We give you hearty thanks, beloved brethren, that you not only address us as your brethren in a letter, but also admonish and exhort us in sadness of heart diligently to beware of false prophets.[251] We for our part, in these parts (*in his oris*), by God's help, have not given nor will we give ear to pseudo-prophets of this sort. Nay rather, as we have once submitted to the word of our God and Father, so we will remain steadfast in this purpose, still, and with assistance of the same most merciful Father we shall give ear to the only Master (*Magistro*) whom he has given and shown us, in order that we may be faithful to our profession. For we are marked with the name of Christians by the Son of God, Christ our Lord.[252] However, since you remind us that it was to come to pass that believers should be disturbed by the doctrines of false prophets,[253] this indeed agrees with the utterances of our Teacher (*Doctoris*). He called those who had come before him and beside him promising men eternal life, false prophets, thieves, and robbers, and taught that his sheep [187] would not hear their voice and would not know the voice of strangers, but would obey and follow only their own Shepherd.[254]

His Gospel is not hidden, save from those who are to perish.[255] Therefore we take no offense at this, nor are we in any way disturbed by what disturbs you, who take too much upon yourselves. For you say that infant baptism is founded on the authority of the word of God, and yet you bring forward from that no proof of it. You cite only this in support of your case, that while teaching that no faith is to be given to false prophets, you yourselves prophesy about things that have never entered the minds either of us or of our ministers. You call this [believers' baptism] the plague and ruin of the Commonwealth and of the Church of God.[256] But we consider this to be an emendation [in restoration of the usage] of the Apostolic Church, so that those who believe and confess their faith and are regenerated may become partakers of the Lord's [two] sacraments.

You admonish us not to be carried about by any wind of human doctrines.[257] And you yourselves, upon human authority, overthrow a thing instituted by the Son of God, as was evident even in the synod lately held.[258] For you sent nothing thither that had been taken from the word of God, but only what you chose for yourselves as witnesses. And you took up stones against the Son of God, when mentioning the rod of the magistrate.[259] But we, with God's help, shall not retreat nor allow ourselves to be frightened by hisses nor scared away from the teaching of the Son of God.[260]

We here are all united by the grace of God, nor are we teaching fierceness, either the abominable deeds of Antichrist or indeed the crimes of Münster, but rather the teaching of Christ, reverence and obedience to the civil government, not only because of fear, but also for conscience's sake.[261]

We also learn to lead a godly life at home with our wives, as we know that God created woman for a single man, and punished those having two wives. This the Scriptures everywhere teach, because the sons of those having two wives either polluted their fathers' beds, or drove them from their homes, or laid violent hands on themselves.[262]

We learn also to provide according to our means for services to the glory of God, knowing that it is right for the brethren to own estates (*praedia*), since the Apostle Paul also collected alms from the rich and gave them to the Church.[263]

Moreover, we attempt, with God's help, to become *spirituales*, and free from all the things with which men used to burden our consciences. But our ministers, whom you point to as "wretched manikins," do not understand this Spiritual perfection as meaning that those who have once submitted themselves to the word of God [188] no longer sin, or are not subject to temptation.[264] For the Lord commanded his elect to pray to their Father without ceasing[265] to forgive them their debts or sins. The Apostles also show that the baptized children (*liberis*) of God, when they sin, have a Mediator and Advocate with God, even Jesus Christ.[266] Nay indeed, the kingdom of Christ given him here must needs fall, unless those who have sinned are encouraged by the hope of remission of sins.[267] For another part of his rule consists in the fact that he acts as Mediator and Propitiator for those who know his care as a shepherd.

At the judgment of God, to which you too appeal, those prophets [of yours] will render to our Lord their account, who having fallen short of the truth and of the certainty of the declarations of God, are resorting to the weapons which Antichrist was accustomed to employ. For though he[268] could not [directly] fault the Gospel teaching, he turned to another strategem, and he charged God's elect with accepting the [unmediated] Gospel in order to fulfil the lusts of the flesh. And we therefore beg you through God not to wage war with the weapons of Antichrist against the Lamb, one foot of whom is stronger than all the weapons of the whole world.[269]

We indeed take it from you with grateful mind that you advise us to embrace the word of God; but we hear with pain that you are obedient to men. Yet verily, by these prophecies of yours you overthrow the teaching of the Lord, and not our faith. For with God's help, as far as we can, we are getting out of the gutters of Antichrist and shall no longer wallow in their mud. We shall also agree, as you say, to the simple Christ and to his simple Gospel, who has sent the scepter of his Kingdom to the elect of his Father in preaching the Gospel.[270] Wherefore, without regard to the subtleties of commentaries, we live content with this simple sincerity, and with God's help shall always show ourselves obedient to the words of our Master. But just as we were before in grief, fearing that our minister[271] was to be called away from us, so now we thank God that he has thought fit to leave that to us, who also congratulates himself that he is clinging to this little flock. We therefore pray you again and again not to impede us in our course, as we are approaching the goal set before us to carry off the prize.[272] Nay rather, you pray God that as he has begun to lead us out of Babylon, so he may complete the work. [189] We too shall not fail to join our prayers to yours. The grace of our Lord Jesus Christ be with us all, Amen.

Given in Brest (*Brestia*), 20 February 1566.

> To all our beloved Brethren in Christ:
> To be delivered into the proper hands of the Church at Vilna
>
> The Servants of Christ, your well-wishing
> brethren in the Church at Brześć [Litewski]

Even in our haste, the memorable case of Nicholas Wędrogowski [pastor in Vilna] demands our attention. *For as death drew near,[273] he confessed to having committed the crime of hypocrisy before God. When asked how, he replied that though he called himself a minister of the heavenly Lord, yet he often taught in hope of winning not His favor, but that of men, and he cried out: "My praise is turned to shame, because I have sought my own glory, and not God's."* So Budziński records it. No wonder that he was omitted by Andrew Węgierski in his *Historia Ecclesiastica*.[274]

[The radical Reformed in Transylvania deplore the
movement toward believers' baptism in the Commonwealth]

When the Transylvanian churches learned that this controversy [over baptism] was being violently carried on by the Poles and the Lithuanians, they several times sent them letters admonishing them not to draw out disputes and quarrels about this matter that seemed to them rather unnecessary, appropriate though it was to those early times and to Jews or pagans converted to Christ. This they set forth in a long writing (*aliquoties datis literis*), in which also appeared onsets of a Judaizing spirit.[275]

They[276] complained, among other things, that the need of salvation was being entangled with the rite of baptism, that baptism was being made a sort of new savior, and even an idol like the brazen serpent; and indeed that those who perform it act the same as if one would seek to get possession of Noah's ark, or Jeremiah's yoke, or the arrows of King Joash.[277] In addition, they thought at length that baptism was suited to primordial Christianity, with a view to the conversion of the Gentiles and ensuing miracles, as was the blood of the Passover lamb and the sight of the brazen serpent; but [that baptism was] not [suited] to later times.[278] For even the Apostles themselves [190] regarded as holy the children born to parents either of whom is a believer. This shows clearly that children born of a Christian parent and brought up in the piety of the Christian religion are saints and believers; and that even if they should not be baptized, will by no means perish.[279] Further, that when the error about original sin is done away with, its [theological and sacramental] consequence, absolution, that is, its being washed away through baptism, is also done away.[280] Such things are all to be taken with a grain of salt.[281]

Nor was this controversy even yet settled between the disputants. Nay, while some with the greatest intensity opposed and others defended infant baptism, the truth about the solemn incorporation (*solemniter inserendis*) of catechumens into the Church [in antiquity] through baptism at length came to light, like fire from the striking of steel and flint. For although this controversy about the necessity and the renewal of baptism was also discussed with restraint in published writings between Martin Czechowic[282] and Faustus Socinus,[283] yet at length both truth and love, that is, candor and good sense, were satisfied, since infant baptism was rejected and the true and primitive baptism of catechumens was restored to the Church and established in it. And an adequate means was found of reconciling differing opinions, so that infant baptism was not altogether condemned, and was tolerated in certain places.

So it was in Transylvania, where yielding to necessity in order to avoid too great offense, children are baptized. This the Brethren in [Royal] Prussia[284] also do during this severe persecution.*[285] But to those who had been deprived of

---

*The Editor of 1685 notes: ''They [the Polish Brethren] did so for fear of their adversaries at the time when the author wrote this in 1665, though some were reluctant and opposed it, and afterwards they did not do it.''

holy baptism in infancy, liberty was allowed either to receive true baptism in adulthood or to omit it, in order that no one's conscience might be burdened.

[Heroes in the struggle against pedobaptism]

Nicholas Szczekocki[286] here deserves the courtesy of mention, distinguished for his noble birth, steadfast piety, and abounding hospitality which he extended in 1564 in the palatinate of Lublin to strangers from Kujawy.[287] Their leaders in 1564 were [Land] Judge John Niemojewski[288] of the palatinate (*terra*) of Inowrocław (of the Rola clan, distinguished by birth, character, and piety), who as a genuine fugitive from a deceitful world resigned his office, though he had discharged it faithfully, and his dearest friend *Lawrence* Brzeziński, Sr.[289] For he [Brzeziński] had been prevented by protracted and serious illness from receiving baptism [in infancy], as was his wish, having long postponed his own baptism according to an old custom.[290]

The first to reject the puerile baptism (which we have stated above[291] ought to be called rhantism rather than baptism, since it is done not by immersion but by sprinkling) [191] and to receive true baptism [i.e., by immersion as a believer] was John Siekierzyński.[292] He was a man of marked simplicity, yet highly accomplished in Holy Scripture, an eloquent preacher, impressive and acute, whom more than one called the axe of his vice[293] (as Demosthenes called Phocion the axe of arguments),[294] a teacher of burning zeal, steadfast in the truth, most attentive to duty, even in attention (*cultus*) to the body, which he held in slight regard and even as vile. When John Sieniński of the Dębno clan,[295] palatine of Podolia, a man most illustrious and an elegant follower of the world, went to hear him [preach] for the sake of diversion, he was so overcome by the moving eloquence and remarkable earnestness that during the sermon he wet several handkerchiefs with his tears. And when he[296] had left the place,[297] and Peter Kazimirski[298] (of the Biberstein clan), whom Otwinowski (in his *Christian Heroes*) compares, as a regenerated soldier, to the pious centurion Cornelius,[299] an ardent confessor of the truth (although his brother was Bishop of Kiev),[300] asked him[301] whether he now felt like laughing, he replied: "Unless we have lived as this pious man taught, we shall all perish everlastingly."[302]

Also to be reckoned among the first [to be rebaptized] is Peter Pulchranin, whom we have mentioned before.[303] For this reason [anabaptism] a certain man of the Łaszcz family, of noble birth but of rude manners, severely beat Peter and threw him into a deep pond, but God nevertheless rescued him from the danger that then threatened his life.

To these [early anabaptists] deserves to be added Andrew Lubieniecki the Elder, son of Stanislas [I], and C[atherine] Sobieska.[304] He had been liberally educated at the expense of King Henry of Valois [1573–74], upon the recommendation of Brudzewski, palatine of Brześć in Kujawy (his native land) since he was his relative and a youth of great promise, and he had been maintained at the University of Paris together with other chosen Polish noblemen, in accordance with an agreement made with the Commonwealth.[305]

He[306] was deemed born for some distinguished career by the great [John] Zamoyski.[307] To him he was also related by blood. Zamoyski used generously to encourage youth of good ability, as is shown by the instance of [his support of] Stanislas Żółkiewski[308] (to whose family Andrew's stepmother belonged), his successor in both the offices of grand chancellor and grand general. And yet for all that, although he[309] also enjoyed the favor of King Stephen [Batory], to whose court he was attached and [where] he might have hoped for distinguished honors, leaving the court at Cracow,[310] Andrew Lubieniecki went to Wieliczka (a town three miles from Cracow). [192] And [there], splendidly clothed, he received the genuine rite of baptism [by immersion] and joined the [Minor] Church, to the great astonishment of the court. Indeed he afterwards even undertook the office of the ministry,[311] and exercised it wholly at his own expense and set his younger brothers Stanislas[312] and Christopher[313] a good example.

The aforementioned Martin Czechowic, having with six brethren removed from Kujawy to Lublin,[314] persuaded many to repeat their baptism, or rather to take it in exchange for [a mere] sprinkling [in infancy]. For he had strongly attacked infant baptism, not only in Polish writings but also in a Latin book entitled *De paedobaptistarum errorum origine, et de ea opinione, qua infantes baptizandos esse in primo nativitatis eorum exortu creditum*, which was printed by Theophilus Adamides in 1575.[315] He had dedicated it to a man distinguished for his very high rank and his very great piety, John Kiszka of Ciechanowiec,[316] captain of Samogitia and cupbearer to his Royal Majesty in the Grand Duchy of Lithuania. This work, which even now is being passed from hand to hand, was written in a rather sharp style, and it brought great ill will upon him and endangered his safety while he was "the target of the rod of magistracy,"[317] as he himself relates in the dedication of his book. With him, his collaboraters were the aforesaid Niemojewski, also Gregory Paul, Sierkierzyński, Kalinowski,[318] and others living at Raków.

[The founding of Raków, 1569, and controversy about
baptism with the advent of Faustus Socinus, 1579]

This town was a town in the palatinate of Sandomierz, the name of which, when its construction started in 1569, was derived by palatine [John] Sienieński from our Polish word *Rak*, that is, Crab. This was [a motif in] the clan coat of arms of his wife, [Jadwiga] Gnoińska.[319] However, Samuel Przypkowski[320] the Great, author of the Life of F[austus] Socinus,[321] remarks that [John] Siekierzyński[322] was the first both to embrace and to defend the views of Socinus, that then others followed, and among them the triplet brothers Lubieniecki,[323] then at length younger ministers who were more apt to embrace the milder and moderate view of Socinus, notwithstanding the authority of the aged and the prejudice of preconceived opinion[324] [**BAnt no. 59**].

[Martin] Czechowic, who was opposed to Socinus and even more hostile to Andrew Lubieniecki on account of their different opinion about baptism, yet when drawing near to death, urged his followers to persevere[325] within the Minor Church. So was ours then called, after the Calvinian Church, called the Major, separated from it.[326]

[193] The repute of Socinus's party [in the Minor Church] was greatly enhanced at that time [c. 1580] by the moderation [on baptism] of Albert Kościeński,[327] minister of the Cracow church. [He was] the successor of Gregory [Paul], when the latter had been driven from Cracow to Raków by the violent and virulent hatred of the Calvinists, who had incited against him the palatine and captain of the city Stanislas Myszkowski, one of their adherents.

[Other episodes in the baptismal controversy, 1566 or 1574, 1653; moderation]

And [Socinus's repute was to be enhanced also] most especially by the influence of Stanislas Lutomirski, superintendent of the churches of Little Poland, a man distinguished by his extraordinary piety, learning, and wisdom. For when the Italian Nicholas Paruta,[328] defending the commonly received (*vulgo recepta*) doctrines, reproached Lutomirski [from Moravia in 1566 or from Transylvania in 1574] in a letter about this controversy,[329] the latter replied, among other things, as follows:

> *Wise lovers of piety do not deny that both the Lord's Supper and [believers'] baptism* (baptismus) *ought to be administered amid the congregation* (*in coetu*) *of the pious.* Yet we know that they are not bound to places and times. Let superstition give way to edification, let all be subject to the peace and quiet of the Church.[330] Paruta [had] meant, in fact, as Budziński notes, that
>
> [A]lthough they [?in Transylvania] considered rebaptism (baptismi iteratio) *necessary to salvation, it should be performed by ablution* (ablutio) *in the church lest by immersing in public they immerse themselves in peril for a mere ceremony.[331]*

But he [?who] did not obtain assent to this.[332] But this restraint (*moderatio*) of the [Minor] Church remains even now on a firm footing, unshaken.[333] Nevertheless in 1653, at Rabkowa in the palatinate of Cracow, liberty of receiving true and genuine baptism was granted to the noble and pious Christopher Wiskowski,[334] cupbearer of Bielsk. He was a sometime member of the court of the Duke Janus Radziwiłł and a strict Calvinist, but afterwards a reborn (*regenitus*)[335] and true Christian, who scorned all the allurements of the world, and the wrath of his wife![336]

CHAPTER FOUR

Of Persecutions Stirred up by Papists[337] and Calvinists[338] against the Confessors of the Truth in Their Impugning the Dogmas of the Trinity and Pedobaptism.

No fair-minded person can but marvel, no pious person can be indignant enough and critical that men who, be they Christian or Catholic, Evangelical or Reformed, all wishing to be called "orthodox," [194] are quite able for religious difference alone to rage inordinately against men differing (*dissidentes*[339]) about matters of faith, even though Christians in religion, in many cases also against their own fellow-countrymen (*populares*), and even kinsmen (*necessarios*). In my judgment, in fact, no more abominable heresy can be found under the sun [than religious intolerance]. This detestable tyranny is indeed a wrong not only against the royal law of love[340] and the majesty of the Divine Being (to whom as the omnipotent and omniscient author and searcher of hearts,[341] and the only King and judge of minds, superior to any exception, belongs rule over consciences), but also against humanity itself and civil society. And so this doctrine, contrary to the Holy Scriptures, to the mild and gentle spirit of Christ, to the teaching and practice of the Apostles, and to the usage of the primitive Church, nay even to that of the first three centuries, has Satan for its author, and Cain, Jews, Gentiles, and the Roman Antichrist for its leaders. With what most shameful and almost exterminatory wars both Germany[342] and the Netherlands,[343] France[344] and England[345] have for this reason been shaken and miserably afflicted, it is for the present not our purpose to treat, especially since we shall elsewhere discharge that duty to later posterity.*

I shall call our Poland happy in times past,[347] since it did not suffer itself to be involved in wicked and destructive wars of this sort, and with the exception of some few private men whom we have noted above, did not descend to bloody persecutions.

[The impetuous Jerome Filipowski, 1566]

Yet ill will of unexampled fierceness fell upon Jerome Filipowski, occasioned by his noteworthy activity in promoting divine truth. Such was their fierceness that indeed all the haters of the truth, though they otherwise strove by turns not so much through petty quarrels as through enmities, could indeed be said to have conspired against him. The controversies that arose about the office of the

---

*In the *Theatrum Cometicum* (Leiden, 1681).[346]

Mediator, about the person of the Son of God begotten before the foundation of the world, and about repeating baptism (*de iterando baptismo*), caused great hostility against the confessors of the truth.

Instigated therefore by adversaries led by the spirit of Rome and Geneva, King Augustus at the Diet of Lublin in [June] 1566 had a law of dreadful character passed and promulgated against the Anabaptists and Tritheists (*Trideitae*) by which they were ordered to leave the realm within a month[348] [**cf. BAnt no. 28**].

And this fell especially upon Filipowski, who at the time was suffering from ill will not only on account of his religion, but also of his marriage that he had contracted with the widow of [Nicholas] Myszkowski [d. 1557], castellan of Wieluń. (His wife [Sophia] descended from the family of Komorowskis, lords of Żywiec). [195] The marriage greatly displeased the Myszkowskis, brothers and relatives of the deceased, famous for their high rank and wealth.[349] Moreover, Filipowski also suffered from envy on account of the treasurership that he held in his native palatinate of Cracow. The citizens of the palatinate had voted a certain tax, but when the King demanded it, the nobles (*primores*) enjoined the treasurer, Filipowski, from turning it over to the King.

Meanwhile those who were ill-disposed to him excited the King's resentment against him on this account.

Therefore they tried to bring it about that by this law Filipowski, as a promoter (*fautor*) of Anabaptists, should suffer capital punishment.[350] Even the deputies of the city (*municipium*) of Cracow[351] deserted him. Alone of them all, Przyłęcki[352] defended the just cause. Such undeserved treatment and injustice greatly moved his noble heart, so that in the council he [Filipowski] burst out in these words: "You are doing me wrong now, wretched man that I am. But the time will come when another King will pronounce judgment, who will defend his people, and his cause will triumph." In this he referred to the heavenly King, as his unsullied loyalty and uprightness and the case itself show. But yet, John Zamoyski, one of the deputies of the palatinate,[353] turned it into suspicion of crime, interpreting it as an allusion instead to Prince John [Sigismund Zápolya] of [Transylvania, claimant to the throne of] Hungary (whom we have mentioned above as son of King Augustus's sister), and taking in a bad sense what had been well intended, nay, adding something of his own in what he told the King in order to incriminate Filipowski, to the effect that the latter had promised (*pollicitus*) that within a year John would come and seize power. This delation[354] disturbed the King, as he had conceived something of this sort in his own mind, addicted to divinations and delusions. Hence he conceived for that reason dislike and displeasure and anger against the innocent Filipowski.

Filipowski for his part conceived righteous indignation and sorrow, and he had it in mind to seek satisfaction for the wrong done him by his malicious accuser, and for the damage to his good name. But Stanislas Cikowski,[355] performing the duty of a good and wise man, dissuaded him from his plan, intimating that Zamoyski was right then so fiercely inflamed with anger against him that he would surely charge him with this [defiance] before the King. So he covered with profuse tears and due silence the anguish that he felt within, and following wise counsel, he abandoned his plan. Nevertheless, being a prudent man, he did not abandon his case in idleness, but went to Zamoyski's father, who already held the senatorial [196] dignity of castellan of Chełm, and poured out his bitter brief into his bosom. The father,[356] upon hearing of the atrocious notoriety of his son as being an informer and a slanderer and knowing full well of what an upright character Filipowski was, sent for his son and reproached him seriously and severely, threatening to disinherit and even kill him if he did not abandon this disgraceful course. So he restrained him by fear of punishment.

Filipowski, nevertheless, vigilant in preserving his own safety, assisted by his friends, had audience with the King, very early in the morning. There he complained of the atrocious wrong done him by ill-disposed men. He also showed sincere sorrow that the disposition of the King, contrary to his native kindness, had been irritated by accusations and slander. He maintained his innocence. He produced authentic documents to refute the malicious charge that he cherished a grudge because [the payment] of the impost had been impeded and reported the deceit of his enemies. And, by proving his fidelity in all respects, he satisfied the King, who accepted what he had said as founded on truth, and confessed not without tears: "Your clan (*gens*) and your people (*populus*), Filipowski, betrayed you to me." He banished anger from his heart. The King having been reconciled, innocence rejoiced: "And this loyalty has attained its end."

Meantime his ill-wishers in large numbers gathered at the palace at the very breakfast hour, daring nothing less than to persuade the King to put Filipowski to death. This they did at an odd time, having snored until broad day to sleep off their excess of wine. Wherefore the King in jest compared their business to the mushrooms of Doctor Miechowita,[357] highly distinguished in the art of medicine, who used to say of those earth ulcers that they should be cleaned in water, boiled in oil, fried in butter, and then thrown out of the window with the frying pan, lest they cause death.

Anger, eager for revenge, consumed all his[358] enemies. Anger set some of them on fire, although bursting forth and glowing for shame, when their malice, even though dashed with cold water, yet for that very reason struggled more and more against it. Thus in the end some were forthwith consumed by their own fire, especially Marshal [Sigismund] Myszkowski of the King's court, Castellan [Nicholas] Wolski of Sandomierz, and *Łukowski*, one of the deputies of the palatinates.[359] But as "wars and struggles are never wanting to the pious, and the pious mind always has something to fight with,"[360] so this pious man was attacked in almost incessant assaults of Satan, as happened indeed a little later.

For when he[361] was giving his brother's daughter in marriage at Piotrkowice to the noble personage Gnojeński[362] [197] of the Rak clan,[363] Simon Zak, minister of the congregation at Cracow,[364] in a discourse (*concione*) spoken at the 14th hour, announced from the pulpit what would be done at a place distant some miles from the city. At the 18th hour, when the young bridal couple were being united by the usual rite with a benediction pronounced,[365] Zak reiterated[366] several times that Filipowski would expose the newlyweds naked to the sight of people in his garden under a fir (*picea*).[367] (The liar ought to have remembered in the old saying, it was a *Juniper*, not a fir.)[368] Budziński, who was an eye-witness of it all and had an important part in it (for he was steward of the wedding),[369] relates that: *Prosper Provana,[370] an Italian by birth, a pious and upright man who had been present at that sermon,[371] wrote Filipowski a letter informing him of this matter. When this was publicly read among the guests at the banquet all of them —whether members of either the Major or the Minor Church or outsiders— could not sufficiently marvel at the man's perversity. Yet this false rumor spread among people, and even insinuated itself at the King's court. Hence Bishop Padniewski[372] of Cracow adjured Budziński, when the latter was paying rent, and seriously asked him whether this was so. But when he had learned the truth, he said:*

> You see, Budziński, that's your Evangelicals (Evangelicos), not my Catholics, who are saying such things of you. How can the rest be trusted, when this minister has lied so, and he an old man?

At this point Budziński adds the exclamation: *And how can the bishops be trusted, who spread such horrid rumors about Arius, as must also be noticed about Paul of Samosata, Photinus, and others, all of whose writings the insolence of the opposite party plunders at will, envying us for having them?[373]*

[The conservative Calvinists turn on the Brethren]

When the Diet of Lublin [1566] was at an end and the atrocious measure against the Anabaptists was passed by the King[374] that had been fathered by the [lay] leaders of the Evangelicals (the latter being instigated by the ministers Sarnicki, Gilowski, Sylvius, and Zak, as well as by [Christopher] Trecy, a scholar of notorious perversity),[375] no innocence was safe, being unarmed and exposed to violence. Indeed it was fiercely attacked by the faction of the adversaries of the truth, as much superior in power as it was furious, and too much given over alike to partisan zeal and to that anger engendered in behalf of [their] favorite errors, which sanction (*patrocinantes*) vices.

In this matter [Stanislas] Myszkowski, captain of the capital of the Kingdom,[376] surpassed the others in cruelty. [198] Since Gregory Paul knew that the latter was hostile to him, he made a timely escape from the threatening danger.[377] Nevertheless, Albin from Iwanowice and some others brought together the brethren, who were like sheep scattered for fear of wolves. To them Albert *Kościeński*[378] was at length given as pastor. Some, allured by love of a quiet life, removed to the country. Budziński also, *who dwelt in the house assigned to Filipowski[379] as [palatinate] treasurer, did not fail to gather the brethren, comfort, and advise them, and invite them to pour out their prayers with him until the time that the fierce storm should cease to rage.* Not without cause did the fierce spirit of Antichrist, armed with the might of violence and secular favor, strike grievous fear into the peaceful flock of Christ, since Geneva had learned from Rome how to maintain its religious tyranny by severe punishments and violent writings.

[Adam Neuser of the Rhenish Palatinate, John Sommer of Lower Saxony, Jacob Palaeologus of Chios converge on Kolozsvár, c. 1572]

Still before their eyes were the recent examples of Servetus, Valentine Gentile, Sylvan,[380] Gribaldi, Ochino, whom the spirit of Geneva, armed with fiery zeal and word, either destroyed or was hounding to their death, heedlessly also threatening with the fatal stroke all those damned as heretics, with whom in the judgment of the Romanists are included not only the followers of Calvin's devices, but also all the others.

Terrifying also was the example of Adam Neuser, who was for ten long years held in confinement in a foul prison at Heidelberg,[381] and whom neither his piety nor his extraordinary learning nor his distinguished merits were able to rescue from such a calamity. But the great and good God, who is wonderful in his works, brought this good man out of prison in a truly admirable way, as though by an angel sent to free him, as we read of the Apostle Paul in sacred history [Acts 16:26]. The story is as follows, and deserves telling, as related by Budziński:

One of the Elector's bodyguards, given him in rotation as watchman, no doubt aware of Adam's piety and pitying him because of his prolonged suffering, when entering the prison to sleep along with him, said to the man instead of greeting him: "Are you still in this prison?" He replied: "Why should I not be here, wretched man, being detained in harsh confinement?" But the other said: "Have you no eyes? Are you not endowed with reason?" Then Adam realized at last that an angel had been sent to him by God to set him free. Then, when the guard had finished his watch and left, he looked about to see whether he could break open the door, which opened upon an arbor and [199] a yard, from which, being a high place, a descent was not easy. At length, with God's help, he found a way of freeing himself from his long misery. The bodyguard who had left was followed by another man of haughty temper and given to wine, and thus minimally fitted to perform the duty of watchman, though eminently suitable for giving a prisoner an opportunity to escape! He entered the prison, and seeing that the bed on which he was to lie with the prisoner was foul, disdained it, saying to the prisoner: "Sleep you here in this filth, while I sleep in the inn." He locked the prison and went away. But the poor prisoner, watching for an opportunity to free himself from the foul prison, tore up into strips all the covers and whatever linen and wool were at hand, tied them together like a rope, then broke open the door and finally let himself down. And so this good man escaped the harsh hands of his adversaries.

Fleeing thence, Neuser wandered through France and Holland, vainly seeking a safe refuge in a world aflame with hatred and religious wars. So he came to Śmigiel,[382] a town in Great Poland, where he stayed for some time. But as he could not safely live even there, he [proposed] to remove to Transylvania, where religious peace prevailed under the pious and truth-loving Prince John Zápolya.[383] He was conducted as far as Cracow by a certain minister of the word of God.[384] There John Sommer, a very learned man (who was also fleeing from the hatred of his ill-wishers), also had arrived on the same day.[385] So on April 15 [1572] they together continued their journey, accompanied for some distance by the brethren.[386]

Soon after reaching Kolozsvár they fell into danger, which is the lot of lovers (cultores) *of the truth. For there was a certain spy who reported them to the authorities. At the time King Stephen [Batory] of Poland held the supreme power there, though he had transferred the rule to his brother Christopher Báthory.[387] Thus Transylvania was at that time ruled under a divided sovereignty; especially since Francis Forgách,[388] formerly a bishop, full of papist spirit which is inimical to the truth and to any equity, had been put in the place of the aged Csáki,[389] who was unwilling to hold the office of chancellor of the principality under a papist prince, and had voluntarily resigned his office. Hence, as religious liberty had diminished and the legal conventions of the country were violated, [200] tyranny was moving unrestrained along the beaten path to banishment, prison, and death. And since this also was threatening Adam [Neuser], the burghers of Kolozsvár, who had come to revere and love him not only for the dignity of his appearance, but also for his unusual learning and purity of character, wished also to protect him from the danger to which his life and person were exposed. Sanctuary was secured for him, though only for a short time.[390] For at the end of three months, threatened with danger from the Emperor's spies,[391] he found it necessary to leave the country and flee to Constantinople. (This, as we have seen above, was also Alciati's lot. So far do the Turks surpass Christians in justice and humanity.)[392] There he was met by Palaeologus, who lamented the man's condition. So far as I[393] know, nothing more has been recorded of him.[394]*

At this point, something should be said with regard to [Jacob] Palaeologus, now that we have mentioned him, although the very subject we have in hand also leads us to him.[395]

"On the life, character, and death of Palaeologus," see F[austus] Socinus, "Against Wujek," 2nd ed., chap. 2, fol. 42.[396] His brief life, as well as a good many things included in this *Historia*, I owe to the especial care of Jacob Ryniewic.[397] On the advice of the brethren, being pressed by the malice of his persecutors, he assumed his mother's name, Trembecki. [He was] a very learned and pious man, to whom the Polish [Minor] Churches are greatly indebted, indeed, even in the dispersion this is so.

Palaeologus was descended from the ancient and distinguished race of the Greek emperors.[398] When he came to Rome and expressed dissent from the dogmas generally accepted, he was brought before the office of the so-called Holy Inquisition (which is the very hangman of Antichrist for minds and bodies) and was thrown into prison.[399] Thence, breaking out of the prison, he fled first to the Protestants in Germany, and from there to our brethren in Poland,[400] with whom, to be sure, he did not agree on certain points of greatest importance, namely, on the divinity and on the invocation of the Son of God, and on the powers of magistracy.[401] From there he went to Moravia, was sought in vain through plots of Pope Pius V, was finally arrested by the Emperor [Rudolph II] at the request of Gregory XIII, and was sent [back] to Rome. Confined there in a foul prison, he remained steadfast in his opinion and was condemned to the stake. But when he saw it and two prisoners bound to posts, he was overcome with the horror of this most painful death, declared that he would recant, [201] and was taken away from the stake. But when in chains he seemed still to persist in holding his original opinion, he was again condemned to the flames and suffered a pitiable death.[402]

CHAPTER FIVE

Of the Open Schism of the Churches That Arose after the Colloquium Held during the Diet of Piotrków in 1565.

During the controversy about the Trinity, which lasted five or six years, the party that sought truth and peace[403] made every effort to prevent its breaking out into an open schism, endeavoring in every way to commend their religious confession by their fairness, moderation, and love. However, it happened opportunely that a great many men of every clan (*generis*) gathered in 1565 at Piotrków to hold a Diet of the estates of the Royal Commonwealth, including also ministers of the word whom the magnates and the knights used to bring with them to the Diet, since liberty was then already flourishing, though guaranteed by no laws.[404] Since Gregory Paul was also among these [ministers], he left no stone unturned to have the old harmony restored by arranging a discussion in the presence of their [respective] patrons, sober and moderate men. And through earnest entreaties this was at length secured by [Jerome] Filipowski, a man burning with zeal for the glory of God, by virtue of the influence that he had with some other men of the equestrian order [the gentry], especially since there were not a few who were unattached to either party.[405]

On the part of the confessors of the truth [**cf. BAnt nos. 26, 27, 55**], Gregory Paul and George Schomann, minister at *Książ*, were appointed disputants (*collocutores*).[406] Present also from the senatorial and equestrian orders were: Castellan John Lutomirski of Sieradz;[407] the speaker of the Chamber of Deputies (the Sarmatian Demosthenes),[408] Nicholas Sienicki;[409] John Niemojewski, judge and deputy of Inowrocław;[410] royal secretary Stanislas Lutomirski, superintendent of the churches of Little Poland; and Jerome Filipowski, who was appointed coordinator (*Director*) of the council (*concilii*) by his party.[411] Also present were

Stanislas Paklepka,[412] minister of the word, as witness (*testis*) and judge (*judex*), together with others. Albert Romeus of Wrzos was appointed the secretary for this side.[413]

On the part of the Trinitarians[414] [202] the disputants and authors of the schism were: Stanislas Sarnicki with his Discordia,[415] Jacob Sylvius,[416] John Rokyta,[417] and Rector Christopher Trecy of the school at Cracow.[418] Their judges and witnesses were John Firlej,[419] palatine of Lublin and Grand Marshal of the Kingdom, Castellan John Tomicki of Gniezno,[420] and *starosta generalny* (*Comes*) Jacob Ostroróg.[421] Their chairman (*praeses*) was Castellan Stanislas Myszkowski of Sandomierz.[422] Their clerk of the proceedings of the discussion was Nicholas Dłuski Jr.

After they came to the appointed place, Gregory [Paul] spoke at the colloquium somewhat[423] as follows:

> I remember some years ago, at the synod of Secemin,[424] I heard from the mouth of Peter of Goniądz (whom I justly hold in high regard as a man both pious and learned, although he differs from me in some respects), by what steps things proceeded beyond the primitive truth so that errors were advanced.[425]
>
> These things, I confess, disturbed my mind at the time, and soon moved me to inquire more carefully into the certainty of the primitive truth. From that time on, I gave myself up wholly to more diligent reading of the Holy Scriptures anew, and to a closer examination of them. I brought together the writings of the Old and the New Instruments: in the former the divine promises of the Messiah, in the latter the fulfillment of them. I compared them all together. I examined also the writings of the early Fathers. But after much labor and effort I found nothing so certain as the reading of the divine Scripture and the genuine sense of it, which the clearest words show well enough. And if I see anything, I see that all things human are justly and rightly to be examined by this touchstone, as the ancients with one mind and one voice agree.
>
> To be sure, what is said of the descent into hell in the very creed called ''Apostolic'' can be reconciled with Scripture, although in so brief a summary of the articles of faith that must be believed for salvation, it does not savor of the apostolic style. Moreover it is not found either in the old Eastern Creed or in that of the Romans,[426] nor even in the Rule of Faith which Tertullian somewhere calls the ''only one unchangeable and unalterable [rule].''* Nor does the third part of the Creed occur there either, which also does not resemble the style of the Apostles in so short a summary of things to be believed, [203] as the thing itself shows although it can be reconciled with Scripture, as the former one also can.[428] But if the Apostles' Creed, in which all of us who bear the name of Christians are baptized, confessing the Father, Son, and Holy Spirit,[429] needs a fair and liberal (*benigna*) explanation, yet more so does the Nicene Creed need one. For in this the expression of τοῦ ὁμοουσίου (consubstantial or coessential) is found, used

---

Liber de virginibus velandis.[427]

of the Son in opposition to Arius. And even though unknown to Scripture, it was nevertheless introduced into the Church despite the opposition of many who rejected the word, and of some who also rejected even the doctrine itself, as many ancient and modern writers freely confess and as no one who is really acquainted with history can deny. Moreover, this newly coined word occasioned so much disagreement that the whole Christian world was engaged in terrible wars on account of a single letter, some making the Son *homoousios* and others *homoiousios* with the Father.[430] To this [former] word indeed, if it had existed in Holy Scripture, an iota would by no means have had to be added.[431] And would that the addition of a strange word, unknown to Holy Scriptures, had never been made! Without it Arius could [never][432] have been convicted of error by the plain teaching of Scripture concerning one God the Father, and his Son Jesus of Nazareth, begotten of the Virgin by the power of the Holy Spirit, the Christ of God, the heavenly King. For that it[433] was done with evil counsel and most unhappy results, history teaches. All the more since they stubbornly defended the newly coined dogma of *homoousia* with armed force, and heaped insults and slanders upon Arius.

And this the Romanist monks even yet do unjustly, and even [so also] those who have abandoned the papacy,[434] though Arius nevertheless followed the Ante-Nicenes (especially Origen, Tertullian, Theophilus of Antioch, Dionysius of Alexandria, Lactantius, all highly renowned leaders)[435] with regard to the Son of God existing before all time or before the world,[436] who in number and substance is other than God the Father. If we swerve a hair's breadth from the truth, none is more ancient than this view.[437]

Of how many evils, unfortunate for Christendom, the arbitrary treatment shown Arius was afterwards the cause. And what party zeal, what hateful names of sects and heresies, what deadly hatred [204] which, alas, still continues, it [the Homoousion] brought forth, is all well known.

By these means the dogma of the [consubstantial] Trinity spread, injurious to God; for that idol no more comports with the word of God than thick darkness with the sun. However, the Creed of Nicaea [325] stops with the words: "believe in the Holy Spirit." To this at length subsequent words were added at the Council of Constantinople [381] and the "Filioque" much later yet.[438] What shall I now say of the Creed that is said to be that of Athanasius?—although strong reasons are not wanting that prove that it was not composed by him, since it both does not agree with the instruction of faith handed down by him in other books, and was published after his time! Hence it is not recorded in the list of his works.[439] For the Nicenes indeed acknowledged one God the Father, creator of all things, together with the Apostles' Creed (although certain learned men, and among them the very distinguished Valla[440] and Erasmus, surmised that the Apostles' Creed was not composed[441] until the Council of Nicaea, and hence in the fourth century), and with all Holy Scripture and primitive antiquity. To be sure, moreover, the Nicenes [of 325] acknowledged that the Son was indeed consubstantial with the Father, though yet "God of God, light of light," ascribing the origin of Deity to the Father. But about the Holy Spirit they said nothing definitely, following the trend of that age, by which the Holy

Spirit either was believed to be the Spirit of God, a power, a gift, the mouth of God, or was confused with the Word of God created, made, begotten before all ages or at the beginning of creation.[442] But [the Holy Spirit was] joined to the confession of the Father and the Son, and not to be separated from the confession of the Father and the Son, nor adored or invoked, but to be gained and sought after. Nay, it was not even to be believed in equally with the Father and the Son, but considered as only something to be acknowledged. For they[443] were unwilling to decide rashly a question that was raised by the curious who were not content with the simplicity of Scripture, and thus was rendered difficult. Hence the complaint of Gregory of Nazianzus to *Cleodonius* that the Nicene Fathers had not handed down a complete doctrine of the Holy Spirit.[444]

Besides, the Creed that commonly passes under the name of Athanasius declares with extreme boldness that Father, Son, and Holy Spirit are one God. Hence anyone sees by what paths men departed from the royal way (*via regia*) of primitive truth and wandered off into byways. Moreover, it is no secret to anyone that the Holy Spirit [205] by the mouth of the Apostles[445] foretold and declared heresies or strange doctrines and corruptions, nay the falling away from the faith. And now it is pointing this out to us as if with finger extended. From this any one who values his eternal salvation is bound to conclude that there must be a return from errors to the primitive truth. Nor indeed can what I am asserting seem [to be merely] my own, new, or recent. But on the contrary I recommend and urge that nothing is more in accord with piety than the primitive simplicity, and doctrine in accord with piety.[446]

And so to conclude, I say that the God who is proclaimed in the Holy Scriptures as the only good, only wise, only powerful,[447] is the God and Father of our Lord Jesus Christ. And I heartily pray and beseech him that through him as the one and only Mediator he may lead back from byways into his straight and plain paths all of us who have been led out of the thick darkness by the bright torch of his word; that he may direct us in them by the power of his Holy Spirit, and bring us thereby to eternal joys, and look with favor on these pious deliberations and efforts, and upon the assembly and discussion designed to this end.[448]

[The schism of the Polish Reformed confirmed; the conservative Calvinists stir the Catholics up against the Brethren, 1565]

Thus indeed did truth then plead its cause in speech and in writing. The other party demanded that a copy of this be made for them, as though they meant to reply to it on the following day.[449] But they did not stand by their promises, showing well the nature of the adversaries of the truth. Lacking in weight of arguments, they took refuge in the vain things of the world, the honor of public offices, the pride of titles, the pretense of antiquity, the boastfulness of power, the philter of promises, the poison of slanders, why, even the parries of persecution. For instead of presenting a reply on the appointed day and a declaration of their view, [cf. **BAnt no. 55**] they enjoined perpetual silence on the confessors

of the truth, a law being passed to have no further discussions of these controversies. Nay, lest any injustice be wanting, they did not even communicate this
conclusion of theirs to the opposite side, nor did they give an opportunity for
any reply or defense, being armed with the authority and power of Firlej, the
mace bearer, who managed the whole Diet.[450]

Moreover, in order to annoy the lovers of the truth, they stirred up their
common enemies [**cf. BAnt no. 55.1**], the Papists, against them as blasphemers
of the Most Holy Trinity, and hence as doing injury to the whole Christian religion. Nay, they even complained of leniency in the Catholics because they were
not punishing them, that is, after the manner of those of Geneva or Bern.[451]
They even took grave offense that Cardinal Hosius acknowledged that the doctrines of the Trinity [206] and infant baptism cannot be proved from the Holy
Scriptures alone.[452] Moreover, they blamed the bishops themselves for neglecting their duty in permitting these blasphemers to ruin so many heedless souls
who had been led astray from their faith in the Most Holy Trinity (*Trias*). They
also employed the usual device of adversaries of the truth by at once publishing
the acts of the discussion and celebrating a triumph before the victory was
won.[453] Thus they imposed on a people (*populo*) inexperienced and laboring
under a preconceived opinion, such that they [the conservative Reformed
divines] might appear as the strenuous defenders of orthodox religion.

They added slanders and with such spots they attempted to stain the unsullied
reputations of Lasocki and Filipowski [**cf. BAnt no. 55.1**], the most upright of
men. Especially [antagonistic were] Sarnicki and Sylvius who, not shrinking
from the abominable fault of ingratitude toward their own patrons and benefac-
tors, charged them with treason against their country. For they said: ''What plot
they formed against their country, the Despot also could tell, were he alive.''[454]
But if, under the principle of the civil law, one is presumed innocent until the
contrary is proven, certainly there could not here be endangered the excellent
reputation of these two men of such approved character that rumor, however
hostile to a worthy man, would always be afraid to lie about them.

And moreover, the history of the Despot related above proves their innocence.[455] Add also that facts themselves, even among the most unfair judges,
free them from all suspicion. For they were far from having any reason for
grudge, and certainly for any disloyalty, toward their country.

In that they had sprung from famous families and were even related by blood
or marriage to the most illustrious men, they were advanced to honorable
offices, and they continually served the Commonwealth in the Diet and elsewhere, enjoying an enviable liberty in religion and possessing great wealth. Or
[far, too, were they from any disloyalty] toward the King, their most happy,
wise, and excellent prince. Neither had they any reasons for devotion to a
foreign prince, a fugitive, grasping after power among a people noted for their
fickle faith.[456] And so the ill-wishers had imprudently thrown the burning mis-
sile of calumny into the water of innocence, where it was immediately
extinguished.

But nevertheless, as a result of this, the [Minor] Church was wretchedly split and was the more liable to insults and exposed to outrages from its common adversaries. A beginning was then forthwith made with three poor brethren who for several years had lived in Biecz,[457] whom the parish priest of this town attacked [207] by virtue of the measure lately set forth by the King against "Anabaptists and Arians" and holders of new heresies.[458] The priest was preparing to banish them from his town, having procured from the King a writ addressed to the local magistrate. But they, though men of the simplicity of doves, showed the wisdom of serpents in avoiding the threatened attack.[459] They said that they were, in fact, neither Anabaptists nor Arians, and were not introducing anything novel, but that they adhered to the primitive and Catholic religion as expressed in the Apostles' Creed, and were not departing from it by a finger's breadth, even if someone should try to lead them away from it by crafty reasoning of the human mind. So without slighting the King's command or refusing to obey the magistrate of Biecz, those good men enjoyed peace and liberty in that town.

CHAPTER SIX

Containing the Last Will and Testament of George Schomann, and the Whole History of His Life and Death, as well as That of More Acts of the Churches.

We have previously spoken of the controversies about the Trinity and infant baptism and the subsequent persecutions, intending soon to treat of the controversies about the deity and invocation of the Holy Spirit. I shall take the opportunity to insert in the midst of all this the last Will and Testment of George Schomann, a man highly distinguished by his learning and piety, and very greatly esteemed by the School[460] and the Church. For it contains not only the whole history of his life and death, but also no small part of the history of our churches. In addition it contains something also about the persecutions of the confessors of the truth.

And Peter Statorius [Jr.],[461] son of the Peter [Statorius, Sr.] who had provoked the controversy about the Holy Spirit,[462] was appointed successor to this Schomann in the ministry of the church in Lusławice.[463] And this writing is indeed in all respects worthy of being remembered by coming generations, since it is an excellent example of both piety and diligence and good sense, as well as of paternal *tenderness*[464] deserving to be imitated by all.

But yet I have a special reason for inserting it [the Testament] in this work nor indeed one that, as it seems to me, should be lightly esteemed. [208] For it was thirty years ago[465] when I was journeying with my father of blessed memory[466] to Kisielin, a town in Volhynia.[467] There, soon, George Czaplic-Szpanowski scion of an ancient and illustrious family (elsewhere, please God, to be mentioned with respect),[468] received the Muses that had been banished from Raków.[469] And my father, that frugal manager of my time and strict accountant of it, had given me this Will [and Testament] composed by the blessed Schomann to be read in the carriage, recommending it to me as of unusual worth. It came to pass that the reading and the summer heat caused me to fall asleep, I being only a lad. So the writing fell from my hands. But when my father discovered this, he bade me get out of the carriage and hunt for the lost writing, while he continued his journey to the place appointed, a mile and a half distant. Obeying my parent, I retraced the way on foot, found the writing, and having met good companions on the way, found my father late in the evening at the appointed place. So much did he value this writing, and so much did the loss of it then cost me!

[Schomann's autobiographical *Testamentum*, originally placed by Lubieniecki at this point, was removed from the *Historia* (1685), because it had already been printed by Benedict Wiszowaty in Christopher Sand, *BAnt* (1684) 3, 191–98, at the same press. This invaluable personal record, 1530–c. 1591, has not, after some deliberation, been restored here to its original place, partly because it recapitulates several happenings already covered by Lubieniecki and Budziński before him, and its parallel accounts have been adduced by cross-reference to our Appendix of Related Documents as *BAnt, RD 3*, nos. 13–43.]

CHAPTER SEVEN

Containing the Controversies about the Person and Deity of the Holy Spirit [1561–65].

We have mentioned above how Spiritus, a native of Holland, gave occasion to reflect upon the invocation of the Holy Spirit,[470] and also how Remigian Chełmski called it in question at the twelfth synod at Pińczów in 1559;[471] how Peter Statorius [Sr.] behaved there; and finally how Gregory Paul and other pious and truth-loving men discussed this matter with mature deliberation, summoning the common doctrine of the Trinity before the scales of judgment and examining it by the touchstone of the word of God. We then mentioned that a reply touching this matter was sent [by the synod] to Chełmski,[472] but that Statorius, who was living with him and had the written opinion in hand, when he intimated, further, at the nineteenth synod held in Pińczów in 1561,[473] that Chełmski was not well satisfied with the reply. [Then] Statorius himself was directed [by the synod] to reply to him more at length, as the Spirit moved.

And he did indeed reply, [209] but in such a way that his own opinion on this subject is not clear, as I learn from a note added by his own grandson, John [Statorius] Stoiński [**cf. BAnt no. 4**], the distinguished minister of the church at Raków. [Peter] Statorius [Sr.] was only saying that Biandrata had been charged by Calvin with cherishing the poison of Servetian wickedness, while his own opinion, which he set forth at the synod, was approved by all, [even] though he was asked whether he held to a plurality of Gods when saying that the Father is unbegotten, and [yet] believing that his only Son was begotten. "In fact"— these are his own words—"all of us who are living with Biandrata come I know not how, under suspicion of heresy. But if those are heretics who believe in the Father, Son, and Holy Spirit, after the precept of the Holy Scriptures, I willingly confess that I am one of their number. That reproach with respect to the Holy Spirit, which that wicked demon had prepared for me, has not yet come, but I am at peace with my own good conscience."[474]

I pass over what Węgierski inserted about Statorius in his *Historia Ecclesiarum Slavonicarum* as being well known to the public.[475] Budziński relates that *[W]hen he [Statorius] was afterwards promoted to the direction of the Pińczów school, he professed the true teaching about the Holy Spirit, namely: it is idolatry[476] to invoke the Holy Spirit before conducting worship in churches and schools so that it may come to them, when not a single word of that it is reported in Holy Scripture, and surely not the invocation of it. Nay it is not even taught in the oracles of God that it is some person in the Divine Being* (in Divinis), *or is even to be believed in.* Add, as we have seen, that this dogma [of the consubstantial deity of the Third Person] was quite unknown to the *doctores* of the Church for some centuries, and was not finally established until late in the fourth century.[477]

When controversy arose between Statorius and certain theologians, he pressed them hard with the authority of Holy Writ, while they endeavored to defend their preconceived opinion under the pretense of some of the more difficult passages of Holy Scripture and on the testimony of the later doctors of the Church. He taught and affirmed against them from the word of God that the Holy Spirit is in no respect a person, but a power and a gift of God which he bestows upon the faithful and divides according to his good pleasure in various measure; but that to Christ, as his only begotten Son and heir of all his good things, he gave a greater abundance of it than to all others, and so anointed him with this oil of gladness above all [210] his fellows.[478] Thus, indeed, of the plenitude (which he wished to have dwell in Christ) all others have received differing portions.[479] Therefore it appears that the Holy Spirit is neither creator of heaven and earth, nor some God, and hence is not to be invoked, since it can be given, measured, and divided into parts, which cannot be said of God.

[The argumentation of the Statorians for a Christ-adorant Ditheism]

Thus from that controversy the truth began to arise more radiantly. For many, even those who held with the party opposed to Statorius and supported that point of faith against him,[480] aroused by his reasons as though from deep slumber, were overcome by their weight and surrendered to the truth. I find it reported in written records[481] that they used these arguments, which I have thought it worth while to add here:

> When Christ asked his disciples whether they believed God or in God, he bade them also to believe in him [cf. John 14:1]; but we nowhere read that he commanded them to believe in the Holy Spirit.[482]
>
> His disciples, when teaching the doctrine of the Holy Spirit, warned the faithful to try the spirits, whether they were of God [cf. 1 John 4:1].
>
> Christ, when teaching the Apostles in what the way of attaining eternal life consisted, said that "the Father is the only true God," but that he, that is "Jesus, is his Christ" and Ambassador, making no mention of the person of the Holy Spirit [cf. John 17:3].
>
> When Christ, risen from the dead, was about to ascend into heaven, he said to the faithful that he was about to "ascend to his Father and their Father, to his God and their God," making no mention of an ascent to the Holy Spirit [cf. John 20:17]. In the same place the holy Evangelist recorded [cf. John 21:25] that Jesus indeed did far more miracles than either he wrote down or the world could contain for their number, but that he had only written down certain ones in the book of the gospel "to the end that his disciples might believe that Jesus was the Christ, the Son of God, and that thus they might attain eternal life." Nor does he here mention the Holy Spirit when he treats of the way of attaining eternal life.
>
> Certainly, it is true that in the Creed that is called the Apostles' Creed we do profess: "And I believe in the Holy Spirit." Yet this makes no reference to adding the prayers that in the churches are commonly directed to the Holy Spirit. For although Christ taught that [211] we must believe also in him, not in God only, yet faith is directed to God in a way different from faith in Christ, since it is through Christ as Mediator that it reaches him and ends in him. But one believes in God much differently from believing in the Holy Spirit. Thus in the same Creed we confess that we also believe in the Holy Church of Christ. Moreover, when the Apostle writes to Philemon [5] that he thanks God because he has heard "of his love and faith towards the Lord Jesus and towards all the saints," it is probable that occasion was taken from this to insert these words about faith in the Holy Church.[483] One ought then first to recognize the fact itself, in order that then the reason and nature of one's faith, or of what is to be transformed into it, may be understood. The holy records also report [cf. Exod 14:31] that the people believed in God and in Moses. But as Moses was different from God, so also was the faith. So then, the faith in Christ as Mediator, and in the Holy Spirit, and in the saints, is different from that which is directed to the Most High God.
>
> For to believe in him is to have faith in all his commands and promises, and to follow his will as he revealed it through angels, prophets, and last of all through his Son.
>
> To believe in Christ is to have faith in him as Mediator and Ambassador of God teaching in the name of his Father, and to imitate[484] him, but also, to

adore and to invoke him as Lord and the Christ made by God to the glory of God the Father, since Christ is to be believed in such a way that we may believe in God through him. And Christ is to be adored and invoked, as Scripture plainly teaches,[485] no matter what this person or that, being led by a half-Jewish spirit, may have yammered as though the worship of the Most High were diminished by the worship of Christ.[486] For it is precisely through him that worship is indeed most firmly established and increased, nay, worship cannot otherwise be rendered under the New Covenant, since Christ himself says [John 7:16]: "My teaching is not mine, but his that sent me," and: "He that believeth in me, believeth not in me, but in him that sent me" [12:24]. This with equal right can and should be said also of the worship and invocation of Christ, while the Apostle [cf. 2 Cor 1:20] also removes all scruple by the words: "to the glory of God the Father."

Moreover, to believe in the Holy Spirit is to believe that it is the inbreathed spirit of God, a power, a gift to be sought from God, which makes believers of those who receive it and consecrates them to divine uses, and thus, by giving them this pledge, confirms to them their inheritance of eternal life.

[212] To believe in the Holy Church is to believe that the Church of Christ ought to be holy, blameless, glorious, having no "spot or wrinkle or any such thing," since Christ shed his blood on the cross to this end that he might make her so for himself, even as the Apostle [cf. Eph 5:27] teaches. Whence it appears that when several gods are brought in to be adored and invoked, this is not done without danger of idolatry, since the Apostle [1 Cor 8:6] expressly teaches the same thing: that "there is one God, God the Father, from whom are all things," and we through him.

Moreover about the Holy Spirit the Apostles [cf. John 14:26] taught by word of mouth and in writing as follows:

'Receive ye (said Christ) the Holy Spirit which after my departure God will send you in place of me, another Comforter and most perfect Teacher, who shall bring all things to your remembrance which ye have heard from me, and shall lead you into all truth.' Therefore it is written [John 1:16]: "Of his fulness have we all received;" and this Holy Spirit is called "the Spirit of Christ" [cf. Rom 8:9]. For Christ so divides it and bestows it as the Spirit of Moses was formerly divided among the elders of the people.[487]

"He in whom the Spirit of truth dwelleth, searcheth the deep things of God" [1 Cor 2:10]. Those in whom it is not are animals who do not receive heavenly things. "For as no one knoweth what is in man but the spirit that is in man, so no one knoweth what is in God but the Spirit of God," as the Apostle teaches [1 Cor 2:10–11], who also says further on [1 Cor 6:17]: "But he who is joined to the Lord is one Spirit with him." It is verily something great when Christ also says [John 14:10; 10:30]: "I am in the Father and the Father is in me: The Father and I are one"; on account, that is, of the very close connection that is formed through the Holy Spirit. That (*Iste*) leads us to every good work [cf. Rom 8:28], and in it [the Spirit] "we cry, Abba (Father)" [Rom 8:15–16]. Therefore our bodies are temples of God and of the Holy Spirit (since God dwells in us through the Holy Spirit which he has given us), so that both our body and our spirit are God's [1 Cor 3:16].

The same Spirit in us [cf. Rom 8:26] "searches all things, and intercedes for us with groanings that cannot be uttered." And God knows what he wants. This "Spirit beareth witness with our spirit, that we are sons of God" [Rom 8:16]. Ananias had no such spirit when he lied [Acts 5:3]. Whoever sins against this Spirit, with the utmost wickedness ascribing its works to an unclean spirit, obtains no forgiveness [cf. Mark 3:29–30]. This Holy Spirit, as Stephen confesses, was always resisted by the [213] Jews [Acts 7:51]. This Spirit revealed that he saw the Lord's Christ [cf. Acts 7:55–56].[488]

This Spirit spoke through the Apostles before kings and judges of the earth. Whoever is not endowed with it is fouler than any beast. Before the Lord Jesus was glorified, the Apostles did not have this Spirit so glowing as afterwards [John 20:22]. Peter did not have it when he denied him [Matt 26:34 etc.]. The Apostles did not have it when they wished to call down fire from heaven to destroy the inhospitable Samaritans, not knowing by what Spirit they were being led [Luke 9:54].

Christ says [Luke 11:13]: "The Father gives this Holy Spirit to those who ask him." "The world does not know it, and will not receive it" [John 15:17], preferring the friendship of Satan to the friendship of God. Impelled "by this Spirit," the Apostles "proclaimed the great things of God" after their disciples learned that it existed [cf. Acts 4:31].

With this [Spirit] God anointed his Son above measure [Ps 45:7; Heb 1:9]. By this the prophets foretold the sufferings that were to befall Christ.

Nor do those know it who sing: "Come, Creator Spirit."[489]

Concerning this, Cardinal Hugo in his explanation of the Mass recorded at the end: "And now why is prayer not directed to the Holy Spirit? Because the Holy Spirit is not God, but is a gift of God. Hence it is not to be directed to the gift, but to him who bestows the gift."[490]

These arguments the confessors of the truth then urged not less with courage than with the power of the Spirit, in order to proclaim the nature of the Holy Spirit, which is the Spirit of God, and not God himself. Statorius then justly said with the poet: "Let me play the part of the whetstone, which is to sharpen the tool, though itself having no share in the cutting."[491]

[Petrus Statorius deserts the Brethren for the Tritheists, 1567]

For his good mind that his initial teaching about the Holy Spirit had sharpened, his love of the world had blunted in him. For at the synod held at Łańcut[492] in 1567 [at n. 512], when there was active controversy about the Holy Spirit, and there was much discussion between the parties not only about the Holy Spirit but also about the Son of God, he took the opposite side and denied that he had ever taught thus about the Holy Spirit, fearing that his adversaries might deprive him of his livelihood. Furthermore, the printer Alexis Rodecki[493] told him to his face that he had learned this article on the Holy Spirit from Statorius, when pursuing his own studies at Pińczów where, as we have said, [214] Statorius was rector of the school.[494] Yet Statorius nevertheless denied this to his face. He [now] said that the Holy Spirit was God, to be worshiped as God, and that whoever teaches otherwise is of his father the Devil.[495] Budziński notes this "unstable faith of his" and hence calls him "Proteus,[496] one from whom this Spirit of God withdrew, who also offered his support to a written error," and adds that "he died shortly afterwards."[497] Even Otwinowski argues that he did not always employ the talents entrusted to him in support of the truth (for he was a very learned man, eloquent and able, as is evident especially from the Polish grammar[498] published by this French native), but that at length he adhered to the more powerful party of the Trinitarians.

CHAPTER EIGHT

Of Efforts for Harmony amid So Many Differences of Opinion and Controversies, Especially of the Synods Held at Łańcut and Skrzynno in 1567.

As we have seen above, many were the measures of restoring harmony and bringing peace back again to the [Polish Reformed] Church of Christ, or at least of introducing Christian tolerance into it. Measures with this in view were often and earnestly attempted in different ways, especially the canons adopted at the synods of *Pińczów* in 1562[499] and of Mordy in 1563.[500] Even though these efforts were frustrated by the patrons of errors, with the power of the carnal arm defending them and daily spreading them, nevertheless the efforts of the lovers of the truth for renewing peace in the Church did not cease. They were much grieved that the Church was so divided, especially by the discussion held at Piotrków in 1565. It is no wonder that Gregory of Nazianzen, writing to Procopius, once complained of the unhappy outcome of all the councils, in which more attention is paid to ambition than to piety.[501]

[The schism of Farnowski and Peter of Goniądz, 1565]

But even more were they ["the lovers of truth"] grieved that while the controversies between the Trinitarians and Unitarians concerning God, the Son of God, the Holy Spirit of God, and those concerning the baptism remained unsettled, a new schism was raised [within the Minor Church] by Peter of Goniądz and Stanislas Farnowski both of whom defended the view of Arius.[502] [These two Ditheists carried on] [cf. **BAnt no. 58**] so bitterly that they uttered many poisonous things against the confessors of the truth,[503] not only in speech but also in writing.[504] [215] And they persisted in this evil course to the end, not employing their excellent talents in the right way. Strange that those who disagreed with the adversaries of the truth in the articles about the Trinity and baptism, yet joined with them in counsels and efforts against the confessors of the truth, as though a conspiracy had been formed.

Both parties[505] indistinguishably imposed upon the confessors of the truth [the Unitarians] the invidious names of Ebionites, Samosatenians, and Arians, despite the fact that those two[506] were [themselves] nothing but new Arians.[507] Peter of Goniądz, who ten years earlier penetrated Little and Great Poland,[508] disturbing them with the view of Servetus about the preeminence of the Father, was no doubt armed by the Wittenbergers against those who honor the truth, as well as by others with whom he conferred orally or by letters.[509]

When a synod had been appointed at Łańcut and the business had been announced, all who had the glory of God at heart were called to assemble there[510] [with Budziński as one of two secretaries].[511]

[The synod of Łańcut: 14 June, 1567,[512] Calvinists, Tritheists, Ditheists, and six Cracow Unitarians]

And accordingly, four [lay] members of the congregation at Cracow went thither: Simon (Ronemberg,[513] *as I suppose*), *an apothecary of Cracow, a man of exceptional piety endowed by God with an unusual gift in offering public prayers, so that it may well be said that he had received the spirit of grace and of prayer, Budziński, Alexis (perhaps the aforesaid Rodecki),[514] and Zalaszowski.[515] And [there were] also two ministers of the word: [John] Siekierzyński the Younger[516] and Stanislas Lutomirski. [The latter] had resisted the truth long and strongly but at length yielded to it. [He had been] mindful of the example of Stanislas Orzechowski who also, after he had long and stoutly resisted his [Lutomirski's] father-in-law, John Łaski, at length publicly took leave of him in these words [in agreement]: "These hands I offer you, O man of God, in submission."[517]*

No doubt these [six from Cracow], too, wished to bear witness that the truth and the glory of God had been their joy and care. But while unexpected [at Łańcut] and unwelcome, they nevertheless came as guests to the place where had gathered those holding diverse doctrines, yet agreeing together in this: that [the unitarian] *confessors of* [merely] *the name of the Son of Man ought to be maligned with bitter hatred.[518]* (Budziński, who had a large part in these matters, observes that) *many of the nobles were more moderate than the ministers of the word, with the sole exception of Ivan Karniński,[519] whom he (taught by his own experience) call immoderately virulent and worse not only than any Calvinist, but even than a heathen. In a sharp encounter with him, a certain nobleman named Sikorski[520] who, though holding a different view than of the Son of God, was yet not so extreme as the rest, began his speech [216] with these words.*

> *"Ye shall know them by their fruits [cf. Matt 7;16] and "Test the spirits, whether they are from God" [1 John 4:1] are admonitions from the Holy Spirit itself, profitable to us all in case of need and everywhere to be employed. Therefore they are now to be applied by me too, Ivan, while I observe that thou art[521] aflame with bitter jealousy. I cannot but say to thee sincerely and earnestly, by way of duty, that thou art not being led by the Spirit of God nor of Christ, which is gentle and humble. For thou hast of thine own accord taken a seat here in the midst of those who have of their own accord also gathered here from places widely scattered. And thou wishest to give them orders and to impose upon them the necessity of believing what thou believest to be true, heaping reproaches upon them, in order that pious hearts, in hope of thy favor, may think, may believe, may speak contrary to their own judgment. Such tyranny has indeed no place even in political affairs among pagans. God forbid that it should have place in religious affairs, where one's eternal salvation is at stake, where the discussion is about the errors from which we are trying to free our feet as from unfriendly and unfordable morasses. Dost thou wish here to win thy cause by a stentorian voice or even by scandals, that is, by the same means by which the Pope of Rome thinks he has won his case against thee? Why, I am ready to die at hearing such things. For I too have come hither, not that someone may overcome me by rude shouts, nor to overcome someone else, but that we may discuss together in love. We certainly are not here submitting our free necks to thine imperious vociferation nor to that of any man, nor to harsh pride, but to the gentle word of God and the mild yoke of Christ.*

Ivan [Karniński] tried by raising his voice to make up for the weakness of his judgment, but ashamed and confused, he was obliged to abandon his purpose and to stop his mouth, being awed into respect by the presence of Bal, Domaradzki, the Gołeckis, and other men prominent by their noble birth and their dignified bearing.[522] Thereupon the brethren from Cracow[523] were bidden to withdraw from the meeting.

Then the rest took counsel whether or not they ought to reconvene with them to discuss the Son of God. Some agreeing and some disagreeing, Peter Statorius[524] who, although a traveling companion of Ivan, was still acquainted with the truth, was unwilling to draw out the opinions (keeping a wicked craftiness in his heart) and opposed the encounter, saying: "They will fall away from their cause, and will withdraw, confused with shame. I know them. I know you. I know what I am saying.''

Then Ivan, immoderate in passion and tongue, attacked him[525] in sharp words, [217] charging him with partiality, and shouting in an angry voice: ''Why not fight with them hand to hand? Have we not oracles of God at hand? We read in Micah [5:2]: 'And his going forth from the days of eternity;' and in 1 John [5:1]: 'Whosoever loveth him that begat, loveth him also that is begotten of him.' ''[526]

But [Stanislas] Farnowski[527] asserted that this passage does not fit the case.[528] Statorius himself snatched it away from him, saying that it treats of the generation of the faithful from the seed of the Word, not of the generation of Christ.[529] So Ivan's eagerness to dispute wore out. Yet he bore it ill that he had been rebuked by others and corrected as to the meaning of the words of Holy Scripture.

But Farnowski, at the same time, encouraged the defense of the preexistence (praeeternitas) of the Son, taking support for this view from the beginning of the gospel of John [1:1] about the Word, or rather the speech, which was in the beginning. Here Siekierzyński[530] asked him where he could show a Word operating from the beginning of the world and declared that he to the contrary would show as clearly as day the Word operating from the beginning of the Gospel, in the time of both Johns, namely, the Baptist and the Evangelist.[531] Thereupon Farnowski, unable to control either his passion or his tongue, tried to wear him down with his shouts and, failing in reasons, descended to insults, as though he were dumping them from a cart. But when the [chosen] arbiters saw this, it seemed to them unfair, indecent, and harmful to cover the matter with silence; and they put a stop to the quarrel and an end to the angry disputes; and by common consent they appointed a synod for June 24 at Skrzynno, a town of Little Poland, and invited to it all concerned for their own salvation and the glory of God and his Christ. Then Ivan alone, being too full of jealousy, swore that he would never assist in holding a discussion with a sect that was, as he said, blasphemous against God, nay, would see to having the synod broken up.

All separated from one another at the synod of Łańcut with love unimpaired, mutually promising that they would cultivate harmony and observe the limits of moderation until the next synod. Here Ivan alone departed from them all, and renounced his friendship with the other party, especially with Filipowski. In this matter he remained firm beyond measure, or to use a more fitting word, obstinate to the very last, driven by the unyielding spirit of Calvin.

[The synod of Ditheists and Unitarians at Skrzynno, 24 – 29 June 1567][532]

Then came the day appointed for the synod, [218] at which gathered one hundred and ten nobles and ministers from Little and Great Poland and from Lithuania, besides a crowd of people of both sexes from the neighborhood,[533] all with minds alert and ears cocked to hear the discussions of religious matters. [Jerome] Filipowski was made (creatus) chairman (praeses) and moderator of

this meeting by general vote, great confidence being placed by all in the wis-
dom, piety, and fairness of this distinguished man. Nor did he disappoint their
expectations.

It was provided for at the outset by this able champion of fairness that in
order to obviate quarrelsome and heated controversies, each party should
observe mildness and modesty and should state its views moderately through
appointed (electi) disputants (collocutores); but that if anyone wished to ask any
necessary question, one should do it with the leave of the one speaking, since in
this meeting very long proceedings were in prospect. Therefore the party that
contended that the Word, or Son of God, existed before the Mother, and together
with the Father created heaven and earth, chose as disputants John Kaza-
nowski, Farnowski, John Niemojewski (judge of Inowrocław, who had already
been baptized by Czechowic), Nicholas Żytno, John Falconius, Martin
Czechowic, Daniel Bieliński.[534] The office of secretaries was entrusted to
Lawrence Krzyszkowski[535] and Thomas Świechowski.[536]

The other party, which defended the primaeval truth handed down in the holy
records that the Son called the Verbum *or* Sermo *of God, because he was the*
interpreter of the Father's will, did not exist before the foundation of the world,
but had the beginning of his existence at a certain time, namely within the life-
time of John the Baptist and the other John, the Evangelist and Apostle, in the
reign of the Roman emperor Octavius Augustus, as the sacred history expressly
states,[537] chose as disputants **[cf. BAnt no. 28]** *George Schomann, Gregory*
Paul, John Siekierzyński, Matthew Albin, John Baptysta [Święcicki] of
Lithuania, Martin Krowicki, Simon Budny, and Jacob Kalinówki. As secretaries
they appointed Albert Kościeński and Stanislas Budziński.[538]

On his word we rely,[539] as that of a trustworthy witness, incorporating it in
this *History.*

Each party conducted the matter exclusively in the words of Holy Scriptures,
without trying to observe the scrupulous carefulness of scholastic procedure in
their debates, which were in any case not about philosophical questions and for
the vain laurel crown that is commonly sought with might and main for fame in
trifles, [219] but rather were about the eliciting of the primitive truth and the
attainment of eternal glory in heaven. Moreover, since [even] those [scriptural]
words admit and seem to bear different explanations, they proceeded so that
when one thing was compared with another, the clear one shed light on the
obscure one, the easy one on the difficult one. And so, accordingly, by the use
of reason, truth was elicited from the darkness of ignorance and was brought to
light. Budziński, a writer of well-known trustworthiness and industry, reports
that *[t]here was almost no passage of either the former or the latter Testament*
that one or the other party did not cite, though it would be a long matter to fol-
low them up.[540]

At length they separated from each other in such a way that each party said
to the other that they would acknowledge no other as Son of God and Saviour of
the world than Jesus Christ crucified, whom God begot in a chaste Virgin by the
Holy Spirit, anointed with the same, whom he sent into the world, raised from

the dead, seated at his right hand in heaven, and sent for himself a messenger for that eternal Word.[541] Of this Word Augustine wrote that if he sent himself, he sanctified himself, himself came from himself and in his own name.[542]

Having left the synod, even if they went away differing in opinions,[543] they yet took no bitterness away, except for Farnowski, who even after this attacked the opposite party with barbed writings.[544] But they,[545] having regard for their own reputation and safety as against the assaults of the three or four sects, namely the Papists, Lutherans, Calvinists, and Ditheists (*Binaturiae*) or Farnovians (although Farnowski agreed with them [the Unitarians] on the one God and as to his preeminence), published the whole record of what was then done. This was edited by Stanislas Cikowski, chamberlain of Cracow, with the addition of the replies to all the objections of the opposite party.[546] Deserving both the special attention of the debater and the retention of the reader is the conclusion or rule and law drawn up by the chairman of the synod [of Skrzynno] with the unanimous consent thereof and adopted by them, although not altogether observed. It is as follows:

> The Trinity is reverently and sacredly to be retained on this condition that brotherly love be continued according to the command of the Son of God, and that all bear with one another's infirmities, but that no one may by any means abuse another.[547] For if one does otherwise, he shall render account to God. Meantime it is allowed to treat of this in writing, but in such a way that one does not misrepresent another, revile him, or condemn him either in private or in public.
>
> [220] They may hear one another's prayers and sermons with the understanding that the prayers are offered in a form that is given in the word of God. But if anyone offers prayers, or in place of a sermon teaches not in the usual style observed in Holy Scripture, in this let each follow the leading of his own conscience. If perchance one is unwilling to hear the prayers or sermons and goes out, it is not to be taken as an offense in him, as though he broke the bond of brotherly love.[548]
>
> Likewise in the baptism of infants and in the act of commemorating the death of Christ the Lord [at the Supper], each one must follow the leading of his own conscience in this difficult confusion of affairs introduced by the Romanists, while all shall wait to see what and how they may prove themselves to one another.[549]
>
> And we shall pour out fervent prayers that we may with one mind employ true instruction in amending our lives to the glory of God and our mutual comfort, no one being willing to lord it over the faith of another, since for each the Lord and Giver is God himself, until in his own time he sends his angels as wiser ministers to pluck up the tares and separate them from the wheat [Matt 13:30, 39]. Meanwhile let us not uproot nor injure one another. For this Christ would not permit to his Apostles, still less does he permit it to us.[550]
>
> Done at Skrzynno, 29 June 1567

And these things were then wisely considered and justly carried through.[551]

[The Ditheist Schism: 1567 – 78][552]

But these things were not observed by those who, having once undertaken the defense of implanted errors [despite the agreements of Skrzynno], left nothing untried to gratify their desire and vex the supporters of the truth. The standard-bearer of the disagreement was Farnowski, [**cf. BAnt nos. 58, 75.1**] the most passionate supporter of the Arian [Ditheist] opinion, puffed up by the pride of ambition. He, having got a patron in [Stanislas] Mężyk, captain of [Nowy] Sącz, took up his residence in that town on the border of Hungary and there opened a school,[553] ardently defending the preeternity or preexistence of the Son before the foundation of the world.[554]

How sharply not only the Papists but also the Calvinists defended infant baptism, and how splendidly the supporters of the truth endeavored to correct this corruption of the Church and rejected it, we have seen above.[555]

[221]CHAPTER NINE

Of the Enmity of the Reformed against the Lovers of the Truth at the Synod of Cracow in 1568, Which Gave Offense to Andrew Dudith, and so Furnished Him an Incentive for Inquiring into the Truth; Also a Brief Account of His Life and Death.

[Christopher Trecy interferes with the Publication in Basel
of the *Sylvae* of Andrew Frycz Modrzewski]

The ill will that Christopher Trecy, rector of the school at Cracow and an adherent of the party of Sarnicki and Discordia, had shown against the confessors of the truth in words and efforts and letters written to the Swiss, he also showed in very deed toward Andrew Frycz Modrzewski.[556] He was a man highly distinguished by his piety and learning, to say nothing of his noble birth and the dignity of his office, and deserving to be named among the first men of his time. King Augustus had commanded him as his secretary to collect all the different views as to the Trinity, or rather to reduce the discordant ones to harmony. This he undertook after the King had gone to the war against Muscovy in 1565,[557] and happily composed that most excellent work of the four *Sylvae*. He completed it in 1569, but for various reasons was unable to publish it in his life-time.[558]

He gives an account of this in the preface of the fourth *Sylvia*, in which he modestly enough refers to the wiles of one of his own countrymen. In fact he means Trecy who, upon coming to Basel whither Frycz had sent this work of his to be printed by his old friend, the skillful printer Oporin,[559] and hearing that such a book of Frycz was being printed by him, asked to be given an opportunity to view it. When the good man,[560] measuring the other's craftiness by his own integrity, had complied with his wish,[561] he [Trecy] got into his net the booty he sought, noticed in it arguments for the truth far stronger than the answers, exceptions, and objections of the Trinitarians, at once left Basel, escaped, broke away, carried off Frycz's book which had been loaned to him in good faith, and so prevented its publication. Then, when back in Poland, he met Frycz at Cracow who asked him whether he had seen [222] Oporin and heard anything of the publication of the book. Trecy replied, although perhaps concealing it [even at that moment] on his person, that he had seen neither Oporin nor the book.[562]

Meanwhile, Oporin, seeing that he had been cheated by an imposter, informed Frycz of Trecy's contemptible fraud. When Frycz saw Trecy, he sharply rebuked him, but found him brazenly shameless. Seeing that he was wasting time, as if in trying to snatch a crumb from Cerberus, he related the affair with due resentment to Stanislas Myszkowski, palatine and captain of Cracow. When he found the latter laboring under a preconceived opinion and too much given over to partisan zeal, he complained to the palatine of the deceit of the thievish Trecy, urgently demanded the return of the book, deplored that the wrong done him was contemptuously belittled even by the palatine, and [thereupon] bitterly sought court action. But at length Frycz yielded before the power of the palatine who protected Trecy.

Finally Frycz searched through his files, and without delay composed the work anew from arguments and drafts that had been all but thrown away, and finished it before death overtook him. And so we have at length that most excellent book of the *Sylvae*, though very small in bulk, preserved from destruction.

[Andrew Dudith Sbardellati at the joint synod in Cracow, 1568;
appealing address of Jerome Filipowski]

Meantime the wise and truth-loving men devoted all their efforts to defending and spreading the truth, paying no attention to their adversaries' insolence, anger, and insults, with which they wickedly strove to hinder the good cause, yet with slight success if any, since all those who revered truth and honor strove the more eagerly for the glory of true praise in the face of all the obstacles in the world.

At that time deservedly first among them was Andrew Dudith Sbardellati,[563] sometime bishop of Knin, afterwards of Csanád [**cf. BAnt no. 60**], and then of

Pécs. Councillor of the three Emperors, Ferdinand I, Maximilian [II], and Rudolph [II], [he it was] who acted at the Council of Trent[564] in the name of the Hungarian clergy, and was permanent ambassador at the Polish court.[565] He was a man deserving, in view of his profound leaning, his knowledge of languages, and especially for the purity of his personal character, to be reckoned among the foremost who have ever lived. I pass over as having been already related by others how from the midst of the Papacy and the allurements of the world he came to the knowledge of the purer truth, and not only honorably resigned his office under the Empire, but also resolutely gave up his rich bishopric, and how he entered upon the state of matrimony as though bidden by heaven, thus bringing upon himself the indignation and anger of the Pope of Rome and all the Papacy. He was burned in effigy at Rome.[566] [223] I cannot [however] leave out what Budziński alone has recorded [as of 1568]:[567]

While residing at Cracow, he used to attend the church of the Calvinists and took careful note of their hatred and of the insults with which they tried to force the lovers of the truth to desert their good cause, and he was of such singular modesty and with the shyness of a matron more than with that of a man (if we may believe Budziński) that he withdrew his sympathy from them.

An especial cause was afforded him [Dudith] at the great synod held by the Calvinists in 1568 at Cracow, in the mansion of Palatine [Stanislas] Myszkowski, to which the confessors of the maligned truth sent as delegates several eminent men, assigning the duty of spokesman to Filipowski as a man of known moderation.[568] Jerome Filipowski is described as speaking in this assembly as follows:

Cause enough has been offered us, most honored brethren and friends in Christ, as being cast out of our common [Reformed] Church, shut out from the society of our brethren, shunned and rejected, so often suffering repulse and shamefully treated on your part—certainly by most of you: let innocent moderation have its reward—to wrap ourselves in our own virtue, being settled within the limits not only of invincible patience and unconquerable modesty, but also of necessary silence.

Nevertheless, a very ardent love for the glory of God, for restoring harmony by every effort, for explaining the truth, for procuring the salvation of you all and of others, has led us, mindful rather of our many duties than of our many wrongs, to attend also this general assembly[569] (Conventum) of yours. We have not come in the character of mischievous busybodies. We are doing nothing rash. We shall do nothing harsh. We are present in this distinguished company as delegates from our brethren who heartily wish and earnestly desire to be yours also, not only in name but also in very deed. We are here to treat decently with public authority and in a public place, not of a light and trifling matter, but of one than which none is more important, none more glorious. Such encomia surely befit Christian charity [as we know] from the mouth of Truth itself. Think not, I beg you, that we shall give you annoyance. We forgive the injuries.

We seek the harmony [224], or at least toleration and moderation of an obliging mind. We shall not disturb the course of your arguments, wishing to bring all within the course of justice. We shall also not disturb your quiet, since we seek nothing but peace in all our desires and efforts. We are not poking into other people's business, but we are mingling in your affairs intending to treat with you of Christ's concerns which are your own. Moreover, we are counting on an equal desire on your part for harmony and observance of justice, unless all things deceive us.

Even the invidious will confess, however reluctantly, that in all the godly gatherings held in this very metropolis of the Royal Commonwealth in 1561, in Książ, Pińczów, and Rogów in 1562, in Mordy in 1563, afterwards in Piotrków in 1565, then in Łańcut [in 1567], and finally in Skrzynno, last year [later in 1567], we observed all moderation, even when fiercely attacked and unfairly treated. But especially have we kept inviolate the measures concerning tolerance that were adopted at the former synod at Pińczów and at Mordy and Skrzynno, being for nothing more renowned than for the afflictions of every sort which we have suffered from all for the sake of the Son of Man.[570]

Whether, therefore, we have performed the duty of true disciples of Christ in trying to keep the unity of the Spirit in the bond of peace,[571] *you be the judges. But in order that we might neglect no part of our duty, there was even yet need that we meet together with you. We bear witness before God the author and searcher of hearts*[572] *that we accept the supreme authority of the Holy Scriptures as the only infallible one, and without any exception, and heartily adhere to their primitive integrity, being devoted to the doctrine and truth which is in accord with piety.*

Nor are we false when we assert that whatever in all antiquity agrees with the unalterable rule of divine truth acts with us, fights for us, excepting the devices of the philosophers. These are unknown to us, rather simple folk that we are, who nevertheless always form the greater part of the Church, notwithstanding that upon those devices Christian doctrine, which commends itself in no way more than by its simplicity, began to weigh down a little after the times of the Apostles. This ''was the first step of the Church in decline,'' as the great Erasmus deservedly and rightly judges in his preface to Hilary.[573]

Thus fully persuaded of the certainty of the truth, and [225] firmly confident in our opinion, we by no means hate, condemn, persecute others in word or deed, or even in thought. Let us leave the decision about hidden things to the judge incorruptible. We beg and exhort you again and again that, mindful of your duty on account of the glory of Almighty God and his only begotten Son our Lord Jesus Christ, you treat with us as brethren and friends about explaining the truth according to the Holy Scriptures alone, about maintaining love, about restoring harmony. We beg and exhort truly that you bid all quarrels, enmities, angers cease, seeking nothing but the glory of God and the edification of one another.

And these are the things that I had to say to you in behalf of my brethren, that is, in behalf of true faith, piety of conduct, harmony, and peace in the Church, to which if you lend willing ears, we shall esteem ourselves happy to have pleaded a good cause not only well but also successfully. But if not, as has happened at other times hitherto, we shall be sorry that of you also is

> true what Erasmus said in the same work: "Riches increased and power
> grew. Then the influence of the Emperors being involved in this business
> did not much promote the sincerity of faith. At length the matter was
> reduced to sophistical quarrels, and countless articles broke out. From that
> it went on to terrors and threats."[574]

Thus did Filipowski speak in that crowded assembly, in the sight and hearing of
a great many others, even Papists, and most opportunely in the presence of
Dudith. Thus did he fulfill all the offices of a man weighty with aged wisdom
and authority. But those whom the love of this world and confidence in their
power had rendered refractory, showing no reverence for a man venerable in
age and also of great influence in the Commonwealth, dismissed him with a
reply full of anger and insult.

By this they offended the minds of all impartial persons, even of the Papists
themselves, who easily judged that they [the Major Churchmen] had forgotten
hospitality itself and the law of nations concerning the treatment and the dismis-
sal of envoys.

And this great wrong certainly cost them dearly in the loss, namely, of the
great Dudith. For how highly he was rated by all the greatest men, such as de
Thou, Lipsius, Crato, Monau, Muret, and indeed even his most important
opponents, Beza and Raemundus,[575] it is not for me [226] to say, since it is
known to the whole world. For certainly he was then concealing his dissent for
the time, but quietly hiding all in his bosom.

Meantime envious men, whose custom it is to claim everything, even the most
foreign, for their party, and to interpret discrete silence as consent, while striving to commend their shameful act by the reputation of this great man, and were
demanding of foreigners (for their great self-confidence would not contain itself
at home) that they should highly praise such great piety in Dudith and stir him
to manifest his zeal. So among many, not however the sharp-sighted, esteem for
his great reputation was much impaired, especially through the agency of Trecy.
[Trecy was] a man of notorious garrulity, fickleness, and ambition, who was
puffed up over his erudition suited to the scholastic arena, over his journey to
Switzerland hardly know to plain people, and over his correspondence carried
on with Calvin, now four years dead (d. 1564),[576] and with Beza and their associates.[577]

Therefore Dudith, a man scrupulously observant of both truth and good reputation, erased with the sponge of discreet writing in his right hand the stain that
the left hand of his detractor had spattered upon him. Henceforth favoring the
better party, [Dudith,] though he indeed did not give his name as to what was
both the Minor and the truer [part] of the Church, yet was its protector, and at
Śmigiel its patron, nay, its founder.[578] For in recognition of his very great services he was admitted to citizenship in 1567 at the Diet of Piotrków,[579] and also
enjoyed the support of distinguished connections. For example, at his second
marriage he espoused Elizabeth Zborowska.[580] She was born of an illustrious
family, whose father was the first lord in the Senate, her four brothers senators

of the royal Commonwealth, and the remaining three were appointed to high offices.[581] And leading a Christian life even to the last, he passed away peacefully at Breslau, confident of his last hour and of a better life.[582] He was a man who by virtue of his ancestry as well as of all his gifts of mind, his distinguished services, the splendor of his offices in church and state, his relationships, his pious life and death, richly deserves to be reckoned among all the foremost men and "Christian Heroes" of the world, even as Otwinowski has done in his poem, though he also deserved to be called the Incomparable.[583]

CHAPTER TEN

Of the Journey to Moravia Undertaken by Filipowski and Schomann, and of the Moravian Brethren [the Hutterites].[584]

The famous synod of Cracow,[585] of which we have treated in the previous chapter and which, as we have said, was hostile to the purer truth, according to the ancient pattern of councils, was followed with no better success by a journey to Moravia made by the same Filipowski and George Schomann.[586] For Luke Mundius [**cf. BAnt no. 30**], a councilor (*senator dignitate*) of the city of Vilna leaving his office and native land and yielding to a pious impulse, used to like traveling through various places, and thus in 1569[587] he came upon the sect of the Moravian Brethren[588] (who ....).[589] Living with them several weeks, he commended the Polish Churches as agreeing with them, save on community of *goods*.[590] So these excellent men learned much by hearsay of the unusual piety, sobriety, mutual love, and moral discipline of these Moravian Brethren. But also in this case experience not a little detracted from reputation. For while these two men found much that was excellent, yet unexpectedly they found them holding obstinately to the common doctrine of the Trinity, and persecuting with hatred any who denied it, and turned from them in horror. For they dared to call us pagan worshipers, who by the grace of God confess the pure truth and believe in one God the Creator and Father, through Jesus Christ as Mediator and Saviour, High Priest, heavenly King, Lord and judge of all men, and in the Holy Spirit. Than this faith none is more catholic, apostolic, Christian, divine. So that the journey and effort of these two men were in vain, for those good men would not depart by a finger's breadth, as the saying is, from their preconceived opinion and ingrained error. Insomuch [ingrained] that even from those who otherwise are hated by the world and condemned by its judgment, we must needs suffer hatred on account of the name of Jesus of Nazareth.[591]

[228]**CHAPTER ELEVEN**

Of the Trinitarian Conflict That Arose in Transylvania,[592] and of the Struggles Undertaken by George Biandrata and Faustus Socinus in Behalf of the Invocation of Christ against Francis Dávid.[593]

The conflict over the Trinity in Poland and in Lithuania was not waged without presently engaging the Transylvanians of the vicinity as well.[594] An excellent occasion both for opposing errors and for defending and spreading the truth was afforded under John [II] Sigismund, Prince of Transylvania [1559–71], who was compensated by the King of kings for the loss of his father's kingdom of Hungary[595] with the knowledge of the mysteries of the kingdom of heaven, being strenuously trained to true piety in the school of patience and led as it were by the right hand of God.[596] He had called to Kolozsvár[597] not a few men versed in the Holy Scriptures, whose religious discussions, held for ten whole days [in Alba Julia in 1568], he diligently attended and presided over[598] [**cf. BAnt no. 57**]. And constantly devoted to these pious endeavors, he exchanged this life so full of tribulations for the happy heavenly one on 14 March 1571.[599]

Under this magnanimous prince, endowed with Christian virtues and therefore distinguished, much was done within those bounds to promote the true worship of the divine name.

And indeed in the year 1578 at Torda in Transylvania [under Prince Stephen Báthory, 1571–81 and his brother, Christopher] three hundred and twenty-two Unitarian ministers met at a synod, at which pedobaptism was rejected, as Valentine Schmalz (Smalcius) recorded in his notebooks (*Adversariis*).[600] But also a veritable tempest in a teacup was raised when Francis Dávid,[601] pastor at Kolozsvár, opposed the invocation of Christ, which the Majesty of the King of Heaven demands in his own right, and that the more because it is offered to the glory of God the Father.[602] The first to oppose him was [Dr. George] Biandrata, whose influence with the prince was great [alike, with Stephen, elected King of Poland, 1576–81, and Prince Christopher, 1581–86].

Both [Dávid, the nonadorant, and the prudent Biandrata] were railed at in violent writings by Theodor Beza[603] [in Geneva] and by George Major, professor at Wittenberg.[604] And the latter indeed, after celebrating a triumph before victory, relapsed into silence in shame and confusion.

There is among the papers of Budziński an extract from a letter from Biandrata to the Churches of Little Poland, written at Segesvár [229] on 27 January 1569,[605] which I am glad to insert here as being pertinent to the matter of which we are treating:

As you were long ago informed of our affairs and those of our churches by our brother, Master Prosper Provana, I shall now touch but briefly upon them all.[606] First, I suppose that you have seen Beza's notorious book, raving against the ashes of Valentine Gentile and against us all in turn, in which big work he praises as divine the act of the Bernese in butchering that man.[607] And that he might bring forth his poison the more fully, he prefixed to it an epistle whose author is evidently a son of Satan. At the same time it was nothing at all relevant to the charge or to the inquest of the case. After this, at the end, he sounds a terrible trumpet, urging the Most Serene King of Poland and the Most Serene King of Transylvania to vent their rage against us [August 1567].[608] It is a shame to report the petulance of a clown and the infamous impudence of a pettifogger. So it will surely be worthwhile for our enemies to write in conformity with their own inborn wickedness. But let us beware of ever seeming to be like them in abuse.

Peter Méliusz,[609] pastor at Debrecen, has issued summons [14 December 1567] for a synod appointed by his party at Debrecen, with these for debate.[610] This the cunning impostor has of course done intentionally, having an understanding with the Germans, in order to take us captive.[611]

Thus he recently betrayed Master Luke Égri, whom he ordered Lazarus Schwendi to throw into prison—the most learned of all the pastors. He is our brother who, although he does not in all points agree with us, was ready even to face death while arguing in debate that before its incarnation the Word neither was nor could be called the Son of God, except by way of predestination [at the synod of Kassa, 27 January 1568].[612] We now hear that he is safe, or at all events has escaped, though proscribed.[613]

This Méliusz slanders us all [in that letter of December 1567], even as Beza does in his introductory epistle, and heaps abuse upon us, and knowing that we can by no means come thither, he boasts at the end: "If they do not come to us, it will be plain to all that they are men who flee the light and are defending a bad cause."[614] Wherefore we are sending by the hand of Valentine [Krawiec], elder of the church at Lublin, [what was enacted at] our synods, with the theses added in forty copies.[615] Pray the Lord that [230] just as he was actively with us in the public debate (in publica illa disputatione Albensi) at Alba Julia,[616] so in this one at Torda[617] he may strengthen and teach us by his spirit through Jesus Christ.

As for the rest, dearly beloved brethren, believe that the Lord now has his champions here who are openly and in private preaching the only and Most High God and his only Son conceived of the Holy Spirit,[618] with such fervor of mind that they cannot be frightened by any torments. You know *that it was ordained of the Lord that a pillar of great strength should be raised here through us and placed in inaccessible mountains [cf. Isa 2:2 and Mic 4:1].[619] Consider, I pray, the beginnings, the means, and the method by which these are now being carried out (*transigantur*).[620]*

I deem myself not quite apart from the number of those who have given occasion for advancing the cause. Meanwhile I freely confess before God that I know not in what way or for what use and end God has wished these things to be furthered by us. It remains for us without ceasing to pray the God and Father of all comfort and mercy that he may accomplish the work that he has begun through us to the glory of his holy name.[621]

*We have a printer who is quite our own,[622] and a Most Serene Prince who is willing to hear, weigh, and justly carry out all things. Nor is it clear why Lucian soldiers or buffoon soldiers [(*thrasones*) of our own party] should insist, with insolence or with the claptrap of showy rhetoric, that Beza, with all his Claudian thunders, cannot move even a hair.[623] Pray the Lord, I beg, that he may at all events preserve this Most Serene Prince to us, if it shall still be his own will.[624]*

From this it is apparent enough with what fierce Trinitarian adversaries the defenders of the truth then contended. For even this Peter Méliusz was bad enough, being the firebrand of the disturbances in Hungary.[625] For this reason action was taken at the synods held at Torda and Alba Julia.[626]

All the proceedings[627] there were published in book form, but have not reached us, except for their titles alone.[628] The one is a *Refutatio* against a Writing by George Major, *in which he has attempted to prove from the puddle of Antichrist that God is triune in persons and one in essence, and then that his Son is single in person and two-fold in nature* [1569]. The other is a *Refutatio* against a Writing by Peter Méliusz, *in which he teaches in the name of the Synod of Debrecen* [1567] [231] *that Jehovality and the Trinitarian God were known to the Patriarchs, Prophets, and Apostles.*

When these two synods were ended, and even a third, by far the most famous,[629] they not a little weakened the false doctrines, especially those of the Roman sect (*the worst and the idol-worshiping,* to use the words of Budziński), since books on religious controversies had been widely spread through Poland, Germany, and Italy . . . .[630]

[Two letters of 15 May 1571 concerning the Trinity, the second signed by John Sommer]

We also transfer here a letter [Leipzig, 15 May 1571] . . . to Hallopegius which speaks both of books to be secretly published and of certain other matters that we hope will not be wearisome to the reader:[631]

> I congratulate you on your present good fortune, and also thank you for kindly congratulating me on mine from God. It is the duty of us both to take care lest we abuse God's great mercy and kindness to us. You need not

have offered me an excuse for your silence. You wrote soon enough. Though had you never done so, it would not have been a sign of disgrace. Yet your great liking for me is pleasing to me, for which I in turn again offer you in your absence what I have at other times offered in your presence, that is, whatever I can and should.

As to the book that you would like to have printed here through my intervention, hear this in brief: You know that men of this class, i.e. printers, are not such as are accustomed to undertake the printing of books at their own expense. When books are offered by authors whose reputation and standing they do not deem well-known to them, or at least to many, they ask themselves one question and nothing more. Unless the book of your fellow-countryman that was recently published at Wittenberg had professed to be a defense of Doctor George Major, certainly even it would hardly have been printed.[632] I do not speak without warrant.

I approve of your purpose, as you are eager to serve God and to have regard for you neighbor (*proximo*) in a matter of such importance, but I beg you not to be an imitator of any. You will surmise what I mean. There are already many things in circulation by the Transylvanians against those people, and by those people and our people against the Transylvanians. Nor do I suppose that more can be said or brought forward by you. Yet [232] to all the arguments of Francis Dávid in his book *De vera et falsa religione*,[633] in reply to Doctor George Major and elsewhere, our brethren have in turn made many replies to Dávid.

See to it therefore that you do not waste your pains, but either make a better reply if you can, or else keep quite silent. You are not one of those, I think who would squeeze a trinity of persons into a unity out of the cockcrow thrice heard when Peter denied the Christ of God,[634] and thus expose it to ridicule greater even than those brethren of ours have done already.

With regard to another thing, we should remember that we were told that in these matters glory is to be given only to the one God, and that we ought not here to be tickled and puffed up by any ambition for our own glory. (What mortal is there who has not been infected by that itching?) A great thing, forsooth, it seems to have our name circulated in print which may however be done with less harm to us if dealing with other subjects; but in these divine matters [this] cannot be done without punishment from the angered Deity. Whatever you do, refrain from those Genevan passions, that is, do not connect the holy knowledge of God with words of abuse. For by no other spirit than the Devil's are those men led who break out in such unholy words concerning these mysteries. Rage does not win over the mind of any adversary. Abuse does not make insults creditable, and does not persuade. These things, declares Aristotle in his Rhetoric,[635] are proper to those whose cause is weak.

Moreover, the words water, fire, sword, halter, are the words of a cannibal, not of a Christian debater; as though a cause, be it true or false, would be burned or perish with the men themselves.

"But if any man obey not our word"—says Paul to the [2] Thessalonians [3:14 – 15]—"note him [. . .] that he may be ashamed. Yet count him not as an enemy, but admonish him as a brother." And writing to Timothy

[2:24 – 25], he describes for us the pastor of the church, when he says: "The servant of the Lord must not strive, but be gentle unto all men, apt to teach, patient with evil men, in meekness instructing those who oppose themselves, if God peradventure may give them repentance to the acknowledging of the truth."

Judgments (*limitationes*) are being brought here from those Genevan tombs, but what they will be worth, God alone will judge, before whose [233] judgment-seat we shall all sometime stand. The tares will be wholly rooted up in due time,[636] but by whom? Christ himself, the Son of the most high God, foreseeing that there would be many in the last age who would be uprooting the wheat instead of the tares from the field of God, commanded that we should not gather them up ourselves, but should let them grow until the harvest. For "then" (he says) "the Son of man shall send his angels"—*these* make no mistake; *we* can be mistaken in telling the wheat from the tares—"who shall gather all things that offend, and shall cast them into a furnace of fire" [Matt 13:41 – 42].

These things, if you would be an acceptable disciple, you will receive from your Teacher (*Praeceptore*) in the spirit in which they are said, that is, candidly and sincerely. Between the righteous and the wicked there is no distinction of wickedness. He who submits to political authority (*magistratui*) in all reverence, whether in gain or in loss, he, as Aristotle quotes from Homer, ἅμα ... καὶ πόλεμον ἐπιθυμήτης ["at the same time is also desirous of war"].[637] But we are not asking this.[638] The question is whether the consciences of men, so far as knowledge (*ad cognitionem*) is concerned, are ever or anywhere to be forced by fire, water, or sword. The question is whether those who profess the ministry of the word of God ought ever to incite the princes of the earth to fire, to water, to sword, to halter.

You might have desired from me to have more clearly set forth certain words taken from philosophy and used by you to explain this revealed mystery of the Trinity. It will be well, my dear Hallopegius, if you pass philosophy by and treat the whole matter theologically. For indeed in this discipline of ours [scriptural theology] there is nothing that would not be diametrically incompatible with this article [on the Nicene Trinity], as well as with these terms: "to differ" or "to be identical," "really" or "essentially," "rationally one," "triple," [or] with "essentia," "hypostases," and others of the sort, of which Luther had somewhere written most justly that they are certainly mere trifles which obscure the Trinity more than illuminate it.[639] And indeed, if I would reduce them to the rules of Aristotelian philosophy, we should be quite finished.

Why then, you will say, do you condemn the opinions of so many and such great men and philosophers and even of those whom you previously praised? This one opinion I certainly condemn as false and chimerical, and abhor as harmful. I formerly praised it because I was blind with the blind. Now [234] it seems to me that I am able to distinguish these things somewhat more sharply in this our native philosophy.[640] Blessed be the name of the Lord.

To conclude briefly what I mean: the more you mix your philosophy with your dispensation (*dispensationi tuae*), the more you will give our adversaries occasion to laugh and to make further replies. Thomas and Scotus before you, what men and how great [were they as philosophers]? You will understand the rest by yourself. Farewell, and I beg you to love me for other reasons, and I beseech you to write me often. Inform me as carefully as you can about the whole state of religion there.[641] Again, farewell.

Leipzig, May 15 in the year of the Lord 1571.

We shall also add another letter of John Sommer, rector of the school at Kolozsvár, prefixed to [Eight] *Theses* [on the "Papal" Trinity],[642] in which he tried to trace the authors of the commonly received dogma of the Trinity, together with the theses themselves:

> There has hitherto been a long and large controversy about the Triune God (*Deo Uno Trino*), and one with the greatest contest of wits, but with like consequence on either side. For as our minds have become not a little more assured, so many of our adversaries have become more obstinate, whether because they are ashamed to yield, or because they know no better. And others, although nothing is found written in the Evangelists and Apostles that goes to confirm the doctrine, are undecided, because they do not well enough know whence their interpretations are drawn.
>
> I have therefore thought that I would be doing something worthwhile, if I showed in the compass of a few theses the [pagan] authors of their doctrine, from whom all these things have been taken. I do this because I have absolutely no doubt at all that even among them there are many for whom nothing is further from their mind than that they are defending Plato's doctrine instead of Christ's. And there are also many among our brethren who are not well versed in the reading of these authors. In the time of Christ and of the Apostles, Greece flourished on account of the study of philosophy, and the principal originators of it [235] were Chrysippus, Plato, and Aristotle. And one who was not acquainted with their views was certainly not accounted among the learned. Many from their schools gave their adherence to Christ.[643] But in order not to hold a doctrine common with the [Christian] multitude, they endeavored to reconcile the Gospel with Plato [cf. BAnt no. 47], which to them seemed very easy, since on both sides they found the same words Λόγος, πνεῦμα, ψυχή, *Verbum*, *Spiritus*, *anima*, *principium*, though with a different meaning. Whence Paul also probably complains that the Greeks sought for wisdom in him [1 Cor 1:24], because it may be conjectured that he read the writings of that Dionysius whom they [Sommer's opponents] wish to make out to have been Paul's disciple.[644] The Platonic philosopher Amelius, a disciple of Ammonius,[645] having read the beginning of the gospel of John, exclaimed: "May I perish if that barbarian (for he himself was a Greek) has not expressed in brief what the divine Plato and Heraclitus taught of the divine reason, in principle and arrangements" as Postel relates in his book, 1.3.[646]
>
> Such were the beginnings. In subsequent times everything became more

and more corrupted, as may be plainly seen even in the books of Lactantius.[647] Farewell, Christian reader. From these few words estimate the whole dogma, from top to toe, as the saying is, and be amazed by it.

Kolozsvár, 15 May A.D. 1571

[John Sommer's *Octo Theses de Deo Papano Trino* (1571), of which the foregoing letter is the preface]

[Thesis I]

God the Father, Son, and Holy Spirit is one, undivided in essence, distinct in three persons, accordingly these three are one.

Proof: Plato in the *Timaeus*:[648] "An indivisible essence, and one that always continues in the same form, and on the other hand mingles together out of a divisible one a third intermediate kind composed of them both, which again is derived from the essence of and the same [end of] the other. For they cling together. And when these are taken, which would be three, he mingles them all together into one idea."[649]

Again Marsiglio Ficino, [Plato's] *Epistle 6*: "Ye adjure God as the Head of all things, then also the Father as Lord of those things that are, and of the Head and cause. And here you have a Trinity: Father, Head (*dux*), and Cause."[650]

[236] [Thesis] II

These three together, and not the Father only, are the author of heaven and earth.

Proof: Aristotle, *Physics*, VIII [5]: "The world is governed by three: the Mover not moved, the Mover moved, and the Mover not moving." That is, as though he said: The uncreated Father begets an eternal Son, from whom and the Father proceeds the Holy Spirit, in whom is the end (*finis*) of divinity. Postel, *De orbis concordia*, I, iii, [supplies an] explanation of Plotinus, *Enneads II*, IX, ii:[651] "There are three elements in things: the good itself, its son, the intellect, derived from the primal brightness of light spreading as is usual, and the soul of the world, derived from the divine intellect, as a Spirit flowing out through all things." Marsiglio Ficino, *Timaeus*, ix:[652] "The Platonists judge that this universe is made by the good itself, through the divine intellect, because it is the son of that good and the soul of the universe." The same [Ficino says] in the *Summa of* [Plotinus'] *Enneads*, V, ii:[653] "The good includes the comprehension (*intellectus*) of paternal fecundity, the emanation of the intellectual son, and the procession of the Spirit includes the soul by means of the will."

[Thesis] III

The eternal Father, looking into eternity (*sempiternum*) brings forth a Son in his own image, light from light.

Proof: Plato, in *Timaeus*:[654] "This maker of the supreme beauty and supreme good [. . .] begot the most perfect God." Plotinus, *Enneads*, III, viii, chap. 10:[655] "One who considers the intelligible world [. . .] ought to inquire carefully into the author: who he is, where or when he brought forth such a son, meaning a child pure and beautiful, a son, I say, full of his father." The same, *Enneads*, VI, viii, chap. 18:[656]

> For of whatever kind is that which is in the mind of just such a kind is that considered to be which is in the One, even though it is much more excellent; just as if a light widely diffused were proceeding from some one thing that remains in itself and is absolutely transparent. For surely what is diffused is the image of the other thing. But that from which this shines forth is doubtlessly real light, yet the diffused image is not a foreign and unlike form.

[Thesis] IV

The Son is light from light, and the image of the prior doctrine (i.e., of God the Father, according to Thesis III) because he is partaker of that essence.

Proof: Plato in *Timaeus*;[657] "It is fitting for an image to take being in something else, so that it may in a certain measure also employ its essence; otherwise it would not be anything at all." [237] Again, in definitions:[658] "Generation is a motion toward essence, assumption of an essence, progression toward the end of taking being." Marsiglio Ficino [comments] in *Timaeus*, x:[659] "The image of the good is derived from what is good, just as light outside the sun comes from light within the sun, which it pours out from itself, just as the light pours out splendor."

[Thesis] V

Since the Son is the beginning, he ought to be eternal without any temporal beginning, not created.

Proof: Plato, *Phaedrus*:[660] "A beginning is not created. Whatever is, must needs take being from a beginning, but especially if it was created from nothing (*ex nullo*). For if it took being from something, it would at any rate take being from beginning, and since it was not made, it also cannot be corrupted."

[Thesis] VI

This Logos created heaven and earth together with the Holy Spirit, and governs all things.

Proof: Plato, *Timaeus*:[661] "The intellect or reason is son of the good, and the architect of the world;" the same [in] *Epinomus*:[662] "The most divine reason for the most divine word constructs the visible world;" the same [in] *On the Laws*, i:[663] "The soul, which is God, joining to himself a mind, which itself is also God, always governs all things justly and faithfully;" the same [in] *Cratylus*:[664] "The mind and soul govern the nature of all other things" [and] in the same dialogue, Anaxagoras says:[665] "The mind, as supreme ruler, and mingled with none, sets things in order, passing through

all things.'' Plato [says in] *Philebus*:[666] "All wise men agree that mind is
the king of heaven and earth" [and] in the same:[667] "We say that mind and
a certain admirable intelligence construct and govern what we call the
universe.''

[Thesis] VII

The Son of God has in one person two natures: the one divine from
his Father, the other human from his mother; of which the former is
immortal, while the latter is mortal.

Proof: 1: On the authority of Homer, *The Odyssey*, book 11:[668] "Hercules is only half dead, and only in respect of his human nature. Its ghost is
among the dead, and only his divine nature feasts with the celestials.''

[Proof] 2: On the authority of Lucian, in his *Dialogues of the Dead*,[669]
where the ghost of Hercules tells the ways in which the two natures were
combined: For Diogenes asks thus: "'By ... Hercules, tell me, pray, when
he was alive were you [238] even then an image existing with him? or were
you indeed one in life, but separated after you departed from life? did he fly
away to the immortal gods, while you became his shade among the dead?'
Hercules: 'Whatever of Amphytrion was in Hercules, that itself was
affected by death; but beyond doubt, all that I am, which was from Jove, has
converse with the immortal gods.' Diogenes: 'Now I understand clearly.
You say that Alcmena bore two sons at the same time, the one from
Amphytrion, but the other from her Jove; whence it came to pass that you
rejoiced as twins in the womb of one mother.' Hercules: 'By no means, you
fool. We were really both the same one.' Diogenes: 'And yet I still do not
understand whether it is easy for two Herculeses to be joined into one,
namely, man and God [. . .]. Hercules: 'Do not men seem to you to be composed in the same way, namely of a soul and a body?' With these things the
Creed of Athanasius agrees, which blossomed out two hundred years later:
"As soul and body are one man, so God and man are one Christ."'[670]

[Thesis] VIII

The Holy Spirit proceeds from the essence of the Father through the
emanation of his love.

Proof: Plotinus, *Enneads*, VI, viii, chap. 16:[671] "Moreover, the same
God within himself penetrates equally throughout the whole, as it were, loving pure light as his very self, being himself the very thing that he loves,
that is, however, bringing himself forth into a hypostatis." The modern
Jehovality and *Eternity* have been born at Debrecen![672] Hence they lack the
testimony of the early writers.[673]

These [Theses of Sommer], and other writings of the same sort did not fail of
their effect. Although condemned and forbidden,[674] yet were they more eagerly
sought for, in the traditional human way, and they led some to tolerance and others to the knowledge of the truth. Nay, even slander and other weapons of persecution had no more power against the truth than mists against the sun.[675]

CHAPTER TWELVE

Of the Foundation of Raków, and of the Synod There That Lasted for Several Years [1567/69]; Of the Conferences Held by Many Godly Men on Matters of Faith; Of Many and Notable Instances of Divine Providence Watching over that Place until Its Ruin, Which Took Place in 1638.

The time and occasion admonish me to put together in this place the history of the celebrated Raków.[676] For in this town not only were married both my grandmother Anna (daughter of Erasmus Otwinowski)[677] and my father with my mother Catherine Filipowska (granddaughter, *neptis*, of Jerome),[678] but also I began my life[679] and [here] made progress however judged in humane studies in the celebrated school founded after the plan of my great-uncle Stanislas [II] Lubieniecki.[680] Thus I cannot, without showing an ungrateful mind, pass over in silence the history of my native place, nor indeed, without sacrilege, the marked proofs of divine providence which so many times quite marvelously preserved that town.

John Sienieński[681] was related to the family of Oleśnicki (who bear the same coat-of-arms as that of the Dębno clan), castellan of Zarnów, afterwards palatine of Podolia, and Reformed as to his confession. In 1569[682] in the palatinate of Sandomierz, one mile from Szydłów, he founded this town named from the coat-of-arms of his wife (who was of the ancestral stock of the Gnoiński clan), namely *Rak*, that is, crab.[683]

The region was very sandy, and thus the soil was not very fertile, but it produced as much as was needed even for comfortable subsistence, and rejoiced also in a mild and healthful air and a pleasant situation, with level grounds, ponds, springs, forests nearby even with trees planted in order, and abounding in meadows. Many of the pious, even from rather distant places, had been attracted to remove and settle there by the convenience of the site and by the very welcome liberty[684] granted by its pious patron. For both Gregory Paul and [Matthew] Albinus[685] removed thither from Cracow. The Kalinowskis, too [Jacob and John], George Schomann, [240] [John] Siekierzyński [Sr.],[686] and others chose this place for their home. [Lucas] Mundius, councilman (*senator*) of the city of Vilna, and other brethren from Lithuania did the same [after the amicable but decisive debate on Christology and socio-economic and ecclesial issues at the Lithuanian synod in Iwie, 20–26 January 1568].[687]

And so they formed there a regular fellowship (*collegium*), and for several years without intermission held a synod there,[688] having leisure for divine matters, and discussing holy things with one another.

[The attempt at communitarianism in Raków, 1569 – 72][689]

But the lovers of the truth could not so happily surmount the initial difficulties but that among so large a number of men differences arose, since the minds of a good many were possessed by superstition with regard to the disparagement of the care of the body[690] and the relinquishment of all public office and every vocation,[691] even that of the ministry as inconsistent with Christian perfection and equality,[692] and with regard to the introduction of the community of goods.[693]

Schomann left on record[694] that God, having mercy on their scattered condition, by the agency of the most excellent man, Simon the Apothecary (I doubt not that he means Ronemberg of Cracow, a man endowed with the spirit of grace and of eloquence) [**cf. BAnt no. 30**], as it were a new Ezra, gathered them together (*in unum*).[695] And as they seemed, humanly speaking, to have fallen into ruin, in the midst of that disorder he instituted a ministry with the baptism of adults, in 1570.[696]

In a letter from Transylvania written to Filipowski, Biandrata admonished them of their duty, namely, to abandon their superstitions and live among men, and by the example of their lives to light their way in the pursuit of truth and piety.[697]

[Lay and clerical leaders of Raków and its Academy][698]

This Church was guided by outstanding men from all quarters: Christopher Ostorodt,[699] Peter Statorius, Valentine Schmalz, the brothers Stanislas [II] and Christopher Lubieniecki, John Crell,[700] Jonas Schlichting,[701] Peter Morzkowski,[702] John Stoiński, Solomon Paludius.[703]

A school founded there in 1602[704] took on an excellent growth [**cf. BAnt no. 62**]. And so within a brief space of time, happily under the direction—besides that of its patron (a man of untiring ability)—of outstanding men from all quarters: Jerome Moskorzowski,[705] Erasmus Otwinowski, Adam and Andrew Gosławski,[706] and others, it was considered as among the most famous schools in all Poland. Hence, many of the papists sent their children thither as to a market of good letters, attracted by the reputation of its teachers: Paul Krokier [1610 – 16], John Crell, Martin Ruar, [Paul Ryniowicki], Joachim Stegmann the Elder, Adam Franck, [Peter Teichmann], George Nigrinus [Schwartz], and Lawrence Stegmann [1634 – 38] (who after the ruin of Raków was called Tribander), who were rectors of the school after [the first: Christopher Brockay, 1603 – 05]), [Martin Borrhaus], George Manlius, and Samuel Nieciecki.[707] [241] Among the Catholic pupils were men recently, even to this day, illustrious in their country and distinguished in senatorial rank: the Leszczyńskis, Branickis, Tarłos, Niezabitowskis, and others. And this [interest in the school arose] certainly because apart from the incomparable devotion of the teachers and the reputation (*auctoritas*) of the academic regulations, the noble youth in this Sarmatian Athens[708] were instructed in good manners.

Jacob Sienieński,[709] son of John, a hero most deserving of eternal remembrance, was—as I have said—moved to establish this school and a press,[710] as well as to grant liberty to the townsmen, by the persuasion of Stanislas Lubieniecki [II], whose friendship he once enjoyed at the court of King Stephen, and who acted as minister of the word in the settlement at Raków, together with Christopher Ostorodt of Goslar, a man exceptionally learned and pious.

There lived at Raków at that time, devoted to holy leisure, two outstanding men. The first was Jerome Moskorzowski[711] of the Pilawa clan, highly distinguished not only by his noble descent (from an ancient and illustrious race and his ties bound him with the Dudiths, the Aborowskis, the lords [*comes*] of Tarnów and other notable families of the Kingdom), but also by his intellectual gifts, services to the Republic, and more important by his matchless courtesy, modesty, and purity of life. The second was Matthew Radecke, distinguished for learning and piety, who before he became a sharer of divine truth, had held the very honorable office of syndic of Danzig.[712]

Faustus Socinus, a man never to be mentioned without praise, in a letter to Ostorodt,[713] given at Lusławice in 1602, congratulates him on his patron Sienieński having joined the Church, so that it appears that the defenders of the truth there had long enjoyed the generous patronage of the Sienieńskis, father and son, although both were adherents of the evangelical Reformed religion.[714]

[Episodes of divine providence in Raków during civil turbulence,
c. 1606–c. 1614][715]

But now I think I shall do something worthwhile if as an example of trust reposed in God I mention some exceptional proofs of divine providence often shown in protecting and preserving that place.

In 1606 a fierce storm of civil war[716] broke in Poland, the people taking up arms for liberty against King Sigismund III, as being too much bound to the Austrians. And to this party, which was believed to be that of the Commonwealth, belonged [Jacob] Sienieński, patron of the Church and school. [242] He was a man who adorned his illustrious lineage by his illustrious services in the Commonwealth and in the Church. When the King, being victorious, passed through the town with his whole army, although many of the magnates and soldiers, incited by priests (*pontifices*) who were aflame with mortal hatred against this place, tried to inflame the mind of the King, and threatened the place with utter destruction, he used his victory wisely and modestly, spared the place, and earned the [monumental] crown famous to this day [with the inscription]: ''For Saving the Citizens.''[717]

It is appropriate that I should also mention here a remarkable favor of divine providence shown at this critical and difficult time to my maternal grandmother (*avia mea materna*) [Sophia Komarowska], the widow of Jerome Filipowski, son's bride (*nurus*) of the *Ciołek* clan.[718] When the inhabitants heard the news of the victory of the royal party [1607], since their patron belonged to the opposition party, they all sought safety in flight and carried their possessions away to a place of greater security. This widow, advanced in years, had with a very few remained in the town, relying only upon God. To her came a certain man, or really an angel in human shape, who addressed her in about these words: "Why is it, my lady, that you are staying alone in this town, when the rest have fled?" She replied that, weakened by old age, she trusted to divine providence for her safety, or really would rather die here between hope and fear than amid all the constant troubles of flight. He encouraged her and promised to defend her. He kept his promise, and so well indeed that when soldiers approached and saw him as though put on guard, as the custom is, to ensure her safety, they always went on without doing her any harm. After all the forces passed by, the widow, having duly thanked God, also paid her respects to the guardian of her safety, and asked him what he wished to be paid as a reward. But he refused it, and declared that he had been sent by God to protect her.

I shall relate below a similar instance elsewhere, in which God chose in a miraculous manner to preserve Licinius the Elder,[719] nay more, Peter Statorius, Michael Gittich Venecius, and my father,[720] each snatched from unforseen evil and the rage of beserk men.

Within the six years following [i.e., c. 1611 or 1612], the confederation of Polish mercenaries serving in Muscovy under the leadership of Joseph Ciekliński,[721] not only brought much harm to the Commonwealth, but also threatened the town with disaster. But the hand of God in marvelous fashion averted a new stroke planned by the camp chaplains (*pontifices castrenses*).[722]

In contrast, confederate soldiers several times quietly held their general [243] councils there. Distinguished among the confederates was *Sienicki*.[723] His leadership and command [unfortunately] were followed by the Lissovians,[724] so called, who through their murders and robberies were [in other places] troublesome not only to their own country, but also to neighboring Hungary and Silesia. One of the colonels (*tribuni*) of the Lissovians was an Oporowski.

[The King's Chamberlain and a German pharmacist are instruments of
Providence, Raków, 1620][725]

[This Oporowski was the one] who [later] pursued Sienieński, the owner of the town, with bitter hatred. Having got the opportunity to wreak revenge, and willing to use it, he stationed some of his best troops in the vicinity overlooking the place and he himself took his stand with two squadrons in the royal borough of Szydłów not far distant.[726] He was intending, as was arranged, on the following day, at the end of the year 1620, to attack the town of Raków which, well supplied with bakers and other tradesmen, also with merchants and rather wealthy citizens,[727] had stimulated the covetousness and fierceness of the soldiers, especially of those who were wanton and obeyed no regular commander.

Among his fellow soldiers was Elias Arciszewski, later celebrated in Denmark and in his native country as an able captain in the Prussian and Muscovite wars.[728] In his heart and when it seemed opportune, he held with the defenders of the detested (*exosa*) truth, in words though not in deeds, as men fare who are by nature devoted to the world.[729] Of his religion nothing was known to Colonel Oporowski.

Elias, being aware of the wicked design, hastened to Raków late in the evening and warned the inhabitants betimes of the ruin threatening them.[730] And the town was indeed protected by the nature of the site and by the work of hands. It was bordered on one side by a deep pond and on the other by a wooden stockade, but, besides, also provided with a goodly number of citizens keeping constant watch and ready to take up arms in the just cause of self-defense and to ward off injury. But all this offered a weak defense against so great a force, and that suddenly rushing on them like a flood. And so they all, putting their reliance (after God) in flight, sought safety in flight on a moonless and hence extremely inconvenient night, especially since its darkness did not sufficiently congeal the rain mingled with snow nor freeze the waters and the marshes. They hurried on, making for the dark of the forests, because hostile soldiers had filled the neighboring villages.

For all who thus either took to flight or girded themselves for it, God provided safety by sending an angel from heaven. For late at night there came into the town a man of eminent nobility, of the Gruszczyński family,[731] chamberlain to the King, speeding day and night with strict orders to Colonel Oporowski [244] to dismiss his troops without a moment's delay. It happened however that the chamberlain, entering with his tired horses the Urzędów quarter of the town,[732] which was not paved with stones and was very muddy, found the going very difficult in the stormy night, and was for some time stuck in the mire.

While struggling with the mire and the horses, the driver and other servants by their repeated shouting aroused the apothecary Daniel Kunau,[733] a rich German, who with others [had stayed behind] to stand watch for the safety [of Raków]. God directed him to bring them [the chamberlain and his men] help.

His arrival [on the scene] and assistance was, accordingly, very welcome to them, and also his kindness in inviting them into his house near by, neat, comfortable, provided with everything, including delicacies. Every act of hospitality was extended to the tired men hastening on their way. And this Daniel did the more cheerfully and carefully and rejoiced the more that a deliverer had been sent there by heaven. For on being asked who he was, the [officer] replied that he was the King's chamberlain sent to bear royal commands for Colonel Oporowski to discharge his unruly soldiers at the earliest moment. For by means of this [disclosure] he was anxious to arouse even more the efforts of the apothecary to help him on his way as soon as possible, being unaware [of how close he was to Oporowski and of the fact] that the druggist and the whole town urgently needed his help in warding off the danger by his swift departure [to execute his commission]. And without delay he inquired as to his fellow-soldiers and where they were stationed. Nay, to stimulate the kindness and diligence of his host in making haste (to whose lot a better service could not have fallen), the chamberlain related how so many desperate complaints of citizens had been piercing the ears and smiting the soul of the King that he had commissioned him to summon Oporowski to dismiss his soldiers instantly on receiving the order, under the penalty of death. (And that [was to be] the most cruel and shameful, such as had been suffered a little while before by one Karwa, a man of the same feather, who had been impaled).

Anyway, in spite of the greatest desire on each side, since not enough haste was being made, the situation was soon reported (as was proper) to the patron, Sienieński. He, like a father, was as anxious for the safety of his citizens as for his own. Other horses with fresh strength were substituted for those worn out, and at the second watch they brought the chamberlain to Szydłów. Upon his arrival there, the King's servant and commissioner betook himself to the town hall, [245] at once delivered the King's orders to the town mayor (*consul*) and to the colonel, and under threat of capital punishment ordered the latter immediately to dismiss his soldiers.

The colonel was astonished, grieved, angry at the unexpected occurrence, asked to be granted a slight delay of at least a few days (of course only that he might plunder Raków, though he did not reveal this plan to the King's servant, but hoped that he might be excused for his religious hatred), pleading that the difficulties were as good as insuperable. The other, on the contrary, very strongly pressed the King's orders, commanded prompt obedience under severe penalty, and threatened him with certain ruin. To the gathered company he read the King's letter, adding threats.

Arciszewski also, secretly inclined to favor the Racovians, urged his fellow-soldiers to obedience and put fear into them. So at length the regiment, upon their discharge, were obliged to disperse hither and thither. Thus the Racovians, relieved of impending danger, extolled the wonderful providence of God in due praises. In solemn thanksgiving they reverenced the confidence they had reposed in God, acknowledged that this had been their temporal salvation, recommended like faith to others, and thereby confirmed themselves therein. And for eight whole days, with all acts of kindness they waited upon the King's chamberlain as their deliverer, a most splendid and noble knight, and sent him away not without gifts in testimony of their grateful sentiment.

[The duel of Lissovian Różycki and the drunken murder of his aged
host Peter Gucci, c. 1620]

A little later, that is, when the rapine of the Lissovian soldiers was on the increase, there appeared a new evidence of divine providence. Two squadrons of them, very famous for the number of soldiers and brave men, the one bearing a black standard, the other a red, took up their station in the town, being attracted by high hopes of plunder, and obeying no particular commander. Then there arose among them strife among the parties of Sieradzki, Zaleski, and Różycki, especially the last. He was of peasant (*rusticus*) origin, though not in cunning (*astus*) nor in mind.[734] Too much given to violent passions and to wine, and hence bold to commit any infamy, he surpassed all both in brains and in ferocity, seeking the honor of colonelcy, alluring his fellow soldiers by gifts and banquets, winning them over to his side. He threatened to hang one of the ministers of the word of God from the ceiling of the church (*aede sacra*), and then to destroy it with fire.

But God, who kept constant watch over his people, in time sent to his faithful ones (overcome with fear) [246] a new defender of their liberty and safety. This was Frederick Iwanicki, descended from a noble family and related by marriage to those Iwanickis who were defenders of the divine truth. He had imbibed knowledge of this truth from one of them whose name was Gabriel [Iwanicki], and who for his proven wisdom and uprightness had been entrusted with the double office of judge and vice-captain of Włodzimierz.[735] As he arrived there with a company of picked soldiers, having been appointed colonel by the King to lead this force of brave men at once against Gabriel Bethlen,[736] prince of Transylvania, he resented Różycki's roughness and abuse (which arose from jealousy), especially since he knew that the latter was a native of the town of Ilkusz.[737]

Therefore, turning to his troops, he shouted that any of them might with his consent engage in single combat with the latter[738] and beat him without fear of punishment. This task and honor (as at least the soldier's mind deems it) was undertaken by one Bejkowski, small in stature, great in courage, and quick of hand. He wounded Różycki severely in a duel, and forced him, [badly] gored, to resort to disgraceful flight. To bind up his wound, the wounded man summoned his host, Simon Polanus,[739] accomplished in drugs and not inexperienced in medicine, assistant to the great to Jerome Moskorzowski who much delighted in such studies.[740] Różycki acknowledged that the punishment had been sent down from above to avenge the crime he had meditated against the innocent, confessed his fault to those present, expressed his regret, begged pardon of his host Polanus, and said: ''It was not without reason that I could not harm them before this misfortune, however much I would: I was as though glued up, or as though some one kept me from doing it.'' Presently Różycki's partisans called upon the colonel, meaning to ask of him the reason for what he had done, but finding him prepared both to give a good reason for his deed and to use arms, they desisted from their purpose.

While these things were thus taking place, the somber news was brought to John Gucci, the colonel's host, that a comrade of Różycki, one Chróstowski of Lithuania, was beating to death their common host, his grandfather Peter Gucci of Florence.[741]

He was a man more than eighty years old, who had left his native land together with other Italians, following Queen Bona, but afterwards followed Christ the King, having come to know the pure truth. As long as there was a flourishing Church at Cracow, he lived there, thence removed to Pińczów, then to Chmielnik, and at length to Raków, [247] following, so to speak, the migratory fortunes of the Cracow church.

The host [John Gucci] at once fell at the feet of the colonel [Fredrick

Iwanicki] and besought his aid, bewailing with tears the fact that his grandfather was being murdered by Różycki's companion. The colonel at first marvelled (*miratus est*) that his host, a man of forty, surrounded by grown children, should be bemoaning the critical situation of a grandfather.[742] Colonel Iwanicki immediately sent his subordinates to rescue the victim and save him from harm. But they found him half-dead, bashed by many and very heavy blows, and since the murderer had stolen away, they for a while took their revenge upon some of the servants.

The murderer, after he had slept off his cups and come to himself, and had learned of the crime he had perpetrated against a harmless, pious, and kind old man, cursed the drunkenness that had been the source of so great a wrong, abominated his crime with tears, and confessed his crime. And, throwing himself at the feet of the old man, who was hardly breathing, nay falling prone, with his whole body lying at the old man's bedside, he[743] humbly and submissively begged for forgiveness, praying also that he should not curse him, but rather beseeching him to show by words or by laying on his hands that he pardoned his crime. And this indeed he obtained, the old men, feeble and wounded as he was, raising his heavy hand to lay it on his head.

The occasion of the crime had been this. Chróstowski, returning to his lodgings quite drunk, violently abused Peter Gucci as a blasphemer of the Most Blessed Virgin Mary. He, being unwilling to dispute with a soldier, and a drunken one at that, yet also unwilling to abandon a good cause by his silence and rather earnestly desiring to appease him by a temperate and civil reply, said that he by no means blasphemed the most Blessed Virgin, nay rather, that being immaculate and blessed, she had borne the only-begotten Son of God, the Saviour of the world conceived by the power of the Holy Spirit. Not content with this, Chróstowski said: "But you do not invoke her and you do not direct prayers to her." Here the old man declined to reply, kept silent, and withdrew. But the other imperiously and insolently pressed for a reply. Then Gucci made it in these words: "Certainly, because God has not commanded us to do so." Here the soldier, as if seized with fury, taking no account of his venerable age, none at all of his hospitality nor of his innocence and respectability, as is usual with drunkards, [248] seized a large roller and beat the feeble old man severely, while his wife, who with her husband had shown the soldier all the offices of hospitality, piteously interceded for him in vain as the heavy blows were raining down. Chróstowski insisted that the old man should invoke the Most Blessed Virgin. The latter recited the angel's salutation [the Hail Mary of Luke 1: 28ff.]. The soldier did not acquiesce at this but vented his rage beyond all reason, while the other bore all patiently for the sake of the truth.

But [now] the colonel described the heinousness of the foul crime to the fellow-soldiers of Różycki's faction who were raising a riot nearby, exaggerated it, even threatened them violently. Then they quieted down. At daybreak the old man rendered his spirit to God, the Creator.

Shortly afterwards the colonel took pity on the Racovians with an expression of his good will, and giving a signal to his fellow-soldiers, ordered them to leave and commanded a new banner to be unfurled, which was decorated with this inscription: "It is an honorable disgrace to die for a good cause,"[744] as though it were a memorial of Gucci's death.

Różycki, discharged from service, ailing and pale from his severe wound, later set off after his troops with a poor lot for company, exaggerating and begging pardon for his fault as he took leave of his host and other people. On the following day funeral honors were paid to the old man. The pious and learned John Crell preached his funeral sermon from the words of Christ [cf. John 21:19] in which after his glorious resurrection, triumphing over death, he indicated to Peter (for the old man, who should be reckoned among the martyrs, had the same name) by what manner of death he would be glorified.

[The grisly end, 1626, of a pupil of Raków turned soldier of
fortune, hanged by his own captain for thievery and treachery.]

After the lapse of no long time, that is, in the year 1626,[745] my father Christopher Lubieniecki, who after the death [1624] of his father Christopher, minister of the Raków congregation, had undertaken the ministry of the congregation at Lublin [1626], came to Raków on his way from Cracow to Lublin. He found soldiers rioting there. The pond being frozen over, they had outwitted the burghers' watch at the gates and burst into the town, opening the way for themselves with arms. He dared not trust himself to the town in its distress, but turned in at the manor (*aula*) of the patron. While all were greatly preoccupied with the fear of the immediately imminent danger, by benign fate, Christopher Wiszowaty[746] came thither, a young man highly distinguished not only by his noble ancestry and eloquence, but also by his services, being treasurer to Stanislas Koniecpolski,[747] grand general of the Royal Commonwealth. Both [Christophers], supported by the general's authority, quieted the soldiers who were threatening extreme measures. [249] Hardly had this storm ceased raging when lo! a new one arose the next year.

The savagery of the lawless soldiers who at that time were roving here and there about Poland, would also sometimes terrify, sometimes [only] disturb the Racovians. For indeed, apart from the avarice of the soldiers eager for a town richly supplied with everything, the religious spite and the hateful incitements on the part of the priests raised dangers for it, although the inhabitants turned away many troops not only by ready and wary watchfulness, but also by bribery.

There was a certain troop which was then threatening. In it a dissolute young man was serving, Stanislas Franconius by name, son of the celebrated and pious poet Daniel [Franconius], who however, had been commonly given the surname of his mother's first husband, namely Krause, an assessor of the honorable Imperial Chamber at Speyer (as indeed even happened for his father).[748] He [Stanislas Krause Franconius] had spent his youth among soldiers, as is often done, and had the more shamefully corrupted it[749] by the basest crime of ingrati-

tude to his native place, having been born, reared, and liberally educated at
Raków. The townsmen did not know that the wanton youth was following the
army, and that very troop. But he had agreed with the soldiers that they, at a
certain hour in the morning, when the cattle used to be driven through the gate
into the neighboring pastures, would [rush] from ambush and take possession of
the gate, while he would be stirring up a dispute and beginning a quarrel with
the watchmen. Thus far fortune favored what he did. The soldiers rushed headlong into every sort of license, as though the town had been captured. The traitor, devoid of all shame and loyalty, laughed not in his sleeve but openly, nay
jeered, and betrayed the names of wealthy persons whom he knew. Hence all
were struck with fear, while the savage soldiers, and the dread they inspired,
spread through the town.

But Punishment ever crouches at the gate. She did not suffer the villainy of
the young man, who rushed into every insolence (being degenerate, wicked, and
ungrateful), to go unpunished. Nay more, she made an example of him, by
which she showed that she sometimes grants evil men a longer impunity and
moves to vengeance with slow step, sometimes even granting them prosperity,
to the end that men may sorrow the more for a change in their fortunes, and may
recognize the mighty hand of God which makes up for its tardiness by the severity of the punishment. That traitor, who held as nought all laws divine and
human, stole a horse from a certain nobleman near Raków. [250] The culprit
was prosecuted and condemned for this base deed. The captain of the troop, an
upright man who observed justice and cherished a good reputation, seeing this
[deed as well as] disloyalty to his native town (as treachery is always appreciated, but a traitor is hated), marched the troop out of town, and ordered him to
be hanged by grooms of his fellow-soldiers from the door of a neighboring barn
opposite the gate at which he had betrayed his native place. [This happened]
even though the townsmen, mindful of the uprightness and worthiness of his
parents, interceded for him. When he was pushed out to hang, the rope broke,
and he fell to the ground and started running away. But he was brought back by
the lieutenant's order, and being better hanged from a fatal tree with a rope, the
wretch suffered a shameful fate, and ended his infamous life with a most
infamous death.

At that time there was present here a famous physician from Germany,
Bartholdus, who begged the magistrate to give him the corpse of Krause. And
when the magistrate had granted the request, he made of it some salve which he
successfully employed to ward off diseases of various kinds, so that as long as
he had this artificial salve, he was considered a fortunate and famous physician.[750] "Let all men take warning and learn righteousness, and not despite the
Deity," as the old saying is. Let young men learn from the uprightness of their
parents not to degenerate, but to follow it with firm step. Let them learn loyalty
to their parents and to their birthplace (*patria*) as well as to God. Let them also
learn a grateful mind, since the earth bears nothing worse than an ungrateful
one.

[The Racovians aid the nearby Catholic royal borough of Szydłów,
burned and plundered in 1630]

That I may discharge the debt of gratitude that I proposed, I shall relate a praiseworthy act of the Racovians in 1630.

And wishing at the same time to perform the duty of a grateful mind, I shall confess that I owe all these things to the extraordinary diligence of the above-mentioned Jacob Ryniewicz,[751] who took his mother's name of Trembecki, a man whose services to the Church, especially during this severe persecution, cannot be sufficiently proclaimed. Indeed, this act of the Racovians that I am about to relate he copied out of a memorandum-book of his father of blessed memory, Nicholas Ryniewicz. The latter was born in decent condition in the district of Łuków,[752] but in poor circumstances. This is the condition of most of the nobles, who live in great numbers in that poor district.

And therefore a relation of his, a bishop[753] (*pontifex*) who was a man comfortably situated, sent him to Cracow to pursue his studies. But God afterwards sent him to Raków to learn His own truth [251] and to deserve well of His Church.

There had come into those parts some troops of soldiers, unrestrained by any discipline, who were wandering like robbers through the whole Kingdom and had been joined by a great crowd of desperadoes and brigands, whom hope of plunder and their eagerness for fighting drew away from husbandry and daily labor, as sometimes used to happen in Gaul, according to Caesar.[754] They fell upon anything that aroused their itch for wanton greediness, and especially upon Raków, where the hope of rich plunder was not uncertain.[755] The inhabitants therefore, being far fewer in number, yet watching carefully alike for their safety and dependents[756] and for their fortunes, did not overlook any approach to peaceful agreement, so that at length they bought peace at a high price.

These plunderers (for so they should be called, rather than soldiers), having left Raków, attacked and assaulted the neighboring town of Szydłów,[757] the royal borough, masoned and surrounded by walls and ramparts, situated on a cliff, hence well fortified by nature and labor, and thus well enough adorned with a castle and churches (*templa*) and other buildings. At this time its royal governor was [Jan Karol] Stanisławski, a man distinguished for his native worth, his rank, and his relationship to the Kazanowski family. He relied on the inhabitants and fortification of the royal borough, but also remembered the example of the town of Raków, which, built of wood and far inferior in troops and in importance, laboring also under hatred of its religion, had warded off their attack though with "silver spears." Accordingly, he ordered the gates of the borough to be closed and barred, and, in fear of an assault, banked up with earth (save only the one leading into the castle), and the walls and ramparts to be guarded by armed burghers. Thus the soldiers, shut out from access to the borough, took their stand in the widely scattered suburbs very near the borough, and from there in their own manner demanded of the burghers money, wine, mead, meat, oats and dealt with them as they had bargained with the Racovians.

The burghers however, relying on their walls, men and forces, and on the authority of the governor, scorned any means of arranging peace. The soldiers, therefore, eager for booty and revenge, pillaged the suburbs and set them on fire. The devouring flames, catching upon the roofs near the borough, consumed the whole town and the castle, because the two wells were not enough to put out so great a conflagration, one of them being in the middle of the market-place, the other in the castle. And [252] as the gates were blocked no water could be brought into the borough from the suburbs. Nay, when things had reached the depth of misfortune, so that all were obliged to seek safety in flight, cruel death could hardly be avoided by all [those escaping] along the difficult exit open through the gate of the castle, itself burning in the conflagration. When this had been done, the infamous incendiaries deserted their standards, scattered [to plunder] wherever chance or fortune led them, and escaped the punishment they deserved.

The Racovians, having [for their part] duly thanked God for his great providence over them and for the safety they had secured, were greatly pained by the bitter fate of a borough that was friendly enough (a rare thing, especially in one so near), prepared all sorts of provisions, dispatched them without delay on the following day, and vied with one another in doing timely services and showing kindness: the patron[758] to the governor, the ministers[759] and townsmen to the priest (*Parochum*) and the burghers, the Jews to the Jews.[760] So they moved the unfortunates to admiration, and drew tears from some for joy, from others out of reverence, from yet others for shame. The priest himself could not refrain from tears. There were even some[761] who said in compunction of heart: "May God reward them and spare us who [so recently] did climb our towers, ramparts, and roofs in the dead of night, expecting to witness their doom when their town was set to flames. And now here we are, fallen all of a sudden from a lofty height, eating their bread and drinking their drink, though they have been summoned by no obligation or entreaties."

But the kind providence of God was also shown at other times in protecting Raków, in which well attended synods of Brethren from all over the royal Commonwealth were held each year for one or even two weeks, until:

[The destruction of Raków, 1638]

At length in the thirty-eighth year of this century it [Raków] suffered a really grievous upheaval by an unjust sentence which left the guilty free, but vented its rage on the innocent; for it proscribed the patron, a matchless hero of the Christian comonweal (*Respublica christiana*),[762] deserving also of the highest honor from the Commonwealth of Poland. Of him you may justly say with Cicero: "He wholly spent himself and squandered a large part of his inheritance in the service of the Republic."[763] Yet in this we have not used the fitting word, for he did not squander it, but spent it in the interest of the [Royal] Commonwealth, of which a shining proof is a part of the public testimonial bestowed upon him at the diet.[764] at the instance of the palatinate of Sandomierz.

The sentence [of 1638] also proscribed the ministers and teachers, breaking up the Church and the school, destroying the refuge of so many exiles, [253] widows, and orphans, and demolishing the seat of piety and of the Muses. Of this we shall take occasion to speak below in the course of time, if the Lord should permit, so that whoever will may learn from history itself that the very eye of Poland was then plucked out.[765]

CHAPTER THIRTEEN

Of the Rise, Progress, and End of the Church at Lublin, as also of the Churches at Gozdów and Zaporów.

As in a good many royal boroughs, so also at Lublin God prepared a place for the heavenly truth in the beginning of the reign of Sigismund Augustus.[766] After this King's death, this church prospered under Kings Henry [1573 – 74] and Stephen [Batory, 1576 – 86], and in the beginning of the reign of Sigismund III [1587 – 1632], although Stephen, by the advice of John Zamoyski, grand chancellor and grand general of the Kingdom, established a supreme Tribunal there in 1578.[767] For the church enjoyed the patronage of distinguished men, from all quarters, highly renowned for their noble birth and character and for outstanding intellectual gifts. Such were Chamberlain (*archicamerarius*) Stanislas Orzechowski of Lublin;[768] cupbearer Paul Orzechowski (afterwards chamberlain) of Chełm, captain of Suraż, marshal of the equestrian order at the electoral diet of Sigismund III;[769] the Niemojewskis, the Lasotas, the Ostrowskis, the Suchodolskis, and the Lubienieckis.[770]

The first to dispense the word of God in Lublin was the above-mentioned Stanislas Paklepka,[771] and inhabitant of the city, an excellently learned and pious man, outstanding as a popular speaker who, as we have said, was among the first to lay bare the errors concerning the Trinity and pedobaptism. After his death [1567] and that of Lord [John Baptist] Tęczyński [d. 1563], *starosta* of Lublin, the first patron of this church, religious meetings were interrupted and the school was removed to Bełyże. The attendants, even from among the burghers, were men of high standing: [Paul] Krokier,[772] [John] Balcerowic,[773] [Noel] Naborowski, the Ciechańskis, [Jerzy] Bach,[774] [Michael] Schürer,[775] [John] Kokot, [Zacharias] Ecker, and others. There were active in it, beside apothecaries, goldsmiths, and artisans of every kind, men distinguished in the practice of medicine, [254] namely: [Peter] Ciachowski,[776] [Paul] Krokier, [John] Tomkowicz, and others.[777]

The congregation had fitted up its first nest in the house of the minister, Paklepka, which stood on the spot where the splendid Jesuit Church (*templum*) is now seen. But from there the congregation removed to the neighboring house of the noble Lady Ostrowska, born of the old and illustrious family of Suchodolski. Her husband, Jacob Ostrowski of the Gryph clan, steward (*dapifer*) of Lublin, was a man of exceptional piety and rare modesty; and her son, Peter Ostrowski, a royal courtier, a man of unusual courtesy and skill in managing affairs, was therefore renowned at home and abroad for discharging with great credit the missions by which he was distinguished, among others one to the Turkish emperor.[778] The congregation met for some time in the house of the noble Andrew Lasota, master of the King's hunt in the palatinate of Lublin.[779] At length it was removed to the house of the famous Stanislas Orzechowski and his wife Sophia Zieleńska,[780] a lady famous for her rare devoutness, burning zeal, saintly character, and uncommon generosity to the ministers of the word of God, to the poor, and toward the printing of many books. This house, dedicated to religious uses by the last will of this devout couple, was maintained, under the right of patronage, by Paul Lubieniecki, [half]-brother of those three [Stanislas II, Andrew, Christopher] ministers of the word of God, though born of a Zółkiewska.[781]

[Paul Lubieniecki was] a man renowed for his merits and services not only in the church, but also in the diet and the Tribunal.[782]

And when John Niemojewski, a man famous in the Commonwealth, removed thither [to Lublin in 1570] from Kujawy[783] with Albert Brzeziński, Simon Siemianowski, [John] Plecki, Bielawski[784] (who died holding the office of deacon), and Martin Czechowic, bearing the torch of a praiseworthy example of devoutness, the congregation, having been revived and strengthened, became prosperous. It was adorned by the distinguished names of Kurowski, Brzeziński, Komorowski, the Otwinowskis, the Suchodolskis, the Kazimirskis, the Wilkowskis, the Lubienieckis, the Lendzkis, the Szezekockis, the Orzechowskis, the [family] Goźdź, the Bieniewskis, the Zieleńskis, the Siestrzewitowskis, the Matczyńskis, the Zaporskis, the Gorzkowskis, the Łepkowskis, and others, not to speak of burghers living in Bełżyce, Piaski, Urzędów, Kraśnystaw, Lewartów, and other towns in the vicinity.[785]

The importance of this church was not a little enhanced by the neighboring [255] school at Lewartów,[786] of which the first rector was Albert of Kalisz. [He was] a man of uncommon learning whose advice and services the great John Zamoyski[787] employed in shaping the academy of Zamość. [At Lewartów he served] under the patronage of the most noble knight, Nicholas Kazimirski[788] of the Biberstein clan, very famous for his services to the Commonwealth. His brother was the Peter [Kazimirski] whom we mentioned above;[789] while another was Bishop Christop of Kiev;[790] and the third was Lawrence, father of triplet brothers, Casimir, Ladislas, and Thomas, who are still living.[791]

At first this church enjoyed not only a minister, but also a patron, in Paklepka. He died [1567] together with his wife and children with no fear of the ever present danger from the plague, having faithfully discharged his sacred office in the face of a great many difficulties which followed this office as a shadow its body, and with no fear of hatred of the world which he lessened by the uprightness of his character.

He was followed by laborers not slothful in the Lord's vineyard: Martin Czechowic, Valentine Smalcius, John Stoiński, men famous for their published writings, Christopher Lubieniecki the Elder, Matthew Twardochleb, a man of singular devoutness and as sparing in food and clothing as he was generous to the poor, and Joachim Rupnowski; and bringing up the rear, Christopher Lubieniecki the Younger [the Author's father],[792] and the Jacob Ryniewicz whom we have mentioned above.[793]

For during the ministry of these latter, this church, though its affairs were still vigorously carried on in the reign of Sigismund III, was destroyed in the twenty-seventh year of this century [**cf. BAnt no. 12**]. Indeed this church, frequented by such members and situated in such a famous place, kindled the envy of its enemies. On account of the magnificence and the lofty towers of the [Catholic] churches (*templa*) of this city, situated on a rather high hill and distinguished as the seat of the Supreme Tribunal of the Kingdom [correctly: of Little Poland], it might fairly be said of this church what the Holy Oracles [Rev 2:13] declared concerning the church at Pergamon, namely that "it was there where Satan's throne was."

[How religions tension mounted in Lublin to 1627]

For in truth and beyond controversy this came to be said after the college of the Jesuits[794] was founded as a refuge for youth ready for any infamous act and stirring up all vicious people to attempt anything whatever on the pretext of religion, and then the Supreme Tribunal, the workshop of all injustice and of all extravagance. It hurt the eyes of the adversaries to see the crowded religious gatherings (*conventus*) that used [256] to be held in this city,[795] at which there came together from various places in the vicinity both ministers, such as Christopher Rudnicki,[796] John Völkel,[797] Andrew Siedlikowski,[798] and others, and also nobles and other participants. It hurt all the more for the reason that the number was increased by knights and other very honorable men coming from all over the Kingdom to the Tribunal from now on [after 1578], as well as noble youths who lived there while studying the law of their country.

Indeed, even from Lithuania, from Samogitia, Volhynia, and other provinces of the Royal Commonwealth, ministers and nobles passed through this city on their way to attend the synods at Raków, though, indeed, a good many synods were also held here.[799]

Nay, [more, there were] even public disputations on religious matters with

Jesuits, Dominicans, and Carmelites [1579 – 1624], by Niemojewski, Czechowic, Peter Statorius, John Stoiński. Some of these were issued in print.[800]

[The last disputation in Lublin and increasing tempo of Catholic persecution there, 1636 – 37]

The last disputation here was by Christopher Lubieniecki [Jr., minister of the local congregation] against the Jesuit Caspar Drużbicki in 1636. This took place at the request of George Niemirycz, a man of wide reputation, who was assessor of the Supreme Tribunal.[801]

For while he was yet a youth, cultivated by education and foreign travels, and with his wealth and splendor comparable to that of princes, the world tried to ensnare him. And it did at last, for when, toward the end of the war with Sweden,[802] Niemirycz was aiming at the highest office in a new Grand Duchy of Ruthenia[803] (*Russia*) and was following the Ruthenian side,[804] the world ensnared him and, as is its wont, miserably destroyed him.[805]

But although all these debates fell out happily for the confessors of the truth, as much to their great reputation as to the confusion of their adversaries, the latter considered the Brethren as flaunting [these forensic victories in their face] even though they were actually peace-loving. And hence, setting at nought all right and justice, these [Catholic adversaries] left no stone unturned to overthrow the church.

They first came forward in fox's clothing, producing an alleged letter, supposed to have been sent to Christopher Lubieniecki by John Stoiński from his sick-bed at Lusławice, and brought from there to Lublin by a young man versed in Jesuit arts and quite ready to practice deceit and to impersonate various men.[806] And it was craftily composed and calculated to deceive, as though Lubieniecki or someone else by word of mouth or in writing were professing sentiment for Prince Gabriel Bethlen of Transylvania, who was then waging war against the Emperor, [257] and also planning revenge on account of the aid furnished to the latter by the Polish King through the Lissovian troops;[807] or else [professing sentiment] for King Gustavus Adolphus of Sweden, who at the same time was overrunning Prussia with a hostile army.[808] This letter related that rumors had been spread there about the confessors of the truth being expelled from Lublin, and about someone being condemned to the stake on account of his religion.

And this, indeed, although invented by way of experiment, bore a certain appearance of truth. For at the time Samuel Bolestraszycki-Świętopełk, a man of very noble family, of the Calvinist profession, had been proscribed [1627]; and a book by Peter du Moulin on the vanity and wretchedness of human life, written in French and translated by Bolestraszycki into his native tongue, had been condemned to the flames.[809]

This letter was brought and handed to [Christopher] Lubieniecki [Jr. at his home in Lublin] while he was occupied after dinner in entertaining friends, whom his relation Stanislas Matczyński had invited, as they were returning to Lithuania and Volhynia from a synod at Raków.[810] But when with keen eye some examined the inscription and others the style of the letter, and questioned the [suspected] impostor about the looks of Stoiński and the fording of the Vistula, the deception at once appeared as clear as the light in a Punic lamp. Yet they practiced a timely concealment and showed hospitality to the pretended courier. When he pressed for an answer, Lubieniecki replied that he was both fatigued by labors protracted during the whole day until the eve of Pentecost, those being in preparation for the Holy Supper, when according to custom an examination is made of the morals of the whole church, and was thereafter occupied with the duties of hospitality; that he could not give a reply in such inconvenient circumstances, but would prepare it during the night, although it was late and now advanced, so that if he returned at daylight or even at early dawn, he would find it finished.

When the impostor had departed and the deceit manufactured in Loyola's workshop had become evident to all, a messenger was sent to show it to Lawrence Dominik, pastor of the Reformed congregation (who lived in the vicinity and cultivated friendly relations with our Brethren, and was besides a pious and upright man), and to ask him whether he had not been approached by a like impostor. He expressed his thanks for the kindly message and warning, and acknowledged that he had already been led by a similar deceit to give a rather frank reply. As this, if shown to the Jesuits, might cause him trouble, he left Lublin for a time.[811]

Lubieniecki therefore used the greater caution [258] in replying to "Stoiński": He is sorry for his illness and his sudden flight.[812] He assures him that nothing has been heard here about disturbances in Hungary; that no one at Lublin has been condemned to death or banished on account of his religion, but that only Bolestraszycki's book has been burned, and he himself heavily fined. Commending the Supreme Tribunal on account of its care for justice and public tranquillity, he wisely admonishes him ["Stoiński"] of his duty. Yet he informs him that they are acting cautiously in the city, and for fear of exciting disturbances on the part of those who are without work and spend their leisure ill,[813] that they are content with scanty household furnishings and are living prepared for flight if occasion demands. And finally, in return for the rumors invented and composed with intent to deceive, he reports the certain and joyful news of the victory won over the Swedes at Hammerstein,[814] adding a prayer which demands loyalty to the fatherland.

The clever impostor came very early in the morning, asked for, and gladly received, the reply. Then as soon as he had left, he was discovered by a spy who followed him from the place to make his way straight to the house where the Jesuit College was. Here he gave Lubieniecki's letter over to Lawrence Suśliga,[815] at that time the superior of the Jesuits and chief enemy of the antipapists (*anti-Pontificiorum*), besides being a man of fierce and violent nature, who was eagerly waiting for it as well as for the prey that he doubtlessly sought. On this very account, indeed, the man, rash and foolish in all his counsels, had

several days before invited hearers on that very day to hear and see something
unusual!

[Michael Gittich Venecius, on a visit from Lithuania, charged with being treasonably pro-Swedish in his sermon in Lublin on Pentecost, May 1627]

But prudence confident in its innocence, disappointed all the gaping ravens.
These, as this way had failed, being as much inclined to deceit as to outright
malice, and always ready, always at liberty, always free to inflict injury, tried
the other way, that of open slander. For on the very next day[816] they haled the
patrons, elders, and ministers of the church before the Tribunal, namely that
illustrious hero [Jacob] Sieniénski, the palatine of Podolia, and his faithful associate in the service of the Church and the Commonwealth, Paul Lubieniecki,[817]
uncle of Christopher,[818] and the minister Venecius and bound them over
together [on bail].

The last of these Michael Gittich[819] was called Venecius from the city of
Venice of which his father was a native, a most faithful pastor of the churches in
Lithuania, a man of rare learning, marked by his dignity of character. The day
before, on the very day of the feast of Pentecost, he had preached a sermon to so
great an audience that, since neither the spacious chamber (*conclave*) nor the
porches (*pergula*) were large enough [259] for it, [only] the removal of a parti-
tion could furnish space for so great a gathering. The adversaries shamelessly
charged that after the sermon he had offered prayers to God for the success of
Gustavus, the enemy of the country.[820] They were rash in their madness. For
what man of sound mind would say this before the eyes and ears of so many
enemies hostile to the truth, or would in the first pace believe that a pious and
learned man had said it—especially while suffering from public ill will?[821]

Sieniénski called upon the presiding justice (*praeses*) of the court, who had
always been a friend of his, and there asked him why Gittich had been haled
before the Tribunal. He called to witness his age, the serious condition of his
health, in particular his innocence, unstained by any crime, and demanded his
discharge. The president charged him with the crime of treason on account of
prayers offered in public for the public enemy. Sieniénski vouched for Gittich's
loyalty and defended his innocence. The president congratulated him on this
and gave him good hope of a discharge.

On the appointed day, which was a Wednesday, Sieniénski and Lubieniecki
appeared in the Tribunal. The gathering of people for a case of such importance
was very large. The case of Venecius was called, as he was held at the pleasure
of the court and hence obliged to appear. The accuser (*instigator*) [Andrew]
Lisiecki,[822] a man of hasty nature, bursting out into passion against the antipapists, pressed upon the accused the crime of treason. This they denied, as was
appropriate. Sieniénski was accused as the patron of Raków, since those ministers[823] coming from there implicated those going thither, so great was the crime.
[Paul] Lubieniecki, for his part, was accused as patron of the church in Lublin in

which this great crime had been perpetrated. Both were like the lamb that muddied the river on the bank opposite the wolf. They denied the fact, and demanded and insisted on being faced by the informer. He did not appear.

Therefore they invoked the penalty of *lex talionis* against the accuser as a calumniator and wanton slanderer.[824] He said he had done nothing except by order of the presiding justice. They, with their legal counsel [Alexander] Rużyński (an adherent of the Reformed confession), stoutly defending their case, demanded according to law that, since there was no one accusing them, they be acquitted, and they insisted on being declared free. But the pettifogger, putting on a bold face, pressed that Venecius [first] be produced. They did not know where he was hidden (which was in the house of Michael Schürer, a burgher and merchant of Lublin).[825] There were some who thought that he ought to be brought before the court to give account of his loyalty (*fides*). Among these at first was even the defender of the case [Rużyński], an upright man. [260] But afterwards he found out that the enemies were bent on destroying Gittich without any regard to justice, with the aid of a certain cleric wickedly and deliberately suborned, who was prepared to prove the calumny on oath, and what is more, to involve all the rest in a common punishment as privy to the crime and accomplices in the treason. Then he himself earnestly and urgently warned the Brethren to get him away from the [burden of] death that was certain and determined upon and that had been also prepared for so many innocent men. And to this proposition they all agreed. But indeed the wickedness of men ready to venture anything had gone too far.

After many insults and accusations, in which the brazen-faced pettifogger (the court being by no means paved with sharp stones, as advised by Cato the Elder),[826] like a viper accustomed to hiss and bite, attacked the good name of the illustrious and innocent men, the verdict was given by the judges that those cited, being duly sworn, should declare that [Gittich] Venecius had not said such things, that they had not been heard by anyone, and that they and he were innocent. When this was done, they were sentenced to pay a heavy fine and thus escaped the unjust judges. And this after Sienieński, being fully conscious of his own great services to the Commonwealth and of his own innocence, pointed out with utmost frankness the atrociousness of the injury and the shamelessness of his malicious and crafty accuser. This [privilege] was allowed [in recognition of] the age and services of the distinguished man whose soul glowed with generous virtue.

[The churches in Lublin of the Reformed and of the Brethren
are destroyed, 1627]

But not even in this way did those men, who had then escaped from so adverse a trial, escape from the cunning of their enemies, who, unrestrained and implacable, rushed on to yet worse. Nay, by the end of the month,[827] as their unbridled license raged along the beaten path, dire calamity wasted not only us but also those devoted to the Reformed confession, and destroyed both churches. For such a terrible wrong there was no cause beyond the malice of the adversaries of the truth and of all right; but the occasion offered was this.

Two of those who liked to be called companions (*socii*) of Jesus, going from Lwów to Warsaw and passing through Lublin, were being escorted out of the city by two associates and several adult students by way of courtesy, their carriage preceding them. They were passing through Czechów, the suburban estate of Lord Raphael [Leszczyński] of Leszno, palatine of Bełz, a man highly distinguished by his senatorial rank and his services to the Commonwealth, and a generous patron of the Reformed Church. As [they progressed,] the students (an undisciplined class of youth, especially in a nation more than free, [261] and encouraged in their fierceness by the loose Jesuit discipline), who wore swords according to a vicious custom, attacked some German soldiers as they were drinking together in an inn. These the palatine, having completed the term (*obitum*) of a judge in the supreme Tribunal of the Royal Commonwealth, was then preparing to dispatch to the war against Gustavus.[828] No cause of offense was given, but even here the proverb seemed to hold true: "whoever wishes to do mischief never fails to find a reason." The students were the first to attack, because the Germans had not been first in paying them the honor of a salute as they were passing by, even while that ceremony by custom was rather incumbent upon the former. Hence on account of a head not being uncovered, the door was discovered for calamity, and one of a wide extent, for it also led to an atrocious wrong not only against the Evangelicals but also against the Unitarians.

The former were innocent indeed so far as having any share is concerned, and the latter were investigated without any pretext of a wrong committed (beyond the bare hatred of truth and innocence). It is helpful to follow conventions not at all [in themselves] useful to life. One of those wild fellows, without regard to propriety, nor yet at an opportune moment, pressing the duty of courtesy upon the drunken soldiers, arrogantly and rashly addressed them thus: "Why do you not show decent respect to the Fathers of the Society of Jesus when they pass by?" The soldiers, though heated with wine, had nevertheless not lost the use of reason, a sense of politeness, and a respect for what was becoming. They therefore retorted, as was fitting: "Still, my good man, it was proper for you as you passed by to take the lead in such a courtesy to us who had been already seated here in our inn." Thereupon it came to a brawl. The wild fellow, alarmed for the safety of his Fathers, drew them away to their carriage with the rest of the crowd, threatening that on his return he would avenge the wrong. This done, the student and (if God likes such) disciple of the Company of Jesus retraced his steps, but overstepping bounds, first with words and then with a sword, attacked a soldier and that a German and full of wine, yet observant of decent manners. When it came to arms, [however,] the wild fellow fell pierced with a sword, and at once died and suffered the penalty of his rashness.

The rest of the crowd forthwith raised the shout of hot-heads: "To arms, men, to arms. Run to destroy the churches of the Lutherans." (So are all those dissenting from the Roman Church commonly called.) ''The Lutherans are murdering the Catholics!'' And this soldier was in fact a follower of the Lutheran camp; but on the estate of his master, he was in the paid service of a hero adhering [262] to the Evangelical [Reformed] confession, and he was more spirited. By ingrained habit, he spurned all delay, being not only rather clever but also of an ingenious fierceness in carrying out wicked designs, often carrying off the palm of bravery in his own class. A vile rabble ran together: students (far removed indeed from the camp of the Muses),[829] artisans, servants, and all those who were abandoned (*perditi*) and inappropriately occupied (*maleferiati*) on the Lord's day. A great many of them, indeed, by a very bad custom (feigning the Christian name and forgetting all shame, and not even fearing the sun from which the day also takes its name), make of it the Devil's day by indulging in drinking, dancing, and lewdness (if we are to believe Chrysostom[830] in respect of the dances alone, not to mention the Apostle and Christ). The same evening vicious crowds attacked the churches (*templa*) of the Evangelicals and of the Christians.[831]

There was in the city at the time among the Evangelical magnates, Andrew Firlej, castellan of Bełz (later palatine of Sandomierz and commander [*rotmistrz*] of the armies of the royal Commonwealth in the recent Cossack War).[832] Since he had a mansion adjoining the house in which their ministers lived, he bolted the doors, together with his household and friends who had taken refuge there in the sudden and serious danger, and defended himself against the fury of those idle loafers (*maleferiati*), nay, thieves plundering in the city. He ordered muskets to be fired forthwith against the attackers, who had indeed been the first to do this, sparing neither their violence nor wantonness, nor even the innocence [of others]. So the night passed, with a noisy attack on the one hand and the needful defense on the other.

Before nightfall, one of the ministers of the Unitarian Church, [Christopher] Lubieniecki, went to the Jabłonna estate, situated about three miles from the city. The other one, [Jacob] Ryniewicz [Trembecki], with some other brethren, was unwilling to be shut up in the mansion of Firlej and to be obliged to repel force by force, or even to witness such things. Therefore, taking thought for his safety in the unexpected danger, he swam across a large pond (since no other way out was open), and thus escaped immediate danger by flight, and spent the short night under the open sky, dripping wet.

When the sun was up and he returned to his post of duty, he did not find the place in which to conduct the usual worship but (I use his own words) ''the abomination of desolation'' [Dan 12:11; Matt 24:15]. For during the night the buildings of both churches (*aedificia*) fell in total ruin. Why, not even their neighbors were spared. The storm broke with special force upon [263] the home of a wealthy burgher belonging to the Reformed confession and deacon of its church, which adjoined the meetinghouse (*aedes*) of the Christians. To him Ryniewicz, together with Andrew Lubieniecki, brother of his colleague, and Alexander Przypkowski, discharged the office of human compassion (*humanae miserationis officio defuncti*). Meanwhile John *Ciechański*,[833] one of the leading burghers and deacon of the Church of the Christians, a pious and clever man, took Rynewicz in good time to Jabłonna. Paul Lubieniecki the Younger,[834] having accompanied him to the bridge, could hardly get back to the house of his uncle of the same name for the tumult, and on his way he rescued from imminent danger his brother Andrew, who barely escaped being crushed in the general ruin together with his companion Nicholas Borzęcki, a noble and wise man.[835] In the morning [the riot] ceased for a while to rage; but within a few hours the whirlwinds, not even fearing the sun in broad daylight, raged against the very ruins and attacked Firlej's mansion, into which the ministers of the Evangelicals had fled for refuge.

While all this was taking place, to the great delight of some, to the grief and horror of others, the judges of the Supreme Tribunal, laughing in their sleeves and repeating the ancient *Euge*! [bravo!] (instead of "for shame") at length for fear of more serious evil, did send some of their number of the clerical and lay orders to calm the riot and disperse the crowd. The disorder was quelled with difficulty, as the hope of plunder had grown. The villainy and rage were dreadful indeed; but what I have told is but little in comparison with what I am about to tell.

For no just punishment or commiseration followed the vileness of such a great crime. Nay, since religious tyranny, cruel and unrestrained, had destroyed all feeling of both [justice and commiseration] and of humanity itself, a cruel punishment was imposed and fell upon the innocent and the unfortunate. Severely afflicted though they were, a far greater affliction was still added, and that a perpetual one. And lest anything be wanting to complete the injustice, it was joined with abuse. The palatine [of Bełz, Raphael Leszczynski], though a judge in the Supreme Tribunal, as well as the castellan and other patrons of both churches, were summoned to the court. The former was compelled to surrender two of those German soldiers. One of them was put to death by the sword, and the other barely ransomed, and at great cost. The castellan was condemned forthwith to pay a fine of a thousand marks. Both churches were abolished and proscribed under a permanent sentence, certainly unjust and severe.[836] No justice, no fairness, no law, no precept, no entreaties, finally, not even [264] satiety with blood, fines, or plunder, which generally moves even tyrants, availed to prevent this consequence hard upon the destruction of both churches, as we have already seen exemplified, at Cracow.[837]

From this atrocious example and others of which we have hitherto spoken and shall hereafter speak, a measure may justly and fairly be taken of the just punishment of God which, though with halting step, did not fail to overtake past crime and made up for its tardiness by the severity of the punishment of internecine wars that arose from this source of savage injustice.[838] After this [1627] one might not safely have a funeral procession, nor go to the residences of illustrious men or nobles to hold divine worship.

Notorious is the grave wrong done to Samuel Makowski [in 1633 in Lublin].[839] This befell verily a doctor of medicine of great experience and renown, and furthermore of upright life, especially deserving very much from the city, the more so when the plague was raging. Although protected by the patronage of the King and declared innocent by the royal commissioners, yet by the judges of the Tribunal he was many times dragged into court, put into prison, condemned to punishment, and after protracted fear of death was barely ransomed at a great price and by earnest entreaties. The Church of the Unitarians assisted the afflicted man by donating a thousand guilders (*librae*).[840] All that could assuage the violent grief of so many wrongs were empty words and nothing more. For the afflicted, filling the dietines of the palatinates and the diet of the Royal Commonwealth with their complaints, obtained sympathy instead of relief.

And in the same year of 1627, and again in 1632 they had laws passed in the Diet abolishing the decrees of the Tribunal which had abrogated at its own discretion the strength of a new law [**cf. BAnt no. 12**].[841] But "what can wrath alone do without any power," as the saying is, the unjust judges replying to the whole Commonwealth after the example of Pompey's soldiers: "How dare you lay down laws for us who are armed with the sword?"[842] The sword, that is of sacred and civil authority, and [also] of the supreme power and fury of the populace!

[The persecution of the Author's father, Christopher Lubieniecki, and others, 1628]

Lubieniecki presided over this [Lublin] church, as also over that situated at Zaporów in the vicinity together with Andrew Siedlikowski, son of Albert, a man learned, eloquent, godly, and of notable hospitality. Lubieniecki was exposed to various insults from the adversaries, among which was prominent the attack made in 1628 by lawless soldiers recently enlisted. In this [attack] both these servants of God, a third, Jacob Ryniewicz-Trembecki, and the whole congregation while at worship incurred imminent risk of life had not divine providence intervened.[843] [265] It happened that Peter Królewski[844] of the Strzemie clan (a man famous for his noble birth and his services to the Commonwealth) unexpectedly came up and was recognized by the leader of that band of thieves and robbers. The leader, thanks to friendship, interceded in the camp. And within a few days this company of wild men was broken upon the vicinity and scattered by Bishop [Remigian] Koniecpolski of Chełm.[845]

I shall rightly and deservedly add here two [further] memorable cases of divine providence. When that cohort of madmen attacked an inn (*diversorium*) in which our people had taken refuge, one of them took my father's hat away from him. This he at once redeemed with a few coins. Hence the ruffian, won by the slight kindness, protected him during the tumult. But when other [ruffians] were beating George Bach almost to death—a German by race, a prominent burgher of Lublin, a godly man well-known for his kindness—one of the ruffians, who had a little before worked as a porter (*bajulus*) in Lublin, asked whether Michael Schürer was among them [too]. He, also, was a German, a wealthy and kind man, one of the first citizens, too, of Lublin. This

Schürer had obliged the porter by many acts of kindness. My mother, sharing the danger with her husband, responded, pointing to Bach, and thereby snatched him from death.[846] Thus virtue sometimes finds place even among thieves.

And thus by such favors of God the Church escaped the impending danger.

[Unitarian John Cichowski's defense before the Lublin Tribunal of his
inheritance contested by Catholic Christopher Ossoliński;
the imprisonment in 1635 of Pastor Christopher Lubieniecki
and others for their support of Cichowski, and their release]

It will not be foreign to my present purpose but rather calculated to produce confidence in what I have said, if I mention [first] some instances of very great wrongs which were passed over by the author of the *Historia Ecclesiarum Slavonicarum*[847] (who labored under partisan spirit and ill will, and who also in this respect merits impartial correction) and also that the laws of the diet may be understood to furnish protection to dissidents in religion.[848] For not only the Evangelicals but also the Arians (commonly and wrongly so called) are included [in the *Pax dissidentium*].

Since he enjoyed the right of nobility and hereditary possession in that palatinate, and thus also that of suffrage in its dietines, Christopher Lubieniecki suffered passionate and extraordinary hatred from the adversaries. Hence he was rather often assailed by wiles and by open force, yet always escaped their hands. But he narrowly escaped being crushed by the misfortune of Cikowski which fell heavily upon many of the Brethren, and especially upon him as a minister of the word of God.

I add a brief account of the affair. Stanislas Cikowski (son [266] of Stanislas, chamberlain of Cracow, grandson of Stanislas, castellan of Biecz and grand general of the Kingdom), having no children by Dorothea Błońska of the Biberstein clan, bequeathed a rich inheritance to his only sister [Zofia Cichowska], the wife of Christopher Ossoliński, palatine of Sandomierz, and to her only son Baldwin.[849] To his paternal cousin John [Cikowski], an adherent of the Unitarian religion, he bequeathed the village of Krzelów with some farmsteads, providing for his rights in every proper way according to the public laws.

Ossoliński, taking great offense at this, after the death of his relation summoned his widow [Stanislas's] and his cousin John into court, and as is usual with adversaries of the truth and of everything just and honorable, fomented ill will, and even trumped up the false charge of Arian heresy, pretending that on account of his wife's Catholic religion the lawful succession had been alienated from her by her relative with the design of spreading the Arian heresy.

[John] Cikowski, well aware that in the supreme Tribunal dissidents from the Roman Church[850] had so often been struck by the thunders of fatal decisions, and seeing that notwithstanding the justice of his case he was running a risk with regard to the succession, begged many of the Unitarians and some of the Evangelicals (among whom was George Rzeczycki, captain of Urzędów, an illustrious man) to aid his cause by their intercession before the judges, that is, that they [the judges] preserve in their fulness and integrity the venerable laws passed with regard to the pact on the *dissidentes de religione* and concerning the right of inheritance, and take no cognizance of an unjust case against an innocent person. He obtained this service from his friends, who were not unwilling, since it was safe and not unusual, according to the wish of the Lublin church itself, which was suffering solely from religious hatred. [And they were the more willing to do this] since before this [a similar incident had] turned out not unhappily, in the case of [Stanislas] Chronowski, a nobleman, both minister and heir of Rąbkowa.

Stanislas Orzechowski, himself deserving well of the Commonwealth in that very Tribunal and in the diet, successfully undertook the duty of pleading the case which had been entrusted to him. He was the son of that Paul [Orzechowski] who was chamberlain of Chełm (a very distinguished man in the Commonwealth, as we have seen) by his wife [Elizabeth] Oleśnicka (sister of the palatine of Lublin).[851] But the boldness with which he was moved to say that if the venerable laws were not effectual, he would appeal the case to the diet, so offended the judges that they shut up fifteen or sixteen nobles in prison, and also condemned the rest to the top of a drafty tower, but thrust [Christopher] Lubieniecki down into the lowest dark and filthy dungeon.[852]

For Lubieniecki this very severe punishment was really almost equal to death, [267] given that he was of frail health and was subject to catarrh. Moreover, he was separated both from the companionship of his devoted wife who lowered herself down into that horrid dungeon repeatedly and only with the greatest of discomfort, and from the pleasant society of his Brethren whom he did not neglect even there and at that juncture of his affairs. He would lead them in prayers and in the singing of psalms. These services, incumbent upon a pastor, angered a number of ill-disposed people, as did also a far-fetched ascription of wickedness: that the prisoners, in order to satisfy their revenge, sang Psalm 79 [:1] in the prison, which begins: "O God, the heathen are come into thine inheritance." This line might indeed have been applied by some to the unjust and cruel judges, but to those men who knew of whose spirit (*cujus*) they were, it was not so applied. For such execrations would have been foreign to the circumstances of the hour, as well as to the spirit of Christian teaching.

After so many noble men had thus for some days been confined in a disgraceful and filthy prison, with great loss of their property and with public disgrace (which however was sweetened by their confidence in having the better cause, and a conscience that paled for no crime), [certain] senators of great influence and of the right mind (*bonarum partium*), Prince George of Zasław[853] and Roman Hojski,[854] castellan of Kiev (who also were assessors of that Tribunal, but were absent from the court when the atrocious sentence was passed against the prisoners), interceded for them with their colleagues and obtained their release, though each of them was fined six hundred marks, which comes to nearly one thousand *librae*.

When released from prison and brought into court, they were obliged to submit at once to the sentence, however unjust and severe. Nevertheless Martin

Czaplic,[855] whose family and distinguished services to the Commonwealth were set off by his unusual modesty in manners and speech, pleaded so eloquently in behalf of the Brethren for a mild penalty that he wrung tears from the eyes of some of the judges. One of them said: "If Czaplic had pleaded for you[856] instead of Orzechowski, you would not have been imprisoned."

But here, in passing, though of importance, is to be noted an instance of divine justice. For indeed the judges, mollified by a fine that was certainly severe, and unwilling to provide an occasion of some great commotion in the Commonwealth over very legitimate complaints, should they overthrow the sacrosanct right of succession and testament which is protected by laws of all nations, [268] left [Jan] Cikowski his right [to Krzelów] unimpaired. Therefore the palatine [Ossoliński], opposing all law and justice, compacted with him about the inheritance (*de successione*) for 12,000 thalers (*Joachimicorum*) and paid this sum of money within a few years, but meantime under the name of interest at once gave Cikowski possession of the estate of Kobylany, three miles from Raków; and he had to leave the widow[857] what is called a "life right (*advitalium*) unimpaired," or possession of Krzelów as long as she lived.

However, neither he [Christopher Ossoliński] nor his wife nor his only son Baldwin entered into the inheritance, because the widow survived him.[858] When Baldwin was about to go to the Tatar-Cossack war in 1649, he asked her forgiveness,[859] renounced all rights [to Krzelów], and asked and obtained her blessing, for she was a lady both devout and possessed of unusual influence, and highly esteemed. Yet nevertheless he [Baldwin Ossoliński] did not escape the divine judgment, of which the royal psalmist [Ps 36:6] sang as of a great deep, and of which the examples of so many kings and kingdoms tell. For he fell at Zborów.[860] His widow,[861] though burdened with great debts, married a second time and transferred to another house the ample property of [Stanislas] Cikowski, which had come to her husband by inheritance and had fallen to her under the marriage title. Only the estate of Krzelów fell to Baldwin [Ossoliński's] paternal cousin.[862]

But to return to the subject [the imprisonment and release of the Lublin dissidents]. When everything was duly finished in court, Prince George very kindly invited all the prisoners to a banquet. The names of so many confessors deserve the perpetual remembrance of posterity. There were thus three of the Szpanowski [branch of the] Czaplic clan,[863] Martin, his brother George, and Martin's son Alexander. They were related to the aforesaid castellan [Hoyski], as well as to the Kierdej family (since they bore the same arms, and so were of the same clan), but also were in kinship with Prince George (as his grandmother will have been of the Czaplic family, and related besides to the princes Wiśniowiecki and Korecki). [Other guests at the banquet were] Peter Suchodolski (of the Janina clan, also related to the Sobieskis), Peter Królewski, John Konarski, Stanislas Orzechowski, whom I have mentioned, George Grek, Stanislas Matczyński, John Łępkowski, Nicholas Rostek.[864]

[Christopher] Lubieniecki, however, was absent, hindered by his infirmity. Indeed the loathsome prison [269] had greatly sapped his strength, so that henceforth he suffered from quartan fever. Also, he was henceforth assailed more often by the hatred of adversaries, especially that of the students reared in the Loyolitic school in craftiness and malice. This [malice] once got him into a snare, for some of their number, audacious fellows, followed him from the city as he was returning to the estate of Jabłonna,[865] nay attacked and wellnigh kidnapped him, when, by a marvelous providence of God, Basil Bieniewski,[866] a noble and God-fearing man, coming up with a numerous retinue of servants, rescued him from imminent danger. From there he went with him and some other friends to the College of the Jesuits, duly reproached [them] in words for the mad conduct of the students who were roving about through the city like brigands, earnestly and seriously admonished the teachers of their duty in respect to such atrocious deeds, and compelled them to apologize for the misdemeanor, and to promise that henceforth they would restrain the youths who under their direction were pursuing humane studies.[867]

CHAPTER FOURTEEN

Of the Same Church of Lublin, Removed First to Piaski, Thence to Siedliska, and Finally Scattered Together with the Rest by the Recent Disaster of the Swedish War.

Being driven from Lublin, the church found a new habitation (*sedes*), or rather lodging place (*diversorium*), three miles from the city at Piaski, where Martin Krowicki, above mentioned,[868] finished his days. This town was owned (after Stanislas Orzechowski, chamberlain of Lublin) by Andrew Suchodolski of the Janina clan,[869] a man not only of illustrious family but also wealthy, godly, and steadfast. At the same time his wife, of the Podlodowski family, adhered to the Reformed religion, being sister of Stanislas, also of the Janina clan, a man noted for his learning, knowledge of civil affairs, wisdom, and above all for his exceptional piety.

For Stanislas Podlowski, having gone abroad for his higher education (*mercatus bonarum artium*), was not ashamed to confess openly the pure truth which he had come to know among the Dutch (*Batavi*) in the midst of Calvinism;[870] [this] as related by the illustrious Christopher Sieniuta[871] and by Daniel Rudnicki, [the latter] a very learned nobleman and [270] sometime professor of theology and philosophy in the center of the papacy at Rome.[872] To the great grief of godly people, Stanislas Podlodowski parted from life in the very flower of his age, having begotten an only daughter, who is still alive, from Sophia, the

daughter of Peter [Suchodolski], steward (*dapifer*) of Lublin. [This Peter
Suchodolski was the] brother of the [Andrew] Suchodolski mentioned above.[873]
But his sister adhered to the Reformed party to the last. Yet after the death of
her husband [Andrew Suchodolski] she defended the confessors of the truth
even to the end, and gave them generous patronage, not forgetting her husband
and brother in equity, though after her death all these were forgotten by her only
son Adam Suchodolski, as we shall presently relate.

[Adam Suchodolski uproots the congregation removed from Lublin in 1633]

As a boy and youth, I saw this church flourishing in its numbers and in the distinction of its attendants under the protection [first] of its patron [Andrew
Suchodolski, then of] the widow [the lady Podlodowska-Suchodolska] and her
son [Adam] while a minor. He had indeed joined our church, and had had as
director of both his studies and behavior at home and abroad Andrew
Wiszowaty, grandson of Faustus Socinus through his daughter,[874] a man of profound learning—but without recompense. For after his return from abroad,
[Adam Suchodolski] neither paid him any salary nor showed any respect for the
shades of his parents and for common justice.

In the year 1645[875] he uprooted the church. And a little later, by a reckless
accident, meaning to frighten his maiden sister with a loaded pistol of which she
was particularly afraid, he killed her. Over [all] this [Christopher]
Lubieniecki,[876] whom his parents[877] as intimate friends had always held in high
esteem, and whose presence Adam knew his mother had greatly desired when
she lay dying, lamented deeply with him over so great a wrong contrary [first] to
that virtue (than which nothing is more admired), [then] to the actual circumstances by which his more than adamantine heart should have been turned
to right and justice by his sister's blood (for a diamond is said to soften by
blood), and [finally] to his ancestral alliances and many relations.

What attitude toward the pure truth and its confessor was held at this time [of
accidental manslaughter] by Stephen Swietlicki,[878] rector of the school at
Bełżyce, formerly his preceptor, is clear from a rather unusual letter, a copy of
which it is right and due that I present from the original in my possession. On
the outside the letter bears this address:

> To a dear soul in sorrow, but soon to enjoy the comfort of Jesus Christ, the
> Noble Adam Suchodolski.

[271] Within it reads as follows:

> Suchodolski, a dear soul as much beloved of God as it is afflicted: The
> great Ruler of the world, "whose judgments are a great deep" [Ps 36:6],
> has wished you to atone (*piare*) for the life of the most lovable Jesus Christ,

most worthy of love, long rejected [by you] but now acknowledged in the death of your dearly beloved sister. Continue suffering and expiating the faults of your youth committed at home among us and abroad, and cry: ''I am unworthy, O Lord, of all thy mercies.'' Perhaps, had our dear sister not thus died, you would have died a second time.

[The church removes to Siedliska, 1645–58]

For the perpetration of this atrocious deed [of recklessness, Adam Suchodolski's], status and reputation suffered not a little. A cousin on his father's side, Nicholas [Suchodolski], son of Peter and Dorothea (a devout lady of the Spinek family),[879] granted the congregation (*ecclesia*) hospitality at the neighboring village [**cf. BAnt no. 95.1**] of Siedliska, which adjoined the ancient seat of the Suchodolski family, and in which the church (*Ecclesia*) once had had its home (*nidus*).[880]

To its ministry, in which my parent of blessed memory had died in 1623, I, too, was attached in 1652 and 1653 as a tyro, being made a colleague with John Ciachowski, grandson of the [George] Schomann mentioned above, and with Joachim Stegmann, men remarkable for their piety, learning, eloquence, and zeal.[881] And [the church] was indeed well-attended to the last.

But a little afterwards, namely in 1655, the storm broke forth on the occasion of the Swedish war [1655–60] and of the violent Muscovite invasion [1655], and when at length on the occasion of the persecution of 1658, even to the public proclamation of the sad banishment by a law of hard tenor passed in the Diet,[882] for its ferocity unheard of among so free a nation—the church was grievously shattered and at length dispersed.

[The flight of the Lublin-Piaski-Siedliska congregation to Transylvania and elsewhere][883]

Even the patron himself [Nicholas Suchodolski] (formerly brother-in-law of George Czaplic Kierdej, then of John Rupniowski of the Śrzeniawa clan, and finally of the great Samuel Przypkowski of the Radwan clan),[884] together with many of the Brethren sought refuge on the border of Hungary, in Mármaros County, by the courtesy and kindness of a famous man, the illustrious Count Francis Rhédei.[885] But great danger arose where safety was hoped for. For all (and the wretched [272] company comprised more than five hundred) were ill-treated by the lawless imperial soldiery and stripped of their possessions even to nakedness [**cf. BAnt no. 110.3**], and finally were treated with almost unbearable mockery by those who were jeering at them with every sort of insult.[886] Thence some fled to Transylvania, others to Prussia.[887] Among the latter was their patron, who amid the bitter misfortunes of exile kept faithful to his Saviour to the end.[888]

CHAPTER FIFTEEN

Of the Churches in the Piedmont, Especially the Very Old and Famous Church at Lusławice in the Palatinate of Cracow; As also an Account of the Death of Faustus Socinus.

Among the first nests (*nidia*) that the Great and Good God built in Poland for the truth and his Church is that at Lusławice.[889] This village is in the palatinate of Cracow, near the town of Zakliczyn; and opposite it, across the Little Danube River (commonly called Dunajec), is the castle of Melsztyn overlooking the river. It lies in a very pleasant place, being in the middle of a plain somewhat extended on all sides, which is surrounded by foothills of the Carpathian mountains as though by a crown. Hence the name of Piedmont is applied to this district.

Its heirs at that time were Stanislas Taszycki of the Strzemie clan (a man who adorned the nobility of his family by his distinguished services not only at home but also abroad, with the most glorious Emperor Charles V, and hence possessed great influence in his native land)[890] and Abraham Błónski of the Biberstein clan.[891] The former had founded a church on his estate which was conducted, among others, by men everywhere distinguished: Peter Statorius, George Schomann, Stanislas Lubieniecki [II], my great-uncle, John Stoiński (grandson of Peter Statorius the Elder, son of the Younger), and by Jonas Schlichting.[892] This church, being situated in a very convenient place, was quite often visited by great men, nobles and others, both young and old, our Brethren, as they were coming from or returning to Transylvania. These men in that country are called Unitarians,[893] as being worshipers of the one God the Father through the only Mediator Christ.

[The School at Lusławice][894]

They [the Transylvanian Unitarians] also used to send their children and young men to Lusławice [273] to learn the Polish language, and to be trained in the liberal arts, especially in religion. In the time of our fathers there was, indeed, a school there, over which learned men from neighboring Hungary were often called to preside, and which grew much after the ruin of the famous schools at Raków [1638] and Kisielin [1655], and under the rectorship of Master Valentine Baumgarten.[895] [He was] a Prussian from Memel, an extraordinarily learned man who departed this life not long since as parish (*plebanus*) minister at

Kolozsvár. The School flourished like a veritable academy with theological, metaphysical, physical, and logical studies and discussions, and with practice in oratory.

[Religion and culture in Lusławice]

Having myself taken part in these things, I am here writing of what I personally know, in reference for those who early formed my mind. There were then living with us some noble ladies, who devoted the remainder of their lives to the practice of religion. There were living there two very eminent chemists, famous throughout all Poland, Martin Wilhelm[896] and Simon Polanus.[897] There were living there also young men cultivated in letters, Christian Pyrner, a Saxon from Magdeburg, and Christian August Frederick von *Höhnstedt*, a nobleman from Brunswick.[898] The rather fine buildings erected for the purpose [of housing the activities of the School] gave to it the appearance of a town. Other attendants, and especially the triplet brothers John, Peter, and Alexander Błonski,[899] used to come from the vicinity to hear the sermons of Schlichting, not only each Sunday but also on Wednesdays and Fridays.[900] And yet, when persecution arose against Schlichting in 1647, the two former went over to the camp of Calvin, while Alexander choked to death at a table which was all the more sumptuous for his having been a childless man.[901]

To celebrate the Holy Supper (*sacra synaxis*) the church [in Lusławice] used to be crowded, as nobles gathered there from near and far: not only from neighboring churches like that of Robków (Rąbkowa), which had been founded by Stanislas Chronowski,[902] a man of ancient nobility, deserving the name of the Christian Cato for the strictness of his morals, who did what was rare, acting at the same time as both the patron and the minister of the word; and like the church of Pielnia, of which the patron was Paul Brzeski Żegota of the very ancient Topór clan, a man equally distinguished for birth and zeal, my father-in-law[903] but also from more distant churches, [such nobles as] the Morsztyns and the Rupniowskis and others who lived across the Dunajec and the Vistula.

Among these [others] were the twin brothers Adam and Andrew [274] Gosławski of the Oksza clan who,[904] besides the splendor of their fathers' race (which reckoned among the family's ornaments Barbara, wife of Valentine Dembiński, grand chancellor and castellan of Cracow),[905] and of their mother's race (she was a Filipowska), were also famous for their services in the Church and in the Commonwealth, and for great excellence of character, being of incomparable courtesy and modesty, treated considerately[906] even by [those] magnates who were otherwise most hostile to the truth. And the former [Adam Gosławski] indeed gave the world uncommon proofs of his exceptional learning in published writings, and would have given more had not his work written against the very famous philosopher Jacob Martini been lost through the carelessness of a friend.[907]

[Andrew Gosławski, Sigmund Taszycki,
and the end of the church in Lusławice]

Andrew [Gosławski] held an estate at Lusławice in the right of his wife, whom
he had married out of the Szczepanowski family. She was the surviving widow
of Cyril Taszycki (grandson of Stanislas, son of Matthew).[908] To her [Elizabeth
Szczepanowska-Taszycka-Gosławska] belonged the use and enjoyment of the
estate for her lifetime.

[The late] Cyril's younger brother, Sigismund [Taszycki], educated from
boyhood in accordance with his parents' wish by Stanislas [II] Lubieniecki the
Elder and distinguished for his piety, might justly and fairly be said to have been
a man of courteous dignity and dignified courtesy (so well were both these virtues combined in him) and gave very high hopes of himself. But he, "a beard-
less youth when at length his guardian was withdrawn"[909] and when both his
parents were dead, being captivated by the enticements of an alluring world,
was twice led astray into marrying daughters of Papists.

I knew his second wife, [Anna] Czermińska, a woman of great ambition and
burning with relentless hatred against the lovers of the truth. Thus for his
absurd love of her and of his mother-in-law (the second wife of his uncle Achatius Taszycki), and under the influence of Bishop Peter Bembicki of Cracow,[910]
Sigismund [Taszycki]—having redeemed the dowry right granted to his
brother's wife [Elizabeth Szczepanowska-Taszycka], now married to [Andrew]
Gosławski—turned away from the [Minor] Church and violated a promise given
to Gosławski and to the Brethren. He was unmindful not only of the promise
given his friends but also of justice and honor, and besides especially of the
solemn entreaty of his pious mother the venerable Lady [Catherine Wierzbięta-
Taszycka] (of the Janina clan), who was buried in the cemetery (*coemeterium*)
of that [Lusławice] church. And before her death she had implored and
besought him to preserve as a treasure the church (*edifice*) established on her
estate, not to suffer it to be taken from him nor to be appropriated by the force
of Satan's wiles. She even threatened every misfortune, especially to his male
descendants, if he should do otherwise. Indeed he repeatedly [275] made a
promise [to do] everything good for his part to the other Achatius and to John,
his own uncles,[911] and to his other relations who cherished the [Unitarian] faith
of their fathers. Among them were also his brothers-in-law, George Czaplic and
Sigismund Zabawski,[912] and the great Samuel Przypkowski.

I remember that I, too, as a young man, being surrounded by the circle of my
comrades, urged them in a congratulatory oration to make the same promise as
that made by Sigismund. But he [Sigismund Taszycki] afterwards despised it
all, contravening all justice, especially after bitter persecutions had been stirred
up so against other patrons of churches, as also against his relation Czaplic (as
we have said and, please God, shall further see below).[913] I have been credibly
informed that after committing this nefarious deed he was never at peace, but
was disturbed day and night by visions of his pious mother reproaching him for
his great wickedness, for his ingratitude toward God and herself, and for his ir-

reverence. Nay, once when he had lain down on his bed and tried to go to sleep at midday, he was greatly frightened by the apparition of his mother, threatening him with blows and pulling off his spread, so that he jumped out of bed and fled half-dead with fear. After this he was constantly driven by the furies of bad conscience, and it is not known in what way he at length perished in the Cossack War.

His wife's sister, Birecka [Czermińska], was divorced by her husband, a noble and wealthy resident of the district of Przemyśl, because, forewarned by someone, he saw a poison to be given to him when he should go to the bath, being prepared by some old sorceresses (*anus venificas*) and two noble maids-in-waiting of his wife. The sorceresses were later condemned to the stake, the noble maids were put to death by hanging in front of their mistress's gate. He made a test of this poison by ordering it to be poured into a wooden bowl which broke forthwith. At length Lady Birecka came to Lusławice and lived with her sister.[914] And when she went up to the holy edifice, saying with a boast that a large inn (*cauponam*) might be built out of it, she experienced the just wrath of the avenging God, and within a few days was deprived of life.

In the part of the district [of Lusławice] that fell to John Błoński, son of Abraham, Faustus Socinus once dwelt, as may be seen from his letters.[915] And he died there on 3 March 1604, and was buried in the cemetery of the church.[916] The funeral sermon for him was preached by Peter Statorius with whom he had daily enjoyed [276] religious conversation, and who followed him within a year, though he had removed to Raków.[917]

It fell to my lot also to live with the Rector Baumgarten in the very place in which Socinus once lived.

CHAPTER SIXTEEN

Of the Churches in the Palatinates of Volhynia and Kiev.

Among extraordinary proofs of divine providence, one may justly mention several churches that were founded with a noble zeal for religion in these two palatinates [of Volhynia and Kiev].[918] This was evident not only in men but also in distinguished women, so that we may learn that divine power is manifested even in the weaker vessels. Among the leading patrons were Gabriel and Roman Hojski, father and son,[919] both adorned with the very high honor of castellan of Kiev, and besides this, the father was captain of Owrucz and Włodzimierz. Under their patronage churches long flourished at Hoszcza[920] on the Horyń and at Zokołowka or at Kurczyca on the Słucz, towns in Volhynia.[921]

The father served some time as marshal of the court of the powerful Prince

Basil Constantine Ostrogski,[922] palatine of Kiev, whose services to the Commonwealth were famous, and whose sons were George, castellan of Cracow, and Alexander, palatine of Volhynia. And I suppose this prince (though himself steadily adhering to the Greek religion as long as he lived) learned from Gabriel [Hojski][923] justice toward those who honored the truth, whom he not only suffered to live quietly at Ostróg, Lubartów,[924] and Ostropol, but also granted the right to found a church at Konstantynów.[925]

Christopher Sieniuta,[926] offspring of a very noble family and comparable to princes in wealth (whose conversion at Rome, as well as that of Daniel Rudnicki, mentioned above,[927] we shall describe elsewhere as being especially deserving of attention), had likewise founded churches on his dominions at Lachowice and Sieniutowice.[928] He suffered many misfortunes on this account, and expended no small part of his yearly income in defending and promoting the truth.

And also the brothers Martin and George Czaplic, already mentioned by us[929] (sons of Theodore [277] Czaplic,[930] land judge of the district of Łuck), having been enlightened by divine truth, provided hospitable shelter for the [Minor] Church at Beresteczko[931] and Kisielin,[932] towns only a mile distant from each other; as also did their uncle Adam at Szpanów[933] and Miłostów.[934]

[The Schools of Kisielin, 1612/38 – 1644, and Czernihów][935]

And indeed the School at Kisielin had grown wonderfully from the ruin of the School at Raków, under the rectorate of Eustace Gizel, Louis of Hohleisen, Peter Stegmann (the distinguished brother of Joachim),[936] and Theodore Simon of Holstein. He [Simon], highly accomplished in Greek letters, wished to be called Phillippus Cosmius for a book once published against the papacy,[937] and who there [in Kisielin] made a Greek translation of the *Janua* of Comenius.[938] And several synods were also held there.[939]

But the peace that God had given us there aroused the hatred and anger of the adversaries of the truth and of everything just and right, so that by an unjust decree of the Tribunal at Lublin these churches at Beresteczko and Kisielin, and the School, were also broken up. Of this matter, please God, we shall treat at length below in due order, in a chapter on the persecutions.[940]

The School at Czernihów was directed by Bartholomew Woch, [John] Debel, a Prussian, and Paul Myślik, a Silesian.[941] The School at Hoszcza [was directed] by Theophilus Młynarz, Daniel Duroski, the later celebrated doctor of medicine Solomon Paludius, and Albert Caper.[942]

The Church had built herself a home, though one of brief duration, at Babin,[943] the hereditary estate of the Babińskis. The Church had erected far larger and more lasting homes (*nidi*) on the domains of the Niemirycz family. A beginning was made by the devoted lady [Maria] Niemirycz of the very noble family of Chreptowic, wife of the land judge of Kiev. Her son Stephen, chamberlain of Kiev and captain of Owrucz, completed the affair by establishing a church in the town of Czernihów.[944] A convenient place for the Church was afterwards assigned at Szersznie[945] and Uszomir[946] by Stephen's son George, who succeeded his father in the office of judge and captain, and protected the Church not without may assaults of persecution and troubles, of which, if God permits,[947] we mean likewise to say more in due place.

[The editorial words of Benedict Wiszowaty[948] for his edition of
the *Historia*, Amsterdam, 1685]

Inasmuch as the most noble Stanislas Lubieniecki was not able to carry his *Historia* through to the end, being carried away at Hamburg in 1675 by poison [administered] by a maid-servant incited thereto by wicked men,[949] it has seemed good to supplement in some measure what is here wanting by adding a letter of the eloquent Polish knight Samuel Przypkowski,[950] in which he relates the calamities with which the Unitarians in Poland were overwhelmed from 1648 until they were banished by royal edicts [in 1658 and 1659].[951]

[These words are placed under an improvised heading for Chapter 17: IN THIS FRAGMENT ARE PUBLISHED SOME THINGS PERTAINING TO THE HISTORY OF SUBSEQUENT TIMES, IN WHICH ESPECIALLY IS RELATED HOW THE UNITARIANS, AFTER SUNDRY PERSECUTIONS, WERE EXPELLED FROM POLAND. This is followed by a letter from Königsberg (pp. 278–85). In an improvised Chapter 18 we find a parallel account, titled: COPY OF A LETTER OF THE UNITARIANS IN EXILE TO N. N. (*pp. 285–305*). As the dates of these two letters are respectively, Königsberg, 23 September 1663, and Kreuzburg, Silesia, 17 June 1661, they have been placed in reversed and hence in chronological order in the translations in *Polish Brethren*, Docs. XXXIII–I and II. The Königsberg Letter is signed by Samuel Przypkowski. The Kreuzburg Letter was signed by many exiles headed by Jonas Schlichting. It is now known from the annotated but never published second edition of the *Bibliotheca Antitrinitariorum* (*BAnt*[2]) of the Library of the University of Leiden, that Stanislas Lubieniecki helped draft the Kreuzburg Letter.]

Related Documents (RD)

Preface

Benedict Wiszowaty appended the *Vita* of Stanislas Lubieniecki and two letters of exiles to his edition of the *Historia* (1685). These may be found in *The Polish Brethren*, Docs. XXVIII and XXXIII – I and – II. Following his editorial precedent, I have also appended documents closely related to the subject of the *Historia*, nine altogether. The majority of these were preserved by Wiszowaty himself as appendices to Christopher Sand, Jr.'s *Bibliotheca Antitrinitariorum* (*BAnt*), which he had just edited (1684). In his edition of *BAnt*, Wiszowaty calls these documents in his subtitle *alia quaedam Scripta* and in his Table of Contents a *series Tractatum*, occupying *pp. 181 – 296*, a substantial body of historiographical documentation.

The full title (Pl. 1) is *Bibliotheca Antitrinitariorum or a Catalogue of Writers, and a succinct Account of those Authors who, in the past and present century, have either impugned the commonly received doctrine concerning three Persons in every way equal in One God, or have taught that the Father of our Lord Jesus Christ is the only True or Most High God: A posthumous work of Christopher Sand, the Son of Christopher Sand. Some other Scripta are added . . . : and all united exhibit a Compendium of the Ecclesiastical History of the Unitarians, commonly called Socinians* (Amsterdam, 1684).

Christopher Sand (Sandius), Jr. was born in Königsberg, 12 October 1644, and died in Amsterdam, 30 November 1680, a scholarly youth who was survived by his scholarly and cosmopolitan father (1611 – 86). Never taking upon himself the name Unitarian, Socinian, or Arian, the compiler of *BAnt* was indefatigable in collecting materials from the traditions represented by these names, while he worked as a corrector at the press in Amsterdam (see more fully RD 5 n. 1). A prodigious writer, Sand compiled this Compendium about 1670. After his death in 1680, Benedict Wiszowaty edited it for publication, supplying names and information on about seventy additional writers, and adding seven related documents (eight counting an appendix).

Several of the *BAnt* documents provide parallel chronological accounts of some of the episodes dealt with by Lubieniecki in his *Historia*.

Of the eight *BAnt* documents, three bearing primarily on the Socinianism of the *seventeenth* century have appeared in annotated translation in *The Polish Brethren*: Documents I (The Life of Andrew Wiszowaty, d. 1678), IX (the martyrdom in Warsaw of John Tyszkowic, 1611), and XXIX (Lubieniecki's *Vindiciae*, c. 1660). The remaining five *BAnt* documents, all of them bearing on the *sixteenth* century, are here vernacularized and annotated for the first time, as part of an Appendix to the *Historia*, Related Documents 1–5.

As several of the eight *BAnt* documents run closely parallel to the text of Lubieniecki and were perhaps in all cases also known to him, references to them are embedded in brackets in his translated text, for example, in Book 1 at n. 68, as the first instance, *BAnt* no. 47. Here the reader is alerted to such a parallel account. The numbering (no.) refers to topical paragraphs within the *BAnt* documents running consecutively through all of them that have the character of chronicles, all of which is editorially intended to target cross-references more specifically than by pagination. These serially numbered paragraphs run from 1 to 120.

The first *BAnt* document so numbered is our Related Document 2, which is an *Epitome* of a longer account by John Stoiński (d. 1654) of an otherwise lost History of the Origin of the Unitarians in Poland (1556–1616), our topical paragraphs nos. 1–12.1 Our RD 3, the autobiographical *Testamentum* of George Schomann (d. c. 1591), also chronicles the general history of the Polish Brethren (1546–91), a record, in fact, preserved for posterity by Lubieniecki by his inclusion of it in his *Historia*, as the main content of his Book 2, chapter 6. Wiszowaty excised it for his edition of Sand's *BAnt*. It, too, has been broken into paragraphs, nos. 13–43. RD 4, evidently put together by Benedict Wiszowaty, is a very skimpy account of Unitarian printing presses in the Commonwealth, nos. 44–46. RD 5 is a Brief Narrative (*Narratio compendiosa*) by Andrew Wiszowaty (d. 1678) about How the Unitarian Christians Separated in Poland from the Reformed Trinitarians (154–619), nos 47–63. First printed by Sand, this *Narratio compendiosa* was reprinted by Bendict Wiszowaty with an appendix in *BAnt*. This appendix is, in fact, an excerpt from one of the *Sylvae* (1590) of Andrew Frycz Modrzewski (d. 1572), recalling the visit of a Netherlandish humanist, Spiritus, to Cracow in 1546/47. This passage might have been included here in its own right from the critical edition of Modrzewski's *opera*, but along with it in *BAnt* Benedict Wiszowaty also excerpted with comment three passages about the same episode in the lost History of Budziński upon which Lubieniecki ackowledged he was drawing. The Wiszowaty appendix thus falls into two topical "paragraphs" and *in situ* would be nos. 64–65. However, under the pressure of sheer chronology, I have displaced this episode forward to constitute RD 1, dropped the otherwise disconcerting serial numbering, and thus assigned the episode the due prominence it had in the idealization of their history alike for Budziński, Lubieniecki, and the Wiszowatys, father and son.

Before characterization of the additional four Related Documents supplementary to the *Historia* from sources other than *BAnt*, a bit more may be said here than in the Introduction about the ways in which *BAnt* is prominently and variously cited in the *Historia* and the annotation throughout. What within the text of the translated *Historia* appears in brackets as *BAnt* no. 47 appears in the cross reference more amply as RD 2, no. 47, etc. In the same annotation the three *BAnt* pieces earlier translated in *The Polish Brethren* (1980) are cited as *PB* with its Roman numeral in that volume and, the case of Document 1 (The Life of Andrew Wiszowaty), with the serially numbered topical paragraphs, nos. 66–120. Sand's work is also referred to, of course, in its own right, in reference to the pagination in his biobibliography as amplified and edited by Wiszowaty, *BAnt*, 1–180. With a view to a second further much amplified edition, Wiszowaty worked on his master copy (Pl. 64), cited in my annotation as *BAnt*.² Benedict Wiszowaty may have toiled on it until death stayed his hand in 1704. This invaluable MS copy of *BAnt* came to scholarly attention only in August 1984, when most of the editing of Lubieniecki's *Historia* and the *Scripta* not published in *Polish Brethren* had been completed. However, some of the most important data from *BAnt*² have been incorporated in my notes.

Now assigned the number Sem. Rem. 5657 in the Library of the University of Leiden, *BAnt*² first came to the attention of Dr. Ronald Breugelmans, curator of Western imprints. It fell within the purview of Dr. Jeremy D. Bangs, archivist in the same Library, who in turn notified his father, Professor Carl Bangs of St. Paul School of Theology in Kansas City. He in turn wrote me of the discovery. This most important information was relayed over the Atlantic from Leiden to Cambridge, and in early October 1984 *BAnt*² reposed, insured by the kindness and curatorial vision of Dr. Maria Grossmann, for a few days in the Andover Harvard Library, where, by dint of photocopying of the loose pages and by the diligent transcription of the others by classicist Christine Krause, there is now a subsidiary copy. There are sufficiently numerous addenda and corrigenda in *BAnt*²' to warrant their publication by Lech Szczucki and Jeremy Bangs in a forthcoming issue of *Odrodzenie i Reformacja w Polsce*.

There are two hands at work in *BAnt*²'. The first hand is on the printed pages of the first edition. Originally they were small addenda and corrigenda, written perhaps primarily for the benefit of the owner, clearly Benedict Wiszowaty. For example, on p. 47 where Sand had given a Polish title by Martin Krowicki, the addendum starts as follows: ''Hunc titulum ex Budzinio *descripsi*: Ejusdem vero libri tertiam editionem tali *vidi* titulo,'' whereupon a fuller title in Polish is given. It is not certain that Sand even read Polish. In any case, ''I have described,'' ''I have seen'' are written into his posthumous publication, by a polyglot corrector who had been able to read a more accurate title out of a *Polish* MS History of Budziński than Sand. This first hand for the second edition was that of a Polish exile and surely of the editor himself of Sand's posthumous work. The second hand, italicizing, has prepared fair copies of the more compact or less legible addenda, which never vary from the original but occasionally make clear to the present reader what was intended by the first hand especially where pages are worn or slightly damaged. All this interleaving has been placed in a pocket of the book, now protectively supplied with a supplementary binding, after it had so long lain unnoticed in the Collection of the Remonstrant

Church, now permanently under the University Library. It is most likely that
this second hand is also that of Benedict Wiszowaty. Probably his also are the
directions to the printer in Dutch, the German script of several new titles, always
rendered and sometimes more fully in Latin, and a good deal of new material in
English on John Biddle, John Knowles, and on translations of works of the Polish Brethren from Latin into English.

Although the title page has *Editio secunda aucta et emendata* written in, it is
not clear that the editing was quite complete. First and second Editor Benedict
Wiszowaty on p. 147 in connection with his father's *Catechesis Ecclesiarum
Polonicarum* has inserted: "Vide Valentinum Smalcium." He has crossed out
and corrected it to: "Benedictum Wissowatium." At no point does he refer to
himself again, which appears as excessive modesty or even self-effacement.

In any case, the surmise of Lech Szczucki stands that Benedict Wiszowaty
almost certainly was the author of two variant MSS of a comprehensive history
of the movement to which he belonged and the records of which he had been so
sedulous in collecting and editing, namely, *Medulla historiae ecclesiasticae*. He
had an opportunity to ascribe it to his father in *BAnt*[2]' but did not. The ascription to Benedict of the *Medulla* is at the center of Szczucki's essay, based itself
on many new findings, "Socinian Historiography in the late 17th Century." See
my Introduction at nn. 9 – 32. Of the *Medulla*, roughly the counterpart of
Lubieniecki's *Historia*, Szczucki prints the chapter headings, 1 – 25, from 1, *De
Nazaraeis et Ebionitis* to 25, *Continens saeculum 16 et 17*, p. 290.

We return from the emendation of *BAnt*, from which five of the Related
Documents of our Appendix are drawn, to the remaining four new ones. As
each Document has its own separate introduction or foreword, suffice it here to
characterize them briefly and justify their inclusion in supplementation of the
Historia. The seventeenth-century Socinians were embarassed by the social and
religious radicalism of the early Racovian commune and Lubieniecki, though
himself born there, slips past its beginnings with evasion (Book 3, chap. 12).
Hence I have included as Related Document 6 an excerpt from his great uncle's
Poloneutychia (Raków, 1616), which condescendingly describes the religious
ferment in the whole Commonwealth in a view highly colored by what Andrew
Lubieniecki knew about the beginnings of Raków itself.

RD 7 is the *Catechesis* of George Schomann, printed in Cracow in the very
year that the elected King Henry of Valois was liturgically anointed in the castle
cathedral above the town. It is the fullest evidence that immersionist Unitarianism under the lordship of Christ in his threefold office of priest, prophet, and
King of kings was a Polish manifestation of what is elsewhere identifiable as the
Radical Reformation.

Under the impact of Faustus Socinus the *Catechesis* evolved into the Racovian Catechism (Polish, 1605) of a different spirit. Although our Lubieniecki
was a *Polish* Socinian, that is, a Socinian who still adhered to believers' immersion against the argumentation of Socinus, he scarcely mentions Socinus himself
in his *Historia*. To make up for this lacuna, I have included as RD 8 the essential
portion of the Life of Socinus written by Samuel Przypkowski, resident on an

estate in palatinate Kiev, just a couple of years before the New Raków of the Socinianized Polish Brethren was dismantled by royal-parliamentary decree in 1638, and when many families of the Polish Brethren, as well as of the Calvinists, were seeking new lands in the Ukraine. Przypkowski's account is marked by more partisanship against Francis Dávid, ''the father of Transylvanian Unitarianism,'' than was displayed by mild Socinus himself, when boarding and debating in the parsonage of Dávid in Kolozsvár, 1578/79.

RD 9, an excerpt from an Elizabethan envoy's report on the whole situation in the Polish-Lithuanian Commonwealth as of 1598, is meant to serve as a new contemporaneous introduction to the *Historia* of Lubieniecki in the very language into which it has now been translated—a report in the cadences and phraseology of a Cornwall gentleman from the same period and the same class of society to which our Author's parents belonged. Sir George Carew's Anglican observations help the reader of Lubieniecki's baroque Latin here anglicized evoke the religio-political and social scene of Poland in the counterpart English of about the year of the death of the former Fransiscan, Stanislas Budziński, Lubieniecki's principal (and vernacular) source.

Related Document 1

Andrew Frycz Modrzewski

A Reminiscence of the Visit of the Dutch Humanist Spiritus [to Cracow, 1546]

(as presented by Benedict Wiszowaty
as an appendix [216]
to his father's *Narratio*, with comment)[1]

Foreword. The Polish Brethren liked to claim Modrzewski, the most renowned publicist of the age, as their own, and in several accounts drew attention to his own recollection of the seminal visit from Holland of Spiritus, from which they liked to date the rise of Anti-trinitarianism in Poland and in the retelling, not incidentally, capture the good will of the Dutch Remonstrants among whom they sojourned in exile. Benedict Wiszowaty supplies the excerpted recollection as an appendix to his father's *Brief Narrative* (our Related Document 5), "containing," as he says, "a fuller history [than his father Andrew gives in no. 51] concerning Spiritus the Dutchman," along with some useful annotation of his own.

Andrew Frycz Modrzewski, in his *Sylvae*, [*quatuor* (Raków, 1590)] 1, Tract 2, 2,[2] relates the following:

> There had come to Cracow, in the year 1546, if my memory does not fail me, a man of the Dutch (*Belga*) nation, apparently well versed in the Holy Bible and very prompt in citing passages from it. He, when staying at Cracow a few days, was invited to a banquet by a certain man of high renown [Andrew Trzecieski, Senior],[3] whose guest I was also. And first, before the banquet had begun, we were taken into the library of our host, which was full of writings of every sort. And when each one (for there were not a few of us) according to his taste perused such books as he pleased, Spiritus (for this was the name of the Dutchman)[4] happened upon a little book of Christian prayers.[5] *And when he found prayers in this, one to God the Father, another to God the Son, a third to God the Holy Spirit, he said, addressing us: "Well, have you three Gods, good friends?" And we

replied: "We have one God, who has three persons in unity of essence."
"But now," said he, "what has, and what is had are different things. He
that has the three is therefore different from the three that are had by him."
"Why, Spiritus," we said, "you are playing the sophist. Our confession is
simple: God is one in essence, threefold in persons." "Is your God, then,"
said he, "both threefold and one?" "Assuredly," we said, "but the one in
one respect, while the other in another." Then said he: "If then this threefold being is one, why do you address *them* with different prayers? Why do
you in these prayers ask from them different blessings they might confer
upon the human race?" These matters were then discussed back and forth
among us. As we believed the matter to be of all things the most certain,
and were forbidden by our religion to engage in debates about it, we turned
the conversation to other matters.** But when I was afterwards pondering
the subject more carefully, I wondered to myself how it happened that [217]
though all the outward actions of the persons were thought to be undivided,
yet we addressed them in different prayers, praying separately to the Father,
separately to the Son, separately to the Holy Spirit, and then beseeching the
aid of the Trinity in one prayer, as though one asked something from Peter,
Paul, Andrew, James, Philip in different prayers, and then in one prayer
begged aid from all the Apostles, whose essences are distinct as well as their
persons. In the common books of prayers there are distinct prayers of this
sort to three persons.*** This and the like in Frycz, *loc. cit.*

Budziński wrote down the same story in his manuscript History, chapter four.
He relates that

> the most mentioned was John [Andrew] Trzecieski,[6] a pupil of Erasmus,
> illustrious for noble birth as well as for his knowledge of the Hebrew,
> Greek, and Latin tongues.

Further, he notes among the guests, besides Frycz already mentioned:

> Bernard Wojewódka, printer and alderman (praetor) of Cracow, also a dis-
> ciple of Erasmus, and Jacob Przyłuski, notary of the Cracow castle, a most
> distinguished jurist.[7]

Budziński adds:

> All were silent at the words of Spiritus the Dutchman, and other subjects
> were introduced until they went into the banquet. But there were those in
> whom that hook was driven deep and who, noting the things that they had
> heard, took this question home with them. This question [about the Trinity]
> was about to spring up in Poland in their time.[8]

But who this Spiritus the Dutchman really was, where he came from, and what
became of him after this, the authors quoted do not tell. I[9] wonder whether
Adam Pastor was not disguised under this name.[10]

Related Document 2

John Stoiński[1] [1590–1654]
Pastor of the Congregation at Raków

[183] An Epitome of the History of the Origin of the Unitarians in Poland:[2]

A Chronology of the Steps by which Heaven's Truth Gradually Reached its Height in Poland, and Especially concerning God the Father, the Son, and the Holy Spirit[3]

Foreword. In the following record, John Stoiński, pastor of the church in Raków (1612–38), tracks the pre-schism debate in the Reformed Church on the doctrine of the Trinity (1555–62), then summarizes the progression toward Christocentric Unitarianism and ends with an account of efforts in Lublin to bring together the Major and the Minor Church congregations there, disrupted by two episodes, the lightning fire of the church of the Holy Trinity in the citadel in 1616 and a decree of the Tribunal in 1627. Stoiński seems to be following the lost Chronicon (at n. 12) of Andrew Lubieniecki, who was likewise in Raków (1616–28).

[Goniądz at the synod of Secemin, 1556]

[No. 1, an editorially assigned paragraph] In the year of our Lord 1556, Peter of Goniądz in Podlasie at an evangelical synod held in January in Secemin[4] (which was the second in order in Poland, after the first held at Pińczów in the reign of King Augustus on the first of May 1555[5]), stated that he was satisfied with the Apostles' Creed alone, but rejected the Nicene and the Athanasian and the rest of the same sort, and this he confessed openly. He denied that the Trinity was the one God, and maintained that the Son was less than the Father, yet was God, while always giving honor to the Father; and that the only true God was he from whom Christ had received all things. He held that no communication of idiomata ought to be accepted. At his examination Gregory Paul, the evangelical minister at Pełsznica, was also present, though he was still doubtless a Calvinist. But although Peter of Goniądz opposed the consubstantiality of the Son with the Father, yet he is said to have maintained that ὁ Λόγος, that is, the invisible *Word*, was changed into flesh in the Virgin; that is, God was changed into man. Among other things, they say he declared that: "One Irenaeus is to be preferred to all the recent writers." [BW: Andrew Lubieniecki, the venerable minister,[6] relates incidentally that at the same synod an account was given of the so-called union formed with the Waldensians[7] at Koźminek;[8] but that after the union was formed, church discipline disappeared.[9]] In the letter of that synod to Philip Melanchthon, in which Peter of Goniądz is recommended [to him], it is stated that he believes that the Logos is less than the Father as to divinity; that his divine nature was changed into a human one; that God actually died. But I should prefer to get this from Peter's own mouth, or from his writings. [184] However, the wonder is that one striving with great and difficult effort to escape from deep mire and labyrinthine darkness should have been able in those first beginnings of the reborn gospel to struggle free at all.

[The coming of Biandrata and the synod of Pińczów, 1558]

[no. 2] In 1558, there came to Pińczów, the town of the Oleśnicki family, George Biandrata, a doctor of medicine, who is said at that time to have held the same view as the Spaniard Servetus about the preeminence of God the Father. And there he found Peter of Goniądz who held the same view, as well as the Italian Stancaro who denied that Christ was Mediator in his divine nature. While these were discussing by turns, now with one another, now with Lismanino of Corfú and [Martin] Krowicki the Pole, a synod was called in November,[10] with the purpose of settling these controversies. At this were present also John Łaski, superintendent of *Little* Poland,[11] Gregory Paul, Stanislas Sarnicki, Felix Cruciger, and not a few others besides, also magnates. Although controversies of this sort were carried on for some days pro and con, yet no conclusion was reached; for those above named persisted in their opinion, while Sarnicki and Lawrence Discordia, together with some nobles who were ill content, as the saying is, withdrew. But [Andrew] Lubieniecki's *Chronicon*[12] adds the remark that this synod made "a large beginning toward demolishing the dogma of the Trinity."

[Controversy over pedobaptism at the synod of Brest, 1558]

[no. 2.2] In 1558, on December 15, at the synod held at Brest Litovsk, a book against pedobaptism, published by Peter of Goniądz, was publicly read there. With almost all trying to refute it, save Jerome Piekarski, who was defending that view, Peter himself openly declared that there were also other things that had crept into the Church from the Papacy, such as the dogma of the Trinity and of the communication of idiomata, that of the two natures in Christ, and not a few others. [BW: This was the ninth synod.] And although he was forbidden to promote such views under pain of excommunication, nevertheless he declared that he could not oppose his conscience. But this synod was held with only the ministers of Podlasie and Lithuania present.

[no. 3.1] At the tenth Polish synod on 25 April 1559 [in Pińczów], Łaski and Sarnicki were present. Yet although it was concluded that an examination [185] of the ministers ought to be set up to ascertain what they were thinking about God, about the unity of the Trinity, and of the persons in the Trinity, etc,[13] nevertheless, by the favor of God, the divine truth, notwithstanding this hindrance [Sarnicki *et al.*], at length shone forth.

[Controversy over the invocation of the Holy Spirit, 1559 and 1561]

[no. 3.2] For in the same year, at a synod at Pińczów on 22 November 1559, there was a long and heated dispute with Stancaro about the Mediator, and no progress was made. To this synod a letter was brought from Lord Remian [BW: or Remigian] Chełmski (though he had not signed his name), in which he called in question the invocation or the addressing of prayers to the Holy Spirit, seeing that the only rule in praying is that we ask all things, including even the Holy Spirit, from the Father through the Son. This was the twelfth synod.

[no. 4] On 30 January 1561 at the nineteenth synod at Pińczów,[14] Peter Statorius, a Frenchman, reported at the beginning that lord Chełmski was not quite satisfied with the reply made by the synod of Pińczów to his letter. Statorius was directed to reply. He replied as prompted by Deity (*numinis*), but in such a way that the meaning he had in mind on this subject was not apparent. He only said that Biandrata had been spoken of by Calvin as one who was carrying the virus of Servetian impiety. Meanwhile, he says that his view, that he put forth in the synod, was well received by all, though he was nevertheless asked whether he asserted a plurality of Gods when he called the Father the only unbegotten and believed that the Son was begotten. "In fact, all of us"—the words are those of the same Frenchman, Statorius—"that are living with Biandrata, come, I know not how, under suspicion of heresy. But if they are heretics who believe in the Father, Son, and Holy Spirit after the precept of the Holy Scriptures, I willingly confess myself one of their number. That ill will that the evil Demon had contrived against me on the issue of the Holy Spirit has not yet come [BW: some read, "has calmed down"], but I am at peace with my good conscience" [cf. 1 Pet 3:21]. In this synod Lutomirski was proclaimed superintendent of Little Poland, though hitherto he was considered only that of Pińczów.

[Controversy over George Biandrata, 1560–62]

[no. 5] At the synod of Książ, numbered the seventeenth, in September 1560,[15] Biandrata began to be called elder (*senior*) of the Church of Little Poland; as also at the nineteenth synod at Pińczów, 30 January 1561, in which mention is first made of Peter Statorius the Frenchman.[16] At the twentieth [synod] at

Cracow, 16 September 1561, a letter of Calvin was brought by Martin Czechowic, in which Calvin urged the Cracovians and the Pinczovians to beware of Biandrata.[17] [186] Jerome Ossoliński there burst out, saying: "Would that no writings on the Trinity had been spread abroad!" By this he showed he wished that things that are not found in the word of God had not been disseminated.[18] Lismanino is reported to have said with Biandrata: "Let all the *doctores* leave me one God, and not divide him. Let them have whatever Mediator they have invented." Biandrata was also ordered to write out and sign his own confession. [BW: *N.B.*] Lismanino was complained of for having written a letter to Lord Iwan Karniński on the preeminence (*eminentia*) of God the Father.[19]

[no. 6] At the twenty-first synod, in the month of March 1562, at Książ,[20] Biandrata presented his signed confession, but this, being approved by some while utterly disapproved of by others, was read only in private. At length, at the twenty-second synod, held at Pińczów in April 1562, it was read through in public, and since it was expressed in the language of Scripture, it met with objections from few; and his reconciliation with Calvin was expected. Nevertheless, he insisted that Calvin permit Christ to be confessed as the Son of God (the Highest and Great God); and that one speak of the one God simply and without qualifications; or that he [Calvin] at least assent to the simple word of God and the Apostles' Creed and retract what he had put in the prefaces to [his *Commentaria in*] *Acta Apostolorum*, dedicated to the palatine of Vilna.[21] At the same synod it was voted that ministers refrain from philosophical ways of speaking of the Trinity, of essence, of generation, of the manner of proceeding, but that each confine himself to the terms of the prophets, the apostles, and the Apostles' Creed.

[Sarnicki attacks Gregory Paul and works for a schism, 1562]

[no. 6.1] Hence it came to pass that in the same year, 1562, after the synod at Pińczów, Gregory Paul, minister at Cracow, complying with its decisions that forbade the *mentio* [invocation] of the Trinity before the sermon, thus preached publicly just as the Holy Scriptures and the Apostles' Creed speak of the one God, and, following the order in which the most holy volume of the New Testament is arranged, he used to read it through in the service and explain it. This so much displeased Sarnicki, a most acrimonious champion of the Trinity, that he did not scruple to demand of Gregory that he should henceforth not detain his hearers with reading the New Testament or the gospels, but should explain the Creed. But when Gregory continued explaining the Gospel of Luke, [187] and preached with Sarnicki present, about God the Father, the Son, and the Holy Spirit, he adhered to the words of the text as closely as could be done. Sarnicki, fearing at that time to engage in a struggle with Gregory, denounced him to the magnates.

[no. 6.2] Hence in July of the same year, 1562, Stanislas Szafraniec, at a synod called at Rogów,[22] endeavored through a joint conference (*colloquium*) to reconcile so serious a quarrel between them. But this was to no purpose, except that it was voted at that synod that the parties should bear with each other and should abstain from terms unknown to the Holy Scriptures. But Sarnicki did not give up denouncing Gregory. Hence in August of the same year they again had a dispute in public at the synod [in Balice].[23] But as Sarnicki also tried to bring about a schism, and presently undertook to have Gregory removed from the metropolitan, that is, the Cracovian church, a synod was called again in August of the same year [1562] at Pińczów,[24] to which however the adversary of the truth, notwithstanding his promise, did not appear with his party.

[no. 6.3] But in the meantime, at Cracow, the gleaming orb (*globus*) at the summit of steeple of a church was hit by a bolt of lightning from heaven and thrown down. This church is commonly called the church of the Holy Trinity.[25]

[BW: Stoiński himself reduced this tract to a summary (1556–62) as follows:]

[no. 7] First, Peter of Goniądz: he comes in January 1556 to Secemin to a synod of the Evangelicals, and teaches this matter of the primacy of the Father over the Son; he also comes to Brest in Lithuania in 1558 and repeats the same things, adding a book against infant baptism, to which Jerome Piekarski gives his assent.

[no. 8] Second, George Biandrata: he comes from Geneva to Pińczów in 1558 with the views of Servetus.

[no. 9] Third, Remigian Chełmski in 1559: he writes to the synod at Pińczów.

[no. 10] Fourth, Francis Lismanino, with his letter to Lord Ivan Karniński of Aleksandrowice, in which he openly disapproves of the Nicene and Athanasian Creeds and shows that they are contrary to the Apostles' Creed; he passionately entreats all the *doctores* to leave him one God, and to acknowledge that He is not divided, and that no dispensation (*oeconomia*) be established within him.

[188] [no. 11] Fifth, Gregory Paul of Brzeziny, appointed Evangelical minister of the church at Cracow: after the decree of the synod at Pińczów in April 1562, he began openly to preach in the metropolis of Poland about God the Father, the Son, and the Holy Spirit, abandoning the commonly employed terms and following the usage of the Holy Scriptures and of the Apostles' Creed; he also waged a spirited fight with Sarnicki.

[The Brethren in Lublin: episodes of 1616 and 1627]

[no. 12] Our Brethren at Lublin in Poland (a city in which the sessions of the Tribunal are held each year), as well as the Evangelicals, for many years used to conduct (*celebrare*) the affairs (*negotia*) of their denomination (*religio*) there publicly until 1627.[26] But in that year, by a decree of the Tribunal, we were with the utmost injustice expelled and driven out [of Lublin] on a certain pretext. First there was a riot of the populace, who in a day and a night destroyed the [two] places of worship (*oratoria*) of the unitarian Christians and of the Evangelicals or Reformed. After this a most unjust decree was passed against us, as the general Diet at Warsaw itself then acknowledged, and it passed a common law: that the decrees of the Tribunal ought not to make new laws, but that they ought to be carried out in accordance with the old ones, already passed and sanctioned by usage.[27]

[no. 12.1] In this city also, in 1616, when there was a conference (*conventus*) of our Brethren with the Evangelicals in the interest of religion, and when the court of the Tribunal was in session with Marshal [Andrew] Zborowski,[28] castellan of Oświęcim presiding—on the very day of the Holy Trinity—when the anniversary (*encoenia*) of dedication, with indulgence fair and kermis,[29] was beginning in the church of the Holy Trinity situated in the citadel of Lublin, the building was struck by lighting and burned down, while the whole city watched the fire with trembling and awe. For a very dense crowd of both sexes from town and country had flocked to the church for the sake of remission of their sins. The falling of the church then caused the deaths of two priests and of some of the people. The greater cause for wonder was given by the fact that at this time our Brethren had begun colloquies with the Evangelicals about entering into an alliance or union with mutual tolerance. In the colloquy the question about the Trinity was among the foremost [issues].[30]

Related Document 3

George (Ciachowski) Schomann

[189/91] The Last Will and Testament[1]
Containing a Brief History of his Life
as well as of sundry things
done in the churches

Foreword. This *Testamentum* was preserved for posterity by Stanislas Lubieniecki, who has a charming introduction to it, an evocation of a moment of his youth (*Historia,* Book 2, chap. 6). It was removed from his work by Wiszowaty because as editor he had already printed it in *BAnt* (1684). Wiszowaty in planning the publications was aware of how much Schomann's narrative interrupted, by its full biographical span, the flow of Lubieniecki's own more comprehensive account. The *Testamentum* is the sketchy but reliable autobiography and last will of a Silesian Polish Anabaptist (1530 – c. 1591), the author of the oldest confession of faith, the *Catechesis* (1574) of the Polish Brethren (RD 7).

[No. 13] George Schomann, a Silesian of Racibórz,[2] prays for his children[3] grace and peace, from God the Father and our Lord Jesus Christ.

[no. 14] Both because we are mortal and because the memory of things past is fleeting, the tongues of men, moved by Satan, are full of venom and since they are wont to blacken and to slander the Christian renown of even the most upright men and thus to obscure the glory of God and Christ by the doings of men [even while they are alive], and to hinder the progress of the Holy Gospel, how, think you, will it be when we are dead and can no longer reply to slanders? For example, while we are still alive and publicly practicing our religion in Cracow, two bishops of the Romanists have not scrupled to spread abroad infamous printed pamphlets alleging that we, forgetting God and all decency, are accustomed to come together in our congregations to perpetrate all manner of shameful things, and to perform the marriage ceremonies naked in public.[4] It has therefore seemed to me necessary to leave you a brief story of my life, simple and plain, written by my own hand, so that you may have ready a proper defense both to encourage you in praising God, and to stop the mouths of foolish men. I pray God the Father of our Lord Jesus Christ, crucified, raised from the dead, and reigning, that he may rule you by his Holy Spirit, that he may make you vessels of mercy unto honor and not unto shame,[5] so that after this mortal life he may give us all an eternal and immortal one, through the same [192] Jesus Christ our Lord, Saviour, and Defender. Amen.

[no. 15] In the year of our Lord 1530 I was born at Racibórz (Ratibor) in Silesia. My father was Stanislas Lössel, commonly called Schomann, native of a German village between Krosna and Rymanowa; and my mother was Ursula, whose father was a noble, Christopher [Ciachowski],[6] chancellor of the prince of Racibórz, bearing the arms *Stary koń z toporem* [BW: *Old horse with an axe*];[7] but she was robbed of the villages and of all her inherited property by her brother, the Canon Christopher [Ciachowski]. As a boy I learned at home the elements of grammar and music, together with the papist (*papistica*) religion.

[no. 16] In the year 1545, I saw great clouds of locusts.

[no. 17] In the year 1546, I came to Breslau, where I dwelt not among the Evangelicals of the city, but with some canons on the island,[8] and began to make a little progress in the arts. And at length, from being a stubborn papist, I became a sort of Lutheran, thanks to our teacher John Cyrus, who was a Lutheran.[9] He, after he arrived in Italy, slipped back to the papacy; and he tried to drag me into the same pit, even pressing upon me a canonry at Breslau; but I, God keeping me, so far from yielding to his enticements, even resigned to him my canonry at Racibórz. But he, disappointed in his expectation of the bishopric of Breslau, out of desperation became a monk and abbot of St. Vincent's monastery at Breslau.[10] And I, having been appointed preceptor to lords Joachim and Francis Maltzan,[11] and expecting to be sent to France, had to return home when King Ferdinand by military force took Wartenberg away from the lords Maltzen on account of a debt.[12]

[no. 18] In the year 1552, I came to Cracow, where I was first at St. Mary's School,[13] next preceptor with Jerome Beck,[14] then at the poor students' Bursa,[15] and finally at St. Anne's School, where I made some progress in the liberal arts and philosophy.[16]

[no. 19] In the year 1554, I came to the salt works of Wieliczka,[17] to Master Jerome Bużeński,[18] the superintendent of the salt works of the palatinate of Cracow, who placed under my instruction his grandsons and some other noble boys. These I faithfully and unremittingly taught for six years [1554–60], receiving [193] both from the master and from the parents of my pupils a gratification not to be displeased with. Yet I was all but sunk in the salt pit, and in the allurements of the world, and in the abundance of things of that sort, had not the mercy of God called me away from salt out of the earth to the salt of heaven [cf. Matt 5:13].[19]

[The conversion of Schomann, 1558–1559]

[no. 20] In the year 1558, I conducted some of my pupils to Pińczów, others to Wittenberg. There [in the first school] the lectures both of Peter Statorius and [in the second] of Philip Melanchthon[20] prevailed upon me not to waste my life in the salt works, for they judged that even then we lacked many things pertaining to true piety.[21]

[no. 21] Returning therefore from Wittenberg, and driven now by the luxury of the court (*aula*),[22] now by dreadful dreams, now by the pricks of conscience and by the word of God, I with difficulty obtained my discharge from the lord superintendent of the salt works, and in the year 1559 I came to that most devout man, Master John Łaski at Dębiany, to make progress in Christian piety (*pietatem*).[23] There, indeed, I should have made great progress, had not death [8 January 1560] snatched away from us that holy man, already worn out by his long labors.[24] This happened while I was in Pińczów. There I lived on intimate terms with Peter Statorius, a Frenchman of Thionville, with John Thenaud, a Frenchman of Bourges,[25] with Master Francis Lismanino, Master George Biandrata, a physician, and Bernardine Ochino;[26] and I learned clearly that any sort of equality of the Persons in the Trinity is an error, and not the Christian faith, but that God the Father is one, the Son of God is one, and the Holy Spirit is one; although until now we did not understand much in regard to this.[27] A little before the death of Master Łaski, we had a dispute with Francis Stancaro on the human nature of the Mediator and the Trinity in God.[28]

[no. 22] In the year 1560, I was placed over the church at Pińczów as minister [1560–61]. But as the gift of continence was not granted to me, I took a wife there, the daughter of a burgher's widow, a maiden of sixteen years, Anna by name, on February 18.[29] Doctor Biandrata set forth before us the errors in the doctrine of the Trinity, and when we had given them to brother [Paul] Gilowski for his judgment, he confessed that he could not reply to them.[30]

[no. 23] In the year 1561, in the autumn, I was sent by the Church and synod to be minister of the church at Ksiż [Wielki], in the domain of the noble lord, John Boner of Balice, castellan of Biecz and governor (*wielkoradaca*) of Cracow, who later [1562] ordered [194] me to be expelled and deprived of all my possessions on account of the Trinity.[31]

[no. 24] In the year 1562, on 15 January, at dawn, my oldest son Paul was born to me, who was baptized in his infancy, as we had up to now no knowledge of true baptism.[32]

[Antitrinitarian Anabaptism: A Visit to the Hutterites]

[no. 25] In the year 1562, I was sent by the Church, together with the noble and most excellent heroes, lord Jerome Filipowski and lord Stanislas Lasocki, to the Diet at Piotrków to preach [in the concurrent synod] the Gospel of our Lord Jesus Christ. There I was soon branded by [Stanislas] Sarnicki and other elders among the brethren with Arianism, a thing of which I had never even thought.[33] And there they openly withdrew from us, without any just cause. Also, lord Lasocki died there, whose body we buried at Pełsznica.[34]

[no. 26] In the year 1564, on 22 January, at sunrise, a daughter was born in Ksiż [Wielki]. She was not baptized in her infancy, because I had already learned and was teaching that infant baptism was a human, not a divine, command.[35] In the same year I was appointed to go with lord Filipowski to the Diet at Warsaw [22 November 1563 – 1 April 1564]. There, when Sarnicki openly called us heretics and blasphemers of the Trinity, a conference was arranged through the agency of the noble Lord Nicholas Radziwiłł, palatine of Vilna. But as Sarnicki with his party professed a triune God, and we one God the Father, we separated.

[no. 27] In the year 1565, I was again appointed to go with lord Filipowski to the Diet at Piotrków, where [in the concurrent synod] a solemn disputation was then arranged between us and the opposite party, and it lasted fourteen days.[36] But as they stubbornly defended the triune God, and we confessed one God the Father, we separated.

[no. 28] In the year 1566, we were again appointed to go the Diet at Lublin with lord Filipowski and lord Stanislas Cikowski. There the opposite party were so strong that we were forced to leave the city. But nevertheless, through the mediation of lord Nicholas Sienicki, we enjoyed the King's promised clemency until his death. From this time on we kept away from the diets. And our opponents had now become so strong that by their pressure upon our patrons we were compelled to yield our places (*loci*), [among the Deputies]. At about this time [195] some of the Brethren learned from the *Rhapsodia [in Esaiam]* of Master Laelius Socinus[37] that the Son of God is not the second Person of the Trinity, coessential and coequal with the Father, but is the man Jesus Christ, conceived of the Holy Spirit, born of the Virgin Mary, crucified, and raised again. Being impressed with this, we were persuaded to search the Scriptures.

[no. 29] In the year 1567, I removed from our dwelling at Pińczów to Chmielnik, to lord John Oleśnicki.[38]

[no. 30] In the year 1569, on 20 August after sunset, Martha was born at Chmielnik. At about this time we had gone with lord Filipowski, master Simon [Ronemberg] the apothecary, and several others, to Moravia, to compare our doctrine and moral discipline and those of the Moravian [Hutterite] Brethren with each other. We found the government (*gubernatio*) of God's people there most excellent, but all the followers of the sect defended with tooth and nail a triune God.[39]

[The Brethren converge on newly founded Raków, 1569 – 72]

[no. 30.1] Also, many Brethren had come to Raków from Lithuania and Poland, nobles as well as ministers, to confer upon the Scriptures. This [spontaneous, local] synod continued for several years and ended in serious disagreements, displayed in their calling one another Pharisees, Saduccees, Jews, or Atheists, which was lamentable. And it came to this, that we almost all gave up the ministry of the word with the exception of Martin Czechowic, which came near to resulting in the ruin of everything. But God took pity on us through that most excellent man, Master Simon the apothecary, as through [another] Ezra, rebuilt our ruined estate, and even during those disorders set up a ministry with the baptism of adults (*Baptismo adultorum*).[40]

[no. 31] In the year 1572, on the last day of August, at the age of forty-two I was baptized at Chmielnik in the name of Christ.[41]

[no. 32] In the year 1573, I was sent to Cracow to be minister of the Minor Church [1573–86]. Since we were to come thither, my wife was baptized in [Casper] *Konarski's* garden.[42]

[no. 33] In the year 1574, on 1 August my wife's mother was baptized at Chmielnik.[43]

[no. 34] In the year 1574, on the last day of August, at daybreak, Peter, afterwards a doctor of medicine,[44] was born at Chmielnik.

[no. 35] In the year *1579,* we had a conference with Master Faustus Socinus on [196] baptism, which he approved in us, but said that in his case this was less necessary, because he had not learned his religion from us.[45]

[no. 36] In the year 1585, our teacher, John Völkel, was sent by the synod at Chmielnik to the school at Węgrów, and in Lithuania was made minister of the word of God.[46]

[no. 37] In the year 1586, at the beginning of January, I was sent from Cracow to be minister at the church at Lusławice.[47]

[no. 38] In the year 1588, by direction of the synod, I came from the Piedmont to Chmielnik, where a terrible hail-storm deprived us of all our crops.

[no. 39] In the year 1589, the alarm of a war with Turkey.[48]

[no. 49] In the year 1590, most merciful God preserved us from fire, when an adjoining house was burned.

[no. 41] These were in general the things, dearest sons and daughters, sons-in-law and grandchildren, that I deemed worthy of relating to you briefly and truly. From this you can judge concerning both our religion and our poverty. Wherefore I beg, admonish, and entreat you, by the Lord Jesus Christ, that you not only do not desert this Church in which I have lived, but also that you go on in it even beyond us, as you hold your eternal life dear. For if I in my lifetime had seen or heard of a purer Church, I should certainly have joined it. But here, as you know from our *Catechesis*, which I first privately compiled for you from the Holy Scriptures,[49] I worshiped in spirit and truth God the Father most high, and the man Jesus Christ, the only begotten Son of God, our Lord; and having been purified by the baptism of repentance (*baptismo poenitentiae*),[50] I labored in the Lord's vineyard together with pious brethren, with prayers, preaching of the word of God, and the practice of the appointed discipline, in proportion to the talent entrusted to me from heaven. For though I was endowed with but ordinary education and grammar, yet by the mercy of God and the knowledge of the uncorrupted word I was both for myself and for others a guide of the way to true piety (*pietatem*). And although many tried to deflect us from our purpose by open force as well as by cunning deceits, defections, and dissensions, yet by the aid of God and of the Lord Jesus Christ we have both continued steadfast up until now, and hope that we shall with his aid persevere even to our life's end. Amen.

[197] [no. 42] Indeed, I would seriously advise you, that if after our death God sees fit, as we hope, at length to open through someone a way to a more

perfect estate for the Church (*status ecclesiae*), you do not hinder the course of the Gospel, whether carried away by ambition or by some carnal desire, or by envy or hatred, but on the contrary that you may pray God, as we used to do, 'that all Israel may prophesy,'[51] and that not only the Lutherans, but even the Papists, may equal or surpass us in all godliness. It is a pity that Papists envy Lutherans, Lutherans Calvinists, Calvinists us, as though striving for preeminence. But let us take pains that out of all sorts of Christians, nay of Gentiles and Jews, we gather a Church for the Lord, that we may also far outdo in uprightness of life those whom we far surpass in the knowledge of truth, that we may inflame them with the fire of charity, and may attract them by words of love, so that whether they will or no, ''seeing our good works they may glorify our Father in heaven,''[52] and our Lord Jesus Christ his beloved Son, so that ''when we have finished our course, we may obtain the crown of life that fadeth not away.''[53] Amen.

[no. 43] However, as far as our wordly goods are concerned, I beg you for the sake of God and his Christ, complain not that we have led a life in poverty, ''for you are going to have many things if you fear the Lord,'' as Tobias [4:23] tells his son. Indeed, out of the little money that I had made in the salt works, I spent at Pińczów, where I served a whole year at my own expense, thirty gold ducats (*aureos*) for a house when I took my wife, and paid forty gold pieces for books. I have never been able to provide anything for you, because out of our daily living I shared not only with you, but also liberally with the poor. But yet I thank my God that through the generosity of the Brethren I so brought you up, and several others to adult life, that you have suffered neither hunger nor shameful nakedness.

Finally, I have married off three daughters,[54] giving each a dowry of ten marks. But how much I spent for woollen, linen, and fur garments, for bedding, and for other personal things acquired as was enough, our household can tell.[55] Indeed, had not our Brethren and Sisters assisted,[56] my means would not have been equal to so many and such great expenses. But since I have nothing else but this domicile and the little plot of ground [198] [here] in Chmielnik, Elizabeth[57] having been settled as best as I could, my daughters and sons-in-law will forgive me if they look for nothing more from our possessions than what they have already received. For my sons will have hardly as much from an equal division of all the property[58] as the daughters themselves have had. But God will be your possession and your great reward, if you cleave to him with all your heart. To your mother, since I have nothing to give, I have given and granted this house and plot of ground for as long as she lives. When she has died, our sons and daughters shall be equal heirs, if God preserves the house and the ground [Chmielnik, c. 1591].[59]

Related Document 4

Benedict Wiszowaty

[199/201] On the Printing Presses Of the Unitarians in Poland and Lithuania[1]

Foreword. It is surmised that Benedict Wiszowaty, indefatigable editor of *BAnt* and the *Historia,* decided to review the imprints in his collection in Amsterdam and then Andreaswalde, and tell the story of their printers as he recalled them. The first Reformed press was in Pińczów and at the close he leafs through a few of these extant *libelli vetusti.*

[No. 44] Our brethren had two printing presses in Poland: one in Poland properly so called, the other in Lithuania adjoining her. The former was removed to Raków from Cracow. The printer was Alexius Rodecki, who dwelt in Cracow and even during the reign of Stephen Batory in Poland followed his trade and printed many books,[2] especially by Socinus, though not under his name.[3] After this, being now advanced in age, he removed to Raków, where among other books, he printed the New Testament translated into the Polish tongue [from the Greek] by Martin Czechowic in 1579.[4] Raków at that time was in the possession of John Sienieński, palatine of Podolia, father of Jacob Sienieński and an adherent of the Reformed religion. But in 1600 the latter at length joined our Church, and greatly strengthened and built up the Christian cause. And in the same town of Raków, which was better supplied than usual with buildings for Church and school, the press also was well equipped, for Sebastian Sternacki married Alexius Rodecki's only daughter [Judith Rodecka] and also received the types by right of dowry. This press continued until 1638.[5]

[no. 45] The Lithuanian press seems to have been still earlier, having been first established by Matthew Kawieczyński.[6] The Polish Bible in Budny's version was printed in Zasław, a town in Lithuania, in 1572, nine years after the Reformed Bible was published at Brest,[7] the expense being met by the same Kawieczyński and his brother, with Daniel of Łęczyca as compositor.[8] This press was removed to the town of Łosk, which was the possession of [John] Kiszka, castellan of Vilna, a man of our confession; afterwards it was removed to Vilna, where the printer's name was [Ian] Karcan; and still later to Lubecz

[This was] a town that was then a possession of the same Kiszka and was situated on the river called Chronus, otherwise the Niemen. When Peter Blastus Kmita[9] married Karcan's daughter, he received the types as dowry. After him the press was run by his son John Kmita,[10] and after the latter [202] by John Lang, a Lutheran.[11] But Lubcz was [by] then already subject to Duke Janus Radziwiłł, palatine of Vilna and grand hetman of the Grand Duchy of Lithuania, who was born of the above-named Kiszka's brother's daughter or grand-daughter.[12] This press lasted longer than that at Raków, for even after the latter was destroyed, the Reply to Meissner's books was finished there, and Schlichting's lengthy preface was printed also.[13] But this press also, partly owing to the terrible plague, partly to the Muscovite invasion, came to an end in 1655 or 1656.

[no. 46] Some ancient books of ours are also to be seen that were printed while Augustus still reigned as King of Poland, one at Pińczów under [Nicholas] Oleśnicki, another at Lusławice. [In Pińczów, for example, was printed] the *Explicatio difficilum sanctae Scripturae locorum* by Gregory Paul,[14] who was minister of the word of God at Cracow, and after that the first one at Raków, when this town was still in the possession of John Sienński of the Reformed Church, though this Sienieński's wife [Jadwiga Goińska] was a member of our Church.[15]

Related Document 5

Andrew Wiszowaty[1]

[208/9] A Brief Narrative (*Narratio compendiosa*)
Of How the Unitarian Christians
Were Separated in Poland
From the Reformed Trinitarians

Written c. [1668]

Foreword. The following is a summary of a now lost larger account of the Minor Church that seems to have broken off in 1612, about the same year to which Andrew Lubieniecki carried his *Poloneutychia* (excerpted as RD 6) and perhaps compiled in the same place, Raków. Perhaps originally put together by Joachim Stegmann, Jr., in its present brevity the *Narratio* comes from Andrew Wiszowaty (1608 – 78), whose Life and Times by his son Benedyct appears as Doc. I in *PB*. The *Narratio* first appeared in print in the *Nucleus* of Christopher Sand, Jr. (Amsterdam, 1668) and was reprinted by Benedict Wiszowaty in *BAnt.*

[No. 47] When sometime after the days of the primitive Apostolic Church, a virgin undefiled, the clear teaching proclaimed by the apostles and professed by simple Christians (such as the Nazarenes and some of the better Ebionites), had already begun to be corrupted by the admixture of strange doctrines, owing to the adherence to Christianity on the part of some of the philosophers, especially the Platonists, there were some who held fast to the original teaching and they resisted and opposed those newer ones that were gaining strength. Such about the year 190 after the birth of Christ was Theodotus of Byzantium; then Artemon with some of his adherents, about A.D. 200; Bishop Beryllus of Bostra, about 240; Paul of Samosata, bishop of Antioch, about A.D. 260, together with his followers; then, after the Council of Nicaea, Bishop Photinus of Sirmium, about 350, with those who espoused his views. Concerning these see such writers of Church history as Eusebius, Rufinus, Theodoret, Socrates, and Sozomen, who traduce them in the usual manner as heretics.

[no. 48] But after that black night of errors, which were gradually introduced into religion, had burdened the Christian world for several generations, the day of divine truth, again returning with the favoring grace of God, began gradually to dawn, as is its wont. The appearance of Luther, Zwingli, Calvin, and Menno [Simons][2] came first, as if daybreak and dawn, and this was then followed by the brighter rays of the returning sun.

[no. 49] About the year 1546 after the birth of Christ, in Italy, in the jurisdiction of Venice [210] near Vicenza, conferences and meetings on the subject of religion began to be held by about forty participants who called in question the accepted opinion concerning the Triune God. And when two of these, Julius of Treviso and Francis of Ruovigo, had been seized and drowned in Venice, the rest left Italy on account of the danger, some going to Thessalonica and Damascus, and putting themselves under the rule of the Turks, where liberty is allowed to any religion, while others went to Switzerland.[3]

[no. 50] Of the latter the foremost was Laelius Socinus of Siena. When he began the study of *Roman* (text: *humani*) law, which was hereditary in his family, he deemed that this must be derived from the fountainhead of divine law, and so applied himself to the sacred books. He noted that the commonly received dogmas of the Church, especially that of the Holy Trinity, disagreed with them, and he rekindled as though it had been buried under the ashes the doctrine about the Son of God Jesus Christ as not existent before his mother Mary. He left Italy in 1547 at the age of twenty-two, and lived in Zurich in voluntary exile. He first came to Poland in the year 1551 and [again] after that in 1558, where he instilled some thoughts against received errors both in Francis Lismanino, who was confessor to Bona Sforza, consort of King Sigismund I of Poland, and in others. From here, passing through Moravia, where his comrades Alciati, Paruta, Ochino, and others were then sojourning, he returned to Zurich, where he died in 1562.

[no. 51] It is said that at about the time when Laelius Socinus left Italy, a certain Belgian, Spiritus by name, came to Poland, and there among some friends at Cracow, taking occasion from a book in which separate prayers were addressed to three separate divine persons, he raised the question whether they had three Gods.[4] Wherewith, having volubly reproved this error, he aroused doubts in some, and among these in Andrew Frycz Modrzewski. He being entrusted with the secret matters of King Sigismund Augustus, by command of the same kind King, who was interested in various subjects, inquired into the controversies about the divine Trinity which were then going on, and wrote on this subject the books entitled *Sylvae*. In the first book of the *Sylvae*, the second tract, he recorded this story about Spiritus the Belgian.[5]

[211] [no. 52] Those in Poland who disagreed with the received view about the Trinity were then called Pinczovians, from the town of Pińczów in which, under their illustrious patron and protector Nicholas Oleśnicki, both Francis Stancaro of Mantua (noted for the famous controversy about Christ being Mediator in his human nature alone) and Lismanino, plus Peter Statorius the French-

man, George Biandrata, the Italian physician, after he left Geneva, and John
Łaski the Pole, after he came back from England, were dwelling along with
several others. There the Polish version of the Bible was made by several
Reformed [translators], which later was printed under the auspices and at the
expense of Nicholas Radziwiłł, duke in Ołyka and Nieśwież, palatine of Vilna,
at the city of Brest in Lithuania, of which he was captain.[6]

[no. 53] The Pole Peter of Goniądz, a native of Podlasie, returning home
from travels abroad, in the synod at Secemin in 1556 brought forward a view
about the preeminence of God the Father before the Son, mostly derived from
the opinions of Michael Servetus and Valentine Gentile; and after this at Brest
in 1558 he also brought forward the view for the baptism of catechumens
against the silly (*puerilem*) baptism of infants, and though opposed by many,
made an impression upon some.

[no. 54] In the year 1562 after Christ's birth, in a synod held by the Reformed
at Pińczów, as a result of the controversy about the Trinity, whether God is one
in essence and trine in persons, it was agreed that preachers of the word of God
should refrain in their sermons about religious matters from expressions foreign
to the Holy Scriptures and the Apostles' Creed, and introduced from other
sources. Complying with this rule, Gregory Paul of Brzeziny, who was serving
as pastor to the Reformed at Cracow, was traduced as an heretical Arian and
Servetian by Stanislas Sarnicki, who envied him his ministry of the church in
the capital city, and was burning with zeal without knowledge.

[no. 54.1] Meantime John Boner, patron of the Reformed church in Cracow,
castellan of Biecz and grand governor of Cracow, suddenly died and his widow
married another. A place for the congregation was then appointed in the house
of Stanislas *Cikowski*, who was then high chamberlain of Cracow, later castellan
of Biecz and commander of the army in the war with Muscovy.[7]

[no. 54.2] Afterwards, Gregory Paul was condemned for heresy. This was
under the direction of Sarnicki and his associate one Lawrence by surname "of
Przasnysz," in fact of "Discordia," whom the former [212] had had appointed
superintendent of the churches of Great Poland although he had previously condemned him for his hardly commendable life. Gregory, though neither summoned nor heard, and denied the exercise of the sacred ministry, was in fact
retained by his patron Cikowski and other hearers. The same Sarnicki, contriv-
ing a schism, arranged with some of the patrons of the Reformed churches to
have other preachers who taught the preeminence of the Father over the Son
removed from office also.

[no. 55] In the year of Christ 1565, at Piotrków, a royal city of Great Poland,
at the time of the Diet of the royal Commonwealth, [an effort was made to
restore harmony] when not a few of the Reformed, even Senators of the Realm,
were present there. Gregory Paul with his associates, namely Stanislas Lutomirski, [later] superintendent of the [Minor] churches of Little Poland and secretary
to the King, his brother John [Lutomirski], castellan of Sieradz, also Nicholas
Sienicki, speaker of the Chamber of Deputies of the equestrian order, John

Niemojewski, judge of Inowrocław, and others, endeavored to bring about harmony in the Church, which had been broken by Sarnicki and Discordia. To this end, an address was delivered in the assembly and a friendly conference requested. This was indeed carried on for a few days. But Sarnicki very strongly urged the authority of the so-called Fathers of the Church. On that occasion the reply promised to Gregory was not made. Indeed, the stronger party and the view more acceptable to the crowd (*vulgus*) prevailing, it was decided without the presence of the other party, no longer to hold conferences with the latter about those issues.

[no. 55.1] Thus, with a schism now openly breaking out, the Church broke into parties, and was split into the Major, which professed the Trinity of the most high God, and the Minor, which upheld his Unity, so that the former deemed it impious to stay in communion with the latter. Nay, even their common adversaries the Papists and their bishops were stirred up by the former, the stronger group, against the latter, the weaker one, as blasphemous Arians. Also a malicious charge of treachery to their country was made on the part of those who differed from them against certain noble patrons, such as Stanislas Lasocki, high chamberlain of Łęczyca, and Jerome Filipowski, treasurer of the palatinate of Cracow.[8]

[no. 56] It was taken for a remarkable omen that in 1562, when that decision against the doctrine of the Trinity was being taken and the schism [213] was impending, in Cracow, at noon on Trinity Sunday itself, while Gregory Paul was preaching against this very opinion of the Trinity, lightning struck Trinity Church and threw down the orb fixed on its steeple.[9]

[no. 57] In the meantime John Sigismund, son of the elected king of Hungary, John Zápolya, and nephew of Sigismund II Augustus by his sister [Isabelle], having arranged in his own principality of Transylvania a ten days' conference in Alba Julia on the principal points of religion, and especially on the Triune God, approved the view of those who confess God most high, one in essence as well as in person, indeed, the Father only and [acknowledged] his only Son [to be] conceived of the Holy Spirit of God and born of the Virgin Mary, and who therefore are called Unitarians in that country and enjoy liberty for their religion confirmed by that prince. He also called George Biandrata, a physician (exceedingly hated by Calvin and his partisans for his opinion about the one God) from Poland into Transylvania to him. These things were done about 1567.[10]

[no. 58] Of those who, rejecting the common view about the Trinity of God, embraced the view about the preeminence of the Father over the Son, some slipped clearly into Arianism, such as Stanislas Farnowski or Farensius, who split off [as Ditheists] from the other Unitarians about 1567. After his death his followers divided, some going to the other Unitarians, some to the Calvinists.[11]

[no. 59] Faustus Socinus of Siena, nephew of Laelius by his brother Alexander, born of Agnes, daughter of Borghese Petrucci, prince of Siena, having spent twelve years in distinguished service in the court of Grand Duke *Cosimo*[12] [of Tuscany (this after the death of his uncle [Laelius], by whom he had been instructed in an extraordinary knowledge of divine things), of his own will [then] turned his back on the favor he had enjoyed with the prince. Spurning both his present fortune and his expectations, and moved by concern for his own and others' salvation, he removed from Italy to Switzerland in the year of Christ 1574. There, while staying at Basel, he began *Disputatio de Jesu Christo Servatore*; but in 1578 he was called to Transylvania by George Biandrata, chief physician to Prince Christopher Báthory, to confute Francis Dávid who, having rejected the error concerning the Son of God as consubstantial with God the Father, fell into another yet worse, [214] that Christ should not be liturgically (*religiose*) honored or invoked.[13] From here [Transylvania] Faustus in 1579 relocated in Poland and there, at the synod at Raków in 1580, he asked publicly to be admitted to the churches that confessed that only the Father of Jesus Christ is God most high. He was, however, rejected for his disagreeing on certain doctrines, which he did not conceal such as on the satisfaction of Christ, on justification without any works, on predestination and free will, and on baptism by immersion. [He felt that the Brethren were Calvinist Baptist Unitarians.] Nor was he admitted to the Holy Supper (*synaxis*). [Half−included] he yet in defense of these churches contended actively in his writings against their antagonists. Among others, he wrote a book against Andrew Wolan, a Calvinist, on the nature (*natura*) of Jesus Christ the Son of God, and also on the atonement of sins through him,[14] which he dedicated to John Kiszka of Ciechanowiec, at the time captain of Samogitia (afterwards castellan of Vilna), the patron of about twenty unitarian churches [in Lithuania].

[no. 60] Andrew Dudith, formerly bishop of Pécs in Hungary, when attending the Council of Trent, noticed the wiles of the Popes and of the Church of bishops there, and leaving it, joined the Reformed. But afterward, moved now by considerations of reason, now by the harshness of the Calvinists against the Unitarians (for he saw how the peace-making deputation of the latter were treated with contempt by the former), he became their patron later, as appears from some of his own letters.[15]

[no. 61] In 1580, when one hundred and fifty Reformed preachers assembled at Lewartów, the Unitarians expected a conference with them, of which hope was held out to them, but the Unitarians, with Socinus present, were disappointed in their hope on coming there, for the Reformed replied that it was a sin for them to have a conference or anything to do with them because they were followers of Ebion, Arius, and the Samosatene, who had been of old excommunicated by the Church.

[no. 62] About the year 1600, Jacob Sienieński of Sienno, son of the palatine of Podolia, owner of Raków, formerly a Calvinist, acknowledging that the views of the Unitarians were more consistent with the truth, adopted them, and built a school and a press in that town for the use of these unitarian churches.[16]

[no. 63] Even after this the Unitarians attempted a reconciliation with the Reformed [215] (who in Poland are called Evangelicals) on this condition, that though a difference of views remained, they might unite in friendship and mutual tolerance. But at the synod of the latter at Lublin in 1612,[17] the Reformed (still needing to be Reformed) refused them, saying that no union could be made so long as the other party retained views opposed to their own concerning the Holy Trinity, the satisfaction of Christ, the mode of justification, and of baptism. Indeed, they presently published a book in the vernacular, entitled *Fire with Water*,[18] by which they meant to say that they could in no wise unite with them. To this book a reply was made by Valentine Schmalz of Gotha,[19] preacher of the church at Raków.[20]

Related Document 6

Andrew Lubieniecki, Senior (I) (c. 1551 – 1623)[1]

Religious Ferment and Factionalism in the Commonwealth, 1562 – 72[2]

A selection from
*Poloneutychia or the Happiness
of the Kingdom of Poland and with It
That of the Grand Duchy of Lithuania
and Then the Impairment of Happiness
in the Year 1612 and 1613*
(MS done in Raków, 1616)[3]

Foreword. Andrzej Lubieniecki, incorporating this religious survey in the larger history of his time, writes about religion in the Commonwealth from both the geographical and the ecclesiological angle of Raków, by then, the flourishing capital of the Polish Brethren, but at a moment when he was painfully aware of the marginalization of his own Minor Church, which he refers to throughout only as the church of "Christians" over against that of "the Evangelicals" and that of the largely Germanic Lutheran. (all at n. 5). He deals with the church of the Czech Brethren only very confusedly (between nn. 18 and 21), but he is diffidently aware that the three "Protestant" bodies have, in fact, achieved a Consensus at Sandomierz in 1570 (Pl. 34) and a Confederation excluding his "Christians." Because he still yearns for a reunion of the Major and the Minor Church (at n. 8) as God's ordained intention and, no doubt because of his nobiliary and theological disdain for some of the early vagaries in Raków itself, he warps his overall presentation by evidently generalizing from the antinomianism of the early Racovian commune (between nn. 21 and 26) before taking note chronologically of its foundation and three year upheaval (between nn. 28 – 29). Indeed he alludes to Raków without naming it already (at n. 16), where he is bringing together various kinds of Baptists, from the Ditheists of two kinds who introduced believers' immersion before his own Racovians, through the Lower Vistula Mennonites, to Moravian Hutterite Anabaptists (between nn. 12 and 16). It is possible that Raków was in its radical phase only representative of a number of less well remembered episodes of religo-social ferment. He reports on two Judaizing trends, one within Eastern Orthodoxy (not thus specified) and the other within the Minor Church itself, the non-adorant, socially conservative scriptural baptist Unitarians (at n. 27).

In any case, this "Socinian" survey of 1613 may be appropriately compared with the "Angelican" sketch of the same groupings in the Commonwealth as seen more from the angle, say of the staple town of Elbing, but earlier, as of 1598, RD 9.

[50] . . . [F]rom the beginning of the world within a period so short, the ten last years only of the Augustan reign [1562–72] and in a corner of the world so small as this our land, we never saw anywhere what we see here in a heap that there should be such varied worship: Roman Catholic, Greek, Armenian, Jewish, Karaite,[4] [Muslim] Tatar, and even pagan, as are in our land.

At that time there were several dozen heretical [groups] and even quite powerful ones that had among them educated and powerful people in their own right, which [however] by the grace of God expired as not having foundations so that only two churches were left on the field, those who called themselves [51] Evangelicals [Calvinists] and those others holding themselves to be [simply] Christians [the Minor Reformed Church]. As then and now these are the only two [Protestant] groups in Poland and Lithuania, besides the religion of Lutheranism in [Ducal] Prussia and Courland among the Germans; and they are united with the Evangelicals.[5] And the heretics say that the two churches must one of these days become a single church (*zborem*) because the times will come when all cults (*nabożeństwa*) must be in a single place (*w jednej matnej*).[6] And "there will be one pastor and one sheepfold" of all people gathered,[7] and they will be easily united in order that they may also uphold discipline in their church, as many of them desire. And so if they become more devout, their union will be easily accomplished.[8]

And it happens between these two churches that the king of Navarre [Anthony of Bourbon (d. 1562)], himself a Calvinist, grandfather of the present French king in Paris [Louis XIII (1610–43)], said to the ambassador of the Danish king [Frederick II (1559–88)], a Lutheran, that "there are forty things in which we heretics differ from the Catholics. First we have to dispute about thirty-nine with the Catholics and when this is done, then the fortieth item [the Eucharist] we will consider among ourselves."[9]

There were at that time [1562–72] quite a few of the Saxon or the Lutheran religion, even among the Senators and the magnates. But there are no more.[10]

There were many Tritheists [among the Reformed] who, having rejected the word "Holy Trinity," [yet] confessed three divine Persons: God the Father, God the Son, and God the Holy Spirit. Such was the Vilna church and other Lithuanian and Podlachian churches. And they are no more.[11]

There were Ditheists [among the Reformed] who did not recognize the Holy Ghost as person and they said that the Son was with the Father of one essence (*z Ojcem jednej istności*).[12] And they did not survive either.

There were those who said that the Son of God was generated from the Father before the creation of the world, while others said that he was generated before time and they recognized the Holy Spirit to be something of a small person (*jakąs osobą małą*). And these [Ditheists] were most markedly split in two, for there were those who [still] baptized infants; and their leaders were [John] Kazanowski, [Thomas] Falconius, [Nicholas] Żytno (*Zitinius*), Thomas in Wysokie [Lubelskie], and [Jacob] Szadurski; and of these men there is no trace. And the second [among the Ditheists] were those who did not baptize infants but adults, and whose leaders were [Stanislas] Wiśniowski, [Stanislas] Farnowski, and [John] Petrycy. They, too, are gone and have, like bees without mothers, dispersed themselves among other cults. Then there were those also in Kujawy who held that the Lord Jesus had been with the Father before ages; they baptized adults and differed among themselves in the doctrine of justification and other things mentioned above and had rigorous discipline among themselves; and their leaders were then John Niemojewski, [Martin] Czechowic, and others. And these are no more either, because their leaders proceeded further [towards Unitarianism].[13]

Besides them [the Polish Ditheists] there were those also who introduced opinions from the Dutch Neo-Baptists (*nowokrzczeńcami*) who had come to settle in [Royal] Prussia;[14] and they[15] desired to inculcate them in the [Minor Reformed] Church. But they did not fare well either.

There were as well those who introduced and propagated Moravian [Hutterite] communalism (*komuniją*) and other opinions; and indeed the Moravian [Hutterites] themselves traveled here [to Raków] and helped them [the Racovians]. But they accomplished little, and are not heard of [among us] any more.[16]

There were those who believed in the Holy Trinity just as they learned in the Roman Catholic religion, adhering in this belief to the doctors [of the Church] and the councils.[17] And these had their own different reasonings. For among them were the Waldenses.[18] Among them were common (*pospolicie*) Czech ministers who maintained the discipline in their church. And they are no more, because, having been drawn into a larger heap (*kupy*), they had both lost their discipline and made themselves invisible.[19] Among them [the Trinitarians] were others who lived without any discipline at all, and accordingly went further than the Waldenses.[20] And meanwhile some of these followed in their doctrines Zwingli, others Melanchthon, still a third group Flacius Illyricus with respect to the Lord's Supper. Thus the first [observed the Supper] with [ordinary] bread; the second, with unleavened bread; and others, with wafers; and some went to the sick with this, others did not. And all these groups came together in one contemporary Evangelical Church and are conjoint with each other (*conformes*).[21]

[52] There were also those who spoke of the Scripture as a dead letter and black ink. They thought that their dreams, visions, and ideas were the thing most necessary in religious practice and for salvation. And in this they desired to imitate [Caspar] Schwenckfeld[22] but they added that they permitted themselves all sins not prohibited by common law and their attendance at services in [Catholic] churches (*kościołach*), in [Byzantine-rite] basilicas (*cerkwiach*), and in synagogues, remarking that "it does not matter what we do it with the body if we have pure spirits" [cf. Rom 8:1 – 17].[23] There were quite a few such, but the

Lord Jesus took them out of the world because none of them wanted to ponder on their way of life.

There were those who condemned all officiating at any religious services, claiming that nobody was fit to officiate or instruct unless he had had a revelation from heaven and had either witnessed miracles or had the power to perform them. Such were [John] Śleszyński, [Daniel] Bieliński, [Basil] Tapiński, [Matthew] Albinus, Jan Baptystya [Święcicki], and many others. And they, too, were rooted out by the Lord Jesus.[24]

There were those also who became rustics, worked with their hands, walked about, lay around, and ate in an uncouth manner, claiming their way to be favored by God; and, having puffed themselves up because of this, thought all other ways undeserving of eternal life. They, too, are gone on their way and are not seen any more.

There were those who incited godly and honest men to relinquish their offices, put away their arms, and forbade recourse to legal self-defense even over the most grievous slander and to the swearing of an oath. And many upright men laid down their landed benefices and the King gave them to some other. Some left their estates and freed their serfs.[25] One Ożarkowski, an upright man, having in the Diet of Lublin [1569] approached the King for counsel, publicly thanked him for his benefice and said that he could [nevertheless] no longer make use of it in good conscience without serving the King or the Commonwealth for it. Having thus spoken, he gave back to the King the privilege of incomes from Przybysławice and three other villages in the land of Lublin, requesting that the King release him from it and that he give it to anyone who could really serve him. The King did not wish to take it from him, but he still did not want it and said: "You are able, my Lord, to take from me whatever you want by force, but you cannot give anything to me by force." And immediately Lord John Firley, Marshal of the Crown, asked about this, observing that this [demesne] once belonged to his captaincy of Kazimierz and he besought the King to return it to this captaincy. And the King so acted and it is thus today joined to the captaincy of Kazimierz in the house of the Lords Firley.[26]

But also there were some and these the worst in their transgression whom Satan strew most thickly throughout Lithuania, White Russia, Podlachia, Volhynia, and the Ukraine, for they did not believe in the Lord Jesus, our Lord. Thus some mingled together the Old Testament and the Gospel; others placed the Old Testament above the Gospel and introduced Judaism. And of these, some had taken to celebrate the Sabbath or did not eat those dishes that Jews do not eat. But these, too, our Lord Jesus Christ not only confounded through his servants but also took away so completely that none of them do we know in our lands. And their leaders were [Jerome] Piekarski, [Jacob] Palaeologus, [Simon] Budny, [Matthias Vehe-]Glirius, [Daniel] Bieliński, [Thomas] Garliński, [Peter] Domaniowski, and many other educated people.[27]

And along with such an outgrowth of different aberrations were countless errors, sprouting from errors, that one could scarcely count them. But the divine will was done in the last days of Augustus's reign with respect to all these sects, sapping the strength of some and destroying others. And this began to happen in the fourth year before the King's death and lasted till his death [1568–72]. For by then people got weary of controversies and quarrels that they had even pursued publicly during the diets. Thus in Piotrków twelve Evangelical ministers [of the emerging Major Church] disputed with those who call themselves Christians [of the Minor Church]—[53] in the presence of many Senators and Deputies and many distinguished people from the royal court [20–30 March 1565]. And they disputed incessantly in the general synods held nearly every year in different places.

There were men[28] who came out to say they had sickened of all wordly affairs and wished to go away some place in a band so as to live together, practice their religion, and await death in peace. At the same time, Lord [John] Sienieński, also castellan of Żarnów, founded by charter the little town of Raków [27 March 1567] in the Land of Sandomierz, to which flocked people from Great and Little Poland of their same practice of faith—noblemen, burghers, ministers and countless others, educated people, some foreigners. And these for a certain time lived in peace, built for themselves residences and houses; and then to them came quite a few of this sect from Lithuania, Volhynia, and from other lands, who exercised themselves in reasoning out the sense of Holy Scriptures and polished themselves through different adversaries, and there were a lot of them of the sects aforementioned who arrived, and to those a hundred other heads arrived with other different questions, some of whom had betaken themselves to Raków to live, others of whom rode there only for an occasion, bothering some people. And such people said that this must be the truth that St. Paul in 1 Cor 11:19 declared there must be such in order that among the people of the Lord there be heresies in order that those who are genuine be recognized. Thus there was no peace, day or night, for three years [1569–72];[29] for the various debates went on without respite among different ones, until finally a fair number were converted through the arguments propounded, while the remainder, unconvinced, went on their way and later perished, and they say this now. It turned out what the Lord and our Saviour replied to Matthew (15:13): "Every plant which my Father has not planted will be uprooted." And this that Gamaliel said in Acts (5:38) that what is not of God will fail but what is of God is hard to ruin. The ones who stayed on in Raków were those known as Christians; they continued to live together in peace for four years [1572–76], having elaborated their doctrine and humbled their hearts, or—as they called it—yielded (*poddane*)[30] them to the Lord Jesus. They submitted their necks to him under his government and discipline with readiness. Among them were scores of ministers later assigned to different places. For example they were brought by Lithuanian Lord Kiszka to his Podlachian and Lithuanian estates; the Ruthenian palatine [Jerome] Sieniawski[31] took some to Ruthenia; Prince Ladislas Zbaraski[32] had others go to Volhynia. Thus various other noblemen divided them in different places throughout their estates as much to Little as to Great Poland and to Ruthenia. Then followed the *interregna* [1572–73].[33]

Related Document 7

The Catechesis of George Schomann, Cracow, 1574

Introduction. In his *Testamentum* George Schomann twice refers to his *Catechesis*.[1] Although the composition of one minister, the *Catechesis* documents the scriptural beliefs and practices of perhaps the majority of the Polish Brethren in Little Poland only a couple of years after the most radical experimentation in Raków, 1569–72, so evasively reported by Lubieniecki in his *Historia* and so partisanly reported by his great uncle Andrew in the *Poloneutychia* (RD 6). It is the earliest unitarian (Baptist) confession of faith in any land, published in Cracow in the sole year of the rule of Henry of Valois, 1574.

The *Catechesis* covers in six sections major concerns of the Minor Church six years before Faustus Socinus assumed leadership of the Racovians and the whole Minor Church in Little Poland in 1580. Although cast almost wholly in scriptural phrasing, the *Catechesis* as a whole reflects the faith, spirituality, and to some extent the structure of the Minor Church in its pre-Socinian, moralistic, sectarian Separatism and constitutes an invaluable witness to the life and mood of that Church at the end of the third quarter of the sixteenth century before it had entered upon its more Evangelical Rationalist phase, that is, before it became partly Socinian. As the *Catechesis*, moreover, served as the model for the Racovian Catechism in Polish of 1605, which embodied much of the teaching and directive of Socinus, including his downplaying of baptism, it is all the more important to include the *Catechesis* here in the Appendix in order to have accessible a quite rare publication that supplies in comprehensive, catechetical form what Lubieniecki sets forth only in polemics, synodal debates, and epistolary reports. It is in fact the deposition of a distinctive kind of Polish Anabaptism of a scripturally grounded, eschatologically intense, Christocentric unitarian immersionist piety and discipline that was to be gradually impregnated with the systematizing scriptural rationalism of Socinus. It may be instructively compared with Michael Sattler's *Brüderliche Vereinigung* of Schleitheim, 1527,[2] widely accepted by the Swiss and South German (Evangelical) Anabaptists with its seven articles (on issues disputed with the emerging establishmentarian churches) on baptism, the ban, the Lord's Supper, separation from the world, pastors, non-resistance, and the oath, which topics the *Catechesis* placed in a more substantial theological context, on God, Christ, justification, and sanctification.

If compared with the somewhat evasive or equivocating Confession of Faith of Laelius Socinus,[3] extracted from him in Zurich in 1555 by Bullinger (Pl. 10A), the *Catechesis* is much more sectarian, although no more intensely eschatological, while if compared with *Confessio fidei*, based on the Apostles' Creed by Jonas Schlichting, 1642

(*Polish Brethren*, Document XXII, that discretely included some of Socinus's most controverted points), it nevertheless has much in common, both being veritable tapestries of scriptural passages. Indeed Schlichting's *Confessio*, personally drafted and furtively printed, is as much a descendant of the *Catechesis* of Schomann as is the more renowned Racovian Catechism in its successive revisions and liberalization, for both the *Catechesis* and the *Confessio* are alike in holding to an inalterable faith once and for all delivered to the saints (Jude 3), while the Racovian Catechism, for all its initially exclusivistic view of revelation and salvation, bore within it the seed of a dynamic relation between reason and Scripture, allowing for more truth yet to be revealed or confirmed.

When Schomann composed the *Catechesis*, he had only two years before (1572) in Chmielnik submitted to believers' immersion in the name of Jesus Christ; and in the preceding year (1573) he had been synodally commissioned "for the ministry" of the congregation of the Minor Church in Cracow, which in the terminology of his *Catechesis* meant that he was not only *pastoral elder* (*senior*) of that congregation but also in effect presumably superintendent, i.e., *episcopus* (see his Section 3), hence the authority with which he writes the *Catechesis* and has it published by the printer of the Church, Alexander Rodecki, right in the capital of the Commonwealth.[4]

Indeed the place and date of publication are noteworthy. In the very year of its publication the *episcopi* of the Realm, all of the Senators, and the mitred abbots participated in the liturgical unction of the elected King-designate, Henry of Valois, in the castle cathedral, 21 February 1574. In the *ordo* for the unction and coronation, Henry in tunic, gloves, alb, dalmatic, and pallium, was asperged with holy water and addressed by Primate Jacob Uchański thus: "God the instructor of the humble, thou who dost console us by the vivid illustration of the Holy Spirit, extend over this thy servant Henry the grace that by him we may sense thine advent present in our midst."[5] One cannot read the Latin *Catechesis* of the Minor Church in Cracow in the context of a dramatic and still parlous constitutional transition without a sense of its having been composed to place the Christology of that Church of the Lord Jesus, the crucified Messiah, in polemical parallelism with that of Primate-Interrex Uchański, all the more intensely felt by the author for the reason of the conspicuously eschatological expectancy of the whole community from which the *Catechesis* issued. Even the replete reference therein to baptism as a dying and rising with Christ, as both an *immersio* and an *emersio*, cannot have been composed in Latin by our sectarian, Restorationist *episcopus* without his sensing however vaguely a parallel with the Latin collect quoted above in the *ordo* of liturgical kingship. Having had himself earlier served as the tutor of the sons of courtiers and palace functionaries, he might not have been aware that some of his phrases evoked the recent memory (or the anticipation) of the long-delayed and elaborate obsequies for the late King (who had died in Knyszyn, 7 July 1572) in the castle church, 4–7 February 1574, whereby Church and Commonwealth celebrated the dying and rising of royal power and hence the *salus populi*: the King is dead (finally buried with due solemnity), long live the (duly elected and consecrated elected) King!

Politically loyal in the sense of Romans 13, Schomann nevertheless does not refer to the principalities and powers of the castle and the cathedral by the Vulgate term *potestas* or *ordinatio* but rather by the term *magistratus* that had evolved as the generic term for the state in Geneva and elsewhere under the impact of Reformed thought about the orders of creation and redemption. It is even possible that Schomann is conscious of the separatist thrust of the polity of his *Catechesis* when he refers to Jesus Christ as *Magister*, when he could have used *propheta/doctor* for teacher/master, and that he intended to suggest that the master was also King of kings, the eschatological Judge/Magistrate (*magistratus*). In the annexed *Oeconomia domestica*, to be sure, Schomann makes clear that the magistrates in his mind are primarily the town magistrates.[6]

It is in any case noteworthy that Schomann preserves the Erasmian/Laskian *triplex munus Christi*, and clearly distinguished the office of Jesus Christ as *Propheta, Sacerdos,* and *Rex*, which threefold office would become structurally even more important in the subsequent Racovian Catechism.[7]

Of the seven articles of the Schleitheim Confession (1527), the article on non-resistance does not come out in the *Catechesis* as an express disavowal of war in the author's own words nor as withdrawal from any public office involving the *jus gladii*, but in quoting the whole of the Sermon on the Mount Schomann makes evident his pacifist intent. It is true, however, that he is, with the sanction and the models of the Old Testament and the New, a proponent of "the natural" hierarchies of ruler over subjects, of lords over servants (and no doubt therefore also serfs), of men over women, of parents over children. The *Catechesis* is not a socially radical manifesto. Indeed, it represents the recovery of many conservative positions temporarily abandoned during the socially and theologically radical phase of Raków, now for him past, when women had gained a voice, for example, and are now here bidden to get back into the kitchen and among the children and to remain silent in the church.

One senses, indeed, in the argumentation style of the *Catechesis* the subsiding swirls of the spirit-driven debates in Raków over the meaning of Scripture, as men and women, idealistic lords and their released serfs, educated pastors and unlettered artisans searched the meaning of the word of God under the sanction of the *lex sedentium*, 1 Cor 14:23ff. This *locus classicus* for free, engaged, mutual inquiry under the guidance of the Holy Spirit is notably missing from the scriptural tapestry held up by Schomann.

Although the *Catechesis* by its very title would seem to be a catechism for children, on reading it one becomes clear that the *pueri* (boys, children) are not being addressed but that the genre of a catechism is employed as a compendium of the main tenets and practices of a disciplined community, all set forth for confirmed fellow believers to strengthen them after a period of turmoil, and for prospective converts. Written in Latin, it is intended for more than Poles, as is at least suggested by the identification of Cracow in the imprint as being in Poland. And Schomann was indeed to be refuted by a fellow Silesian, by the Breslau-born Zacharias Ursinus of the orthodox Reformed position in Heidelberg, in the posthumous *Explicationum cathecheticarum . . . absolutum opus* (Neustadt, 1603).

The *Catechesis* is printed in a booklet along with the *Oeconomia Christiana seu pastoratus domesticus*, a manual for the *paterfamilias* leading in family prayers, instruction in the Ten commandments (in the Reformed, not in the Catholic/Lutheran, numeration) and for the pastor in the house church. This is cast in instructional language and formularies that go far beyond the almost exclusively scriptural phrasings of the *Catechesis*; and in the pastoral prayer of several folios, Schomann does clear up his sense of the state as ordained of God: "And especially we implore Thee, King of kings and Lord of lords, who dost alone establish Kings and Magistrates, that thou wilt deign to govern with thy divine hand and protect their hearts, minds, counsels, health, life of all princes, so especially of our most benign King of Poland and the Queen[8] and of all councilors and magistrates of the towns, our lords, rule them with thy princely spirit, and defend them from all threats and perils for the good order and public tranquility of this whole Commonwealth of Poland. . . ." (going on to include Magistrates again and prefects and to implore protection from natural disasters, external war and internal sedition).[9] In many ways the *Oeconomia Christiana* is more revealing of the actual thought and practice of the Minor Church, c. 1574, than the *Catechesis* proper.

The translation was made by T. Corey Brennan from a copy of "the first unitarian Confession of faith," as it is inscribed by the donor, in the Andover Harvard Library (see Pl. 31). The author used the Vulgate, often quoting from memory. In translation the Revised Standard version has been employed with only an occasional Douai rendering where that reading could better catch the intention of Schomann. Where Schomann conflates texts, reverses sequence, lets a few phrases stand for the whole locus, the editing brings out the texts and occsionally amplifies where necessary in bracks. Thus the dots in the text do not imply editorial ellipsis. The only part of the *Catechesis* not reproduced in its entirety is the amassing of prooftexts under I. A, On God the Father as the only true God of Scripture, the determinative tenet of the fully unitarian Polish Brethren as of 1574, but predictable and fully treated by Lubieniecki in his *Historia.*

Catechesis and Confession of Faith
Of the Congregation Assembled Throughout
Poland in the Name of Jesus Christ Our
Lord, Crucified and Resurrected

Deut 6[:4] "Hear, O Israel: The Lord our God is one Lord."
John 8[:54] "Jesus said 'It is my Father . . . of whom you say that He is your God'."

At the press of Alexander Turobińczyk
[Rodecki in Cracow] in the year of the birth of
Jesus Christ, the Son of God, 1574

Eccl 11[:7]: "Do not find fault before you investigate; first learn, then justly reprove."
1 Cor 4[:5] "Do not pronounce judgment before the time."

Preface to the Reader

The congregation (*coetus*) throughout Poland, baptized in the name of Jesus Christ the Nazarene, though meagre and distressed, sincerely prays for grace and peace for all those who thirst after eternal salvation from the one God the Father, who is most high, through his only-begotten Son our Lord, Jesus Christ crucified.

Because the name of the Anabaptists,[1] due to certain accursed men, is so disreputable and hated among all (just as it was among us a few years ago) so that as a result even the holy and salvation-giving oracles of God Himself and His Christ clearly do not have a place among many men—even those who are not the worst sort—merely because [a3] the Devil, that old imposter, besmirched the hated name of Anabaptism, and lest we appear to fail ourselves and yourselves before God and His Christ, we therefore present to you a confession of our faith and a catechism of our children (*puerorum*), frank and simple, produced insofar as it was possible from His Holy Scripture. We call to witness God, the Saviour of hearts, and Jesus Christ, the righteous and terrible judge of the living and the dead, that we are not acting in a fraudulent, haughty, and high-handed manner, but do all things with a good conscience [cf. 1 Pet 3:21], as God inspires us with his Holy Spirit, and as far as Holy Scripture allows us, and we do this to the glory of God and His Son our Lord, for the correction of our life, and to attain eternal life. Moreover, if there is anything which escapes our notice, or "if in anything we are otherwise minded, God will reveal that also to us," as it says in Phil 3[:15]. Indeed, these things which we now present to you we have drawn not from the cisterns of men that can hold no water [cf. Jer 2:13] but from the very clear fountains of the Saviour. We are so sure and confident of these things that even [Gal 1:8] "if an angel should try to thrust anything contrary on us, let him be accursed."

We make solemn appeal and entreaty to all by God and [for] your salvation to examine these [teachings] against the rule of the divine oracles and flee from a Babylonian faith and a life of Sodom, "having boarded the Ark of Noah" (1 Pet 3[:19]).[2]

For the Lord is in a short time going to exact punishment from this accursed and ungrateful world, by means of a final flood, not of water, but of fire which will devour all those who are sinful and know not to repent [cf. Luke 12:49; Heb 10:27]. May God our Father who is most merciful avert this evil from us, for his own sake through the agency of His most charitable Son Jesus Christ, who was crucified and resurrected for our sake, and is now exalted above all the angels and blessed for ever and ever. Amen.

Written at Cracow, Poland, in the 1574th
year after the birth of Jesus Christ.

Catechism and Confession of Faith
of the Congregation Gathered Throughout Poland,
in the Name of Jesus Christ Our Lord
Who Was Crucified and Resurrected

Q. Tell me, what things are especially necessary for the Christian man to know for salvation?

A. First and foremost is to know [A] the only true God, and [B] Jesus Christ whom He has sent ... and this is Eternal Life, [C] and the Holy Spirit, John 17[:3]; second, [to know] about our justification; third, discipline; fourth, prayer; fifth, baptism; sixth, the Lord's Supper.

[A] [On the only true God, the Father
on Jesus Christ, and on the Holy Spirit][3]

Q. What and what kind of God is it of whom Moses says [Deut 6:4]: "Hear, O Israel, the Lord your God is One"?

A. The One God is Spirit [John 4:24], Creator of heaven and earth [Gen 1:1], our Father [Genesis 32; Matthew 19], God of gods, Lord of lords, King of kings [Dan 2:47], "the one, only, wise God, immortal, [invisible]," [1 Tim 1:17]; Head, God, and Father of Christ, to whom the Son and all are subject, He however to none [1 Cor 11:3; 15:27 – 28]; our Life, in whom as our God, with our whole heart, we ought above all to fear, to love ardently as our Father, to hear, to adore, to invoke, and with our lips and our pious life constantly to confess. [The remainder of the section amplifies these ardent affirmations scripturally, a5 – b3 omitted.]

[B] On Jesus Christ

Q. What is Jesus Christ, the Son of God?

A. He is a man, our mediator with God, promised in the past to [our] fathers by the prophets, and born at last from the seed of David. God the Father made Him Lord and Christ; that is, a most perfect Prophet (*Propheta*), a most holy Priest (*Sacerdos*), a most invincible king (*Rex*). Through him [God] created a new world, restored, reconciled with Himself, and pacified all things, and granted Eternal Life to those chosen by Him. Thus let us believe Him, most high after God. Let us adore Him, let us invoke Him, let us hear Him, let us imitate Him in our own small measure, and in Him let us find rest for our souls.[4]

Q. Where does Holy Scripture call the Son of God a man?

A. 1 Tim 2[:5] "For there is one God and there is one mediator between God and men, the man Christ Jesus"; Rom 5[:12] "As sin came into the world through one man, . . . [:15] so much more is the grace of God, . . . which is of one man, Jesus Christ." 1 Cor 15[:20] "As by a man came death, by a man has come also the resurrection of the dead. For as in Adam all die, so also in Christ shall all be made alive. . . . [:45] The first man Adam became a living being; the second man, the last Adam, became a life-giving spirit." And the Lord Jesus said of Himself in John 8[:37] "'You seek to kill me, a man, because I speak the truth to you. . . . [:28] When you have lifted up the Son of a man, etc.'" Matt 16[:13] "'Who do men say that the Son of man is?' . . . [:16] 'You are the Christ, the Son of the living God.'" Dan 7[:9] "As I looked, thrones were placed and one that was Ancient of Days took his seat; . . . [:13] I looked then, and behold with the clouds of Heaven there came one like the Son of man, and to Him the Ancient of Days gave dominion and glory and kingdom, that all peoples, nations and languages should serve Him; His dominion is an everlasting dominion, which will not pass away, and His Kingdom one that shall not be destroyed."

Q. Where is He called the mediator of God and men?[5]

A. 1 Tim 2[:5] "There is one God and there is one mediator between God and men, the man Christ Jesus." John 14[:6] "Jesus Himself said 'I am the way, and the truth, and the life; no one comes to the Father, but by me!'" Eph 2[:18] "Through Jesus we have access in one spirit to the Father." Rom 8[:34] "It is Christ Jesus, who died and was raised from the dead who is at the right hand of God, interceding for us.'' 1 John 2[:1] ''My little children, . . . do not sin; but if any one does sin, we have an advocate with the Father, Jesus Christ the righteous; [:2] and He is the expiation for our sins, and not for ours only but also for the sins of the whole world.''

Q. To which fathers was Christ promised?

A. To Adam, Abraham, David, and all of Israel.[6]

Q. Where is He first promised to Adam?

A. Gen 3[:14] ''God said to the serpent. . . [:15] 'I will put enmity between your seed and her seed; he shall bruise your head, and you shall bruise his heel'.''

Q. Where are these things made clear?

A. 1 John 3[:8] ''He who commits sin is of the Devil; for the Devil has sinned from the beginning. The reason the Son of God appeared was to destroy the works of the Devil.'' Heb 2[:14] ''Jesus through death destroyed him who has the power of death, that is, the Devil, [:15] and deliver all those who through fear of death were subject to lifelong bondage.'' Rev 12[:7] ''Now war arose in heaven, Michael and his angels fighting against the dragon; and the dragon and his angels fought, [:8] but they were defeated and there was no longer any place for them in heaven. [:9] and the great dragon was thrown down, that ancient serpent, who is called the Devil and Satan, the Deceiver of the whole word—he was thrown down to earth, and his angels were thrown down with him. [:10] And I heard a loud voice in heaven, saying, 'Now the salvation and the power and the Kingdom of our God and the authority of His Christ have come.'''

Q. Then how was Christ promised to Abraham?

A. Gen 12; 18; 22; 26 [22:18] '''By your descendants shall all the nations of the earth bless themselves'.'' Gal 3[:16] ''Promises were made to Abraham and to his offspring (*semen*). It does not say 'and to his offsprings,' referring to many; but referring one, 'and to offspring,' which is Christ. . . . [:19] The Law was added because of transgressions, till the offspring should come. . . . [:24] [c1] The law was our custodian until Christ came.'' Gal 4[:4] ''When the time had fully come, God sent forth His Son, born under the Law, to redeem those who were under the Law.''

Q. Where was He promised to all Israel?

A. Deut 18[:15] ''Moses said, 'The Lord your God will raise up for you a prophet like me from among you, from your brethren—Him you shall heed . . . [:18] and I will put my words in His mouth, and He shall speak to them all that I command Him. [:19] And whoever will not give heed to my words which He shall speak in My name, I Myself will require it of him'.'' Acts 3[:20] ''God sent to you the one before promised for you, Jesus Christ. [:22] For Moses said to your fathers, 'Your Lord God from your brethren has raised up a prophet similar to me. . . .'' [:26] God having raised up His Son Jesus, sent Him to you first, to bless you in turning every one of you from wickedness.''

Q. But where was He promised to David?

A. 2 Sam 7[:12] ''The Lord of Hosts said 'When your days are fulfilled and you lie down with your fathers, I will raise up your seed after you, who shall come forth from your body, and I will establish his eternal Kingdom. . . .' [:14] 'I will be His father, and he shall be my Son.' Psalm 89 and Isa 7[:14] "Hear then, O House of David! Your Lord God will give you a sign. Behold, a virgin shall conceive and bear a son, and shall call his Son Emmanuel." 9[:6] "for to us a child is born, and to us a son is given . . . and his name will be called 'wonderful counselor, mighty God, everlasting father, Prince of peace.' [:7] Of the increase of His government and of peace there will be no end, upon the throne of David, and over His Kingdom He will sit for evermore, . . . the zeal of the Lord of Hosts will do this."

Q. In whom were all those things made complete?

A. In Jesus Christ our Lord, just as it was written in Matt 1[:1] "The book of the genealogy of Jesus Christ, the Son of David, the Son of Abraham.. . . . [:20] An angel of the Lord said, 'Joseph, son of David, do not fear to take Mary your wife, for that which is conceived in her is of the Holy Spirit. [:23] She will bear a son, and his name shall be called 'Emmanuel' (which means, God with us)." Luke 1 is even more expansive: [:26] "the angel Gabriel was sent from God to a virgin betrothed to a man whose name was Joseph, of the House of David. . . . [:31] And he said, 'Behold, you will conceive and bear a son, and you shall call his name Jesus. [:32] He will be great, and will be called the Son of the most High, and the Lord God will give to Him the throne of His father David, [:33] and He will reign over the House of Jacob forever, and of His Kingdom there will be no end.'" Luke 2[:1] "In those days a decree went out from Caesar Augustus that all the world should be enrolled . . . [:4] and Joseph also went to Judaea, to the city of David, which is called Bethlehem, because he was of the lineage of David . . . [:5] with Mary, his betrothed, who was with child. . . . [:7] And she gave birth to her first-born son. . . . [:10] And behold, an angel of the Lord said to shepherds, 'Be not afraid, I bring you good news of a great joy . . . [:11] to you is born this day in the City of David a Saviour, who is Christ the Lord'. . . . [:25] And Simeon, looking for the consolation of Israel . . . [:26] received a revelation from the Holy Spirit that he should not see death before he had seen the Lord's Christ. . . . [:27] And when the parents brought the child Jesus into the temple,. . . [:28] he took him up in his arms and blessed God and said. . . . [:30] 'Mine eyes have seen Thy salvation, . . . [:32] a light for revelation to the Gentiles, and for glory to Thy people Israel.'"

Q. Where is God said to have created this Jesus Lord and Christ?

A. Ps 45[:7] "Your God has anointed you with the oil of gladness above your fellows." Isa 61[:1] [and Luke 4:18] "The Spirit of the Lord is upon me because God has anointed me to bring good tidings to the poor." Luke 4 and Dan 9 [:26] "A most holy man, Messiah and Prince, will be anointed, and the Messiah will be killed. John 3[:34] "It is not by measure that God gives the Spirit to this Jesus." Acts 2[:36] "God has made Him both Lord and Christ, this Jesus whom you crucified." Acts 10[:38] "God anointed Jesus of Nazareth with the Holy Spirit and with power." And Jesus Himself said at Matt 28[:18] "All authority in heaven and on Earth has been given to me." Phil 2[:5] "Jesus Christ, [:6] though He was in the form of God, . . . [:7] took the form of a servant ... [:8] and being found in human form He humbled Himself and became obedient unto death, even death on a cross. [:9] Therefore God has highly exalted Him and bestowed on Him the name which is above every name, [:10] that at the name of Jesus every knee should bend, in Heaven and on Earth and under the Earth, [:11] and every tongue should confess that Jesus Christ is Lord, to the glory of God the Father.''

Q. Where is Jesus said to be a *Prophet* Most High?

A. A little above something was quoted from the Deuteronomy of Moses, chapter 18. But God Himself, the heavenly Father, proclaims concerning Jesus: Matthew 3 and 17 [Matt 17:5] '''This is My Son, with whom I am well pleased. Listen to Him.''' John 1[:1] ''In the beginning was the Word. ... [:17] No one has ever seen God; the only Son, who is in the bosom of the Father, He has made Him known.''[7] Matt 23[:10] ''You are not to be called masters, for you have one master, the Christ.'' Rev 19[:11] ''I saw a white horse, and He who sat upon it is called faithful and true. ... [:13] He is clad in a robe dipped in blood, and the name by which He is called is the Word of God.'' Heb 1[:1] ''In many and various ways God spoke of old to our fathers by the prophets; [:2] but in these last days He has spoken to us by a Son.''

Q. Where is the *priesthood* of Christ written about?

A. Ps 110[:4] ''The Lord has sworn and will not change His mind, ''You are a priest forever after the order of Melchizedek.''' Heb 4[:14] ''Since we have a High Priest who has passed through the heavens. ... [:16] Let us then with confidence draw near to the throne of grace.'' Heb 5[:7] ''In the days of His flesh, Christ offered up prayers and supplications, with loud cries and tears, to Him who was able to save Him from death, and He was heard for His [Godly] fear.'' Heb 9[:11] ''Christ, the High Priest of good things to come,. .. [:12] taking not the blood of goats and calves but His own blood, entered once for all into the holy place, thus securing an eternal redemption. ... [:14] Christ, who through the eternal Spirit offered Himself without blemish to God, will purify our conscience from dead[:11] ''Every works to serve the living God.'' Heb 10[:11] ''Every priest stands daily at his service, offering repeatedly the same sacrifices, which can never take away sins. [:12] But when this man has offered a single sacrifice for sins, He sat down at the right hand of God, . . . [:14] for by a single offering He has perfected for all time those who are sanctified.''[8]

Q. What is the benefit which derives from His priesthood?

A. It is most great, concerning which there is 1 Pet 2[:9] ''You are a chosen race, a royal priesthood, a holy nation, a people for God's possession.'' Rev 5[:5] The lion of the tribe of Judah, the root of David, has conquered. ... [to whom the twenty-four elders sang] [:9] 'Worthy art thou to take the scroll and to open its seals, for thou wast slain and by thy blood didst ransom men for God, and hast made them a kingdom and priests to our God.'''

Q. Where is it written concerning the Kingdom of Jesus Christ?[9]

A. Dan 2[:44] ''And in the days of those kings the God of Heaven will set up a Kingdom which shall never be destroyed, nor shall its sovereignty be left to another people. It shall break in pieces all these kingdoms and bring them to an end, and it will stand for ever.'' Ezek 34[:24] ''I, the Lord, will be their God, and my servant David shall be prince among them.'' 37[:24] ''My servant David shall be king over them.'' Zech 9[:9] '' 'Rejoice greatly, O daughter of Zion! . . . Lo, your king comes to you; triumphant and victorious is He, humble and riding an ass, on a colt the foal of an ass'.'' Matt 21[:7] ''The disciples brought the ass and put their garments on it, and sat Him thereon. . . . [:9] and the crowds that went before Him and that followed Him shouted 'Hosanna to the son of David!' Blessed be He who comes in the name of the Lord!'.'' Ps 2[:2] ''The kings of the earth set themselves, and the rulers take counsel together, against the Lord and His anointed. . . . [:6] 'I, [the Lord], set my king on Zion, my holy hill. . . . [:8] I will make the nations your heritage.' '' Acts 4[:27] ''There were gathered together against they holy child Jesus, whom thou didst anoint, both Herod and Pontius Pilate.'' John 1[:49] ''Nathaniel said to Jesus, 'Rabbi, you are the Son of God! You are the king of Israel.' '' John 18[:33] ''Pilate said to Jesus, 'Are you the king of the Jews?' Jesus answered, ''Do you say that I am a king? . . . [:36] 'My kingship is not of this world.'' John 19[:19] ''Jesus of Nazareth, the King of the Jews'.'' Col 1[:13] ''Give thanks to the Father, who has delivered us from the dominion of darkness and transferred us to the Kingdom of His beloved Son, in whom we have redemption, through His blood, and the forgiveness of sins.''

Q. But where is it written concerning this ''new creation'' of which you speak?

A. Isa 65[:17] ''For behold, I create new heavens and a new earth; . . . [:18] for behold, I create Jerusalem a rejoicing, and her people a joy.'' 66[:22] '' 'For as the new heaven and the new earth which I will make shall remain before me,' says the Lord.'' Ezek 36[:26] ''A new heart I will give you, . . . and I will take out the heart of stone.'' Ps 51[:10] ''Create in me a clean heart, O God, and put a new and right spirit within me.''

Q. Where is it written that all things have been created anew, restored, reconciled, and pacified by Jesus?[10]

A. John 1[:3] ''All things were made through Him.'' 2 Cor 5[:17] ''If any one is in Christ, he is a new creation; the old has passed away, behold the new has come. . . . [:18] God, through Christ, reconciled us to Himself; [:19] God was in Christ reconciling the world to Himself.'' Heb 2[:2] ''Through a Son God created the world.'' Col 1[:16] ''In Him all things were created, in heaven and on Earth, visible and invisible. . . . [:17] In Him all things hold together. [:18] He is the head of the body, the church; He is the beginning. . . . [:20] Through Him He reconciled to Himself all things, whether on Earth or in Heaven, making peace by the blood of His cross.'' Eph 1[:3] ''Blessed be the God and Father of our Lord Jesus Christ. . . . [:10] who in the fullness of time unites all things in Christ, things in Heaven and things on Earth.'' 2[:3] ''And we were by nature children of wrath. . . . [:5] but God made us alive together with Christ. . . . [:10] for we are His workmanship created in Christ Jesus for good works. . . . [:15] He created in Himself one new man in place of the two, so making peace, and reconciled us both. . . . [:18] For through Him we both have access in one spirit to the Father.'' Eph 4[:22] ''Put on the new nature, created after the likeness of God in true righteousness and holiness.''

Q. Where is it written that God shares eternal life with us through Jesus?

A. John 5[:26] '' 'As the Father has life in Himself, so he has granted the Son also to have life in Himself. . . . [:24] Truly, truly, I say to you, he who hears my word and believes Him who sent me, has eternal life; he does not come into judgment, but has passed from death to life.' '' John 6[:47] '' 'He who believes in me has eternal life'.'' John 10[:28] ''To my sheep I give eternal life.'' John 11[:25] '' 'He who believes in me shall never die.'' Col 3[:3] ''Your life is hid with Christ in God. [:4] When Christ who is our life appears, then you also will appear with Him in glory.'' 1 John 5[:11] ''God gave us eternal life, and this life is in His Son.''

Q. Where is it written that we, after God the Father who is most high, ought to believe in Christ Jesus the mediator?

A. Ps 2[:11] ''Kiss the Son, lest He be angry, and you perish in the way; blessed are all who take refuge in Him.'' Isa 28[:16] ''Behold, I am laying in Zion for a foundation a stone, a precious cornerstone. . . . 'He who believes will not be in haste','' [quoted with slight variation in the New Testament] Rom 9[:33] '' 'Behold I am laying in Zion a stone that will make men stumble, a rock that will make them fall; and he who believes in Him will not be put to shame';'' 1 Pet 2[:6] '' 'Behold, I am laying in Zion a stone, a cornerstone chosen and precious, and he who believes in Him will not be put to shame.' [:7] To you therefore who believe, He is precious, but for those who do not believe. . . . [:8] He is 'a stone that will make men stumble'.'' John 9[:35] ''Jesus said, 'Do you believe in the Son of God?' [:36] He answered, ''And who is He, Sir, that I may believe in Him?' [:37] Jesus said to him, ''You have seen Him, and it is He who speaks to you! [:38] He said, 'Lord, I believe; and he worshiped Him.'' 14[:1] ''Christ Himself said to His Disciples, 'Let not your hearts be troubled; you believe in God; believe also in me.' '' 6[:29] ''This is the work of God, that you believe in Him whom He has sent. . . . [:47] Truly, truly, I say to you, he who believes in me has eternal life'.'' 11[:25] '' 'I am the resurrection and the life; he who believes in me, though he die, yet shall he live, [:26] and whoever lives and believes in me shall never die'.''

Q. Why must one believe in Christ?

A. Matt 28[:18] ''Because all authority in heaven and on Earth has been given to Him.'' Heb 1[:3] ''He upholds the universe by his word of power.'' Matthew 12 and John 2 'He knows the thoughts of men.' Rev 2[:23] ''He searches mind and heart.'' Heb 7[:24] ''He holds the priesthood permanently, because He continues for ever. [25] He is able for all time to save those who draw near to God through Him, since He always lives to make intercession for them.''

Q. Where is it written concerning the adoration and invocation of Christ?

A. Dan 7[:9] ''As I looked, thrones were placed and one that was Ancient of Days took His seat. . . . [:13] I also saw come with the clouds of heaven one like a Son of Man, and He came to the Ancient of Days. [:14] And to Him was given dominion and glory and kingdom, that all peoples, nations and languages should serve Him; His dominion is an everlasting dominion, and His Kingdom one that shall not be destroyed.'' John 20[:28] ''Thomas said to Jesus, 'My Lord and my God!'' Luke 23[:42] '''Lord, remember me when you come into your Kingdom.''' Luke 24[:50] ''Jesus blessed the Apostles, and was carried up into Heaven. And they worshiped Him, and returned to Jerusalem with great joy.'' Acts 7[:55] ''Stephen, full of the Holy Spirit, gazed into Heaven and saw the glory of God, and Jesus standing at the right hand of God; [:56] and he said, 'Behold I see the Heavens opened, and the Son of Man standing at the right hand of God. . . . [:59] Lord Jesus, receive my spirit.' [:60] And he knelt down and cried with a loud voice, 'Lord do not hold this sin against them.''' And Paul always asks for ''grace and peace from God the Father and Lord Jesus Christ.'' Phil 2[:5] ''Jesus Christ, [:6] who, though He was in the form of God (that is, ''although He was the image of the invisible God'' Col 1[:15]; and ''He reflects the glory of God and bears the very stamp of His nature,'' Heb 1[:3]) did not count equality with God a thing to be grasped, [:7] but emptied Himself, taking the form of a servant, being born in the likeness of men. [:8] And being found in human form (that is, ''For our sake He made Him to be sin who knew no sin 2 Cor 5[:21], ''Having become a curse for us'' Gal 3[:13]), He humbled Himself and became obedient unto death, even death on a cross. [:9] Therefore God has highly exalted Him and bestowed on Him the name which is above every name, [:10] that at the name of Jesus every knee should bow, in Heaven and on Earth and under the Earth, [:11] and every tongue confess that Jesus Christ is Lord, to the glory of God the Father.'' Ps 72[:9] ''May those who dwell in the wilderness bow down before Him, and His enemies lick the dust. . . . [:11] May all kings fall down before Him, all nations serve Him!'' Heb 1[:6] '''Let all God's angels worship Him'.'' Rev 5[:11] ''I looked, and I heard . . . the voice of many angels . . . [:12] saying with a loud voice, 'Worthy is the lamb who was slain, to receive power and wealth and wisdom and might and honor and glory and blessing.' [:13] And I heard every creature in heaven and on Earth and under the Earth and in the sea, saying, 'To Him who sits upon the throne and to the lamb be blessing and honor and glory and might for ever and ever, Amen!' ''

Q. What is the most important thing that we shall ask of the Son of God?

A. What He Himself gave the commandment to be asked, and what His true worshipers once asked of Him, that is, that He might forgive our sins. Matt 9[:2] ''The Lord Himself said, 'Take heart, my son; your sins are forgiven. . . . [:6] The Son of man has authority to forgive sins'. . . . [:8] Although the crowds were surprised at this, they glorified God, who had given such authority to men.''

[We shall ask Him] ''to build His own Church, according to His promise Matthew 16; 'I will build my Church, to collect the sheep that are scattered into one fold' John 10; '' 'to gather the children of God.''' John 11[:52].

[We shall ask Him] ''to sanctify His Church, having cleansed Her by the washing of water with the Word'' Eph 5[:26].

[We shall ask Him] "'not to desert us but to be with us always, to the close of the age'" Matt 28[:20].

[We shall ask Him] "to send the promise of the Holy Spirit which He has received from the Father" John 15 and Acts 2[:33].

[We shall ask Him] "to give the Church suitable ministers of the Word" Eph 4:11, and "to give rest to all who labor and are heavy-laden" Matt 11[:28], [and] "'to increase our faith'" Luke 17[:5], [and] "'bless us and turn us from our wickedness'" Acts 3[:26], [and] "to reveal the gospel to us just as He revealed it to Paul" Gal 1[:12], [and] "to change our bodies on that day" Phil 3[:20], [and] "to help us in our temptation" Heb 2[:18], [and] "to heal us in our sickness" Matthew 9 and Acts 9, [and] "to raise up those who believe on the last day" John 6[:40], [and] "to forgive our enemies for their wrong and to take our spirit into His hands" Acts 7; and finally, "to give us the crown which does not languish on that day" 2 Tim [:8].

Q. Why have all these things been written concerning the Son of God and why must they be believed?

A. In order that we may hear Him teaching, the only Master (*Magister*) from God; and trusting in Him and imitating His steps, in proportion to His giving that we may find rest for our souls.

Q. Where is this commandment made?

A. Matt 17[:30] and 2 Pet 1[:17] "We heard the voice of God the Father, "This is my beloved Son, in whom I am well pleased.'" John 3[:16] "God so loved the world that He gave His only Son, that whoever believes in Him should not perish but have eternal life."

Q. Where has instruction been given on imitating the Son of God?

A. Christ the Lord Himself said, at Matt 11:28 "'Come to me, all who labor and are heavy-laden, and I will give you rest. [:29] Take my yoke upon you, and learn from me; for I am gentle and lowly in heart, and you will find rest for your souls.'" 1 Pet 2[:21] "Christ suffered for us, leaving us an example, that we should follow in His steps. [:22] He committed no sin. No guilt was found on His lips. [:23] When He was reviled, He did not revile in return; when He suffered, He did not threaten; but He trusted to Him who judges justly. [:24] He Himself bore our sins in His body on the tree, that we might die to sin and live to righteousness."

[C] On the Holy Spirit[11]

Q. Now discuss the Holy Spirit, because we are not able to cry, "Abba! Father!" without the Holy Spirit [Rom 8:15], and "He who does not have the Spirit of Christ does not belong to Him" Rom 8[:9].

A. "The Holy Spirit is the power of God, whose fullness God the Father gave to His only-begotten Son, our Lord, in order that we may take, as adopted sons, from His fullness' John 1:3. The identity and character of the Spirit of God will be apparent from His names, which follow.

1) He is "The Spirit of God" because He is from God, or rather, proceeds from God the Father. John 15[:26] "The Spirit of truth, who [necessarily: qui] proceeds from the Father." 1 Cor 2[:11] "We have received not the Spirit, which is from God."

2) He is called "The gift of God." Acts 2[:38] "'You shall receive the gift of the Holy Spirit.'" Eph 4[:8] "[When] He ascended on high, He gave gifts to men."

3) He is called "The finger of God." Exod 8[:19] "The magicians said to the Pharaoh, 'This is the finger of God.'" Luke 11[:20] "'It is by the finger of God that I cast out demons.'"

4) He is called the "energy" or "power" of God. Luke 1[:35] "'The Holy Spirit will come upon you, and the power of the Most High will overshadow you.'" Acts 1[:8] "'You shall receive the power of the Holy Spirit, who will come upon you.'" Acts 10[:38] "'God anointed Jesus of Nazareth with the Holy Spirit and with power.'"

5) He is called "fire". Matt 3[:11] "'He will baptize you with the Holy Spirit and with fire.'" Acts 2[:3] "There appeared to them tongues as of fire, distributed and resting on each one of them, and they were all filled with the Holy Spirit."

6) [He is called] "water." Isa 44[:3] "I will pour water on the thirsty land . . . and I will pour my Spirit upon your descendants." Ezek 36[:25] "'I will sprinkle clean water upon you; . . . [:26] a new heart I will give you, and a new spirit I will put within you.'" John 7[:38] "He who believes in me, as the scripture has said, 'out of his heart shall flow rivers of living water.' [:39] Now this He said about the Spirit, which those who believed in Him were to receive."

7) He is a seal and a guarantee of our inheritance. Eph 1:[13 – 14] "You who have believed in Him were sealed with the promised Holy Spirit, which is the guarantee of our inheritance." 4[:30] "Do not grieve the Holy Spirit of God, in whom you were sealed for the day of redemption." 2 Cor 1 and 2 Cor 5 [2 Cor 1:21 – 22] "But it is God who establishes us with you in Christ, and has commissioned us; He has put His seal upon us and given us His Spirit in our hearts as a guarantee."

8) He is said to be "the anointing of God." Ps 45[:7] "Your God has anointed you with the oil of gladness above your fellows." 1 John 2[:27] "The anointing which you received from Him abides in you . . . and His anointing teaches you about everything."

9) He is called "our counselor and teacher." John 14[:16] "'I will pray the Father, and He will give you another counselor, to be with you for ever. . . . [:26] The counselor, the Holy Spirit, whom the Father will send in my name, He will teach you all things, and bring to your remembrance all that I have said to you.'" 16[:7, 13] "'If I do not go away, the counselor will not come to you; but if I go, I will send Him to you. . . . When the Spirit of truth comes, He will guide you into all the truth.'"

Q. Why then does Saint Paul call Him "the Spirit of Christ" and "the Spirit of the Son"?

A. Because God gave to His Son the fulness of the Holy Spirit to distribute to those who were chosen. John 1[:14] "We have beheld His glory, glory as of the only Son from the Father . . . full of grace and truth. . . . [:16] And from His fullness have we all received. John 3[:34] "'It was not by measure that He gave the Spirit to Him!'" Col 1[:19] "In Him all the fulness of God was pleased to dwell." Col 2[:3, 9] "In Christ are hid all the treasures of wisdom and knowledge. . . . In Him the whole fulness of deity lives bodily."

Q. Does there exist in scripture a commandment and an example for worshiping and invoking the Holy Spirit?

A. In neither the old nor new covenant is there any mention of this matter. But Christ gives the commandment that God the Father is to be asked for the Holy Spirit: Luke 11[:13] "'The Heavenly Father will give the Holy Spirit to those who ask Him. He likewise orders that God is to be worshiped in spirit: John 4[:24] "'God is spirit, and those who worship Him must worship in spirit and in truth. . . . [:23] For such the Father seeks to worship Him.'" Rom 8[:11] "The Spirit of God dwells in you. . . . [:15] Through whom we cry, "Abba! Father!" 1 Cor 12[:3] "And no one can say 'Jesus is Lord,' except by the Holy Spirit."

II On Our Justification Before God[12]

Q. What is justification?

A. It is the forgiveness in living faith of all our past trespasses by the pure grace of God, through the agency of our Lord Jesus Christ, regardless of our works and merits; [it is also] the most certain expectation of eternal life, and a true, not artificial, correction of our life by the aid of the Spirit of God, to the glory of God the Father and to the edification of our neighbors.

Q. Where has it been written concerning our sin?

A. Gen 6[:5] "The Lord saw the wickedness of men on Earth, and that the imagination of the thoughts of his heart was only evil continually." 8[:21] "'The imagination of man's heart is evil from his youth.'" Job 15[:14] "What is man that he can be clean? Or that he is born of a woman, that he can be righteous? [:15] Behold, God puts no trust in His holy ones, and the heavens are not clean in His sight, [:16] how much less one who is abominable and corrupt, a man who drinks iniquity like water!" Ps 14[:2] "The Lord looks down from Heaven upon the children of men, to see if there are any who act wisely, that seek after God. [:3] They have all gone astray, they are all alike corrupt; there is none that does good, no, not one." Ps 51[:5] "Behold, I was brought forth in iniquity, and in sin did my mother conceive me." Ps 130[:3] "If Thou, O Lord, shouldst mark iniquities, Lord, who could stand?" Ps 143[:2] "Enter not into judgment with thy servant; for no man living is righteous before Thee." Isa 53[:6] "All we like sheep have gone astray; we have turned every one to his own way." Rom 3[:23] "All have sinned and fall short of the glory of God. . . .

[:19] So that every mouth may be stopped, and the whole world may be held accountable to God. [:20] For no human being will be justified in his sight by works of the law since through the law comes knowledge of sin." Rom 5[:12] "Sin came into the world through one man and death through sin, and so death spread to all men."[13] Eph 2[:3] "We were all by nature children of wrath, like the rest of mankind." 1 John 1[:8] "If we say we have no sin, we deceive ourselves, and the truth is not in us.... [10] If we say we have not sinned, we make Him a liar, and His word is not in us." Rom 7[:7] "If it had not been for the Law, I should not have known sin. I should not have known what it is to covet if the law had not said, "You shall not covet".... [:12] So the law is holy, and the commandment is holy and just and good.... [:14] The Law is spiritual, but I am carnal, sold under sin. [:15] I do not understand my own actions. For I do not do what I want, but I do the very thing I hate.... [:17] Sin dwells within me: for I know that nothing good dwells within me, that is, in my flesh.... [:21] I find it to be a law that when I want to do right, evil lies close at hand. [:22] For I delight in the law of God, in my inmost self, [:23] but I see in my members another law at war with the law of my mind and making me captive to the law of sin which dwells in my members. [:24] Wretched man that I am! Who will deliver me from this body of death? [:25] Thanks be to God through Jesus Christ our Lord!"

Q. Where has it been written concerning the grace of God and the forgiveness of our sins?

A. Num 14[:18] "The Lord is slow to anger, and abounding in steadfast love, forgiving iniquity and transgression." Ps 103[:8] "The Lord is merciful and gracious, slow to anger and abounding in steadfast love. [:9] He will not always chide, nor will He keep His anger forever. [:10] He does not deal with us according to our sins, nor requite us according to our iniquities. [:11] For as the heavens are high above the Earth, ... [:12] as far as the East is from the West, so far does He remove our transgressions from us. [:13] As a father pities his children, so the Lord pities those who fear Him. [:14] For He knows our frame; He remembers that we are dust." Isa 43[:11] "I, I am the Lord, and besides me there is no Saviour.... [:25] I, I am He who blots out your transgressions for my own sake, and I will not remember your sins. [:26] Put me in remembrance, let us argue together; set forth your case, that you may be proved right." Isa 42[:1] "Behold my servant, ... my chosen, in whom my soul delights; I have put my spirit upon Him, He will bring forth justice to the nations.... [:13] A bruised reed He will not break, and a dimly burning wick He will not quench; He will faithfully bring forth justice." Isa 49[:3] "You are my servant Israel.... [:6] It is too light a thing that you should be my servant to raise up the tribes of Jacob.... I have given you as a light to the nations, that my salvation may reach to the end of the earth." Isa 53[:11] "By His knowledge shall the righteous One, my servant, make many to be accounted righteous. [:5] He was wounded by our transgressions.... [:6] The Lord has laid on Him the iniquity of us all .... [:10] He made His soul an offering for sin.... [:12] and made intercession for the transgressors." Jer 31[:34] "The

Lord says 'I will forgive their iniquity, and I will remember their sin no more.'" 23[:5] "Behold, the days are coming, says the Lord, when I will raise up for David a righteous branch. . . . [:6] In His day Judah will be saved. . . . And this is the name by which He will be called: "The Lord is our righteousness." Ezek 18[:21] "If a wicked man turns away from all his sins which he has committed and keeps all my statutes and does what is lawful and right, he shall surely live; he shall not die. [:22] None of the transgressions which he has committed shall be remembered against him. . . . [:23] Have I any pleasure in the death of the wicked,' says the Lord God, 'and not rather that he should turn from his way and live?'" 37[:23] "I will save them from all the backslidings in which they have sinned, and will cleanse them; and they shall be my people, and I will be their God. [:24] My servant David shall be king over them; and they shall all have one shepherd. They shall follow my ordinances and be careful to observe my statutes. . . . [:25] David my servant shall be their prince forever." Rom 3[:23] "All have sinned and fall short of the glory of God. [:24] But they are justified by His grace as a gift, through the redemption which is in Jesus Christ, [:25] whom God put forward as an expiation by His blood, to be received by faith. This was to show God's righteousness, because . . . He had passed over former sins. . . . [:28] A man is justified by faith apart from works of Law." 5[:1] "Since we are justified by faith, we have peace with God through our Lord Jesus Christ." 1 Cor 1[:30] "Christ Jesus, whom God made our wisdom, our righteousness and sanctification and redemption." Eph 2[:4] "God, who is rich in mercy, out of the great love with which He loved us, [:5] even when we were dead through our trespasses, made us alive together with Christ. . . . [:8] by whose grace you have been saved by faith; and this is not your own doing, it is the gift of God [:9] not because of works, lest any man should boast." Tit 3[:3] "We ourselves were once foolish, disobedient, led astray, slaves to various passions and pleasures, passing our days in malice and envy, hated by men and hating one another; [:4] but when the goodness and loving kindness of God our Saviour appeared, [:5] He saved us, not because of deeds done by us in righteousness, but in virtue of His own mercy, by the washing of regeneration and renewal in the Holy Spirit, [:6] which He poured out upon us richly through Jesus Christ our Saviour, so that we might be justified by His grace and become heirs in hope of eternal life." 1 John 1[:9] "If we confess our sins, he is faithful and just, and will forgive our sins and cleanse us from all unrighteousness. . . . [:7] And the blood of Jesus His Son cleanses us from all sin." 2[:1] "My little children, . . . do not sin; but if any one does sin, we have an advocate with the Father, Jesus Christ the righteous; [:2] and He is the expiation for our sins, . . . and for the sins of the whole world."

Q. Where has instruction been given concerning the correction of our life?

A. John the Baptist said at Matt 3[:8] "Bear fruit that befits repentance. . . . [:10] Even now the axe is laid to the root of the trees; every tree therefore that does not bear good fruit is cut down and thrown into the fire." Matt 5 Jesus said to his disciples [:16] "Let your light so shine before men, that they may see your good works and give glory to your Father who is in Heaven. . . . [:17] I have come not to abolish the Law but to complete it. . . . [:20] Unless your righteousness exceeds that of the scribes and Pharisees, you will not enter the Kingdom of Heaven.''

1) "[:21] You have heard that it was said to the men of old, 'You shall not kill; and whoever kills shall be liable to judgment.' [:22] But I say to you that every one who is angry with his brother shall be liable to judgment; . . . and whoever says, 'you fool!' shall be liable to the Gehenna of fire.''

2) [:27] "You have heard that it was said to the men of old, 'You shall not commit adultery.' [:28] But I say to you that every one who looks at a woman lustfully has already committed adultery with her in his heart.''

3) [:33] "You have heard that it was said to the men of old, 'You shall not swear falsely, but shall perform to the Lord what you have sworn.' [:34] But I say to you, do not swear at all, either by Heaven . . . [:35] or by the Earth. . . . [:37] Let what you say be simply 'yes' or 'no'; anything more than this comes from evil.''

4) [:38] "You have heard that it was said, 'an eye for an eye and a tooth for a tooth.' [:39] But I say to you, do not resist one who is evil. But if any one strikes you on the right cheek, turn to him the other also; [:40] and if any one would sue you and take your coat, let him have your cloak as well; [:41] and if anyone forces you to go one mile, go with him two miles. . . . [:44] Love our enemies, and [Luke 6:28] bless those who curse you. . . . [:27] Do good to those who hate you . . . [:28] and pray for those who abuse you.'' Gal 5[:16] "Walk by the Spirit, and do not gratify the desires of the flesh. . . . [:19] Now the works of the flesh are plain: immorality, impurity, licentiousness, [:20] idolatry, sorcery, enmity, strife, jealousy, anger, selfishness, dissension, party spirit, [:21] envy, murder, drunkenness, carousing, and the like. I warn you . . . that those who do such things shall not inherit the Kingdom of God. [:22] But the fruit of the spirit is love, joy, peace, patience, kindness, goodness, faithfulness, [:23] gentleness, self-control; against such things is no law. [:24] And those who belong to Christ have crucified the flesh with its passions and desires.'' Eph 2[:10] "We are the workmanship of God, created in Christ Jesus for good works, which God prepared beforehand, that we should walk in them.'' 4 and 5 [4:17] "This I testify in the Lord, that you must no longer live as the Gentiles do. . . . [:22] Put off your old nature which belongs to your former manner of life. . . . [:24] And put on the new nature, created after the likeness of God in true righteousness and holiness.''

1) [:25] Therefore, putting away falsehood, let every one speak the truth with his neighbor. . . .

2) [:26] If you be angry, do not sin. . . . [:31] Let all bitterness and wrath and anger and clamor and slander be put away from you, with all malice,

[:32] and be kind to one another, tenderhearted, forgiving one another, as God in Christ forgave you. . . .

3) [:28] Let the thief no longer steal, but rather let him labor, doing honest work with his hands. . . .

4) [:29] Let no evil talk come out of your mouths, but only such as is good for edifying. . . . [5:4] Let there be no filthiness, nor silly talk, nor levity. . . .

5) [5:3] Impurity or covetousness must not even be named among you, as is fitting among saints. . . .

6) [5:18] Do not get drunk with wine, for that is debauchery; but be filled with the Spirit. . . . [5:5] No immoral or impure man, or one who is covetous (that is, an idolater) has any inheritance in the Kingdom of Christ and of God. [:6] Let no one deceive you with empty words, for it is because of these things that the wrath of God comes upon the sons of disobedience. [:7] Therefore do not associate with them, [:8] for once you were darkness, but now you are light in the Lord.

7) Tit 2[:11] "The grace of God has appeared for the salvation of all men, [:12] training us to renounce irreligion and worldly passions, and to live sober, upright, and godly lives in this world, . . . [:14] as a people of His own who are zealous for good deeds." 1 Pet 1[:15] "As He who called you is holy, be holy yourselves in all your conduct. . . . [:18] You know that you were ransomed from the futile ways inherited from your fathers, not with perishable things such as silver or gold, [:19] but with the precious blood of Christ, like that of a lamb without blemish or spot." 2[:21] Christ suffered for us, leaving us an example, that we should follow in His steps. . . . [:24] He Himself bore our sins in His body on the tree, that we might die to sin and live to righteousness." 1 John 3[:1] "Beloved, what love the Father has given us, that we should be called children of God. . . . [:3] and every one who thus hopes in Him purifies himself as He is pure. . . . [:7] Little children, let no one deceive you. He who does right is righteous, as He is righteous. [:8] He who commits sin is of the devil. . . . the reason the Son of God appeared was to destroy the works of the devil." Jas 2[:14] "What does it profit, my brethren, if a man says he has faith but has not works? Can his faith save him . . . ? [:19] Even the demons believe— and shudder. . . . [:26] For as the body apart from the spirit is dead, so faith apart from works is dead."

III On Ecclesiastical Discipline[14]

Q. What is discipline?

A. It is the frequent recital of the duty (*officium*) of individuals, and the duty of those sinning against God or a neighbor, first in private, then also in public, before the whole congregation having been called together, and finally the duty of those stubborn men who are alienated from the communion of the holy, in order that they, one filled with shame, may change, or, if they are unwilling to do this, be damned for ever [Matt 18:15–18].

Q. What is the office of the bishop (*episcopus*)?[15]

A. 1 Tim 3[:1] "If any one aspires to the office of bishop, he desires a noble task. [:2] Now a bishop must be above reproach, temperate, sensible, dignified, hospitable, an apt teacher, [:3] no drunkard, not violent but gentle, not quarrelsome, and no lover of money. [:4] He must manage his own household well, keeping his children submissive and respectful in every way; [:5] for if a man does not know how to manage his own household, how can he care for God's Church? [:6] He must not be a recent convert, or he may be puffed up with conceit and fall into the condemnation of the slanderer; [:7] moreover he must be well thought of by outsiders, or he may fall into reproach and the snare of the devil."

Q. Where is the duty of deacons (*diaconi*) described?

A. Acts 6[:1] "Now in those days when the disciples were increasing in number, the Hellenists murmured against the Hebrews because their widows were neglected in the daily distribution. [:2] And the Twelve summoned the body of the disciples and said, 'It is not right that we should give up preaching the Word of God to serve tables. [:3] Therefore, Brethren, pick out from among you seven men of good repute, full of the spirit and of wisdom, whom we may appoint to this duty. [:4] But we will devote ourselves to prayer and to the ministry of the Word.' [:5] And what they said pleased the whole multitude. . . . [:6] They set the men whom they chose before the Apostles, and they prayed and laid their hands upon them." 1 Tim 3[:8] "Deacons must be serious, not double-tongued, not addicted to much wine, not greedy for gain; [:9] they must hold the mystery of the faith. . . . [:10] And let them also be tested first; then if they prove themselves blameless let them serve as deacons. [:11] The women likewise must be serious, no slanderers, but temperate, faithful in all things. [:12] Let deacons be married only once, and let them manage their children and their households well."

Q. Where is the office of elders (*seniores*) described?[16]

A. 1 Tim 5[:17] "Let the elders who rule well be considered worthy of a double honor, especially those who labor in preaching and teaching; [:18] for the Scripture says 'You shall not muzzle an ox when it is treading out the grain,' and 'the laborer deserves his wages.' [:19] Never admit any charge against an order except on the evidence of two or three witnesses. [:20] As for those who persist in sin, rebuke them in the presence of all, so that the rest may stand in fear."

Q. Where has instruction been given concerning widows?[17]

A. 1 Tim 5[:5] "She who is a real widow, and is left all alone, has set her hope on God and continuous in supplications and prayers night and day. . . . [:9] let no one be enrolled as a widow who is under sixty years of age, or has been married more than once; [:10] and she must be well attested for her good deeds, whether she has brought up children, shown hospitality, washed the feet of the saints, received the afflicted, and devoted herself to doing good in every way.... [:14] I would have younger widows marry, bear children, rule their households, and give the enemy no occasion to revile us.... [:16] But if any believing woman has relatives who are widows, let her assist them; let the Church not be burdened, so that it may assist those who are real widows.''

Q. Where has the commandment been made concerning husbands and wives?

A. Eph 5[:22] ''Wives, be subject to your husbands, as to the Lord. [:23] For the husband is the head of the wife as Christ is the head of the Church, ... [:24] As the church is subject to Christ, so let wives also be subject in every-thing to their husbands. [:25] Husbands, love your wives, as Christ loved the Church and gave Himself up for her .... [:28] Even so husbands should love their wives as their own bodies.... [:29] For no man ever hates his own flesh, but nourishes it and cherishes it.... [:31] 'For this reason a man shall leave his father and mother and be joined to his wife, and the two shall become one....' [:33] However, let each one of you love his wife as himself, and let the wife see that she respects her husband.'' 1 Tim 2[:8] ''I desire then that in every place the men should pray, lifting holy hands without anger or quarreling; [:9] also that women should adorn themselves modestly and sensibly in seemly apparel, not with braided hair, or gold or pearls or costly attire [:10] but by good deeds, as befits women who profess religion. [:11] Let a woman learn in silence with all submissiveness. [:12] I permit no woman to teach or to have authority over men; she is to keep silent. [:13] For Adam was formed first, then Eve. [;14] And Adam was not deceived, but the woman was deceived and became a transgressor. [:15] Yet woman will be saved through bearing children, if she continues in faith and love and holiness, with modesty.''

Q. Where are old men and women, girls and boys taught their office?

A. Tit 2[:1] ''Teach what befits sound doctrine. [:2] Bid the older men be temperate, serious, sensible, sound in faith, in love, and in steadfastness. [:3] Bid the older women likewise to be reverent in behavior, not to be slanderers or slaves to drink; they are to teach what is good, [:4] and so train the young women to love their husbands and children, to be sensible, chaste, domestic, kind, and submissive to their husbands that the Word of God may not be discredited. [:6] Likewise urge the younger men to control themselves.''

Q. Where has a statement been made concerning the office of children and parents?

A. Eph 6[:1] ''Children, obey your parents in the Lord, for this is right. [:2] 'Honor your father and mother; (this is the first commandment with a promise), [:3] 'that it may be well with you, and that you may live long on the earth.' [:4] Fathers, do not provoke your children to anger, but bring them up in the disci-pline and instruction of the Lord.''

Q. Where have commandments been given concerning servants and mas-ters?

A. Eph 6 says also [:5] ''Slaves, be obedient to those who are your earthly masters, with fear and trembling, in singleness of heart; ... [:6] not in the way of eyeservice, as men-pleasers, but as servants of Christ, doing the will of God from the heart, [:7] rendering service with a good will as to the Lord and not to men, [:8] knowing that whatever good any one does, he will receive the same again from the Lord, whether he is a slave or free. [:9] Masters, do the same to them, and forbear threatening, knowing that He who is both their master and yours is in Heaven, and that there is no partiality with Him.''

Q. And how ought those who are subjects behave toward the magistracy (*magistratus*)?[18]

A. Rom 13[:1] ''Let every person be subject to the governing authorities. For there is no authority except from God, and those that exist have been instituted by God. [:2] Therefore he who resists the authorities resists what God has appointed, and those who resist will incur judgment. [:3] For rulers are not a terror to good conduct, but to bad. Would you have fear of him who is in authority? Then do what is good, and you will receive his approval, [:4] for he is God's servant for your good. But if you do wrong, be afraid, for he does not bear the sword in vain; he is the servant of God to execute his wrath on the wrongdoer. [:5] Therefore one must be subject, not only to avoid God's wrath but also for the sake of conscience. . . . [:7] Pay all of them their due, revenues to whom revenue is due, respect to whom respect is due, honor to whom honor is due.''

Q. Where are commandments laid down concerning wives, widows, and unmarried girls?

A. 1 Cor 7. Read the entire chapter.

Q. Where is instruction given concerning the office of the rich as regards those who are truly poor?

A. Luke 6. ''Jesus said, [:30] 'Give to every one who begs from you. . . . [:35] and lend, expecting nothing in return; and your reward will be great. . . . [:36] Be merciful, even as your Father is merciful. . . . [:38] Give, and it will be given to you.'' And Matt 25[:34] ''Come, O blessed of my Father, inherit the Kingdom prepared for you; . . . [:35] for I was hungry and you gave me food, I was thirsty and you gave me drink, I was a stranger and you welcomed me, [:36] I was naked and you clothed me, I was sick and you visited me, I was in prison and you came to me. . . . [:40] Truly, I say to you, as you did it to one of the least of these my brethren, you did it to me.'' 1 Cor 16[:1] ''Now concerning the contribution for the saints; as I directed the churches [of Galatia] so you also are to do. [:2] On the first day of every week, each of you is to put something aside and store it up.'' 2 Cor 9[:6] ''He who sows sparingly will also reap sparingly, and he who sows bountifully will also reap bountifully. [:9] Each one must do as he has made up his mind, not reluctantly or under compulsion, for God loves a cheerful giver.'' 1 Tim 6[:17] ''As for the rich in this world, charge them not to be haughty, nor to set their hopes on uncertain riches but on the living God. . . . [:18] They are to do good, to be rich in good deeds, liberal and generous, [:19] thus laying up for themselves a good foundation for the future, so that they may take hold of the life which is life indeed.'' Jas 1[:25, 27]

''Religion that is pure and undefiled before God and the Father is this: to visit orphans and widows in their affliction, and to keep oneself unstained from the world.''

Q. Finally, how ought individuals behave toward their neighbor?

A. Rom 13[8] ''Owe no one anything, except to love one another; for he who loves his neighbor has fulfilled the law. [:9] The commandments, 'You shall not commit adultery, you shall not kill, you shall not steal, you shall not covet' and any other commandment, are summed up in this sentence, 'You shall love your neighbor as yourself [Lev 19:18].' [:10] Love does no wrong to a neighbor; therefore love is the fulfilling of the law.''

Q. What must be done if one does not behave according to the rules which have been ordained?

A. This must be done, what Christ the Lord has ordered: Matt 18[:15] ''If your brother sins against you, go and tell him his fault, between you and him alone. If he listens to you, you have gained your brother. [:16] But if he does not listen, take one or two others along with you, that every word may be confirmed by the evidence of two or three witnesses. [:17] If he refuses to listen to them, tell it to the church; and if he refuses to listen to the church, let him be to you as a Gentile and a tax collector. [:18] Truly, I say to you, whatever you bind on Earth shall be bound in heaven, and whatever you loose on Earth shall be loosed in Heaven. [:19] Again I say to you, if two of you agree on Earth about anything they ask, it will be done for them by my Father in Heaven. [:20] For where two or three are gathered in my name, there am I in the midst of them. [:21] Then Peter said to Him, 'Lord, how often shall my brother sin against me, and I forgive him? As many as seven times?' [:22] Jesus said to him, 'I do not say to you seven times, but seventy times seven.'''

Q. Where have His disciples carried out this commandment of the Lord?

A. 1 Cor 5[:1][19] ''It is actually reported that there is immorality among you. . . . [:2] And you are arrogant! Ought you not rather to mourn? Let him who has done this be removed from among you. . . . [:3] I have already pronounced judgment, [:4] 'So that when you are assembled in the name of our Lord Jesus Christ, . . . with the power of our Lord Jesus Christ, [:5] this man who has done such a thing is to be delivered to Satan for the destruction of the flesh, that his spirit may be saved in the day of the Lord Jesus. . . . [:11] If any one bears the name of brother, if he is guilty of immorality or greed, or is an idolater, reviler, drunkard, or robber—do not even eat with such a one.'' 1 Cor 6[:9] ''Do you not know that the unrighteous will not inherit the Kingdom of God? Do not be deceived; neither the immoral, nor idolaters, nor adulterers, nor homosexuals, [:10] nor thieves, nor the greedy, nor drunkards, nor revilers, nor robbers will inherit the Kingdom of God.''

Q. What is the destruction of the flesh?

A. It is the same as the death of the old man. Rom 6[:6] ''Our old self was crucified with Christ, so that the sinful body might be destroyed, and we might no longer be enslaved to sin.'' Col 3[:5] ''Put to death what is earthly in you:

immorality, impurity, passion, evil desire, and covetousness, which is idolatry. [:6] On account of these the wrath of God is coming upon the sons of disobedience.''

Q. Are there not more examples pertaining to this matter?[20]

A. 1 Tim 1[:19] ''Certain persons have made shipwreck of their faith, among them Hymenaeus and Alexander, whom I have delivered to Satan so that they may learn not to blaspheme.'' Tit 3[:10] ''As for a man who is factious, after admonishing him once or twice, have nothing more to do with him.'' 2 John 1[:10] ''If any one comes to you and does not bring this doctrine, do not receive him into the house or give him any greeting; [:11] for he who greets him shares his wicked work.'' 2 Thess 3[:6] ''Now we command you, brethren, in the name of our Lord Jesus Christ, that you keep away from any brother who is living in idleness and not in accord with the tradition that you received from us. . . . [:11] For we hear that some of you are living in idleness, mere busybodies, not doing any work. [:12] Now such persons we command and exhort in the Lord Jesus Christ to do their work in quietness and to earn their own living. . . . [:10] [But] if any one will not work, let him not eat.''

Q. But what ought to be done, if a fallen brother should change his ways?

A. The church ought to do what the Lord Himself did, who rejoiced after finding His sheep which was lost [Matt 18:12−14; Luke 15:4−7], and what the father did after his prodigal son returned and found welcome [Luke 15:11−32].

Q. Where is this commandment?

A. 2 Cor 2[:6] ''For such a one this punishment by the majority is enough; [:7] so you should rather turn to forgive and comfort him, or he may be overwhelmed by excessive sorrow, [:8] so I beg you to reaffirm your love for him.''

Q. What must be thought of a man if right up to the time of death he does not come to his senses?

A. [Matt 26:24] ''It would have been better for that man if he had not been born,'' for to him will apply that commandment stated above in Matt 25[:41] ''He will not inherit the Kingdom of heaven, but he will be sent into the eternal fire, . . . [:30] where there will be weeping and gnashing of teeth.''

IV On Prayer[21]

Q. What is prayer?

A. It is the serious and ardent conversation of a faithful believer, when he or a neighbor is in need, with God the Father. That is to say, prayer is either a giving of thanks for benefits received in the past, or a plea for help in time of distress, with the full assurance of faith that God wishes to help (as the Father is most loving of us), that He knows how to help (as He alone is wise), and that He is able to help (as the Lord is all-powerful).

Q. Who has taught us this?

A. ''We by nature do not know how to pray as we ought'' Rom 8[:26]. But God Himself, our Father, and His beloved Son, our Lord Jesus Christ commanded this to us, promising that we will surely be heard and made free.

Q. Where has this been written?

A. Ps 50 "Says the God of gods [:14] 'Offer to God a sacrifice of thanksgiving; . . . and call upon me in the day of trouble. I will deliver you, and you shall glorify me.'" And this Son of God says in Matt 7 [:7] "Ask, and it will be given you; seek and you will find; knock, and it will be opened to you." Ps 145[:18] "The Lord is near to all who call upon Him, . . . in truth [:19] He fulfills the desire of all who fear Him." Isa 65[:24] "Before they call I will answer, while they are yet speaking I will hear." Ecclesiastes 35 "The prayer of a man in distress passes through the clouds."

Q. Yet because "The one God is a terrible God" (Deut 7:2)[22] and "He dwells in unapproachable light" (1 Tim 6[:15]), how shall we approach Him?

A. Through the one mediator, the man Jesus Christ, our Lord, 1 Tim 2[:5]. And the Lord Himself says at John 14 and 10 "I am the way [14:6] and the door [10:9], no one comes to the Father but by me. [14:6]." John 16[:23] "If you ask anything of the Father, He will give it to you in my name."

Q. What is "to pray in the name of Jesus?"

A. Our Lord Himself explains at John 15[:7] "If you abide in me, and my words abide in you, ask whatever what you will, and it shall be done for you." Heb 10[:19] "Since we have confidence to enter the sanctuary by the blood of Jesus, [:20] by the . . . way which he opened for us, . . . [:22] let us draw near with a true heart in full assurance of faith, with our hearts sprinkled clean from an evil conscience and our bodies washed with pure water. [:23] Let us hold fast the confession of our hope, . . . for He who promised is faithful; [:24] and let us consider how to stir up one another to love and good works, [:25] not neglecting to meet together, . . . but encouraging one another."

Q. Therefore "God does not listen to sinners, but if any one is a worshipper of God and does His will, God listens to him" John 9[:31]?

A. Most certainly. For so it is written in Ps 50[:16]: "to the wicked God says 'What right have you to recite my statutes, or take my covenant on your lips? [:17] For you hate discipline, and you cast my words behind you. [:18] If you see a thief, you are a friend of his; and you keep company with adulterers. . . . [:19] and your tongue frames deceit.'"

Q. Therefore what qualities does one especially need for prayer?

Q. Faith in God, and love toward [one's] neighbor.

Q. Where is instruction given concerning faith?

Q. Heb 11[:6] "Whoever would draw near to God must believe that He exists. . . . and without faith it is impossible to please Him." Jas 1[:5] "If any of you lacks wisdom, let him ask God . . . and it will be given him. [:6] But let him ask in faith, with no doubting, for he who doubts. . . . [:8] must not suppose that, . . . he will receive anything from the Lord."

Q. Where is instruction given on charity towards one's neighbor?

A. Matt 5[:23] "If you are offering your gift at the altar, and there remember that your brother has something against you, [:24] leave your gift there before the altar and go; first be reconciled to your brother, and then come and offer your gift.'' Isa 1[:15] ''Even though you make many prayers, I will not listen; your hands are full of blood.''

Q. How must we feel about those who are ''weak'' and ''frail''?

A. The Lord does not reject their prayers if they do not indulge in a sin in violation of their conscience, but having fallen, grieve in earnest and raise themselves up again. Thus the case of the taxpayer in Luke 18 and that of Cornelius in Acts 10.

Q. What about the place and time of prayer?

A. John 4[:21] ''Neither on this mountain nor in Jerusalem. . . . [:23] but in spirit and in truth . . . will true worshipers worship the Father.'' 1 Tim 2[:8] ''I desire that in every place the man should pray.'' Concerning the time, the Lord says: Luke 18[:1] ''They ought always to pray and not lose heart.'' 1 Thess 5[:17] ''Pray constantly, [:18] give thanks in all circumstances.''

Q. For how long must one pray?

A. Although the Lord prohibits at Matt 6[:7] ''heaping up empty phrases,'' yet if the need be pressing and the heart is in agony it is permitted to pray more urgently, as the Lord Himself does at Luke 22[:44].

Q. What things ought to be asked of God in prayer?

A. Good things which pertain to both the spirit and the flesh. These things are spiritual: the forgiveness of sins, the gift of the Holy Spirit, increases in the glory of God, good order in the church, a good conscience, a correction of [one's] life, and eternal life. These things pertain to the flesh: peace in the state, good magistrates, a fair amount of money, success in crops, food, friendship, freedom from enemies. We ought to ask for the spiritual things without using a condition: John 12[:28] '' 'Father, glorify Thy name.' Then a voice came from heaven, 'I have glorified it, and I will glorify it again.' '' But the things of the flesh must be sought conditionally, [with the formula] ''if God be willing''. As David says: 2 Sam 15[:25] ''If I find favor in the eyes of the Lord, He will bring me back. . . . [:26] But if He says, 'I have no pleasure in you,' . . . let Him do to me what seems good to Him.'' Dan 3[:17] ''Our God . . . is able to deliver us from the burning fiery furnace; . . . [:18] but if not, be it known to you . . . that we will not serve your gods.'' Matt 26[:39] ''My Father, if it be possible, let this cup pass from me; nevertheless, not as I will, but as Thou wilt.''

Q. With what words must one pray?

A. It is best that Christian boys be trained in the prayers of the prophets, Christ, and the apostles, but the adult Christian ought to pray as he is inspired by the Holy Spirit, who, Rom 8[:26], ''helps us in our weakness . . . and intercedes for us with sighs too deep for words.''

Q. In what manner must one pray?

A. God is mindful of the heart, but in order that the heart may be stirred up, it is best, when [our] conscience calls us to account, to lower our eyes and beat our breast, as the taxpayer does in Luke 18. When we cast ourselves down before God, it is best to raise our hands, as Moses did in Exodus 17.[22] When we prostrate ourselves [falling] onto our knees and face, it is best to let the hands fall, as the Lord Jesus did in the garden Matt 26. When we are joyful in spirit, it is best to lift the hands up to Heaven as the Lord does in John 17.

Q. Ought a man pray alone or with another?

A. Both alone and with the congregation. The Lord speaks about private prayers at Matt 6[:6] "When you pray, go into your room"; and public prayer at Matt 18[:19] "If two of you agree on Earth about anything they ask, it will be done for them." Acts 1[:14] "All these with one accord devoted themselves in prayer."

V On Baptism[23]

Q. What is baptism?

A. Baptism is the immersion (*immersio*) and emersion (*emersio*) of a man believing in the gospel and doing penance in the name of the Father and Son and Holy Spirit, [Matt 28:19] or in the name of Jesus Christ [Acts 2:38], in which he publicly declares that he has been cleansed of sin by the grace of God the Father, in the blood of Christ, by the assistance of the Holy Spirit, that, having been introduced into the body of Christ, he will put to death the old Adam, and will be transformed into the heavenly Adam, certain that after the resurrection he will gain eternal life.

Q. Who instituted baptism?

A. It was God our Father, who instituted baptism and His beloved Son, our Lord Jesus Christ [who] confirmed it.

Q. Where is this written?

A. Matt 21[:25] "The baptism of John was from Heaven." Luke 7[:29 – 30] "The baptism of John was the purpose of God." Luke 3[:2] "The word of God came to John the son of Zechariah in the wilderness [:3] and he went . . . preaching a baptism of repentance for the forgiveness of sins." John 1[:6] "There was a man sent from God, whose name was John."

Q. But where is Christ, the Son of God, said to have confirmed baptism?

A. Matt 28[:18] "Jesus said 'All authority in Heaven and on Earth has been given to me. [:19] Go therefore and make disciples of all nations, baptizing them in the name of the Father and of the Son and of the Holy Spirit, [:20] teaching them to observe all that I have commanded you; and lo, I am with you always, to the close of the age.'" Mark 16[:14] "Go into all the world and preach the gospel to the whole creation. [:16] He who believes and is baptized will be saved; but he who does not believe will be condemned."

Q. Where do we read that John and the apostles followed these mandates?

A. Matt 3 Mark 1 Luke 3 [Matt 3:5, Mark 1:4, Luke 3:3] "John appeared in the desert, preaching a baptism of repentance for the forgiveness of sins. [Matt 3:6] And all went out to him . . . [Matt 3:6, Mark 1:5] and were baptized by him in the River Jordan, confessing their sins. [Matt 3:7] And he said to them, [Matt 3:8, Luke 3:8] 'Bear fruit that befits repentance. . . . [Matt 3:10, Luke 3:9] Even now the axe is laid to the root of the trees; every tree therefore that does not bear good fruit is cut down and thrown into the fire.' [Luke 3:10] And the multitudes asked him, 'What then shall we do?' [:11] And he answered them, 'He who has two coats, let him share with him who has none; and he who has food, let him do likewise.' [:12] Tax collectors also came to be baptized, and said to him, 'Teacher, what shall we do?' [:13] And he said to them, 'Collect no more than is appointed you.' [:14] Soldiers also asked him, 'And us, what shall we do?' And he said to them, 'Rob no one by violence or by false accusation, and be content with your wages.' ''

Q. So even Jesus himself has been baptized?

A. Most definitely. Matt 3[:13] ''Jesus came . . . to John, to be baptized by him. [:14] John would have prevented Him, saying, 'I need to be baptized by you, and do you come to me?' [:15] But Jesus answered him, '' 'Let it be so now; for thus it is fitting for us to fulfill all righteousness.' Then he consented. [:16] And when Jesus was baptized, he went up immediately from the water, and behold, the Heavens were opened to Him, and he saw the Spirit of God descending like a dove, and alighting on him; [:17] and lo, a voice from Heaven, saying, 'This is My beloved Son, with whom I am well pleased.' ''

Q. So were the apostles also baptized?[24]

A. Most definitely. Acts 2. The extensive speech of Peter, which was given to him as a gift by the Holy Spirit, who, by the agency of God through Jesus of Nazareth, had filled the apostles, concludes [:36] '' 'Let all the House of Israel therefore know assuredly that God has made Him both Lord and Christ, this Jesus whom you crucified. [:37] Now when they heard this they were cut to the heart, and they said . . . 'What shall we do?' [:38] And Peter said to them, 'Repent, and be baptized every one of you in the name of Jesus Christ for the forgiveness of your sins; and you shall receive the gift of the Holy Spirit' . . . [:41] So those who received his word were baptized, and there were added that day about three thousand souls. And they devoted themselves to the apostles' teaching and fellowship, to the breaking of bread and the prayers.''

Q. Christ commands that baptism be made in the name of the Father and the Son and the Holy Spirit; the apostles however baptized only in the name of Jesus. What is the significance of this difference?

A. There is no difference for . . . Jesus did not come on His own accord but the Father sent Him. . . . John 8[:42] 'He does not seek His own glory, but that of His Father' John 7[:18]. Finally, at John 12[:44] He cries out in a deep voice ''He who believes in me, believes not in me, but in Him who sent me. [:45] And he who sees me, etc.''

Q. Therefore what does it mean to be baptized in the name of the Father and the Son and the Holy Spirit, or in the name of Jesus?

A. It means to believe and to confess that God is your father, [and to believe] in His beloved Son Jesus Christ who gives to you the Spirit of sonship, through whom we cry ''Abba! Father!'' Rom 8[:15].

Q. Therefore all ought to be baptized, and ought to hear the word of God, and ought to believe, confess, and do penance?

A. Most definitely. Acts 8. ''Philip told the Eunuch of the good news of Jesus reading from a passage of Isaiah [53:7 – 8]. And [:36] as the eunuch and Philip came to some water, the eunuch said . . . 'What is to prevent my being baptized?' [:37] And Philip said, 'If you believe with all your heart, you may.' And he replied, 'I believe that Jesus Christ is the Son of God. . . .' [:38] And they both went down into the water, . . . and he baptized him.''' Heb 6[:1] ''Let us leave the elementary doctrines of Christ and go onto maturity, not laying again a foundation of repentance from dead works and of faith toward God, [:2] with instruction about ablutions, the laying on of hands, the resurrection of the dead, and eternal judgment.'' Gal 3[:26] ''In Christ Jesus you are all sons of God, through faith. [:27] For as many of you as were baptized into Christ have put on Christ.'' Acts 8[:12] ''The Samaritans believed Philip as he preached good news about the Kingdom of God and the name of Jesus Christ, [and] they were baptized, both men and women.''

Q. But did they baptize whole families by the faith of the heads of the families?[25]

A. No, for the righteous man lives by his own faith, not another's. In Acts 16, where they are said to have baptized families, they only baptized those hearing the word and believing. [:14] ''The Lord opened the heart of Lydia to give heed to what was said by Paul. [:15] And she was baptized, with her household, and the jailor said [:30] ''Men, what must I do to be saved?'' [:31] And they said, ''Believe in the Lord Jesus, and you will be saved, you and your household.'' [:32] And they spoke the Word of the Lord to him and to all that were in his house. . . . [:33] And he was baptized at once, with all his family. . . . [:34] And he rejoiced with all his household that he had believed in God.

Q. Where is it written concerning the death of the old Adam through baptism?

A. Rom 6[:3] ''All of us who have been baptized into Christ Jesus have been baptized into his death. [:4] We were buried therefore with Him by baptism into death, so that as Christ was raised from the dead by the glory of the Father, we too might walk in newness of life. . . . [:6] We know that our old self was crucified with Him . . . so that we might no longer be enslaved to sin. . . . [:12] Let not sin therefore reign in your mortal bodies, . . . [:13] Do not yield your members to sin as instruments of wickedness, but yield yourselves to God as men who have been brought from death to life, and your members to God as instruments of righteousness.'' Col 2[:11] ''In him you were circumcised with a circumcision made without hands, by putting off the body of flesh in the circumcision of Christ; [:12] and you were buried with him in baptism, in which you were also raised with him through faith in the working of God, who raised him from the dead.'' 1 Pet 3 [:21] ''Our baptism, which corresponds to the Ark of Noah, now saves us, not as a removal of dirt from the body but as an appeal to God for a clear conscience.''

Q. What must a man do if he sins after baptism?

A. He ought not despair of the grace of God in Christ, but ought to pray fervently "Forgive us our sins." And the church ought to deal with him as was stated above on discipline.

Q. How must one feel about the man who renounces faith in God and Christ?

A. This is what is said in Heb 6[:4] "It is impossible to restore again to repentance those who have once been enlightened, who have tasted the heavenly gift, and have become partakers of the Holy Spirit, [:5] and have tasted the goodness of the Word of God and the powers of the age to come, [:6] if they then commit apostasy, since they crucify the Son of God on their own account and hold Him up to contempt. 10[:26] For if we sin deliberately after receiving the knowledge of the truth, there no longer remains a sacrifice for sins, [:27] but a fearful prospect of judgment, and a fury of fire which will consume the adversaries. . . . [:29] How much worse punishment do you think will be deserved by the man who has spurned the Son of God, and profaned the blood of the covenant by which he was sanctified, and outraged the spirit of grace . . . ? [:31] It is a fearful thing to fall into the hands of the living God."

VI On the Lord's Supper[26]

Q. What is the Lord's Supper?

A. It is the holy action, instituted by Christ the Lord himself, in which proven disciples of Christ sitting at the table of the Lord in holy congregation, sincerely give thanks to God the Father for His benefits in Christ, and breaking bread eat it, and they drink from the chalice of the Lord, to the devout recollection of the body of Christ our Lord, handed over to death for our sake, and of His blood poured out in the forgiveness of our sins, stirring ourselves up in turn to constant endurance under the cross and to sincere brotherly love.

Q. Where is this taught?[27]

A. Matthew 26. Mark 14. Luke 22. [Luke 22:14] "And when the hour came, Jesus sat [at the table] and the twelve Apostles with Him. [:15] And He said to them, 'I have earnestly desired to eat this Passover with you before I suffer; [:16] for I tell you I shall not eat it until it is fulfilled in the Kingdom of God. . . .' [:19] And he took bread, and when he had given thanks he broke it and gave it to them, saying " 'This is my body, which is given for you. Do this in remembrance of me.' [:20] And likewise the cup after supper, saying, 'This cup which is poured out for you is the new covenant in my blood.' [Matt 26:29] 'Truly, I tell you I shall not drink again of this fruit of the vine until that day when I drink it new with you in my Father's Kingdom.' And all drank from it. [Mark 14:23] And he said [Luke 22:28] 'You are those who have continued with me in my trials; [:29] as my Father appointed a Kingdom for me, so do I appoint for you [:30] that you may eat and drink at my table in my Kingdom, and sit on thrones judging the twelve tribes of Israel.'" Acts 2[:42] "The baptized devoted themselves to the Apostles' teaching and fellowship, to the breaking of bread and the prayers." 1 Cor 11[:20] "When you meet together, it is not the Lord's Supper that you eat. [:21] For in eating, each one goes ahead with his own meal, and one is hungry and another is drunk. [:22] What! Do you not have houses to eat and drink in? Or do you despise the church of God and humiliate those who have nothing? What shall I say to you? Shall I command you in this? No, I will not. [:22] For I received from the Lord what I also delivered to you, that the Lord Jesus on this night when He was betrayed took bread, [:24] and when He had given thanks, He broke it, and said, 'This is my body which . . . is broken for you. Do this in remembrance of me.' [:25] In the same way also the cup, after supper, saying, 'This cup is the new covenant in my blood. Do this, as often as you drink it, in remembrance of me. [:26] For as often as you eat this bread and drink this cup, you proclaim the Lord's death until he comes. [:27] Whoever, therefore, eats the bread or drinks the cup of the Lord in an unworthy manner will be guilty of profaning the body and blood of the Lord. [:28] Let a man examine himself, and so eat of the bread and drink of the cup. [:29] For any one who eats and drinks without discerning the body eats and drinks judgment upon himself.'''

Q. But why is the remembrance of the body and blood of Christ made with bread and wine?

A. Because just as ''Bread strengthens man's heart, and wine gladdens it'' Ps 104[:15], so Jesus Christ our Lord is given to us starved sinners by God the Father, as a bread which nourishes us to eternal life.

Q. Where is this written?

A. John 6[:27] ''Do not labor for the food which perishes, but for the food which endures to eternal life, which the Son of Man will give to you; for on him has God the Father set His seal. . . . [:35] I am the bread of life; . . . . [:50] which comes down from heaven, that a man may eat of it and not die, ... [:51] but will live forever; and the bread which I shall give for the life of the world is my flesh. . . . [:53] Truly, truly, I say to you, unless you eat the flesh of the Son of man and drink his blood, you have no life in you; [:54] he who eats my flesh and drinks my blood has eternal life, and I will raise him up at the last day. [:55] For my flesh is food indeed, and my blood is drink indeed.''

Q. What is it, to drink and eat Christ?

A. Hear the Lord Jesus Himself speaking: [John 6:63] ''The words that I speak to you are spirit and life. . . . [:29] This is the work of God, that you believe in him whom He has sent. . . . [:35] He who comes to me shall not hunger, and he who believes in me shall not thirst. . . . [:40] For this is the will of my Father, that every one who . . . believes in the Son should have eternal life; and I will raise him up at the last day. . . . [:47] He who believes in me has eternal life. . . . [:56] He who eats my flesh and drinks my blood abides in Me, and I in him. [:57] As the living Father sent me, and I live because of the Father, so he who eats me will live because of me.''

Q. Is not this action, then, a sacrifice for sin?[28]

A. No. But it is the grateful remembrance and a commemoration of that sacrifice once offered, on which there is Heb 9[:25] ''Christ has entered, not into a sanctuary made with hands, a copy of the true one, but into Heaven itself, now to appear in the presence of God on our behalf. [:25] Nor was it to offer himself repeatedly, ... [:26] for then he would have had to suffer repeatedly since the foundation of the world, but as it is, he has appeared once for all at the end of the age to put away sin by the sacrifice of himself. . . . [:28] So Christ, having been offered once to bear the sins of many, will appear a second time, not to deal with sin but to save those who are eagerly waiting for him.''

Q. How is Christ present at this action, when ''heaven must receive him until the time for establishing all things?'' Acts 3[:21] ''And He will come in the same way as He was seen to go into Heaven?'' Acts 1[:11]

A. He is most certainly present to His faithful, as Matt 28[:20] promised ''Lo, I am with you always, to the close of the age.'' I say that he is not present in the flesh, but by his Holy Spirit, as John 14 states [:16] ''I will pray the Father, and He will give you another counselor, to be with you forever. . . . [:18] I will not leave you desolate. . . . [:26] The counselor, the Holy Spirit, whom the Father will send in my name, he will teach you all things.'' John 16[:8] ''When the counselor comes, he will convince the world of sin. . . . [:13] He will guide you into all the truth. . . . [:14] He will glorify me.''

Q. Where does Christ at the Supper rouse His followers to steadfastness and endurance?

A. John 16[:1] ''I say this to you to keep you from falling away. [:2] They will put you out of the synagogues; indeed, the hour is coming when whoever kills you will think he is offering service to God. . . . [:20] You will be sorrowful . . . you will weep and lament, but the world will rejoice . . . but your sorrow will turn into joy. . . . [:22] I will see you again and your hearts will rejoice, and no one will take your joy from you. . . . [:33] I have said this to you, that in me you may have peace. In the world you have tribulation; but be of good cheer, I have overcome the world.'' John 15[:18] ''If the world hates you, know that it has hated me before it hated you. [:19] If you were of the world, the world would love its own; but because you are not of the world, but I chose you out of the world, therefore the world hates you. . . .'' [:20] ''A servant is not greater than his master. If they persecuted me, they will persecute you; . . . . [:23] He who hates me hates My Father also.'' Luke 22[:31] ''Jesus said 'Simon, Simon; behold, Satan demanded to have you, that he might sift you like wheat, [:32] but I have prayed for you that your faith may not fail; and when you have turned again, strengthen your brethren.' ''

Q. Where in the Supper does the Lord command brotherly love?

A. John 13. ''Jesus said to his disciples [:14] 'If I then, your Lord and teacher, have washed your feet, you also ought to wash one another's feet. [:15] For I have given you an example, that you also should do as I have done to you. . . . [:34] A new commandment I give to you, that you love one another, even as I have loved you. . . . [:35] By this all men will know that you are my disciples.' '' 1 Cor 10[:16] ''The cup of blessing which we bless, is it not a communion of the blood of Christ? The bread which we break, is it not a communion in the body of Christ? [:17] Because there is one loaf, we who are many are one body, for we all partake of the same loaf. . . . [:21] You cannot drink the cup of the Lord and the cup of demons. You cannot partake of the table of the Lord and the table of demons.''

Q. What is a worthy preparation and examination (*probatio*) for the Lord's Supper?[29]

A. The church ought to keep careful watch lest it admit to the sacred meal anyone who has been contaminated with manifest crimes and does not do penance. [The section] above, ''On Discipline,'' is more expansive on this matter. But if anyone is not notorious for a heinous crime, the Holy Spirit commands him to put himself to this test:

1) If he believes with his heart and confesses with his mouth that he is a sinner before God the Father, and by nature a son of wrath, and a slave of death. [The section] above, ''On Justification,'' is more expansive on this matter.

2) If he believes that ''God so loved the world that He gave His only Son, that whoever believes in Him should not perish but have eternal life,'' John 3[:16].

3) If he has resolved for the future to conduct a pious and guiltless life. 1 Pet 4[:1] ''Since therefore Christ suffered in the flesh for us, arm yourselves with the same thought; for whoever has suffered in the flesh has ceased from sin, [:2] so as to live for the rest of the time in the flesh no longer by human passions but by the will of God.''

Q. Must absolute perfection in this test of faith be expected?

A. There will at last be absolute perfection in the other life. ''For here our knowledge is imperfect'' 1 Cor 13[:9]; and often we are compelled to shout, with the apostles, ''Lord, increase our faith'' Luke 17[:5]; 1 Cor 5[:7] ''Cleanse out the old leaven that you may be fresh dough, as you really are unleavened. For Christ, our passover lamb, has been sacrificed. [:8] Let us, therefore, celebrate the festival, not with the old leaven, the leaven of malice and evil, but with the unleavened bread of sincerity and truth.' Thus, if we handle even one talent faithfully, to the glory of God, to the one who has will more be given, and we will hear that most joyful voice, ''Well done, faithful servant . . . enter into the joy of your master'' Matt 25[:21]. May God, our one Father, through Jesus Christ His Son our Lord, grant this to us. Amen.

Related Document 8

Samuel Przypkowski

The Life of That Incomparable Man Faustus Socinus of Siena (Kiev, 1636)

Introduction. The *Vita* was written in the palatinate of Kiev c. 1631 by Samuel Przyp-kowski (1592–1670), a major spokesman of the Minor Church of the Polish Brethren. The *Vita* is filled with considerable detail, as the author was remotely related to Faustus Socinus by marriage into the Wiszowaty family. Przypkowski differed sometimes from the Brethren themselves, on a number of issues being closer to the Remonstrants, with whom he had studied; and from them and from Socinus also he differed specifically on Christology, holding that the Son was begotten from the very essence of the Father but not from eternity. He was thus a true Arian, like Sand (Introduction at n. 30) in the fourth-century sense. Pryzpkowski was the husband of one of the granddaughters of Andrew Wiszowaty (d. 1678), whose mother was Agnes Socina, the only child of Faustus; and in the Life of Wiszowaty a portion of the *Vita*, respectively the lineage and early life of Wiszowaty's Sienese grandfather, was copied out. As this had been printed in *Polish Brethren*, Document I, I have seen fit here to leave out the Life of Socinus before his departure from Italy in 1574.

The *Vita* was first published anonymously as by "a Polish Knight" in 1636 without place, again in 1651. It formed the basis for a German Life by Joachim Pastorious (1637), the English translation by the Father of English Unitarianism, John Biddle (London, 1653), and a Dutch version of the *Vita* (1664). In due course the *Vita* was repub-lished at the beginning of the collected works of Socinus in *BFP* 1 (Amsterdam, [1668]). The *Vita* of 1653 was the basis of the edition by E[mily] S[harpe], *The Life of Faustus Socinus of Siena: The unitarian Reformer, as written in Latin by Samuel Przipcovius, Polish Knight in the Year 1636, with English Annotations* (Manchester, 1912). She dedi-cated the edition to Bishop Joseph Ferencz of the Unitarian Church in Hungary, oblivious of the degree to which Przypkowski's disparagement of Francis Dávid and her assump-tion that Socinus was a father of Transylvanian Unitarianism would have had to be swal-lowed with episcopal grace. In her helpful paraphrases of the fulsome *Vita*, she follows the translation of Biddle but makes her own alterations in the light of the change of English over two and a half centuries and her own informed reading of the Latin text. I have chosen to give the full Biddle translation, as the archaic style and intention of the author are appropriately evoked in the preservation of his spelling and capitalization (not always his punctuation). I have, however, brought the spelling of the proper and geographical names into conformity with the usage elsewhere in the edition of the *Historia*. As the original Biddle text is not readily accessible, I have used instead the reprinting of it from the library of Edward Harley, second Earl of Oxford, *Harleian Miscellany: A collection of scarce, curious, and entertaining pamphlets and tracts . . . found in the library of the late Earl of Oxford*, with an introduction by Samuel Johnson, 8 vols. (London, 1744–46) 7.213–25. The translation, checked against the Latin, has been occasionally modified and only modestly annotated; and the part of it has been cut where Przypkowski reflects on renown in general and brings in Ignatius of Loyola as another kind of saint remembered in a different cycle of honor and devotion in the Catholic Church.

Every modern Life of Socinus must return to Przypkowski's text. Ludwik Chmaj, who edited the two-volume calendared translation of the letters of Socinus, *Listy* (Warsaw, 1959), preceded them with a succinct updated biography, 1.13–30 and chronology, 2.342–46, expanded this as the definitive interpretation to date in the posthumous *Faust Socyn (1538–1604)* (Warsaw, 1963). The most recent presentation in English with the literature to date is that of Zbigniew Oginowski, "Faustus Socinus," Jill Raitt, ed., *Shapers of Religious Tradition in Germany, Switzerland, and Poland, 1560–1600* (New Haven: Yale University Press, 1981) chap. 12. For the place of composition of the *Vita*, see Orest Levysky (Lewicki), "Socynjanie na Rusi," *RwP* 2 (1922) 231–34; translated as "Socinianism in . . . South-West Rus," Ukrainian Academy in the U.S.A. Annals 30 (1953) 485–508, p. 492; Ludwik Chmaj, *Samuel Przypkowski* (Cracow, 1927) 24; for the genealogy of the Family Przypkowski, see Włodzimierz Budka, "Przypkowski i rola ich w rucha reformacyjnym," *RwP* 4 (1926) 60ff. with a genealogical table. Samuel Przypkowski is the author of three writings included in *Polish Brethren*, Documents XI–I and XXXIII–II, and also in Document I, nn. 15–17. Pls. 47 and 48 are devoted to Socinus.

The Life of Faustus Socinus

. . . It was in the Year of our Lord 1574, and the five and thirtieth of his Age, when he [Faustus Socinus] retired out of Italy into Germany. At his Coming he was entertained by Basel, that courteous Receiver of Christ's Exiles, which had long since learned to cherish in her Lap endangered Innocency. Where he studied Divinity full three Years and upwards, being chiefly intent upon the Sacred Scriptures, to the sincere Understanding whereof whilst he aspired with daily Vows and Prayers, he was much helped with a very few Writings of his Uncle Laelius, and sundry scattered Notes left by him. Which Thing, though it was in his Power to suppress it, yet did he always ingenuously own and profess. As he lived at Basel until the Year 1575, he detained not, within the Closet of his private Breast, the Truth that had been deposited with him. And therefore, whilst he endeavored to propagate unto others the Light that was risen to himself, he proceeded by Degrees, from Reasoning with his Friends to discourse with Strangers, and, having begun his Disputation concerning Jesus Christ the Saviour by Word of Mouth, he afterwards comprised it in Writing. Which before he could finish, being first excluded by Sickness from his Studies, then by the Pestilence from his Books left at Basel, he in the mean Time dispatched at

Zurich, in the Beginning of the Year 1578, another Disputation with Francis Puccini,[1] and afterwards in the same Year, being returned to Basel, he put the last Hand to his Book, *Concerning the Saviour*.[2]

At that Time the Transylvanian Churches were extremely infested with the Opinion of Francis Dávid and others, touching the Honour and Power of Christ.[3] To remedy which Mischief, George Biandrata, a Man very powerful in those Churches, and with the Báthory Princes, who had there ruled, in that very Year of the Lord invited Socinus from Basel,[4] to the End that he might draw the Ringleader of the Faction, Francis Dávid, from so gross and pernicious an Error; which that it might the more commodiously be effected, having at a great Rate hired a Lodging for Socinus with Francis Dávid, he would have them both for above the Space of four Months to use the same House and Table. But the said Francis took far greater Care how to retain his Credit amongst those of his Party than how to seek after the Truth. Whereupon adventuring not only to spread his Error in private, but publickly to proclaim it in the Pulpit, he drew present Danger on himself, being soon cast into Prison by the Command of the Prince of Transylvania, where he shortly after ended his Life.[5] Of whose Death, though Socinus was altogether guiltless, yet did he not escape Blame. As if he were not able to vanquish the said Francis with other Weapons, when notwithstanding the Disputations of both are published: *Or* that the Magistrate was so addicted to the Cause of Socinus as to employ the Weapons of his Authority for him, or any one of his Party.[6] But, if perhaps some Person, who favoured the Cause of Socinus, did incite the Princes to deal roughly with the said Francis, whereof nevertheless I am not certain,[7] yet let not Socinus be blamed for him, inasmuch as he could neither know his Counsel, nor approve his Deed. For, to omit sundry Considerations, there could not happen any Thing more contrary to the Mind of Socinus than that such a Doctrine as could not be defended with the Words and Wit of the said Francis, whilst he lived, should seem to be confirmed by the mute, but efficacious Testimony of his Death: Especially because, carrying the Face of a Martyrdom, it presently turned the Eyes of all Men to it. The Disputation of Socinus with him,[8] though written, whilst the said Francis was alive, could notwithstanding hardly [barely] come to Light fifteen Years after [1595].

When this Disputation was finished in May, Anno 1579, and presented to the Transylvanian Churches, Socinus could not long tarry there by Reason of a Disease then raging, which they commonly call the Cholick. Wherefore in the same Year, being now forty Years old, he traveled into Poland, where he made Suit publickly to be united to the Polonian Churches, which acknowledge none but the Father of the Lord Jesus Christ to be the most High God: but, not concealing his Dissent in certain Doctrines [notably on baptism], here suffered a Repulse very roughly and for a long Time.

Nevertheless he, being composed unto Patience, not so much by his natural Inclination, as by the Resolution of His Mind, was no Whit enraged with this Disgrace, nor ever gave any Signs of a disaffected Mind, but rather undertook to repel with his Wit the Incursion of divers Adversaries, who then infested those Churches. And first of all he received the Charge of Andreas Wolan, by reselling his *Paraenesis*.[9] And upon the same Occasion, at the Request of Niejmo-jewski *[On the place of Paul in] the Seventh Chapter of the Epistle to the Romans* was explained.[10]

Afterwards it pleased him to assail Jacob Palaeologus, whose Reputation and Authority did at that time cherish the Relicks of pernicious Errors in Men otherwise well-minded.[11] He being somewhat roughly handled, not out of Hatred, but [out of] Advice [consideration], he always excused. A little after, when Wolan had renewed the Fight, he was again encountered, and withal an Answer made to the Positions of the College of Poznań.[12]

Whilst Socinus undergoeth so much Fighting and Hatred for the Patronage of the Truth, amongst so many Enemies there wanted not some Calumniators. Stephen was then King of Poland. A Pickthank [self-ingratiating *accusator*] blows his Ears with the Report of a Book written against the Magistrate; adding that it would be a very dishonourable thing to suffer a wandering Italian Exile to escape Scot-free (*impune*) with so bold an Enterprise. He hinted at the Book against Palaeologus, which, though it required no other Testimony of its Innocency than the Reading, yet did he think good to decline the Danger.[13]

Whereupon, he departed from Cracow, where he had now lived four Years [1583 – 87], to a Nobleman, named Christopher Morsztyn, Lord of Pawlikowice in which Place he defended his Innocency, not so much by Skulking, as by the Privilege of Nobility in our Nation. For that Suburb-farm is a few Miles distant from Cracow. It seemed a wiser Course to clear himself from the Crimes laid to his Charge, rather out of that Place, than out of Prison. Nor was he entertained in that hospitable House for that Nick of Time only, but there cherished for above three Years. And to the End that the Courtesy shewed to an Exile and Stranger might be more abundant, a little While after, the Daughter of the Family,[14] a noble Virgin, was, at his Suit, given him in Marriage so that, being of a Stranger become a Son-in-law, he seemed to have established his Security in those Places by Affinities and Friendships.

Whilst he lived in the Country, he wrote many notable Pieces, and chiefly that against [Gabriel] Eutropius, constantly defending the Fame and Cause of that Church, which had, with most unjust Prejudice, condemned him, and caused him, though innocent, continually to suffer many Indignities.[15]

His Daughter Agnes was born to him around Pentecost in the Year of our Lord 1587, and forty-eighth of his Age. Of her, being, after her Father's Death, married to Stanislas Wiszowaty [grandfather of Benedict], a Polonian Knight, there are as yet remaining Nephews and Nieces. In September the Same Year, he lost his Wife Elizabeth. This sad and disastrous Chance was followed with a grievous Fit of Sickness so obstinate that, for certain Months, it caused the use of his Studies to cease. And, that no Kind of Calamity might be wanting, almost about the same time, by the Death of Francis, the Grand Duke of Tuscany, the Revenues of his Estate, which he received yearly out of Italy were quite taken away from him. Indeed, a little before, by the Bitterness of Accusers and Threats of Popes, his Estate came into Danger; but by the strenuous Endeavours of Isabella de' Medici, the Grand Duke's Sister (who was married to the aforesaid Paul Jordan Ursini[16]) whilst she lived, and afterwards by the Favor of Francis the Grand Duke, it came to pass, that, during his life, Socinus received the yearly Income of his Estate. For, indeed, his old Deserts were still so fresh in Memory that those Princes, though long since forsaken, and oftentimes rejected, did yet, in a most difficult Matter, gratify the Letters and Prayers of a condemned and exiled Person. Yea, Letters full of Courtesy were sent unto him, and he bidden to be of Good Chear for the future, as long as they lived, so that, in setting forth Books, he suffered not his Name to appear. But those Princes were then taken away by a Destiny disastrous to Socinus. And, that all Things might seem to have conspired to the Perplexity of the Man, being a Widower, sick, and stripped of all his Fortunes, he was molested with the very Times of our Commonwealth, which were then exceeding turbulent, because divers did contend who should be the King of Poland;[17] so that the Adversaries thereupon took greater License to themselves.

Socinus was now returned to Cracow[18] and sought Solace, in the Midst of so many Evils, from the Employment, which God had imposed on him to purge the [Minor] Church of such Errors as were then rife in her. Wherefore, although he had been formerly accustomed to frequent Ecclesiastical Assemblies, yet, in the Year 1588, in the synod of Brest (which is a Town on the Borders of Lithuania) he disputed with greater Earnestness and Fruit than before, touching the Death and Sacrifice of Christ, touching our Justification, touching the Corrupted nature of Man, and, finally, with the Davidians and Budnyites, touching the Invocation of Jesus Christ. This was the Year, wherein the Care and Charge of the Church at Lusławice was committed to Peter Stoiński, Son of Petrus Statorius of Thon-ville, whose Family, having heretofore been naturalised into the Nobility of our Nation, hath, even at this Day, some Men surviving, who have been invested with great Honours, in our Country. He, being no less sharp in Judgment than ready in Speech, being once admitted into the Friendship of Socinus, yielded willingly to his Opinion. A little before also he had privately drawn many of the chief ones into his Opinion, and there was daily an Accession made of such Men as complied with them. Nevertheless, certain Men of very great Authority still stood off, as Niemojewski and Czechowic, together with the greatest Part of the ancient Ministers. The report is that [John] Siekierzyński was the first that adventured openly to maintain the Tenets of Socinus, to which he had assented. Not long after, others followed. This Party was exceedingly strengthened by the Accession of the three brothers Lubieniecki: Andreas, Stanislas, and Christo-pher, who being Brethren of noble Descent, and born to very great Hopes, and brought up partly in the King's Court and partly in the Society of the greatest Peers, were, by a sacred Instinct, transported from the Midst of the Allurements of this Life to the Care of Religion.[19] These men, as they had, by a most inflamed Zeal, trodden under Foot all the Impediments of Piety, so, with an equal Candour and Greatness of Mind, they subscribed to the Known Truth.

And now others of the Pastors came earnestly to the Party, especially the Juniors, who were less retarded with the Prejudice of inveterate Opinions and Authority; and that, by Reason of an Accident very notable for the Newness thereof, which gave a memorable Proof how great the Force of the Truth is. Amidst a great Jarring of Opinions this was a laudable Agreement of that Church, that those Men contended only with Arguments, and not with Hatred; and, though they detested one another's Opinion, yet did they not condemn one another; and therefore, keeping mutual Tolerance entire, they oftentimes disputed very eagerly. And this was the chief Work of their Synods.

Wherefore, Anno 1589, in the Synod of Lublin, the Opinion of Socinus, touching the seventh Chapter of *Romans*,[20] was exceedingly agitated. There were some that defended it; but as great a Number of Pastors that opposed it. One whereof, named Nicholas Żytno, being willed by others of the same Party to explain that Chapter contrary to the Mind of Socinus, and having, to that Purpose, stoutly managed the Matter, falling in his Discourse upon those Words, wherewith the Apostle giveth Thanks to God for his Freedom [Rom 7:25] stood like a Man amazed. And by and by, ''What is That Benefit, which drew from the Apostle so great Thanks? Was it that he was of Necessity detained in so great a Servitude of Sin? Certainly such a Thing as this can, at no Hand, gain Approbation with me. I therefore,'' saith he [Żytno], ''in like Manner give very great Thanks to the Father of Lights in that he would have the Light of his Truth arise unto me, who am now freed from Error.'' Afterwards, entering upon a contrary Way of Explaining, he accurately disputed for the Orthodox Opinion. When they, whose Cause he had [first] undertaken, being amazed, did rebuke him, his Answer was That he could not resist the Judgment of a convinced Mind.[21]

This Business was of great Moment for the Propagation of the Truth. Nor did their Endeavors less conduce thereunto, who had lifted up the Standard unto others to embrace it. Amongst them the Eloquence of the foresaid Peter Stoiński did excel. That elegant Toungue God only had bestowed on those Churches [a tongue] equal to the Wit of Socinus and able to deliver, in a popular Manner, his [Socinus's] subtle Senses that were above the ruder Sort, and to commend them unto all by his flexanimous Speech. Him [Peter Stoiński], therefore, as the chief Interpreter of his Mind, did Socinus make Use of, to the notable Advantage of God's Church. And, indeed, certain Things happened, which did inforce a stricter Union with him.

Socinus sojourning at Cracow [1588 – 98] began, long since to be environed with such Dangers on every Side, as are, for the most Part, wont to accompany the faithful Servants of Christ. How great an Indignity was there offered to him by that indolent Soldier Wiernek (Vernecus), he himself signifieth in a certain Letter?[22] But above all, after the Printing of his Book, *Concerning the Saviour* [Cracow, 1594], the Adversaries again began to shew the Rancour of their Hatred. Whereupon, in the Year 1598, the Scholars (*scholastici*), having stirred up the Dregs of the Rabble, took Socinus, being then sick and minding the Recovery of his Health, and pulling him out of his Chamber half naked, dragged him in a contumelious Manner through the Market, and the most noted Streets, the greatest Part, in the mean Time, crying out, To have him brought to Execution. At length, having been grievously handled in that furious Rout, he was, with much ado, rescued out of the Hands of the raging Multitude by Martin Wadowita, Professor of Cracow. The Plundering of his Goods and Household stuff, together with other Things liable to Spoil, did not so much grieve him as the irreparable Loss of certain Writings, concerning which, he often did profess, that he would redeem it with the Expense of his Life. Then perished together a notable Labour of his *Against Atheists,* which he had undertaken to refute the ingenious Devices of a certain great Man.[23]

But when to so barbarous an Example of Cruelty, Threats were also added, he departed from Cracow to Lusławice unto a certain village, famous for his last Habitation and Death, and distant about nine Miles from Cracow, where having, for certain Years, used the Table and House of a Nobleman, named Abraham Błoński, he lived a Neighbor to [Peter] Stoiński. Both, therefore, affording mutual Help near at Hand in Chasing away the Relicks of Errors, had now brought almost that whole Church to an unanimous Consent in all Opinions.

For even Niemojewski himself, having in most Things already given Assent to Socinus, condemned his own Mistakes with such Ingenuity, as can never sufficiently be extolled. Czechowic only could not be removed from his Opinion Who as, the better Part prevailed, conniving, though with much ado at other Things, a little after began to make a Stir about the Opinion concerning Baptism, which nevertheless being suddenly, according to the Wish of Socinus, laid asleep, did afterwards vanish of its own Accord. [24]

Having thus fully purged the Church from Errors, as if his Life had been prolonged hitherto for this Purpose only, he was at the End of Winter, in the sixty-fifth Year of his Age, taken away at Lusławice by a Death not so untimely to himself, as sad to his followers. His last Words at his Death were these, namely, that he no less full of Envy and Troubles than of Days did, with a joyful and undaunted Hope, incline to the Period of his appointed Time, which shewed to him both a Discharge from his Sorrows and a Reward of his Labours.

Peter Stoiński, who had been the Associate of his Life and Labours, was also the Praiser, and in the Year following, the Companion of his Funeral. For, as if he had already ended the appointed Task of his Life, he followed Socinus, being hardly forty Years old.

Having passed over the Race of Socinus's Life, through which we have made a short Cut, it remaineth, that we stop a While in considering what he did and performed.

No Man in our Memory did better deserve of all the Christian World, but chiefly of the Polonian Churches. For first, by setting out so many Works, he opened the genuine Meaning of the Holy Scriptures in innumerable Places.

Next he only shewed how to confirm with solid Arguments, and skilfully to defend from subtle Cavils and Sophisms, those Opinions touching the Person of God and Christ, which he found already rife in Poland. After that he happily extinguished some impious, other profane Opinions, whose deadly Poison did by Stealth insinuate itself into the Bosom of the Church. No Man did more vigourously quell Judaizers. He also exploded the Opinion of the Chiliasts, and many other fanatick Dreams besides. As for the Errors, received from the

Reformed (*Reformatis*) Churches, which did in a great Number as yet reign in that Church, he did with a marvelous Felicity root them out. Such were that of Justification, that of Appeasing the Wrath of God, that of Predestination, that of the Servitude of the Will, that of original sin, that of the Lord's Supper and Baptism, together with other misconstrued Doctrines. Finally, having taken away pernicious Errors, that he might not also leave any Fopperies in the Church, he exterminated very many Superstitions about indifferent Things: Of which Sort was the over-much Affectation of mean Clothing, and the Eschewing of Magistracy, and Refusing to prosecute one's own Right, even without a Desire of Revenge, and what other like Spots (*naevos*) there were, caused by the inconsiderate Zeal of their first Fervor.[25]

Having explained the Order of his Life and his Actions, it remaineth that we add a few Things concerning the Habit of his Mind and Body. To relate the Praises of his Wit and Judgment is a superflouous Labour, inasmuch as there are so many Monuments thereof extant. As for his Learning, the more pertinaciously he hid it, the more impatiently it breaketh out. It was somewhat late but more solid. Nor are there wanting in his Writings the Footsteps of a happy Memory also.

I cannot pass by one Proof thereof, which he gave in his *Disputation* [on the adoration of Christ] with Christian Francken. This Fellow, in the Session of the synod of Chmielnik, desiring to shew a Proof of his Learning and Wit did, in a more arrogant Manner than was meet, challenge those Pastors to dispute, slighting the mean Learning of every one. And that he might with very Plenty puzzle and overwhelm him that was to dispute, having beforehand provided himself, he together proposed fifty Arguments, against the Adoration of Christ.[26] This Matter troubled some, and they, though the Church had so often rejected Socinus, did yet enjoin him to make an Answer. He, attentively hearing the Man who had on a sudden entered upon an unjust Way of arguing and did, with one Breath almost, pour out so many prepared shafts, was admonished to take in Writing, at least, the Heads of the Reasons, to which an Answer was to be returned. But he [Socinus], in Confidence of his Memory, slighted the Assistance of his Pen and patiently heard the Man uttering those Reasons of his, as long as he pleased. And by and by, in the same Order, repeating the long series of his Arguments, [Socinus] gave such a solid answer to each of them that the Adversary had hardly any Thing to mutter against him. Whereupon having professed that he was unskilled and unprepared, he went away confounded to the Admiration of all.

And, because we have touched the Endowments of his Nature, if any Man be curious to know the Figure of his Body also, let him know that he wanted not a Form answerable to his Disposition, being of such a Stature as exceeded not the just Size, yet was nearer to Tallness. The Habit of his Body was somewhat slender, yet within Measure; in his Countenance, the Dignity of his high Forehead and masculine Beauty of his Eyes did cast a Glance. Nor did the Comeliness and Grace of his Look diminish the Vigor and Majesty thereof. He was somewhat sparing of Meat and Sleep, and abstinent of all Pleasures, without

Affectation; only, in the Conservation of his Health, he seemed scrupulous, and oftentimes over-diligent. Yet was he, for the most Part, of a prosperous Health, but that he was sometimes troubled with Pains of the Stone and with the Cholick. Moreover, being grown somewhat old, he complained of the Dimness of his Sight, contracted with over-much studying by candlelight. The Genius of his Life was gentle and innocent. There was a marvelous Simplicity in his Manners, which was so tempered with Gravity that he was free from all Superciliousness. Whence it came to pass, that you would sooner reverence him than you could fear him. He was very affable, giving Honour to every one exceedingly; and would you desire to reprove any Thing in him, there was nothing nearer to Discommendation than the over-much Debasement of himself. The Clothing of his Body was modest, but yet neat and spruce; and, though he was at a remote Distance from Bravery,[27] yet was he less averse from slight Ornaments.[28] He was officious[29] towards his Friends, and diligent in all Parts of his Life.

He had so won the Affection of the Princes, in whose Service he spent Part of his Life, that neither could long Absence extinguish the Desire of him, nor manifest Offence obliterate the Favour to him. Having shewed all Manner of Officiousness towards his Uncles, Brethren, and Male kindred, he chiefly regarded and reverenced Laelius [Socinus, Pl. 13].

Among his Female kindred, besides his grandmother Camilla [Salvetti, mother of Laelius Socinus], a most choice Matron, he exceedingly loved his Aunt Portia [Sozzini Pecci], and his Sister Phyllis, and that according to their Deserts. The former of which twain, being, whilst she lived, an Example of most commendable Chastity, did by her Discretion, and incredible Gentleness of Manners, so gain the Affection of her Husband Laelius Pecci, a Man of Rank and Quality, that he would often say with Tears, that he was unworthy of such and so great a Wife. The latter, by the Sanctity of her Manners and Discipline in governing the House had so approved herself to her Husband Cornelius Marsili, a great Nobleman, that, at her Death, she left behind her an immortal Desire of her Company.[31]

And, forasmuch, as we are long since slipped from the Endowments of Nature to those which he acquired by his own Industry, we must not pass over in Silence some of his Virtues, whereby he was eminent above many. I cannot easily say whether there was more Fire or Wit in so vehement a Disposition, so prone to Choler had Nature framed him, before he had allayed those violent Motions with Reason. Nevertheless, he did so break and tame his cholerick Temper that the Mildness, which afterwards shined forth in him, seemed to very many to be the Praise of Nature, not of Industry. The Commendation of his Patience likewise is enhanced, as by the Indignity of his Fortune and Injuries, so also by his delicate (*irritabilis*) and consequently touchy Disposition. No Evil is wont to happen unto such Persons, without an exquisite Resentment; nor is it so much to be wondered at that oftentimes a larger Wit (*ingenium*) is capable of more Sorrow.

But he in this fight also appeared Conqueror of his Fortune and Nature, after he had, with a Christian Greatness of Mind, borne and undergone so many Calamities from Strangers, so many Injuries from his Countrymen, Perils from enemies, Ingratitude from Friends, Envy from the Learned, Hatred from the Ignorant, Infamy from all, Poverty from Fortune, in fine, a continual Repulse, not without Ignominy from that very Church which he had chiefly beautified.

I have almost done an Injury to Fortune in seeming to have ascribed unto her the Cause of his Poverty. But I have not now accused her Fault, but intimated her Condition which Socinus might, perhaps, by Fortune's Means have escaped, would either his Conscience or a certain Generosity of Mind, have permitted him. Certainly he never sought after the Fame of Holiness by Beggary. Nevertheless, as often as he was able to sustain his Condition with the smallest Means, he could not be brought to take such Gifts as were freely offered him. Yea, he did of his own Accord expend his Means on the Poor. Nor was he only conversant in every Kind of Alms, but in every Kind of Liberality also; so as you may thereby understand that his Charity was inflamed with the promiscuous Love of all Men. Likewise he published certain Books at his own Charges that he might omit nothing for the Accomplishment of his ardent Zeal to promote divine Truth, which he had undertaken to propagate with what so many Writings; what with so many Letters; what with so many private and publick Disputations; what with so many Informations of them, who were in all Places the Interpreters of his Mind; what with so many long Journies, most of them from the utmost Border of Silesia to the midst of Lithuania; what with the Loss of Health, Fame, and Fortunes; what, finally, with the Hazard of his Life. That very thing, which had been the only Solace to sustain him in the Midst of so great Labours and Perils, did he continually inculcate to the whole Church, as the only Remedy to lead a holy Life, namely, a continual Hope of Immortality, which he thought was to be carefully and delicately cherished. So that when a certain old Man shewed a tomb built for himself in Token of Piety, saying, that he did perpetually meditate on Death: Socinus replied, that he would do more rightly, if he did meditate on the Reason of the Resurrection.[29]

Certainly his Prudence shined forth in all Parts of his Life, but chiefly in his Judgment of Spiritual Things, and was, as it were, a certain Fruit of his Humility and Modesty, a Virtue so inbred and peculiar to his Nature that, in other Virtues, he may seem to have vied with others; in this with himself. He never despised any Man, never attempted any Thing, but with Advice and Circumspection. In his very Studies also he was so far from all Self-confidence that he never essayed to write any Thing, but what had been concocted with long and mature Meditation. And this may easily be discerned in his Works. How often did he go very gingerly through those rough Ways, which others would have securely trodden? So that no Man seemeth to have distrusted another's Wit, as he did his own, which as we have said, was then the Reward, and now the Token of his singular Modesty. But especially his Faith did much shine forth amongst other Praises. [The praise of Socinus continues, moves into a comparison of Uncle Laelius and Nephew Faustus and proceeds to reflection on fame in the Minor and the Roman Catholic Church, St. Ignatius Loyola adduced in comparison.]

Related Document 9

George Carew (d. 1612)

Society and Religion in the Polish-Lithuanian Commonwealth, an excerpt from

A Relation of the State of Polonia and the United Provinces of that Crowne Anno 1598

Introduction. The *Relation* or Report, written about the time of the death of Stanislas Budziński, Lubieniecki's chief source, was anticipated in our Introduction (at n. 64). Our two selections from it here jointed together from the 165-page critical edition of the invaluable text,[1] were there recommended as a supplementary introduction to the *Historia* itself in that they are chock-full of constitutional and economico-social details presumed by Lubieniecki. Composed by a keen English observer of approximately his class and education,[2] in the very language of our translation, only at its Elizabethan stage, it authenticates commensurably late feudal English terms for the Commonwealth classes, offices, economics, warfare,[3] and political institutions.

The Excerpt has the unique merit of introducing readers in the idiom of their own language, as of the sixteenth century, to the great differences between England and Poland even then noted by an Englishman who was also sufficiently concerned with religion on his tour of diplomatic duty to seek permission, for example, for his fellow countrymen stationed in Elbing and perhaps other places to worship according to the Book of Common Prayer. He was patently astonished by so many religions, schisms, and sects; and when reporting on the lords and on the Polish constitution he makes clear how different even in his age were the social arrangements and temperament of the Poles and those of the English and how relatively weak was the central authority over against the bishops, princes, lords, and knights in this vast and heterogeneous state, the second largest geographically of Europe in the sixteenth century, larger than the Holy Roman Empire, on which its constitution was in some respect modeled, rivaling that of Muscovy, whose Grand Duke Ivan IV assumed the title of Tsar only in 1547. The Excerpt imparts at once a sense of the daily world of the father of Stanislas Lubieniecki, a knightly minister among knights and lords, who clad in armor into the eighteenth century elected from horseback their King and who entered into constitutionally recognized armed confederations to secure among other privileges that of religious toleration, most notably in 1573.

Envoy Carew filed his Report just three years after Stanislas Budziński signed his name to a legal document in Cracow (Pl. 1) and could just possibly even have met there the former Franciscan author of the MS Polish History drawn upon so heavily by Lubieniecki.

Despite the eccentric Elizabethan spelling, syntax, punctuation, and occasional prejudice, close attention to this fascinatingly accessible *Relation* of the Anglican envoy opens to us the whole range of society in which three-fourths of the narrative of our *Historia* unfolded. To facilitate comprehension I have no more than eliminated a few intrusive commas, intercalated a few others in brackets, placed also in brackets or in the annotation the modern sense of some obsolete words and also the modern equivalent of many place names, and italicized Carew's Latin and other foreign words.

For all the verisimilitude, the account, it should be noted, fails to point up adequately the political distinction within the *szlachta* as between the Polish magnates and the Lithuanian princes with whom, along with the Hanseatic patricians also of the north Carew seems to have had the most converse, and whom he constitutionally characterizes as the "chief publicke nobility," and the middle and lower *szlachta* the "gentry" and the "gentlemen" of his account, whom he thinks of as "the private nobility" (cf. at n. 7 and after n. 11); and he never really explains the latter apart, or their distinctive institutions.[4]

He scarcely intimates, moreover, that a powerful, socially turmoiling "movement for the Execution of the laws" from 1505[5] into the period of his mission to the Commonwealth was primarily fostered by the gentry against the magnates, the lesser nobles exerting themselves in *Sejm* and *sejmiki* primarily against the magnates of the senatorial class to implement the reformatory laws that would prevent the alienation of the royal demesnes and many appointive offices (like that of *starostwo*) from becoming virtually hereditary among the magnates for services already performed for the King or for loans and other favors for him and hence the consequent hazard for the commonweal that the King might come to lose his fiscal autonomy and also his far-flung command and would then emburden the gentry with increasing taxes.

In the opening paragraph, Carew vividly and for the most part appreciatively characterizes the members at all levels of the *szlachta* (both gentry and magnates) who entertained him lavishly. Then, after a very substantial account (here omitted) of the economy, constitution, and history of the Commonwealth through the reign of Stephen Batory (d. 1586), not without identifying and vividly characterizing the townsmen[6] and the serfs (far more that does Lubieniecki: *kmiecia*, *Bauwers*, villeins, plebeians) over whom the gentlemen (and all the magnates) had "absolute and insolent power" as nowhere else in Western Europe, Carew then goes on to describe the multifarious religious scene largely patronized by the "private nobles" of the *sejmiki* and the Chamber of Deputies, including in his religious survey the senatorial Roman bishops, the Uniates (Vladitians), the remaining Orthodox, the Armenians, Jews, Tatars, idolatrous pagans, and various Protestants, including "Trinitaries",[7] although nowhere in the entire *Relation* does Carew appear to have consorted with any professed Socinians, writing though he did in the very year of the elimination in their stronghold of Lublin of the leadership of the Anabaptist Unitarians by Socinus in 1598, RD 8, n. 24.

[3] . . . They [the Polish nobles] are large of body, tall, uprighte, and personable. The gentry [are] full of ceremonies, civill and curteous in enterteinement,

bountifull at table, costly in dyett, greate gourmandes, and quaffers, not sleepy, nor heavy in theire drunkennesse, as the Dutche, but furious, and quarrellsome, highe-mynded, and proude, but in a iollity, and not so surly, as the Germans. Apert [open] in theire dealinges, so liberall, that they are rather prodigall, and hating avarice, they distaste the artes [crafts and business] and trouble of gayning, great shifters [contrivers] to lyve bravely [showily] (which they muche affecte) and therefore badd payemasters, highly conceipted of themselves, and so the more easely ledd, and cousened by Parasites, whoe adoring them, stripp them of theire wealthe. Theire nature being suche, and so well knowne to the Italians, hathe drawne greate nombers of them into Polonia, whoe partly followe greate men, and partly trade, both [groups of Italians] working uppon the magnificency of the Poles. In Italy, theire carelessnesse, and symplicity in gyving, and bargayning, hath allmost silenced the [deprecatory] proverbe of Fresco Tudesco [*I'm not a gullible German*] and brought in use *Non sono Polacco* [*I'm not a (gullible) Pole*]. Theire travailing into foraigne contreys (to which they are muche gyven) for knowledge of state and languages, makes them now begynn to looke better to theire purses. . . .

[62–68] The title of kinge [of Poland] was first graunted to Boleslaus Chabri Anno 1001 by Othe the third Emperour, forfeited 1082 by ecclesiasticall censures, pronounced by Gregory the 7 against Boleslaus the second for killing St. Stanislaus bishopp of Cracow at the altar (for which it is allso thoughte that the Poles were enioyned the shaving of theire heades used yet by them, though (I thinke it is to be attributed to some other cause synthence the Hungarians, Dalmatians and Sclavonians doe the lyke). The title was restored 1320 by John the 22[,] Pope[,] with the consent of the Emperour [Louis the Bavarian, 1314–47] (Polonia being then an arrierefiefe of the Empyre. . . .) For the restitution of the regall dignity the Poles were bounde to paye a yearely tribute to the Churche of Rome, which was called Peter pence. . . .

The greate [e]state [*stan*, order] of the lande which with the kinge, and in the vacancy[,] absolutely possesseth the Soveraignety, is the Nobilitie, which is eyther proper or by union, [as in the case of] Cracow, and the 3 Cityes of [Royal][1] Prussia united and incorporated with the Nobility in the Dyets, Conventes [martial assemblages] and the whole government. The proper is called Equestris Ordo [nobility], holding theire landes onely by the service of the sworde and allmost absolutely free, saving that in 3 cases they acknowledg the Crowne. Fyrst that theire Bawres [serfs] pay the Fumalia for theire proper Coppyholdes.[2] Secondly, as tyed to the Courtes of Justice. Thirdly, as bounde to service of the defensive warre. [63] Thys came by the liberality of the kinges, who did not onely make them partakers of the governement, and graunte them theire lande in inheritance, but also allmost made them absolute lordes over theire possessions, and subiectes in so muche that no prynce in Europe hath so absolute power over hys subiectes, as the gentlemen of Polonia have over theires, bothe for goodes and lyfe, the villanes [Bawres/serfs] being accounted in theire lordes chattells, which makes the Gentry (*szlachta*) allmost as insolent over the plebeians as the Mamelukes were over the Egiptians.

The priviledges of the Nobility (*szlachta*) are theise. Fyrst, immunity from all paymentes, services, greivaunces, customes, etc. Secondly, that they onely by lawe exercise armes. Thirdly, that they have all the honours [,] prefermentes, offices, magistracyes, and advauncementes (excepting the Burgerly)[3] by that meanes possessing both the military and Civill estate. Fowrthly, they onely possesse Mannors and landes called Bona terrestria, that is, belonging to the terrestriall Judgementes. For that by Statute Burgers and Plebeians may not holde any suche eyther in propriety or by morgage for 2 reasons. Fyrst because the Burgers would not suffer gentlemen [*szlachta*] to possesse howses, or landes of the Burgerly tenure, and that secondly for that Burgers possessing terrestriall landes tyed to military service to the greate preiudice of the lande, as making a profession different from armes[,] founde meanes to free themselves from personall service in military expeditions.[4] Notwithstanding after that by Sigismundus [II Augustus] statute of 1550 gentlemen were admitted to the righte of Burgerly tenure upon condition of subiecting themselves to the lawes of it. Burgers have ben allso permitted to enioye the other upon the lyke conditions. Fyftly, the Nobility is greately priviledged in villany, if that may be called a priviledge, and not a dampnable licentiousnes preiudiciall to itselfe.[5] Sixtly and lastly (to omitt the more petty) the Nobility conioyned hath the soveraignety and disposition of the Crowne arbitrarily, tyed in it no wayes to the other members of the lande, and in the Interregnum[6] the making of lawes, which allso bynde the future kinge (whoe is sworne to them) so that then they may gyve themselves what authority or priviledge they will, and alter the very forme and administration (if they please) [therein being obnoxious] to no man.

This Nobility is devided into publike and private persons. The *publike* are suche as have parte of the publike charge, whether it be in commaunde or onely in administration. Theise are eyther Senators, or other inferior magistrates, and offices.[7] The Senators charge is eyther ioyntly in counsaile, or particuler to eache mans office. The first is doubly considered as ioyned with the kinge (whoe then is theire heade in particuler, as in [64] generall he˙ is of the whole realme) or in the Interregnum, theire president then being the Archebishopp of Gnesna cheife man of the lande.

Theire office with the kinge is to procure the publike good in all matters, to mannage the whole state, to heare and decide causes, to gyve audience and dispatches to embassadors, to conferre the olde fiefes, and allso those of newe conquestes, etc, to gyve theire direction and advice for the Dyet, place, tyme, and matters to be therein propounded. All which they doe onely as the kinges assessors, and Counsellors, the kinge communicating by lettres, matters of ymportance with them which are absent uppon theire charge, for onely parte of them followe the Courte. In the wydowehoode of the realme theire charge and care is greater. They take order for the securing of the confynes against externall force, looke to the peace of the land, constitute extraordinary judgementes, appoynte the tyme, place, and order of the election and in generall see *Ne quid Respublica detrimenti capiat.*[8]

The Senate consistes of 140 persons. Was devided into twooe by Sigismundus Augustus viz. the grande Counsaile and the privy Counsaile, there being out of thys excluded the 50 Castellani minores, which he did for the many inconveniences in communicating matters of sodayne execution, and to be passed with greate secrecy to suche a multitude. Thys moderne Senate is according to Sigismundus constitution at Lublin [1569]; when he incorporated Lithuania with Polonia and made one common Senate of bothe, whereas before they helde severall[9] Dyetts, and were distinguished in all matters, save that being under one heade, they weare combyned by a perpetuall league. The persons [of the Senate] are eyther spirituall or secular. The spirituall are the 2 Archebishopps[10] and 13 Bisshopps. They in the Senate and Dyet representing the whole clergy have the charge of the religion, in which regarde that State is considerable in thys place.[11] [At this juncture Carew expatiates on the diversity of religion without his taking up *directly* that sector of the nobility he distinguished above as "private" persons under whose patronage the ensuing denominations abounded.]

Religion in thys lande is manifold, bothe for manyfest opposition and diversity of sectes, which commes, for that it confynes with[12] nations of most contrary rites, all men drawing by nature some novelty from theire neighboures. And therfore borderers uppon severall religions doe never syncerely observe that of theire contrey, but mixe it with borrowed superstitions. Theise we see in the confynes of Polonia [along the borders with] Wallachia[13], Moldavia etc., where besydes the wonderfull nombers of heretikes, especially in the capitall article of the Trinity,[14] there are many Qui aut nullos, aut Deos tantum colunt impios,[15] the collission of dyvers opinions easely corrupting, if not altogether extinguishing the religious affection of mans mynde.[16] [Faith and confusion][17] doe generally distinguish the religions of thys kingedome. The first[18] is devided uppon difference about the Messias into Christianisme, acknowledging Christ, Turcisme, Mahumet[,] and Judaisme, in expectation [of the Messiah][,] theise twooe last retayning circumcision though diversly.[19] [65] The Christians are subdevided into the Latyne and orientall Churche. Thys latter into the Greeke and the Armenian. The Latyn into suche as have publike churches and those which eyther communicate in conventicles, or privately mainteyn, and propagate theire opinions. Those which have publike churches are the Papistes, Calvinistes[20] and Lutheranes. The first are onely allowed of the State, and the Clergy of it admitted to the Senate, the other twooe tollerated by articles of publike peace,[21] and the Layemen of them capable of all publike offices though Massovia suffers no religion but Popery.

Of Protestantes the Calvinistes in Polonia are in greatest nomber. In Prussia and Livonia the Lutheranes (Lutheranisme being allmost onely proper to the Germanes through all Europe). Theise twooe are most rooted in Prussia (the

Ducall being alltogeather Evangelical)[22] and Livonia, where the Eastlanders retayne some dregges of the Romish superstition, otherwise without religion for wante of clergymen. In bothe Poloniaes[23] are some store of Calvinistes, but most in the Lesser, where they had in Cracow itselfe a publike churche, destroyed by the studentes 1587, and lastly 1592. In [the palatinates of] Lithuania and Samogitia,[24] they have made meetely progress, and would have don more, yf the Cardinall Radzivil,[25] and hys three bretheren had not defected from theire fathers profession. Thys howse[,] cheife for authority and mighte in Lithuania[,] planted the [Reformed] religion in it. For the twooe Cozen Germanes bothe called Nicholas[,][26] being Commanders of Lithuania (for that the one after the other was palatyne of Vilna, generalls of the forces and Chauncellors of Lithuania)[,] made profession of the Ghospell.[27] The one (thys moderne Cardinalls father) defended the Evangelical[28] openly, and caused the byble to be translated into Polish, which cost hum 10000 florins.[29] The other was father of the present palatyne of Vilna.[30]

In theise contreys are also greate stoare of Anabaptists,[31] Osiandristes,[32] Ebionites,[33] and of all sortes of Antitrinitaries.[34] The Romish religion[35] is held upp by twooe meanes, the kinges[36] hott profession, whoe perswaded by the Jesuites[37] preferreth not (if he can choose without too greate inconvenience) any other then of the Romishe Churche, or yf he doe, it is with an intent to weaken hym, as he served Leschinczky, whome he made Palatyne of Brzestye,[38] which office hath not above 300 florins yearely profitt, that thereby constrayned to maynteyne the greater state after the Polish fasshion, he should be forced to spend hys inheritance, and therefore gave hym not for hys helpe in that charge any Captayneshipp or other office of proffitt, as commonly those greate Dignitaries have. Thys did he, for that Leschinczky was bothe of a fayre lyving, and a man of a greate courage and zealous in hys profession. The second meanes is the care of the Byshopps and dilligence of the Jesuites, whoe nestle themselves everywhere in that lande, growing very riche, that being lykely to worke theire ruine, for that they become now odious to the Catholikes themselves for invegling and fetching in gentlemen to endowe theire Colledges with theire inheritances to [66] the prejudice of theire howses. Theire cheife[39] colledges are at Bransperg,[40] in Prussia, founded by Cardinall Hosius, besydes a seminary there instituted by Gregory the 13. In Livonia at Riga, suppressed by the Burgers 1587 and restored by Parliament 1591, and at Derpt, bothe founded by kinge Stephan; at Calisia[41] in the Greater Polonia, founded by the Archebishopp of Gnesna, Stanislaus à Carnków;[42] at Vilna founded by Gregory the 13, Polotia by kinge Stephan 1579, bothe in Lithuania. And at thys present the kinge for all hys povertie, builds at Cracow very stately for them.[43] Besydes theise they [the Jesuits] have many schooles, preache at Dantzig, and would fayne have the inspecting of the Universities, but neither Zamoysky[44] whoe doth not greatly fancy theise busybodies will committ hys universitie to them, nor the Schollers of Cracow by any meanes admitt them, it being aunsweared by the Rector, Professors and studentes [of the Jagiellonian University] that they would not alter theire founded state nor subiect it to them, which are onely good in Pedantery, and never yet in Polonia made sounde clerkes as the Universitie had don, which furnisheth the whole realme bothe with Churche and Statesmen. Theire aunsweare [is thus] much agreeing with the motion of the University of Padova to the seignory of Venice, for the excluding of Jesuites from schoole governementes.[45]

Polonia receyved the gospell [under Duke Mieszko I][46] Anno 966 the Nones of Marche, and therfore in remembrance of the destroying of the Idolles, on that daye the boyes cary about Images, which they throwe into the water, and synge songes of the expelling of the Devill, muche after the olde rite of the Romanes.

Lithuania receyved it [the Gospel in] 1386 uppon convenante with the Poles, whoe gave Jagello Duke of Lithuania the kingdome in dowry with kinge Lewes [of Hungary's] daughter [Jadwiga].[47] He to drawe hys subiectes to the same profession graunted dyvers greate priviledges to the Christians, whereas before the Lithuanians as theire other Northern neighboures were allmost sclavishly subiect to theire princes. Those were, fyrst, that the Churches Catholicall, Barons and Nobles should have lyke privilegdes, Immunities etc with the Polonians, onely that those lay states should be bounde to the service of building, and repayring the Princes Castles, and high wayes, and to paye theire ordinary tribute. Secondly, that they should succeede theire fathers in theire possessions, as the Poles doe, have power to sell, exchange or morgage them, but with the princes consent, and by resignation before the Prince and hys officers, according to the custome of Polonia. Thirdly that Vilna and Troky should be erected into palatinates and Castellanyes and other offices should be instieued after the forme of Polonia, all to be bestowed onely uppon the Catholikes. By thys [67] tearme of Catholike the Evangelicall[s today] are not excluded, for that by it was understoode the latyn Church, which had then no disunion.[48]

The Greekish religion prevailes universally in Russia alba,[49] and for the most parte in Lithuania, Russia rubra, Volhinia, Podolia etc. In the Polish allegiance[50] onely the Gentry followeth the Romish, the Evangelicall, hereticall, and some fewe the Greekish.[51] It is also spredd in Samogitia and some provinces of Livonia, peopled by the Moschovites when they were lordes of it.[52] The cheife prynce of thys religion is the olde Duke of Ostrog, palatyne of Kiovia,[53] whoe notwithstanding suffers hys twooe sonnes to follow the Romish. Thys [Byzantine-rite] churche [in the Grand Duchy of Lithuania] and [the] Moschovitish [each] acknowledgeth for theire heade the Patriarch of Constantinople.[54]

That [Byzantine-rite Church] of the Crowne of Polonia is governed by twooe Archebishopps and 6 byshopps, whome they call Vladikes,[55] the 2 first are of Leopolis, the Metropolitane, and Vilna, the other 6, Polotia, Wlodomiria, Liveoria, Pinsko, Kiovia and Praemisla,[56] but they are not Senatours, neyther meddle they with any parte of the State. The Russians[57] were converted by Basilius Archebishopp of Constantinople,[58] which, as also theire continuall commerce with the Gretians, of whome they borowed theire characters,[59] hath kept them from ioyning with the Latyn Churche.

Theire trade was by the Maesians[60] and Illyrians, bothe as well as themselves Sclavonians by originall, and from Kiovia, which by the Boristhenes[61] communicates with the Euxine.[62] At thys daye in both the [Russia] alba and the rubra[63] the rites are somewhat different from the Greekish altered by tyme, and the Metropolitanes yealding and applying themselves to the princes, so that now in the Polish State the Vladitians begynn [since 1595] to acknowledge the Popes Supremacy.[64]

The Armenians subiect in spirituall matters to theire owne Patriarche, whose seate is at Leopolis, dwell most parte there, and in Camieniecz[65] in Podolia. They are most skillful and riche marchantes, have greate trade in the remotes (sic) contreys of Turkey, Egipt, Persia and India, which commes for that they are muche favoured by all Mahumetanes and greately priviledged amongest them being free from toll and custome by Mahumetes lawe, which he made in thankfullnes for benefittes receyved of them.

[68] The Mahumetanes descended from the Tartarian horde transplanted 1396 upon theire captivity by Vitoldus, Duke of Lithuania and placed not farr from Vilna, were priviledged with liberty of religion, which they still retayne, and serve the kinge for wages against any enemy whatsoever.[66]

The Jewes have theire chiefest residency at Cracow, Leopolis in Russia,[67] and Troky in Lithuania, where they use greate trade of furres, those which dwell in the townes and villages are artisans and husbandmen. The gentlemen[68] may have of them in theire townes, but suche are not in the kinges protection nor have benefitt of the lawes passed in theire favoure, except the kinge have some commodity by them.[69] Those lawes or priviledges, more in favoure of the Jewes then Christians, were graunted by Boleslaus [the Pious] Duke of the Greater Polonia 1264 and confirmed by Casimire the greate 1363 onely for that province, because Boleslaus not being monarche could not gyve them more largely.[70] By them [the royal laws] according to the civill, and Canon lawes they may onely lend upon pawnes, and not uppon bills or bondes. They make a greate parte of the inhabitantes that be comming to passe for 3 causes. Fyrst allmost all trade is in theire handes, the Poles esteeming it sordide. Secondly theire usury is not limitted. Thirdly the princes sufferance for the greate benefitt of the Crowne by theire extraordinary payements. At one tyme they were chardged with 40000 Crownes for a present sent to the Emperor of Constantinople, for the kinge may at hys pleasure impose upon them extraordinary tribute.

Those which retayne Polytheoticall Idolatry are the pagans dwelling in Livonia, Samogitia, Lithuania, and at Ceremissa on the borders of Russia,[71] whoe worshipp severall creatures, and idolles, retayning still Ethnicall rites and sacrifices. For theise there are not statutes or lawes written, onely in those vast regions they lyve at theire pleasure, not forced to Christianity, no man being over hasty to instructe them, or seeke theire conversion, save that of late the Jesuites begynn to teache, and wynn those which are neighboures to theire stations.

To returne to the Clergyman of the Romish churche, which are partakers of the governement: the[y] possesse in the kingdome 76560 villages or Mannors (though they are not the 200th parte of the people) besydes theire tythes, offerings, and other fees, whereas the whole secular nobility possesseth only 140000.[72] The praediall tythes[73] are in some places exacted manipulatim, that is, in specie, and in some places in money, viz. 36 kreutzers uppon the Laneus,[74] but lesse in Pomerania.

The heade and Metropolitane is the Archebishopp of Gnesna, *Legatus natus*,[74] by the Popes graunte about Anno 1200, second person of the realme and cheifest authority in the Interregnum.

NOTES TO THE INTRODUCTION

1. The *Vita* by his son/sons, covering in *HRP* folios 2r.–7v., has already appeared in translation in my *The Polish Brethren: Documentation of the History and Thought of Unitarianism in the Polish-Lithuanian Commonwealth and in the Diaspora, 1601–1685*, Harvard Theological Studies 30 (Missoula, Montana: Scholars Press, 1980), Doc. XXVII.

The set of two consecutively paginated volumes is now distributed by the present publisher of *HDR* and *HTS*: Fortress Press, Minneapolis. Scholars Press moved to Chico, California, and is now in Atlanta, Georgia. *Polish Brethren* appeared concurrently with the same title in *Proceedings* of the Unitarian Historical Society, volume 18:1 (1976–77); volume 18: 2 (1978–79), 773 pp., 17 plates, pullout map, 4 indices, and errata slip.

This indispensable slip with addenda (!) is available upon request from the publisher. *The quite detailed indices are, alas, off by 4 pp. in reference to the second, consecutively paginated, volume.* (Hence, e.g., the opening document of the second volume— Document XV—appears on printed page 359, while the indices to it and the contents of that page are all to the ghostly original, 363.)

Besides the *Vita*, there are two biographies: Janusz Tazbir, *Stanisław Lubieniecki: Przywódca ariańskiej emigracji* (Warsaw: PAN, 1961) and the Danish Lutheran pastor-scholar and ecumenist, K. E. Jordt-Jørgensen, who was able to use the preceding (and also Tazbir's other preliminary studies and text editions), *Stansław Lubieniecki: Zum Weg des Unitarismus von Osten nach West im 17. Jahrhundert* with an extensive *Litera-turverzeichnis* of MSS still unpublished and of the secondary literature, Kirche im Osten, Monographienreihe, 6 (Göttingen: Vandenhoeck & Ruprecht, 1968); while Tazbir puts it altogether again succinctly in his entry in *Polski Słownik Biograficzny (PSB)* 17 (1972) 603–7.

2. In Polish usage, instead of the maiden name, the family name is commonly given in the plural in the form, e.g., as here: *z Filipowskich*, "of" or "from the Filipowskis." For non-Polish readers I have throughout the text and the annotation given the simple maiden name and have commonly used it even after marriage, for in this way it is possible to keep the *feminine* ending and the various pluralizations of family names when referring to both spouses.

3. Tazbir presents in his book a pullout genealogical table of the extensive and distinguished Lubieniecki Family. In an earlier work, and also in the present annotation, I have assigned roman numerals to distinguish the many namesakes, who in the sources and in scholarly Polish usage, are at most identified as junior/senior; młodszy/starszy.

4. Janusz Tazbir, "Księgozbiór Stanisława Lubienieckiego," *Rocznik Biblioteki Narodowej* 4 (1968) 197–217.

5. *Fidelis relatio rerum Thorunii 10 Octobris anni 1644 peractarum, in Colloquio Charitativo, instituto inter Romano-Catholicos et Dissidentes in religione ab ecclesia*

eorum. The MS was printed by Friedrich S. Bock, *Historia Socinianismi Prussici* (Königsberg, 1753) 115–21. The earliest bibliography of Lubieniecki's works is *BAnt,* 165–68.

6. This has been translated and annotated in my *Polish Brethren,* Doc. XXII. Subsequently I brought together additional material in my "The Place of the *Confessio Fidei* of Jonas Szlichtyng in the Life and Thought of the Minor Church," in Lech Szczucki, ed., *Socinianism and its Role in the Culture of the XVIth to XVIIIth Centuries* (Łódź: PAN, 1983) 103–14.

7. The Berlin MS is edited by K. E. Jordt Jørgensen in two volumes with an introduction in German and a useful conspectus of all figures referred to in the colloquy and the Latin text (Copenhagen: Akademisk Forlag, 1982). See further in Bk. 1, n. 93.

8. *Compendium Veritatis* 2.358; noted by Jørgensen, *Lubieniecki,* 24–29, 31–32, "'Das liebreiche Gespräch' zu Thorn." See further Section III D, final paragraphs.

9. The set was initiated by Andrew Wiszowaty and his son Benedict, editor of *BAnt* and *HRP.* This set is made up of two volumes of Faustus Socinus, four volumes of Johannes Krell, one volume of Schlichtyng in two parts, one volume of Johann Ludwig von Wolzogen in two parts, to which series after a substantial interval was added one volume of Samuel Przypkowski.

10. For the sojourn of Lubieniecki and other Poles in France and particularly in Paris, where Hugo Grotius facilitated their way to liberal Protestant salons, see Jean Moreau-Reibel, "Sto lat podróży różnowierców polskich do Francji," *Reformacja w Polsce* (*RwP*) 9–10 (1939) 1–27, on Lubieniecki, particularly 22–26. Heinsius reappears in our Introduction between nn. 24 and 25.

11. In MS 527 of the Remonstrant Library in Rotterdam are about 170 works in Latin and Polish describing in verse the characteristics of various European peoples. Among these is one ascribed by Andrew Lubieniecki to his nephew, our Author, "Stosowanie Francuzów z Hiszpany," printed along with several others from the same MS by Stanisław Kot, "'Descriptio Gentium' di poeti polacchi del secolo xvii," *Ricerche Slavistiche,* 6 (1958) 150–84. Our Author's poem deplores intolerance and absolutism wherever found and evidences his unfavorable observation of the French as impetuous, excessively verbal, inconstant in love, and indiscrete in their drink, '*Descriptio Gentium,*' 170–77. It is possible that Lubieniecki visited Italy and England during his three years of the grand tour. In exile from Poland, however, he would later be highly supportive of the effort of Louis XIV to be elected Holy Roman Emperor to replace the Hapsburgs.

12. For Niemirycz in support of the Union, see *Polish Brethren,* Doc. XXVII. A convoluted memoir of André de Tabac (probably a pseudonym), recalling the family history of the Lubienieckis (to whom he was related) from the point of view of the paintings of two of our Author's sons, and referring to some documents in the possession of his grandfather, seems to preserve authentic, even though confused, memories of the association of Lubieniecki as even an envoy in Berlin of Hetman Bogdan Chmielnicki and then of Ivan Vyhovskyi. It is a photocopied typescript in the Widener Library of Harvard University, *Lubinetzki: Geschichte einer arianischen Familie von Malern und Politikern* (no place; c. 1970). There it is said that Lubieniecki's second son, born according to de Tabac in 1653, was named Bogdan after the Hetman, also that in the family archive was a long letter (which he, de Tabac, had once perused) from Zofia Brzeska Lubieniecka (our Author's wife), addressed to one Pani Strzykowska, in which she recounted her harrowing trip with a Tatar escort, prompted by longings for his husband, to join our Author in Berlin in 1653, carrying secret instructions of the Hetman (and possibly Niemirycz) to him. *Lubinetzki,* 11.

It is possible that this memoir stems from a descendent of Stefan Niemirycz, who settled in Neudorf (near n. 22.)

The family reminiscences of de Tabac, composed before he was introduced to the standard sources of the life of Lubieniecki, says that with his son Bogdan he made a trip into Poland to "seine Schwester, Frau [?Anna] Horodyska in Lubinec . . . vermutlich um die ausbleibenden Rente [for property turned over to her when he had to leave Poland]." *Lubinetzki*, 19. The same writer says that Lubieniecki's widowed mother (d. 1663), remaining behind in Poland, had sent abroad to her son the remains of her late husband's library. *Lubinetzki*, 52.

13. This was edited by Janusz Tazbir, "Dariusz drogi krakowskiej i legacyjej krystyańskiej do krola JM Karola Gustawa anno domini 1655 octobris," *Odrodzenie i Reformacja w Polsce* (*OiRwP*) 5 (1960) 201 – 21.

14. The speech is imbedded in a work of Lubieniecki, dealt with as Doc. XXV in *Polish Brethren*, 578 – 79.

15. In the *Historia* Lubieniecki is evasive about the details of the theology and practice of believers' immersion. In the manuscripts examined by Jørgensen the usage of the Polish Brethren and of Lubieniecki himself comes up several times and the phrasings in quotation are respectively from Stettin in 1661 in relation to his newborn son and from Hamburg in 1667, replying to the city senate, *Lubinetzki*, 77, 110. The account here of the two memorials in defense of Unitarians in Poland is drawn from the same, *Lubieniecki* 45 – 51. The observations of Photinianism are substantiated in the annotation to the *Historia*.

16. *Polish Brethren*, Doc. XXIX; *BAnt*[2] verifies his authorship; see further n. 31. Lubieniecki's *Vindiciae* has much of importance for the sixteenth century, as it deals extensively with the constitutional freedoms, notably with those consolidated in the Warsaw Confederation of 1573, whereby the Protestants, on conditions made even more explicit in the IV Henrician Articles, acceded to the election of Henry of Valois in 1574 (Section III D and Pls. 35 – 37).

17. When mentioning the edict against heretics of 1424, Lubieniecki alludes (*Historia, 33*) to this projected work: "Quod in historia civili, Deo volente, demonstrabimus," and dealing with the activity of Nuncio Lippomani at the Diet of 1556 he remarks (*Historia, 76*): "Quid ea de re in comitiis actum fuerit, tomo 2 cum Bono Deo dicemus." The two references are brought together by Barycz (my note below, 35 "Lubieniecki jako historyk," 85, n. 8), who holds that something like the *Legal Claims* was in Lubieniecki's mind (translated in *Polish Brethren*, Doc. XXIX), not a purely political history, which has been the view of Janusz Tazbir.

18. Jordt-Jørgensen, *Lubieniecki*, 74.

19. *Brevis et fidelis relatio colloquiorum inter D. Hieronymum Mulmannum, Soc. Iesu theologiae et philosophiae doctorem, et Stanislaum Lubieniecium, in Regia Hafnensi, anno 1661, 12 Februarii habitorum*, *BAnt*, 167, with a still accessible MS, a copy thereof in the Remonstrant Library in Amsterdam.

20. The work in the German edition is edited by Arnold Starke, *Jahrbuch des Theologischen Seminars der Unierten Evangelischen Kirche in Polen*, 3 (Poznań: Lutherverlag, 1937). Noted by Jørgensen, *Compendium Veritatis Primaevae*, 2 vols. of annotated text and an extensive introduction in German (Copenhagen: Academisk Forlag, 1982) 1: 7. For the Synod of Czarków, 1654, Jørgensen brings together a notice of the East Prussian historian of Socinianism, Friedrich Bock, and the records of the earliest Arian synods compiled by Stanisław Szczotka, "Synody Arjan Polskich," *RwP* 7 – 8 no. 1 (1935/1936) 21 – 100, specifically pp. 94 f.

21. *BAnt*, 165; a copy exists in the Bodleian Library, Oxford, Pol. B14. Another presumably related work in quarto but without date is mentioned by Sand, ibid., *Morientis Poloniae conservandae ratio certissima*, under the name of Brutus. These works are not cited by Adam Kersten in his otherwise comprehensive article on Lubomirski, *PSB*, 18 (1973) 14–21.

22. Matthias Scheitz (1625–1700) painted a picture of Lubieniecki in Hamburg possibly in 1664 when he was forty-one. Lambert Visscher (1633–90) used this painting as the basis of his copperprint for the *Theatrum Cometicum*, for which he provided other illustrations, including the view of Hamburg with comets of 1664 and 1665 on the skyline. This painted portrait, by way of Gerard van Papenbroek, came into the possession of the portrait gallery of the University of Amsterdam. The copperprint, commonly reproduced, is also found in *Polish Brethren*, Pl. M.

23. Jørgensen, *Lubieniecki*, 112–16. This author has almost certainly established the improbability of the later rumor that the family was conspiratorially poisoned at the behest of the Lutheran divines.

24. Sigismund II Augustus personally approved the decrees of Trent in 1564, but they were not adopted by the Diet until under Stephen Batory in 1577.

25. This term of Czech scholarship is not congenial in Lutheran and general Reformation scholarship, since, of Luther's three reformatory principles, *sola scriptura, sola fides, sola gratia*, Hussitism, largely a moral and popular reformation, did not clearly articulate either of the last two.

26. Janusz Tazbir, *State without Stakes* (1967: Warsaw: PIW, 1973).

27. On the *Nucleus*, see further RD 5, n. 1.

28. The "Medulla" is extant in two slightly variant MSS (Hamburg, Cluj). It is dealt with in the Dutch context by Lech Szczucki, "Socinian Historiography in the Late Seventeenth Century: Benedict Wiszowaty and his '*Medulla historiae ecclesiasticae*,' " in F. Forrester Church and Timothy George, eds., *Continuity and Discontinuity in Church History: Essays presented to George Huntston Williams*, Studies in the History of Christian Thought, 19, series ed. by Heiko Oberman (Leiden: Brill, 1979) 285–300. See further RD 5, n. 1.

29. *BAnt*, 167.

30. In the year of the completion of this Transylvanian chronicle (Pl. 64) much used by Wilbur, Friedrich Samuel Bock (1716–86), polymath, professor of theology at Königsberg, and castle librarian, published his biobibliography based on *BAnt* but by arranging alphabetically rather than chronologically his amplified and accrued entries, *Historia Antitrinitariorum, maxime et Socinianorum* 2 volumes (incomplete) (Königsberg/Leipzig, 1774/76). For his life, see *Allgemeine Deutsche Biographie* (*ADB*) 2:766. The first historian to place the pre-Socinian Antitrinitarians in the context of the Reformation era was Friedrich T. Trechsel (1805–85), docent of the Bern Academy, *Die Protestantischen Antitrinitarier vor Faustus Socin*, 2 vols. (Heidelberg, 1839/44).

31. "Dziejopis polskiej Reformacji," chap. 9 in Tazbir, *Lubieniecki*, 304–43.

32. See Jørgensen, *Lubieniecki*, where the form, style, and motivation of Lubieniecki in *HRP*, *Theatrum Cometicum*, and the *Compendium* are treated systematically in the second half of the book under the general heading "Der Schriftsteller und Theologe."

33. "Lubieniecki jako historyk Reformacji," in Lech Szczucki, *Wokół dziejów i tradycji Arianizmu* (Warsaw: PAN, 1971) 77–94; more fully in the context of general Polish historiography, "Stanisław Lubieniecki—Historyk Reformacji polskiej," *Szlakami dziejopisarstwa staropolskiego: Studia nad historiografią w XVI–XVIII wieku* (Wrocław: Ossolineum, 1981) 243–65. See further at n. 89.

34. Szczucki, "Benedict Wiszowaty," p. 288.

35. *BAnt*, 55.

36. Otwinowski composed in Polish *Christian Heroes* on the lives of Protestant patrons and ministers. His *vita* of Budziński is summarized in *BAnt*, 55; cf. the much reduced summary of *Heroes* in Węgierski, *Slavonia Reformata*, 535. On the age of Otwinowski, see *BAnt*, 83; *PSB*, 24.

37. "Stanislas Budziński (c. 1530–1595): The First Historian of Unitarianism," *The Papers on the Conference on Unitarian History*, Kalamazoo, Michigan, May 1984, ed. by John C. Godbey, *Proceedings* of the Unitarian Universalist Historical Society, 20:2 (1985) 77–93; cf. above at n. 30.

38. The very act of translation from the Polish into Latin was no doubt in part a paraphrase by Lubieniecki and, as I may not have always been sure what was from Budziński when our Author failed to acknowledge his probable dependency, it remains for another scholar to study all the surviving Latin texts of Budziński in Lubieniecki and compare them with the total of about a page and a half of additional or overlapping material from Budziński converted into Latin by five other historians and assess further this first historian of the movement in his own right. An independent study of Budziński is foreseen by Z. Pietrzyk in *Bibliotheca Dissidentium*, 8.

39. Of importance, perhaps, is the fact that both Socinus and Budny were mortalists, holding with close scrutiny of Scripture to the death or sleep of the soul at the death of the body, and disavowing immediate immortality and stressing rather the resurrection. Under the heading of "psychopannychism" I have dealt with this as a usual trait of many radicals, including the Anabaptists, *Radical Reformation*, 3 passim.

40. In this quasi-Gnostic notion Socinus held that Jesus after his baptism at Jordan was taken up into heaven by God the Father so that he might ascertain what of the Old Testament should be discontinued, what confirmed, and what was to be distinctive of his own God-willed saving Gospel. See on this further, *Polish Brethren*, 85–86. That Jesus' commission to teach came from God precisely after his baptism is what made Socinus minimize its importance, the more so for the reason that there is no *effectual* scriptural account of Jesus' baptizing (John 4:2 prevails over 3:22), not even of his apostles, while Paul, the chief apostle, largely eschewed the practice, leaving it for others.

Throughout my work here and elsewhere I have opted for one of two usages among Baptists in North America: believer*s'* baptism and believe*r's* baptism, the former registering the objective historic communal character of the ordinance, the latter its subjective character as resulting from personal adhesion to the community of faith by conscious choice. Each usage can be theologically and otherwise defended. Two Southern Baptists historians of Christian thought and practice, with doctorates from Harvard Divinity School, Professors Samuel Leo Garrett of Southwest Theological Seminary, Fort Worth, Texas, and Timothy George, Dean of Samford University Divinity School, Birmingham, recognize both usages as current, the first favoring the objective, the second, the subjective aspect of baptism by immersion of the adult believer.

41. This is accessible in a facsimile edition by Janusz Tazbir (Warsaw: PAN, 1973) with a summary of the life of Węgierski and a very good summary in Latin of antecedent and related ecclesiastical histories in Czech, Polish, and Latin, and an index, henceforth cited *Slavonia Reformata*.

42. See Szczucki, as cited in n. 29. Although most publications centered in Holland, other centers of the diaspora were Transylvania and East Prussia.

43. Cf. above in connection with Hegesippus, near n. 43.

44. Cf. Harry A. Wolfson, "Trinity and Incarnation in the Kalam," *The Philosophy*

of the Kalam (Cambridge: Harvard University Press, 1976) 304 – 54.

45. The rise of Unitarianism among the English Nonconformists of congregational and presbyterian polity is set forth succinctly by Wilbur, *Transylvania and England*, 254 – 64.

The emergence of Trinitarians and Unitarians among the Noncomformists in England began with the division at the Salter's Hall Conference in 1719 (Presbyterian, Independent/Congregational, and Baptist) into Subscribers (to the Westminster Assembly's *Catechism* on the doctrine of the Trinity) and the Non-subscribers, most of whom or their congregations eventually became explicitly Unitarian by the end of century. The rupture was replicated still again notably in the gradual schism within the (Congregational Puritan) Standing Order in Massachusetts, in its province of Maine, and in New Hampshire, beginning in 1805, i.e., into trinitarian Congregationalists and Unitarian congregationalists, with the latter carrying with them most of the professors of the Puritan's oldest College, Harvard University, all its presidents, clerical and lay, Unitarians, 1805 – 1933. Although the first expressly Unitarian congregation in America was that of Anglican King's Chapel in Boston (1785), Unitarianism was primarily a movement within the *town* theocracies of New England of congregational polity after much of their eastern seaboard leadership had first passed through an Arminian/Enlightenment phase. C. Conrad Wright, famous for his aphorism that "the father of New England Unitarianism was John Calvin," went beyond Wilbur in detailing this development in *The Beginnings of Unitarianism in America [1735 – 1805]* (Boston: Starr King Press, 1955). The liberal movement in New England away from the Calvinist orthodoxy out of the original congregational Puritan theocracies was by way of Arminianism, with but isolated episodes of Arianism before the general wave of scriptural Unitarianism that swept up into its movement most of the first parishes or congregations of the semi-Erastian "Standing Order" in the eastern seaboard towns of Massachusetts, Maine, and New Hampshire and with it the oldest college. Although the minister of King's Chapel who shifted theological allegiance evidently had a set of the *Bibliotheca Fratrum Polonorum* and other *Sociniana*, neither Wilbur nor Wright regarded the currents from Poland or Transylvania, chronicled by Lubieniecki, as having been decisive in the New England development. Within the self-limiting scope of congregational polity, the Association of Unitarian ministers, laymen, and congregations (1825), forerunner of the organized denomination, became, in the terms of the presbyteral/synodal Reformed in Poland and Transylvania, the "Minor" Church with respect to theology but culturally for a century the dominant community in the region of its first emergence in America. A succession of nine clerical and lay presidents of Harvard University, 1805 – 1933, was Unitarian. Dr. Wilbur, magisterial historian of Antitrinitarianism, himself shifted his allegiance from the trinitarian Congregationalism of his native Vermont to congregational Unitarianism while a student of the Harvard Divinity School (class of 1890).

For the history of Harvard, with some of the themes of this note expanded, see G. H. Williams, ed., *Harvard Divinity School* (Boston: Beacon Press, 1954); *Divinings: Pointers from Harvard's Heritage* (New York: Pilgrim Press, forthcoming).

46. "Studies in the Radical Reformation (1517 – 1618): A bibliographical survey of research since 1939," *Church History* 27 (1958) 46 – 69; 124 – 160.

47. Although identified by me in the preface as the definitive version, coming to 1060 pp., it has not, when reviewed, been always recognized to have dealt extensively with the scholarship and source collections appearing in the preceding score of years; but see Arnold Snyder, *The Catholic Historical Review* 73:4 591 – 92; Paul Knoll, *The Sixteenth Century Journal* 19: 296 – 97 (Summer 1988).

The Spanish edition had been preceded by a very substantial revision for an Italian edition (translated by Albano Biondi) to have been published by Einaudi Press in Turin.

I rehearsed the development of my conceptualization of three interrelated movements of the sixteenth century (Anabaptist, Spiritualist, and Evangelical Rationalist) in the Cyril Richardson memorial lecture, "The Radical Reformation Revisited," *Union Theological Seminary Quarterly Review*, 39:1 and 2 (1984) 1–24. Professor Milan Opočensky announced a Radical Reformation Consultation in Prague, 23–27 January 1986. The theme was addressed in the Sixteenth Century Studies Conference in St. Louis, 24–26 October 1986 and its papers published by Hans Hillerbrand, ed., *Radical Tendencies in the Reformation: Divergent Perspectives*, Sixteenth Century Essays and Studies 9 (Kirksville, Missouri, 1988). The *Radical Reformation*, embodying all the addenda and corrigenda of the Spanish edition, appears in the foregoing series 10 (Kirksville, 1990).

48. Heiko Oberman, in the context of the tripartition of the modalities of the Reformation, by princely territory, by city councils, and by refugees, gives a perceptive overview of Nicodemism as "Ausharren statt Flucht," in his larger collection *Die Wirkung der Reformation: Probleme und Perspektiven*, Institut für Europäische Geschichte, Mainz, Vorträge no. 80 (Stuttgart: Steiner, 1987) 32–46 with the recent literature. On Italian Anabaptism, see my "Two Social Strands in Italian Anabaptism ca. 1526–ca. 1565," in Lawrence P. Buck and Jonathan W. Zophy, eds., *The Social History of the Reformation: In honor of Harold Grimm* (Columbus: Ohio University Press, 1972) 156–207; much of this and additional material are included in my *La Reforma Radical*.

49. Such is the fortifying observation of Lech Szczucki in his *Marcin Czechowic (1532–1613)* (Warsaw: PWN, 1964) and in connection with his discovery in a Swedish Library of Czechowic's *Trzech dni rozmowa* (Pl. 27), on baptism, written in 1564, published in Łosk in 1578 by Szymon Budny with a short critical comment, discussed in two articles, the first edited by Jean Rott in Strasbourg, the second in *OiRwP* 31:1 (1986). Szczucki's identification of the baptist synod of June 1565 in Brzeziny near Łowicz, the birthplace of Grzegorz Paweł, firms up what is said in *Historia*, Book 3, n. 203 and elsewhere.

50. With respect to the Polish Brethren within their homeland and the Transylvanian Unitarians until c. 1700, I have made some general comparisons in "Unterschiede zwischen Polnischen Brüdern und den siebenbürgischen Unitariern," Papers of the Tagung in Hamburg, 13–14 June 1985, *Der Einfluss der Unitarier auf die europäisch-amerikanische Geistesgeschichte*, ed. by Werner Erdt and Wolfgang Deppert, *Kirche im Osten*, Publikationsreihe der Unitarismusforschung, ed. by Róbert Dán, Deppert, Erdt, and A. de Groot.

A fundamental difference between the Transylvanian Unitarians and those elsewhere was that precisely the leading lights on Kolozsvár were escaped biblical Unitarians from the Reformed Rhine Palatinate, who already belonged to the *Erastian*/Antidisciplinarian (anti-Calvinist) party in Heidelberg.

51. The single English term "magisterial" can combine allusion to both the *magister* and the *magistratus*, in other words to the *magisterium* of duly educated and ordained clerics (bishops, abbots, or university professors on the basis of Scripture, the Fathers, canons, and councils) and to the magistracy or rule in or over the church on the part of kings, princes, or town councils, the latter on the basis of distinctive urban law. This double connotation is not easily taken up in a single comparable term in several languages other than English, attested from 1632 for authoritative teaching and from 1660 in the political sense (*Oxford Dictionary*, 16). In an intercalated new section of my *La Reforma Radical*, 32.3, I have further defined "Reforma Magisterial y Reforma

Radical,'' 933 – 40, noting that "antimagistratical" was used specifically and polemically of Independents (Congregationalists) as of 1645.

52. A major study in English on the pacifist and semi-pacifist patrons of Poland is that of Stanisław Kot, *Ideologja polityczna i społeczna Bracia Polskich zwanych Arjanami* (Warsaw, 1932), translated by Earl Morse Wilbur as *Socinianism in Poland* (Boston: Beacon Press, 1957). Another even more comprehensive in coverage is that of Peter Brock, *Pacifism in Europe to 1914* (Princeton: University Press, 1972) chap. 4.

53. Janusz Tazbir brings out the ruthlessness and greed of some Protestant lords in their espousal of the break from the control of bishops and who then inculcated fear and resentment in their peasants and serfs. He warns against any idealization of the whole nobiliary class because of the exceptional magnanimity of some few, mostly Unitarian, lords, "Ze studiów nad stosunkiem polskich Protestantów do chłopów w XVI wieku," *RwP* 11 (1953) 32 – 61.

54. *Sixteenth Century Journal* 16:2 (1985) 228 – 56. A comparable introduction to the rally of the church and her orders in Counter-Reform, including the Uniates, for the whole of the period covered by Lubieniecki and in the background of the *Historia* is that of Jerzy Kłoczowski, "Catholic Reform in the Polish-Lithuanian Commonwealth," in *Catholicism in Early Modern History 1500 – 1700: A Guide to Research*, ed. by John O'Malley, S.J. (St. Louis: Center for Reformation Research, 1988).

Perry Anderson as a Briton and a Marxist is especially helpful in the attention he gives to the distinctiveness of the nomenclature of feudal society in Poland in the larger context of the evolution of noble classes from antiquity into the age of absolute monarchy, through which Poland never passed, in two related works, *Passages from Antiquity to Feudalism* and *Lineages of the Absolutist State*, both (London, c. 1974).

55. J. K. Zeman, "The Rise of Religious Liberty in the Czech Reformation," *Central European History* 6:1 (1973) 128 – 47; Peter Brock, *The Political and Social Doctrines of the Unity of the Czech Brethren in the Fifteenth and Early Sixteenth Century* (The Hague: Mouton, 1957); Edmund De Schweinitz, *The History of the Church Known as the Unitas Fratrum* (2nd ed, Bethlehem, Pa.: Moravian Publishing House, 1901).

56. Quoted by Zeman, "Rise."

57. Ibid.

58. Sándor Szent-Ivanyi, *Freedom Legislation in Hungary 1557 – 71* (New York: Hungarian Inter-Faith Brotherhood, 1957).

59. Ibid.; Pl. 40.

60. G. H. Williams, *The Radical Reformation* (Philadelphia/Mexico City: Westminster/Fondo de Cultura Económica, 1962/1981) passim, indexed under *Sitzerrecht*.

61. Charles O'Malley, *Jacobo [Giacomo] Aconcio*, tr. by Delio Cantimori (Rome: 1955). See also Bk. 3, n. 385.

62. Edited by Růžená Dostálová, Iacobi Chii Palaeologi, *Catechesis Christiana dierum duodecim*, Biblioteka Pisarzy Reformacyjny 8 (Warsaw: PAN, 1971).

63. De Schweinitz, *Unitas Fratrum*, chap. 34.

64. Węgierski, *Slavonia Reformata*, 215; quoting Stanislaw Sarnicki, *Annales Polonorum*. When early in his reign as Catholic prince of Transylvania, he was urged not to show so much favor to Protestants, he replied with the same religio-political aphorism, often quoted to his credit, an axiom which must have often been given voice in the dining halls of his fellow lords and magnates: Wilbur, *Transylvania* 38; Haner, *Historia*, 295; Lampe, *Historia*, 281; Bod, *Historia*, I, 429; Uzoni, L. 192.

65. Ambroise Jobert, *Luther à Mohila: Pologne dans la crise de la Chrétienté 1517 – 1648* (Paris: Institut d'Etudes Slaves, 1974), chaps. 14 and 15. Lubieniecki

criticized the effort to exclude Unitarians from the electorate in 1632, above near n. 20.

66. Notable here was the provisional independence of the Polish Primate and the episcopal bench from the papal legate and the Holy See in seeking an internal confessional settlement on the basis of construing the three Sandomierz Protestant synods as schismatic rather than heretical (Magni). Anything comparable would have elsewhere only happened theoretically in time of papal schism with more than one obedience. In fact, along with the role of Primate-Interrex Uchański at the end of the Jagiellonian dynasty and of the Pacification of the Ruthenians, the Colloquim falls into a Polish tradition of popular and hierarchial loyalty to Rome reaching into the twentieth century when the Polish bishops (under Cardinal Hlond and Archbishop Sapieha) assertively chose to meet apart from the affronted papal nuncio (the later Pius XI Ratti) in their organization meeting under the II Republic at Częstochowa or when in a series of self-disciplined and hazardous actions, bringing him to house arrest, Primate Stefan Wyszyński on his own then dealt with the United Workers Party and government (1951), dealt reconcilingly with the conforming bishops who had taken an oath to the People's Republic, and who then brought to Rome in 1957 representative conforming and martyr prelates, saying to Pius XII Pacelli: "We are the united Polish Church," and who took the leadership in the Polish episcopal conference to extend a reconciliatory gesture to the Germans, independently of the government and of the Holy See.

67. Edited in *Elementa ad Fontium Editiones*, 13 (Rome: Institutum Historicum Polonicum, 1965).

68. Several letters of Carew in English and Latin concerning Poland are published or calendared (if published elsewhere) by the same editor in the same series, volume 17 (1967), nos. 117–125.

69. Cf. n. 1. Hungarian names as printed regularly reverse Hungarian usage by giving the family names last instead of first, and in the case of Stephen Báthory, his name is spelled in the Polish manner, Batory, on his becoming King.

70. See the tribute by Jan Szeruda, "Edmund Bursche (1881–1940)," *RwP* 11 (1948–52) 131–33.

71. In a letter to Duncan Howlett from Berkeley, 28 September 1949, Dr. Wilbur said: "I made the translation in the first instance for my own sake, a dozen or more years ago, thinking I ought not to write the Polish section [of his two–volume *Unitarianism*] without first mastering the chief original sources, which meant, if I were to do a thorough job, making the translation." In recalling in an address before the Unitarian Historical Society "How the *History* came to be written" (1950), he said: "Another task of drudgery now faced me [after translating two fundamental works of Servetus, 1932]. The only contemporary history of our movement in Poland is Lubieniecki's *History of the Polish Reformation*, 1685, a rare book to find, and when found a hard one to read, but it is an invaluable source book for mastering early Unitarian history, and without mastering that I could not hope properly to write our history in Poland. That, too, I must [I had to] put into English [c. 1938]. The unpublished manuscript of my translation awaits the favorable attention of some patron." Unitarian Historical Society, *Proceedings*, 9:1 (1951) 5–23, esp. p. 14.

Dr. Duncan Howlett, Harvard College and graduate schools, A.B., 1928; J.D. 1931; S.T.B., 1936, kindly made available to me his Wilbur File in photocopy with his own covering letter of 6 December 1985. Wilbur's recollection here of the date of his translation is confirmed by the datings of letters and advertising on the back of his recycled pages on which he had typed it in the smallest elite typeface any of us had ever seen, the venerable typewriter evidently inherited from his father's law office in Vermont.

72. The citation read:

Earl Morse Wilbur, D.D.,

Founder and builder of the Starr King School for the Ministry, scholar extraordinary, builder of a library of *Unitariania* unique in the world, author of what is universally acknowledged to be the definitive *History* of the Unitarian movement.

This has been the work of a lifetime, and was written from original sources, many of them now perhaps forever lost, which he traveled to Europe many times to consult.

To write this history, he had command of nine languages—English, French, German, Latin, Dutch, Spanish, Italian, Polish, and Hungarian.

Now at the age of 84, he is hard at work upon the second volume which will bring his History of our movement down to date.

We salute Dr. Wilbur who has done as much as, perhaps more, than any contemporary to advance our cause, by showing the deep historical roots which nourish us and by searching out the spiritual substance of the Unitarian movement as it emerges in the long course of our history.

The denomination later struck a medal in his honor as the Unitarian of the year, 1955.

73. Reduced to its core, the Earl Morse Wilbur Collection of Socinianism and Unitarianism is housed (in part) in the library of the ecumenical Graduate Theological Union, Berkeley. Of the Collection there are 9 reels of 16 mm. film available in several research libraries. His son-in-law, Newell Nelson, has inventoried the Wilbur papers in his home and made the list available to several libraries.

74. In the Earl Morse Wilbur Lecture in Berkeley for 1984, I brought together a great deal of his life and bibliography in ''Wilbur's Vision: Freedom, Reason, and Tolerance Reglimpsed,'' *Unitarian Universalist Christian*, 42:2 – 3 (1987) 43 – 62.

75. His was a review essay on Kossowski's *Protestantyzm w Lublinie i w Lubelskim* (1933) in *RwP* 6 (1934) 243 – 252 and on his ''Zarys dziejów protestantyzmu na Wołyniu w XVI – XVII wieku'' in *Rocznik Wołyński* (1933) *RwP* 7/8 (1935/36) 409 – 10. Although Wajsblum became a member of the Communist party, there is nothing in his critique of Kossowski nor in the notes I received from his widow that suggests, for example, a Marxist interest in theological and synodal quarrels as disguised contests of class interest. My own annotation may still suffer, indeed from insufficient attention to class factors and class struggle in the *Historia*.

Dr. Werner Erdt, in his habilitation thesis submitted to the University of Hamburg, ''Der polnische Sozinianismus: Eine kirchen- und dogmengeschichtliche Studie zu einer kirchlichen Randgruppe der Reformation in Polen'' (1986), dealing with the Polish Protestant scene primarily during the lifespan of the Lubieniecki of the *Historia*, held that Socinianism could be seen as the religious expression of the lower and the middle *szlachta* in the context of their socio-economic and political displacement in the Counter-Reforming Commonwealth of the magnates.

76. The first tribute to Dr. Wajsblum after his death was written by Wiktor Weintraub. This minute and others were brought together in ''Marek Wajsblum (1903 – 1962): Historian of Polish Culture,'' *Polish Review* (*PR*) 11:2 (1966) 3 – 10, with his bibliography. The earlier obituary by Weintraub in *Rocznik Polskiego Towarzystwa Naukowego na obczyźnie* 12 (1961/62) 18 – 20 mentioned the edition of the *Historia* as virtually completed!

77. The several studies of Dr. Wajsblum relevant to the *Historia* are cited by me at the appropriate places, notably his ''Dyteiści małopolscy,'' *RwP* (1935 – 39), dealing with certain family archives bearing mostly on the seventeenth-century history. None of

the specific wording of his survives in the present edition: still the onerous task of complete annotation that I have accomplished would have been even more arduous but for his robust explorations. And his substantiated findings, along with *all* his (often spirited) *corrigenda* of the lucubrations of his peers, remain intact. Several of his *excursus* have been broken up and distributed to appropriate points in the annotation, some summarized, and a very few omitted. (All his handwritten notes in Polish and English have been deposited with my own papers relating to the edition in the Andover Harvard Library, although one substantial sheaf of them, in Book 3, were somewhere lost in the transmission to me.)

78. See above, n. 39.

79. See above, Part I.

80. See above nn. 1, 2, and 29.

81. See above n. 72.

82. See above n. 73–76.

83. See below at nn. 87 and 90. For all the works on Barycz to date, see the volume in his honor, *Studia i Materiały z dziejów nauki polskiej*, series A, no. 14 (Warsaw: PAN, 1978).

84. For the latest assessment of the literature on Comenius and Harvard, see my *Divinings*, chap. 1, and for the possible Polish origins of the seal, *ibid*, chap. 2.

85. The speakers were graduates Thomas Danforth, John Gorham, and Bradstreet Story who held a French conference "Upon the comparative importance of the American, French, and Polish revolutions to mankind," 19 July 1792, reported in *Dunlaps American Daily Advocate*, 28 July 1792. This information was included by Miecislas Haiman in his survey of American Opinion on the Great Diet and the Constitution of May 3 in his *The Fall of Poland in Contemporary Opinion [1791–98]* (Chicago: 1935) 69. The episode was kindly brought to my attention by Professor Józef Andrzej Gierowski, sometime rector of Jagiellonian University.

86. The tract was commissioned and published by the American Unitarian Association's *Tracts*, Ist Series, no. 47; most accessible in Sydney E. Ahlstrom and Jonathan S. Carey, *An American Reformation: A Documentary History of Unitarian Christianity* (Middletown, Conn: Wesleyan University Pres, 1985), 136–50. The editors, following C. Conrad Wright, *The Beginnings of Unitarianism* (1955, n. 47), hold that Ware's essay represents only a retrospective appropriation of a spiritual pedigree rather than being in any way testimony to some local continuity by way of Arminianism of the Socinian impulse. It could be otherwise. For the latest assessment and the literature, see my *Divinings*, chap. 1.

87. *Loc. cit.*, p. xxxvi.

My further emended and corrected working copy of the facsimile edition of *HRP*, after a score of years of work, slipped unheard into a full wastebasket in my office and was carried off in April 1985. All of my corrigenda, identifications, and surmises have fortunately been largely taken into the translation and annotations. Dr. Wajsblum did not have access to the facsimile edition with its invaluable index, but he appears to have had, through correspondence, advance copies of certain entries in the *Polski Słownik Biograficzny*, still in progress.

88. These related writings in order of publication are (1) "Anabaptism and Spiritualism in the Kingdom of Poland and Grand Duchy of Lithuania," *Studia nad Arianizmem* (Warsaw, 1958) 214–62; (2) "The Sarmatian Myth Sublimated in the *Historia Reformationis Polonicae* (1664/85) of Stanislas Lubieniecki and Related Documents," in Victor Erlich, ed., *Essays in Polish Literature, Language, and History* offered to Wiktor

Weintraub on his 65th Birthday (The Hague: Mouton Publishers, 1974) 567–579; (3) "A Colonial Rector of Harvard University and Stanislas Lubieniecki: A note on one of the first books written by a Pole known to have been read by an American, 1689," in Henryk Zins, ed., *Studia Anglistyczne*, Lubelskie Towarzystwo Naukowe (Warsaw: PWN, 1975) 41–47; (4) "Erasmianism in Poland 1518–1605," *Polish Review*, 22 (1977) 3–50; (5) "Socinianism and Deism: From Eschatological Elitism to Universal Immortality," *Historical Reflections/Réflections Historiques* 2 (Winter 1975) 265–290; (6) "Stanislas Hosius 1504–1579" and (7) "Peter Skarga, 1536–1618, S.J.," in Jill Raitt, ed., *Shapers of Religious Traditions in Germany, Switzerland, and Poland, 1560–1600* (New Haven: Yale University Press, 1981) 159–171; 175–194; (8) "Protestants in the Ukraine during the 'Superintendency' of John Laski, 1556–1560," *Harvard Ukrainian Studies*, in two installments, 2: 1 (March 1978) 41–72; 2: 2 (June 1978) 184–210; (9) "Francis Stancaro's Schismatic Reformed Church Centered in Dubet'ko in Ruthenia, 1559/61–1570," in Ihor Ševčenko and Frank E. Sysyn, eds., *Essays Presented to Omeljan Pritsak on his Sixtieth Birthday by his Colleagues and Students* (Cambridge: Harvard University Press, 1979–1980) 931–952; (10) *The Polish Brethren: Documentation of the History and Thought of Unitarianism in the Polish-Lithuanian Commonwealth and in the Diaspora*, 1601–1685, Harvard Theological Studies, 30 (originally Missoula, Montana: Scholars Press; now: Philadelphia: Fortress Press, 1980); (11) "The Polish-Lithuanian Calvin during the 'Superintendency' of John Laski, 1556–1560," in Brian A. Gerrish, in collaboration with Robert Benedetto, ed., *Reformatio Perennis: Essays on Calvin and the Reformation in Honour of Ford Lewis Brattles*, Pittsburgh Theological Monographs Series, No. 32 (Pittsburgh: Pickwick Press, 1981) 129–158; (12) *The Mind of John Paul II: Origins of his thought and action* (New York: Seabury Press, 1981, now distributed by Harper and Row), map, 415 pp; (13) "The Christological Issues between Francis Dávid and Faustus Socinus during the Disputation on the Invocation of Christ, 1578–79," in Robert Dán and Antal Pirnát, *Antitrinitarianism in the Second Half of the 16th Century* (Budapest/Leiden: Hungarian Academy of Sciences/Brill, 1982) 287–321; (14) *La Reforma Radical*, corrected, enlarged, definitive edition, tr. by Antonio Alatorre (Mexico City/Madrid: Fondo de Cultura Económica, 1983) map, 1053 pp; (15) "The Place of the *Confessio Fidei* of Jonas Szlichtyng in the Life and Thought of the Minor Church," in Lech Szczucki, ed, *Papers of the International Conference: Socinianism and its Role in the Culture of XVIth to XVIIth Centuries.* (Warsaw/Łódź: PAN, 1983) 105–114; (16) "The Radical Reformation Revisited," The Cyril Richardson Memorial Lecture, Union Theological Seminary, New York City (21 March, 1983), *Union Theological Seminary Quarterly Review*, 39 1:2 (1984) 1–2; (17) "Stanislas Budziński (c. 1530– c. 1595): The First Historian of Unitarianism," Unitarianism in its Sixteenth and Seventeenth Century Settings, Papers delivered at meetings for the Society for Reformation Research, May 1984, *The Proceedings* of the Unitarian Universalist Historical Society, 20: 2 (1985–1986) 77–78; (18) "[Earl Morse] Wilbur's Vision: Freedom, Reason, and Tolerance Reglimpsed," The Wilbur Lecture for 1987, Berkeley, *The Unitarian Universalist Christian* 42: 2–3 (Summer/Fall 1987) 43–62; (19) *Protestants in the Ukrainian Lands of the Polish Lithuanian Commonwealth*, combining items 7 and 8 with a preface by Frank Sysyn, the Millennium of Christianity in Rus'-Ukraine Series (Cambridge: Harvard Ukrainian Studies Fund, 1988) 86 pp; (20) "Strains in the Christology of the Emerging Polish Brethren," in Samuel Fiszman, ed., *The Polish Renaissance in its European Context*, Papers of the International Conference honouring Jan Kochanowski, May 1982 (Bloomington: Indiana University Press, 1988) 61–95; (21) "Religion, Law and Revolution in the Shaping of Harvard College, 1636–1708," expansion of "Religio et Veritas," a lecture at the 350th anniversary celebration of Harvard University, in John Watts, Jr. and Frank S. Alexander, eds, *The Weightier Matters of the Law: Essays on Law and Religion in Honor of Harold Berman* (Atlanta: Scholars Press for the American Academy of Religion, 1988) American Academy of Religion Studies in Religion, 51: 123 – 162; (22) "Die Unterschiede zwischen dem polnischen und siebenbürgischen Unitariamus und ihre Ursachen," paper read in Hamburg before the international Tagung on the history of Unitarianism, June 1985, to be published with the other papers by Werner Erdt and Wolfgang Deppert.

89. The autobiographical material of Wiktor Weintraub (1908 – 88) is printed in Twórczość 42:9 (1986) 75 – 93. An author in Polish literature, he wrote a dissertation under Stanisław Kot on the influence of Ducal Prussian Lutheranism on the Polish Reformation, *Historia*, Bk. 1, n. 159, and comprehensively surveyed the scholarly literature on "Western Studies of Italian-Polish Literary Relations during the Renassaince Era," in Sante Graciotti and Emanuela Sgambati, eds., *Rinascimento letterario italiano e mondo slavo* (Croatian, Hungarian, Czech, and Polish only]: *Rassegna degli studi dell'ultimo dopoguerra* (Rome, 1986). In his essay Weintraub alludes to the anticipated American edition of Lubieniecki's *Historia* and has much to say on the one prinicipal exception to the otherwise "artificial isolation" of Poland from general works on the impact of the Renaissance and Reformation, namely, the extensive studies of Polish Antitrinitarianism, which he assesses, among them the achievement of Earl Morse Wilbur. A major assessment of his own life and work, especially at Harvard, appears in *Harvard Ukrainian Studies* 13 (1989).

NOTES TO BOOK ONE
THE GREETING

1. The editor of the book and the author of this Greeting was Benedict Wiszowaty, editor also of *Bibliotheca Antitrinitariorum* of Christopher Sand, Jr. See Preface to the Appendix of Related Documents and Book 1, n. 68. The identity of the purported publisher, Johannes Aconius, has not been established. The text shows that it was composed by a non-Polish compositor who in many cases was unable to identify the Polish names. It seems that Wiszowaty had no time to supervise the printing since in the autumn of 1684 at the latest, he had to go to Electoral Prussia for the synod of Rutów, 14 October 1684, at which he was ordained.

2. These two letters of 1661 and 1663 are printed in *The Polish Brethren* Doc. XXXIII, 635 – 69.

3. The term *Antitrinitarius* is not used within the *Historia* itself, suggesting that its appearance in the book's printed subtitle is due to Benedict Wiszowaty.

4. The Life is printed in *Polish Brethren* as Doc. XXVIII, 516 – 41 with portrait. Wiszowaty placed the account of Lubieniecki's life after the Greeting and preceding the Index Capitum.

NOTES TO THE FOREWORD

1. The use of *Antitrinitariorum* suggests that the headings are not from Lubieniecki.

2. Lubieniecki presupposes the centrality of religion for state and society, and he means Christianity. It was his deep conviction that there is a "Catholic" Christianity, which for him Unitarianism most clearly approximated, because it alone of the rival versions rests solely on Scripture and the Apostles' Creed, what he called *Veritas primaeva* (see further Plate 1 and Book 1, nn. 11, 93). But he would like to consider in his *Historia* the whole of religion in Poland, not merely his own group, and would like to think that the presentation is sufficiently fair to be worth the testimony of a thousand. As a restorationist of Apostolic Christianity, he recorded what he considered the account of the climax of the Reformation/Restoration among a kind of Chosen People, who, like their antecedents of the Old Covenant, must ponder adversities as God's instruction and chastisement. The *Historia* abounds in references to providential coincidences. The rationalist interpreter of comets in human history (Plate 63) and among court astrologists in *Theatrum cometicum* (3 vols., Amsterdam, 1666 – 68) here seeks to descry the workings of the Lord of history. His account of the Primitive Church, of patristic sanctions for the Minor Reformed Church, of medieval dissenters, and of the Reformation beyond the Polish-Lithuanian Commonwealth is derivative but takes up much of Book 1.

Lubieniecki means by *Reformatio Polonica* in his title the Reformation among Polish-speaking people, mostly in Poland and in the lands ceded by the Grand Duchy of

Lithuania to the Crown in the Union of Lublin of 1569 (Plate 32), especially in Podlachia (Podlasie) and Volhynia. Yet he does deal some with developments in Transylvania and even episodically in Moldavia. Except for Podlachia and the palatinate of Vilna, he does not go much into the Protestant developments in the Grand Duchy, nor in Great Poland. And he scarcely refers to the Czech Brethren in Great Poland, with whom the newly Reformed Poles sought to establish synodal and confessional unity (the latter realized to some extent by the Consensus of Sandomierz of 1570, Plate 34, not even alluded to by Lubieniecki).

Much in the *Historia* could be classified as regional or local and family history. Some of it unfolds like the tale of a lordly raconteur at a manorial hall after dinner. On this cadenced telling of family tales with some of the original allusions lost to modern readers, as on a leisurely river, float documents and fragments of compact narrative from other sources that make the whole *Historia* a strange mingling of precious documentation, useful comment by the author himself, highly partisan accounts, genealogy, and gentlemanly gossip.

It is not here the place to give Lubieniecki's sources or even the secondary literature, except for a few preliminary titles, for in the notes that follow references are made to several modern treatments of Church history in the Polish-Lithuanian Commonwealth in the period actually covered by Lubieniecki, roughly from 1540 to 1650.

The most recent treatment of Polish Church history in general is the collective enterprise, edited by Jerzy Kłoczowski of the Catholic University of Lublin (KUL), *Chrześciaństwo w Polsce 966–1945* (Lublin: KUL, 1980), with a bibliographical essay. For just the Catholic Church and in the period of the Commonwealth there is Janusz Tazbir, *Kościół Katolicki w Polsce (1490–1795)* (Warsaw, 1968). A lesser period is covered in admirable detail and with ecumenical comprehensiveness by Jobert, *De Luther à Mohila.*

For the general Protestant development only there are Theodor Wotschke, *Geschichte der Reformation in Polen* (Leipzig, 1911), Karl Völker, *Kirchengeschichte Polens* (Berlin/Leipzig, 1930), Paul Fox, *The Reformation in Poland: Some Social and Economic Aspects* (Baltimore, 1924), and K. E. Jordt-Jorgensen, *Ökumenische Bestrebungen unter den polnischen Protestanten bis 1645* (Copenhagen, 1942).

In the foregoing titles "Poland" includes to some extent the Grand Duchy of Lithuania, only a portion of which was ethnically Lithuania, roughly the area of the Soviet Republic of Lithuania, except for Vilna (Vilnius, Wilno) and environs with its then strong German, Jewish, and Polish populations, as in the palatinate in general. Three treatments of the Reformation in the Grand Duchy are Józef Łukaszewicz, *Geschichte der reformirten Kirchen in Lithauen* 2 vols. (Polish: Poznań, 1842–43; Leipzig, 1848), Marceli Kosman, *Reformacja i kontrreformacja w Wielkim Księstwie Litewskim w świetle propagandy wyznaniowiej* (Wrocław: Ossolineum, 1973), and Semen Aleksandrovich Podokshin, *Reformatsiia i obshchestvennaia mysl' Belorussii i Litvy* (Minsk: Nauka i Teknika, 1970). The last two are concerned with socio-economic aspects of the Reformation.

For the Polish and Lithuanian Brethren and the Transylvanian Unitarians, seen in a pan-European Reformation context (with little reference to antiquity and the Middle Ages), the standard still are the closely interrelated works of Earl Morse Wilbur, *A History of Unitarianism: Socinianism and its Antecedents* (Cambridge, 1945) and *A History of Unitarianism: In Transylvania, England and America* (Cambridge, 1952).

Following the example of Christopher Sand, Jr., *Bibliotheca Antitrinitariorum* (Amsterdam, 1684), Robert Wallace, drawing upon the subsequent scholarly efforts, composed his still very useful *Antitrinitarian Biography or Sketches of the Lives and Writings of Distinguished Antitrinitarians; exhibiting a view of the state of the Unitarian doctrine and worship in the principal nations 'of Europe, from the Reformation to the close of the seventeenth century,* 3 vols. (London, 1850). The first vol. is a *History of Unitarianism in England during the same period.* Vols. 2 and 3 are cited without any title in the ensuing notes.

Frequently cited in the nn. that follow are *Podręczna Encyklopedja Kościelna* (henceforth *PEK*), 44 vols., but bound together in alphabetical clusters (Warsaw, 1904 – 15); *Encyklopedja Katolicka,* in progress, 3 vols. to date (Lublin: KUL, 1973, 1976, 1979); and *Polski Słownik Biograficzny* (henceforth *PSB*), in progress, 29 vols to date (Cracow, 1935 –).

NOTES TO CHAPTER ONE

1. Cf. Peter's sermon at Pentecost, Acts 2:14 – 40.
2. The Author refers to the Apostles' Creed in use among the Polish Brethren.
3. Acts 20:28; 2 Tim 3:1.
4. The Author gets ahead of himself. He must first illustrate corruption in the "Jewish Church."
5. Eusebius of Caesarea *Hist. eccl* 4. 7.
6. The text wrongly says III, xxix. See Migne, *Patrologia Graeca,* 20, cols. 281 – 84. Lubieniecki quotes Eusebius in the Latin in the Latin translation of Tyrannius Rufinus. The final phrase is from 1 Tim 6:20 on the false *gnosis.*

References in the following nn. to critical editions where available would be pedantic because Lubieniecki sometimes quoted from the Fathers from Synodal acts, collections, and patristic *florilegia* assembled by his own party, some of whom knew well the Greek texts.

The Polish Brethren are almost unique among the groupings of the Radical Reformation in that they eagerly used the testimony of the first age of the Church, even into the fourth century, e.g., Hilary of Poitiers. Yet they did not share the view of Eusebius of Caesarea in his observation of the *Praeparatio Evangelii* among the Greek philosophers. Even Justin Martyr and other Apologists beloved by the Polish Brethren had also perceived the universal *Logos spermatikos.* Still it was in the classical pagan writings that the Polish Brethren found their sanction and testimony for a universal morality. And the testimony of the Ante-Nicene Church reinforced the New Testament moral code congenial to them.

But as for high doctrine, they were by the end of the sixteenth century immersionist Christocentric Unitarians with a deep sense of Holy Communion, who remained faithful to the Apostles' Creed, even though they came to recognize its late date, and baptized their catechized offspring in the name of the Father and the Son and the Holy Spirit (Matt 28:19). Though using the trine formula, the Polish Brethren were confident that they had peeled away the patristic and particularly the scholastic terminology with respect to God the Father, Jesus Christ the Redeemer, and the Holy Spirit as Gift.

Lubieniecki's predilection for Hegesippus (known almost exclusively from the *Historia* of Eusebius) is explained by the fact that he wrote his work in defense of the primitive tradition. Lubieniecki may well have noted also that Eusebius tended to subordinate the Son of God to the Father, a position similar to that of some early Polish Brethren before the definitive formulation of their Unitarianism.

7. The Author does not complete his thought.

8. The Author here postulates that the Church was implicitly ''instituted'' at the birth of Jesus, which he knows was some months ''B. C.''

9. The Author regards Luther as only a forerunner of the decisively fundamental reformation in Poland. He deliberately turns 35 into 5 X 7 to ease over the slight disparity with his 30 for the fulfillment of Luther's reformation in Poland in 1550.

10. Neither Johann Funck nor Johann H. Alsted, the two historians quoted by Lubieniecki himself in his introductory chapters (*p*. 7 at n. 64), provides a direct clue to his chronological speculation. According to Alsted's *Thesaurus chronologiae* (Herborn, 1650) 34 – 35, the first interval would be either 1494 or 1496 years long, while according to Funck's *Chronologia* (Nuremberg, 1545), 62 and 134, it would be 1509 years long. In the *Tabula Chronologica Mathematicorum Viennensium* of 1571 (quoted by Alsted, *Thesaurus*, 35) the interval was 1519 years long. This would agree with Alsted's periodization of history of the New Testament, according to which the fourth period of universal history started in 1519, ''qui potest appellari tempus revelationis Antichristi et Reformationis Ecclesiae,'' Alsted, *Encyclopaedia* (Herborn, 1630) 1992. Lubieniecki might have followed Alsted's general conception, but introduced his own chronological calculation, the better to fit the symmetrical scheme of his own history.

Notes to Chapter Two

11. Cf. Matt 25:36. The Author wrote a *Compendium Veritatis Primaevae* as complementary to his *Historia*. See further Introduction, nn. 57, 93, and Book 3, n. 425.

12. The following persons (pp. 6 – 8) might have been taken up by Lubieniecki from any of the numerous ''Catalogues of the witnesses of truth,'' so popular in Protestant works on chronology or Church history aimed at establishing a new conception of the tradition against that promoted by the Roman Catholic Church. Lubieniecki supplements the series of witnesses with a few Antitrinitarians, whom he may have had occasion to discuss by correspondence with Benedict Wiszowaty, Introduction at n. 31.

13. The Author is singling out amid alleged corruption of theology through secular and priestly power the ancient theologians he regarded as most akin to the views of the Polish Brethren in faithfulness to the ''Primitive truth'' of the Apostolic Age.

14. The council of Ancyra (modern Ankara) was held at Easter, 314, and promulgated 24 canons; that of Gangra in Paphlagonia, c. 345, passed 20 canons against a false asceticism which condemned marriage.

15. The I Council of Toledo, 400, was a national council of Spain directed against Priscillianism. Its twenty canons tend to be rigoristic, with the clergy set apart. The canons presuppose the possibility of clerical marriage and sexual intercourse only *after* ordination.

16. The Author implies that all the councils cited condemned clerical celibacy, which was scarcely true of I Toledo or Elvira.

17. The council of Elvira (near Granada), c. 306, passed 81 severe canons. Canon 33 required continence of all the clergy. Canon 36 opposed pictures in the church for fear of veneration.

18. Lubieniecki, probably by way of a *florilegium*, refers to the third council of Carthage under Primate Aurelius of 397, canon 23: *Et cum altari asistitur, et semper ad Patrem dirigatur oratio*. Giovanni Domenico Mansi, *Sacrorum conciliorum nova et amplissima collectio*, amplified by Phillipe Labbe and Gabriel Cossart, 31 vols. (Lucca,

1759–98); carried forward to Vatican I in cumulatively 55 vols. by B. Martin and L. Pettit (Paris, 1899–1927) 11, col. 1403. Without having perhaps the date of the council, Lubieniecki could have thought of it as in the time of the Donatists who insisted on rebaptism in the tradition of St. Cyprian. In any case, Lubieniecki shows an interest in the two ordinances of his church, believers' baptism and the Eucharist during which prayer is directed to God the Father, all with ancient conciliar sanction.

19. Lubieniecki understood Augustine on the preexistence of Christ the mediator and on the session of Christ at the right hand of the Father and his endorsing presence during communion, through the instruction of Calvin. In his few references to Augustine in the *Historia*, Lubieniecki may also resort to patristic *florilegia*, as elsewhere. As to the conviction concerning the *corpus Christi caelestibus spatiis contentum*, while it is probably compatible with the view of Socinus on the session of Jesus at the ascension, the phrasing is very much like that of the non-Adorant Ferenc Dávid and it does not suggest Christ's vicegerency in heaven.

20. Epiphanius of Salamis (c. 315–403) wrote two epistles preserved in Latin by Jerome, 51 and 91. The first was written to John of Jerusalem in 393, among other things, describing how he had come upon a church curtain in a village named Anablatha that bore an image of Christ or of a saint and in iconoclastic anger tore it (Migne, *PG*, 43, cols. 379–92). Soon after the Epistle to John, Epiphanius wrote three treatises against images. Karl Holl, ''Die Schriften des Epiphanius gegen die Bilderverehrung'' (1916), *Gesammelte Aufsätze*, 2 (Tübingen, 1928) 351–98.

21. The life of Aerius of the 4th century, a presbyter of Pontus, an associate of Eustathius (355, bishop of Sebaste), is preserved by Epiphanius, *Haereses*, 75, who considered him an Arian. His followers, Aerians, are mentioned by Augustine, *De haeresibus*, 53. Lubieniecki faithfully records that Aerius considered prescribed foods as Judaizing and that he made no distinction between *presbyter* and *episkopos*; he also opposed prayer for the dead.

22.The text has incorrectly *Eustachius*. Eustathius, (c. 300–c. 377), archbishop of Sebaste, who studied under Aerius in Alexandria and had been drawn to Monasticism, figures modestly in the condemnation of Macedonius, bishop of Constantinople (342–48; 350–60). The Macedonians or Pneumatomachi, while accepting the creed of Nicaea as of 325, opposed ascribing personhood to the Holy Spirit as in the Nicene—Constantinopolitan formulation. Eustathius is only a name Lubieniecki has pulled out of some larger work, perhaps of Sand or even B. Wiszowaty. As for *Trinitarii*, he here uses it for the ancient Nicene party, here contrasted with the Macedonians, in effect, the adherents of the original Nicene formulary that was silent on the deity of the Holy Spirit.

Elsewhere in his *Historia* Lubieniecki uses the term for the contemporary adherents of the Nicene-Constantinopolitan Creed (Bk. 2 at n. 506; Bk. 3 at nn. 118, 414, 561, and 635). As for the counterpart term, *Unitarii*, Lubieniecki employs it in the text only three times for his grouping (Bk. 3, near nn. 828, 832, 840, 849, 850, 893). These instances late in his narrative and connected with his father's congregation in Lublin sound a little out of place and may be introduced by Wiszowaty, as also in the chapter titles more than once. Lubieniecki freely uses *Unitarii* in his polemical works.

23. The text has *Euphratantion*. Lubieniecki probably intends the bishop of Balaneae in Syria to whom Eusebius of Nicomedia wrote, saying that Christ was ''no true God.'' Athanasius, *De synodis*, 17.

24. Marcellus, bishop of Ancyra (d. c. 374), was an embarrassing ally of Athanasius in supporting the Homoousion of I Nicaea. He taught that in the unity of the Godhead the

Son and the Holy Spirit only become independent entities for the purposes of creation and redemption. He held with 1 Cor 15:24 that Christ would deliver his kingdom to God the Father. The clause in the Nicene-Constantinopolitan Creed, "Whose kingdom shall have no end," was inserted to combat Marcellus. Evidently Lubieniecki liked in Marcellus the final subordination of Christ to God the Father.

25. Photinus, a pupil of Marcellus of Ancyra, was the scholarly and eloquent bishop of Sirmium (in Pannonia), c 344. He held to some form of Modalistic Monarchianism, and the death of the soul pending the resurrection. Photinians were condemned by 1 Constantinople in 381, canon 1.

26. Vigilantius, a presbyter of Aquitaine (Barcelona), survives primarily in an attack on him by Jerome, *Contra Vigilantium* (406).

27. The Author links the Arians and the Donatists as together opposing the Nicene formulation of the Trinity. Arius of Alexandria (d. c. 336), though the traditional archheretic, Lubieniecki here in passing rehabilitates by linking him with Donatus the Great of Carthage, after whom the rigoristic North African Schism took its name. The Donatists regarded the persecution as stamping them with the mark of the true Church, and the support of the imperial rulers as proving the opposite for their adversaries.

Lubieniecki not only does not employ the term *Ariani* for the Polish Brethren but also claims that the appellation is inappropriate. He is uneasy with it [cf. below at n. 121]. In point of fact, in the devolution of the received dogma of the Trinity among the radical Polish Reformed, few of them passed through a recognizably Arian phase with respect to the intradeical Logos/Son: "there was when He was not" (ἦν ὅτε οὐκ ἦν), "brought out of nothingness" before the creation of the world (ἐξ οὐκ ὄντων).

In Polish historical scholarship, for reasons of Polish history, the term *Ariani/Arjanie* is used in a factual sense for the theological left wing within the Reformed Church in Poland even in incipient stages of expressed uneasiness with the Nicene-Constantinopolitan Creed. This usage, however, sometimes leads to anachronism when referring to theological positions and not to groupings. More recently, usage has firmed up in more frequent reference to emergent (subordinationist) Tritheists, Ditheists, and Unitarians. Since all the Polish Brethren became (Christocentric) Unitarians whether in the Transylvanian or the Socinian sense, the theologically radical party within the Reformed Church before it became the schismatic Minor Church could be called on occasion proto-Unitarian. Unitarianism in Poland seems to have developed out of reflection on Christ the Mediator rather than out of the ancient conciliar problem of Father and Logos/Son.

On this see my article in n. 170, and "Strains in the Christology of the Emerging Polish Brethren," and the parallel theological strand in my *Divinings*.

28. Pelagius, a British monk and exegete, taught in Rome, c. 390–410, thereafter in Africa and Palestine. He vindicated asceticism against the charge of Manichaeism by stressing man's freedom to choose good by virtue of powers untouched by original sin which he minimized. Pelagius won adherence among aristocratic circles in Rome and, by contagion, in Sicily. Pelagianism constituted a major thrust in the eyes of Augustine. A council of Carthage in 411 condemned Pelagius as also that of Ephesus 431, canon 4 in the person of Celestius, companion of Pelagius, and more radical in his renunciation of original sin. Pelagianism and Semi-Pelagianism have frequently cropped up in Church history. The Polish Brethren were in the end Pelagian or Arminian.

29. Duns Scotus (d. 1308) of Oxford, Cambridge, and Paris, Doctor Subtilis, was the founder of a major late medieval scholastic system that combined Aristotelianism and

selective Augustinianism, in which primacy was given to love and the will over and against that of reason in Thomism.

30. Samson of Cordova.

31. Serlo not identified.

32. Ratramnus (in the text *Bertramus*; d. 868), monk of Corbie, defended double predestination and in *De corpore et sanguine Domini* attacked the realist or metabolic view of Paschasius Radbertus on the sacrament of the altar.

33. Berengar of Tours (d. 1088) was condemned for his doctrine of the Real Presence over against the metabolic view defended by Archbishop Lanfranck of Canterbury.

34. Peter of Bruys (d. c. 140) rejected infant baptism, the Mass as commonly observed, church edifices, prayers for the dead, and the veneration of the cross. He was condemned by II Lateran and thrown to the flames near Nimes by people infuriated by his burning of crosses. His followers were Petrobrusians. Unfamiliar with this term, Lubieniecki simply pluralizes Petrus.

35. In the text *Baillardus*, a medieval form for Peter Abelard (n. 39).

36. Henry of Lausanne (d. after 1145), a precursor of Peter Waldo, was a monk turned itinerant preacher. He upheld the ideal of absolute poverty. He understood the efficacy of the sacraments as based on the moral probity of the priest (Donatism). He recanted at the synod of Pisa, 1135, but resumed his anti-clerical preaching. He was opposed by Bernard of Clairvaux. Henricians arose in Tour under Henry's influence in the twelfth century. The facsimile edition of the *Historia* mistakenly identifies the *Henricus* as Henry of Ghent.

37. Arnold of Brescia (d. 1155), a student of Abelard, a neo-Donatist, was condemned with Abelard at the synod of Sens in 1140. In Rome, he supported a movement to eliminate the temporal power of the papacy, whereupon he was excommunicated by Eugenius III in 1148. He was captured by Frederick I Barbarossa (who had in the meantime himself come to terms with the papacy), and he was executed.

38. Peter Waldo (d. between 1205 and 1218). Once a rich merchant of Lyons, on hearing from a jongleur the story of St. Alexis, Roman patrician who gave up all for a life of mendicancy, Waldo did something similar and followed the Dominical words in Matt 14:21. Providing for his wife and daughters, he became an itinerant, mendicant preacher. Waldo sought approval for "Poor men of Lyons" at III Lateran in 1179; but, although the vow of poverty was approved, preaching without permission of resident clergy was forbidden. The Waldensians were excommunicated at the synod of Verona in 1184 and evolved into an important, widespread medieval sect, which gave prominence to preaching, stressed the vernacular Scripture, renounced both oaths and judicial and military killing. A. Lubieniecki may allude to the survival of Waldenses on Polish soil, *RDFR* 6.

39. Peter Abelard (1079–1143), renowned for his Sic et non, applied the dialectical method to his inquiry into the dogma of the Trinity, which he clarified in *Theologia Christiana* after his condemnation. In his *Commentary on Romans* he expounded his exemplary theory of the Atonement. Bernard of Clairvaux (d. 1153), arbiter of his age, preacher of the Second Crusade, was the opponent of Abelard and Henry of Lausanne.

40. *Epistola CXCII ad Magistrum Guidonem de Castello* (1140; *PL* 182) cols. 358–59. Lubieniecki wrongly has *Epistola CXCIV*.

41. Caesar Baronius (1538–1607) replied to the Magdeburg *Centuries* in his *Annales Ecclesiastici* (1588–1607).

42. Amalric of Bène, near Chartres (d. c. 1204), trained at Paris, influenced by John Scotus Erigena, held that God is the underlying *essentia* of all creatures and that those

who remain in his love cannot sin. His thesis and the Amalricans were condemned by IV Lateran in 1215.

Lubieniecki, even in his survey of witnesses, leaves unnoticed the major antagonist figures of this Lateran council, Peter Lombard and Joachim of Fiore, on Christ the Mediator. See Intro., IIIA.

43. William of Occam (d. 1347).

44. Paul Alvaro of Cordova.

45. John Tauler (d. 1361) was a Dominican mystic of Strassburg.

46. John Wycliffe (d. 1384), Oxford reformer and theologian; defended civil dominion over the Church, holding that clergy not in the state of grace should be deprived of benefices. He began the translation of the Bible into English, attacked the dogma of transubstantiation, opposed the mendicants. His followers were the Lollards.

47. John Hus (d. 1415), developed in the University of Prague the ideas of Wycliffe, insisting on communion for the laity under both species (*sub utraque specie*). Hence his followers, after his condemnation by the Council of Constance, were called Utraquists. The Utraquists and Czech Brethren, widespread in the Polish-Lithuanian Commonwealth, particularly in Great Poland, become prominent in the ensuing annotation.

48. Wessel Gansfort (d. 1489), educated at Deventer by the Brethren of the Common Life, studied and then taught in Paris. A nominalist, he was a forerunner of the Reformation.

49. Bartholomew Platina (d. 1481), from near Mantua, student of Greek in Florence. In and out of favor with a succession of popes, he was made librarian of the Vatican in 1475. In his *Lives of the Popes* (Venice, 1479) he mentioned the prayers and curses of Callistus III in 1456 against the Turks. In this context he mentioned Halley's comet almost as if it, too, had been papally excommunicated. It would have been as author of *Theatrum Cometicum* (Amsterdam, 1667) that Lubieniecki came in contact with Platina and includes him here for good measure. Perhaps the Sozzini family had had memorable contact with him, his fame thus relayed to Raków, where Lubieniecki was born.

50. Jerome Savonarola (d. 1498) was the rigoristic Dominican reformer of Florence, the assailant of debauched Popes.

51. Emperor Philip the Arabian (244–49) celebrated in 248 the millennium of Rome. Eusebius records (*Hist. eccl.* 6.33) that he was debarred from a church (in Babylas of Antioch) until he had done penance for his sins.

52. Emperor Leo III the Isaurian [the Syrian] (717–41) published an edict declaring all images of Christ and the saints idols and instituting their destruction and thereby initiating the Iconclastic Controversy.

53. Emperor Constantine the Great (306–37) called the Council of I Nicaea, 325; but Lubieniecki may have included him because he was baptized by immersion by Eusebius, bishop of Nicomedia, a correspondent and friend of Arius.

54. Charlemagne, king of the Franks, first emperor of the "restored" Empire (771/800–14), may have been mentioned by Lubieniecki because he did not accept II Nicaea (787) which restored image veneration.

55. Otto I the Great (936–73) was the restorer of the (German) Roman Empire. It is notable that with this entry and that preceeding and following it, Lubieniecki reveals how naturally the knightly Pole felt himself to be wholly of the western tradition.

56. Emperor Louis I the Pious (814–40) was the son of Charlemagne, under whom some theological developments congenial to Lubieniecki occurred.

57. The Author again alludes to his *Compendium veritatis primaevae*. It is this truth

of the Primitive Church that he has always in mind when he speaks of the defense of truth. See n. 93.

58. John 2:18. Lubieniecki in his own manner and proportion recognizes the Catholic appeal to the authority of Scripture, Reason, and *Patristic* Tradition.

59. The account speaks of the Antichrist as coming and of many antichrists as having come already.

60. It is not clear which Nicephorus is meant. None of the historians of this name wrote a work which would have a Book 41. However, Nicephorus Callixtus Xanthopoulos, a Byzantine historian of the fourteenth century, develops this argument in his *Ecclesiastical History* (3.16), known since 1553 in a Latin translation, and comments on the well-known paragraph of Hegesippus (Migne *PG* 145 cols. 927–30). Cf. *Historia 3*.

61. Michael Neander, *Chronicon, sive epitome historiarum* (Eisleben, 1582).

62. *Centuria* was the common title for the great *Ecclesiastica Historia secundum singulas centurias per aliquot studiosos et pios viros in urbe Magdeburgica* (Basel 1559–74), a collective work of Lutheran scholars initiated by Matthias Flacius Illyricus (d. 1575) and largely edited by Johann Wigand (d. 1587). The leading idea of the work was to demonstrate the decline of the truth and the corruption of the Church after the times of the Apostles until the restoration by Luther. The enormous work was impressive by the scope of its sources, covering also political history, and by the critical treatment of these sources, although there was also a tendentious inaccuracy in some texts adduced, especially against the papacy.

63. Jean Daillé, *De vero usu Patrum* (Geneva, 1656). Lubieniecki evidently approves of Daillé's critical appreciation of the Fathers as historical sources and his criticism of the orthodox Lutheran treatment of historical sources by the authors of the *Centuria*.

64. *Chronologia Joanne Funcio authore* (Nuremberg, 1545), numerous later editions. For the addition quoted here, see the Basel edition of 1554, p. 296; the *Commentariorum in praecedentem Chronologiam libri decem*, p. 94; Alsted, *Encyclopaedia*, p. 1997 gives the year 192, not 194.

65. Theodotus the cobbler, a Dynamic Adoptionist Monarchian, came from Byzantium to Rome under Victor (c. 189–98). He was succeeded by Theodotus the money-changer.

66. The preexistence of Jesus Christ is asserted or implied in several ancient Jewish Christian strata in the New Testament, e.g., Phil 2:6f. (*kenosis*). These passages became problems for Nicene and Post-Nicene Fathers who had to circumvent the subordinationist implications. These orthodox Fathers came to speak interchangeably of the eternal Word and the eternally engendered Son, and generally thought of the Word/Son incarnate as Jesus Christ, eventually defined as in two natures (Chalcedon, 451). Lubieniecki is not consistent christologically. At n. 19 he seems to approve of Augustine when holding to the preexistence of Christ the mediator, while here he approves of Adoptionism and observes that "many dared" to express the view seemingly approved above in Augustine.

67. Artemon, who developed the teachings of the two Theodoti (n. 65), was excommunicated in Rome, c. 235. In this school of Christology Jesus was proclaimed as a man anointed with the Holy Spirit at his baptism, whereupon he became the Christ. Lubieniecki was evidently drawn, as were other Polish Brethren, by this ancient school in Rome, since they, too, practiced adult baptism by immersion and held the Spirit to be the confirming Gift.

68. From this point on there will be recurrent references to parallel but often slightly

divergent records and transcriptions in one or another of the documents printed by Benedict Wiszowaty in his edition of Christoff Sand's *Bibliotheca Antitrinitariorum* (Amsterdam, 1684), abbreviated *BAnt*. These documents are described in my Preface to the Appendix of Related Documents. In the translation of these documents, I have broken up the long paragraphs into smaller paragraphs; and these I have numbered consecutively through the set of closely related historiographical documents to facilitate access to something more specific than the page in the Latin text. The reference here is, e.g., to Related Document (*RD*) 5, the opening paragraph, as it happens, no. 47. Paragraph no. 46 in this system is the final paragraph in the preceding document as arranged in *BAnt*, namely *RD* 4. In the main text I have only alerted the reader of Lubieniecki to the presence within the same covers of the writings of other historians who may have drawn upon the same sources as he and rendered them in fuller or slighter form, in many cases, from the lost MS History of Stanslas Budziński.

When these same documents are referred to in the notes, they are more fully identified as to which document. *BAnt* paragraphs beyond 65 are to The Life of Andrew Wiszowaty by his son, which, being primarily of the seventeenth century, has been printed in *Polish Brethren*, 15 – 66 (serving in that collection as its Doc. I).

N.B. A reference in my annotation to *BAnt* followed by a number (not a numbered paragraph), e.g., *BAnt* 23, is to a page in the main biobibliographical text of Sand, edited by Wiszowaty, in which, as e.g. here, Sand refers to a passage in Budzińzki's lost History (incidental to his account of Laelius Socinus).

69. The document preserved in excerpts by Eusebius is the *Little Labyrinth*, which modern scholars have ascribed with probability to Hippolytus.

70. Paul of Samosata, a Dynamic Monarchian, held that the Godhead was a Trinity of Father, Wisdom, and the Word, a single hypostasis until the creation. In Christology he was a precursor of Nestorius in that he held that at the incarnation the Word rested on Jesus. He was procurator ducenarius of Queen Zenobia of Palmyra and overthrown with her in 272. Earlier he had been condemned but not effectively deposed as bishop of Antioch by a synod there in 268. In the Augsburg Confession (1530) Pars 1, art. 1, the neo-Samosatenes are condemned. Michael Servetus did not publish his *De Trinitatis erroribus* until 1531. Possibly Hans Denck and Ludwig Haetzer were embraced under the term at Augsburg.

71. Mentioned above at n. 25.

72. The reference is to the establishment of Nicene Christianity under Constantine and some of his successors.

73. The phrasing is not a direct quotation from the Apostles' Creed, which the Polish Brethren used at believers' baptism (cf. *Polish Brethren*, Docs. XXII and XXIII), nor quoted selectively from the disavowed Nicene Creed. It has an echo of a credal formulary in the subtitle of the book (1646) by Piotr Morzkowski (*Polish Brethren*, Doc. XXIII) ''of those who confess one God the Father through His only begotten Jesus Christ in the Holy Spirit.'' Distinctive in Lubieniecki's formula here is that God the Father as Creator of all things raised up and exalted Jesus Christ who thus is passive, whereas in the Apostles' Creed he actively on his own rises and ascends to heaven.

74. The Author refers to the Nicene Creed and other symbols.

75. A fully Socinian affirmation of faith is here being set forth by Lubieniecki as his own in the form of a rhetorical question, here broken down into two queries. The one God of the Polish Brethren has sent his only Son begotten of the Virgin by the power of the Holy Spirit, fully Man, Jesus Christ, who preached a Gospel confirmed by miracles,

the interpreter of the Father's will and Mediator between him and men, and this same God, Creator and sustainer of the universe, further confirmed the unique role of his human messenger by resurrecting him from the dead and raising him to his right hand, where in heaven he discharges the office of King-Judge, having on earth as *propheta* discharged the office of *doctor Ecclesiae*. The rhetorical question implies the *Triplex munus Christi*, the threefold office of Christ, a formula made prominent in the Polish Reformed by Jan Łaski from the moment of his return to Poland in 1556 and destined to become distinctively prominent in the catechisms of the Polish Brethren. On the *triplex munus Christi*, see further n. 56. On the distinctive stress of Faustus Socinus within this context of Christ's High Priesthood discharged only after the Ascension rather than on the cross, see *Polish Brethren*, Doc. III with preface, pp. 83 ff.

It is noteworthy that in place of *mediator* Lubieniecki chooses the more classical word *sequester*, intervener, hence secondarily mediator.

76. Although the Author here uses *eligere*, he construes election not as predestination to salvation but as the inclusion of all those who believe and perform good works, whereupon they are accorded the promise of eternal life (after the Second Advent). Lubieniecki is Hebraic, Pelagian, Erasmian as to free will unto salvation. However, he preserves without explanation, the concept of imputed righteousness, justification by faith. As this theme is not much discussed later in his *Historia*, attention may be drawn here to the fact that at this point Lubieniecki is rendering in a generalized way the teaching on justification by faith reasserted among the Brethren by Faustus Socinus. On this further, see John Godbey, "Fausto Sozzini and Justification," *Continuity and Discontinuity in Church History*, ed. by F. Forrester Church and Timothy George, *Studies in the History of Christian Thought*, ed. by Heiko Oberman, 19 (Leiden: Brill, 1979), 250–64; *idem*, "Fiducia: A Basic Concept in Fausto Sozzini's Theology," *Socinianism and its Role in the Culture of the XVI-th to XVII-th Centuries,* ed. by Lech Szczucki in cooperation with Zbigniew Ogonowski and Janusz Tazbir (Warsaw/Łódź, 1983), 59–67. See n. 104.

77. Here is the Author's distinctive wording of the *Acceptilatio* theory of the atonement of Faustus Socinus, to be appropriated at believers' baptism. See n. 78. For Socinus on the atonement, see *Polish Brethren*, Doc. X.

78. The Polish Brethren were generally baptized in adult believers' immersion with the trine formula of all Christians, Matt 28:19, but see details, esp. in Bk. 3, n. 238.

79. Their confession at baptism was the Apostles' Creed. Cf. *Polish Brethren*, Doc. XXII.

80. The Author uses the classical *piacularis* to avoid the common idea of "a full and sufficient sacrifice" of the orthodox of all traditions instead of the Socinian token.

81. It is not clear why the Holy Spirit understood as Gift is given only in the eschatological future rather than at baptism and during the Lord's Supper.

82. Here the Author uses *mediator*, whereas above (at n. 75) he has *sequester* in line with his tendency to use classical Latin terms. In his reference to the Holy Catholic Church he employs a phrase from the Apostles' Creed and interprets it in a universal sense. The Polish Brethren held that there was salvation in all churches, in their own Church the simple scriptural truth being only more clearly set forth for sustaining of the holy life in Christ.

83. The Author makes a similar reference to dogmatic appendages as fish-tail decorations in his *Compendium Veritas*, 383; K. E. Jordt-Jørgensen, Stanislas Lubieniecki: *Zum Weg des Unitarismus von Ost nach West im 17. Jahrhundert* (Göttingen, 1968), 130, 134.

NOTES TO CHAPTER THREE

84. The Author evidently refers to the Apostolic Fathers, but these were given that name in the collection of Jean Baptiste Cotelier only in *SS. Patrum qui temporibus Apostolicis floruerunt opera*, Paris, 1672. Some of the Fathers would have come to the attention of Lubieniecki and disturbed his idea of plenary and primal simplicity in the New Testament, hence his disparaging reference to what presumably he had no curiosity to read. Of the two letters ascribed to Clement of Rome (d. c. 95), only the first, actually from Clement, would have been acceptable to Lubieniecki. However, he had probably heard of the Pseudo-Clementine letters, which could well have alarmed him. They appeared as decretals in Pseudo-Isidore and were printed separately as sub-apostolic.

85. This is the *Quicunquevult*, a wholly Western creed of the fifth century.

86. Joachim Camerarius the Elder, Κατήχησις τοῦ χριστιανισμοῦ ἤγουν κεφάλια τῆς ὑγιοῦς διδαχῆς Χριστοῦ τε αὐτοῦ καὶ τῶν Ἀποστόλων (Leipzig, 1547; 2nd ed., 1575). Camerarius was the first to raise serious doubts as to the authorship of the Athanasian Creed.

Camerarius was involved ironically in the Osiandrist Controversy and in 1568 urged upon Maximilian II a Catholic-Protestant reunion. For his work on Slavic Reformation history, see Introduction near n. 32.

87. Ambrosius Pelargus (Storch) of Nidda, a Dominican, in 1541 published a critical edition of the Creed with notes.

88. Gerhard Johannes Vossius, *Dissertatio de tribus symbolis, Apostolico, Athanasiano et Constantinopolitano* (Amsterdam, 1642).

89. On the controversy concerning the eucharist for infants, see A.Vacant, *Dictionnaire de Théologie Catholique*, 3, col. 495 – 96 and 563 – 65. Lubieniecki returns to this problem.

90. Pope Gregory I the Great (590 – 604) is quoted here for his stand in the conflict with John IV the Faster, Patriarch of Constantinople, about the title "Ecumenical" which he refused either to grant to the bishop of Constantinople or to claim for himself. He took instead the still current papal title *servus servorum Dei*.

91. In *De consideratione*, Bernard instructed Pope Eugenius III (1145 – 53) in papal restraint.

92. Eberhard, archbishop 1200 – 1246, was a staunch supporter of the Hohenstaufens against the Popes.

93. *Compendium Veritatis primaevae [sive nova, facilis et certa Catholicae Christianae confessionis demonstratio per brevia amica quindecim colloquia: inter Politicum Christianum, Romanum Christianum, Gracecum Christianum, Lutheranum Christianum et Catholicum Christianum, Arianum vulgo dicunt]* exists in a unique MS, Westdeutsche Bibliothek, Marburg, MS theol. lat. Quart., 225. It was Lubieniecki's principal theological work in the form of a dialogue among George, representing spiritualized lay Christianity adaptable to any religio-political situation; Faustus, representing "Catholic" Christianity on the basis of the Bible and the Apostles' Creed ("the truth," Socinianism); Adrian, representing Roman Catholicism; Cyril, representing Orthodoxy; Martin, representing Lutheranism; and John, representing Calvinism. The work is large (535 quarto pages), unfinished, and of unknown date. It is discussed by K. E. Jordt-Jørgensen, *Lubieniecki*, 101, 120 – 23, 125 – 26; and now edited by him in two volumes, Copenhagen: Akademisk Forlag, 1982. The George here may represent a vague conflation of Dr. Giorgio Biandrata, Jerzy Schomann, and Jerzy Czaplic, Iuri and Stepan Niemirycz, and King Frederick III the Wise, cf. Introduction, at n. 9, again near n. 22, *cf. BAnt* 167.

NOTES TO CHAPTER FOUR

94. Martin Luther (1483–1546) inspired many burghers of German ethnicity in Poland, and Lutheranism was first anywhere established, 1525, as the religion of state in Ducal Prussia, a fief of the Polish Crown. Lubieniecki, however, looked upon Luther only as the forerunner of the final Reformation, that effectuated by the Polish Brethren, cf. above, at n. 9. Several pastors and lords patron studied in Wittenberg and heard Luther lecture and one, Krowicki, modeled his *Napominianie* (1554) on Luther's *Address to the German Nobility*, Bk. 2, n. 153.

95. Philip Melanchthon (1497–1560), professor of Greek at Wittenberg and chief author of the Augsburg Confession, 1530, was preferred by the Polish Brethren to Luther.

96. Martin Bucer (1491–1551), Dominican turned Lutheran, was the chief reformer of Strassburg.

97. Andreas Bodenstein von Karlstadt (c. 1480–1541), Thomist Augustinian turned supporter of Luther's reform, he became more radical than Luther on the Mass. He espoused the peasants while remaining pacifist. He ended up as professor of Bible in Basel. See Calvin Augustus Pater, *Karlstadt as the Father of the Baptist Movements: The Emergence of lay Protestantism* (Toronto: University Press, 1984), which gives attention also to the radical Lutheran career in Livonia of Melchior Hoffman, an ally of Karlstadt, and a major figure in Dutch Anabaptism, Chap. 6.

98. Johann Bugenhagen (Pomeranus; 1485–1558), former Premonstatensian canon, became pastor in Wittenberg, acting as Luther's confessor. He went on a leave of absence to help organize the Lutheran Church of Denmark, crowning Charles III and his Queen in 1537. Lubieniecki knew Denmark well.

99. 1 Tim 2:5.

100. Luther held that Christ is present *corporaliter* along with the bread and wine, a view sometimes retrospectively called consubstantiation.

101. The Author is critical of Luther's justification *sola fide* and understands it as a divinely permitted provisional extreme to overcompensate for the works righteousness of medieval Catholicism. See n. 76.

102. As to undue influence in government, the Author could only have in mind unusual practices in Lutheranism away from its centers, but he is wrong about Luther and Electoral Saxony. On auricular confession he is partly correct in that the Augsburg Confession, Pars 2, art. 4, legitimates confession but holds "that the enumeration of sins is not necessary."

103. The Author is somewhat confused here with his *missae memoria*, and again a few lines below at n. 109. He is right in saying that the Reformed divines mentioned above eliminated Luther's consubstantiation. Going beyond Zwingli's purely memorial and eschatological interpretation of the observance of the Lord's Supper as *commemoration*, Calvin sought to develop a doctrine of the Real Presence. Cf. n. 111. Luther himself grouped together his eucharistic opponents to the left as "Sacramentarians," a somewhat misleading term sanctioned by long usage to designate all those who found in the observance of the Supper only a solemn commemoration. On the evolution of the term, see Douglas Shants, *Valentine Gentile Crautwald: Theologian of the Royal Way between Catholic and Lutheran*, Bibliotheca Dissidentium (1989) in interpretation of *CS* 9, Doc. 436.

104. Like the Catholic opponents of Lutheranism, Lubieniecki commonly embraced under the concept of solafideism not only justification by faith alone but also predestina-

tion and penal atonement. Lubieniecki was also concerned with sanctification. Hence his appreciation of the Reformed tradition as represented by figures below. On solafideism as his generic concept for Lutheranism, see nn. 76 and 101, Jordt-Jørgensen, *Lubieniecki*, 52.

105. Huldreich Zwingli (1484–1531), more of a humanist than Luther, initiated in Zurich and the Swiss Confederation a movement partly independent of that in Luther-dominated Saxony. Luther grouped him with Oecolampadius, n. 106, Karlstadt, n. 97, and also the Anabaptists, not here mentioned, as *Sakramentierer*, i.e., opponents of his idea of the sacrament of the altar (n. 103). For Zwingli on baptism, see Bk. 3, n. 238. At a Colloquy at Marburg, 1529, the Swiss and Saxon opponents met and, in the face of reprisals from the Old Believers, agreed on all points of reform, except on the Lord's Supper. In the Commonwealth Reformed churches, rising well after the death of Zwingli, were in lively contact with his successor, Heinrich Bullinger.

106. Johann Oecolampadius (1482–1531) from the Palatinate, cathedral preacher of Basel, was the reformer of the canton, participant in the Marburg Colloquy of 1529.

107. Jean Calvin (1509–64). In his correspondence with his followers in Poland he addressed them as *Fratres Polonici*. The Polish Brethren of the Minor Reformed Church, for a period thinking of themselves as faithful followers of Calvin against Stancaro (n. 237), came to monopolize the embracing term for themselves as distinguished from the *Kalwini* of the Major Church. Lubieniecki, by way of Budziński, preserves some letters or full versions of letters uniquely in the *Historia* and this is noted in the *Opera* of Calvin.

Calvin's first communication to the Poles was addressed to King Sigismund II Augustus, 23 May 1547, in his letter dedicating his *Commentary on Hebrews* to the King, *Joannis Calvini opera quae supersunt omnia*, 59 vols., ed. by H. W. Baum et al. (Braunschweig, 1863–1900), cited *OC*, 13, nr. 1195. The correspondence of all the Swiss to the Poles is calendared and where not conveniently accessible printed or reprinted by Theodor Wotschke, *Der Briefwechsel der Schweizer mit den Polen* (Leipzig, 1908), *ARG*, Ergänzungsband 3, where Calvin's letter to Sigismund is calendared as nr. 11, p. 19.

This entry is intended to stress the point early in the annotation that, although the orthodox followers of Calvin in Poland became known as Calvinists or Evangelicals (in Transylvania as first "Catholics" and then as Calvinists), the Polish Brethren felt that they were his true heirs in Poland even though his name was gradually preempted by the Major Church after the schism of 1563/65.

Although Calvin and the Swiss Reformed had some teaching about natural revelation and natural theology, the Polish Brethren took over from the stress on the uniqueness of revelation in Scripture and felt that they were truest to Calvin when they scorned patristic and scholastic efforts to ground the dogma of the Trinity in the language of *philosophia perennis* and in the legitimation of its technical terms in the patristic doctrine of the *praeparatio Evangelii* among the Gentiles. The Polish Brethren in the end used the Fathers only when they themselves had used scriptural (revealed) language. They felt that they were "consequent Calvinists" in their adherence to Scripture only and the testimony of the Primitive Church. Since they baptize by trine immersion, they are not often called in the subsequent notes Arians, Unitarians, Antitrinitarians, or Socinians, although Lubieniecki himself was a rationalist, immersionist, Socinian, therefore Christocentric Unitarian. See Preface, n. 3; Foreword, n. 1; and nn. 120, 121, 123.

108. Pietro Martire Vermigli (1499–62) was named after the sainted inquisitor of Verona by his father, Stefano Vermigli. Pietro, a follower in Florence of Savonarola, was an Augustinian monk when converted by reading Bucer and Zwingli. He fled Italy within a day of Ochino (n. 172) to Basel, whence, after a brief stay in Zurich, he left for

Strassburg, residing with Bucer until November 1547. Invited by Thomas Cranmer, Martyr resided at Lambeth Palace from December of 1547 until March of 1548 when he became canon of Christ Church, then Regius professor, Oxford. Lectures there on 1 Cor 10 and 11 became the flash point in 1549 as Martyr held a euharistic debate. Private lectures on Romans were given publicity in Strassburg, whither he had come as Marian exile, and where they were polished for publication. In Strassburg, 1553 – 56, he served as professor of theology. A biblical scholar, he was professor of Hebrew in Zurich, 1556 – 62. It was mostly from this post that he advised the right wing of the Polish Reformed synods about Christ the Mediator against what he considered the deceptive simplification of his fellow Italian so influential on the theological left in Poland and Transylvania, Dr. Giorgio Biandrata. For the correspondence of Vermigli with the Poles beginning in Strassburg, see Wotschke, *Briefwechsel* pp. 45 – 424 passim, and for the impact of Vermigli in the synods, 1559 – 62, see Sipayłło, *Akta* 2: 2 – 151 passim. Marvin Walter Anderson, who is preparing a second edition of his *Peter Martyr: A Reformer in Exile (1542 – 1562)* (Nieuwkoop: De Graaf, 1975), has dealt with Cranmer, "Rhetoric and Reality," *Sixteenth Century Journal* 19 (October 1988), and with Vermigli's relations, among others, with the Poles, "Vista Tigurina: Peter Martyr and the European Reformation (1556 – 62)," submitted to *HTR*.

109. The Author persists in his confusion (see n. 103) in wording, at least. By *memoria missae* he means the opposite of what *memoria* meant to Zwingli. Lubieniecki intends by the word, unless he is truly mistaken (which is inconceivable in a pastor of his training), the Catholic idea that the sacrifice of Calvary is replicated at each Mass. Lubieniecki is wrong about Luther, however, whose German Mass, though it retained most of the Roman Mass, omitted all phrasing which deflected thought from the once-for-all sacrifice on Calvary.

110. The Reformed, the Author rightly observes, gave increased attention to sanctification (advance toward personal perfection) as a consequence of justification alone, stressed by Luther.

111. The Author is in general right but, standing himself in the Reformed tradition, should have stated clearly that Calvin went behind Zwingli to insist on the Real Presence by faith. Through his doctrine of the ubiquity of Christ, Luther was able to insist on the literal sense of the eucharistic words of Dominical institution in every liturgy, *hoc est corpus meum*. Calvin, insisting on Christ's bodily presence at the right hand of God the Father after the ascension, worked with what the Lutherans called disparagingly *illud extra Calvinisticum*, that extra of Calvin by which he managed to assert Christ's intended presence for the faithful at communion.

112. In classical Latin, *sacramentum* denoted a military oath of allegiance; the word was taken over by Tertullian and others as the Latin equivalent for the Greek μυστήριον, cf. 1 Cor 4:1, etc.

113. Andrew Frycz Modrzewski (Modrevius, 1517 – 72) was a major publicist of European renown. See, amid a vast literature, Konrad Górski, "Ewolucja poglądów religijnych Andrzeja Frycza Modrzewskiego," *Studia nad Arianizmem*, ed. by Ludwik Chmaj (Warsaw, 1959) 9 – 47; the comprehensive *A. F. Modrzewski: Bibliografia* (Wrocław, 1962); and Wacław Urban, *PSB*, 21 (1976) 538 – 43. See also nn. 114, 175.

114. *Sylvae quatuor* (2nd redaction of the author, Raków, 1590). For this imprint, see Alodia-Kawecka Gryczowa, *Ariański oficyny wydawnicze Rodeckiego i Sternackiego: Dzieje i Bibliografia* (Wrocław: Ossolineum, 1974), nr. 39 (henceforth *Gryczowa* and the numbered item). For an account of the origin of this book, see below Book 3, 9, *pp.* 221ff. The critical edition of the works of Modrzewski appears in a Latin and a Polish

series, each set in 5 vols., *Opera omnia*, ed. by Kazimierz Kumański and *Dzieła Wszystkie*, ed. by Łukasz Kurdybacha (Warsaw, 1953–60). The passage quoted is in this edition, *Opera omnia*, 5, p. 216.

115. The sacramental ubiquity of Christ.

116. The Author again misunderstands Zwingli, whose eucharistic theology was really close to his own. By "newly invented sacramental presence," Lubieniecki is referring to Calvin's views, n. 111.

117. Ebionites were "Poor Men" (Hebrew), Jewish Christians, widely documented in anti-heretical sources. They purportedly "reduced" (hence the term "poor") the doctrine of Christ, such that Jesus was the wholly human son of Mary and Joseph. Theirs could also have been a survival of a primitive view. They upheld the binding character of the Mosaic Law.

118. Paulians, or better, Paulianists, were the same as the Samosatenians, n. 119.

119. The Samosatenians were the followers of Paul of Samosata (n. 70), and Lubieniecki thinks well of him.

120. The Polish Brethren were called "Socinians" mostly outside of Poland and especially after the publication of the *Bibliotheca Fratrum Polonorum* (henceforth *BFP*) in Amsterdam, 1665–85, the first two volumes of which were the collected works of Faustus Socinus (1539–1604). The Reformed pastor, active in Chmielnik, used the term in his polemical *Antilogia et absurda Socinianorum* in 1623. *Polish Brethren*, 199. Martin Ruar documents the fact that the Polish Brethren were "unfairly" called "Socinians" even in 1643. Cf. *Polish Brethren*, Doc. XXIV–II. The fact that Socinus almost single-handedly tried to do away with the believers' immersion of the Polish Brethren accounts for the fact that "Socinianism" as a term never implies this distinctive baptismal practice. Lubieniecki evidently feels quite strongly that the name of Socinus should not replace that of Christ for the Church and group he defends as the climax of the Reformation of Christianity, its return to primordial truth and apostolic practice. On the *Bibliotheca*, see *Polish Brethren*, Doc. XXXV–II, Preface and esp. n. 10.

121. The charge of their being "Arian" lay ready at hand for all who in the sixteenth century and thereafter departed from the received Triadology, although Servetus was not so charged. The imprecision of the term bothered Lubieniecki and all the Polish Brethren. Few in the Polish-Lithuanian Commonwealth espoused the position of any of the Arians and Semi-Arians of the fourth century.

122. There were followers of Photinus (n. 25) in antiquity but no self-acknowledged Photinians in the Reformation Era. The term in the writings of opponents intended to stress only one of the tenets of Photinus, namely, the death or the sleep of the soul pending the general resurrection (psychopannychism). The Polish Brethren for the most part held this view and were therefore with some plausibility called Photinians, and also with respect to their Christology and doctrine of the Godhead.

Of the distinctive eschatology of the pre-Socinian Brethren and of the Sozzini themselves there are few traces in the *Historia*, except for Lubieniecki's strong sense of God's providence in general history and in the shaping of the Reformation in Poland. On personal immortality and on the second advent of Christ neither Budziński, as preserved here, nor Lubieniecki has much to say. On the views of Faustus Socinus on Christian mortalism or psychopannychism, see *Epitome Colloquii Racoviae habiti anno 1661*, ed. by Lech Szczucki and Janusz Tazbir (Warsaw, 1966), parts of which are translated in *Polish Brethren*, Doc. III. See also my *The Radical Reformation* (Philadelphia, 1962), *La Reforma Radical* (2nd and definitive ed., Mexico City/Madrid: Fondo de Cultura Económica, 1983), chap. 5. 4 and passim.

Of Budziński himself it is known that he wrote *De regno Christi millenario tractatus*, c. 1590, a lost MS, *BAnt* 55. At an unspecified date, our Author's great uncle and historian, Andrew Lubieniecki (c. 1550 – 1623), wrote a work of the same title and wrote a lost Commentary in Polish on the Apocalypse of St. John, *BAnt* 83. It is known that the uncle departed from his millenarianism under the influence of Faustus Socinus. Janusz Tazbir, one of the editors of the critical edition of Andrew Lubieniecki's *Poloneutychia*, n. 126, on which his grand-nephew, our Author, draws from time to time, notes that none of the older millenarianism (of the early Polish Brethren) survived in *Poloneutychia* (pp. ix, n. 21). Tazbir (p. vii – xiii) takes note of the theodicy of Andrew Lubieniecki and compares it with that of Piotr Skarga, S. J. (1536 – 1618): the latter, twenty years before, as a prophet had condemned the rulers of the Polish-Lithuanian Commonwealth for the toleration of heresy and saw in its tribulations the punishment of God, while Andrew Lubieniecki saw in the restrictions on toleration, especially since the martyrdoms of Franco di Franco and Iwan Tyszkowic in 1611 (*Historia, 168, 175*), the occasion of God's anger against Poland.

123. In several of their confessional documents the Polish Brethren called themselves simply "Christians."

124. In this phrasing, the Author is echoing the titles of several catechisms and confessions of faith of the Brethren.

125. The Author here allows the confessions of "the truth" and the Church he defends to collapse into one entity as if the Reformation began in Poland. What he intends, of course, as a Polish nationalist, is that the perfection of the Reformation was consummated in Poland, thus enhancing the unique mission of the Polish nation (actually the *szlachta*) at this juncture in world history. Cf. my "The Sarmatian Myth Sublimated in the *Historia Reformationis Polonicae* (1664/85) of Stanislas Lubieniecki and Related Documents," in Victor Erlich, ed., *For Wiktor Weintraub: Essays in Polish Literature* (The Hague: Mouton, 1974) 567 – 79; Stanislas Cynarski, "Sarmatyzm—ideologia i styl życia," in Janusz Tazbir, ed., *Polska XVII wieku: Państwo, społeczeństwo, kultura* (Warsaw: PAN, 1977).

NOTES TO CHAPTER FIVE

126. The first paragraphs of this chapter (*pp.* 14 – 16) are a summary of the historical work of the Author's great-uncle, Andrew Lubieniecki the Elder, *Poloneutychia*, ed. by A. Batowski (Lwów, 1843); by Lech Szczucki, Janusz Tazbir *et al.* (Warsaw: PAN, 1982), pp. 45ff. Although a general history, the work stresses the "happy times" before religious intolerance and the consequences thereof. It is divided into three parts: From the Piasts through the reign of Sigismund III to 1612; From 1612 to 1613; Reflections on God's punishment, particularly of Poland-Lithuania, for the persecution of the pious. At this particular point, Lubieniecki is making use of Jan Dymitri Solikowski (1539 – 1603), archbishop of Lwów, *In funere D. Sigismundi Augusti oratio* (Cracow, 1574), *Poloneutychia* p. 48. See further, Marcin Kromer (1512 – 89), *Polonia* (Cologne, 1589) 701 ff.

127. *Deus Optimus Maximus*; a Ciceronian phrasing used by Jan Łaski and other Reformers.

128. The Author says, less accurately, Walachia. Stephen IV Rareş (1551 – 52) of Moldavia, supported by the Hapsburg Emperor, was indeed supplanted, after the short reign of John I Joldea, by Alexander II Lăpuşneanu (1552 – 61), supported by Poland and the Turks and specifically by Mikołaj Sieniawski (1489 – 1569) Grand Hetman of the

Crown. Polish diplomacy aimed at peaceful coexistence with the Ottoman Empire and at the containment of Hapsburg expansion eastward. It tended to support Turkish partisans in the three lower Danubian principalities. Cf. A. Lubieniecki, *Poloneutychia*, 47. For Moldavia see further *Historia, 153 – 57*.

129. The conflict in Danzig between the "third estate" and the merchants entrenched as an oligarchy in the town council grew throughout the century. In July 1552, Sigismund went there to personally investigate the situation. Although he did not give in to the demand of the burghers for a larger participation in the town government, he considerably curtailed the abuses of the oligarchy and gave the burghers some form of control in the financial administration. Paul Simson, *Geschichte der Stadt Danzig*, vols. 1, 2, 4 (Danzig, 1913 – 18) 2. 125 – 137 and 4. 160 – 167.

130. Henry II the Younger, duke of Braunschweig-Wolfenbüttel (1489 – 1568), leader of the Catholic League in Germany, married Sophia (1556), daughter of Sigismund I the Old. In 1554 he planned an invasion of Ducal Prussia, Lutheran since 1525 and fief therewith of the Polish Crown. By diplomatic action Sigismund II averted war and safeguarded Lutheranism in his Ducal fief. A. Lubieniecki, *Poloneutychia* 43.

131. Johann Funck, a Lutheran theologian and chronicler, was court preacher and adviser of Duke Albert of Prussia and leader of the Osiandrist party on the issue of justification. Andreas Osiander, preacher in Nüremburg, had converted Albert of Hohenzollern to the Reformation during a sojourn there.

Osiander (1498 – 1552) was professor at Königsberg (1549 – 52), publishing his revisionist *De justificatione* in 1550. On his dispute with Francesco Stancaro, see *Historia*, 30 – 33 and n. 256. As a politician, Funck supported the Duke and the court party against the Prussian Estates. In 1566 the old Duke annulled his testament of 1555 which appointed the Land officials guardians of his heir, Albert Frederick, and appointed as sole guardian and alternative heir John Albert I, Duke of Mecklenburg, his son-in-law. John Albert was suspect at the Polish court because of his involvement in the affairs of Livonia, and suspect in the Prussian Estates because of his conflicts with his own Mecklenburg Estates. The Prussian gentry appealed to Sigismund II as the sovereign of the Duchy. The royal commissioners restored the rights of the Estates and handed Funck over to the City Court of the Kneiphof (Königsberg), by which he was sentenced to death. *Allgemeine Deutsche Biographie (ADB)*, 56 vols. (Berlin, 1875 – 1912) 24: 473 – 88; Marcin Bielski, *Kronika polska* (Cracow, 1597) 599; Gottfried Seebass, *Das reformatorische Werk des Andreas Osiander* (Nuremberg, 1967) and for what came to three professorial disputations arousing the controversy, see *De lege et evangelio* (April 1549), *De justificatione* (October 1551) the second *De justificatione* (November 1551), Gottfried Seebass, *Bibliographia Osiandrica (1496 – 1552)* (Nieukoop: DeGraaf, 1971) items 49.1.1, 48, 491.1, 56.1.

132. The Teutonic Order of Livonia was founded in 1202 under the name of the Sword Knights by Albrecht von Buxhövden, the first bishop of Riga, to assist him in the Germanic Christianization of the region. From its capital, the castle of Wenden (Kieś), the Order joined forces with the Teutonic Order of Prussia (1237) to secure independence from the bishops.

In the sixteenth century the struggle between the Order and the gentry and burghers who inclined toward Lutheranism rendered Livonia helpless against the growing pressure of Muscovy in her drive toward the sea. The last Catholic archbishop of Riga, Wilhelm of Brandenburg (1529 – 63), the brother of Albert of Prussia, sought Polish support against the order but was suspected of planning to convert his archbishopric into a secular duchy. In the ensuing Livonian War (1557 – 82), the Order, led by the coadjutor of the

Grand Master, Johann Wilhelm von Fürstenberg, soon Grand Master himself (1557–87), won the day; but, unable to withstand the Muscovites, he had to submit to Sigismund II and restore Wilhelm of Brandenburg to his see. (Lubieniecki reverses the facts here.) Fürstenberg endeavored to counterbalance Polish influence by connections with Denmark and Sweden; but, failing to repel the Muscovite invasion, he was forced to resign. For his successor, see n. 135.

133. Ivan succeeded his father, Basil III (1505–33), at age three. His regent until 1538 was his mother, Lithuanian Helena Glinska, thereafter the boyar families Shuisky and Belsky. On assuming direct control, Ivan had himself crowned Tsar in 1547 by the Metropolitan of Moscow, whose successor was elevated by his son as Patriarch Job (1589–1605). Lubieniecki, *Poloneutychia*, 47, reported the new title.

134. Aleksander Iwanowicz Połubiński (d. 1607/8) was captain of horse and led a detachment of Lithuanian Tatars against Gotthard Kettler, whose castle in Courland fell to Sigismund, 31 August 1559. Pro-Polish, he became a Polish vassal in 1561, n. 135. The reference in the text is to the operation of the King against Ivan, who held Pskov and in 1564 threatened Marienburg and Dorpat. Marek Plewczyński, *PSB*, 27 (1982) 356–58.

135. The last Grand Master of the Order, Gotthard Kettler (1517–87), was the leader of the pro-Polish party supported by the gentry. In 1561 the Order was secularized. Kettler embraced Lutheranism and became Duke of Courland as a Polish vassal, while Livonia (Latvia) north of the Duna (Dzwina) River became a Polish province (1562) with wide liberties for the Estates and the free exercise of the Augsburg Confession secured. Estonia, however, was occupied by the Swedes.

From then on the antagonism of the three Baltic powers—Poland, Sweden, and Muscovy—centered upon Livonia, occasioning a number of wars. Cf. *Poloneutychia*, 48.

136. What Andrew Lubieniecki, our Author's source, understood under this term, was the victory of the ''execution-of-the-laws''party. From the very beginning of the reign of Sigismund I the Old (1506–48) the financial and administrative weakness of the state and of the feudal rule of the magnates had been revealed. Backed by his Queen Bona Sforza d'Aragona (1494–1557), a talented politician and administrator in her own right, Sigismund I attempted reforms aimed at strengthening the central political power and its financial foundations, but he ran into the passive resistance of the magnates and the active opposition of the gentry. The gentry, whose economic strength was rising with the mounting demand for agricultural products, started a struggle for political power. A program of ''the execution of laws'' was formulated. This legalistic formula, implying interpretation of the extant laws only, covered a program aimed at breaking the rule of the senatorial oligarchy (the magnates in and out of the Senate), circumscribing the royal prerogative, securing full domination of the numerous gentry (lower *szlachta*) in the House of Deputies and in the elective dietines, and transforming the loose Polish-Lithuanian-Prussian federation into a more homogeneous parliamentary commonwealth with a fully elective monarchy as of 1572.

The domination of the gentry over the peasants was achieved by turning them into serfs (1519/20), and over the burghers by extruding them from the Diet, by minimizing their town rights, and by depriving them of the right to possess landed property (1536–39). The result of the restriction was that a great many of the patrician burghers who had heavily invested in land deserted the burghers and, by nobilization, joined the landed gentry—in some cases the senatorial oligarchy—and thereby deprived the towns of social leadership and of capital. Such ennobled families were prominent in the history of the Polish Reformation, e. g., the Boners (Calvinists), and the Morsztyns (Unitarians).

The legalistic program against royal absolutism at the expense of the rights of peasants and burghers, initiated by the diet of 1520, was embodied in a demand for a *conventus justitiae*. This resulted in the unsuccessful attempts at codification (1526, 1532). The legalistic call for "the execution of laws" (purportedly *all* traditional) soon grew into a movement for overall administrative and political reform in the interest of the gentry alone. It was the diet of 1534 which switched over from the *correction-of-laws* to the *execution-of-laws* program, eagerly debated at the subsequent diets of 1536, 1538, 1538/9. The Church was an autonomous power in her own right with vast holdings, and bishops were *ex officiis* Senators, supportive of the senatorial oligarchy. Some of this material was anticipated in my Introduction, III C. There are further details in RD 9, nn. 5 and 6.

137. Stanislas Leśniowolski, twice noted in A. Lubieniecki, *Poloneutychia*, 47, 58, died in 1565.

138. The Muscovites actually numbered 24,000, observes the editor of A. Lubieniecki, *Poloneutychia*, 47; 181, n. for line 27.

139. He was Hetman from 1566, dying in 1572. A. Lubieniecki, *Poloneutychia*, 47.

140. This Lithuanian prince is a major figure in the *Historia*. The name in Lithuanian is Radvila. Among the sons of Mikołaj Radziwiłł (d. 1509) were Jan Mikołaj (d. 1522) and Jerzy (d. 1541). Jobert, *De Luther à Mohila*, 415, gives a genealogical chart of the Radziwiłłs.

Of the four children of Jerzy, notable in history were Mikołaj R. the Red (1512–84), who died a Protestant, and his younger sister Barbara Radziwiłłówna. Barbara (1520–51) was first married to Stanisław Gasztołd, who died 18 December 1542. Against the intentions of his mother Bona Sforza, Sigismund II Augustus married Barbara secretly, 28 July 1545, before doing so publicly, 6 August 1547. Of the immense literature, cited only is the story as recounted empathetically by Roland Bainton, *Women of the Reformation from Spain to Scandinavia* (Minneapolis: Augsburg, 1977) 135–55, with pictures of both Bona and Barbara, and Władysław Pociecha, "Barbara," I *PSB* (1935) 294–98.

Of the ten children of Jan Mikołaj R., outstanding in the *Historia* was Mikołaj the Black Radziwiłł (1515–65). A correspondent of Calvin, he was a major supporter of the Reformation from his seats at Ołyka and Nieśwież and as Grand Chancellor of Lithuania as of 1550 and a palatine of Vilna as of 1551. His life is written by Józef Jasnowski (Warsaw, 1939).

141. The reference is to Szymon Starowolski, *Sarmatiae Bellatores* (Cologne, 1631) 175, 179–80, 200–201, etc.; cf. A. Lubieniecki, *Poloneutychia*, 47.

There were two battles on the Uła (n. 141), the decisive one on 26 January 1564. The Uła flows into the Duna River south of Połock. In 1563, the Muscovites had taken Połock and threatened Vilna. An attempt at retaking Połock failed in 1567. The recapture of Uła was no compensation for this grievous loss of Połock. Under Sigismund II the Grand Duchy of Lithuania was so exhausted by the Livonian wars against the Tsar that an armistice had to be signed in 1570.

142. Stanisław Cikowski was Deputy Treasurer of Cracow. He died in 1617.

Filon Czarnobylski Kmita (c. 1530–87), captain of the horse of Smolensk, features several times in A. Lubieniecki, *Poloneutychia*.

143. Lubieniecki took this sentence "... Moscoviam perdomuit" from A. Lubieniecki's *Poloneutychia* 48, lines 2–3. In the fuller account there is ambiguity.

144. Roman Sanguszko (1537–71) was Lithuanian Field Hetman as of 1567.

145. Andrzej Sapieha (d. 1611) was castellan of Witebsk. This information is not in

A. Lubieniecki, *Poloneutychia*. Wenden is the German name for Kieś in Latvia.

146. Olbracht Łaski (1536–1605), son of the adventurer and diplomat Hieronym Jarosław Łaski, and brother of Jan the Reformer. Olbracht is mentioned in the *Historia*, 15, 153–57. There is a genealogy of the Łaski family in Jobert, *De Luther à Mohila*, 413.

147. The Author uses the classical terms for the geographical designation, in *Pontium Euxinum*.

148. Suleiman II the Magnificent (1520–66) was followed by Selim II (1566–74). Hapsburg pressure notwithstanding, Sigismund I the Old and Sigismund II followed a steady policy of peace toward the Ottoman Turks, especially with a view to securing the peaceful colonization of the southeastern frontier provinces of Poland-Lithuania, the benevolent neutrality of Turkey in the Lithuanian wars with Muscovy, and the support of Hungary under the Zápolyas against the Hapsburgs, without however implicating themselves in an active military cooperation with the Turks. In 1553 the old Polish-Turkish treaty of peace and friendship was renewed.

149. During the Union Diet of Lublin in May, 1569, a Turkish embassy led by Ibrahim Bey proposed a Polish-Turkish alliance against Moscow. Ibrahim Bey had been a Polish nobleman, Joachim Strasz, who, taken prisoner by the Tatars, had embraced Islam and risen to be one of the foremost Turkish diplomats of the century. The alliance was not concluded. Because of Lithuania's exhaustion in the wake of the wars, Sigismund II aimed at peace with Muscovy. An armistice of three years was concluded in Moscow in 1570.

150. John II Sigismund of Szépes/Spisz/Zips, Prince of Transylvania (1559–71), was the son of Isabella (sister of Sigismund II Augustus) and ruler of Transylvania (1541–56; 1556–59) and John I Zápolya (Szapolya), elected national king of Hungary (1526–40). (On Spisz, see Book 2, n. 698.) The peace of 1538 between John I Zápolya and Ferdinand I of Austria had secured the Hungarian crown for the latter should Zápolya die first. However, on the death of John I Zápolya his son, John II Sigismund, was instead proclaimed king-elect of Hungary in 1540 under the protection of Suleiman. The ensuing wars between the contenders, John II Sigismund and Ferdinand I (later Maximilian I/II), were terminated by the treaty of 1570 wherein John renounced title to the kingdom of Hungary for the title of merely Prince of Transylvania. He died in 1571 (to be succeeded by István/Stephen Báthory). The peaceful initiative was undertaken by Sigismund II Augustus, himself without a direct heir, in order to secure for his nephew a chance of succession to the Polish throne upon his own death. With this in view the last Jagiellonian King agreed to the otherwise disadvantageous treaty for the sake of his sister's son. Moreover, Prince John II Sigismund died a year before his Polish uncle. See *Historia, 170*. The tripartition of the Kingdom of Hungary, 1526–71, that is, from the defeat at the Battle of Mohács to the election of István Báthory as Prince of Transylvania, elected King of Poland in 1586, is treated in broad lines, with very useful maps for the boundaries of the Ottoman conquests of 1544 and of 1576, in the collective work István Barta *et al.*, *Historie de la Hongrie des origines à nos jours* (Budapest: Horvath, 1974) and in appropriate detail also with maps by László Makkai *Historie de Transylvanie* (Paris, 1946).

151. Lubieniecki refers here to John III Vasa (1568–92), second son of Gustavus I (1532–60), in whose line the kingship had been declared hereditary by the four-house Rikstag and who had broken with the Holy See over his replacement of a rebellious primate of Upsala. Gustavus was succeeded by his oldest son, Eric XIV (1560–68), who imprisoned John, then duke of Finland, and his spouse, Catherine Jagiellonka, sister of

Sigismund II Augustus. After the murder of his insane half-brother, to secure his new position, John terminated a war with Denmark started by Eric over Swedish interests in Livonia. Władysław Czapliński, *PSB* 12 (1966–67) 218–20.

Sigismund II Augustus' peaceful initiative aimed at general pacification in the Baltic to keep Muscovy from access to the sea and to secure Poland's own position in Livonia. At the Congress of Stettin in 1570, with the participation of all interested states, including Lübeck, a peace between Denmark and Sweden was concluded, which, however, ran against Polish interests by acknowledging the Emperor's arbitration in the Livonian question and by keeping open the commercial traffic with Moscow.

Independent of this was the three-year truce with Muscovy (n. 149), not Lubieniecki's *amplius decennio.* Stephen Batory undertook his first expedition against Moscow, 30 August 1579, taking Połock.

The son of John III and Catherine Jagiellonka was Sigismund Vasa, duke of Finland, brought up in his mother's faith. Within days of the election of the Catholic duke of Finland in 1587 in succession to Stephen Batory as King Sigismund III (Bk 3 n. 716), John and his now regal son and his own dynastic successor to the Swedish throne agreed in the Articles of Kalamar that the two kingdoms in personal union and prospectively in perpetual alliance would retain their separate religions and their constitutional and economic identities and that when King Sigismund should become sole ruler, in his absence from Sweden, the realm would be governed by seven Swedes, six appointed by the Polish-Swedish King and one named by Duke Charles of Sudermania (the youngest son of Gustavus I, Charles, a strong Protestant.)

152. The Union of Lublin, 1569, changed the personal union between Poland and Lithuania into a federal union, providing for a common Diet, with separate administrations for the Crown and the Grand Duchy, which ceded to the Crown the palatinates of Podlasie (Podlachia), Volhynia, and the Ukraine. Administrative unity had been one of the goals of the ''execution-of-laws'' program (n. 136). Further, Royal Prussia with its German colonizers, provisionally united with the Crown by the Diet of 1562–63, was fully united with Poland in 1569; but it, too, retained a distinctive administration. Royal Prussia was made up of the prince-bishopric of Warmia (Ermland) and the palatinates of Malbork (Marienburg), Chełmno (Kulm), and Pomerelia with the free city of Danzig.

The Polish kingship had always been elective, the Grand Ducal dignity hereditary. The Grand Duke enjoyed extensive power, limited only by the Council of Princes, while the gentry was virtually deprived of political rights. Under the impact of the Polish gentry movement, the Lithuanian gentry had also started a campaign for political reform, consummated from their side also in the Union at the Diet of Lublin, 28 June 1569.

153. Cf. the earlier action at Urła, n. 141; *Poloneutychia* 48.

154. Both these men were preachers to Prince Sigismund in Cracow and Vilna in 1544. Both were alumni of the University of Cracow from the time of Jakub of Iłża the Younger, *Historia 23.* Of Wawrzyniec Niezgoda (Discordia) of Przasnysz there is much in *Historia* beginning Bk 2 at n. 619. Some basic sources are first adduced before further identification of Jan Koźminczek, (¶¶ 3–5). On Discordia, see further Bk. 2, n. 619. Jan drops out of the *Historia,* at this point.

The mention by the Author of these two first figures of the Reformation in Poland and Lithuania requires reference here to Andrew Węgierski, who under the name Adrianus Regenvolscius, wrote *Systema historico-chronologicum Ecclesiarum Slavonicarum per provincias varias* (Utrecht, 1652). This was republished with addenda evidently by Benedict Wiszowaty as *Libri quatuor Slavoniae Reformatae* (Amsterdam, 1679). This was published in a facsimile edition under the care of Lech Szczucki, with a *Praefatio* by him and an index (Warsaw: PAN, 1973). Henceforth the 2nd ed. is cited as *Slavonia Reformata*. Lubieniecki himself cited the work under the title accessible to him. Both Jan and Discordia are dealt with by Węgierski, pp 74 passim. With the same two Theodor Wotschke deals and supplies documents in "König Sigismund August von Polen und die evangelischen Hofprediger," *Archiv für Reformationsgeschichte* (henceforth *ARG*) 4 (1906/07) 329–69, as also Henryk Barycz, *Historija Uniwersytetu Jagiellońskiego w epoce humanizmu* (Cracow, 1935) 108–10; *idem*, "Discordia," *PSB* 5 (1939–46) 171–74; *idem*, "Jan z Koźmina," *PSB* 10 (1962–64) 458–60. Barycz brought together these and many related Reformation age essays in *Z epoki renasansu, reformacji i baroku: Prądy, idee, ludzie, książki* (Warsaw: PIW, 1971). Węgierski, *Slavonia Reformata*, 74 dates Jan's preaching to 1542; and Discordia's preaching to 1544, but elsewhere, both as *doctores Evangelici* in 1544 perhaps more carefully: "Prolegomena" to the synodal protocols, apud Maria Sipayłło, *Akta synodów Różnowierczych w Polsce 1 (1550–59)* (Warsaw 1966) 1. 1. This critical edition of the synodal acts is continued by her: 2 (1560–70) (*ibid*: Warsaw University Press, 1972); 3 (1571–1632) with map (*ibid*: Jagiellonian University Press, 1983) henceforth *AS*, 1, 2, or 3.

Jan was born in Koźmin before 1510, studied at Cracow, 1525/26–31, and received his *magister* along with the future leader of Calvinism in Lithuania, Szymon Zacius, *pp.* 29 passim. A classical humanist, he taught Latin and Greek at the Lubrański Academy in Poznań, where the three sons of Jędrzej Górka, captain general of Great Poland, studied, as also did Stanisław Sarnicki, who was destined to be a major leader of Calvinism in Little Poland, *pp.* 58 passim. By this time Jan was drawn to the new reforming ideas in church and society. It is possible that Jan studied briefly in Wittenberg. There is a letter 1536 to him as a fellow Pole, Melanchthon, *Opera omnia* 5, no. 1432. He and Discordia may have been at the court in Cracow as early as 1542 in some capacity. On the recommendation of Jakub Uchański (1502–81), later bishop of Chełm (1551–61), at the time secretary to Bona Sforza, Jan and Discordia received positions as court preachers to Prince Sigismund, 9 April 1545. They were with him as effectual governor (*wielkorządca*) (1544–48) of Lithuania in Vilna. He had borne the title of the Grand Duke as of 1522 and more solemnly after his elevation to the throne in Vilna as a boy in 1529 . His two preachers reached out to the burghers and the Lithuanian gentry, and Jan established contact with the Lutherans in Königsberg. As the old King declined, the bishops became alarmed that the heir would be dangerously sympathetic to Protestantism and sought to have the preachers removed, for example, in deliberations at the provincial synod of Łęczyca, 1547. The bishop of Cracow, Samuel Maciejowski, Grand Chancellor, intervened with Grand Duke Sigismund and sent the learned Marcin Kromer with a commission to restrain the Prince from making any religious innovations.

After the death of Sigismund I, 1 April 1548, and the accession of his son, the bishops again exerted pressure on Sigismund Augustus against the two preachers during the Diet of Piotrków, October to December 1548. Jan considered leaving to study further in Königsberg, but the new King confirmed him and Discordia in their positions as court preachers, so long as they refrained from assailing any Catholic dogma. Cf. Bk 2, n. 619 ¶2. Jan entered into a relationship with Stanisław Orzechowski, n. 270, who was fighting against clerical celibacy, and won over to the Reformation movement Stanisław Zamoyski, *Historia, 195–96*, father of the later Grand Chancellor Jan Zamoyski. Amid student unrest Jan had printed his zealously reformatory *Epistola ad ministros verbi Dei*, 24 May 1549. He wrote an anonymous appeal (lost) to Julius III to call a free and catholic council for canonical reform, 1550. Keeping in contact with Königsberg, Jan proceeded to administer communion in both kinds to the faithful secretly gathered in

Cracow, Easter 1551. The report of this action prompted the new bishop of Cracow, Andrzej Zebrzydowski (1551 – 60), to cite him before the episcopal court, 11 April 1551. He was imprisoned in Lipowiec and may have died there. He is mentioned again by Lubieniecki at nn. 194, 202.

155. The year 1543, said by Lubieniecki to be the starting date of the spread of the new teaching, was marked by the Diet of Cracow's demand for freedom of exit from the Kingdom. At the Diet there in 1545 the deputies of Great Poland directly demanded the freedom to send sons to foreign schools and to read foreign books. At the same time the foundation of the Lutheran University of Königsberg created a new scholarly center accessible to Poles. Renewed edicts against the importation of heretical books (e.g., 10 July 1544) remained ineffectual.

156. The Author readily grants that Jan Łaski (1499 – 1560) promoted *the truth*. On him more fully, see *pp.* 64 – 66, 78 – 91, and passim.

The preeminent Polish Reformer's daughter, Barbara Łaska, would marry Stanisław Lutomirski (d. 1575), a major figure in the early Minor Church. Many of the emphases and traits of Łaski's version of the Reformation persisted in the Minor Church: the yearning for a national or territorial reform, a more Erasmian view of the freedom of the will than in most major Reformed divines; concern for internal church discipline; satisfaction with the Apostles' Creed as containing the essentials of Triadology and Christology; stress on the Erasmian *triplex munus Christi* (nn. 75, 170).

In his ecumenical confessional nationalism, the Polish Reformer would after 1556 express his overiding concern to bring Lutherans, the Reformed, and the Czech Brethren together in a Commonwealth-wide synodal reformed Church. He would have in mind the reformed Anglican Church under Edward VI (1547 – 53) which he knew at first hand at the invitation, 1548, of Archbishop Thomas Cranmer, served him as advisor, and during his second sojourn, 1550 – 53, as superintendent of the Strangers' Church, actually a clustering of foreign Protestant congregations in London, linked synodally. He would also have been influenced in his vision of the reform of his native land by the very role itself of his uncle, Primate Jan Łaski (1510 – 31). For his superintendency of the Strangers' churches, see Andrew Pettegree, *Foreign Protestant Communities in Sixteenth Century London* (Oxford: Clarendon, 1986) 26 – 74.

The basic life of the reformer before his return to Poland in 1556 is that of Oskar Bartel, *Jan Łaski, Część I, 1499 – 1556* (Warsaw, 1955), trans. with the same title (Berlin: Evangelische Verlagsanstalt, 1981). Part 2 was carried on by Halina Kowalska, *Działalność reformatorska Jana Łaskiego w Polsce 1556 – 1560* (Wrocław: Ossolineum, 1969). These replace of earlier standard work of Hermann Dalton, *Johannes a Lasco: Beitrag zur Reformationsgeschichte Polens, Deutschlands und Englands* (Gotha, 1881; photocopy, Nieuwkoop: De Graaf, 1970). Abraham Kuyper edited in 2 vols. *Joannis a Lasco, Opera tam edita quam inedita* with a *vita* (Amsterdam/Utrecht, 1866).

157. The Author seems reluctant to say it clearly that the King actually sought to smash the Reformation in Danzig in 1526.

In the continuous struggle between the community of Danzig and its council, Sigismund I supported the community against the council. Then, in 1522 the program of the community started showing a strong Protestant trend, and the first Lutheran preachers appeared openly. Attempts to stem the agitation provoked a number of riots. In 1525, a revolution ensued against the council, and the new government began reforming the parishes. In April, 1526 the King occupied the city with his forces and restored the old order. The leader of the revolution, Johann Schulz (Scholt), a boatsman, and a few of his followers were sentenced to death and beheaded in June, 1526. To prevent further conflicts, the King issued on 20 July 1526 the basic statute which remained the constitution of the city for many years. Simson, *Geschichte der Stadt Danzig*, 2. 40 – 95.

158. Lubieniecki glosses over the attitude of Sigismund I the Old towards the Reformation. Three years after Luther proclaimed his 95 Theses, Sigismund I issued an edict, dated Toruń, 24 May 1520, in which the importing and spreading of Luther's works was prohibited under forfeiture of estate and banishment. However, as in contravention to this edict Luther's books were spreading and his opinions were defended in public, other edicts followed on 15 February 1522 and 7 March 1523, the latter threatening preachers of heresy with the stake. A further edict of 22 August 1523 bestowed vast authority on the episcopal inquisitors and introduced a censorship of books, printed or imported, by the rector of the Jagiellonian University. In 1525 the last prince of Masovia, Janusz, issued an edict against the importation of Lutheran books and forbade the spreading or confessing of the new teaching.

In the early period the new teaching spread mostly among the German burghers in Cracow and in Poznań, but there were sympathizers of Lutheranism among educated Poles. It was, however, only after 1530 that the Lutheran movement gathered strength. Lubieniecki is right in asserting that the Augsburg Confession of 1530 exercised a deep impression in Poland, mainly among the magnates. The universities of Wittenberg and Leipzig attracted an increasing number of Polish students, in spite of the renewed royal edict of 4 February 1535 which threatened students at a Protestant university with banishment. *Volumina Legum: Prawa, Konstytucje y Przywileie Królestwa, y Wielkiego X. Litewskiego*, 10 vols. (Cracow, 1889), I. p. 448. For the place of this collection, see Peter Siekanowicz, *Legal Sources and Bibliography of Poland* (New York, 1964), item 5, p. 8.

159. Albert Hohenzollern (1490 – 1568) was the son of Sophia, daughter of the King Casimir Jagiellonczyk (1447 – 92), and Margrave Frederick the Old of Ansbach. Their son Albert was thus the nephew of Sigismund I. Elected Grand Master of the Teutonic Order in 1511, Albert embraced Lutheranism and secularized the Order, proclaiming himself hereditary prince of Ducal Prussia under Polish sovereignity (1525). Married twice, he had no heirs. For the influence of Albert in spreading the Reformation in Poland proper, see Wiktor Weintraub, "Udział Prus Książęcych w reformacji polskiej," *Reformacja w Polsce* (henceforth *RwP*) 6 (1939) 38ff.

This periodical was founded by Stanislas Kot, vol. 1 (1921) through vol. 12 (1953 – 55). It was continued under the auspices of PAN as *Odrodzenie i Reformacja w Polsce*, vol. 1 (1956) (henceforth *OiRwP*).

160. Jan Seklucjan (1498? – 1578), a German from Bamberg, started preaching Lutheranism in Poznań in 1525, under the patronage of Jędrzej Górka (n. 154). In Königsberg he printed c. 1544 the first Protestant confession in Polish, *Wyznanie wiary chrześcijańskiej*, ed. by Halina Kowalska and Stanisław Rospond, with something on his life (Warsaw/Łodź: PAN, 1972). His *Katechizm prosty dla ludu* (Königsberg, 1545, 1547, 1549, 1568) was based on Philip Melanchthon's *Short Catechism* of 1524 (Königsberg, 1545) and is ed. by Stanisław Rospond (Olsztyn, 1948). He published the Gospels in Polish (1551), the rest of the New Testament (1552), and the entire New Testament (1552). He published hymns (1547, 1559) and his domestic sermons, *Postylla polska domowa* (Königsberg, 1556), photocopy available from the Biblioteka Narodowa in Warsaw. Ignac Warmiński, *Andrzej Samuel i Jan Seklucjan* (Poznań, 1906) includes the *Wyznanie* and deals with Seklucjan's place in the heresy trial of the Dominican Andrzej Samuel, 1541 (Poznań, 1906).

Seklucjan's *Wyznaie* (1544), based on Luther's *Small Catechism*, (1529), went beyond it in mentioning Anabaptists (*nowokreczency*) as evidently present in Royal and

Ducal Prussia, and Selucjan is aware of baptism by sprinkling, pouring, and immersion/emersion (*zanorzanie/wynorzanie*), *op cit*, 14 – 15; noted by Darek Jarmola, ''The Origins and Development of Believer's Baptism among the Pre-Socinian Polish Brethren,'' doctoral thesis, Southern Baptist Theological Seminary, Louisville, Kentucky, due in 1990, chap. 5.

161. The reference seems to be to *A Conversation on the Christian funeral and the Popish one* (1547), *A short and simple dispute on some ceremonies and church statutes* (1548), *Dispute of a [Roman] Priest with a [Greek] Priest on celibacy* (1548), etc. Seklucjan was mostly a publisher, not an author. See I. Warmiński, *Samuel i Seklucjan* (Poznań, 1906).

162. The Author erroneously gives Vogel. Katarzyna was born Zalaszowska. She married Melchior Weigel, a city councillor. In the sources she is called Zalaszowska, Weiglowa, or Melcherowa (-*owa* means ''wife of,'' -*ówna* means ''daughter of ,'' *owska* does not show the difference).

Some of these sources have disappeared, but survive in excerpts from the acts of the trial in Polish translation, Julian Bukowski, *Dzieje Reformacji w Polsce* 1 (Cracow, 1883) 176 – 79. Wojciech (Adalbert) Węgierski, pastor of the Cracow District of the Reformed Church, preserved in Polish and Latin important documents in the archive of the Cracow congregation; *Kronika zboru krakowskiego* (Cracow, 1817), most accessible in the German edition of C. F. Wilhelm Altmann, *Chronik der evangelischen Gemeinde zu Krakau von Anfängen bis 1657* (Breslau, 1880), including item 3 on Katarzyna Weiglowa. See also n. 163. Bainton makes the episode vivid with translation of the excerpts in *Women: Spain to Scandinavia*, 156 – 59.

It is clear that there was an early Sacramentarian trend of the iconoclastic thrust; cf. *Radical Reformation*, chap. 2. But she was put to death *ob Judicam religionem* (version of Budziński by Sand, n. 163 and by Górnicki, an eyewitness, n. 167). It is possible that a local Judaizing current had set in, and also that there were Antitrinitarian impulses from Bohemia. Wacław Urban deals with the rise of Unitarianism among the Czech and Slovak heirs of Hussitism, *Der Antitrinitarismus in den Böhmischen Ländern und in der Slowakei in 16. und 17. Jahrhundert*, Bibliotheca Dissidentum, Scripta et Studia, ed. by André Séguenny and Marc Lienhard (Baden-Baden: Koerner, 1986). In the later tradition of the Polish Brethren Katarzyna is retrospectively the first Christian Unitarian martyr.

Wacław Sobreski accepts, with Górnicki, the episcopal charge of her apostary to Judaism, ''Propaganda żydowska w 1530 – 1540,'' *Przegląd Narodowy* 21 (1921) 24 – 42.

163. The *MS* History of Stanisław Budziński (Budzyński) (d. after 1595) in Polish was extensively used and excerpted by Lubieniecki, Andrew Węgierski (n. 154), and by Christopher Sand in *BAnt*. Because it was lost, the present edition of the *Historia* draws attention to the fragments of the History surviving through italic font.

Of this particular account in Budziński's History, there are at least two transcriptions in Latin, that here of Lubieniecki and that of Christopher Sand in his *Nucleus* (1679) and *Appendix* (n. 178), the latter reprinted in *Slavonia Reformata* (1679) 527 – 28. In the latter transcription Budziński acknowledged Łukasz Górnicki as a source, mentioned by Lubieniecki as a source only at n. 167, who correctly reported that Górnicki said he was an eyewitness of the burning of the eighty-year old Katarzyna Zalaszowska Weiglowa. (folio 7. 12).

164. The author here voices the unfavorable and unfair opinion of the ''republican'' propaganda of the sixteenth century. Piotr Gamrat (1487 – 1545) was a Renaissance prelate who joined magnificence of life with a love of letters and scholarship. An astute politician, he supported with a firm hand the endeavors of Queen Bona Sforza to strengthen

the royal power at the expense of the Senate and to oppose the Hapsburgs. Gamrat was an enemy of Jews and heretics and attempted to establish the inquisition, but he understood the necessity for reforms in the Church and vigorously promoted them. The adverse opinion of the senatorial nobility, the Hapsburg propaganda, and the memory of his anti-Protestant measures have combined to transmit a thoroughly unfavorable image of Gamrat.

165. It is not certain that the inset material comes verbatim from Budziński. Węgierski, *Slavonia Reformata*, 207, also citing Budziński, has *tamquam epulas*, where Lubieniecki has *tamquam ad nuptias*: 'together, the wedding feast.'

166. Faustus Socinus and his heritage are dealt with more fully, *pp. 190–93*. Here, as often elsewhere, Lubieniecki sees the hand of Providence in chronological coincidences.

167. The eyewitness of the martyrdom in Cracow was Górnicki, on whom Budziński himself depended. Cf. n. 163. It is not certain here whether Lubieniecki also read Katarzyna's answer to the episcopal court concerning the Creed, as given by Łukasz Górnicki (c. 1533–73) in his *Dzieje w Koronie Polskiej od roku 1538 aż do roku 1572* (History in Crown Poland) (Cracow, 1637), ed. in modern spelling with notes by Henryk Barycz (Warsaw, 1953) folio 7.12–13:

> Why, the Lord had no wife nor son, nor is He in need of it; for those only need sons who die, but the Lord is eternal; and, as He was not born, so neither can He die. Us he has for His sons that follow the ways directed by Him.

Katarzyna Weiglowa was suspected of heresy even in 1529. Summoned to the episcopal court, she had replied to the questions put to her "that she was unable to comprehend by her reason the belief in the divine unity of the three persons, confessing that she believed in one God only, but could not understand the three persons of Father, Son, and Holy Spirit." In 1530 she had recanted; but she then reverted to her former conviction. See Bukowski, *Dzieje Reformacji w Polsce* (Cracow, 1883) 1. 175–79.

In Lubieniecki's text it is not clear whether the second personal reference, "I understand" (*credo*), comes from Lubieneiecki or was copied by him inadvertently from Budziński, who (at n. 163) had done the reading in Górnicki. In that case the first personal reference, "I do not conceal" (*Non dissimulo*) would then be, of course, from Budziński, which seems likely and in which case the material down to the intercalated caption should be in the italicized Budziński font. There are only a few instances where we have two Latinized transcriptions of what was in Budziński's MS Polish History and here we have reference to a printed source, clearly read by Budziński only in MS and which could have been, indeed, consulted by Lubieniecki in print as of 1637, but probably not.

168. Stanisław Orzechowski, *Annales Polonici ab excessu divi Sigismundi Primi* (1554; edition of Dobromil, 1611) 89 continues:

> for which some people assert that he [Maciejowski] had swirled close to the Lutheran heresy in his diocese, which however was not so, neither can it be ever proved.

On Orzechowski, a major Catholic publicist, see n. 270, and *Historia, 22, 30–32*, and on Maciejowski of Cracow, *Historia, 20–28* passim.

The primatial succession in Gniezno includes Jan Łaski (1510–31, cf. n. 156); Maciej Drzewicki (1531–35); Andrzej Krzycki (1535–38); Jan Latalski (1537–40); Piotr Gamrat (1540–45, n. 164); Maciejowski Mikołaj Dzierzgowski (1546–59, *pp. 35, 61, 93*); Jan Przerębski (1559–62, *Historia, 59* passim); Jakub Uchański (1562–81, n. 184); Stanisław Karnowski (1581–1603).

169. Jan Andrzej Trzecieski (d. 1547), once a student of Erasmus of Rotterdam,

learned Greek and Hebrew abroad. He identified himself with the Reformation.

Jan Andrzej was a correspondent of Erasmus and Melanchthon. He wrote Erasmus from Breslau, 28 October 1527. Erasmus, *Opus Epistolarum*; ed. by P. S. Allen, 11 vols. (Oxford, 1906–47 and index 1958) 7. nr. 1895, 218–20.

For the resonance of Erasmus in Poland and for the beginnings of the Reformation currents in the Commonwealth, only intimated by our Author in his haste, see in the collection of his own studies, Henryk Barycz, *Z epoki renesansu, reformacji i baroku*, esp. "Sladami Erazma z Rotterdamu w Polsce" and "U narodzin ruchu reformacyjnego w Małopolsce"1–41; 219–42.

Trzecieski was the father of one of the greatest writers in Poland in the sixteenth century, Andrzej (c. 1530–84), whose *Carmina* and *Dzieła wszystkie* have been edited critically in 3 vols. (Wrocław, 1958, 1961). See further Jerzy Krolowski, *Andrzej Trzecieski: Poeta-humanista i działacz reformacyjny* (Warsaw, 1954) 15–25.

Jan Andrzej was a correspondent of Erasmus and Melanchthon. Jan Andrzej wrote Erasmus from Breslau, 28 October 1527. Erasmus, *Opus Epistolarum*; ed. by P. S. Allen, 11 vols. (Oxford, 1906–47 and index 1958) 7. nr. 1895, 218–20.

Bernt Wojewódka was not a typographer at that time. On this, Lubieniecki seems to be following Węgierski, *Slavonia Reformata*, 124. A humanist himself, a pupil of Erasmus, Wojewódka had in 1545 already started translating the *Postilla* of Joannes Corvinus (1501–53) of Braunschweig, then the New Testament, then the Psalms. In 1550 he was appointed *wójt* (bailiff) of Cracow. Mikołaj Radziwiłł the Black commissioned him and Andrzej Trzecieski to establish a press at Brześć-Litewski (Brest Litovsk) to publish Protestant literature in Polish. There, 1553–54, he published three translations. He drowned in July, 1556. K. Budzyk, R. Pollak, and S. Stupkiewicz, *Bibliografia Literatury polskiej okresu Odrodzenia* (Warsaw, 1954) 348, 369. Cf. RD 5, no. 50, RD 1, no. 65.

Wojewódka and the press, founded by Radziwiłł in Brześć, 1553, is seen in the larger setting of Polish printing by Alodia Kawecka-Gryczowa, *Drukarze dawnej Polski od XV do XVIII wieku: Wielkie Księstwo Litewskie* (Wrocław, Cracow, 1959) 65; the next vol. is subtitled: *Małopolska-Ziemie Ruskie* (ibid., 1960).

170. Desiderius Erasmus (probably 1469–1536) was a major influence in Poland, beginning in Cracow. Jan Łaski, the future reformer, sojourned with Erasmus in Basel and arranged for the sale of his library, later conveyed to Cracow by Frycz Modrzewski. From Erasmus, rather than indirectly from Calvin, Łaski evidently took over the idea of the *triplex munus Christi*, first developed by Erasmus in his Commentary on Psalm 2, a formula that would become a *topos* for the Polish Brethren, the threefold office of Christ, an all the more precious legacy from Erasmus and Łaski as they became Christocentric Unitarians by the close of the sixteenth century. For this theme and the relevant literature in Polish to date, see my, "Erasmianism in Poland 1518–1605," *Polish Review* 23 (1977) 3–50 and n. 169, ¶2.

171. Francesco Lismanino (1504–15), a major figure, is dealt with below, esp. *Historia, 40–44, 67–70*, and *168–70*. He was born of Greek parents on Corfu under Venetian control and brought by his parents to Cracow as a boy. He became provincial of his order in 1538.

Henryk Barycz summarizes his eventful, indecisive, and sad life in *PSB* 17 (1972) 464A–570B, which cites works to be adduced and subsequently in my own annotation: idem *Historia Universitetu Jagiellónskiego*, about Lismanino as doctor theologiae, from 1545 lector in theology and Scripture (Cracow: University Press, 1935) 408–10, idem, "Meandry Lismanianowskie," *ORwP* (1971); and idem, *Z Dziejów w polskich wędrowek naukowych za granicę*, about Lismanino's sojourn in Switzerland (Geneva, Lausanne, Zurich, and Geneva again, and full conversion to the Reformation, 1553 – 56 (Wrocław: Ossolineum, 1969) 253 – 56.

172. Bernardino Ochino (1487 – 1564), a native of Siena, joined the Observantine Franciscans and rose to be their general. He transferred to the Capuchins in 1524 and was twice elected their vicar-general (1538 – 41). Reputed to be the most moving preacher in Italy, in August, 1542, he left Italy for Geneva. He was minister of the Italian congregation in Augsburg (1545 – 47). For his later story, see *Historia, 29*, and in context, Ronald Bainton, *Bernardino Ochino* (Florence, 1940).

173. Jakub Przyłuski (1554) was a universal Renaissance humanist, linguist, and poet. The codification of laws was one of the political programs of the nobility which aimed at incorporating their own interpretation of the social and political structure of the country. Their first attempt, initiated in 1532, failed. See n. 136. Przyłuski, encouraged by his patron, Piotr Kmita (n. 175), undertook the work and attempted to bring it to the attention of the first diet of Sigismund II in 1548. The gentry supported him in his endeavor. The work, however, was a failure. Instead of a useful codification, it turned out to be a legal and political encyclopedia. Although he was in a clerical order, Przyłuski married and actively opposed the Roman Catholic Church. B. Ulanowski "Jakob Przyłuski i jego statut," *RwP*, 2 (1926) 240 – 55.

174. *Statuta Regni Poloniae methodica dispositione conscripta* (Cracow, 1548); 2nd amplified edition, *Leges seu statuta ac privilegia Regni Poloniae* (1553). Siekanowicz, *Legal Sources of Poland*, item 9, 9.

175. Andrzej Frycz Modrzewski of Wolbórz (Andreas Fricius Modrevius) (1503 – 72) was a humanist, a member of the early Erasmian circle in Cracow, and the foremost Polish political writer of his century. He served in the chancery of the Primate Archbishop of Gniezno Jan Łaski (1510 – 31)—the uncle of the Reformer—and then served other members of this powerful family on their diplomatic missions, mainly in Germany, where he was in contact with leading Protestants.

The struggle of the gentry for political and economic domination and their discriminatory measures against both burghers and peasants provoked him to a sustained literary campaign in defense of the rights of the lower estates (from 1543 on). In this connection his main work was *Commentarium de republica emendanda libri quinque* (Cracow, 1551). The work, supplemented in 1553 (full edition 1554) and soon to be translated into German, French, Spanish, and Polish, was put on the Index in 1557. Modrzewski supported the program of "execution-of-laws" as interpreted and promoted by the moderate wing of the gentry, led by Mikołaj Sienicki (below, *p. 201*) primarily against the bishops and the magnates, but in the economic and social sphere he followed the old line of defense of the burghers and the peasants. He advocated a centralized state, based on Roman legal conceptions, with a strong and efficient administrative and fiscal apparatus, but tempered by parliamentary procedures.

In international politics, in accordance with the program of the gentry, Modrzewski advocated peace and an ordered community of states, including non-Christian ones. His ideas to a great extent became an inspiration for the moderate, humanist-educated wing of the gentry. Modrzewski contributed to the formulation of the "execution-of-laws" program at the diets of 1552 and 1553. Also his religious ideas greatly influenced the party of reform.

In 1545 Modrzewski started advocating the right of laymen to take part in the Council of Trent (Period I, 1545 – 47; II, 1551 – 52; III, 1562 – 63); and in 1546 he was appointed secretary to the Polish delegation to the Council. In his *De ecclesia*, already composed in

1551 but (owing to the opposition of the bishops) only published in full in the second edition of 1554, he subjected the Church to severe criticism. He advocated the complete separation of church and state, the participation of laymen in church administration on a democratic basis, the congregational election of the clergy, the use of the national language in worship, and lay communion in both kinds.

From 1547 Modrzewski served as secretary in the royal chancery. In 1552 he was again appointed secretary of the Polish delegation in Trent, who had agreed to seek the abolition of clerical celibacy, the adoption of the national language in worship, communion in both kinds, and other reforms.

However, attacked by the leaders of the hierarchy, Modrzewski had to leave Cracow and settled in Wolbórz where he was appointed bailiff (*wójt*). Here he enjoyed the protection of its owner, Jan Drohojowski, bishop of Kujawy (1551–52). Of Orthodox parentage, once bishop of Chełm (1546–51), Drohojowski was himself suspected of Protestantism (n. 184). The pressure of the bishops grew so great that Modrzewski had to flee and took refuge with Grand Hetman Jan Tarnowski (1488–1561). Secundio Curione in Basel had dedicated to Tarnowski his *Schola sive de perfecto grammatico*, August 1555. On Tarnowski, see *Historia, 65–66*. Modrzewski returned when the King, under pressure from the Diet of Warsaw (1556/57), granted him a safe-conduct. After that he enjoyed the protection of Bishop Jakub Uchański (1557/61–62), controversial successor of Drohojowski and whose friend and trusted councillor he became. In his own fight against Rome Uchański availed himself of Modrzewski's services. In *De primatu papae* (1558), anonymously attacking the interference of bishops in state matters and defending the political independence of the state, Modrzewski influenced the Diet of Piotrków of 1558/59 in the direction of a reformed national Catholic church (n. 184).

The enlarged edition of *De republica emendanda* (Basel, 1559), including several additional treatises, marked his sharpening opposition to the Church. Nevertheless, in that period in his theological writings Modrzewski drew nearer to the Reformed Church of Little Poland or rather to its lay patrons, the leaders also of the "execution-of-laws" party.

When asked by his friends to do so, Modrzewski took part in the controversy against Francesco Stancaro on Christ the mediator (see *Historia, 116–47*) in order to help preserve the unity of the Protestant movement, but he did not identify himself with the distinctively Calvinian thrust in the Polish Reformed Church. He was still thinking in terms of a national church as a constituent part of the Church universal; and, when disappointed by the Council of Trent, he became one of the leading intellectuals of the party of the national council (1562–65). This party was led by Uchański, archbishop and primate (1562–81), fully supported by the King. It was the King who commissioned him to elaborate a program for unifying the Protestant forces. Four treatises resulted, in which Modrzewski developed his program of the national council (n. 177).

176. Piotr Kmita (1477–1553), Grand Marshal of the Crown, *starosta* of the Wawel and palatine of Cracow, fought against the Tatars, 1509; against Moscow, 1514; and against the Teutonic Order, 1520. His seat at Wiśnicz was a center of Renaissance culture. Halina Kowalska, *PSB* 13 (1967–68) 96–100. As Marshal he issued, 7 November 1533, an edict against Anabaptists from Moravia settling around some thirteen towns between Cracow and Pińczów, *Edictum contra Anabaptistas*, cited by Kot/Wilbur, *Socinianism* 11.

177. *Sylvae quatuor* (Cracow, 1590), critical edition, 5. 109. The first *Sylva* treats "De tribus personis et una essentia Dei."

Modrzewski developed marked antitrinitarian tendencies. The Calvinists were appalled and prevented his manuscript of *Sylvae* from being published. See *Historia, 22ff.* Modrzewski reworked his manuscript, and it was posthumously published in 1590 by the Minor Church. Persecuted by the Catholic clergy, Modrzewski in 1568 had to leave his seat in Wolbórz, and he retired to a little estate bought by him in Małecz nearby. There he died from the plague in 1572 and was buried.

Another work of Modrzewski also came into print because of the radical Reformed. His *De Republica emendanda* was translated into Polish by Bazylik Cyprian and printed at the press established at Łosk (1573) by Jan Kiszka in 1577 as *O poprawie Rzeczypospolitej*, with a dedicatory *carmen* of Szymon Budny and a Latin dedication written by Andrzej Wolan to the palatine of Polock Mikołai Dorohostajski (d. 1597), who bore the expense. This was noted by Benedict Wiszowaty, *BAnt²*, 36. A copy of the first Polish edition that had come to his attention is reproduced by offset with a preface by Julian Krzyżanowski (Warsaw, 1953). For Bazylik Cyprian (c. 1535 – after 1591), owner of the press in Brześć, 1562? – 70, see Gryczowa, *Drukarze: Księstwo Litwewskie*, 45 – 52.

178. The Brethren attached considerable importance to the Dutch guest and perhaps found in the purported visit of Spiritus Belga some sanctions from the native land of Erasmus, while in the festive library setting there could also have been some allusion to the arrival of Erasmus's library purchased by Łaski and conveyed to Cracow by Modrzewski (n. 170). Spiritus Belga could have been a fictional personification of Modrzewski's own views. However, in the passage Modrzewski clearly distinguishes himself as "I . . . pondering."

The advent of Spiritus in Cracow from the Netherlands is dated in the sources as of 1546 or 1547; and he himself has been variously conjectured in these sources to have been a figure in the *Dialogues* of Ochino (below 3), the Unitarian Mennonite Adam Pastor (RD 1, n. 10), and one Everhard Geesterhans (*spiritus* in Dutch: *geest*, ¶5).

As for the date, perhaps of no great moment, Modrzewski, whose reminiscence in his *Sylva* 1:2 (no. 177; RD 1) has 1546, is followed by Lubieniecki. Andrew Wiszowaty, however, in *Brief Narrative* (RD 5, no 51) implies that the visit was in the same year as the departure of Laelius Socinus from (Vicenza/Bologna), that is, 1547. There is one more testimony to 1547. The *Narrative* was printed three times in the seventeenth century (RD 5, n. 1), first by Sand in his *Nucleus*. Right after it Sand printed a sketchy chronology, 1547 – 67, beginning with the Spiritus episode. This chronology is now most accessible in the facsimile edition of Węgierski, *Slavonia Reformata*, 508-10. It opens: "In about the year 1547 a certain Dutchman, whose name was Spiritus, came to Poland, etc." The chronicler refers to *Sylva* 1:2, having nevertheless emphatically shifted the date, and speculates on the visitor: "*Nescio vero annon hic Spiritus sit ille, qui in* Dialogus *Occhini (qui etiam fuit in Polonia) introducitur, differens.*" The Speculator could, of course, be Sand himself rather than the author of the snippet. The next entry in this sparse Chronicle is for 1553: "Francesco Lismanino is regarded in Poland as an Arian, and his secretary Budziński is likewise said to be and Arian, who wrote an ecclesiastical History of the so-called Arians of his time, to a great part of which he was eye-witness." *Loc. cit.*, 508. While the Chronicler himself could not have been Budziński, referred to in this distinct way in the second entry, the Chronicler's first entry "Anno 1547, Circiter . . ." could nevertheless have stemmed from Budziński's History. The Speculator could, of course, in that case be Budziński himself, saying in effect that he thought Modrzewski's Spiritus was a literary figure, like one in Ochino's humanistic dialogues. Although Ochino published *Dialoghi sette* (Venice, 1542), the Speculator had probably in mind Ochino's *Dialogi triginta* in two books dedicated to Francis (Russell) 2nd Earl of Bedford and Prince Mikołaj Radziwiłł (Basel, 1563), which, to be sure, could have been familiar to a Speculator of an earlier date through an Italian MS circulating before Curione's translation in Basel. In any case, the snippet and the speculation might come from Budziński's MS History, 1.4. (cf. RD 1, no. 65, near n. 6) and the date 1547 seems to authoritatively independent of Modrzewski's "*Anno Christi 1546, misi memoria me fallit.*"

Aware of the importance of Spiritus for the Polish Brethren and aware, too, that their practice of baptismal immersion spread by way of the Rynsburger spiritualized Remonstrant Collegiants to the sojourning English Baptists, Dutch scholars have been attentive to Spiritus and may have found his grandson in Johannes Geesteranus, pastor in Alkmaar, the first candidate to be baptized by the Rynburgers in 1620 and called to serve in Poland in 1622. On Spiritus/Geesteranus, see *BAnt*, 113–14; *BAnt²*, 114; J. C. Van Slee, *De Rijnsburger Collegianten* (Haarlem, 1895) 377; W. C. Kühler, *Het Socinianisme in Nederland* (Leiden, 1912) 5, 28; Stanisław Kot, *Modrzewski* (2nd ed.; Cracow 1923) 73; Wilbur, *Socinianism*, 284, nn. 5–6.

179. Adam Drzewicki appears as a member of this circle also in Węgierski, *Slavonia Reformata*, 124, and in Wojciech Wengierski, *Kronika*, 5. However, there was no canon of Cracow of this name otherwise attested. Cf. Ludwik Łętowski, *Katalog Biskupów, Prałatów i Kanoników krakowskich*, 4 vols. (Cracow, 1852–53) 2. 212–13. There were brothers Jan and Mateusz Drzewicki, sons of Adam Drzewicki, castellan of Radom and nephew of the late Maciej Drzewicki, archbishop of Gniezno, who in 1542 were canons of Cracow and royal secretaries. Mateusz studied in Leipzig in 1528, but as canon of Cracow, parson of Włocławek (cathedral see of Kujawy) and verger of Łęczyca, he was known as an orthodox Roman Catholic and an adversary of Uchański, and died in Rome in 1575. Nothing is known of Jan, canon of Cracow and scholastic of Łęczyca, who died in 1554. One of their brothers, Adam, with another brother, Jakub, studied in Leipzig in 1556 and then in Padua in 1540, but this Adam was a layman. Thus again the context of the visit of Spiritus Belga remains obscured. For the above information, see George Erler, *Die Matrikel der Universität Leipzig*, 3 vols. (Leipzig, 1895–1902), 1. 599, 620, where the names are misspelled. Adam Boniecki, *Herbarz Polski*, 10 vols. (Warsaw, 1901–13) 5. 55–56.

180. Andrzej Zebrzydowski, newly arrived from Kujawy, was bishop of Cracow, 1551–60. Lubieniecki's opinion of him is supported by contemporaries, both Protestant and Catholic. It was common knowledge that he bribed his way to the bishopric. Archbishop Gamrat, himself not free from faults, used to call Zebrzydowski the "Beast." Stanisław Górski, canon of Cracow, highly praised for his archival work, considered him "a man unfit, a liar, and a soured man." He was known as greedy and avaricious, an oppressor of peasants. The chapter of Cracow called him in 1551 a man "of no religion or faith." The general opinion was that by his often injudicious persecution of heretics he simply wanted to restore his shattered reputation. However, his efforts were in vain. In 1555 Rome instructed the nuncio, Girolamo Lippomani, to investigate the accusations of grave lack of faith against the bishop. See Władysław Wisłocki, ed., *Andrzeja Zebrzydowskiego Korespondencyja 1546–1553* (Cracow, 1878), *Acta Historica Res Gestas Poloniae Illustrantia, 1507–1795*, 12 vols. (Cracow, 1878–1909) 1. 3–4.

181. Samuel Maciejowski, translated from Chełm, was bishop of Cracow, 1546–50.

182. *Kronika polska Marcina Bielskiego: Nowo przez Joachima Bielskiego syna iego wydana* (Cracow, 1597) 599, 608. This was part of the *Kronika wszystkiego Świata* (1st ed., Cracow, 1551). Bielski stressed the innovative attitude of Uchański. On Marcin Bielski himself (1495–1575) see Ignacy Chrzanowski, *PSB*, 2 (1936) 64–66.

183. Jan Drohojowski (1505–57), born Greek Orthodox, was converted to Roman

Catholicism in his youth. A humanist and lawyer, he entered upon a church career in 1532. In 1533 he was appointed canon of Cracow. A cousin of Stanisław Orzechowski (n. 270), and the lifelong friend of Andrzej Frycz Modrzewski, he was one of the foremost partisans of the reform of the Church in Poland. Appointed bishop of Kamieniec in 1545, in the same year he was promoted to the see of Chełm. In 1546/47 he was the prospective leader of the Polish delegation to the Council of Trent where he was expected to promote his program. Sigismund II, himself a partisan of reform, promoted him in 1551 to the see of Kujawy (n. 175). He settled in Wolbórz, where Modrzewski also lived, and made it into a center of the Catholic reform movement. One of his secretaries was Szymon Zak (Zacius), later superintendent of the Reformed Church in Lithuania, *Historia, 29, 43, 177, 197.* In 1552 Drohojowski was again appointed to lead the Polish delegation to Trent. Attacked by the conservative Polish bishops and the nuncio, he seemingly yielded.

Modrzewski and Orzechowski were present as he lay dying. It is possible that on his deathbed he regretted his weakness and that this is the substance behind the spurious *Narzekanie* in which he confirmed "his will to confess the Reformed faith." Stanisław Kot *PSB* 5 (1939–46) 380–82; idem, "Opposition to the Pope by the Polish Bishops 1557–1560," *Oxford Slavonic Papers* 4 (1953) 46–55; 62–70. Kot prints the whole of the unique Lament of Drohojowski, *Narzekanie* (Brześć-Litewski, 1557?), 56–62, which he ascribes to Stanisław Lutomirski, 43 passim.

184. Paweł Piasecki, bishop of Przemyśl, *Chronica gestorum in Europa praesertim in Polonia singularium 1575–1644* (Cracow, 1645; 2nd ed., 1648) 49. Lubieniecki has correctly *Uladislavensis*, but the see of Kujawy (Cujavia) was at the time Włocławek.

Jakub Uchański (1502–81), born in the Land of Chełm, canon of Cracow, a member of the humanist circle and friend of Modrzewski (n. 178), was well acquainted with the Byzantine Church. This had bearing on his later reformatory tendencies. Although without higher education, he was a good lawyer and widely read, especially in Protestant literature. He served as a lawyer for Queen Bona, and through her influence was appointed canon of Cracow in 1539, as well as crown referendary. Notwithstanding his connection with the humanist circle, he enjoyed the full confidence of the Cracow chapter.

During the crisis of 1549/50, provoked by the King's marriage (n. 140), Uchański acted as intermediary between the parties and as his reward was nominated bishop of Chełm in 1550. Under the pressure of the Inquisitor General, Oliviero Cardinal Caraffa (later Pope Paul IV), he was denied a licence to preach, and a canonical examination of his beliefs was ordered. The provincial synod of Piotrków in 1551 refused him admission to its deliberations. This provoked a conflict between Sigismund II and Rome about the right to nominate bishops. As the bishops were Senators *ex officiis*, the King claimed the right of nomination for himself. The Pope, fearing an open break, yielded, and Uchański obtained his confirmation. However in 1555 the new bishop, under the influence of Modrzewski, openly sided with the campaign for a national council of the Polish Church, worship in the national language, communion *sub utraque specie*, and abolition of clerical celibacy, and he demanded a reconciliation with the Protestants.

In 1557, against the opposition of Stanisław Hosius, bishop of Varmia, the leader of the conservative Catholics, Uchański was nominated bishop of Kujawy in succession to Drohojowski (nn. 175, 183). Paul IV refused to allow him to preach. A conflict again ensued between the King and Rome. Backed by the lay Senators, the King refused to yield. His position was taken up by the Protestants in a pamphlet, *De primatu papae*

(October 1558, probably in Brześć Litewski), anonymously written by Modrzewski, which attacked the political activities of the papacy and the oath of allegiance to the Pope required from the Polish episcopal Senators. The Author adduces in support of his charge the papal oath of allegiance as it was sworn by Primate Mikołaj Dzierzgowski (1546–59), reproduced by Kot, "Opposition to the Pope," 62 ff. It was at this interval in the career of Uchański that the Swiss Reformed pressed him. Calvin wrote him from Geneva, 19 November 1558, and from Zurich, Heinrich Bullinger, 28 November 1558, Wotschke, *Briefwechsel*, nos. 155 and 158. Calvin's letter is in *OC*, 17, n. 2983. Cf. Calvin's earlier allowance for a reformed national hierachy (1554), Bk 2, n. 61, ¶ 2. Bullinger's letter is in *Uchańsciana czyli Zbiór dokumentów wyjaśniających życie i działalność Jakóba Uchańskiego*, ed. by Teodor Wierzbowski, 5 vols. (Warsaw, 1884–95) 1, no. 17, 32–34. Wierzbowski gives the old date of 18 November; he supplies a register of all the correspondence of Uchański, 1, 1–xliv; and in vol. 5 he presents an historical monograph. As for the critical edition of the letters of Bullinger—whose correspondence is larger than that of Calvin—his epistles to the Poles are not yet included in the ongoing *Werke*, ed. by Fritz Büsser, with *Briefe*, now into 3 vols. up to 1533 (Zurich: Theologischer Verlag, 1972–).

The reformatory ideas of Modrzewski's *De primatu papae* and the collected invectives of the married-priest publicist, Stanisław Orzechowski (n. 270 and *Historia, 17* passim) in *Repudium Papae Romani*, who threatened to join the Byzantine-rite Church, reechoed at the Diet of Piotrków of 1558/59, notably in the speech there of Hieronim Ossoliński. Uchański himself openly joined the Protestant-led party of the "execution-of-laws" and promoted the idea of a national council with the Pope's permission, but with the King as arbiter. Under the pressure of the gentry, a national council was indeed promised by the King.

Backed by the King and public opinion, Uchański took his place in the Senate and as bishop of Kujawy took over his see. Paul IV retorted, 9 May 1559, by a summons to the Roman Inquisition. The summons was issued in clear contradiction to the privilege obtained by Sigismund II from Paul III, on the strength of which no royal subject could by summoned to Rome, especially by the Inquisitors, without the King's knowledge. Uchański retorted by an appeal to a universal or national council and then by a Polish pamphlet, *Jednyna obrona/ The Sole Defense—Truth Divine—of the Rev. Jacob Uchański, by the grace of God Bishop of Kujawy, against the Rumors of the priests reckoned as Roman Inquisitors*, Raciąż, 8 July 1559, and probably written by Modrzewski. *Uchańsciana*, 2. nos. 64, 114–34. The new Pope, Pius IV Medici, seeing the dangerous situation, yielded on all points in 1561. The reconciliation among the King, Rome, and Uchański struck a heavy blow at the high hopes of the native and foreign Protestants, who had maintained contact with the reform-minded bishop. Wierzbowski devotes a full chapter to the place of Uchański in the idea of a national Church in Poland, 1548–74, *Uchańsciana*, 5. 268–379.

At the provincial council in 1561 at Warsaw, Bishop Uchański resumed a leading Catholic role and was chosen a delegate to Trent. Nevertheless, he did not give up his reformatory ideas; and, influenced in this by his friend Modrzewski, he promoted the idea of reunification of the Protestants with the Church on the ground of reasonable compromise based on free discussion. This openess did not prevent his being appointed Primate in 1562, in succession to Dzierzgowski. Kot, "Opposition to the Pope," 46–55, 62–70, n. 183.

185. Kasper Cichocki, *Alloquiorum Osiecensium sive variarum familiarum sermonum*

libri V (Cracow, 1615). This work gained attention for having prompted the English ambassador to seek redress for the pictures given therein of Elizabeth I and James VI/I. *PEK*, B-D 98.

186. Mikołaj Pac, bishop of Kiev, resident in Vilna, was the only member of the Catholic hierarchy to join the Calvinists. He retained his episcopal title and properties until 1580 when he joined the ranks of the temporal Senators. He was one of the named executors of the testament of 27 May 1563, left by Prince Mikołaj Radziwiłł, patron of the Reformed congregation that met in his palace (Gasztołd) in Vilna. Pac wrote with the help of Georg Weigel and Andrzej Wolan, against the radical leadership, in Vilna, 1563–66, calling it Arian Anabaptist, in his own *Orthodoxa fidei confessio* (Königsberg, 1566) which he dedicated to Jan Chodkiewicz, the *starosta* of Samogitia, who sustained the costs. Pac also wrote *Epistola ad veros Christi fideles* (Königsberg, 1579). *PEK*, N-R, 296; Stanisław Kot, "Opposition to the Pope," 55; see n. 196.

187. In *Sylvae quatuor* IV: *De Homousio ad Jacobum Uchanorum Archiepiscopum Gnesnensem*, Modrzewski addressed a plea, dated June 1569, to the Primate "as second to the King in this Republic" to support an assembly to discuss Triadology. *Opera*, 5. 236–38.

188. Erazm Otwinowski (c. 1528–1614), pupil of Marcin of Opoczno, and protegé of Piotr Kmita, palatine of Lublin, from 1556 took an active part in the Reformed Church. A member of the embassy to Turkey in 1557, he left an interesting history of this. A servant of the powerful Tęczyński family, as secretary to Jan Baptista Tęczyński, Otwinowski took part in several diplomatic missions, and in his master's unfortunate expedition to Stockholm in 1561 to marry the Princess Cecilia Vasa. In the Cracow synod of 1563 he sided with the emerging Minor Church, belonging to the Lublin group, and he eventually settled in Raków. Among other things, he published his rhymed *Bohaterowie chrystiańscy* [Christian Heroes] about 126 patrons of congregations and 44 ministers (surviving only in summaries) and his rhymed *Przypowieści Pana naszego Jezusa Chrystusa* (Raków, 1599). Stanisław Kot, "Erazm Otwinowski," *RwP* 6 (1939) 1–37; Henryk Barycz, *PSB* 24 (1979) 641–45. See further, Book 3, at n. 140.

189. The material on Falconius, incidental to the point made about Bishop Drohojowski, is taken by Lubieniecki, as on several occasions in the *Historia*, from the lost MS of *Bohaterowie*, n. 188. This work is summarized in *Slavonia Reformata*, 529–38, where the summary of Falconius (537), as in Lubieniecki, speaks of Falconius as a priest (*Mysta*) of the cathedral church in Lublin, thrown into prison for his change of religion, freed, and in Lithuania called by Prince Mikołaj Radziwiłł to preach the Word under his patronage. Lubieniecki should have known that Lublin was not a cathedral see. Thomasz (Falconius) Sokołowicz wrote *Sprawy y Słowa Jezusa Krystusa* [Acts and words of Jesus Christ the Son of God, written for the eternal comfort of the elect] and *Wtóra Księga Łukasza świętego* (Second Book of St. Luke, the title of which is History or Acts of the Apostles), both published in Brześć Litewski in 1566. They give the Protestant text of the Gospel according to the Bible of Brześć of 1563 (n. 266) with commentaries. The Harmony mentioned by Lubieniecki is a chronicle of the life of Jesus Christ compiled from the three harmonized synoptic gospels, contained in the first of Sokołowicz's two books. The commentaries embody the tenets of the Tritheist current among the Polish and Lithuanian Brethren. On Sokołowicz, see further *Historia, 43, 166; BAnt*, 4; Konrad Górski, *Studia nad dziejami polskiej literatury antytrynitarskiej XVI wieku* (Cracow, 1949) 129–40.

190. As of the primacy of Uchański (1562–81) there was not yet a patriarch of Moscow (est. 1589), and Orthodox Kiev under the Crown had only a metropolitan. There

was clearly a possibility of a national church, perhaps under a primate patriarch (n. 184, ¶¶ 3, 8).

191. This would be Adam Drzewicki (n. 179) or possibly this is a misprint for Drohojowski. The words ''he steadfastly befriended the truth [that of the Minor Church] to the very end'' especially fit Drohojowski, as witnessed by the *Narzekanie* (n. 183).

192. It seems likely that the whole paragraph depends upon Budziński. Friars of ''the Franciscan *familia*'' could include Bernardines or Capuchins. Few of them mentioned here are identifiable. They are not reported by Węgierski, *Slavonia Reformata*. Opoczno is mentioned twice. See *Historia, 23*. From the two notices, we know that he was an intimate friend of Lismanino and that he eventually returned to his order.

193. The text reads Sigismund I.

194. For Jan of Koźmin, see n. 154

195. Discordia, already introduced along with Jan Koźminczek, Augustus in Vilna (1545–50) at n. 154, is here retrospectively diparaged by Lubieniecki as his source.

After receiving his Cracovian A.B. (c. 1533), he was ordained priest (before 1541) and became a prebendary of St. Barbara's in Cracow and came under the proto-Evangelical preaching of Jakub of Iłża, lector in the Academy and popular preacher at St. Stephen's (n. 202). In 1541 Discordia got involved in canonical litigation; after paying a fine, left as wandering preacher against the faults of the Church in the diocese of Jan Dziaduski, bishop of Chełm (1543–45), later bishop of Przemyśl (n. 170 ¶ 3), expelled from his jurisdiction. On the recommendation of Mikołaj Radziwiłł the Black, Discordia, and Jan Koźminczek received salaried appointments, as of 9 April 1545, as court preachers. We next come upon Discordia in the *Historia* in Bk. 2, at n. 619. 143, 164–68.

196. The pontifical dates in Cracow were Tomicki (1523–35), Jan Latalski (1536–37), Chojeński (1537–38), Maciejowski (1546–50) (n. 181), and Andrzej Zebrzydowski (1551–60; n. 180).

197. Sigismund II had three queens. The first was Elizabeth, daughter of Ferdinand I Habsburg. The second was Barbara Radziwiłłówna (n. 140), the mistress of Sigismund from 1543. His love for Barbara is legendary. After her death, 8 May 1551 he followed her hearse on foot to Vilna. His third queen was Catharine, sister of his first wife, widow of Francesco III of Mantua.

198. On Leonard Słonczewski, see n. 205. He was absent at the diet and thus could not take part on the King's behalf. See *Diaryusze Sejmów koronnych 1548, 1553, 1570 w.*, ed. by J. Szujski, *Scriptores Rerum Polonicarum*, I (Cracow, 1872) 168. Lubieniecki follows here the discrepant narrative of Stanisław Orzechowski (n. 168), written in 1554, *Annales Polonici ab excessu divi Sigismundi I* (Dobromil, 1611) 30; repeated in Marcin Bielski, *Kronika Polska*, 589.

199. Orzechowski, *Annales* 26–27, from the debates of the Diet of Piotrków in 1548. The King spoke 13 November 1548. He had secretly married Barbara 28 July 1547, publicly 6 August 1547. The marriage was very unpopular both in Lithuania, where the powerful Radvilas were feared, and in Poland, where it almost provoked a rebellion on Sigismund's accession to the throne in 1548. The Diet of Piotrków (31 October–12 December 1548) was a scene of sharp conflict between the estates and the King. Even Primate Dzierzgowski advised divorce. One of the most vehement leaders of the gentry's opposition was Hieronim Ossoliński, later leader of the Protestants. The excitement was so great that Sigismund, fearing a revolution, concluded on 2 July 1549 a secret treaty with Emperor Charles V, that secured his assistance against rebellious subjects at the price of his renunciation of the hereditary rights (through his sister) to the crown of Hungary. The struggle continued at the diet of 1550, but more weakly because of fear of

Austrian intervention. The King acquired the support of the bishops for his marriage by promising them a decree against heretics, cf. Book 2 at n. 148. The Primate, himself one of the original leaders of the opposition, thereupon crowned Barbara on 7 December 1550. See Szujski, *Diaryusze sejmów*, 160 ff., esp. 183, 187, 276; *PSB*, 294 – 98.

200. For Krupka, see *Historia, 51 – 52*. An important treatment of the lay patrons of the Polish Reformation is that of Gottfried Schramm, *Der polnische Adel und die Reformation, 1548 – 1607* (Wiesbaden, 1965) with a good map of the palatinates.

201. A major patron, see *Historia, 52 – 54*. The *vita* to which Lubieniecki refers as his source, was in the lost *Bohaterowie* (n. 188).

202. Jakub of Iłża became a student of the University of Cracow in 1509 and received his M. A. in 1516. He was at the *collega minus* in the faculty of philosophy and preacher at St. Stephen's. Given to humanist studies, he eventually turned to theology and earned a B. D. A good preacher, he started spreading Evangelical opinions, and in 1528 he was summoned to the episcopal court. He denied the accusation. In 1534 he was again tried for spreading heresy from the pulpit and in private meetings. He turned anti-intellectual, urging that boys be trained for good jobs as more conducive to savlation than liberal arts preparatory to becoming priests of privilege. His written defense was declared heretical. He promised publically to recant, but by the end of October 1534 he fled to Wrocław. He was formally proclaimed a heretic on 24 May 1535. Barycz, *Historia Universytetu*, 102 – 5.

The Samuel of Pińzów is not otherwise attested unless he be identical with Andrzej Samuel, O. P., Węgierski, *Slavonia Reformata*, 74, 381.

203. Stanislovas Rapolionis (Rafałowicz; c. 1484 – 1545), a Lithuanian from a noble family near Kaunas (Kowno), studied theology at the University of Cracow, 1528 – 32. By 1542 he had followed his relation Dr. Abrahamas Kulvietis (Kulwa; c. 1510 – 45) to Königsberg. Duke Albert financed his studies in Wittenberg (1542 – 44), where he graduated with a D. Theol. In Königsberg he took a leading place among the professors of the new university and was a driving force of the Prussian Lutheran Church. He took part in the creation of Lithuanian literature as translator of hymns into the vernacular, and cooperated in the literary activities of the group of Polish writers resident in Königsberg. See P. Tschackert, *Urkundenbuch zur Reformationsgeschichte des Herzogthums Preussen*, I (Leipzig, 1890) 258 – 64, 288 – 93, 339. See also articles in *Lietuviu Enciklopedya*, 36 vols. (Boston, 1953 – 69) 24, 491 and in the parallel—*Encyclopedia Lituanica*, 6 vols. (Boston, 1970 – 78) 4. 436 – 37.

204. The Author has 1547. Rapolionis's untimely death was a heavy blow to the young university. The epitaph in the Lutheran church next to the University attests to his role: ''Here lies a great man, an honor to the Lithuanian nation.''

205. Leonard Słonczewski, D. D. (d. 1562), called *Altipolita* (i.e., of Wyszogród in Mazovia), a commoner, had studied in Wittenberg. In 1543 he was preacher at St. Mary's Church in Cracow, and in 1544 he started attacking the dissolute clergy and even the papacy. The popularity of his sermons among the burghers and gentry caused an alarm among the clergy, who suspected him of heresy. However, with the protection of Queen Bona, he was in 1546 appointed bishop of Kamieniec in Podolia, to the great astonishment of the clergy. He retired from the court and was the first bishop of Kamieniec to take up permanent residence in the see, where he distinguished himself. W. Abraham, ''Leonard Słonczewski,'' *RwP* 4 (1926) 121 – 27.

206. The Franciscan convents in Cracow and in Vilna were in a low state. On Lismanino, provincial, see esp. *Historia, 40 – 44*.

207. The sometime Franciscan Aleksy here, following Lubieniecki, could be

identified as Aleksy Rodecki, the printer who was later active in Raków. The ex-Franciscan Aleksy is attested at the synod in Pińczów, 25 April 1556. Sipayłło, *AS* 1. 55. However, the later printer was a student in the Pińczów school, probably in 1561. This raises the question of whether Lubieniecki confused two Aleksys. Alodia Kawecka-Gryczowa so holds, *Ariańskie oficyny wydawnicze* (Wroclaw: Ossolineum, 1972) 25 ff. on the life of Rodecki the printer, with the literature.

208. This Hieronim might be that Spinella (given name unknown) who preached anti-trinitariansim to the Italians in Cracow and was followed as minister of the Italian congregation by millenarian Giambattista Bovio. See Delio Cantimori, *Eretici italiani del Cinquecento* (Florence, 1939), *Italienische Haeretiker der Spätrenaissance* (Basel, 1949), p. 322; and Domenico Caccamo, *Eretici italiani in Moravia Polonia, Transilvania (1558 – 1611)* (Florence: Sansoni; Chicago: Newberry Library, 1970) 58, 95, 98 (Boviso, no mention of Spinella).

209. See above at n. 192.

210. Lord Stanisław Iwan Karniński became an elder of the Cracow district of the Reformed church, which broke from the liberal wing in 1567. See further *Historia* *25 – 29.*

211. This canon is supplied with his Christian name in the facsimile *Historia* index. He might be the convert of Iwan featured in the unit from Budziński beginning at n. 219. The index of the facsimile edition of Węgierski's *Slavonia Reformata* 125 identifies a Cracovian canon in a similar relationship to Lismanino as Jerzy; cf. *Historia, 23.*

212. This episode, drawn expressly from the Budziński MS, is given in similar wording by Węgierski, *Slavonia Reformata* 124 – 25. Here it is said that Lismanino recommended Maciejowski to Queen Bona for the see of Cracow, and also that it was Bishop Maciejowski who invited Francesco Stancaro at the beginning of 1550 to teach Hebrew at the Jagiellonian University.

213. On Jakub Przyłuski, see *Historia, 18.*

214. Stanisław Bojanowski.

215. This sentence comes from Budziński and the whole paragraph must be a summary of what this ''member of the household'' of Lismanino would have recounted. The Paul in direct discourse could be either Paul of the Gentiles, the Apostle par excellence for Luther and Calvin and their reformation, or just possibly Grzegorz Paweł, who studied seven years in Cracow and later became the first minister of the first Reformed congregation of Cracow in 1557 (n. 262).

''M. K.'' could read either Miłościwy Księże (Reverend Sir) or Miłościwy Książę (Serene Duke). The bishops of Cracow were dukes of the petty Silesian principality of Siewierz, purchased in 1448 by Bishop Zbigniew Oleśnicki (1423 – 55) who in 1451 had been named Poland's first cardinal.

216. In translating from the Polish, Lubieniecki turns the text of Budziński into indirect discourse and the first person into the third. It would be precarious to attempt a restoration of the Budziński text.

217. Giovanni Maria Cardinal del Monte was elected Pope Julius III, 8 February 1550.

218. Andrzej Czarnkowski, scholar of Cracow and royal secretary, and been sent by the King in September 1550 to make his obedience to Julius III. He returned to Poland in February 1551. Since Bishop Samuel Maciejowski of Cracow had died 26 October 1550 and his successor, Andrzej Zebrzydowski, had been appointed in December 1550, the meeting with Lismanino probably took place in January 1551. Czarnkowski, an ecclesiastical careerist, rather indifferent in religious matters, discredited by his cupidity,

dissolute life, and a disgraceful conflict with the University of Cracow (1549) had just been frustrated by the King and the Pope in his expectations of the bishopric of Cracow. He probably wanted to ingratiate himself with Queen Bona, then in open conflict with her son and the new queen, Barbara. Czarnkowski became bishop of Poznań in 1553. See Wierzbowski, *Uchańsciana* 5. 90 – 2, 513; 4. 216 – 17.

The chapter of Cracow cathedral complained in May 1551 about the heretical leanings of Lismanino and his friars, but the new bishop, Zebrzydowski, continued to protect him well into 1553. Zebrzydowski, *Korespondencyja,* 392, 425, 488.

219. Karniński (n. 210) is suddenly introduced here simply as Iwan. The text of this whole unit here and the next are very close to that of Budziński, perhaps verbatim, hence the *in ipso Ivano vivo* and *ac pagi illius* which presuppose a fuller reference to Iwan and to his estate in the preceding lines, absent however here.

The story from the household of Lismanino in Cracow gives a good glimpse of reformation ferment, vacillation, ecclesiastical threat, and the magnanimity of both the bishop and the proselytizing lord. Since Iwan is the hero of the story, we are not told who the vacillating priest was, although just possibly Canon Stanisław Podalowski (at n. 221). Perhaps the preacher returned well, a second time, to the obedience of the bishop of Cracow.

220. Adam Gosłowski died on 12 August 1642 and was buried in Czarkowy. *BAnt²*, 108. He could have been personally acquainted with Lubieniecki. On him, see also *Historia, 274.*

221. This unit is continuous with the preceding and must also stem from Budziński and the episode cannot be dated later than 1550. For Maciejowski's pontifical dates, see n. 181. Grzegorz Paweł was pastor of the Cracow Reformed congregation only in 1552.

222. In the text it is *obseptus*, corrected in the facsimile edition to *obreptus.*

223. This unit must come also from Budziński.

224. Seweryn Boner/Bonar (d. 1592) was the third son of Seweryn, Sr. (1486 – 1549) banker to Sigismund I. He was not so prominent in the Reformed movement in Little Poland as his oldest brother, Jan (d. 1562), on whom see *pp.* 48 passim, and for the illustrious family, see Table 124 in *Genealogia: Tablice,* ed. by Włodzimierz Dworzaczek (Warsaw, 1959).

225. *Evangelica* is the adjective for the Reformed, not the Lutherans.

226. It will not have gone unobserved that the Reverend Sir Stanisław, our Author, mentions the killing of horses before their coachman. In the divine vindication of Lord Karniński the deaths of a man and beasts are counted as minor losses.

227. Szymon Zak (Zacius) of Proszowice, M. A. of the University of Cracow in 1531, was ordained priest and made lecturer there in mathematics and astronomy, 1532 – 39. Later he went into Latin literature. He was probably pastor in Krzyżanowice, 1539 – 49. In 1549 he began preaching the new faith and married. Excommunicated, he sought shelter with Bishop Jan Drohojowski in Kujawy (n. 183). Mikołaj Radziwiłł, palatine of Vilna, took him to Lithuania. In 1553 he appeared in Brześć. In 1555 he was appointed minister in Vilna and elected superintendent of the Lithuanian churches. See further *Historia, 43, 177, 197.* See W. Budka, "Simon Zacius," *RwP* 2 (1922) 288 – 96; Barycz, *Historia Uniwersytetu,* 106ff.; *Lietuviu Encycklopedija* 35. 157. See Book 3, n. 197.

228. Marcin of Opoczno, M. A. of Cracow in 1537, *extraneus* of the faculty of philosophy, 1539 – 43, teacher of the author of *Bohaterowie,* was connected with the court of Piotr Kmita, palatine of Cracow. In 1542 he was priest in the diocese of Przemyśl, pastor of Babice. He began preaching the new faith in 1547. Imprisoned by Bishop Jan Dziaduski in 1550, he was rescued by the gentry and attained as minister of the synod of

Pińczów, 1550. See Sipayłło, *AS* 1. 2; Węgierski, *Slavonia Reformata* 536; and Barycz, *Historia Uniwersytetu* 111 – 12; *Zepoli* 305 – 6.

229. He is mentioned as present at synod at Pińczów, 1550, and thereafter (Sipayłło, *AS* 1.2, 80, 172) as minister in Solec under Marcin Zborowski as patron, 1556, then as minister to Jan Bonar.

230. Węgierski, (*Slavonia Reformata* 249, 536) preserves more from Otwinowski than Lubieniecki. Mikołaj was a vicar near Lublin, preaching against "papal superstitions." Between 1551 – 53, he was condemned to prison by Zebrzydowski when he refused to foreswear the new faith and died of hunger, hence *martyr*.

231. Feliks Cruciger (Krzyżak) was a student of the University of Cracow from 1529 to 1535. All the early reform leaders mentioned on *Historia, 23, 29 ff.*, such as Jan of Koźmin, Szymon of Żak, Marcin of Opoczno, Feliks Cruciger, belonged to the period in which Jakub Iłża was teaching, and were probably his disciples. See Barycz, *Historia Uniwersytetu*, 111.

232. See n. 172.

233. Marcin Krowicki (1501 – 73), a major figure in the Polish Reformation, was a nobleman born in Lubawa, Pomerania. He matriculated at the university in Cracow, but it was not primarily from there that he acquired his deep knowledge of the Greek and Latin classics nor his emerging competence in theology and vehemence and precision in disputation. It was rather at the brilliant humanistic court of Piotr Kmita in Wiśnicz (n. 176), palatine of Cracow, starosta of the same, of Przemyśl, and two other palaces. Krowicki served him succesively as secretary and as ordained chaplain. At the diocesan synod of Przemyśl in 1550 he openly criticized the corruption of the clergy and clerical celibacy, and he asked for communion in both kinds for the laity. With the support and indeed connivance of Stanisław Orzechowski (n. 270), he seems to have been the very first priest to have entered wedlock, though without the awareness of what he was doing on the part of the priestly celebrant (nn. 239, 274, Bk. 2, n. 155), 13 December 1550. Lubieniecki or his source should really have included the Krowicki marriage along with the other two firsts that he adduces at n. 270.

For many in Poland, among priests, even bishops, nobles, and townsmen, reformation at first concerned three major changes, all of them already achieved by the Czech Brethren, namely, 1) communion *sub utraque specie,* 2) marriage of the clergy, and 3) vernacularization and simplification of the liturgy and freedom from external controls.

234. Lubieniecki refers frequently to Krowicki, but despite his own "parochial" proximity to Krowicki's final ministry (Piaski, Bk. 3, n. 868), he never really makes clear his eminence and his several roles; and this slighting of him could be due to the Author's awareness that on the issue of the sword and public office debated within the Minor Church, Krowicki came to side with Budny and Budziński. It may be surmised that Krowicki bulked larger in Budziński's History than in the *Historia*: e.g. we know Budziński had preserved in it Krowicki's letter to himself on the very issues of the sword, dropped in Lubieniecki's appreciations of his predecessor's work.

The reference in the text is to Krowicki's *Obrana/Apologia* (1560), n. 289. The sermon "On the Cross of the Lord Christ and of his followers," preached at the general synod of Książ, September 1560, constituted a short chapter in the *Obrona*.

235. Budziński or Lubieniecki has apparently crossed names here, giving to Mikołaj of Kurów, mentioned above, the name Marcin by confusion with Krowicki's.

236. Piotr Zborowski, castellan of Biecz, was appointed castellan of Wojnicz in 1568 and palatine of Cracow in 1574. Budziński must refer instead to his father, Marcin Zborowski, then palatine of Poznań and the leader of the militant Protestants.

237. In introducing a passage from Orzechowski, Lubieniecki overlooks the fact that he alludes in a quotation to a major figure, Francesco Stancaro (1501 – 74), whom he has himself not hitherto mentioned, assuming perhaps that the mere surname, as here, would suffice for the reader.

Fiery and visionary, a Christian Hebraist with substantial knowledge of patristic and scholastic theology, Stancaro held to a view of the atonement in consonance with conciliar and scholastic theology, notably with Petrus Lombardus. The virtual founder of the Polish Reformed Church at Pińczów, 1550 (Book 2, n. 420), he presently involved Lutherans in Ducal Prussia, and the Reformed in both Poland and Transylvania in the protracted controversy over Christ the Mediator (Book 2, n. 425). The literature on Stancaro is extensive. It is drawn together by Lorenz Hein, *Italienische Protestanten und ihr Einfluss auf die Reformation in Polen* [to 1570] (Leiden: Brill, 1974) chap. 3. See further my "Francis Stancaro's Schismatic Reformed Church in Ruthenia, 1559/61 – 70," *Harvard Ukrainian Studies* 3/4 (1979 – 80) 931 – 57; and, forthcoming, Wacław Jan Urban, *Francizek Stancaro i Polska*.

Stancaro came to Cracow from Alba Julia, where at the court of Transylvania (1548 – 49), he had won the admiration of Queen Isabelle and her son (Book 2, n. 128, ¶¶ 4 – 5.) and carried with him her letter of recommendation for the lectorship in Hebrew at the Jagiellonian University.

Born in Mantua of possibly Sephardic Jewish antecedents, he studied in the cloister school the Church Fathers, the scholastics, and the humanists of his day, became a priest, and published his first work, *De modo legendi Hebraice institutio brevissima* (1530). About 1540 he was lector in ancient languages in Padua and married a girl beneath his station. Caught up in the Reformation, he was imprisoned by the Venetian Republic for 14 months and 6 days (as he later wrote out for his protector Górka). He was released and left Italy with the establishment of the Roman Inquisition, staying in Chiavenna in the Rhaetian Republic, where he engaged in controversy with both the local Reformed pastor Agostino Mainardo and Camillo Renato, a kind of anabaptist with an unusual rite of communion. (For this figure, connected indirectly with several Italian radicals in Poland, see my "Camillo Renato c. 1500 – c. 1575," *Italian Reformation Studies in Honor of Laelius Socinus*, John Tedeschi, ed., [Florence: Le Mounier, 1965] 103 – 83, 195, unnoticed by A. Gordon Kinder in his essay, among others, *Bibliotheca Dissidentium* 4 [Baden Baden: Koerner, 1985], and his collected works, Rotondò, *Opere*.) Because of Renato he was bitterly opposed to Anabaptists. He became lector in Hebrew at Vienna (1544 – 46), ordered out by King Ferdinand. He participated in the second Religious Conference of Regensburg of January 1546, along with Ochino, the two Italians staying together in Augsburg until Stancaro went to Basel to get his doctorate in theology. Here he published his *Della Riformatione* (April, 1547), addressed to the Signoria of Venice, quoting on the title page Rev 5.5: "Behold the Lion of the tribe of Judah [in pointed allusion to the lion of the Piazza di San Marco], the Root of David, so that he can open the scroll and its seven seals." The work was a call to all princes to undertake the reformation of doctrine and the sacraments on the basis of Scripture and the Church Fathers without tarrying for the Pope to call a council.

The above mentioned Camillo Renato could well have been another seminal figure, at length from his congregation in Caspano. He wrote his "Trattato del battesimo e dell santa cena" in 1547, quite possibly sent to Mainardo, ed., by Rotondò, *Opere*, 91 – 108. Renato was innovative in that he opposed the very term "sacrament" for the two Reformed ordinances, so different in intent and engagement as baptism and the eucharist.

He opposed the Zwinglian and hence Mainardian view in Chiavenna of pedobaptism as a continuation of circumcision (Bk. 3, n. 239, ¶¶6, 7), insisted that instruction precede baptism, and noted that the Greek word implied "la immersion e la emersione" without saying that his own congregation had introduced immersion, although he did significantly change the character of the Lord's Supper (*epulium*). On both, see my "Camillo Renato," pp. 153-56. Jarmola, *op. cit.*, appendix D, suggests a connection between Renato and both immersionist ideas in Poland and indifference to baptism in Faustus Socinus and some Transylvanian Unitarians. He suggests that Laelius Socius and Ochino may each have been influenced by Renato and that through these two plausibly encountered by Czechowic on his mission for Prince Mikołaj Radziwiłł to reconcile Calvin with Biandrata in 1561.

238. In the first sentence ("After Stancaro . . . families"), Lubieniecki alters that of Orzechowski, *Annales* (1611) 86. The relapsed Catholic calls the Reformed Church of Poland, beginning in Pińczów in 1550, a *secta*.

239. For the bride, see Bk. 2 n. 155. A relation was Wacław Pobiedziński, master of the horse; and Marshal of the armed confederacy (1612 – 14). See also A. Lubieniecki, *Poloneutychia*, 200.

240. By 1535 Krowicki had joined the court of Kmita, palatine of Cracow, and its humanist circle in Wiśnicz (n. 176). He served Kmita as secretary, later as steward of his estates. Through the latter's influence, he was appointed parson of two churches in the diocese of Przemyśl, of which Jan Dziaduski was bishop, 1545 – 59. The influence of his neighbors Marcin of Opoczno, Stanisław Orzechowski, and Jakub Przyłuski, pushed Krowicki into opposition to Rome. See further at Bk. 2. nn. 153 – 56. The Reformation came to Little Poland first in imitation of Wittenberg, then of Zwingli's Zurich, then of Calvin's Geneva.

241. Mikołaj Oleśnicki (d. c. 1567) was a deputy in the diet, a follower and defender of the Reformation.

242. Lubieniecki here confuses the sequence, which should be the professorship in Cracow, the composition of *Canones* (n. 243), the gathering of the church in Pińczów (1550), and the printing of the *Canones* (1552).

243. This account is set forth by Wengierski, *Chronik*. The reference is to Stancaro's *Canones Reformationis Ecclesiarum Polonicarum* (Frankfurt/Oder, 1552). The *Canones* were written in 1550, allegedly in the prison of Lipowiec. They were modeled on the *Einfaltiges Bedenken einer christlichen Reformation* (1543) of Archbishop Hermann von Wied (1477 – 1552) of Cologne, elaborated by Bucer and Melanchthon and published as the *Reformatio Coloniensis* (1545). The sharp attacks against the Roman Catholic Church and the quasi-legislative form of the *Canones*, joined to only moderate reformatory measures, displeased not only Roman Catholics but also the emergent Protestants. Stancaro's book was largely suppressed.

An enlarged Polish version, *Porządek naprawienia*, incorporating a new second book "On the Emendation of Lay Government," was printed in Cracow in 1553 at the expense of Hieronim Filipowski. However, this edition, too, met with strong opposition at the synod of Słomnicki on 25 November 1554. For reasons yet to be recounted, some Evangelicals feared that Stancaro's name on the preface would endanger the reform. Nevertheless, his order of service was accepted. See Sipayłło, *AS* 1. 3. The Polish edition was burned on the advice of Stanisław Stadnicki, so that no *complete* single copy survives.

See Hermann Dalton, *Lasciana. Nebst den ältesten evangelischen Synodalprotokollen*

Polens 1555–61 (Berlin, 1898) 397 ff; Józef Lukaszewicz, *O Kosciolach Braci Czeskich w dawnej Wielkopolsce* (Poznań, 1835) 36–7, 43–44; Kazmierz Piekarski, "Nieznane druki reformacyjne z 16 w.," *RwP* 3 (1924–25) 143–44.

244. The *Succamerarius (Podkomorzy*, i.e., sub-chamberlain) had become, in spite of the prefix, a higher office than that of *camerarius (komornik*, i.e., Chamberlain).

On Stanisław Lasocki, see n. 278.

245. Andrew (c. 1530–84) and his father Jan Andrzej Trzecieski are mentioned above, n. 169; by Węgierski, *Slavonia Reformata* 77 passim and attested at Reformed synods. He participated in the first observance of the Lord's Supper at Pińczów 25 November 1550 and is reported as sending his greeting from the synod of Pińczów, 30 January 1561; Sipayłło, *AS* 1. 2; 2. 90.

246. Krzysztof Gliński (d. c. 1600) is not mentioned by Węgierski or A. Lubieniecki, but is attested as present at synods in 1556, 1557, 1561, 1562; Sipayłło, *AS* 1. 31, 217; 2. 125, 139.

247. On 25 November 1550, the first Reformed service was celebrated in Pińczów by Jakub Sylviusz. Dalton, *Lasciana* 397–98; Sipayłło, *AS* 1. 2.

248. Zbigniew Oleśnicki (1389–1455), as bishop of Cracow, 1423, had been the leader of Polish politics under Ladislas II and Ladislas III the Varnian.

249. For the full account of Stancaro's vicissitudes and the quotation, see Orzechowski, *Annales* (1611) 79–80.

250. Lubieniecki, not following the Vulgate, uses perhaps more than one Protestant version of Scripture in the *Historia*, but his usage has not been given attention in these notes.

251. The Author refers to Paul's familiar image of spiritual armor of Rom 13:12 and Eph 6:13 and applies it to lordly Oleśnicki.

252. Lubieniecki here repeats Orzechowski, *Annales* (1611) 78:

Erat hic (Oleśnicki) in Sienensium familia natus, unde multi clari viri in Polonia fuerunt, lex quibus Sbigneus Cracoviensis Episcopus et urbis Romae Cardinalis.

Lubieniecki mistook the name of the clan Sienno for the name of the family Sienieński, prominent in the history of Polish Unitarianism. All these families shared the Dębno coat of arms. For Cardinal Zbigniew Oleśnicki, see n. 248.

253. The text has mistakenly 1524. The statute of Wieluń of 1424 was published against the Hussites. *Volumina legum* 1. 85–86. The statute was not revoked by Ladislas II Jagiełło (1386–1434). Lubieniecki may allude to the charter of Jedlnia of 1433 which provided that no inhabitant of the realm would be either imprisoned (with the exception of four reserved crimes) or would forfeit his estate without due process of law (ibid. 1. 93). As the statute of Wieluń ordered any heretic, or anyone suspected of heresy, or his patron, to be captured by the captains or magistrates and banished with forfeiture of their estates, the charter of Jedlnia seemed to abrogate the former statute. Lubieniecki stressed the "abrogation" and invalidity of this statute because it was quoted as the legal basis of the statute of 1658 which banished the "Arians" from Poland.

254. Planned by Stanislas Lubieniecki, probably under the influence of the *Poloneutychia* of his great uncle Andrew Lubieniecki, but it was never written. However, *The Legal Claims for the Freedom of the Religion of Unitarians* embodies much of the constitutional history he may have envisaged, *Polish Brethren*, Doc. XXVIII.

255. The decree of Parczów of 7 August 1564, pressed for by the Calvinist party, banished all "foreign innovators" as of 1 October 1564.

256. Andreas Osiander (1498–1552), from Nuremberg, became professor at Königsberg, where he published *De justificatione* (1550), (n. 131). In order to solve the

problem of sanctification in the Lutheran context, Osiander developed the distinction between the problem of Christ's justifying action on Calvary and the substantial transference of this righteousness to the believer in faith. He held further that Christ's ubiquitous divine nature (Luther) was involved in this mediation. Stancaro assailed this innovation in terms of the scholastic and patristic view of Christ the Mediator in his human nature alone (cf. 1 Tim 2:5), *Von dem einigen Mittler* (Königsberg, September 1551).

257. Matthias Flacius Illyricus (1520–75), professor of Hebrew at Wittenberg, 1544–56, left for Jena and subsequently developed a nearly Manichaean view of evil. A Genesio-Lutheran, he opposed Crypto-Calvinism. He was a leading spirit among the Magdeburg Centuriators and was the author of the *Catalogus Testium Veritatis* (1556).

258. Jan Łaski, the preeminent Polish Reformer, in effect general superintendent from his return to Poland in 1556 to his death in 1560, was first mentioned by Lubieniecki at n. 156, (with bibliography). Halina Kowalska who in *Działalność reformatorska Jana Łaskiego w Polsce 1556–1560* (1969) picked up where Bartel left off, admirably puts the whole life together in *PSB*, 18 (1973) 237–44; and for the related interpretation of Calvin's counsel to the Poles, see my ''Polish-Lithuanian Calvin,'' and my ''Christology of the Polish Brethren.''

259. Giorgio Biandrata (Latin: Blandrata) (1516–88), court physician in both Poland and Transylvania, was hitherto theological adversary of Calvin from his base in the Italian congregation in Geneva. His first attendance at a Polish synod is attested for that at Pińczów, 22 November 1559. Sipayłło, *AS*, 1. 315. The monographic literature on this major personality is brought together in a fresh authoritative article by Antonio Rotondò, *Dizionario Biografico degli Italiani (DBI)* 34 vols. to date (Rome, 1960–) 10 (1968), 257–64.

260. Petrus Statorius (d. 1591), born presumably Pierre Pfoertner of ''Thionville'' in Luxemburg, was a major educator in the Reformed tradition in Poland. For his origins, see Lismanino to Calvin, 15 April 1556, *OC*, 16. 108, and André Mazon, ''Pierre Pfoertner = Petrus Statorius Gallus,'' *Revue des études slaves* 14 (1934) 82–84. See also Bk 2, n. 646. That Statorius brought with him the works of Michael Servetus is stated in Lubieniecki in *Historia, 148*.

261. Jerzy (Georg) Schomann (Szoman) (1530–91), became a major figure in the later settlement of Raków Schomann left for an exchange with the Hutterites in Moravia. Lubieniecki preserved his *Testamentum*, cf. *BAnt*, RD 3, nos. 13–45. *BAnt*[2] 47 supplies the firm date of his birth. On him, there is much more below, *Historia, 152* passim.

262. Grzegorz Paweł of Brzeziny (c. 1525–91), with an M. A. from Cracow, studied in Königsberg, 1547–49, and became rector of the school of St. Mary Magdelene in Poznań under the patronage of Andrzej Górka (n. 282), 1549–50. Forced out by his bishop, he left for Wittenberg where he attended the lectures of Melanchthon, but he returned to Poland committed to Calvinism under the patronage of Stanisław Lasocki (n. 278). Minister successively in Brzeziny, Pełsznice, and Cracow, he was a major figure of the Polish Reformation, on whom there is much more below, *pp. 38* passim. The basic study is that of Konrad Górski, *Grzegorz Paweł z Brzezin: Monografja z dziejów polskiej literatury Arianskiej XVI wieku* (Cracow, 1928) and idem, *PSB* 9 (1960–61) 82–83.

263. Petrus Brelius is mentioned by Węgierski, *Slavonia Reformata* 528, 532.

264. Andrew Trzecieski helped Stancaro out of prison (n. 245).

265. Raków, founded in 1569 (see Book 3, ch. 12), in due course would acquire the title of ''Sarmatian Athens,'' hence here the ''then.'' Sarmatia was a classical name which the Poles took up as an ancient designation of the ancestors of the *szlachta*. Pińczów owed the name ''Sarmatian Athens'' to its excellent school, which was

organized in 1551 by Grzegorz Orzak (Orsatius). Lismanino, while abroad, was invited by the synod of Little Poland to investigate the school systems in the Protestant centers of Switzerland and Germany. After an attempt to secure Sebastian Guldibeck as rector of the school of Pińczów failed, Lismanino persuaded Petrus Statorius Sr. to move from Geneva to Pińczów 1556. In turn Statorius brought his friend Jean Thénaud of Bourges. Under the leadership of Orsatius, Statorius, and Thénaud, the school won widespread praise but the Catholic synods of 1556 and 1557 asked the King to close it.

In 1558 Statorius published *Gymnasii Pinczoviensis institutio*, a monument of human-ist pedagogy, partly modeled on the statutes of the college of Lausanne (where Statorius had studied). The gymnasium of Pińczów was not only the first modern school in Poland, but also the first school consciously to promote a program of national Polish cul-ture as formulated by Statorius in his statutes and in his *Polonicae grammaticae institutio* (Cracow, 1568), the first Polish textbook of grammar. The gymnasium attracted the cul-tural activities of the Reformed Church. Stanisław Kot, ''Pierwsza szkoła protestancka w Polsce,'' *RwP* 1 (1922) 15 – 34.

266. The magnificent Brześć (or Radziwiłł) Bible of 1563 was the result of a collec-tive translation, starting with the New Testament, authorized by the synod of Włodzisław, 4 – 15 September 1558 (Sipayłło, *AS*, 1. 273). Originally under the leadership of Orsa-tius, 1558 – 61, it was continued by Petrus Statorius with the participation of a number of others. In theory the Old Testament version was based on the Septuagint, but it actually followed the Geneva Bible. Soon after its appearance it met with strong criticism, voiced at the synod of Skrzynno, 24 – 29 June 1567, which gave impulse to new attempts at translation, with a clearly antitrinitarian thrust. For Skrzynno, see Sipayłło, *AS*, 2. 213; cf. Marek Wajsblum, ''Dyteiści małopolscy,'' *RwP* 5 (1928) 66 – 67. The Brześć Bible, however, was in use in the Reformed Churches in several emended editions throughout the seventeenth and eighteenth centuries (Danzig, 1632; Amsterdam, 1650; Halle, 1726; Königsberg, 1738, 1779). See also Bk. 3, n. 133.

267. On Bernard Wojewódka, see n. 169.

268. The book of hymns cited was *Pieśni chwał Boskich* by Jan Zaremba of 1558.

269. Only at the beginning was this true. In Poland Lutherans of Germanic ethnicity were commonly referred to as adherents of the Augsburg Confession. According to the provisional statistics of Henryk Merczyng, *Zbory i Senatorowie Protestanccy w Dawnej Rzeczpospolitej* (Warsaw, 1905), in 1591 the proportion of Major and Minor Church congregations to Roman Catholic parishes in certain districts of the palatinate of Cracow, Sandomierz, and Lublin was very high.

270. Stanisław Orzechowski, already encountered in *Historia*, 17 and 22, and at n. 168, was grandson of a priest of the Byzantine rite. He studied in Vienna, Wittenberg, and in Italy and was the favorite of several cardinals, identifying himself as *gente Ruthenus, natione Polonus*. Through the influence of his father, a writer, he was made a canon of Przemyśl. He promoted in his letter to Bishop Gamrat, *Baptismum Ruthenorum* (Cracow, 1544), the idea of the reunification of the Greek Orthodox and Roman Catholic churches by means of the mutual recognition of their distinctive baptismal rites granting of communion in both kinds to laymen.

On the issue of baptism he could adduce in his favor the bull of Alexander VI Borgia of 1501, *Non sine grandi*. Addressed to the Latin bishops of the the Grand Duchy through the bishop of Vilna, Alexander had upheld the canon of the Council of Florence, whereby the baptism of the eastern churches was deemed valid, so long as the formulary be triune and even though, as with the Ruthenians it be bestowed in the third person declarative. Alexander had made the concession that Ruthenians desirous of coming under the Latin rite might publicly abjure whatever was false in their old way but would not be baptized a second time. Giovanni Domenico Mansi, *Sacrorum Conciliarum nova et amplissima collectio*, 31 vols. (Lyons, 1748–52) 11 item XXXVII, pp. 373f. Orzechowski actively campaigned for the abolition of the celibacy of the Catholic clergy in *De lege coelibatus*, 1547, cast in the form of a conversation among participants in the Council of Trent. Summoned by Jan Dziaduski, bishop of Przemyśl, (1545–59, n. 194) Orzechowski abjured his writings and promised silence in 1547, only to resume his efforts in 1548. From 1549 on he gained popularity by formulating in his writings the political program of the gentry. He provoked condemnation by arranging in 1550 the marriage of the priest, Marcin Krowicki of Wisznia Sądowa (nn. 233, 234, 239), and by his open avowal of his own plan to marry Magdalena Chełmska.

Orzechowski's case raised a tempest at the diet of 1550. Supported by the gentry against the hierarchy, he married in 1550, and, despite excommunication in 1551, he addressed the Pope with open defiance. The diet of 1552 rose to his defense. The bishops, terrified, cancelled the excommunication and sent the case to Rome.

Orzechowski then published a confession of faith that cut himself away from the mostly Protestant reform party, and he found himself isolated. He tried to gain the King's favor by his *Annales* (n. 168), but in vain. His temporary absolution was withdrawn in 1556. He replied with a threat to join the Greek Orthodox Church and with a defiant satire. His *Repudium Papae Romani* (n. 184, ¶6, probably not printed) was directed against both Lutherans and the Papacy. It was only in 1560 that Pius IV authorized the lifting of the excommunication. The question of his marriage was left pending. His *Chimerae* (Cracow, 1562) was directed against Stancaro and Modrzewski. Thereupon, Orzechowski started a violent campaign against all Protestants, promoting a Catholic theocratic system of government, based on the middle *szlachta*, with the consecrated King under the Primate, and the Primate under the Pope, *Quincunx* (Cracow, 1563).

T. Śliwa, *Rozwój protestanckiej reformacji w diecezji przemyskie* (Przemyśl, 1977); Jan Ślaski, "Polskie dialogi polityczne Stanisława Orzechowskiego," *OiRwP* 12 (1967) 47–86; Hanna Świderska, "Stanisław Orzechowski: The Uneasy Years, 1550–1559," *PR* 8 (1963) 3–50; *PSB* 24 (1979) 287–92. See also Bk. 3, n. 517.

271. Mikołaj Rey (c. 1505–69), major Polish poet, owner of Nagłowic and Oksza, is attested several times at synods, e.g., in the company of Andrzej Trzecieski, among the patrons of the synod in Secemin, 21–29 January 1556, Sipayłło, *AS*, 1. 46.

For the family of the poet in the Polish Reformation, see Henryk Merczyng, "Rejowie z Nagłowic jako członkowie polskiego kosciola ewangelickiego," *Z wieku Mikołaja Reja: Księga jubileuszowa 1505–1905* (Warsaw, 1905) 49–58.

272. Remigian Chełmski, owner of Włoszowa, nephew of Marcjan (d. c. 1575), husband of Katarzyna Szafrancówna, was prominent at the synods. See further, *pp. 48* passim.

273. Piasecki, *Chronica gestorum* 49 (n. 184). Lubieniecki's quotation is not verbatim. The same material was excerpted by Węgierski, (*Slavonia Reformata*, 209).

274. Lubieniecki fails here to elevate the importance it deserves, the marriage of Marcin Krowicki before Orzechowski and at his urging, Bk. 2, n. 155.

275. Marcin Białobrzeski (d. 1586) was abbot of Mogiła, outside Cracow, in 1559, titular bishop of Laodicea in 1566, bishop of Kamieniec in 1576, a counsellor to King Stephen Batory, and the author of a catechism and various polemical works against the Polish Brethren. His brother Stanisław was abbot in Jędrzejow in 1571 and died in Mogiła in 1585. Neither of them is known to have married. They were both active in

fighting the dissenters. Lubieniecki took this story from Węgierski's *Slavonia Reformata*, 220. The two abbots might have been confused with Mikołaj and Hieronim Białobrzeski, two brothers known after 1620 who married two sisters. See Julian Bukowski, *Dzieje Reformacji w Polsce*, (Cracow, 1883–86, with genealogical tables, 2 vols.) 1. 215–16.

276. The constitutions of the provincial synod in Piotrków of 16 June 1551 prescribed the form of an oath to be taken by all priests, of which one point is ''I believe that the marriage of priests is not allowed, is indeed heretical.'' The bishops had to take an oath proving their adherence to celibacy at the synod itself on 14 June 1551. The canon was probably a reaction against the vote of the gentry of the district of Nowokorczyn who at the Diet of Piotrków in 1550 asked for the abolition of clerical celibacy and for the cup for the laity. See Zebrzydowski, *Korespondencja* 499 n., 525.

277. Marcin Stanisław Zborowski (d. 1565) was palatine in Kalisz, 1550, in Poznań, 1557, and castellan of Cracow in 1562, mentioned below, *pp. 50* passim. He is simply listed in Węgierski, *Slavonia Reformata*, 532; he was prominent at the synods.

278. Stanisław Lasocki (c. 1521–63) mentioned at n. 244, studied with his older brother Jakub in Leipzig, 1532–33. He supported the reform movement as early as 1545. At first desirous of the federation of the Reformed with the Czech Brethren, he became a supporter of the Minor Church and is several times noted by Węgierski, *Slavonia Reformata*, and is attested frequently at the synods. See further at n. 286, and Halina Kowalska, *PSB* 16 (1971) 548–49.

279. Hieronim Filipowski (d. before 1574), owner of Krzcięcice, where his predecessor had founded a congregation as early as 1547, was a major patron of the Polish Reformation, then of the Minor Church. On him further and comprehensively, see Book 2. n. 105. Filipowski's great grand daughter, Katarzyna Filipowska was the mother of our author, who undoubtedly draws on family lore as well as documentations as he weaves the careers of the two boon companions throughout the *Historia*, almost always together in one cause or another. It is here in place to characterize Hieronim Filipowski as a rigorist or puritan, hence his early support of union with the highly disciplined Czech Brethren (Koźmenck, 1555; Lipnik, 1558), his critique of Krowicki and others for spreading too wide the communion table without moral monitoring, and his enthusiasm for the Hutterite communes and the Racovian commune.

280. Stanisław Mateusz Stadnicki (d. 1563), husband of Barbara Zborowska, was also the owner of Dubiecko in Ruthenia, where he was patron of Francesco Stancaro, as schismatic, 1559/61–70, and his school. See *Historia, 48, 117* and my ''Reformed Church of Stancaro.''

281. Mikołaj Dłuski (c. 1540–84) was son of Andrzej, who turned the local church at Iwanowice into a Reformed congregation in 1551, and of Agneszka Myszkowska Dłuska (*p. 65*), who after the death of her husband, sent Mikołaj and his brother Wojciech to study in Zurich, fall of 1555. Mikołaj would later join Stadnicki (n. 280) in sponsoring the Stancarist Schism. On him see further *Historia, 48, 52,* and Henryk Barycz, *PSB* 5 (1939–46) 195–97.

282. Andrzej Górka, Sr. (c. 1500–51), magnate and protector of Protestants, is only mentioned here by Lubieniecki, but several times by Węgierski, *Slavonia Reformata*. Jan of Koźmin, c. 1542, taught his sons (n. 154). He protected Lutheran Seklucjan (n. 160), refugee Czech Brethren in 1548, obtained the benefice of St. Mary's in Poznań for Grzegorz Paweł, 1549 (n. 262), received Wawrzyniec Discordia, 1550 (n. 154), and supported Orzechowski. He died within the Catholic Church, himself still straining for

reform of the Church while on his deathbed. See Włodzimierz Dworzaczek, *PSB* 8 (1959–60) 401–5.

283. Jakub Ostroróg (c. 1516–68), owner of Ostroróg, was the protector of the Czech Brethren in Great Poland. He was made in 1566 *starosta generalny wielkopolski*. He features in Węgierski, *Slavonia Reformata*, is attested frequently at the synods, and mentioned *pp*. 66, 116, 202. See Maria B. Topolska, *PSB* 24 (1979) 500–502, in the midst of articles on other members of the distinguished Ostroróg Family to whom in 1953 the Polish Academy of Sciences (PAN) erected a commemorative obelisk.

As protector, Jakub and his brother Stanisław (1510–68), feature in Rudolf Bidlo, *Jednota Bratrská v prvním vyhnanstvi* [1548–95], 4 vols. (Prague, 1900), I 1548–61, esp. pp. 87–92, 109–11; II 1561–72. Rudolf Ričan, *Dejiny Jednoty Bratrské* (Prague, 1957), trans. as *Die Böhmischen Brüder: Ihr Ursprung und ihre Geschichte mit einem Kapitel über die Theologie der Brüder von Amadeo Molnár* (Berlin, 1961), Edmund Alexander de Schweinitz, *The History of the Unitas Fratrum* (Bethlehem, PA, 1885).

The arrival of refugee Czech Brethren in Great Poland under the protection of the Ostroróg Family is an important event in Polish Church history not adequately noticed by Lubieniecki. There was early groping among the Reform-minded Poles around 1550 as to whether they should join the ethically and ethnically congenial synodal structure already quickly in place (and with intact settlements surviving in Moravia, if not in Bohemia proper, after 1548) or create their own synod on the model of the Swiss.

The followers of Jan Hus already in the fifteenth century were divided into the conservative Utraquists and the Unity of the Brethren. But even the latter by c. 1490 had undergone a partial separation into the Major Party mostly of townsmen and the mostly rural Minor Party over the issue of the oath, the magistracy, arms, and participation in public affairs. Peter Brock deals with the struggle monographically in *Social Doctrines of the Czech Brethren,* and succinctly in a larger context, ''The Czech Brethren,'' *Pacifism in Europe*, chap. 1.

The Protestant Schmalkald League (1530), headed by John Frederick Elector of Saxony and Margrave Philip of Hesse, evoked the first princely armed conflict in the Empire, within months of the death of Luther, the Schmalkald War, 1546–47, which would alter forever the status of the Czech Brethren in Bohemia. When it broke out, King Ferdinand, as an elector of the Empire and as brother of Charles V, secured troops from his diet for a limited period. When he asked for a new levy, a resistant counterpart Bohemian League made up largely of Utraquist nobles and patrons of the Unitas sent troops to join the Protestant forces. In the defeat at the decisive battle of Mühlberg near Torgau, 24 April 1547, came the loss of territory and the Electoral dignity for John Frederick. In Bohemia there followed, 27 August 1547, the execution of four nobles, one of them of the Major Unitas Party, the definitive split between the Utraquists and the Unitas, the former finding common ground with the Catholics, and the renewal, 8 October 1547, of the Edict of St. James (1507), a mandate made unequivocal in application in 1548 and which obliged the Brethren to convert to Catholicism or go into exile.

Resistance of the nobles of the Margraviate of Moravia spared the Czech Brethren there, who eventually took on the name of Moravian Brethren, and upheld episcopal oversight of the brethren in the diaspora. From Bohemia proper most of the Brethren fled in three main wagon trains by way of Silesia (then under Bohemian Hapsburg suzereignty) into Great Poland with Lutheran Ducal Prussia their goal. Bishop Jiri Israel led one of these bands to Poznań and was welcomed in 1555, to the protection of Jakub Ostroróg. So great was the concentration of Czech refugees on his and related estates that eventually Israel would join the succession of Presidents of the Executive Council of the Unitas in which stood Lukáš of Prague (1517–28), Martin Škoda (1528–32), Jan Roh (Horn; 1532–47), Jan Augusta (1547–72), Israel (1572–88). As Jerzy Izrael, he is prominent in certain phases of the Polish Reformed synodal records, having been present first at a meeting in 1555 at the residence of Hieronim Filipowski at Krzcięcice (n. 279), Sipayłło, *AS* 1. 5 and n. 2.

284. Rafał Leszczyński (c. 1526–92), opponent of the King's marriage to Barbara, defender of the priestly marriage of Orzechowski (n. 270), was one of the leaders of the "execution-of-laws" movement, who resigned his senatorial office of palatine of Brześć in Kujawy (1545–50), seeking instead election, in the dietine, to the chamber of deputies as a "commoner." By this act he won enormous popularity and confidence among the gentry (the middle and lower *szlachta*). He is several times mentioned, along with his namesake nephew and great nephew, Węgierski, in *Slavonia Reformata*, and frequently attested at the synods. See Maria Sipayłło, *PSB* 17 (1972) 132–350.

285. Krzysztof Lasocki (d. c. 1580), brother of Stanisław (n. 278), founded the church in Brzeziny, to which he called Grzegorz Paweł (n. 262) and the former Augustinian Stefan of Cracow, although he opposed Modrzewski as vicar there. He moved with the theological left wing of the Reformed into schism. See Irena Kaniewska, *PSB* 16 (1971) 540–41.

286. Bielski, *op. cit.,* 591ff.

287. This is the Konrad Krupka-Przecławski, above *p.* 22, below *pp.* 50–52, 116.

288. Orzechowski, *Annales,* 69 ff. A great part of the *Annales* (n. 168) deals with the vicissitudes of Orzechowski caused by this marriage.

289. Rather, Bielski, without giving the specific date, puts the coronation at the end of 1550, *Kronika Polska*, 592.

290. The Primate officiating at the wedding was Archbishop Mikołaj Dzierzgowski (*p.* 15). The text has *Pontifices* which could be rendered "bishops" or "Papists." The episode is unclear. Even though Lasocki complied and withdrew from his proper place, he evidently remained close enough to provoke the interruption of the liturgy long enough for Lubieniecki to interpret the episode as a victory for the Protestant cause at court.

291. After the death of her husband, Queen Bona retired to an estate in Masovia, but she lived mostly in Warsaw.

292. See above at nn. 217, 291.

293. *Qui tibi cunque Bonae sacris dum tingeris undis Imposuit nomen, omnibus imposuit.*

294. Barbara fell grievously ill soon after the coronation. In view of her imminent death, Queen Bona reconciled herself with her daughter-in-law on 31 March 1551. Barbara died on 8 May 1551. The reconciliation was only superficial, and a false rumor soon started spreading that Bona had had Barbara poisoned (her relation spoke of syphilis). This caused a new break between the King and his mother, who would eventually leave Poland, in February 1556. In this period Lismanino's influence with the King reached its apogee, especially after he rendered important services to the King in the negotiations about his third marriage to Catherine, daughter of Ferdinand Hapsburg (n. 197 and Bk. 2. n. 25).

295. Jan Ocieski (1501–63), already Vice Chancellor, 27 July 1550, assumed the full duties of Samuel Maciejowski on his death, 26 October 1550. For his life and sources, see Anna Sucheni-Grałowska, *PSB* 23 (1978) 507–13.

296. Lubieniecki goes on, indeed, from the Easter Tuesday reconciliation of the Queens, 31 March 1551, to the death of Queen Barbara, 23 May 1551 (Bk. 2. chap. 2).

Notes to Book Two
Chapter One

1. There may have been a manuscript *Life of Laelius*, written by Andrew Wiszowaty, but the reference by Lubieniecki to a *vita* probably means what was known from the epistles and *vita* of his uncle Faustus (below). The first printed *Vita* is that of Friedrich Illgen, *Vita Laelii Socini* (Leipzig, 1814). For updating material on him with special reference to the genealogy of the two Sozzini, see John Tedeschi, ed., *Italian Reformation Studies in Honor of Laelius Socinus (1562–1962)* (Florence: Collana di Studi "Pietro Rossi," 1965), esp. his own, "Notes toward a genealogy of the Sozzini family," 245–311. See, comprehensively, Rotondò, *Opere*, who anticipated this major work on the seminal Laelius in his polemical "Sulla defusione clandestina delle dottrine [esp. the interpretation of John I] di Lelio Sozzini, 1560–68," *Studi e Ricerche di storia ereticale italiana del Cinquecento* (Turin: Giappechelli, 1974), 87–116. Rotondò, using nine references to Laelius in the epistles of Faustus and new archival sources, places Laelius in a wider Sienese/Bolognese/Paduan stream of thought that till the close of Trent I (1545–47) hoped for radical humanist reforms within the Church; for the places in Faustus, see Wilbur, *Socinianism*, 247, n 40; for the new setting, *Opere*, 15–22. It is the well argued and documented view of Rotondò in his critical edition of the works of Laelius Socinus that the radical Christology of his *Brevis explanatio in primum Iohannis caput* (1555) —was a major, new, non-Servetian fountainhead of proto-Unitarianism in the eastern realms. It may well have circulated in MS in Poland and Transylvania or kindred writings (cf. Bk. 3, n. 531) even before its anonymous two sixteenth century printings. Laelius construed the *mundus* of John I not as the cosmos but as the world of human beings to be redeemed and the Logos as God's *sermo* in the teaching of Jesus Christ. Laelius understood him to be the Messiah and the Virgin-born Son of God who had, however, no pre-mundane existence as cosmological and soteriological principle or as eternally begotten Son of God. As God's saving and recreative word to humankind, Christ is at once *rex, sacerdos, propheta, magister, pastor, servator*. The *Brevis explicatio* is critically edited from two texts in *Opere*, 103–28, annotated, 340–71. The two anonymous texts for the critical edition are in Giorgio Biandrata, *De falsa et vera unius Dei Patris, Filii et Spiritus Sancti cognitione libri duo* (Alba Julia, 1568) and François du Jon of Bourges (Junius), *III Defensio catholicae de S. Trinitate in unitate esesentia, adversus Samosatenicas interpretationes ... et ... Brevis explicatio in primum caput Evangelii Ioannis, sine auctoris nomine* (Heidelberg, 1591).

In the *Vita* of Faustus Socinus (RD 8) composed by Samuel Przypowski in the palatinate of Kiev in 1636, and printed with the *Opera omnia* in the *BFP*, I, there is preserved an admonitory letter from Calvin to Laelius, 1 January 1552, reprinted in *OC* 17, Ep. 1578. Translated by Emily Sharpe (Bk 3, n. 321 and *RD* 8) alongside the original text as *The Life of Faustus Socinus of Siena* (Manchester, 1912), this *Vita* gives the letter from Calvin to Laelius, pp. 10–11. See also "Four Letters from the Socinus—Calvin

Correspondence (1549)," translated and edited by Ralph Lazzaro, *Laelius Socinus*, ed. by Tedeschi, 215 – 41.

For the nonconformist context of the Sozzini family, see Valerio Marchetti, *Gruppi ereticali senese del Cinquecento* (Florence: La Nuova Italia, 1975). The father of Laelius and grandfather of Faustus, namely jurisconsult Marianus, Jr. (1482 – 1556), despite his European fame, was discretely interrogated by the Inquisition and obliged to recant his heretical view. Tedeschi, "Genealogy," *Laelius Socinus*, 292 – 98. Laelius Socinus is placed in the context of the Polish sector of the Italian diaspora by Hein, *Italienische Protestanten*, 140 – 48.

2. Perhaps supplemented by oral tradition in the family, Budziński's MS account was first printed in *Narratio compendiosa* by the grandson of Faustus Socinus, Andrzej Wiszowaty. Christopher Sand appended the *Narratio* to his *Nucleus Historiae Ecclesiasticae* (Cologne, 1676; 2nd ed. 1678) 86 – 90. Benedict Wiszowaty, son of Andrew, printed it again in *BAnt*, *RD* 5, the account of the Vicenza circle (and of Laelius) being nos. 49f. Lubieniecki's text is closer to the original in being the fuller transcript, whether or not compacted or edited is not certain. But the inclusion of the millennialist passage at n. 5 suggests that Lubieniecki has no more than translated the Polish of Budziński. Observe, however, that Andrew Wiszowaty says that Laelius left Italy in 1547 at age twenty-two.

For some time, however, the authenticity of the Socinus-Budziński tradition concerning the Vicenza circle has been doubted by a number of German scholars from G. G. Zeltner (1729), through J. L. von Mosheim (1741), to Friedrich Trechsel (1839). Rehearsing the scholarship to date (1945), Wilbur was very certain in his reconstruction of what must have been the original and valid components of the half-legend, and in his scholarly dissolution of the Vicenza academy as a phantom (*Socinianism* 80 – 84). See also, with special reference to one alleged participant in the Vicenza fellowship, my "Camillo Renato c. 1500 – c. 1575," *Laelius Socinus*, 172, n. 1.

A succession of Italian scholars, however, have persisted over the years in attaching considerable importance to the tradition. The following were inclined to accept the essential validity of the later Socinian tradition, which recalled as in one grouping in Vicenza persons who were later counted respectively as Socinians and Hutterites: Cesare Cantù, *Gli eretici d'Italia*, III (Turin, 1866) 156; Emilio Comba, *I nostri protestanti*, II: *Durante la Riforma* (Florence, 1897) 485; and with important qualifications, Cantimori, *Eretici Italiani* 53 and n. 3. Cantimori conjectured that the grandson of Faustus could be expected to have had a reasonably accurate oral tradition about Faustus' uncle Laelius, given the great learning in the family. Aldo Stella, on the basis of freshly exploited archival material, was prepared to substantiate the Budziński tradition in *Dall'Anabattismo al Socinianesimo nel Cinquecento Veneto: Ricerche storiche* (Padua, 1967), 57 – 61, 64. See also more recently, idem, *Anabattismo e Antitrinitarismo in Italia nel XVI Secolo: Nuove ricerche storiche* (Padua, 1969) and "Gli eretici a Vicenza," *Vicenza Illustrata* (1978) 253 – 61, which is evidently preliminary to a fuller study of the Socinian tradition about the *collegia Vicentina*. These he regards as "sufficientement documentabile," twice mentioned in his study of the influence of the University of Padua among Anabaptists, Poles, Transylvanians, and others, "Influssi culturali Padovani sulla genesi e sugli sviluppi dell' Antitrinitarismo cinquecentesco," in Robert Dán and Antal Pirnát, eds., *Antitrinitarianism in the Second Half of the Sixteenth Century*, Studia Humanitatis, 5, ed. by Tibor Klaniczay (Budapest: Hungarian Academy of Sciences, 1982) 203 – 13, the anticipatory references to the *Collegia*, nn. 26, 34. Not entering into the debate with new data, Massimo Firpo is nevertheless also inclined to hold that the tradition of the *collegia Vicentina* has some validity for retrospective Socinian historiography. See his *Antitrinitari nell' Europa orientale del c. 500: Nuovi testi di Szymon Budny, Niccolò Paruta e Iacopo Paleologo* (Florence: La Nuova Italia, 1977) 192–94. Partly independent of the foregoing Italian scholars, Hein (1974) upholds the essential validity of the Polish connection with the *collegia Vicentina*, 118–23; now, definitively, but in a broader context, Rotondò, *Opere*, 22–30.

Given the sedititious implication of the Anabaptist name, it would appear unlikely that Budziński would gratuitously invent in Poland four Anabaptist associates of Laelius Socinus, all the less likely for the reason that *Faustus* Socinus in any case opposed the practice of believers' baptism and occasional anabaptism which he found among the Polish Brethren. Moreover, the *four* names of four Anabaptists preserved by Lubieniecki from Budziński would not have been otherwise well known in Poland, although the memory of two (Giulio Gherlandi, Francesco della Sega) was preserved among the Hutterites in Moravia, whom Jerzy Schomann, among others, visited. The presence of these names in the tradition of the Polish Brethren as reflected in Budziński's sources suggests that the *collegia Vicentina* took place c. 1546, even if that tradition had inflated the number of participants and unduly stressed the formality of the gatherings.

We have evidence that Laelius was still in his home in Bologna: a letter from Florence, 1 April 1547, was addressed there by Antonio Francesco Doni. Tedeschi, "Towards a Genealogy," *Laelius Socinus*, 306. For the *collegia Vicentina* and the Italian Hutterite martyrs, see *Radical Reformation*, chap. 22: 3 and 4; Stella, "Influences and Developments of Hutterian Anabaptism in Italian Nonconformist Conventicles," *MQR* (1988).

3. The received form of the Apostles' Creed, to which the Polish Brethren gave assent at baptism, makes the simple statement that Jesus Christ "rose . . . ascended." Faustus Socinus insisted here on the passive voice, namely, that he "was raised . . . exalted," the Father-Creator having thus confirmed the Son's mission. Budziński is reported to have placed this language on the lips of the members of the *collegium* in Vicenza in 1547.

4. Cf. 1 Cor 15:45.

5. This asservation is scriptural but wittingly directed against the phrase in the Nicene Creed that affirms Christ's "kingdom shall have no end," in its time, directed against Marcellus of Ancyra (*Historia, 6*) in the revision of 381 and thereafter.

Most notable in this eschatological section is that Lubieniecki preserves without comment the chiliasm of Budziński himself ascribed to Laelius Socinus and his circle in Vicenza.

6. Girolamo Busale (also: Buzzale) was a Neapolitan Benedictine abbot who, after acquiring Hebrew at the University of Padua, became an Anabaptist. *BAnt*, 18, wrongly calls him Leonardo. See Stella, *Dall' Anabattismo* passim; my *La Reforma Radical*, 612–15; and Rotondò, ed., Sozzini, *Opere*, 24–26.

Busale is also mentioned in another Polish source. Running parallel to Lubieniecki's *Historia* and largely dependent upon the MS History of Budziński, to the point he leaves off, is the unique Lambeth palace MS no. 935, *Nieznana Kronika Ariańska*, which evidently reached London by way of Danzig. It is not reliable as to dates and spellings of names but it occasionally provides supplementary information or confirmation. It has been published in two parts. Part 1: edited by Lech Szczucki, covers the years 1539 to 1569 with some items of later date out of chronological order, with the MS title, "Nomina illorum, qui ab initio, relicto Papatu puriorem religionem profiteri coeperunt et illorum quoque, qui ex Italia, Gallia, Germania etc. propter religionem exules in

Poloniam venerunt," *Wokół dziejów i tradycii Arianismu*, Part I (Warsaw: PAN, 1971) 165–72. This postdates the edition of what at the time was considered the more valuable Part 2 of the MS, ed. by Kazimierz Dobrowolski, "Nieznana Kronika Ariańska, 1539–1605, *RwP*, 4 (1926) 158–72, wherein the origin and authorship (possibly Maciej Radecke of Danzig, once rector in Raków) of the *Kronika* are discussed. Henceforth the printed MS will be referred to *Nieznana Kronika Ariańska*, Parts I and II. Abbot Busale is referred to as one of the circle in Vicenza and as himself going to Thessalonica, *Nieznana Kronika Ariańska*, Part I, ed. Szczucki, 171.

7. Giulio Gherlandi, known also among the Hutterites as Julius Klemperer, was born near Treviso c. 1520, went to Thessalonica, and was drowned as an Anabaptist in Venice in 1562. Much about him survives in Joseph von Beck, ed., *Die Geschichts-Bücher der Wiedertäufer in Oesterreich-Ungarn* (Vienna, 1883) 239; *The Chronicle of the Hutterian Brethren* (Rifton, New York: The Plough, 1987), 379 n, 383. See *Radical Reformation*, 572–623 passim and Stella, *Dall' Anabattismo*, esp. 104–12.

8. Francesco della Sega (also Saga) of Rovigo (Lubieniecki has Franco de Ruego) was born either in 1528 or 1532 in Rovigo, studied law at Padua, but on becoming a Hutterite, he worked as a tailor, and was drowned as an Anabaptist in Venice in 1565. See my *RR* 572–77, 620–23; Stella, *Dall' Anabattismo*, esp. 110–19.

9. Jacopo of Chieri has not been identified. The sometime Anabaptist Pietro Manelfi in his depositions knew of an Anabaptist Jacopo, a tailor, in Vicenza. See Carlo Ginzburg, ed., *I constituti di don Pietro Manelfi* (Florence/Chicago: Sansoni/Newberry, 1970) 74.

10. At Venice drowning in the sea or strangulation was substituted for burning as the punishment of heretics. Since these methods were less conspicuous, they were less likely to have an unfavorable effect upon the large and profitable trade of Venice with Protestant Germany.

11. One strand in Italian Anabaptism was made up of Marranos, initially converted from their nominal Catholicism to "Lutheranism," who soon became unhappy with it also. That forty of the pious society in Vicenza went to Thessalonica and Damascus reflects an historic flight of Italian Anabaptists to these two centers of Sephardic Judaism. See my "Italian Anabaptists." For the general non-conformist Italian diaspora, see Domenico Caccamo, *Eretici Italiani in Moravia, Polonia, Transilvania (1558–1611)* (Florence/Chicago: Sansoni/Newberry, 1970).

12. Some of the distinguished heritage of Faustus Socinus is mentioned above, *Historia, 17* at n. 166.

13. Laelius was in Wittenberg from July 1550 to June 1551; he reached Cracow by way of Vienna and Prague. From the second visit to Cracow and Vilna (1558–59) there are two letters, one from Jan Utenhove, 13 January 1559, directed to Laelius in Vilna, the other from Laelius in Cracow, 23 January 1559, directed to Bullinger. After returning via Vienna to Zurich, 17 August 1559, he wrote Calvin two letters describing his visit. Letters 47–52, *Opere*, ed. Rotondò. The tradition ascribing an influence on Lismanino to him is not confirmed by any other historical record; *Opere*, ed. Rotondò, 270 n. 3.

The parallel account based on Budziński in A. Wiszowaty, *BAnt*, *RD* 5, nos 49–50, gives the number of the circle in Vicenza as forty and speaks of a second visit of Laelius in 1558.

A correspondent writing, April 1547, to Laelius in Bologna anticipates meeting him there; *Opere* ed. Rotondò, 133. Another correspondent writing, 10 October 1548, from Bologna to Duke Ulrich of Würtenberg and Christopher reports that Laelius had involved himself in a dispute with the Council Fathers of Trent, who had reconvened in Bologna,

11 March 1542, on the pretext of a few cases of the plague, but principly to distance themselves from the agenda of Charles V gaining ascendency in the Schmalkald War (1546 – 24 April 1547). The Council Fathers threatened Laelius with fire. The same German letter reports that Laelius went from Bologna to Augsburg, seeking out Ochino there. Whence he went to Strassburg, Basel, England, Paris, Geneva, and Zurich. The German account from Bologna is printed in full, *Opere*, ed. Rotondò, 31 – 32.

14. Laelius Socinus died in Zurich and left his papers to his nephew Faustus.

15. Niccolò Paruta, a wealthy Venetian refugee who settled first in Geneva, then in Moravia, protected Bernardino Ochino on his Moravian estate. Bainton, *Bernardino Ochino*, 158 – 60; my *Radical Reformation*, esp. 690 – 92, 753ff.; Caccamo, *Eretici*, 47 – 49; Firpo, *Antitrinitari nell' Europa*, which prints Paruta's *De uno vero Deo Iehova* 329 – 60.

16. Giovanni Valentino Gentile, a follower of Mofa Matteo Gribaldi and an opponent of Calvin on the doctrine of the Trinity, was executed for heresy by Bern (n. 351). Wilbur, *Socianism*, 81, passim, and my *Radical Reformation*, esp. 635 – 38 and 703 – 7.

17. Dario of Siena may be also Dario Scala, commonly thought to have been identical with Darius Socinus, brother or kinsman of Laelius. See Tedeschi, "Toward a Genealogy," *Laelius Socinus*, 301 – 2, no. 45; Cantimori, *Eretici*, 232, 236, 287 – 90, 295; *Haeretiker*, pp. 226, 273 – 74, 454 – 55, 466 – 68. He reappears in Bk. 3 at n. 1.

18. Giampaolo Alciati. See n. 353; Bk. 3, n. 2.

19. Francesco Negri (Niger), an associate of Camillo Renato in Chiavenna and an antagonist there of Augustino Mainardo, was the father of Giorgio Negri, Reformed and Minor Church pastor in Pińczów. It is quite possible that Camillo Renato was an important mediator of the idea of Christian mortalism (psychopannychism) to the Polish Brethren. See my "Camillo Renato (c. 1500 – c. 1575)," in Tedeschi, *Laelius Socinus*, pp. 103 – 83, 195, and Antonio Rotondò, *Opere*, ed. by Camillo Renato (Florence/Chicago: Sansoni/Newberry, 1968). Francesco Negri published *La libertà, o sia del Libero Arbitrio* (Poschiavo, 1546, 1550), and the Latin edition (Zurich, 1559) with a *carmen* by Giorgio dedicated to Mikołaj Radziwiłł. *BAnt*[2], 28; Wilbur, Socinianism, 107.

20. Sand/Wiszowaty, *BAnt*, 25 and Bock, *Antitrin.*, 2.653 thought the Budziński/Lubieniecki *Theses* and *Voces ambiguae* might well be from Laelius Socinus, from a portion of Biandrata's *De falsa . . . cognitione* (1567), 2, chap. 2. Rotondò, ed., *Opere*, 306 – 97, withdraws them from Laelius. The reference may be to the some twenty theses of Darius Socinus and even to the eleven *Theses de Deo trino et uno* of Paruta, published by Szymon Budny in 1566 and edited by Valerio Marchetti, "Ricostruzione delle tesi antitrinitarie di Niccolò Paruta," *Movimenti ereticali in Italia e in Polonia nei secoli XVI – XVII* (Florence: Instituto Nazionale di Studi sul Renascimento [1974]) 211 – 68; the *Theses*, 259 – 68.

NOTES TO CHAPTER TWO

21. The main bases for the claim that Laelius influenced Lismanino are Lubieniecki here and above at n. 13 and the related references in *BAnt*. Although not stated as such, the information stems from Budziński, and could be important, as Budziński was secretary to Lismanino.

22. Lismanino resigned his office of provincial in the autumn of 1554. At the suggestion of Calvin and Socinus (cf. n. 13) he married a Huguenot, Claude, at the end of the

year in Geneva. Her family residing in Zurich, the couple moved there. There he intensified his relations with Laelius Socinus. Henryk Barycz, *PSB*, 17 (1972) 466B; below at n. 45.

23. On Sigismund Augustus' first and second wives, Elizabeth (d. 1545) and Barbara (d. 1551), respectively, see Bk. 1, nn. 197 and 294. Catherine, Elizabeth's sister, married him in 1553. The King repudiated her in 1566, and sent her back to Austria, where she died in 1590. Lismanino's weakening influence with the King, and his final disfavor, might have been linked with the failure of this third marriage.

24. Francesco I Gonzaga died in 1550.

25. The author dealt with the same topic in Bk. 1, at n. 216. They probably read from the 1539 edition of the *Institutes*. Hein, op. cit., p. 35.

26. The reference is to the Chronicle attributed to Nestor, monk of Kiev of the eleventh into the twelfth century, edited by S. H. Cros, *Harvard Studies and Notes in Philology and Literature*, 12 (1930) 77 – 309.

27. Either by author's error or because of a misprint, the text has 983. St. Vladimir of Kiev (956 – 1015) was baptized upon his marriage in 988 (traditional date; perhaps 987) to Anne.

28. These were Emperors Basel II Bulgaroctonus (963 – 1025) and Constantine VIII (963 – 1028).

29. The Author follows here the historians and geographers of his century who, combining the *Odyssey* XI. iv and Herodotus, *History*, described the ancient Cimmerians as a people dwelling between the Dnieper and the Don, plunged in darkness and unblessed by the rays of Helios. W. Smith, *A Dictionary of Greek and Roman Geography*, I (London, 1878) 623 – 24.

30. Lubieniecki has taken in his Latinized source the Ruthenian word for a messenger as a surname for an already fictious Ivan Smera.

Lubieniecki was aware of a letter of Ivan Smera. See Jan Malyszewski, ''Podlozhnoye Pismo Polovtsa Ivana Smeiry k vielikomu kniazhu Vladimiru sviatomu,'' *Trudi Kievskoi Duchovnoi Akademu* 3 (1876) 141. This letter had been turned from Bulgarian into Ruthenian and Polish by Jakub Ryniewicz-Trembecki, particularly pp. 262 – 64. This letter came into the hands of Benedict Wiszowaty who translated it into Latin in 1677 and made it available to Christopher Sand.

Sand in his *Nucleus Historicae Ecclesiasticae, Appendix* (Cologne, 1678) 61 – 65, printed from Lubieniecki's MS *Historia, 41 – 42* (from *Reperimus* to *continentur*), as an introduction to the epistolary forgery of his overzealous countrymen, Andrzej Kołodyński, Szymon Budny, and Stanislas Budziński. Vladimir's messenger signed himself: ''Your physician and rhetor, Ivaniets Smera Polovlanin.'' Sand added that other authors have ''Ivan Smera Poloviets, which means the same.'' A. Lubieniecki, who also knew of the letter, called the messenger ''Jolacz,'' *Poloneutychia*, 125, 205. B. Wiszowaty and Sand did not suspect a forgery. It is to the historiographical credit of Lubieniecki that he did not reproduce the letter as a document, but he took it seriously enough to summarize it. It is not certain that the four Brethren identified as the forgers, including Budziński, wove their tendentious yarn out of their heads, although this is the view of Janusz Tazbir in his preface to the facsimile edition of the enlarged Węgierski, *Slavonia Reformata*, xix.

The forged letter of Smera is known not only from Sand but also more accessibly from Benedict Wiszowaty himself, who in the expansion of the *Systema* of Węgierski of 1652 (cited here throughout as *Slavonia Reformata* of 1678), printed the whole of Sand's

Appendix to the *Nucleus* with his own Latinization of the letter which clearly he perceived to be authentic, *Slavonia Reformata*, 499–503.

31. The letter to Vladimir is given in part in n. 33. The presumably Coptic Christians with their very simple, Judaizing liturgy, are perhaps wholly imagined and appear like Polish Brethren and Sisters. The Czech Brethren had sent missions to Constantinople and elsewhere, the possible inspiration of the spurious letter. The letter with its appreciative references to synagogues in Alexandria reflects a positive attitude towards Jews and perhaps particularly toward Judaizing impulses in sixteenth-century Kiev and Moscow. On Judaizers in the Ukraine, see, with the literature and sources, my ''Protestants in the Ukraine,'' Some of the recent literature and sources respecting the rise of the Judaizers appears in a numismatic study by A. V. Chernetsov, *Types on Russian Coins [and other artifacts] of the XIVth and XVth Centuries*, translated by H. Bartlett Wells, and not yet in Russian. British Archaeological Reports, International Series, 167 (with an extensive errata slip because of mutilation by the word processor) (Oxford, 1983).

32. The Poles were converted to Roman Catholic Christianity in 966. On Lubieniecki's reading of the letter, it prophesied the Minor Church of 1565.

33. Ivan Smera, wrote about the evangelical group in Alexandria thus:

> Here I saw sumptuously built synagogues, in which were men of the manners of the great basilicas. I also saw Christian congregations not a few where there are no idols, but a table and benches only. And these men are theologues (in Polish *Bogomówcy*, i.e., speaking of God), honest, loving peace above all. In short, they are like the Lord's angels. And they come together for worship every day, according to God's command, and also for prayers before the break of day, again after sunset, sometimes at the third and fourth hour of the day. And everywhere men call them God's new Israelite people, or Israel. And this teaching here is followed even by some kings with their sages (*doctoribus*) and I myself always used to go to them for the sake of their teaching. And I have been reborn among them already by water and spirit [cf. John 3:5], in the name of almighty God the Father, and of his Son Jesus Christ, and of the Holy Spirit proceeding from the same God. Therefore, I send you, Prince, their book called Gospels that you may learn. But of this also may your majesty know, that to these good and pious men great injury is being done in Caesar's jurisdiction: for Greeks, being of sly and arrogant speech, can turn a lie into a just thing, imitating in this some Roman teachings and institutions, and by their cunning [they] draw simple people into their synagogues and churches. [Węgierski], *Slavonia Reformata*, p. 500.

The letter makes clear that the forgers were distrustful of Caesar (the Sultan?) and the cunning Greeks and Roman teaching (the Patriarchs and the Pope) and that this messenger had submitted to believers' baptism in Alexandria by immersion like the forgers.

34. The whole unit may well depend on the MS History of Budziński, once a student in the Franciscan school of St. Andrew in Cracow, along with an Aleksy Rodecki (not identical with the later printer for the Polish Brethren), and then personal secretary to Lismanino. However, only a portion of the unit has been printed in inset italics as presumably straight translation of Budziński's Polish text. The unit begins right after Lubieniecki summarizes the spurious Letter to the Prince of Kiev. The rationale of this unit is not stated by Lubieniecki clearly even with the help of the editorial insertions, namely, that just as Prince Vladimir sent an envoy in search of religious truth in several

ancient Christian centers and, in effect, founded a new and true church in Kiev, close in spirit and manners to the Apostolic Church, so King Sigismund sent Lismanino abroad for the sake of renewal in Cracow.

The itinerary of Lismanino, if it depends upon Budziński, is valuable but sketchy.

Some of the dates and data in the following nn. are based upon Henryk Barycz, *PSB* 17 (1972) 465–70, with the literature to date. But see also the sketch of Lismanino and bibliography in Rodolphe Peter and Jean Rott, *Les lettres à Jean Calvin de la collection Sarrau* (Paris: Revue d'Histoire et de Philosophie Religieuses, 1972) Cahier 43, 51, n. 3. See also Bk. 1, n. 171.

35. Lismanino traveled in Franciscan habit. Before Venice, Lismanino visited in Přerov (Przerów, Prerou) in Moravia, where he was probably engaged in exchanges with Jan Augusta (Blahoslav) (1523–71), whose family originated there. In the history of the Czech Brethren the period, 1547–72, is set apart as a distinct episode when the Unity was under the guidance of Jan Blahoslav and Mattěj Červenka. See Bk. 1, n. 183, Jarold Knox Zeman, *The Anabaptists and the Czech Brethren in Moravia 1526–1628* (The Hague: Mouton, 1969) 25, 249–50. Already in 1536 Lismanino had been impressed by the confessional statement of the Unity. Moreover, his authority as Franciscan provincial included Bohemia, homeland of the Unity, and hence Moravia.

36. It appears that he had earlier studied at the university of the Republic of Venice and there received his doctorate in theology.

37. Ferrante I Gonzaga (1539–57), Prince of Molfetta, was imperial governor of Milan, 1546–55. It is hard to picture the provincial of the Franciscan order in Poland and Lithuania, and Bohemia, with a safe-conduct from the Polish King, being arrested by the authority of this Hapsburg governor of the Duchy of Milan on delation by ''monks,'' presumably Franciscan friars with whom Lismanino had spoken too confidentially.

38. Rudolf Gualther (1519–86), pastor of St. Peter's in Zurich, succeeded Bullinger in 1575 as chief pastor (*antistes*). He edited the works of Zwingli.

39. Konrad Pellikan (Kürsner) (1489–1556), a former Carmelite of Alsatian origin, was in Zurich from 1525 as professor of Hebrew and Greek, also as librarian.

40. Johann Heinrich Bullinger (1504–75) was chief pastor in Zurich in succession to Zwingli from 1531 to his death. In 1549 he had joined Calvin in producing the *Consensus Tigurinus* on the Lord's Supper. He was a much respected correspondent with the Poles. He is frequently mentioned in their synods. Lismanino embraced the *Tigurinus* in 1555.

41. Theodor Bibliander (Buchmann) (1504–64) succeeded Zwingli in 1531 in the chair at the Academy of Zurich. He published a Hebrew grammar (1535) and an edition of the Koran (1543).

42. Leo Jud (1482–1542), an Alsatian, pastor of St. Peter's, became the second pastoral figure in Zurich, from 1523, first in relation to Zwingli, then Bullinger.

He would not have been there when Lismanino visited Zurich. This fact casts some doubt on the reliability of the other names in the cluster.

43. Konrad Gesner (Gessner) (1516–65) was a prodigious Zurich-born polyhistorian.

44. Lismanino lived in Geneva from November 1554 to February 1555, where he listened to the lectures of Calvin.

45. A letter from Laelius to Bullinger documents him as present in Geneva 19 April 1554. Laelius could indeed have been a factor in the marriage.

46. The Author could well have had in mind an admonitory letter of Calvin of 1 January 1552 once in the possession of Samuel Przypkowski (n.1 § 3). In it Calvin concluded: ''A time will come, I hope, when you will rejoice that you have been thus

chastized.'' *OC* 14, est. 1578, col. 259–60. For the date, see therein n. 5.

47. This and the next sentence could be from Lubieniecki. Budziński no doubt remained true to his own clerical vows longer than Lismanino and evidently was more conscientious about the promise to the King.

48. The whole of this text would appear to come from Budziński: There is not enough of his History extant, however, even in translation, to be sure that he everywhere referred to himself in the third person. In a different Latin version the opposition of Budziński to the marriage of his master is also preserved, Węgierski, *Slavonia Reformata* 127. Here the rendering of the Polish is *famulo ejus Bodrino* where Lubieniecki has *Budzinio*, *ministro suo*. Węgierski acknowledges his dependence on Budziński's History, 110 in the margin.

49. Lismanino comes as close as any to being the Father of the Minor Church of the Polish Unitarians. Yet despite his centrality, he has never been so regarded. He was the most Polonized of all the Italians who contributed to the unraveling of the received doctrine of the Trinity and could be taken to summarize in himself their influence. Yet he had been remarkably close to the royal court, to both the King and the Queen Mother, and could have been a Polish Thomas Cranmer to Sigismund. But despite his professorship at the university, he seems to have lacked the drive of the usual national reformer. Perhaps this lack was not only temperament but was due to his being of mixed foreign origin, both Italian and Uniate Greek, without full identification with the Polish nation. As a sometime Franciscan provincial, he did not have the base of a bishop in the tradition of the prince bishops of Cracow, so often also chancellors. In the following pages it will be seen how unobtrusively he becomes a recessive figure, not because he must await the glare of the King's displeasure with his former confidant. On Lismanino, besides the article (1972) of Barycz of n. 34, and literature cited therein, see further, Hein, *Italienische Protestanten*, chaps. 1 and 5 on Lismanino, and my ''The Polish-Lithuanian Calvin,'' 129–58 (the account there begins actually in 1550.)

50. Piasecki, *op. cit.* 41, remarks that Sigismund II Augustus ''was rather lax in observing the Catholic religion'' and that he was also interested in ''curious sciences.''

51. The figures mentioned in the next paragraph particularize the reference to ''the incandescent torch of great examples.'' Only those not already encountered in Lubieniecki's *Historia* are identified briefly in the nn. Węgierski has much fuller and annotated lists, *Slavonia Reformata*, esp. 308–454.

52. Johann Brenz (1499–1570), reformer of Württemberg, a recorder of the University of Tübingen, would have been appreciated by Lubieniecki for his moderate espousal of religious toleration. Brenz had a conference with Jan Łaski in 1556 and in 1558 was engaged in controversy with Bishop Stanisław Hosius of Varmia.

Pietro Vermigli is already identified in Bk. 1, n. 108.

53. Augustin Marlorat du Pasquier (1506–63) was a French Augustinian friar and renowned preacher, who became a Calvinist in 1533, and sought refuge in Geneva. He was sent by the consistory to Paris in 1559 and was called to Rouen as the first Protestant pastor there. He prepared a concordance to the Bible, *Thesaurus* (London, 1574). He was hanged on the charge of treason although he had actually sought to quell the passions of his own people.

54. Thédore de Bèze (1519–1605) was the associate and successor of Calvin, a correspondent of the Poles.

55. Pietro Paolo Vergerio (1498–1565), born in Capodistria, studied law in Padua, married Diana Contarini on whose death he entered upon an ecclesiastical career. He was by 1533 papal nuncio to King Ferdinand in Germany and sought Protestant participa-

tion at the Council of Trent and was rewarded with the bishopric first of Modrusz in Croatia, then of his native Capodistria. Suspected of Protestant leaning, he left Italy forever in 1549. He was in Königsberg, 1556–59, becoming involved in the controversy over Christ the Mediator. He was in Cracow in 1559. He died in Tübingen. For his career in Ducal Prussia and Poland-Lithuania, see Hein, *Italienische Protestanten* chap. 6. See also Jan Sembryzcki, *Die Reise des Vergerius nach Polen*, 1556–59 (Königsberg, 1890).

56. Aloisius Italus is mentioned in *Slavonia Reformata*, 538, as minister of Italians in Cracow.

57. These figures have been met before, except for Dudith (*Historia, 106, 22, 225–26*), and Stanislas Lutomirski, eventually first Unitarian superintendent (*Historia, 133* passim). These are names mostly of the first generation of the Reformation in the Kingdom of the Two Nations, except for Dudith, who was Italo-Hungarian and cosmopolitan. Several are notable primarily for having openly taken wives as priests, but they are also representative of regions of the whole realm. Although he ended his brief career as professor at Königsberg, above *p.* 23, St. Rapolionis is perhaps here included as an ethnic Lithuanian. He was a consistent Lutheran. A *baccalaureus* of Cracow, in his promotion, with Theodor Fabricius, to the doctorate in theology in Wittenberg, 23 May 1544, he was Stanislaus *Lituanus*, with *28 Theses de Poenitentia*. *Luthers Werke*, Weimar Edition, 39:2, 258–83. Others in the series, although not ethnically Lithuanian, were most active in the Grand Duchy; others in Great Poland and Ruthenia, as well as in Little Poland.

58. The three Emperors whom he served were Ferdinand I, Maximilian II, and Rudolf II. On Dudith at Trent, see Lech Szczucki, "Między Ortodoksą i nikodemizmem," *DiRwP*, 29 (1984) 49–90.

59. Lismanino sent the books and letters of the Swiss Reformers to the King with the help of Budziński, who evidently recovered the autographs c. 1602.

60. The Author alludes to *Joannis Calvini epistolae et responsa: Quibus interiecta sunt insignium in ecclesia Dei virorum aliquot epistolae* (Geneva, 1575, 1576, 1597) and also possibly also to T. Beza, *Epistolarum theologicarum liber unus* (Geneva, 1573, 1575).

61. *Joannis Calvini epistolae et responsa*, ed. Théodore de Bèze (Geneva, 1575) 139–40; *OC* 15, no. 2057, cols. 329–36, where the editors acknowledge at n. 2 in the complete edition that Bèze indeed dropped Lismanino's name after *venerandus frater noster* in the opening sentence; Wotschke, *Briefwechsel*, no. 19.

Here Calvin allows for a national episcopate, with the primate as only *primus inter pares* to preside at the national synod and to exhort his colleagues and the faithful to unity, while the bishops themselves should not be of fixed places but collegial overseers for the maintenance of the common good.

62. This letter is printed in *OC* 15, no. 2362, cols. 892–95 with but slight variation from Lubieniecki's version. See also Wotschke, *Briefwechsel*, no. 33.

63. The address has been removed from its original place at the end of the letter.

64. The reference is to the Diet of Piotrków in Great Poland of 3 May to 15 June 1555. See my "The Polish-Lithuanian Calvin," esp. 131–32.

65. The letter of n. 61. Calvin had also earlier dedicated his *Commentaries in epistolam ad Habraeos* to the King, 22 May 1549, and accompanied it with an exhortation to reform the Commonwealth, *OC*, 13, no. 1195; Wotschke, *Briefwechsel*, no. 11.

66. The letter of Sigismund to Calvin has been lost. Calvin refers to it again in a letter to Jan Łaski, 7 cal. Ian 1555, *OC*, 15, no. 2041 at n. 3.

67. Ps 2:11.

68. That is, any *metus* or *dubitatio* on the part of the King.

69. Lubieniecki's version of the letter uses *eum*, in reference to *totus orbis*, whereas the *OC* version has *eam*, in reference back simply to *Polonia* in the previous sentence.

70. Ps. 132:3 – 5.

71. David's son Solomon (971 – 31 B.C.E) built the Temple (967 – 60), 1 Kgs 6:1; 6:28. Hezekiah of Judah (719 – 691), facing the threat of Assyria under Sennacharib and the prophetic demands of I Isaiah and Micah, undertook religious reform, 2 Kgs 18:2 – 8. Josiah (638 – 609) repaired the Temple under the scribe Shaphan who received from the priest Hilkiah a book of the law (Deuteronomy), which, authenticated by Huldah the prophetess, became the basis of the centralization of worship in the Temple and its reform, 2 Kgs 22:1 – 20.

72. The last two paragraphs were omitted, in the de Bèze edition but *OC* supplies them, indirectly, from Lubieniecki, their n. 5.

73. It is not clear whether *experientia ipsa*, perhaps intentionally ambiguous, refers to Calvin's contact with Lismanino or the King's.

74. The letter ends with the address, in the translation transferred to the beginning. Although Lubieniecki publishes the whole letter to show that de Bèze had seriously tampered with it in publication, he would not have included it at this point but for his own sense that Lismanino was the great Reformer manqué of Poland.

75. The editors of *OC*, 15, col. 893, n. 4, indicate at this point that their search in several cited places has been in vain.

76. Wotschke, *Briefwechsel*, no. 29.

NOTES TO CHAPTER THREE

77. This is a general reference to the program of ''the execution-of-the-laws,'' sponsored by the middle and lower *szlachta* against royal centralism.

78. Jost Ludwik Decjusz (Dietz, son of the humanistic royal mintmaster of the same name, d. 1545), master of the three classical languages at the Jagiellonian University, is documented at several synods from his congregation in Wola. He was a member of the committee (1557) for the publication of the Bible in Polish. He remained strictly Calvinist. Bk. 3, n. 76. Władysław Pociecha, *PSB*, 5 (1939 – 41) 45 – 46.

79. The first preacher of the Reformed church in Cracow was probably Stanislas Sarnicki, *Historia, 58* passim. Beginning in 1552 Grzegorz Paweł preached for this congregation sporadically coming in from Brzeziny and Pełsznica. He was appointed regular preacher of the congregation only in 1557 when the meeting place was moved to Boner's garden near the St. Nicholas gate. An assistant was Stanisław Wiśniowski (*Historia, 141 – 42, 163*) from 1557 until 1559. In 1558 Daniel Bieliński of Silesia (*Historia, 80, 218*) was appointed preacher for German members of the congregation. The site was later occupied by the Carmelite cloister. Wengierski, *Chronik*; Górski, *Grzegorz Paweł*, 42ff.

80. On Remigian Chełmski, see *Historia, 34*. His estate was near the salt mines of Wieliczka.

81. This is close to the account in Wengierski, *Chronik*, 6 – 8.

82. The Latin here is quite different from Vulgate Ps. 83:5 – 8.

83. Jan Boner (Bonar), (d. 1562), son of Seweryn, studied classical languages at the University of Cracow. He was a major figure in the early development of the Reformed

church in Cracow in 1562, Krystyna Pieradzka, *PSB*, 2 (1936) 299–300. He was one of
nine lay leaders to whom Calvin wrote 29 December 1555. Wotschke, *Briefwechsel*, nos.
34–42. See *Historia, 65* passim.

84. Cf. Wengierski, *Chronik*, 8.

85. On his dates in Cracow, see n. 79; for a fresh assessment of Grzegorz Paweł as
the Polish follower of Gribaldi, Gentile, and Biandrata, see Hein, *Italienische Protestanten*, 195–202.

86. *Psia Góra*.

87. Mikołaj Dłuski, Sr. (d. 1551; also *Historia, 48, 52*), may have been the brother of
Andrzej, husband of Agnieszka Myszkowska Dłuska, whose sons Mikołaj and Wojciech,
with their tutor Jean Thénaud, were received in the home in Zurich of Johann Wolph,
referred to in his letter of 23 January 1556. Wotschke, *Briefwechsel*, no. 57. Agnesżka
(*Historia, 65*) was one of the nine lay persons mentioned above, n. 83, as recipients of a
letter from Calvin, and Bk. 1, n. 281.

88. The following unit, with purported exchanges in direct discourse, must stem from
Budziński who once lived on *Ulica Bracka*.

89. The family Jeleń (Gieleń) were rich burghers of Cracow, possibly Czech, and
adherents of the Reformed Church. Bartłomiej and Józef Jeleń, both of them goldsmiths,
are named in 1565 as Calvinists in an episcopal visitation. J. Bukowski, *Dzieje Reformacji w Polsce*, 1. 622, n. 1.

90. I.e., *Ulica Bracka*, Franciscan street, of the Brethren (Friars).

91. Ovid *Fasti* 3. 21.

92. Stancaro was there confined, see *Historia, 31*. The ruins of the castle are still
standing, some twenty-five miles west of Cracow.

93. Almost unique among Polish prelates, the bishop of Cracow was also a prince by
virtue of a small temporality in Silesia, Siewierz, owned since 1443.

94. Cf. Horace *Ars poetica* 5.

95. Cf. Virgil *Aeneid* 4. 93.

96. A good deal preceding this section, although not in special font, obviously also
comes, perhaps verbatim, from Budziński.

97. Throughout the sixteenth and seventeenth centuries many wrote about the treatise
De tribus impostoribus, which allegedly maintained that the founders of the three great
religions (Moses, Jesus, and Mohammed) were impostors, but nobody seems to have seen
it. There are few outstanding critical or liberal authors form the Middle Ages to whom
this legendary book was not ascribed, from Peter de Vineis, the chancellor of the
Emperor Fredrick II Hohenstaufen, to Benedict Spinoza. The legend probably originated
in Gregory IX's encyclical of 1239 alleging that Frederick II declared Jesus, Moses, and
Mohammed to have been impostors. An imprint allegedly of 1598 is suspected of being a
forgery of 1743. Jacob Presser, *Das Buch "De tribus impostoribus"* (Amsterdam, 1926).
It was generally recognized in Poland already in the sixteenth century that Ochino was
not the author of the work. That the treatise was ascribed to Ochino in the sixteenth century we know from Stanisław Reszka (Rescius) in his *D. Stanislai Hosii Vita* (Rome,
1587) 168. Berating Ochino for denying the divinity of Jesus Christ, Reszka wrote:

> Sic fecit alter ille impostor nequissimus, cuius nomen scriptum est in inferno, qui
> librum edidit de tribus humani generis impostoribus, Moyse, Christo, and Mahometo.

In the seventeenth century the scholarly opinion outside Poland almost unanimously
agreed with Reszka on this point: Sir Thomas Browne (d. 1682), *Works*, ed. by Simon

Wilkins, 4 vols. (London, 1835–36), 1. 359–60, 2. 128; Johann Deckherr, *De scriptis adespotis, pseudepigraphis et suppositiis conjecturae* (3rd ed. Amsterdam, 1686) 119; Joannes Rhodius, *Auctorum suppositorum catalogus*, ed. by Vincentius Placcius (Hamburg, 1674) 33–37.

98. Andrew Patrycy Nidecki (1522–87), born in Oświęcim, was a classicist in the Franciscan school. Lismanino was responsible for his being called by Zebrzydowski as his secretary (c. 1546–59), first when bishop in Kujawy, then in Cracow. Nidecki would end his life as bishop in Wenden, Courland. Leszek Hajdukiewicz, *PSB*, 72 (1977) 712–14. He composed Zebrzydowski's *Reply* to Krowicki, n. 288.

It is quite plausible that Nidecki, once in the service of Zebrzydowski, disclosed these tales to Budziński, his former pupil. As of 1545, Budziński was in the service of Lismanino, both men now secretaries to prelates.

99. By espousing the Reformation, the nobility and gentry hoped to gain freedom from episcopal courts and escape from a quasi-vassal status. In the Senate magnates and bishops sat on either side of the chamber as Senators. One of the protectors of Krupka-Przełaswki was Mikołaj Lutomirski, n. 147.

100. Marcin Stanisław Zborowski (d. 1565) was successively palatine of Kalisz (1550), and Poznań (1554), and castellan of Cracow (1562). He is several times attested at the synods.

101. Lubieniecki approved of the execution of a royal mandate through Palatine Marcin Zborowski to punish Dymitr Sanguszko (Lubieniecki says wrongly Wiśnowski). Zborowski may have sought the propertied Halszka (diminutive for Elżbieta) Ostrogska (1530–82) for his own son in marriage.

Halszka was the daughter of Beata Kościelska, who was early widowed by Prince Eliasz Ostrogski (1510–39), palatine of Bracław, natural brother of Prince Konstanty Wasyl Ostrogski (c. 1526–1608). This Konstanty was marshal of Volhynia and palatine of Kiev, a major figure in relations between the Orthodox, Catholics, and the Judaizers within Orthodoxy in Kiev and Moscow. See my ''Protestants in the Ukraine.'' Konstanty was the designated guardian of Halszka, sometimes at cross purposes with her ambitious mother Beata. It was with Konstanty's approval that Halszka was betrothed to Prince Dymitr Sanguszko. Because King Sigismund II desired that Halszka's vast properties in the Grand Duchy come under a husband especially loyal to the Polish Crown, he placed Prince Sanguszko under an edict that intended his death. Sanguszko escaped with Halszka dressed as a page into Bohemia. Pursued by a posse of noblemen, he was cruelly killed by Zborowski in Jaromeř (Jaromierz), 3 February 1554. Halszka was obliged to marry one of her husband's assailants, Łukasz Górka (c. 1533–73), who had become the leader of Lutherans in Great Poland by his concern in 1553.

For Łukasz and Halszka Górkowa, see Włodzimierz Dworzaczek, *PSB* 8 (1959–60) 412–14; 424–26. Halszka became a figure in drama by three Polish playwrights.

Halszka is anachronistically pictured in a painting by Jan Matejko (reproduced in *Polish Brethren*, 194–96) where she is mistakenly said to be the daugher of Konstanty, her protector.

102. In *Heroes*, rhymed Polish account *Bohaterowie* (Bk. 1, n. 188) in the possession of the Lubienieckis but surviving only in listings in Węgierski, *Slavonia Reformata*, 532.

103. Piasecki, *op. cit.*, pp. 49–50.

104. This would mean the great poet, Andrew Trzecieski (above, Bk. 1, nn. 169, 245, 265, and *Historia, 23* near n. 202), conducted the funeral serving for Dłuski, who died in the same year he reformed his village church. It survived as a congregation of the Minor Church until 1624.

Most of this paragraph is in inset italics because it is only a longer version of what Węgierski acknowledged was taken "from Budziński, ch. 5, p. 28," *Slavonia Reformata*, 229.

105. She was Regina Glińska. Her first husband (1538 – 49), Jerzy Niemsta, was one of the first promoters of the Reformation, who in 1547 reformed the church of Krzczęcice. She married Hieronim Filipowski sometime between 1550 and 1552.

The episode of 1557 juts chronologically forward and may represent a family reminiscence of the proud author from his own great grandfather.

Hieronim Filipowski was mentioned in Bk. 1 at n. 279. A major figure in the *Historia* he is dealt with here, *pp. 52 – 54*, as the target of episcopal harrassment as of 1557, and, linked with Lasocki, *pp. 63, 65*. His protection of Stancaro up till 1555, joined by Stadnicki and Oleśnicki, comes at p. 117. Lubieniecki passes over the role and the recorded speech of Filipowski at the synod of Koźminek in 1555 at n.120.

In this decisive exchange between the Polish Reformed and the Czech Brethren Filipowski was one of the three lords on the Reformed side, along with his friend Stanisław Lasocki and Jędrzej Trzecieski, in a delegation headed on the clerical side by Cruciger. In one intervention Filipowski uses ecclesiological language later rare in the Reformed tradition in Poland, speaking of "the church government" (*rząd cerkwie*) with the Polish word usually employed for *church* of the Orthodox. The church of the Protestants is generally the Polish word usually used only for the Catholic Church is here applied to themselves as the Church universal, called also the "people of God, *Kościół albo lud Boży*." Sipayłło, *AS*, 1, p. 34.

Lubieniecki deals with the support by Filipowski and Lasocki of the Despot of Moldavia in 1561, *pp.* 152 – 53 (nn. 696 – 97); mentions Filipowski as present at the synod of Rogów, 1562, *p.* 133; mentions him at the Diet of Piotrków, 1562, *p.* 152 (nn. 680, 684); applauds him as protector of Ochino in 1564, *p.* 110, n. 385; mentions him with Lasocki at the Diet of Piotrków, 1565, *p.* 157, n. 757, *pp.* 201ff. (3, ch. 5); notes his election as moderator of the synod of Węgrów, 1565, *p.* 189 at n. 211; devotes a section to him as impestuous in mortal danger because of his anabaptism, 1566, *pp.* 194 – 98.

The life of Filipowski is brought together by Stanisław Szczotka, *PSB* 6 (1948) 457 – 60.

106. The great Sigismund Bell of the Wawel castle, cast in 1520 (245 cm in diameter and 195 cm high), was sounded only on very exceptional occasions.

107. Of this Hieronim Filipowski, Jr. (1556 – 87), Lubieniecki holds a rather unfavorable opinion probably because he did not follow in his father's footsteps, but remained in the Reformed church; and on his deathbed he embraced Roman Catholicism. *PSB* 6 (1948) 495B – 50A. See also Bk. 3, n. 718.

108. The Filipowskis and Koniecpolskis shared the coat-of-arms Pobóg. Some of the Koniecpolskis were Evangelicals. They were a senatorial family of the Ukraine and grew in wealth and power during the seventeenth century.

109. The embassy was to Sultan Amurat in 1582. Lubieniecki incorrectly says he was barely thirty years.

110. Silus Italicus (d. c. 101), *Punica*.

111. The funeral of Regina (n. 105) took place 19 October 1557. Wengierski, *Chronik*, 7.

112. Lubieniecki erroneously has Wrowecki. Węgierski has it correctly from the same acknowledged source, Budziński (chap. 5. 18), *Slavonia Reformata*, 229 – 30. There was a Nicholas Wrovicius who was inscribed at Wittenberg. Wotschke, *Briefwechsel*, no. 21a.

113. Lubieniecki gives Marcin of Kurów. Lubieniecki or his source, Budziński, seems to have mutilated the account of the death of Mikołaj. According to a narrative by Feliks Cruciger about the persecution of Protestant clergy, written in 1555 for the Czech Brethren, Mikołaj was imprisoned in a dungeon for a few days. When he did not die of hunger, the bishop ordered the burgrave to have him killed. The burgrave sent one of his servants, who strangled Mikołaj with a rope and broke his head with an iron rod. J. Łukaszewicz, *Dzieje kościołów wyznania helweckiego w dawnej Małej Polsce* (Poznań, 1853) 12 – 15. This account squares with the closing passage of Lubieniecki's narrative.

114. Juvenal *Satirae* 13. 184 – 87. In the thirteenth Satire one Calvinus has suffered the loss of money deposited with an unfaithful friend. Juvenal holds that philosophy teaches that thought of revenge is the pleasure only of a stunted, feeble, and petty mind and adduces here in support three Greek philosophers, including Socrates ("nursed on sweet Hemettus").

115. Pliny the Elder, *Naturalis Historia* 263.

116. The reference is to the conspiracy against Julius Caesar, the ides of March 44 B.C. Marcus Antonius was not part of the conspiracy of fifty republican aristocrats headed by Marcus Junius Brutus. As consul, Antony took possession of Caesar's papers and assumed uncontrolled power, the immediate beneficiary of the assassination. Nero's ferocity was that of one who had directly ordered the torture and death of Christians in the circus.

117. Luke 10: 29 – 37.

NOTES TO CHAPTER FOUR

118. Examples are Calvin's letter to Sigismund II of 24 December 1555 and others mentioned or printed above, *Historia, 44 – 47*, and letters to nine other lay persons in Poland of 29 December 1555, n. 83.

119. As the terms *conventus, conventio, congregatio, synodus* were in the beginning fluid, except that the last would most clearly intend a gathering of lay and pastoral elders from several congregations, it is not certain whether the meeting in Słomniki of 25 November 1554 or that of 1 May 1555 is entitled to the appellation of "first *synod* in Little Poland."

There has been some uncertainty as to whether there was a synod of 1 May 1555. It is also mentioned by Węgierski, *Slavonia Reformata*, p. 230. Maria Sipayłło, "W sprawie synoda pińczowskiego z 1. V. 1555," *OiRwP* 10 (1965) 213 – 21, argues compellingly for its historicity, even though not noted by Jakub Sylwiusz, the first synodal protocolist, but she herself does not give it a separate page without protocol, as she does for other synods and gatherings of which the protocol as been lost, though she does list it in the synoptic register of *AS*, 1. 2. She holds that Lubieniecki discusses the Unity of the Brethren at this point in his *Historia 56 – 58*, because this was the matter discussed there in his sources. See further, n. 136.

120. Synod of Koźminek, 24 August – 1 September 1555. Sipayłło, *AS* 1. 18 – 43.

121. In the historiography of the Czech Brethren and of their interpreters all these names were indeed used. Lubieniecki here displays a strange remoteness from a church of importance in Poland, to be compared with the use of *Valdenses* by his great uncle.

Lubieniecki does not explain that there was once a defensive Hussite invasion of Silesia and Poland nor take note of why the Czech Brethren were in exile in Great Poland after 1548 (cf. n. 126).

In both Poland and Bohemia-Moravia the Czech Brethren knew that they had an authentic late, medieval Waldensian strand in their history. Poor Men of Lyons was another name for Waldensians. Outside of Bohemia they were often called disparagingly also *Picardi*. But these were, correctly, pantheistic medieval sectaries of Picardy and Walloon territory, some of whom in 1418 fled to Bohemia, where they were received by the martial Hussites at Tabor, the Taborites. On this see further the words of the superintendent of the Czech Brethren in attendance at a Polish synod, Sypayłło, *AS* 1. 54 (*Picardi-Adamitae*). The Albigenses were Cathars, radical dualists of Provence. Largely extinguished in the crusade against them under Innocent III (ending only in 1215), remnants coalesced with some Waldensians. Lubieniecki no doubt held them in respect as medieval non-conformists without knowing much more than the name. See the extraordinarily comprehensive bibliography *raisonnée* of Jarold Knox Zeman, *The Hussite Movement: A bibliographical study guide* (Ann Arbor: Center for Reformation Research/Michigan Slavic Publications, 1977).

The Czech Brethren retained all seven sacraments. Of significance for the prominence of believers' immersion and not infrequent testimonial adult rebaptisms in this manner among the Polish Brethren is the baptismal usage of the Czech Brethren. At their synod in Lhota in 1467 all the elders were solemnly rebaptized (not, however, by immersion) and while rebaptizing future converts to the Unity from among Catholics and Utraquists, they continued the practice of solemn pedobaptism for their own progeny. Then at their synod of Jablonek (Jungbunzlau) in 1534, the Czech Brethren under the influence of Luther and the notoriety of Münster, disavowed their rebaptism of converts, only one elder resisting the consensus, and embodied this suspension of an earlier practice in the *Confessio* presented to King Ferdinand in 1535. Although when the Czech Brethren in Great Poland began their parleys with Reformed Church in Little Poland, culminating in the provisional federation of Koźminek in 1555, the older members would have recalled their own practice of rebaptism suspended only a score of years earlier; and it is likely that several of the Unity congregations beyond the administrative center in Morvia, notably in Silesia under the Bohemian crown, persisted in the sectarian, exclusivist believers' baptism that would have fused with the Germanic Anabaptist impulses in the same region. De Schweinitz, *Unitas Fratrum*, 136–37, 204, 246, 254.

The idea of union with the Czech Brethren was first promoted by Feliks Cruciger, superintendent of Little Poland, who, in 1551, while a refugee in Great Poland, made their acquaintance. The problem of union was debated at the synod of Słomniki (n. 108) and at a colloquium in Krzczęcice (18 March 1555), as well as at the synod of Gołuchów in Great Poland (24–27 March 1555), preparatory to the synod of Koźminek. At this provisionally successful synod (n. 120) of the Czech Brethren participants were, among others, Jan Czerny of Boleslav, co-bishop (1553–65), Jan Lorenc (later pastor in Koźminek), who together had been formally received on legation by Duke Albert in July 1555, and Jiří (Jerzy) Izrael, the head of all Czech Brethren in Greater Poland.

In view of the divergent social outlook of the members of the two churches and the preservation of clerical celibacy on the part of the Czech Brethren, the movement toward union would never be wholly successful even after the Consensus of Sandomierz of 1570. Hermann Dalton, *Lasciana* (Berlin, 1898) 410; Bidlo, *Jednota Bratrská*, 1. 109ff.; Amadeo Molnár, *Boleslavští Bratři*, with a chap. on the fortified town of Mladé Boleslavé by F. M. Bartoš, and with substantial *resumés* (Prague, 1952).

Neither at this point in his narrative nor elsewhere does Lubieniecki give his reader any sense of the near merger of the Reformed with the Czech Brethren. Łaski oriented the Reformed Church to the Swiss and, in effect, opposed what got started at the synod of Koźminek before he arrived. Without using Polish works or sources, A. A. van Schelven, *Het Calvinisme gedurende zijn bloeitijd*, vol. 3: *Polen, Bohemen, Hongarije en Zevenburgen* (Amsterdam, 1965) nevertheless sees clearly how Łaski resisted what he feared would be the further ascendancy of the Czech Brethren, so rigoristically and internationally disciplined, over the nascent Polish Reformed synod, 29–30.

122. This account of a sudden death seems to be the author's vague reference to the Roman patrician, St. Alexis, *Historia*, see Bk. 1, n. 38.

123. The author wrongly assumes a continuity between Waldo and Wycliffe in England and exaggerates the number of Wycliffe's writings.

124. A pupil of Hus, Hieronymus afterwards studied (1398) in Oxford. With freshened convictions, he discussed Wycliffite principles at Budapest in 1412 with the reform-minded Sigismund of Luxemburg, king of Hungary (1387–1437) and accompanied Grand Duke Witold of Lithuania from Cracow to Moscow, where he aroused suspicion in looking favorably on the Old Slavonic liturgy. He was almost condemned with Hus at Constance. After two trials and a partial abjuration, he died at the stake with great courage, 1416. J. Pilny, *Jerôme de Prague* (Geneva: Perret-Gentil, 1974).

125. The principle was the basis for the repudiation of the safe-conduct of Hus at Constance. Lubieniecki uses the phrase in his *Legal Claims* (c. 1560), *Polish Brethren*, 583, n. 33; cf. nn. 34–37.

126. In this unit Lubieniecki partly rehearses what he said in Book 1, chap. 4 on Luther in the stage of the Reformation. In that context he saw Luther as the climax of reform movements within medieval Christendom and then moved over to show how this impulse was picked up in Poland and destined under Providence to be the fulfilment and perfection of that Reformation, chap. 5. Here in Book 2 he has presented Italy as at once the "factory ... of the engines of so many errors and superstitions" and of the very "arms of the heavenly truth cast there" against Rome by God himself, chap. 1. It is almost as if Luther were only one of two almost equal impulses to the Polish Reformation alongside Laelius Socinus, whose reform was taken over in Poland by Faustus Socinus. But then, besides Germany and Italy there is also Bohemia Slavica. Although Lubieniecki gives not hint of a flood of Czech Brethren in Great Poland as refugees of 1548, he is still susceptible to their medieval beginnings, stressing Waldensian, Wycliffite, and even Picard impulses, while saying almost nothing about the Unitas Fratrum as such, from 1467 on, or about them as survivors of the persecution of 1547/48 in Moravia and Great Poland. On the phases of the history of the Unitas, see Bk. 1, n. 283.

127. In his exchange with Johann Eck at the Leipzig debate of 1519 Luther vindicated Jan Hus, and by 1523 he was drawn to write his *De institutendis ministris ad senatum Pragensem Bohemiae*. Historians of the Utraquist Church and of the Unitas Fratrum agree that they came under the dominance of "the Second Reformation," that of Luther from c. 1525 to c. 1575, after which Calvinist influence was strong. With this new perspective it was not difficult in piety, historiography, hymns, and iconography to draw connections between the close of the Council of Constance in 1417 that had put to death Hus and elected Martin V and the dramatic emergence of Luther in 1517. For the literature on Luther and the Utraquists, see Zeman, *Bibliography*, 232–35, and on the Unitas, 249–53.

128. Johann Tetzel (d. 1519) preached the indulgence (for the building of new St. Peter's Vatican) in Juterbog just outside Electoral Saxony. After hearing him Luther was promopted to challenge the system with his Ninety-Five Theses, 31 October 1517.

129. Leo X Medici (1513–21) excommunicated Luther, 1520.

130. Polydorus Virgilius, *De inventoribus rerum* (Venice, 1499). Lubieniecki probably used the edition of 1671 and gives the page as 622.

131. Jacob Augustus Thuanus (de Thou), *Historiarum sui temporis ab anno Domini 1543 usque ad annum 1607 Libri CXXXVIII* (Geneva, 1620), 1. 12–13.

132. Laurentius Surius the Carthusian, *Commentarius brevis rerum in orbe gestarum ab anno salutis 1500 usque ad in annum 1568* (Cologne, 1568) 122. Lubieniecki gives 92–93 as the pagination in the edition used by him.

133. Even with slight emendation this "namely" clause is not so clear as it could be. Lubieniecki, though a minister, does not sharply distinguish between salvific faith on hearing the Word of God expounded in preaching (cf. *fides ex auditu*, Rom. 10:17) and priestly absolution at the confessional or during the purchase of an indulgence for others in Purgatory.

134. Frederick III the Wise (1463/86–1525) founded the University of Wittenberg, 1502, and protected its most illustrious professor at the Wartburg after the diet of Worms.

135. The fact that the author used *Respublica* instead of *Sacrum Imperium Romanum* suggests that he thought readily of similar benefits for the magnates of the Polish-Lithuanian *Respublica*.

136. The synod was mentioned first at n. 119.

After a discussion of the First Reformation in Bohemia under Hus and of the Second under Luther, Lubieniecki returns to the synod of Pińczów of 1 May 1555, where presumably the problematic name of *Picardi* (Beghard, in the mandate against the Unitas in 1508) was discussed as union with the Unitas Fratrum, mostly of Great Poland, was on the agenda of the Reformed.

Following Sipayłło, (n. 119, ¶2), against Wotschke and Górski, the letter of invitation, written by Feliks Cruciger, was indeed sent to Lismanino from this synod. It and Lismanino's reply are repinted as annexes to *Brevis explicatio de sanctissima sancta Trinitate* (Könisberg, 1565), of which there are few copies. On this book, see more fully, Bk.3, n. 106. Lismanino to the end denied that he was an Antitrinitarian. T. Wotschke translated the annexes into German in "Francesco Lismanino," *Zeitschrift der Historischen Gesellschaft für die Provinz Posen*, 18 (1903) 213–32, wherein the undated letter is ascribed to the synod of Pińczów of 21 September 1555, that is, after the protracted colloquy with the Czech Brethren in Koźminek of 24 July to 2 September 1555, which Sipayłło (cf. n. 119) rightly says does not make sense. Her argument changes the usually accepted chronology for the travel of Budziński as bearer of the letters.

137. See *Historia, 131–34, 138–44*, etc.

138. One has not come to expect Lubieniecki to be impartial!

139. See *Historia, 55* and also Wotschke, "Lismanino," 226 and *Briefwechsel*, nos. 25–27.

140. Walenty z Brzozowa, *Cantional [Kancjonal] albo ksiágy chwał Boskych to iest Pieśni duchowne Kościoła swiętego podług Ewangeliei y prawdziwego Pisma swiętego złożone; a teraz z Czeskiego ięzyka na Polsky nowo przełożone* (Könisberg, 1554). The Czech original of the hymnbook by Lukáš of Prague had been published in 1541. The Polish edition of 1554 reappeared in 1569 and 1684.

141. At the synod of Pińczów, 24 April–1 May 1556. Some of the Polish Brethren requested insistently that nothing be published under the names "Picard" or "Waldensian," seeing that these names were scandalous to the Poles. Sipayłło, *AS* 1. 54, *tertio loco*.

142. Both Lubieniecki and Węgierski (*Slavonia Reformata*, 230) mention the intervention of the armed forces of the bishop of Cracow and the latter says there were thirty horsemen galloping up with an allegedly royal mandate; and Sipayłło (n. 119, *loc. cit.*, 214, 216) supplies the name of the bishop's chancellor and argues that there was also an episcopal effort to come to grips with the synod in Pińczów, 21 September 1555, but in a less aggressive manner. The situation for the bishop and for the Reformed had changed since the close of the Diet of Piotrków, 15 June 1555.

Although neither historian acknowledges Budziński as the source, it is only their silence that inhibits the Editor from putting much of the material on the synod of Pińczów, 1 May 1555, in inset italics as essentially from Lismanino's secretary. It is the kind of anti-episcopal story to the glory of the stalwart Reformed noblemen that he had preserved among his letters.

143. Bishop Zebrzydowski is even held responsible for the wenching by his predecessor, Zawisza (1381 – 82), chancellor from 1374. Lubieniecki derives the account from A. Lubieniecki's *Poloneutychia*, 11: "Zawisza z Kurozwęk, climbing a haystack to a peasant wench, pushing off the ladder by the same, he fell and broke his neck." Stanislas Lubieniecki must have known the location from family tradition, for Dobrawoda is not in his source. This episode is not included in *Sacrum Poloniae Millennium*, I. 595.

144. Jan Przerębski, from 1550 to 1559 Vice-chancellor of Poland, was then a canon of Cracow and in this capacity administered the bishopric of Cracow *sede vacante* between the death of Maciejowski (1550) and the appointment of Zebrzydowski. Przerębski became bishop of Chełm in 1558, Primate, 1559 – 62. *Sacrum Poloniae Millennium*, I. 542 – 43.

145. Łowicz belonged to the archbishop of Gniezno. There was a provincial synod held there, 6 – 11 September 1556, under the presidency of Nuncio Aloiseo Lippomano, *EK*, S – U, 322B, but this may not be the reference, which would not fit in with either synod of Pińczów, 1555, n. 142. See *Historia, 76*.

As for *conventiculum*, Lubieniecki uses the term in the perjorative sense it had acquired in Gratian's *Decretum*, *PL*, 187, col. 1507B.

146. The author dealt with this at nn. 140, 199, 294.

147. The dietine convened at Praszowice, December 1551. Zawichost is on the Vistula below Sandomierz. Mikołaj Lutomirski (c. 1495 – 1566), who owned a house in Cracow next to Krupka-Przełtawski, joined other nobles in protecting him in 1551 (n. 99). See Halina Kowalska, *PSB*, 18 (1973) 142 – 43.

148. This acknowledgment comes in the text at the end. Undoubtedly much of the preceding unit came also from Budziński.

149. Pagans presumed still to survive in Lithuania; not Jews or Muslims.

150. The date would be 12 December 1550. The dating "of our reign the twenty-first" refers to the election of Sigismund II in 1529 as prospective king of Poland *vivente Rege*, i.e., during the life-time of his father Sigismund I who thereafter began to be called "the Old." The actual reign of Sigismund II Augustus started in 1548 on the death of his father. The decree was sharply attacked by the Diet of Piotrków in 1552, both by the Protestants and by the Roman Catholics, as being contrary to the liberties of the nobility.

151. The speaker seems to have had at hand John Gratian (d. c. 1159), *Corpus Iuris Canonici*, perhaps as ed. by Paolo Lancelotti (Lyons, 1614), cols. 873 – 78. The whole of *causa* 24 is devoted to heresy and schism in 40 chapters, chapter 39 presenting authoritative chracterizations of heresies and heretics, a dictionary of errors. One of the chapter headings of patristic and papal citations partly supports Lutomirski's discourse (*PL*, 187,

cols. 1292–1318) namely cap. 28: "Haereticus est, qui . . . novas opiniones vel gignit, vel sequitur," col. 1306B. Lutomirski implies that papal institutions and dogmas are the innovation.

152. The records of the diets are not complete. What there is for 1548, 1553, and 1570 is published in *Scriptores Rerum Polonicarum*, I, without index. The name of Lutomirski has not been found, nor his speech here as excerpted by Lubieniecki. Among the notes to the Sejm of 1553 (*Scriptores*, 23, n. 40), materials are adduced on religion, 1549–55. Here *Scriptores*, 94–95, n. 3, is a "Memoriałe o stanie Kościoła w Polsce r. 1551." At the end of it there is the statement that there was turbulence in the diet of 1552.

153. From internal evidence much of this unit draws heavily on Budziński. Much herein is expressly ascribed to Budziński in the parallel Latinizing of his Polish text by Węgierski (*Slavonia Reformata*, 229–30). However, the two accounts do not fully overlap.

The Author's vivid account deriving from Budziński is not the only nor perhaps the most accurate account of the bolder efforts of Bishop Zebrzydowski to apprehend the dangerous publicist sheltered by Oleśnicki. But entering into this episode with Lubieniecki, the reader should know what happened after Krowicki refused to appear before the diocesan court of Przemyśl for his having uncanonically married (Bk. 1, nn. 233, 234, 239, 274).

On the strength of the royal edict against the innovators of 12 December 1550 (n. 162) and the Cracow chapter it had proceeded against, Stancaro left for Konigsberg, Feliks Cruciger sought refuge with Jakub Ostroróg in Great Poland, and Jakub Sylvius of the town church in Pińczów , pursued by his former patron, Kmita, sought refuge in Silesia. Krowicki had taken the place of Stancaro as chaplain in the castle above Pińczów, Węgierski, Slavonia Reformata, 229; Barycz, *Z Epoki*, 318. Then he descended from the castle and took over the pastorate in the Hospitaler church and then in that central to the town, the church of the Pauline Hermits (n. 154), the center of Polish Protestantism. But with direct pressure on his patron from Cracow, he encourged Krowicki to get away. Taking with him his wife, Magdalena, he matriculated in Wittenberg, 13 October 1553, Barycz, *Z Epoki*, 329. Befriended by Melanchthon, he was under consideration for a mission over the Bohemian border, where through the similarity of languages he could preach the Gospel to the Czechs in the villages of the Erzgebirge. Instead, he worked on his Polish counterpart to Luther's *Address to the German Nobility* (1520), his *Napominianie* (Magdeburg, 1554), having made the acquaintance and gained the support of Flacius Illyricus (nn. 158, 289). With a letter of recommendation from Melanchthon, 4 February 1554 stopping over in Breslau, he returned to his vacated post in Pińczów, and would stay there through most of 1555. It was because of the inflammatory *Napominianie* and the dissolution of the monastery of the Pauline Hermits that Bishop Zebrzdowski made his attempt on the Evangelical pamphleteer and restored pastor in Pińczów. For the other sources, metropolitical and parliamentary, besides the *Historia*, see Barycz, *Z Epoki*, 328, n. 35.

The full title of this address to the Polish King with an incendiary critique of the institutional Church is *Chrześciańskie a żałobliwe napominanie do Najaśniejszego Jego Królewskiej Miłości Majestatu i do wysztkich panów wielkich, małych, bogatych i ubogich, na sejmiech bywających tey sławnej Koronyy Polski, Aby Pana Jezus Christusa pryheli i ewangelią świetą, i bałofalstwa antichristowe i sług jego* (Magdeburg, 1554). Krowicki prepared with the Croatian Centuriator, Matija Flačič Illyricus (Bk 1, nn. 62,

257), a shorter Latin version for possible absorption in the Magdeburg Centuries: *Adhortia ad Regem, proceres et nobilitatem omnesque Christianos Regni Poloniae ad accipiendam*. Stanisław Kot, after discovering this work in Wolfenbüttel, wrote about it and the reformatory role of Flacius, "Odnošiácev Matije Flaciji Ilirika prema Reformacji u Polskoj," in a collective work, *Šišićev Zbornik* (Zagreb, 1929) 149. In the foregoing Latinized title of Krowicki's *Napominiani/Adhortatio* in partial imitation of Luther's *Address* but without Luther's nationalism (*mutatis mutandis*) singles out in exhortation for ecclesiastical and societary reform alike "the lords great and small, rich and poor." Something of its specific content is noted in n. 288. For the modern editions, see n. 158.

154. Aleksander Witrelin (d. c. 1586) is not recorded as minister in Pińczów until 1558. Sipayłło, *Akta* 1.367. Witrelin was one to whom Calvin was expected to write, according to a list drawn up by Lismanino, *OC*, 15, no. 2350, col. 869. This much of the account with less detail is found also in Węgierski (*Slavonia Reformata*, 231), said to be taken from Budziński, 5. 28.

The presumably aged *Monachus* surviving in the *coenobium* was a Hermit of St. Paul. The Paulists were founded in Hungary in 1250, priests and brothers living according to strict observance of the Rule of St. Augustine. Their monastery was established in Częstochowa in 1382. Their library at Pińczów will have served well the debaters at several synods and also, to a lesser extent, the new academy there. See "Paulini" and "Paulini w Polsce," *Ek*, N – P, 395 – 404.

155. Krowicki features in Bk. 1, at nn. 233 and 240. His wife as Magdalena Pobiedzińska, sixteen-year-old daughter of a noble of Sanok, joined in the first public clerical marriage in Poland. However, the celebrating vicar was unaware of the clerical status of the groom. Moreover, the marriage took place in the home of Orzechowski (Bk. 1, n. 270), who himself did not regard his own espousal of clerical marraige and communion in both kinds for the laity as disqualifying him from the priesthood and who married also in 1550. He had, moreover, earlier opposed Catholic rebaptism of converts from Orthodoxy. Henryk Barycz, *PSB*, 15 (1976) 350 – 53.

156. He had been summoned by Bishop Dziaduski to appear before his diocesan court, 7 January 1551, charged with uncanonical clerical marriage, Lutheran hersey, and blasphemy, cf. Bk. 1 at n. 274.

157. By alluding to the arrival of Krowicki at the castle of Oleśnicki (April 1551) Lubieniecki confuses the sequence of events at Pińczów (1551 – 55).

158. Lubieniecki put the prison scene into too close chronological sequence with the two attempts of Zebrzydowski to break up the synod of Pińczów in May and again in September 1550, above n. 142. He scarcely alludes to the charges preferred against him by his bishop in Przemyśl (n. 156) for his marriage of 1550 (Bk. 1, at nn. 239, 274) nor his *Admonition* (*Napominianie*). This book has been republished with two other works of Krowicki by B. Otwinowska and Janusz Tazbir, *Chrześciańskie a żałobliwe napominianie* [1554], *Adhortatio* [1560], *Obraz a kontrefet własny Antykristów* [1561] (Warsaw, 1969).

159. Virgil *Aeneid* 2. 49. The reference is not wholly apt except that to apprehend a person as honored guest, presumably of the lone monk, was especially reprehensible.

160. Marcin Mazowiecki. The parallel in the account in this paragraph and the next is so close to that of Węgierski (*Slavonia Reformata*, 231) that it is here printed in italics as virtually a translation from Budziński.

161. Baltazar (Balcer) Łukowski (d. after 1570), brother of Kasper and Kilian, is documented as present at several synods. A Łukowski appears in Bk. 3 at n. 359.

162. Lubieniecki is here scrunching together almost a single episode in the antagonism between Zebrzydowski and Krowicki, as though c. 1551, a good deal of what may well have been stretched out in the narrative of Budziński, namely, the development of the Evangelical movement in and around Cracow and also in the biography of Krowicki himself. In dealing here with Krowicki's preaching in the town house of Lasocki in Cracow, Lubieniecki is aware that he has already recounted several episodes about Cracow and environs, *pp.* 22–23, 25—29, 35, 50–56. Indeed he has told of a sad episode in the life of his own ancestor, Hieronim Filipowski, that gets ahead of his main account, to 1557, at nn. 52-53. But the immediate background of the present episode is that up to now the Evangelicals had been meeting in the summer homes or at the courts of noblemen resident outside the walls of Cracow, e.g. at Aleksandrowice as guests of Krupka, at Chełm, as guests of Marcjan, at the summer house of Jan Boner beyond the walls. Now at this juncture the Evangelicals with their several nobiliary patrons were emboldened to meet in the town house of Lasocki. The preacher was Krowicki. He had in the meantime removed from Pińczów (succeeded by Witrelin) to Włodzisław in the autumn of 1555, where its owner Jan Lanckoroński had converted the village church to Reformed usage in 1551, which was replaced in turn during Krowicki's tenure by a model Reformed church edifice with plain walls and a pulpit centered between two clear windows. This picture is in *Polish Brethren*, Plate G; see further Tadeusz Przypkowski, "Dysydenckie zabytki Kielecczyzny," *OiRwP* 1 (1956) 214; Barycz, *Z Epoki*, 331, n. 28. At the synod of Pińczów, April 1556, he would be elected one of two clerical and two lay (nobiliary) deacons, among the latter, Lasocki, the quadrumvirate having oversight of the philanthropic concerns of the burgeoning Reformed synod of Little Poland. It was thus as a guest preacher in the center of the capital that, in Lubieniecki's skimpy account, Krowicki drew a second time the ire of the bishop. Moreover, Zebrzydowski's own determination to rid the capital and his diocese of the Evangelicals was given impetus by the arrival of the severe nuncio, Aloysius Lippomino (n. 212), with instruction from the new Paul IV Caraffa to crack down on temporizing with the Reformation leadership on the part of any Polish bishop. Barycz, *Z Epoki*, 332.

163. The same person and the characterization following are found in Węgierski (*Slavonia Reformata*, 229). He there gives as his source, Jan Łasicki, *De origine e rebus gestis Fratrum Bohemicorum, quos ignari rerum Waldenses, mali autem Picardos vocant* (1585).

Although not cited by Lubieniecki, this Jan Łasicki (c. 1534–after 1599), deserves further mention here as having in the sixteenth century a pan-European status comparable to that of Modrzewski, Hosius, and Jan Łaski in religion and historiography. An older work on him (1925) by the veteran historian of Polish Church history, Theodor Wotschke, has been superseded by that of Henryk Barycz, *Jan Łasicki: Studium z dziejów polskiej kultury naukowej XVI wieku*, with substantial summaries in French and Russian (Wrocław, etc.: Ossolineum, 1973), also *PSB*, 18 (1973) 218–22. Łasicki remained with the Reformed Church, wrote an account of the rise of the schism of the Minor Church, *De diis Samogitarum caeterorumque Sarmatorum et falsorum Christianorum* (Basel, 1615), *De Russorum Moscovitarum et Tartarum religione* (1582), and against the head of the Jesuits, Antonio Possevino, *Pro puriore religione* (1584). Born in Masovia, a student under Grzegorz Paweł in Poznań, he spent most of a quarter century abroad, 1556–81, in France, Italy, Heidelberg, Basel, Geneva, Paris, England, Heidelberg again, in Wittenberg, and Padua. He ended his years in Lithauania under the patronage of Jan Hlebowicz, castellan of Minsk. A friend of Beza among others, he was a liberal Calvinist. He and his friends arranged for the honorable burial of Curione, also his friend, a gesture that had obliged him to leave Switzerland. On Łasicki, see further nn. 383, ¶5; 391, 399.

164. Piotr Kmita had formerly patronized Krowicki, the palatine of Cracow and *starosta* of Przemyśl, Bk. 1, nn. 176, 233.

In the text, the name of the second in command, Secygnowski, appears without a capital, which is noted in the supplementary *errata* of the facsimile edition, but does not appear in the modern index. This may be Paweł Secygnowski, royal master of the horse in the Cracow militia, attested at the synods.

Lubieniecki postpones to n. 288 mention of Zebrzydowski's Reply to Krowicki's *Napominianie* (Magdeburg, 1554) and to n. 289 Krowicki's masterful *Apologia* (cf. nn. 234, 289).

165. Mikołaj at first authorized, 1553, a Reformed service in his private chapel in the palace at Vilna opposite the former St. John's Church. This service became public when it was established on one of his neighboring estates outside the walls; Łukiszki. In 1562 the service was again transferred, back to the palace chapel. Łukaszewicz, *Lithauen*, 2.73.

Of Radziwiłł the papal nuncio Giovanni Francesco Commendone, accredited to Poland, 1563–64, wrote: "Die katholische Religion weiß gegenwärtig in Polen wie ausserhalb des Landes vielleicht keinen grösseren Verfolger." Karl Völker does not adduce his source for this, *Kirchengeschichte Polens* (Berlin/Leipzig, 1930) 161. Some of the nuntial documentation has now been lost, Adam Penkalla, "C," *EPK*, 3 (1979) 554. Commendone's predecessor, Aloiso Lippomano, writing to Pietro Contarini in Rome, 8 April 1556, was content to call Radziwiłł "the most important patron of the Lutherans." E. Rykaczewski, *Relacye nuncyuszów apostolskich i innych osób o Polsce od roku 1548 –1690*, 2 vols. (Berlin/Poznań, 1864) 1.13.

166. The theology of history connecting the two Augusti and respectively the birth of Jesus and the rebirth of the Primitive Church among the Polish Brethren was expressed earlier in *Historia, 42*.

167. Jan Łaski (1499–1560) was the nephew of Primate Jan VIII Łaski (1510–31), who at the V Lateran was declared *legatus natus* for Poland.

168. Łaski had no theological degree, although he had studied in Vienna (1514), Bologna (1515–18), and Padua (1518–19). He studied in Basel and lived with Erasmus (1525). At this time he made arrangement for the purchase of the humanist's library, which would be taken to Cracow. It was possibly his strong ethical and disciplinary emphasis, his mediating position on the freedom of the will, his irenicism on theological niceties, and his major stress on worship and polity that fitted him to be the leader of the Reformed Church in Poland, 1556–60. Besides the principal biography by Oskar Bartel, above, Bk. 1, n. 156, which was completed by Halina Kowalska, *Działalność Reformatorska*, who also wrote the article in *PSB* 18 (1973) 237–44, see also my "Erasmianism in Poland 1518–1605," "The Polish-Lithuanian Calvin" (much on Łaski) and "Protestants in the Ukraine," (further identification of "six traits" of his reform) 57–60.

169. He had the benefice of guardian of Łęczyca, a canonry in Płock and Cracow (the latter as of 30 November 1517), and of the coadjutorial deanery of Gniezno (30 December 1517). Veszprém is in Hungary, at the time under the Turks. He was ordained priest in 1521. On Erasmus's hopes in 1527 for him in Poland, see *Epistolae*, ed. Allen, no. 1805.

170. Łaski was in 1543 the selected reformer of East Frisia under Countess Anna of Oldenburg. His *Epitome doctrinae ecclesiarum Phrisiae Orientalis* (1544) helped shape

his idea of reform and organization later in Poland. He engaged in christological discussion with Menno Simons, his ideas set forth in *Defensio vera doctrinae de Christi Domini incarnatione* (Bonn, 1545).

171. Łaski sojourned in England twice, 1548–49, 1550–53. There he was superintendent of the Strangers' Church in London and wrote his *Forma ac ratio*, dedicated in 1555 to Sigismund. See Fredrick W. Norwood, "The Strangers' 'Model Churches'," in *Reformation Studies in Honor of Roland Bainton* (Richmond, Va.: Knox, 1962) 181–96.

172. In 1540 in Louvain Łaski married the daugher of a tailor from the circle of the *Devotio Moderna*, possibly a Margaret, and then later, 1553, in London, a Catherine.

173. Stanisław Myszkowski (d. 1570) was a major Reformed lord and courtier. Son of Marcin (burgrave of Cracow and castellan of Wieluṅ and Zuzanna Łaska, d. after 1557), sister of the Reformer, Stanisław M. was carver of the Lesser Crown 1551, of the Great Crown 1556, castellan of Sandomierz and general *starosta* of Cracow 1563. See Dworzaczek, *Genealogia*, table 130; Halina Kowalska, *PSB*, 22 (1977) 394–99.

174. Olbrecht Łaski (1536–1605), not *frater* of the Reformer, above, Bk. 1, n. 146, palatine of Sieradz, owned many estates in Poland and Hungary, and features in chap. 9.

175. Lismanino arrived in Little Poland in March 1556. *PSB* 17 (1972) 467A.

176. Łaski participated in a synod, in progress, of patrons and ministers at Iwanowice, 1 January 1557. Sipayłło, *AS* I. 173, line 3.

177. The royal decree came in May 1556 and considerably hampered Lismanino's effectiveness. *PSB* 17 (1972), 467A.

178. She is mentioned above, Bk. 1, n. 281. In a letter of 27 December 1555, Calvin commended her for sending her two sons to Zurich for their education, *OC*, 15, no. 2367, cols. 903–4. She is several times mentioned in relation to the synods.

179. They dominated Vice-Chancellor Przerębski.

180. Jan Amos Tarnowski (d. 1561) was a correspondent with the Swiss. Secundo Curione wrote Tarnowski, August 1555; Calvin wrote him on 29 December 1555, Wotschke, *Briefwechsel*, nos. 21a, 40, etc.

181. Stanisław Lasocki (*Historia, 31, 35–36, 43–44, 48*) was a strong supporter of a union of the Reformed and the Czech Brethren, an interest of both Lismanino and Filipowski.

182. This could not be the Stanisław Tarnowski (after 1541–1618), castellan of Sandomierz from 1582, mentioned by A. Lubieniecki, *Poloneutychia*, 74, 194. He is not attested in the synods nor in the correspondence of the Swiss with Poles.

183. Spytek Jordan (1518–68) became palatine of Sandomierz only in 1561. He was a correspondent of several Swiss Reformers. Wotschke, *Briefwechsel*, nos. 22–24.

184. The sentence may be taken over from Budziṅski who is most likely to have been the collector of these letters.

185. The letter is not extant and the reference to a confession of faith must be to an expression of support for the Reformation. At this juncture the major confessions considered by the Poles in synod would be the Augsburg Confession and that of the Czech Brethren. Cf. Sipayłło, *AS* I. 21–41.

186. The Lutherans called the Swiss Reformers by this pejorative name primarily in reference to the sacrament of the altar. The term may have been first used by Carlstadt in *Von dem Neuen Testament* (1525), where he called Luther a *Sacramentler*. Luther himself gave universal currency to the word in a sense negative for him in calling Carlstadt and the Swiss, notably Zwingli and Oecolampadius *Sakramentirer* (with variants). After the *Consensus Tigurinus* of 1549, Calvin and the German Swiss, too, held to the Real Presence at communion and were not properly called Sacramentarian, although the

Reformed did not have the Lutheran "consubstantiation." On the term, see Bk. 1, nn. 103, 105.

187. This is a reference to the call of the synod of Pińczów of 1 May 1555 and letter of Feliks Cruciger "ex convocatione Pinczoviensi 1555" to Lismanino, n. 119. On 24 January 1556 during the synod of Secemim, it was deliberated where Lismanino could be appropriately and safely lodged. Sipayłło, *AS* I. 48.

188. Zator is a town south of Oswięcim and west of Cracow. Myszkowski had received form the King the administration and benefice of these two small towns in 1551, partly in recognition of his leadership in support of the marriage with Barbara Radziwiłłówna. *PSB* 22 (1977), esp. 378 A.

189. Balice was a village, down river from Cracow, owned by Jan Boner (above, n. 83) and where he established a Reformed congregation. From a university-educated patrician family of Cracow, Boner wrote in several capacities, among them as Senator. During this period, Boner was the patron and protector of the Reformed congregation in Cracow where Grzegorz Paweł, commissioned by the synod of Pińczów, was pastor, 1552–61, along with Stanisław Wiśniowski, preaching in Boner's garden in the suburb of Wesoł.

190. Cruciger refers to the bishop.

191. The text has *coetu*, not corrected in the original or in the facsimile edition. Cruciger turns from *coetus* (*zbór*, congregation) in the singular to a verb in the plural, either the members of the congregation or the various congregations.

192. Matt 25:14.

193. Cruciger, unlike Krowicki (n. 158), had not studied in Wittenberg, but at Cracow (Bk. 1, n. 231). He had taken refuge in 1551 with Jakub Ostroróg (Bk. 1, n. 283) in Great Poland, who was a supporter there of the Czech Brethren, headed by Jerzy Izrael. Ever thereafter he would tend to favor the integration of the Polish Reformed under this late medieval reformed church. On him, see further Stanisław Szczotka, *PSB* 4 (1938) 107–09, Łukaszewicz, *Lithauen* 2. 63–69.

"Germany" in this letter would not have meant Bohemia, but the whole of the Holy Roman Empire, including Bohemia and even the Netherlands and the Swiss Confederation. Cruciger meant here primarily the Swiss and the Strassburgers.

194. In 1553 lord Stanisław Szafraniec (d. 1595), palatine of Sandomierz and owner of Secemen, turned the local Catholic edifice into a Reformed church with Cruciger the minister and a deacon to help. See Michał Rawita Witanowski, "Ogniska reformacji: Secemin," *RwP* 3 (1924) 132 At the synod of Słomniki, 25 November 1554, Cruciger was elected superintendent of all the congregations of the synod of Little Poland. At least he is already called superintendent at synod of Krzcięcice, 18 March 1555. Sipayłło, *AS* I. 2, 2–4; *PSB* 4 (1938) 107A.

195. See n. 194.

196. The dogma of Transubstantiation was given conciliar formulation by Pope Innocent III in the IV Lateran (1215) without yet the technical term.

197. The Author uses *sacramenta* in the sense of *signa*, signs.

198. Tertullian (d. c. 225) first took over into Christian usage the term which originally meant the soldier's oath, *Ad martyres*, 3. See also Bk. 1, n. 112.

199. Here the Author writes as a seventeenth-century minister of the Minor Church, in which believers' baptism had indeed become a young recruit's experience. For adult baptism among the later Brethren, see Bk. 3, esp. n. 238, and *Polish Brethren*, "Concerning the Baptism of Water," 446–57.

200. The Author puts the following specific references all within square brackets, his

way of annotation. It is quite likely that he swept them all up together form a secondary work. However, as several of the items deal with the sacrament of baptism, it is possible that Lubieniecki read some of them directly, while others he drew from *florilegia* of the seventeenth-century Brethren, who had to defend their practice of believers' baptism by immersion.

201. The older numbering, 23, has become *Ep.* 98 in Pl. 33, cols. 94 – 98. It deals with the faith of parents effectual in the baptism of infants.

202. The reference spelled out clearly suggests a *summa* as the source. The abbreviation for Augustine's opponent is Maximin. There is no Maximinus in the extensive works of Augustine, nor a *Contra Maximinum*. Maxianus, schismatic bishop of Carthage *within* the Donatist grouping, is at the center of Book 3 of Augstine's *De baptismo contra Donatistas libri vii* of c. 400, Pl. 9, cols. 33 – 108. This is a treatise made up of related writings. Book 3 is indeed a letter addressed to (another) Boniface, *Comes* of Africa under Valentinian III. The abbreviation in the *Historia* could be a slight error. Distinctio 2, "de consecrat. C. Sacrificium" does not correspond to anything at the appropriate place in *De Baptismo*, 3.

203. John Chrysostom (d. 407) preached 90 homilies on Matthew, c. 390, the oldest complete commentary on the first gospel. There are two numberings off by one in *PG*, 57 – 58, cols. 757/53 – 751/52, in which a symbolic eucharistic reference is not obvious.

204. Theodoret of Cyrus (d. c. 466) was the last great theologian of the school of Antioch. The reference is to *Eranistes seu Polymorphus* (c. 447) in four books against the Monophysites. The first three are in one form of dialogue between the orthodox believer and a beggar (the Monophysite). The first dialogue is about the unchangeable character of the divinity of Christ, but the Liturgy/Mass comes up and Theodoret does speak of the symbolic character of the eucharist. *PG*, 83, cols. 55/56.

Vermigli (N. 108) supplied Archbishop Cranmer with this very text, which then became central in his own eucharistic *Defensio* (Zurich, 1559) against catholicizing Bishop Stephen Gardner of Winchester (d. 1555), Lord High Chancellor under Mary Tudor.

205. See n. 196.

206. The reference has not been identified.

207. Joannes Eusebius Nieremberg, S. J., *Panegyrica narratio de tribus martyribus Societatis Jesu qui 1621 in Paraquaria passi sunt* (Lyons, 1628).

208. The episcopal succession in Cracow after Zebrzydowski (Bk. 1, n.196) included Filip Padniewski (1560 – 72), Franciczek Krasiński (1572 – 77), Piotr Myszkowski (1577 – 91), Jerzy Radziwiłł (1591 – 1600), and Bernard Maciejowski (1600 – 05).

209. Lubieniecki here, as elsewhere, is clearly addressing his *Historia* to Protestants to the west of Poland. The *populus* is, of course, the *szlachta*, not the burghers, peasants or artisans. On Lubieniecki's Sarmatianism, See. Bk. 3, n. 708.

210. This may be an illusion to what eventuated as the *Vindiciae, Polish Brethren*, Doc. XXIX.

With the pride of Lubieniecki in the Polish constitution expressed immediately above, one may here recall his twofold reference to the Kingdom/Commonwealth of the *polulus/szlachta as embodying Jesus Christ a second time, as it were , under a second royal Augustus, Bk. 1 at n. 127, Bk. 2 at n. 166. The idealization, among the Polish Brethren, of the electively royal Respublica* (Commonwealth) of the gentry found notable, even though incidental, formulation in the Racovian Catechism (1609), where in an answer to the question about Christ's having been lifted up to heaven, the Latin version responds: "Because that is the seat of immortality, and there is the mansion and *Respub-*

lica of all God's children.'' (with allusion to Phil 3:20), *Polish Brethren*, Doc. VIII, 237.

211. The episode here recounted on the basis of what Lubieniecki says is Budziński's ''eye-witness account'' is recounted in greater and more plausible detail in a MS ''Rerum memorabilium liber V'' of a Carmelite Rovero Pontani preserved in the archives of the Theatines in Naples under date of 1556. This is edited by Erazm Rykaczewski, *Relacye nuncyuszów apostolskich i innych osób o Polsce od roku 1548–1690*, 2 vols. (Paris, 1864) 1. 60–61. The account of Budziński/Lubieniecki has independent value, as it gives many details of its own not given by Pontani. The episode with the date 1557 is summarized by the *Nieznana Kronika Ariańska*, Part I, ed. Szczucki, 169.

212. Luigi (Aloysius) Lippomano (1500–59) was one of the first of the new type of papal nuncio, pastoral more than political. Coadjutor bishop of Bergamo in 1538 and bishop of Verona in 1548, ordinary of Bergamo in 1558, he was successively nuncio in Portugal (1542–45), the Empire (1548, 1555), and then Poland (1555–58). There he set up a permanent nunciature. Lippomano presided at national synods in Łowiz (c. 1556) and Warsaw (1557), *EK*, 21–22 (1910) 353. He was one of the presidents of the Council of Trent, Period II, 1551–52.

213. Claudian, *In Etropium*, 181. The quotation is not apt for Lismanino.

214. Lismanino came from a distinguished Venetian family.

215. The term *dissidentes* is anachronistic, the *Pax dissidentium* was agreed upon in 1573. The term as of that date meant ''those differing concerning religion and originally therefore included the Catholics.'' As of 1556 the Protestants still had high hopes for the reformation of all of Poland.

216. Horace *Carmina* 3.16.9.

217. No doubt, a proverb.

218. The reference is to Stanisław Borek called *tribunus et capitaneus* of Sochaczew by the King. See n. 222.

219. The fuller account of a Catholic partisan (n. 211) makes clear that there were more Jews involved than Budziński/Lubieniecki indicate and their names are given, although not consistently in the partisan source and in the King's letter (n. 22).

Dorota Łazięcka of Sochaczew may have been of the humble class, for she is said to have been a servant of Benedict, no doubt a Gentile servant on Sabbaths for a substantial Jewish family of Besheim. But it is quite possible that she had some standing. She may have been a Judaizing ''sacramentarian'' like Katarzyna Zalaszkowa Weiglowa of Cracow, *Historia, 17* and n. 223. She had a child of Benedict's son, buried unbaptized.

Her conduct, in showing perhaps the Jewish household what the Host was, may in fact be at the core of the episode—not, of course, any request by Jews for it. Nor could she have sold it. She at most showed it, evidently not herself believing in Christ's presence in it. The rest, to her painful exit from life and that of her Jewish friends, is palpably a compounded fabrication, based on rumor and perhaps a specific tradition of anti-semitic tales of atrocities. That Dorota could have displayed to Jewish friends the Host borne as recounted seems all the more plausible in that in the same year a canon of Kalisz, Stanisław Golański, informs the Primate, that recently in nearby Chełmce a village priest himself sold two Hosts to local Jews. They were punished by death. The canon asks the Primate to intervene and order the same punishment for the cleric. Rykaczewski, *Relacye nuncyuszów*, 59–60. Again, it is inconceivable that there would be a sale or a purchase. But rumors of such dealings were in the air.

220. Myszkowski is identified as captain of Marienburg at n. 173. He was *krajczy*, carver, not cupbearer.

221. The Rev. Vice-Chancellor was at once confident in the alleged miracle of the

vial of blood from the allegedly boughten Host and in the plan to punish the three Catholic women who sold the Host.

The fact that so eminent a prelate and statesman as Przerębski, Vice-Chancellor (1551 – 58), later Primate (1559 – 62), believed in the alleged miracle shows how widespread and deeply believed in were the anti-semitic legends. It is a strange perversion that it was out of the Host of flour, as the Jewish defendants implied, that Jews, not Christians were thought to be able to extract a vial of blood for their purposes.

Lubieniecki seems to wish to hold Lippomano responsible for what Przerębski seems to have initiated: the royal mandate of death to the three Jews. Cf. Jan Igancy Korytowski, *Prałaci i kanonicy kapituły metropolitanej gnieznienskiej od 100 r. do dni naszych*, 14 vols. (Gnesen, 1883) 3. 229 – 71.

222. Budziński/Lubieniecki are right about the attitude of the King. His letter of 8 June 1556 addressed to Stanisław Borek or his deputy, is extant. Rykaczewski, *Relacye nuncyuszów*, 60 – 61.

223. The quite plausible testimony of the Jews and the use of hot pitch are among many details unique to the Budziński/Lubieniecki account. Budziński was a millennialist and conceivably had eschatological as well as simply humane affinities with the Jews. That Dorota was also put to death is stated expressly by Rovero Pontani, *loc. cit.*, 61. Dorota and Benedict the Jew were buried 17 May 1556. Two other named Jews and a third, the son of Benedict, who had had an infant from Dorota and had buried it without benefit of baptism in his father's sepulchre, were burned in Płock some distance away, 1 June 1556.

224. No account is found in the nuncio's own *Relacya* on Poland, 1556. Translated from a Vatican MS into Polish, it reveals an interest primarily in the social, constitutional, and military situation in Poland over against Muscovy. There are a few words about the many sects. Rykaczewicz, *Relacye nuncyuszów* 1. 64 – 68. It is true that Rovero Pontani (n. 211) praises God for the miracle of the blood from the Host. Lubieniecki will have had this kind of report in mind.

225. Mikołaj Rudy (the Red) was the brother of Queen Barbara and thus very close to the King (Bk. 1, n. 140). The Author was evidently aware of the published exchange of letters in 1556 in Latin between the Nuncio and the Prince, *Dwa listy na polski język właśnie wyłożone* (Brześć Liteweski, 1559).

226. See *Historia, 64 – 66.* Lubieniecki does not mention the major letter of Łaski to the King from Frankfurt on the Main, 6 September 1555, accompanying his *Forma ac ratio tota* of 1550, which contained his arrangement for the Strangers' Church in London (Frankfurt, 1555). The dedicatory letter to the King is reprinted by Kuper, ed., *Opera* 1 – 36. Łaski also wrote to the King from Frankfurt, 31 December 1555, as also to the Senators and the *szlachta, Epistolae tres* (Basel, 1555), the three reprinted together by Kyuper, *Opera*, 1. 347 – 88; to the King, 349 – 52.

227. This letter, taken from Lubieniecki, is reprinted in Kuyper's calendered edition of Łaski's correspondence, *Opera*, 2, *Epistola* 125, 738 – 46 with 16 small notes.

228. Stanisław Myszkowski (*Historia, 65 – 66*, n. 173) was made *starosta* of Marienburg 5 October 1565, to the great displeasure of Bishop Stanisław Hozjusz of Warmia (Ermland), on whom see my "Stanisław Hosius, 1504 – 1579." In December 1554, along with some senators of Ducal Prussia, Myszkowski requested Bishop Jan Lubodzieski of Chelmno not to remove the rector of the Lutheran school there as Hozjusz desired. *PSB* 22 (1977) 395 A.

229. Łaski's first letter to the King was indeed from outside the Commonwealth, 6 September 1555. He had been dismissed as "ephor" in charge of reform in Emden and

had left in April for Frankfurt. Here, he came in charge of a fourth congregation of Dutch and German Reformed. He was charged by Johann Brenz with being a Sacramentarian. In his last months in Frankfurt, Łaski devoted himself to the theology and practice of the Lord's Supper, all the more problematic by reason of the fallout of the debate of Reformed and Lutherans, convened by Duke Christopher of Württemburg and the Prince Elector of the Palatinate, Ott Heinrich (1549–76), in Stuttgart, 22 May 1556. On the dispute, see John T. McNeill, *Unitive Protestantism* (Richmond, Va., 1964), 205–6, where he places the debate in the context of the ''Union Activities of Beza and Farel.'' McNeill characterizes Łaski as ''one of the most irenical and constructive minds of the age, despite misfortunes that largely nullified his efforts'' (205).

In this atmosphere of failed colloquy, Łaski produced his own eucharistic formulation, *Purgatio ministrorum* (Basel: Operius, 28 December 1556), reprinted by Kuyper, *Opera* 1. 243–67. He avowed it was true to the Augsburg Confession and yet had the approval of Calvin, who was in Frankfurt in September 1556. Łaski had worked on it in Wittenberg, where he conferred with Melanchthon. Passing through Breslau, he reached Jan Boner in Rabsztyn. His letter to the King from Balice where he was resident during the synod of Iwanowice, 1 January 1551, was occasioned by the earlier receipt of a letter from the King, restricting his activities, presumably drafted by the bishops (''Pharisees''). For Balice, see n. 189. For his first public appearance in synod, see Sipayłło, *AS*, 1. 173. For a compact coverage of the events leading up to Łaski's letter, see *PSB* 22 (1977) 241 B. The King's letter to Łaski is summarized below.

230. The reference is to the master of bishops, the Pope, by implication also Antichrist.

231. This was Stanisław Budziński. See n. 235.

232. Mikołaj Radziwiłł.

233. St. Bartholomew's Day is 24 August. The Diet had been called by the King for Warsaw, and it actually sat between 6 December 1556 and 14 January 1557. Łaski would wait in relative obscurity three days after the dispatch of his letter before appearing in synod.

234. Łaski had done this in his *Purgatio*, n. 229.

235. On Łaski's synodal call, see n. 187. For kinsmen supporting the call, see among others, n. 174. Mikołaj Radziwiłł had written him to this effect quite early, as is evident from the letter to the Prince from Łaski, London, 16 December 1552. Kyuper, *Opera*, 2, no. 90, 674.

236. Kuyper suggests the emendation *Historia, 80*, line 3 from bottom: ''estimarem: [ita tamen] ut . . . .''

237. Łaski here testifies rightly to his strenuous efforts for a pan-Protestant ecclesio-political concert of energies, and he understood that the crux for a unitive Protestantism was clarity and charity as to Communion. The topography of his reforming activity includes England, the Netherlands, Switzerland, parts of the Empire, even a passage to Denmark, a visit to Ducal Prussia and Lithuania, and activity in both Great and Little Poland. The princes to whom he refers are Elector Palatine Ott Heinrich, Duke Christopher of Württemberg, Landgrave Phillip of Hesse, John Frederick, Elector (to 1547) of Saxony, and Duke Albert Hohenzollern of Prussia.

238. There were four such churches in Frankfurt.

239. Łaski refers to his *Purgatio*, n. 227. As he wrote, the work had come from the press. The MS thereof would have been brought to the King by Budziński. It is reprinted by Kuyper, *Opera* 1. 243–344.

240. Kuyper amended the text, reflected in the translation. By *observantio* Łaski

means the observance of the Lord's Supper in churches under his reforming direction.

241. For the actual dates, see n. 233.

242. Łaski hoped that aging King Sigismund would be like young King Edward, that all of Poland with Ducal Prussia and large parts of Lithuania would join the Protestant camp. He signed his Latin messages as *Baro*, not as *pastor*.

243. Cf. Ps 101:7. Łaski in his letter to the King of 31 December 155 (n. 226), had, using Psalm 2, envisaged the King as a new David, and he had thought of himself in the new situation as discharging the office of *propheta* in reference to the *triplex munus Christi* (Bk. 1, n. 170).

244. Łaski, something of a nationalist, convinced that the bishops weaken royal authority by their loyalty to the Pope, understands the Protestant mission in Poland to be the strengthening of royal authority. He seems to be saying that the bishops are not only pharisiacal but also deceptive in pointing to himself in his ministry rather than to themselves in their machinations as the problem for royal rule.

245. Cf. John 3:9 and 10:1 etc.

246. Cf. John 3:19–20.

247. Mordantly ironic.

248. Mikołaj Radziwiłł.

249. See *Historia, 48*, specifically n. 225.

250. Kuyper makes the abbreviated *et* of line 11 from the bottom into *ut*, here reflected in the translation.

251. The words of God the Father about the Son at the Transfiguration, Matt 14:5; Mark 9:7; Luke 9:35. They are printed in solid capitals in the text.

252. Cf. Rom 3:4. In his straining of this text Łaski reveals how desperate he feels. An Erasmian, he should have not been so pessimistic about his fellow men. In this section of the letter Łaski gives expression to his thoughts about original sin, sins, and forgiveness more fully than in his tracts on theology and reform.

253. Łaski reflects Swiss usage: The institution of (the true) religion. He eschews here *restauratio* and *restitutio* because of their sectarian implications, but also *reformatio* because this would in Poland mean the inclusion of the national hierarchy. Cf. Calvin, n. 61, ¶2 and Primate Uchański's temporary vision of a national Church, Bk. 1, n. 184, ¶¶ 3–7.

Łaski here means what he says: An *institutio* of the Church in its pre-Constantinian plenitude understood as a synodal national Church *without* bishops, or with bishops understood as synonymous with presbyters, but also an *institutio* of such a Church with the help of a new Constantine, Sigismund II, whom he presently asks personally to embrace the "true religion." Further on in the letter he also uses the more sectarian *restitutio*.

254. The bishops.

255. The traditional word here would be *innovationes*, which from classical Roman times suggested even revolution. Łaski, in using the simpler Latin word, suggests at once reformation and a fresh start without incurring the charge of seditious innovation, pressed against him by Lippomano and several bishops. For Lippomano's view of all Protestants and perhaps some sympathizing bishops, see briefly in his largely political survey, "Relacya," Rykaczewski, *Relacye nuncyuszów*, I, p. 67: "In one house you could encounter three different faiths, *cum tamen sit unus Deus, una fides, et unum baptisma* [Eph 4:5]." Lippomano quite despaired of the Poles!

256. Łaski did not have a clear picture of Eastern Church history and thinks of

several *regna* as having at length submitted to papal control, wherewith the fall of Orthodoxy ensued. He, of course, ironically calls the union Council of Ferrara-Florence, 1438 – 39, a *novatio* shortly before the fall of Constantinople, 1453.

257. The *novatio*, innovation, Łaski fears most is that that began with the appointment of Lippomano as nuncio, authorized to reorder the Church of Poland.

258. Surely the bishops, at least superficially, were right about Germany, better: The Holy Roman Empire. But as for the Apostolic Kingdom of Hungary, its "tripartition," 1526/41, was primarily due to the Turkish onslaughts, although the strong adherence in the Principality of Transylvania to Lutheranism on the part of the Saxons and to the Reformed faith and polity on the part of the Magyars accounts in part for the independence of this third of the kingdom.

259. Łaski found it difficult to accept the enormous cleavage in the Empire and beyond between the *instauratio* of Lutheranism and that of the Reformed Church. He calls them together "the true religion."

260. Cf. 1 Sam 7:3.

261. *In toto corde*, 1 Sam 7:3.

262. The allusion is to Dan 11:38, where *mayzzim* is now translated "the god of forces/fortresses," namely the pagan deity obtruded upon the Jews by Antiochus Epiphanes. Łaski refers to the Pope.

263. Cf. John 3:19.

264. Łaski at this point suggests, though he does not expressly state, that as the power of God is reflected in the state, so the image of God is reflected in the royal father of the fatherland.

265. In his epistle to the King of 31 December 1555 (n. 226), Łaski had developed the Erasmian conception of the threefold office of Christ as Prophet or Teacher (*Doctor*), King, and Priest. He suggests here and elsewhere that his own authority is that of a *propheta/doctor* addressing as a new Samuel a new Saul or David.

266. Melanchthon wrote three letters to Sigismund. See *Opera*, ed. by Karl Bretschneider and Heinrich Bindseil, 28 vols. (Braunschweig, 1838 – 60) 28, 328. The letter of 18 October 1556 is given in full, at n. 268.

267. At the close of this hortatory letter to the King, a word on the ideal of polity is appropriate. See esp. the careful analysis of Łaski's polity in East Frisia, London, Frankfurt-on-the Oder, and Poland as worked out by O. Naunin, "Die Kirchenordnungen des Johannes Łaski," *Deutsche Zeitschrift für Kirchenrecht*, 3rd series, 19 (1909): 23 – 40, 195 – 236, 347 – 75. Naunin observes that Łaski brought the *seniores* and patrons to a very high level of authority in the Church, especially in synod, where pastors were disciplined on preaching and doctrine no less than on pastoral care and personal behavior. Naunin disagrees with Johannes Kurske, *Joahnnes a Lasco und der Sakramentsstreit* (Breslau, 1899), that in giving such prominence to the elders and patrons Łaski was influenced by the usage of Menno Simons, with whom he was once engaged in debate on another issue. Naunin holds, rather, that the lay control of the parish priest had been vigorously and widely preserved from early times in East Frisia, precisely where Łaski first labored as a reformer, and that it was from the usage in this region that he appropriated his henceforth distinctive principle of polity. In any case, *Baro a Lasco*, as he often identified himself, was a royalist with full appreciation of how certain great lords could advance Protestantism under Edward VI. In Poland, he could readily defer to the lesser lords, once a Commonwealth-wide Reformation was seen as unrealistic. Łaski would find in Dr. Giorgio Biandrata a layman of similar views on polity, different from those of

Calvin, and this could in part explain Łaski's initial welcome of the Italian proto-Unitarian. For Łaski's welcome of Biandrata to Poland in 1558, see n. 438, for Biandrata's view of polity, n. 447, ¶ 6.

268. The letter is reprinted from Lubieniecki in Melanchthon, no. 6092, *Opera*, 8, col. 869–70. It would appear that Budziński obtained his copy from Łaski.

269. The last Tatar invasion would be in 1624 reaching as far West as Przemyśl and Rzeszów. In 1241 the Mongols/Tatars had defeated the coordinated resistance at Liegnitz/Legnica of the Polish and German cavalry. However, on their own they withdrew.

270. Melanchthon refers to the struggle over Italy, 1494–1516 and its sequel.

271. Wisdom of Solomon.

272. Stanisław Hosius (Hozyusz) bishop of Chełmno, 1549–51, was at the time bishop of Ermland (1551–79), later Cardinal (1561). Surrounded by Lutherans, he published his *Confessio Catholicae Fidei Christiana* (1552–53), to which Melanchthon primarily refers, a Catholic *apologia* of pan-European resonance.

273. The Augsburg *Confession* of 1530.

274. The letter of Melanchthon, the MS copy of the *Purgatio*, and Łaski's severe, ''prophetic'' letter were brought to the King by Stanisław Myszkowski. See n. 173. For the context, see further Kowalska, *Działalność*, 128–29.

275. Lismanino and Łaski were comparable figures, potential rivals for the leadership of a greater Reformed Church in the Commonwealth. Because of Lismanino's previous relationships with the King, not because he was of foreign origin, he had incurred a mandate against his person, while Łaski, more than a score of years out of his native land, yet nephew of a former Primate, enjoyed a status and seems to have also displayed a reforming energy that Lismanino lacked.

276. Jan Utenhove (d. 1565/66), a patrician of Ghent, expelled by the Peace of 1544, sojourned in Strassburg and became an elder in his Strangers' Church under Łaski in London, and accompanied him to Poland, appearing with him in the midst of the synod in progress at Iwanowice, 1 January 1557. This is stated (as of 1556) by Węgierski, *Slavonia Reformata*, 412 (see also 410 and 531—at Pińczów) but not confirmed by Sipayłło, *AS* 1.173. Utenhove is first attested at the synod of Pińczów, 10–17 August 1557, as a minister, listed right after Łaski and before Superintendent Feliks Cruciger (*AS*, 1, 217), and in the same order at the synod of Włodzisław, 4–15 September 1558 (*AS*, 1. 265. For the whole of the life, see F. Pijper, *Jan Utenhove* (Leiden, 1883). He wrote Socinus from Poland, 13 January 1558, *Opere*, ed. Rotondò, no. 48, and *The Life of Łaski*, see Plate 1.

277. The Author does not give this important letter but accurately characterizes it. It is printed in *OC*, 16, 2599, col. 415.

278. The last diet in Warsaw was in 1529. Budziński's ''first'' is in reference, perhaps, to the era of reform.

279. The usual listing of the four Latin *doctores* includes Gregory the Great and does not presume to take over the Greek Father, John Chrysostom.

280. Horace *Epistolae* I. 7. 23.

281. Translating the *incedendum* of the text as *incendendum*.

282. Cf. Virgil *Aenid* 2. 49.

283. Documentary parallels to the Budziński/Lubieniecki account of the proceedings of the Diet are difficult to come by. Mikołaj Rey (c. 1505–68), the great poet, was close to the Protestants (Bk. 1, n. 271). He charged Szafraniec with spoliation sanctions by reformation.

284. Mikołaj Kossobudzki.

285. Stanisław Szafraniec (d. 1598), owner of Secemin, features several times later in the *Historia* and at the synods.

286. Col. 3:14.

287. The Author seems to be following Stanisław Orzechowski, *Annales*.

288. Ths was a reply, *Krótka odpowiedź*, written for Zebrzydowski by his secretary, Nidecki (n. 98) (hence *Pontifices*, § 3) and directed against Krowicki's *Napominianie*, (n. 158). Zebrzydowski/Nidecki assailed Krowicki for his affrontery in dedicating his work to the King and, to reply, summarized Krowicki's charges against the papacy: (1) that it teaches the remission of sins, not in the name of Christ, but in the name of the dead, in paid masses in the names of the saints of various orders; (2) that the Pope is the God of this world; (3) that the Pope in his Mass blasphemes and crucifies Christ; (4) that the Church keeps the ordinary good people away from the blood of Christ; (5) that they teach that there are as many mediators (*jednaczków*) and intercessors (*przyczyńców*) without Christ; and (6) that they teach a hypocritical moral purity. Quoted and characterized by Barycz from two examplars in the Czartoriski library, *Z Epoki*, 333. Zebrzydowski proudly sent a copy of the Reply to Rome.

289. The *Obrona/Apologia* is a response to Zebrzydowski's *Reply*. Bock, without explanation dates it as 1557. Barycz uses a copy that makes if an imprint (cf. ¶2) of Daniel of Łęczyca (Pińczów, 1560) and discusses it as of that date, *Z Epoki*, 342–45. Wiszowaty gives an earlier (first) printing, 1556 (possible another work). Wiszowaty in *BAnt²*, 45 and in the fair copy, knows, besides the *Obrona/Apologia* given by Sand without place or date, of an edition with a slightly different title, *Obrona Braciey Zboru Christusowego, przeciw fałszywey nauce Andrzeia Zebrzydowskiego Biskupa Krakowskiego, ktorą wydal gaiąc prawdziwey nauce Słowa Bożego, i szczypiąc Marcin Krowickiego*, 1556; authorship: Bracia Zboru wiernego Christusowego z Samuelem Kinearthem; printed *in quarto* and dedicated to the same Kinearth. Wiszowaty then mentions another edition with a letter of dedication, Königsberg, 18 June 1560. What he calls a third edition is entitled *Apologia więtrza; to iest Obrona Nauki prawdziwey y wiary starodawney Krzesciánjskiey, ktorey uczyli Provocy, Krystus Syn Boży y Apostolowie swięci. Na przeciwko nauce fałszywey y wierze nowey, ktorey uczy w koscielech swoich Papiesz Rzymski*, dedicated to Jan Hlebowicz, castellan of Minsk and treasurer of the Grand Duchy of Lithuania, by Stanisław Niniński, 1 January 1584. The above spelling here is not as it is in *BAnt²* but as in the plate of the title page of an edition of 1560, Lech Szczucki and Janusz Tazbir, eds., *Literatura ariańska w Polsce XVI wieku: Antologia*, illustrated documents, some in translation and with short biographies of the authors ([Warsaw], 1959), p. 3. As this title page does not include the four words above before *Obrona*, Wiszowaty undoubtedly had another edition before him as he supplemented Sand.

The edition of Szczucki and Tazbir critically sets forth only Part Three on the twofold cross, ''O Krzyżu Pana Krystusowym i zwolenników,'' ibid., 4–14, which the editors connect with a sermon on the cross given in the course of the general synod of Książ, Sunday, 15 September 1560. See the interesting setting, Sipayłło, *AS*, 2. 51, where the synodal record interestingly recalls the spirited discussion as to whether only the synodists or also *chłopięta, i dziewki, i niewieścianki* (boys, girls, women) might participate and they did.

Evidently successive editions of the *Obrona* after 1556 carried supplementary material.

290. Michael Servetus was burned in 1553.

291. The reference is to Calvin's *Defensio orthodoxae fidei contra prodigiosos errores Michaelis Serveti Hispani ubi ostenditur haereticis jure gladu coercendos esse* (Geneva, February 1554), well dealt with by Wilbur, *Socinianism*, chap. 13.

292. The reference is to Théodore de Bèze's defense of Calvin's action, against the cogent assault on it by Sebastian Castellio under a pseudonym, namely, *De haereticis a civili magistratu puniendis libellus* (Geneva, 1554); *Traité de l'authorité du Magistrat en punition des hérétiques* (1560). See Wilbur, *Socinianism*, chap. 14.

NOTES TO CHAPTER FIVE

293. Actually most of Lubieniecki's discussion of Servetus is in the present chapter.

Several of Servetus's writings have been reprinted and in some cases translated, stimulating fresh research. John F. Fulton in *Michael Servetus, Humanist and Martyr* (New York, 1953) supplies a clear account of the works of Servetus and a census of all known copies. Angel Alcola updates the works of and on Servetus in *Servet, el hereje perseguido* (Madrid, 1973), the Spanish translation of Roland Bainton's *Hunted Heretic* (Boston, 1953; in French, Geneva, 1953). Four other revisionist writers analyse Servetus's thought, José Barón Fernández, *Miguel Servet: su Vida y su obra* (Madrid: Espasa-Calipe, 1970); Claudio Manzone, *Umanesimo ed eresia: Michele Serveto* (Naples: Guida, 1972); Francisco Sánchez-Blanco, *Michael Servets Kritik an der Trinitätslehre: philosophische Implikationen und historische Auswirkungen*, Europäische Hochschulschriften, series 20, vol. 28 (Frankfurt a/M: Lang, 1977); and Jerome Friedman, *Michael Servetus: A case study in total heresy* (Geneva: Droz, 1978). Lech Szczucki has edited a collection of translated selections, *Michal Servet, 1511–53: Wybór pism i dokumentów* (Warsaw, 1967).

For the diffusion of the thought of Servetus see Stanisław Kot, "L'influence de Michel Servet sur le mouvement Antitrinitarien en Pologne et en Transylvanie," in Bruno Becker, ed., *Autour de Michel Servet et de Sebastien Castellion* (Haarlem, 1953) 72–115; Mihály Balázs, "Die osteuropäische Rezeption der *Restitutio Christianismi* von Servet," in Dán and Pirnát, eds., *Antitrinitarianism*, 13–23.

294. On Johann Sylvan, see Bk. 2, nn. 362, 364; Bk. 3, n. 380.

295. On Matteo Gribaldi, *Historia, 108*; on Alciati, n. 353.

296. On Adam Neuser, n. 364.

297. Lubieniecki has incorrectly Rennes, as does also *BAnt*, 6.

Servetus was born in 1511 in Villanueva de Sijena (Huesca). Juan-Manuel Palacios Sanchez, *El ilustre aragonés Miguel Servet: Breve biografia del sabio españo, descubridor de la circulación de la sángre* (Huesca, 1956). In *Radical Reformation* and *La Reforma Radical* there are, alas, traces of an older view that Servetus was a Basque, cf. chap. 23:3 n. and en passant on p. 3/15. In this older work and its revision, Servetus was treated somewhat as a great but idiosyncratic figure. The influence of his writings, as well as the impact of his steadfast martyrdom are evident in Lubieniecki's account of developments in the Commonwealth and in Transylvania, as communicated especially by Italian sojourners. The practice of immersion among the Polish Brethren may have in part come from him. His distinctive triadological language, however, does not become prominent, Gribaldi having been more influential.

298. In this statement Lubieniecki was possibly independent of N. Lindanus who says the same thing in *Tabulae grassantium hereseon* (Paris, 1562); see Wilbur, *Socinianism*, 52, n. 13.

299. These are references to a Latin verson of the Zohar.

300. Justin Martyr of Samaria and Rome (d. c. 165) wrote in Greek.

301. Hilary of Poitiers (d. 367) in his *Epistola ad Constantium* suggested that the solution to all the conflicting conciliar creeds would be a return to the Apostles' Creed. *PL*, 10, col. 559. See *Polish Brethren* 358, n. 5.

302. Michael Servetus, *De Trinitatis erroribus libri septem* (Hagenau, 1531), translated by E. M. Wilbur, *The Two Treatises of Servetus on the Trinity*, *HTS*, 16 (1932).

303. The Author no doubt alludes to the dying words of Servetus: "O Jesus, Son of the eternal God, have mercy on me." Mino Celso, *In hereticiis coercendis* (1547) 109, quoted by Wilbur, *Socinianism*, 181 at n. 93.

304. Most of the information and some of the phrasing of the preceding was taken from "Lyncurius's" preface to the *Declaratio* and what follows inset was taken *verbatim* from the same. "Lyncurius" said that Servetus was intending to go to Venice. On "Lyncurius"; see nn. 305 and 306. Servetus had already published his *Biblia Sacra ex Santis Pagnini tralatione, sed ad Hebraicae linguae amussim novissime ita recognita, et scholiis illustrata*, 6 vols. (Lyons, 1542; Frankfurt a/M: Minerva, 1972); reprinted in Lyons, 1545 and in still a third edition in the same year in 7 vols. Thus correctly, Servetus was in Geneva en route to Spanish Naples to practice medicine. Bainton, *Hunted Heretic*, 168; Barón, *Miguel Servet*, 226.

305. The identity of Alphonsus Lyncurius Tarraconensis, the self-stylized compatriot of Servetus, was long controversial. "His" only known work was the *Apologia pro Michaele Serveto* (published in 1555), accessible in *OC*, 15. 52–63. Giorgio Biandrata, in *De falsa et vera unius Dei Patris, Filii et Spiritus Sancti cognitione libri duo* (Alba Julia, 1567) E2, mentions Lyncurius as the author of a work of five chapters, *De uno Deo et unico eius filio*. On the strength of this note, the name "Lingurius" appeared in *BAnt*, 40. Celio Secundo Curione has been thought to be the author, also Laelius Socinus. The author of the *Apologia* now appears to have been Matteo Gribaldi, n. 365. See discussion and the later literature in my *La Reforma Radical*, 688–89 and n. 16, and esp. Rotondò, ed. Sozzini, *Opere*, 311–30.

306. The inset listing with introductory sentence is copied from the "Lyncurius" preface to Servetus's *Declaratio Jesu Christi filii Dei*.

The Latin MS of the *Declaratio* is in the Württemburg Archives in Stuttgart (A 66, B 25). A copy of it is in the Roland Bainton Papers, Sterling Library, Yale University. He was not able to use it for his biography of Servetus (1953). Stanisław Kot sought to identify the whole *Declaratio* of "Lyncurius" as the work of Servetus, "L'Influence de Michel Servet sur le mouvement antitrinitarien en Pologne et en Transylvanie," in Bruno Becker, ed., *Autour de Michel Servet*, 86. It is now proposed that the author of the *Declaratio* was not Servetus, as Kot had thought, but Gribaldi. Curione merely provided the work with a preface. In the preface possibly Antonio Curione listed other works in MS known to him. The *Declaratio* with Curione's preface spread through Poland in manuscript, one of the many "Sermones," prepared by "Servetus" and to a large extent known to Curione and specifically mentioned by him in his preface. Lubieniecki, for his list of prospective "discourses," had at hand one of those MS copies of the *Declaratio*, current among the Polish Brethren, including one of them in his *Historia*, at n. 312. The exact list from Curione's preface is printed by Kot, ''Michel Servet,'' 144; Barón, *Miguel Servet*, 320; Rotondò, ed. Sozzini, *Opere*, 313.

307. This is precious testimony. Besides the Servetian items of nn. 302 and 306, Lubieniecki would probably have had *Dialogorum de Trinitate libri duo*, bound with *De institia regni Christi* (Hagenau, 1532; reprinted, Frankfurt a/M: Minerva, 1965), translated by Carl M. Wilbur, ''Treatises on the Trinity.''

Lubieniecki would not have had access to *Restitutio Christianismi* (Vienna, 1553). Only three copies escaped the Inquisition in Lyons: in Edinburgh, Paris, and Vienna. The original was newly printed by von Murr (Nuremberg, 1790), reprinted (Frankfurt a/M: Minerva, 1966). Bainton, *Hunted Heretic*, 166–67; 221–22.

308. These three propositions are stated at the beginning of Servetus's *De Trinitatis erroribus*.

309. Servetus was a kind of Monophysite. He held to a variant of the doctrine of the celestial flesh of Christ. See next n. and further, *Radical Reformation* chap. 11. There is no trace of this doctrine among the Polish Brethren or Transylvanian Unitarians.

310. In Servetus's Triadology there was God the Father, the Word, and the Spirit. Together the last were the two hands of God. *Restitutio*, 694–95, 698. Friedman, *Servetus*, makes this basic to his clarifying chap. 5, where he points out that the Word gives structure to the world, while the Spirit is poured out only on human beings. Jesus, only borne by Mary, took nothing of her characteristics, for the Messiah was sired through the ministry of the Spirit by God the Father in a quasi-physical fashion so that the Saviour has the substance of the Father.

311. For Lubieniecki the prelates were Calvin and the Swiss and other divines he consulted before the trial of Servetus. But Servetus was also concurrently tried *in absentia* in Lyons.

312. This ''Discourse'' is the fourth of the ''Sermones'' of ''Servetus,'' as enumerated by ''Lyncurius'' in his preface to the *Declaratio* (n. 304). Lubieniecki, misled by the term ''sermo,'' perhaps also mindful of the statement of Faustus Socinus that Servetus, being led to the stake, refused to call Christ the eternal Son of God, but called him Son of the eternal God, was prompted to set forth the ''Sermo'' as a speech of Servetus from the pyre. Cf. Wilbur, *Socinianism*, 180–81. The ''Discourse,'' taken from Lubieniecki, was reprinted H. van Allwoerden, *Historia Michaelis Serveti* (Helmstedt, 1727) 131–38, and by Johann Lorenz Mosheim, *Anderweitiger Versuch einer Ketzergeschichte* (Helmstedt, 1748) 451–56; translated into English by Richard Wright, *Apology for Servetus* (1808) 244–55. In his introduction to the document, Mosheim was quite certain that it was not from Servetus or from anyone who knew his theology well. Lyncurius may have been Matthew Gribaldi (n. 305, 306). There is a pertinent reference to him in Bk. 3, near n. 509.

313. The exact Nicene formulation would be *substantia*; in the course of scholastic and Reformation thought *substantia* (Greek: *ousia*) was also rendered *essentia* and less frequently *natura*. Notably IV Lateran, 1215, in the canon *Firmiter* against Joachim of Fiora in support of Petrus Lombardus, declared: ''tres quidem personae, sed una essentia, substantia seu natura simplex omnino.'' Heinrich J. D. Denzinger and successors, *Enchiridion symbolorum, definitionum et declarationum de rebus fidei et morum* (Freiburg, 1932) 17. 188. Subsequent editions preserve the sequential numbering.

314. Vergil in *Eclogue* 1. 6–8, says: ''O Meliboee, deus nobis haec otia fecit; namque erit ille mihi semper deus'' and explains this god further in lines 42ff.

315. Cicero of P. Lentulus Spinther says in *Oratio post reditum ad Quirites (Oratio*

cum populo gratais egit) 5.11: ''. . . P. Lentulus consul, parens, deus, salus nostrae vitae, fortunae, memoriae, nominis. . . .''

316. ''Servetus'' quotes correctly Exod 21:6, instead of Exod 22:28 which also refers to gods or judges.

317. Correctly: Exod 22:29.

318. The use of *autographum* here makes it probable that Lubieniecki is not transcribing from Budziński's MS History of 1593 but from his own MS copy. Cf. n. 307.

319. The text has incorrectly Heb 1:8.

320. The Author or his source incorrectly gives Wis 24:16.

321. The Author refers evidently to the Greek Orthodox and the Catholics but his point is unclear or even wrong. Could this be evidence of a Polish Armenian source? There was an Armenian cathedral in Lwów.

322. The text has incorrectly Eph 1:22 – 23, and adds *piety*.

323. Although purporting to be the words of Servetus, the *florilegium* of texts suggests the hermeneutical contouring of the age of Faustus Socinus, who paid particular attention to Hebrews 1 and esp. v. 3 that seems to place the atoning act in heaven standing up, wherupon Jesus Christ is ''begotten this day'' and takes his seat at the right hand of Majesty.

324. Cf. John 5:23.

325. The Author feels comfortable in his swift transition, because he is confident that he has transcribed the ''sermon'' of ''Servetus'' from the pyre (n. 312).

326. Mark 3:14; Luke 9:52 – 56.

327. The letter to Simon Sulzer, minister in Basel, is dated 9 September 1553; *OC*, 14, no. 1790, cols. 610 – 14.

328. The Author quotes here from *Joannis Calvini epistolae et responsa* (Geneva, 1575); *OC*, 15, col. 614.

329. Guillaume Farel (d. 1565), student of Jaques d'Étaples, introduced the Reformation at Neuchâtel, 1530, and at Geneva, 1535. He was responsible for bringing Calvin to Geneva.

330. Writing in Geneva to Farel in the same, Calvin is referring to messengers to the German Swiss.

331. Calvin to Farel, 26 October 1553; *OC*, 14, no. 1839, col. 657.

332. In an earlier letter to Farel of 20 August 1553, Calvin had said that while he desired capital punishment, he desired that Servetus not undergo ''poenae vero atrocitatem.'' *OC*, 14, no. 1772, col. 590. Lubieniecki appears to have read this phrasing alluded to in parentheses.

333. Farel to Calvin, 8 September 1553; *OC*, 14, no. 1792, cols. 612 – 14.

334. These letters, numbered as in the edition of 1575, are here adduced in nn. 331 and 332.

335. *Joannis Calvini Vita a Theodoro Beza* was originally attached to Calvin's *Commentary on Joshua* published posthumously, Geneva, 1564. This *Vita* was prefixed to the edition of Calvin's letters, 1575, used by Lubieniecki. See n. 328; and in the *Vita*, *sub* 1553. The *Vita* is available in English, T. F. Torrance, ed., *Calvin's Tracts and Treatises*, 3 vols. (Edinburgh, c. 1958) 1.

336. *Theodori Bezae Epistola ad Clarissimum et ornatissimum virum D. Andream Duditium* (Geneva, 28 June 1570); Théodore de Bèze, *Correspondance*, 11 vols. to date (Geneva: Droz, 1960 –), 11, no. 780, pp. 168 – 85. Andreas Dudith (d. 1589), successively bishop of three Hungarian sees (Knin, Csánad, Pécs), would become in 1565 per-

manent ambassador of Emperor Maximilian to the Polish Court, patron of the Minor Church, correspondent of Faustus Socinus. See above at n. 58 and further *Historia, 222ff.*

337. Hugo Grotius (de Groot = Great), (d. 1645), was a Remonstrant, much esteemed by the Polish Brethren, although he wrote against Faustus Socinus on the Atonement. *Polish Brethren*, Document X.

338. *Non inveni.*

339. Calvin, *Defensio orthodoxae fidei Serveto*; see n. 291.

340. Beza, *De haereticis a civili magistratu puniendis libellus, adversus Martini Bellii farraginem et novorum academicorum sectam* (Geneva, 1554). "Martinus Bellius" was the pen name of Sébastien Castellio/Châteillon, *De haereticis, an sint persequendi et omnino quomodo sit cum eis agendum* (Magdeburg/Basel, 1554), tr. in extensive excerpt by Roland Bainton, *Concerning Heretics, whether they are to be persecuted and how they are to be treated*, with related documents (New York, 1935).

341. Matt 22:37–40, etc., and cf. Lev 19:18.

342. The reformers, respectively of Zurich and Basel (Bk. 1, nn. 105–6), both died in 1531 and therefore had nothing to say about Servetus in 1553. Oecolampadius was perhaps more tolerant than Zwingli, who was severe on Balthasar Hubmaier and other Anabaptists.

343. Matt 5:44.

344. Jude 15.

345. Matt 18:17.

346. Calvin, *Commentarii integri in Acta Apostolorum*, 20, ß28 (in the Geneva edition of 1584), 210: "neque tamen imaginanda nobis est duplicis naturae confusio ... qualem Hispanicus canis Servetus hoc tempore fabricavit" ("we must not imagine a confusion of the two natures ... which the Spanish dog, Servetus, has at this time invented").

347. Lubieniecki had a copy.

348. Lismanino's copy has the following distich:

> Cur tibi Calvine canis? tuus efficit ardor
> Ne canis heu dicar, sed miseranda civis.

The copy was given by Lismanino to Jerzy Schomann. Benedykt Wiszowaty, the editor of Lubieniecki's *Historia*, copied the distich and may have inserted it in the present text. S. Kot, "Michel Servet," 91 (see n. 306).

349. Daniel Chamier (d. 1621) was a Reformed logician. The quotation is from his *Panstraticae Catholicae*, 4 vols. (Geneva, 1626) II: *De Deo et Dei Cultu: De Sancta Trinitate*, I, v 4. 18.

350. Ibid., II, I, 4, ß 20. 13.

351. Giovanni Valentino Gentile (c. 1520–66), a disciple of Gribaldi, was a major questioner of the received doctrine of the Trinity, a second Servetus as to his martyrdom, and a reviver of ancient Tritheism as to doctrine.

Early sources for the life and martyrdom are Théodore de Bèze, ed. *Valentini Gentilis teterrimi haeretici impietatis ac triplici perfidiae et periurii brevis explicatio, ex actis publicis Senatus Genevensis optima fide descripta* (Geneva, 1567) and Benedetto Arezzo (Benedicturs Aretius), *Valentini Gentilis iusto capitis supplicio Bernae affecti brevis historia* (Geneva, 1587). From Arezzo's *Historia* it is known that in Lyons Gentile published the (lost) *Antidota*, dedicated to Sigismund II. In it he assailed Calvin's

Triadology in the *Institutes* of 1550 and appealed to [Pseudo-]Ignatius, Justin Martyr (from whom he properly withdrew the Ἐκθέσις), Tertullian, and Hilary of Poitiers, *Historia, 11, 42*.

Budziński had access to a MS copy of the *Liber Antidotorum*, perhaps that of Biandrata, and summarizes it more fully than does Lubieniecki, *BAnt*, 27.

The Tritheism of Gentile was structurally and terminologically quite different from the Triadology of Servetus, who had idiosyncratically sought to reaffirm the received doctrine of the Trinity in terms congenial to the Renaissance. His Triadology sought to preserve an intradeical Trinity not merely an economic Trinity. In his Christology Gentile thought of the flesh of Christ as issuing from the divine Seed introduced into the blood system of the Virgin through the ear (on the manner of conception, the view also of Menno Simons). The Tritheism had none of the complications of Servetus's view, and more than it could appeal to post-Nicene was well as ante-Nicene Fathers. Tritheism was worked out in Christian antiquity by Monophysite John Philoponus, commentator on Aristotle in the sixth century. In Tritheism the Three divine Persons differ also as to substance in descending degrees of potency from Father to Holy Spirit. The philosophical basis of medieval Tritheism was Nominalism, first associated with Roscellinus. Of the three most original Romance recasters of the doctrine of the Trinity, Servetus, Gribaldi, and Gentile, only Gentile was briefly in Poland, n. 359. The tritheist phase in Polish Reformed thought on the way to Unitarianism owes probably more than is commonly stated to Gentile. His use of Semi-Arian Pseudo-Ignatius of fourth-century Antioch probably gave circulation to this ancient testimony.

On how Lubieniecki himself understood the term *Trideitae*, as he has it (consistently translated Tritheists), see *Historia, 170*, esp. at n. 122 in Bk. 3.

See especially T. R. Castiglione, "Valentino Gentilis antitrinitario calabrese del XVI secolo," *Archivo storico per la Calabria e Luciana*, 8 (1938) 109ff.; 9 (1939) 41ff.; 14 (1945) 101ff.; idem, "Valentino contro Calvino: Il processo del 'secondo Serveto' nel 1558, a Genevra," in Ludwik Chmaj, ed., *Studia nad Arianizmem* (Warsaw, 1959) 49–71; idem, "La 'Impietas Valentini Gentilis' e il corrucio di Calvino," in Delio Cantimori, ed., *Ginevra e l'Italia* (Florence, 1959) 149–76. See also Wilhelm Niesel, "Zum Genfer Prozeß gegen Valentino Gentilis," *ARG*, 26 (1929) 270ff. For his career, especially in Poland, see Hein, *Italienische Protestanten*, 169–84.

352. The Author has *but* instead of *for* to smooth out a long sentence in which his attitude toward Chamier is obscured. Chamier, a moderate Calvinist, was critical of his own group and showed that in some instances the Catholics were more humane. Lubieniecki was so anti-Catholic and anti-Calvinist that he was ill at ease with Chamier's concession and comparison.

353. Giovanni Paolo Alciati Della Motta (c. 1520–73/81) probably went to Poland as early as the middle of 1561. He lived with Prospero Provana on his arrival. See Marek Wajsblum, "JA," *PSB*, Domenico Sella, "GA," *DBI*, (1960) 68; 353, I.56–57, Hein, *Italienische Protesten*, pp. 169ff. For Alciati and Gentile conferring with pious Poles, see n. 359; for his later life, Bk. 3. n. 2, 392.

354. The Author used, among other sources, Calvin, *Epistolae* (1575), the letters under the years 1558 and 1561. The account is skewed by the impatience of the Author to put several parts of a complicated life into parentheses.

Gentile fled from Geneva in 1558 and for a time dwelt with Gribaldi in Farges, then in Lyons and Grenoble. In 1561, on his return journey to Farges, he was arrested by Simon Wurstenberg, bailiff of the land of Gex, subject of Bern. (Wurstenberg was successively bailiff of Moudon, 1551, Gex, 1557, and Baden, 1569, and thrice member of the Little

Council of Bern and died in 1577.) Wurstenberg required him to set forth his views on the Trinity in an extant MS *Confessio* (see n. 355). Freed by Wurstenberg, Gentile returned to Lyons, but there persecuted by authorities, he went to Poland (1562) (nn. 359 and 62). After the edict of Parczów, 1564, against foreign heretics Gentile went to Moravia. In 1566 he returned to Switzerland, where he was arrested by Wurstenberg, tried in Bern, and decapitated, 10 September 1566. See Friedrich Trechsel, *Die protestantischen Antitrinitarier*, I.331ff. and 355ff.

355. Valentino Gentile, *Domini Jesu Christi servi de uno Deo, de unius Dei Filio et de Spiritu Sancto Paracleto catholica et apostolica Confessio* (''Antwerp,'' 1561). The *Confessio* concludes with annotations on the Athanasian Creed. it was printed in Lyons through the effort of Paolo Alciati but does not survive as an imprint. However, the original MS survives in the Bern Archives, printed by Trechsel, *Die protestantischen Antitrinitarier* 2.372–79, along with the item in n. 356. Calvin used the slightly variant printed text. On this, see Hein, *Italienische Protestanten* 170, n. 243.

356. This is the *Piae et doctae in Symbolum Athanasii adnotationes*, printed along with the *Confessio* in Lyons and reproduced by Trechsel, *Die protestantischen Antitrinitarier* 2.480–86.

The Bern MS, Codex 122 has a second appendix to the *Confessio*, ''Euisdem protheses theologiae,'' *Die protestantischen Antitrinitarier*, 2.48ff. Gentile's critique of Triadology is admirably clarified by Hein, *Italienische Protestanten* 169–84, who uses also the MS ''Protheses.''

357. The ''I'' here may be Budziński. This paragraph, the preceding, and the next are closely related to quotations from Budziński's History, chap. 27, converted into Latin in *BAnt*, 26–27. In the second paragraph of this unit Lubieniecki acknowledges quoting or paraphrasing Budziński.

358. This is an accurate quotation, cast, however, in indirect discourse, from Calvin's *Impietas Valentini Gentilis breve scripta detecta et palam traducta* (Geneva, 1561). This was a refutation of Gentile's ''Protheses.'' See *OC*, 9, cols. 375, Thesis 10. Hein (*Italienische Protestanten* 172, n. 245) observes that in reaction from Gentile's levels of divine potency, Calvin reasserts insistently here and in the *Institutes* (1559; 1.13.25) the unity of the divine substance/essence expressly against Gentile: ''una essentia, substantia seu natura quaedam'' – all three persons unbegotten, as with Peter Lombard. Luther, not having been so challenged, differentiated within the *Summa res* of Lombard a begetting and being begotten and expressly sided in 1544 with Joachim of Flora against Lombard. (Werke 39:2, p. 287)

359. There were synods in Pińczów, 4 November (14 November: Gregorian dating) and in Cracow 14 November (24: Gregorian dating) 1562. In Sipayłło, *AS* 2.141–43, there is no record of Gentile's presence or to the discussion of his ''confession.'' Nor does Stanisław Sarnicki mention Gentile in his nearly identical letters to Calvin and Bullinger of 6 November (Julian) 1562, *OC* 19, nos. 3873 and 3874. But Sarnicki does mention him, Gribaldi, and Alciati with many more in the letter of approximately the same date to Krzysztof Trecy (d. 1591), rector of the Reformed school in Cracow, with the inscription, ''Historia perturbati status polonicarum ecclesiarum propter introductum Servetianismum,'' *OC* 19, no. 3875, esp. cols. 576, 580, sufficient to confirm the doctrinal phrasing at Pińczów reported by Lubieniecki on the basis of Budziński. The nearly identical Latin transcription of Budziński on Gentile at Pińczów, 4 November 1562, is preserved in *BAnt*, 26: that ''Deum creavisse in latitudine aeternitatis, Spiritum quendam excellentissimum, qui postea in plenitudine temporis incarnatus est (MS, chap. 27).''

The formulation of Budziński in *BAnt* and Lubieniecki about the ''Spiritum quendam excellentissimum incarnatum'' is Paulinian/Samosatene. Gustave Bardy in his *Paul de Samosate* (Bruges, 1923) has a useful chapter 3, ''Souvenir de Paul de Samosate dans les temps modernes,'' with special attention to Servetus, Socinus, and the Polish Unitarians (pp. 491 – 515), a chapter not included in the revised edition of 1929.

Wiszowaty in *BAnt*², pp. 26, 42 adds two items about Gentile, namely that Stanisław Lutomirski wrote a *Scriptum*, ''De adventu Valentini Gentilis et Pauli Alciati in Poloniam,'' that ''when he was a *Trinitarius* he had, c. 1562, a colloquy with Gentile concerning God, his Son coeternal, and the Holy Spirit but had heard nothing impious from his lips,'' and also, not directly related, ''that he wrote a letter to Jakub Sylvius in which he admonished him to present reason for his faith before the church as not being immune to the errors of Stancaro.'' Gentile had evidently served as a counterpoise to Stancaro.

There was an ''ecclesiola italica'' at Pińczów, according to Lismanino in his letter to Johann Wolph of 27 April 1563, wherein he also mentions both Ochino and Gentile. See Wotschke, *Briefwechsel*, 277.178 – 80, esp. 179; Caccamo, *Eretici*, 93. The authoritative presence of Gentile as an observer at a Polish synod seems plausible.

360. Although Lubieniecki is following Budziński closely, this historical assessment would appear to be his own and it is not necessarily made in approval of Arius, from whom, as the traditional archheretic, the Polish Brethren commonly worked to dissociate themselves. Yet Lubieniecki has already favorably mentioned Arius (*Historia, 6, 7, 10*) and he clearly approves of Justin and Lactantius, both of whom subordinated the Logos/premundane Son to God the Father.

361. The preknowledge of the Messiah or the preexistence of Christ in the mind of God was an ancient rabbinical and an early Christian view represented in several primitive Christologies.

362. Johann Sylvanus (d. 1572, n. 364) from the Tyrol was not superintendent of Heidelberg, but rather of Kaiserslautern, later of Laudenburg. The main source for Sylvanus, Vehe-Glirius (n. 364), and Adam Neuser (n. 364) in the Heidelberg episodes is edited by Hans Rott, ''Neue Quellen für eine Aktenrevision des Prozeßes gegen Sylvan und seine Genossen,'' *Neues Archiv für die Geschichte der Stadt Heidelberg*, 8 – 9 (1910 – 11); W. Seeling, ''Johannes Sylvanus, Matthias Vehe als Pfarrer in Kaiserslautern,'' *Blätter für pfalzische Kirchengeschichte*, 32 (1963) 134 – 45; C. Horn, ''Johann Sylvan und die Anfänge des Heidelberger Antitrinitarianismus,'' *Neue Heidelberger Jahrbücher*, 17 (1913) 236 – 50; see also further Wilbur, *Socinianism*, 259 – 66; Róbert Dán, *Matthias Vehe-Glirius: Life and Work of a Radical Antitrinitarian with his Collected Writings*, Studia Humanitatis, 4 (Budapest/Leiden: Hungarian Academy of Sciences/Brill, 1982) 15 – 34. See also Plate 43 and 44.

Lubieniecki's assertion that Sylvanus was a tutor of Frederick III the Pious of the Palatinate is not supported by his biographers. Cf. *ADB*, 37.385 – 86.

363. The argument of the Jewish multitude to Pontius Pilate, John 19:12.

364. Of a triumvirate of radically Reformed in the Rhine Palatinate, Lubieniecki gives here the names of two only, Sylvanus (n. 362) and Neuser, omitting the most important Matthias Vehe-Glirius. Of Adam Neuser (d. 1576) Lubieniecki writes again, Bk. 3, n. 381, while his chapter 11 on Transylvania can only be understood in relation to the radically Judaizing role there of Vehe-Glirius.

Matthias Vehe-Glirius (c. 1540 – 90) was a Judaizing Christian Hebraist of the Palatinate, influential in Transylvania, Poland, Lithuania, and East Frisia under at least five names. Robert Dán includes major documents in his biography and theological analysis, *Matthias Vehe-Glirius*, with 8 of his writings, including his autobiographical Apologia, and a facsimile edition of a major work published by him under the name of Elias [Elijah] Nathanael [the true Israelite praised by Jesus, John 1:45 – 51], *Mattanjah* [Gift of God/ Gift necessary to understand God], *das ist, Ein kurtzes unnd nutzliches schreiben sehr notwendig einem jeden Christen der die lust und lieb zur warheit hat zulesen, dan in im viel und mancherlei stuck und puncten, die ware Christliche Religion aus der Bibel recht zu finden, sehr notwendig in dieser itziger zeit da mancherlei Lehr unnd secten sich erheben, aus Hailiger geschrifft grundlich tractirt werden* (Dansenbrugk [probably Cologne], 1578), discussed by Dán in chap. 3, esp. p. 67.

Sylvanus, Neuser, and Vehe-Glirius should first be seen in the evolution of Protestantism in the Rhine Palatinate and in the context of the confessional and political role of the Palatinate within the Empire and in the cause of pan-European Protestantism and particularly of European Calvinism. Of the seven lay and spiritual Electors of the Emperor, the Elector palatine stood next in dignity to the elected King/Emperor. The Lutheran Elector palatine, Otto Henry, had been foremost in demanding Protestant rights in the Imperial Diet of 1556/57, although he and the other Lutheran princes and imperial cities had agreed to the Peace of Augsburg, 1555, whereby Protestants had renounced any alteration in the religious status of ecclesiastical territories (*Reservatio ecclesiastica*). Mostly at issue was whether the concession of Ferdinand had the force of the treaty, the *Declaratio Ferdinandea*, which permitted nobles and cities within ecclesiastical territories to practice Protestantism. The new Elector palatine, Frederick III (1559 – 76), espousing Calvinism as of 1562, became the proponent of militant pan-European Protestantism against the Holy League and eventually sought in the Cologne War to Protestantize the vast Electoral Archdiocesan territory of Cologne. The University of Heidelberg, Protestantized by Otto Henry in 1558, under Frederick rapidly became the academic center of European Calvinism. Within the University and with the Church Council and the Council of State there developed the conflict between the Antidisciplinarians, or Erastians (Thomas Erastus) and the high Calvinists on sacramental discipline and the role of the Church as coordinate with the government of the Palatinate. Sylvanus, Neuser, and Vehe-Glirius were among the low Calvinists or Erastians. Claus-Peter Clasen, *The Palatinate in European History 1555 – 1618* (Oxford: Blackwell, 1963).

Sylvanus, born in the Tyrol and serving as superintendent in Laudenburg, was under pressure in 1567 to comply with the request of Wenzeslaus Zuleger of the palatine Church Council and of the Dutch court preacher Petrus de Berghen (Dathenus) to refute Antitrinitarianism on a scriptural basis. Zuleger and Dathenus were responding to a synodal delegation from Poland made up of the historian of the Czech Brethren, Jan Łasicki (d. after 1599; Bk. 3, n. 314) and Krzysztof Trecy, rector of the school in Cracow. Łasicki had been on earlier like mission c. 1564/65. Some Antidisciplinarians had evidently already become Antitrinitarian, partly on the basis of agitation in Heidelberg from Italian and Eastern European students, notably one or two Polish and Silesian students. One of these was the (later) Polish Ditheist Stanisław Farnowski; another, Martin Seidelus who, as a teacher in the middle school, was expelled for doubting the authority of the New Testament and would end up as a disputant with Socinus, holding that even in the Old Testament only the Decalogue is valid as the true revelation of God. On this see Dán, *Vehe-Glirius*, 176 – 77.

The Polish emissaries had originally stopped off in Geneva and were advised to proceed to Heidelberg. These Poles, just as Péter Méliusz of Debrecen (n. 709) from an earlier concerted attempt, had been disappointed in the requested defense of the Trinity and of the divinity of Christ by Josias Simler, *De aeterno Dei filio Domino et servatore nostro Jesu Christo adversus veteres et novos Antitrinitarios* (Zurich, 1568), as they felt it was not sufficiently grounded in the Hebrew Bible and that it depended too much on *patrum consilia*. The lost terms and assessment is from Matthias Vehe-Glirius himself namely, in his Apologia (c. 1570), first edited from the Zurich MS by Hans Rott (1910) and reprinted by Dán, *Vehe-Glirius*, text 7, 271 – 87, specifically 280; discussed by Dán, pp. 24 – 25, who dates it c. 1590, p. 12, n. 1. The scholarly Sylvanus, at the time of the visit from the Polish delegation suspect in the Antidisciplinary or Erastian controversy, felt obliged to comply with the Heidelberg request. Vehe-Glirius professed not to know where his superintendent got all his books from "Adam Pastors Volk," Apologia, 280 – 81 and 285, a curious and yet insistent phrasing. Vehe-Glirius goes so far as to speak of the books brought from Poland for scrutiny and refutation as having been those of "Adam Pastor's people."

Adam Pastor, born in Dorpen in Westphalia (c. 1510), laid down the Catholic priest-hood in 1533, joining the Anabaptists, probably at Münster, for he was one of Jan Bockelson's emissaries, but he converted to the pacifistic cause of Menno Simons by whom he was ordained an elder c. 1543 and became active in Lübeck. He entered into controversy with the Jorist Nikolaas van Blejsdijk in Lübeck in 1546, and was present at conferences in Emden and Goch in 1547 with Menno present. In Lübeck in 1552 he debated against Menno on the deity of Christ and the Trinity and was excommunicated by him for his *Underscheit tusschen rechte leer unde falsche leer der twistigen articulen*. The last is edited with introduction by Samuel Cramer, *Bibliotheca Reformatoria Neerlandica*, 5 (The Hague, 1909) 361 – 81, along with *Disputation van der Godheit des Vaders, des Soens unde des hilligen Geistes*, and an excellent introduction, 317 – 59. See also *BAnt*, 38 – 40; Wilbur, *Socinianism*, 40 – 48; but Vehe's testimony in the Apologia alone places Adam Pastor and "his people" in Poland and even Hungary on an international plane of influence. cf. RD 1, n. 10.

It is not wholly clear how the scholarly Sylvanus and his associates became Antitrinitarian under impact of reading the books of "Adam Pastor's people" and books known to have been sent also by Biandrata, as Bullinger learned, 1 September 1570; but when the radical triumvirate set off on 10 July 1570 to meet Gáspár Békés, as a Unitarian and the delegate to the Imperial Diet of Speyer for King John Sigismund, they were seeking to prepare the way for the emigration of Antidisciplinarian (Antitrinitarian) ministers like themselves in the Rhine Palatinate to serve among the Saxons in Transylvania. Neuser, Sylvanus, and Vehe established contact with the Transylvanian envoy Gáspár Békés, a major patron of Ferenc Dávid (Bk. 3, n. 387, ¶3). They gave him letters to the Sultan and to Dr. Biandrata that alleged that many princes and theologians of Germany sided with the Unitarians and Muslims in their teaching about God. When Emperor Maximilian II refused to give his daughter in marriage and to conclude an alliance with John II Sigismund of Transylvania on the pretext that all his people denied the Trinity, the unitarian envoy Békés surrendered these letters to show good faith. The Emperor in turn handed them over to Elector Frederick III who had no choice but to institute proceedings. Neuser was arrested but escaped (n. 380) Sylvanus, on the opinion of the Heidelberg divines, was sentenced to death and beheaded 23 December 1572, (Bk. 3, n. 380). Vehe, after sojourning in Cologne and elsewhere, learning more Hebrew from the rabbis and publishing there his *Mattanjah*, (¶2) arrived by way of Poland in Transylvania, 1578 (Bk. 3, n. 593).

365. Gribaldi died in his manor of Farges in September, 1564. Born of a patrician family in Chieri near Turin, professor of jurisprudence in Padua in 1548 – 55, he had come to Geneva where he got into difficulty with Calvin because of his sympathy with Servetus. He proceeded to Tübingen where he had been invited to become professor of

jurisprudence. See Wilbur, *Socinianism*, 214–23. He may have been the author of the Binitarian *sermo* presented by Lubieniecki at n. 312.

366. The writing has not been identified. What is here reported by Lubieniecki sounds like Gribaldi, when not under constraint. See preceding note. In the Polih context the formulation here attributed to Griblaldi would be high Tritheism. However, the known *confessiones* extracted from Gribaldi under duress are all more or less consonant with Reformed formulations, "Carissimi in Cristo Iesu fratelli," September, 1554, *OC*, 15, no. 2018, cols. 246–48; *Confessio* in Geneva, with copy in Zurich, 7 November 1555 (date: 7 Idus Nov., supplied by Trechsel, *Die protestantischen Antitrinitarier*, 2.461, from unidentified source), *OC*, 15, no. 2341, cols. 855–57; and *Professio fidei* in Bern, September 1557 where he expressly denied holding to three distinct subordinate deities, *OC*, 16, no. 2719, cols. 636–38. He is the author of the *Apologia* for Servetus, n. 305.

367. The Author has in mind the premundane existence of the Logos/Son (John 1:1) and of (Jesus) Christ the Mediator (1 Tim 2:5). The Church Fathers commonly understood the Logos/Son philosophically without the anthropomorphic lineaments of the incarnate Logos. All Reformation divines, eschewing philosophical terminology when they could, in connecting John 1:1 to Christ the Mediator, spoke of a preexistent Christ in ways often guarded against by the Fathers.

368. Cf. at n. 367. The epistles of Alciati to Grzegorz Paweł are not extant. Austerlitz is Slavkov. In the letters Alciati may have written favorably of Hutterite Anabaptism. On the possibility that Alciati here reflects acquaintance with Laelius Socinus on John 1, see Bk. 3, n. 531, ¶5. On Alciati in Poland, see Bk. 3, n. 2.

369. The *inventurum* of the text has been read as *inventum*: stopped. Lubieniecki appears to be reporting, perhaps on the basis of Budziński's letter collection or History, evidence that Gentile encouraged Grzegorz to consider Muslim Christology, Jesus the Virgin-born Prophet. The text could also be rendered: "he [Gentile] had preferred Mohammedanism to this [trinitarian] doctrine, but this was contrived by Calvin...." The Author perhaps reflects only what is excerpted from the *De falsa et vera cognitione Dei*, lib. 11, cap. 6, in *BAnt*, 27. From this work of the ministers of Sarmatia and Transylvania (Alba Julia, 1567), Lubieniecki could have known of Gentile's interest in the Latin Koran of Zurich.

370. The Author presumably refers to Elijah's slaying the priests of Baal after his contest with them on Mount Carmel, 1 Kgs 18:40.

371. Jerome wrote *Homilia in Psalmos*, edited only in 1897, and *Breviarium in Psalmos*. A few phrases like those Lubieniecki appear in *PL*, 26, cols. 834–37, including references to heretics, but the passage and the main points are not there. The passage must be a false attribution. Cf. n. 374.

372. *Non inveni*.

373. *Non inveni*. To give over to fire would not have occurred to Jerome as punishment for either a crime or a heresy.

374. This Anti-Donatist work was written c. 406, *PL*, 43, col. 526, cap. 50:55. Lubieniecki may well have gotten the passage from a collection, but the Polish Brethren were interested in Augustine's writings on rebaptism, the general problem of *liber* 3. As for the Fathers mentioned by Lubieniecki below, he adduces them on non-coercion in matters of faith in *Vindiciae*, *Polish Brethren*, Doc. XXIX at nn. 36–37, 111–14.

375. Bernardino Ochino (1487–1564), *Historia, 2–6*, appears here as a figure in Polish history. "In review," Lubieniecki gives more details. In the preaching career of Ochino as Capucin (1534–42), his most decisive episode was in Venice in 1541, where his sermon and the reaction thereto caused him to be summoned gently but firmly to

Rome. He may earlier have been heard by Popes, surely by cardinals, but Lubieniecki seems to refer to the last encounter with the hierarchy in Italy. Ochino went no further than Bologna where he had a colloquy with the benevolent Gasparo Cardinal Contarini near death and with Pietro Martire Vermigli in Florence. Ochino was not a confessor to any Pope, nor was his confrontation with the Papacy so dramatic as here depicted. See Bainton, *Ochino*, 49 – 57.

376. It appears that Lubieniecki had at hand the second edition of *Epistolarum theologicarum Theodori Bezae Bezelii liber unus*, edited by the Author himself (Geneva, 1575), p. 330.

This epistle was addressed to all Christians upholding the dogma of the Trinity, Geneva, 5 August 1567, and served as a preface to Beza's critique of Gentile, "Christianis et orthodoxis omnibus ecclesiis in Domino nostro Iesus Christo, aeterno aeterni Patris Filio coessentiali." This extremely valuable account of the role of Italians like Laelio Sozzini, Giorgio Biandrata ("if I know him, he always has a Thesis"), and Gentile in Poland and Transylvania is critically edited in *Correspondance*, 8 (1967), Appendix III, 234 – 58, wherein the sentence quoted by Lubieniecki is on 339. The critical editor rightly observes that in the second edition of his own correspondence (that used by Lubieniecki) Beza amplified his list of specific addresses, the *pii doctores*, whom he appealed to by name toward the close of the epistolary preface at n. 107, to include, besides Łasicki, Trecy, Sarnicki, the new allies: the Magyars Petrus Melius and one Szegedinus.

The correspondence of Beza and the rich annotation of its modern editors invites a thorough exploration under the heading: "Beza and the Poles and Hungarians."

377. The text ends just this way: *Ipse scripsit*. Either Lubieniecki, Wiszowaty, or the printer allowed something to drop out. The fulle title of Ochino's *Dialogi XXX in duos libros divisi, quorum primus est de Messia . . . Secundus potissimum de Trinitate* (Basel, 1563), translated from the Italian by Sebastien Castellio. The second book was dedicated to Mikołaj Radziwiłł, palatine of Vilna. In analysing the *Dialogi* theologially with special reference to Poland, Hein describes Ochino as having a Triadology akin to that of Gentile, "emanationist-subordinationist," and finds in him a kind of Spiritualist like Caspar Schwenckfeld, op. cit. 184 – 95, esp. 190 – 91. In *Correspondance* 11 (1570) 83, n. 32, all of Beza's references to Ochino are brought together.

378. Pietro Perna was typesetter in Basel, printer of the *Dialogi* without clearing with the censor. Bainton, *Ochino*, p. 140.

379. Marcin Czechowic (1532 – 1613), born in Zbąszyn in Great Poland, studied at the Lubrański school in Poznań (c. 1549), at Leipzig (1554), and on his return (c. 1559), became a teacher in the Calvinist school in Vilna, founded by Prince Mikołaj Radziwiłł the Black. In 1561 he was Radziwiłł's envoy in Switzerland, where he was unsuccessful in his attempt to persuade Calvin and Bullinger of Biandrata's orthodoxy. After the death of Radziwiłł in 1565, Czechowic moved to Kujawy. See Lech Szczucki, *Marcin Czechowic: Studium z dziejów antytrynitaryzmu polskiego XVI wieku* (Warsaw, 1968).

380. The text has, incorrectly, 1569. Identified as an error by Szczucki, *Czechowic*, 231, n. 81.

381. The *Sed* suggest that Lubieniecki may have been truly misled by the date in his source (cf. n. 380) and comes in what follows to state another view about the itinerary of Ochino which is, however, faulty. Ochino went to Moravia from Poland, not directly from Venice.

382. The sentence has been cut here. As so often Lubieniecki tries to gather up too much before he comes to his principal point. On Sarnicki, see n. 531.

383. As for the three groupings in 1564, we know that a perceptive orthodox Calvinist, Paweł Gilowski (n. 612) writing Bullinger as of 1568, distinguished three sects or factions alongside the main body of Calvinists, in addition to the schism of Stancaro, also mentioned. See Wotschke, *Briefwechsel*, nos. 378, 290 – 93. The three are not given labels. The first "denies the eternity of Jesus Christ, the Son of God" and holds that Jesus first became the Son and the Christ at baptism. Cf. Matt 3:17 and parallels. The second group confesses that the Son is coeternal with the Father and they invoke and adore all three Persons but speak of them as *unum*, not *unus*. The third group is derived from Gentile, especially prominent in Lithuania, according to whom the Son is *essentiatus* "by a certain propagation of the wills or hearts of men."

This characterization of Gilowski of three factions of Antitrinitarians as of 1568 may be compared with that of Krzysztof Trecy to Bullinger of 1565, dealing with the Major and the Minor Church; see Wotschke, *Briefwechsel*, no. 343, esp. p. 248: the orthodox supported by the senatorial class.

The second are the *Tritheistae* or *Trideistae* or *Trinitarii*. But cf. n. 351 and Lubieniecki himself, Bk. 3 at n. 118. After a while they give way to the *Ditheistae* who hold out for the preexistence of Christ against outright Unitarianism.

The first grouping were most disposed to stress baptismal immersion on the model of Jesus at the Jordan. They were also called by the same names as the second.

The first are differently characterized by Jan Łasicki in a letter to Beza from Cracow, 30 May 1566, *Correspondance*, 7 (1566), n. 470, 107 – 10, which supersedes Wotschke, *Briefwechsel*, nos. 350, 270 – 72. However, on p. 272, n. 1, Wotschke quotes a related passage from Lublin, 31 May 1566, from Andrzej Krajewski to Hosius. On Krajewski's letter, see further n. 398.

384. There were two edicts, effective as of 1 October 1564; but their effect was much restricted to the point of nullification by 2 November 1564. Lubieniecki comes back to Parczów (Bk. 3, at n. 137). Sarnicki (on whom see more fully at n. 531) and Trecy, among the orthodox Calvinists, were conspicuous in pressing for the edicts. At this point in his narrative Lubieniecki is dealing with constitutional events in advance of his ecclesiastical and theological account.

385. Hieronim Filipowski (n. 105) was owner of Krzcięcice, where Ochino presumably stayed.

386. Ochino was by this time a widower, his plight all the more poignant.

387. Wiszowaty corrects *Slavoniae* as *Slavcoviae*, *Historia*, *306A*. Slavkov is called by its German name, Austerlitz, at n. 368. Ochino, not a Tritheist nor an Anabaptist, came nevertheless under the ban of Parczów and stayed with Niccoló Paruta. See Bainton, *Ochino*, 152 – 59.

NOTES TO CHAPTER SIX

388. In the heading, which seems not to come from Lubieniecki, reference is made to the *sententia* of Servetus, defended by Biandrata and Lismanino. Although Servetus has been given considerable prominence (*Historia*, 96 – 99), Lubieniecki expressly states his differences "from us" and it seems scarcely possible that he would have called the Minor Church "Servetian" *per sententiam*. In any case, this opinion was not expressly defended by Biandrata, who was more of a Tritheist, and surely not by Lismanino.

389. Mantuan Stancaro clearly aroused Biandrata and Lismanino. It is noteworthy that the superscriber, whether Wiszowaty or Lubieniecki, places Biandrata first, although

he has thus far been mentioned only once, *Historia, 33*, in contrast to Lismanino who has been featured. Lubieniecki himself seems to regard native Gonesius as the father of Polish/Lithuanian Unitarianism. Gonesius was born in Lithuanian Podlachia, and was minister in Węgrów, an estate of the Lithuanian magnate Jan Kiska, *tritheita et Anabaptista,* Wotschke, *Briefwechsel*, 346. Gonesius was minister there from 1558 until his death. See next n.

390. Lubieniecki here introduces Gonesius, a major figure of his narrative and of the left wing (theological and social) of the Reformation in the Commonwealth. Yet as integrated into the *Historia* as he is, Piotr [?Giezek] of Goniądz (c. 1530 – 73) was a figure apart. His ''teaching was already formed by the end of the 'fifties, and—in contrast to the view of other Polish Antitrinitarians—did not undergo fundamental evolution, although in a few small matters Piotr clearly changed his position. . . .'' (Lech Szczucki, ''Piort z Goniądza,'' *PSB* 26 (1981) 398 – 401, esp. 400A). Highly qualified philologically (Greek, Latin, and some Hebrew), Piotr was, indeed, a major figure in the radical current, but he was atypical and not wholly in the main stream of the Polish Reformed, whose participants were centrally concerned with the problem of Christ the Mediator as provocatively propounded by Stancaro. With Stancaro he is here linked in the same chapter heading, and yet who seems to have developed his conception of the Three from impulses in Gribaldi, alongside the parallel progression reflected in the *Historia* from Tritheism, through Ditheism, to Unitarianism. The next major n. on Gonesius is 624.

Gonesius studied at the University of Cracow, where in 1550 he distinguished himself by a protest against Stancaro's teachings as Hebraist. About 1551 he was sent to study at Padua by Bishop Paweł Holszański of Vilna (1536 – 55). He was a student of Gribaldi and from him learned about Servetus. In Padua Gonesius lectured in 1554 on the *Sophistics* of Aristotle. See Węgierski, *Slavonia Reformata*, 125, whose information expressly comes from the Budiński MS; W. Przałgowski, *Dzywoty biskupów wileńskich* (Petersburg, 1860) I.142; A. Riccoboni, *De Gymnasio Patavino* (Padua, 1598) 28; Józef Jaśnowski, *Piotr z Goniądza: życie, działalność a pisma* (Warsaw, 1935).

391. Lubieniecki undoubtedly draws this information about Gonesius in Moravia from his principal source, the History of Budziński, chap. 20. See Sand, *BAnt*, 41 at the end of the main paragraph. Szczucki conjectures that Gonesius might well have come into contact with Italian Hutterites while in Padua and in the circle of Gribaldi without his having come back to Lithuania by way of Moravia (*PSB*, 26.398A). Lubieniecki has Gonesius himself alluding, at least, to a visit to Moravia en route home in his speech, at n. 399. But Jan Łasicki, an authority on the Czech Brethren, in a letter (n. 399), confirms the Moravian Hutterite connection.

392. The synod in Secemin, 21 – 29 January 1556, was preceded by a synod in Pińczów 21 September 1555. Gonesius came to Secemin with letter from Prince Mikołaj Radziwiłł the Black. On the second day, 22 January, he offered a confession written by himself ''full of blasphemies against the Son of God and his glory.'' Sipayłło, *AS*, 1.47. The protocol summarizes the confession in six points. Gonesius is dismissed from the church, in the sense perhaps only of the synodal gathering, for his confession is discussed the next day. Gonesius after farewells leaves turmoiled and crying, all the brethren wishing for him a change of mind. Sipayłło, *AS* 1.47 – 48.

The speech appears to have been a reconstruction by Budziński or Lubieniecki but based on notes taken by hearers of it at the synod and reminiscences. The girding with a wooden sword (at n. 399) could not have been an invention. Towards the end there is, however, the evident anachronism of the reference to all being baptized into the Church according to the Apostles' Creed, the immersional practice of the Minor Church of

Lubieniecki himself but at issue in the days of Gonesius. The stress on salvation *sola fide* and *sola scriptura* has the ring of the onset to regional reformation but it is hard to imagine that Piotr would have been so overweening as to suggest (at n. 394) by his conversion to a radical Reformation, a status for himself and his theology in the synod comparable to that of Saul/Paul returned form Damascus.

Darek Jarmola in his dissertation conjectures that in the original speech Gonesius introduced his views on baptism, drawing on both Servetus and Gentile and cites Wiszowaty, Doc. 5, no. 53, brought into relation with n. 442 below.

393. The references to Hannibal and Carthage are noticably frequent in Lubieniecki and not always as enemy. Here, of course, it is Gonesius as preserved or reconstructed by Lubieniecki.

394. See n. 390. Gonesius is not generous to his episcopal benefactor here.

395. Gonesius in his reference to Wittenberg and Geneva is not implying his study in either place. Sand (*BAnt* 41) errs in asserting that he studied in Wittenberg. His bishop would never have been so unwise. Gonesius is here announcing his understanding of the emergent Minor Church with its Moravian Anabaptist link as a third manifestation of the Reformation, alongside Lutheran and the Reformed Church with believers' baptism a note.

396. *Non inveni*.

397. Gonesius could have many places in mind in Paul but 2 Corinthians 13–15 on deceptive apostles and servants comes close to his intent.

398. See at *Historia, 2–3, 7, 112*.

399. There is independent attestation of the *ligneus ensis* of Gonesius in the letter of Jan Łasicki to Beza, Cracow, 30 May 1566. Wotschke, *Briefwechsel*, no. 350, p. 271. On the reliability of Łasicki's letter, see Bk. 3, n. 314. On this cosmopolitan Reformed humanist and historian, see nn. 162, 383, 391. Łasicki was commissioned to help refute (cf. n. 415) the Unitarianism of Adam Neuser and Vehe (*Historia, 96, 98, etc.*).

The use of a side sword suggests that Gonesius was of the *szlachta*, although students not of that estate also wore swords. It is noteworthy that his new practice had already made him "better known *per totam patriam*" than his new theological view, which suggests that he may have been in Lithuania longer than is suggested by his sudden appearance at Secemin. In the letter, Łasicki is said to have written a book, *De magistratu*, otherwise unknown, ibid., 271, n. 5. Lech Szczucki suggested that Gonesius assimilated the pacifist ideal of the Moravian Hutterites from Italian Anabaptists in league with them, *PSB*, 26 (1981) 398–401.

Slavkov (Austerlitz) was a center of the pacifist Anabaptists. Lubieniecki refers to the place as both Austerlitz (*Historia, 109*) and Slavkov (*Historia, 111*). A major settlement of Anabaptists was in Moravia and around Mikulov (Nicolsburg) under the leadership of the Balthasar Hubmaier from Ingolstadt and Waldsburg. Among evangelical Anabaptists he was notable for upholding the legitimacy of the sword of magistracy, of war taxes in the context of the protection of the refugees by the Lord of Liechtenstein. *Radical Reformation*, chap. 9.

In the controversy over the sword, a minority of the refugees under Hubmaier had left for Slavkov in mid-March 1528. They were called by the remaining majority *Stäbler* in reference to their adoption of the staff as the outward sign of their consistent pacifism. It is quite probable that they were following the practice of the Minor Party of the Unitas Fratrum. See Peter Brock, *Social Doctrines of the Czech Brethren*. But there is no Czech quivalent of the term *Stäbler*. Although the secessionist *Stäbler* of 1528 were in the minority, they were the prototype of what would become, by 1566, the mainstream of

Anabaptism in Moravia, communitarian Hutterites. On this and on the *Stäbler* and the interrelations of German-speaking Anabaptist and the Unity, see J. K. Zeman, *Anabaptists and Czech Brethren in Moravia*. On communism and pacifism the work of Johann Loserth has value, "Der Kommunismus der mährischen Wiedertäufer," *Archiv für österreichische Geschichte*, 81 (1894) 135–322, esp. 148–49.

It is not certain whether the Hutterite *Stäbler* actually wore a wooden sword, as the members of the Minor Party of the Czech Brethren may have. The use of the wooden sword by Gonesius, the nobleman Jan Niemojewski, and others in Poland is likely to have had a Slavic Moravian model as well as the putative Germanic Hutterite one.

There were two Hutterite Bruderhofs, founded 1535–37, headed by Ulrich Stadler (d. 1540), which may have had some influence on the emerging Polish Brethren. Brixen-born Stadler, a capable theologian of Christian communism, wrote four letters from there, "Ladomir aus Podoliagen Crasnicktau auf grenzen Polen." Three of these letters, concerning the theology of the two colonies, are edited by Lydia Müller, *Glaubenszeugnisse oberdeutscher Taufgesinnter, I, Quellen und Forschungen zur Reformationsgeschichte*, 20 (1938) 228–36; for the place, 236. Ladomir would appear to be Włodzimierz in Lithuania, near the Polish border in Volhynia, Crasnicktau, to be Krasnikόw in Podolia, although it has also been taken for Kraśnik, near Lublin. The fourth letter, as yet unprinted, only in the *Geschichtsbücher* of Hutterites in Canada, is addressed "to the authorities, in Poland." Robert Friedmann, "Stadler," *The Mennonite Encyclopedia*, 4 vols. (Hillsboro, Kansas, etc. 1955–59) 4.607–8, does not print the fourth letter in *Glaubenszeugnisse*, II, *Quellen zur Geschichte der Täufer*, 12 (Heidelberg, 1967). Another writing of Stadler on the Community of Goods has been translated by me, *Anabaptist and Spiritual Writers*, The Library of Christian Classics, 25 (Philadelphia, 1957) 272–84.

For Lubieniecki the *fratres Moravi* may have included both the Hutterites and the Czech Brethren. The *denominational* as distinguished from regional sense of Moravian Brethren largely dates to the revival of the Czech (Bohemian) Brethren under Pietist Count N. L. Zinzendorf in 1722.

400. He is apologizing for taking too much of the time of the synod. The protocol shows that the whole of the day and part of the next was taken up with Gonesius's address and *confessio*.

401. In the eighth century Gregory I (590–604) the Great began to be ranked with Ambrose, Jerome, and Augustine as *doctor* of the Western Church.

402. Epistola 31, *Ad Cyriacum Episcopum*, 7; *PL*, 77, col. 889. Editor Wiszowaty has *Epistola* 38, 6.

403. Patriarch John IV the Faster (582–95) was succeeded by Cyriacus (595–607). Already in the Acacian Schism of the sixth century the bishop of Constantinople was referred to as the "Ecumenical patriarch." See *Historia, 113, 142–43 and 146*.

404. *Non inveni*.

405. *PL*, 2, col. 47. Lubieniecki or the printer carries the italics of quotation from Tertullian a sentence further into his own wording. Jerzy Miziurek, *Chrystologia Braci Polskich: Okres przedsocynianskie* (Lublin: KUL, 1983), begins his chap. 2 on the preexistence of Christ in the thought of the Brethren with a sentence further on in this speech.

406. *PG*, col. 897.

407. Deut 6:4. Eph 4:6. Gonesius is also thinking of 1 Tim 1:17.

408. In the penultimate paragraph of the speech (as here edited) it is possible to see how Lubieniecki, lacking a document, improvised a speech but not without some source. He does not acknowledge a source here; but Sand (*BAnt* 41; adduced also above, n. 395)

has a roughly parallel but fuller, though still compact account of Gonesius's doctrine expounded at Secemin, expressly drawn from the MS *Chronicon* of A. Lubieniecki. This was in Polish. The translation into Latin would account for some variations between Sand's rendition of a synodal resume and Lubieniecki's retroversion of the same Polish text into direct discourse. Other variations and omissions could be explained by Lubieniecki's preferred emphasis, since here he was dealing with Gonesius as an esteemed forerunner of the Minor Church of which he was the chronicler. A. Lubieniecki, as preserved by Sand/Wiszowaty, summarized the synodal heads against Gonesius thus (the inserted brackets being the numbering of the items stated somewhat differently in Sipayłło):

> [12] That he approved the Apostolicum but rejected the Nicene Creed and the Athanasium, [3] that the Trinity is not God and [4] that the Son of God is indeed God but less than the Father; . . . that the Son of God always showed honor to the Father and that Christ received all things from the Father . . . , and asserted that God the Father is the only true God (John 17:3); that [5] the λόγος i.e., the invisible Word immortal was changed into flesh in [the fullness] of time in the womb of the Virgin: that the invisible Word was the seed (*semen*) of the incarnate Son; that [6] he denied the [christological] *communicatio idiomatum*; that he asserted that there is only one substance or nature in Christ; especially however he opposed the consubstantiality of the Son with the Father; he said additionally, that Christ the Man was changed into God and God or the Word into Man.

It would appear that Lubieniecki rearranged this synodal record and transformed it into Gonesius's speech minus some of the points like the Monophysitism that Lubieniecki did not find congenial. It would be good if all his improvisations elsewhere in the *Historia* were as close to the original as this section, and perhaps they were.

Within the speech but not in the synodal summary is a bit of Angel Christology that Lubieniecki is not likely to have improvised and that must have stood in his source, A. Lubieniecki, not preserved by Sand either, and wholly consonant with Gonesius's understanding of the Three wholly in terms of Scripture and the Primitive Church. In the paragraph of the speech so replete with authentic reminiscences of what is likely to have been said by Gonesius is the term *Legatus*. Hilary of Poitiers, among the favorite Nicene Fathers of the Polish Brethren before they became explicitly Unitarian, could have been a remote source for the transitional revival of the very ancient Angel Christology, *De Trinitate*, 4.23; *PL*, 10, cols. 113–14 (n. 480). Therein he cited the christological prophecy of Isa 11:6: "Angel of great counsel" (LXX). Hermas of the Shepherd referred to Christ as Angel, also Justin Martyr (at n. 488). See further, Wilhelm Michaelis, *Zur Engelchristologie im Urchristentum* [against Martin Werner] (Basel, 1942).

409. Grzegorz Paweł (*Historia*, 33, 38, 48, 109), at the time pastor of the village church of Pełsznica, is listed right after Cruciger, pastor of Secemin, and superintendent. Hieronim Filipowski, once host of Ochino (at n. 385) was the elected moderator. See Sipayłło, *AS* 1.46.

410. The letter presumably of January 1556 is probably lost. That Gonesius was entrusted with it is notable. This may be the basis of the later statement of Sand in *BAnt* (n. 395) that Gonesius studied in Wittenberg.

Lubieniecki's summary, presumably, of the synodal letter to Melanchthon sets forth a position more extreme (that God died) than that in the extant synodal protocol, points 4–5, Sipayłło, *AS*, 1.47; cf. A. Lubieniecki preserved by Sand, above. It is therefore likely that Lubieniecki is here quoting from a portion of the lost synodal letter as preserved by Budziński, who, as Sand acknowledges, was his source (History, ch. 20) for some related material (the Moravian visit of Gonesius) in his account, *BAnt*, p. 41.

It is of interest that as of 11 November 1556 Jan Łaski was in Wittenberg, spending a whole day with Melanchthon, who wrote to Landgrave Philip of Hesse about it, 21 November 1556. See Melanchthon, *Opera*, 8, no. 6122, cols. 91–92 and for Łaski's arrival in Wittenberg, *Annales Vitae*, 1556, p. xvi. Łaski's plan for a national synod, also prospective hazards in his return to Poland, are dealt with in the letter.

The edition of Melanchthon's letters does not include letters to him , as in the case of Calvin's *Opera*; hence the uncertainty about whether the synod's letter fo Melanchthon of 1556 is lost.

411. Eutyches (d. 454) was the Monophysite archimandrite at Constantinople who occasioned the Dyophysite (orthodox) formulation of Christ as one person in two natures at the Council of Chalcedon in 451.

412. Tertullian charged the Modalist Monarchian Praxeas with interpreting God the Father as suffering in his "mode" as Christ.

413. Juan Maldonado, S.J. (d. 1583), Spanish theologian and exegete, taught at the Sorbonne. He was cleared of the charge of heresy by the Archbishop of Paris in 1576. His works may well have entered Poland with the returning legation after their greeting of Henry of Valois in 1573. His principal work, widely popular, was *Commentaria in IV Evangelia*, 2 vols. (1556–57). He was esteemed by the Polish Brethren, *Polish Brethren*, 594, 613, 628. The Brethren may also have known by name another Juan Maldonado, vicar general of Burgos and Erasmus's letter to him (1527), lauding the young Łaski, *Epistolae*, ed. Allen, 7, no. 1805.

Lubieniecki's reference has not been tracked down. Here is the first time that Lubieniecki speaks positively of the "Arian" view and here suggests that it was the regnant view through most of the first four centuries.

414. At the synod of Pińczów of 25 April 1559 among the examined questions was "quomodo intelligant verba Christi in Cena: Hoc est corpus meum." Sipayłło, *AS*, 1.298. The index has many references to *Wieczerza Pańska* after this date. The Polish Reformed in general do not seem to have referred to the intra-Swiss debate between Zurich and Geneva, which eventuated in the *Consensus Tigurinus* of 1549, dealing primarily with the Lord's Supper and more in the sense of Calvin than Zwingli.

415. Josias Simler, *De aeterno Dei Filio Domino et Servatore nostro Jesu Christo et de Spiritu Sancto, adversus veteres et novos Antitrinitarios libri quatuor* (Zurich, 1568), fols. 27ff (n. 364, ¶5). The book had been written by Simler at the urging of Jan Łasicki and Krzysztof Trecy, commissioned by the Polish Calvinists who supplied the author with the writings of Polish and Transylvanian Antitrinitarians. The preface was written by Bullinger. Dań, *Vehe-Glirius*, 24–25, 173–76.

Here Lubieniecki has mentioned for the first time Ferenc Dávid, who comes up for special attention in Bk. 3, ch. 11. At this point the Author surely has in mind the importance of the development, partly parallel to his *Historia*, in the Principality of Transylvania. There is a fundamental note on this region, Bk. 3, n. 128.

416. Parts of the following unit, unacknowledged, come from Budziński, acknowledged by Węgierski (*Slavonia Reformata*, 229, 250). Lubieniecki would not have called Cruciger *pius* if it had not been in his source. An awkward sentence between notation 420 and 422 has been substantially reconstructed for the sake of coherence.

417. See *Historia, 30–33*.

418. The text has 1553, but this must be a printing error, as he gives the correct date on *Historia, 30*.

419. Jakub Ostroróg (c. 1516–68) (*Historia, 35–36*), *starosta generalny* of Great Poland, was the protector of the Czech Brethren and an advocate of their becoming independent of the Mother Church in Moravia and an advocate of union of the Unity of Great Poland with the emerging Reformed Church of Little Poland. His younger brother, Stanisław O. (1519–68), was protector of Lutherans. Jakub O. matriculated at the University of Leipzig in 1532 and was drawn to the Reformation. His wife, 1545, was Barbara, sister of Stanisław Stadnicki of Dubiecko and Niedźwiedź, one of the first lords in Little Poland to support the Reformation. Barbara became a convert to the Church of the Czech Brethren (Unity) who were settling near Ostroróg in 1548. In this adherence Barbara was following the lead of Katarzyna, sister of Jakub. Under the influence of the sisters Katarzyna and Barbara, Jakub participated in the celebration of worship of the Czech Brethren in his residence in Poznań.

It was as a sympathizer with the Unity that Jakub O. in June 1551 personally conveyed to his estate Feliks Cruciger, pastor at Niedźwiedź, owned by his brother-in-law Stadnicki. Maria Topolska, "J.O.," *PSB* 24 (1949) 500–2.

420. Stancaro in 1550/51 wrote *Canones reformationis Ecclesiarum Polonicarum* (Frankfurt a/0 1552). See Bk. 1, n. 243; not mentioned there is the fact that the *Canones* drew from the *Einfaltiges Bedencken* (1543) of the Archbishop Elector of Cologne, Hermann of Wied, available in excerpt in Aemilius Ludwig Richter, ed., *Die evangelischen Kirchenordnungen des 16 Jahrhunderts*, 2 (Leipzig, 1871), 2.30–54, as *Deliberatio qua ratione Christiana Reformatio instituenda sit* (Bonn, 1545), known in English as the *Didagma*, drawn upon by the compilers of the Prayer Book, *A Simple and Religious Consultation of us, Herman, by the grace of God*, Archbishop of Cologne (1548). Jan Łaski was independently influenced by tall, kindly white-haired Archbishop Hermann, Dalton, *A Lasco*, 284, 288, 304.

421. Bk. 1, n. 235, Bk. 2, n. 113.

422. Walenty's marriage as an occasion of uproar is mentioned by Lubieniecki *Historia, 34, 43*.

423. The Author confuses things. Contrary to our text, at that time Stancaro did not need any protection, since the royal decree of 12 December 1550 against the Evangelicals and the specific decree of banishment against Stancaro were virtually abolished by a decision of the Diet of Piotrków, 13 March 1552. At the seat of Ostroróg, Stancaro met Cruciger who had been living there since his escape in 1551. See n. 419. Ostroróg did not "dismiss" Stancaro, since the latter had already been called by the gentry of Little Poland in the summer of 1552. See Wotschke, "Fr. Stancaro," *Altpreussiche Monatsschrift*, 47 (1910) 475–76, 488, n. 1; 487–89.

424. As for "enmity," Stancaro goes down as much scorned in Lutheran, Calvinist, and Unitarian historiography, whether the last originated in Poland or Transylvania. Antisemitism played a role. Lismanino who shared with Stancaro in Italianiate culture, called him an *ebreo* and *miserus Judaeus*, Wotschke, *Briefwechsel*, 117. Stancaro's family may well have been of Sephardic Jewish origin, but he himself was admirably schooled in patristics, conciliar history, and scholastic theology, even though he was professionally a Hebraist, successively at Vienna, Cracow, and Königsberg.

425. Except for this diffuse allusion, Lubieniecki makes no reference here to Andreas Osiander (but see *Historia, 33*, Bk. 1, n. 256) in Germany and Ducal Prussia.

The controversy over Christ the Mediator first centered in Königsberg, eventually between Stancaro and Osiander, and at length there were repercussions beyond Ducal

Prussia in the Empire. One can distinguish a Prussian, a Polish, and a Transylvanian phase of the controversy.

Lutheran Osiander who was forced from Nuremberg by the Augsburg Interim came into Königsberg 27 January 1549 at the invitation of Duke Albert who regarded him as "Vater in Christo." His inaugural address, *De lege et evangelio* of 5 April 1549, called forth alarmed opposition from fellow Lutherans. Osiander was trying to interpret Luther's doctrine of justificaiton in such a way as to involve the Glorified Christ (fully God and fully man) in the experiential transaction of justification-sanctification in the believer's appropriation of the benefits of the atonement and this required a fresh clarification of Christ as soteriological and then also as cosmological Mediator.

In defending purely forensic justification *sola fide* Luther had eventually found a prophecy of the righteousness of Christ as that alien righteousness appropriated by faith, Jer 23:6, "The Lord is our righteousness." Osiander came to alter the forensic view with precisely this text and others, stressing the content of justification as the righteousness of Christ *according to his divinity* dwelling in the believer through faith. Osiander retained thus the fundamental Lutheran and indeed classical Protestant tenet of *sola fide* but advanced a participatory justification that went far beyond Catholic sanctification as experiential and objective holiness. As on this view the Person and divine nature of Christ were involved in justification (sanctification), the problem of Christ the soteriological, then as cosmological, Mediator emerged as a distinctive topos in which Stancaro and the Polish and the Transylvania Protestants were intensely engaged. On the issue of participatory justification, see Pelikan, *The Christian Tradition*, 4.150–52; on Christ the Mediator in Osiander, Hein, *Italienische Protestanten*, 73–78; on the whole of his life and thought, Gottfried Sebass, *Das reformatorische Werk des Andreas Osianders* (Nuremberg, 1967).

426. Obliged to leave Königsberg, Stancaro sought out old friends among the nobles in Little Poland, who esteemed him as theologian and physician, then crossed over into Upper Hungary, sojourning under the protection of Peter Petrovics at Bártfa, where he disputed with the Lutheran pastor Leonhard Stöckel over Christ the Mediator. Thereupon he was forced to betake himself to Transylvania, first to Kolozsvár, where in 1553 he debated the same issue with then Lutheran Ferenc Dávid. In Wilbur's treatment of the sources and the secondary literature there remained a discrepancy as to the chronology of Stancaro: in *Socinianism*, 298, Stancaro is reported as leaving Poland late in 1554; in *Transylvania*, 23, Stancaro is already at work in Transylvania in 1553. The earlier arrival is consonant with two venerable secondary accounts, Georg Haner "of Schässburg (Sighişoara) in Saxon Siebenbürgen," *Historia Ecclesiarum Transylvanicarum, Inde a primis Populorum originibus ad haec usque tempora* (Frankfurt/Leipzig, 1694), 222–40, and Friedrich Adolf Lampe, *Historia Ecclesiae Reformatae in Hungaria et Transylvania* (Utrecht, 1728) 106–16. The former Hermannstadt pastor and Reformation historian Karl Reinerth gives quite precise dates for Stancaro, *Die Gründung der Evangelischen Kirchen in Siebenbürgen*, Studia, Transylvania, 5 (Cologne/Vienna: Böhlau, 1979) 211 passim, fixing the date of arrival in Kolozsvár as 22 March 1553.

Stancaro was formally condemned at the synod of Ovár, 1554. He obtained a teaching post in Hermannstadt (Sibiu), where Protestantism in its Lutheran aspect was first manifest in all Transylvania in the new service of worship conducted in the home of the town councilor there, Johann Hecht, in 1520. (Stancaro had lived there before, during his first sojourn in Transylvania, 1549–50.) Expelled from Hermannstadt, he returned to Kolozsvár at the end of 1557 and was challenged by the ministers there to debate. They made use of Melanchthon's *Responsio de controversiis Stancari* (Wittenberg, 1553;

Kronstadt/Braov, 1554; Pińczów, 1559). For his part, the future Unitarian Dávid had already defended the Melanchthonian view of Christ the Mediator against him in *Dialysis scripti Stancari contra primum articulum synodi Szekiensis* (Kolozsvár, 1555). Therein Dávid coped with the syllogism of Stancaro that would evidently prepare the way for his own eventual Unitarian position but for the time being directed against the Lombardian/Stancarist Christology: "Quidquid non est minus Patre, id non potest esse Mediator. Sed *persona* Christi non est minor Patre coelesti. Ergo *persona* Christi non potet esse Mediator." The syllogism is from Stancaro's *Apologia contra Osiandrum*, as reported by Johann Wigand, *De Stancarismo* (Leipzig, 1585), 69–70, and set in the Transylvanian context by Reinerth, *Evangelische Kirchen*, 213.

In the new debate, alongside Dávid were Kaspar Helth (Gáspár Heltai) and Matthias Hebler. Stancaro prepared a stinging assault upon them and their distant mentor Melanchthon, in which passages from Augustine's *Contra sermonem Arianorum* (*PL, 42*) were arranged over against Melanchthonian statements, as *Collatio doctrinae Arrii et Philippi Melanchthonis...et reliquorum Saxonum doctrinae de Filio Dei, Domino nostro Jesu Christo una est et eadem*, 1559. For the Transylvanian context and Dávid's role, see Bk. 3, n. 129. Smarting from defeat, Stancaro boldly addressed Isabelle Jagiellonka to order her council of state to condemn the Kolozsvár pastors to death for blasphemy, beginning with the words "Hear, O Israel, the precepts of the Lord." Lampe, *op. cit.*, 116. Worried, the Kolozsvár pastors printed their response, an *Apologia adversus malidicentium et calumnias Stancari* (Kolozsvár, 1558). This was known to Wilbur (*Transylvania*, 23, n. 3), but not included among the imprints of *Régi Magyar Könyvtar*. Stancaro left for Little Poland. For more on Stancaro, see nn. 431 and 435.

Stancaro's *Collatio* was printed by Daniel of Łęczyca, complying under pressure from Grzegorz Orsacius. All copies were presently to be burned by order of the synod of Włodzisław, 26–28 June 1559. Cf. Sipayłło, *AS*, 1.309, n. 2. One exemplar survives in the State Archive of Zurich. Hein excerpts and discusses, *Italienische Protestanten*, 97–99.

See also my "Francis Stancaro's Schismatic Reformed Church centered in Dubets'ko in Ruthenia, 1559/61–1570," *Eucharistarion*: Essays presented to Omeljan Pritsak on his Sixtieth Birthday, *Harvard Ukrainian Studies*, 3/4 (1979–80) 931–57, esp. 936. Stanisław Mateusz Stadnicki (d. 1563) had founded a Reformed church at Dubiecko perhaps as early as 1546, and patronized the Stancarist gymnasium and seminary there, H. Smyczński, "O szkole kalwińskiej w Dubiecku w XVI wieku," *Kwartalnik Rzeszowski*, 1 (1966).

427. Wilbur, *Transylvania*, 23. Hein, *Italienische Protestanten*, who devotes the whole of ch. 3 to Stancaro, admirably analyses his severe Triadology and its impact on his understanding of Christ the Mediator. Stancaro was following many of the Church Fathers and Petrus Lombardus. Joachim of Fiore had criticized him and was himself condemned on the issues by IV Lateran in 1215 in the canon *Firmiter*, 2, and Lombardus vindicated. Denzinger, *Enchiridion*, 431. Hein shows how Luther and Melanchthon departed most clearly from *Firmiter* on both the Trinity and Christ the Mediator, Calvin remaining closer to Lombardus (*Enchiridion*, 79, 91, 94–95, 105, 118, 172). Stancaro counted on the support of Calvin and the Swiss divines (against Luther, Melanchthon, and Osiander), but Calvin, with certain safeguards, was much closer to Melanchthon than to Stancaro. Jaroslav Pelikan does not deal with Christ the Mediator as a marked emphasis, not to say as something of a departure from medieval Catholicism on an authoritative definition in his authoritative *Christian Tradition*, 4 (1984). This work in

Dogmengeschichte has the merit of taking seriously some of testimony from Slavic Christendom and has a whole chapter (6) on "Challenges to Apostolic Continuity," including therein a subsection on "Repudiation of Trinitarian Dogma," 323–31, dealing mostly with Faustus Socinus.

428. The complement of this text and more decisive is 1 Tim 2:5: "For there is one God, and there is one mediator between God and men, the man Jesus Christ."

429. Far removed from the issues of the controversy and, as here, from the Chalcedonian presuppositions of all orthodoxy on Christ, Greek, Roman, Lutheran, and Reformed, Lubieniecki says correctly *ut ajunt*, which applies to what goes before, not to what follows, which is precisely at issue as between Stancaro and the Reformed.

430. At this synod of 25 November 1554, the recorded action was the acceptance of the *Porzdek* of Stancaro without reference to his *name*. Sipayłło, *AS*, 1.2–3.

431. Lubieniecki is not much interested in Stancaro, except as he occasioned theological problems, and he moves easily from the rejection of Stancaro's name at n. 430, to the condemnation of his doctrine *de Mediatore* "at Sandomierz in 1559." There is no otherwise recorded synod there, but Hieronim Ossoliński (d. 1571), castellan of Sandomierz, was the lord who moved at the synod of Książ, 13–19 September 1560, that there be silence imposed on all for four months, during which time they would send Stancaro's *confessio* and the *Confessio de Mediatore* of the synod (n. 452, ¶3) to Calvin, Vermigli, Beza, and Bullinger as "judges." Lord Iwan Karniński protested this action heatedly, lest the freedom of the Church be abused while Stancaro was free "to sell" his *Collatio* against Melanchthon (n. 426, ¶3). It was indeed to these very judges that Stancaro addressed his own letters, except that for the one to Beza, he chose Musculus, n. 435, ¶3. Sipayłło, *AS*, 2.42–43.

In any case, whether there was a synod at Sandomierz in 1559, there was one in Książ in 1560 and under the influence of Castellan Ossólinski the opposition against Stancaro was actually held up. To him, Frycz Modrzewski dedicated his *Liber secundus de Mediatore*, as to a friend, June 1560, with a postscript, 12 September 1560, after two of Stancaro's followers, Przechadzka and Orsacius, were barred from "Evangelical congregations" by the synod of Włodzisław, June 1560. On this and them, see n. 446, ¶4. Modrzewski's third, largest, and last book, *De Mediatore*, was dedicated to Stadnicki, 9 September 1561, and finished 15 September 1561, *Opera omnia*, 4.19–76. For his first, see n. 434.

432. Lubieniecki refers again to a synod in Pińczów in 1558 at n. 438, ¶2; cf. n. 445.

The issue of Stancaro, *De Mediatore*, was prominent in synod in Poland; it was at Pińczów, 25 April and 7–8 August 1559: at the former not by name, only in anticipation of his return from Transylvania that May, and in the latter, when Stancaro was present in his own defense and where his view was condemned as Nestorian, cf. n. 435. Sipayłło, *AS*, 1.298, 311.

433. The synod of 1 May 1555 is mentioned in *Historia*, 56.

Of 88 synods or meetings of elders edited by Sipayłło in *AS*, 22 were at Pińczów. She does not number these gatherings consecutively in her second volume and does not make anything of the consecutive numbering employed by A. Lubieniecki in his lost *Chronicon/Acta* that survives in incomplete snippets from it in Lubieniecki and Stoiński.

434. Andrzej Frycz Modrzewski, *Sylvae*, 3.1; *Opera omnia*, 5.176, where he writes of the doctrine "Jesus Christ the Son of God and of Man, at once God and our Lord." After the synod of Włodzisław of 26–28 June 1559 had censured the local printer of Stancaro's *Collatio* (n. 426, ¶3), Modrzewski, aware of the rising importance of the issue

raised, addressed his own *Liber primus de Mediatore* "to the Fathers and Brethren, and their Patrons to be gathered in Włodzisław or wherever," *Opera omnia*, 4.11. For two other books *de Mediatore*, see n. 431, ¶2.

As for "Pinczovians," lord Mikołaj Oleśnicki, mentioned by Lubieniecki several times, most recently near nn. 422 and 424, granted a privilege to noble settlers on his estates in Pińczów in 1559, even "omnibus peregrinis nobilibus et civibus cuiuscunque status et conditionis ex quocunque regno venientibus et puram Christi doctrinam profitentibus." All issues of the new community were to be referred *ad censuram ecclesiae*, Wotschke, *Briefwechsel*, no. 175, 97. The church intended was the former Pauline cloister, the already gathered Reformed congregation (*zbór*), and the emerging synodal structure. The *privilegium* attracted many Italian Protestants, who established there an Italian-speaking congregation, of which Giorgio Negri (*Historia, 119, 125*) was the first pastor.

The Italian "noble pilgrims" of faith and citizens of all stations and conditions soon became so influential, much out of proportion to their number, that by the synod of Pińczów of January 1561 it was agreed, first, that as much as God was to be praised for sending so many of them, "nevertheless it is not acceptable that those foreigners/visitors/wayfarers of faith have any prerogative in the Church of God and be superior to us, but be equal brothers with us and co-workers (*socii*) in laboring together in the vineyard of the Lord; and next, when they come to us, that they first present their *confessio* to us before they join our churches, lest the churches of Christ in Poland be turmoiled by foreigners (*peregrinos*)." Sipayłło, *AS*, 2.73.

Alodia Kawecka-Gryczowa convincingly shows that the initiators of the foregoing agreement were Stanisław Sarnicki (n. 531) Sarnicki and Jakub Sylvius (n. 501), by now suspicious of Lismanino's dependence on Biandrata, "Jakub Sylwiusz a rozłam w zborze małopolskim," *RwP* 9–10 (1937–39) 28–63, esp. 30. The *privilegium* of Oleśnicki explains not only why there were so many Italians among the Pińczóvians but also, given its grant of *iudicium* in most matters to the discipline of the church (*censura ecclesiae*), why confessional statements became unusually prominent in Pińczóvian/Little Poland synodal history—not only the evolving *confessio* of Biandrata himself, so prominent and yet evasive in Biandrata and somewhat confused in Lubieniecki's accont of it. To be banished from the protection and pleasantness of the Pińczów colony or settlement was an ordeal. There is reference to the congregation of Pińczów exercising the ban in accordance with the *privilegium* as it came to be interpreted, below n. 446, ¶2 (Orsacius a "pestiferous vine").

Patron Oleśnicki died in 1566/67. In 1586 the properties were acquired by Bishop Piotr Myszkowski of Cracow, who turned the Protestants out of Pińczów.

For the use of the term "Pinczovians," see the text in RD 5, n. 20.

435. The first *schism* in the Reformed Church of Little Poland and Ruthenia is that of Stancarian Church centered in Dubiecko, 1559/61–70. See n. 426, ¶5. Against Stancaro (and now his *Collatio*) the main body of the Reformed under Łaski prepared their *Confessio de Mediatore* (n. 452). Before its actual publication they convened in synod at Pińczów, 7 August 1559; Stancaro was present in his own defense. Sipayłło, *AS*, 1.310–14. There his view *de Mediatore* was formally condemned (n. 432) as Nestorian, 311. When their own *Confessio de Mediatore* was about to be printed, the main body met in synod at Pińczów, 20 and 22 November 1559; Pierre Statorius cleared himself of all errors, including the Arian, Servetian, Eunomian, and *Stancarist*, there was a long discussion of Stancaro *de Mediatore*. Sipayłło, *AS*, 1.314; 315. Then at the synods of Pińczów of 13–16 January 1560 and 29 January–1 February 1560 followers of Stancaro

were singled out, Grzegorz Orsacius, Marcin of Lublin, Erazm Gliczner, and somewhat later Krzysztof Przechadzka of Lwów, for grilling and finally extrusion as Stancarists.

On 3 June 1560 at Dubiecko Przechadzka finished his *Okazanie i pan Krystus pośrednikiem jest Boga i ludzi* (Pińczów, 1560) in defense of Stancaro's understanding of 1 Tim 2:5 that supplied the Polish title of the book and dedicated it to their common patron Mikołaj Stadnicki. The extant copy exists in the Czartoryski Collection in Cracow. Przechadzka, while in Switzerland on his mission for Stancaro and Stadnicki, writes Calvin, 25 February 1561, explaining his intentions. *OC*, 18, no. 3345, cols. 371–76. Therein he summarizes the position of Stancaro in which the formulation of the VI Ecumenical Council is decisive (cf. n. 435, ¶9) and then adduces many Fathers, Anselm, and contemporary Reformers, including mostly isolated statements, because most of the Reformers had, in fact, come to make of the topos of Christ the Mediator something different from what it was in antiquity when the Logos speculation linked with other originally philosophical concepts inhibited the emphases now common in Melanchthon, Bucer, and the Swiss divines. It is quite possible that the location of Dubiecko in the border terrain of Byzantine-rite Christianity and the attraction of some of the once Orthodox landlords/boyars and even magnates to the Stancarian Christology is related to the Christos Pantocrator tradition of their iconography of Christ.

After meeting defeat for his idea and for his disciples in the synods of Pińczów and Włodzisław in May and June 1560 (n. 446, ¶¶2–4), Stancaro, still confirmed as to his triadological and christological orthodoxy, against what he considered as Polish Arianism, Eutychianism, and Tritheism, wrote from Dubiecko, 4 December 1560, identical letters to Wolfgang Musculus, Pietro Martire Vermigli, Jean Calvin, and Heinrich Bullinger in defense of orthodoxy. (These were the same Swiss ''judges,'' addressed by the synod of Książ, on the intervention of Ossoliński, except Musculus. See n. 431.) He enclosed some kind of *historia* to be interpreted by Przechadzka, the bearer of the four letters and presumably of the letter of Stadnicki himself of 11 December 1560 to Calvin, recommending his protegé Stadnicki. Wotschke, *Briefwechsel*, nos. 208–9; *OC*, 18, nos. 3288 and 3290. He wrote in facile or perhaps only boldface confidence of Swiss solidarity with himself:

> The Arians here teach that the Father, the Son, and the Holy Spirit are not one God but three gods as separate from each other as three men are separate from each other and that these three gods are three separate substances, three wills, and three operations as you will see more clearly and distinctly in the account I am sending to you. Further they hold that the Son of God, our Lord Jesus Christ, is less than the Father in the divine nature or according to divinity and according to the same nature that He was without beginning (*sine principio*), that is, from eternity, is now, and will be, that is, without end (*sine fine*) Priest, High Priest, Mediator (*sacerdotem, pontificem et mediatorem*), according to his humanity of course the victim and the sacrifice. *OC*, 18, cols. 260–61.

He goes on to deplore the fact that ''this faith or rather these heresies and this madness or even blasphemies'' are being declaimed in the name of his addressees. Noting that he himself has been proscribed and three of his followers with B.A. degrees along with him, he says evidently confident of warm Swiss resonance:

> I defend this doctrine and catholic faith concerning the Trinity and the Mediator that the whole word [*ubique*] not simply one received and approved but does now receive and approve [*semper, per omnia*], namely, that the Father, the Son, and the Holy Spirit are the one only true God, of one essence, of one will, and of one operation

[IV Lateran, Lombardus], and that our Lord Jesus Christ, very God and true man, is
our High Priest, Priest, and Mediator only according to his humanity. According to
his divinity, along with the Father and the Holy Spirit, he is at once the Author of
both the high priestly office and the mediation, as is clearly stated in the VI [Ecumeni-
cal] Council of Constantinople [III of 680–81 against Monotheletism], action 4, 8, 10
and 18.

The main reference here is to the Letter of Pope Agatho (678–81) and the Roman Synod
that served as instruction to his legates and was embodied in the acts of the Council, *PL*,
87, cols. 1215–16; Philippe Labbe and G. Cossart, *Sacrosancta Concilia*, 15 vols., 5,
cols. 677–78. Denzinger, *Enchiridion*, 289; and in the opening lines it is clear in the
approximating bracketed words that Stancaro is also appealing to the Vincentian Canon
(n. 447, ¶ 9).

Stancaro shows no awareness in his letter to the Swiss that Calvin and the Genevan
divines had already written the first of two treatises about him for the Poles, *Responsum
ad fratres Polonos ad refutandum errorem Stancari*, 9 June 1560; Wotschke,
Briefwechsel, no. 195; *OC*, 9, cols. 353–42; the second, *Responsio ad nobiles Polonos et
Franciscum Stancarum Mantuanum de controversia Mediatoris*, would appear in March
1561; *OC*, cols. 347–58. Cf. Tylenda, "Biandrata," (n. 436, ¶5) 39, n. 53.

That Calvin and the Swiss divines in general opposed Stancaro so fiercely and without
any reservations made many of the Polish divines and patrons feel that they were still
loyal to the Swiss when, in opposing Stancaro and his VI Ecumenical Council and Lombardus, they were presently drawn into "further clarification" of Triadology and Christology by Biandrata and Lismanino. See further my "Strains in Christology," also
"Stancaro's Schismatic Church," 933–41.

436. The thrust of this long sentence is that no one, from Łaski to Biandrata, could
prevail upon the stubborn and disliked Stancaro. The death of the great Polish Reformer
is only caught up in this general thrust. The funeral service for him was the occasion of
the synod of Pińczów, 29 January–1 February 1560. First there was an exhoration in
Polish by Sylvius as the body was brought in, then two orations in Latin, by Sarnicki and
then Pierre Statorius, teacher at Pińczów, and a closing address in Polish by Cruciger. He
was buried where once had been the high altar in the formerly Pauline cloister church, the
very center of the Reformed Church of Poland as of the moment. Sipayłło, *AS*, 2, 8–12,
with some unpleasant charge of Orsacius (n. 446, ¶2) as to the cause of the death and a
reexamination of the body.

Giorgio Biandrata (Dr. Blandrata) was mentioned on *Historia, 33*, Bk. 1, n. 259, and
now appears here as though a quite familiar figure, a savior from Stancarism. He is rein-
troduced as among others at Pińczów, *degentes vel illuc venientes*. A bit further near
n. 445, Lubieniecki writes of this very year, presumably from the context, 1558, *cum ven-
isset Pintzoviam Blandrata*. And it was in November 1558, on which see further, nn.
438, ¶2. Physician at two courts, with a doctorate in philosophy and another in medicine
from study in three universities, Dr. Biandrata was a towering figure, more highly
esteemed by most of the Reformed nobles and ministers in Poland (and Transylvania)
than Stancaro with his doctoral specialities in Hebrew, patristics, and scholastic thought.
Each proud man had perhaps come to think of himself as destined by Providence to be
the principal instrument in the establishment of a Reformed Church in Poland and to a
lesser degree in Transylvania. This vision appeared to Stancaro earlier, who was in fact
the first synodist in Poland and was on the point of organizing his own schismatic
Reformed Church (1559) when Biandrata entered Poland for the second time in 1558.

Biandrata seems to have had almost as good a command of the technical terms of Triadology and Christology as Stancaro, although he was not anywhere near so earnest about it all as Stancaro. Because of Stancaro's charge of Arianism at the core of the Reformed Church of Little Poland, Lismanino, the preeminent Italian of half-Greek ancestry, himself so long in the country as to be a major religious figure, yielded to the theological blandishments of Biandrata and even personally despised Stancaro. The persevering, strict Polish Calvinists called their internal foes Blandratists far more often than Servetians.

Biandrata had studied medicine in Montpellier, 1530–33, where he was a fellow student of François Rabelais, physician and satirist. He continued his medical studies in Padua where he received the *laura* in 1534, confirmed in Bologna in 1538. His *Gynaecorum ex Aristotele et Bonaciolo* [Ludovico Bonacioli] *exerpta* (Strassburg, 1539) was dedicated to Bona Sforza and her daughter, Isabelle Jagiellonka, mother of the future voivode of Transylvania, John Sigismund. For the documentation of his doctorates in philosophy and medicine, see Henryk Barycz, "Doktorat Jerzego Blandraty," *RwP* 12 (1956) 215–16.

In 1540 Biandrata was called to Cracow by Sigismund I to serve as physician to Bona Sforza where he remained till 1544. Thereupon he went to Transylvania as court physician, 1544–52, to Isabelle Jagiellonka, widow of national King John Zápolya (1526–40) as Queen Regent, 1541–51. From 1551 to 1556 the Hungarian and Transylvania realms were reunited; and Isabelle with her heir John Sigismund returned to Poland, while Biandrata in Vienna carried on delicate negotiations in her interest.

He went on to Padua, where he was especially drawn to theology when his fellow physician, Servetus, was burned in Geneva in 1553. He left for there in 1556. He became a citizen as esteemed physician, a member of the Italian congregation, where he was elected one of the four lay presbyters with Celso Martinengo the pastor; and he proceeded to engage in controversy with Calvin. Cf. n. 506 below. For the conflict between Calvin and Biandrata in Geneva, 1556–58, and thereafter in counsel to the Poles, with documentation, see Joseph N. Tylenda, S.J., "The Warning that Went Unheeded: John Calvin on Giorgio Biandrata," *Calvin Theological Journal* 12 (1977) 24–62; "Christ the Mediator: Calvin versus Stancaro," ibid., 8 (1973) 5–16; "The Controversy on Christ the Mediator: Calvin's Second Reply to Stancaro," ibid., 8 (1973) 131–57. Tylenda sides with Calvin on the christological issue. What has been said above in this n. in a different emphasis from that of Tylenda is stated more fully in my "Strains in the Emerging Christology." See also E. David Willis, "Calvin and the Italian Anti-Trinitarians," *ARG* 62 (1971) 279–82. His distinction between the Arianism of Servetus, the Sabellianism of Biandrata, and the Modalism of Stancaro does not seem apt, but very useful in his demonstration of the degree to which there is a permanent deposit of the controversy of Calvin with "the Antitrinitarian" Italians and with the baffled Poles as Calvin reconsidered and compacted his asseverations for the final version of the *Institutes* of 1559, *Calvin's Catholic Christology: The Function of the So-Called Extra Calvinisticum* (Leiden, 1966).

Biandrata left Geneva, as unsafe, for Farges to seek out Gribaldi, then for Zurich and Basel. Lubieniecki has his own retrospective acount of Biandrata in Switzerland, *Historia, 126*, beginning after n. 505.

The substantial article by Antonio Rotondò, "G. B.," *DBI* 10 (1968) 257–64, supersedes even for things Polish Marek Wajsblum, "J. B.," *PSB* 2 (1936) 118–20. Rotondò corrects where necessary Delio Cantimori, "Profilo di Giorgio Biandrata saluzzese," *Bollettino storico-bibliografico Subalpino*, 38 (1936) 352–402.

As for his appearance in Poland, it is known that Calvin warned of his ''serpentine'' ways in the postscript of a letter to Lismanino, 20 December 1558, as if informed of his itinerary, *OC*, 17, no. 2981, cols, 378 – 79. Rotondò, ''Biandrata,'' *DBI* 10.258B, says of Biandrata that he was already in Pińczów in November 1558. His evidence would not come directly from Lubieniecki but rather from the *Epitome* of Stoiński, *BAnt*, no. 2. Lubieniecki uses the same source, at nn. 438 – 39.

437. Andrzej Lubieniecki the Elder (c. 1550 – 1623), author of *Poloneutychia*, wrote a Polish MS *Liber continens Acta et Conclusiones Synodorum a primordiis reformationis in Polonia celebratarum: a cuius obitu continuata haec sunt*. *BAnt* 89. This has perished. Janusz Tazbir, ''A.L.,'' *PSB* 17 (1972) 595 A.

438. The November in brackets (cf. n. 432) is supplied from the *Epitome* of Stoiński, *BAnt*, no. 2, where the Epitomizer (B. Wiszowaty) writes of the arrival of Biandrata in Pińczów in 1558 (cf. n. 436, ¶8) and of a *synod* there in November. Sipayłło, *AS*, does not credit this ancient reference to the extent she does more reliable allusions to non-extant protocols by assigning it a nearly empty page. She records no synod or synodal gathering in Little Poland between that of Włodzisław, 4 – 15 September 1558, and that of Pińczów, 13 March 1559. Lubieniecki/Wiszowaty/Stoiński could have been right about the year/month/ but not the thrust of the proceedings. For the proceedings, see next n.

Although otherwise unnoted, there could have been a synod or perhaps simply a local church session at Pińczów in November 1558, at which Biandrata was welcomed by Łaski and presented an orthodox *confessio*. As late as the synod of Pińczów, 25 – 30 January 1561, Biandrata himself would offer his guarded wording of the Nicene-Constantinopolitan confession of faith, which he would say had been approved by Calvin and then by Łaski, respectively 3 March and 7 November 1558. Sipayłło, *AS*, 2.84. Górski (*Grzegorz Paweł*, 5, n. 3) having come to regard A. Lubieniecki's date of November 1558 for a synod of Pińczów as a mistake, copied by S. Lubieniecki and Stoiński, still conjectured that at some unrecorded gathering (*konwent*) somewhere other than Pińczów Biandrata offered his deceptively orthodox *confessio*, 7 November 1558. That Łaski festively welcomed Biandrata (in 1558) is attested in other sources. See below, nn. 517, ¶5; 518, ¶3; also n. 447, ¶9. Lubieniecki's year and place, presumably also the month from the same source, may well be validated by Biandrata's own specificity; but the Epitomizer and S. Lubieniecki hastened the synodal onset of Biandrata's radicalizing disclosures.

439. The phrasing ''a large beginning *ad demoliendum dogma Trinitatis*'' is from A. Lubieniecki (n. 437), on whom Lubieniecki may, and Stoiński does (n. 438) depend, and the chronicler uncle connected it with a synod in Pińczów, November 1558. If A. Lubieniecki could have been right on Biandrata's appearance before Łaski (with an orthodox *confessio*) in November 1558, the Epitomizer of Stoiński, or Stoiński himself, and Lubieniecki could have been confusing this action with that *ad demoliendum* in a synod in the same place a year later, 22 November 1559.

Biandrata and most of the others to whom Lubieniecki refers were indeed present at the synod of 12 November 1559. Sipayłło, *AS*, 1.314. But then Jan Stoiński, evidently using A. Lubieniecki (*BAnt*, no. 3.2), deals with this 1559 synod and supplies details, corresponding to those preserved by the protocol, namely, about the controversy over a letter of Remigian Chełmski, who had raised a question about invoking the Holy Spirit. (This letter and Pneumatology are discussed, n. 649.) Having suspected that Grzegorz Paweł, pastor of the Reformed congregation for Cracow but lodging outside with Remigian in Chełm, was the drafter of the offending letter, Sarnicki eventually printed it in his

Collatio in qua aperte demonstratur, blasphemias Gregorii Pauli conformes esse doctrinae Arii (probably 1564). A variant of this synodal letter is critically edited by Sipayłło as part of the synodal protocol. *AS*, 1.314–18. Indeed it bulks so large in the record that A. Lubieniecki's *ad demoliendum* seems out of place.

However, this protocol is in the Vilna codex and there is no Kolozsvár counterpart. Lubieniecki preserves the evidence from "his" side that the synod of Pińczów of 1558 and hence perhaps also of 1559 divided and that Sarnicki and Discordia went their separate way (*BAnt*, no. 2; in reference, to be sure, to 1558). It is possible that the Vilna protocol for 1559 correctly preserves the names of participants, including Biandrata and Grzegorz Paweł, but that A. Lubieniecki and his nephew preserve something of the resonance of the radical side, although it would have been Grzegorz and not yet Biandrata who would have been in the lead.

440. No reference to a preceding month has been made. Lubieniecki means here December 1558, since the preceding (Stoiński) date is [November] 1558.

441. The synod of Brest-Litovsk, December 1558. Lubieniecki returns to his source and this synod in *Historia, 144* at n. 623. See further, *Historia, 145–47*, *BAnt*, 41, also nos. 2.2 and 53; Bock, *op. cit.*, 1.1.108. The treatise of Gonesius was read and examined, 15 December 1558.

In general our Author avoids dealing with baptism until Bk. 3, chap. 3 and thus obscures in his *Historia* the extent to which baptismal radicalism within the Reformed churches of the Commonwealth developed first in the Polish-speaking palatinates of Lithuania, beginning evidently in Vilna, with its German quarter and quite possibly Mennonite presence. In effect, Lubieniecki shows his awareness in his sources of the emergent sequence, in Lithuania and adjacent palatinates of Great Poland, from antipedobaptism to believers' immersion—this by a few scattered references from "the ninth synod" of the Reformed Church in Lithuania in Brest-Litovsk, December 1558. But, as in Book 2, he is concentrating on the devolution of the dogma of the Nicene Trinity, and only picks up the development in Book 3 a bit before he deals with the important synod on baptism at Brzeziny, June 1565. As even there he passes over almost five years of baptismal thought almost without details, they may be appropriately discovered, which besides an imaginary colloquy by the author, contains the *Wotum* of Mikołaj Wędogowski, another lost account of the development by Szymon Budny. All three of these are to be found in *Trzech dni rozmowa*. Czechowic succeeded Budny in the Vilna church and school, while Wędrogowski was the senior minister there. Lech Szczucki uses these sources in a preliminary way in his article, "The Beginnings of Antitrinitarian Anabaptism in Lithuania and Poland in the Light of a So Far Unknown Source," in Jean-Georges Rott and Simon Verheus, eds., *Anabaptistes et dissidents au XVIe siècle* (*Bibliotheca Dissidentium*, Scripta et Studia 3; Baden-Baden: Koerner, 1987) 348–56, the subsequent Polish version of which is "Szymona Budnego relacja o pocztkach i rozwoju anabaptyzmu w zborze mniejszym," *OiRwP* 31 (1986) 93–109, which includes excerpts from Budny's recently discovered *O dzieciokrzczeństwie krótkie wyspanie* (Bk. 3, n. 99, ¶ 2).

In amplifying our Author, where he passes over so much of importance in Lithuania, it may be here noted that Gonesius, prominent in Lubieniecki's text, although seminal, was not so active a figure as Czechowic. Soon after his replacement of Budny in the Vilna church, Czechowic was entrusted by their common patron, Prince Mikołaj Radziwiłł, with the delicate mission of visiting Switzerland in July 1561 with a view to persuading Calvin from disparaging Giorgio Biandrata, so much esteemed by both the Lithuanians and the Little Poles, on the issue of the Nicene formulation of the dogma of the Trinity. With memories of encounters there with the major figures and also Ochino and Laelius Socinus, Czechowic returned to his post in Vilna with a report of Calvin's adamance as to the person and theology of Biandrata. In 1563 Czechowic was the first in Lithuania publicly to proclaim his refusal to baptize children. Wędrogowski, his senior in the ministry of the Vilna church, while himself disposed to the views of Gonesius and hence also Czechowic, felt it impolitic to identify himself publicly. Czechowic's refusal to baptize infants even of believing parents called out the indignation of two lay elders, Jan Katerla and Jakub Kurnicki, who restrained Wędrogowski. When Czechowic remained obdurate, a synod was called in Vilna in January 1564. At it Kurnicki rose and asked: "Is it a sin to baptize infants or not?" Of the twenty-six ministers present, thirteen were opposed to pedobaptism, Wędrogowski, voting with the other thirteen, wrote it out with his reasons, the now recovered *Wotum,* with the reply to it of Czechowic. The synodists agreed that there should reign mutual toleration on baptism until a new synod could be convened to decide the issue. Prince Radziwiłł, who hoped to avoid schism in the Lithuanian Reformed Church over both the Trinity and baptism, warned two synodists prominent in the recent debate on baptism, Budny and Wawrzyniec Krzyszkowski, that they might be deprived of their posts for their antipedobaptism, while Wędrogowski wrote to the Prince demanding that he use the *virga magistratus* on Czechowic, his colleague. Czechowic wrote a warning to Wędrogowski and his *Wotum* and prepared his *Three-Day Colloquy (Discourse),* set in the castle of Nieśwież. He took high ground in this *Trzech dni rozmowa* in the person of "the Christian" in colloquy with an Evangelical (Calvinist) and a Papist.

He makes clear that his anabaptism has little in common with the revolutionary and seditious Anabaptism of Münster, that it is wholly biblical and of the primitive Church. His single quotation from a Germanic Anabaptist is from Balthasar Hubmaier. Czechowic defines faith as derived from hearing the Word of God (*salus ex auditu,* Rom 10:17) and acknowledges as licit evangelical discipline only the ban (Matt 13:36–42) and opposes the view of Wędrogowski and the others that a Reformed lord could use coercion with peasant fathers on their estates, "hardened in sin," and bring their infants under Reformed tutelage. He expressly opposed Augustine's *Compelle intrare* (originally against the Donatists), leaving it to God's predestination and the awakened faith of these peasant children when they should come to the age of believers'

According to Budny, Prince Radziwiłł read the first version of *Trzech dni rozmowa,* prior to that of Łosk, and modified his opposition to the anabaptist current ("became somewhat kinder") and decided to convene a "great synod" for all Lithuania in order to decide the issues. He died 27 May 1565, a few days before the projected synod.

442. The *libellus* (cf. n. 624) was written in Latin. Its content no doubt reappears in the Polish version, *O ponurzaniu chrystyjańskim przeciwko chrztu nowochrzczeńców niedawnym (De baptismo christiano adversus baptismum recentiorum)* (Węgrów, 1570), critically edited by Halina Górska *et al.* (Warsaw, 1960). The scriptural motto of the book is Mark 16:16: "He who believes and is baptized [immersed: *ponurzon*] will be saved, but he who does not believe will be condemned." Gonesius is thought to have first introduced the Polish term for immersionist baptism, title p. and p. 85, later extensively used among the Polish Brethren. As for the title used by Lubieniecki, he may have known by name the Gonesian *Scriptum ad Laurentium Orisovium* [Krzyszkowski], *Contra paedobaptismum,* 1562: BAnt n. 41.

Hein deals with Gonesius and his Paduan doctorate in philosophy under the rubric: "Ein polnischer Verteidiger des Matteo Gribaldi," (*Italienische Protestanten,* 135–40) with special reference to his *O Trzech* (Węgrów, 1570) (full title, Latinized: *De Tribus, id est de Deo, de Fiio eius et de Spiritu Sancto adversus Trinitatem Sabellianorum* [Stancarists]), ed. by Lech Szczucki (Warsaw, 1962).

443. The author means the first in Little Poland. Within the Commonwealth, Polish-speaking Lithuania seems to have led the way. See Bk 2, chap. 9. On Albin, see nn. 604, ¶3 and 687; also Bk. 3 at n. 190.

444. Hieronim Piekarski (d. after 1585) had been a vicar in the diocese of Przemyśl, where he was twice charged with heresy. The second time, 31 January 1550, he cleared himself by oath of all "innovations" before the provost in Chyrów. In 1554 he went to Podlasie and there married, joining the Protestant movement. Charged by the bishop of Łuck with heresy, he was haled before the synodal court at Janów, accompanied by lordly supporters, and despite their aid and the intervention of Radziwiłł the Black, he was formally excommunicated as a heretic, 1 July 1558, and deprived of his benefice and status in Przemyśl. He thereupon became the minister in Biała in Podlasie, 1556–65, under Radziwiłł's protection. He and his deacon Jan Falconius came under the influence of Gonesius as early as 1556. Only Lubieniecki (here and *Historia, 118* at n. 625) reports that Piekarski took part with Gonesius at a synod in Brześć in December 1558.

At the synod of Włodzisław, 14 September 1558, Piekarski, Falconius, and another minister, Walenty Brzozowski, were charged with "the heresies of Arius, Cerinthus, Servetus, and Gonesius." Evidently Piekarski attached importance to Irenaeus, an express opponent of Cerinthus. Apart from labels, the synod found that the three Podlachians affirmed that "Christ the Son of God suffered in his divine nature," that "the *communicatio idiomatum* [in respect, here, to the two natures of Christ] is a human figment," "that the Son is less than the Father and there was an interval when there was no Son," that "Christ is an adoptive Son of God, even as we." Sipayłło, *AS*, 1.280–81. These characterizations may be as much of the ancient heresies as of the specific tenets of the three under synodal scrutiny. In any case, they were readmitted to the ministerium by the right hand of fellowship after they had reaffirmed their belief "in the Son of God according to the confession of the Nicene, the Apostolic, and the Athanasian Creed" and disclaimed the errors of Gonesius, promising to go through a public renunciation of the heresies charged against them in their own *templum* in Podlasie, the procedure being spelled out. On Piekarski, see further Wacław Urban," "H.P.," *PSB* 26 (1981) 65–66 and below at n. 625.

445. Lubieniecki has not lost sight of his own date, based on his uncle's synodal records ultimately, and therefore means 1558 (nn. 437, 438, ¶2). But he has prematurely advanced the direct influence of Biandrata in the Polish synods. Cf. nn. 446–47.

446. As an intellectual historian, Lubieniecki is right about the enormous influence of Biandrata on Lismanino, but he is thin here on biographical details. Biandrata left for Transylvania in June 1559 to help dying Queen Isabelle (n. 436, ¶4), but he was back in Poland in time to attend the synod of Pińczów, 22 November 1559 (nn. 438–39). He is next attested at the synod of Pińczów of 5–9 May 1560, where on 6 May he is noted as having come to "our churches from Upper Germany [Switzerland]." The *seniores* took counsel with him and entrusted him with a mission to Mikołaj Radziwiłł the Black in Vilna in support of Lismanino. See further at nn. 503–4. (Perhaps it was this trip that had earlier prompted Lubieniecki to confuse his narrative somewhat at n. 440 in his mentioning the synod in Brześć *in Lithuania* in 1558.)

At this same synod of Pińczów the former physician to Queen Bona Sforza was charged with the task of persuading Mikołaj Oleśnicki "by the word of God" that as lord of Pińczów he should no longer tolerate Grzegorz Orsacius (c. 1520–67), "pertinacious" in his Stancarist heresy, and that he should rid Pińczów of him "as a disturber of the Christian Commonwealth and as propagator of the Stancarist blasphemy.'' Before Biandrata could act the synod itself was emboldened to do so. Szymon Zacius, the super-intendent of Podlachia (Podlasie) and other ministers of Lithuania having arrived on 7 May and having agreed about Orsacius, the synod was closed with a kiss of peace. Thereupon, after some synodists had left for Cracow, Orsacius was asked to appear before the seniorate. This was a joint session of the higher authorities beyond the local presbytery, and like it made up of lay and clerical *seniores*, *starszy*. Orsacius was queried as to whether he persisted in his Stancarist error *de Mediatore* and he responded ''that he believed that Jesus Christ the Son of God is the Mediator in human nature only.'' Thereupon the elders promptly proceeded to a public convocation of the church of Pińczów. A signal being given, a large multitude of people along with ministers con-vened in the church. And the superintendent (unnamed: possibly Zacius) pronounced the ban upon Orsacius as ''a pestiferous vine.'' Sipayłło, *AS*, 2.15–22, esp. 16–17, 211–22. This scholarly rector of the *gimnazjum* at Pińczów (1551–60) is not mentioned by Lubieniecki. On him see further, Henryk Barycz, ''G. Orszak,'' *PSB* 24 (1979) 260–63.

On the same day, 6 May, 1560, when the intervention of Biandrata had been author-ized, the synod moved also against another Stancarist, Marcin of Lublin, pastor at Włodzisław, who was severely grilled. He said that he consented to the opinion of Cal-vin on Christ the Mediator in the *Institutes* (of 1550 or of 1554), summed up evidently as: ''Christ in his whole Person insofar as he is God and man is the Mediator according to both natures (*utramque naturam*).'' Sipayłło, *AS*, 2.17. He was even willing to subscribe to the faith of Bullinger and Calvin, but he did not wish to formulate his own view as such and evidently did not agree with the *Confessio de Mediatore* of Pińczów, 10 August 1559 (n. 452). Sipayłło, *AS*, 1.312, n. 1; 313 at n. 1.

A disciplinary synod convened in Włodzisław, 12 June 1560, and Marcin of Lublin, with a B.A. from Cracow, defended himself in the presence of his lord, Jan Włodzisławski-Lanckoroński, master of the royal hunt for Sandomierz. Although the inquiry does not report Marcin's own words *verbatim*, there is quite sufficient detail to see where Stancaro's doctrine *de Mediatore* could lead a follower to sound both Sabellian and Nestorian, as he was charged. He said ''that he does not know how the one divine essence is divided in persons, but believes that God is wholly (*totum Deum*) in Christ, that is, that the Father, the Son, and the Holy Spirit are in the humanity'' and, further on, ''that the Son of God has spoken through the flesh, not in the flesh,'' and, in reference to Phil 2:7, he denied ''that Christ had emptied himself according to his divinity, but rather according to his humanity.'' Obliged by the synod to pack up and leave in four days, he was given a chance to think it over with Stanisław Lutomirski in Kazimierz, but he said he intended to proceed to Dubiecko. His lord agreed with the synod's decision and turned the key to the church over to the presbyters who in turn entrusted it and the care of each believer and the custody of church articles to the deacons. Sipayłło, *AS*, 2.27–28.

Stancarism aroused strong emotions. A transitional form of Blandratism that preserved the *divine* Suffering Christ, Tritheism seemed to many a solution. Cf. Hein, characterizing of Biandrata's Christology, n. 447, ¶7. At the disciplinary synod, Grzegorz Paweł had evidently preached from Marcin's own pulpit on Christ the Mediator according to the Apostles' Creed, and Marcin found it unconvincing.

447. ''From now on.'' Lubieniecki is evidently in haste, passing over many events and synods in order to demonstrate his major thesis that Biandrata helped Lismanino cope with the theological challenge of Stancaro (actually by way of Tritheism; see n. 351).

On *Historia, 118* Lubieniecki mentions Pińczów five times as a domicile or site of a synod. There was no synod recorded there in 1558 except by Lubieniecki himself and his sources (nn. 438 – 39); there were six synods there in 1559; in 1560, three. With so many synods in Pińczów alone, Lubieniecki could have been confused in his narrative, but there is a sense in his text that he may wish to avoid some of the synodal controversy, desiring to preserve the memory of Łaski intact for his side. His chronological coverage is especially obscured in chapter 6 by the changed density letters and speeches interspersed amid narrative and interpretation. Between *Historia, 111* and *118*, of the many synods in Little Poland alone, he mentions only that of Secemin, 1556, that alleged (and probable) of November 1558 (*Historia, 117*), that not otherwise documented of Sandomierz of 1559 (*Historia, 117*), and he is about to quote a decisive letter from Lismanino to Karniński, which, however, he incorrectly dates as 10 December 1561. He mentions the synod of Włodzisław of 21 – 25 September 1561 (*Historia, 126 – 29*).

Since Lubieniecki neglects development on the conservative side of the Reformed Church and too eagerly awaits the emergence of his own preferred formulations, it is desirable at this point to note the synods after Łaski's death (incidentally inscribed, *Historia, 117*).

The first was at Pińczów, 13 – 16 January 1560, with Lismanino, Cruciger, Grzegorz Paweł, Sarnicki, Sylvius listed in that order first among the ministers; Biandrata and other laymen are not mentioned. Already noted was the move evidently of Sarnicki and Sylvius to restrain the Italian peregrine like Biandrata, n. 434, ¶3. Important theological liturgical, and administrative decisions were here made: that litanies for Sunday prayer from the *Liber antiphonarum* should be discontinued because they were instituted by Pope Gregory I; that baptism might be observed in homes so long as convivial "adversaries of the Word of God" were not invited; that the Polish version of the Bible be expedited by the more specific assignment of parts and translators; and that Stancarism be rooted out. On the problem of Christ the Mediator in the Stancarist sense, Marcin of Lublin, Erazm Gliczner, and esp. Grzegorz Orsacius were under suspicion for heresy. Sipayłło, *AS*, 2.1 – 6. Two of these ministers have already been mentioned (n. 446, ¶¶2, 3). The next synod was called to solemnize the burial of Łaski, 29 January 1560, although other important matters were transacted (n. 436). After an April synod for the Lublin district alone came the May synod in Pińczów with Biandrata prominent (n. 446).

Passing over most of the eight synods recorded by Sipayłło between Pińczów, May 1560, and Włodzisław, September 1561, mentioned in passing by Lubieniecki (at n. 503), the reader must be alerted to two of them in order to assess the importance of the long letter of September 1561 by Lismanino to Karniński preserved in Lubieniecki's text.

The synod of Książ Wielki, 13 – 19 September 1560, was an important constitutional synod. Dr. Biandrata spoke up frequently, e.g.: "Magnificent and generous lords, understand that the ministry of the word is the most outstanding and highest office in the Church of Christ and that the ministers are the principal members of the Church of God. But truly, for solving of political affairs (*ad componenda negotia politica*) presbyters from among the people (*plebe*) should be joined to the ministers seeing that it is not permitted that ministers get involved in those matters, as "coadjutors" to the ministers as *doctores et pastores*. Sipayłło, *AS*, 2.32 – 68, esp. 36. This indeed represented moderation in comparison with what had just been said by four or more lords in response to an earlier intervention of Biandrata to the same effect, namely, Hieronim Ossoliński, Baltazar Łukowski (*Historia, 63*), and two or more of the Myszowskis present (ibid., 33, 35): "Look, they [the ministers] seek to dominate, they desire to dominate us as once the Pope did with his bishops." On the following day the lords Ossoliński and Myzowscy presented a written plan to be read and deliberated on. Then, excluding the ministers, the landowners drew apart and divided up the Little Polish Church into districts with elected lordly *seniores* for each, all ''without the vote of the ministers.'' Thereupon, Feliks Cruciger was confirmed as superintendent and assigned two coadjutors: ''Francesco Lismanino of Corfù and Giorgio Biandrata, physician, who recently came to Poland.''

As the subdivision of the general synod of Little Poland was not meant necessarily to hold after the next general synod, the details are not all given here, but they are of interest. The first district mentioned was that of Pińczów with five churches and four lay *seniores*, headed by Mikołaj Oleśnicki, patron of the central church and town. Although the District I was part of palatinate Sandomierz, the action of the lords in synod turned secondly to the delineation of two palatinate Cracow districts, then the Włodzisław district, back to the district of the capital plus Wieliczka (with three lords as *seniores*, headed by Jan Boner), and finally still within the palatinate of Cracow, the district of Podgórze, south of the city. Then come two more districts in palatinate Sandomierz, besides District Pińczów, namely, that of the palatine seat and that of Radom. The last district formed was that of the land of Sanok, one of four subdivisions of palatinate Ruthenia. Dubiecko, Stadnicki's seat, was in this district but neither it nor he is mentioned, for the Stancarist schism was already in progress. Biandrata's proposal could have led to the complete control of the synod and each local church by the lay patrons. Biandrata had a fresh memory of the syndics of Geneva and perhaps feared the repetition of Pastor Calvin's control of the lay presbyters encompassing the death of Servetus. For Biandrata in Poland, see Hein, *Italienische Protestanten*, 148–68. He notes that Biandrata observed that Jesus himself never called himself *deus*, only *filius Dei*, that Biandrata upheld the ideal of the *Christus pauper*, of a simple lay Christianity as he himself pictured the Primitive Church, not excluding its community of goods, although Biandrata clearly looked out for himself and his own well-being.

The other synod selected for notice, although unnoted by Lubieniecki, is that of Pińczów, 25–30 January 1561. Sipayłło, *AS*, 2.72–91. This, too, has already been mentioned (n. 438, ¶2) only to establish the date and place of Biandrata's reception by Łaski and the submission of an orthodox *confessio*. At this point more should be said.

On the morning of the 27th the synod deliberated on how to deal with Stancaro and his protector at Dubiecko, Mikołaj Stadnicki. Letters from the divines of Geneva, Basel, and Strassburg (probably also Zurich) demonstrate clearly that all these Reformed churches agreed with the Polish Reformed on their *Confessio de Mediatore* (n. 446) expressly against Stancaro. Sipayłło, *AS*, 2.82–83 and 38 (synod of Ksiaż, mentioned above, of September 1560), n. 1 (on the foreign correspondence). The doctrine common to these distant divines and that of their own *Confessio* under Łaski was now summarized: ''That Christ according to his two natures divine and human is from eternity High Priest (*summus Pontifex*) and Mediator between God and men. For in what manner did he fulfil the parts of a Mediator, who has his being [a little] below the angelic order [cf. Ps 8:5]? For to conquer death, sin, and the devil, to acquire justice and gain eternal life is not the work only of a man but of God. And therefore he is called Priest forever because he is not simply assumed out of humanity (*ex hominibus assumptus*), but rather by the decree of the Father he [the Son] became man (*hominem assumpsit*) for the expiation of sins [Heb 5:1–6 compacted]. For unless the Mediator had been called the Son of God in power there would be no Mediator.'' Cf. the similar formulation of an earlier synod, n. 446, ¶3. After Stancaro's teaching was again condemned, the synod went on to handle the threat of Grzegorz Orsacius and Marcin of Lublin, already condemned but now active respectively as teacher and pastor in the Stancarist center in Dubiecko, whither some nobles were sending their sons for education. See my "Stancarist Schism." Thereupon several gentlemen were entrusted with seeing to this problem, among them Biandrata; but he was by now also presenting the synod with the startling problem of his being rumored to be tainted with Servetianism, although all synodists were eagerly disposed to receive his denial.

In this atmosphere benign toward him Biandrata professed the brief *Confessio* that Lubieniecki chooses to put on his lips at a later synod (at n. 523, ¶12), a *Confessio* supplied verbatim by the protocol of Pińczów. Sipayłło, *AS*, 2.84. After this and his assertion that it was the same *Confessio* lauded by Calvin and then Łaski (n. 438, ¶2), Biandrata went on to say suavely: "We receive/accept the symbols of faith: the Apostles' Creed, the Nicene, the Athanasian," with a perhaps subtle resonance of the Vincentian Canon in his explanation. Vincent of Lérins (d. before 450) in his *Commonitorium libri*, 2.2, said that the threefold test of Catholicity was "quod ubique, quod semper, quod ab omnibus creditum est,' "what has been believed everywhere, always, and by all." Biandrata changed *ab* to *per* and omitted *ubique* to say:

> We receive the symbols of faith ... [as received] *by all* in that sense which the catholic church *always* uses, and we repudiate the dogmas concerning the Holy Trinity and the incarnation of Christ of all heretics, especially indeed in this age of Servetus and of his followers. When I showed this my written [brief] *Confessio* [at n. 523], Master Łaski gave me a clean conscience (*paratam reddidit meam conscientiam*). Now therefore I pray that you deal most benignly with me, seeing that I subject myself wholly to this Church and wish to be obedient to her. Do not have any trouble in this Church because of me, by all means even I seek with my ignominy the peace of this Church. But this I ask of you, that letters be written by you to the Lord palatine of Vilna and to master Calvin that I am alien to the doctrine of Servetus and recoil from all his heresies, which he in his writings seems to hold.

Although the brethren expressed satisfaction with Biandrata, some evidently pierced the suavity of his blandishments enough to procure a conference with him "in a private place concerning the Holy Trinity." The interrogators were headed by Lismanino, Cruciger, Stanisław Lutomirski, Sarnicki, and Grzegorz Paweł, enough of his kind to ensure a favorable report that nothing was found in him "that is alien to Holy Scriptures, prophetic and apostolic." But even then the synod desired that Biandrata submit at a subsequent synod a written *Confessio* before a letter would be written exonerating him to Calvin, while in the meantime they were willing to report to Radziwiłł what had been ascertained in the satisfactory private assurances.

Among many other important things transacted by the synod was the acceptance of eighteen articles concerning the doctrine and discipline of the Church, the last being the promotion of Lutomirski, on whom see further at n. 552, to the rank of full superintendent. Sipayłło, *AS*, 2.76–78, 91.

448. Stanisław Iwan Karniński (d. 1603) (*Historia, 25–29*; Bk. 1, n. 210) was a correspondent of Calvin as early as 1555. See further n. 449.

449. This valuable document, only made public at the synod of Władysław (n. 503), was perhaps obtained by Budziński from Grzegorz Paweł who had been absent from the synod. See further n. 502, Górski, *Grzegorz Paweł*, 75.

The letter had not been set in italics as from Budziński because here, as in several other instances, Lubieniecki makes no such reference himself: my principal criterion for my conservative italicizing to flag the Budziński source. The contents of the letter are thoroughly discussed by Hein, *Italienische Protestanten*, 203–7. The letter catches the argumentation of Lismanino in the moment when the larger body of the Polish Reformed faced the charge from Stancaro that they were Arianizing. The letter is of special interest because Lismanino, of Uniate Venetian Greek origin, and capable of reading Greek, cites and quotes in this long letter only Greek Fathers, except for Hilary of Poitiers who knew Greek, namely, in chronological order, Pseudo-Ignatius (actually, between 364–76), Justin Martyr (c. 165), Athanasius the Great (d. 373), Pseudo-Athanasius, Basil the Great (d. 379), and Gregory, bishop of Nazianzus (d. 389). Lismanino freely adduces the Uniate Greek formula of the Holy Spirit proceeding from the Father and *through* the Son, and he uses other terms than the traditional Latin *processio/processus*. Presently in letters to Calvin and Johann Wolph of December 1561, Lismanino will detail his extensive reading in the Fathers *de Trinitate* (n. 517).

Against Stancaro who evidently had a powerful grip on several Reformed lords, as this letter attests, Lismanino wishes to uphold the distinctiveness of the eternally begotten Son. His use of especially early Greek Fathers before the conciliar clarifications of the fourth century and, unwittingly, of two pseudonymous fathers somewhat weakens his own triadological position or, better: his view of the Trinity is already rapidly moving in the new direction, all in an attempt to "escape" Stancaro's charge of incipient Arianism. Stancaro was not far from the fact.

It would be fascinating if Lord Iwan (to whom Lismanino addressed himself) were himself from the Byzantine-rite territory of the Commonwealth with an awareness of the Greek formula. He was not. He befriended Lismanino in 1550, through whom he then came into epistolary contact with Calvin. He gave refuge to Lismanino on his estate at Aleksandrowice in 1556 and, with other lords invited Łaski to Poland at the synod of Pińczów in April 1556. Sipayłło, *AS*, 1.54, 63, and n. 2. Lord Iwan had studied in Leipzig in 1531 and could presumably follow the patristic arguments of Lismanino.

Calvin and Melanchthon would have found the spirited and patristically resourceful argumentations of Lismanino for the most part congenial. To be sure, he eschews the terminology of *hypostasis/persona*. Cf. his own assessment fo the thrust of the letter at n. 516. Hence the presumed preservation of the letter by his secretary-historian and especially its inclusion, evidently unabridged in his *Historia*, by Lubieniecki testify at once to the animus felt by so many Poles toward Stancaro, and the intended trustworthiness of the unfolding record; for this letter, among the four or five largest documents transcribed by Lubieniecki, still falls within the range of orthodox classical Protestant, not to say more specifically, Reformed theology.

450. Referring here to himself in the third person, Lismanino has in mind Stancaro and his lordly patron. Lismanino and his party had him charged with incipient Arianism. It is his view that Stancaro does not make sufficient distinction among the Three Persons and is therefore guilty of Sabellianism (see next n.). It is clear why Lismanino found Biandrata a congenial ally in that he seemed, as almost a Tritheist, sufficiently to distinguish the Three Persons.

Stancaro held with most of the Fathers and with Lombardus that (Jesus) Christ could not have been a Mediator before the incarnation, since it was precisely in his manhood, in his human nature, that he was Mediator. Lismanino with almost all others felt that Christ's mediatorship was jeopardized by Stancaro. See nn. 452 and 455. For this whole problem see further Hein, *Italienische Protestanten*, chap. 5 and my "Strains in Christology," and my "Stancaro's Schismatic Church." Hein sees Lismanino bound to Biandrata out of theological deference and medical dependence (for his epilepsy). Calvin was indeed somewhat closer than Melanchthon to Lombardus in locating the sacrificial action of Christ in the human nature rather than with the Second Person in his divine *substantia/essentia/natura*. Calvin did not sufficiently gratify the Polish Reformed in their importunate requests for guidance in withstanding the specific charge from Stancaro (the virtual founder of the Polish Reformed synod) that their view of Christ as Mediator even before the incarnation of the Son of God, in their deference to the Swiss divines, was Arian in the sense of antiquity, a charge so compelling that there indeed emerged a Stancarist synod and school in Dubiecko even before the schism of the Major and Minor Reformed, both of these parties opposed to Stancaro.

451. Sabellius, a Libyan of the Pentapolis, (c. 215), became leader of the Modalist Monarchians in Rome, his name preserved in Sabellianism. Tertullian attacked Sabellius also as Patripassian, that is, as so minimizing the persons of the Triad as modes of divine appearance that the Father-Creator would seem in the system to have suffered on the cross.

Lismanino and his party within the Reformed Church of Poland, assailed by Stancaro and hurting from his charge of Arian subordination of the Word/Son/Christ to the Father/Creator, sought to distinguish the three Persons as eternally and almost separately subsistent. Lismanino thought that in Stancaro he was fighting a Sabellian. See n. 517, ¶6.

452. The reference is to the lost *"longa" Confessio*, drafted by Łaski, and approved by the synod of Pińczów in August 1559.

Just as Lubieniecki hastens over the formative synods of the undivided Reformed Church of Little Poland and which, for that reason, have been summarized in n. 447, so here with the allusion of Lismanino to one synodal confession, a conspectus can be given on the transitional *synodal* confessions of faith passed over by Lubieniecki in contrast to his attention to *personal* confessions, like the progressive stages of Biandrata's theological views.

Several of the synodal confessions are lost and they and the extant ones and fragments can get confused. Stancaro in his *De Trinitate et Mediatore* (Cracow, 1562), in a special section, "Examinatio Pinczovianorum super confessionem fidei eorum," reports that: "Multas confessiones scripserunt et impresserunt Pinczoviani"; he distinguished the now lost *"longa" Confessio* by Łaski discussed beginning at 8 o'clock, 8 August 1559 (printed, 1561) and the ["parva"] *Confessio [de Mediatore]* of the same synod of Pińczów, discussed 7 August 1559, composed 10 August, presented to Patron Oleśnicki, and a copy sent to Switzerland. For Stancaro's testimony, see Wotschke, *Briefwechsel*, 92, n. 1 and Domański and Szczucki, "Miscellanea arianica" (to be fully cited, n. 604, ¶9), 228, n. 2 (on the Cracow synod of 1562), all three scholars having had access to Stancaro's volume. Wotschke prints a copy of the *parva Confessio* sent to the Swiss, *Briefwechsel*, no. 172, 92–95; reprinted by Hein, 259–62, with a German translation, 101–4, and placed in the historical context, 89–115, with careful theological analyses. Domański and Szczucki print a fragment of the *longa Confessio* cited by Sarnicki, this in the critical edition of the conservative *Consensus* prepared at Cracow in 1562 (nn. 616–17). That the *longa Confessio* was drafted by Łaski and printed after his death is known from the same composite letter of Sarnicki (*OC*, 19, col. 580). For a conjecture as to its disappearance, see n. 617, ¶7.

Pierre Statorius in his letter to Calvin of 20 August 1559 from Pińczów, right after Stancaro's "raving" at the synod, which he would later discuss, made very clear the issue as he perceived it: "Although you here and there in your books clearly teach that the Son of God, to be sure (*nempe*), the Second Person of the Holy Trinity already discharged the office of μεσίτης, first to the patriarchs before the Law was given, then after the Law to the prophets, i.e., before ὁ λόγος σὰρξ ἐγένετο," *OC*, 17, no. 3098, cols.

60–61. (For Christ as the Mediator of the law itself, see for example, the testimony of Jerzy Fredro *et al.* from Cracow, 1562, n. 617, ¶2.)

The Pinczovian *parva Confessio de Mediatore* and *longa*, drafted by Łaski, should be distinguished, of course, from the later Pinczovian *Confessio de Trinitate*.

453. Cf. 1 Chr 13: 9–10.

454. The correspondence of the Swiss and other divines, Calvin foremost.

455. For Lismanino Stancarism was tantamount to Modalism and hence Patripassianism. But Stancaro himself in his MS *Confessio* of 1570 clearly sought to avoid precisely the direct involvement of the Godhead in humiliation, suffering, and death. He insisted that the ransom/offering, of 1 Tim 2:6 (next after the verse that is the *locus classicus* for Christ the Mediator) and of its counterpart in Heb 9: 13–14, was to God, not to the Father, and hence as much also to God the Son and God the Holy Spirit. *Confessio*, 4, is printed by Hein, *Italienische Protestanten*, 256–57, and rendered in German with discussion, 91–93. Lismanino might have called Stancaro more nearly accurately, in Christology, a Nestorian, which he does in his letter to the Zurich divines, 1 September 1559, Wotschke, *Briefwechsel*, no. 174, 96.

456. In *Firmiter*, 2 of the IV Lateran (n. 427) upheld Lombardus against Joachim, asserting that *Deus*, Father, Son, and Holy Spirit, are together *summar quaedam res* that *non est generans, neque genita, neque procedens*. Stancaro followed *Firmiter*, when Luther and Calvin expressly departed from it. Hein, *Italienische Protestanten*, 172, n. 245.

457. Son of Francesco Negri, *Historia, 40*, Giorgio Negri (d. 1570), became deacon in Łętkowice in 1558, minister in 1559, then pastor in Iwanowice. See Bk. 3, n. 57.

458. In the ensuing quotations from Basil Lismanino confuses notes excerpted from two different editions of Basil's works: the first, edited by Wolfgang Musculus, *Opera D. Basilii Magni Caesariae Cappadociae Episcopi omnia* (Basel, 1540), and the second, *Omnia D. Basilii Magni Archiepiescopi Caesareae Cappadociae, quae extant, opera*, edited by Ianus Cornatius (Basel, 1565). The first quotation below, from *Lib.* I.134, refers to the Musculus edition. All the other references are to that of Cornatius. For the quotations from the *De Trinitate*, see the Cornatius edition, 343 (although Lismanino probably took them from the Musculus edition).

459. *Contra Eunomium*, 1,20; *PG*, 29, cols. 557/58. It is likely that Lubieniecki rather than Lismanino himself left out "according to the difference." The Greek has φύσις where οὐσία could have been expected.

460. John 14:28; *Contra Eunomium*; *PG*, 29, col. 567.

461. *Contra Eunomium*, 1, 25; *PG*, 29, cols. 567/68. Lubieniecki puts in italics as direct quotation from Basil only that through the second question. But the whole is Lismanino's rendering in Latin of the Greek. Bursche noted *minorem* as a mistake for *majorum*.

462. *Contra Eunomium*, 3, 1; *PG*, 29, cols. 653/54. Basil is turning into a question what Eunomius has just said, that the saints had always taught that the Holy Spirit was third in dignity.

463. *Contra Eunomium*, 3, 1; *PG*, 29, cols. 655/56. Lubieniecki separates from the quotation the last two sentences. Only the last is Lismanino's own summary.

464. *Homilia contra Sabellianos, et Arium, et Anomoeos*, 4; *PG*, 31, cols. 605/6. Right after this (in Latin) Basil continues: "Etenim si una est divinitas ingenita, una vero genita, tu es qui deorum praedicas multidudinem, cum Ingenitum Genito contrarium dicas, statuasque essentias etiam plane contrarias: siquidem essentia οὐσία Patris esset

ingeneratio, essentia vero filii, generatio.'' Although not quoting this, Lismanino, half-Greek, was very close here to the issue that divided himself from Stancaro, who upheld *Firmiter* nn. 427, 456, 470), as Lismanino, not referring to it, did not. At this point Lismanino was Greek Orthodox but not Lateran Catholic.

465. *Contra Sabellianos*, *PG*, 31, cols. 607/8.

466. Gregory is reconciling John 14:28 and 20:17; *Oratio* 4.7; *PG*, 30, cols. 111/12.

467. Basil is quoting John 10:30.

468. Gregory, *Oratio*, 4.7; *PG*, 30, cols. 113/14. Bursche sees the initial *neque* of the paragraph as *nempe* (''surely'' instead of ''for.'')

469. Desiderius Erasmus, ''Apologia ad Jacobum Fabrum Stapuleum,'' Louvain, 5 August 1517; *Opera* (Basel/Leiden, 1540), 9, col. 35. Johann Sturm, rector of the academy of Strassburg, whom Lismanino met there, February 1556 (Hein, *Italienische Protestanten*, 46), is several times mentioned in the correspondence with the Poles and himself wrote to them. Wotschke, *Briefwechsel*, index.

470. The challenge of patristic-Lombardian Stancaro with his charge that the main body of the Polish Brethren were being deceived by external Protestant advisors at the risk of being Arian is explicit here. Cf. n. 427.

471. Lismanino quotes from Hilary's *Lucubrationes* (Basel, 1550). The text has *liber* VII. He may refer to *De Trinitate*, 4.7, where, however, it is not *fiat Lux*, but *fiat firmamentum*. *Pl*, 10, col. 110. See nn. 477–78, 480.

472. The two quotations cannot be traced in ''the seventh book'' (n. 471). The matter is treated in the fifth and sixth books.

473. Col 1:15.

474. 1 Cor 8:6.

475. 1 Tim 2:5.

476. The scriptural support for this final phrasing is given in the original as John 20:17 where Christ says: ''I ascend unto my Father and your Father and to my God and your God,'' and 1 Cor 15:28 on the delivery by Christ of his Kingdom to God the Father that ''God may be all in all.'' The Nicene-Constantinopolitan Creed in the phrase ''and his kingdom shall have no end'' (cf. Luke 1:33) is directed against Marcellus of Ancyra and the implication of this scriptural passage was hard for Athanasian orthodoxy in that the Son appears at the Eschaton to be subordinate to the Father.

Lismanino could not know that he was quoting from pseudo-Ignatius, Epistle to the Ephesians (2 and 3), part of the Long Recension of thirteen Epistles. It and one to the Virgin Mary were composed by a Semi-Arian of Antioch. See James D. Smith, III, ''The Ignatian Long Recension and Christian Communities in fourth-century Syrian Antioch'' (Ph.D. diss., Harvard University, 1985). The excerpt has been edited with ellipses, etc. against the Greek in *PG*, 5, cols. 891/92B.

477. *De Trinitate*, 4, 16; *PL*, 10, col. 109.

In this same section 16 Hilary makes an important statement about the role of the Son as *cosmological* as distinguished from *soteriological* Mediator. After adducing John 1:1–3 about all things made through the Logos, Hilary takes up Gen 1:6: ''Let there be a firmament.''

> You observe that it does not say they [all things/ the firmament] came into existence, because it was His pleasure. In that case there would be no office for a Mediator between God and the world while awaiting its creation. God, from whom are all things, gives the order for creation which God [the Son] through whom are all things [1 Cor 8:6] executes.

478. *De Trinitate*, 4, 16; *PL*, 10, col. 104.

479. Cf. John 5:46.

480. *De Trinitate*, 5, 23; *PL*, 10, cols. 113–114: "Moses, indeed, will refute you with the whole volume of the Law, ordained through angels, which he received by the hand of the Mediator." Hilary held that the Son of God, as the Angel of great counsel (Is 9:6 LXX), appeared to Moses on the Mount.

481. The following seven quotations are to be found in Greek and Latin columns, *PG*, 6 cols. 597/98, 599/600, 601/2, 605/6, 607/8, 613/14.

The *Dialogus*, which purports to represent an exchange in Ephesus during the Bar-Kochba Revolt, 132–35, was in its final form set forth after Justin's I *Apologia*, c. 150/155, with three main ideas: the transitoriness of the Old Covenant and its precepts; the identity of the Logos with the Old Testament theophanies and callings; and at length the vocation of the Gentiles to replace Israel. The definitive appearance of the Logos with precepts is in Jesus Christ with his new commandments. A Polish translation appears to have been the first vernacular version in Europe, *Świętego Justyna Filozofa Rozmowa z Tryfonem Żydem* (Nieśwież, 1564). It was the work of Wawrzyniec Krzyszkowski, who, first converted to the confession of the Czech Brethren in Great Poland, had been called by Mikołaj Radziwiłł the Black to serve as pastor in Nieśwież. In an appendix the translator stresses the role of Justin in the development of ideas among the Polish and the Lithuanian Brethren. On what little is known of the pastor-translator, who was helped by Szymon Budny, see Konrad Górski, *PSB*, 15 (1970) 562–63; on the distinctiveness of the pioneer Polish rendering, A. Lisiecki, introduction, *Dialog i Apologia* (Poznań, 1926); on the press at Nieśwież, Alodia Kawecka-Gryczowa, *Drukarze*, 190–91.

482. *Dialogus*, 56, the bracketed subordinating phrases being omitted, presumably by Lismanino. *PG*, 6, col. 597.

483. The references which follow are to the appearance of the Second Person in the guise of an angel to Abraham and Sarah, n. 486.

484. *Dialogus*, 56; *PG*, 6, col. 600.

485. Through David, i.e., in Ps 110:1; 14:6–7; *Dialogus*, 56; *PG*, 6, col. 601.

486. The passage is in the context of the appearance of three men or angels to Abraham and Sarah at the oaks of Mamre, Gen 18:1–2, in *Dialogus*, 56; *PG*, 6, col. 605. The translation conveys Lubieniecki's Latin. The material in parentheses comes from him. But the correct renderings of the original Greek behind his Latin rendering is as follows:

> And now have you not perceived, my friends, that *one* of three, who is both God and Lord, and ministers to Him [the Father] who is in the heavens, is Lord of the two [other] angels?

487. *Dialogus*, 57; *PG*, 6, col. 605.

488. *Dialogus*, 58; *PG*, 6, col. 608.

489. *Dialogus*, 60; *PG*, 6, col. 613.

490. As with Lombardus, God is *suprema res* (cf. at n. 496), the relationships of Father, Son, and Holy Spirit being in the Persons, not in the *substantia/essentia/res*, the Godhead as distinguished from the Persons, a view that seemed to Lismanino to undercut the distinctive role of the incarnate Son as soteriological Mediator.

491. *De aeterna filii et spiritu Sancti cum Deo existentia, et contra Sabellianos* is among the *dubia* of Athanasius; *PG*, 28.

492. *Contra Sabellianos*, 12; *PG*, 31, col. 116.

493. *Contra Sabellianos*, 12; *PG*, 31, cols. 116–17: "unam in tribus *forman*...non unam *rem* ex tribus."

494. *Contra Sabellianos*, 12–13, *PG*, col. 117.

In transcribing Lismanino's letter, Lubieniecki perhaps misread Lismanino's Latin of Pseudo-Athanasius: "Nec tamen ideo in unum illa verba complico: *ex quo, per quem, et in quo* [hoc est, patrem, Filium et spiritum Sanctum] ut *Trinitatem nitar unitatem efficer*." *Contra Sabellianos*, 12–13, *PG*, 31, col. 117B. Lismanino probably himself added the clarificatory words in brackets, but he would not have made *per quem* into *per Deum*, as in the Lubieniecki text.

495. Lismanino makes the italicized phrasing of Pseudo-Athanasius (n. 494) his own as he turns from quoting "Athanasius" (already in the first person) to attacking himself the Sabellius of his own time, as Lismanino perceives Stancaro.

496. Whatever the terminology of Sabellius, Lismanino is again at the center of his concern with Stancaro in whose doctrine of the Trinity the *res* of the Godhead is conceptually resistant to any meaningful differentiation of Personal roles of relational modalities and thus appears to Lismanino to become in effect Unitarianism, although he sees Stancaro as Sabellian with only one *Persona*. For a possibly typical expression of his kind of Stancarism in an excommunicated pastor, see the charge against Marcin of Lublin, n. 446, ¶3.

497. This is presumably the *Apologeticus de fuga* (abbreviated in Lubieniecki); Gregory of Nanzianzus, *Oratio* 2; *PG*, 35.

498. After the differentiation between the Greek and the Latin text of the Niceno-Constantinopolitan Creed by the interpolation of the *Filioque* at the III Council of Toledo (589), the ecumenical interchange of the Greek and Latin theologians at the 17th Ecumenical Council of Ferrara-Florence (1438–89) made formal that in the Union the *Filioque* was authoritative and that the new variant Greek phrasing Latinized *ex Patre per Filium* was to be understood in the Latin sense. Denzinger, *Enchiridion*, 691.

499. From *Epistola* 38.1 to Gregory of Nyssa on the difference between οὐσία and ὑπόστασις quoting 1 Cor 12:11; *PL*, 32. The letter is not authentic. A. Cavallin, *Studien zu den Briefen des hl. Basilius* (Lund, 1944). In the next line, with Bursche, "indignis" is conjectured.

500. To virtually the end of his life Lismanino asseverated his belief in the Trinity, in the Greek Uniate manner, i.e., holding to the procession of the Holy Spirit from the Father and *through* (*per*) the eternally begotten Son/Logos, *Brevis explicatio doctrinae de Sanctissima Trinitate* (Königsberg, 1565); Hein, *Italienische Protestanten*, 44, n. 90 and passim. It is not certain whether in the foregoing paragraph Lubieniecki or the printer has accurately rendered the technical terms. Clear it is that Lismanino sees the creatures (all things of Col 1:15–17) as created *ex nihilo* so that they be not seen to emanate from eternal being, from God, and that *Ingenita potentia* in the Godhead presides over the creative act of the eternally *Genita potentia*. Lismanino here uses *potentia* where in the debate presided over by Luther on the same issue, with the terminology of Lombardus expressly employed and disallowed, the terms are *Generens* and *Genita essentia* or *Persona* (at issue) and *Genitus* as the Second Person. Cf. the paraphrased speech of Lismanino at Włodzisław, where Lismanino expressly opposed Lombardus and cited Luther in support, esp. at n. 515. The debate over Lombard and the Trinity at Wittenberg and Włodzisław were much less than a score of years apart.

501. Jakub Sylvius (Sylwiusz) (d. after 1583), minister in Krzcięcice, then Pińczów, mentioned several times below by Lubieniecki, several times already in the nn., prominent in the correspondence of the Swiss and Poles, was the owner of Calvin's *Opuscula*

omnia in unum volumen collecta (Geneva, 1552), purchased from Lismanino in 1556. Sylvius preserved the *Acta* of some synods from 1550. Sipayłło, *AS*, 2.XV.1.xxiv; 2.73–88. Sylvius may have been *filius* to Lismanino but he was not in agreement with him. His life and role in the emergent schism is told by Kawecka-Gryczowa, "Sylvius a rozłam w zborze małopolskim," n. 434, ¶3. For Negri, above, n. 457.

502. Lubieniecki erroneously gives the date as 10 December 1561. Dalton (*Lasciana*, 550) and Bock (*op. cit.*, I. 437) tried to explain this discrepancy by assuming that Lismanino wrote two letters to Karniński. But see *BAnt*, 35. A copy of this letter exists in the palatine archive of Gdańsk. Sipayłło, *AS*, 2.119, n. 1.

503. This important and well attended synod deliberated in Włodzisław, 21–25 September 1561. Sipayłło, *AS*, 2.115–23. Among the ministers Lismanino, Biandrata (!), Cruciger, and Krowicki are listed first. Sarnicki was the local pastor. Jan Boner leads the list of lordly gentlemen.

Superintendent Cruciger introduced the items of business: (1) church discipline, (2) the erection of a school at Książ for the training of youths, some of whom would go on to the ministry, (3) the establishment and direction of a bank for the poor (*mons pietatis*), on a Catholic model, and (4) a consultation "on common necessities of the Church."

Discipline at this moment had to do with communion and the terms of excommunication, the lesser and the great ban. The problem of the Stancarist school in Dubiecko and of the nobles sending their youths there was in the background of both items 1 and 2, while a major concern of some nobles is evident in the appeal that Stancarists be reconciled if possible, lest Catholics take advantage of the public acrimony among Protestants.

In this larger framework, which was not wholly held to, Biandrata resigned his lay eldership (cf. n. 447, ¶12), but after Mikołaj Oleśnicki criticized fraternally the alliance between him and Lismanino, the landlords by vote restored him to the eldership. Lismanino was dealt with more severely. Some regarded him as the author of the new doctrine of the Trinity. His letter to Lord Stanisław Iwan Karniński, given *in toto* by Lubieniecki immediately above, first became a synodal issue at Włodzisław, where it was read and discussed. The ministers asserted that because of the importance of "the unity with the other Churches, the Helvetic, the Bohemian, and Lithuanian" it was necessary for Lismanino to submit in writing a further clarification of his position at a future synod, and he promised to do so. Ibid., 119.

504. The date of this synod in Cracow is given as 16 September 1561 by Stoiński (*Epitome*, *BAnt*, RD 2, no. 5). But besides Lubieniecki here and Stoiński, there are materials from Kolozsvár and A. Węgierski. Szczucki, (*Czechowic*, 232) shows that Lubieniecki's date is correct, followed by Sipayłło, with all the evidence, *AS*, 2.124–26.

505. This action is confirmed by the records. Sipayłło, *AS*, 2.125. But there were perhaps two letters of Calvin read, according to Lismanino, an angry one from Calvin to Cruciger about the impossibility of his being reconciled to a wolf in charge of the sheep (*OC*, 19, no. 3561), and perhaps one addressed to Prince Radziwiłł. Lismanino to Calvin, after the Cracow synod, 14 December 1561; *OC*, 19, 3561), and perhaps one addressed to Prince Radziwiłł. Lismanino to Calvin, after the Cracow synod, 14 December 1561; *OC*, 19, n. 3649, col. 170 at n. 4.

In his dedication to Radziwiłł of his new edition of *Commentaria in Acta Apostolorum*, 1 August 1560, Calvin had attacked Biandrata, saying that he was more dangerous than Stancaro. *OC*, no. 3232; Tylenda, "Warning," 40. The synod of Pińczów, 27 January 1561, had sided with Biandrata and asked Radziwiłł to help reconcile him and Calvin. (This synod was mentioned in nn. 438, 447, ¶6.) Radziwiłł, accordingly, wrote Calvin and Bullinger, 14 July 1561, and the ministers of Vilna added their letters to Calvin, 23 July 1561. Marcin Czechowic was sent with these letters and, on his way, he picked up another letter privately from Cruciger to the Swiss divines, dated 3 September 1561, attesting to Biandrata's orthodoxy, and also privately a letter of Sarnicki against Biandrata. Wotschke, *Briefwechsel*, nos. 222, 223, 224, 226, 227. Calvin, in letters dated 9 October 1561, replied to Sarnicki, Cruciger, the ministers of Vilna, Lismanino, and Radziwiłł with a further warning against Biandrata. Wotschke, *Briefwechsel*, nos. 233, 234 (*OC*, no. 3561 mentioned in first paragraph of this note), 235, 236 (correctly: *OC*, no. 3564), 237. Bullinger wrote, 30 September 1561, to the same effect to Radziwiłł and Cruciger. Wotschke, *Briefwechsel*, nos. 230–31.

506. Deut 6:4: "Hear, O Israel: The Lord our God is one Lord."
The paraphrase recalls wording in the Polish *Akta* according to which Biandrata is reported specifically in Geneva to have criticized with force the *Institutes*. Sipayłło, *AS*, 2.125. But Lubienieckis' *Trinitarii* represents seventeenth-century usage.

In Geneva, 1556–58, after epistolary exchanges and discussions with Calvin, notably in a public dispute held at the Italian Church, Biandrata had been required to subscribe to the official confession of the Church, 15 May 1558, in the presence of Calvin. For Biandrata in Switzerland, see n. 436, ¶¶5–6. As early as November 1558, Calvin had warned Lismanino against Biandrata (n. 436, ¶8).

507. For the letters, see n. 505.

508. This was a letter of Martyr to Calvin, in which he confided that the Italians in Poland fostered a plurality of deities by insisting on diversity of the persons and thereby imperilling the unity of substance (*essentia*). This notice is preserved in Martyr's *Loci communes ex variis authoris scriptis in quatuor classes distributi* (Zurich, 1588). It is mentioned and discussed in context by Marvin Walter Anderson, *Peter Martyr: A Reformer in Exile (1542–1562): A chronology of biblical writings in England and Europe*, Bibliotheca Humanistica et Reformatorica, 10 (Nieuwkoop: De Groot, 1975) 443. This work carries on from Philip McNair, *Peter Martyr in Italy: The Anatomy of an Apostasy* (Oxford, 1967).

Vermigli was in frequent contact with the Poles or with fellow Swiss divines concerning them. His communication to the Poles from Strassburg, 14 February 1556, dealing with 5 points of Christology, was printed as *Ad ecclesiam Polonicam* (Pińczów, 1559), listed by Anderson, *Peter Martyr*, 546, among early imprints. The publisher of Vermigli's *Ad ecclesiam* was Daniel of Łęczyca (near Kutno), referred to by Węgierski, *Slavonia Reformata*, 252. Anderson's *Register epistolarum* of Vermigli (*Peter Martyr*, 467–86) does not list the letter mentioned by Lubieniecki, who may well have himself had at hand a copy of Vermigli's *Communes loci*. Vermimgli addressed the problem of the Poles in his preface, directed against Stancaro, 15 August 1561, *Dialogus de utraque in Christo natura, quomodo coeant in unam Christi personam inseparabilem*. Wotschke, *Briefwechsel*, no. 225. For Vermigli's larger relationship with the Poles, see Anderson *Peter Martyr*, esp. 439–54.

509. Sipayłło supplies a sparse record of this synod. *AS*, 2.124–26. In his ensuing account Lubieniecki supplies speeches for Biandrata, Ossoliński, and Lismanino. Sipayłło raises the question as to whether these interventions are authentic. *AS*, 2.126, n. 1. Places for them can be found in the meagre record. Lubieniecki indeed may have known this very text and amplified it, possibly from independent records. He and the *Akta* agree that Lismanino's letter to Iwan was examined.

510. Cf. 2 Tim 4:4, Titus 3:9.

511. In the *Akta* (in Polish) Biandrata is reported to have talked about Satanic

"craftiness" and to have assessed the three creeds. In the Latin source for the synod Biandrata was expressly "arianismi sive servetianismi suspectus." In this synod it was summarized that "Arianorum sive Servetanorum factio augebatur." *AS*, 2.126. Lubieniecki's speech for Biandrata sounds authentic. It was agreed that Biandrata should write "swoję konfesyją" for presentation at a future synod set for 10 March 1562 at Książ. This same synod records the presence of a letter of impressive recommendation for Stanisław Paklepka signed by Pietro Martire Vermigli, not known to Anderson, *Peter Martyr*.

512. Hieronim Ossoliński (d. 1576), later castellan, was married to Katarzyna Zborowska. Note the connection at n. 513. The *Akta* refer briefly to his intervention. Sipayłło, *AS*, 2.125–126. But Lubieniecki's speech for him, so very plausible and characteristic, could not have been a mere simplification of hints in the synodal record.

513. The palatine of Poznań, 1557–62, Marcin Stanisław Zborowski (d. 1565). His wife was Anna Konarska, niece of the bishop of Cracow. Zborowski, a correspondent of Calvin, gained Commonwealth-wide notoriety/fame for having killed cruelly in 1553 Prince Dymitri Sanguszko, first husband of Halszka Ostrogska (*Historia, 51*). The episode features in the protocol of the embassy of the Czech Brethren to the Reformed of Little Poland, 29 November–16 December 1556. Sipayłło, *AS*, 2.82–171, 125. Ossoliński's disparaging remark about the capacity of Zborowski's wife to understand Stancaro, at n. 513, is the belittling reference of a brother-in-law (n. 512). He himself had made an effort to hear Stancaro out; and a *Liber de Mediatore* by Frycz Modrzewski sympathetic to Stancaro had been dedicated to Ossoliński as recently as September 1560 (n. 431).

It is not clear what book was presented to Anna K. Zborowska. It could have been the *Collatio* (Pińczów, 1558) above n. 426, ¶3, but it is not likely Lismanino would recently have been handed it. She could have had a manuscript of *De Trinitate et Mediatore Domino nostro adversus Henricum Bullingerum, Petrum Martyrem, et Joannem Calvinum, et reliquos Tigurinae ac Genevensis ecclesiae ministros* (Cracow, 1562). This was written after the failure of his identical letters to these Swiss divines, quoted in part, n. 435, ¶3. The preface is dated 1 June 1561. Karol Estreicher, *Bibliografia polska XV–XVI stólecia: Zestawienie 7200 druków w kształcie rejestru do Bibliografii* (Cracow, 1875); reprinted (New York, 1964); 29, 174–75 supplemented by *Polonica XVI do XVII wieku nie znane Bibliografii Estereichera ze zbiórów Biblioteki Gdańskiej*, ed. by Anna Jędrzejowska *et al.* (Gdansk, 1968).

514. The second alternative was the view of all the Swiss divines and Melanchthon but not of Lombardus and the majority of Fathers (n. 427).

515. It is strange that Lismanino would attribute the entire vocabulary for Triadology and Christology to the inventions of the Schoolmen. In his authentic letter quoted *in toto*, *Historia, 119–26*, and alluded to in his speech below, Lismanino adduced many patristic texts with philosophical terms not found in Scripture. Evidently this paraphrase (not wholly an invention) owes much to Lubieniecki by way of simplification. Lombardus here stands for scholasticism, but Lismanino is quite right that Luther opposed Lombardus and favored Joachim, e.g. in his interventions as chairman of the promotional debate of Georg Major and Johann Faber for their doctorate in theology, Wittenberg, 12 December 1544. There were 47 theses distributed between the candidates to defend, no. 14: "Quin Magister *Sententiarum*, no satis recte docuit, Essentiam divinam nec generare nec generari," *Luthers Werke*, Weimar Edition, 39:2, 287. The terms *genita* and *generens* with respect to the divine *essentia* or *persona* (under debate) are of the same problematic as with Lismanino, at n. 500. In several interventions Luther supports

Joachim against Lombardus for fear of a Quaternity of four substances, e.g., ibid., 314. Cf. Hein, *Italienische Protestanten*, n. 245; Luther, however, does not expressly mention *Firmiter* (n. 427). Johann Bugenhagen, the promotor, adds that since the Pope had not understood the point of Joachim, the abbot should not have been condemned. For an assessment of how in Wittenberg the relative authority of the Church Fathers, conciliar creeds, and the Schoolmen over against the Scripture was worked through, see Reiner Jansen, *Studien zu Luthers Trinitätslehre* (Bern/Frankfurt: Europäische Hochschulschriften, 1976). On Luther and the Trinity, see further Bk. 3, n. 125.

516. Lismanino, as here paraphrased perhaps, seems to be insisting on the toleration of an optional use of traditional terms in the group over against the radical scripturalists of his party who would press for their total elimination. In his authentic letter to Iwan he employed traditional terms, *Historia, 119–26*.

517. The reported speech of Lismanino seems to be close to what he actually said and this versimilitude enhances the approximation to authenticity of the other two interventions (Biandrata's and Ossoliński's). In the *Akta* Lismanino is reported to have responded to Ossoliński concerning Stancaro, *De Trinitate*, and then to have said: "Let it be that all *doktorowie* leave me One God, let them not divide Him or make in Him a dispensation (*ekonomijej*); when they leave God whole (*cało*), let them have whatever Mediator they wish to devise." Sipayłło, *AS*, 2.126. Theologians have traditionally made a distinction between the intradeical and the economic (dispensational) Trinity. Lismanino as reported in the *Akta* seems to place the dispensational *within* the Godhead. Cf. n. 639.

Of interest for Lismanino's intention in his reported intervention and for authenticating it is the fact that Benedykt Wiszowaty in his *Epitome* of the original Stoiński/Lismanino (*BAnt*, no. 5) quotes part of the above translated from the Polish of the *Akta*: "Reliquant mihi omnes Doctores unum Deum," where Lubieniecki has: "Reliquant mihi *antiqui Ecclesaie Doctores* Deum unum." There is a slightly different meaning possible, also, this time in favor of Lubieniecki's Latin version "Deum unum" with the *unum* in this position being plausibly adverbial and thus like the Polish text of the *Akta*: "To [that God] gdy oni cało zostawią." It is likely that Stoiński had no more before him than the present *Akta* and that his sentence and the Polish protocol are correct, and that Lismanino's *doctores* refer to diverse Reformation divines. For it is hard to imagine that the dexterous adducer of patristic triadological texts in the letter to Iwan (*Historia, 119–26*), itself referred to constructively by its author two months later, would be now enjoining the same Fathers to set forth only what he is now proclaiming. In that letter he had surely been absorbed in the varied ancient triadological testimony. Interesting is the degree to which his synodal formulation comes close to that of Stancaro and actually stands further from Biandrata's transitional Tritheism, though both men be in agreement on the Apostles' Creed.

Surely no parties wished to be called Tritheists. The charge could be leveled against anyone or a grouping that deviated from the traditional defense of Christian monotheism, the unity of the Godhead in Three Persons. To many among the Polish Reformed Stancaro's orthodox formulas in patristic and scholastic terms (e.g. in n. 435) seemed stark, especially in the light of the regained plenary authority of the revealed language of Scripture and of the explicit instruction of Melanchthon and the Swiss divines, that of the latter directed expressly to the Poles in their quandaries and scruples and perhaps in a special way in their emotional attachment to the Suffering Christ. Against the starkness of Stancaro's alleged orthodoxy in his schismatic church, Lismanino could find in the philosophically or more specifically ontologically unspecific triadological formulation in the Apostles' Creed a received, *traditional*, surely apostolic safeguard of the unity of God and the plenitude of the Person and Work of Christ and sufficient concerning the Spirit.

However this may be, the reported speech of Lismanino does not stand by itself as witness to what he held, at least when explaining the synod of Cracow himself quite soon afterwards to Calvin, Bullinger, and Johann Wolph, December 1561. Wotschke, *Briefwechsel*, nos. 244–46, the last two printed by Wotschke, the first in *OC*, 19, no. 3649, cols. 170–75. What Lismanino says in all three in denigration of Sarnicki and Sylvius and in spirited self-defense as to his own intended orthodoxy does not invalidate what Lubieniecki or the tradition he represents recorded or remembered of Lismanino's intervention at the synod.

In two of three (to Bullinger and Wolph) Lismanino says: "Errare possum, hareticus esse non possum (nec volo)." *Briefwechsel*, 142, 145. In two of them (to Calvin and Wolph) he reveals the impressive extent of his reading in the Fathers *de Trinitate* (well documented in his letter to Karniński, *Historia, 119–26*). *OC*, 19, col. 174; *Briefwechsel*, 145. What he recounts to the Swiss divines is somewhat different from what he stressed in the letter to Karniński, n. 449. The three letters are personal to the point of expressing anger, distress, and tenderness (mentioning the need to dictate rather than himself to write because of his affliction, epilepsy: to Calvin, col. 175; to Wolph, pp. 144, 145; and in this third letter turning from an initial section in Italian and returning to it briefly at the end). In all three letters he fulminated against Sarnicki, who had written against him to Calvin and Bullinger in September (*Briefwechsel*, nos. 226, 228) and against Sylvius. In two letters (to Calvin and Wolph) he assailed Stancaro to defend Biandrata, pressing the fact that Biandrata had been welcomed by Łaski. With Calvin he was evasive and circumspect, since Calvin had earlier rebuked him, 9 October 1561 (*OC*, 19, no. 3564) for his sponsorship of Biandrata, while he called Stancaro a "mad dog" and his messenger, Krzysztof Przechadzka (n. 435 ¶2) as futile in his mission.

Although in this nervous reply to Calvin he says it uniquely, the characterization here of the four positions Lismanino opposes may be considered representative of his mood in synod and in his three letters of December 1561: "the Servetian impiety, the Arian insanity, the Sabellian foolishness, the Stancarian madness," *OC*, 19, col. 174. By Sabellianism he means Stancarism, which he makes clear to Wolph imagines "one person or substance . . . as Father, Son, and Holy Spirit, of that person three names," *OC*, 19, 145. In his most defensive letter to Calvin he is most clear in explaining the course of theological thought among the Reformed in Poland. Right after his characterization of Sabellianism/Stancarism as he understands Stancaro under the ancient appellation, he tells Calvin that the Apostles' Creed could in time of misunderstanding suffice and appeals to Hilary of Poitiers (*De synodis*, 27, 63) and boldly notes (col. 174) that Calvin has himself suggested the same thing in the *Institutes* (1559:1, 13, 5). He alludes to the following:

> Hilary accuses the heretics of a great crime, that by their [the Arian's] wickedness he is forced to submit to the peril of human speech what ought to have been locked within the sanctity of men's minds; and he does not hide the fact that this is to do things unlawful, to speak things inexpressible, to presume things not conceded [*De Trinitate*]. . . . And elsewhere [*De synodis*] he pronounces the bishops of Gaul happy because they had neither wrought out, nor received, nor known, any other confession at all than *the ancient and very simple one* that had been received among all churches *from the Apostolic Age*.

From the edition of John T. McNeill and Ford Lewis Battles in two continuously paginated vols, Library of Christian Classics, 20 (Philadelphia/London, 1960) 127, emphasis editorially supplied here. Calvin has been quoted at length because Lismanino sanctions the practices and beliefs of the emergent pre-Socinian Minor Church, the church that would presently become fully Unitarian, with an appeal to Calvin and to the sources to which Calvin had appealed—Hilary and the Apostles' Creed. Retaining the Creed for trine believers' baptism by immersion, the Minor Church claimed that they consistently represented the Reformed Church of Poland and that Poland was the final theater of the Reformation—the almost explicit claim of the *Historia*.

As to how Calvin felt about Lismanino, there is *inter alia* the passing remark by Calvin in a letter to Bullinger, about a year before, wherein he disparagingly referred to Lismanino as *Graeculus* who had fostered (reading *fovet* for *sonet*) Biandrata. In the same letter of 1 February 1561, Calvin also made disparaging remarks about Łaski, deploring his having brought his own personal domestic problem for synodal discipline and his having taken delight in Biandrata. *OC*, 18, no. 3332, col. 349.

518. Three letters were dated from the Cracow synod, 13 December 1561. Wotschke, *Briefwechsel*, nos. 241–43; *OC*, 19, nos. 3647 and 3648. They are markedly different, although signed by (nearly) the same five pastors and four elders, among the latter Iwan Karniński and Biandrata. Besides misspellings and somewhat different identifications of the signatories, there is the discrepancy in the surname of two *seniores* Adam (A. Swierczkowski in the first version, A. Spinkonsvus in the second). One letter may be a spurious substitute for the other, or they may be two quite variant drafts with a common purpose.

The first of the two as printed in *OC* sets forth a *Credimus* that, while it has phrasings in common with the brief *Confessio* of Biandrata of the synod of Pińczów, 27 January 1561 (Sipayłło, *AS*, 2.84), is identified by Lubieniecki, at n. 523, as the *Confessio* presented by Biandrata and discussed at Książ and Pińczów, 10 March and 2 April 1562. In presenting the *Credimus* here, phrasing close to, and probably distinctive of, that of Biandrata in his brief *Confessio* (given in the Latin by Hein, below n. 523), is italicized:

> ... Agnoscimus patrem verum Deum esse, Christum quoque filium Dei esse verum Deum, spiritum quoque sanctum esse verum Deum. *Pluritatem deorum destamur*. *Unum esse Deum*, non persona, sed indifferenti natura credimus. Contra Arium credimus ὁμοούσιον filium patri. Contra Servetum credimus aeternum ex aeterno patre genitum filium, omnipotentem ex omnipotente, perfectum ex perfecto. Item Verbum quoque suo tempore factum hominem, non mutata natura Verbi in carnem, sed carni in unam hypostasim unita (*OC* 19, col. 167).

The letter goes on immediately to express a preference for the *Apostolicum*. Yet the *Credimus* can be construed as Nicene-Constantinopolitan and Chalcedonian. Where it asserts "God to be one, not by Person but by undiffering nature," Biandrata on his own had simply "one God ... indivisible by essence." The *Credimus* is close to what Lismanino argued for in this three communications after the synod, set forth in n. 517, ¶¶4–6.

The second letter from the Cracow synod to Calvin more openly defends Biandrata, pointing out that he had been received into fellowship by Łaski (the same is said by Radziwiłł to Calvin, n. 522), that he is the open enemy of Arius and Servetus.

A third letter, that of the Cracow synod to Bullinger, was preserved in copy by

Lismanino in his *De Trinitate*; Wotschke, *Briefwechsel*, no. 243, printed by him in his "Lismanino," 317 – 18 (n. 136).

519. Sarnicki and Sylvius, not mentioned by name in the two *OC* letters of n. 518.

520. Lismanino and Biandrata.

521. In the three letters of the Cracow synod (n. 518), Sarnicki and Sylvius are only alluded to, as also in Radziwiłł's letter to Calvin of n. 522. But in the *libelli* of these two theological conservatives of 1562, see n. 529, ¶4.

522. Radziwiłł to Calvin, 14 July 1561; *OC*, 18, no. 3443. Thanking Calvin for his dedication of the *Commentarius* but spiritedly defending Biandrata, whom he calls *archipresbyter* (= perhaps *coadjutor*), against "the contention and assault of two most distinguished men" (Sarnicki and Sylvius, presumably), Radziwiłł observes that the doctor, his doctrine and his life, was once *viva voce* accepted by Łaski, later by Lismanino. Probably with the help of Czechowic, bearer of the letter, Radziwiłł adduced in support of simple formulations Hilary of Poitiers and Gregory of Nazianzus, *Oratio* 32, *De moderandis disputationibus* (in which Gregory had once denounced the passion of the Constantinopolitans in their bitter dogmatic argumentation). Having sent with Czechowic a fur mantle in token of appreciation for Calvin's gift to him of the dedication, the palatine clearly expected to be heeded by the distant Reformer. For the messenger of Radziwiłł on this mission, see Szczucki, *Czechowic*, 38 – 39 and for the whole context of the palatine's theological and reforming activity, Józef Jasnowski, *Mikołaj Czarny Radziwiłł* (Warsaw, 1939) 188 – 234.

523. The texts of the (brief) *Confessio* are identical in Węgierski, *Historia/Slavonia Reformata*, 86, and Lubieniecki, except that the latter inserts after *Fateor: esse*.

Węgierski, over against Lubieniecki/Budziński, places these words *verbatim* at the synod of Pińczów, (25) 27 January 1561 (nn. 438, ¶2; 447, ¶9; 518; 524, ¶3); and, in fact, the protocol for Pińczów preserves them, also verbatim. Sipayłło, *AS*, 2.84. For want of a speech from Biandrata at the decisive synod of Książ, 10 March 1562, Lubieniecki evidently quotes Biandrata from the earlier synod. Hein usefully discusses the brief *Confessio* as though it were of 1562 and notes that Biandrata's basic conviction is that "unus nobis sit tantum deus essentia indivisibilis," the rest, he says, being terminological camouflage (*Italienische Protestanten*, 160 – 61). But the subtle *Confessio* with its use of traditional language belongs to Pińczów, 1562.

The Blandratan *Confessio* of Książ, 1562, was so radical that it has not survived. It is described at Książ and at Pińczów, 2 April 1562; Sipayłło, *AS*, 2.129 – 30, 132 – 33. It was "long, smoothly written, scriptural." Biandrata presented it, as requested by the synod of Cracow, to be read publicly but quite a few ministers and nobles preferred that it not be so read but rather examined by, as it turned out, eleven ministers and Biandrata himself as author and lay elder (*senior* in the records always means lay elder) ("między ministrami i starszymi wyższej mianowanymi"). On the non-participation of Sarnicki and Sylvius, two of the eleven, see n. 529, ¶5. In the end no resolution came and it was agreed to take *skrypt* (perhaps it was not so long but what copies for all could be made) to their homes to deliberate over and ponder until the foreseen synod at Pińczów. On what happened there, see at and in n. 529. Because of the importance of this lost *skrypt*, efforts have been made to interpret the brief *Confessio* reported by Lubieniecki as all of it or part of it or to locate it elsewhere.

On the role of Stanisław Lutomirski and Książ and Pińczów, see n. 552.

Delio Cantimori, e.g., thought he had identified the much pondered full *Confesssio* of Biandrata at Książ. This was published by H.P.C. Henke, *Georgii Blandratae confessio antitrinitaria* (Helmstadt, 1694). Cantimori presented his view in "Profile," *Eretici Itali-*

ani. Wilbur accepted this, *Socianinism*, 309, also n. 13; I followed him in *Radical Reformation*. Lech Szczucki is credited with having noted that the *Confessio* of Henke/Cantimori is in any case after the preface to Beza's *Valentini Gentilis perfidiae brevis explicatio* (Geneva, 1567), to which this *Confessio* refers and which is therefore probably to be situated in Transylvania, 1568/69. Sipayłło, *AS*, 2.129, n. 4; Rotondò, "G.B.," *DBI*, 259A.

524. This is the first edition of *Slavonia Reformata* (1652). For the place and year of the brief *Confessio*, Węgierski was evidently correct, not Budziński. See preceding n.

525. The letter to Radziwiłł, signed by Cruciger, was dated Pińczów, 13 March 1561; *OC*, 18, no. 3359. It speaks of a *Confessio* surely larger than that offered by Węgierski/Lubieniecki (at n. 523) and urges Radziwiłł to resume the efforts at reconciling Calvin and Biandrata, "in whom we have a son of the orthodox Church," *OC*, 18, no. 3359, col. 402.

526. Budziński is confirmed by the synodal record as to dates and agenda, but he scarcely conveys any sense of the ever more radical evolution of Biandrata's *Confessiones*, resulting in the veritable revolution in synodal doctrine consolidated at Pińczów. Sipayłło, *AS*, 2.129; 132. In the translation, for the *Illum, Jezuza* (it could have been *Christum*) has been supplied in brackets from the *Akta*, as well as *great* (*wielkiego*) for Budziński/Lubieniecki's *wiecznego/aeterni*. As to the last, it is possible that Budziński's was the original reading in the protocol, transcribed as *Wielki* in the Unitarianizing Kolozsvár MS as the only source for the critical edition. Szczucki with a fuller synodal record before him than Lubieniecki discusses Książ and Pińczów, characterizing Biandrata's tactic at the latter synod "as none other than an intentional, conscious gibe at Calvin," even while the brothers in synod were promising to do everything in their power by writing to Calvin to reconcile the two, *Czechowic*, 40.

527. The synod was under pressure from Biandrata, on the offensive and possibly infused with his own vision of a congeries of doctrinally and liturgically simplified Reformed Churches in Lithuania, Poland, Transylvania (and perhaps also Moravia and Moldavia), all under the protection of puissant princes, voivodes, and lords of the Eastern marches of Latin Christendom on the frontier of Orthodoxy (without an *Athanasium*, a *Filioque*, and a plethora of scholastic terminology for the doctrine of God), and with its Tartar and Ottoman Islam (with its sheer monotheism). He requested almost impudently that Calvin retract (*retraktował*; Lubieniecki has for Budziński's Polish, which may have been precisely this, *revoceret*) the offending dedicatory epistle in his *Commentarius* or at least henceforth to omit the hostile reference in it to Biandrata. For the *Commentarius*, *OC*, 48, cols. 1–574; for the dedicatory letter alone, *OC*, 18, no. 3232; for the action of the synod, Sipayłło, *AS*, 2.132 and n. 4. The Epistle dedicatory to Prince Radziwiłł is printed in the standard English version of the *Commentary upon the Acts of the Apostles*, translated by Christopher Fetherton (London, 1585), somewhat modernized in the edition of Henry Beveridge, reprinted in the Eerdmans edition (Grand Rapids, 1949) xv–xxiv, wherein the offending section reads:

> First, although no foreign enemy troubles you [O Prince], you shall have business enough to withstand those evils which are at home with you. You have sufficiently tried [experienced] with how may sleights Satan is furnished that he may work some policy to overthrow that holy concord amongst the brethren wherein consisteth the safety of the [Reformed] Church [in the Grand Duchy]. . . . So, whilst that Stancaro, a man of a troublesome nature, doth, through that ambition wherewith he is wholly set on fire, spread amongst you his dotings, hereupon brake out that contention which threateneth some scattering abroad; and you were laid open unto the landers of many,

because it was thought that this sect [of Stancarists] did spread itself farther. Behold, on the other side, a certain physician, called giorgio Biandrata, worse than Stancaro, because his error is more detestable, and because he hath in his mind a secret poison. For which cause these aso [unnamed Lithuanian and Polish Reformed leaders] are the more worthy to be reproved, at whose hands the ungodliness of Servetus hath found such favors of such a sudden. For although I am persuaded that they [the tolerant leadership] are far from those perverse and sacriligious [Servetian] opinions, yet they should have taken better heed, and not have suffered this fox [Biandrata] craftily to creep into their company. *Loc. cit.*, p. xx – xxi (the Latinized Italian names restored to the vernacular).

528. The completion of Lubieniecki's should be: 'And I do not find in this epistle directed to King Christian anything about Biandrata.' The first edition of the *Commentarius*, part 1, was dedicated Christian III, 28 February 1552; and part 2, to his son Prince Frederick, 25 January 1554; and in such a dedication Calvin would have had no occasion to mention Biandrata.

In the next sentence the phrasing "in aliis Commentariis MSS" is misleading as seeming to refer to other versions of Calvin's *Comentarius*, but Lubieniecki means MS accounts of the synods.

529. The reference is to John 14:28.

In this paragraph on Pińczów, Lubieniecki is drawing upon, not only the account of Budziński, acknowledged at n. 526, but also evidently the source common to Andrzej Wiszowaty and to his son, Benedykt, namely, the MS *List of Stages* by Stoiński, of which Benedykt made the *Epitome*, RD 5, no. 54. There is also a snippet of the record of Pińczów preserved uniquely by Lismanino (below, ¶5), in addition to the scanty protocol, edited by Sipayłło, *AS*, 2.132 – 33. From all this it is possible to add *seriatim* some details related to Lubieniecki's information. Górski (*Grzegorz Paweł*, 85 – 86) says clearly: "The April synod of 1562 played the role of the pointer on the scale that decided on victory as between the tendencies long struggling with each other in the [Reformed] Church of Little Poland: traditional and revolutionary."

That the ministers should henceforth abstain from the use of non-scriptural, philosophical terms, *Trinitas*, *essentia*, *generatio*, *processio*, marked the beginning of Unitarianism in Poland. At Pińczów, 2 April 1562, the Radical Reformation became theologically explicit synodally in thus registering the first moment in the final descent of a reasoning together about the Godhead, from the received Triadology, through various formularies of Nicene and Ante-Nicene Fathers, down and back to Scripture alone and the testimony of the apostles in "their" *Apostolicum*. Previous affirmations of the wholly undefined Triadology of the baptismal formula of Matt 28:19 and of the Apostles' Creed had been accomplished by quite idiosyncratic and earnest speculators like Servetus, Gribaldi, and Gentile, or by the virtual repudiation from the start of all formulations not clearly supported by revelation in Scripture or even in the New Covenant alone, as with many Anabaptists and others. The Polish Brethren of Pińczów by virtue of this process therefore still considered themselves as truly and completely Reformed, Catholic, Apostolic, as well as scriptural.

Moreover, in appealing to the one received creed, the *Apostolicum*, the Brethren at Pińczów, without knowing it at the time, also fixated their movement at this point. In Britain in the seventeenth century Puritans, whether Congregational, Separatist, or Baptist, would readily let go the *Apostolicum*, and the Presbyterians scarcely appealed to it. But Jan Stoiński of the *Epitome* would compose a *Hymnus in Symbolum Apostolicum* printed in the Hymnal and Psalter which the Polish Brethren in the seventeenth used in their churches, *BAnt* 122; and one of their great theologians and apologists, Jonasz Szlichtyng, would ornament the *Apostolicum* with festoons of scriptural *loci* and present it ecumenically as the testimony of the apostolic faith and polity of the Brethren in his *Confession* of 1642, *Polish Brethren*, Doc. XXII. The various Racovian Cathechisms in succession would serve as preparatory to believers' immersion, not as replacement of the *Apostolicum*, except possibly the editions of the Catechism published *after* the exile.

Lubieniecki writes disdainfully of the defeated minority as made up of *turbidis ingeniis* and suggests that the power of the world (*potentia seculi*) (cf. 1 John 4:5: simply *mundus*) induced them to espouse the opposite of what was agreed to by the majority of perhaps by all present at Pińczów. Lubieniecki preserves the residue and basic thrust of an agreement between Lismanino and Biandrata against Stancaro, their *bête noire*. Górski (*Grzegorz Paweł*, 85, n. 1) prints a portion of the diminished protocol of Pińczów that survives only in Lismanino'as rare *De Trinitate*, C3–C4. From this it appears that, while Sarnicki and Sylvius (n. 523, ¶3) may have been presented with copies of Biandrata's long *Confessio* from the synod of Książ, they did not attend it; and only Sylvius attended the synod of Pińczów of 2 April 1562. Each had prepared *libelli*, which, leaving off their attack on Biandrata, went after Lismanino himself for being so supine and dependent on him. The attack took the form of a commentary on Lismanino's *Epistola* of 10 September 1561 to Jan Karniński (*Historia, 119–26*). When Aleksander Witrelin, pastor of Goźlice under Hieronim Ossolińksi, read from both the *Epistola* and Sarnicki's *libellus* in a high voice, the brethren recognized that Lismanino was being assailed with great insults and calumnies. The *libellus* of Sylvius, evidently first intended for the synod at Książ, was only read in part, when the author himself acknowledged that he had not understood Lismanino's *Epistola* and publicly apologized.

The identity of the authors of the two *libelli*, referred to in Lismanino, is inferred from the corresponding account (date mistakenly 1561) in *Annales Calvini*, *OC*, 21, col. 746. Feliks Cruciger also states that Sarnicki was ''in Padua'' during the synod of Książ, and that Sylvius kept his distance from it, though only two miles from the place, but that he was present at Pińczów, and there acknowledged his error.''

NOTES TO CHAPTER SEVEN

530. This title, whether from Wiszowaty or Lubieniecki, testifies to the sense the Polish Brethren had to the end of their existence as an organized Church that they not only carried out the reformation implicit in the achievement of Luther and Calvin but also the primary, if not the more puissant, thrust in the Reformed movement in the Commonwealth with Lismanino and Łaski as respected forefathers. See comment in n. 517.

531. Stanisław Sarnicki (c. 1532–23 September 1597) was a major chronicler of Polish history and a more important divine than he appears in Lubieniecki's pages. To a small manor born near the village of Lipsko near Chełm, Sarnicki descended from Jakub Sarnicki from Ruthenia, who, knowing their language, was sent on legations to the Tatars by King John Albert (1492–1501). As a martial and studious youth, Stanisław came to the attention of Duke Albert of Prussia who enabled him to study at Cracow, along with the sons of Andrzej Górka. Thereafter he went on the grand tour west in the company of Leonard Górecki, returning to Poland as a determined follower of Calvin. He was successively minister to Boner in Biecz, to Stadnicki in Niedźwiedź (as successor to Cruciger), 1556–57, then (indirectly) to Włodzisław-Lanckoroński in Włodzisław (as successor to Marcin of Lublin), 1557. In 1563 he was named superintendent of the Cracow

District. After the synod of Sandomierz of 1570 he retired to his family estate in Lipsko to write and publish his histories. Niesiecki, *Herbarz Polski*, 8, 280–81.

Among his theological writings, besides his correspondence with the Swiss, are *Judicium et censura Ecclesiarum piarum de dogmata in quibusdam provinciis septenrionalibus contra adorandam Trinitatem per quosdam turbulentos noviter sparsa* (Cracow, 1563), *O uznaniu prawego w Trójcy jednego Boga kazań troje* (Cracow, 1564), *Collatio* against Grzegorz Paweł (n. 605), three sermons concerning the *Confessio* of the One God in the Trinity, and *Colloquium Piotrkowskie* (Cracow, 1566). Among his historical writings, besides his parliamentary *Oratio pro lege electionis ad Majestatem regiam* (Cracow, 1575) at the election of Stephen Batory, there are *Descriptio veteris et novae Poloniae* (Cracow, 1585), *Annales sive de origine et rebus gestis Polonorum et Lithuanorum libri viii* (Cracow, 1587), and *Statuta i przywilejów koronnych* (Cracow, 1594).

In Bk. 2, he has been thus far mentioned by Lubieniecki on *Historia, 127* in connection with his opposition to the synod of Cracow, 10 December 1561, and in an anticipatory fragment, *Historia, 110*, at n. 382. Near n. 535 at the end of *Historia, 131*, Lubieniecki evokes the memory of Sarnicki when still minister in Niedźwiedź, frequenting Cracow. He was ousted from Niedźwiedź by its owner Stadnicki, a partisan of Stancaro, and perhaps only briefly replaced an ousted Stancarist minister at Włodzisław. It would appear that Sarnicki at some point made a trip to Venetia. In the calendared correspondence with the Swiss there is a gap between his letter from Cracow to Calvin in April 1558 and his next to Switzerland, also to Calvin, of 1 September 1561, Wotschke, *Briefwechsel*, nos. 128, 226. Evidence of his having been specifically in Padua comes *inter alia* in a letter of Jan Lusiński (Łużyński), in an important letter of Sarnicki himself (*OC*, 19, no. 3874), below, n. 604, ¶2, in a letter of Lismanino (*OC*, 19, no. 3649, col. 171), the whole letter discussed in n 517 and n. 537, and in a letter of Cruciger, preserved in the *Annales Calvini* (*OC*, 21, col. 746), mentioned in n. 529, ¶6. The entry in *PSB* can make all this clear. Sarnicki assembled c. 1577 *Exempla et formulae electionum Pontificum romanorum, Imperatorum, et Ducum Venetorum*. Niesiecki, *Hebarz Polski*, 8.281. The examples of the formularies, among others, for the election and installation of the Doges of Venice does suggest a disposition towards "Italian" constitutions.

But he was certainly not well disposed toward the heterodox Italian *peregrini*, like Biandrata and even Lismanino. See, for as early as January 1561, n. 434, ¶3. From this synodal intervention and, more overtly, from his letter to Calvin of 1 September 1561 to the close of the interconfessional gathering at Sandomierz climaxing in the *consensus* of 1570, Sarnicki was a major figure of the conservative Reformed, alongside Krzysztof Trecy, in resisting the confessional blandishments of Italian humanists and their native allies. However, Trecy himself, as of 18 February 1570, would be willing to write of him somewhat like Lubieniecki, as a "hypocrite who by his ambition disturbs good order," as "ambitious," "inexperienced," as having some kind of "semipapist" tendency. Wotschke, *Briefwechsel*, no. 407a, 314.

On the last charge, Trecy had in mind Sarnicki's seeming to favor the traditionalist elements in the Church of the Czech Brethren and he would favor them at the parley at Sandomierz. But for most of the crucial decade, Sarnicki was a protagonist of the Helvetic position, upon which the higher *szlachta* relied for acceptability in the Commonwealth. Indeed, Schramm, noting that Sarnicki was himself of noble birth in contrast to most of the ministers, considers him the theological spokesman of the higher *szlachta* (the greater landlords, the senatorial class, the magnates), who, mostly in and around Cracow, were in significant numbers *seniores* and patrons of the Reformed, whereas beyond the district of the capital and in the other palatinates of Little Poland it was the gentry or lesser *szlachta* (lesser landowners) who patronized the Reformation. The program of "the execution-of-the-laws" was that of the gentry (*szlachta* in narrowed sense). And Schramm gives a socioeconomic and political as well as theological interpretation to the eventuating schism (cf. inserted subtitle at n. 616):

> In der Tat setze er [Sarnicki] sich in der vom Hochadel beherrschten Krakauer Gemeinde am raschesten durch. Von dort aus vordringend triumphierte die reformierte Orthodoxie bald in der Umgebung der Hauptstadt, wo allein es ja seit 1560 magnatische Laiensenioren gab. Man wird von hier viellecht eine Verbindungslinie ziehen dürfen zum Ausbruch der Woiwodschaft Krakau aus der kleinpolnischen Exekutionsfront im Jahre 1565. In diesem Gebiet war der Anteil der Magnaten am Boden höher als in der übrigen Provinz, und hier formierten sich zuerst die durch als siegreiche Vordringen der Szlachta zunächst gelähmten Kräfte der Magnatenschaft *neu* und begannen, die Masse des Adels zu beeinflussen. Das zeigte sich im politischen Leben, aber wohl auch im evangelischen Kirchenwesen. Die Mehrheit der Pfarrerschaft war empört, dass sich Sarnicki über die legitimen Instanzen der Bekenntnisbildung, die nach vereinbarter Ordnung zusammenzurufenden Synoden, hinwegsetzte, und hielt zu [Gregor] Paulus: selbst nachdem dieser deutlicher als vorher zu erkennen gegeben hatte, dass er Kalvin nicht als unbedingte Autorität anerkannte. So ging das Gros der mühevoll gesammelten Intelligenz des kleinpolnischen Protestantismus den Weg zum Antitrinitarismus mit.... Hier eine kleinere Gemeinschaft, der sich kein einziger Magnat, dafür aber eine stattliche Zahl geistig regsamer Prediger anschloss.... Die von keiner starken, die Synoden regierenden Prediger anschloss.... Die von keiner starken, die Synoden regierenden weltlichen Autorität gebremsten Antitrinitarier bauten in wenigen Jahren immer mehr an herkömmlicher Christologie ab. Mit der aus humanistischer Wurzel stammenden Dogmenkritik verband sich sogleich die rigoristische Sektenethik und Weltachtung der Wiedertäufer zu einer eigentümlichen Mischform radikaler Reformation.

Der Polnische Adel, 47–49. The compacted excerpt, without the original paragraphing, does not include Schramm's nn. and generalizes beyond the immediate occasion of this n. He could have adduced Lubieniecki himself, at n. 127, on Sarnicki and the senatorial nobility, c. 1563. In his insightful characterization of a nodal point, Schramm points to Sarnicki's special synod of Cracow "of September 1561" (p. 48) but surely means the October synod of 1562 at n. 616.

532. This whole unit appears to be a paraphrase from the Polish of what was recorded in the Kolozsvár copy of the dispute in Balice, 11 July 1562, and the synod in Rogów, 20 July 1562. Sipayłło, *AS*, 2.134–35. Although the account therein and that of Lubieniecki do not wholly coincide, each supplies something distinctive. The episode is discussed by Górski, *Grzegorz Paweł*, 31ff.

533. Grzegorz Paweł was appointed minister of the Cracow congregation by the synod of Pińczów, 17 August 1557, the first Protestant minister to be appointed for Cracow.

534. In the partly parallel account in Polish, "Grzegorz Chrystusa oddziela od Boga." Sipayłło, *AS*, 2.135.

535. The congregation used to meet in the garden of Jan Boner near the St. Nicholas Gate, not in the castle.

536. The text has *magnus arcis procurator*, which in the old Polish *Akta* was *wielki rządca*.

537. Sarnicki in 1561 may still have regarded Grzegorz as only a misguided upholder

of Calvinist orthodoxy. Therefore, he was the more disappointed with him when Grzegorz went along with the decisions of the April Pińczów synod. Dalton, *Lasciana*, 442–43; Wotschke, *Briefwechsel*, no. 228, 132. Sarnicki's opposition was ascribed by Lismanino as well to his envy and disappointment at not being re-elected senior (elder). See Lismanino to Calvin, 14 December 1561; *C0*; 19, no. 3649.

538. This person is wrongly identified as Erazm Aichler in the index of the facsimile edition. The author was Dr. Stanisław Eichler (d. 1585), doctor of both laws from Bologna, city notary. He is attested as having pledged 2 gulden in 1568 toward the expenses of the Cracow congregation. He was married to Krystyna, daughter of Jost Ludwik Decjusz. Sipayłło, *AS*, 2.135. Wengierski, *Chronik*, 11. Eichler is no. 36. In the list of 68, interestingly as many as 14 donors were women.

539. Walerian Pernus (d. 1569), an artisan citizen of Cracow, was an elder who pledged 44 gulden for the congregation in 1568. Wengierski, *Chronik*, 14; Sipayłło, *AS*, 2.135, 141, 148.

540. Given in full at *Historia, 119–26*.

541. These youths were the offspring of Jan Myszowski (d. 1555), castellan of Oswięcim, and Anna Komorawska, namely Jan and Mikołaj. On their father's death Anna remarried Stanisław Cichowski. A sister of Anna, Zofia Komorowska, was married to Mikołaj Myszkowski (c. 1511–57), and she on his death also remarried: Hieronim Filipowski. The two brothers were sons of Wawrzyniec Myszkowski (c. 1486–46), castellan of Oswięcim. Sipayłło, *AS*, 2.135 and n. 2; entries on the Myszkowski family in *PSB*, 22 (1977) 368–407. Both Stanisław and Zygmunt Myszkowski are attested as having pledged money in 1568 to the Cracow congregation. Wengierski, *Chronik*, 13. The preservation of the record of family relations suggests that the bulk of the material in Lubieniecki on the conflict in the Cracow congregation goes back to Budziński, who was in the service of Stanisław Myszkowski. See n. 545.

542. Stanisław Cichowski, Sr. (d. 1576), already encountered on *Historia, 15*, one of the most important military figures in the Poland of his time, was from 16 September 1560 an elder of the Cracow district. Stanisław Bodniak, "S.C.", *PSB*, 4 (1938) 72–75.

543. Why Grzegorz chose Luke for expounding is not evident except for its link to Acts and the early Church, to the standards of which he was appealing. The Creed preferred by Sarnicki was probably the Niceno-Constantinopolitan Creed, as the Apostles' Creed is not in the Nicene sense explicitly trinitarian. The Brethren would continue to the end to baptize in the name of the Father, the Son, and the Holy Spirit, Matt 28:19. Of the four Gospels only two have genealogies, and of these two Luke is fuller than Matthew in regard to the annunciation, the nativity, and the adoration. Further on, from another source, Lubieniecki gives the date of the exposition with Sarnicki present as the sixth Sunday after Trinity, on the octave of the feast of the Nativity of St. John the Baptist; and the Wednesday preceding the exposition had been feast of the Visitation of Mary. The two opening chapters of Luke were rich in the Catholic liturgical atmosphere and in the awareness of Grzegorz and Sarnicki brought up in that tradition, even though as Reformed they had moved on to a simplification of the liturgical year. Grzegorz would soon return to the Lukan material in his polemic with Sarnicki at synods in Cracow and Pińczów in October 1563 and later publish his thoughts in *Krótkie wypisanie sprawy, która była o prawdziwym wyznaniu i wierze prawdziwego Boga* (Nieśwież, 1564) 384–407, wherein his arguments from Luke were taken from chaps. 1, 3, 10, 20. Noted by Sipayłło, *AS*, 2.135, n. 2.

544. *PL*, 2, cols. 157–58. A bit left out by Lubieniecki for the sake of his sentence has been restored in brackets. Interestingly, Tertullian continues "are startled at the

dispensation [of the Three in One], on the ground that their *regula fidei* itself withdraws them form the world's plurality of gods to the one true God.''

545. Stanisław Myszkowski (d. 1570) was made palatine of Cracow and at the same time *starosta* of Malbork in 1565. Budziński was in his service at some point (*Historia*, 77) and the information in this section evidently comes from him (n. 541).

546. Although governor of the Wawel and a castellan, Boner exercised his authority as a member of the Senate to convene a gathering of the Reformed as his estate at Balice.

547. In the account in Polish the date for the dispute in the manor house of Boner in Balice is given as 11 July which Sipayłło takes as more authoritative, *AS*, 2.135, n. 3. Hein accepts Lubieniecki's date, *Italienische Protestanten*, 162.

548. Sipayłło (*AS*, 2.134–36) covers the synod of Ragów mostly on the basis of the Kolozsvár MS with a paragraph from Vilna, dealt with by Lubieniecki from more than one source rather amply, *Historia, 131–41*. It was preceded by a diputation at Balice, 14 July 1562, in my annotation, n. 604, ¶¶3–5.

In the Kolozsvár record, Sarnicki is mentioned among participants at the head of the protocol but not Grzegorz; in the few lines from the Vilna record he is mentioned clearly as reproached (''Wytkniony''), although this could refer to him without his presence being thereby attested. However, from internal evidence in the longer record, from what Lubieniecki himself says, and from *BAnt*, no. 6.2, it is clear enough that he was present. Górski, who deals with the evidence, does not raise any question about the presence of Grzegorz, notes that both he and Biandrata, the latter heading the list of those present, are not recorded as having said anything at Rogów, Biandrata having found in Grzegorz a temperamentally more forceful exponent than indecisive Lismanino of ideas he had himself put forward with more suavity and tact than now Grzegorz. Górski regards the ensuing speeches of the two antagonists as authentic, because Grzegorz ''does not yet go beyond Tritheism.'' Górski, *Grzegorz Paweł*, 88–91, esp. 89, n. 3. On authenticity of the interventions, Sipayłło holds that this is ''doubtful,'' but for the general course of argumentation they are plausible for this stage of the debate, *AS*, 2.136, n. 2. Annotation in the speeches that follow presumes that they are not wholly inventions of Lubieniecki.

549. Stanisław Szafraniec (d. 1598) (*Historia, 95*), was owner of Rogów, where he had founded a Reformed congregation in the village in 1550, and of Secemin, where he had founded a congregation in 1553, with Cruciger its pastor in 1556.

550. The records (n. 549) bear out this claim.

551. The poet, mentioned also *Historia, 34, 94*.

552. Of this series, new in the text is Pustelnik, Jan of Chęciny, who was minister in Książ, then from 1558, in Rogów (*Historia, 158–59*).

It is to be noted that Stanisław Lutomirski appears in Lubieniecki and his source at this point as simply a *senior* of the Pińczów district, after Cruciger as *superintendens Ecclesiarum Minoris Poloniae*. *Senior* could include in Reformed usage both the lay elder and the pastor. In any case, in Lubieniecki's source on Rogów the designation for Lutomirski is minimalist, while in the always slightly tendentious Kolozsvár MS, both Cruciger and Lutomirski are each equally *superintendens*, and the proto-Unitarian is listed first. Sipayłło, *AS*, 2.134. Lutomirski was given his rank by article 18 of the synod of Pińczów, 30 January 1561. Sipayłło, *AS*, 2.91, noted above, n. 447.

Lutomirski was evidently rising to importance at the synods of Książ and Pińczów in the spring of 1562, n. 523. Given their decisive importance theologically, it may here be observed that the two synods of Książ and Pińczów were also important for polity and emergent leadership, foreshadowing the Schism. At Książ, 10 March 1562, Stanisław Lutomirski was listed first among the eleven numbered ministers, along with ''other brethren of different classes," and for the first time in the synodal records styled *superintendens* of the Pińczów district, Feliks Krzyżak (Cruciger) following in second place, simply as *superintendens*. In the two divergent letters of the earlier synod of Cracow of December 1561 to Calvin (n. 518), the theologically more conservative letter was signed by Lutomirski simply as *ecclesiae Dei minister*, while the more radical of the two, in extended defense of Biandrata, was signed by Lutomirski as *superintendens ecclesiarum dioecesis Pinczoviensis*. In both letters Cruciger appeared as *superintendens ecclesiarum Minoris Poloniae* and preceded Lutomirski. In a letter to Geneva the title of "Pińczów diocese" might have been thought to appear impressive, even if there were no Catholic countepart; even Lublin stood under Cracow. In the Cracow synod record Lutomirski was only scribe in charge of the *liber actorum synodalium*. Sipayłło, *AS*, 2.12–13. Thus there is evidence of Lutomirski's being rapidly put forward. Up through the definitive Schism in the Reformed Church, the double listing of superintendents persists. Actually for Pińczów, 2 April 1562, there is no full indication of participants. For Lutomirski in Podolia, see n. 762, ¶ 2.

Lutomirski was destined to become the superintendent of the Minor Church of Little Poland. An ex-priest, canon of Przemyśl, royal secretary, he was married to Barbara Łaska, daughter of the Reformer. Jobert, *op. cit.* appendice 3, "Généalogie des Łaski." This relationship and the fact that her father was remembered as having welcomed Biandrata in Poland (n. 438, ¶ 2), as having himself stressed the *Apostolicum*, as having been attracted to the Erasmian (Calvinist) formulary on the *triplex munus Christi*, a subsidiary way of sorting out the attributes of God revealed, go far in explaining how Lubieniecki (or more likely Wiszowaty) could speak in the heading of chap. 6 of "the Schism made by Sarnicki," as though the Minor Church were palpably in the direct succession. See the related annotation in relation to Lismanino, n. 517.

Lutomirski has been mentioned only once before in the *Historia, 43*; but he has already appeared frequently in the annotation. The fullest account of him is that of Theodor Wotschke, "Stanislas Lutomirski," *ARG*, 3 (1905/6) 105–42.

553. That the priest Aaron, probably brother of Moses, had sons is stated frequently, Exod 38:1 passim. The allusion here is to Aaron's idolatrous making of the golden calf, Exod 32, in which his (priestly) sons were presumably involved, and hence to the alleged idolatry of the Mass.

An allusion at the opening of the paragraph to security "abroad" remains obscure.

554. The text incorrectly says chap. 29.

555. This very passage from Hegesippus is quoted by Lubieniecki himself at the opening of his first book, *Historia, 4*.

556. Grzegorz stresses the scriptually revealed God of Israel in contrast to the divinity of pagan philosophy.

557. The stress on the Jesus of the Synoptic Gospels is characteristic of the emergent Minor Church.

558. In the use of *resuscitatum* Grzegorz is stressing the initiative of God (the Father) in effectuating the resurrection in contrast to the *resurrexit* of the Apostles' Creed, which suggests the initiative of Christ himself, along with *ascendit*, instead of as here *exaltatum*, again passive. This stress on Christ's passivity in resurrection and exaltation was made by Faustus Socinus; and the speech of Grzegorz may have therefore been modified according to standards of the age when Lubieniecki was writing. Górski (*Grzegorz Paweł*, 89–90) summarizes the whole speech of Grzegorz and that of Sarnicki which follows and holds to their authenticity, 89, n. 3; see n. 549. But this proto-Socinian trait, not in the *Apostolicum*, along with the references below to Christ ascended as King and

Priest, drawn from Hebrews, an epistle given central importance by Socinus, points to unwitting alteration of whatever notes or summaries Lubieniecki had for his expansion.

559. Grzegorz could have said, in order to render the patristic position accurately, ''in one *substantia*,'' but scholastic and even Calvin's usage permitted this reading.

560. Grzegorz could better have said ''one person in two natures.''

561. The peculiar people of Christ are the Poles in this proud speech with some allusion to 1 Pet 2: 5, 9.

562. By insisting that the revealed God of Christians remains the God of Israel Grzegorz eliminated the philosophical God of intradeical potencies or persons and a common substance and yet strangely he does not appear to be repudiating the consubstantiality of the Son at Nicaea, only interpreting it in his own way without further explanation.

563. Athanasius came to this position in his struggle with the Pneumatomachoi and Macedonians. After his return from exile under Julian the Apostate, he called a synod in Alexandria in 362. Gregory of Nazianzus deals with the deity of the Holy Spirit in the fifth of his Five Theological Orations (27–31), delivered in Constantinople in 380, *PG*, 36.

564. The three parties have been called Semi-Arian, Macedonian, Neo-Nicene.

565. Hilary of Poitiers, writing *De Trinitate* in an exile (356–59) in Asia Minor imposed on him by Arian Emperor Constantius, prepared the way for the union of the Neo-Nicenes and the Semi-Arians (Homoiousians). He held that ὁμοιούσιος could be understood in an orthodox sense and admitted that the ὁμοιούσιος could be misunderstood. He tended to be more scriptural and less philosophically disposed than his party and in *De Trinitate*, 2, 1, expanding on the baptismal commission of Matt 38:12–20 wrote: ''[T]his is the confession of the Creator (*Auctoris*) and of the Only-begotten (*unigeniti*) and of the Gift (*doni*).'' *PL*, 10, col. 50. The Polish Brethren moving to tritheism and ditheism and the unitarianism liked this passage in Hilary and there were many others that seemed sufficiently subordinationist for their sensibilities.

566. John Chrysostom.

567. Probably Cyril of Jerusalem rather than Cyril of Alexandria.

568. John of Damascus.

569. Theophylact was a medieval archbishop of Ochrida, whose Greek commentaries and also polemics against the Bogomiles (called Manichaeans) were commonly in the sixteenth century thought to be ancient!

570. All the Greek Fathers wrote of θέωσις/deification and both Athanasius and Gregory of Nazianzus stressed participation in the divine as the modality of salvation in both faith and sacrament. However, this was not the way they understood the divinity of Christ.

571. This can be inferred also even from the skimpy record of the synod. Sipayłło, *AS*, 2.136. Grzegorz evidently had not reached the point where he felt that he could not read the traditional symbols in his sense.

572. See the synod of Pińczów, 2 April 1562, *Historia, 130–31*. At the earlier synod of Cracow, 10 December 1561, Lismanino had argued for the necessary toleration of the traditional terms without compulsion to subscribe, *Historia, 127–29*.

573. The Tower of Babel, Gen 11:7–9.

574. The threefold *sanctus* of the angels in the vision of Isaiah in the Temple, Isa 6:3.

575. The baptism Jesus received from John, Matt 3:13–17 and parallels, and the baptism commanded by Jesus, Matt 28:19–20.

576. I John 5:8.

577. As an orthodox Calvinist, Sarnicki, in his reference to the One Holy Catholic

Church, ignored the Church still flourishing within range of his voice, to postulate the invisible Church of the elect among the Reformed; and, like the Reformed in Transylvania, he assumed that the Church reformed in Poland and Switzerland constituted the true Catholic Church.

578. Ebion, meaning *poor* men, was the supposed founder of the Jewish Christian Adoptionists, Ebionites, who lived East of the Jordan. They held that Jesus was the human son of Mary and Joseph and that over him the Holy Spirit hovered at his baptism, authorizing his messianic mission. They are mentioned by Justin Martyr and Irenaeus. Ancient heretics and heresies were often known from collections and *catenae haereticorum* with acquired specialized meanings in scholastic and reformation polemic. One very accessible source was the *Decretum* of Gratian, Pars secunda, causa xxiv, quaestio 3; *PL*, 187, cols. 1310 – 11, itself based upon Isidore of Seville, *Etymologiae*, viii, c. 5. The heresies, briefly characterized, are in little order. In the *catena*, the Ebionites are numbered §35.

579. Cerinthus, an early Gnostic, flourishing around A.D. 100, held that the world was created by a Demiurge, not by the Supreme God. In Gratian, Cerinthians are held to practice circumcision and as millenarians to await a voluptuous kingdom under Christ.

580. Paul of Samosata, spokesman of the Dynamic Monarchians (*Historia, 8*, Bk. 1, n. 70) is mentioned by Gratian as heresy 28, where the *Pauliani* are reduced to believing that Christ came into existence with his birth from Mary. For the historic personage, see Gustave Bardy, *Paul de Samosate* (Bruges, 1923), of which there is a 2nd ed., 1929, that expands and corrects the first but leaves out the valuable excursus on "Le souvernir de Paul" with useful treatment of what "Samosatene" or "Paulinian" meant in the Reformation Era, particularly in Poland, 493 – 514.

581. Bishop Photinus, ultra-Arian who also disavowed the immortality of the soul as distinguished from the final resurrection of the body and reanimation thereof, is mentioned *Historia, 6, 8*, Bk 1, n. 25. In Gratian under heresy 36 he is limited to the charge of having revived Ebionism and asserted that Christ was born of nuptial coition. The Polish Brethen, insofar as they would later adopt the position of Laelius and Faustus Socinus (who, however, held to the Virgin Birth) on death and resurrection, could be called also Photinian.

582. The words of the Lesser Doxology, the *Gloria Patri*, of very early origin.

583. John 10:12; Titus 1:11; Rev 13:11 ff.; cf. Acts 20:29, alluded to by Grzegorz in his speech, *Historia, 134*.

584. Acts 8:9 – 24; Gratian, *Decretum*, heresy 1, with a specialized meaning.

585. There were in Christian antiquity those whom modern scholarship distinguish as Dynamic and as Modalistic Monarchians. Among the first were the Adoptionists, among the second the Sabellians.

586. The *Alogoi* of Asia Minor, c. 170, were opposed to Montanus and ascribed the Gospel of John and the Apocalypse to Cerinthus. They therefore rejected both from their canon.

587. Although in writing to Calvin, Sarnicki could have been more forceful, here in the divided synod he remained orthodox, even though his formulation is not detailed and his characterization of his principal opponent as to the monotheism of the Father ("de unica Deitatis persona") is a bit strange.

588. In contrast to the first speech of Grzegorz this second one bears ever more marks of the rhetorical improvisation of Lubieniecki. Here, for example, the reference is to the baptismal formulary common to all Christians, Matt 28:19, where it seems to be introduced as though to show that the Minor Church so long as it survived, as also in the

Unitarian Church of Transylvania, continued to use scriptural terms in their ordinances. But such a reference as of 1562 seems anachronistic, and as though written back from a later phase when believers' baptism by immersion had become common among the Polish Brethren.

589. Bishop Theodoret (d. c. 466) of Cyrrhus supplemented the *Historia ecclesiastica* of Eusebius by carrying his down to 428. Therein (ii, 19), he says that Flavian of nearby Antioch noticed that when the clergy and the rest of the people of God were divided in two groups when singing the *Gloria*, one group using the conjunction "and", the other using the preposition "through" of the Son, and applying "in" to the Holy Spirit. Grzegorz is wrong that the *Gloria* in some triadological form began only at this time. *PG*, 82, cols. 157–58.

590. The reference could be to St. Niceta or to Nicetas Acominatos (d. after 1210). if the latter it could be to his θησαυρὸς ὀρθοδοξίας in 27 books, on contemporary heresies. St. Niceta (d.c. 414), bishop of Remesiana (Bela Palanka in Yugoslavia), did not write a *Historia* but commented on the Apostles' Creed, *Explanatio Symboli*, and may have composed *Te Deum laudamus*, a kind of symbol; but it is surprising that Grzegorz could have adduced him as little known in the sixteenth century.

591. Bishop Flavian of Antioch, only belatedly recognized by Rome, died in 404.

592. Rev 5:13.

593. 1 Tim 1:14.

594. 1 Tim 2:5.

595. The synodal records from two sources and the conflated account of Lubieniecki leave some obscurity about the succession of events. But the Kolozsvár MS does say that Sarnicki and Grzegorz went after each other *na podpór*, after a break, and adduces the very text of John 14:1 as part of the final argumentation.

596. Rev 5:13.

597. The argument about the quaternity may be taken from *Gentili Confessio evangelica* (Lyons, 1561). See Trechsel, *Die protestantischen Antitrinitarier* 335, 472. But it is more likely that Grzegorz knew that Joachim of Fiore had charged Petrus Lombardus with formulating a *quaternitas*, and that his own work was instead condemned at IV Lateran Council, 1215. See nn. 313 and 427 *passim*.

598. The references are not particularly compelling and suggest that in a possible transcription of the speech scriptural references became partly lost and jumbled.

599. For the canon, see *Historia, 141*, n. 529; for the renewed decision, see the retrospective account in connection with the dispute in Cracow, 5 August 1562, Sipayłło, *AS*, 2.137.

600. In the conference the *fortiora pars* was surely that of Grzegorz Paweł. Lubieniecki is, however, thinking of his grouping as *infirmiora* in the larger context of the Helvetian churches in Poland. He could be alluding to the social distinction between the magnates and the middle/lesser gentry, whose clerical spokesman here was Grzegorz. Sarnicki was of the higher *szlachta* (n. 531).

601. Some record of the dispute in Cracow of 5 August 1562 is preserved, Sipayłło, *AS*, 2.137.

As for Stanisław Wiśniowski (incorrectly indexed in the facsimile edition of the *Historia* as Wiśniowiecki), although not much about his life is known, he was an important figure, vacillating among the winds of doctrine.

He is earliest attested as a representative of the congregation in Cracow at the synod of Pińczów, 24 April–1 May 1556. At that time he gave the extravagant estimate of adherents in Cracow of a thousand (more like two hundred) and asked the synod to appoint a minister for them, expressed his own ardent intention to serve, and then had a third matter, the disposition of the manuscripts left to his widow Dorta by the Cracow printer Bernard Wojewódka. Sipayłło, *AS*, 12.58. After serving as deacon in Solec, owned by Marcin Zborowski, he became in 1559 minister in the royal town of Wieliczka, in which capacity he appears in the *Historia*, upholding the invocation of Christ (as divine). He is indeed fixed in the text by Lubieniecki in a characteristic stance as an upholder of mutual toleration in the community of faith and as a defender of traditional devotional practices with respect to Christ. He moved to the side of Grzegorz Paweł but appears next in Lubieniecki's account only incidentally as signatory of the letter of Stanisław Lutomirski from Cracow, May 1563 (Bk. 3, n. 44).

Wiśniowski would become an ally of Stanisław Farnowski, leader of the Ditheists, and move from Wieliczka to Lusławice in the service of Stanisław Taszycki, *Historia, 272, 274*. With him he would go over to the consequent Unitarians, then return to Farnowski's group. Two of his works have been excerpted in modern Polish in the *Antologia* of Szczucki and Tazbir, *Okazanie sfałszowania i wyznanie prawdziwej nauki pana Krystusa* (Lusławice, 1572) and *Rozmowa o szczerej znajomości Boga Ojca, Syna jego i Ducha Świętego* (Lusławice, 1575), *Antologia*, 423–38; 489–315; short life of author, 651–53; cf. also *BAnt*, 53.

602. This is confirmed by the narrative account, which again suggests that Lubieniecki had access to perhaps the original behind the Kolozsvár MS, printed by Sipayłło, *AS*, 2.137–38. After the dispute with Wiśniowski rallying to the support of Grzegorz, the elders of the Cracow congregation rebuked Sarnicki: "You seek a schism in the congregation, stir up unrest, turmoil and incite the lords (*pany*), unheeding of the injunction of the Lord Jesus, who commanded us to live in love and harmony in the bearing by each other's burdens."

603. Sipayłło, *AS*, 2.137–38. Among the ministers was Schomann. Darek Jarmola, *op. cit.*, adduces as evidence that he declared himself at the moment a follower of Gonesius on baptism as well, a letter of Sarnicki to Trecy, November 1562; *OC* 19, col. 574, and identifies Balice as the synod referred to by Lutomirski, Bk. 3 at n. 316. He also holds that two synods otherwise known only from Sarnicki and dated by Sipayłło, *AS* 2 to 1563, actually took place in Kościelic and or Książ between January and August 1562 where opposition to pedobaptism was raised and the Lithuanian baptismal theology was adopted by Schomann and Paplepka of Lublin. This surmise is based upon Sarnicki's *Collatio* (1563; n. 605) and his *Colloquium Piotropowskie* (1566; n. 605)

604. Sarnicki is not fairly represented by Lubieniecki theologically at least and perhaps not also in terms of his character and motivation. (Cf. n. 531.) Here, both the followers of Lismanino and of the conservatives were at one against the Stancarists about differentiation in the roles of the Three Persons of the Trinity. At issue among all three major groupings within the Reformed Church already schismatic with respect to the Stancarists of 1559/60 was the way in which Jesus Christ as the incarnate Word in hypostatic (personal) union with the man Jesus was cosmological and especially soteriological Mediator and then especially how his distinctive role was reflected in the definition of the primordial Godhead or the intradeical status of the Persons in respect to the divine *essentia* (in the ancient creeds: *substantia*/οὐσία). The Stancarists held to the Lombardian position which had ancient conciliar support (n. 427). This view was held to be "scholastic" and "Papist" by both Sarnicki and Grzegorz and thus Sarnicki, in the *entirety* of his Triadology/Christology, opposed what is here ascribed to him by Lubieniecki.

Sarnicki's views on what happened at Balice survive in two writings from his hand. In his book against Grzegorz (n. 605), he preserves the *Credo* of Grzegorz in Polish.

Then in a series of letters he tells much about the general situation to Calvin, Bullinger, Krzysztof Trecy (in Switzerland at the time and the designated interpreter of the letters), and still another one to Bullinger, the four written 6–19 November 1562; Wotschke, *Briefwechsel*, nos. 259 A and B, 260, 263, in *OC*, 19, nos. 3883 and 3874, 3875, and 3878. Sarnicki reports on Balice of 12 August 1562 in the third letter in this series, the one to Trecy. By far the most important in any case, it is undated. It looks to be a composite letter composed over some weeks, at least. At the beginning Jan Boner is referred to as one of two nobles (the other Stanisław Myszkowski) holding back "the deluge inundating our whole *patriam*" (col. 575), while deeper into the letter he is referred to as recently deported (575). As Boner died suddenly, 15 September 1562 (n. 613), it would appear that the editors of *OC* have placed it at the proper place in the Swiss-Polish correspondence.

Near the beginning of this letter Sarnicki sets forth Twelve Blandratist Articles (cols. 573–74). Although describing them thus systematically in propositions as presumably set forth by Grzegorz et al. at Balice, in their present state they are not wholly coherent with each other and in any case contain narrative and descriptive material from Sarnicki himself, although perhaps the more valuable for that reason. That he calls them Blandratist rather than Gregorian articles fits well into the situation at Balice where Biandrata, though not a minister, is listed first among the ministers as "senjor zborów w Małej Polsce" in front of Lutomirski and Cruciger as superintendents, and quite apart from the magnates (Myszkowski and Boner) and lesser lords and Cracow citizens. Sipayłło, *AS*, 2.134; the disputation at Balice and the synod in Rogów in *Historia* at n. 549.

Although the Twelve Articles represent the cumulative impressions of the views of his opponents, Sarnicki may well be right that something like the twelve points were dealt with perhaps even seriatim under the moderatorship of Biandrata. In the twelfth article Sarnicki's opponents in Balice are said to be willing to accept Christ's mediatorship in Calvin's sense if they understand him correctly. In the seventh article they approve of the (Uniate) Greek opinion that the Spirit proceeds from the Father and through (*per*) the Son, although they thought that whole issue had been buried (at Florence). This would suggest Lismanino's input. In the ninth article Eccl 12:1 with its assertion that the Creator is one is adduced to affirm that it applies to God the Father alone, in accordance with the general thrust of Sarnicki's opponents to make more of a distinction among the Three than did Stancaro or, in his own way, Sarnicki. The eleventh article reads in full: "*Trinitas, personae, essentia* are papist words. Even in Vilna they are rejected. And that Jerzy Schomann publicly in a sermon in Cracow assailed the word *Trinitas* and with a big mouth (*plena bucca*) called it a papist figment to the scandal of many." After the twelfth article it goes on: "All these items have been faithfully written down. And Schomann approved of the teaching on the Trinity there in Balice before all auditors. On this there was a colloquy at Balice. As to peace the colloquy was in vain. For Schomann publicly proclaimed that he would prefer to carry on the trade of a cobbler or to suffer whatever rather than to desert that purity [of the Apostles' Creed]."

The quotation of the whole of one article sufficiently displays the character of the Twelve Articles—they were not formal propositions of the Blandratist party, but they supply valuable information, however biased. And the asseveration of Schomann, a major figure also of the written legacy of the Polish Brethren (*Testamentum*, the first Racovian Catechism, RD 3), in Cracow, then in Balice, seems wholly consistent with other sources.

The next sentence in Sarnicki's letter to Trecy (col. 574) leads to a letter by "our [Jan] ·Lusiński, bishop of Moldavia under the Despot." On him under the Despot, see esp. n. 762, and in general, Halina Kowalska, *PSB*, 18 (1973) 135–36. He had been the tutor of the two Długi sons and visited Basel, came to know Calvin and others in Geneva, Bullinger and especially Johann Wolf in Zurich. It was Wolf who held high hopes for him in Moldavia and by way of Trecy sent him plans for organizing the Reformed Church in Moldavia, for erecting a humanistic school and publishing the Heidelberg Catechism of 1562 in Romanian. Lusiński (Łużyński) and his wife left his parsonage in Iwanowice in 1562 for Cotnari in Moldavia. But it was evidently before leaving Poland that he wrote, not to Sarnicki himself but to a friend, as Sarnicki is referred to therein. The text is a bit garbled but is of interest, produced by Sarnicki as further testimony for Trecy in Switzerland as to how things were going in Poland in the absence of each. (There is other evidence that during a crucial period Sarnicki was out of the country n. 529, ¶4.) Lusiński writes in part:

> However, [as for] the matter of Biandrata, which has never been clear and understood by me, because of the difficulty of the material itself and because of the distance of the place that separates me from them. Nevertheless, what happened among us you know, namely, that besides Sarnicki, Jakub Sylvius, [Maciej] Albinus [Lusiński's successor in Iwanowice], [Erazm] Gliczner, all ministers have [by now?] defected to the Biandrata party. And this thing forced Sarnicki to leave his ministry and go away, up to this time we don't know where, whether to us, or to Italy, or to France. What followed afterwards I don't know. After this action at Balice by a mandate of the nobles they had to call a general synod [Pińczów, 18 August 1562], but they did not call more than a few ministers, where they wrote out a certain confession (*schedam*), which they issued in the name of all ministers. This development moved many of the *szlachta* (*ordinem equestrum*).

The transcribed letter goes on and concludes that at that time Lismanino and his allies "lost faith and authority among the major part of the *szlachta*." The letter is further testimony from a responsible Polish minister, an important correspondent of several Swiss divines and at the point of becoming the superintendent of a new Reformed Church in Moldavia, that social and theological conservatism were somewhat linked, even though all of the radical Italians in the Polish synods ranked with most of the *szlachta* and were so esteemed.

Sarnicki then goes on to describe his own conservative synod in Cracow of 16 October 1562, *Historia, 143* at n. 617, and follows this up with a fuller *Consensus catholicus*. This part of Sarnicki's letter to Trecy is critically edited by Juliusz Domański and Lech Szczucki, "Miscellanea Arianica," *Archiwum Historii Filozofii i Myśli Społecznej*, 6 (1960) 199–288, the *Consensus*, 217–19. See further at n. 617.

605. Another formulation by Grzegorz in this same discussion, based on 1 Cor 8:6, ran:

> Also St. Paul teaches me the same creed, saying: "But for us there is but one God who is the Father, from whom are all things, . . . and one Lord through whom are all things, [and, Rom 8:15] one Spirit, in whom we call Father, Father." And as the three are not three Gods, but one God the Father, his one Son God of God, one Holy Spirit God, so also I do not ever want to mix these three or to confuse them so that the three be one.

S. Sarnicki, *Collatio in qua aperte demonstrata blasphemia Gregorii Bresinensis* (1564/65), fol. B1. As here quoted Grzegorz Paweł is still a tritheist.

The word is not ever used by Lubieniecki but it abounds in the scholarly literature in the identification of a stage through which the prospective members of the Minor Church passed. The term was applied by the contemporaneous critics, derived perhaps, from the *catena haereticorum* of Gratian (n. 578), heresy 68 (*Tritheitae*). For the succession and classificaiton, see Misiurek, *Chrystologia*, 28–43.

606. In this generalizing, Lubieniecki prematurely unitarianized Grzegorz who, as of the moment, still upheld some kind of Triadology, cf. quotation in preceding n. "Loose" and "tight" are scarcely appropriate terms in reference to the Godhead but they might be used here to make clear how intensely Grzegorz with his allies were still struggling against the "tight Triadology" of Stancaro, the *deus "confusus"* and how he was opposing Sarnicki with an anti-Stancarist thrust and fervor. In his quoting in item 3 from Gal 3:30: "Mediator . . . unius non est: Deus autem unus est" (Lubieniecki has this in the subjunctive of report), Grzegorz was perhaps repeating the argument that had seemed to himself convincing against Stancaro that one divine Person (or Hypostasis) cannot mediate with another divine Person. Mediation, according to Paul, implies more than one, God is one, and therefore Jesus mediated with God the Father. Grzegorz held to the Apostles' Creed and in his "loose Triadology" he found the divine unity in the action of Three called God, in the single Personhood of God as Father, that is a moral unity in the one divine soteriological transaction of Christ's atonement.

607. For an omen of the Triadological struggle, see *BAnt*, RD 2, nos. 6.2, 56.

608. The Kolozsvár MS of Antitrinitarian synods gives 28 August 1562. See Sipayłło, *AS*, 2.139–40, and determination of the date, 139, n. 1. There are still two superintendents. Lutomirski is identified as of the Pinczovian *trakt*, i.e., "way" and area. In the listing lay *senior* Biandrata precedes Grzegorz Paweł, clerical *senior* (*minister*).

609. The reference to the public authority and *Seniores* bears attention. In the protocol in Polish the lay elders of the Cracow congregation are listed as *Senjorowie* without names after several lords (*Panowie*), headed by Mikołaj Oleśnicki as host, followed by the chamberlains of Cracow and Łęczyca. For Lubieniecki the public authority would be represented by the patrons of various stations and properties, some of whom, like Biandrata (cf. preceding n.), were also lay *seniores*. See further on *seniores* in n. 612.

610. At stake in the controversy was, more specifically, the title "Oecumenical Patriarch," claimed by John IV. In comparing Gregorius Paulus to Gregorius Magnus, Lubieniecki is reaffirming his appreciation of Pope Gregory I as a great but humble preacher. See *Historia, 10, 113, 146*. Note also that Lubieniecki disparages Patriarch John not only for ecclesiastical pride but also for encroachment on imperial (or royal) power.

611. The Pinczovian *Confessio de Trinitate* was printed by Daniel of Łęczyca, 20 August 1562. A copy survives in the Zurich Archives. It was reproduced by Lismanino in *De Trinitate* (1565) and by Girolamo Zanchi, *Epistolarum libri duo* (1613) 1ff., where it is wrongly dated 22 August, inconsistent with the fact that a letter with the same *Confessio* enclosed was sent to the Strassburg divines, 21 August 1562. Wotschke, *Briefwechsel*, no. 255. Sipayłło reprints the *Confessio de Trinitate* of 1562, *AS*, 2.323–34. It can now be conveniently compared with the Pinczovian small *Confessio de Mediatore* of 1559 (n. 452).

The *Confessio de Trinitate* is made of five paragraphs as edited. The first paragraph proclaims the intention of the document as being directed against those who accuse the Reformed churches of Little Poland of holding to Arianism and a plurality of Gods. Thus it is directed at once against Stancaro, who had been making the charge of Arianism and had organized his own schismatic Church at Dubiecko, and Sarnicki, who was making the charge of Tritheism. The second paragraph gives preeminence to the Apostles' Creed but includes the creed of Nicaea against Arius lest the church fall under suspicion. The third paragraph is, in fact, the Creed of Nicaea of 325, without reference to the consubstantiality of the Holy Spirit, conventionally held to have been formulated at Constantinople in 381.

The fourth paragraph begins with the concluding anathemas of 325. The received Latin version of this creed goes back to Hilary of Poitiers, *De synodis*, §84, wherein the original Greek of the anathemas, ἐξ ἑτέρας ὑποστάσεως is rendered *ex alia substantia*, that is, ὑποστάσις in the primary meaning of οὐσία. The Pinczovians have *ex alia subsistentia*, which suggests a direct translation from the Greek, but the Greek here means what Hilary said and not subsistence = *persona*. The Pinczovians were evidently anathematizing Stancaros' insufficient distinction among the Three Persons in his allegedly "deus confusus." In the same paragraph the so-called Athanasian Creed is rejected because it insists on "the unity of divine nature of Father, Son, and Holy Spirit" in such a way as to contaminate the purity and truth of the Apostles' Creed and to risk Sabellianism (the recurrent charge against Stancaro).

Then the true Athanasius is adduced in his *Epistola ad Epictetum* in support of their contention that the Three can be distinguished in several ways. In this long *Epistola* to Epictetus, bishop of Corinth, which once nearly gained canonical status during the later christologial controversies, Athanasius argued mordantly and almost too vividly against the Docetism of Apollinarian and even certain Arian groups, insisting that the eternally begotten Son of God, *qui desendit de caelis, incarnatus est*, brought down no celestial body or flesh. *PG*, 26, cols. 1049–70. The final paragraph holds the names of the many ministerial signatories, who were surely also in attendance two days before, although unmentioned in the protocol.

Among the participants in the synod and signatory of the *Confessio* was Stanisław Paklepka, who signed himself as "superintendent of the churches of his sort (*suae sortis*) in the land of Lublin." He similarly signed his name in a letter from Pińczów, 18 August 1562, addressed to Vermigli. Earlier he had earlier written to Vermigli, a participant in the Colloquy of 1561 at Poissy, summoned by Catherine de'Medici and led on the Protestant side by Beza and which prepared the way for the measure of freedom accorded Protestants in France by the edict of 1562. Paklepka's letter makes vivid the theological anguish of the Polish Reformed in the face of the Stancarist challenge. Wotschke, *Briefwechsel*, no. 253, 151–53. Paklepka writhes in desperation as he appeals to Vermigli to set it all right by further explanation. He abhors "the abominable school of the papists that contrives a monster of an *essentia, non generans, non genitum, non procedens*" and the schismatic school of Stancaro at Dubiecko persisting in the error. Over against such a "confused" Trinity without sufficient differentiation, Paklepka appeals in confidence to Vermigli as to the rightness of the Apostles' Creed wherein God is *separatus*, namely, "the eternal God the Father, the eternal God from God, the Son, and the eternal Holy Spirit, in whom/which we cry Abba." This represents as full a form of Tritheism as is encountered, as each of the Three is expressly eternal, which was not claimed expressly by Grzegorz Paweł in his Tritheist Credo in Polish (given in full n. 605). Paklepka's testimony makes clear the degree to which the emergent Minor Reformed regarded themselves when resorting to the Apostles' Creed as the best or only formulary for themselves as still fully in a triadological tradition. Paklepka in this letter and presumably therefore at the synod, as signatory of the *Confessio*, was a Tritheist, not a Unitarian.

612. Here Lubieniecki introduces one of the big three of the emerging Major Church,

alongside Sarnicki and Trecy. Of the lower *szlachta*, Paweł Gilowski (c. 1534–95) had been a priest, then provost of Wojnicz, before joining the Reformation at the synod of Iwanowice in 1556. At the request of Zygmunt and Krzysztof Myszkowski he was appointed minister at Polanka Wielka and Przeciszów in 1557 in the Silesian principality of Oświęcim-Zatór (which in 1569 was united with the Crown), later in Spitkowice. He became superintendent of the Reformed of that principality but by the synod of Książ of September 1560, some of the possibly less able pastors in his district agitated the cause of getting out from under his discipline and coming under the superintendent of the capital. Already Gilowski had shown a disposition to open the right of voice and vote to the whole *coetus* whether the synod or congregation (*zbór*). During the synod of Włodzisław of 26–28 June 1559, several important measures had been voted to establish order and advance "the Kingdom of God in our Polish *patria*." Then, on his own, he thereupon moved further that "the superintendent and *seniores* be elected not only by the *seniores* themselves but also by the whole congregation (*coetus*) of the church." Sipayłło, *AS*, 2.45; 1.308. Ministers and laymen were alike members of the presbytery (*senatus*), by election, the ministers not *ex officiis* as in most Reformed polities.

Gilowski was a signatory of the *Confessio de Trinitate* of 20 August 1562 and would persevere in this upholding of the Helvetic position but with moderation or at most condescension. He dedicated to his patron, Myszkowski, his defense of the received doctrine of the Trinity, *Okazanie że Ociec, Syn i Duch Święty są jeden prawdziwy Bóg* (1566).

For the whole life, see Stanisław Szczota, "P.G.," *PSB*, 7 (1948–58) 471–72.

613. Jan Boner died at the dinner table in the presence of several friends. Lubieniecki gives the date *17 September* 1562, as does Wengierski, *Chronik*, 10. Krystyna Pieradzka, "JB," *PSB*, 2 (1936) 301, on the basis of more sources, gives the date as 15 September and Sipayłło agrees, giving the date of burial 16 September 1562, *AS*, 2.141, n. 3.

614. Katarzyna Bonarówna, née Tęczyńska, on the very day of the funeral, married Stanisław Barzi (1529–71), captain of Śniatyzi, later palatine of Cracow and captain general of Cracow, an ardent Catholic and partisan of Cardinal Hosius. As a result of this precipitous marriage, all the evangelical churches on the extensive estates of Jan Boner reverted to the Catholic Church. Thus began the decline of the already riven Reformed Church in Little Poland.

615. The site was at the southwest corner of Szpitalna and Sw. Tomasz streets, where St. Thomas' Church now stands. The "cathedral church" of Lubieniecki is not that of the Wawel but rather Great St. Mary's at the corner of the Rynek, not properly called the cathedral. Of this congregation Grzegorz Paweł was pastor. With the transfer of the Reformed congregation from the house of Boner to the house of Cichowski, November 1562, the new synod of the emerging Minor Church began. Cf. Sipayłło, *AS* 2.143.

616. Sarnicki in a letter to Trecy, freighted with documentation, adduced in n. 604, ¶5, supplies the exact date of Sarnicki's synod and provides the *Consensus catholicus tam primitivae quam recentioris ecclesiae in sua particulari synodo Cracoviae xvi Oct. A.D. 1562 celebrata*, critically edited by Domański and Szczucki, *loc. cit.* (nn. 604, 217–19). For its components, see following n.

617. The *Consensus*, preceding n., of Sarnicki's synod of Cracow affirmed the three ancient Creeds, the Zurich Articles, Łaski's Confession, Beza's Confession, and the Pińczów Confession printed in 1561 lost, except for its section here against Stancaro, *loc. cit.*, 219 and n. 2, 228–29.

The critical edition of the orthodox Cracow *Consensus* is included with other items of a MS of Jan Osmolski (1525–c. 90) of the Lublin district, which can be best noted here. Following it comes (220–21), the letter of Stanisław, Krzysztof, and Jerzy Fredro to the

Calvinists of Lublin and Chełm, dated Cracow 18 October 1562, where they had evidently attended Sarnicki's synod there. They supply five testimonies from Scripture proving that the received dogma of the Trinity is satisfactorily demonstrated from Scripture alone. The second testimony, e.g., is that of 1 Cor 10:9, where Paul is construed as having placed Christ in the place of the God of Moses in Num 21:5–6: "We are not to put *Christ* to the test as some of them [the Israelites in the desert of Sinai] did and were destroyed by serpents." This is a Vulgate reading but most ancient authorities have Κύριος instead, and the verse was not used thus during the ancient triadological debates.

Following this document in "Miscellanea Arianica," 222–27, is a letter of the conservative Calvinists of Lublin to the Zurich divines, November 1562. Not unlike that of Sarnicki to Trecy (n. 604), it contains several articles of Triadology and Christology adhered to by two parts of the local synod. The conservatives, "One part of the Church in the province of Lublin" who compiled the letter, adduce the trinitarian formulations of Geneva, of Zurich as summarized from letters to the Poles, of Poissy, 1561, and of the *Augustana*, to which they add four articles of their own consonant with the above. They contrast this with ten articles of their adversaries, presumably drawn from authentic utterances of the dissenting part of the Lublin group, "who seem to follow the opinion of Valentino Gentile." The dissenters are restrained. *Their* articles are written up by the conservatives who may well catch the beliefs of an emerging Minor Church, when the dissenters still imagine that their views are consonant with the original Nicene Creed of 325 in opposition to Arius (art. 3) in respectful appeal to Athanasius (art. 7), for they hold that the Son is begotten not made. They do reject the *Athanasium* as patently "supposititious." They profess to wish to use only scriptural language, although inadvertently much of the traditional vocabulary survives. They insist against the heresy of the "the Neogreeks" that the Holy Spirit proceeds from both the Father and the Son (art. 8). They know they are not Eutychians, they say, because they hold that "Christ is Saviour, that is, God and Man: est salvator [Mediator], sed secundum divinam naturam qua nobis remittat peccata; . . . Christus est passus, Deus homo, sed in humana natura" (art. 7). They base this clarification of 1 Tim 2:5 in appeal to John 5:27: "The Father gave the Son the authority to execute judgment insofar as he is *Son of man*" (art. 7). Although Stancaro is not named, he appears under the reference to the perceived Sabellian schism of a *confusus Deus ex tribus* (art. 5), and yet the Adversaries agree with him that Christ suffered only in his human nature and seem to be sensitive to his charge of Eutychianism against the main body of the Polish Reformed in following the Swiss on Christ the Mediator, saying expressly that they are not Eutychians (art. 7).

It is of note that the Adversaries employ *salvator* for *Mediator*. In 1574 Faustus Socinus would write his major contribution to the Reformation Era discussion of the atonement, on Christ the Redeemer, using a kindred word without the recently acquired partisan connotations of *Mediator* (with its use only twice in the New Testament), *De Iesu Christo Servatore, hoc est, Cur et qua ratione Iesus Christus noster servator sit*, published by Rodecke in Raków in 1594, fitting in appropriately in the very region of Europe so long torn by theological despair over Christ the Mediator as between Stancaro and Lismanino. Gryczowa, *Ariańskie oficyny wydawnicze*, 181–82, nn. 67. It was a third Italian's "solution" that wholly accepted the view of Stancaro as to the locus of redemptive suffering without explicit reference to his extraordinary role in Polish Protestant thought and at the same time fully satisfied the advanced "Adversaries," by this point, of course, the Minor Church as it had emerged. The *De Servatore*, thought through by Socinus in Basel against the arguments of the Huguenot minister Jacques Couvet, 1574. For the Polish Brethren it was one with the *scriptural* sensibility of the

Reformation Era, of which Calvin was the chief exponent, in adherence to Jesus Christ as suffering in some ultimate way different from countless other examples of enormous human suffering. On the original setting, see Wilbur, *Socinianism*, 391–92. The Polish Brethren/Socinians would come to think of this interpretation by Socinus as more than an Exemplary Theory of the atonement, traditionally associated with Abelardus. The Remonstrant jurist Hugo Grotius would in his turn find it inadequate in his own defense of what he considered the Catholic or Satisfaction Theory of both Calvin and the Tridentine Church but would thereby set forth what is called the Rectoral or Governmental Theory of the atonement. Since Lubieniecki does not elsewhere deal with this central transaction in Christian thought, the excursus is made here and reference made also to a condensation and annotation of Grotius *vs.* Socinus (1617) in *PB*, Doc. X.

To return to the *Confessio adversariorum* as preserved by the conservative Reformed in Lublin, it may be ascribed by the authors of the letter to Zurich to Gentile (and back of him to Servetus), but this *Confessio* is far more testimony to the challenge of Stancaro in the face of Calvin's insufficiency of argumentation on Christ the Mediator. The "Adversaries" have in fact retained Calvin's relatively new formulation concerning the Mediator but they have dropped to a wholly scriptural Triadology, in effect, to a ditheism with the Holy Spirit *donum*, not *persona*.

On two points at least, it is of importance to compare the *Confessio* of the Adversaries in Lublin with the testimony of kindred adversaries as characterized by Sarnicki at about the same time. In a letter to Jan Rokyta of the Czech Brethren from Piotrków, 14 December 1562, Sarnicki set forth in ten points what his adversaries are spreading "in the churches being renewed" in Poland, which show the extent to the opponents of Sarnicki had come to think of him and his fellows in the Reformed Church as no better than having "a Turkish God, a conflated God and as being Stancarists and Jews." This is the thrust of item 3. Sipayłło, *AS*, 2.324–25. They construe the Shema of Israel (Deut 6:4–9, 11, 13–21; Num 15:37–41), summarized for Christians by Jesus, Mark 12:29: "Hear, O Israel: The Lord our God, the Lord is one," to mean: "One therefore is God the Father truly God, the God of Israel" (item 4) and that "The Father alone is Creator of things visible and invisible" (item 8). They hold further that "From Him alone proceeds the Holy Spirit *per* the Son, as the Greeks and Ruthenians teach" (item 7), that "He sends the Son, commands, hears his prayers; He alone is reconciled, not the Son nor the Holy Spirit" (item 8).

In his letter to Trecy of the same year (nn. 604, 616–17), Sarnicki had seen fit to include, among several Reformed *confessiones*, a portion of Łaski's *Forma ac ratio* of the London Strangers' Church, 1550; *OC*, 19, col. 579; Domański and Szczucki, "Miscellanea arianica," 219. Quoted by Sarnicki *verbatim* from Łaski's *Forma* are *interrogationes* 21 and 22 and their *responsiones*. Kuyper, ed., 2.131. Łaski here had used the unusual Latinized Greek for monad, *henas*, to refer to the unity in substance of the Three Persons, itself a possible indication that Łaski was not secure in Triadology. (Indeed, this insecurity of formulation may explain the strange disappearance of the Pinczovian *longa Confessio*, drafted by Łaski and printed, n. 452, ¶3.) In any case, Sarnicki in repeating this clearly misspells the decisive word, *Responsio* 21: "Credo ... est in una atque eadem divinitatis *haenade* distinctionem prorsus trium personarum etiam discrimen agnoscam, juxta quod videlicet in nomen, et patris et filii et spiritus sancti baptizamus."

It can be here noted that, as not in the *Forma*, 1550, so also in neither the *Compendium doctrinae* nor *De Catechismus, oft Kinder leere*, both in Latin and Dutch/Flemish (London 1551), did Łaski himself ever include *verbatim* any ancient creed besides the *Apostolicum*, which, in fact, became the basis for *Catechismus* or *Confessio* from *interrogatio* 120 on. Kuyper, ed., 2.408. In the *Forma* he also displayed a marked interest in the threefoldness of Christ's offices (Bk 1, n. 156) as King, Teacher, and Priest, e.g., in his prayer to Christ at the ordination of elected ministers: "Domine Deus, fili Dei vivi, Jesu Christe! . . . . Te jam supplices deprecamur, Domine Rex, Doctor, ac Pontifex noster aeterne! ut hosce viros fratres nostros, per nos ad verbi ministerium in tuo sancto nomine electos, Spiritu sancto tuo replere digneris. . . ." Kuyper, ed., 2.72.

The Adversaries of Lublin and the opponents of Sarnicki, could easily have found ample sanction in Łaski's Triadology as of London, 1550, 1551, e.g., where he wrote, as self-evident, that God the Father is the Creator and that it was an incomparable consolation to hear "that the Supreme God, the Father of our Lord Jesus Christ, wishes to be also our father." Kuyper, ed. 2.410, items 121–26.

It is of interest that in *Responio* 22, Łaski adduced 2 Cor 10:5, "We destroy arguments and every proud obstacle to the *scientiam Dei* and take every *intellectum* captive to obey Christ." The Reformed Church in Poland might be said to have divided over the meaning of precisely this text in dealing with the divine Mystery.

618. Virgil *Aeneid* 9.73.

619. The place name evidently could not be read in MS by the editor who prints 5 asterisks.

Wawrzyniec Discordia (Niezgoda) of Przasnysz entered Lubieniecki's narrative in Bk. 1 at nn. 154, and now near the close of his erratic career (d. c. 1566). After coming to the throne in Cracow, following the death of his father, Sigismund II called two maverick preachers, Discordia and Jan Koźminczek, to him during the Diet of Piotrków in 1548. Despite episcopal entreaties to the new King to rid his court of them, Sigismund permitted them to continue their evangelical Catholic preaching and propaganda at the court in Vilna, so long as they did not offend against any Catholic dogma. News of the propitious development at the royal court reached the ears of Łaski on a visit to Duke Albert in Königsberg, whence he wrote Discordia, July 1549: "I hear that you, disgusted I suppose with the court [at Vilna], are preparing your departure from there, which I beg you, Brother, do not do." Łaski went on to urge him to make the most of his position to advance the Reformation. Kuyper, ed., 2: part 3, *Epistolae*, no. 56, 623–24. But pressures were too strong fo him to stay on. Between 1550 and 1554 Discordia was successively under various lordly protectors in the borderlands of Masovia and Ducal Prussia (he was once interviewed by Lutheran superintendent Paulus Speratus), escaping diverse episcopal efforts to lay hands on him. He was once nearly imprisoned.

In March 1555 Discordia appeared for the first recorded participation in a Protestant synod, the one in Golulchów, where the Calvinists and the Czech Brethren were in preliminary discussions that would led to the temporary merger at Koźminek, Bk. 1, n. 120. Among the differences were observance of the Lord's Supper. This was undertood, however, on both sides as the renewal of the Dominical covenant (in the Czech text, *úmlova*). Whereupon worthiness to receive communion became an issue and hence church discipline. The Calvinists upheld some degree of privacy and inwardness, testing of the conscience. But standing among the Reformed, Stanisław Lutomirski in the lead and Andrzej in his own native town, Discordia differed from all the rest in holding that the profession of faith should not be a part of the act of repentance or penance, that confession should be in the face of the congregation (*facies Církve*) or in a special assembly for the purpose along with the express repudiation of the papal system of private confession and penances imposed by the priest. Some of the discussion of penace/repentance seems to be linked to the rebaptism of converts by the Czech Brethren, though formally renounced in 1535. Sipayłło, AS 1. 1, 6, 14–15. In 1555 Discordia established contact with the Reformed in Poland proper, attending the synod of Gołuchów in Great Poland in 1555. Sipayłło, *AS*, 1.6.

About this time Discordia became minister in Podlasie; but then, in the company of others from this Lithuanian palatinate (Polish after 1569), for reasons of his pastoral behavior and views as expressed in his manuscript on faith and penance, he submitted respectively to the discipline and to the *censura* of the synod of Włodzisław, 14 – 15 September 1558. His book was to be dedicated to Radziwiłł the Black, *Nauka o prawdziwej i o fałszywej pokucie* (1559). It was to be examined for Reformed orthodoxy by Aleksander Witrelin, pastor in Pińczów, and Grzegorz Orsacius, who presumably found in the MS attacks on the hierarchy and on penitential practices, intercession of the saints, and Purgatory reminiscent of the young Luther. Sipayłło, *AS*, 1.277 – 78. Superficially integrated into Reformed thought and practices, he was made minister to the courtier Kacper Smolik at Brzeziny near Chęciny. He participated in four synodal gatherings in Little Poland in 1559 without the usual indication of his pastorate in the protocol. By 7 August, he appears replaced in Smolik's service. With blandishments he got a synodal letter of recommendation to Radziwiłł the Black; but, back in Lithuania, he was soon charged with vagrancy and deportment inappropriate to any member, not to say a minister; and a complaint was lodged against him with the Little Poland synod that had commissioned him, formally received at the synod of Pińczów, 1 February 1560. Discipline was meted out by the synod of Włodzisław, 8 May 1560, where Discordia was suspended from the ministery for misbehavior and required to do public penance. Sipayłło, *AS*, 2.12, 23; Barycz, *PSB*, 5, 172.

620. On Jakub Sylvius, referred to in *Historia, 126, 133*, and more frequently in the nn., see n. 501.

621. For the protocol of this synod, based on the Kolozsvár MS, see Sipayłło, *AS*, 2.141 – 43. In Polish, it says that there were 18 ministers and educated men present, 13 lords, all unnamed. Lubieniecki mentions this synod three times, drawing on sources different from the Kolozsvár MS or its source, namely, on *Historia, 107* at n. 359, and *144* at n. 621 and *162* at n. 29.

In the first of these snippets Lubieniecki preserves the notice not only of Gentile's presence at Pińczów but also of his triadological position in summary. The two quotations there from Gentile (n. 358, Lubieniecki's own recolleciton of something read, and 359) suggest Sabellianism, namely, the ancient view of Sabellius that God is successively present as Father, as Son in the lifetime of Jesus, and as the Holy Spirit. But in Poland in 1562 Stancro was, incorrectly, charged with being the principal Sabellian. The Tritheism of Gentile (n. 351, ¶4) could be used as an antidote to Sabellianism, even though Lubieniecki's single quotations from Gentile (at nn. 358 – 59) themselves sound slightly or very much Sabellian But the authentic influence of Gribaldi and Gentile by way of Gonesius, Petrus Statorius, and Biandrata would have been as scriptural-patristic defenders of the separate identities of Father, Son, and Holy Spirit in the spirituality of the Polish Brethren. At intervals, the annotation of the *Historia* observes that overt or more commonly a Tritheism camouflaged for critics but also obscure even to the proponents is an improtant interval in the emergence of Unitarianism. In antiquity Christians defended their monotheism against religious pagan charges of polytheism, then in light of philosophical considerations. In the era of the Reformation the Polish Tritheists considered themselves monotheists, henotheists with respect to God the Father as Creator of the universe, henotheists, too, when they expressed their devotion to Jesus Christ their only Saviour.

622. 3 John 9 – 10.

NOTES TO CHAPTER EIGHT

623. In chap. 8, covering events from 1558 to 1562, Lubieniecki chronologically overlaps his earlier narrative. Indeed, he mentioned the synod of Brześć back on *p. 118*. It is evident that he finds in Gonesius a congenial theologian, especially perhaps on adult immersion. Lubieniecki evidently feels also that the issue of the Third Person justifies a reprise of some synodal history. Writing from the point of view of Little Poland, Lubieniecki does not make clear that the initial opposition to pedobaptism in the Commonwealth was in Polish-speaking Lithuania, notably Vilna. See Jarmola, *op. cit.*

624. Gonesius has been met in this narrative, particularly in n. 390, up through his own speech at Secemin in 1556 (*Historia, 111–15*, esp. n. 408), then again briefly on *Historia, 116* n. 414 on his trip to Wittenberg. Then on *Historia, 118* quite incidentally he was brought up in connection with the defense by Piekarski of his book against pedobaptism at the synod of Brześć in 1558, esp. in n. 442.

The literary legacy of Gonesius is *Doctrina pura et clara* against Sabellians (Catholics and Calvinists), Ebionites, (Budnyite Unitarians), and Nestorians (Stancarists) (Węgrów, 1570, unique copy in Paris), made up of four tracts that may well represent revisions of 'antecedent Latin versions, that in any case substantially differ from three of them published at the same time and place in Polish. The three Polish versions of the Latin tetralogy were critically edited in a series, 1960–62, n. 442: (1) "De Deo et Filio eius Christo Iesu et Spiritu Sancto:" *O Trzech*; (2) "De uno vero Deo, Patre Domini nostri Iesu Christi;" (3) "De unigenito Filio Dei," evidently adapted as *O Synu Bożym*; and (4) "De baptismo Novi Foederis:" *O ponurzaniu chrystyjańskim* (n. 442, where Lubieniecki gives the title as "Contra paedobaptismum.")

It was the Latin version of item 3 that was the object of concern when the synod of Pińczów, 24 April–1 May 1556, dealt with Gonesius's "Arian error, because his book against the Lord Christ, written in Latin, was published in Cracow." Sipayłło, *AS*, 1.72, item 4. It was agreed that he should be refuted and that two lords should be dispatched to the bishop of Cracow who should inform him that "none of us is or ever was a heretic, etc." Ibid. There was a royal edict against Gonesius in 1556. Józef Jaśnowski, "Dwa edykty Zygmunta Augusta przeciwko Piotrowi z Goniądza i Janowi Łaskiemu," *RwP*, 9–10 (1939) 442ff. See further Bk. 3, nn. 503–4.

625. Piekarski appeared also at nn. 444 and 642. For the *libellus* see n. 442; on him, further Bk. 3, n. 193.

626. Although in the style of his age Lubieniecki could have created the speech, it is too long for such a purpose and carries a load of theological technicalities with which he in his account of synods readily lets go with generalizations. See e.g. at n. 639, clear evidence that Lubieniecki in setting forth a speech by Piekarski in defense of Gonesius was drawing upon authentic Gonesian sources; cf. nn. 441, 639. In the first paragraph the decisive phrase is probably "really suffered," as against the ancient Docetists unnamed but perhaps preeminently in defense of *Christus patiens* against the tendency most extremely expressed in Stancaro (Lombardus) to dissociate the divine from the suffering of the cross. Piekarski, ardent follower of Gonesius, may well have known "De unigenito Filio Dei" later: *O Synu Bożym* (above n. 624), in some stage of its transformation from Latin MS to Polish book, and certainly would have known that his mentor had been charged with holding that Christ personally suffered, n. 408 (with a synodal summary of 6 items of Gonesian belief) and esp. in the text at n. 410, a proposition evidently preserved uniquely by Lubieniecki.

The whole speech of Piekarski in defense of Gonesius should be compared with that of Gonesius himself at Secemin, beginning at n. 392. Although there are Lubieniecian traits and components in both, they both in some ways not fully clarified, preserve authentic reminiscences, issues, phrases.

627. Constantine I the Great (306–37) and Licinius (207–25) were co-Augusti from 307 and co-Emperors from 313, when the two agreed about religion in the edict of Milan. Constantine was victorious over Licinius in 324 and this victory led to Constantine's call for the council of Nicaea of 325.

628. The Homousians were the Nicene Party, holding to the common *ousia* of the Father and the Son.

629. "Nimium altercando amissa est veritas," Pubilius Syrus, first century B.C., *Sententiae* 326.

630. Hilary, cited at *Historia, 97* and at several other times, was a post-Nicene favorite of the Polish Brethren because of despairing reference to the succession of synodal creeds and his willingness to settle for the Apostles' Creed. He was also their patristic sanction for the Holy Spirit as *Donum* rather than *Persona*.

631. The speaker/editor is not clear as to when he thought the Pope arrogated to himself improper power and authority. Hilary died in 367.

632. *Non inveni*.

633. Innocent III, after his opening sermon for the IV Lateran Council (1215), ordered that his *Capitula 70* be read before the whole council. Herein a verbal form of transubstantiation first appears. The chapters were approved with discussion and were only subsequently ascribed as canons of the council. Canon 1, among many other important matters, dealt with the Eucharist, Canon 21 enjoined the faithful to go to confession at least once a year. Mansi, 22, cols. 982–83.

634. Piotr is reported to have made the same point in his speech at Pińczów in 1556, *Historia, 111*.

635. Boniface III received this title from the Byzantine emperor Phocas in 607. *Liber Pontificalis*, ed. Theodor Mommsen, *M.G.H. Gesta pontificorum Romanorum*, I 164. Phocas I (602–10) was an untutored soldier, cruel, and utterly incompetent who captured and executed his predecessor (582–602) and his sons.

636. Bernard of Clairvaux, addressed to the Cistercian Pope, Eugenius III (1145–53), *De consideratione*; *PL*, 182, col. 776.

637. Mentioned in Homer, the Cimmerians emerged into history only in the 8th century BC when they were driven by the Scythians from their former home in Crimea and came to the region around Lake Van (in modern Turkey). The Latins described them as a Thracian people living on the Dnieper. In mythology they were portrayed as inhabitants of caves in a remote realm of perpetual mist, gloom, and darkness—the abode of Sleep.

The Mongols were known to their invaders as Tatars, a word of Mongolian origin, easily assimilated in Europe to Tartarus, hence *Tartari*, as here in Lubieniecki. Under the grandson of Genghis Khan, Batu (1236–55), the Golden Horde almost defeated Latin Christendom as they had riven the Eastern Slavs (Kiev, 1240; Moscow, 1328), defeating in 1241 the combined German and Polish knights at Liegnitz in Silesia, Bohemian King Wenceslas I at Wahlstat, and King Bela IV of the Apostolic Kingdom of Hungary at Sajo River in Walachia. The Golden Horde was nominally Islamized c. 1300. The last Tatar invasion of the Commonwealth was in 1624, although Tatars allied themselves with the Cossacks in the Chełmiński Uprising of 1654–56.

638. The three centuries are those before the Council of Nicea (325), which promulgated the creed with the consubstantiality of the Father and the Son affirmed in

opposition to the view of Arius that the preexistent Logos/Son was created, not begotten.

639. The reference here to the intradeical and to the economic or dispensational is clearer in the speech of Piekarski in support of Gonesius than in the undoubtedly faithful transcript by Lubieniecki of the response of Lismanino to Ossoliński in synod, 1561. See at n. 517. The *communicatio idiomatum* in the speech refers to two natures of Christ, the more ancient christological sense, rather than to the Body and bread in the eucharistic sense. These two phrasings in the speech show that Lubieniecki is here very close to an authentic source, not improvising.

640. Tertullian, *De Baptismo*, 18; *PL*, 1, cols. 1220–21.

641. *PL*, 20, 592 AB.

642. At its *sessio* XXI of 16 July 1562 the Council of Trent in its doctrine on communion, cap. 4, merely stated that *parvuli* were not obligated to take communion. Jedin, ed., *Decreta*, 703. But *parvuli* are not *infantes*. First communion had generally been deferred after baptism to the years of discretion. Ex-priest Piekarski would have been alert to the canons of Trent, but the Tridentine date suggests that there is editorial updating, if indeed there was at this point an original transcript.

643. In the Byzantine Church (and in the Latin Church until the close of the twelfth century), infant baptism was at once followed by the administration of confirmation (chrismation) and holy communion.

644. Ambrose was as yet a catechumen when the Catholic laity of Milan pushed forward his candidacy to fill the vacant see. With hesitation he accepted the call, was baptized, and then ordained.

645. There are two accounts of eight questions examined by this synod, item 2 in each list being "Quid sentiant de unitate divinitatis et de trinitate personarum." Sipayłło, *AS*, 1.298, 299.

646. Pierre Statorius (his offspring Polonized the name as Stoiński), who was mentioned as head of the school in Pińczów (Bk. n. 260), was also a leader among the translators of the Bible into Polish (n. 266). On him, see more fully Bk. 3, n. 474.

Lorrainer, Statorius Gallicus, was long enough in Geneva to be up on what Calvin thought of Biandrata there (and in Poland) and to have brought with him the book of Servetus (at n. 651), perhaps those published at Hagenau, above n. 302.

In what follows, from Lubieniecki largely dependent upon Jan Stoiński (n. 653 and Bk. 3, n. 474) and Budziński, there is very valuable testimony to Statorius's Pneumatology specifically and to his theology in general; but it would appear that Lubieniecki conflated his sources such as to obscure the probability that the first testimony from 1561 is followed without notice by Lubieniecki by another testimony evidently from an earlier moment in the unfolding of Statorius's thought, from 1559, as here conjectured, n. 656.

647. Cf. Ps 92:12. Actually, once cut, a palm tree does not flourish.

648. Sipayłło, *AS*, 1.315–16. This synod was preceded by a gathering of elders, 20 November 1559, just prior to the synod and at which Statorius had cleared himself with reluctant recantation (discussed out of the putative chronological order n. 656). In neither the gathering nor the synod proper is there deposit in the protocol of a dispute *diu mutumque*. The protocol of the synod is largely taken up with the synodal letter to Remigian Chełmski (following n.).

649. That Chełmski did not sign his name is mentioned for some reason in the small notation on him in *BAnt* 48. Here the Latin has simply "sine nomine auctoris." In "the source material," probably Jan Stoiński (n. 653), Sand says there is Chełmski's letter of 25 January 1561 to Petrus Statorius. The letter is printed with the protocal by Sipayłło, *AS*, 2.89.

Chełmski's letter and the role of Petrus Statorius are rehearsed by Lubieniecki in Bk. 3, nn. 472–74.

650. In Acts 2:38 (etc.), important for Servetus (and Hilary of Poitiers), the Holy Spirit is the *donum*. Here Chełmski asks for the *dona* of the Holy Spirit from the Father through the Son.

651. The text has mistakenly *Paulus*. In the sixth act of the presbytery in Pińczów, 20 November 1559, Orsacius (n. 447, ¶2) was threatened with public excommunication within three weeks if he would not repent of error in favoring Stancaro. Sipayłło, *AS*, 1.314.

652. This letter is preserved in the synodal protocol and in Sarnicki's *Collatio* against *Grzegorz Paweł*. This work is cited fully in n. 439. Sarnicki published the synodal letter as though it had been composed and even signed only by his opponent. The Sarnicki version is printed as an appendix by Górski, Grzegorz Paweł, 284–85. The synodal protocol has the letter (with minor variants duly considered in the critical edition) signed by Cruciger in his own hand, then Grzegorz, followed by Sylvius and Lismanino. Sipayłło, *AS*, 1.318. It is commonly thought that Sarnicki was right about the real drafter of the synodal letter but Lubieniecki, with Budziński and perhaps also the synodal MS of his great uncle behind him, surmised that it was Statorius who raised with Lord Chełmski the issue (in sentence right after n. 650). In any case, both Grzegorz and Statorius had the same questions in mind. Górski (*Grzegorz Paweł*, 58–62) has a lucid account of the controversy over the Holy Spirit, but he sees only two possibilities for the vacillation and fall of Statorius: Biandrata or Stancaro. But although unapologetic about his association with Biandrata, Statorius, a biblical scholar, had philological and other resources for independent inquiry; and the argumentation that follows, unique to the *Historia*, suggests a quite capable theologian. Górski rightly holds (*Grzegorz Paweł*, 59–60), however, that the whole Polish Reformation from the beginning unfolded largely on the level of personal and social ethics and the upgrading of moral conduct in scriptural terms.

653. The sentence was absorbed by B. Wiszowaty from the margin of Lubieniecki's MS into the text and rendered in italics. The translation here gives precedence to any variant reading in the Jan Stoiński text, *Epitome*, RD 2, *BAnt*.

654. Calvin warned Poles of Biandrata as bearing the poison of Servetus, in the several letters of 6 October 1561. Wotschke, *Briefwechsel*, nos. 233–37. But already Statorius, mentor of Lord Chełmski, had received a response from Calvin to his own (lost) letter of 9 June 1560. Therein Calvin chided Lismanino and thereby indirectly Statorius for preferring ''Servetus's disciple [Biandrata], so crammed full of venom, and error, to me.'' *OC*, 18, col. 102; Tylenda, ''Calvin on Biandrata,'' *Loc. cit.*, 39.

655. The last phrase evokes 1 Pet 3:21.

Lubieniecki had before him, as he says, the MS copy of Statorius's letter from Pińczów to Chełmski, 30 January 1561. The whole letter is printed with the protocol by Sipayłło, *AS*, 2.89–90. Statorius's letter had been requested by the syod in response to that to Statorius from Chełmski, from the village of Lścin (near Jędrzejów), 25 January 1561, expressing concern lest the fire (over Pneumatology) within the fellowship break out into public view. Ibid., 89. In the part of Statorius's reply not included by Lubieniecki as not germane to Pneumatology there is reference to the petition of Wojciech Biskupski (Episcopius), who had been synodally appointed at the request of Chełmski to become his minister in 1559 in Włoszczowa (near Chęciny) and who also asked Statorius to intervene.

656. There follows a long excerpt from Budziński. His History evidently itself included paraphrases of, then apparently substantial direct quotations from, the speech of

Statorius quite possibly at the gathering of elders in Pińczów, 20 November 1559, where he had been informed against by several for opposing the invocation of the Holy Spirit. From the record elsewhere of this gathering it is known that he defended himself, saying that it was not the invocation as such that he opposed but rather the order of ever invoking the Holy Spirit before the Father and the Son. Sipayłło, *AS*, 1.313–14. If the paraphrase/quotation is from the self-defense before the signing of the *confessio*, ibid., 314, Lubieniecki should have alerted his readers to his dropping back chronologically from the synod of January 1561. Lubieniecki, following Budziński, seems to be referring indeed precisely to the gathering of elders (*colloquium*) of 20 November before the synod proper of 22 November when, after finishing off his long quotation at the top of *Historia, 152* he says: "Sed Statorius haec pulcre et solide dicta post haec *negavit*." The text goes on: ". . ., ut infra videbimus." This phrasing may even come from Budziński rather than Lubieniecki, who occasionally transcribed absent-mindedly. See n. 677, ¶4. The retracting *confessio* is known in full from the synodal acts, also in part from Węgierski, *Slavonia Reformata*, 85–86. That Statorius's speech on the Holy Spirit comes earlier rather than later is suggested further at n. 677, ¶2. Obliging Statorius, by way of a retractation, to fall in line with the majority of elders was the fifth act of the *zjazd/colloquium* of 20 November. The sixth was the solemn warning of Orsacius as a Stancarian (nn. 651; 446, ¶ 2).

657. Heb 1:9, with allusions to Ps 45:7, Ps 89:19–20.

658. According to Acts 1:3,9 the Ascension of Christ took place forty days after the resurrection Sunday, and according to Acts 2:1 the Holy Spirit descended fifty days after a Sabbath Passover.

659. Perhaps Acts 17:27–28, Ps 145:18, Jer 29:13.

660. Acts 18:24–26.

661. Statorius is here alluding to the Vincentian Canon of Catholicity, "*quod ubique, quod semper, quod ab omnibus creditum est*," n. 447. Statorius has *illa quae ab initio semper et ubique fuerit recepta, et ab omnibus intellecta*.

662. The quotation is italicized as though perhaps taken from an early *Confessio* of the Brethren, e.g., Jerzy Schomann, ed., *Catechesis* (Cracow, 1574), but is from 1 Cor 8:5–6, the two verses reversed with only insubstantial divergence from the Vulgate.

This *Catechesis et confessio fidei, coetus per Poloniam congregati, in nomine Jesu Christi Domini nostri crucifixi et resuscitati* is included in the appendix of Related Documents. For discussion of its structure and contents, a forerunner of the Racovian Catechism, see *Radical Reformation*, chap. 27:4 and *Polish Brethren*, 183–85.

663. John 14:26; 16:7.

664. John 20:22.

665. John 15:26.

666. Perhaps 2 Cor 3:17; Rom 8:9.

667. 1 Cor 2:10–16.

668. The argument here used is that just as a man's spirit is not a person distinct from him, neither is God's.

669. Rom 7:6–8:27; 2 Tim 1:7; 1 Pet 1:2.

670. Rom 8:26–27; Gal 4:6.

671. Matt 12:32; Mark 3:29; Luke 12:10.

672. John 8:45–47; Acts 13:46.

673. Acts 5:1ff.

674. Perhaps Rom 1:18–32, 3:9–20.

675. Luke 9:52–55.

676. John 18:17, 27; Matt 26:56, 70, 72, 74; 10:17–18; Luke 12:11; 21:12.

677. The hymn *Veni Creator spiritus*, commonly ascribed to Rabanus Maurus (776–856), abbot of Fulda and archbishop of Mainz, was used from the tenth century as the vespers hymn of the feast of Pentecost. It came to be used at the ordination of priests and the consecreation of bishops. The critical edition of it is by G. M. Dreves, *Latein-ische Hymnendichter des Mittelalters*, 2 (*Analecta Hymnica Medii Aevi*, I) (Leipzig, 1907) 193–94.

At the synod of Pińczów, 13–16 January 1560, prayers and hymns from the *Liber antiphonarum* and presumably other liturgical books were formally eliminated from the evolving Reformed liturgy (n. 447, ¶4). This would suggest the general context of this point in Statorius's argument. It is true that in the context, Statorius's thrust is against Catholics and he doubtless alludes the John 3:8: "The wind [but often taken as the spirit] bloweth where it listeth," over against the ecclesiastical imperative: *Veni!*

It would appear that at this point Lubieniecki leaves off his transcription from Budziński's History as well as that of the speech of Statorius contained therein. His references in what follows up to the action of Sarnicki are obscure and the progression of thought not clearly motivated. But it would appear plausible that Lubieniecki, himself quite forthcoming about his own attachment to believers' baptism by immersion as apostolic, moved from Statorius's paragraph on the Holy Spirit as a gift of God to the believer (who properly does not summon a *gift* in routinized sacrament) to anticipatory remarks about anti-pedobaptism in three regions because for him believers' baptism under the open sky, as with the Son of God himself at the Jordan, is a major—if not epiphany—then at least experienced manifestation of the Holy Spirit in the Christian life.

It is possible that some of the paragraph following Statorius's speech owes something to Budziński's MS. On *p. 152* near the top, "ut infra videbimus" is followed at the end of the next sentence with the same anticipatory "videbimus."

678. Hugh of St. Cher. On him and his *Expositio*, see Bk. 3, n. 490.

679. For the conflict between Statorius and Grzegorz Paweł at this point, see Wilbur, *Socinianism*, 311.

680. The Diet of Piotrków (30 November 1562 to 25 March 1563) is remembered as the *Sejm egzekucyjny*. It returned to the Crown all properties which had been appropriated by the magnates since 1504 without the consent of the Diets The King agreed to devote a quarter of these revenues to the creation of a standing army. The Diet marked a rapprochement between the King and gentry. Francis Dvornik, *The Slavs in European History and Civilization* (New Brunswick, 1962), 253–54. See n. 684 and cf. at n. 404. and Bk. 3, n. 46.

681. Sarnicki held a semi-synod in Piotrków in January 1563 and an anti-synod in Cracow, May 1563. See Bk. 3, n. 17.

682. As recently as 21 (or 23) November 1563, three leaders soon to become leaders of the Unitarian Minor (Reformed) Church, Paclesius (n. 685), Krawicki (n. 684, ¶5), and Mikołaj Żitno (Bk. 3, n. 218) had professed in a letter to Zurich that in an outrage at Stancaro, their subscription to the ancient creeds, including the *Athanasium*, Wotschke *Briefwechsel*, no. 264. Despite his excommunication for immorality, Discordia (*Historia, 16, 143*, esp. n. 619) stood with Sarnicki on the dogma of the Trinity and pedobaptsim. Lubieniecki's account here is partisan and confused. A synod in Piotrków in Great Poland (December 1562 or January 1563), reported by Lubieniecki, is said here to have made Discordia "superintendent of Great Poland" only by inference from the location of

Piotrków; but it was rather, of Little Poland; and he did not discharge the office. A. Wiszowaty, *Narratio compendiosa*, RD 5, *BAnt*, no. 54.2, also says "superintendent of Great Poland." Barycz, *PSB*, 5, col. 173B.

683. The Author suggests a connection between the person of discord and the schism of the Minor and Major Church the schism being retrospectively dated to the definitive dissociation in theology and polity during the debates and discussion at the Diet of Piotrków and at the associated synod of the Reformed churches. For the socio-political basis of the schism, see the observation of Trecy to Bullinger, see, n. 383, ¶2.

684. At the point in his narrative Lubieniecki allows the reader to confuse events of the Diet of Piotrków of 1562/63 and that of 18 January–14 April 1565. He takes up Piotrków 1565 at *Historia, 201*, Bk. 3, chap. 5. Jan Stoiński (*Epitome*, RD 5, *BAnt*, nos. 55, 55.1) puts his emphasis on Piotrków 1565, and only alludes to Piotrków, 1562 in no. 34.2. Schomann (*Testamentum*, RD 3, *BAnt*, no. 25) makes it clear that he preached at the Reformed synod at the Sejm Egzekucyjny of 1562/63, whereupon he was branded among others by Sarnicki with Arianism. He says he was sent by his church to Piotrków together with lords Lasocki and Filipowski. The pair had once been co-commissioned to represent the lordly patrons for the finalization of the decision of the Reformed to unite with the Czech Brethren at the Synod in of Koźminek, 155, Bk. 1, n. 120. Both lords espoused the Biandratan/Statorian interpretation of the Trinity. Lasocki died in Piotrków in January 1563. Halina Kowalska, "S. L.," *PSB*, 16 (1971) esp. col. 549A. On Filipowski comprehensively see n. 105; on the Diet of Piotrków 1565, Bk. 3, n. 405.

For the prominent role of Deputy Niemojewski at the Diet of Piotrków 1562/63, see Lech Szczucki and Janusz Tazbir, "J.N.," *PSB*, 23 (1978) 13–16, esp. col. 14A. It was presumably precisely during the Diet that he was named district judge, the position once held by his father Mikołaj.

Jan Kazanowski (d. 1591), who was district judge of Łuków, is attested several times at the synods. He may have joined the Reformed earlier in 1557. In 1564 he had printed his *Krótka odpowiedź*, a defense against Calvin of the *Tabula de Trinitate* of Grzegorz Paweł. See Bk. 3, n. 406, ¶2 and *Historia, 218*. Wacław Urban, "J.K.," *PSB*, 12 (1966) 255–56.

Stanisław Lutomirski, who was concerned for the unity of the Reformed Church (cf. his *O jedności Kościoła*, 19 June 1560), nevertheless supported the line of thought leading to the schism of the Minor Church, of which he would be the first superintendent. Kowalska, *PSB*, 18, col. 145B.

For Krowicki, superintendent of the Reformed congregation in and around Lublin, and for Paklepka (n. 685), the shift at Piotrkow was decisive and sudden (cf. n. 680, ¶2), and Krowicki's rigorous adherence to the received formulations in his *Obrona* (1560), n. 289. Lubieniecki last mentions Krowicki in reference to his death, 1573, Bk. 3, n. 868.

685. Stanisław Paklepka (Paclesius, d. 1565) studied at the Jagiellonian University, 1551, and from 1558 to 1560, he was in charge of a group of Polish students in Basel, among them two Lutomirskis, then studied on his own. On his return, he became minister for Jan Lutomirski, then the first Reformed pastor in Lublin. At his death, the Lublin congregation was split until 1570: Stanisław Tworek, *Zbór Lubelski* (Lublin, 1966); Maria Sipayłło, "S.P.," *PSB*, 25 (1980) 36–37. See also Bk. 3, n. 146.

686. For Erazm Otwinowski (also *Historia, 171–73*), see Stanisław Kot, "Erazm Otwinowski," *RwP*, 6 (1934) 1–37 and Henryk Barycz, "E.O.," *PSB*, 24 (1979) 641–44. Kot regarded Otwinowski as the author of an anonymous booklet of vernacular verse of c. 1590. Barycz takes note of the inconclusive argument against such authorship of Rafał Leszczyński (1961). Otwinowski, of the Reformed movement since 1554,

identified himself with the emergent Minor Church in Cracow in the synod of Cracow in 1562. On his involvement in an iconoclastic episode in Lublin, see Bk. 3, at nn. 140–45.

687. Maciej Albinus, a deacon in the service of Stanisław Lutomirski in Kazimierz mentioned (*Historia, 118*, n. 443) as first to speak up against pedobaptsim. He served as pastor in Włodzisław, then in Iwanowice.

688. *Historia, 175ff.*

NOTES TO CHAPTER NINE

689. The ensuing episode, evidently of great interest to Lubieniecki, is based in part on Budziński, who preserved a letter from the *Despota*, copied out by Lubieniecki (*Historia, 155–56*), but for the most part the chapter is of interest primarily as evidence of how the personality of the *Despota* and his daring attempt to bring Moldavia under the influence of the Reformation were understood by Lismanino, whom Budziński served as secretary, and who was indeed invited to Moldavia (in the text *Valachia*). The chapter is of special interest in revealing how Lubieniecki himself assessed a fascinating episode of the political history of the Commonwealth and in the spread of the Reformation.

Lubieniecki would not have found interesting or pertinent the distinction between the Magisterial and the Radical Reformation. He saw in the voivode of Moldavia only a more puissant patron of the Reformation than any single Polish palatine under the King or even than a major Commonwealth prince. But for a growing number of those whose story Lubieniecki chronicles there would be an increasing disposition to see the Minor Church without magisterial sanction, whether of the King in diet or under the Major or Minor patrons. Schramm has called the Minor Church ''a peculiar mixed form of the Radical Reformation,'' n. 431. The terminology of ''magisterial'' and ''radical'' is discussed in *RR*, Spanish edition, chap. 32:3. For an explicit reference to the congregation independent of the magistrate, see the whole letter of the congregation of Brest Litovsk to the congregation in Vilna, 1566, *Historia, 186–89*, esp. Bk. 3 at nn. 231, 259–60 and the text at n. 317.

690. In the Latin the title is *Despota Princeps*. The Latinized Greek title represented the ancestral claim of Jacob Heraclides Basilicus to the rule of the Aegian islands of Samos and Paros. *Princeps* here renders Voivode. Voivode in its several Slavic forms is modeled on *Herzog*, although the voivodes (hospodars) of Moldavia, Walachia, and Transylvania were often rather grand dukes whenever they renounced a vassal relationship (to the Turks, Tatars, Poles, Hungarians). The Hungarian rendering of the Slavic word as *vajda* is sometimes reflected in the English specialized spelling for the prince of Transylvania as *vaivode*. The Polish *wojewoda*; Romanian *vodă* (Czech *vĕvoda*) is rendered in Lubieniecki and elsewhere *palatinus* and by convention *palatine* in English. The three ''Romanian'' voivodes in the sixteenth century were much more autonomous than the *wojewoda* in the Commonwealth.

691. Jacob Heraclides (1520–63) was born probably simply Ἰάκωβος possibly on Rhodes. To the Christian name he eventually added three titles that served as surnames, all with royal pretension: Basilicus, Despota, Heraclides (descendant of Ἡρακλείδης). He first studied medicine in Crete before launching his career in Europe, eventually fluent in six languages.

Throughout the chapter Lubieniecki refers to Walachia, meaning Moldavia, which term was commonly used in Poland for both voivodeships indifferently.

692. The term Walach is Slavic in origin (*Vlach, Voloch, Włoch*) for the peoples of

Romance (or "foreign") speech surviving within or beyond the confines of the ancient Roman empire, comparable to the Germanic Welsh, Walloon, Welsch, and Wallache. The Slavic word for the Romanians, as they call themselves, was taken over as Βλάχιοι which when Latinized and Anglicized becomes Walach (Walachian).

The two voivodiates, Moldavia and Walachia, became only in the mid-nineteenth century the United Kingdom of Walachia [with a single diet]; and after World War I it was given Transylvania. The older name of the state of "foreigners" was replaced with the proud name of the principal ethnic group, Romania.

693. Jacob Basilicus is reported by Melanchthon to have come to Wittenberg from France in the company of Count Volrad of Mansfeld, and to have stayed part of "the ten months," roughly from September 1555 into May 1556 "und ist der Lehre in unsern Kirchen zugethan." This in a letter of recommendation to King Christian of Denmark, 1 June 1556. *Opera Melanchthonis*, 8, no. 6005, cols. 770–71. The letter of the same date, no. 6006, in Latin to Henricus Busoducensis largely overlaps. Although Melanchthon considered Jacob Basilicus a Lutheran, the Despota was converted to the Reformation, not specifically to the way it worked out in Wittenberg, Copenhagen, Königsberg, which he successively visited. He was in Poland drawn to the Laskian ideal of a national reformation (England, Poland) and he came to feel most congenial with those among the Polish Reformed whom Lubieniecki identifies as the upholders of "the [primitive] Christian Truth." But at the time of his effort with Olbracht Łaski (n. 698) morally and religiously to reform Moldavia, 1561–63, he would have said publicly "Reformed Orthodox" and privately Laskian, meaning both Jan Łaski and his martial nephew.

694. In what follows two phases in the "restoration" of Jacob Basilicus to rulership in Moravia are not made distinct and Lubieniecki says little about his effectual rulership, 1561–63.

695. The sources for the life of Jacob Basilicus are adequate to establish an unbiased biography and the chronology. He is commonly regarded as a genial adventurer and imposter, from the vantage point of Orthodox, Catholic, and even early Protestant historiography, and later Walachian (Romanian) interpretations.

There are two contemporary lives, one by Johann Sommer of Pirna (Bk. 3, nn. 385 and 642), *Vita Jacobi Despotae, Moldavorum Reguli* (Wittenberg, 1587), and the other by Nuncio Antonio Maria Graziani, "Jacomo Basilio," first published in Latin as *De Joanne Heraclide Despota Vallachorum Principi* (Warsaw, 1759), along with another biography by the same author from the same Bibliotheca Zalusciana. The *vitae* by Sommer and Graziani have been published with related documents by Émile Legrand, *Deux vies de Jacques Basilicos* (Paris, 1889), respectively 1–59 and 149–216. The Italian original is found in the Vatican Archives, in the correspondence of Commendone, *Nunciatura de Polonia*, 10, 302ff. A copy close to Graziani's original was published, by N. I. Jorga, *Nouveaux Matériaux pour servir à l'histoire de Jacques Basilikos l'Heraclide dit le Despot, Prince de Moldavie* (Bucharest, 1900) 1–20, along with documents transcribed in Königsberg from the Ducal correspondence with Poland and Hungary. Legrand did not vouch for the reliability of Graziani, whereas Jorga, who projected a modern biography himself, gave credence to Graziani of whom he sketches the life in his preface. Jacob Basilicus, vaunting a lineage in Homer, published his Pedigree in Transylvania in 1558 to make good his claim to a relationship with Heraclis Ruxanda and others in the Moldavian voivodial houses. This is reprinted by Legrand, *Jacques Basilicos* 62–63. Sommer also composed fifteen elegies evoking the Moldavian tragedy, *De clade moldavica*, ibid., 67–128.

Other material on Jacob Basilicus is in Docsachi Hurmuzaki, *Documente privitore la Istoria Românilor* 2:1 and 2 (for 1518–1814) in one vol. (Bucharest, 1891). This is rich in documentation unexplored for this note. There is further documentation in modern Romanian from all sources *Documente privind Istoria Românilor, Veacul XVI, A. Moldova*, vol. 2 (1551–70) (Bucharest, 1951). This popular series, of which this one volume, is being published alongside the more ample *Documenta Romaniae Historica: A. Moldova*. The latest vol. in this series within a series is 2 (*Moldavia, 1449–86*) (Bucharest, 1976).

Theodore Wotschke gives a German translation of the *Vita* by Sommer, along with other documentations and notes made in Königsberg and Romania, "Kirchengeschicht-liches vom rumänischen Kriegsschauplatz," *Theologische Literatur-Bericht*, 1917. For the secondary literature, see esp. Pfarrer Hans Petri, Bucharest, "Jakobus Basilikus Heraklides, Fürst der Moldau, seine Beziehungen zu den Häuptern der Reformation in Deutschland und Polen und seine reformatorische Tätigkeit in der Moldau," *ZKG*, 46 (1927) 105–43, with all the antecedent literature in his first n.; Ernst Benz, who with confidence broke through the pretentions of the printed Pedigree created by Jacob for his religio-political purpose in Moldavia and from the suspected biases of Sommer and Gra-ziani to rehabilitate the Jacob the Voivode-Reformer, admirer of Melanchthon, all in the ecumenical expectant context of the first Assembly of the World Council of Churches in Amsterdam, "Melanchthon und Jakobus Hieraclides Despota," *Wittenberg und Byzanz* (Marburg, 1947; 2nd ed. with new preface, Munich: Fink, 1971), revised from *Kyrios*, 4 (1939–40) 97–128; and Şerban Papcostea, "Nochmals Wittenberg und Byzanz: Die Moldau im Zeitalter der Reformation," *ARG*, 61 (1970) 248–62, which updates the literature on Jacob Basilicus (only indirectly) and, adducing an anonymous letter of 1553 in the *Acta Tomiciana*, 14 (1952) 203, reveals that a scholar from Moldavia sought in Wittenberg to prepare a trilingual version of the gospels and Pauline epistles.

The Hapsburg Archives bearing on the Despot and Moldavia were first edited by Andreas/András Veress as *Acta et epistolae relationum Transylvaniae Hungariaeque cum Moldavia et Valachia*, as part of Fontes rerum Transylvanicarum, 4 (Budapest, 1914). The project was resumed by Andrei Veress in 9 vols. as *Documente privitoare la Istoria Ardealului* [Transylvaniae], *Moldovei şi Ţării-Româneşti* (Bucharest, 1929–37). In vol. 1, acts and writers (1527–72), many of the items between 220 and 290 are written by the Despot or about him.

696. Stanisław Lasocki, *Historia, 31* passim, especially n. 684. His religio-political role as supporter of Jacob Basilicus is summarized in a phrasing in a larger sentence in the entry in *PSB*, 16 (1971). See also next n.

697. The theologically and politically spirited Hieronim Filipowski, treasurer of Cracow, above *Historia, 35* passim, esp. n. 105. The synodal *Akta* note the absence of Lasocki and Filipowski from the general synod of Ksiąž Wielki of 13–19 September 1560. They had just recently left with "the Walachian voivode, the Despot of Walachia that they might help him in that palatinate so that the gospel would be received there." Sipayłło, *AS*, 2.51. Lutomirski, a major spokesman at the synod, wrote to Calvin about the venture, 5 November 1560 *OC*, 18, no. 3275.

698. Olbracht Łaski (d. 1605) (Bk. 1, n. 146), nephew of the Reformer, was son of Hieronim and Anna Kurozwęcka, born in one of the family seats, Kieżmark (Kézsmárk) in Spisz (Zips), Hungary (now Kéžmarok, Slovakia). From 1412 to 1796 Spisz was on lease to the Polish Crown. Kieżmark and a dozen other towns were organized as a dis-trict (*starostwo*) and as part of the palatinate of Cracow. Young heir, after his father's death (1541), of many mortgaged estates in both Poland and Hungary, Olbracht Łaski

was a politically ambitious adventurer. After a humanistic education and service in the courts of Charles V and King Ferdinand of Hungary, he married the wealthy widow of a Hungarian lord in 1558, his eyes already on the voivode's throne of Moldavia. He was by place of birth a Hapsburg Hungarian and by intention an expansionist Pole, as he campaigned for the installation of Jacob Basilicus whom he may have first learned about in Charles's court in Brussels (where he was created court palatine by the Emperor in 1555). Roman Zelawski, "O. Ł.," *PSB*, 18 (1973) 246–50.

699. Sieradź is on the Warta in Great Poland. His father had been palatine before him. The castellan of Sieradź was Jan Lutomirski, brother of Stanisław, destined to be superintendent of the Minor Church. Cf. RD 5, nos. 55 and 55.1.

700. The chronology for Jacob Basilicus remains to be clarified. Budziński's notice is accurate in that Jacob arrived in Ducal Prussia in November 1556.

In his itinerary before entry into the Commonwealth, Jacob is penultimately attested in Wittenberg, 28 June 1556, after returning from Copenhagen. Jacob Basilicus had returned from (cf. n. 693) Copenhagen by at least this date, for it was then in Wittenberg that he for the first time exercised his right (bestowed on him by Charles V for military service in Flanders) to crown laureates, two Latin students from Mansfeld. One of them, later pastor in Heckstadt, Zacharias Praetorius, supplies Melanchthon with the Greek words used by Jacob Basilicus. *Opera Melanchthonis*, 8, col. 770, n. and no. 6065, cols. 638–37; Petri, "Jakobus Basilikus," 111. The last attestation for him is at Rostock, where he crowned the poet Zacharias Orthus of Straslund. Legrand, *op. cit.*, 273; cf. Petri, "Jakobus Basilikus," 114. He may have sailed from near Rostock or from Stralsund, and by way of Danzig, arrived in Königsberg. He was there about two months. He is reported to have had his greeting conveyed to Duke Albert, along with that of Pierpaolo to Vergerio (whom he had come to know in Wittenberg), 2 November, 1556. The account by the Duke's physician, Andreas Aurifaber, is printed from the Königsberg archives by T. Wotschke, "Kirchengeschichtliches," 30; quoted and discussed by H. Petri, "Jakobus Basilikus," 114.

701. In 1554 Tsar Ivan IV the Terrible had obliged the Livonian branch of the Teutonic Order, headed by Wilhelm Fürstenberg, to enter into a treaty, in which among other provisions the Knights renounced for fifty years any political association with Poland-Lithuania. Then the King of Poland, by the treaty of Pozwol (Poswol), north of Kaunas, 14 September 1557, entered onto an alliance with the Knights to protect Livonia (Inflanty) from Ivan. That the reasoning on chronology comes from Lubieniecki is evident, for Budziński, living in the time of the Treaty of Pozwol would not be trying to figure out his own surmise.

702. Ivan IV Vasilivich (1533–84) assumed the style of Tsar in 1547. Budziński would have still, c. 1590 more understandably, referred to him as Grand Duke. Lubieniecki, writing two generations later, is still a political Catholic (Westerner) and patriotic Pole in not acknowledging in the Muscovite titulature Tsar, a Caesar in Moscow as the Third Rome, even while he writes approvingly of the Despota who took the style of βασιλεὺς Μολδαβίας and even though he regularly calls in Latin the Sultan in Constantinople *imperator Turcarum*.

703. Lubieniecki is unaware of the fact that Jacob Basilicus first appeared in the Commonwealth in the ducal court in Königsberg, whence he could have traveled to Vilna. Duke Albert wrote a letter of recommendation for him to the King (n. 706), 22 January 1557, and another letter of recommendation of him to *Dux* (Mikołaj Radzwiłł) in his seat at Ołyka, 8 July 1557. Jorga, *Jacques Basilikos*, 23–25.

704. Truth means for Lubieniecki that of the Minor Church. Cf. nn. 693 and 763.

There are two letters by Jacob Basilicus from Cracow to Duke Albert, commending Jan Łaski and Jan Utenhove, dated respectively 2 and 3 January 1558. Jorga, *Jacques Basilikos*, 28 – 33.

705. Jacob Basilicus was possibly twice in Vilna, before and after his participation in the Livonian wars. Cf. Lubieniecki, not reliable for the chronology, at nn. 703 and 711.

706. A letter of Duke Albert Hohenzollern from Königsberg, addressed to the King of Poland, 22 January 1557, is printed from the archives by Jorga, *Jacques Basilikos*, 21 – 23, and reprinted by H. Petri. "Jakobus Basilikus," 115 – 16, in the context of an account of a presumably some two-months stay in Königsberg. At the time of this letter, the King had left Warsaw after the Diet there, 6 December 1556 to 14 January 1557, to be in Vilna. The letter recommends Jacob Basilicus for his military skills, also as a writer on martial matters. But Lubieniecki, presumably with the History by knowledgeable Budziński before him, specifies that the Despota left Cracow for Vilna "cum letteris electoris Brandenburgici." This would be the Kurfürst Joachim II Hohenzollern (1505 – 71). In 1535 he had taken as second wife Jadwiga, daughter of Sigismund I the Old. Lubieniecki might here be supplying information not otherwise available.

707. This was the poet Andrzej Trzecieski *filius*, *Historia, 31, 33, 52*.

708. Jacob Basilicus in his two letters (n. 704) to Duke Albert speaks of the Reformer as *in Christo pater et propheta*, Jorga, *Jacques Basilikos*, 29, cf. 31 – 32. See more fully T. Wotschke, "Johann Łaski und der Abenteurer Heraklides Basilikus," *ARG* (1920) 51ff.

709. Among the *szlachta* Jacob Basilicus became acquainted with the Filipowskis, Łaskis, Lasockis, Lutomirskis, and Zborowskis. He knew Jan Boner (to whom posterity owes some things of the Despota), Francesco Lismanino (a fellow Greek, whom he would later invite to Moldavia), Stanisław Budziński (who preserves a letter of his to lord Stanisław Lasocki, *Historia, 155 – 56*), and Jan Lusiński (whom he would invite with his spouse to serve as the first Protestant bishop in Cotnari). On Lusiński, see n. 604, ¶6 and n. 763, ¶¶2, 3.

710. There was war over Livonia, 1558 – 82. The Muscovites took Narwa in Estonia and Dorpat in Livonia in 1558, despite the efforts of the Polish fleet. Then on 31 August 1559 the estates of Livonia submitted to Sigismund II in exchange for defense against Muscovy. By the treaty with Vilna, 28 November 1561, Livonia became a fief of the Polish Crown, Livonian Teutonic Knights having been secularized and Courland became a more integral part of the Commonwealth, preserving the privilege and the free exercise of the evangelical religion.

In any great conflict such as this the Voivode of Moldavia, a protectorate of the Crown, had the obligation to send armed forces. It has been conjectured for this reason that perhaps even Voivode Alexander IV Lăpușneanu of Moldavia was himself on the field with Sigismund in Livonia. Wotschke, "Łaski und Basilikus," 51; questioned by H. Petri, "Jakobus Basilikus," 116, n. 1. Perhaps already thinking of the Moldavian throne, Jacob Basilicus may have had an additional reason for displaying his military powers on the battlefields with King Sigismund.

711. Jacob Basilicus could not have been long in Livonia.

712. It would appear that Sigismund rewarded Jacob Basilicus for his military service with a letter to the Sultan in which he would have perhaps nominally supported the Despot's claim to Samos or indemnification but perhaps more seriously have made some proposal regarding the Despot in Moldavia. Some clues might be found in several letters on trade between Poland and the Walachians in 1559 – 61 (Lwów the entreport), transcribed in Königsberg and summarized in his long n. by Jorga, *Jacques Basilikos*, 29 – 34

(and there said to be published by him in full in *Economia naṭionalǎ* [Bucharest, c. 1900]), and in seven letters of 1561 of several writers, including Jan Boner, published in extract, ibid., 49–52 (in a continuous footnote).

713. Lubieniecki's references are to an itinerary for the first and non-military descent into Moldavia from presumably Little Poland, through the palatinates of Crown Ruthenia. Jacob Basilicus wrote Duke Albert from Jassy, 25 May 1558 (viii kall. Junii), filled with expressions of pleasure in his reception at the court of voivode Alexander, noting the renown of the Duke in Moldavia, and asking for arms to recover his patrimony, Jorga, *Jacques Basilikos* 34–36. The Duke replied 24 July, sending two falcons and thirty pistols with powder and bullets to defend himself, expressing the hope that the Despot might be able to recover his Aegian patrimony. And in the same post, he commended the Despot to the voivode Alexander and expressed the same hopes for the restoration to the Despot for the common good of Christendom. Ibid., 36–39. H. Petri, "Jakobus Basilikus," 123, surmises that Jacob already had the idea of gaining control of Moldavia by force in order to reinforce his project in the Aegian against Suleiman. But if Albert was aware of the double strategy, his gift of thirty pistols would suggest he may have been indulging Jacob's fancy.

714. The reference, as elsewhere, is to Moldavia and "the good will" is Lubieniecki's benign interpretation. Here and later Lubieniecki's imprecise geographical terminology is retained. The first rule of Voivode Alexander IV Lǎpuṣneanu (1552–61) followed that of the murdered Voivode Ṣtefan Rare (1552–52). Although the Walachs, Bulgars, and Greeks in Moldavia and their boyars and elected voivodes were Orthodox, the Saxons, Poles, Magyars interspersed among them had been traditional Catholics. There were also Armenians and refugee Hussites among them. A report of a Moldavian functionary under Voivode Petru Ṣchiopul (1582–91) to the nuncio in Poland, Bartolomeo Brutti, observed that because of "gli falsi predicattori, fuale gia 50 anni hanno smembrato questi popoli del grembo della santa chiesa romana." Hurmuzaki, *Documente privitore*, 3.96. Relevant here is a letter of 1535 from King Sigismund I to Palatine Piotr Kmita of Sandomierz that barred transit to Walachia and Moldavia of all "perniciosae sectae homines" entering his Kingdom, *Acta Tomiciana*, 17 (Poznań, 1966), and other evidence. Papcostea ("Nochmals Wittenberg," esp. 251–53) holds that by c. 1535 the Saxons and Magyars of Moldavia had converted to Protestantism, that Ṣtefan Rareṣ intended to convert or drive out all heretics and heretical settlers, that Alexander, although of a different temperament and interest (cattle raising), nevertheless continued the policy, and that this harsh policy explains the temporary acceptance by most parties of "ecumenical" Jacob Basilicus (1561–63) before the redoubled Orthodox reaction and restoration.

715. The account of a conspiracy against Alexander sealed in an Orthodox edifice may be unique to Lubieniecki.

716. This appears to be Mircea III Ciobanul (January 1558–September 1559), voivode/hospodar of Walachia with claims to Moldavia, the two areas having been sometimes claimed competitively by one or another rival hospodar. For the probable date of the attempt on Jacob's life, see following n.

717. Without this specificity Graziani reports the attempt to poison Jacob. He escaped Mircea and fled to Kronstadt (Braov), protected by the mother of Voivode John Sigismund Zápolya (1559–71), namely by Dowager Queen Izabel Jagiellonka, daughter of Sigismund I. Graziani in Italian, Jorga, *Jacques Basilikos*, 3; Graziani in Latin version, Legrand, *Jacques Basilicos*, 164 (just the attempt mentioned, not place or persons). In Kronstadt Jacob had his Pedigree printed, 1558 (Legrand, *Jacques Basilicos*, 59–62),

with its claim to relationships not only to Homeric Heracleides but also to two voivodial houses. His purported cousin, Heraclis Ruxanda, was the spouse of Voivode Alexander III (IV) Lăpușneanu (1552–61). Ruxanda was the sister to the two preceding voivodes, Elias II (1546–51), who had converted to Islam and who was replaced by his brother Stephen VI Rareș (1551–52). Stephen was murdered by the boyars who placed Alexander Lăpușneanu on the throne in a camp "with support from the Poles." After the coup savagely cruel Alexander blinded Ruxanda's *vir* (unnamed) and married her in 1553, thereby enhancing his dynastic legitimacy. On this contemporaneous history, one can surely trust the Despot's Pedigree.

718. This line with reference (tripartitioned) Hungary is best read as a generalization about the sojourn in Transylvania when he would have been close to, but safe from, the boyars of Moldavia (*Proceribus Vlachiae*).

719. Lubieniecki has chosen to report another poison plot, failing to place the episode in its context, which may have been during an escape to the protection of the palatine of Ruthenia. Palatine Mikołaj Sieniawski was also Grand Hetman for Crown Ruthenia. He was perhaps at the time at Kamieniec just across from the Moldavian border. A letter of Duke Albert to the palatine, 10 December 1558, commends the Despot, who has sought the palatine's protection "propter orthodoxam religionem." Albert, without knowing the whole situation, undoubtedly refers to the Orthodox bishops and boyars, who sympathized with Alexander's attempt to coerce the Magyars and Saxons back into Catholicism and rightly suspected Jacob of sympathy with these ethnic elements and their Protestantism. H. Petri, "Jakobus Basilikos," 126.

720. This edict was issued by the King after the alliance of Olbracht Łaski and Jacob.

721. Although Jacob might well have informed Lasocki by letter, it is clear (at n. 730) that Lasocki and Filipowski were with him in Upper Hungary. The memoirs of these two lords may be the Polish source on which Budziński or Lubieniecki drew for whatever is unique in the *Historia*. See n. 748.

722. See n. 698.

723. In the Laskian residence in Kieżmark in Spisz (Zips), n. 698.

724. Lubieniecki writes as though it was by the intervention of Lasocki with Jan Łaski that Jacob first came into contact with nephew Olbracht Łaski.

The following sentence repeats this and intensifies the degree to which Lasocki and now also Filipowski had given detailed counsel. See nn. 698, 730. The two lords are reported as boon companions earlier in the text, near n. 111.

725. Emperor Ferdinand I (1556–64) was restrained by a treaty of 1559 to keep peace with the Sultan and not change the status of the Moldavian protectorate, but his son, Archduke Maximilian, was favorable to Protestantism. He openly disapproved of the work of the Council of Trent that would end in 1563, and on becoming Emperor, king in Bohemia and king of Hungary (1564–76), he would have the Mass omitted at his coronation rather than partake of communion in one kind, sensitive to conservative heirs of Hussitism, the Utraquists, although he would reluctantly consent to the closing in 1566 of the churches of the Czech Brethren.

While still only Archduke he supported Jacob Heraclides in the Moldavian venture. Jacob, from Kieżmark, residence of Łaski, wrote to Emperor Ferdinand, 1 March 1560, on matter relating to the venture; Łaski himself wrote from the same place to Archduke Maximilian, 2 April 1560; and Jacob followed this with a letter to the Archduke, 9 April 1560. In his letter Łaski said that the claimant to the Moldavian throne had sworn that he desired to see that the Gospel be taught throughout Walachia and that all refugees for reason of conscience would receive his protection. On the very day of this letter of Łaski,

9 April 1560, Ferdinand confirmed the privileges granted to Jacob by Charles V. Jacob wrote to Maximilian from Kieźmark, 4 May and again 25 June 1560, expressing appreciation, speaking disparagingly of Voivode Alexander, and styling himself "Moldaviae Terrarumque Walachiae legitimus Dominus, ac electus." This title could have been intended to embrace Moldavia, Transylvania, and Walachia in the narrower sense. Hurmzaki, *Documente*, 2, 1, nos. 350–53, pp. 375–78; *Documente*, Veress, nos. 220, 223, pp. 172–74; dealt with by Jorga, *Istoria Românilor*, 5 (Bucharest, 1937), chap. 2; quoted and placed in context by Petri, "Jakobus Basilikus," 127–28.

It has been shown that some of the Moldavian adventurers had much more in mind than the enthronement of Jacob and his welcoming of Protestant refugees. Antal Pirnát suggests, in another connection, that the aim was a united Greater Walachia under Hapsburg sway, "Il martire e l'uomo politico (Ferenc Dávid e Biandrata)," in Dán and Pirnát, eds., *Antitrinitarianism*, 174–77. Indeed, he suggests that Maximilian foresaw the overthrow of John II Sigismund in Transylvania, who would not renounce his claim to the Hungarian throne until 1570 (Bk. 1, n. 150), and the establishment of a substantial bulwark, under a client of the Hapsburgs, against the Ottoman Empire, as also a second base from which to force his election as succesor of Sigismund II Augustus.

Since the King of Poland had his own interest in Moldavia and in peace with the Porte, it is understandable that the Polish noblemen involved in this politically Protestant venture would become suspect in the Polish court and in the Polish diets among even Calvinist, not to say Catholic, lords.

Olbracht Łaski, the leading Polish nobleman in the adventure, was probably not as much interested in religion personally as was Maximilian, but his two Polish allies, Lasocki and particularly Filipowski, could be said to be very much concerned for the extension of a theologically liberal Protestantism. The Hungarian associates of the Despot in his Moldavian venture were the prefect of Kassa, Ferenc Zay, the political adventurer, Menyhért Balassa, and Tamás Arany of Köröspeterd, the first Magyar to preach against the dogma of the Trinity. On the last, see Wilbur, *Transylvania*, 31. Having written a book denying the Trinity in 1558, Arany proclaimed his views in 1561 in Debrecen in debate with Péter Méliusz there for five days but was obliged to recant. Łaski at the time of the Moldavian venture made claims to being the noble patron of Debrecen, as it had been given to his father Hieronim by King John I Zápolya.

726. Hurmuzaki, *Documente*, 2:1.371ff.; Petri, "Jakobus Basilikus," 126, n. 2.

727. Lubieniecki in his *restituendum* assumes at this point that Jacob had already ruled as Voivode.

728. This letter not found.

729. That is, into Moldavia. The invading forces had two possible routes into Moldavia, one along the Commonwealth side of the Carpathians through the palatinates of Ruthenia and Podolia, the other of greater difficulty, but more surprise, over passes in the southern Carpathians (Transylvanian Alps) among Walachian shepherds and villagers.

730. This is perhaps the only text attesting, insofar as accurate, the presence of Lasocki and Filipowski in Upper Hungary to help in the plan for the taking of Moldavia.

731. Sigismund Augustus's opposition to any strengthening of Hapsburg Hungarian influence in Moldavia may have been pro forma while the two Polish Reformed lords, surely not privy to any plan to unseat Protestant John II Sigismund (n. 725, ¶3), felt that they were patriotic so long as the expedition did not challenge Polish sovereignity and yet sought to extend to the Black Sea the benefits of the (Polish) Reformation.

732. Evidently Lasocki and Filipowski went through the palatinate of Ruthenia into

that of Podolia with the intention of joining forces with Łaski and the Despot on the field of battle after entering Moldavia from the north.

733. By way of Ruthenia and Podolia.

734. The fear was for the reputation of the Reformed Church, seeking independently of the King to extend Polish and Protestant influence in Moldavia.

Jan Boner, writing to Duke Albert, 8 October 1560, expressed dismay at the armed expedition to dethrone Alexander but seems to be thinking more of the martial and political peril of it for his co-religionists. He does not expressly mention Lutomirski and Filipowski, or Olbracht Łaski. Jorga, *Jacques Basilikos*, 55–56. In December 1560 Stanisław Ostoróg writes to the same effect to the Duke, mentioning by name Łaski, Lasocki, and Filipowski ''nostrae religionis,'' and sees the peril of disobeying the general law of the Commonwealth that prohibits any lord from using a force of a hundred cavalry against another in a private action. He fears that the bishops will incite the King to be drastic in punishment. Jorga, *Jacques Basilikos*, 44–45 (mentioned in footnote).

735. The letter of Duke Albert to Sieniawski is noted above, n. 719.

736. Lasocki and Filipowski felt constrained to explain to Sieniawski that they had expressly counseled Jacob and Łaski not to march through royal territory. Cf. the Despot's own statement exonerating them, at n. 751.

737. The itinerary of the armies and of the Palatine are not clear from other sources.

738. Crown Ruthenia consisted of the palatinates of Ruthenia, Bełz, and Podolia that bordered Moldavia on the north. After 1569, it included two more: the whole of Volhynia and the palatinate of Kiev, transferred from the Grand Duchy to the Crown. The palatinate of Ruthenia was itself divided into lands: Sanok, Przemyśl, Lwów, Halicz (which later gives its name, by extension, to a much larger area, Galicia, namely, the Austro-Hungarian third of the tripartitioned Commonwealth, minus Cracow), and Chełm. On the Byzantine-Latin-rite border in the Commonwealth see Bk. 3, n. 98, also *Polish Brethren*, foldout map.

The lords of Crown Ruthenia were prevailingly of the Byzantine rite, among whom there were a few converts to Catholicism (the Union of Brześć-Litewski would come in 1595) and to the Reformed Church, and also lordly Polish colonists of the Latin rite, Lwów, the palatine seat, having been a royal Crown Polish city with a charter based on Magdeburg law (1349) and a Catholic archepiscopal see (1412). On the attraction of some Ruthenian lords and boyars to the Reformation see Schramm, op. cit., chap. 2, ''Kronpreussen,'' 60–76.

Besides the confessional ambiguity of Jacob's plans and the presence in Ruthenia of the polyglot armed force recruited by Łaski, the Despota in Imperial territories seemed now a double threat to most of the Orthodox Ruthenian lords. That some Ruthenian lords called him to their palatinate is stated by Jacob himself at n. 751.

739. The two Reformed lords grieved because they feared that they might appear to have been implicated in the armed march of the forces of Despot Jacob presumptively devoted to their own emergent Minor Church party, as a show of force to further their own religious goals within the Commonwealth, which for them was the stabilization of the Protestant forces, not simply of the Minor party.

740. Palatine and Grand Hetman of the Crown Sieniawski was primarily charged to defend the Commonwealth from Tatars and Muscovite invasion. Crimean Tatars had penetrated the palatinates of Kiev and Bracław in 1558.

741. The Polish effort to gain control over Livonia, 1558–61, was reinforced by sustained battles till 1582.

742. Jacob implores Lasocki and Filipowski to exercise the office of mediators with Alexander in the interest of Jacob now temporarily checked and humiliated, but not daunted.

743. By *tyrannus Valachiae* Lubieniecki means the voivoide of Moldavia, but with execration as a tyrant; cf. at n. 750. Lubieniecki has not told enough to explain exactly the reconciliation with Alexander *damnis reparatis*.

744. The King's order prohibiting transit. See at n. 720.

745. Jacob persevered to show how well disciplined were his mercenaries and adventurers.

746. Hetman Sieniawski could not permit a largely foreign force, however well disciplined, to fight any of the King's foes as targets of opportunity.

747. Combat on Ruthenian soil was avoided by the parley, and Jacob's withdrawal into the forest held the worst consequences for Lasocki and Filipowski.

748. Budziński was evidently in possession of the autograph letter given to him expressly for the History, perhaps.

749. This is perhaps the sole basis for Lubieniecki's generalization about Ruthenian support at n. 738.

750. To betray Jacob to "Tyranno Christianitate toti insenso," means to Voivode Alexander, not the Sultan; but Jacob surely exaggerates the general notoriety of Alexander.

751. It seems plausible that the Łaski-Jacob expedition through Ruthenia into Moldavia had the expressed support of some, perhaps Orthodox, Ruthenian lords. Jacob was crafty enough not to share the letter with Lasocki.

752. Thus ended Jacob's first armed assault upon Alexander. He withdrew into Upper Hungary. Ferenc Zay (nn. 725, ¶5, 754) reports on the incursion to Emperor Ferdinand, twice, 25 December 1560 and more fully, 1560 (without the month). Hurmuzaki, 2, nos. CCLV and CCCLVI, 380–84. He gives many clear accounts on the encounter with palatine Sieniawski, including the fact that Jacob declined to accept in marriage Sieniawski's widowed sister about whom he allegedly had "some suspicion." It is clear from this report that Łaski did not accompany the Despot into Ruthenia.

753. Here is further evidence that Lasocki and Filipowski were indeed primarily concerned with consolidation of Protestantism in Moldavia. At the end of the same year, from Vaslui, 11 December 1561, the Despot wrote his dearly beloved lords Lasocki and Filipowski, apprising them of what in general they already perhaps knew, namely, that he was opening up his realm to settlement by "the exiles because of the word of God from France, Spain, Germany, and other places" with promised lands and help in constructing new towns with charters of Christian liberty. Veress, *Documente*, I, no. 251, pp. 201–2. On the hazardous repercussions of the involvement of the two proto-Unitarian lords in the Moldavian venture, see Bk. 3, nn. 454–56.

754. That Filipowski would have his own copy of a letter addressed to two lords and that he would turn it over to Budziński for his archive is quite plausible. The prefect of Kassa, whence the letter came, was Ferenc Zay (n. 725, ¶5).

755. Lubieniecki, looking back at what he had himself written and has before him in Budziński (which could well have been only a segment of the whole saga of the Despot), tries to persuade himself that the letters of the Despot must have been sent shortly after his sojourn in Cracovia, 1557–58. But he is wrong.

756. These are the leaders of the emergent (Calvinist) Major Church, who edited the Colloquium (in Polish), following n. At the definitive schism, revealed as fundamental at

this Colloquium, the Minor Church and its leaders were all called by their opponents "Arians" and this appellation for the Polish Brethren would survive to the present.

757. *Colloquium Piotrkowskie* (Cracow, 1566). See further Bk. 3, n. 405 for the full title and the event. N. 454 has a taunting quotation from it. This printed report by the conservative Reformed party cofirmed the permanent division of the Reformed Church in Poland.

758. The battle took place near the village of Verbia on the Jijia River between Hîrlău and Iai (Jassy). Jorga assigns only a few pages to this battle in his well documented multivolume *Istoria Românilor*, 5.61–65. Fewer pages are devoted to the episode in the collective and multi-volume *Istoria Româei*, 2 (Bucharest, 1962) 906. Both accounts have together illustrations relating to the Despot not found in Legrand, *Jacques Basilicos*, namely an additional medallion and a coin of 1563.

759. The Despot ruled as Voivode, November 1561 to November 1563. For achievements of his reign, see nn. 753–63.

760. Olbracht Łaski reverted to Catholicism in 1569. He printed two letters to the Reformed, *Responsum ad letteras haereticorum*, 1570 (printed 1578) and *Epistola ad novas in Polonia ministros responsoria* (1561).

761. The Latin spelling is corrected by B. Wiszowaty, *Emendanda*, 196.

762. The chapter ends abruptly without full awareness on the part of Budziński or Lubieniecki of the career of Voivode Jacob, "Vindex et Defensor libertatis Patriae." So reads the reverse legend of the medallion of 1563, the obverse of which carries the crowned head and arms of the Despot. Legrand, *Jacques Basilicos*, plate. His chief seat was in Vaslui near Iai.

The new Voivode founded an academy in Cotnari on the river up from Iai in what had been the summer residence of Voivode Stephen the Great (1447–1504). Johann Sommer, the later biographer of Jacob (n. 695) 2, presided over a humanistic academy open free to qualified youths, It was in the present ruins of the Catholic cathedral church in Cotnari that Jan Lusiński, once pastor in Iwanowice (n. 604, ¶¶6, 7), served as Protestant bishop for the principality, living nearby with his wife. For the ruins of the cathedral, see Jorga, *Istoria Românilor*, 5.70. On 2 January 1562 Stanisław Lutomirski, later superintendent of the Minor Church, wrote to Duke Albert from Kamieniec Podolski about the religious disposition of the Despot which he intended by his visit to confirm, if possible, Jorga, *Jacques Basilikos*, 6; H. Petri, "Jakobus Basilikus," 130–32. Later Johann Wolph wrote in Zurich, 23 August 1563, to Lismanino, who had been invited to Vasilui, saying that he had heard much good about Voivode Jacob, especially from Andrzej Trzecieski, *filius*, also that he had himself written directly to "his Bishop Lusiński, from whom I expect a letter. Of news from these parts, as I write, I have nothing (as yet)." Wotschke, *Briefwechsel*, no. 519, p. 432.

Bishop Lusiński died of a fever and was buried by his widow in the church in Iai. But she herself was caught up in the ferocious reaction to the Despot and was seized at her estate given them near Cotnari and strangled; Sommer's eleventh Elegy is for Bishop Lusiński (and his widow), *Vita*, by Sommer, ed. by Legrand, 35. *De clade moldavica*, 106–09.

John Sigismund's age convinced the Hungarian soldiers under Zay to withdraw their support from the despot. Surrounded by the forces of the restorationist boyars, Jacob Basilicus was put to death, 9 November 1567, by order of his successor facing him, Stephen VII Tomaşa (1563–64), to be followed by Alexander IV for his second time (1564–68).

A later Moldavian chronicler, Grigore Ureche (c. 1590 – 1647), once a student at Lwów (the first to write of the unity of the three Walach peoples and of them as descended from the ancient Romans), treating Moldavia, 1359 – 1594 not too far after the event, retrospectively looked upon Jacob Basilicus "as a Socinian." H. Petri, "Jakobus Basilikus," 132. His *Letopisețul Țării Moldovei (1359–1594)*, the first chronicle in Rumanian, was partly based on Joachim Bielski (Bk. 1, n. 182).

It perhaps goes beyond the annotation of Lubieniecki to remark that concerted research in the still incompletely exploited rich and unsynthesized documentation on the Despota could establish him as tolerant and humanistic and Reformation-inclined Voivode of Moldavia (1561 – 63), roughly corresponding in policy to Voivode John Sigismund of Transylvania (1559 – 71), the one in an Orthodox, the other in a Catholic principality. The Despota is referred to once again, *Historia, 206*.

763. Budziński perhaps gets his false dating from misreading the imprint of Olbracht Łaski's *Exhortatio ad milites in expeditione Moldavica, cum Jacobum Basilicum Despotam introduceret* (1567). Żelawski mentions this without paying as much attention to the Moravian expedition as to later events, *PSB*, 18.246 – 50. Schramm, *Der polnische Adel*, does not mention the Moldavian incident, neither Lusiński nor Basilicus, although the other principals are dealt with in other connections. The severed head of Basilicus was sent as a trophy to John Sigismund.

NOTES TO BOOK THREE
CHAPTER ONE

1. Probably Dario Scala, a relation of Laelius Sozzini, see Bk. 2, n. 17. He incurred the censure of the Italian church of Chiavenna for his defense of Alciati, Gribaldi, and Biandrata. See on him and substantial letters *Reflective of the Christology of L. Socinus* written for a synod in Chiavenna, 2 January 1561, Rotondò, ed. L. Sozzini, *Opere*, 363 – 70. Dario had previously been construed as the writer of the letter and as the person referred to by Lubieniecki (cf. index to the facsimile edition of the *Historia*).

2. On Alciati, see Bk. 2, nn. 353, 368, Bk. 3, n. 392. Obliged to leave Poland for Moravia by the edict of Parczów of 1564, he wrote a letter from there to Grzegorz Paweł, denying the preexistence of Christ. From Slavkov (Austerlitz) he made his way to Danzig and practiced medicine there, dying in 1573. *BAnt*, 27 – 28.

3. Sand and Wiszowaty do not mention this work of Dario Sozzini or Scala in twenty propositions in collaboration with Niccolò Paruta. Cf. my *Radical Reformation*, 622, and esp. Bk. 2, n. 20.

4. The Piedmontese family Provana were all active in the court at Cracow. Traiano Provana was secretary to Bona Sforza, the wife of Sigismund I. Prospero Provana (d. 1584) was organizer of the royal post with Venice and administrator of the salt mines at Wieliczka and Bochnia, in association with his brother. The brothers Provana are dealt with by Henryk Barycz, *W blaskach epoki Odrodzenia* (Warsaw, 1978) 238 – 39; and the role of Prospero Provana, appointed by Stephen Batory in 1577 in succession to Hieronim Bużeński (Schomann, *Testamentum*, *BAnt*, RD 3, no. 19), in the efficient exploitation of the mines and in the protection of heretics is dealt with by Aleksander Bocheński, *Przemysł Polski w dawnych wiekach* (Warsaw: PAN, 1984), esp. 152 – 54, with the earlier more specialized literature on the mines. Prospero married Elżbieta Jerzykowiczówna and became *starosta* of Bozentyn. He is attested at the synod of Książ, 26 July 1558, and there asked that Giorgio Negri be designated pastor for himself and his brother at Traiano's seat in Łętowice. (See Sipayłło, *AS*, 1.263 – 64 and n. 57.) When Biandrata left in 1562 for Transylvania, Prospero was entrusted with at least two books by Servetus. Caccamo, *Eretici*, 75 – 79. Biandrata himself says in a letter from Alba Julia, 18 September 1565, to Grzegorz Paweł, that "Prospero ... possesses all my books." Wotschke, *Briefwechsel*, no. 348, p. 168; critically edited by Sipayłło, *AS*, 2, Dodatki, 353, correcting the date. Besides the Servetus books Biandrata said he left with Prospero Provana, in the same letter to Grzegorz he said that he had left his miscellaneous papers, letters, and no doubt some of his own *scripta* with Petrus Statorius (n. 474), Sipayłło, *AS*, 2.353. Rotondò (*Opere*, 356, n. 123) has adduced further evidence and argumentation for the likelihood that Biandrata and Statorius were theologically akin. He is later attested as present with Budziński at the synod of Skrzynno, 24 June 1567; *Nie-*

znana Kronika, I, ed. Szczucki, 171. Provana had a home in Cracow, Pod Różą, 14 Floriańska Street, where he would host a debate between Jerzy Schomann and Piotr Skarga, S.J., in 1580. Provana would eventually conform to the Catholic Church, being buried in the Church of the Dominicans in Cracow.

5. Stanisław Szafraniec was owner of Secemin and Rogów. See Bk. 2, n. 285, Sipayłło, *AS*, 2.135.

6. Sipayłło, *AS*, 2.134–36.

7. This Jan of Chęciny (Johannes Heremita), as ex-priest, was deacon in 1557 in Kazimierz (n. 73), minister in Książ, then in Rogów under Szafraniec as of 13 September 1558. Sipayłło, *AS*, 1.279. He is mentioned in *Historia, 133*, as a supporter of Szafraniec in his effort to stave off schism at the friendly conference at Rogów (Bk. 2, n. 552).

8. Budziński's text may well have continued to this point, because the reference to Piotrków is not a lead into what follows.

9. The author gives prominence to Feliks Cruciger as a link between the undivided Helvetian Church in Poland and the emergent Minor Church. He was one of the first Polish priests to become Protestant, 1546. Educated at the Jagiellonian University, he negotiated for Union with the Czech Brethren in Great Poland. He had been elected the first superintendent in Little Poland. In this capacity he corresponded with the Swiss divines and defended Biandrata. Evidently a weak person, he conformed to strong personalities about him; and when his patron, Szafraniec, began to side with Sarnicki, he lost heart. Although the querulous spirit self-displayed in the farewell sermon, below, is petulant as much as poignant, he is evidently being set forth by Budziński/Lubieniecki as a reverend father of the Minor Church of the truth.

10. Feliks Cruciger died 11 April 1563. The source for this circumstantial description and following reflection on clerical marriage may come from Budziński.

11. Secemin, a town near Chęciny, was owned by Szafraniec. Cruciger had been minister there since 1553. The Easter sermon prepared by him was to presumably also be his farewell sermon. He had evidently been dismissed by Szafraniec as being theologically too indecisive. See nn. 13, 17.

12. Of the spouses, only the wife of Szafraniec is known by name, Anna Dembińska.

13. According to Sarnicki, it was Szafraniec himself who dismissed Cruciger for his favoring Biandrata. Cruciger fell paralyzed after his sermon and died on Easter Monday. *OC*, 19, no. 3938, col. 723. The view here expressed of a happy life *immediately* beyond death was not that of most followers of Faustus Socinus.

14. Lubieniecki places the sentiment on the lips of one representative of all those who attend church but are really preoccupied with their wordly affairs.

15. Matt 6:33.

16. Of all the speeches recorded by Lubieniecki, himself a minister, this would have been one of the easiest for the author to improvise. But it may come from Budziński and be an approximation of what was said.

17. This date is definitely correct for the synod of "our side." Sipayłło, *AS*, 2.149–51. But it was the announced date also of Sarnicki's synod. The orthodox Calvinist synod appears first to have been made up of about ten ministers and also lords, originally in attendance at the Diet of Piotrków, meeting about December 1562; and, separately, the leaders of the two Reformed factions, tilting toward schism, announced at Piotrków a synod for 14 May 1563. The "liberal" faction, among them Lutomirski,

specified Cracow as the place. The Diet closed 25 March 1563. Sarnicki evidently planned his synod for Secemin, owned by his lordly supporter Szafraniec. It is possible that the "liberal" pastor of Secemin, Feliks Cruciger, prevented its being held there. This would explain the mood of his Easter and farewell sermon of 11 April 1563 (nn. 9 – 13). The conservative synod was thereupon assembled in Cracow "in these days" (at n. 22) and perhaps on precisely 14 May also. On the semi-synod during the Diet at Piotrków, see Sarnicki to Bullinger, 23 January 1563; Wotschke, *Briefwechsel*, no. 268, as well as an account from the "liberal" side of their synod in Cracow, 14 May 1563. Sipayłło, *AS*, 2.149, also n. 3.

That Sarnicki called a conservative synod for 14 May 1563 is clear from the invitation to the Czech Brethren to attend it. See the whole letter of Sarnicki, signed also by palatine Jan Firley of Lublin, Stanisław Myszkowski, and Joachim Lubomirski, dated Cracow 10 April 1563. The letter is printed as an extended n. 3, in Wotschke's edition of no. 268 (above). See further Book 2, n. 681.

18. Lutomirski identifies himself at the end of the letter of May 1563 as simply the elder with its special meaning in Polish Reformed polity; one of the seniorate modeled perhaps on the *Sejm*. But already, as Lubieniecki intimates, he was superintendent in Little Poland (Bk. 2, n. 552), and Lubieniecki is here casting him as in effect the successor of Cruciger, whose eulogy by Szafraniec has been given uncommon attention along these lines. Cf. Lutomirski's actions, nn. 30 – 31.

19. A record of this gathering of 14 May 1563 is in Sipayłło, *AS*, 2.149 – 51. Lutomirski's gathering of 23 ministers is not the same as the synod (of September) to which he invites participants in the two following letters. In these letters he also describes his gathering.

20. What follows is addressed to the Sarnicki synod gathered in Cracow.

21. Triadological phrasing of this important letter of 1563, on the eve of schism, explains why the editor is reluctant to prematurely call the emerging Minor Church "Antitrinitarian" or "Arian." Arius could have subscribed to the wording of Lutomirski but the wording does not contain terms distinctive of him nor of the Nicene orthodox. Here the eternal and only begotten Son is equal to God (the Father) but without reference to *substantia*. The formula is loose, rather ditheistic than unitarian, but the intention is to be apostolic. See the variant formulary at n. 35.

22. Cf. n. 17 and extensively at n. 69.

23. Paweł Gilowski (Bk. 2, n. 612), former priest, was minister to Krzysztof Myszkowski in Polanka Wielka in Silesia, and at the same time minister to Stanisław Myszkowski of Przeciszów. He was at the synod following the death of Jan Boner (n. 28). Being a known conservative who took part in the earlier exclusionary synod in Cracow, Gilowski is reliable when he avows that the one now in progress is irregular. Stanisław Myszkowski, palatine of Cracow, nephew of Jan Łaski, is several times mentioned by Lubieniecki, e.g., Bk. 2 at nn. 173, 545, 612, Bk. 3, n. 74.

24. Partisan of Sarnicki but agreeing that the meeting called by him was irregular, Paweł Gilowski would presently serve as elder of the Cracow district of the Helvetic confession and as minister of their church, the Brog, on Św. Jana street in Cracow, 1573 – 78, in charge during the first assault on the edifice in 1574. He would serve from Łańcut as his base as superintendent/elder of the Ruthenian district, 1578 – c. 1595.

25. The text has only *At*.

26. Lubieniecki offers two words (*processus*, *sententia*) for the Polish of Budziński.

27. Lutomirski evidently said synod and Budziński followed him, even though precisely the canonically synodal character of Sarnicki's assembly is being contested. Lubieniecki seldom uses *synodus*, instead *pius conventus*, etc., cf. *Historia, 158*.

28. Lutomirski presumably refers to the partisan "synod" (of ten ministers) held in Piotrków, possibly in December 1562, and to that in Cracow 16 October 1562.

Taking advantage of the funeral of Jan Boner (Bk. 2, at nn. 613, 616, *Historia, 143*), Sarnicki had similarly organized an exclusionary synod in Cracow, 16 October 1562, in which a few of the nobles, some Cracow burghers, and about a dozen ministers took part. This exclusively conservative synod deposed all the elders of the province and published a conservative confession. For the sense of outrage, see the account of it in the record of the synod of Pińczów of 4 November 1563. Sipayłło, *AS*, 2.141. The argument of Lutomirski is that, in effect, three assemblies of Sarnicki (Cracow, Piotrków, Cracow) were not canonical synods because they were not open to all Reformed ministers.

29. Reference is to the synod in Pińczów, 4 November, followed by that of Cracow, 14 November. Sipayłło, *AS*, 2.140 – 143.

30. Lutomirski proposes a duly convened general Reformed synod from all appropriate parts of the Commonwealth. He is probably aware of Sarnicki's invitation of the Czech Brethren of Great Poland to face the crisis with the conservative Reformed in Cracow, 14 May 1563 (n. 17). The "liberal" Reformed were pan-Commonwealth, as had been Jan Łaski, latitudinarian and consensual in their desire to include all parties of the Reformed. They were also at least as much dependent upon the authority of patrons and pastors as were the conservatives, except that the greater lords were usually conservatives. Cf. Bk. 2, nn. 447, 531, Bk. 3, n. 40.

31. The ideal of a Reformed synod of the whole Commonwealth persisted even for the Major and the Minor Church after the schism of 1563/65. Indeed, the Minor Church carried out the comprehensive impulse well into the seventeenth century, seeking "ecumenical" contacts beyond the Commonwealth with the Hutterites, Mennonites, Remonstrants, and several times they attempted reunion with the Major Church.

32. Lubieniecki renders the Polish of his text with the same two words as at n. 26.

33. John 7:24.

34. Cf. Exod 23:2 "Thou shalt not follow the crowd to do evil."

35. Holding that the word of God, Scripture, is the ultimate authority, Lutomirski regards his formulation of Triadology as even more concordant with Scripture than that of the conservative party. But the formulation at the beginning and the end of the letter differ. To contrast the two: Here on *Historia, 162* at n. 35 it is: *gloria Dei viventis, et ejus aeterni unigeniti Filii, ei aequalis et similis, tum et Spiritus* and on *Historia, 161* at n. 21 in the same letter: *per Deum vivum Patrem nostrum aeternum, et ejus unigenitum Filium et Spiritum Sanctum*. Cf. also the formulation in n. 63.

Since this is a Latin translation of what was probably Polish in the Budziński MS, one can only observe that the variation in the received text of Superintendent Lutomirski at the very point of visible schism in Cracow, May 1563, reveals both the unclarity of the native Polish leadership as to the scriptural doctrine of the Trinity and the quite plausible fluctuations tolerated. Yet the first triadological formulary of Lutomirski above with its *Filius aeternus*, could have been a tolerable compromise formula (to the "left") even in the mid-fourth century.

More than they could have been conscious of, they were all dealing with the politics of the universe.

36. Friday, 14 May 1563. Bronisław Włodarski, *Chronologia Polska* (Warsaw, 57)

388. The concordance attests to the reliability of Lutomirski's address.

37. Joachim Lubomirski (also *Historia, 165*) was a gentleman of the royal court. The conservative synod thus met in his residence, 14 May, and probably it closed on or before 17 May 1563.

38. Lutomirski must be referring to the recent synods wherein the two parties had met separately and the Latin *colloquia* may reflect his avoidance of the formal word, suggesting that each of these on either side was, a *zjazd* or *rozmowa*, not a proper *synod*.

39. Grzegorz Paweł, a signatory of the address and invitation, is here held free of theological suspicion, despite the daring of his (lost) *Tabula de Trinitate* (Cracow, November 1562).

40. This was on a Monday. The signatories below may be regarded as making up the first association clearly emerging as the Minor Church, still with a wide spectrum of theological views over against the strict Calvinism of the other party that met at the same time in Cracow. The ministerial signatories are for the most part in the service of the lower *szlachta*. The ministers to the great (senatorial) *szlachta* are on the other side.

Only the signatories who have not, or only by a marginal mention, thus far appeared in the *Historia* are identified below.

41. Zielenice, owned by Mikołaj Stadnicki. Jerzy is attested at several synods.

42. Wojciech Biskupski, once deacon in Secemin, was then minister since 1559 to Remigian Chełmski in Włoszczowa. See Bk. 2, n. 655.

43. As Cristianus twice attested at the synods.

44. Deacon in Solec under Pastor Aleksander Witrelin, then deacon in Cracow, Stanisław Wiśniowski was minister in the royal city of the salt mines, 1559, disappearing from the synodal records after the synod in Pińczów, 1563; Sipayłło, *AS*, 2.351.

45. For Jan Pustelnik of Chęciny, see n. 7.

46. Melchior Palipowski (Philipovius) was many times attested at synods, pastor in several places, including Pińczów.

47. Tyburcjusz Borzyszkowski, former priest, was first minister to Stanisław and Maciej Bal in Hoczew near Sanok, then after 1559, in Siekluka for Hieronim Filipowski.

48. Attested at the synods.

49. Marcin of Łasko, attested at the synods.

50. Piotr Fredrich Martyr, deacon in Brzeziny, minister in Szczekoziny (owned by Maciej Szczepanowski, who founded the congregation there in 1556), is attested at the synods.

51. This is Jan Siekierzyński, Jr., of Bobin, owned by Kacper Smolik, a protector of Discordia (Bk. 2, n. 619, ¶3). He is said to have been "the first Polish Anabaptist," Węgierski, see n. 292; on his first post as deacon, see n. 73. Jan Siekierzyński, Sr., (*Historia, 191* passsim) was minister in Iwanowice, succeeding Grzegorz Paweł there in 1557, then in Pełsznica, owned by Stanisław Lasocki who had founded the congregation about 1550. Father and son are attested at the synods. See on each resp. *Historia, 191–92* and *215, 217*.

52. Jakub Zygmunt Megalius is attested at the synods. See also n. 73.

53. Bartłomiej Łuczycki, formerly vicar in Dzrekanowicz, then its Reformed pastor, is attested at the synods.

54. Jakob of Przeczyca, later minister Łańcut, became superintendent of the Podgórski district, attested several times at the synods.

55. Text has *Pharnesius*. Stanisław Farnowski, leader of the Ditheists, reappears at nn. 502 and 528.

56. Marcin of Kalisz, minister in Secemin is several times attested at synods.

57. Text has incorrectly *Gregorius* Niger. Jedlińsko is near Radom. See Bk. 2, n. 457.

58. Stanisław of Mojcze, scribe at Pińczów, then minister there, is attested several times at the synods.

59. Not attested at the synods.

60. Text has Marcus Victor. Marek is attested at synod of Pińczów, 7–14 October 1563. Sipayłło, *AS*, 2.51.

61. Although not addressed or mentioned, the superintendent of the Reformed Church in Vilna was Szymon Zacius/Zacjusz/Zak/Ż (c. 1507–91, *Historia, 29, 43*). With an M.A. from Cracow, he had been professor there, 1532–39. Abandoning thereafter a decade of priesthood because of his marriage (to Katarzyna Pakłotka), he had to leave Cracovia in 1549, became minister in Brest Litovsk from 1555, also superintendent in Vilna and presumably Brest and Podlasie. He edited the *Akta* of the synod of Vilna on December 1557. See further n. 197. Under the influence of Jan Łaski, Mikołaj Radziwiłł had been turned from Lutheranism to the Reformed view. Under him Zacius had set forth *Wyznanie wiary* (1557) in the aforementioned *Akta* (1559), the first public manifestation of Calvinism in Vilna. Włodzimierz Budka, "Szymon Zacius pierwszy superintendent zborów litewskich," *RwP* 2 (1922) 288ff., esp., 290; Szczucki, *Czechowic*, 17 and 48–50, for the situation at the receipt of Lutomirski's letter.

Lubieniecki treats only here and there of the Reformation in the Grand Duchy of Lithuania. Vilna (Vilnius, Wilno), capital of the Duchy and of the palatinate up the Viliva River from Troki, was the natural center of Protestantism, at first Lutheran, then Reformed, and for a decade strongly under the influence of the radically Reformed (antipedobaptist, anti-Trinitarian). The Catholic structure, of course, remained intact. Besides the palatinate of Vilna and that of Podlasie (n. 98), four others were drawn into the Reformation, in towns among burghers or in the private chapels on estates. These four other palatinates were, between the palatinate of Vilna and Ducal Prussia, that of Troki, and to the north to the coast, Samogitia (Żmudź), the heartland of ethnic Lithuania. To the south of palatinate Vilna were the palatinates of Novogorodok (with Nieśwież a printing center), of Brest Litovsk, and Volhynia, all of them ceded to the Crown by the Union of Lublin in 1569, with Volhynia destined to become a second homeland of the Racovian community after 1638.

Developments in the Lithuanian palatinates, apart from Podlasie, have been touched upon by Lubieniecki in Bk. 2 at nn. 162–65, 441, 505, 521, 624–26, and further in the annotation. Besides the source collections and secondary literature previously cited, mention may be made of the incomplete *Monumenta reformationis Polonicae et Lituanicae (MRPL)*, ed. by Henryk Merczyng *et al.* and originally projected in 12 series (Vilna, 1911–13) and the inventory and description of MSS held in the Public Library of Vilnius, *Opisanije rukopisnogo Otdelenija Vilenskoj Publičnoj Biblioteki*, 5 vols. (Vilna, 1895–1906). Jobert, *De Luther à Mohila*, does not deal much with the Reformation in Lithuania but supplies a good genealogical chart of the Radziwiłłs, nor does Schramm for different reasons, although, since his approach is in part systematically regional, he has a good bibliographically updated section on the Lithuanian nobility, chap. 2:6. Stanisław Kot says the most from a specialized perspective in "La Réforme dans la Grande-Duché de Lithuanie: Facteur de l'occidentalisation culturelle," *Annuaire de l'Institut de philologie et d'histoire orientales et slaves*, 12 (1952), published also separately (Brussels, 1953). For further bibliography see n. 196.

Sipayłło gives the bibliographical details of *MRPL* and surveys the synodal records, noting that the tumult in Vilna in 1611 (n. 166) destroyed the Vilna MSS dated earlier. *AS*, 1.x, xii. Marek Wajsblum prepared for publication with valuable annotation two copies of codices from Vilna, still in MS form in Cracow, ibid., xii, n. 4. Szymon Żak edited *Akta tho iest sprawy zboru krześciańskiego wileńskiego, które się poczęli roku pańskiego 1557, miesięca decembra, dnia 14* (Brześć, 1559); republished in the series *MRPL* (Vilna, 1913).

62. The Latin *Scrinium*, capitalized, suggests that at this point Lubieniecki has access to a book or box of papers related to Budziński's History, for he otherwise indicates the relevant chapter.

63. The greeting is modeled on the formula common to most of Paul's letters.

64. Following a scriptural and patristic sanction (1 Cor 8:6), Lutomirski distinguishes between the Father as the source and the Son as the agent in the creation.

65. The *per quem omnia* (reflecting 1 Cor 8:6) of the Nicene-Constantinopolitan Creed remains in Lutomirski as descriptive of Jesus Christ, except that in that Creed the role of agent in creation is carefully ascribed to the Son, *natum ex Patri ante saecula*. Cf. the quotation from Hilary, Bk. 2, n. 477.

66. The term *Electi* is not common in the writings and the synodal acts of the Polish Reformed, including those of Jan Łaski, who was something of an Erasmian on free will, after his return to Poland.

67. Lutomirski's definition goes beyond the received Latin text of the Nicene Creed of 325 in speaking of the Holy Spirit as *coessentiale*, perhaps conscious of some difference from *consubstantialis*, said here of Jesus Christ (rather than of the eternal Son only).

68. Rom 8:15, Gal 4:6.

69. At n. 17 and thereafter.

70. The lay elders (*seniores*) and the ministers elected to the seniorate.

71. Marcin Zborowski.

72. Jan Firlej, as major Calvinist magnate, see at *Historia, 202, 205*.

73. Mikołaj Lutomirski (c. 1495–1566) was a cousin of Stanisław and Jan Lutomirski. Educated at the Jagiellonian University, he had a congregation at his property in Kazmierz Wielki, 1554, where Jakub Megalius (at n. 52) was minister in 1556, thereafter his cousin Stanisław Lutomirski. To Mikołaj was dedicated the *Acta* of the Church in Vilna of 1559 (Brest Litovsk, 1569). In the same congregation served successively as deacon, Jan of Chęciny, 1557; Jan Siekierzyński, Jr., 1558; Maciej Albinus, 1559.

Despite his family relationship with Superintendent Stanisław Lutomirski, Mikołaj would host the conservative Reformed in his Cracow residence in October 1563. For his conservative political and economic position at the Diet of Piotrków, 1562/63, see Halina Kowalska, ''M.L.,'' *PSB* 18 (1973) 142–43.

74. Stanisław Myszkowski, n. 23.

75. The host for the Sarnicki synod, see at nn. 17 and 37.

76. Jost Ludwik Decius (Decjusz; c. 1520–67), humanist (mentioned *Historia, 47*), was elected member of the synodal commission at Włodzisław, 15 June 1557, to translate the Bible into Polish. He took part in the conservative synod of 17 October 1562 in Cracow, which moved against the emergent Minor Church.

77. The four burghers have not been identified. That any of them would have been Catholic in the sense of heeding the bishop of Cracow seems wholly implausible.

78. Grzegorz Paweł.

79. The emerging Minor Church stressed personal morality. Discordia had been under synodal discipline since 1559 for his behavior. See Bk. 2, n. 619; Barycz, *PSB* 5, 173A.

80. The ministerial brethren of what Lutomirski calls the pseudo-synod.

81. The presence of the superintendent of Little Poland would have given full canonical status to Sarnicki's synod.

82. Marcin Zborowski.

83. Jan Firlej.

84. The Feast of St. Stanisław, bishop of Cracow, was observed on 8 May, thus in 1563 on Saturday. Włodarski, *Chronologia*, 257, 388.

85. Stanisław Myszkowski.

86. Lutomirski looks forward to a pan-Commonwealth general synod with the Lithuanian Brethren present and as of 20 May 1563 thinks of the Major Church, yet to be so designated, as breaking away from the Minor Church.

87. The text has *ventos*, in allusion to the winds of doctrine by which some are blown about, Eph 4:14.

88. The emerging Minor Church wished to think of Calvin as only misinformed.

89. Josias Simler, *Responsio ad maledicum Francisci Stancari Mantuani librum adversus Tigurinae Ecclesiae ministros, de Trinitate et Mediatore Domino nostro Jesu Christo* (Zurich, 1563). Grzegorz outlined his doctrine in a long letter to the Zurich divines, Cracow, 20 July 1563. Wotschke, *Briefwechsel*, no. 297, pp. 197–202.

90. This characteristically generous phrase is noted in context by Szczucki, *Czechowic*, 49–50.

91. Mikołai Wędrogowski belonged for a period to the radicalizing Reformed circle under Falconius (n. 92) in Vilna, including Szymon Budny and Gonesius, cf. *Historia, 166* at n. 91; *177–79*.

92. Tomasz Falconius (Sokolowski), former priest in Lublin, a Bible scholar, was the preacher to Radziwiłł. He is attested at several synods in Poland. For his activity in Vilna, see Szczucki, *Czechowic*, 17 passim.

93. See *Historia, 110* and passim.

94. Stanisław Paklepka, *Historia, 152* and *172–73*.

95. Marcin Krowicki (d. 1573) Bk. 1, nn. 233, 234, 239, 274; Bk. 2, nn. 155, 158, 233, 289. From his new base in Brzeziny (1557), Krowicki was elected superintendent of Podlasie at the ensuing synod of Mordy, 9 June 1563. Sipayłło, *AS*, 2.326. On the significance of which, see n. 98. Krowicki is next mentioned at the synod of Brzeziny (1565), n. 220.

96. As Lubieniecki turns presently to the reaction to the letter in Lithuania, he must intend here the still not officially divided Reformed Brethren in Little Poland, who will have been made aware of the contents of both letters of Lutomirski.

97. Sipayłło, *AS*, 2.153, 225–26. There were 42 persons present. Aleksander Witerlin (*Historia, 62*) writing to Bullinger, from Orańsko, 24 June 1563, mentions briefly the counter synods in Cracow under Sarnicki and Lutomirski, then the synod in Mordy. Wotschke, *Briefwechsel*, 294, p. 193. From some source Wotschke gives the dates for Mordy, 4–9 June 1563 in a n.

98. Podlasie (Latin: Podlachia) was part of Masovia. Masovia (Mazowsze) was once a principality. By the opening of the sixteenth century two of what would be counted as its four palatinates were already under the Crown, Płock and Rawa. In 1526/(29), one year after newly Ducal and now Lutheran Prussia became a fief of the Crown, the palatinate of Masovia proper, with its chief city and eventual national capital, Warsaw, was incorporated into the Kingdom. The fourth palatinate, Podlasie, was not part of Poland proper until ceded to the Crown by the Union of Lublin of 1569. It was a corridor between the palatinate of Lublin in Little Poland and a stretch of the Ducal Prussian

border; and, of all the socially conservative palatinates of Masovia, it was the most open to the Reformation and it has already been featured as a place of synods and interchanges.

The Latin-Byzantine-rite boundary (in terms of village churches) extended northward from the Hungarian (Slovakian) boundary near Sanok, through the eastern half of palatinate Lublin (between Lublin and Chełm) and through the center of Podlasie, slightly curving northeast through the Lithuanian palatinates of Troki and Vilna (with the villages around both these palatine seats included within Byzantine-rite territory), but then turning north on the Dvina (Dzwina) River (between Połock and Riga). The Byzantine rite from Kiev, Muscovy, and Novgorod did not extend into Samogitia, Livonia, and the other Baltic regions were converted to Latin Christianity by the Teutonic Order and its successors.

Podlasie with its mixed Catholic/Orthodox population, with the Orthodox brotherhoods and very weak episcopal oversight providing models of lay participation and with their married Orthodox priests vividly reminding the Latin-rite reformers of another apostolic usage than that of Gregory VII, was a lively corridor between two centers of Reformation, Lublin and Königsberg. Linguistically the palatinate of Podlasie was mixed: Polish and Byelorussian insofar as these terms can cover the regional dialects.

Politically Podlasie stood somewhat apart during the Reformation century and by 1569 was directly under the Crown; but a score of years before that Podlaise featured in the synods of Little Poland as a full participant, therein in a way different from delegations from other Lithuanian palatinates.

99. The lesser lords among the *szlachta* took a major part in directing their estates and the serfs serving them on the farms and fields. Only here and there did the Reformed landowner draw into the fellowship of new *zbóry* (*ecclesiae* also *coetus*, never in the *Historia: parochiae, greges, congregationes*)—the peasants and villagers under the Reformed lord.

The number of 42 persons (confirmed by the record printed by Sipayłło, *AS*, 2.152) would have been made up of lords and ministers.

100. The synod spoke of ''the excesses of Sarnicki and of his fellows.'' Sipayłło, 2.152.

101. The Kolozsvár record printed by Sipayłło (*AS*, 2.152) gives the same text, except that probably it preserves more faithfully *verbum hominum*, the word of men, man collectively, in council and tradition. The synodists of Mordy retained what they considered a scriptural Triadology and some clearly preferred to drop *Trinitas* as nonscriptural, although to the end of the Brethren and Sisters as a Church they would always baptize in the name of the Father, the Son, and the Holy Spirit (Matt 28:19).

102. Wawrzyniec Niezgoda (Discord) is throughout made by Lubieniecki to carry the full burden of the literal meaning of his ''surname.'' He has in mind Discordia's advancement under Sarnicki despite his having been synodally disciplined for immorality (n. 79).

Notes to Chapter Two

103. The water of mutual toleration or enjoined silence created explosive steam. Lubieniecki in this reading in physics has picked up the word *reactio*. In France of the same century there was the same issue as between Catholics and Huguenots of mutual toleration or theological concord as sought at the Colloquy of Poissy, 1561. Cf. Mario Turchetti, ''concord ou tolerance à la veille ou guerres de religione en France?'' *Revue de théologie et de philosophie*, 118 (1986), 255–56.

104. The three options, not entirely distinguishable, are those of the brethren of the emerging Minor Church.

105. This striking phrase, *Res publica ecclesiastica*, brings together intentions and expectations that had been in the Reformed Church from Stancaro's Canons on the model of Archbishop Hermann von Wied, Prince Elector of Mainz, through the death of Łaski, nephew of the Polish Primate, i.e., from 1550 to 1560, during which time some thought of the emerging regional synods as meeting with sufficient representation to have Commonwealth-wide import. Their Seniorate was instinct with traits and gestures of an idealized Diet, of a Senate without bishops, only lords and superintendents! Cf. observations in nn. 18, 28, 30, 31, 38, also in Bk. 1, n. 175 (the vision of Modrzewski). Sipayłło has a full index to all references to the evolving Seniorate (*AS*, 2.405), the *Senjorowie* being different from presbyters and syndics in Geneva, or presbyters and lairds in the Assembly of the Kirk and in the Scots Parliament.

As he alludes to the restrictive edicts of Parczów of 1564, already mentioned in Bk. 2 at n. 834, and to be presently treated at n. 137, Lubieniecki for the first moment in his *Historia* acknowledges that his "true Church" was severed from the Royal Commonwealth and even suspect. Lubieniecki was temperamentally a would-be religiously tolerant "Magisterial Reformer" as to polity, craving some benign relationship of the Crown and the Commonwealth institutions, like the dietines, with his "truly Reformed" Church.

106. *Brevis explicatio doctrinae de sanctissima Trinitate*, finished January 1563; published in Königsberg, 1565, referred to in the present nn. as *De Trinitate* (Bk. 2, n. 136, ¶3). The same four *doctores Ecclesiae* are mentioned in Bk. 2 at n. 279. In part 2 Lismanino's work contains a compilation from patristic sources, e.g., excerpts from a letter of Basil and from his sermon on Job 1:1; from Aquinas, *Summa*, quaestio 31, second article after Hilary and Ambrose; from Augustine, *De fide et symbolo*, 9; and from Hilary, *De Trinitate*, 4, on Deut 32. See Wotschke, "Lismanino," 296–97, 306.

107. *Historia, 109*, etc.

108. The reference is to *De Trinitate alias in Symbolum Apostolorum tractatus*, which is not actually from Ambrose. There is no division into books; in chapter 3 it is stated "Quod autem natum est, et factum non est, filius est. . . ." Migne, *PL*, 17, cols. 511–12.

109. In *De Trinitate* 2.1. Augustine does not appear to have used *Deus genitus* although in context it could be orthodox.

110. Not identified in *PL*, 35 cols. 1906–8. *De agone christiano*, 20; "Mediator Dei et hominum homo Christus Jesus," *PL*, 40 col. 301.

111. Not found in *Enarratio in Psalmum*, 37, *PL*, 4, cols. 396–412.

112. *Retractationes*, I, 24: "propter substantiam vero naturae humanae, in qua ascendit in coelum, etiam nunc mediator Dei et hominum homo Christus Jesus (I Tim 2:5), *PL*, 32, col. 623.

113. Jerome in reference to the kenosis and humiliation of Christ Jesus in Phil 2:5–11.

114. God as God the Father was regarded by Origen, *De principis*, as the primordial Ἀρχή and in John Chrysostom Lubieniecki's quotation is plausible, as it is close to John 10:29, 14:28, etc.

115. Lubieniecki has quoted the four Doctors where they were themselves closest to Scripture. His examination was not thorough but programmatic. He was looking in the Fathers for such texts as 1 Tim 2:5.

116. Lismanino adduced the Johannine Comma, which was noted as a textual prob-

lem by Erasmus and is recognized as an interpolation in the Vulgate. Of North African or Spanish origin, 1 John 5:7–8 is an important triadological locus in the history of Latin Christendom. The interpolation is italicized, 5:7: "Quoniam tres sunt qui testimonium dant *in coelo: Pater, Verbum, et Spiritus sanctus; et hi tres unum sint.*" The interpolation continues in the next verse through "*in terra.*" But Lismanino is concerned only with the close of verse 7 and observes that *unum* can mean adverbally one or as one man and not as one *essentia* or *substantia*. Lubieniecki goes on to reinforce the adverbial sense of *unum* with reference to the analogy of believers in Christ.

117. The masculine *unus* is in references to the divine Person as *testis*. The orthodox argument presupposed here is that the Witnesses are three and yet one Witness (*unus*).

118. Lubieniecki's usage here of *Trinitarii* (cf. Bk. 1, n. 22) is that of the Unitarian Transylvanians in reference to the orthodox Calvinists after they had themselves become explicitly Unitarian, although the latter designation came first into official use c. 1600. See n. 123. In Poland the Catholics, no less than the conservative Calvinists, rightly called the anti-Nicene party of the Reformed Church, 1562–65, though strange to modern ears, *Trideitae* (at n. 121), since in a transitorial phase the view was episodically in the ascendant that there were three divine beings, God the Father, the Son, and the Holy Spirit without clarification of their voluntary or ontological unity in what was therefore an unresolved tritheism. Wilbur, *Socinianism*, 344. Tritheism had an ancient representative in Philippoponus, a scholastic antecedent in Roscellinus, and an Italian Reformed ally in Gentile (Bk. 2, n. 351).

119. See n. 116.

120. Johann Bugenhagen (Pomeranus) (1485–1558) was pastor in Wittenberg for life and was Luther's confessor (*Historia, 11, 43*).

121. Lubieniecki in a generalizing statement has primarily in mind Lutherans and Calvinists (as by his time the Major Reformed Church were called).

122. In paraphrasing 1 Tim 2:5 in a clarified unitarianism of the Father as alone God, with Jesus Christ being the Mediator between that God and men, partly through the Gift of the Spirit, Lubieniecki here insufficiently acknowledges the phase in Polish Reformed history (already recorded in part by himself) when his antecedents in faith and provisional formulation were, in fact, Tritheists, then some of them Ditheists. See n. 118.

123. The term "Unitarian" seems to have originated in the great dispute at Alba Julia, 3–12 March 1568, where Péter Méliusz, debating against Ferenc Dávid, reached the conclusion: "Ergo Deus est trinitarius." Thereupon his opponents may have began to be called Unitarians or devotees of God as *unitarius*. Wilbur, *Transylvania*, 47 n. 12. The term, however, spread only gradually. The earliest documented use of the term is in a letter of 1585 from King Stephen Batory to his youthful nephew, Sigismund, at the court in Alba Julia, alerting him to the hazards of consorting with *Unitarii* at the Jesuit college there and in Kolozsvár. The letter is presented by Ferenc Pápai, *Rudus redevivum* (Cibinii, 1684) 157–58; picked up by Lampe, *Historia*, 313; noted and discussed by Wilbur, *Transylvania*, 93, n. 31. The designation appeared for the first time as the name of the Transylvanian radical Reformed Church in an official document in the records of the diet in the Szekler village of Léczfalva in 1600. Possibly the first use of *Antitrinitarian* was in 1564, n. 452.

The *Complanatio Deesiana*, defining the distinctive doctrine of the radical Reformed Transylvanian Church, authorized as licit by the synod and the diet of Dées (Dej) in 1638 (thirty miles north of Cluj) as indeed Unitarian, promoted the growing use of the term as official for the *Unitaria recepta religio*. The term later spread to Poland, as evidenced here (but not common), then to Holland and England. Not until most of the Minor

Church was disbanded in exile after 1660 did the Polish Brethren call themselves Socinians, seldom Unitarians, unlike their Transylvanian allies and opponents and others. Wilbur, *Transylvania*, 100, 118.

124. The Major Reformed, who also postulated the sole authority of Scripture.

125. Lubieniecki's observation would find confirmation in Luther's own commentary, *Die Drei Symbole* (Wittenberg, 1538), wherein he expressed a preference for the Apostles' Creed, always accepted by the Minor Church, and wherein he thus dealt with the *Quicunquevult*, with the *Te Deum laudamus* (traditionally ascribed to Ambrose and Augustine), and only as an appendix with the Nicene(=Constantinopolitan) Creed. Weimar Edition, 50.262–83. On Luther in a speech by Lismanino, 1561, see Bk. 2, n. 515. For Luther elsewhere, see Bk. 2, near n. 128, Bk. 3 at n. 639. Willis indirectly gives much attention to the Italian and Polish dissenters on the dogma of the Trinity in *Calvin's Catholic Christology* (Bk. 2, n. 436, ¶5). For emphasis on Calvin's "snatching away" inadvertently (Lubieniecki) of crucial triadological Bible passages, see my "Strains in Christology." This was written without the benefit of the systematic study of the Rev. Jerzy Misiurek, *Chrystologia Braci Polskich: Okres przedsocyniański* (Lublin: KUL, 1983), esp. 26–34. With respect to the Polish Brethren even more than the Transylvanian Unitarians, the discussion of the dissolution of the dogma of the Trinity is subsumed under Christology in response, as it were, to the Apostolic question, "What think ye of Christ?" (Matt 22:42).

126. That is, Lismanino's patristic *Brevis explicatio*, n. 106; but perhaps Lubieniecki alludes also to Lismanino's letter in Bk. 2 at n. 449.

127. Lismanino attended the synod of Mordy, 6 June 1563. Seeing his impending defeat, he considered going to Moldavia to serve Voivode Jacob Basilicus (Bk. 3, chap. 9); he went on to Vilna, where he received a pension from Chancellor Mikołai Radziwiłł, who also gave him leave to go to Moldavia. But news came of the coup against the Voivode and thereupon Lismanino went to Königsberg, October, 1563, where he was appointed councillor to Duke Albert. In the autumn of 1564 he fell seriously ill, compiled his *De trinitate* (Bk. 2, n. 136) and wrote a *Testamentum*, published by Wotschke, "Lismanino," *Zeitschrift der historischen Gesellschaft für die Provinz Posen* 18 (1903) 221, 305–8. Either at the end of April or at the beginning of May, 1566, he fell or jumped into a well and was drowned, perhaps in a fit of epilepsy. His unusual death gave rise to rumors eagerly spread by his opponents. According to one account, preserved by Budziński (*History*, chap. 26), he had committed suicide in despair over the adultery of his wife, Claudia. *BAnt*, p. 35. According to another account he committed suicide in a fit of frenzy caused by his "disappointed avarice." Wotschke, "Bericht über Lismaninos Tod," *Briefwechsel*, no. 349, p. 269–70; Barycz, *PSB* 17.469; Rott and Peter, eds., *Lettres à Calvin*, 51, n. 3.

128. Lubieniecki refers to Voivode John II Sigismund (1559–71; Bk. 1, n. 150) and supplies the salient dynastic facts, Hungarian, Hapsburg, Polish, and Ottoman. It is here and in n. 129 the place to say more of the land and religious situation to which Biandrata was returning for a second time and where he would die, almost to the end a cosmopolitan visionary and schemer for liberal Protestantism in tolerant Eastern lands, esp. Little Poland and Transylvania, the latter a vassal state on the border of the Ottoman Empire.

When Biandrata came to Transylvania in 1563, John II was roughly one third the way through his reign as voivode (for the term, see, Bk 2, n. 690) and as claimant (till 1570) to the Crown of Hungary, portions of which (*Partium*, see further in this note) he actually governed. When Lubieniecki turns to Transylvania in a chapter of its own (chap. 11) as of c. 1578, John's immediate successor, Stephen Báthory, will have already been elected King of Poland (1575/76 – 86).

The references to Hungary and Transylvania (on the distinctive constitution of this frontier palatinate/voivodeship and eventually independent principality and its early Reformation, see n. 129, ¶¶4 – 6) in the prospective chapter and elsewhere in the text and annotation are to territories, even when taken together, that were of much less geographic scope than the vast polyglot Apostolic Kingdom of Hungary shattered by the immense Ottoman victory at Mohács in 1526. Yet Suleiman the Magnificent (1520 – 66) had left much of this under the two claimants to the Crown of slain Louis II Jagiełło (1516 – 26): Ferdinand I Hapsburg (1526 – 64) and John Zápolya (Szapolyai), voivode of Transylvania (1520 – 26), who was elected by the Hungarian estates as the national king (1526 – 40). The newly elected voivode, Péter Perényi (1526 – 29), custodian of the Crown of St. Stephen (977/99 – 1038), betrayed John in ceding it to his rival.

In a coup d'état in 1528 John had to flee to Cracow, taking refuge with Sigismund I, whose first queen had been Barbara Zápolya (d. 1515). In exile, John engaged, among others, the Croatio-Italian Paulist monk György Martinuzzi (1482 – 1551) as his chief advisor. Dedicated to the reunification of Hungary against the Hapsburg claimant, John was prepared to negotiate with both anti-Hapsburg Francis I of France, who had a secret understanding with the Porte, and the Sultan himself. For the mission to Istanbul, he chose Hieronim Łaski (1496 – 1541), palatine of Sieradź, older brother of the Reformer and the father of Olbracht Łaski of Bk. 2, chap. 9. In 1529 Suleiman marched up the Danube for the third time, formally installed John in Buda, received his homage, and adopted him as son, in effect as vassal; and then he proceeded to the terrible but for him unsuccessful siege of Vienna in September 1529. After confused fighting between Hapsburg and disparate Zápolyan and pro-Hapsburg forces in Transylvania, John regained the voivodeship of Transylvania and the royal title over annexed territory, while Ferdinand allowed himself also to be adopted as son of the Sultan, the rival kings of Hungary having recognized the territorial status quo, 1533, Pozsony (Pressburg) and Alba Julia (n. 129, ¶5) their respective (provisional) capitals. Then by the secret treaty of Várad of 1538, it was agreed that on the death of John all Hungaria including the voivodeship of Transylvania would come under Ferdinand as sole King or his successor. Despite his age, John married in 1539 Isabelle Jagiellonka, daughter of Sigismund I, from whom issued John (II); and the proud father reconsidered the secret treaty. On his deathbed, July 1540, John I convened his council of state, notably Martinuzzi, bishop of Várad, treasurer of the realm but in effect chief minister, to charge them to break the treaty and unify all Hungaria under the infant son, Isabelle to become regent.

Appealing to the terms of the treaty of Várad, Ferdinand besieged Buda. After his defeat, Suleiman incorporated Lower Hungary along both banks of the Danube as a military province of the Ottoman Empire in 1541, the *Beylerbeyilik* (*beger beglik*) of Buda, while the voivodeship of Transylvania was placed under Isabella Jagiellonka (1541 – 51) as queen regent for her minor son. Ferdinand retained a remnant of territory from Fiume in the Adriatic, along the outer rim of the Holy Roman Empire and then along the crest of the Carpathian frontier with the Commonwealth beyond Spisz as far as (on the Polish side) the source of the Wisłok, a territory that dipped south to include (up to 1596) Eger. Under the guidance of her ministers, Isabelle sought to preserve for John (II) the *partes regni Hungariae* (for short: *Partium*) that, annexed to voivodal Transylvania, much enlarged its bounds beyond the Tisza to make good the Zápolyan claim to the whole of non-Ottoman Hungary. After contesting Isabelle's grasp on about half of *Partium*, Ferdinand by 1547 acquiesced in the tripartition of the ancient realm to the extent of agreeing to pay tribute to the Sublime Porte of 300,000 ducats annually. By this treaty of which the Emperor Charles V, the Pope, the King of France, and the Republic of Venice were also parties, Suleiman loomed on the border of the Empire and from across the Adriatic as the Lord of his Age (*Sahibi Kiran*).

In 1551 Ferdinand, limiting his own hopes for reunification to the annexation of at least (Greater) Transylvania, sent General Giambattista Castaldo, with a force too large to be a legation, too small to succeed as an army, to force Queen Isabelle to abdicate. This she did after the assassination of György Martinuzzi, bishop of Csnanád and Várad, (1534/36–39/51) who had once accompanied her late husband during exile in Poland; and Transylvania was temporarily united with Hapsburg Hungary, 1551–56. Biandrata, who had had to leave court, negotiated in her interest in Vienna (Bk. 2, n. 436, ¶4).

At the head of separate armies the Beylerbey of Buda and the Grand Vizier routed the Hapsburgs and restored Isabelle, 1556–59, to a much reduced Transylvania, while a new *beylerbeyilik* of Temesvár was consolidated. At the same time, in the contested area of the *Partium*, Hapsburg Hungary organized a captaincy of Upper Hungary with Eger and Kassa, Sárospatak (seat of displaced Moravian Brethren), Munkács, and Szatmár among the royal boroughs. Debrecen, the Reformed capital of the valley of the Tisza, was at times part of Transylvania, of the captaincy, and of the Beylerbeyilik. It was in this context that Isabelle issued in 1557 her edict of toleration, Introduction at n. 60, also Pl. 39.

On his thirteenth military campaign in 1566 Suleiman received John II, "my dear son," in Belgrade and promised to enlarge his realm at the expense of the Hapsburgs (cf. n. 354). He died shortly thereafter of apoplexy in his tent during the siege of Szigetvár on the Drave (defended in epic valor by Miklós Zrinyi). The embalmed body was carried in the imperial litter during the remainder of the campaign, orders were still given in the name of the deceased Sultan, and the army was kept unaware of the death until after the descent to Belgrade, where his son Selim II officially succeeded (1566–74).

Selim II would attack Venetian-held Cyprus, inspiring the Holy League under Pius V and Philip II of Spain, whose forces under Don Juan of Austria, with a Venetian fleet, defeated the Ottoman armada off Lepanto, 7 October 1571. Under Selim (and his successor, Murad III, 1574–95), John II Sigismund ruled in Transylvania as voivode, and in *Partium* as claimant to the national Crown (Bk. 2, n. 364, ¶2; Bk. 3., n. 598, ¶2), not only as dutiful vassal but also evidently as spirited ally, not renouncing the royal claim until 1570 (n. 39) when he made an overture through Gáspár Békés to negotiate a marriage with the daughter of the emperor, Bk 2, n. 364. For the voivodial succession after 1571 and for the changing boundaries of Transylvania, see n. 387.

Hungarian history in the sixteenth century was the scene not only of massive Ottoman incursion and hegemony and of dynastic conflict between the Hapsburgs and the Zápolyans of Polish connection (and their princely successors) but also of religious toleration on all sides in the service of practical politics. Stephen Alexander Fischer-Galati carries his account, *Ottoman Imperialism and German Protestantism* (Cambridge, 1959) only from 1521 to the Peace of Augsburg in 1555, touching upon Hungary only incidentally, but concluding: "The Turks diverted the attention of the Hapsburgs from German affairs and made them dependent on Protestant cooperation for the realization of their secular ambitions in Europe, particularly Hungary. The consolidation, expansion, and legitimizing of Lutheranism in Germany by 1555 should be attributed to Ottoman imperialism more than to any other single factor" (*Ottoman Imperialism*, 117). Similarly, although never so acknowledged by its proponents, proto-Unitarianism in Transylvania, where the Saxon towns had been drawn to the cause of Luther as early as 1520

(n. 129, ¶6), cannot be seen but as the partial consequence of the religious toleration that was itself an Ottoman policy in occupied and vassal territories, as well as of sympathetic vibration with the simpler monotheism of the dominant religio-political power—an analogy tauntingly raised by the foes of Unitarianism—and yet also a partial consequence of the Reformation quest for the simplicity and verity of primitive Christianity. Although the radical Reformed Church counseled by Biandrata in Little Poland and that in Transylvania (in both he was a prime mover and a ranking Elder) were in communion and close correspondence, the "Anabaptist" marks of believers' baptism, of socio-economic egalitarianism and the community of goods, of reserve in respect to magisterial authority in doctrine and discipline, and disposition toward pacifism were never so prominent in Transylvania as in Little Poland and in affected palatinates of Lithuania; and, of the three or four ancient symbols, the Unitarian Church in Transylvania abandoned all, while the Polish Brethren retained the Apostles' Creed on Polish soil (although it came to be increasingly overshadowed by a succession of Racovian catechisms).

Except for the preceding paragraph much in the note is drawn from Halil Inalcik, "The Heyday and Decline of the Ottoman Empire," in P. M. Holt, Ann K. S. Lambton, and Bernard Lewis, *Cambridge History of Islam*, 2 vols (Cambridge: University Press, 1970) I.324 – 30; and Makkai, *Transylvanie*, chaps. 8 – 10. Jan Reychman, with a map and many illustrations, recounts for a general readership *Historia Turcji* (Wrocław, etc.: Ossolineum, 1973) and makes especially clear the role of Poland in the period of Ottoman rule. Much more detailed is Janusz Pajewski, *Węgierska polityka Polski w połowie XVI wieku (1540 – 71)* (Cracow, 1932), while Endre Kovács places Hungarian-Polish cultural and political relations from 1364 to 1580 in the special context of the role of the Jagiellonian University in Hungarian culture, *A Krakkói Egyetem és a Magyar mübelödés* (Budapest, 1965), translated by Eugeniusz Mroczko as *Uniwersytet krakowski a kultura węgierska: Przyczynki do historii węgiersko-polskich stosunków kulturalnych wieków XV i XVI* (Budapest: for Ossolineum, 1965).

129. Isabelle Jagiellonka died 15 September 1559. Lubieniecki seems to be confusing the summons of her son to hasten to her bedside (Biandrata returned to Pińczów after her death) and the invitation in 1563. Biandrata had left Poland before 5 September 1563. This is known from a letter of Jan Łasicki to Bullinger of that date, saying that Biandrata had proceeded to the court of the Despot Jacob Basilicus of Moldavia (Bk. 2, chap. 9). Wotschke, *Briefwechsel*, no. 307, p. 211. It is quite plausible that the Despot would have extended an invitation to so distinguished a physician, but after the Despot's assassination, it appears that John II Sigismund (Jacob's foe) urged Biandrata to return to Transylvania and to serve as privy councilor. His departure from Pińczów had marked the close of his second major sojourn in Poland (1558 – 63), the first sojourn having been that in Cracow as court physician (Bk. 2, n. 426, ¶¶3 – 4). In establishing the dates Rotondò uses the Łasicki letter but has no conjecture about Moldavia, "Biandrata," *DBI*, 10 (1968), col. 259A. Dr. Biandrata in his second Transylvanian sojourn, 1563, until his obscure death in 1588, was perhaps the chief architect of the emergent territorial christocentric Unitarian Church, *as it would survive radicalization* under its driven, scholarly, temperamental, and prophetic superintendent and charismatic preacher Ferenc Dávid (n. 601), who had begun to radiczalize the Reformed church's scriptural message from his pulpit in Kolozsvár by 1565. By this date, as in the Reformed Church in Poland, the problem of an "antischolastic" scriptural Trinity had come to the fore. I have not consulted the article on Blandrata in Jenö Zoványi, and Sándor Ladanyi, eds., *Protestáns Egyháztörténe Lenkon* (Budapest, 1977) 81 – 82.

Transylvania could never be marginal to Lubieniecki, who was keenly conscious that

Voivode/Prince King Stephen Báthory/Batory once ruled both the Commonwealth and Transylvania, 1571/76/86 (n. 387, ¶2) and, within his own direct experience (n. 285), that Calvinist Prince George II Rákóczi (1648–60) had invaded Poland in 1657 as an ally of Lutheran Charles X Gustavus (1654–60) of Sweden. It is here in place to encapsule further (cf. n. 128) the development of the Reformation in progress in the Transylvania to which Biandrata went in 1563 and where before he had already discharged an important role (1544–52; Bk. 2, n. 436, ¶2), and whence in 1564 he would write back enthusiastically to Prince Radziwiłł (n. 132).

There is a small subsection on Transylvania in Bk. 3 (*Historia, 189–90*), esp. n. 280 (on baptism, c. 1565); a snatch on Adam Neuser en route from Cracow to Kolozsvár in 1572 (Bk. 3, nn. 383–95); and there is yet to follow a whole chapter 11 on the intra-Unitarian debate on the adoration of Christ in Transylvania, mostly from 1565 to 1579. There are incursions by Lubieniecki into Transylvania earlier in its history, notably, the second sojourn there of Stancaro (1553–58; Bk. 2, n. 426).

Transylvania as a voivodeship (the palatinate, containing several counties), apart from the contested *Partium* (n. 128, ¶5), was a geographically unified but ethnically disparate region, of three major ethnic stocks: Hungarian (Magyar), Walachian (Romanian), and Saxon. Among the Hungarians were the quite distinct Szeklers (the German for *Székely*; Latin: *Siculi*). From nomadic times they inhabited the easternmost marches (counties) of the voivodeship in villages and pastures of a culturally compact region known to the Saxon colonists on their periphery as Szeklerland. Proud yeomen, preserving their communal laws and liberties from their nomadic period, they were represented in the voivodal diet by their noble chieftains, while their customary law was usually confirmed by successive voivodes in diet, and when not, restiveness and revolt could ensue. Cf. n. 387, ¶3. The Walachians of a strongly Slavicized Romance speech and of the Byzantine rite in a Cyrillic text, although numerous, are scarcely heeded in Hungarian and Saxon records of the centuries within the purview of Lubieniecki.

The Saxon colonists, the first to be touched by the dawning rays of the Reformation, had been originally invited by the Hungarian kings into Mongol-devastated terrain where they organized themselves with royal charters in the early thirteenth century in seven free walled cities. Saxon burghers, with their own confederational body, the *universitas Saxonum*, and the Szekler and Magyar nobility were represented in the voivodial diet from 1229. (Walachian representation would not come until all ethnic, as distinguished from confessional, privileges were leveled in the *Ausgleich* and the reunion of Transylvania and Hungary under the Dual Monarchy of the Hapsburgs, 1867–1918.) Transylvania ("beyond the forest:" Hungarian: Erdely; Rumanian adapted as: Ardeal), in its German designation Siebenbürgen (Polish: Siedmiogród), was, as a voivodeship, much more than the confederation of the seven Saxon royal boroughs, as constitutionally progressive as these were. In the languages of the three linguistic groups these boroughs were: (1) Kronstadt (Brassó, Braov); (2) Hermannstadt (Nagyszeben, Sibiu); (3) Klausenburg (Kolozsvár, Cluj); (4) Mediasch (Medgyes, Media); (5) Schässburg (Segesvár, Sighioára); (6) Bistritz (Beszterce, Bistriţa); and (7) Mühlbach (Szászebes, Sebeş). Of these, boroughs 1, 2, and 3 feature most prominently in Reformation history. The third town, extruded fom the Seven and replaced, became Magyarized by the beginning of the seventeenth century (n. 597). The court of the voivodeship/realm/principality was, not in the same linguistic order, Alba Iulia (earlier: Julia)/Gyulafehérvár/Weissenburg/Seograd (Serbian)—not one of the Saxon Seven. Important also was Thorenburg (Torda, Turda), one third of the way south from Kolozsvár to the court capital. For the changing boundaries of Transylvania, see n. 387.

The Reformation first reached Hermannstadt, c. 1520. It spread from the Saxons to the Magyars but scarcely reached the pastoral Walachs of Orthodox allegiance (but see Bk. 2, chap. 9). The first theological leader of the Reformation in Transylvania was Johannes Hunterus of Kronstadt, who had studied at Vienna, Cracow, and Basel. In 1544 the confederational assembly of the Saxon body politic (*universitas Saxonum, Sachsenuniversität*), seeking to establish a common polity and liturgy for the villages and towns under their sway, adopted the *Augustana* and called for the election of a superintendent by the chapters of the seven main borough churches; and the following year the desire was expressed to separate from the jurisdiction of the archbishop of Gran and the bishop of Alba Julia and to come together as "members of one religion and body." Paul Wiener, pastor of Kronstadt, became the first superintendent. He was succeeded in 1556 by Matthias Hebler (from Spisz), a fellow-student of Ferenc Dávid in Wittenberg.

For the role of Stancaro on the issue of Christ the Mediator among the Transylvanian Saxons, 1553–57, see Bk. 2, n. 426. The first publication of Dávid, and as a Lutheran, was the *Dialysis Scripti Stancari* (Kolozsvár, 1555), the first article of the synod in Szék (Sic, northeast from Kolozsvár toward Dées), where Stancaro's issue of Christ the Mediator had been raised. Károly Szabós and A. Hillebrant, *Régi Magyar Könyvtár ar. 1531–1711* (Early Hungarian Bibliography), 3 vols. (Hungarian, Latin, and Latin published outside Hungaria; Budapest, 1879–96) 2, no. 65. Although Wilbur held with Uzoni, 1776, and with Haner, 1694, that Stancaro's "error faded away more quickly than even a shadow," *Transylvania*, 13–14, it is noteworthy that Dávid would be still instinct with the Stancarist theme even as late as in his *De Mediatoris Jesu Christi hominis divinitate, aequalitateque libellus* (Alba Julia, 1568), to which is appended *De restauratione Ecclesiae* by the Hebraist Martin Borrhaus (Cellarius 1499–1564), *Régi Magyar Könyvtár*, 2, no. 115. Cellarius had been a temporary convert to the way of the Zwickau prophets. See my *Radical Reformation*, 47, 251, etc., and monographically, Irena Dorota Backus, ed. Martin Borrhaus, *Bibliotheca Dissidentium* (Baden-Baden, foreseen for 1981).

Until 1556 the Magyars were one with the Saxons in the espousal of the *Augustana*, where in Debrecen its pastor, Márton Kálmáncsehi, on the rising issue of the Lord's Supper, openly espoused the Swiss view and was pilloried by the Saxon Lutherans as a Sacramentarian. At the Diet of Torda in 1557 religious toleration was accorded all (Pl. 39) It was precisely in defense of the Lutheran doctrine on the Lord's Supper that Dávid, younger colleague of Kaspar Helth (in the Saxon church) in Klausenburg, composed and co-signed with him the *Consensus* of the Lutherans of both nations in Lower Hungary and all Transylvania at the synod in the town of 13 June 1557, indeed as "pastor ecclesiae Claudiopolitanae ac *superintendens ecclesiarum* Christi *nationis Hungaricae* in Transsilvania," *Consensus doctrinae de sacramentis Christi* (Kolozsvár, 1557); *Régi Magyar Könyvtár*, 2, no. 76. The phrasing may be a scribal retrojection of his superintendency; but, whatever may have been the exact dates, Dávid was considered superintendent of the Magyar Lutherans and may have, as of the *Consensus*, sustained the hope of a united Protestant diocese or province, whatever the doctrinal accommodations necessary, "that all Transylvania become Lutheran." The decree of toleration of the Diet of Torda of 1557 (n. 599) had provided for a Transylvanian national synod, and its presupposition was the preservation of the unity of Christianity ("quaevis fides christiana una sit"). Co-signer Helth (Heltai), who had studied with Melanchthon in 1543, would later translate the New Testament into Hungarian (Kolozsvár, 1562; *Régi Magyar Könyvtár*, 1, no. 51), become a Calvinist, direct the press in Klausenburg, and later, 1572, become a Unitarian (n. 598).

By 1564 it had become evident that there were not only two nations of Protestants in Transylvania but also, in effect, two confessions, Lutheran and Reformed, initially divided over the issue of the Lord's Supper. At the Diet of Schässburg/Segesvár early in the year it was decided that there be a synod of Transylvanian Protestants at Enyed (near Alba Julia) to achieve a *modus vivendi* for the two parties. John Sigismund sent Biandrata as his ecclesiastical negotiater (and afterwards rewarded him for his successful efforts with the ownership of three villages near Kolozsvár that had belonged to the cathedral chapter of Alba Julia) to work out an amicable separation of the national synod roughly along ethnic-sacramental lines. Sometime Lutheran Superintendent Dávid became henceforth the (Magyar) Reformed superintendent, Biandrata a major ally and collaborator. For the calling of the synod of Enyed in 1564, see Georg Haner of Schässburg, *Historia ecclesiarum Transylvanicarum* (Frankfurt/Leipzig, 1694) 274–77; Friedrich Lampe, *Historia Ecclesiae Reformatae in Hungaria et Transylvania* (Utrecht, 1728) 123–24; another venerable source and account is that by Péter Bod (1712–90), *Historia Hungarorum ecclesiastica* 3 vols, ed., by L. W. E. Rauwenhoff assisted by Károly Száláy (Leiden, 1888); Wilbur, *Transylvania*, 26–27, who himself much used the MS "Historia" of Stephanus Uzoni (1776; n. 600). As many Transylvania Protestant divines were of mixed lineage or at least bilingual, as well as competent in Latin in their synods and tracts, the Lutheran-Reformed schism of 1564 was still felt to be in part only pragmatic, linguistic for purposes of worship and church discipline, and not yet decisively confessional. In any case, the separated Saxon synod of 1564 only confirmed their acceptance of the Augsburg Confession in 1572 (cf. ¶6).

For the dividing of the Protestant Church during the superintendency of Matthias Hebler, see Karl Reinerth, *Die Gründung der evangelischen Kirche in Siebenbürgen*, Studia Transylvanica, 5 (Cologne/Vienna: Bühlau, 1979), "Trennung der beiden evangelischen Kirchen," and "Annahme des Augsburger Bekenntnisse," 229–303; 304–22; esp., 222, 237 (for some of the date above); and, in a Reformed perspective covering briefly the whole of Hungarian Church history, see Mihály Bucsay, *Geschichte des Protestantismus in Ungarn* (Stuttgart, 1959). So complete was Protestantization of Transylvania, especially under the Calvinist princes, 1604–91, that there was no bishop of the see of Alba Julia from 1556 to 1716, the last bishop having been Paul II Bornemisza (1553–56); Gams, *Series Episcoporum*, 382.

130. On Biandrata, see at *Historia, 118–19, 126–31, 148–49*. Lubieniecki deals further, not in chronological consistency, with Biandrata at *209, 228* (his role in the debate of Socinus and Dávid, 1579), *229–30* (a letter from him to the Polish Brethren, 1569), and at *249* (his opposition to believers' baptism, 1570).

131. *Biblia święta, tho iest, Księgi Starego y Nowego zakonu, własniez Żydowskiego, Greckiego y Łacińskiego, nowo na polski ięzyk z pilnścia y wiernie wyłożone* (Brest Litovsk, 1563). The translators were Szymon Zacius, Petrus Statorius, Jean Thenaud, Grzegorz Orszak, Andrzej Trzecieski *filius*, and Jakub of Lublin. Węgierski, *Slavonia Reformata*, 142. See Bk. 1, n. 266.

Petrus Statorius was responsible for the strong dependence of the Old Testament on the French version of Geneva, the basis of the ensuing "disparagement from adversaries" mentioned in the next sentence. On him, see further, n. 476.

132. Mikołaj Radziwiłł, patron of inchoate Unitarianism in Vilna, would die in 1565 (n. 222), deploring some of its local excesses. With the reference on the same page to the departure of Biandrata to the court of another patron of Unitarianism in Transylvania, a few related points about Radziwiłł's life can be gathered up here.

His conversion from Lutheranism to the Reformed position under Łaski was mentioned in n. 61. His calling of the synod of Mordy in 1563 was mentioned by Lubieniecki at n. 97.

From Transylvania Mikołaj Radziwiłł received letters of encouragement from Biandrata and also from Ferenc Dávid, no doubt at the cosmopolitan physician's instigation. Of them there is a summary in the letter of the private secretary to the Prince, the lexicographer Jan Mączyński, to Hosius, 9 December 1564. This letter is printed in Hosius, *Epistolae* (1564) 5, ed. by Alojzy Szorc, *Studia Warmińskie* 13 (Olsztyn, 1976) 565–66, no. 423. Attention was drawn to this letter by Lech Szczucki, "Polish and Transylvanian Unitarianism in the Second Half of the 16th Century," in Tibor Klaniczay, *Antitrinitarianism in the Second Half of the 16th Century*, Studia Humanitatis, 5 (Budapest: Hungarian Academy of Science/Leiden: Brill, 1982) 231–41, esp. n. 4. In reporting Biandrata's letter to the Prince, Mączyński with considerable exaggeration tells Hosius, according to it, "That all the Evangelical churches throughout Hungary and Transylvania have embraced this same confession of the one true God the Father and of his only begotten Son, having repudiated the term 'Trinity' as a human invention," and "that his Highness the King [John II Sigismund] himself has gone over to the full profession of the Gospel and likewise also repudiated the papacy," Hosius, *Epistolae*, 567.

In the course of the year Prince Radziwiłł with his theological advisers wrote four extant letters in defense of an ante-Nicene Triadology: to Calvin from Brest, 6 July 1564 (*OC*, 20, no. 4125, cols 328–50); to the divines in Zurich from Brest, 14 September 1564; to the same from Wolpa, 10 October 1564 (Wotschke, *Briefwechsel*, nos. 328–29); and to Hosius from Niechniewicze, 10 December 1564 (Hosius, *Epistolae*, 5, 570–80, no. 426). In all but the third Radziwiłł appeals to Hilary, *De Synodis*, 38; *PL*, 10, col. 512: "Si quis innascibilem et sine initio dicat Filium, tanquam duo sine principio, et duo innascibilia, et duo innata dicens, duos faciat deos, anathema sit." He holds that Justin Martyr also saw things correctly and encloses a copy of the Polish translation of the *Dialogus* patronized by him that very year (Bk. 2, n. 481; Bk. 3, n. 192).

To the letter of Radziwiłł to Calvin, Beza replied, 19 March 1565, a full defense of the received dogma of the Trinity, *Correspondance*, 6 (1565) 277–85.

133. *Biblia tho iest księgi starego y nowego przymierza*, (1570–72). The first two volumes were of the Old Testament Apocrypha and of the New Testament (Nieśwież, 1570). Then followed the Old Testament (1572). The Brest Bible of 1563 was criticized at the synod of Skrzynno in 1567 (Bk. 1, n. 266). See the two secondary references for the synod, of which the protocol has not survived. Sipayłło, *AS*, 2.214.

Entrusted with the task of the revision of the Brest Bible of 1563, Szymon Budny produced the first Polish translation from the original Hebrew and Greek. His far-reaching critical commentaries followed, H. Merczyng, *Szymon Budny jako krytyk tekstów biblijnych* (Cracow, 1913). Although Faustus Socinus and his followers would reject Budny for his radical doctrines, his Bible would command respect among them.

134. *Nowy Testament: Tho iest Wszystkie pisma nowego Przymierza z Greckiego ięzyka na rzecz Polska wiernie y szczerze przełożone* (Raków: Radecki, 1577). Gryczowa, no. 4, pp. 142–43. Czechowic introduced Polish terms consonant with his Antitrinitarian and (ana)baptist interpretation. Estreicher, 13.13,16–18, 30.

135. *Historia, 153–57.*

136. Stanisław Cichowski, *Historia, 15, 132, 143*. In a letter to Bullinger from Cracow, 1 August 1565, Trecy refers to the Cichowski youths as having been "benignly educated" in Zurich but as now, alas, ensconced at Pińczów "in the church and the school of the Arians," and then to Cichowski himself as "up till now the head of the Arians." Wotschke, *Briefwechsel*, no. 343, p. 250.

137. In what follows the chronology and nomenclature are confused and the interpretation erroneous. The Diet of Parczów extended from 24 June till 12 August 1563. Lasocki indeed died in 1563. The decrees of Parczów were published 7 August 1564.

Stanisław Myszkowski, castellan of Sandomierz, the leader in the Diet of the conservative Calvinists, had promoted a decree against the emerging Antitrinitarians. A draft of such a decree was ready in May 1564, but was opposed by Cardinal Hosius and the Legate Giovanni Francesco Commendone as likely to unify the remaining Protestant groupings, and at the same time to accord them political status which would in the end harm the Catholic Church. The prelates at first urged the King to exile simply all Protestant ministers, or at least all the foreigners among them (measures which had already been proposed at the provincial synod of Warsaw in 1561). At the Diet of Parczów, June 1564, the efforts of the legate were frustrated by the opposition of the Senate. Eventually, after the Diet disbanded, two royal decrees were issued. The first, very indefinite, appealed to all subjects of the realm to submit to the Roman Church under the threat of penal measures yet to be decreed. The second ordered all foreigners "who separated themselves from the universal Christian faith" to leave the country before 1 October 1564. The text of both edicts are printed by Wincenty Zakrzewski, *Powstanie i wzrost reformacji w Polsce 1570 – 1572* (Leipzig, 1870) 271 – 74.

That the two royal edicts were issued without the full knowledge of the Diet, and that thereafter attempts were made to persecute the resident alien Czech Brethren caused such an uproar among the gentry and some magnates that in the edict of Piotrków of 2 November 1564 the King declared that the two Parczów decrees concerned the Antitrinitarian innovators only. The foregoing modifies Wilbur, *Socinianism*, 318 – 22.

138. Acts 5:29; 4:19.

139. Lubieniecki always puts the best interpretation on the person and acts of Sigismund II.

140. Lubieniecki anticipated this episode (*Historia, 152*; Bk. 2 at nn. 685 – 86). It is treated briefly by Tworek, *Zbor Lubelski*, 32 – 33 and by Aleksander Kossowski, *Protestantyzm w Lublinie i w Lubelskim w XVI – XVII wieku* (Lublin, 1933) 30 – 31.

Notice is here given to this pioneer regional study of Polish Protestantism in Lublin and the palatinate by Kossowski, a professor of Catholic University in Lublin, because of the importance of Lublin in the *Historia* and because Marek Wajsblum, *RwP* 6 (1934) 242 – 52, thoroughly reviewed Kossowski's book in a spirited and substantive *Auseinandersetzung* with the author that not incidentally sets forth Wajsblum's own vision of the appropriate historiography of Protestantism in Poland. Based on unusually rich regional archives, including those of the Tribunal of Lublin and the dioceses of Cracow and Lublin, Kossowski's work, although less often cited in the annotation than that of Tworek, is still very useful, esp. for the towns and villages of the palatinate, with a map.

141. Bk. 2, n. 686.

142. *Bohaterowie Chrystiańscy* (Bk. 1, n. 188) survives only in a much reduced summary in the 2nd ed. of Węgierski's *Slavonia Reformata*, 529 – 38.

143. Jerzy Otwinowski became abbot of the Benedictine monastery at Tyniec, near Cracow, but later joined the Brethren and died in Raków in 1608. His work is lost. See Stanisław Kot, "Erazm Otwinowski," *RwP* 6 (1934) 2, 34, 35.

144. *BAnt*, p. 84.

145. *Dysputa piekarza z malarzem o swych bogach*, written in verse, now lost. Estreicher, 23.530.

146. The Jesuit church, as of the beginning of the seventeenth century, may be seen as figure 2 in a copperprint of Franz Hogenberg in Georg Braun, *Civitates orbis terrarum*

(Cologne, 1617). Begun in 1580, as of 1805 it became the cathedral church of St. John the Baptist, Bronisław Natoński, "Katedra Lublina 1580–1625," *Nasza Przeszłość*, 27 (1967) 63–133.

The first meeting place of Protestants in Lublin was in the residence of Jan Baptistu Tęczyński, *starosta* of Lublin. See below near n. 771. Here Paklepka dwelt and kept school. After the death of Tęczyński the Jesuits acquired the property and there built what is now the cathedral, Kossowski, *Protestantyzm w Lublinie*, 29. The third home of the congregation was the residence of Stanisław Orzechowski and his wife, Zofia Zielińska, the present episcopal palace, ibid. 29, n. 3.

147. Piotr Ostrowski is not attested at the synods. That he was ambassador to the Sultan is mentioned in the summary of *Heroes* in Węgierski, 553, and also that he was at one time in Raków. L. Szczucki has references to him at a later date (*Czechowic*, 196, 198). Several members of the Suchodolski family on his mother's side are referred to in the *Historia*. For Zofia Suchodolska O. and her son, see *Historia, 254*.

148. *Historia, 253–72*.

149. 1 June 1564.

150. In the sixteenth century St. Michael's in Lublin was made a collegial church and its archdeacon was *ex officio* a canon in the cathedral in Cracow, under which Lublin stood canonically until 1805 (n. 146).

151. In the Latin text *Burgrabium*. The merchant burghers of many Polish towns in the sixteenth century, like Cracow and Lublin, were German. The drinking room below street level of the town hall in Lublin has German and Latin inscriptions on its walls.

152. *Propraefectus* Piotr Suchodolski, a Catholic, urged his fraternal nephew, Piotr Suchodolski (who was accustomed to meeting for Reformed services in the home of quite likely the Reformed sister of the *Propraefectus*, namely Zofia Suchodolska Ostrowska, at n. 147) to apprehend the blasphemer/iconoclast Otwinowski.

153. The deputy captain demanded a word of honor from Otwinowski that he would surrender to the King's order.

154. At the Diet of Piotrków, from November 1562 until March 1563, a statute was issued forbidding the captains to carry out any sentences against the nobility except those issued by the land courts. Another statute abolished the legal effects of ecclesiastical excommunication. See *Vol. Legum*, 2, no. 50, p. 621 and no. 68, p. 625. The Diet of Piotrków of 1565 voted the statute abolishing all summonses issued by the clergy against the captains who had refused to execute the sentences passed by an ecclesiastical court. See ibid, 2, no. 74, p. 692.

155. The Diet of Parczów, 24 June–12 August 1564. The poet Mikołaj Rey (1505–69), who defended the iconoclast Otwinowski (*Historia, 34, 94, 133*).

156. In the text *Municipii* is an error since Rej, a nobleman, was not a burgher of Cracow. However, at the Diet of Parczów, where the case was debated, June 1564, Rej was deputy of the palatinate of Ruthenia. See Ludwik Kolankowski, "Posłowie Sejmów Zygmunta Augusta," *RwP* 5 (1928) 129.

157. As a matter of fact, under the pressure of the papal legate, Commendone, the King submitted the case to the Senate where, however, the law *Neminem captivabimus nisi iure victum* was quoted, and the King promised to bring the culprit to the royal court. Kot, "Otwinowski," 13.

158. Rom 12:19 and Old Testament antecedents.

159. Num 16:25–33.

160. The description of the defense that Lubieniecki adduces may be unique to him. *Listy i materiały* under Otwinowski and Rej in *Nowy Korbut*, 3.74, 160–61.

161. The iconoclastic act took place in Lublin, the Commonwealth regulation was enacted at Parzów, and Lubieniecki describes the after effects from the point of view of Cracow.

162. The occasion was evidently the procession for the feast day of the Invention of the Cross, May 3. A crucifix seems to figure in the account.

163. Semion presumably implied that the defiled crucifix of the procession would be in the meantime spirited from the sanctuary.

164. The priests, evidently informed of what Semion had said at his banquet.

165. The source of this account for Lubieniecki may have been Budziński. In any case, Lubieniecki seems to be compacting one of several stories of the clever lordly disbelievers, who, not unlike himself, enjoyed tales of priests and bishops outwitted.

166. Franco de Franco from Friuli was nephew of Pietro Franco, administrator of the royal salt mines in Poland. Valerio Marchetti, "Una tarda consequenza della 'questione della fuga': il martirio del calvinista Franco de Franco in Lituania nel 1611," *Bolletino della Società di Studi Valdesi*, 89/124 (1968) 14–23; Caccamo, *Eretici*, 169–70, 271–73. On these last pages, he reproduces part of a letter and the whole of another from Francesco Simonetta, bishop of Foligno, to Scipione Borghese, Vilna, 2 and 3 July 1611. In the fragment Franco is said to have been condemned to the gibbet, his body cut up into pieces, and his tongue cut out. In reaction to Franco's blasphemy, Catholics, most of them pupils, in a procession from St.Mary's of Troki, broke up and set on fire "the synagogue of the Calvinists." This was the large edifice in which Marcin Bielecki served as pastor. Janusz Radziwiłł protested the burning of the church and the property of Bielicki. Janusz Tazbir, "Die Hinrichtung des Calvinisten Franco de Franco in Wilna 1611," *Jahrbücher für Geschichte Osteuropas*, 34 (1986).

167. The author's untimely death prevented the fulfillment of this plan. Wiszowaty shortened and edited in Latin (*BAnt*, 405–6) a substantial account in Polish of this tragedy. This is translated as "A Brief Account of the Martyrdom of John Tyszkowic," 1611, in *Polish Brethren*, Doc. IX. Stanisław Kot found in Rotterdam and edited the longer original with annotations by Andrzej Lubieniecki, Jr., as of 1656, "Relacja o Iwanie Tyszkowicu," *RwP* 9/10 (1937–39) 464–69.

NOTES TO CHAPTER THREE

168. Even modern scholarship remains divided in the contrast of Joachim Jeremias, *Die Kindertaufe in den ersten vier Jahrhunderten* (1958; English 1960) and Kurt Aland, *Die Säuglingstaufe im Neuen Testament in der Alten Kirche: eine Antwort an Jeremias* (1961; English, 1963). In the New Testament and Christian antiquity there was the tradition of baptism as personal repentance after circumcision in the wake of John the Baptist and the other tradition of the Jewish cleansing baptism for female proselytes. The example of Jesus in submitting to the baptism of John and his injunction as the resurrected or ascended Christ to his disciples to baptize in the name of the Father, Son, and Holy Spirit with variants (Matt 28:19; Luke 24:47; Mark 16:15–16 — part of a harmonizing addendum, 9–19; and Acts 1:5,8) and the example of the Apostles in Acts and elsewhere obscured the residual proselyte baptism of infants along with their family when it converted to Judaism and then when it entered into the New Israel, the Church. The practice of pedobaptism did not become general until the fifth century and the rite of baptism, East and West, long preserved language that presupposed the child's responding to words addressed to an adult believer.

169. Lubieniecki refers to the correspondence of Bishop Cyprian of Carthage (d. 258). This consists of 81 pieces, 65 from his pen. Letters 67–75, written during the pontificate of Stephen of Rome (254–57), insist on the rebaptism of heretics. Lubieniecki may have in mind, however, *Ep.* 64 or even the Pseudo-Cyprianic *De rebaptismo*, which distinguished between baptism of water and baptism of the Spirit, conferred by the bishop.

170. Lubieniecki may be referring to the Donatists, although the moralistic view of ministry among the Brethren could have been called Neo-Donatism, as was that of the Czech Brethren.

171. Gregory of Nazianzus, the Theologian (329–89), son of the bishop of Nazianzus, was with many others in the fourth century encouraged to postpone cleansing baptism until after the fires of youth had subsided.

172. The catechetical instruction of John Chrysostom (c. 347–407) in Antioch presupposed a needed preparation for children and older converts for the by now elaborate rite of baptism, often in a separate edifice, the baptistery.

173. Martin of Tours (d. 397) was only a catechumen when he served in the army. A vision of Christ at the sight of a beggar with whom he shared his cloak at Amiens impelled him to a delayed baptism.

174. Constantine convoked the Council of Nicaea in 325 but was not baptized (by Arianizing Bishop Eusebius of Nicomedia) until death approached, 337.

175. Constantius II (337–50/61), eventually sole ruler, followed his father's practice of delaying baptism, supporting various Arianizing compromises.

176. Orthodox sole ruler Theodosius I the Great (379–95) also delayed baptism.

177. Valentinian I (364–75) co-ruled with Arian Valens (364–78) in the East.

178. Ambrose, son of the pretorian prefect of Gaul, was a catechumen when, as governor of Milan, he was acclaimed bishop and only then underwent baptism, 374.

179. Nectarius was praetor in Constantinople, where he was selected by Theodosius I in 381 to succeed Gregory of Nazianzus (n. 171), and was thereupon baptized and consecrated.

180. Theologically orthodox Valentinian II (383–92) was never baptized; at the funeral following his murder, Ambrose of Milan said that his piety and desire for a baptism had cleansed him ("hunc sua pietas abluit et voluntas").

181. The three successors of Constantine I the Great were Constantine in the prefecture of the West (337–40), Constans in the prefecture of Italy and Illyria, and Constantius (n. 175).

182. Canon 5 in Ep. "Inter ceteras Ecclesiae Romanae," 5, 27 Jan 417; *PL*, 20, col. 592 AB and 56, col. 470. Cf. Ep. 182 of Augustine, *PL* 33, col. 784 (*CSEL*, 44.720–21).

183. Lubieniecki seems to bear some animus toward Africa. See at n.170. Cf. his reference to "Egyptian godlets."

184. Innocent I (401–17), Ep. 2, "Etsi tibi," 15 February 404, wherein he defends the validity of baptism by heretics (Novatianists), "since they are baptized in the name of Christ." Denzinger, 594.

185. Augustine in his anti-Donatist writings theologically undercut the Donatists in their practice of rebaptising Catholics admitted to their schism. In defending the acceptance of converted Donatists without baptism, he appealed to the perfection of the Dominical sacrament itself rather than to the personal probity of the priestly celebrant, a principle later formulated as sacramental validity *ex opere operato*. Cf. Ep. 182, *PL*, 33, cols. 784–85. For the scholastic and early Reformed controversies on baptism, see bk. 3, n. 239.

186. The practice of infant baptism with confirmation followed immediately by communion became widespread in Byzantine territory and was administered by a priest, usually married. In Latin territory the practice of infant communion was restrained by the emergence of confirmation as a distinct sacrament after baptism to be administered only by bishops.

187. *Sessio* 21, 16 July 1562, chap. 4: "Denique eadem sancta synodus docet parvulos usu rationis carentes, nulla obligari necessitate ad sacramentalem Eucharistiae communionem, si quidem baptismi lavacrum regenerati (Tit 3:5) et Christo incorporati adeptam jure filiorum Dei gratiam in illa aetate amittere non possunt. Neque ideo tamen damnanda est antiquitas, si, eum morem in quibusdam locis aliquando servavit." C. J. Hefele/Henri Leclerq, *Histoire des conciles*, 10/1 (Paris, 1938), "Les décrees du concile de Trente," 419; Hubert Jedin, consultant, *Conciliorum Oecumenicorum Decreta* (Basel, etc. 2nd ed., 1962) 703.

Lubieniecki may here also allude to the Eastern Orthodox and, for his own time, the Uniate Byzantine (since 1595) usage of administering communion to infants after baptism, combined with confirmation, although he almost never looks in the Orthodox direction.

188. Lubieniecki pulls together an account of the antipedobaptist impulse in the Reformed churches in both Poland and the Grand Duchy of Lithuania that led to the practice of believers' baptism by immersion and with some outstanding instances of anabaptism, which may indeed have been much more frequent than recorded. As for the areas covered in the ensuing account, Lithuania always refers to a vast jurisdiction with its own diet, court, army, and with its official language, not Lithuanian but chancery Byelorussian. But the language *of the Reformation* in the several subdivisions of Lithuania (except for the fully ethnic principality of Samogitia), namely in the palatinates of Troki, Vilna, Novogorodok, Brest Litovsk, Polock, Minsk, and, before 1569, Podlachia, Volhynia, and Kiev), that is, the language of synods and most books, was either Polish or Latin, even among Byelorussian and Ruthenian burghers, boyars, and magnates until after the story recounted by Lubieniecki. Educated ethnic Lithuanians used both Latin and the lingua franca, Polish, in epistles and discourse. Moreover, there was among the Reformed, perhaps more than among Catholics, some sense of a Church of the whole Commonwealth of the Two Peoples, even though jurisdictionally the Grand Duchy would remain quite distinct even after its truncation by the Union of Lublin.

In what follows Lubieniecki himself suggests that believers' baptism first cropped out in Kujawy (at n. 194); cf. the text at n. 287 (where the Kujawy of Niemojewski and the Lublin of the Author's own family are dramatically linked), although he has already dealt with tritheist, baptist Gonesius, the Pole, who, to be sure, first came prominently to attention in the *Historia* at precisely Brest Litovsk, Bk. 2, chap. 8 and is noted again here at nn. 192, 195. It is possible that, himself a convinced baptist, with a sense of the providential role of Polonia as an instrument of God in the completion of the Reformation, Lubieniecki did not care to emphasize precisely the role of Lithuanian lands in "the restoration of believers' baptism," as he could have put it.

189. Lubieniecki refers to Bk. 2, chap. 8.

Writing as an immersionist (baptist) Unitarian Pole (n. 188), Lubieniecki does not follow Faustus Socinus, who opposed the immersionist practice of the Polish Brethren (at n. 283). His collected *opera* in two volumes, among them writings against baptism (cf. n. 238), head the *Bibliotheca Fratrum Polonorum* and this way could suggest that all Socinians, insofar as this term is ever used by non-Poles to embrace the Polish Brethren in their native lands before and after Socinus's arrival among them, could have been indifferent to baptism.

Lubieniecki was not indifferent to baptism. He gives quite a bit of attention to it, to the pedobaptist view of Biandrata, to whom he remained partial, and to that of others in Transylvania and even Lithuania, like Budny and Palaeologus, alluded to only (*Historia, 189–90*), but he obscures the role of Socinus, when he reintroduces him at the top of *193*.

190. See Bk. 2, at n. 443. Szczucki mentions all named here and in *Historia 118, 176, 191* as among the first Poles to be rebaptized; he adds Jan Siekierzyński, Jr. (*Historia, 163* and at n. 292), as the very first; Szczucki, *Czechowic*, 56.

191. See *Historia, 191*; he is attested at the synods; Wilbur, *Socinianism*, 332, n. 21 with references.

192. Wawrzyniec Krzyszkowski (Krzyzkowski), M. D. (d. c. 1563), minister in Nieśwież, shared the ministry with Budny, who had been transferred from Vilna, Bk. 2, n. 441. He published a translation of Justin Martyr, *Justyna Rozmowa z Tryfonem Żydem* (Nieśwież, 1564, Bk. 2, n. 491). See Bk. 2, n. 442.

193. Hieronim Piekarska is mentioned on *Historia, 118, 144*. See Bk. 2, nn. 444, 625.

194. A. Lubieniecki makes this observation (*Poloneutychia*, p. 51, line 28). There could have been a Mennonite influence on the Cujavians. Dutch Anabaptists had been settling in the two Prussias and Danzig since 1530. *Radical Reformation*, chap. 15.2.

The lands of an earlier principality, Kujawy, comprised in the sixteenth century two palatinates, associated with Great Poland, namely, the palatinate of Inowrocław with the Land of Dobrzyn, together athwart the Vistula near Toruń, and further up on the left bank of the Vistula, the palatinate of Brześć (Kujawski) and Kujawy (in the narrower sense). Lubieniecki is speaking of the Cujavian palatinate of Inowrocław as bordering on (both Royal and Ducal) Prussia.

195. The antipedobaptist lord, Jan Niemojewski, made the acquaintance of Marcin Czechowic in 1561, after the latter had returned from his mission in Geneva to defend (in vain) Radziwiłł's protegé, Biandrata, before Calvin and resumed his post in the Protestant school in Vilna (c. 1559–65). On the death of Radziwiłł, Czechowic settled in Niemojówka, the estate of Niemojewski, on whom see further at n. 288.

196. For the sources, problems, and achievements of the Reformation in the Grand Duchy, see Marceli Kosman, who reviews the literature, 1919–69, ''Badanie nad reformacją w Wielkim Księstwie Litewskim,'' *OiRwP* 16 (1971) 162ff. His *Reformacja i Kontrreformacja w Wielkim Księstwim* (Wrocław, etc., PAN in 1973) stresses developments after 1570, the year in which the Jesuits began winning over the magnates with their college in Vilna, and the year in which in the Lithuanian response to the Agreement of Sandomierz, the conservative Reformed organized themselves into a province with five districts, each one headed by a superintendent, with whom a synod of ten Lutheran congregations was affiliated. See also bibliography and sources in n. 61. The remnants of the Reformed, the antitrinitarian baptists became about this time, in effect, the ''Minor Reformed Church'' in the Grand Duchy. For the emergence and decline of antipedobaptism in Vilna, see Stanisław Kot, ''Ausbruch und Niedergang des Täufertums in Wilna (1563–1566),'' *ARG* 49 (1958) 12–26, and now Lech Szczucki and Darek Jarmola, cited in Book 1, n. 161. Among many new observations one may be noted here, namely, in the correspondence and other papers of Legate Commendone, that he wrote in 1564, again in 1565, that ''many *Trynitarjusze* [Trinitarians in the Catholic sense of anti-

Nicene] openly teach circumcision, and many had been circumcized, including the ruler of Vilna" and that there were indeed "sects of newly circumcized (*nowych obrzezańców*), that is Anabaptists, who do not want to baptize children before they turn thirty, just as Christ did" (*Commendone*, 1, 23, 267).

197. Szymon Zak (nn. 61, ¶¶3, 327, 364) burgher by origin, began preaching the Reformation in Lithuania, c. 1549. He seems never to have settled down permanently, serving in and around Brześć, superintendent of Podlachia (and presumably of the neighboring palatinate of Brześć). Kosman, *Reformacja*, 43 – 44; *Historia, 29, 43, 177*.

198. *Wyznanie wiary zboru wileńskiego z Księdzem Simonem z Proszowic Superintendentem y ze wszemi Ministry wespołek przyięte y pochwalone* (Brest Litovsk, 1559). The first chapter is devoted to the question of baptism.

199. Czechowic was established in Vilna in 1569 as headmaster of the new school and Budny was reassigned as minister in Kleck. In July, 1561 Czechowic was sent by his patron to Switzerland in order to reconcile Calvin with Biandrata, whom Mikołaj so highly esteemed. Szczucki, *Czechowic* 231 – 32. On his return Czechowic carried Antitrinitarian and antipedobaptist views, the first in Vilna publicly to declare himself against pedobaptism and in favor of his own rebaptism (1564). The famous colloquy on baptism took place in the palace of Mikołaj the Black in Nieświez in January 1565.

Czechowic, having debated with Wędrogowski, printed an account of three days of colloquy and dedicated it to the memory of Prince Mikołaj Radziwiłł (d. 28 May 1565). Till recently known only by its Polish and Latin titles, a unique copy has come to light in Sweden: *Trzech dni rozmowa o niektorych artykułach tych czasów wzroszonych [?] a zwłaszcza o Nurzaniu niemowiatek y innych nierozumnych dziatek: w której się wiele potrzebnych rzeczy (nie jedno ktemu Sakramentowi, ale i ku innym sprawom należących) z pisma św a nadto z dawnych Teologow i z rozmaitych Autorów przywodzi i rozbiera*. This was composed in Lublin in 1564 and printed with the permission of Prince Jan Kiszka by Jan Karcan of Wieliczka at Łosk in 1578. (Karcan was printer there, 1576 – 80, in Vilna, 1580 – 1611. Kawecka-Gryczowa, *Drukarze: Wielki Księstwo Litweski*, 107 – 16.) To this Budny added, by leave of Mikołaj Wędrogowski, his *Wotum* [May 1564] his rationale for his synodal vote in favor of pedobaptism *o Chrzcie dziatek malych*, with the Warning and Admonition (*Przestroga i Napominanie*) concerning this by Marcin Czechowic dated in Lublin, 29 May 1564. (A photocopy of the title page was kindly sent to me by Lech Szczucki, while I was reading page proof of the nn. for the *Historia*. He quotes passages from *Trzech dui rosmowa*, yet to be critically edited by him in "The Beginnings of Antitrinitarian Anabaptism in Lithuania and Poland in the Light of a So-far Unknown Source," *Sixteenth Century Anabaptism and Radical Reformation*, ed. by Jean-Georges Rott and Simon L. Verheus, Bibliotheca Dissidentium, Scripta et Studia 3 (Baden-Baden adn Bouxville: Koerner, 1987). Sand had given the full title in Latin as *Trium dierum colloquium* [*in quo* Christianus, Evangelicus, *et* Pontificius introducuntur loquentes*] de quibusdam articulis fidei, praecipue vero de paedobaptismo*, *BAnt*, pp. 50 – 51. In the printed Colloquy Czechowic drew a sharp distinction between the "evil neobaptists" of Münster and the Evangelical "good neobaptists of the severely simple, separationist life style," *Trzech dni*, p. 351.

Sand conjectured that an anonymous work against pedobaptism in Polish, *O dzieciochrzenstwie krotkie wypisanie, De Paedobaptismo brevis relatio, de origine contentionis et politura adhibita primo sacramento i.e. baptismo in Magno Ducato Lithuaniae et postea quoque in Polonia, 1565* (Nieświez, 1564?; *BAnt*, 174), was to be ascribed to Czechowic, although Czechowic himself never referred to it. However, with the discovery of the *Trzech dni*, it is clear that *O dzieciochrzenstwie* is from Budny, Bk. 2, n. 441, ¶2.

200. Mikołaj Wędrogowski was a key figure. He was a general superintendent and the minister of the Reformed congregation of Vilna, which met in the Gasztołd Palace under the protection of Prince Mikołaj Radziwiłł the Black. The palace housed also the minister's family and the school. Wędrogowski early came to the antipedobaptist position under the influence of Grzegorz Paweł and esp. Czechowic (cf. n. 91), but then he drew back evidently under pressure from the conservative theologians and his patron (n. 22). His absence from the synod of Węgrów that endorsed believers' baptism occasioned at least four letters from them to him, all but one (Żytno) deploring his defection from their ranks and still hoping for his reconversion to the radical positions on the Trinity and baptism. For the letters to him, see nn. 210 and 228. He frequented some of the Polish synods after 1560. Lubieniecki presently notes Wędrogowski's acknowledgment of hypocritical conformity under pressure, *Historia, 189*.

201. Paweł of Wizna (in Masovia, on the Narew) minister for Dávid Jeśman, attested at Polish synods after 1560, was superintendent in Vilna, not of all palatinates in Lithuania, as the slack reference suggests.

202. That is, Żak, Wędrogowski, and Paweł opposed Czechowic. As for the title *Superintendens Ecclesiarum Lituanicarum*, in Lubieniecki it seems to be fluid. What palatinates and districts are embraced in the oversight is not always clear, except surely Vilna itself.

Our Author passes over important episodes on the Lithuanian scene between 1559 and 1565 in the next paragraph. Legate Commendone reported from Warsaw, 7 February 1563, that a Reformed synod in Vilna (thus late 1562 or early 1563) had recommended that children not be baptized until age seven, but then in effect resumed to allow the slight majority of the synodists to continue with pedobaptism, *Commendone* 1, p. 55, while Jakub Sylvius in *Pociecha pobożym ludziom* (Cracow, 1564) reported that the radicals, among whom were fourteen ministers (including Gonesius, and of Vilna itself three: Czechowic, Wędrogowski, Wojciech Kościenski), "opened the doors for the anabaptists (*nowokrzczenców*)," quoted by Alodja Budny (*O dzieciokrzczeństwie*, 105) reports another synod, that of Vilna, 26–27 January 1564, attended by twenty-six ministers, of whom half opposed pedobaptism. The Prayer Book of 1563 of Nieśwież (destined to become a cultural center for Lithuanian Brethren), edited by Budny, Czechowic, Krzyszkowski, T. Falconius, and Wędrogkowski, contained strong antipedobaptist sentiments among its hymns and catechisms, e.g., the hymn on Holy Baptism (*O krzcie świętym*), Alodja Kawecka, "Kancjonały protestanckie w. XVI," *RwP* 16 (1926) 128–39.

203. There is a Brzeziny in palatinate Kujawy, another in palatinate Łęczyca. For the location of the second, see the map in Sipayłło, *AS*, 3, pocket; for the record of the synod, *AS*, 2.193; for the location of Brzeziny in Kujawy, where it is shown that the meeting place could not have been the royal town of Brześć Kujawski (as I conjectured in "Anabaptism in Poland and Lithuania," 235), nor Brześć-Litewski on the Bug, as Wotschke conjectured, Trecy to Bullinger, Cracow, 1 August 1565, *Briefwechsel*, no. 343, p. 251, n. 1. The owner of Brzeziny in Kujawy was Wawrzyniec Brzeziński, boon companion of Jan Niemojewski, whom he accompanied to Lublin in 1570 (n. 289). However, on the basis of testimony closer to the event than Lubieniecki (who would have had family reasons to connect baptismal innovation/restoration with the migration of Cujavian Niemojewski with Czechowic to Lublin), Jarmola, *op. cit.*, chap. 5, decides for Brzeziny in

Great Poland on the river Mrożyca near Łowicz, citing Budny (as treated by Szczucki, *O dziecokrzczeństwie*, 107) and Legate Commendone (*Commendone* 2, 217)

Although the protocol of the synod of Brzeziny does not supply the names of the participants, said in the record to have been 32 ministers and 18 noblemen (*szlachta*), Sipayłło (*AS*, 2.193, n. 2) is able to assemble several names drawn from the retrospective account of the synod from Lutomirski, preserved by the *Historia*, Bk. 3, nn. 218–20, and from the report of the synod of Węgrów, *AS*, 2.197: Lutomirski as in charge, then, alphabetically: Bieliński, Czechowic/Codecius, Grzegorz Paweł, Krowicki, Paklepka, Paweł of Wizna, Wędrogowski (his last time among the radicals), and Żytno.

In the wide-ranging letter of Trecy, there is an evident reference to the synod of Brzeziny suggesting that among the participants were Anabaptist observers from Moravia and elsewhere: "Verum quoniam in proxima synodo Arianica, in quam confluxerunt complures anabaptistae ex Lituania, Moravia, aliisque partibus, conclusum est apud eos idque firmiter, ne pueri eorum baptizarentur et quaedam alia fortasse et de rebaptizatione," Wotschke, *Briefwechsel*, no. 343, p. 251, where the editor incorrectly identified the synod as at Brest Litovsk. Wotschke prints in n. 2 portions of a letter of Mikolaj Żytno (while still a pedobaptist) to Mikołaj Wędrogowski of Vilna, wherein he describes the extent of the Anabaptist fervor at Brzeziny, now more fully accessible (n. 218). Żytno does not mention what Trecy says about the presence of Moravian Anabaptists at the synod. This letter from Cracow of August 1565 should not be confused with another of his of 1566 and one by Łasicki, also referring to immersionism (n. 314, ¶¶1–3). I may have made too much of Trecy as witness to a Moravian influence in Brzeziny in "Anabaptism in Poland," 237.

Wacław Urban is most helpful in bringing into one place all the known and conjectured contacts between Moravian Anabaptists, not only Hutterites, and the Reformed in the Commonwealth, "'Calendarium' kontaktów anabaptystów morawskich z Rzecząpospolita," *Małopolskie studia historyczne*, 9 (1966) 57–70, for Brzeziny, 59.

204. Andrzej Cizner is not otherwise identified.

205. The reference to sisters, also at n. 208, is an indication of the importance of women in the Reformed churches. In her topical index of the *Akta*, in *AS*, 2 for vol. 1 and 2, and in 3, Sipayłło offers many entries under *Kobiety w zborze*.

206. Jan Katerla was a barber and lay elder (*senior*), S. Kot, p. 219, identical with Joannes Katerla in attendance at the synod of Pińczów as of 7 May 1560. Sipayłło, *AS*, 2.18. Others present from churches of Lithuania and Podlasie in the same delegation were Żak, Wędrogowski, Piekarski, Andrzej Trzecieski, Bazyl Drzewnicki, and Jakub Kurnicki. Ján Katerla is mentioned in Bk. 2, n. 441.

207. Jakub Kurnicki was a merchant and lay elder of the Vilna congregation. Kot, "Ausbruch," 219.

208. Cf. n. 205.

209. Phil 4:5.

210. The thrust of Lutomirski's letter, expressive of the whole synod of Brzeziny, was in the name of mutual toleration to gain the time to make the antipedobaptist standard prevail throughout the Lithuanian and Podlachian churches. At this stage they were primarily concerned for the postponement of baptism until the age of seven or eight and wanted to avoid conspicuous controversy. Cf. Szczucki, *Czechowic*, 58. From Alba Julia came a long letter to Grzegorz Paweł, 21 September 1565 (n. 23), warning him not to get bogged down in so secondary an innovation as believers' baptism, which could bring upon the progressive movement in the Lithuanian churches the invidious label of "Anabaptist," and urging him to concentrate on ridding them of Nicene dogma.

It is likely that in the interval here in the *Historia* between the synods of Brzeziny and Węgrów is to be placed the polemics against the anabaptist menace addressed in three documents mentioned in n. 236, one of which alone is dated 14 December, 1565.

211. Sipayłło, *AS*, 2.197–200.

212. The text implies incorrectly that Lady Kiszka (Polish: Kiszczyna) and Hanna Radziwiłłówna were two different women. Hanna Radziwiłłówna (d. 1600), next oldest daughter of Mikołaj the Black and brother of Mikołaj Krzysztof "the Orphan," married ca. 1552 Stanisław Kiszka (d. 1554), palatine of Vitebsk. Hanna R. Kiszka converted to Calvinism. She became a supporter of the radical Reformed in 1563. In that year, on the advice of her brother, Prince Mikołai, the widowed Hanna sent her son Jan to study in Basel where he matriculated and was under two preceptors, one of them Georg Weigel, an exiled Philippist among Lutherans, a spirited opponent of Anabaptism in Vilna. Jan Kiszka became a defender of the radicals. On the disentangling of the names of his mother, garbled in *BAnt*, 54 (under Falconius) and also here in the *Historia*, see Szczucki, *Czechowic*, 239, n. 143. On Anna and her son, Janusz Tazbir, "J.K.," *PSB* 12 (1966–67) 507–8.

213. *Piedmons* in Latin, in Polish *Podgórze*, the southern part of the palatinate of Cracow. For it as a synodal district, see Bk. 2, n. 447.

214. To understand this second communication of Lutomirski, preserved by Lubieniecki, one has to have in mind the positions of what seemed to have been three parties, never clearly distinguished and characterized. Presumably a minority of six to eight ministers held to pedobaptism as a matter of faith and venerable usage among Catholics and Protestants alike. They were led by Mikołaj Żytno. Then a majority of the synod were apparently open to the idea of postponing baptism until the completion of religious instruction of the young, as catechumens, without thereby intending to invalidate the baptism already received in infancy by all the members of the synod. Lutomirski presumably counted himself among this group (cf. *Historia, 182*) until his own immersion in 1573 (n. 330). Then, thirdly, a small but almost as vigorous a minority as that of the pedobaptists were inclined to invalidate pedobaptism retroactively (*Historia, 282–83*) and to call for believers' baptism, in effect, rebaptism for the current generation, but they shunned the term. When the spectre of Münster was brought up, the Polish Reformed "Anabaptists" dissociated themselves vigorously from the Münsterites by professing their loyalty to magistracy as ordained by God. The third group was headed by Grzegorz Paweł.

215. The text mistakenly reads 10 December. For the sense of the "true baptism," see n. 221.

216. See Bk. 2, n. 442 (Gonesius), and Bk. 3, nn. 624, etc. Darek Jarmola, *op. cit.*, conjectures that the obscure reference is to the synod of Balice. Bk. 2 at n. 603.

217. Christmas, 25 December 1565. Among the Reformed the festivals of the liturgical year had retreated in favor of an increasing emphasis on Sunday, but in this and other communications of the Brethren the calendar is still thought of in the old way for purposes of reckoning. In the present letter the significance of each liturgical feast is in fact brought out: the Holy Spirit a gift of Christ, Jesus Christ born of Mary (not of an eternal engendered substance).

218. Mikołaj Żytno, minister in Pustotew, a village in the Land of Chełm, over which he served as superintendent, is first recorded at the synods, 14 January 1560. Sipayłło, *AS*, 2.7. For his position on the Nicene Creed as of 1562, see Bk. 2, n. 681. At Węgrów Żytno remained an opponent of the majority, a pedobaptist. In a letter, 29 December 1565, to Wędrogowski, who had once been reluctantly drawn to the radical position and

reverted, he expressed appreciation for his shift, regret that he had not been present, and urged him to hold fast to his regained orthodoxy and orthopraxis. The letter is printed by Domański and Szczucki, "Miscellanea Arianica," 232–33. See further Budny's acoount apud Szczucki, "Budnego relocji." For a summary and the context, see S. Kot, "Ausbruch," 221. Later Żytno himself reversed himself and became a supporter of rebaptism and a major thinker of the Minor Church in the circle of Czechowic in Lublin.

219. Daniel Biliński (Bieliński, etc.; d. 1590), of Silesia, a former priest, served as a Reformed deacon in Brzeziny, then in Cracow as minister of the German congregation, then in Olkusz. He was eventually excluded from the Minor Church. See also *Historia, 218*. He is dealt with among others by Wacław Urban, *et al, Bibliotheca Dissidentium*, 8 (Baden-Baden, 1986).

220. Of the remaining participants, Bartłomej Codecius attested only at the synods of Brzeziny and Węgrów. Sipayłło, *AS*, 2.193, 197. Of Krowicki, Paklepka, and Żytno, it is recalled that as late as 1563, they joined in a letter to Zurich, asseverating their subscription to all the ancient symbols, Bk. 2. 681. The absence of Czechowic would explain the prominence of Grzegorz Paweł.

221. The strategy is clear: At the call of the named superintendents with authority to convene in most parts of the Commonwealth several local synods see to it that the problem be ventilated but muted, namely: the restoration of scriptural *Baptismum/ponurzenie* (both words used in the Polish synodal account of Węgrów) without any theological synodal, or social disorder; the discreet baptism of the most conscientious already baptized in infancy; as well as the postponement of baptism/immersion for the offspring of members until they had finished the catechism, the principle of toleration in the coexistence of and the defense of two routes to the agreed upon ideal of believers' baptism.

222. Mikołaj Radziwiłł the Black died 28 May 1565. That he had once written expressly about the synods in Poland being attended by Lithuanians but not the other way around is also mentioned in the account of the synod at Węgrów. Sipayłło, *AS*, 2.198.

He left a testament that suggested his growing impatience with the anti-pedobaptist and possibly egalitarian social thrust among the antitrinitarians he had been protecting, the more unsettling for its imperilment of the federation of the Reformed forces. That the patient protector of the congregation in his Gasztołd Palace in Vilna had become alarmed by the socially radical thrust is evidenced by a few words from a letter embedded in the funeral oration for one of his sons, Mikołaj Krzysztof Radziwiłł the Orphan (1549–1616). In the *Kazanie na pogrzebie* (Cracow, 1616), 22, Marcin Widziewicz, S.J., in speaking of the deceased's having renounced Calvinism, indirectly adduces words from the father: "Thereto [the renunciation contributed] a letter written by his father (of glorious memory) before his death, in which he complained of his pastors for having gone so far in deceiving him in his faith that he no longer knew what to believe." S. Kot quotes from the Polish imprint in "Ausbruch," 217, n. 8.

223. As for the location of a general synod, Węgrów was at least in a Lithuanian palatinate; but, at the southeast border of Masovia: Węgrów in Podlasie was a proprietary town of the Kiszka family. The local minister was Marcin Krowicki.

224. The palatinate of Ruthenia, Red Russia (Rus Czerwona) with its chief city Lwów, was wholly within Byzantine-rite territory. Lwów was a major royal Polish fortification; Polish lords owned many manors throughout the palatinate, and even the lords of the Byzantine-rite tradition spoke and many wrote Polish and Latin.

The Latin, Ruthenian, and other service books are referred to also in the account of Węgrów. Sipayłło, *AS*, 2.198. All older church orders of baptism preserved archaic formularies attesting to their primordial use in relation to believers assenting in faith.

225. Armenians fled from the eastern part of their ancestral lands when invaded by the Tatars in 1243 and settled among earlier colonists in the Crimea, concentrated in Kaffa (Teodosiia), a Genosese city-state. With the fall of the Armenian state in Cilicia in 1375 and a century alter the fall of the Crimea to the Turks, the inrush of Armenians on the territory of the Polish-Lithuanian Commonwealth was considerable. The seat of the Armenian bishop was Lwów/Lviv as of 1365 with a cathedral built by an architect from Kaffa. The bishop stood under the Catholicos in Echmiadzin until 1667, when Bishop Michael Torosowicz (c. 1604–81) led his people into union with Rome. The first beatified Polish Jesuit, the young Stanisław Kostka (1550–68), was of Armenian ancestry. Lubieniecki mentions an Armenian merchant unfavorably in Bk. 2 at n. 719, probably from Kamieniec Podolski, one of the some 70 Armenian colonies in the palatinates of the Ukraine, self-governed by the Armenian Statute, approved by Sigismund I in 1519. On Armenians in Poland and the Ukraine, see B. Struminsky, "Armenians," *Encyclopedia of Ukraine*, ed. by Volodymyr Kubijovyč, in progress, 1 (Toronto: University Press, 1984), 113f. with bibliography; "Ormanie w Polsce," *EK*, N-P, 241–44.

226. The Czech Brethren (in Great Poland especially), with whom the Polish Reformed had once developed close association and would again in 1570, had in the fifteenth century acquired such service books on their visits to Constantinople.

227. Under Luther's influence, the order of baptism was enhanced in the vernacularization of the service, the elimination of several medieval features, and the relocation of its observance in the parish church.

228. The account of Węgrów also mentions a communication from the conservative Reformed in Vilna, who defended pedobaptism in appeal to tradition and to the arguments of the Reformers (*neoteryków*). Sipayłło, *AS*, 2.198. Żytno in his letter to Wędrogowski, December 1565 (nn. 218, 238), speaks of the addressee as the author of this communication (*scriptum et litterae*). His authorship had been all the more painful to the radical majority in Węgrów for the reason that he had once gone along with them reluctantly (above, n. 200). In his own collecting of modern views, Lutomirski himself in his letter of the same time to Wędrogowski mentioned, besides Cyprian and Augustine of antiquity, Calvin, Bullinger, Musculus, and Melanchthon and then revealed how "the unconquerable truth of our unique Master" turned all this collected chaff into the glowing spark of conviction as to believers' baptism. Domański and Szczucki, "Miscellanea Arianica," 236.

229. This whole paragraph is so worded as to situate the practice of restored believers' baptism (with eventually some rebaptism) in the mutually tolerant community of baptists and pedobaptists. Anabaptism among the Polish-speaking Reformed in Lithuania, Great Poland (Kujawy), and Little Poland made its appearance without an abrupt break. In contrast, the Swiss Anabaptists broke cleanly on this issue, c. 1525, from the Reformed cantons of Zurich, etc. The gradualism and tolerance in "Polish Anabaptism" (at first antipedobaptism) was attended by not only some of the social radicalism of Germanic and Italian Anabaptism but also, as with the Italian Anabaptism, a pre-Nicene Triadology well on its way toward a Christocentric Unitarianism. For the last, see my "Two Social Strands," esp. on the Anabaptist synod in Venice, 1150, 180ff. In "Anabaptism in Poland and Lithuania," I made perhaps too much of the influence of Germanic Anabaptist influence on antipedobaptism/believers' baptism in the Commonwealth by way of the Hutterites and other Anabaptists in Silesia, Moravia, and Slovakia and by way of the Mennonites, just as most scholars have perhaps overstressed the foreign influence (Servetus, L. Socinus, Biandrata, Gentile) in the declension of the dogma of the Trinity among the Polish Reformed.

In the letter of Lutomirski and in related documentation it is clear that "Lithuanian-Polish" "Antitrinitarian Anabaptism" was as much the consequence of carrying out the principle of *sola scriptura* in the Commonwealth context as of assimilating views worked out elsewhere or by influential foreigners sojourning in Poland-Lithuania. The decisive synod of Węgrów is, except for an obscure phase in the history of Transylvanian Unitarianism, the most notable instance of a Church's adopting believers' baptism as most clearly scriptural while tolerating received usage.

It was at the synod of Torda, March 1578, that the Transylvanian counterparts of the Polish Brethren (provisionally) rejected pedobaptism. Cf. Dávid, n. 280, ¶3. Wilbur, *Transylvania*, 69. For the resumption of pedobaptism in 1638 see n. 280, ¶4.

230. The polygamous Anabaptist theocracy of Münster was ended under a joint Catholic and Lutheran siege of the city in 1535.

231. In this affirmation of loyalty to the higher power ordained of God, certain antipedobaptist synodists of Węgrów were asserting what all Germanic Anabaptists agreed to as scriptural, but at Węgrów the terms were no longer the Vulgate *princeps* and *potestas* but the Genevan *magistratus*, even though the Reformed of both groupings were in fact protected by *principes* and *domini* as their lay patrons and who were in some cases lay *seniores*. In the Polish account the term is sovereignity (*zwierzchność*) with reference to the Crown, definitely not in reference to the patrons. Sipayłło, *AS*, 2.199. In the appeal to conscience (Rom 13:5) lay, however, the seed that would presently sprout as scriptural pacifism and in the varied quests for the literal *communio sanctorum* as the socially radical *communio bonorum* (e.g., Raków, n. 590).

232. In this section both in the Latin text and its Polish parallel in Sipayłło (*AS*, 2.49), the emphasis is surely on mutual warning on obedience to the higher power and order even while the synodists were taking the new step towards personal *vera regeneratio/prawdziwe odrodzenie* and *pietas/żywót pobożny* associated with rebaptism or, more often at this early stage, the consent to postpone the baptism of one's children until they could themselves affirm faith. The wording is in keeping with the sense of a significant advance in the restoration of apostolic Christianity.

233. The Roman Church. The feeling is strong in the superintendent that the synodists who resist the recovery of believers' baptism have failed to complete their break from the old order.

234. Lutomirski summarizes well the succession of issues and rightly places the problem of Christ the Mediator as leading into the devolution of the dogma of the Trinity.

235. The Polish parallel of this paragraph from Kolozsvár in Sipayłło is no clearer than the Latin, but it has, for Lubieniecki's martial *castra nostra*, simply "nie są z nami." Sipayłło, *AS*, 2.199. Lutomirski probably refers to the defection of Wędrogowski, pastor in Vilna, and those under him and around him in the conservative restoration. See below, n. 239.

236. At this point the Kolozsvár record of the synod mentions the receipt of a letter, briefly summarized, from the Transylvanian churches. Sipayłło, *AS*, 2.200. In her n. 1, Sipayłło draws attention to the similarity between the synodal summary of the Transylvanian communication on baptism and what Lubieniecki gives in more detailed summary as also from the Transylvanians, *Historia, 189–90*, esp. n. 275.

The authorship of this possibly identical communication, one version preserved in the protocol, the other by Lubieniecki, is under discussion. It is clear that Biandrata wrote from Alba Julia to Grzegorz Paweł, 21 September 1565; printed by Wotschke, *Briefwechsel*, no. 348, pp. 263–68 (here dated 30 November, corrected by Wajsblum, "Dyteiści," *RwP* 5 (1928) 42, n. 9) and by Sipayłło, *AS*, 2.352–59, Appendix 7.

Szczucki was not sure whether the summary in the Węgrów protocol and that, undated, preserved by Lubieniecki were residues of a single letter, when he wrote *Czechowic*, 241, n. 162. But subsequently when he returned to the problem in a different context, Szczucki distinguishes helpfully but not entirely clearly "three" letters from Transylvania to the Poles after Biandrata's departure from the Commonwealth, "Polish and Transylvanian Unitarianism," *Antitrinitarianism*, 233, not counting letters of Biandrata and Dávid to Radziwiłł of 1564 (n. 132, ¶3): (1A) the letter of Biandrata of 1565 to Grzegorz Paweł; (1B) the letter of "the Transylvanian churches" to the synod of Węgrów of 1565, here under discussion; (1C) a letter of "the Transylvanian churches to the Polish churches," expressly on baptism, *Historia, 189−90* (also n. 275, ¶2); (2) the letter of Biandrata of 1568 (actually 1569) to the Polish churches, *Historia, 229−30*; and (3) the letter of Biandrata from Kolozsvár to the Poles of 31 October 1569, ed. by Theodor Wotschke, "[Quellen] zur Geschichte des Antitrinitarismus," *ARG* 23 (1926) 82−100, esp. no. 4, pp. 94−97, which deals with the six-day debate at Várad of October 1569 under the king as judge, Gáspár Békés as moderator, with Péter Méliusz (n. 609) and Dávid the antagonists debating four triadological and christological issues. Wilbur, *Transylvania*, 39−46.

The letter of Biandrata to Grzegorz Paweł as is now understood by Firpo, (*Antitrinitari*, 20,) and with further documentation and argumentation by Rotondò (ed. *Opere*, 354−59) to be primarily significant for relaying or reinforcing the radical Johannine Christology of Laelius Socinus (n. 1, ¶3) that presumably circulated in MS version before its first anonymous appearance in print (Alba Julia, 1568). On the issue of baptism alone only items 1A−C need to be focused on; and only 1B and 1C are of controverted authorship. Without delaying with item 1C, Szczucki now holds that Biandrata also wrote 1B; and he is surely right that Biandrata "did not grasp the sense of immersionist practices," *Antitrinitarianism*, 237. But Szczucki notwithstanding, it seems highly improbable that Biandrata could have been the author or inspirer of both the letter to Węgrów or its seemingly displaced parallel in the *Historia, 189−90* (nn. 275−80), for Biandrata conformist or conventional in what he took to be relatively unimportant would surely not have endorsed the virtual suspension of baptism as meaningless after the apostolic age, when in the same year as the synod of Węgrów he urged Grzegorz Paweł to retain pedobaptism and keep to the central issue of the Trinity, well aware that indifference to baptism and ancient customs related to the consecreation of infants could be upsetting in every village of Transylvania and of Poland and imperil the toleration of the new churches. The authorship of items 1B and 1C is suggested in n. 275.

237. Lutomirski, with the synod, places in an eschatological framework the solemn step they have taken together.

238. At least four other letters were written from Węgrów about this time, all of them to Wędrogowski. They are accessible in the edition of Domański and Szczucki, "Miscellanea Arianica": from Żytno, 29 December 1565, 232−33; from Lutomirski, two letters, one official and personal, one wholly personal, 30 December, urging him not to be so attentive to learned theologians, 234−36; and from Hieronim Piekarski, 31 December, 238. These letters, referred to by Kot, "Ausbruch," 215, n. 5, are printed from the Vaticans MS Ottoboniana, Lat. 3076 P. II, which bears on Reformation currents in Lithuania, 1550−69. The editors of "Miscellanea Arianica" express their intentions (231) of publishing other documents of this loose bundle of pages, specifically a letter of Georg Weigel (see n. 239, ¶4).

At the end of the letter in the name of the synod of Węgrów, decisive in both Poland and Lithuania in consolidating and setting the further course of debate and practice concerning baptism, the reader of the *Historia* is entitled to some retrospective and anticipatory summation of the distinctiveness of Polish-speaking Anabaptism, for here as in other documentation the Polish Brethren not only disclaimed any connection with (revolutionary Germanic) Anabaptism but also proposed for themselves a generic name that called no direct attention to their being baptists. In what follows reference is being made not only to places within the letter but also to places within the following two letters, closely reflecting the deliberations of Węgrów, and within the summary of a letter from the Transylvanian churches to Węgrów.

Polish allows for two generic designations for a Christian: *chrystyjanin* (from Christ, a modern word) and *chrześcijanin* (from *chrzest:* baptism, the christened one); and the Polish Brethren made clear to themselves first and sometimes to others that they were *Christiani* as well as *fratres in Christo,* whereas the Germanic Anabaptists, while they also called themselves *Brüder,* came to think of themselves as simply and biblically *Täufer* or *Taufgesinnte* in rejection of the capital charge of being *Wiedertäufer.* Although Polish Anabaptists did not and would not (until 1660) stand under such a threat as Wiedertäufer/Anabaptistae stood in the Empire under the imperial mandate of 23 April 1529 that expressly appealed for precedent to the Theodosian and Justinianic codes that embodied ancient punishment for Donatista as rebaptizers (Williams, *RR*, 238), it was for more than this reason that the emerging anti-Nicene Polish Brethren largely eschewed both *anabaptista* and its analogue in Polish (*nowochrzczeniec*). It was at Węgrów that they for the first time synodally used their own distinctive word for "true" or believers' baptism, *ponurzenie* (the Polish word only in Sipayłło, *AS*, 2. 127), destined to become standardized after several similar verbal formations would become marginalized. In calling themselves *Christiani,* the Polish Brethren would be setting themselves off from all pedobaptists, whether Catholic, Protestant, or even Orthodox (who, though immersionists, confirmed and gave first communion to the infant at baptism),—as "the [merely] christened, *chrześcijanie* (*krześcijanie*) or nominal or conventional Christians without the Dominical and Apostolic ordinance of immersion and communal discipline, and who might or might not have inward faith. The Brethren dismissed the appeal of all pedobaptists to Acts 8:6 (the baptism of whole families and hence, by the inference of pedobaptists, of minors in those families) and interpreted Matt 19:14 (Jesus' calling of little ones to himself) as his pointing to models of receptivity and trust (Gonesius) or precisely as his giving of a blessing and not dispensing baptism (Czechowic). This passage, indeed, later became the scriptural warrant in Socinian households for a pre-baptismal blessing of young children (cf. the practice of our Author himself, Introduction at n. 17).

Because of the importance of "the baptism of John" as distinguished from "the baptism of Christ," as the paradigm of baptism by full immersion, our Polish *Christiani* had to deal with the relationship of the two and that of circumcision and baptism (whether largely pedobaptist *chrzest* by sprinkling or *ponurzenie*). Scripturally in focus were two *loci* involving disciples of John the Baptist. In Acts 8:16 several Samaritan disciples of John, who had been baptized in the name of the Lord Jesus, on the occasion received from the apostles only the laying on of hands (not rebaptism) and with this touch reportedly received the Holy Spirit, later to be called by the Polish Brethren the gift of the Holy Spirit, which as the accompaniment of baptism (although thought to precede the external action) they considered to be the essence of "the baptism of Christ" in whose name and on whose petition the Father sends the Spirit as comforter (John 14:17; 16:26). In the other scriptural *locus,* Acts 18:24 – 19:7, Apollos of Alexandria and then twelve others who had received "the baptism of John" were evidently differently treated: the twelve in Ephesus were [re]baptized in the name of the Lord Jesus by Paul, while Apollos, who taught about Jesus with ardor and accuracy, seems to have been exempted from rebaptism

(19:1), instructed as he already had been in the way of the Lord (18:25). Known as he was in Ephesus, he was pointedly in Corinth (19:1) when Paul baptized the other twelve Johannite Ephesians. These texts involving the two baptisms and rebaptism are alluded to in the letter from Wrów at the bottom of *p. 181* under ''Gospel history,'' Acts, and Epistles.

Peter Lombard assessed the commentary and opinions of the Fathers about the two baptisms and rebaptism in the New Testament in his *Sentences* (IV, d. 2, q. 2) and made the clarifying distinction that the Samaritans, having a knowledge of the triune God, needed only the laying on of hands to receive the Holy Spirit, while the twelve Ephesians, not having had such knowledge, were in need of the baptism of Christ. In the immediate background of all Reformation thought on the issue of the two baptists was the *Collectorium* of Gabriel Biel (d. 1495) of Tübingen, whose work was a compend of late medieval opinions about Lombard's *quaestiones*. As David Steinmetz has brought to view, Biel rejected Lombard's distinction of two classes among John's disciples, who included all of the Apostles (none of whom was otherwise known to have been expressly baptized) as well as the Samaritans and the Ephesians of Acts. (It is notable that the exegetical tradition allowed John 4:2 on not baptising to suppress, even among Anabaptists, that Jesus was baptising more disciples than John, 3:22.) In scholastic terminology Biel recognized that the disciples of John had indeed faith (*fides*) that was prospectively valid, that they had been laved with the proper matter (*res*), but that the *forma* of John's sacramental was defective, wanting the salvific Dominical formula (Matt 28:19), and that this baptism was thus primarily God's means of transition from circumcision under the Old to baptism under the New Covenant.

In the period of the Reformation, Lutherans continued to subordinate the baptism of John to that of Christ, while the Reformed, beginning with Zwingli, preferred to equalize the two as interchangeable in the interest of establishing the continuity of the People of God of *one* covenant in two dispensations and therefore they sought to make the baptism of John transitional from circumcision to pedobaptism, without their subordinating the baptism of John. The Radical Reformers were similarly divided. Among the Anabaptists, Hans Hut, Hans Denck, Szymon Budny (also Faustus Socinus, although not himself willing to submit to believers' baptism) upheld the virtual identity of the two baptisms, while Balthasar Hubmaier, Gonesius, and Czechowic insisted on the distinction; and, with a concern for immersion, different from that of the Germanic Anabaptists, they developed new features. The issue of the two baptisms was first raised in the Reformation era in 1525 between Zwingli and Hubmaier, as Steinmetz as shown in ''The Baptism of John and the Baptism of Jesus,'' in George and Church, eds., 169–81.

The debate over the two baptisms raged from May to November 1525, between the father of the Reformed tradition, Zwingli, and the eventual leader of the Anabaptists in Moravia, Hubmaier. The exchange was carried out in three works by Zwingli and two booklets by Hubmaier, who therein set the prevailing pattern for Anabaptism in both Germany and Poland. Zwingli laid down the basis of the debate in his *Commentarius de vera et falsa religione* (Zurich, 1525), wherein, concerning baptism, he denied the *ex opere operato* character of any sacrament and hence dismissed the argumentation of both Lombard and Biel, thus also any fine points about *res* and the proper *forma,* and he placed the efficacy of the ordinance instead in the prior election and in faith (hence also in the implicit faith of infants), holding that the sacrament is only a sign of an inward action of the Spirit. (For his view on the sacraments Zwingli was soon to be pilloried by Luther as a ''Sacramentarian.'') Zwingli, still directing his attack on the medieval consensus about the two baptisms, sought in *Von der Taufe, von der Wiedertaufe, und von der Kindertaufe* to cope with the rebaptism of the twelve Johannites in Ephesus. He strainingly resorted to an assignment of four different *scriptural* meanings for baptism: water, Spirit, teaching, and faith; and he defended pedobaptism against the emergent Anabaptists, who as of 1525 were simply emphasizing the necessity of accordant faith in the adult baptizand and the nullity of one's christening in infancy. It was Hubmaier, scholastically trained at Ingolstadt, rather than some Catholic theologian of the school of Johann Eck, who in *Von der christlichen Taufe der Gläubigen* upheld the scholastic distinction between the two baptisms, even though he was in accord with Zwingli on any sacrament as only a sign of an inward grace, the consequence of faith. But Hubmaier understood John's baptism in confession of sins as being filled with the curse of the Law and which therefore simply had to be replaced with Christ's baptism in forgiveness of sins through grace and the Spirit, although Hubmaier appreciated the example of the Forerunner in that he limited baptism to repentant adults—which baptism, nevertheless, lacked the Dominical formulary. Hubmaier preferred in practice the version of Mark 16:15, which, going beyond all medieval precedent, fixed the sequence as teaching (preaching), faith, baptism (for most Germanic Anabaptists by sprinkling). Zwingli angrily replied in his *Antwort,* appealing to Eph 4:5 (one Lord, one faith, one baptism), written supposedly by Paul to the very Ephesians who must have known Apollos and the other twelve disciples of John in their city. Hubmaier responded confidently in his *Gespräch* on the issues raised, agreed with Zwingli (and the later Reformed view) of baptism as having the character of a covenant, the one thinking of it as comparable to the taking of the cowl by the novice (Zwingli) or to the monastic vow (Hubmaier), but then with the commitment to follow not the rule of an order but the Rule of Christ.

The Polish-speaking Anabaptists in general developed their baptismal theology and practice more in line with Hubmaier and perhaps even partly dependent upon this highly trained martyred leader of the Germanic Anabaptists in Miuklov (Nicolsburg), as, e.g., by Czechowic, who cited him. They understood believers' immersion not as rebaptism but rather as true baptism in exchange (*commutatio,* at n. 314) for their nonparticipatory pedobaptism. But they understood both scriptural baptisms as permanently revelatory of God's mandate, that of John as to the mode (matter), namely, immersion in water, and as to appropriate recipients, namely, adult believers; and yet they regarded the baptism of Christ as distinguishable and definitive, its essence being the antecedent and accompanying gift of the Holy Spirit, perhaps also of Fire, and of freedom in grace from some aspects of the Law. As Jesus at his baptism received the Holy Spirit, so all who followed his immersionary example and express mandate receive the same Spirit. Hence the "emerging *Christiani*" were taunted by the pedobaptists in Vilna as *Spirituales.* Like the Germanic Anabaptists they preferred to Matt 28:19 the Domninical formulary of Mark 16:15 because it corroborated their understanding of a divinely fixed sequence: teaching (preaching, catechetical *rudimenta fidei*), faith engendered (in the elect) by the hearing of the Word, repentance, Christ's gift of the Spirit, immersion itself as a dying and rising with Christ, one's becoming a new creature bound in a new pact or covenant or oath as a fresh recruit of the *militia Christi spiritualis,* one's enrolling under a new *capitanus/hetman,* one's being thereby a Spiritual man or woman, *Spirituales,* judging all things, to be judged by none. The immersion took place in a stream or pond (the synodists of Węgrów had for the most part not reached this stage), the candidates clothed, and the service evidently taking place under the cover of twilight.

The Polish *Christiani,* who immersed either in the name of the Father, the Son, and the Holy Spirit or in the name of Jesus, would continue their catechetical or adult believers' baptism, despite the objection of Faustus Socinus, whose view happened to be reflected in the letter from certain Transylvanians, and who later expressed himself systematically in his *De baptismo aquae disputatio,* Cracow, 15 April 1580 (Raków: Sternacki, 1613), where he remarks that the Brethren nevertheless persevere in their wonted baptismal practice and do not take up his arguments, noting that Czechowic, their leader, expressly differentiates the water baptism of John and the Spirit-water baptism of Christ; cf. the baptismal service as of 1646 in *PB,* Document XXIII.

The foregoing synod of Pińczów was much more important politically, organizationally, and theologically than Lubieniecki brings out. And already an important synod had taken place in the home town of its superintendent, Cruciger (Book 1, n. 231), in Secemin, 21 – 29 January 1556, Sipayłło, *AS* 1. 46 – 52. Here the provisional Polish version of the Czech *Confessio,* which had been accepted at Koźminek, was read. The synodists joined in condemning Gonesius as Arian and Servetian, agreed about the ordination of their new ministers and ex-priests by the laying on of hands (1 Tim 5:22), proposed a national council of which there were rumors, and considered having Calvin, Melanchthon, or their own Łaski come and head up the uniting Polish Reformed Church. But not all synodists were sure that they wanted their united Church to be in any supervisory control from outside—from Moravia.

At the synod of Pińczów, beginning 24 April 1556, the first order of business revolved around the Polish version of the *Confessio.* Hieronim Filipowski was elected moderator and he entered very much into the questioning. Present from among the Czech Brethren were Matthias Červenka (Czerwonka), the (presiding) bishop of the Unity; Jiři Israel (Jerzy Israel), their bishop in Great Poland and later president of the executive council of the Unity (1572 – 88); and Jan Rokyta (Rokita), all ready to respond to questions. Many of these related to liturgy, choirs, and unfamiliar customs, concerning which some of the synodists were reserved. One larger issue was whether the synodists should be raising any questions at all about a *Confessio* that they had already accepted in principle, and the Latin version of which had been endorsed by such lights of the Reformation as Luther, Melanchthon, Buder, Capito, Peter Martyr, and Calvin. Concerning the two themes of the *Historia,* the Trinity and baptism, the synodists took the occasion again to dissociate themselves from Gonesius, already restrained by a royal edict, along with Łaski. Józef Jasnowski, ''Dwa edykty [1556] Zygmunta Augusta przeciwko Piotrowi z Goniądz i Janowi Łaskiemu,'' *RwP* 9 – 10 (1937 – 39) 442 – 43. The synodists asked the Czech delegates about marriage of partners from within and without their Unity and about their practice (nominally abandoned since 1534) of repeating baptism (*powtarzanie krstu*) for converts from the Catholics and Utraquists. Both Červenka and Israel seemed to defend rebaptism. The synodists voted that all mention of it be left out of the final Polish version of their *Confessio.* Their own formalization of one's becoming a member (*initiatio*) was by solemnly giving and subscribing one's name, called variously *sacramentum, vinculum, signum oboedientiae.* And they drew up articles about government and church order. The synod was aware that the King suspected the nobles among the synodists of Koźminek, Secemin, and now Pińczów of being engaged in conspiracy, perhaps even treason, and they repeated their expressions of patriotism, insisted that their synods dealt only with doctrine and church discipline, not with political matters, deferring to the magistracy in all such matters, while they looked forward to a national reform council, and had big ideas about the possibility of Calvin, Lismanino, or Łaski being invited to give leadership to the emergent federated Reformed Church of the Commonwealth.

239. Lubieniecki probably means by Vilna Lithuanian delegates in general, Żytno, Bartłomej Codecius, Paweł of Wizna, Piekarski among them. Altogether there were eight. Kot, ''Ausbruch,'' 221. Lubieniecki passes over the development in Vilna where

orthodox Calvinism prevailed, as in Cracow, and the overall picture is obscured. The reception of and reaction to the report of the radical synod of Węgrów, along with the execution of the will of Prince Mikołaj Radziwiłł (n. 222), occasioned much of the documentation.

Executors of the great patron's will who had shortly before this come to despair of the radical tendencies in the congregation he had been supporting were Mikołaj Pac, Jan Krzysztof Tarnowski, Mikołaj Radziwiłł the Red, at the time palatine of Troki and Hetman of the Duchy (soon thereafter, 1566, palatine of Vilna and Chancellor), Prince Konstantin Ostrogski, and Ostafi Wołowicz, deputy treasurer of the Duchy. To them Pastor Georg Weigel directed his fierce and fearful "Necessaria consideratio" concerning the religious situation especially in Vilna, and to all Reformed magnates of Lithuanian he directed a similar memorial, "De confusionibus et scandalis excitatis in hoc Ecclesia Ecclesia Vilnensi." These two undated memorials, throwing considerable light on the situation and embodying the worst fears of the conservatives, are printed by Kot, "Ausbruch," 224–26, along with a summation of a third document form the same source, a letter of Weigel to (Reformed) Bishop Pac, 14 December 1565, that is, less than a week before the synod in Węgrów (219). All three documents are discussed by Kot, "Ausbruch," 216–20, by Szczucki, *Czechowic*, 50–60 with substantial and clarifying nn.; in n. 166 (*Czechowic*, 241–43), Szczucki prints, thanks to Kot, the whole of the letter of Weigel to Pac, Weigel signing himself "minister Verbi et professor Theologiae."

Wotschke discovered Georg Weigel. Born in Nuremberg, he had been court preacher in Königsberg, became involved in the Osiander Controversy (Bk. 1, nn. 186, 256; Bk. 2, n. 425) and was dismissed as a Philippist and Sacramentarian. "Georg Weigel: Ein Beitrag zur Reformationsgeschichte Altpreussens und Lithuaniens," *ARG* 19 (1922) 22–29. In Vilna Weigel took the lead in the restoration of strict Calvinism in association with Mikołaj Pac (*Historia, 20*, Bk. 1, n. 186). Eventually he would return to Catholicism.

In his three communications Weigel raised the specter of Münster and ascribed to the synodists of Brzeziny (Wędrogowski had, of course, recanted his antipedobaptism) and of Węgrów (perhaps partly in anticipation) social egalitarianism in the use of Brother and Sister for all ranks, non-observance of social ranking at communion, the practice of *communio bonorum*, an exaltation of prophesying over against formal preaching (cf. 1 Cor 14:6 14:22, 1 Thes 5:20) and possibly even the institution of polygamy. See the articles ranged against the radical synodists in the two memorials, Kot, "Ausbruch," 224–26. Weigel in his outrage against all factions and persons in the sequence from antipedobaptism to believers' baptism did not distinguish among them, all being pilloried as "Anabaptists."

240. Lubieniecki here and elsewhere makes it clear that the letter is to *Brestia*, not *Braesinia*, Brześć, not Brzeziny. This could not be the royal town of Brześć Kujawski where Sebastian Mielecki, a Catholic, was *starosta*. The letter of the congregation of Vilna would, in any case, have gone more appropriately to the large congregation in Brest Litovsk on the Bug, capital of the palatinate between Podlachia and the Land of Chełm, than to the small manorial congregation of Brzeziny in Kujawy. The author of the letter was probably Żytno, who also wrote to Wędrowski, 29 December 1565, to the same effect, "Miscellanea arianica," ed. Szczucki, p. 232. There are fragments of the same letter of the ministers in Vilna to Brest Litovsk in Łukaszewicz, *Dzieje Kościoła wyzania helweckiego w Litwie* 1, 30–31.

241. Matt 24:5, 23–24; Mark 13:21–22; 2 Tim 4:3–4; 1 John 2:18, 22; 4:3, 2 John 7; Rev 19:20–21, etc.

242. The reference to the baptism of the children (*liberi*) of *infideles parentes* suggests that some of the social radicals among the Reformed may have questioned not only the received Catholic baptism but perhaps also the reception into membership of the offspring of nobles who remained Catholic (or Orthodox).

243. Eph 4:14.

244. The spokesmen for the congregation in Vilna evidently thinking territorial terms in that (involuntary) pedobaptism links families and regions into a church (not sect) coterminous with the larger political entity. The reference to this *Res publica*, commonly rendered in translation Commonwealth could in Vilna mean the Kingdoms of the Two Peoples or for the moment only the Grand Duchy.

245. A reference to baptism in 1 Pet 3:21, a favorite text of all Anabaptists.

246. The conservative Reformed spokesmen of Vilna are saying that the (pedo) baptism received from their Catholic infancy or as observed in modified form in their own Reformed tradition is truly regenerative and its validity should not be questioned and hence not repeated (anabaptism).

247. This is probably an ironic allusion to 1 Cor 2:15: "Spiritualis autem iudicat omnia: et ipse a nemini iudicatur." The writers have only pluralized it, the Spiritual Brethren who allegedly have been given the gift of the Holy Spirit in believers' baptism. They may also allude to the coming of deceitful spirits, 1 Tim 4:1, and may allude, also, to them as Spiritual Libertines, analogues to those in Calvin's Geneva.

248. Believers' baptism was in part modeled on the baptism of Jesus by John the Baptist, who preached concurrently with an innovative practice, the repentance of sins, Matt 3:2, 13 – 14 and parallels.

249. 1 Pet 2:16. The reference to Paul is erroneous.

250. Brest Litovsk.

251. Matt 7;15, 24:11; cf. Gal 2:4.

252. Cf. Acts 11:26 and Rev 14:1.

253. See n. 250.

254. John 10:1 – 12.

255. This is more likely an admonition than an allusion to predestination to election.

256. Near nn. 242 and 244.

257. At n. 243.

258. The reference is to the synod at Węgrów and the letter sent to it in the name of the congregation of Vilna by Wędrogowski, at n. 228.

259. The letter of Wędrogowski with its *verga Magistratus* is implicitly opposed by the spokesmen of Brest who may have in mind not only Jesus' teaching on the proper things of Caesar but also such a passage as Rev 2:27, wherein the *verga ferrea* is placed in an eschatological context, in any case not to be used by the magistrate for the coercion of Christians.

260. Perhaps an allusion to Matt 22:21 and Luke 20:25.

261. Rom 13:5. See at n. 231.

262. Gen 7:24; 1 Cor 5:1; 7:2; 1 Tim 3:2, 12; Titus 1:6.

263. Acts 19:21; 20:7; 4:17; Rom 15:26; 1 Cor 16:1 – 3; 2 Cor 9:4 – 5.

264. Cf. at nn. 245 and 247.

265. Matt 6:12; Luke 18:1,6; 11:4.

266. 1 Tim 2:5; 1 John 1:7 – 9. The *baptizati liberi Dei* (the context must be Jn 1:13) here are not children of God in the sense of *parvuli* but *liberi*, as the regenerate progeny of God.

267. That is, after the repentance at believers' baptism (anabaptism).

268. That is, Antichrist, the Papacy.
269. Cf. Rev 17:14.
270. See at n. 259.
271. The minister remains unidentified.
272. Phil 3:14; 1 Cor 9:24.
273. The date of his death is unknown. As of 19 December 1565, that is, even before Węgrów, Weigel was still lumping Wędrogowski with the lay elders of Vilna, Kurnicki and Katerla, as tacitly anabaptists. His letter is in Szczucki, *Czechowic*, 242.
274. Węgierski only mentions Wędrogowski, *Slavonia Reformata*, 146. After the synod of Węgrów and the angry exchanges, Vilna consolidated its Reformed pedobaptist position; and the movement toward a radical baptismal theology and practice shifted to Little Poland, many of the Lithuanian anti-pedobaptists settling there and in Volhynia. Budny, *O dzieciokrzczeństwie, loc. cit.*, p. 109
275. The annotation at this point falls into two parts: the identification of the letter of the Transylvanian churches and the clarification of Lubieniecki's characterization of the latter as a display of *Judaizantis Spiritus indicia* and the meaning of Judaizing in the text and the annotation.

A communication of the Transylvanian churches to the synod of Węgrów of December 1565 is discussed in n. 236. Known by a title only in *BAnt* is also a possibly distinguishable anonymous "Epistola Ecclesiarum Transylvanicarum ad Ecclesias Polonicas, de Baptismo: in qua late proponunt sententiam suam de hoc ritu (contrariam sententiae Fratrum Polonorum) probantes, Christianos eo nunc amplius non obligari," written in 1566. Budziński exhibited this in his History, chap. 45; *BAnt*, 173. Lubieniecki may here be giving the thrust of it. Right after the entry in *BAnt* among *Auctores Anonymi*, Sand or Wiszowaty goes on: "Conclusiones, Baptismum non successerit circumcisione, in Polonia scriptae: quas anno 1567, 25 Julii refutavit Benedictus Aretius." It would appear then that there was a refutation of the position in the form of conclusions, among them, that the classical Reformed and perhaps specifically Bullingerian connection made between circumcision in the Old and pedobaptism under the New Covenant, as against the Anabaptists, was disavowed by someone in Poland writing presumably for the synod. Cf. n. 238. These *Conclusiones* were then supposedly refuted in turn by the Benedictus Aretius who wrote against Gentile (Geneva, 1567; Bk. 2, n. 351), Wilbur, *Socinianism*, 257–58, and *Transylvania*, 230. But Wiszowaty in *BAnt*[2], 156, conjectures that the writer wa instead "Benedictus Arcosi, Hungarus, Lector Gymnasii Claudiopolitani." This is valuable testimony to the possible origin of other communications to the Polish Brethren, here and at n. 236, namely, the school in Kolozsvár, the more radical counterpart in Transylvania of the school at Pińczów. Cf. Bk. 2, n. 351. (In another connection, Rotondò mentions Aretius/Marty, L. Sozzini, *Opere*, 345, n. 85.)

Among the influential resident aliens who attached no importance to baptism as the rite of entry into the community of faith or to its postponement to mark adhesion to a resolute community of faith were Johann Sommer and Jacobus Palaeologus. We have encountered Sommer as the biographer of the Despot (Bk. 2, chap. 9) and will meet him again as a classicist and pedagogue (n. 385) and as radical Antitrinitarian (Bk. 3, chap. 11). He and Palaeologus (nn. 395, 401) were both influential in the radicalizing of the Reformed Church in Transylvania and both in pressing for consistent Unitarianism and also in the diminishment of baptism as an unnecessary ceremony for those who no longer retained the doctrine of original sin while adhering to predestination and justification by faith. For Sommer, Palaeologus, and others (cf. n. 280), baptism was at best something for converts from paganism, but not for children born of Christian families. In this regard they were akin to F. Socinus, but precisely on this they and Biandrata evidently differed (nn. 236, 280). Admirably discussed, with fresh source materials by Massimo Firpo, *Antitrinitari neff' Europa orientale del '500: Nuovi testa de Szymon Budny, Niccolò Paruta e Iacopo Paleologo* (Florence: La Nuova Italia, 1977), 52ff.

Palaeologus, who was only intermittently and briefly in Transylvania, was nevertheless much more influential among Transylvanian Unitarians than among those in Cracovia (n. 400, ¶4). He expressed himself most fully on baptism in *De baptismo* (1573) and in *Catechesis Christiana* (1574) ed., by Dostálová (n. 400, ¶4), 197–219. Here the figure of the discussant Pastor is at once Ferenc Dávid and Palaeologus, while Samuel represents the Jew converted to (Unitarian) Christianity; Telephus, an Indian of the New World joins the colloquy as a convert from paganism, but as also a fill-in for the ideal convert to (Unitarian) Christianity from Islam, participating with a Papist, a Lutheran, and a Calvinist, and a Chorus of general observers. As a nonadorant Unitarian the ''Pastor'' sees the whole history of salvation in terms of God's Elect People, who were given after the expression of Abraham's faith and his circumcision the whole Law and the promise of a Messiah. Palaeologus takes up into his system the concept of the threefold office of the Messiah, indeed, of three kinds of anointed figures in the history of the Elect People, kings, prophets, and priests. Undoubtedly he thought of himself primarily as a prophet and never became a full member of any Unitarian church. Full salvation for the Jews is the recognition of Jesus as their rejected Messiah and that he will come in vindication of his own, Jews and Gentiles. The acceptance of Jesus as the eschatological Messiah does not dispense with the observance of the Law and does not require Jews to be baptized, although for the sake of general conformity Samuel has in fact received baptism. For Jewish converts the four Gospels are their part of the New Testament, whereas for pagans and Muslims the core of the New Testament is in the Acts of the Apostles and the Pauline Epistles. Converts in any era and generation are to be baptized, but the progeny of Christians, whether of old Christian lines or of the newly converted need not be baptized, as through their parents they already belong to the Elect People of God. The Pastor, in response to queries from several sides, allows for the continuance of pedobaptism and the introduction of adult baptism, depending of the situation in the town or villages, but in any case the rite is not of much importance. Baptism, as understood by Palaeologus and perhaps to some extent by Dávid under his influence, is admirably set in context by Szczucki, *W kręgu myścicieli heretyckich*, 85–96.

As for a *Judaizans spiritus*, the verb ''Judaize'' and its related forms generally has a negative meaning, as here in Lubieniecki, or a positive meaning for the persons or groupings said to be Judaizing, though they are often indisposed to take over the term from their opponents. A not wholly positive locus in the Old Testament is Esth 8:17: ''And many from the peoples of the country [Persia] declared themselves Jews for the fear of the Jews had fallen upon them.'' A not wholly negative locus in the New is that of Paul against Peter in Gal 2:4. Róbert Dán ''*Judaizare*—the Career of a Term'' (Dán and Pirnát, *Antitrinitarianism*, 25–34) traces the term and concept from antiquity and notes the varied application in exegesis, ceremony and morality, theology, and social behavior. Embracing in his survey trends in all of Europe especially in the sixteenth century, Dán proposes that the always ambiguous term be, in scholarly literature, confined to those trends among Christians who retain the minimal creed in the acceptance of Jesus in some sense as the Messiah but who also hold ''to the priority of the Hebrew Bible and rabbinical writings and of their unchanged validity for all peoples of the world,'' ''*Judaizare*,'' 33. Dán's proposal may be too narrow. Although Lubieniecki's usage is here negative, it is not so used in my nn., without my always following Dán's definition, even though Dán includes within his purview the Commonwealth and Muscovy, with recent literature, in n. 287. In his most recent report on his findings based on newly discovered archival material, he grounds his view with an astonishing range of documentation, "Der Einfluss des Judentums auf die antitrinitarische Bewegung des 16. Jahrhunderts," Die erste deutsche wissenschaftliche Tagung zur Unitarismusforschung, Hamburg, 13 and 14 June 1985. For Judaizing Sabbatarianism in Transylvania, see further nn. 615, ¶5; 675, ¶7. For Judaizing in Lublin, see nn. 287, 779.

276. The writers of some letters "from the Transylvanian churches" might be Sommer, Palaeologus, Arcosi (nn. 275; 385, ¶2; 393ff.).

277. Jer 27:2; 28:10–13; 2 Kings 13:14–17.

278. This was indeed the view of Faustus Socinus and at this stage of certain radicals in Transylvania (n. 275, ¶2).

279. The Transylvanian writers had in mind such passages in the New Testament that possibly imply that children were included physically or implicitly in the baptism of households, as in Matt 19:14, Acts 16:33, 1 Cor 1:16, and 1 Tim 2:4. In classical Protestantism, once the identification had been made between circumcision and pedobaptism (n. 275), baptism could be seen as not always physically necessary, since circumcision itself was not practiced during the forty years of wandering in the wilderness. The suspension or marginalization of baptism among certain radicals, mostly in the Reformed tradition, is indeed one of the consequences of raising the issue of believers' baptism.

Although Giorgio Biandrata is not mentioned at this point by Lubieniecki, he did write *De paedobaptismo* about this time with seventeen theses in favor of infant baptism and thirty-six arguments against it. Although he may have understood the view of Sommer and Palaeologus, at least for tactical reasons and probably quite sincerely, he did not intend to join those who would disturb the tolerated status of the Unitarian Church and its "territoriality" in Magyar/Szekler regions, village as well as towns. Wiszowaty's addendum to the original information of Sand (*BAnt*[2], 33) seems to indicate that a quarto edition in Polish of Biandrata's *De paedobaptismo* was confined to thirty-four arguments *against* pedobaptism, out of the original thirty-six. For more on the baptismal positions in Transylvania, see n. 314, ¶7.

It may be noted here that another work of Biandrata, known to Sand, *Antithesis in primum Johannis caput*, was known by Wiszowaty (*BAnt*[2], 34) to have been published *in quarto* in Polish, no place, no date.

280. There are three records on the Polish sources of how some radical Transylvanians felt about the preoccupation of the Polish/Lithuanian Brethren with baptism: the present account; a final paragraph of summary in the report on Węgrów; and a final paragraph in the letter of Biandrata to Grzegorz Paweł (n. 236).

In his own words, Biandrata at this juncture (21 September 1565) was concerned to preserve pedobaptism, important in the Transylvanian situation, lest the counterpart of the Minor Reformed Church, under Dávid, be regarded once again as innovative and thus risk its tolerated status. The two summaries of Transylvanians, including the report here of Lubieniecki, both appear to go much further in belittling baptism, whether of infants or assenting believers, than what most radically Reformed Transylvanians as of 1566 were considering.

Although Anabaptists had so far penetrated (Upper) Hungary that a mandate was issued against them by the Diet of Pozsony (Pressburg) in 1548 (Haner, *Historia*, 108), Wilbur was of the view that Germanic Anabaptism played no such role in Transylvania, as he acknowledged it had in Poland (*Transylvania*, 24). Though the problem was raised about pedobaptism c. 1570 on the proto-Unitarian side of the Reformed Church and though pedobaptism was rejected at the synod of Torda of March 1578 (nn. 229, ¶ 3; 600, ¶2), it is indeed true that under pan-Protestant pressure pedobaptism in the traditional formula (Matt 28:19) would be accepted by the Unitarian Church at the Diet and joint synod of Dées of 1638 as the only basis of continued toleration by the Lutherans and the Calvinists (n. 123, ¶2).

Nevertheless, there was an anabaptist publication in Transylvania, closely associated with Ferenc Dávid himself, which significantly links Flemish anabaptism by way of a conventicle in Warsaw with developments in Kolozsvár, c. 1570. On 19 August, 1569, a physician in Warsaw, Dr. Sándor Wilini, addressed Dávid in Hungarian, urging him to print in both German and Hungarian a substantial anabaptist dialogue, which indeed appeared in both languages as *A Booklet concerning the True Christian Baptism and the Pope's Likeness to Antichrist* (Kolozsvár, 1570). Daniel Liechty prints Wilini's letter, a summary of the Hungarian edition, and his interpretation of the origin and transmission of this some 300-page book with some 770 biblical references, *MQR* 62:3 (1988) 332–48. Antal Pirnát updates the scholarship on the *Booklet* in two versions, reclaiming from Gáspár Heltai for Dávid the translation into Hungarian, "Dávid Ferenc 'Könyvecske,'" *Irodalmotörténeti Közlemények* 57 (1954) 299–308; cf. Pirnát on baptism in n. 314, ¶¶ 6, 7 and his incidental reference to the *Booklet* in "Il matire e l'uomo politico," 170 n. 14.

The *Booklet,* surviving only in the German and the Hungarian, was written in a circle of Flemish Anabaptists, who were familiar with patristic sources and knew Latin and possibly some Greek. Liechty, who once singled out as possibly sole author Jakob de Roore (Keergieter) of Courtrai/Kortrijk, baptized by Gilles van Aken, and burned at the stake in Bruges, 10 June 1569, now thinks of a circle of writers, of whom Herman van Vleckwijk, martyred with de Roore would be another. The latter, leaning to Unitarianism (like Adam Pastor), is recorded in *BAnt*, p. 60. M. J. Reimer-Blok deals with the de Roore circle in "The Theological Identity of Flemish Anabaptists: A Study of the Letters of Jacob de Roore," *MQR* 62:3 (1988) 318–31. The dialogue between the Master and the forthright Disciple originally dealt with the violence of the Münsterite theocracy, with the maddening diversity of claimants to the true believers' baptism even after the defeat of the Münsterites in 1535, and with the Spiritualizing of all ordinances by David Joris. Although the baptismal theology and discipline that emerges in the dialogue is different from that of Menno Simons, it is not incompatible with it and is likewise marked by an extensive use of the New Testament as taking precedence for Christians over the Old (a view later to be abandoned by the translator, Dávid).

The transmitter of the lost and probably only MS *Booklet* in Flemish, Dr. Sándor Wilini, appears from his letter to have been the lay patron of a congregation of christocentric Unitarians in Warsaw, which as of his writing in 1569, was a small Masovia town (only in 1611 destined to become the capital), and which hosted Protestants only when a Commonwealth diet occasionally took place there, remote from the main currents of the Reformation in the Commonwealth. His might have been a Germanophone congregation, with some Dutchmen, for the Flemish tract is said by Wilini to have "given me and many other Christian brethren great spiritual joy." There would appear to be a significant Magyar component of the congregation because it was the recent visit of "the Reverend Wolf (Farkas) Gyulay" that had apprised "us" of "what wonderful works the Father of our Lord Jesus Christ has been doing in Transylvania and Hungary. Liechty has proposed that the writer's surname suggests birth in Vilna. Dr. Wilini himself knew several languages and asks Dávid to send him with a bill any comforting works from Transylvania "in German or the classical languages" on "the Father of our Lord Jesus

Christ, his blessed crucified Son, the true Messiah, in whom we alone have eternal life (John 17)." It is quite plausible that a congregation of the size, ethnic composition, and intellectual level suggested by Wilini's letter would nevertheless have escaped the records of both the Major and the Minor Church in Poland, since there were no other congregations of this kind at the time in all Masovia, the most Catholic cluster of palatinates in the Commonwealth.

There is only one extant copy of Wilini's German translation from the Flemish. It is the basis for the work of Pirnát in showing that Dávid and not Heltai was the translator of the Hungarian version and that Dávid both shortened and expanded on Wilini's German MS and that he underscored it in the alleged, decisive role of Victor I as the first to introduce pedobaptism, in 193, hence his "likeness to Antichrist." In any case, as of 1570, Dávid was espousing believers' baptism, also rebaptism for the sake of "true baptism" against the usage of the papal Antichrist.

281. The remark about taking baptism with "a grain of salt" appears to conclude the summary of communications from certain Transylvanians and leads into Lubieniecki's rather forced generalization about the Minor Church in the Commonwealth and the Unitarian Church as pluralistically established in Transylvania. Lubieniecki holds to "the solemn incorporation" into the Church by the ordinance of immersion and regeneration. But that there was also a disposition to deal lightly with the practice is evidenced in an important and probably representative visitation of three pastors of piedmont churches, among them that at Lusławice, written up evidently by Stanislas Lubieniecki (d. 1634), the Historian's great uncle. Otherwise more important for its extensive treatment of ethical standards in the churches of the period, the *Księga wizytacji zborów podgorskich*, 1612, nevertheless testifies to the persistence, after the death of Socinus, of the practice of the baptism of catechumens, although the stress here is on the understanding and experience of "regeneration or renewal, then death [to sin], then doctrine, and at the end water." The *Księga* is printed from a Budapest MS by Szczucki and Tazbir, *Archiwum Historii Filozofii i myśli społecznej* 3 (1958) 127–72, esp. 130, 153.

282. The work of Czechowic, *De Paedobaptistarum errorum origine*; see n. 315.

283. Lubieniecki refers to Socinus's reply to Czechowic's position in 1580 in *De Baptismo aquae disputatio* (Raków: Sternacki, 1613); Gryczowa, no. 258, pp. 299–300 and specifically to *Responsio* 2 in this work, Socinus's "Ad M.C. notas in appendice libri eius de Paedobaptismo."

284. The reference is less to Lutheran Ducal Prussia than to Royal Prussia. For the administrative components of Royal Prussia, see Bk. 1, n. 152, ¶1.

Merczyng reports the death of the last immersed Polish Brother, Karol Henryk Morsztyn, in Andreaswalde, East (Ducal) Prussia, 1852; *Zbory i Senatorowie*, 88; Wilbur, *Socianism*, 521.

285. Lubieniecki left Cracow with the evacuation of Swedish forces in 1657 (*Polish Brethren*, 523). The decrees of expulsion of the Brethren or forced conversion (*Polish Brethren*, Doc. XXVI and XXX) were completed in 1660.

286. Stanisław Tworek mentions him with his brother Krzysztof as co-owners of parts of the village of Bogucin near Lublin, *Zbór Lubelski i jego rola w ruchu ariańskim w Polsce w XVI i XVII wieku* (Lublin, 1966) 132, but does not mention his hospitality extended to the Cujavians.

287. Concerning the beginning of the important Minor Reformed community in Lublin, with which the Lubieniecki family had close connections and of which presumably also records or reminisces, our Author is strangely reticent. He only touches upon it here in his survey of episodes about the introduction of believers' baptism. He will pick up

the account of Lublin in some detail only after 1570, in chaps. 13 and 14. but at n. 766 he says that Jan Baptista Tęczynski (c. 1540–63), palatine of Bełz and *starosta* of Lublin, was their first patron. About the minister of Lublin, Stanisław Paklepka, our Author is again confused or misleading at n. 406. Of the theology of the Lubliners as of 1562, see Bk. 2, nn. 611, ¶5, and n. 617.

Here in the present context, thinking back about the eminent Cujavians, Lubieniecki wrongly dates the arrival of these Ditheist baptists to 1564, perhaps unwittingly associating them in his mind with the iconoclastic episode in Lublin of that date at n. 140. He will presently allude to the presence of the patron of the immersionist Cujavians, Jan Niemojewski, at the Diet of Lublin, at nn. 348, 375. A Polish MS in Kolozsvár provides some clues as to the developments between the death of Paklepka, pastor in Lublin, in 1565, and the independently ascertained date of the settlement of the Cujavians in 1570. This source is printed by Sipayłło, *AS*, 2.216–17. It reports that after the death of Paklepka the congregation was "orphaned, without a pastor," and that "Satan sent two false prophets among them" (for the date of Paklepka's death, see further n. 406). One of the "false prophets" was evidently their own elder, the Lublin wine merchant with commercial and religious ties with Transylvania, Walenty Krawiec, and the other *Pop* Ezaijasz Moskwiciny, one of seven Muscovite priests (*popów*) of socially and theologically radical teachings. Sipayłło adduces a related statement from Andrzej Węgierski, *ibid*, 217, n. 1, which says that Paklepka died in 1567 from bad weather and that the Cujavians, whom he calls "Servetians or Arians," settled in Lublin in 1570.

Mindful of the Węgierski annotation and holding to 1570 as the date of the final settlement of the immersionist Cujavians in Lublin, though noting Niemojewski's attendance at the Diet there in May 1566 (nn. 348, 375), Szczucki has much more on the career of Niemojewski between 1564 (Lubieniecki's evident misdating of the migration) and 1570. See his *Czechowic*, 74–83, on Czechowic and Niemojewski to their settlement in Lublin in 1570. For the baptism of Niemojewski by Czechowic in 1566, see n. 534.

Walenty Krawiec, whom the Polish Kolozsvár MS villifies as "infected by Hungarian and Lithuanian Judaism," is mentioned by Lubieniecki at n. 615, ¶5 as bearer of letters from Biandrata in Transylvania in 1569. See also nn. 275, 616, 779.

Pop Ezerjasz is said in the Polish Kolozsvár source to have escaped from the Grand Duke of Muscovy with seven other priests to Poland and that he became minister of one Wołozka, patron of Świerze (on the Wieprz), before becoming involved in affairs of the orphaned church in Lublin.

Not mentioned in the Polish Koloszvár MS, unless he was the second of the two "false prophets" (the source is unclear whether Krawiec is the second), was a Russian peasant leader, Feodosii Kosoi, of considerable influence in Muscovy, Lithuania, and Poland, who is given some prominence by A. I. Klibanov, *Reformatsionnye dvizheniia v Rossii vXIV–v pervoi polovine XVIvv* Реформационные движения в России в XIV-в пер-вои половине XIV вв (Reforming Movements in Russia from the Fourteenth through the First Half of the Seventeenth Century), (Moscow: Publishing House of the Academy of Sciences of the USSR, 1960), reviewed by Oswald P. Backus III, American Historical Review, 68:4 (1963) 1060–62. Kosoi escaped from his courtier lord (*gospodin*) in Muscovy in 1547 or at least in 1551, (p. 270), taking refuge with the Pskovian monk Artemii at a hermitage on the shore of White Lake (Beloozera), where he absorbed the monk's anti-clerical teaching in hte spirit of Nil Sorsky and the non-possessors. He was arrested in 1554 and brought to Moscow but escaped the same year, ending up in Lithuania and Poland (272–74) attested there as late as 1575. An antagonist among the Orthodox had a high estimate of his impact when he said: "The devil corrupted the West by Martin the German, and Lithuania through Kosoi'' (272). Kosoi and his Feodosians taught that Jesus taught that only God is above people, that Jesus was against human dominion, including that of the Orthodox priests and bishops. Jesus came, he said, to destroy all temple worship and that his apostles, following his instructions, met in simple rooms (296). Kosoi married a Jewess in Vitelsk. It is plausible to think that in Lublin some of the Feodosian spirit reached Ezaijasz and Krawiec. The Feodosian spirit called forth a major refutation from Zinovii Otensii, *The Evidence of the Truth, for those who Inquire about the New Teaching*. George Vernadsky places Kosoi in the Muscovite setting, *The Tsardom of Moscow, 1547–1682*, Part I (New Haven: Yale University Press, 1969) 68–78, as does Georges Florovsky, *Ways of Russian Theology*, Part I, tr. by Robert L. Nichols, (Belmont, Mass.: Nordland, 1979) 31.

For the Judaizing interlude in Lublin after the death of Paklepka and in 1565 the reorganization in 1570, see Szczucki, *Czechowic*, 84–85. The synod of Cracow, November 1566, reprimanded the Lublin congregation for the new Judaism of not invoking Christ in prayer. Cf. *RD* 6, n. 27. Tworek deals with the same episode, including Ezaijasz, and cites Soviet literature on the Muscovite and Novogorod Judaizers, *Zbór Lubelski*, 34–37. He does not cite the substantial collaborative work of Nataliia A. Kazakova and Ia. S. Lurie, *Antifeodal'nye ereticheskie dvizheniia na Rusi XIV – nachala XVI veka* Антифео-дальные еретические движения на Руси XIV-начала XVI века (Moscow/Leningrad, 1955). With many illustrations and documentation from 1416 to 1505, this work is important for the Orthodox background of the Judaizing priests who made their appearance in the Byzantine-rite parts of the Commonwealth in the sixteenth century, reaching among other places Lublin. See further Lurie, ''L'héresie des judaisants et ses sources historiques,'' *Revue des études slaves*, 45 (1966) 49–67. Lublin, with its own large Jewish community, a commercial entrepot and after 1569 a judicial seat, was a point of convergence of possibly three Judaizing impulses. Besides the Judaizing Orthodox priests and monks like *Pop* Ezaijasz, and some local Jewish proselytism and interfaith dialogue, there was the impulse from Judaizing Unitarianism in Transylvania (n. 275, ¶¶4, 5). The key figure in transmission here is Walenty Krawiec, wine merchant of Lublin (n. 615), on whose travels and notorious escapades Kossowski has written ''Judaizantyzm w Lublinie,'' in *Protestantyzm w Lublinie*, 34, n. 5. There was Sabbatarian and, to this extent, Judaizing Anabaptism in both Silesia and Slovakia. The literature for the first of the three impulses is surveyed by Jan Juszczyk, ''O badaniach nad Judaizantyzmem,'' *Kwartalnik Historyczny*, 76 (1969) 141–51; and I have a section, ''Judaizers in the Grand Duchy of Lithuania, ca. 1530–69/77,'' in my ''Protestants in the Ukraine,'' 1.41–72, esp. 50–56, 2.184–210. Here in n. 11 I have taken seriously the argument of Edward L. Keenan (1971) that the correspondence between Prince A. M. Kurbskii (1538–84) and Ivan IV the Terrible (Bk. 1, n. 133) may be aprocryphal, although valuable with respect to the dozen letters about Judaizers in the Commonwealth. On the neutral use of the term ''Judaizer,'' see at conclusion of paragraph on Róbert Dán, n. 275, ¶5.

In Little Poland and Lithuania (Vilna in particular) Jewish proselytism and particularly interfaith dialogue was mostly connected with the Karaites who did not follow the Talmudic tradition of the majority, ''the Rabbinites.'' Among the devotees of the Hebrew Bible alone was Isaak ben Abraham of Troki (c. 1533–c. 1594). See also Jakub of Bełżyce, to whom Czechowic replied in 1581 (n. 779). See Marek Wajsblum, ''Isaak Troky and the Christian Controversy,'' *Journal of Jewish Studies*, 3 (1952) 62–77. See further, Dán, *Vehe-Glirius*, chap. 8, ''Vehe-Glirius and the Polish Antitrinitarians,'' 173–201; and for the literature, nn. 8–9.

288. The text has *Judex terrae Inovroclavienis*; cf. n. 410. Inowrocław was the seat, southeast of Toruń, of the palatinate, one of two Cujavian palatinates (n. 194).

Niemojewski was converted to Protestantism by Discordia c. 1558. He served as deputy: in the Diet of Warsaw, 1556/57; of Piotrków, 1562 – 63, where he was a tireless member of the commission of inquiry on the execution of the laws respecting the royal demesne; and of Piotrków, 1565, where with Mikołaj Sienicki he fought hard against the spiritual and temporal lords (bishops and magnates) in the Senate. In the meantime, he had founded his own manorial church, c. 1563, and at Piotrków in March 1565 he sided with the Tritheists (see *Historia, 152*). In May 1565 he gave up his two pieces of Crown land; and, when he appeared at the Diet of Lublin in May 1566, it was with a wooden sword and without servants. In April 1566 he was rebaptized at the hands of Czechowic. For the fact that he was rebaptized in his home and hence perhaps in the Mennonite manner of pouring, cf. Zachorowski, "Najstarozy synody," 233. See Józefat Płokars, "Jan Niemojewski: Studjum z dziejów Arjan Polskich," *RwP* 2 (1922) 41 – 117; Szczucki, *Czechowic*, 6 passim (cf. n. above) and for the date of the baptism, 234 – 44, n. 8; Wilbur, *Socianism*, 336 passim; Szczucki and Tazbir, *PSB* 123 (1978) esp. 14A and n. 534.

289. The text has *Valentinus* as also does the Kolozsvár account, but Węgierski's annotation (n. 287, ¶1) has Laurentius and mentions also Szymon Siemianowski among the radical Cujavians joining the congregation in Lublin. Tworek, even without aware- ness of the Węgierski n., has Walenty Brzeziński and, like Lubieniecki, mentions also his brother Wojciech.

It was on the estate of Walenty Brzeziński that the antipedobaptist, anti-Trinitarian synod of Brzeziny of June 1565 met (n. 203).

It is likely that it was the son of one of these who, after the Lublin congregation was deprived of its meeting house in 1627, *chaps. 13 – 14*, gave over his house on *ulica* Olejnej to them: Kasper Jaruzel Brzeziński. Aleksander Kossowski, "Materjały z życia Arjan polskich w Lublinie," *RwP* 5 (1928) 77 – 80.

290. The "old custom" may refer to continuous regional usage or to the apostolic and patristic period (nn. 168ff.). Lubieniecki, a proponent of believers' immersion, is distracted from specifying where and when Brzeziński was baptized, perhaps along with his boon companion Jan Niemojewski.

291. *Historia, 177* near n. 195.

292. That Jan Siekierzyński was "primus in Polonia baptistarum" is stated by Węgierski (*Slavonia Reformata*, 537), no doubt from the same source, Budziński. Szczucki identifies this as Jan Siekierzyński, *Jr.* (*Czechowic*, 56, n. 136); although the index to the facsimile edition of the *Historia* identifies him as *senior, p. 325*.

293. Siekierzyński (Latinized form *Securinus*) derives from the Polish *siekiera* (axe). Jan Siekierzyński is a signatory (n. 51). He would become co-worker with Stanisław Far- nowski, leader of the Ditheists, who as a group within the anti-Trinitarian Reformed, would be the next after the Cujavians to practice as a grouping believers' baptism by immersion, where the Cujavians mentioned above were the first to introduce believers' baptism on the model of the Mennonites. Cf. Doc. 5, n. 20, and below, n. 534. In the context Lubieniecki seems to imply that believers' immersion on professed faith is "*the genuine baptismum*."

294. Phocion, Athenian general and statesman, often opposed by Demosthenes, and condemned to death 318 B.C., is described as prudent and responsible by Plutarch, *Life of Phocion*.

295. Jan Sieniński (Sienieński; d. 1600), castellan of Zarnów, 1588 palatine of Podolia, was a convert to Calvinism. His wife Jadwiga Gnoińska, sympathizing with the radicals, persuaded him to found Raków (*Historia, chap. 12*).

296. Sieniński.

297. Bobin (n. 51) was the place where Siekarzyński had preached.

298. Piotr Kazimirski (c. 1540–after 1598), royal captain of horse, fought a major battle with the Swedes at Weissenstein in 1562 and against the Muscovites under Mikołaj Radziwiłł the Black in 1564. Henryk Kotarski, *PSB* 12 (1966–67) 294–95.

299. A Roman centurion, converted in Caesaria, Acts 10:1–31.

300. Krzysztof Kazimirski, successor of Mikołaj Pac (Bk. 1, n. 186; Bk. 3, n. 239, ¶2) as Catholic bishop of Kiev, appointed 1599. *SPM* 1 (1954) 601.

301. Sieniński.

302. In the much reduced *Heroes* of Otwinowski in *Slavonia Reformata*, 535, Piotr Kazimirski is reduced to his mere name.

303. *Historia, 176*.

304. Katarzyna Sobieska died in 1562. The text erroneously gives the initial N. See *Life of Lubieniecki*, *Polish Brethren* 2.534, n. 11.

305. Although writing about his great uncle, Lubieniecki probably errs here. A. Lubieniecki is mentioned often earlier (Bk. 2, n. 437).

The Brudzewski family of the Pomian clan in Kujawy numbered a few Senators in the fourteenth and fifteenth century and during the reign of Sigismund I, but declined in the latter part of the sixteenth century. In any case it was Palatine Jan Słuszowski of Kujawy who was delegated by the Interregnum Diet to greet the King-elect, Henry of Valois (1573–74). Boniecki, *Herbarz Polski* 2.152–53; *Vol. Legum*, 2.858. Andrzej remained in Paris studying at the expense of King Henry on the basis of a provision of the *pacta conventa* worked out by a Confederation of Warsaw; see *Polish Brethren*, 2, Doc. XXIX, esp. preface, 545 and nn.

Henry, son of Catherine de'Medici, in France succeeded his brothers Francis II (1559–60), husband of Mary Stuart of Scotland, and Charles IX (1560–74), as Henry III (1574–89).

306. Andrew Lubieniecki.

307. Jan Zamoyski (1545–1605), who was responsible at the Election Diet of Warsaw for the provision that every knight (*szlachic*) had the right of electing the King (*virum*), founded Zamość.

308. Stanisław Żółkiewski (1547 or 1550–1620) from his earliest youth at the court of Zamoyski, filled his place as Grand Hetman of the Crown in 1613 and as Chancellor in 1618.

309. Andrew Lubieniecki.

310. He may have been received at court after the election of Stephen Báthory (1576–86). He left c. 1577.

311. He first served in Śmigiel, succeeding Jan Krotowski there in 1585; two years later by appointment of the synod in Chmielnik, he was pastor in Goslar on the Margraviate of Brandenburg near Wolfenbüttel.

312. Stanisław II (c. 1558–1633) was his older brother, married to Urszula Otwinowska.

313. Krzysztof I (1561–1624), married to Anna Otwinowska, was the grandfather of the Author.

314. The removal of Jan Niemojewski to Lublin as new base was made in 1570, anticipated with a date at n. 287 of the arrival there of Szczekocki in 1564.

However, Niemojewski conspicuously attended the Diet of Lublin, 7 May to c. 21 August 1566. His ditheistic pacifist anabaptism drew attention and served as occasion for several letters from Poland describing Polish anabaptism. Of these one was written from Cracow, 30 May 1566, by Jan Łasicki to Beza, Wotschke, *Briefwechsel*, no. 350; Beza, *Correspondance*, 7 (1973) no. 470, gives a valuable overview of anabaptism in the Commonwealth.

Łasicki connects the immersionist practice with Servetus and is the sole witness to the role of Stanisław Kokoszka in the transmission of Servetian ideas. He was a Cracovian student matriculated in Basel, 11 June 1557, who, for a season in the service of Laelius Socinus, helped transmit Servetian writings to Poland (*Correspondance*, 7.109, n. 3). Łasicki accents the teaching and practice of Grzegorz Paweł and Gonesius and is specific about the baptizands entering a river for immersion, *Correspondance*, 271; 108. Rotondò holds that he also transmitted the MS writings of Laelius himself, perhaps notably *Brevis expicatio* (Bk. 2, n. 1, ¶2), *Opere*, 355, n. 118.

Wotschke conveniently excerpts the relevant portion of a letter from Lublin itself, 31 May 1566, by Andrzej Krajewski to Bishop Hosius (*Briefwechsel*, p. 272, n. 1). Krzysztof Trecy wrote letters about Lublin to Bullinger (*Briefwechsel*, 273, n. 1) from Cracow, 1 August 1566, no. 351 (only general remarks on Anabaptists and Arians dealt with more fully in the lost letter), and another to Beza, also lost, but an earlier response of Beza, 1 November 1565, indicates that Trecy had already told him that, according to the innovators, ''repetendus erit necessario Baptismus in omnibus sub Papatu baptizatis, quoniam in falsum Patrem, Filium et Spiritum sanctum fuerint baptizati.'' *Correspondance*, 6, no. 428. For the earlier letter of Trecy to Bullinger, also referring to immersion, see n. 203, ¶3.

It is true that the letter of Łasicki to Beza of 30 May 1566, cited more than once in the present annotation and in the scholarly literature, is not regarded by Pirnát as valid testimony to the practice of believers' immersion among the Brethren of Little Poland until after the synod of Pełsznice of October 1568, where ''not a little hilarity broke out'' when the participants, among them Grzegorz Paweł, had it brought home to them that, despite several years of discussion, no one had yet among them submitted to immersion. Sipayłło, AS, 2.220–21; Pirnát, ''Il martire e l'uomo politico,'' 172 and nn. 19 and 31. Pirnát holds that therefore even Grzegorz had not yet acted on his own principle and that Łasicki, for his part, in writing to Beza had access to Biandrata's monitory passage on believers' baptism in the letter of 21 September to Grzegorz (n. 236, ¶3) and that he only intended to alarm the Genevese about an imminent development. But surely the evidence of Lubieniecki himself makes clear the extent, before October 1568, of antipedobaptist thought, of the disposition to postpone the baptism of progeny, and of actual rebaptism in some cases by immersion. Cf. instances around n. 443 in Bk. 1 and around nn. 186 and 190 in Bk. 2.

Pirnát may not sufficiently distinguish among ''Latin-rite'' use (1) the late medieval conventional, usually festive *domestic*, pedobaptism; (2) Protestant infant baptism in the church; (3) baptism delayed into childhood; (4) (re)baptism of adult believers by sprinkling; (5) (re)baptism of adult believers by immersion, whether indoors or without, a tactical matter; (6) believers' baptism of the catechumens but without the enforcement of rebaptism on adult adherents; and (7) the suspension of baptism as an ordinance, except for converts from non-Christendom. The last was the view of Socinus. Before he aroused a new baptismal controversy in the Commonwealth, the persons and groups reflected on the pages of Lubieniecki went through positions 2, 3, 5. The position of the German Anabaptists was mostly 1. The position of the English Baptists who arose in the seventeenth century was 5. Their mode of baptism derived from the Polish Brethren in exile in Holland.

The Transylvanian Unitarians moved from 2 (n. 279) through 3 (n. 280, ¶3), back to 2, with some at 7 (n. 275, ¶3). The fact is that Paruta's letter to Lutomirski of 1574, as interpreted by Budziński, (nn. 328, 331), could even testify to the practice of rebaptism (5) inside some of the local churches of the Transylvanian Unitarians (n. 378) as of that date (cf. for c. 1570 n. 280, Torda, 1578, n. 600), though later abandoned as an unacceptable innovation (n. 280, ¶4).

Although there was some amusement at the synod of Pełsznica about how long believers' baptism had been discussed and how few synodists had actually submitted to rebaptism, it is very likely that this synod had been called together by Hieronim Filipowski to unite the Ditheist Cujavians and Farnovians and the fully Unitarian Brethren (Wajsblum, ''Dyteiści,'' 68). The synod was socially radical and may well mark the moment when baptism was subsiding as an issue in Little Poland and the mood was forming for a Polish counterpart at Raków of the Hutterite *Bruderhof.*

315. Lubieniecki evidently picked up from his own library shelf this important book (anticipated at n. 282) on the origin of the errors of the pedobaptists and on the opinion that infants should be baptized at the earliest age. The date 1575 has passed into the scholarly literature, but Gryczowa, no. 13, pp. 148f., on the basis of the research of Szczucki (*Czechowic*, 278), describes the book in its printed form as that of the printer Aleksander Rodecki in Cracow between 1580 and 1583, antedated for publication.

316. Jan Kiszka (d. 1592) was the son of Anna Radziwiłłówna K. mentioned at n. 212.

317. Cf. with a letter of the brethren of Brest at n. 259.

318. Jakub Kalinowski attended the synod of Skrzynno in 1567. Kalinowski was an associate of Grzegorz Paweł in a collective work of the Raków community *Adversus Jacobi Palaelogi scriptum* 1573. See *BAnt*, 48 for the book, 45 for the synod; Szczucki, *Czechowic* 49, passim.

319. On Jan and Jadwiga, see n. 295.

Lubieniecki defers to chap. 12 his fuller account of the founding of Raków, intercepting it here on the sole issue of immersion, a practice particularly associated with the utopian settlement and one vigorously opposed by Socinus, who refused to submit to its baptismal order.

320. Samuel Przypkowski (1593–1670) is represented in *Polish Brethren* with three Documents (XI-1 and 2, XXXIII-2). The last is his letter of 1663 added to the *Historia* by B. Wiszowaty as its original editor.

321. Fausto Sozzini, nephew of Lelio, arrived in Cracow in 1579.

The anonymous *Vita Fausti Socini Senensis descripta ab Equite Polono* (1636) appears in translation as RD 8.

322. ''After a time Securinus came forward as the first to defend the opinion of Socinus.'' This would be Jan Sierkierzyński Jr., the first to have been rebaptized among the Poles (n. 292). Sharpe, ed., *Vita*, 37/36.

323. The three were: Stanisław (II), Andrzej the Elder, and Krzysztof, the three sons of Stanisław (I) by his first wife, Katarzyna Sobieska L., n. 304. Sharpe, ed. *Vita* 37/36; *BAnt*, 227.

324. Lubieniecki here seems to be as positive as his aforementioned three great uncles about Socinus, who was opposed to believers' baptism; but our Author evidently remained loyal to his tradition on toleration, having embraced, rather, ''the milder and moderate [societary] views of Socinus.''

325. Cf. *Vita* of Wiszowaty, *BAnt*, 227; *Polish Brethren, Doc. I*, 23 (no. 75.1). In contrast to the author of the *Vita* of Wiszowaty, Lubieniecki expressly states his view that the Major Church separated from the Minor, which Lubieniecki treats in his *Historia* as continuous in the Reformation impulse that started with Luther and in Poland with the Reformed Church in Little Poland and that carried the principles of Calvin, according to Lubieniecki, to their logical conclusion in restoring "the truth of the Primitive Church."

326. Lubieniecki is here thinking of the Minor Reformed Church as continuous with the synod first established in Pińców and hence of the Stancarist synod of 1561 and the Major Reformed synod in 1565 as "schismatic" with respect to his own tradition running through Łaski.

327. The minister of the conservative Reformed congregation in Cracow was, as of 1562, Szymon Żak, formerly superintendent in Podlachia. The smaller Reformed schismatic congregation was under Grzegorz Paweł, who had been minister of all the Reformed in Cracow from 1552 to 1562. He was obliged to leave Cracow in 1566 and was succeeded from Vilna by Wojciech Kościeński, on whom see further *Historia, 193, 218*.

328. Niccolò Paruta, mentioned in *Historia, 40*, one of the presumed members of the Vicenza circle, lived in Slavkov (Austerlitz, where Ochino died in 1564). From 1571 to 1581 he lived in the home of Biandrata in Transylvania. His letter may have been prompted by his host. It is dated by *BAnt*, 25–26 as of 1574. Paruta's relationship with Biandrata and the baptismal issue are touched upon by Pirnát, "Il martire e l'uomo politico," 166. The same letter is carefully analysed by Firpo (*Antitrinitari*, 232–34), who recognizes that the Paruta letter, transmitted from Budziński in two variant snippets by Sand and Lubieniecki, is obscure, as is also Lutomirski's response as reported by Lubieniecki as though it came after the arrival of Socinus and Socinus's challenge to the immersionist practice of the Polish Brethren (n. 282).

Related testimony can at this point be introduced. Jacobus Palaeologus, who had been a guest of Dudith in Cracow, 1571–72, writing in 1580 in his Defense of Dávid (nn. 401, 602) against the synodal *Judicium* of the Polish Churches of 1579, refers, in connection with the controveresy over the adoration of Christ, to how when he was there it was reported by Niccolò Paruta that prayers were directed to Jesus Christ when some were being baptized according to the practice introduced by Grzegorz Paweł ("Nam cum Cracouiae essem, in publica actione cume essent aliqui de more introducto a Gregorio baptizandi a Nicolao Paruta audiui, publicas preces & quidem longas directras fuisse ad Iesum Christum . . ."), Palaeologus, *Defensio*, ed. Dán, p. 341. It would appear from this recollection that Paruta was, like Palaeologus, present in Cracow and in this case actually an observer of the immersional practice of the Polish Brethren in Cracovia and that his communication, reported by Budziński, was thus in the context of a visit and not a letter from Transylvania or Moravia.

329. The controversy was evidently over whether believers' baptism should take place in the meeting place or at a stream *in public*. Immersion would have been hard to effect for an adult in a parish church baptismal font and many of the meetings of the Brethren took place in new structures without any such provision. Lubieniecki is reticent about making clear to his readers that his "true baptism" is, in fact, immersion in flowing water.

330. There is nothing in this passage that could suggest that Lutomirski and his wife had been recently baptized naked and that this could only have been at a stream or pond. Firpo, aware of this passage (*Antitrinitari*, 230–31, n. 143), adduces a letter in Italian of Biandrata to Andrea Dudith, 22 November 1573: "Mi scrivono ch'el nostro Lutomirsky

(*sic*) cum la moglie nudi sono immersi nel aqua cum parecchi voti e giuramenti fatti.''
A. Veress, ed., *Documente privitoare la istoria Ardealului, Moldavei și Țării-Românești*, 16.

Lutomirski, writing c. 1575, commenting on that part of Paruta's text excerpted by Budziński, seems to be calling for moderation as to the *meaning* of baptism for salvation, as once in writing from Węgrów in 1565 (*Historia, 179*) he called for "moderation" on the form of baptism. But given the fact of his own dramatic anabaptism, it would appear that he is actually calling for the *general* observance ot believers' baptism in the Minor Church. In support of this interpretation, note Lubieniecki's own *Sed* at n. 332.

As for places, Lutomirski with respect to baptism probably meant immersion in ponds or rivers and at baptismal fonts within sanctuaries. As for times, he probably meant that the ancient baptismal occasions of Easter and Pentecost needed not be the only times.

331. Sand (*BAnt*, p. 26) dates the letter 1574 and quotes from about the same place in Budziński's History as Lubieniecki, rendering the sense of the Polish somewhat differently, namely that those "approaching the church (*ad ecclesiam accendentes*) in order to avoid perils on account of the ceremony, are not to be asked as to whether this *rebaptisatio* be necessary for achieving salvation.'' It is just possible that Wiszowaty, as editor of Sand, or Lubieniecki, intentionally obscured his Latin transcript of Budziński's rendering in Polish of Paruta's original in Latin, although this seems utterly foreign to the self-effacing editor. As the transcript stands, *ablutio* is a synonym for *rebaptisatio*, or believers' baptism of catechumens, but *inside* the meeting house.

The unidentified locale of *rebaptisatio* inside a church would appear to be, not Slavkov but Kolozsvár (nn. 314, ¶7 and 328). However, Jarmola, *op. cit.*, suggests that Paruta wrote from Moravia in 1566 and that Lutomirski's letter of 1566 (*BAnt*, p. 42) may well be the response of Lutomirski.

332. The referent would better be Lutomirski rather than Paruta. Lutomirski did not prevail with his desire for general observance of believers' baptism.

333. Lubieniecki seems to be intentionally inexplicit. The next sentence with a late example suggests a mixed practice of the ordinance of baptism in the Minor Church, more the consequence of Socinus than of Paruta.

Lubieniecki was very conscious of Socinus as he finished his chapter on baptism and of the debate between Czechowic and the Italian controversialist of 1580 (n. 682). As for the debate of 1578/79 in Transylvania (n. 602), Lubieniecki undoubtedly sympathized with Socinus on Christology and the adoration of Christ, although in the conflict with Dávid (*Historia, chap. 11*), he would be similarly unclear about the fateful contest, but he opposed Socinus on baptism/believers' immersion, without wishing to say so. Indeed, Lubieniecki's *own* view of baptism is put on the lips of an irenic Faustus representing liberal Protestantism in an ecumenical colloquium among Hadrian, Cyril (for the Orthodox), Martin, and John, guests of their genial host and occasional moderator and intervener, the layman George, in his *Compendium Veritatis Primaevae*, ed. by Jørgensen, 2.103–16, these views on baptism being succinctly set forth by the editor in his introduction, 1.70–71. From the main text it is clear that "Faustus"/Lubieniecki holds to baptismal position 6, not the position 7 of the historical Faustus (n. 314, ¶6). "Faustus," speaking for Lubieniecki, (cf. n. 425) observes that the immersionist Polish Brethren (only temporarily thrown off by Socinus) are in communion with the Transylvanian Brethren who by then have wholly reverted to Reformed pedobaptism.

334. Wiskowski was rebaptized as late as 1653 (hence the *verum tamen*) at a time when it was increasingly difficult to be an "Arian," not to say also an Anabaptist, and all

the more notable and perilous for a nobleman with more than manorial responsibilities in the Royal Commonwealth.

335. Janusz Radziwiłł (1612–55) became palatine of Vilna in 1653, Grand Hetman of Lithuania a year later.

336. Lady Wiśnowska presumably remained Calvinist. Lubieniecki more than once refers to wives disparagingly; even when it is the "Arian" wife of a Calvinist lord who induces her husband to found Raków, Lubieniecki does not deign to give her more than her clan name at n. 319.

NOTES TO CHAPTER FOUR

337. Thus far Lubieniecki has used the term *Pontificii* primarily for prelates, seldom for parish priests, never for the Catholic King or Catholic magnates. The chapter heading is in any case probably from Wiszowaty. Henceforth the term includes members of the orders and sometimes parish priests.

338. Thus far in the main text Lubieniecki has used this term *Calviniani* for mèmbers of the Major Church. The same term for the conservative Reformed evolved as the basic nomenclature also in Transylvania (n. 132, ¶1). Members of the Minor [Reformed] Church regarded themselves as *cultores* or *confessores Veritatis*, as consequent or consistent Calvinists or simply and (a bit presumptuously) as *Christiani*, e.g., Lubieniecki in the opening sentence below as even, as here, *Catholici*. The Brethren also always rejected the designation of their Calvinist and Catholic detractors, "Arians," and "Anabaptists." In the opening sentence below Lubieniecki refers to the Calvinist detractors as *Reformati* or *Evangelici*; the usage of Bishop Padnewski at n. 372.

339. The term "dissidents" differs from that of "Dissenters" from the Established Church in England by the Act of Uniformity of 1662. The special Polish usage of the term first appeared in the Covenant of Warsaw of 1573, "*dissidentes de religione*." Those disagreeing concerning religion implicitly included also Catholics, and when the term appeared in the Henrician Articles of 1574, it even more strongly presumed that alike the Roman Catholics and the Protestants were part of the Latin community of faith. This was also stressed by the interregnum covenants of 1586 and 1587 which spoke of the Warsaw Covenant/Confederation as a covenant *inter dissidentes de religione*. It was only the General Confederation of the interregnum of 1632 that narrowed the meaning of the term to the Protestants, including the Polish Brethren. During the interregnum of 1648 attempts were made to exclude the Brethren as Arians from the scope of this term. The statutes of 1659, 1660, and 1661, expelling the "Arians," achieved this effect. All of this history in passionate and learned rhetoric Lubieniecki himself (anonymously) rehearses in *The Legal Claims for the Freedom of the Religion of Unitarians in Poland* (*BAnt*, 265–76; *Polish Brethren*, Doc. XXVIII).

The demotion from the rank of licit *dissidentes* was not expressly formulated constitutionally until 1696, when it was stated that neither "Arians and apostates [i.e. from the Roman Catholic Church] nor Quakers nor Mennonites shall be embraced within this covenant." After the treaty of 1768 the term "dissidents" comprised all non-Catholic Christians, such as Protestants and Greek Orthodox. See. E. Bursche, "Z dziejów nazwy dysydeńci'," *Przegląd Historyczny* 25 (1926); Józef Siemienski, "Dysydeńci w ustawodawstwie," *RwP* 5; 2 (1928) 81ff.; Marek Wajsblum, *Ex Regestro arianismi* (Warsaw, 1948) 28 passim.

340. This *regalis caritatis lex* was appealed to by the Silesian Spiritualist as the *lex regia* first in his *Admonition to All the Brethren in Silesia*, 11 June 1524, *Corpus Schwenckfeldianorum*, 2.62. See also my *Radical Reformation*, 107.

341. Cf. Rom 8:27.

342. The Thirty Years War, 1618 – 48.

343. Evidently the War of Liberation, 1568 – 1648.

344. Probably he means more than the eight Civil Wars of Religion, 1562 – 98.

345. The Civil Wars, 1642 – 49.

346. Stanislas Lubieniecki, *Theatrum Cometicum*, 6 vols. (Amsterdam, 1668: 2nd edition, Leyden, 1681). This work preserves the engraving of the Author, *Polish Brethren*, 516. In correspondence with Johann Ernst Rautenstein, diplomat in the service of Philip Wilhelm of the house of Neuburg (1664f.), Lubieniecki protested against wars originating from *cupiditas* and denounced specifically the contemporary wars between England, France, and Holland as occasioned by competition for markets, colonies, and domination of the sea. See *Theatrum Cometicum*, 1.36, 49, 89, 93, and 116, and Tazbir, *Lubieniecki*, 200 – 02, esp. n. 51.

347. In his "olim nostra Polonia Felix" the author surely alludes to the work of his great uncle, *Poloneutychia*.

348. By fixing upon a personal episode, Lubieniecki misrepresents the general facts, apparently confusing the so-called decree of Lublin of 13 June 1566 with the earlier decree of Parczów of 1564, which had been virtually abolished by the opposition of the gentry. See Bk. 1, n. 255, Bk. 3, n. 137. At the Diet of Lublin in 1566, the conservative Reformed and the Lutherans, led by Stanisław Myszkowski, tried to pass a decree proscribing all *Trideitae* and *Anabaptistae*, both clerical and lay. To gain the support of the bishops, they agreed that every suspect should abjure trinitarian and baptismal heresies before an episcopal court. However, the Catholic bishops refused to be drawn into what they understood as an implicit recognition of other Protestant tenets, while a large part of the Deputies (including Mikołai Sienicki) under the leadership of Filipowski, likewise denounced these moves. Thereupon the representatives of the Major Church attempted to have at least the preachers among the Anabaptist Tritheist Reformed exiled. This attempt likewise failed. In the upper House, Sigismund II Augustus, under the pressure of the lay Senators, declared that "Arians and Anabaptists" should not be tolerated, but banished on the basis of old statutes voted in the defense of the common peace. However, this declaration in its turn was opposed by the episcopal Senators and never became a decree.

Among "the adversaries" on the ministerial side was Trecy, who recounts his role in the effort of the Calvinists to rid Poland "by water and fire" of the Reformed schismatics and heretics—this in a letter to Beza, Cracow, 12 July 1566, *Correspondance*, 7 (1566), no. 482, pp. 177 – 80, esp. at n. 6. See also the already cited letter of Łasicki to Beza, 30 May 1566, ibid., no. 470, pp. 107 – 10, esp. at n. 8. See Stanislas Bodniak, "Sprawa wygnania Arjan w roku 1566," *RwP* 5 (1928) 2.52 – 59; Wilbur, *Socinianism*, 340, n. 3; and esp. Pirnát in n. 354, where he holds that there is little evidence for such a parliamentary action and that in any case Filipowski was not yet himself immersed and that his real danger lay in his having indirectly sought to support the succession of John Sigismund to the Polish throne.

349. Mikołaj Myszkowski, burgrave of Cracow, died in 1557. Dworzaczek, *Genealogia*, table 130. Halina Kowalska, "M.M.," *PSB* 22 (1977), 397B, doubts that the envy because of the marriage caused the conflict among the surviving Filipowskis and Myszkowskis.

Although by n. 369 our Author acknowledges that he is drawing on Budziński, it is plausible that some of this narrative, dealing as it does with a crisis in the life of his own grandsire, Filipowski, comes to his pen out of his own family lore.

350. Anabaptism was a capital offense in the Codex of Theodosius II and that of Justinian, but capital punishment had not been proposed by the Polish Diet.

351. The six other Deputies of the Palatinate of Cracow were all members of the Reformed Church. Ludwik Kolankowski, "Posłowie Sejmów Zygmunta Augusta," *RwP* 5 (1928) 131.

352. Marcin or Marcian Przyłęchi, member of the Major Church, was against the capital threat. Przyłęchi was the castle judge of Cracow, and a Deputy to all the Diets of Sigismund Augustus beginning with the Diet of Warsaw 1563/4. See Kolankowski, "Posłowie," 127–138; Dalton, *Lasciana*, 512, where his name is misspelled.

353. As of 1566 Jan Zamoyski (n. 307) was also Deputy Chancellor of the Treasury.

354. The text reads *dilatio* (deferral), but it probably intended *delatio*, although even *dilatatio* (exaggeration) is a possibility.

Pirnát places the whole paragraph, with its reference to John II Sigismund Zápolya (Bk. 1, n. 150, Bk. 3, ch. 11), in the setting of Transylvanian history, "El martire e l'uomo politico," 178. He sees the episode as not unconnected with Lasocki and Filipowski's support of the expedition of Jacob Heraclides into Moldavia through Commonwealth territory (Bk. 2, chap. 9). These two boon companions would not have been made privy, in any case, to any ultimate scheming of Maximilian in 1561 to have had John Sigismund dethroned in the interest of the Despot's ruling over a greater Walachia (Bk. 2, n. 725, ¶3) and thus a threat to the Commonwealth. Pirnát also holds that the charge in 1566 against Filipowski as a Tritheist and Anabaptist *as of 1566* was invalid, only the second possibly so after the synod of Pełsznica of 1568 (n. 314, ¶5), and that Lubieniecki was seeking on this pretext to draw the attention of the reader from the prophecy of Filipowski that John Sigismund might eventually succeed his heirless uncle, Sigismund II, as an elected (Unitarian) King of Poland. After quoting at length a portion of *Historia, 195*, Pirnát notes the pretext of Suleiman's thirteenth and final expedition (n. 128, ¶8) against Emperor/King Maximilian II/I, in 1566 was to check any further "private" Hapsburg expeditions, like the adventure of Jacob Heraclides, directed against his vassal. To this end he had asked his client Voivode John Sigismund, himself a claimant to the Hungarian throne, to meet him, which he did, at Belgrade, 29 June 1566. In the meantime the Transylvanian estates at the Diet of 28 May–3 June voted to declare war against Maximilian. As a courtesy, John Sigismund had informed his royal Polish uncle of his intended audience with the Sultan. Pirnát finds it therefore quite possible that Filipowski really prophesied the election of John Sigismund, but for the death of Suleiman during the seige of Szigetvár. Pirnát also substantiates his surmise that Sigismund Augustus was quite ready to make up with Filipowski, as he was considering letting go his third queen (Bk. 1, n. 197), Catherine, the sister of his first, Hapsburg, wife, and that in any event he had no intention of joining Maximilian and becoming involved in war against the Turks and his own nephew (and plausibly electable successor).

355. Stanislas Cichowski, Sr., protector of Grzegorz Paweł in Cracow, is mentioned in *Historia, 15, 132, 143, 171*; by Schomann in connection with the Diet of Lublin, 1566, (RD 3, n. 28); and by Biandrata in a letter to Dudith, 1575, (n. 718, ¶2)

356. Stanislas Zamoyski (1519–72) was castellan of Chełm in 1566.

The account here of Filipowski, of Zamość, of angry son and reprimanding father, of Sigismund Augustus whatever the historicity of the encounters, displays the sense of fierce fraternal loyalty, of which the members of the *szlachta* were capable of whatever rank, thinking of each other as brothers (or fathers) in the knighthood. Psychologically the episodic account, disproportionate to the often spare theological accounts of the *historia Reformationis*, illuminates the author and his intended loyalty to the King of Poland, even to his own John Casimir under whom he had left Poland in 1657.

357. Maciej of Miechów (Miechowita), M.D. (1457–1523), was a canon of Cracow, professor of medicine, a prominent historian and geographer of international fame. He was the author of *Chronica Polonorum* (Cracow, 1519), the first history of Poland to be printed. Leszek Hajdukowicz, *PSB* 19 (1974) 28–34.

358. Filipowski's enemies.

359. The text reads *Zucovius* (Żukowski). There were three Łukowskis: Balcer, judge of Sandomierz (*Historia, 63*), Kacper, and Kilian (Bk. 2, n. 160). Balcer and Kilian both appear as Deputies of the Palatinate of Sandomierz at the diets of Sigismund Augustus. Both were Calvinists. Probably Balcer is here meant, for he was a leader of the Calvinist gentry and took a prominent part in the life of the Major Church. Dalton, *Lasciana*, 410, 440, 478, 514.

Mikołaj Wolski is not further identified, evidently on the same side as "Mareschalcus" Myszkowski. Lubieniecki in the chronological context could only mean the courtier Zygmunt Myszkowski (d. 1578), married to Beata Przerębska, a cousin of Mikołaj M., whose widow married Filipowski (at n. 349), and a cousin also of Stanislas Myszkowski, most prominent of his clan in the *Historia*. On him, see Bk. 2, nn. 173, 220. But Lubieniecki surely errs in calling this Zygmunt M. "Marshal of the Court." He has read back that honor from the homonymic son Zygmunt Myszkowski (1562–1615), who was indeed Marshal of the Great Crown, 1603. Dworzaczek, *Genealogia*, table 130.

360. There is some similarity to 2 Tim 3:12. The quotation has not been otherwise identified.

361. Hieronim Filipowski.

362. This may be the son of Andrzej Gnojeński (d. 1572), burgrave of Cracow.

363. A relation of Jadwiga Gnoińska, foundress of Raków (n. 295).

364. On Zak (Zacius), see Bk. 1, n. 227; Bk. 3, nn. 61, 197, 327. He had returned from service under Mikołaj Radziwiłł, who was dissatisfied with his severe Calvinism, to serve as pastor in Cracow and district superintendent, 1563–70, whereupon he removed to the salt town of Bochnia, where he occasionally preached to the miners. For his dates in Cracow, see Wengierski, *Chronik*, ix. In Bochnia, under the name of his half-illiterate wife, Katarzyna Przekłotówna, he acquired landed property, which she energetically managed. Zak died in the winter of 1576/1577; she in 1595, and she left his library to the Calvinists. See the note of Wacław Urban, drawing upon an important but obscure article of S. Warcholik (1959), "Spuścizna Szymona Zacjusza," *OiRwP* 19 (1977) 201.

365. The wedding seems to have occurred on a Sunday. It is unlikely that Zak would have been preaching (and also haranguing) from two to six p.m. on any other day. His discourse was a *concio*, a sermon.

366. From his conservative Reformed pulpit in Cracow.

367. Zak was purveying excitedly a notion that probably drew its plausibility from tales of the Adamite extremists among the Czech Brethren. See my *Radical Reformation*, 208, 507, 511 for a recurrent theme about radicals in different periods appealing to prelapsarian Adam and Eve. Lubieniecki seems willing enough to retell the tendentious tale, secure in the subsequent refutation of Budziński, eyewitness.

368. Lubieniecki capitalizes the name of the tree in reference to Juno, goddess of women in their sexuality, and perhaps alludes to Dan 13:54, 58, where, however, it is *sub schino*.

369. Budziński after the death of Jan Łaski (1560), whom he had served, successively served Prospero Provana and Hieronim Filipowski.

370. *Historia, 158*.

371. The sermon of Zak in Cracow.

372. Bishop Filip Padniewski (1560–72). There is no further explanation for Budziński's *tributum* by Zelewski who has no record of Budziński in his *Materiały w Krakowie*.

373. This stray material from Budziński on dissenters of the patristic age shows the context in which he preserved the false account of an "Adamic" or paradisaic wedding. He evidently, like Lubieniecki after him, sought to show the lack of probity in opponents of the Brethren, in this case Zak, as three (approved) ancients were vilified by the orthodox.

374. *Historia, 194* at n. 348.

375. All these conservative ministers had appeared in the text before except Krzysztof Trecy (d. 1590). Already prominent in our nn., he was the intellectual leader of the Calvinists in his time, rector of the school in Cracow, soon to be a major figure in the Union of Sandomierz of 1570. Jan Czubek, "K.T.," *RwP* 1 (1921) 35–42.

376. The text has *N. Myscovius metropoleos regni praefectus*. But this is surely Stanislas (Bk. 2, n. 173). He was also palatine of Cracow, appointed 17 June 1565. Merzyng, *Zbory i senatorowie*, 130; Dworzaczek, *Genealogia*, table 130. For the role of Myszkowski in Lublin, 1566, see n. 348.

377. Grzegorz Paweł left Cracow about 1566. See n. 327.

378. The text reads *Coscenius*, mentioned at n. 327.

379. Budziński perhaps left the service of Provana precisely when Filipowski became palatine treasurer.

380. Johann Sylvanus, one of the three Palatinate Unitarians, was decapitated in Heidelberg, 1572 (Bk. 2, nn. 362, 364).

381. Lubieniecki mentioned Neuser above, Book 2, at n. 296, n. 364. He errs here on the duration of imprisonment. Neuser escaped prison and made his way to Hungary; but, finding the further way to Transylvania barred, he returned to the Palatinate and was arrested, 25 November 1570 at Amberg. He was transported to the Tower of Heidelberg, the dungeon of Seltenleer. He escaped 14 May 1571. He made his way probably by sea to Poland, thence to Transylvania. Head of the School in Kolozsvár in 1572, he advocated nonadorantism of Christ and is said to have influenced Ferenc Dávid. Neuser died in Istanbul 1576, a convert to Islam. Wilbur, *Socinianism*, 260–61. Pirnát, *Ideologie*, 19–20, Dán, *Vehe-Glirius*, 126–36 and text 7.

382. The radical Reformed minister of Śmigiel (Schmiegel) at the time may have been Jan Krotowski, predecessor of Andrzej Lubieniecki the Elder (n. 311). Of the Polish itinerary of Neuser preserved by Budziński/Lubieniecki, Dán seems to have been unaware, as he summarizes the career of Neuser, *Vehe-Glirius*, 35–36. It seems unlikely that Neuser would have gone to France and the Netherlands when he was so well acquainted with and welcome in the Unitarian Church in Transylvania.

383. John II Sigismund Zápolya, however, had already died in 1571 to be succeeded by the tolerant Catholic Stephen Báthory. See n. 387.

384. In the spring of 1572, Krzysztof Trecy, rector of the Calvinist school of Cracow, denounced Neuser to the local captain, invoking the edict of Parczów of 1564. Wotschke, "Die Reformation in Kosten [Kościan near Śmigiel]," *Correspondenzblatt des Vereins für die Geschichte der evangelischen Kirche Schlesiens* (Liegnitz, 1905) 9.174–75.

385. This is the first mention by Lubieniecki of the outstanding classicist of Transylvania. However, Johann Sommer was mentioned in our annotation as a major source of the life of the Reformed voivode of Moldavia, Jacob Heraclides (1561–63) (Bk. 2, n. 695). He is brought in at this chronological point that is hard to reconcile with the known outlines of his life and movements, for he signed his most important theological work, the *Refutatio* against Károlyi, in Transylvania, 24 June 1572, and he died there of the plague, 8 August 1574 (n. 632; Dán and Pirnát, *Antitrinitarianism*, 189, n. at bottom). From all that is known of his life—and a true biography is difficult, despite the survival of many of his writings—it is not at all likely that he would have been in Cracow between the dates aforementioned. Thus the date 15 April 1572 has been inserted on the basis of an entry in the *Nieznana Kronika Arianska* and on the assumption that Budziński was well informed of the situation in Transylvania and that his notices of regnal and other developments are plausible and that Neuser would have had to take some time for his escape from Heidelberg, 14 May 1571 (n. 381), to travel as extensively as indicated by Budziński. Under the date of 1571 *Nieznana Kronika*, I, ed. Szczucki, 171, reports that in Germany Adam Neuser, pastor in Heidelberg, Sylvanus, and Vehe (alias Glirius) were thrown into prison and that Neuser escaped. In the same *Nieznana Kronika*, II, ed. Dobrowolski, 166, it goes on, under the date of 1572, to report that after being incarcerated also in Transylvania, Neuser, tipped off, escaped, wandered extensively in France and Lower Germany and then "*iterum* in Transylvaniam abiit *cum Joanne Sommero*, qui matrem in Germaniam inviserat, Cracoviam venerat, et cum Adamo Claudiopolin discessit." It is quite plausible that Sommer would have found time to visit his mother and may have even discussed, possibly with Budziński, (the possible ultimate source of this information), the publication of his *Refutatio* in Cracow, but which would in the end only be published there by his erstwhile fellow prisoner in Heidelberg, Vehe. See nn. 631, 632.

The fullest account of Sommer with special reference to his career in Eastern Europe is that of Pirnát, *Ideologie der Siebenbürger*, chap. 1, which supplies the earlier literature, nn. 1–5, but not expressly, Bock, *Historia, 1, 888–94*. Born in Pirna on the Elbe in (then) Ducal Saxony c. 1540, the town having become Lutheran a year before, he acquired a fundamental classical education, for which he was admirably suited, becoming a master of several forms of Greek and Latin prosody. He joined the expedition of Jacob Heraclides and became rector of the humanistic academy and the library established by the voivode at Cotnari. After the murder of his patron, Sommer fled to Transylvania, establishing himself as headmaster in the school in Kronstadt (Braşov), where he wrote the two works relating to the Moldavian episode (the *Vita* published there, Corona, 1567), and *Reges Hungarici* [through Ferdinand and John I Zápolya] *carmine elegiacio*, BAnt, 57; Pirnát, *Ideologie der Siebenbürger*, 19. From 1567 to 1570 he was headmaster of the school in Bistritz. In the fall of 1569, suffering severely from colic, he imitated Lucianus in his *Colicae et podagrae tyrannis* and sent it, dedicated to the court physician in Alba Julia, 1 January 1570. It is thus plausible that Dr. Biandrata was instrumental in procuring the services of the accomplished classicist and Siebenbürger patriot for the school at Kolozsvár. George Haner of Schässburg speaks of him as already rector of the school by 1570, *Historia* 286. As lector there, however, he signed his creative reworking of *De strategematibus Satanae* in 8 books (Basel, dedicated to Queen Elizabeth, 1565) of the Italian humanist and protagonist of toleration, Jacob Acontius, namely, into 5 books augmented and stylistically improved, Kolozsvár, 1570. Thus a great classic of religious toleration was introduced into the relams of Transylvania and Poland.

Born of an aristocratic family in Trent (or nearby Ossana), Acontius (Giacomo Aconcio) (1492/1520 – c. 1566) at first studied the law. He was at the court of Archduke Maximilian in Vienna where he wrote two MSS of an ironic Lutheran-Valdesian persuasion, evidently hoping to convert the Archduke, c. 1550, later published under fuller titles *Dialogo di Giacopo Riccamati ossanese nel qual si scuoprono le astutie con che i Lutherani si sforzano di'ngannare le persone semplici & tirarle all lor setta* and *Dialogo nel quale in proposito del giorno del Giudicio alcune cose si considerano* [earlier: *Somma brevissima della dottrina christiana*] (Basel, 1565), printed by Pietro Perna, *Historia, 110*. In that year and place Acontius also published anonymously his new logic for all sciences including theology, *De methodo, hoc est de recta investigandarum tradenarumque scientiarum ratione*. In the meantime, he had served, 1556 – 57, as secretary to Cristoforo Cardinal Madruzzo, governor of Milan, and then visited the leading humanists in Basel, Zurich, and Geneva. By way of Strassburg he went to London, where he became a member of the Spanish congregation under the Strangers' Church, and served widely in England (1558 – 64), primarily as engineer and inventor, continuing to defend religious toleration, and writing twice to Edmund Grindal (Bishop of London, 1559 – 70), in defense of Anabaptists and critics of the Trinity. In his major work, many times reprinted and translated, mediated in the East through the version of Sommer, Acontius set forth his conviction that all doctrines necessary to salvation were in Scripture, that Protestantism, having acknowledged this, had through the pride, vanity, and self-service of the new clergy repeated the mistakes of the Catholic priesthood and hierarchy, Satan tempting them to use the coercive power of princely states in confessional controversy. He defended the freedom of engaged discussion on disputed points, confident that the saving truth would emerge, and to this end elevated to prominence the *communis prophetia, lex sedentium, Sitzerrecht*, extrapolated from 1 Cor 14:23ff., already used much earlier by the Anabaptists, whom Acontius often referred to favorably. On this, see my *Radical Reformation*, 214, 273, 282, 830; on it synodal recognition among the Transylvanian Unitarians, see n. 600, ¶2. For the life of Acontius, see Delio Cantimori, ''Aconcio,'' *DBI*, 1 (1960) 154 – 59, with the literature, including the critical edition of the *Strategemata* by Walther Köhler (Munich, 1927); for an appreciative assessment of the *Strategemata* and Sommer's changes, see Pirnát, *Ideologie der Siebenbürger*, 22 – 28.

Very soon after his arrival in Kolozsvár, c. 1570, Sommer engaged in conversation in the spirit of *communis prophetia* but also in resolute opposition to the traditional views of the dogma of the Trinity. This can be inferred from a composition of Palaeologus, *Disputatio scholastica* of 1575, in *Catechesis*, ed. by Dostálová, ''Conspectus,'' 11. In the historical conversations behind this literary account, it would appear that Sommer with Palaeologus and Paruta sought to dismantle the received Triadology by arguing against the patristic formulators of it, as in Sommer's *Theses* preserved by Lubieniecki at n. 642.

Soon after the death of John Sigismund, Sommer composed an *Oratio funebris*, meant to be studied as a mirror of princes, which reflected and idealized the tolerant reign and piety of the protector of Unitarians, including an *apologia* for his pro-Turkish policy against the Hapsburgs in the interest of religious toleration. Soon thereafter Sommer completed the *Refutatio* against Károlyi, published posthumously by Vehe-Glirius-Schimberg (n. 632, ¶2).

386. This is a plausible detail that could only have come from Budziński, but the presence of Sommer in Cracow in April 1572 is hard to fit into his known *curriculum vitae*, n. 385, ¶1.

387. After the death of John II in 1571, the Transylvanian Diet elected Stephen Báthory as voivode (1571 – 75/86), the position his father of the same name had held

(d. 1534). The Báthorys were one of a group of eight noble families in Transylvania who had remained faithful to Rome, although the new voivode in the circumstances willingly attended Protestant services and upheld the principle of religious toleration. See his famous axiom, *Polish Brethren*, 565 at n. 47. He dismissed John's counselors except Biandrata.

Elected King of Poland in 1575, partly through the influence of Biandrata among Protestant lords who remembered him favorably, (n. 393), Stephen appointed his older brother Christopher as his deputy in Transylvania (1576–81) with the old title of voivode, while as King of Poland he assumed the style of Prince of Transylvania so long as his brother lived. For Stephen in Poland, see n. 767.

In 1575 Gáspár Békés, major patron of Dávid, counselor of the late voivode-king, his envoy in Speyer (Bk. 2, n. 364), undertook a rebellion against Stephen, seeking to be elected at least co-voivode with him with the support of the Szeklers, many of whom by 1570 had become Davidian. Defeated, nine of his fellow Szekler chieftains were beheaded in Kolozsvár, but Békés escaped, fleeing to Poland, where he was imprisoned, but then, on the magnanimous entreaty of Christopher Báthory, was pardoned by his brother, King Stephen; and he joined him in the campaign against Muscovy. It was in the Commonwealth that Békés received (c. 1578) at the hand of Pál Gyulai (Paulus Julianus) a copy of what is known only as the *Libellus parvus* of Dávid, in which the radical Superintendent had set forth his views on non-adorantism, the future role of Jesus as Messiah, and his rejection of the views of Luther and Calvin on predestination and justification by faith. Palaeologus, *Defensio*, ed. by Dán, 232 and xxviii in the Introduction by Balázs. Békés, faithful Davidian to the end, died in Grodno in November 1579 as did Dávid.

Christopher Báthory was succeeded in Transylvania by his minor son as Prince Sigismund Báthory (1581–98), his uncle Stephen in Cracow yielding the title of Prince in 1583. In 1595 Prince Sigismund entered upon a treaty of reunion with the Emperor as King of Hungary and assumed the new style of Prince of the Holy Roman Empire. Emperor Rudolph Hapsburg, successor of Maximilian, in any case considered himself King of Hungary, 1576–1608. On good terms with Sigismund III Vasa of Poland (cf. n. 716, ¶1), Rudolph and Sigismund joined forces against the Turks in what is known from the Hapsburg perspective as "the Long War" (1595–1606) and from that in Transylvanian historiography as "the Fifteen Year War." At first successful, the allies defeated General Sinan Pasha at the Battle of Giurgiu, 29 October 1595. Sigismund won back lands for the Principality on either side of the lower Maros almost to Szeged, while Moldavia and Walachia became momentarily vassal states of Transylvania. See the map as of 1596 drawn by Makkai, *Transylvanie*, 192. Transylvania was briefly under the domination of Voivode Michael the Brave of Moldavia after the Battle of Suceava, 1600. Rudolph, through his imperial general Giorgio Basta, instituted a reign of terror in Transylvania, 1601–1604, against whom the Unitarian chieftain Mózes Székely rose and also against Voivode Michael, with whom the largely Unitarian Szeklers had at first been sympathetic.

Against the same ruthless Basta, István Bocskai led the war of independence, becoming himself Prince (1604–06). With him began a succession of Calvinist Princes. After the election of Sigismund II Rákóczi (1606–08), came Prince Gabriel Báthory (1608–13) and Gabriel Bethlen (1613–29), the latter mentioned by Lubieniecki at n. 736. Gabriel Bethlen married the widow of Székely. Then followed George I Rákóczi (1630–48) and his son George II Rákóczi (1648–60), who entered the Commonwealth in force as an ally of Charles X Gustavus (*Polish Brethren*, 723).

Gyula Szekfü and Bálint Hóman in *Magyar történet*, 8 vols. (Budapest, 1928–34) in vol. 4 (by Szekfü) have a good map of all *Hungaria* at the end of the rule of Sigismund Rákóczi in 1606, which shows the counties of the *Partium*, partly under the Hapsburgs, partly under the princes of Transylvania, opp. 384. Makkai, *Transylvanie* (opp. 240) shows the considerable scope of Transylvania in 1657 during the rule of George II Rákóczi, whose domain included all of the *Partium* until 1649, and who held suzerainty over the voivodeships of Walachia and Moravia, thus at the time of Lubieniecki's compositions a major state. In the boundary changes, the Reformed capital of Debrecen, under Queen Isabelle in 1547, was directly under Ottoman rule in 1576 but again within Transylvania in 1606 and 1657. Wilbur admirably interweaves the history of the Unitarian community in the aforeoutlined dynastic frame in two chapters, ''The Unitarian Church under the Báthorys'' and ''The Unitarian Church under Calvinist Princes,'' *Transylvania*, chaps. 6 and 7.

388. Ferenc Forgách (1510–72), educated at Padua, was bishop of Várad (Grosswardein/Oradea), 1556–67 (successor of Martinuzzi, n. 128) and chancellor of Transylvania, 1571–75. He was the author of *De statu reipublicae Hungaricae...commentarii, Monumenta Hungariae Historica, Scriptores*, 16 (Pest, 1866).

389. This appears to have been the aged canon, Chancellor Miklós Cáki (older spelling, Csáky; in Lubieniecki's text, *Czascius*) under Isabelle, then John II. Makkai refers to him up to c. 1570 (*Transylvania*, 141, 145, 148) and does not mention his kinsman Pál Czáki, who of the two is alone mentioned in *Révai nagy lexikona*, 4 (Budapest, 1914), col. 741B, item 17; and in the index to the facsimile edition of the *Historia*, 314, reference is (mistakenly) made to this Pál.

390. Evidently as a teacher in the school in Kolozsvár.

391. The reference is to Maximilian II. Neuser is dealt with in Bk. 2, n. 364 and Bk. 3, n. 381.

392. Budziński/Lubieniecki follow here the tradition originated by Gentile's angry words during his trial in Geneva: ''Factus [Alciatus] est Mohammetanus, nec mihi iampridem ullum commericum fuit.'' Gentile meant only that Alciati had become a Unitarian. However Johann Wigand, *De Servetianismo seu de Antitrinitariis* (Königsberg, 1575) fol. 89, accepted this allusion to Islam as literal; and out of this the legend arose that Alciati even went to Constantinople. Actually, Alciati went to Danzig and lived there till his death, perhaps sometime after 1581. Wajsblum, ''Dyteiści Małopolscy,'' *RwP* 5 (1928) 41, n. 6; also idem, *PSB* 1.56

393. The ''I'' here is most likely Budziński, although the sentence could be a transitional line of Lubieniecki, as he turns to Palaeologus from another source.

Here at the conclusion of the excerpt from Budziński, going beyond developments in Transylvania yet to be dealt with by Lubieniecki in chap. 11 (c. 1567–79), is a place to bring together certain developments with reference to Biandrata after the death of John II Sigismund, namely, from 1571 to 1588 as these stood in the penumbra of Lubieniecki's awareness when he composed his *Historia*.

After the election of Stephen Báthory as Voivode (n. 387, ¶¶1–3) and the establishment of new council of government, Biandrata did not lose his influence at a recatholicized court, but he was obliged to be more cautious under a tolerant but Catholic prince in preserving the status of the proto-Unitarian Church of Transylvania under Superintendent Dávid (n. 601) who was by now the main Protestant bishop over the territory of the medieval diocese of Alba Julia, over against orthodox Reformed bishop Méliusz in Debrecen, in effect spokesman of the Reformed churches of Upper Hungary (*Partium*), Ottoman Hungary, and also of the minority of the Reformed in Transylvania who had not been swept into Dávid's movement. Biandrata returned to Poland briefly to speak in behalf of the election of his voivode as King of Poland. After the unhappy experiment with the brief reign of the first elected King on the extinction of the direct Jagiellonian line, namely, of Henry of Valois (1573–74) (*Polish Brethren*, 550–55, etc.), the *szlachta* were drawn to the dynastic claim of Anna Jagiellonka, sister of Sigismund II Augustus (d. 1572). Although Stephen was elected in 1575, he became King only on 16 January 1576 after marriage to Anna and in part crowned King as her spouse. Biandrata had some influence on the election of Báthory among the *szlachta* who remembered him as the distinguished elected archipresbyter of the Reformed Church before the schism and once physician to Anna's mother, and he could plausibly have had influence on Stephen himself accentuating the tolerant spirit in religion, of the puissant and martial King *Dobrze*, remembered thus for his having seemed to master only the one word of his new subjects' language, "Thank you," "Good."

On his return to his estates (n. 129), Biandrata dealt tactfully with Christopher, older brother of the new Polish King, who served as his deputy in Transylvania, 1576–81, and in his own right as voivode, 1581–86. Under him the Counterreformation surged. The Jesuits at court became friendly with Biandrata and tried to convert him. More and more out of things, he died at 72 in May 1588. Wilbur, *Transylvania*, 89–90. On the voivodial/princely succession, see n. 387, ¶¶4–5.

Because of his role in restraining his longtime collaborator, Dávid, 1578/79, and indirectly compassing the death of the father and martyr of Transylvanian Unitarianism (n. 601), Biandrata has not been dealt kindly with or even fully by historians in this tradition or sympathetic with it. Hence the titles of the two recent revisionist articles by Antal Pirnát, "Per una nuova interpretazione dell'attività di Giorgio Biandrata," *Rapporti veneto-ungheresi all'época del Rinascimento*, Atti del II Convegno di studi italo-ungherese (1973), Studia Humanitatis, 2, ed. by Tibor Klaniczay (Budapest: Hungarian Academy of Sciences, 1975) 361–7, and "Il martire e l'uomo politico (Ferenec Dávid e Biandrata)," *Antitrinitarianism*, 157–87, with a letter from Biandrata in Alba Julia to Dudith, 5 June 1575, 187–190. In these two articles Pirnát expresses the view that Biandrata was at the time "l'unica persona in Europa che avesse una visione globale della letteratura clandestina" ("L'uomo politico," 169) with a comprehensive vision and indeed plan for a tolerated liberal Protestant Church in Transylvania under John II Sigismund (d. 1571), in Little Poland under the patronage of lords like Hieronim Filipowski (d. 1574), in Lithuania, or at least the Palatinates of Vilna and Podlasie, under Mikołaj Radziwiłł (d. 1565, n. 131), and perhaps elsewhere, as in Slavkov in Moravia, all these theologically scriptural churches to be affiliated and in synodal communion. Precisely because scriptural, Biandrata knew that these churches had to come to terms with pedobaptism, but moderation was his emphasis, as Prinát substantiates with integrated new and familiar material. Wilbur averred that Biandrata's "share in the propagation of Unitarian belief in Transylvania has been overestimated," *Transylvania*, 30. My own estimate is much closer to that of Pirnát; and surely for the pluralistic state-church system that was incubated in increasingly harsher climate, 1579–1638, from Biandrata's synod to replace Dávid with Demeter Hunyadi, to the compromises accepted for Unitarianism to be recognized under a Calvinist Prince as a licit religion at Dées, Biandrata was in effect the rebuilder of a Unitarian polity and cultus on the slope and around the rim of the volcanic upthrust that was Ferenc Dávid; cf. n. 675.

394. Dán says, on the basis of H. Rott, *op. cit.* (n. 381), 7, pp. 250f., that Neuser had to leave Transylvania for Turkish Hungary, became a Muslim, and died in Istanbul, 1576, *Vehe-Glirius*, 36.

395. Jacob Palaeologus (nn. 399 and 400 for a summary of his life), a Greek-Italian

theological radical but a defender of the orders of society like any magisterial Protestant, as an interfaith covenantal theorist of ''the three peoples'' (n. 275), was never a communicating member of the Unitarian churches of Cracow, Transylvania, Lithuania, or Moravia. He stood in relation to the Unitarian Church in Transylvania, where the major portion of his MSS survive, somewhat like Socinus in relation to the Polish Brethren. (Each resisted the baptismal theology and practice of the ambient Church). Besides works on Palaeologus mentioned in nn. 275, 397, 400, the principal secondary studies are those of Antal Pirnát, ''Jacobus Palaeologus,'' *Studia nad Arianizmem* (1959) 72 – 129 and in *Ideologie der Siebenbürger* (1961), chap. 2; Gerhard Rill, ''Jacobus Palaeologus (c. 1520 – 1585): Ein Antitrinitarier als Schützling der Habsburger, *Mitteilungen des Österreichischen Staatsarchivs* 16 (1963) 28 – 85; Firpo, ''Problemi e sviluppi dell'Antitrinitarismo,'' *Antitrinitari* (1973) chap. 1 and passim with documents. In a major essay based on the documents, published and mostly still unpublished, Lech Szczucki surveys the research to date (thus not Firpo's) in *W kręgu myścieli heretyckich* (Wrocław etc.: Ossolineum, 1972), dividing his essay into two main parts, on the life and politics of Palaeologus, 1 – 83, and his radical theology and conservative politics and social and ethical thought, 83 – 121.

The second essay in this book is on Christian Francken (c. 1552 – 1602), not mentioned by Lubieniecki. Born in Mark Brandenburg of Lutheran parents, Francken became a Jesuit and was converted to nonadorant Unitarianism at Altdorf. Francken arrived via Breslau in Cracow in 1583. He debated Socinus on the honor due to Christ, Krzysztof Pawlikowski, 14 March 1584, *Disputatio de adoratione Christi habita inter Faustum Socinum et Christianum Francken* (in the hall of Raków, 1618); Gryczowa, no. 268; *BFP* 2.767 – 777. Szczucki holds it most unlikely that *BAnt*, 83, had it right that Francken became rector of the school of the Brethren in Chełmnik, although there was some disputation there between him and Schomann, et al., *W kręgu myścieli heretyckich* 143, n. 90; but notes his brief visit in Lublin, before going to Transylvania, where he was received by Palaeologus's patron, Gerendi (n. 400, ¶4). Francken, publishing two works in Kolozsvár during his two-year stay there, converting again to Catholicism in a ceremony in court in the presence of Voivode Sigismund Báthory, 16 April 1591. Despite his recantation, he ended his life as a Carthusian in prison in Rome, c. December 1602. The book makes available in *Materiały* six documents, mostly of Palaeologus and Francken.

396. Lubieniecki refers to *Responsio ad libellum Jacobi Wuieki Jesuitae Polonice editum, De Divinitate Filii Dei, et Spiritus sancti* (Raków: Sternacki, 1624). Gryczowa, no. 278, pp. 319 – 20; no. 71, pp. 185 – 86. The first Latin edition was printed by Rodecki in 1594. It is republished in *BFP* 2.538ff.

397. Jakub Ryniewic was an anabaptist, son of Mikołaj. He served in Lublin (nn. 75ff. and 792). His mother's patronymic was Trębecka, *BAnt*, 142 – 43.

It is noteworthy that Lubieniecki does not purport to have any information on Palaeologus (n. 392), from Budziński. Yet Budziński, like Budny, was a supporter of Palaeologus, theologian of ''dogmatic radicalism'' (Lech Szczucki), and would plausibly have something on him in his MS History. In the published correspondence several letters of Budziński survive; Karl Landsteiner, *Jacobus Palaeologus: Eine Studie...mit noch nicht gedruckten Urkunden und Briefen aus dem Archive des k. k. Ministeriums des Innern*, Separat-Abdruck aus dem Programme des Josefstädter Gymnasiums (Vienna, 1873).

398. Cf. the Homeric and royal claim of another Greek Jacobus Basilicus (Bk. 2, chap. 9). Palaeologus was born in Chios, Giacomo/Ἰάκοβος son of a Genoese mother, Tommasina di Chiavari, and a Greek father of the Uniate Church, a mason, Θεόδωρος

Ὀλυμπιδάριος. Chios would be under the Genoese until 1566. Giacomo would make the claim to an imperial pedigree only in Prague, c. 1562.

399. Giacomo (n. 398) was educated as a boy in the convent of the Observantine Dominicans. He then studied philosophy and theology in Genoa, Ferrara, and Bologna. He was early implicated in charges of heresy by the Inquisition and was twice imprisoned and in one place tortured. He was in the Dominican convent of St. Peter's in Constantinople, 1554 – 55. Back in Italy he was again arrested. As a consequence of the angry assault upon his Roman prison by the tumult after the death of Paul IV in 1559, he and the other prisoners were freed. He made his way to France and attended the Colloquium in Poissy, January 1562. He then sought out his Dominican superior at the session in Trent, April 1562, seeking to clear his name of the inquisitorial charges. From there he went to Vienna to seek Hapsburg protection, then to Prague, where he was urged by the Neoutraquist party to consider election as their bishop, impressed as they were by his alleged doctorate and imperial pedigree. In Prague he married Eufrosyna, the daughter of the Prague historian, M. Kuthen. In some ways Bohemia would be his true new homeland more than either Cracow or Transylvania.

400. Palaeologus was for the first time in Cracow during the fall and winter, 1571 – 72, in part at the residence of András Dudith, with whose reforming views he had presumably become acquainted while at the session in Trent and who, like himself, was pro-Hapsburg in Eastern politics vis-à-vis the Ottoman Empire and who in Cracow was the authorized spokesman of Hapsburg interests. In a letter from Warsaw of 29 November 1571 to Palaeologus in Cracow, the chamberlain (*praepositus/podkomorzy*) of Sandomierz, Piotr Zborowski (d. 1581), encouraged him in seeking a position in the court of Sigismund Augustus. Evidently out of his long reflections the sometime Dominican wrote out in Cracow his programmatic *De tribus gentibus*. Szczucki, *W kręgu myścieli heretyckich*, 61 – 62 and n. 209 (the whole letter of Zborowski).

In February 1572 Palaeologus went to Transylvania, more to make there preparations for his projected return to Chios than to promote his vision of an interfaith Unitarianism.

He returned to Cracow probably in April 1572 and composed his works arising from polemical discussion with Socinus and the Racovians, *De discrimine Veteris et Novi Testamenti* and *De bello sententia*.

He went to Kolozsvár in January 1573 and then to Chios and Constantinople. He left Constantinople, 8 July 1573, in the company of the ambassadors or the voivode of Moldavia. Back in Kolozsvár by 12 August, he had finished his account of the journey and shared his sense of the imminent threat of the Ottoman Empire to that of the Hapsburgs, 10 December 1573, *Epistola de rebus Chii et Constantinopoli cum eo actis lectu digna*, 1st edition, no place given, 1592; 2nd ed. along with a German translation, Ürsel in Flanders, 1594. Palaeologus's interfaith ecumenism or "the three peoples" of his non-adorant Unitarianism was his theologically radical way of dealing with the presence of Muslims throughout the East living among Christians, but Palaeologus remained vigilantly anti-Ottoman and pro-Hapsburg in his geopolitics in contrast to most of his Transylvanian Unitarian associates. He was briefly head of the academy in Kolozsvár, where he finished his *Catechesis Christiana dierum duodecem*, 1 August 1574, edited from the Kolozsvár MSS by Růžena Dostálová (Warsaw: PAN, 1971), with the life briefly recounted in Latin and with a conspectus of the three Kolozsvár MSS containing most of the works of Palaeologus, 7 – 11. Palaeologus withdrew to the court of the Unitarian magnate János Gerendi in Alţina near Kronstadt, where he composed his *Commentarius in Apocalypsin, Theodoro Bezae pro Castalione*, and *Disputatio scholastica*. These and other works are projected for publication by Szczucki and Juliusz Domański. Despite his many friendships in Transylvania among Unitarians, Palaeologus, unsettled by the collapse of the revolt of Gáspár Békés against Stephen Báthory (n. 387), and after the death of his daughter, Despina, left Transylvania in September 1575 by way of Moldavia for the Commonwealth: Podolia (with Mikołaj Jazłowiecki), Lithuania (with Kiszka and Budny), and eventually Cracow. In Cracow, 30 April 1576, he completed his *Assertionum Johannis Simleri de duabus in Christo naturis confutationes* (Łosk, 1578), reprinted by Massimo Firpo, *Antitrinitari*, 365 – 99, with related documents.

During the lively and hazardous machinations leading to the election of a successor of Henry of Valois, the Greek-Italian Unitarian Palaeologus took the side of contender Maximilian II, while the Italian-"Polish"-"Transylvanian" Unitarian Biandrata took the side of voivode Báthory (n. 392).

After the election of the Transylvanian, Palaeologus regarded the Commonwealth as in the Ottoman camp and he withdrew to the castle of Jetřich of Kunovice at Hluk in Moravia on the left bank of the Morava below Kromříž. There he composed his work *Adversus Pii V proscriptionem Elisabethae Reginae Angliae*. Under pressure from the papal nuncio in Vienna after Maximilian's death (1576), Rudolph II eventually acquiesced in the apprehension of Palaeologus, who was turned over to the bishop of Olomouc, 20 October 1581; and Jetřich did not seek to protect him. Szczucki, *W kręgu myścieli heretyckich*, 69, 73.

401. Lubieniecki refers to the *Defensio Francisci Davidis* by Palaeologus, published twice in Cracow by Vehe-Glirius (n. 602) and to the *De bello sententia* (1572), n. 400, ¶3, and *Defensio verae sententiae de magistratu politico* (Łosk, 1580), against which Socinus wrote *Ad Jacobi Palaeologi librum pro Racoviensibus responsio* (Raków: Rodecki, 1581); 2nd ed. (Raków: Sternacki, 1627); Gryczowa, nos. 62 and 243; and for the whole setting and argumentation, see Kot, *Ideologja polityczna/Socinianism in Poland*, chaps. 5 – 8.

402. He was beheaded and burned in Rome, 23 March 1585. On the basis of a letter of Ostorodt in German, *BAnt*[2] (58 and fair copy) has it that with the urging of the Jesuits he renounced his view *de Uno Deo* for fear of being burned alive but was nevertheless, after detention in prison for some time, killed and burned.

NOTES TO CHAPTER FIVE

403. This "fair," "moderate," and "charitable" party is, of course, none other than Lubieniecki's own Minor Church. The schism with the Major Church of consistent or conservative Calvinists has already been presupposed in much of the narrative in the preceding chapters.

404. The statutes of 1563 did not secure the liberty of religion. They merely refused to allow ecclesiastical courts jurisdiction in matters deemed beyond their competence. The Minor Church especially was in a precarious position, because the decrees of Parczów were still a danger to it. See Bk. 1, n. 255 and Bk. 3, n. 137. "After the severe edict and royal mandates passed in Parczów," wrote the scribe of the Kolozsvár MS, "Our people did not dare hold synods in 1564, until the King made a gracious declaration in Pinczów [error of copyist for Piotrków] concerning that edict; after this the lords convoked the synod. . . ." Sipayłło, *AS*, 2.175, with n. 4 giving the date of the mitigation, 2 November 1564.

405. The disputation of Piotrków took place 22 – 30 March 1565. It was mentioned in Book 2, at n. 757; cf. n. 864, ¶1. Lubieniecki's account here is unreliable. It runs

parallel to that of Węgierski (*Slavonia Reformata*, 87), who acknowledged his indebtedness to Antonio Possevino, S.J. (1583–1611), *De Atheismis haereticorum sui seculi*. Lubieniecki may not have consulted the Calvinist account, *Colloquium piotrkowskie, To iest rozmowa, którą mieli wyznawce prawdziwey wiary starodawney o Panu Bodze w Tróicy iedynym z stroną' przeciwną, w Piotrkowie w Seym, roku przes*, 1565; *Tamże o krzcie dziatek y o nowokrzczeństwie* (Cracow, 1566), nor the Kolozsvár account in Zachorowski ("Najstarsze Synody," 221–29, and fully annotated by Sipayłło, *AS*, 2.175–92). See also Antonio Possevino, *Atheismi Lutheri* (Vilna, 1586), also under the title familiar to Węgierski, *De sectariorum nostri temporis atheismis* (Cologne, 1586), chap. 13, fol. 55. For an English account, see Robert Wallace, *Antitrinitarian Biography*, 3 vols. (London, 1850) 2.184–47.

The disputation in Piotrków took place 22, 25, 28, and 30 March 1565. Lubieniecki's list of participants differs from that in the Kolozsvár MS. The list of the Kolozsvár MS, based on the original minutes, must be given preference over that of Lubieniecki. But both Unitarian sources may represent retrospective and tendentious harmonization of the make-up of the *theological* leadership on the Unitarian side. Cf. nn. 406 and 412.

406. The text has Schomann as "Minister Lublinensis." From Schomann's own *Testamentum*, RD 3, nos. 26–27 we know that he was at the time minister in Książ (hence corrected by me to that extent). From Jan Kazanowski (Bk. 2.685, ¶3), we know from another of his works, *Contra duas epistolas Calvini ad Fratres Polonos* [against Biandrata], that there were four clerical disputants on the side of the emerging Minor Church at Piotrków: Grzegorz Paweł, (Stanislas) Lutomirski, (Stanislas) Paklepka (Paclesius *of Lublin*), and Jerzy Schomann (Homanus). These four names together as disputants are preserved in a citation of Kazanowski by the Sorbonne Benedictine Hebraist Gilbert Génébrard (d.1597), *De S. Trinitate libri tres contra huius aevi Trinitarios, Antitrinitarios et autotheanos* (Paris, 1569) — the *autotheani* being an early design for believers in the One self-subsisting God (Unitarians). These four names are given in the note by Sipayłło, *AS*, 2.176, where she observes that the parallel Kolozsvár MS version of the same synodal acts altogether suppresses the name of the first Reformed minister in Lublin (Bk. 2, n. 685). Lubieniecki (whose family will have surely recalled the name of the first minister of "their" Lublin) preserves the surname but by some scribal or typographical or intentional error gives the Christian name as *Johannes* (n. 412). It is evident that the two parallel synodal records and Lubieniecki (less grievously) have intentionally confused the record of the delegation of Minor Church clerical disputants and judges at Piotrków, the synodal records assigning Niemojewski a quasi-clerical role so that there would be at least three theologians. The tendentious marginalization of Paklepka is not wholly clear. He had been involved in support of Otwinowski in the iconoclastic episode in Lublin on Corpus Christi Day in April 1564 (approved by Lubieniecki at nn. 149), already having been obliged to leave the residence of Stanislas Tęczyński after his patron's death in 1563 and to organize his Minor Church elsewhere separate from the ongoing Major congregation of Lublin. One of the four clerical discussants at Piotrków, 1565, Paklepka became ever more radical on the Christian use of the sword and believers' baptism. There was a confusing interruption in the Minor Church in Lublin from his death in 1565 to 1570, when Judaizing currents swirled in 1565 (n. 287). The dating of his death rests on two places in Budny, *O urzędzie*, 19 and *O dzieciokrzeństwie*, 107, apud Szczucki, "Szymona *Budnego relacja*," who anticipates an edition in *OiRuP* by Borys Ploria of the discovered *Testament* of Paklepka (ibid., n. 18), and on a Kolozsvár synodal MS above, n. 287, ¶2.

407. Jan Lutomirski (d. 1567) was a cousin of the Minor Church superintendent, Stanislas, and of Mikołaj Lutomirski.

408. The Brethren were fond of thinking of the *szlachta* as a race apart going back to the classically observed Sarmatians. Probably Lubieniecki is comparing Sienicki (next n.) to the Athenian orator and statesman by reason of his position as Speaker of the House. Elsewhere he likened Jan Siekierzyński as preacher to Demostenes (nn. 292 – 94).

409. Mikołaj Sienicki (d. 1582), chamberlain of Chełm, several times attested at the synods, represented in the Diet between 1550 and 1578 the interests of the higher and middle *szlachta* in favor of the central authority and the royal insistance on the implementation by the magnates of their duties to the common good. See Stanislas Grzybowski, ''Mikołaj Sienicki—Demostenes sejmów polskich,'' *OiRwP* 2 (1957) 91 – 132.

410. Jan Niemojweski, the theological and socio-political radical (*Historia, 152, 190, 192*), is sometimes confused with his nephew and namesake, Jan Niemojewski, son of a brother Wojciech. Our Jan Niemojewski was indeed deputy to the Diet of 1565, but it was his Calvinist nephew who was the castle judge of Inowrocław; cf. Bk. 2, n. 684, ¶2. Kolankowski, ''Posłowie sejmów Zygmunta Augusta,'' *RwP* 5 (1928) 130; J. Płokarz, ''Jan Niemojewski,'' *RwP* 2 (1922) 70 – 71. The Kolozsvár MS makes Niemojewski one of three disputants. Although quite theologically articulate, Niemojewski was more likely among the designated arbiters.

411. In the *Akta* Filipowski is one of two *moderatowie*, the second referred to only as *Pan sądomirski*, namely Castellan Stanislaw Myszkowski. Sipayłło, *AS*, 2.176.

412. The text reads *Joannes Paclesius*, presumably an error for Stanislas Paclesius (Paklepka), Bk. 2, n. 685, first minister in Lublin (d. 1565), cf. n. 406. His attendance is uncertain. He was neither a judge (*sędzia*) nor a formal witness (*świadek*) since these roles were reserved for the nobles. The corresponding Kolozsvár MS completes the list of arbiters with Superintendent Lutomirski, Paklepka, and Stanislas Lutomirski, who were quite likely among the four Antitrinitarian disputants to correspond to the four on the Calvinist side.

413. Lubieniecki has Albertus Romeus Breszensis, while the Kolozsvár MS calls him Albertus, minister of Wrzesz. Górski (*Grzegorz Paweł*, 134) makes this Wrzeszcz, but Sipayłło is almost certain it is ''of Wrzos.''

414. In Reformed schisms the group emerging Unitarian commonly comes to call the conservative Calvinists *Trinitarii* (and these reserve for themselves, sometimes into the present, the official description, Calvinists); e.g. in the synodal Churches in Poland and Transylvania and in the congregational Churches of New England (after c. 1805). At the same time Catholics, observing the theological route taken by the conservative Reformed could call even these conservative Reformed mistakenly, *Trinitarii*. Cf. the very title of Génébrard's book, n. 406.

415. Wawrzyniec Discordia (*Prasnitius*, of Przasnysz) (prominant *Historia, 164 – 68*), is not mentioned in the Kolozsvár MS, where there is instead Andreas *Prasmovius*, minister in Radziejów, who could have been confused by Lubieniecki with Discordia. Sipayłło, *AS*, 2.176. Andrzej Prasmovius is frequently attested at the synods.

416. Jakub Sylvius, *Historia, 126, 133, 143, 164, 197*; A. Gryczowa, ''J.S. a rozłam w zborze małopolskim,'' *RwP* 9 – 10 (1937 – 39) 286 – 63.

417. Jan Rokyta (Polish: Rokita), the representative of the Czech Brethren, was present at the Diet where he tried to promote the Augsburg Confession as a common base for Polish Protestantism (Bohemian, Lutheran, Calvinist, and even the Czech Minor

Party). He certainly was concerned with the outcome of the Trinitarian controversy (as evidenced by his polemics against Tomasz Falconius). He was probably present at the Piotrków colloquium as an observer. He is not mentioned in the Kolozsvár MS. See Bidlo, *Jednota Bratrská*, 2.58–59.

418. First mentioned by Lubieniecki on *Historia, 197*. Theodor Wotschke, "Christoph Threcius," *Altpreussische Monatsschrift* 44 (1907).

419. Jan Firley (c. 1521–74), palatine of Belsk in 1556, of Lublin in 1561, was the ranking noble in support of the conservative Reformed. Thrice married, first to Zofia Bonerówna of Cracow, he was in 1563 Grand Marshal of the Crown and was also palatine and *starosta* of Cracow in 1572. He entered into the epochal Warsaw Confederation and as ranking Protestant Senator joined in the delegation to greet the elected Henry of Valois in Paris, 1573. Stanislas Bodniak, *PSB* 7 (1948–58) 1–6; *Polish Brethren*, 2.554–55.

420. Jan Tomicki (d. 1575) was castellan of Gniezno in 1564.

421. Jakub Ostoróg (c. 1516–68) was in 1566 *starosta generalny* of Great Poland and protector of the Czech Brethren (*Historia, 35, 66, 116*).

422. Myszkowski (*Historia, 195–97*, etc.) and Filipowski were in effect co-moderators. Cf. Sipayłło, *AS*, 2.176.

423. There is much of Lubieniecki in the following speech attributed to Grzegorz Paweł. Sipayłło may be going too far, however, in characterizing the intervention as wholly "the creation of the fantasy of Lubieniecki," *AS*, 2.177, n. It is not at all certain that Lubieniecki could have himself marshalled as many patristic *loci* and Renaissance arguments as here adduced. Cf. observations in nn. 437, 442, 448, 449.

424. Grzegorz Paweł was present at the synod of Secemin, 21–29 January 1556, as pastor of Pełsznica (1555–57). Sipayłło, *AS*, 1.46. Gonesius's written confession is summarized, ibid., 47. On its reported effect on Grzegorz, see Lubieniecki's rather free reconstruction, *Historia, 133–40*; more reliably Dalton, *Lasciana*, 403–09.

425. Lubieniecki again uses the parole of his Church and alludes to his work complementing the *Historia*, his *Compendium Veritatis Primaevae*, ed. by Jørgensen (Bk. 1, n. 11), in which, among the four confessional discussants as guests of "the political Christian" Georgius, is "Faustus, Catholicus Christianus, Arianus." Such is the title as given, not in the printed edition, but in Sand's characterization of the MS in *BAnt*, 167, where an earlier and similar MS is listed, "Tractatus pro illustranda et demonstranda primaeva veritate," and given its proper name by Jørgensen, who has examined it in the Royal Library in Copenhagen: "Veritatis primaevae prodromus." Its full title is "Precursor of the Primitive Truth or commentary on the faith of the early Christians along with that of the Apostles and the martyrs before and after the Ascension of the Lord and of the ancients who lived around the time of the Council of Nicaea and of the corruption of the Church succeeding thereto and of its Reformation," 1.3. For Lubieniecki the primitive or ancient truth once for all delivered to the saints was more in the New Testament than in the Bible as a whole, for he does not often cite the Old Testament; in contrast to the Germanic Anabaptists, among others, he believed it also to be found in the Ante–Nicene testimony and practice (e.g. baptism by immersion), and even in the testimony of some dissenters in the fourth century and thereafter. Cf. n. 333, ¶2.

426. The earliest Greek form of the Apostles' Creed is in Epiphanius, *Panarion, apud Haeres.* 72; *PG*, 42, cols 385/92. Here where the Old Roman has *sepulta*, it has ταφέντα.

The *Forma Romana Vetus* of the Apostles' Creed (before 341) indeed does not have *descendit*. Tyrannius Rufinus, *Expositio Symboli Apostolici* (partly based on the Catechetical Discourses of Cyril of Jerusalem) gives the earliest Latin text of Aquileia and Rome. Accessible in C.A. Heurtley, *De Fide et Symbolo* (Oxford, 1864).

427. *De virginibus velandis*, 1: "regula quidem fidei una omnino est, sola immobilis, et irreformabilis, credendi scilicet in unicum Deum omnipotentem, mundi conditorem, et Filium ejus Jesum Christum, natum ex virgine Maria, crucifixum sub Pontio Pilato, tertia die resuscitatum a mortuis, receptum in coelis, sedentem nunc ad dextram Patris venturum judicare vivos et mortuos per carnis etiam resurrectionem." *PL*, 2, col. 889.

428. Lubieniecki/Grzegorz are right. The development of *sepultus* into *descendit ad infernum* (consistent with *resurrexit a mortuis*) is first attested c. 570 in the *Apostolicum* of the Italian Venatius Fortunatus, later bishop of Poitiers. Heurtley, *De Fide*, 54–567. The belief in the literal *descensus ad inferos* was characteristic of the Germanic Anabaptists who also gave it significance in the mystical tradition, for each believer in daily humiliation. The classical Protestants interpreted the *Apostolicum* nonliterally. Although the *descensus ad inferos* is not mentioned in the Niceno-Constantinopolitan Creed, *descendit ad inferos* appears in the Western (Athanasian) Creed, *Quicunque vult*, §38. See further Erich Vogelsang, "Weltbild und Kreuzestheologie in den Höllenfahrtsstreitigkeiten der Reformationszeit," *ARG* 38 (1961) 40–232; GHW, *Radical Reformation*, 71–72; 840–44. Grzegorz was like the Germanic Anabaptists.

429. By Christians here is meant the birthright members of the Minor Church, who used precisely the Apostles' Creed at their immersion. Cf. Piotr Morszkowski, *Ecclesiastical Polity*, "Baptism," *Polish Brethren*, Doc. XXIII and Jonasz Schlichtyng, *Confessio*, ibid., Doc. XXII (an extensive largely scriptural commentary on and annotation of the *Apostolicum*). The Andover Harvard Library has recently acquired copies of the second edition of the *Confessio* of 1651 and of 1652; Janina W. Hoskins, *Early and Rare Polonica of the sixteenth and seventeenth centuries in American libraries* (Boston: Hall, 1973) nos. 956, 957.

430. The iota by which some orthodox Christians, along with the "Semi-Arians," intended to preserve in their formulation a distinction within the Godhead between Father and Son by understanding the latter as eternally begotten and as "of similar substance" to the Father instead of "of the same substance." There were indeed wars among the heirs and successors of Constantine up through the Council of I Constantinople 381. There the Nicene Creed is, retrospectively, considered to have been revised in the interest of asserting the full Deity of the Holy Spirit. Hence the term Nicene-Constantinopolitan Creed, although modern scholarship somewhat relocated the final Greek formulation.

431. If either technical term had been scriptural, the Homoiousians would not have even considered a compromise with "the moderate Arians, the Homoiousians." Most of the latter came over to the fully orthodox formulation of 381, helped thereto by the Cappadocian Fathers.

432. Grzegorz is saying that the unscriptural *homoiousia* made possible the conviction of Arius. The negative necessary for the sense of the sentence is omitted in the text as printed.

433. The condemnation of Arius at the Council of Nicaea, 325.

434. The classical Protestants and now specifically the Calvinists.

435. Origen, *Historia, 119*; Tertullian, *Historia, 109* passim.; Theophilus, bishop of Antioch in the later second century, was the first to use Τριάς of the Godhead in his *Ad*

Autolycum; *PG*, 6, cols. 1025–1168; St. Dionysus the Great, pupil of Origen, bishop of Alexandria in 247, assailed Sabellianism and was in turn accused of Tritheism by Dionysius of Rome (d. 268); *PG*, 10, cols. 1233–1344; Firmian Lactantius, a kind of Christian deist, more concerned with Christian morality and theodicy than the Trinity, is thrice mentioned by Lubieniecki, here and in *Historia, 107, 235*.

436. The text has *de filio Dei ante seculari vel antemundano*. The anathema of Nicaea against Arians reads in part in Latin: "Eos qui dicunt: 'erat quando non erat [Filius]', et 'antequam nascaretur, non erat' . . . hos anathamazat catholica ecclesia."

437. Literally, "si latum *unguem* a veritate discedamus." The truth referred to is scriptural *veritas* without the formulation of Nicaea; but Grzegorz, in contrast to Lubieniecki, evidently regards the view as scriptural.

438. Grzegorz was correct about the simplicity of the original creed of Nicaea. The double procession of the Holy Spirit was added at the Third Hispanic Council of Toledo, 589. It became integral to the Latin version after 800 and the *Filioque* became a major issue between the Churches, East and West.

439. Grzegorz was, of course, right in his surmises that the Creed was pseudo-Athanasian. It was composed in Latin after 428. The German Gerhard Jan Vosa, a Remonstrant in Holland, showed decisively that the Creed was not from Athanasius, *Dissertationes de Tribus Symbolis* (Leiden, 1642). Lubieniecki himself may have been acquainted with this work. The Brethren were in contact with the Remonstrants. But Grzegorz could just as well have known of the humanists' earlier surmises.

440. Lorenzo Valla (d. 1457), an Italian humanist who also challenged the authenticity of the Donation of Constantine.

441. The Apostles' Creed was first so entitled by Ambrose, c. 390, *EP*, 42, 5.

442. Grzegorz was correct on this. Several Old Testament texts on both Wisdom and the Spirit of God were used in support of the consubstantiality of the Son and by 381 were used selectively in support of the consubstantiality of the Holy Spirit as a Person/Hypostasis of the Godhead. It is unlikely that Lubieniecki would have been so attentive to the history of dogma.

443. At the approach the council of Constantinople in 381, many Nicenes were only gradually aroused to define further the Holy Spirit merely mentioned in 325: Πιστεύομεν καὶ εἰς τὸ Ἅγιον Πνεῦμα.

444. *Ad Cleodonium Presbyterum*: "Nimium nos fidei Nicaenae, quae a sanctis Patribus . . . edita est, nec quidquam numquam praetulisse . . .; illud insuper explicantes, quod ab illis minus plene de Spiritu sancto dictum est . . . .'"; *PG* 36, col. 193/194.

445. Cf. 1 Cor 11:19; 2 Pet 2:1.

446. In this redundance Grzegorz wishes to interrelate simple scriptural truth (*simplicitas*) and virtuous behavior (*pietas*).

447. 1 Tim 2:5.

448. Grzegorz's intervention, as given by Lubieniecki, is not wholly consistent with opinions expressed at approximately the same stage, recorded in verifiable writings, although it is possible that in addressing a mixed assembly, Grzegorz could have conceivably argued in this manner. Lubieniecki's version differs from the short summary of arguments on this occasion, as given in the Kolozsvár MS. That Grzegorz is remembered to have been the chief spokesman of the Minor party at Piotrków is witnessed by Wiszowaty, *BAnt*, 55. The speech, as it appears in the *Historia*, is a "reconstruction" after classical models, as with Lubieniecki's great uncle Andrzej Lubieniecki, but pos-

sibly drawing upon an earlier collective effort to "summarize" the Antitrinitarian position at Piotrków restrospectively (cf. next n.). There are clearly some elements in the long address that could not be Lubieniecki's alone.

449. The speech of Grzegorz may represent the collective effort to respond to the conservative party with a written summary of the views of the Minor party.

450. Firley's symbol of the office of the marshal was actually a baton, not a mace. The grand marshal was responsible for the order and security of the locality where the Diet took place, and his court held the "right of life and death." He commanded a marshal's guard of 150 men.

451. The reference is to the execution of Servetus in Geneva in 1553 and of Gentile in Bern in 1566.

452. The conservative Reformed found themselves compelled to base their defense on post-scriptural sources, and this was exploited by Stanislas Hosius in his *Catholici cuiusdam et orthodoxi judicium et censura, de judicio et censura ministrorum Tigurinorum et Heydelbergensium, de dogmate contra adorandam Trinitatem in Polonia nuper sparso* (Cologne, 1565). Attacking both the contention that the Papacy had corrupted the primitive faith and the Protestant scriptural principle, Hosius asked where in Scripture were to be found such terms as "Trinity," "person," and "essence," and whether or not the tradition of councils and Papacy were not essential for the plenitude of Christian doctrine. See his *Opera omnia* (Cologne, 1639), 1.675. Bullinger replied to Hosius in his preface to Josias Simler, *De aeterno Dei Filio adversus veteres et novos Antitrinitarios* (Zurich, 1568) fols. A6ff.

453. The *Colloquium*, n. 136.

454. Despot Jacob Basilicus (d. 1563), Bk. 2, chap. 9, esp. n. 754. Lubieniecki is quoting from the hostile *Colloquium Piotrkowskie*. Lasocki and Filipowski were involved in Olbacht Łaski's scheme to place the Greek pretender on the throne of Moldavia. See next n.

455. Lubieniecki (Bk. 2, chap. 9) exonerated them. Indeed, his concern for the memory of Filipowski in particular may explain why he included so large and yet incomplete account of the Despot. His mother was a Filipowska (n. 466).

456. The disparaging reference is to the Romanian Orthodox in Moldavia and Walachia. The Polish Brethren tended, in contrast, to be positive toward the other Slavic *Orthodox* churches, especially after the Concordat of Brest Litovsk of 1596 that, bringing most of the Byzantine-rite as Uniates under Rome, left the autonomous Orthodox an insecure minority in a largely Catholic-Uniate Commonwealth. And the Calvinists of Lithuania and the Orthodox resistant to the Union signed together a general confederation in Vilna, 30 May 1599. Domet Oljančyn, "Zur Frage der Generalkenföderation zwischen Protestanten und Orthodoxen in Wilna 1599," *Kyrios* 1 (1936) 29–46, with plates.

Lubieniecki in his account of the Despot (n. 454), with whose career he was fascinated, largely left out of his account the attempt of the Voivode (1561–63) to introduce the Reformation among Magyar and Saxon settlers (cf. Bk. 2 at n. 753) with the counsel of Stanislas Lutomirski.

457. Biecz is near the upper Wisłok.

458. The reference could be either to the edict of Parczów of 1564 or the King's clarification of 1566. The Biecz incident could thus have taken place either about 1565 or 1566.

459. Cf. Matt 10:16.

NOTES TO CHAPTER SIX

460. The School at Raków.

Jerzy Schomann (Szoman) (1530–1571), born at Racibórz in Silesia, was minister in Książ (*Historia, 201*), and then of the Minor congregation in Cracow, 1573–85.

461. Petrus Statorius, Jr. was appointed to succeed him in Lusławice. Bock, *Antitrin.*, 2.826, 922. Faustus Socinus lived in Lusławice, 1598–1604. A son of this Statorius, Jan Stoiński, wrote the *Epitome*, BAnt RD 2.

462. *Historia, 148ff.* and *208*, at n. 166.

463. Schomann was minister at Lusławice, 1586–88. In 1588 he returned to Chmielnik, where he died in 1591.

464. The text has στοργή.

465. The charming episode that follows, said by the author to have taken place *thirty* years before, is also a valuable attestation as to the date of the composition of the *Historia*. Since the academic activity of Raków would not have been transferred to Kisielin before the autumn of 1638, the journey referred to as "thirty years ago" must have taken place in 1638/39. Thus Lubieniecki will have written the reminiscence about 1668/69. He had probably started compiling his *Historia* in 1668. He would have already had historical materials at his disposal as early as 1665. Cf. *Theatrum Cometicum* (1668), part 1.83.

466. Krzysztof Lubieniecki (c. 1598–1648) was husband of Katarzyna Filipowska (d. after 1663).

467. The garbled *Rybelino* of the text is corrected by editor Wiszowaty on p. 307 as Kisielin and he had added *mox* in the sentence, appearing in translation in the following sentence as *soon*.

The Brethren were driven from Raków to Kisielin in 1638. See *Polish Brethren*, Plate B. Lubieniecki was a student in Raków, then at Kisielin, until he was eighteen years old.

468. Jerzy Czaplic-Szpanowski had a center to which the fleeing Racovians could repair. He comes into the narrative more fully at *Historia, 268*.

469. The Muses of Raków indeed took up residence in Kisielin.

Lubieniecki elsewhere refers to one of his teachers at Kisielin, Theodor Cosmius (Simenis) of Berchsted in Holstein, *Theatrum Cometicum*, part 1.125.

In 1640 Cosmius was still living in Danzig. The synod of Kisielin in 1640 commissioned Marcin Ruar to bring Cosmius to Kisielin as rector, where he is attested as of 1641, but in the same year the synod at Piaski appointed Ludwig Hohleisen rector of the Kisielin school. See Bock, *Antitrin.*, 2.113, 133, 136, 417. Thus Lubienieckis were in Kisielin at least by 1640. Stanislas himself may have been enrolled there as a student into 1642.

NOTES TO CHAPTER SEVEN

471. At the gathering of elders in Pińczów and the formal synod there, 20–22. November 1559 (*Historia, 148–49*).

472. Lubieniecki dealt with the controversy over the Holy Spirit, involving Petrus Statorius and Chełmski, Bk. 2, nn. 648–678. Grzegorz Paweł was commissioned to write the reply to Chełmski. His response written in Pińczów, "Nomine ecclesiae contra

Arianica principia, ex synode Pinczoviensi ad quendam nobilem prope Pinczoviam [Remigian Chełmski] qui iam principia hauserat harum blasphemiarum,'' was published by Sarnicki in his *Collatio* of 1561 [Bk. 2, n. 653), fols. H3 – H5; reprinted by Górski, *Grzegorz Paweł, 284 – 85.* See also Bock, *Antitrin.*, 1.606.

473. The acts of the synod of Pińczów, 25 – 30 January 1561, do not mention this controversy. The Kolozsvár MS, in which the synod is dated 30 January 1561, gives Chełmski's letter to Petrus Statorius, Loszczyn, 25 January 1561, and Statorius' reply, Pińczów, 30 January 1561. Sipayłło, *AS*, 2.39 – 40. It is possible that the problem was discussed after the formal synod, at a gathering of ministers, and that the author of the Kolozsvár MS dated the whole synod after the date of Statorius' letter.

474. Statorius seems to be alluding to the unpardonable sin against the Holy Spirit, Matt 12:31. Lubieniecki quoted these same words from Jan Stoiński of Raków in Bk. 2 at n. 653.

At this point, somewhat arbitrarily, the life and work of Petrus Statorius, can be brought together and subsequent references to him in Lubieniecki's text also anticipated. A very important figure in the Reformed community of Poland, he has been partly lost from view by both the conservatives and the progressives in the historiographical tradition.

Lubieniecki first mentioned Statorius *Historia, 33* (Bk. 1, n. 260), and quoted extensively from him on the Holy Spirit (1559 – 61), *Historia, 148 – 49* (Bk. 2, n. 646). Some of this is indeed rehearsed in this chapter even *verbatim* (nn. 47 – 74). In 1568 he would publish a Polish grammar for foreigners (n. 498). In connection with this achievement Étienne Descaux brings together the disparate data on Petrus Statorius Gallicus, Pierre de Tonneville (the name as *boursier* in Lausanne, in Polish sources usually Thionville, cf. *Historia, 148*, Bk. 2, near n. 650), Piotr Stojeński (the name he used for his Polish grammar), although his descendants spelled the name Stoiński, ''Il y a quatre cents ans paraissait sous la signature d'un français la première grammaire polonaise,'' *Revue de l'école nationale des langues orientales*, 5 vols. (Paris: Presses Universitaires, 1964 – 68) 5 (1968) 153 – 62, with a summary of his life, 154 – 57. Although his Tonneville is not the Thionville of Luxemburg (Bk. 1, n. 260) and has not yet been located for certain, Petrus clearly regarded himself as Gallicus, not Germanicus. After studying under Beza at the academy in Lausanne in 1551, and going on to Geneva, he left there at the call of Lismanino in June 1556 and arrived for his new duties in Pińczów in October, but dissatisfied left for Germany and returned in 1558, proposing a complete overhaul of the curriculum (n. 494), replacing Grzegorz Orsacius as rector in 1560 (n. 494). He had on 29 January 1560 given the second funeral oration for Jan Łaski, *BAnt*, 47; Sipayłło, *AS* 2.9. In the meantime he had been working on the Brest Bible of 1563 (Bk. 1, n. 266, Bk. 3, n. 131, ¶2).

Statorius stood close to Biandrata (n. 4, ¶2), and both defended the adoration of Christ (cf. also the undated Argumentation of the Statorians, *Historia, 210 – 13.*

He married Małgorzata Czarnowski, possibly the daughter or sister of Andrzej Czarnowski, attested as minister at the synod of Mordy, 9 June 1563. Sipayłło, *AS*, 2.326. There are commonly thought to have been three sons who were ennobled in 1591 under the Polish surname Stoiński, one of them was Piotr Stoiński, (d. 1605), who married the daughter of Grzegorz Paweł, and from them issued Jan Stoiński (1600 – 64), pastor of Raków. *BAnt*, 121.

Petrus Statorius died in 1570. Perhaps confused with his namesake son, Petrus Statorius, Sr. is sometimes listed as having died in 1591. Cf. Sipayłło, *AS*, 1.361A.

Descaux argued ("Il y a quatre cents," 156) for an earlier date in the 1570's; and Aleksander Brückner held that death overtook Statorius "a bit after 1568," *RwP* 6 (1934) 199. This surmise is based on a letter from Pińczów by Thenaud to Beza, 1 June 1568 (n. 615). Three letters of Beza in response to him and critical of him are extant, 1 November 1565, *Correspondence*, 6 (1565) no. 430, pp. 194–95; 12 July 1567, ibid., 8 (1967), pp. 242, 256, no. 561, pp. 138–41; and 9 March 1570, ibid., 11 (1570) no. 751, pp. 85–86; and in his letter to the pastors and the faithful in Poland of 15 August 1570, he mentions Statorius in parentheses among "those, by the just judgment of God, dead," ibid., appendix 4, p. 321. There is no mention of him as alive after 1570, although indeed he is dealt with in that year at the synod of Sandomierz, where Aleksander Vitrelinus, once minister in Pińczów, was under criticism for his role in the ordination of Statorius to the ministry (*in superintendentem*). Sipayłło, *AS*, 2.256–57, 261–61.

475. The text has Regenvolscius, the name used by Węgierski for his *Systema* of 1652, quoted in the present annotation as the *Slavonia Reformata* of 1679 wherein (84–85) he denounced Statorius as a hypocrite.

476. Statorius, as reported by Budziński, was quite extreme in calling *idolatria* the nonvisual invocation of the Holy Spirit at worship.

477. The II Ecumenical Council of Constantinople in 381 ascribed consubstantiality to the Third Person as the I Ecumenical Council of Nicaea in 325 had ascribed it to the Second, n. 430.

By this scriptural challenge to the Tritheists among the anti-Nicene Reformed Brethren, the scholarly Frenchman became in Poland the first proponent of Ditheism (Bk. 2 at n. 646), although he "for the sake of his stomach" presently renounced Ditheism to rejoin the Tritheists (at n. 492) and eventually the Calvinists.

The party designations, Tritheist and Ditheist, were freely used within the anti-Nicene Reformed community of the Commonwealth almost to the end of the century as well as against them from the strict Nicene Calvinists, Catholics, and Lutherans. The terminology has perpetuated itself in Polish scholarship in the field. In the ancient Church and particularly in the ante-Nicene period before the entry of imperial conciliar authority in credal formulation, the Ditheist positions are commonly referred to retrospectively in patristic scholarship as Binitarianism, which, while acknowledging the scriptural and pentecostal Spirit, was preoccupied with understanding God or God the Father as supreme and at once related to the preexistent Messiah/Christos, whether merely premundane or with God even before creation, and parallel with that, the preexistent Logos, whether created in externalization for the creation of the world (λόγος προφορικός) or in the finally prevailing formulation, the uncreated Logos, coeternal with God (λόγος εὐδιάθατος). The Polish parties, although aware of such distinctions among such anti-Nicene (hence for them ante-Nicene witnesses of the primitive faith) as Justin Martyr and Theophilus of Antioch, themselves eschewed in general all but scriptural *topoi* and were evidently uninhibited about relinquishing in their very nomenclature the formal monotheism of the received dogma of the Trinity (Catholic, Protestant, and Orthodox alike) in their preoccupation to establish a plausible and distinctive role (Mediator) and divine identity for Jesus Christ as their Lord above the sovereigns and *panowie* of the world. For the way these parties were named at the end of the century, see the translation of a portion of an old chronicle, RD 4, n. 20. See also n. 502.

478. Heb 1:9.

479. John 1:16.

480. The Tritheists, Biandrata originally among them. The Statorians were Ditheists.

The record, quoted by Lubieniecki, may have been edited to tone down distinctively Ditheist formularies. (n. 502).

481. Lubieniecki does not further identify ''the written records'' that he extensively quotes, but the ''they'' refers to the Statorians. Some of the argument and the citation below of Cardinal Hugo (n.490) are common to what Lubieniecki reported above from Jan Stoiński (n. 474) as of 1561 (*Historia, 148 – 50*). What follows is perhaps a reworking of the original statement to oppose the nonadorants of Christ of n. 486.

482. See further John 6:29; 7:38; 8:24; 11:25ff.; 13:19; 17:20.

483. The argument of the Statorians in the written record being transcribed by Lubieniecki appears to assume some genetic connection between an elementary formulation of belief on the part of Paul (which has reference only to God, Christ, and the saints) and the expanded Creed, supposedly of all the Apostles, through an extension of the foregoing series by the insertion of *Sanctam Ecclesiam* as though implied in the Pauline ''saints.''

484. The *imitatio Christi*, as a phrasing, is not common in radical Reformed writings in Poland.

485. This was the position, here asserted without scriptural citations, of F. Socinus in his debate with F. Dávid in 1579.

486. The Statorian argument in full support of the adoration of the ascended Christ and of prayer directed to him suggests that the document transcribed, belonging to the Statorian group within the Minor Church, was probably formulated later (cf. nn. 485, 492) than Lubieniecki suggests, when the adoration of Christ became an issue in Transylvania, in that case directed presumably against the nonadorants of Christ among the Polish Brethren, as well as against the Transylvanian Unitarians under Dávid, and the semi-Judaizing Budnaeans (after Szymon Budny) in Lithuania (n. 733). The source of the argumentation here is not likely to be Budziński who became an ally of Budny; cf. n. 30, ¶3 and Introduction.

487. Num 11:17, 25; 2 Kgs 2:9 – 10; 1 Cor 12:4 – 11.

488. At the moment of his martyrdom, Stephen, the first to die because of loyalty to Jesus, *filled with Holy Spirit* (vs. 55), beheld in the heavens God (here: the Lord) and his Christ.

489. The liturgical hymn ''Veni Creator Spiritus,'' ascribing a role in creation to the Holy Spirit (cf. Gen 1:2), is regarded here by the Statorians as even blasphemous, perhaps as invalidating worship among Catholics and Calvinists.

490. Hugh of St. Cher (c. 1200 – 63). See Bk. 2 at n. 678. The often reprinted *Expositio Missae Domini Hugonis Cardinalis, O.P.* was later known in Poland from an edition by Melchior Mościcki, Dominican Provincial, published in Cracow in 1584. The passage referred to occurs not at the end of the work, but rather at the beginning: ''Et notandum quod omnis oratio dirigitur ad patrem, vel filium, nulla autem ad spiritum sanctum. Huius ratio est. Quia spiritus sanctus est donum et a dono non petitur donum, sed ab largitore doni . . . . Unde ad patrem et filium dirigitur oratio tanquam ad alicuius datorem, et non ad spiritum sanctum qui est donum.' In the Nuremberg edition, 1507, fol. A iii verso. On Hugh, see Vacant, *DTC*, cols. 221 – 239.

491. Horace *Ars poetica* 11.304 – 05.

492. On this synodal gathering, for which there is no extant protocol, see Sipayłło, *AS*, 2.213 and then *Historia, 215 – 17*.

493. This is the first certain attestation of the printer Aleksy Rodecki, born in all probability in Turobin near Krasnysław in the Land of Chełm; *BAnt*, no. 44. He printed

for the Brethren in Cracow until c. 1600 when he removed to Raków and set up the famous press there. Lubieniecki thought that a former Franciscan Aleksy, mentioned in Book 1 at n. 207, was the printer as a youth. For the literature on the two Aleksys, see n. 207.

494. Statorius started teaching in the Pińczów academy (founded in 1551) in 1556, and reorganized it in 1558 after the model of the school of Lausanne. The interesting feature of his *Gymnasii Pinczoviensis Institutio* (no imprint, c. 1560; ed. by A. Karbowiak, Cracow, 1912) was the use of Polish in the teaching and the cultivation of appreciation of national culture.

495. Cf. 1 John 3:10.

496. This epithet would link Statorius with a satirical poem in Polish: "Proteus albo odmieniec" (1564), apparently written by an Antitrinitarian tending towards Unitarianism, in the spirit of a non-philosophical conception of Christianity. Estreicher, 8, p. 53B. Descaux, "Il y a quatre cents ans," 155.

497. Budziński is evidently referring to Statorius's subscription to the *Confessio* of the Calvinist Major Church. Cf. final sentence of the chapter.

498. The words in parentheses are from Lubieniecki, the rest a summary of Otwinowski on Statorius. The word *Trinitarii* is unusual in the body of Lubieniecki's text. It may even in Otwinowski have been *Tritheistae*, as it was the party of the Tritheists that Statorius rejoined at the synod of Łańcut in 1567, only then finally the strictly Nicene Reformed, i.e. the Calvinists.

Both the needs of the academy and of adult immigrants prompted Statorius to compile his *Polonicae grammatices institutio* (Cracow: Maciej Wirbięta, 1578) in 216 pages. It was prepared with the encouragement of Prospero Provana, was dedicated to Andreas Dudith, and drew examples of Polish from Mikołaj Rey, Descaux, "Quatres cents ans," *loc. cit.*, pp. 153 passim.

It is possible that Statorius wrote his grammar prompted by Theodor Bibliander, *De ratione communi omnium linguarum* (Zurich, 1548). Bibliander, the Polish lexicographer, wrote (p. 15) about Polish:

> Apparebit linguam istam . . . copia, vi, flexibilitate, elegantia, omnibus denique virtutibus certare cum cultis istis linguis et quae solae quibusdam non barbarae sed humanae videntur.

Similarly, Statorius challenged the prevailing foreign opinion that Polish was "vaga et inconsistens, nullisque regulis comprehensa."

Jan Mączyński (c. 1515 – before 1584), who influenced Bibliander on the Polish language, and perhaps also Statorius, became identified with the Minor Church. He was present at the synod in Cracow, 10 December 1561, and the large synod of Bełżyce in March, 1579. Sipayłło, *AS*, 2.124, 222. See further *BAnt*, 83; Bock, *Antitrin.*, 1, p. 465; and Henryk Barycz, *PSB* 20 (1975) 336 – 39.

NOTES TO CHAPTER EIGHT

499. Lubieniecki erroneously has Piotrków instead of Pińczów. The synods of Pińczów held on 2 April 1562 and 28 August 1562 (*Historia, 142 – 143*, has 18 August 1562) both voted not to use "philosophical" terms but only the words of the Bible.

500. The synod of Mordy, 6 June 1563, established rules of discussion. See *Historia, 130–31, 142–43*, 167; Sipayłło, *AS*, 2.152.

501. Among his 244 extant letters, there are four to the prefect of Constantinople, Procopiuis. What is here alluded to about the unhappy outcome of all councils is not clear. Cf. *PG*, 37, cols. 164, 222, 316.

502. Lubieniecki here turns on two anti-Nicene Brethren (the same at n. 506) who at this juncture are respectively the spokesman of Lithuanian and Little Polish Ditheism (cf. n. 477). Lubieniecki had earlier lauded Gonesius as a brilliant pioneer of the movement he chronicles, making him prominent in Book 2, chapter 6. Gonesius's distinctive doctrine there of the Three essential (substantial) *res* without claiming consubstantiality had by now yielded to the Ditheist solution (cf. the possibly edited down formulation at n. 481). Until his death in 1573 Gonesius and the scholarly Stanisław Farnowski (n. 526) sustained the sense of some pan-Commonwealth party holding out between the strict Calvinists and the outright Christocentric Unitarians, in this phase sometimes designated in dictinction to the Cujavians, impregnating the anti-Nicenes in around Lublin, and the "Cracovians." Jerzy Schomann, first a Pinczovian, then a Racovian, and in the present context a Cracovian, having himself been possibly the first native Ditheist (Wajsblum) to follow the lead of French Statorius (Bk. 2 at. n. 646), may be taken here as a representative of the eventually prevailing party. As the chroniclers and historians of this party of Unitarians/Socinians are largely responsible for the historiography of the last third of the Reformation century among the anti-Nicene Reformed, the eminence of Farnowksi among the Ditheists/Binitarians might have otherwise passed largely unnoticed but for the monograph of Marek Wajsblum who, concertedly exploiting all the resources with sinewy energy, including regional archives, presents the most solid theological and ecclesiastical account of Ditheism to the death of Farnowski (c. 1615), "Dyteiści małopolscy (Stanisław Farnowski i Farnowianie)," *RwP* 5 (1928) 63–97, compactly presented with further clarifications by Stanisław Szczotka, "S. F.," *PSB* 6 (1948). For a brief contemporaneous taxonomy and chronology of the anti-Nicene parties and synods, 1567–1614, see translation in RD 5, n. 20, and for Polish Ditheism in a systematic theological context, Misiurek, *Chrystologia Braci Polskich*, chap. 2.

503. It is distressing to readers of the *Historia* with an interest in the rise of interconfessional toleration in Poland amid strongly held conviction (a stance expounded by the author himself in the perilous seventeenth-century context) to come upon Lubieniecki expressing himself with such animus against two fellow pilgrims on the anti-Nicene, ante-Nicene way, Gonesius and Farnowski, who still clung to the intermediate Binitarian position, as now, baldly, opponents of "the confessors of the truth" (the consequent Christocentric Unitarian, still not so designated).

504. Gonesius separated from the Minor Church ;and in Węgrów in Podlachia, under the protection of Prince Jan Kiszka (d. 1592), nephew of Prince Mikołaj Radziwiłł, he concentrated on his publication, dying there in 1573.

His comprehensive work was *Doctrina pura et clara de praecipuis Christianae religionis articulis* (Węgrów, 1570), of which there is a unique surviving copy in the Bibliothèque Nationale in Paris. It is made up of four tracts of earlier composition, (1) *De Deo et Filio eius Christo Iesu et Spirito Sancto*, (2) *De uno vero Deo Patre Domini nostri Iesu Christi*, (3) *De unigenito Filio Dei* (first ed., Cracow, 1556 (n. 509), and (4) *De baptismo Novi Foederis*. In the same year he printed also in Węgrów Polish versions of 1, 2, and 4 above, of sufficient difference from the Latin to require further study as to the interrelationship. These three are edited under the scholarly, scientific direction of Lech Szczucki (who also succinctly discusses the relationship between the earlier Latin and the Polish versions, *PSB* 26.399A), as Gonesius's *Dzieła Polskie* in 3 volumes, by Halina Górska, Konrad Górski, and Zdisław Zawidzki, *O Trzech* (Warsaw: PAN, 1962), *O Synu Bożym* (ibid., 1961), *O Ponurzaniu chrystyjańskim* (ibid., 1960).

O Synu Bożym was dedicated to Prince Kiszka, appealing to his protection from the Unitarians, for the Prince himself had come to favor them. The subtitle of *O Synu Bożym* makes clear the author's belief concerning the Son "that he was before the creation of world and that he is through whom all things were made: against the Ebionite subterfuges," namely, against the arguments of the Christocentric immersionist Unitarian majority of the Minor Church. Gonesius places on his title page the passage (in Hebrew font) from Zechariah 6;12 which he renders in Polish, "Behold, the Man, whose name is Branch, and who shall grow up from his place." The tract is clearly directed specifically at the anonymous *Brevis explicatio in primum Ioannis caput*, by now ascribed to Laelius Rotondò (Bk 1, n. 1) Socinus. It appeared in the collection of pieces published on the initiative of Biandrata in *De falsa et vera unius Dei cognitione* (1567). See the substantial n. in the critical ed. of *O Synu Bożym*, 94, and on *De falsa et vera cognitione*, see nn. 531 and 610. Gonesius polemicizes against the (Socinian mis-)use of John 3:13 as a central christological topos: "No one ascended into heaven but he who descended from heaven, the Son of Man." Critical ed. of *O Synu Bożym*, preface to Kiszka, 13, line 5 and thereafter. In his defense of the preexistence of the Son against the interpretation of Laelius Socinus, Gonesius does not appear to make use of anything like Servetus's doctrine of the heavenly *flesh* brought down by the Son at the incarnation.

505. For Lubieniecki at this juncture the two parties opposed to what he considers the mainline of the Polish Brethren (he is thinking more of Little Poland than of Lithuania) are the Farnovian Ditheists and the (Servetian) Gonesian Tritheists; cf. following n.

506. Lubieniecki has *illi duo* referring to Farnowski and Gonesius. Cf. at n. 502. It is notable that Lubieniecki would turn with such animus on former associates of the early anti-Nicene Reformed and even use pejoratively of them the term "Arian."

507. Lubieniecki is confusing here, but he doubtless reflects the confusion in his own party. Since Arius of Alexandria was traditionally the archheretic, for a while both parties *within* the Minor Church could use "Arian" and "new Arian" pejoratively of each other. Cf. at n. 502. For Ebionite, etc., see Bk. 2, nn. 246, 248.

508. Lubieniecki dealt with Gonesius on *Historia, 111, 144, 146, 176, 202* who was given special attention in Bk. 2, nn. 390, 624. Lubieniecki refers here to the impact of Gonesius after his return from Padua in the two Polands and in Lithuania, under the protection of Mikołaj Radziwiłł the Black. With a letter from this prince Gonesius appeared at the synod of Secemin, 21 January 1556, Lubieniecki having included "his" speech there (*Historia, 112–15*).

509. Lubieniecki here turns on a major theologian with whom he had earlier dealt as with a pioneer spirit of the movement being chronicled. As a Ditheist, actually as a defender of the mysticism of the Three (as distinguished from the Trinity), Gonesius is therefore about to recede from the Author's view and favor. Lubieniecki seems to be ascribing the failure of Gonesius to come along with the main party of the Minor Church to the ongoing influence presumably of Melanchthon as a result of Gonesius's visit to Wittenberg in 1556 (Bk. 2, n. 414) and to his unclarified exchange with presumably the conservative Reformed beyond the circle of the Tritheists/Ditheists. Gonesius at Secemin (n. 508) had indeed expounded his conviction that the term *Trinitas*, being a *novum* beyond Scripture, could not be retained except as the doctrine of the Three, the second being the immortal, invisible Λόγος/*Verbum* as the seed of the incarnate Son. Sipayłło,

AS, 1.47. Budziński, History, chap. 31, had reported that Gonesius denied that the Son of God existed before his mother, *BAnt*, 42; but Budziński could have misunderstood him. The date of the characterization is, in any case, not preserved.

After Gonesius conferred with the divines in Wittenberg, in two letters of February 1556 Melanchthon, only incidentally touching on Gonesius, characterized him unkindly as "fecundus καί σκωπτικός and dismissed both his *libellus* and the letter delivered by him from the pre-schism Polish synod that had been intended to reassure Melanchthon that they did not themselves depart from "our common consensus." In the *libellus* of "the *Lithuanus*" Melanchthon quickly recognized "Servetias reliquias." Melanchthon, *Opera*, 8, nos. 5929, 5930. Specialized scholarship has thought to identify the *libellus* proffered for inspection as the lost *De communicatione [idomatum,] nec dialectica nec physica, ideoque prorsus nulla*; but given the reason for his having been sent to Wittenberg, Gonesius might well have brought a first draft of his *"De unigenito Filio Dei"*, to be his first published book (Cracow, March/April, 1556). Gonesius returned to Lithuania by way of Frankfurt on the Oder and Poznań. He was excommunicated for his *De unigenito* by the synod of Pińczów of 24 April–1 May 1556, and specifically for being a "Servetian who confuses the Persons of the Trinity and denies the true humanity of Christ." Sipayłło, *AS*, 1.72, 74; Bk. 2, n. 624. Servetus, but not Gonesius, did hold to something like the celestial flesh of Christ; see n. 504, ¶3.

510. "All," that is, all members of the Minor Church, now divided into two parties, the Ditheists or Farnovians/Gonesians and Lubieniecki's "pure" Unitarians. Of this synod there is no protocol. For the marshaled secondary literature, see Sipayłło, *AS*, 2.213. In the opening paragraph of the chapter, the schism referred to is presumably that of the Major and the Minor Churches within the Reformed movement. The debates at Łańcut are difficult to follow in the ensuing records. Filipowski presided at the stormy session. The congregation in Łańcut on the Wislok in Ruthenia had been founded by Krzysztof Pilecki.

511. That Budziński was one of two secretaries is noted at the end of this documentation, *Historia, 218*. It is here in place to note that Budziński in his History, book 1, chap. 15 mentioned Gonesius as a student in Hebrew of Stancaro in Cracow and in chap. 20 his return to the Commonwealth via Moravia with his wooden staff. *BAnt*, 40–41.

512. The synod of Łańcut was a separatist gathering of Ditheists with Tritheists and conservative Reformed, many of them lords. Szczucki, *Czechowic*, 74–75.

513. An elder of the church in Cracow, he is mentioned in *Historia, 227* and by Schomann in his *Testamentum*, *BAnt*, RD 3, no. 30, as one of the delegation to confer with the Hutterites in Moravia in 1569.

514. The printer, *Historia, 213*. The words in parentheses seem to be introduced by Lubieniecki into his Budziński text.

515. Perhaps some descended in the family of Katarzyna Weiglowa Zalaszkowska, the Sacramentarian martyr, *Historia, 14*. The words in parentheses are the surmise of Lubieniecki.

516. Minister in Bobin, the first to be baptized in Poland. Węgierski, *Slavonia Reformata*, 537.

517. This must be a faultily transcribed sentence from Budzinński that may indeed put into question the date and intent of the whole excerpt. Lutomirski as of 1567 is strangely characterized as having long resisted the truth, which even if that means Unitarianism, makes him scarcely different from many others in the text. Stanisław Orzechowski,

whether the Catholic publicist (*Historia, 17 passim*) or the Lublin burgher (*Historia, 253, 266*) or another, seems out of place and a comparison with Lutomirski on either tardiness or on affirming something to a father-in-law is unclear. In any case, whatever Lutomirski said to his *socer* would have been well before Łaski's death in 1561.

518. Lubieniecki here preserves Budziński's surely partisan characterization of the main body in Łańcut as agreeing in one thing only: to malign the christocentric unitarian Reformed in Cracow and elsewhere ("confessors of the name of the Son of God," with allusion to Luke 6:22).

519. Iwan Karniński, one of the circle of Cracow humanists, and one of the first noblemen to join the Reformed Church, of which he became an elder (*Historia, 23, 25 – 29*, passim) was at Łańcut angered by what he regarded as the blasphemies of both factions.

520. Perhaps Iwan Sikorski.

521. Sikorski is addressing Iwan Karniński, rebuking him for presuming to interpose his authority at a synod made up largely of Minor party representation well to the east of Cracow.

522. Possibly Maciej Bal (d. c. 1575), possibly Jakub, Jan, or Stanisław Golecki.

523. The Brethren from Cracow were the aforementioned two ministers (Lutomirski and Siekierzyński) and the four laymen. Budziński does not mean the irate nobleman of the Cracow district, Iwan Karniński, who in anger at both factions at Łańcut, withdraws after the rebuke from Sikorski.

524. Petrus Statorius, Sr., who had by now left the Minor Church to rejoin the Calvinists. See at n. 497.

525. Budziński probably means Sikorski.

526. These two scriptural *loci* could have been quite plausibly adduced by Karniński in support of the eternity of the Son. The Latinized Budziński text for Mic 5:2 is no stronger than the Vulgate: "*parvulus* es ... *et agressus eius ab initio, a diebus aeternitatis.*" 1 John 5:1 begins: "Whosoever believeth that Jesus is the Christ is a child of God and whosoever loveth . . . ."

527. Not clear what the case is.

528. We have come upon Stanisław Farnowski (d. c. 1615 or 16) at n. 55, then with Gonesius at n. 502. He is attested (*Historia, 164*) among the 22 signatories protesting Sarnicki's synodal actions in Cracow, May, 1563. He was at that time minister for Joachim Lubomirski at Tarnowa (1560 – 63). He had been educated abroad and had been a Calvinist minister in Spisz or Transylvania, 1556 – 57. He matriculated at the University of Marburg, 4 October, 1563, leaving after the death of his principal professor, Andreas Gerard of Ypres, 1 February 1564; and he settled in Heidelberg (Bk. 2, n. 364) in the spring of 1564, matriculating there in May 1564. He had to leave the university because of his heterodox views of the Trinity, July 1564, studied for a while in Zurich at the Carolineum, then returned to Poland at the end of 1566, well versed in the classical languages of Scripture, including Aramaic and Syriac, the peer of Czechowic, inferior only to Budny among Commonwealth scriptural scholars.

It was at Łańcut that Farnowski emerged as the articulate spokesman of the Ditheists in his angry thrusts against the Unitarians but also against by now orthodox Calvinist Statorius, who sided with Karniński. Stanisław Szczotka, in his article in *PSB* 6 (1948), gives not only a full account of Farnowski but also clarifies considerably the otherwise obscure record of the intemperate synod of Łańcut of 1567 (n. 510). See further the major piece by Szczotka, "Synody arian polskich od założenia Rakówa do wygnania z kraju" (1569 – 1662), *RwP* 7/8 (1935/36) 21ff.

529. Statorius evidently joined with Farnowski in taking away from Karmiński the second text, 1 John 5:1, as primarily applicable to the rebirth of Christians in Christ, loving God as the Father through regeneration. But in general the now conservative Statorius was presumably supportive of Karmiński and opposed to Farnowski. Cf. Szczotka, "F.S.," *PSB* 6 (1948) n. 189–382, esp. 373B.

530. Evidently the four Cracovian Brethren and their two ministers have been readmitted.

531. Jan Sierkierzyński is here promoting an interpretation of John I that Laelius Socinus also expressed in the anonymous *Brevis explicatio in primum caput Iohannis* (1555), printed twice in the sixteenth century, first in Alba Julia, 1568, the second in Heidelberg, 1591. This evidently circulated in MS before it was printed in 1568. See Bk. 2, n. 1; Bk. 3, n. 610. Sierkierzyński's confidence in the revolutionary exegesis, toppling the main New Testament *topos* for the premundane Logos in relation to Jesus, may well rest upon his reading the work of Laelius circulating in manuscript. Supportive of this surmise is the fact that Schomann reports for 1566 that some of the Brethren were learning of this novel interpretation of John 1 from *Rhapsodia [in Isaiam]*, which he expressly ascribed to Laelius, *Bant*, RD 3, no. 28.

To ascertain the influence of Laelius Socinus in Poland and Transylvania before his principal work was printed, each time (1568, 1591) without proper attribution, the identity and authorship of *Rhapsodia* and also the relationship of titles on the same chapter of John by both Laelius and Faustus Socinus need to be clarified, even through a discussion of the latter at this point is chronologically somewhat premature. But Faustus himself is an independent source as to the transmission of a central idea of his uncle. His own similarly entitled work was the posthumous *Explicatio primae partis primi capitis Joannis* (Raków, 1618).

As for the *Rhapsodia*, Rotondò, although the whole thrust of his critical edition of the works of Laelius Socinus is to underscore his decisive role in the emergence in Poland and Transylvania of a biblical Unitarianism, does not accept Schomann's ascription of this work to him, lending his weight rather to a venerable conjecture that it was not from Laelius but rather an excerpt from the unedited repertory of Andrzej Wojodowski, *Elenchus locorum S. Scripturae Novi Testamenti quae pro asserenda SS. Trinitate et Aeterna Filii Dei deitate adferuntur.* Lelio Sozzini, *Opere*, p. 304. Another work, representative of what was circulating in Poland when Sierkierzyński was arguing for a Socinian interpretation of John 1, was that of Grzegorz Paweł, *Wykład na pierwszą kaptiułę Jana Świętego Ewangielicy* (1567–68), identified by scholars from Sand/Wiszowaty, *Bant*, 23–24, 44, 65–66, to Górski, as a Polish version of an early version of the work of Faustus Socinus. However, in the light of a critically edited text of Laelius by Rotondò, it would appear that *Wykład* was a Polish version of the work of Laelius, which is what Sand put down (p. 44), in fact, only to be "rectified" by Wiszowaty. Rotondò himself does not make a judgment about *Wykład*, whether it was Laelian of Faustian.

With the text of Laelius's original work of 1555 critically established (Bk. 2 n. 1), Rotondò is in a solid position to assess the testimony of Faustus Socinus about his own and his uncle's writings on John 1 and the subsequent scholarly surmises about the impact of the two similarly entitled, revolutionary readings of John 1.

Faustus himself composed a somewhat variant *Explicatio* (above ¶2) in Basel, c. June 1563. When Ochino in his *Dialogi* (Basel, 1563) comes with his interlocutor, "Spiritus," Bk. 1, n. 178, to the revolutionary new reading, he expresses shock at "the blind arrogance" of the novel interpretation of John 1, without precedent on the theme. This assertion by Ochino is regarded therefore by Rotondò as the earliest notice of the circulation of the two similar but distinguishable anonymous works of the Sozzini, uncle (1555) and nephew (1563). Several Swiss and other Reformed theologians immediately sensed the hazards to their churches in Transylvania and Poland, notable among them, Beza, Josias Simler, Girolamo Zanchi, and at length Junius (d. 1602), who printed the *libellus* of Laelius, acknowledging that its authorship remained unknown. Rotondò recounts the alarm of the Reformed divines and their various efforts to distinguish the two treatments and to refute the novel interpretation, *Opere*, 349–71, all as an important episode in the consolidation of Reformed Triadology. He also reinforces the surmise of Massimo Firpo that Biandrata was in possession of the *libellus* of Laelius already when he wrote from Alba Julia to Grzegorz Paweł, 21 September 1565, urging the Polish divine to divert the argumentation in the Polish Synods from the, as he held, inconsequential or perhaps even socially hazardous issue of believers' baptism to the more substantive issue of the person and role of Jesus Christ solely in scriptural terminology. For Biandrata's letter, see Wotschke, *Briefwechsel*, no. 348, critically edited in Sipayłło, *AS*, 2. 352–59; and for Firpo's original surmise, see *Antitrinitari nell'Europa orientale*, 18–21. Firpo only hints that Giampaolo Alciati, writing to the same Grzegorz Paweł from Moravia in 1564–65, in correpsondence known only from our *Historia* (Bk. 2 at n. 368), may also have been drawing on Laelius's *libellus*. Sierkierzyński and Grzegorz Paweł could also have had direct access to some of the writings of Laelius known to have been circulated in Poland by his friend and disciple, Stanisław Kokoszka (Rotondò, *Opere*, 355, n. 118; Firpo, *Antitrinitari*, 18, n. 58).

The ongoing interrelationship of two Socinian *libelli* (1555/63) and their reappearance in varying versions, Latin and vernacular, still awaits a clarification to be based on careful attention to the stages through which the *libellus* of Faustus of 1563 went in the lifetime of its author in order for us to discriminate between the effluvium of the pure Laelius on John 1 and te influence of Faustus in his evolving thought based on his uncle out by his own testimony at points divergent from him.

532. Near Radom. Without protocol, enhancing the value therefore of the following account. Sipayłło, *AS*, 2.214.

533. One of the few references in Lubieniecki to the common people. See Tazbir, *Lubieniecki*, 321. Cf. *Historia, 254*, where the small townsmen in the vicinity of Lublin are mentioned.

534. All these have been previously mentioned by Lubieniecki except for Jan Falconius (Sokolowski), minister in Mordy, a frequenter of the synods.

As to the baptism of Niemojewski, our Author, quoting from Budziński, who may have told of this decisive event in an earlier portion of his History has therefore in the *Historia* only reported that in Kujawy Niemojewski belonged to an evangelical church in 1564. The baptism took place in his residence in Niemkówka near Toruń, c. April 1566. This date is based upon Reszka, *De atheismis* (1596) 255, who says that Niemojewski appeared at the Diet of Lublin just recently baptized. That Czechowic baptized him *in his house,* surrounded by members of the church he had gathered on his estate in 1563, is based upon Zachorowski, "Najstarsze synody," 233. The Cujavians were the first to rebaptize, then the ditheist Farnovians, and then the Racovians, cf. *RD* 4, n. 20. That the mode of rebaptism was that of the nearby Mennonites rather than by immersion, is suggested by Jarmola, chap. 5.

535. Minister in Nieśwież, frequenter of the synods.

536. A Świechowski is attested in Sipayłło, *AS*, 2.116.

537. Luke 2:1. The position is identifiable with that of Laelius Socinus.

538. All of these have appeared in the *Historia*, except for Jan Baptysta Święcicki, minister in Kiejdany in Samagitia (ethnic Lithuania).

Of Krowicki it may be here noted that, standing on the fully Unitarian side with Budny and Budziński, he later, 11 August 1569, would be debating at his town, Mordy, with an old archbishop of Lwów, Jan Dymiter Solikowski. The latter, at one time open to Protestantism, was even now prepared for a full and resourceful defense of the received dogma of the Trinity. By this time Krowicki had come to the same view as Budny, that Christ was begotten by Joseph, although unlike Budny and his Transylvanian colleagues, Krowicki remained an adorant of the Ascended Christ. Solikowski preserved a record of the debate in a MS in the Jagiellonian Library. Barycz, *Z epoki*, 358–60.

Faustus Socinus himself states that Laelius wrote a paraphrase of John 1:1 in 1561, claiming for him priority in that interpretation. See his posthumous *Defensio animadversionum adversus Gabrielem Eutropium (Raków, 1618) 67–68; Gryczowa, no. 266. Faustus in his own Explicatio* (Raków, 1618) 6–7, says that although Laelius disliked publicity and was opposed to publishing his works, some of them appeared in print soon after his death c. 1565. However, this does not dispose of the question of the authorship of the treatise that exercised an influence on the development of the Polish Brethren. Faustus was indebted to the ideas of Laelius (*Explicatio*, 5) taken from conversations with him and from his manuscripts after the uncle's death (1562). However, Faustus was critical of aspects of Laelius's interpretation of John 1, as known from the 1591 edition by Junius of his *Defensio adversus Europium*, 67. Moreover, in 1580 and later Faustus claimed the authorship of the anonymous Latin treatise on John 1 that circulated in Poland by 1566, translated into Polish, and ascribed to Beza and Zanchi to Laelius, as may be seen in Faustus's letters to Dudith, 9 December 1580, and to Krzystof Morsztyn, *BFP, Opera Socini*, 1.456. Faustus claimed that earlier version was much shorter than, but essentially identical with, his own *Explicatio*, in his *Fragmenta duorum scriptorum* (Raków, 1619) 3.

As the known printed version of the novel interpretations of John I prior to the *Explicatio* of Faustus differ considerably, at least those containing the interpretation rejected by Faustus must indeed belong to our or derive from Laelius. The problem, already discussed by Bock, *Antitrin.* 2.649–50, 728–29, was raised also by K. Górski in his "Graegorz Paweł jako tłumacz Blandraty i Fausta Socyna," *RwP* (1926) 21–22, and his *Grzegors Paweł*, 19–5, as well as by Wajsblum, "Rhapsodie Laeliusza Socina," *RwP* 5 (1928) 140-44. Górski reassigned all known versions to Faustus. Wajsblum maintained that the authentic Laelius survived in the versions of Biandrata and of Junius and in Grzegorz Paweł's translation. Much of this argumentation is marginalized by Rotondò's critical edition of the authentic *Brevis explicatio* of 1555.

The upshot of this note is that Sierkierzyński in synod, June 1567, was more likely to have been drawing on some form of Laelius's *Brevis explicatio* (Zurich, 1555) than some early version of Faustus's *Explicatio* (Basel, 1563).

539. Budziński. Lubieniecki renders Budziński's word *Instrumentum*.

540. Tyrannius Rufinus (d. 410) first used *Instrumentum* for the two Testaments together.

541. With the Budziński text before him, Lubieniecki, now presumably resumes a nearly verbatim citation of an important credal formulary, but the print is not in italics; and at the end it reads obscurely: "nuncium se mittere verbo illi prae aeterno," yet no doubt referring to the Holy Spirit. But if the translation renders the intended sense, the formulary represents a compromise in favor of the Ditheists, the acknowledgement of an eternal Logos.

542. *Non inveni*. The referent is to *Verbum* neuter, not *Filius*. The reference to Augustine seems to be from Budziński, a patristic comment that would evidently nullify the preceding statement with which it is known that Budziński disagreed.

543. As a result of the conflicts that surfaced angrily at Łańcut and Skrzynno in June 1567, the Minor Church in the western palatinates of Little Poland split into Unitarians and Ditheists, among them most prominent members, Farnowski, Bieliński, Czechowic, and Żytno. But on the social implications of Ditheism soon Czechowic, Piotr of Goniądz, and Niemojewski were also separated from the Farnovians. See n. 552.

544. It is not clear what work of Farnowski is meant. His first printed works were *Nauka prawdziwa o karności christiańskiey* (Lusławice, 1573) and *O znajomości i wjznaniu Boga zawżd jednego Stworzyciela i jednego Ducha Bożego* (ibid., 1573). In this second book about God the Father and Creator, the preexistent Son of God, and the one Holy Spirit, Farnowski addressed "the most noble of all, the Polish People": "And just as, O Poles, your forefathers once worshiped the three pagan gods, Jove (Piorun), Pluto, and Mars, having then renounced them, ultimately embraced the Triune God of [the Roman] Antichrist, so now, today, knowing and understanding the truth, strip away this offensive, this false basis for you, which up until now you have had for this holy, great, and hidden mystery. . . . It is your primary, highest wisdom, O Poles, that you may in this life know God well and love him and his only Son. This glory Poles never understood for felt before." In the subordinationist Binitarianism of this book the Holy Spirit is understood as the only one through whom the regenerate call unto the Father. See Wajsblum, "Farnowski i Farnowianie," *RwP* 5 (1928) 78–80, where he suggests that the reference here in Lubieniecki is probably only to handwritten leaflets and letters.

545. Lubieniecki's true believers are by 1567 conscious of themselves as distinct from two other groupings who had by now differentiated themselves within the Reformed movement in Poland-Lithuania: the Trinitarian, pedobaptist Calvinists and the Ditheistic, largely adult baptist Farnovians. They themselves were now wholly unitarian, partly pedobaptist, partly adult baptist, and preserved the trine baptismal formula, Matt 28:19–20. Unlike the half-way Farnovians, they denied the preexistence of the Son as well as the deity or personhood of the Holy Spirit.

At the end of the line Wiszowaty probably misreads Lubieniecki to say *Binaturae* for the Ditheists when everywhere else it is *Bideitae*, cf. RD 5, n. 20.

546. For Stanisław Cichowski, Sr., see n. 355. The reported imprint is unknown. Bock, *Antitrin.* 1.102, quotes it as "*Acta synodi colloquiique Skrynicensis A. 1567 celebrati, cum omnibus responsionibus eorum, qui negabant Verbum S. Filium Dei mundum hanc visibilem cum Deo creasse; sed asserebant, initium suum habuisse tempore Joannis Baptistae et Joannis Evangelistae, ad obiectiones adversae partis.*" The descriptive character of the alleged title suggests that it was Bock's deduction from Lubieniecki's text.

547. Similar was the conclusion of the synod of Mordy, 6 June 1563, embodied in the letter to Mikolaj Radziwiłł the Black, above, nn. 95, 97.

548. The Farnovians apart took seriously the injunction of Jesus about praying in secret, when he proffered an example of private prayer, Matt 6:6, although evidently Farnowski discussed prayer and composed hymns for his simple services with only cross and pulpit at Nowy Sącz, the lay members having been encouraged to participate in exchanges during the service, according to the *lex sedentium* (cf. 1 Cor 14:23ff.). Szczotka, "Farnowski," summarizing Wajsblum *PSB*, 374A; *Radical Reformation*, chap. 10.3.

549. Pedobaptism and believers' baptism by immersion coexist and are mutually

tolerated. The intent of the reference to the commemoration of the crucifixion is not clear. Both pedobaptism and the Good Friday observance were held to be Roman Catholic (and Greek Orthodox) alterations of practices in the ancient Church and the synodists were all trying to return to the understanding of their own baptism as a replication of the baptism of Jesus by John and the dying with him to the world (Rom 6:3, etc.).

550. The synod alludes to the request of the mother of the two apostolic sons of Zebedee, Matt 20:20–28, esp. 25–26.

551. The synod also voiced dissatisfaction with the Brest Bible. See Bk. 1, n. 267.

552. Lubieniecki fails to mention two synods that convened to hold together the various anti-Nicene Reformed parties: moderate Calvinists, Tritheists, Ditheists, and Unitarians. His own grandsire Hieronim Filipowski was the instigator of the one at Pełsznica, October 1568, on the estate near Cracow of his deceased friend Lasocki, Sipayłło, *AS* 2. 220–221; discussed by Wajsblum, ''Dyteiści,'' 68–69, where he emends the Kolozsvár MS to show that Farnowski was a major participant. It was at this synod that Lukasz Mundius of Vilna reported on his visit to the Hutterites, at nn. 587, 687, and that the practice of immersion, long discussed, was pressed toward implementation. The same discussion of theology, church ordinances, and the social implications of the Gospel was continued at the synod near Lublin at Bełżyce, March 1569, *AS* 2. 222–25. Here the agenda among the four groupings placed all topics under the main heading of God the Father as the one God, of the Messiah as the Lord Jesus, of the kingdom of the Lord Jesus, the Anointed of God, and of the duties of the disciples of the same. It is evident from the prominence of Grzegorz Paweł and Jerzy Schomann that they must have set the agenda, which in all its points, including immersion, and the social implementation of the Gospel among the Brethren, lordly, clerical, and common, anticipates the topics of the *Catechesis* of 1574 (RD 7).

553. The Ditheists under Farnowski, hence Farnovians, enjoyed the protection of Stanisław Mężyk. The services under Farnowski were attended by gentlemen of the area and townspeople. In the castle chapel cleared of all ornamentation except for the pulpit and a cross the services were informal without prayer. Under the protection of Mężyk a synod of Ditheist churches soon included another major center, Lusławice, where a school was established and nearby a printing press under the protection of lords Stanisław Taszycki and Piotr Błoński Biberstein. Children came to this new moderate Reformed School from Hungary and Transylvania. Stanisław Wiśniowski was the second ranking minister of the synod. By the agreement of Lusławice of 1578, under the pressure of the two lords aforementioned, most of the Ditheist synod rejoined the by now Unitarian Minor Church of the ''Racovians.'' For parallels and further developments to 1614, see Chronicle, RD 5, n. 20; *BAnt*, RD 5, no. 58; RD 6, between nn. 11–15.

553. This would have been the Ditheist counterpart of the Stancarist school in Dubieniecko, the Calvinist school in Lubartów, and the Unitarian school in Raków.

554. It is characteristic of often theologically inexact Lubieniecki to make *praeexistentia* synonymous with an illogical *praeaeternitas*. These terms were employed also in the synods which strove to distinguish between the eternally begotten Son as consubstantial with the Father in the Godhead before creation and the simpler and undefined preexistence of the Son before the incarnation, whether in the mind of God or as the Logos of God instrumental in creation or as the preexistent Messiah destined to come in the fullness of time. Lubieniecki pillories Farnowski with the same heretical identification that the main body of the Reformed who became the Minor Church sought to avoid for themselves form their Calvinist, Stancarist, and Catholic opponents. Far-

nowski and Wiśniowski would not have considered themselves followers of Arius in the precise terms mentioned by the learned Alexandrian presbyter. Misiurek brings the Christology of the Ditheists together briefly, *Chrystologia*, 126.

555. The final paragraph may be making clear that the Minor Reformed Church was approaching the eventual baptist position but nothing is said about the practice of the Farnovians who, in fact, synodally adopted the practice of believers' baptism, though *after* the Cujavians (who relocated in Lublin), yet *before* the Racovians. See the excerpt of a chronicle classifying the groupings, RD 5, n. 20.

NOTES TO CHAPTER NINE

556. The great publicist, who would die in the company of friends in the Minor Church, appears in *Historia, 13, 18–20, 117.*

557. This is in reference to an episode in the Livonian War, 1557–71. Lubieniecki alludes to what Modrzewski himself said in his preface about the origin of the *Sylvae*. Ivan IV seized Polock, 15 February 1563, and annexed the whole palatinate bordering on Livonia and more, holding it until 1570. Sigismund prepared for war against Muscovy in 1565. The date is supplied by Lubieniecki from the *Sylvae*.

558. This major work is quoted in *Historia, 13*. Andrzej Frycz Modrzewski (1503–72) wrote *Sylvae quatuor: I De tribus personis et una essentia Dei; II De necessitate conventus habendi, ad sedandas religionis controversias; III De Jesu Christo filio Dei et hominis eodemque Deo et Domino nostro; IV De homousio et de iis, quae huc pertinant* (Cracow, 1590); reprinted and critically edited by Kazmierz Kumaniecki, *Opera omnia*, 5 vols. (Warsaw; PAN, 1953–60) 5; the same in Polish in 5 vols., Łukasz Kurdybacha, *Dzieła Wszystkie* (Warsaw; PAN, 1960–69), 5, with an extensive introductory essay, ''Początki Antytrynitaryzmu w Polsce'' (5–36), placing the *Sylvae* in context. There is an excerpt of *Sylva* I in *BAnt*, RD 1.

559. Johannes Operinus.

560. Modrzewski.

561. Trecy.

562. The date 1571 is given, no doubt from Budziński, for Trecy's deceitful act in Basel by *Nieznana Kronika Ariańska*, ed. by Szczucki, 1.171.

563. András Dudich/Dudith was born in Budapest of an Italian mother, Magdelena Rizzoni, and of a Hungarian nobleman. On the death of his father he was placed under the care of his uncle Bishop Augustine Sbardellati, and he studied as a youth in Breslau with the humanist Johann Henckel. His extensive humanistic studies and court assignments found him successively in Vienna, Verona, Padua, London (under Queen Mary Tudor), Paris. Returning home in 1557, he received orders with a prebend in Felheviz. Again in Padua, 1558–60, he returned to his native land to serve as secretary of Archsbishop Olah and was named bishop of Knin (Tina), 19 December 1561, by Emperor Ferdinand. See Pierre Costil, *André Dudith, humaniste hongrois, 1533–1589: sa vie, son oeuvre et ses manuscrits grecs* (Paris, 1934); Henryk Barycz, *PSB* 5 (1939–46) 445–448; Lech Szczucki, ed., *Epistolae*, Andrea Dudith Sbardellati (1533–1589), announced at Villa I Tatti, Florence, 11 June 1985.

564. It was as bishop of Knin under Turkish rule (in a diocese beyond even the boundaries of the Apostolic Kingdom of Hungary) that, along with the Bishop John VIII of Csanád (from Kolozsvár), Dudith represented the Hungarian hierarchy during Period III (1562–63) of the Council of Trent. He there supported the chalice for the laity in his

address *Sententia de calice laicis permittendo*, published later in Padua in 1563. On the death of his colleague, Dudith succeeded him as bishop of St. George's cathedral in Csanád, 1561 – 63, and was translated to Pécs (Fünfkirchen), 1563 – 65 (in Ottoman Hungary since 1541, n. 128).

565. Dudith was the diplomatic representative in Cracow, 1563 – 67, of Hapsburg imperial, royal Bohemian, royal Hungarian concerns. Costil, *Dudith*, 117 – 136. He remained in Cracow even after his second marriage.

566. Dudith informed Maximilian, April 1567, of his intention to marry and renounce his ecclesiastical dignities and diplomatic position. Costil, *Dudith*, 128. Gams, *Series Episcoporum*, gives 7 February 1565 as the date when he ceased to be bishop of Pécs.

567. The dating comes by inference from references to synods and *anno superiori*, *Historia, 224*.

568. The synod is known only from the *Historia*. Sipayłło, *AS*, 2.119.

569. The expression *magna Synodus* introduces this material from Budziński, here called *conventus*, and may reflect Budziński's *zjazd*.

570. That is, for Jesus Christ, the Son of Man, not the preexistent Son of God; cf. Luke 6:22.

571. Eph 4:3.

572. Cf. Rom 8:27.

573. Erasmus, *Opera Hilarii*, 2 vols., I: "Doctrina Christi, quae prius nesciebat λογομαχίαμ, coepit a philosophiae praesidii tendere: hic erat primus gradus ecclesiae ad deteriora prolabentis . . . ."

574. Ibid., a paraphrase.

575. On Jaques de Thou, J. Crato von Crafftenheim, Jacques and Pierre Monau, M. A. Muret, and Florimond de Raemond, see Costil, *Dudith*, 1 passim, and for Justus Lysius, ibid, 211. The last was author of *L'Histoire de la naissance, progrès et décadance de l'héresie de ce siècle*, 2 vols. (Paris, 1605; 2nd edition, 1610); Latin edition, *Historia de ortu, progressu et ruina haereseon huius saeculi* (Cologne, 1614), 1.578 – 79.

576. This would indicate that Budziński composed this part of his History in 1568.

577. Trecy, as *vir pius et eruditus*, is first mentioned in Wotschke, *Briefwechsel*, 119 (in a letter to Johann Wolph) by Lismanino, 21 Oct. 1560, as being in charge of a delegation leaving for Switzerland. Thereafter the *Briefwechsel* is filled with references to him or letters from or to him.

578. Dudith founded a Reformed church in Śmigiel before 1580. By 1586 the congregation had changed its theological position and became the main center of the Polish Brethren in Great Poland. See Merczyng, *Zbory i senatorowie*, 118. The somewhat awkward wording of the text as been preserved in translation to bring out Budziński's feeling for the Reformed Church as an ideal unity, of which his Minor Church was the purer form.

579. In the text erroneously 1565. Dudith was recognized as *indigena* and thus as a Polish noble. Costil, *Dudith*, 128, n. 5. Andrzej Lubieniecki the Elder was later pastor in Śmigiel.

580. Elżbieta Zborowska was a widow. Her father, Marcin Zborowski, rose to be castellan of Cracow in 1561, the highest senatorial dignity, and died in 1565.

Dudith's first wife was Regina Strass of the court of Cracow, whom he secretly engaged as early as 1565. Costil, *Dudith*, 127.

581. Of the seven sons of Marcin Zborowski, there were not four but rather three, Marcin, Piotr, and Jan who were Senators. The other four sons (Lubieniecki says three)

held high offices also. See Kasper Niesiecki, *Herbarz Polski*, 10 vols. (Leipzig, 1839 – 46) 10.129 – 30; Merczyng, *Zbory i senatorowie*, 137.

582. He died 23 February 1589. His tomb, with a mural monument, is in the right aisle of St. Elizabeth's in Wrocław. His portrait in the city library is reproduced by Costil, *Dudith*.

583. Otwinowski praised him in his *Heroes*, though only a few lines of summary survive in Węgierski (*Slavonia Reformata*, 533), where he is mentioned as ambassador of Emperor Maximilian II, King also of Hungary (1564 – 76).

NOTES TO CHAPTER TEN

584. The Minor Party within the Unitas Fratrum in Moravia bore similarities to the Minor Church. But Lubieniecki means the Hutterites who were communitarian Anabaptists of German and Austrian-Tyrolese origin. See Jarold Knox Zeman, *Anabaptists and the Czech Brethren in Moravia*; Leonard Gross, *The Golden Years of the Hutterites* (Scottdale, Pennsylvania: Kitchener, Ontario: Herald Press, 1980), with two maps showing the Hutterite settlement; 151 – 61 on Polish-Hutterite contacts, also in my *Radical Reformation*, chap. 27:2; and cf. above n. 203.

585. The reference is to the synod of 1568 in which representatives of the Minor Church made one last effort to cooperate fraternally with the Major Church, *Historia, 222 – 23*. The Polish Brethren of the Minor Church now make overtures to the Hutterite communitarian Anabaptists in Moravia. Lubieniecki chooses to minimize this exchange. It is quite likely that Editor Wiszowaty chose to cut the Author's narrative. I have compensated for this sketchiness by adducing a description from his great uncle's *Polyneutychia*, RD 6.

586. Lubieniecki or, much more likely, editor Wiszowaty, misnames the German-speaking refugees (Hutterites) in Moravia.

The following lacuna in the text was originally intended, no doubt, to characterize them, a lacuna of almost two full dotted lines, possibly omitted by the final editor as inaccurate (or illegible).

587. The date 1569 should be 1568 (n. 588). Perhaps our Author wished to credit his grandsire, Filipowski, with the initiative; for 1569 is the correct date of the first journey of Jerzy Schomann *et al.* to Moravia, *after* the report of Mundius immediately dealt with in Chapter Ten.

However, we know from the Hutterite Chronicle, *Die älteste Chronik der Hutterischen Brüder*, ed. by A.J.F. Ziegelschmid (Ithaca, N.Y., 1943): *The Chronicle of the Hutterite Brethren* (Rifton, New York: Plough Publishing House, 1987) 441/411, that is is recorded that Hieronim Filipowski (Janckowsky in the German text) arrived with three preachers and the apothecary of Cracow, Simon Ronemberg, on 25 January 1570, and that among their beliefs and practices was immersion (*untertauchen ins wasser*) and their understanding of "baptism by the pouring on of water as insufficient." The same Chronicle contains a letter from Walpot to the Polish Brethren (Bartłomiej [Codecius], Jan Święcicki, Adam Mendicus, Szymon Ciechanowski, and Jakub Livius, pp. 443/413, and a second letter in 1571 from Walpot just to Ronemberg 446/415. Robert Friedman deals with this second letter of Walpot in "Reason and Obedience," *MQR* (1945) 27 – 40.

588. Lubieniecki and Budziński before him did not find the overtures to the communitarian and Anabaptists of Moravia congenial, and hence the details are minimal. The chronology here is slack, off even from what is now ascertained. The report to the synod

of Dr. Mundius (n. 589) of October 1568 at Pełszixa (modern Pałecznica, near Miechów, n. 687) was what presumably stimulated a formal delegation to visit the Hutterite communes in August 1569 as reported by a participant, Jerzy Schomann, *Testamentum*, RD 3, no. 30.1. Here it is indicated that he, the apothecary Szymon Ronemberg, Hieronim Filipowski, and others made up the delegation, taking with them several Polish youths. A second delegation, made up of the same with three ministers of Poland and Lithuania, participated in a synod in Nové Mlýny (Neumühl), 25 January 1570, and returned with the Polish youths by 18 February 1570. The Hutterite sources are replete with the visits from the Polish Brethren and are no kinder to them than Lubieniecki in this assessment of the Hutterites. Wacław Urban,'' 'Caldendarium' kontaktów,'' 60–62.

589. Łukasz Mundius was a city councilor and burgomaster of Vilna, who had perhaps as early as 1557 received the title of doctor of medicine by authority of Jacobus Basilicus (Bk. 2, chap. 9) who made him agent in Vilna for the plan to colonize and reform Moldavia, 1561–63. Pirňat, ''Il martire e l'uomo politico,'' Dan and Pirňat eds., *Antitrinitarianism*, p. 173. He became involved in a suit against the *wójt* (*Vogt*, the head municipal functionary) of Vilna, Augustyn Rotundus Mieleski, and he left his city with wife and fled into voluntary exile in the autumn of 1563. He was able to bring his cause to the favorable attention of Maximilian as King of Bohemia, and Emperor Ferdinand I, who wrote letters to him and to King Sigismund in his behalf, 4 and 6 September, 1563. The Duke of Prussia and the King are known to have intervened in his behalf at least for clarification (although in the end he would be deprived of his properties and imprisoned in 1578). During his self-exile he evidently became acquainted at first hand with the Anabaptists in Moravia, especially in Slavkov (Austerlitz), where many foreign heterodox Protestants foregathered, 1564–68, when banished from Poland by the edict of Parczów. Dr. Mundius undoubtedly moved into the heterodox Reformed congregation in Vilna that is known to have existed, 1567–69. Wacław Urban, ''Losy Braci Polskich ad założenia Rakowa do wygnania z Polski,'' *OiRwP* 1 (1956) 139.

Mundius may have been a representative of this congregation when he appeared with some authority at the synod of Pełsznica, October 1568. Sipayłło, *AS*, 2.220–21. Cf. n. 676. Wajsblum conjectured that the initial purpose of the synod was to reunite the Ditheists of Cujavia and the Unitarians of Little Poland. Here social issues were raised about pastors working by the sweat of their own toil (like the Czech Brethren), of landowners not living by the sweat and blood of their serfs, and of giving up the right even to ownership of lands once won by bloodshed. At Pełznica Mundius, having recently visited the Moravian communities, ''recommended admirably the communist sect for their government, and because they had the same understanding with us about God and Christ, and for their piety.'' Discussion arose, but was put off by Mundius, who promised the arrival of Hutterite delegates. Sipayłło, *AS*, 2.21; Urban, '''Calendarium' kontaktów,'' 59–60. Dr. Mundius as of 1569 is characterized as ''civis Vilensis et consul, homo levissimus'' by *Nieznana Kronika Ariańska* I, ed. by Szczucki, 172, probably reflecting the view of Budziński.

590. In the text erroneously *honorum* instead of *bonorum*.

591. While the author here emphasizes doctrinal difference as the chief obstacle to union, contemporary evidence serves to show that a deeper cause lay in the wide difference in education, social culture, and general social customs. The Polish churches, gathering many of the intellectual elite from among nobles and burghers, intent upon free investigation of religious questions, were unable to subscribe to the communitarian ideas of the peasant and artisan communities in which intellectual life was subordinated to economic and social discipline. But the community of goods of Acts 2:44; 4:32, etc.,

crops up in all efforts at apostolic restitution, and the direct influence of the Hutterites on Raków was greater than acknowledged by Lubieniecki in this chap. or in that on Raków, chap. 12.

The Author interrupts his account of the beginnings of Raków (without the name) in order to look at the counterpart of his Minor Church in Transylvania and quickly come to the culminating struggle there, which prepared Faustus Socinus to take over the leadership of the Racovians in 1580.

NOTES TO CHAPTER ELEVEN

592. The inclusion of the following material is the clearest evidence of how in the conceptualization of the "History of the Polish Reformation" Lubieniecki thought of the Unitarian Reformed Church in Transylvania as the "major" church there until the death of Dávid in 1579 and yet as the development most akin to his own Minor Church in Poland. As the reference to diets, disputations, and synods in Hungary are not given by Lubieniecki and his documents in chronological order, all such references in the text and nn. are listed for the convenience of the reader at the end of chapter 11, n. 615.

593. In the title editor Wiszowaty promises an account of the debate of Socinus and Dávid in the home of the latter (1578/79), but the text only alludes to the fact, and never observes directly that Biandrata invited Socinus to defend his side in the fateful debate against Dávid. Chapter 11 is confusing chronologically, with its inclusion of an excerpt of a letter of Biandrata that appears to be misdated by a year (n. 605), and which in any case makes retrospective allusions to events and persons not wholly identifiable. Moreover, the close reader of the *Historia* is aware that in his earlier inclusion of an excerpt from Budziński (*Historia, 198–200*; nn. 383–94) Lubieniecki has already given glimpses of happenings in Transylvania, c. 1572–1613, while in the second half of chapter 11 he presents two documents of 1571, the first a letter reflecting on recent events in Transylvania, to that date, the other Sommer's letter originating in Kolozsvár, introducing his Theses against the dogma of the Trinity.

The close reader is also aware that Transylvania and Hapsburg and Ottoman Hungary, particularly in respect to the Reformation movements, have been mentioned in the notes several times episodically or tangentially prior to the present chapter. In Bk. 1, n. 150 and Bk. 2 nn. 364 and 426, John II Sigismund and Dávid were mentioned. In Bk. 3, n. 118 supplies the decisive dates for the usage of *Unitarius* (1568/1585/1638); n. 128 carries the military political account of all of Hungary to the Battle of Lepanto and the death of John II Sigismund, 1571; n. 129 rehearses the ethnic, constitutional, and controversial development of Transylvania to 1564/72 (respectively for the Reformed and the Saxon Lutherans); nn. 132, 236, 275 concern letters received in Poland-Lithuania from Transylvania on the Trinity and baptism (1565–69); n. 280 mentions Dávid's translation c. 1570 of a Flemish work against pedobaptists; nn. 282 and 714 concern a wine merchant Krawiec, an intermediary between Transylvania and Lublin, c. 1569; and n. 385 deals with the Transylvanian sojourn of Johann Sommer (1567–74). Then, in n. 387, with the mention of Stephen Báthory in the text, the voivodal succession in n. 128 is carried forward from 1571 to 1660, thus going far beyond the decade of chapter 11, itself chronologically confusing and theologically evasive, while in n. 343 Biandrata's relation with the Báthory is discussed.

Because editor Wiszowaty announces the Socinus-Dávid disputation in the title, I have set forth further in this note the two major sources stemming from either side, in this case from Socinus himself and from Palaeologus as defender of Dávid, as these two publications, particularly that of Palaeologus, gathered up earlier documentation that must be cited from near the beginning of the annotation. The benign reader will understand that the ensuing annotation is not intended as a consecutive narrative of the Transylvanian decade 1569 – 1679, but merely an identification and clarification of what Lubieniecki narrates and includes in his own documentation. In this way the reader of the notes starts here with the Disputation and returns to it and its aftermath, nn. 629 – 30.

Socinus arrived in Kolozsvár in late October 1578, and Matthias Vehe-Glirius (Bk. 2, n. 364) (the second his name in Transylvania) had preceded him by a few weeks, a major counselor of Dávid; Dán, *Vehe-Glirius*, 130, 133 – 34. On him see esp. nn. 601, 615, 629, 632, 642.

Szczucki clarifies the succession of events that led to the disputation, the trial of Dávid, and his death in 1579, the implication in it of Biandrata, the damaging role of the Polish Brethren, and the resultant ''grievous shadow which it cast over the relations between Polish and Transylvanian Unitarians for a lengthy period to come'' (''Polish and Transylvanian Unitarians,'' Dán and Pirnát, *Antitrinitarianism*, 238 – 41). Just as Szczucki lifts some of the burden from the Polish Brethren, so Pirnát (''Il martire e l'uomo politico,'' esp. 165, 184 – 88) in dealing with influence of the Christian Judaizer on Dávid (in the strict sense of Róbert Dán, ibid., 33 and in n. 629), Matthias Vehe-Glirius, tempers the traditional Unitarian judgment against Biandrata in suggesting that he acted in great personal peril and to save his cosmopolitan pan-Unitarian plan, not intending to compass Dávid's death.

The protracted debate between Socinus and Dávid, referred to in the title (n. 594), is trivialized or at least minimalized by Lubieniecki here as ''a storm in a teacup;'' and he fails to mention in the text that Socinus went to Kolozsvár (n. 600). The debate is recorded in two principal publications, along with related and antecedent material bearing on the whole decade covered in Lubieniecki's chapter. In chronological order of publication the first is the *Defensio Francisci Davidis in negotio de non invocando Jesu Christi in precibus*, edited by Jacobus Palaeologus (Basel [Cracow: Rodecki], 1581). A second edition followed (Cracow, c. 1582), which included a composite work from Dávid without date, *De dualitate*, Gryczowa, nos. 52 and 53, pp. 170 – 71. The second edition in both parts has been edited in facsimile by Róbert Dán, with an index and an introductory analysis of the complex book, with its parts and documents, by Mihály Balázs, Bibliotheca Unitariorum, I (Utrecht: De Graaf, 1983). At issue for Dávid was not only whether Jesus as the Messiah by designation was entitled, as only a human prophet, to adoration but also whether he as only *designatus rex* was in fact still in heaven, after the merely confirmatory Ascension, to harken to a prayer of invocation, prior to his awaited Second Advent.

As Palaeologus had reproached Socinus as implicated in the death of Dávid, Socinus replied on the basis of his own documentation and recollection in *De Ieus Christi invocatione: disputatio, quam Faustus Socinus per scripta habuit cum Francisco Davidis anno 1578, et 1579, paullo ante ipsius Francisci obitum* (Cracow: Rodecki, 1595), composed sixteen years after the event. The basic texts of the house disputation were written out by May 1579. Also with this collection a second edition followed in Raków, 1626, Gryczowa, nos. 66 and 261. The *Disputatio* is printed in *BFP*, the *Opera* of Socinus, 2.709ff. The non-adorants in Transylvania and the Commonwealth accepted the biblical account of the Ascension of Christ to the right hand of God the Father forty days after Easter (Acts 1:9), but some regarded this as comparable to that of certain Old Testament worthies, like Enoch and Elijah, and even to that of Paul lifted upon the road to

Damascus (2 Cor 12:2–3) and as provisional only, even though Dávid advanced several reasons why even a provisional ascension and a passive waiting role were important. Socinus was undoubtedly hard-pressed to clarify his views of Christ as vicar of God the Father in the rule from heaven of the world and of the church. The debate had thus its sequel in the developing Christology of Socinus. This was stressed in my "The Christological Issues between Francis Dávid and Faustus Socinus during the Disputation on the Invocation of Christ, 1578–79," Dán and Pirnát, *Antitrinitarianism*, 287–321. This study did not include arguments about the reliability of Socinus over against the evidence of the *Defensio* and the evidence there with issues other than adoration.

Socinus brought in November 1578 a letter for Biandrata, his sponsor, in which Grzegorz Paweł urged that Dávid be excommunicated for nonadorantism as the Polish Brethren had done to a certain Daniel, in 1576, *Defensio*, 228, 232, 235. This is thought by Balázs to refer to Daniel Bieliński. He once stood very close to Grzegorz Paweł in the Minor Church, but was readmitted as minister of the Major Church at its general synod in Cracow, of May 1576. Sipayłło, *AS*, 3.15–16, esp. n. 2; Wengierski, *Chronik*, item 21. Wilbur with reference to Uzoni, "Historia," identified the person excommunicated as Budziński, *Transylvania*, 40–41, n. 52, and mentions also Szymon Budny, but he sensed some confusion in dates. Budziński was indeed excommunicated in 1576. This information, with reference only to the date of readmission, is given by *BAnt*, 55. There is no record of it in Sipayłło, *AS*, 3, this volume primarily of Major Church synods. Possibly two sons, Budziński, Stanisław and Daniel, were present at Calvinist synods respectively in 1631 and 1632, ibid., 564, 580.

Although Lubieniecki declines to get into details and calls the controversy over nonadorantism "a storm in a teacup," he is evidently reluctant, in the middle of the seventeenth century, to have the principal spokesman of the Polish Brethren appear as an opponent of Dávid, in whom seventeenth-century Transylvanian Unitarians retrospectively saw their prophet, defender, and martyr. Lubieniecki declines to clarify the differences between "his" Socinus and "their" Dávid, except as he elsewhere refers to "a Judaizing spirit" evidently in his mind only on the margins of the Unitarian Church in the Transylvania of his day; cf. n. 675.

Socinus is already aware of the *Libellus parvus* by Dávid (n. 630), but the formal response of the Polish Brethren to it and their response to the formal request to enter into the Transylvanian controversy was not the (judgmental) private letter of Grzegorz Paweł but the *Judicium* (1579/80) would not, however, in fact affect the outcome of the trial (n. 630). On the personal rather than synodal character of the letter brought by Socinus, see Szczucki, "Polish and Transylvanian Unitarians," 239, nn. 29–30.

594. Lubieniecki may be thinking of the Polish Reformation as having kindled the development in Transylvania. Dr. Giorgio Biandrata had, after all, served in both the royal and the voivodial court and had spoken in behalf of Voivode Stephen Báthory, before his election as King of Poland, 1576–1586. Lubieniecki's great uncles, Stanisław and Andrzej, had briefly been courtiers under Báthory in Cracow. In what follows our author sometimes confuses the issues and the data at least in the opening part.

595. John Sigismund and his parents are mentioned *Historia, 170, 195, 199*, esp. Bk. 1, n. 150.

596. John II Sigismund, with his claim to the Hungarian Crown, has been looked back upon as "the Unitarian King" as of the debate at Alba Julia, 3–13 March 1568, in which he took part (n. 598). Biandrata, in a letter to Mikołaj Radziwiłł already in 1564 counted him as on the side of Dávid (n. 131).

For his edict of toleration, January 1568, see Introduction at n. 61 and Pl. 40.

597. Kolozsvár as Klausenburg had been one of the seven formative towns of Siebenbürgen. In the main square, beginning in 1568 the smaller church became the Saxon parish church, and the larger, St. Michael's was the Magyar parish, with Dávid's pulpit (from 1568 till 1716). After a six-day debate with Péter Méliusz (n. 609) on the Trinity at Várad in October 1569, Klausenburg was extruded from the Saxon Confederation (n. 129) and replaced by Broos (Szászváros, Orăştie). The intellectual center of Transylvanian Unitarianism, with school, library, and press, was Kolozsvár. On the debate and the extrusion, see Wilbur, *Transylvania*, 39 – 42. In the Counter-Reformation, St. Michael's reverted to the Catholic Church and the small church was given to the Unitarians. In this church was preserved the boulder in the square of Kolozsvár on which Dávid is remembered as having stood above the throng after his triumphant return from the ten-day debate with Méliusz in Alba Julia, March 1568.

Kolozsvár, the westernmost of the seven original Saxon boroughs, was rapidly Magyarized after its exclusion from the *Sachsenuniversität*. It may be here in place to anticipate the connections with it and the Polish Brethren. After the condemnation and death of Dávid, Demeter Hunyadi was forced upon the city as pastor of the Kolozsvár church and on the synod as the new superintendent (1580 – 92) (n. 601), to be succeeded by György Enyedi (1592 – 97), to be succeeded by Mátyás Toroczkai, also rector of the academy (1601 – 16), a fugitive in Poland (1603 – 04) from the fury of Basta (n. 387). There he made the acquaintance of Maciej Radecke, son of Matthias Radecke, secretary of the town council of Danzig. He was appointed pastor in the smaller Saxon church in Kolozsvár in 1605, returning to Raków in 1608 and again in 1612. He induced Toroczkai to translate the Racovian Catechism, published in two versions, 1632; *Res litteraria Hungariae vetus operum impressorum*, 2, for the years 1601 – 35 (Budapest: Akadémia Kiadó, 1983) nos. 1542 and 143; Uzoni, "Historia," 21.963 – 64; Budapest copy, MS Ab 70, 1.400. After Toroczkai's death Radecke succeeded him as superintendent (1616 – 332), although unable to speak Hungarian. *BAnt*, 106 – 7, greatly amplified from all sources by Wallace, *Biography*, 2.495 – 96; Wilbur, *Transylvania*, 104; 109, n. 23; 123, n. 62. When the refugees from Poland reached Transylvania in 1660, they were given a still extant house at 13 strada Memorandului near the main square for their worship. It was from among these refugees that came the Kolozsvár records of the synods often cited by Sipayłło, *AS*.

When Stanisław Lubieniecki wrote rules for the Polish exiles of 1660, seeking refuge among the Transylvanian Unitarians, he advised: "To procure exemption from any military service, the general levy included, and to give up the noble title and the rights of citizenship rather than to be obliged to go to war for them. Our people should not accept offices either in towns or in the country, because different activities connected with the office constitute a danger to one's conscience." Stanisław Kot quoted from MS K 30, fol. 68, in Uppsala, "Observanda Fratribus Polonis Unitariis in Transylvania receptio" (1660), quoted here from the English version, *Socinianism in Poland*, 204 – 05, n. 18.

598. The ten days of debate at Alba Julia (n. 596) was primarily between the two factions of the Reformed within Transylvania and from Hapsburg and Ottoman Hungary: on the one side Ferenc Dávid, Biandrata, et al., on the conservative side Péter Méliusz of Debrecen (n. 609), in the presence of Lutherans and even Catholic lords, mostly observers. John Sigismund acted as judge and Lord Gáspár Békés, a partisan of Dávid, was moderator.

Wilbur writes (*Transylvania*, 36, n. 27) of two eye-witness accounts, the one compiled or signed by the elders and minsiters on Dávid's side, *Brevis enarratio disputationis Albanae* (Alba Julia, 1568), and the other by Calvinist Kaspar Helth (Hungarian: Heltai,

n. 129 ¶8), *Disputatio in causa sacrosanctae Trinitatae* (Kolozsvár, 1568); *Régi Magyar Könyvtár*, 2, no. 117. When Helth came to his second edition of 1570, he acknowledged his conversion to Dávid's position. The secondary accounts, based on the primary documents, are those of Haner, *Historia*, 282–87; Lampe, *Historia*, 169–70); Uzoni, "Historia," 1.133–41; and Bod, *Historia Hungarorum ecclesiastica*), who supplies conveniently the preliminary articles of faith on both sides, Uzoni, "Historia," 1.409–12. Dávid signed himself "servus Ecclesiae Jesu Christi crucifixi" on the side of the ministers of the "Professio Evangelica," while the others were to become known often as of the "Professio Catholica," i.e., the orthodox Reformed. In the interval between Helth's two printings of the *Disputatio*, Dávid, working no doubt with a copy of Servetus's *Christianismi Restitutio* in the possession of Biandrata, reprinted some 265 of its 350 pages as two books, each with an appended tract on baptism, *De Regno Christi* and *De Regno Antichristi* (Alba Julia, 1569); *Régi Magyar Könyvtár*, 2, item 120; István Borbély, *A Magyar Unitárius Egyház hitelvei a xvi. században* (The doctrines of the Unitarian Church in the 16th century) (Kolozsvár, 1914), 42; noted by Wilbur, *Transylvania*, 41, n. 42.

599. John II Sigismund (n. 595) died in 1571. Lubieniecki gives the date incorrectly as 1579 and may have confused it with the death of Dávid in that year.

At the beginning of his reign, John was disposed to carry and extend the tolerant principle of confessional pluralism that his Polish mother had fostered in the first decree of toleration of 1557, confirmed in 1563 and notably at the Diet of Torda in January 1568 (n. 610). It was only, however, at the conclusion of the great debate of Alba Julia of March 1568 that John openly sided with Dávid and proposed mutual toleration and he confirmed the principle at successive diets. Decisively at the Diet of Maros-Vásárhely, 6–14 January 1571, only two months before his death, Voivode John Sigismund extended to the radically Reformed under Superintendent Dávid the principle of toleration and expressly acknowledged them as one of the "received religions"alongside the Calvinist Reformed. For a consecutive account in English of the various decrees with documentaiton, see Alexander (Sándor) Szent-Iványi, *Freedom Legislation in Hungary*, and his related *A Magyar Vallásszabadság* (Hungarian Freedom of Religion), (South Lancaster, Mass., 1964); Wilbur, *Transylvania*, 48.

For the political succession after John II, see n. 387; for the religious and constitutional situation after 1571, nn. 385 and 393.

The reader is aware that Lubieniecki passes over, largely unnoticed in this chapter, a decade of turmoiled debate in Transylvanian Reformed synods between the debate at Alba Julia in 1568 at nn. 596, 598, and the synod of Torda of 1578 at n. 600, except as he inserts Biandrata's letter of 1569 at n. 605, and two other documents respectively of 1571 at n. 631 and of 1572 at n. 642. See n. 629.

600. Lubieniecki is here using the *Chronica*, which he ascribes to Walenty Schmalz (1572–1622), who was at Raków, 1606–09. It is discussed as a source in the introduction to Dobrowolski, ed., *Kronika Ariańska*, Part 2, 163. On Schmalz, cf. *Polish Brethren*, Doc. V-1.

The main sources for the synod of Kolozsvár/Torda of March 1578 is the *Defensio*, 220–36 (the variant accounts of Socinus-Biandrata and of Palaeologus himself) (n. 602) drawn upon with other sources by Bod, *Historia*, 1.430–35, with the 16 Theses of Dávid and the 16 Antitheses of Biandrata, the two former allies now antagonists. At this synod with 322 ministers present infant baptism was rejected, and the *communis prophetis* of Acontius by way of Sommer (and of the Anabaptists), based on 1 Cor 14:23 ff. (n. 385), was authorized outside the formalities of synodal debate. It was in this "liberty of prophecying'' (the term in Puritan English) that Dávid raised in his home discussions the question of whether Christ should be invoked in prayer. He would presently argue that Jesus was only Messiah by designation, *designatus rex*. Other issues related to predestination and justification.

He then convened another synod in this spirit in Torda, ''after the harvest,'' 1578, after which he set forth three theses: that Jesus Christ is not God, that he may not be invoked in prayer, that the Elect are the gathered church. To these Biandrata responded with thirty antitheses.

To these in turn Dávid responded in his *Libellus parvus* (n. 630) a copy of which was forwarded to exiled Békés in Lithuania (n. 387) and thereafter to the Polish Brethren. The appearance of the *Libellus parvus* and what it signified in theological, tactical, and perhaps moral rupture (cf. assessment of Wilbur, *Transylvania*, 68, n. 43) between former collaboraters (charismatic superintendent and courtly archpresbyter), led Biandrata to summon Faustus Socinus from Cracow to debate with Dávid, precisely in his home as private, on the invocation and adoration of Christ, n. 602.

On antipedobaptism and liberty of prophecy, see further the denominational history by Stephanus Uzoni, ''Unitario-Ecclesiastica Historia Transylvanica,'' 2 vols. in MS (4 July 1783), 1.243. Wilbur frequently follows his interpretation of events, *Transylvania*, 68–69. There are three copies of the ''Historia'' as ascribed by Wilbur to István Uzoni-Fosztó, ibid., 12, n. 22, where the date given near the end, 2.1262, is 1775; on p. 1274, 4 July 1783. The foregoing reference is to the pagination in the copy on permanent loan to the Houghton Library, part of the Harvard library system, Cambridge. The three copies differ substantially from each other; they are known to be the work of four Unitarian minsiters besides Uzoni-Fosztó: János Kénosi-Tözser, Miklós Kozma Jr. and Sr., and János Kozma; Pirnát, *Ideologie der Siebenbürger*, 202, n. 55; Alexander Szent-Ivanyi, *The ''Historia'' and its Authors*, American Hungarian Library, 3 (New York, 1960).

As for the summons to Kolozsvár, Socinus himself, long after the event, recalled in *De Jesu Christi invocandi disputatio, BFR*, 2.711, that Biandrata wrote him while he was still in Basel, offering to defray his expenses as paying guest in Dávid's house. But Socinus was already in Cracow for his own reasons and his presence precisely there made it opportune for Biandrata to extend the invitation (n. 602). Before the formal disputation Socinus revealed the general position of the Polish Churches (n. 630); and he and Biandrata agreed to a preliminary exchange in the presence of ten ministers in the neighborhood of Kolozsvár, soon after 11 November 1578; *Defensio*, 235.

601. Dávid Ferenc (in Hungarian the patronymic or surname comes first) (1510–79), son of David Hertel of Saxon lineage, successively superintendent of the Transylvanian Magyar Lutherans, of the Magyar Reformed, and of the Unitarians, was mentioned above as *Servetus illustratus* (Simler), Bk. 2, n. 415 and in Bk. 3, nn. 129, 131, 236. The standard life of Dávid is that of Elek Jakab, *Dávid Ferencz Emléke* with a separately paginated volume with fully calendared documentation (Budapest, 1879). This is basic to Wilbur's account, *Transylvania*, 24–80. Some of the more recent literature on Dávid is brought together by János Erdö, ''The Biblicism of Ferenc Dávid,'' Dán and Pirnát, *Antitrinitarianism*, 47–55, and passim in the same volume.

Dávid was thrice married. On the death of his first wife (1557–72), he married the young daughter of the burgomaster of Kolozsvár, Kató (Catherine) Barát, who in 1574 sued for divorce, which was granted by a severe mixed Lutheran-Reformed synod for the special purpose summoned by the voivode in Enyed in 1576. Bod, *Historia*, 1.347–49. His third wife is mentioned in a letter of Biandrata of 3 August 1578 to Palaeologus,

Wilbur, *Transylvania*, 59–60, n. 12. It was thus as one newly wed that Dávid received the still bachelor Faustus Socinus and the Hebraist Vehe-Glirius as guests. Socinus stayed there from the beginning of October 1578 until May 1579. Cf. Wilbur, *Transylvania*, 70, n. 50; Dán, *Vehe-Glirius*, 120; see also n. 702 and n. 630, which supply further details on the sojourn and activity of Socinus.

For the exact date of the death of Dávid in the dungeon of Déva, 7 November 1579, see the diary of the poet Miklós Bogáti Fazakas, interpreted by Géza Szabó, ''A Hungarian Poet and Theologian,'' Dán and Pirnát, *Antitrinitarianism*, 47–55.

602. In this phrasing Lubieniecki is reflecting his own identification with the view of Socinus.

603. Beza attacked Biandrata in the prefatory epistle of 5 August 1567 against Gentile, the *Brevis explicatio* (Bk. 2, n 351), reprinted in *Correspondance* 8 (1567), appendix 3, from nn. 56 passim. Beza still spared Dávid by naming only Biandrata, with merely allusions to his Transylvanian collaborator, ibid., nn. 81, 88, 103. Beza said the same of Transylvanian foes in his edition of István Kiss of Szegedin, *Assertio vera de Trinitate* (Geneva, 1573).

604. Georg Major, *De uno Deo et tribus personis adversus Franciscum Davidis et Georgium Blandratam* (Wittenberg, 1579) and *Commonefactio ad Ecclesiam Catholicam contra Blandratam* (Wittenberg, 1569).

605. Except for this letter of 1568/69, with its retrospective and anticipatory glances, this is all there is in Lubieniecki's chapter on Transylvania of events in the decade 1568–78; cf. n. 599. The following letter from Segesvár is very close to the pen and almost the voice of the real Dr. Giorgio Biandrata confiding the latest theological intelligence to a *trusted* ally in Poland, though it is addressed to the whole Minor Church in Little Poland.

From internal evidence the letter is almost certainly misdated, perhaps in a slip of the writer himself. One event mentioned in it in fact took place in far-off Kassa (n. 612) on the same day given for the letter. It should probably be dated 27 January 1569. In his chronologically confusing but spirited Calvinist chronicle Bod uses the letter twice in his narrative but does not question the date, *Historia*, 1.398, 408. Wilbur (*Transylvania*, 37, n. 20) seems aware of some problem of the date but only cites it incidentally.

Court physician with a cosmopolitan concern and strategy for the consolidation of liberal Protestantism in Eastern Europe, Biandrata, in a letter of 1564 to Prince Radziwiłł, had already counted John Sigismund on the side of Dávid (n. 131). Notice has also been taken of his letter to Grzegorz Paweł of 21 September 1565 (n. 236), and of another one written after the one before us, namely, that to the Minor Church of 31 October 1569 (n. 236).

606. On *Historia, 158* Prospero Provana is mentioned as the recipient of Biandrata's books when he took leave for Transylvania. Biandrata here refers to the letter addressed to the synod of Węgrów, 1565 (Sipayłło, *AS*, 2.200), to his own letter to Grzegorz Paweł (*Historia, 189–90*), and perhaps indirectly to that of Niccolò Paruta (also connected with Biandrata) to Lutomirski (*Historia, 193*, nn. 318–32).

607. *Valentini Gentilis teterrimi haeretici impietatum . . . explicatio* (Geneva, 1567).

608. In the prefatory letter to the *Brevis explicatio*, Beza, *Correspondance*, 8 (1567), appendix 3, p. 24 at nn. 105–106, Voivode John Sigismund is exhorted as *Rex Transylvaniae*, not *Hungariae*, along with his uncle, Sigismund II Augustus, to check the heretical rampage in their lands.

609. Péter Méliusz (1515–72) from a petty noble family of Horhi, successor in Debrecen of the first Hungarian Calvinist, Kálmáncsehi (n. 129), was ''the Calvin of the

Hungarian-Transylvanian Reformation.'' Such is the title of the most recent portrait of him by László Makkai, "Méliusz Juhász Péter: Magyarország Kálvinja,'' *Theológiai Szemle* (1973) 65 – 72. The spelling of his name above represents the Latinized Greek Melius for Juhász in Hungarian orthography, the added ''z'' insisting on the simple ''s'' of most alphabets, since the letter by itself in Hungarian is pronounced ''sh'' (English) or ''sz'' (Polish). Melius without an accent is quite correct. Beza in a letter of 9 March 1570 refers to Méliusz as "fortis in Transylvania *et Polonia* Dei nostri athleta,'' *Correspondance* 11 (1570) n. 748 at n. 6. He had been a factor in the conversion of Dávid from his original Lutheranism to the Helvetic position. Elected superintendent of the Tisza region, from his new base in Debrecen in 1562, he corresponded, debated, and published extensively. He is said to have acquired some Turkish and Arabic, besides Latin, Greek, Hebrew, and German. Méliusz attributed defeat at Mohács (1526), tripartition of the Apostolic Kingdom of Hungary, and further Turkish conquest to God himself in punishment of national sin. He soon came to interpret the conversion of John Sigismund to Antitrinitarianism (cf. nn. 596, 599) as consistent with that divine punishment (cf. n. 628). In his apocalyptic and prophetic sense he was representative of his age and people. Méliusz placed over the customary law of Hungary, advantageous to the noble classes (sanctioned by the decree of Werhböczi in 1514 as the *Opus iuris tripartitum*) the revealed law of God in the Old Testament, including the prophetic ideal of the Law for the poor and the downtrodden; and his own ideal was posthumously embodied in extracts of relevant biblical passages in the *Lex politica Dei* (Debrecen, 1610). In his theocratic intent Méliusz is seen as the Hungarian counterpart of Frycz Modrzewski (*Historia, 13* passim) by László Makkai in his *État des ordres et théocratie calviniste au XVIè siècle dans l'Europe centro-orientale*, Studia Historica, 99 (Budapest: Hungarian Academy of Science, 1975). Bod brings together (*Historia*, 1.257 and 167, item 2) two accounts of the name Melius (the original name Juhász means shepherd; the Greek used is from μέλω; and Bod gives other biographical details.

Méliusz has been encountered in *Historia*, Bk. 2, n. 363, in a pan-Calvinist effort to refute Antitrinitarianism *on wholly* scriptural grounds and especially with Old Testament *loci*. There is a letter of Méliusz from Debrecen to Bullinger, 27 April 1569, in which he speaks of his opponents as *Francisco-Blandratici* and of his MS refutation of ''340 Serveto-blandraticarum hereseon'' and of his desire to get it published along with his work against Rabbi Joseph Albo on the Trinity (1485, Paris; Latin, 1566); Wotschke, *Briefwechsel*, no. 402, pp. 307 – 08. Bullinger reports on this among other things in his letter to Beza, 17 September 1569; *Correspondance* 10 (1569) no. 703, pp. 185 – 87 with nn.; and Beza writes to Méliusz, 9 March 1570, ibid., 11 (1570) no. 750, pp. 83 – 84.

610. The convocational summons here is the same as the letter quoted from at n. 614. The date appointed for the synod in Debrecen was 2 February 1568. Its impact was displaced by the ten-day debate at Alba Julia of March 1568, at nn. 596 and 598 and for Wilbur on Biandrata's reference, n. 605. The letter was originally dated Várad, 14 December 1567, but within it is a reference to the inclusion of (24) *Propositiones* set forth at Szikszó, 6 January 1568; Lampe, *Historia, 176 – 78, 180 – 87*, these propositions being probably the *theses* referred to by Biandrata. In the meantime there were two developments located disparately in *Historia*, at nn. 613 and 633.

An anti-Blandratan *Christianus consensus de Trinitate* in 13 articles had been produced by the pastors of Hungary and Transylvania, most of them worked out at the synod of Maros-Vásárhely, 19 May 1566, confirmed at Várad, 6 June 1566; Lampe, *Historia, 159 – 63*. In the face of this *Consensus* and other developments (cf. at n. 633) Biandrata and Dávid compiled in 1567 their *De falsa et vera unius Dei Patris, Filii et Spirtus sancti sognitione* (Alba Julia, 1568). It consists of two books in 24 chapters, dedicated to John Sigismund, the first on false understanding of God. Within it chap. 4 is entitled "De horrendis simulachris Deum Trinum et Unum adumbrantibus" with 8 illustrations, some from the Commonwealth, some from Italy. The whole book is described by Wilbur, *Transylvania*, 34–35 with a clarification of them in n. 22. Several of them are reproduced by Górski, *Grzegorz Paweł*, 202–07, his plates 1, 2, and 6 corresponding to the items of description in Wilbur, his 3 being Wilbur's 4, his 4 and 7 (a detail enlarged) being Wilbur's 4. In the second book is printed anonymously the decisive work of Laelius Socinus, Bk. 2, n. 1.

At the Diet of Torda of January 1568 John II Sigismund confirmed the decree of toleration of 1557 and 1563 (n. 599), in further specificity: "Our Royal Highness . . . together with the Diet . . . now confirms that in every place the preachers shall preach and explain the gospel each according to his understanding of it, and if the congregation like it, well: if not, no one shall compel them, but they shall keep the preachers whose doctrine they approve. Therefore none of the superintendents or others shall annoy or abuse the preachers on account of their religion, according to the previous constitutions, or allow any to be imprisoned or be punished by removal from his post on account of his teaching, for 'faith is the gift of God' [Eph 2:8]; and this 'comes from hearing, and hearing by the Word of God' [Rom 10:17]." These last two texts were fundamental for Luther; and, when in his speech before the Diet, Dávid espoused this principle in a constitutional context, something of his memories of student days in Wittenberg resonated. The climax of his address is idealized in the painting of Aladár Körösföi-Kriesch commonly seen hanging in Unitarian homes in Transylvania and in some Unitarian church parlors in the United States. The edict grants not only freedom of the pulpit but also congregational authority within the synodal system. The full text of the edict is in *Monumenta Hungariae Historica (Emlékek)*, 2 (Budapest, 1860) 267, 343. Wilbur (*Transylvania*, 38) quotes more fully from the edict. The edict, in effect, legalized Unitarianism which had become the preferred formulation of the majority of lordly and burgher Reformed in Transylvania, while in Hapsburg Hungary and such border cities as Debrecen orthodox Calvinism prevailed.

In such an atmosphere and emergent constitutional situation Méliusz summoned Dávid and Biandrata to his bastion in Debrecen in December 1567, scrutinized the *credo* of Égri at Kassa in January 1568, at n. 613, and faced, with Károly and four other conservatives, both Dávid, Biandrata, and three other debaters at Alba Julia in March 1568, at nn. 596 and 598.

611. The *Germani* here are the imperial and royal Hapsburg forces of Maximilian II (Maximilian I of Hungary) (1564–76).

612. Lukács Égri (of Éger, Erlau), educated in Wittenberg, was a leader of the radical Reformed in Hungary.

On petition of the orthodox Reformed, 16 November 1567, General Lazarus von Schwendi, a Lutheran, the commander of the Hapsburg forces in Hungary, convened a synod in Kassa (Košvice/Kauschau), 27 January 1568, where Égri defended 27 articles on Triadology and Christology. These were much different in theological density from the scriptural and apostolic formularies preferred by Biandrata. Méliusz suspected that he could reduce what he had said to conclusions embodying his "genuine view." Evidently in his third conclusion Égri accepted the Logos of the fourth gospel and of the Apologists but held that the Word of God the Father was Son of God only at the incarnation, the Word made flesh dwelling among humankind, and that only in the *predestinatio* of the Father could the pre-mundane Word that spoke through the prophets be called prospectively the son. This second part of the foregoing sentence is not, however, expressly a part of the conclusions. The seven *propositiones* of Égri at Gönc, 22 January 1566, and the *responsiones* of Károly, and the *responsio* of Égri are given by Lampe, *Historia*, 139–46; see further the twenty-seven *propositiones* and three *conclusiones* of Égri at Kassa, and the orthodox *responsio*, ibid., 187–211, followed by the orthodox *confessio* of Hungary expressly against the confession of Égri, Dávid, and the ministers of Kolozsvár, ibid., 211–14.

In a letter from Gönc of 1 May 1566, Gáspár Károly (1529–92), its pastor, and two other ministers report to Beza on Égri and the general situation, *Correspondance*, 9 (1566), appendix 4b, 235–39.

613. Égri, arrested, sent another *confessio*, January 1573; Lampe, *Historia*, 215–17. He died still in prison in 1574. Pirnát prints a letter of Dudith of 12 March 1568, in which he wrote of Égri as condemned to the flames and suggesting moderation because so many of his view among the nobles in Poland would take offense, "Il martire e l'uomo politico," Dán and Pirnát, *Antitrinitarianism*, 169–170 and for the death, 9.

614. Biandrata accurately, if not verbatim, renders the taunt of Méliusz in his letter of convocation, referred to at n. 610; see Lampe, *Historia*, 178; Bod, *Historia*, 1.407.

Before the quotation from Méliusz, Biandrata, in passing, refers again to Beza's epistolary introduction to the *Brevis explicatio* against Gentile (n. 608). It is true that Beza therein "heaps abuse" on him and others in Transylvania; but, even as of August 1567, Beza still spares mentioning Dávid, evidently feeling indebted to him for having wrested the cause of the Reformation in Transylvania from the Lutherans and perhaps still hoping that he would halt. See in the critical edition of the letter, *Correspondance* 9 (1566), nn. 80–81, 103.

615. The synods and theses to which Biandrata refers as of January 1569 appear to stem from the opening debates on the Trinity in 1566. The shift in mood and scriptural conviction among the following of Dávid is vividly reflected in a *Catechismus* for use in the training of children in "the Church of God of the Hungarian nation," that, having left "the papist Quaternity," have embraced the word of God concerning the Holy Triad, one true God the Father, and his Son the Lord Jesus Christ, and the Spirit of them both" (Kolozsvár, 1566); *Régi Magyar Könyvtár*, 2, no. 99. Bod covers the developments compactly in *Historia*, 1.399–405, and reprints, of the *Catechismus*, the spirited prefatory address to John Sigismund, fiercely anti-Catholic in its return to Scripture alone. With fervor the dedicatory letter upholds the eschatological image of the fully reformed Church as a bride descending from heaven, Rev 21:2, a possibly distinctively Davidian emphasis, as was also the prominent retention of the role of Jesus Christ as Mediator as the (adoptive) Son of God. In response to the implied question of the King and the community at large, "Will there be no end of innovations?," the undaunted compilers of the *Catechismus* and its preface impetuously insist that for the *Electorum Ecclesia* Scripture alone be "the sole norm and the proper gnomon to guide the bark of salvation" without any "commentaries of men or their traditions," just as in their final submission in faith Augustine, Bernard of Clairvaux, and Luther alike had thrown themselves in simple trust upon the sole Word of God in Scripture. Hence in this *Catechismus*, differing from anything of the Polish Brethren in a comparable "Tritheist phase," the Apostles' Creed was not even mentioned.

Two years before the decisive ten-day debate in Alba Julia of March 1568 (nn. 596, 598), Dávid had ordered the first disputation expressly on the Trinity, at Alba Julia, 24 February 1566. Méliusz was generally considered to have come off the victor. *Disputatio prima Albana* (Kolozsvár, 1566), *Régi Magyar Könyvtár*, 2 no. 100. Following this,

Biandrata presented seven theses and antitheses at a synod in Torda, 15 March 1566, Lampe, *Historia*, 147–50. The first of these is that the true *Trias* is that of baptism based on Mat 28;19; the last is that the Logos is embodied (*corporatus*) in the unique Son of God. At a synod in Alba Julia, 25 April 1566, these theses were modified and evidently enlarged by one and supplied with *limitationes*, i.e., the mild criticisms included by local ministers taking part in the synod. Thereupon Superintendent Dávid called a general synod at Maros-Vásárhely for 19 May 1566. To the now eight *theses/propositiones* with provisional *limitationes* were added the *sententiae*, the judgments of the synod. These eight sets of reflection now had full synodal status and were printed as *propositiones in Disputatione Albensi coram Regia Majestate a D. Georgio Blandrata et Francisco Davidis propositae*, including the judgments of Maros-Vásárhely, the *Sententia concors pastorum ecclesiae Dei nationis Hungaricae in Transylvania* (Kolozsvár, 1566); *Régi Magyar Könyvtár*, 2, no. 101, p. 24; under the heading of *Sententia concors* "of the pastors and ministers of the Church of God of the Hungarian nation," reprinted by Bod, *Historia*, 1.399–405. Not from this *sententia* but from other sources Lampe (*Historia*, 149–58) gives the same materials (consistently seven, not eight *propositiones*, however), and then he (*Historia*, 159–62) prints the *Christianus consensus* in thirteen articles as the authentic agreement of the same synod. This *consensus* was not sufficiently conservative for Méliusz, for he was recoiling from what seemed unacceptable credal impoverishment. In any case, it is in fact not made prominent in either confessional historiography. Cf. the account of Wilbur, *Transylvania*, 32, esp. n. 17.

Of the foregoing items it is not clear which was the *libellus* that Biandrata sent to the Poles in forty copies; cf. n. 1.16. He may also have sent copies of his own original theses of Torda as most in concord with the position reached as of even 1565 by the Minor Church in Poland.

He may well have sent also copies of *De falsa et vera unius Dei patris cognitione* (1568) (nn. 538 and 610), as Jean Thénaud, writing to Beza from Pińczów, 1 June 1568, was greatly alarmed at the assault on the old creeds of the Church at the ten-day debate in Alba Julia in March 1568 and referred quite clearly to what he called "the lacerations" of the gospel of John in one publication, clearly the collection of Biandrata and Dávid containing the *Brevis explicatio* of Laelius Socinus. *Correspondance* 9 (1568) no. 609, pp. 75–77. (In the letter Petrus Statorius is referred to as near death from several diseases.)

As for the bearer of Biandrata's letter and the forty copies, Walenty Krawiec has already been identified as a Judaizer who, with *Pop* Ezaijasz from Muscovy, promoted a radical trend in the Lublin congregation, 1567–70, after Pastor Paklepka's death (n. 287). Budziński, who preserves the letter here (and hence the name of Krawiec), was himself sympathetic with the non-adorants of Transylvania (n. 630) under the influence of Vehe-Glirius and Palaeologus. The synod of Cracow in November 1568 opposed the group in Lublin around Krawiec; Sipayłło, *AS*, 2.216 and n. 1; Szczucki, *Czechowic*, 84, 257–58. But for the moment, Krawiec probably had nothing in his hands from Biandrata or Dávid that would have been yet called in Transylvania "of a Judaizing spirit." The phrasing is Lubieniecki's and intended by him in a negative sense. Lubieniecki could have had in mind also the Sabbatarians (n. 675).

616. This would appear to be a reference to the disputation in Alba Julia of 1566 (n. 615), appearing in the title of the copies of the *libellus* being sent by the hand of Krawiec.

617. This is a reference to the ten-day debate at Alba Julia (nn. 596, 598), *not yet con-*

summated and originally called for *Torda*. It was changed from Torda to the capital. See Dávid's *Literae convocatoriae* (Alba Julia, 1568); Jakab, *Emléke*, 2.51, n. 18.

618. Although the formulation is also susceptible to orthodox interpretation, by it Biandrata may have been accommodating himself to the distinctive view of Servetus as to the spiritual conception of Jesus by the Virgin by her breathing the divine cloud of dew hovering over her. Mentioned, with the sources, in my *Radical Reformation*, 335–36, 350–51.

619. Here Biandrata attributes to emergent Unitarianism in Transylvania, partly surrounded by mountains and thought of perhaps as a new Zion, a special eschatological role in the purificaiton of the Reformation. See my *Radical Reformation*, 710. Transylvanian non-adorantism with respect to Christ at the right hand of God was informed also by a sense of God's imminent recall of Jesus Christ to judge the nations. Cf. the different theodicy and eschatology of Méliusz (n. 609).

620. In the following sentence, the subject of *transigantur* is not certain: whether Biandrata's *Theses* were being progressively implemented or, more plausibly in the context, the prophecies about the eschatological role of Transylvania were supposedly being played out.

621. With the resonance of phrasings from 2 Cor 1:3 and Phil 1:6.

622. Unitarian publications in Alba Julia of 1567 were printed by Raphael Hoffhalter, the royal printer. *Régi Magyar Könyvtár* 1, nos. 61, 62 and 2, nos. 107, 111.

623. Filled with classical allusions, the sentence is not entirely clear. "Claudian thunders" refers to the theatricality of Emperor Claudius. The allusion to soldiers of Lucian could be translated a "militia of scoffers," because in this period Lucian (d. after 180) had come to be identified with scoffing. *Thrasones* could well mean braggart soldiers after Thraso in Terence *Eunuchus*.

624. From this letter of Biandrata, preserved among Budziński's papers and incorporated into his narrative of Transylvanian Unitarianism by Lubieniecki, it is especially clear that Unitarianism in the Principality was as "magisterial" in disposition as any Lutheran or Reformed establishment. However, the confessional-constitutional principle of *cuius regio, eius religio*, prevailing in the empire since its adoption in the religious Peace of Augsburg of 1555 (Bk. 2, n. 364) was not imitated either in Transylvania or the Commonwealth. See n. 599.

625. Lubieniecki is probably thinking of Méliusz at Debrecen as a combination of Discordia, Sarnicki, and Trecy, "a firebrand" in the developing harvests of liberal Protestantism in Hungary and Transylvania.

626. Dependent on his immediate sources, Lubieniecki is probably intending to allude to the two events just mentioned in Biandrata's letter, in effect the I and the II Disputations on the Trinity at Alba Julia, 1566, 1568 (Torda becoming Alba Julia).

There followed the six-day disputation of Várad, 10–16 October 1569, with John Sigismund present as voivode and claimant to the Crown of Hungary and lively participant. Dávid called the synod in the fortified town belonging to the voivode but within Hapsburg Hungary. Dávid's call, his nine propositions, the response and conditions laid down by Méliusz, and the four basic issues actually discussed are to be found in Lampe, *Historia*, 224–62; Bod, *Historia*, 1.413–22; discussed by Wilbur, *Transylvania*, 39–40.

In his letter to the Minor church from Kolozsvár after the disputation (n. 236) Biandrata vividly describes the progression of the debate at Várad and circumstances, even though some of the discourse was, at the request of Dávid, in Hungarian. Biandrata reports that on the morrow after the debate on the divinity of Christ, Méliusz appeared in the midst of the disputants and audience, addressing them thus: "Hear me Your Majesty, and all you who are present! For last night the Lord newly revealed to me both who is his proper Son and how constituted, to whom therefore I give eternal thanks." To which John Sigismund responded: "Master Péter, if in this night he taught you who is the Son of God, what, I ask, were you preaching before?" *ARG* 3 95–96.

627. Not in possession of the subsequently mentioned books, Lubieniecki is unaware of the fact that they are not synodal *acta* but indeed, as they say, *gesta* in general on the issues agitated in Transylvania.

628. Lubieniecki, not aware of it, drops back from where the letter of Biandrata has brought the narrative, namely almost to the ten-day disputation of Alba Julia, March 1568, to adduce material illustrative of an antecedent phase of debate. Moreover, he has reversed the order of the two following *Refutationes*.

The second mentioned came chronologically first, Dávid's *Refutatio scripti Petri Melii, quo nomine synodi Debrecinae docet Jehovalitatem et trinitariorum Deum Patriarchis, Prophetis et Apostolis cognitum* (Alba Julia, 1567). It was aimed at the *Confessio Pastorum ad Synodum Debrecii celebratur 24, 25 et 26 Februarii A.D. 1567 convocatorum*. The first two theses of this Trinitarian *Confessio* ran "De uno Jah" and "De Jehova Elohijm seu de Triade." These synodal theses were later separately developed by Méliusz in his (no longer extant) pamphlet, *Propositiones de jah et Jehova, seu de Unitate et Trinitate in Deo vero; Item de Christi aeterna generatione ibi 2 die Augusti disputandae* (Várad, 1568). Under discussion here were the three names of God in the Pentateuch, Yah, Yahweh, and Elohim (the last the plural of El), which in the ancient Triadological debates seldom featured since the Fathers used only the Septuagintal text. Several of the debates in Transylvania worked with the Hebrew text. Róbert Dán has as the first dealt with the role of the Hebrew text in the emergence of Antitrinitarianism in the Hungarian Reformation, 1528–89. *Humanizmus, reformáció, és a héber nyely Magyarórs zágon*, Humanizmus és Reformáció, 2 (Budapest: Hungarian Academy of Sciences, 1973), with a summary of each chapter in English, 253–64. It is here in place to observe that, as much as the Unitarians were interested in the Old Testament, the first translation of the New came from Heltai in 1562 before the schism in the Reformed Church was fully evident (n. 129) and the first translation of the whole Bible was accomplished by Calvinist Gáspár Károlyi (n. 612) and printed in 1590 in the small town of Vezsoly in Hapsburg Hungary between Debrecen and Kassa (Košovice); *Régi Magyar Könyvtár*, 1, no. 236.

The first book mentioned by Lubieniecki in the text was by both Dávid and Biandrata, *Refutatio Scripti Georgii Majoris in quo Deum trinum in personis et unum in essentia, unicum deinde eius Filium in persona et duplicem in naturis ex lacunis Antichristi*, starting out with John 5:43 (Kolozsvár, 1569); *Régi Magyar Könyvtár*, 2, no. 121. It had been aimed at Major's *De uno Deo et tribus personis* (Wittenberg, 1569). Major replied to the *Refutatio* and indirectly warned his own party in *Commonefactio ad ecclesias Catholicas orthodoxas* (1569).

Superintendent Méliusz prepared *Ax igaz Hitnek (A True Confession)* (Debrecen, 1569) with the hope of reconverting Sigismund to the true faith. László Makkai, in reflecting on the critical edition of this confession recently come to light in a unique exemplar, illuminates the theological situation at this juncture and supplies the recent specialized literature on Méliusz, "Un catechisme hongrois contre les Antitrinitaires," Dán and Pirnát, *Antitrinitarianism*, 90–95.

629. By a third "most famous synod" Lubieniecki could mean the ten-day debate of

Alba Julia of March 1568 with which his chapter began (nn. 596, 598). Lubieniecki could not have had a clear picture of the progression of synods, disputations, and diets in Transylvania and in Hungary. But with even minimal awareness of the fateful consequences of the synod of Torda of February 1579, Lubieniecki could surely not have here been referring in his text to it; quite probably he refers to that of 1578. For a chronological listing of all the diets and synods mentioned by Lubieniecki in chap. 11 or in the annotation, see n. 675.

After the house disputation of Dávid (nn. 600 and 602), Dávid called a synod at Torda, 24 February 1579, in defiance of his opposition, including Biandrata, and he intended to get substantial support for nonadorationism before the arrival of any further counsel from the Polish Brethren; cf. n. 630.

The attentive reader is entitled to know in brief what happened between the defiant synod of Torda of February 1579 and the trial of Dávid. After Dávid's arrest, Biandrata called 7 April 1579, for a synod in Torda. Pirnát reprints (''Il martire e l'uomo politico,'' 160 – 63'') the call and the sixteen Theses of Dávid over against the corresponding Antitheses of Biandrata. The prince called for a concurrent Diet in Torda 24 – 26 April 1579. The issue was no longer whether Dávid's new teaching at the earlier synod of Torda was true or scriptural but whether it went beyond what King John had deemed a licit Christián *varia* among his subjects. The sixteen Glirian theses were ascribed to Dávid. Dávid was evidently kept in a prison during the deliberations. There seems to have been advice from on high not to get into another public debate.

With Vehe-Glirius removed in May 1579 and Dávid arrested, Socinus rapidly prepared to assemble fifteen theses, purportedly representing the nub of Dávid's positions on more than the invocation of Christ, central to the disputation. Socinus's document survives in two versions: *Theses quibus Franciscus Davidis sententia de Christi munere explicative, una cum antithesibus Ecclesiae conscriptis* (later published with *De Jesu Christi invocatione*, 1593) and a version with a Josephite thesis added to make the sixteen theses even more frightening to the conventional. The theses, however, analyzed by Dán in their relationship to Vehe-Glirius and his *Mattanajah* (*Vehe-Glirius*, 137), are not Davidic, but pseudo-Davidic, representing the more extreme views of Vehe-Glirius (*Vehe-Glirius*, 131 – 41). On these sixteen theses, see further n. 675.

The fateful Diet of Alba Julia and the trial began on 1 June 1579. Calvinist Sándor Kendi spoke for the Prince. Lukács Trausner, son-in-law, spoke for Dávid, too ill for direct encounter. The nobles and ministers supporting Dávid were required in the presence of the prince to affirm four articles purporting to summarize the faith of the scriptually Reformed Church; see n. 375. The estates were given three questions: (1) whether Dávid acknowledged as his the nonadorant and other theses, (2) whether these were new articles and hence innovations, and (3) whether what Dávid taught was blasphemous.

Wilbur recounts (*Transylvania*, 75 – 77) the trial on the basis of standard sources including the embittered account of Lukács Trausner (n. 675), preserved in the *Defensio*. Dávid's son-in-law himself almost shared the same sentence but escaped to Ottoman Turkey and was rehabilitated as a lawyer in Kolozsvár having first conformed to Catholicism under General Basta and then to Calvinism under Prince Sigismund Rákóczi. Pirnát set the pattern for fresh research in his ''Der Process gegen Franz Dávid,'' *Ideologie*, chap. 5. A newly accessible source is that of the Jesuit observer and participant who wrote down the record 9 June 1579, János Leleszi, S.J. His ''Historia actionis contra Franciscum Davicem trinitarium'' (in the Catholic sense; see n. 118) was made readily accessible by Henryk Barycz, *Studia nad Arianizmem*, edited by Chmaj, 489 – 530. Pirnát, originally without the benefit of this documentation, makes Leleszi's report his point of departure (without altering his previous observation) in "Il martire e l'uomo politico," 157ff. With the reliable data of the Jesuit participant-observer, Pirnát shows that some eight to ten Unitarian nobles, despite the prince's pressure, held fast to Dávid who, though sick and weak, persisted in defending his theses at the Diet of Alba Julia, with Biandrata in the end feeling that either he himself or Dávid would have to die, "Il martire e l'uomo politico," 148 – 49. In defense of Dávid it was argued that his views could be seen in the MS version of Sommer's "Refutatio Scripti Petri Caroli" of 1572 (later printed by Vehe-Glirius in Cracow, n. 632), composed right after the death of John Sigismund. The accusers advanced the possibility that Dávid had written a German book. In any case, the Glirian sixteen articles ascribed to Dávid were probably the most decisive, because they were not so extreme in thrust as the views of Glirius on his own; and with some of them Dávid probably did not feel comfortable, and rightly repudiated them in any case as not his own.

Dávid's own sober *Confessio* from prison survives in several versions, some preserved for vindicating his memory, precisely as not being so extreme or consequent as the views of Vehe-Glirius himself. Dávid nevertheless evidently remained close to the counsel of Matthias Glirius.

Benedykt Wiszowaty in *BAnt*[2], 57, adds a word about Dávid's *Confessio* prepared in prison and later attached by Matthias Glirius to his book, *Wahre und kurze Verteidigung der Bücher Francisci Davidis und der seinen, von dem einigen Gott am Wesen und Person*. This *Confessio* of 17/27 April 1579 was brought to the Diet of Torda: "Confessio de Jesu Christo, quam germanice libello subjunxit Dietericus Dorschius seu Matthias Glirius ... missa ab eo ex carcere ad ordines Transylvaniae congregatos Tordae paulo ante mortem suam (ut idem Dorschius testaur) die 17 aprilis anno 1579." The *Confessio* would be the same as that printed by Elek Jakub, *Emléke*, 2, no. 50, pp. 74 – 75. Wiszowaty's testimony shows once again how close Glirius was to Dávid; but Dán shows that only on the single issue of nonadorantism was Dávid in the authentic *Confessio* a true Judaizer: in Dán's sense fully applicable to Vehe-Glirius, Dán, *Vehe-Glirius*, 143f., but yet that Dávid was condemned for essentially Glirian theses ascribed to him by Socinus and Biandrata; *Vehe-Glirius*, 142 – 44 and 461. Dávid died in Déva in November 1579, n. 601.

Here it is in place to summarize Wiszowaty's characterization in Latin of the whole publication, *Wahre und kurze Verteidigung*, that appears to have been different from the seven texts printed by Dán (*Vehe-Glirius*, part two), even though it contains the authentic *Confessio* of Dávid, as in the *Refutatio Scripti Petri Caroli* (Cracow, 1582). It contains (1) an introductory letter in the name of Dorschius, "Gnade, Fried, etc., i.e. Gratiam, pacem et misericordiam a Deo nostro Patre et Domini nostri Jesu Christi, precatur Dietericus Dorschius omnibus suis Fratribus dispersis per totam Germaniam, qui verum et unicum Deum in essentia et persona Patrem nostri Domini Jesu Christi ... invocant et colunt." Therein he relates what he has seen while living in Great Poland, Lithuania, Transylvania, and Poland. The prefatory letter closes with Dávid's *Confessio*. After the main tract comes (2) Christian Francken's *Enumeratio praecipuarum causarum, cur Christiani circa alios multos Religionis articulos inconstantes tam constantes sint tamen in dogmate Trinitatis retinendo* (cf. wording in n. 642), then follows (3) *Theses Johannis Someri et carmen ejus admonitum*. Wiszowaty ends his annotation with: "see further under Sommer," n. 631.

630. There is a break in the text indicated by three asterisks. It may represent a substantial omission, perhaps by Benedykt Wiszowaty.

Dávid, according to Palaeologus, had sent his *Libellus parvus XXX thesibus Blandra-*

tae oppositus to the Polish Brethren in the summer of 1578, and they appear to have promptly taken the side of their old *archipresbyter* and theological advisor, Biandrata. One of their number had written a letter, carried by Socinus to Kolozsvár (n. 593). With this *Libellus* against Biandrata before them, and perhaps the sixteen Glirian theses ascribed to Dávid that had accompanied a letter of 17 June 1579, the Polish Brethren proceeded to formulate their assessment of Dávid and the assessment of the procedures against him, at their synod in Bełżyce, 24 August 1579; reported only by Palaeologus, *Defensio*, 285; not noted by Sipayłło, *AS*, 3.xvii. They in any case embodied their findings in a synodal letter, signed by Aleksander Witrelin, that was printed in Kolozsvár the following year (1580), as *Judicum ecclesiarum Polonicarum de causa Francisci Davidis* with an anonymous scriptural compendium, ''Loci aliquot,'' probably by Biandrata, unfairly accusing Dávid of unprincipled synodal procedure, *Defensio*, 121–219. The Brethren gathered at Bełżyce said in the *Judicium* that they would have preferred not to become involved, appealing to the Dominical example of obedience and meekness under Pontius Pilate and to the Petrine and Pauline injunctions of obedience to the king or the authorities that be of God, mindful that they were under Stephen Báthory, royal brother of Christopher, who was only deputy voivode (until 1581) in issuing the verdict against Dávid as an innovator against the terms of confessional and political toleration. Briefly, on purely scriptural grounds, the synod of Bełżyce defended the adoration of Christ, with Biandrata, although they seem to have disapproved of Biandrata's resort to trial and of Christ; Szczucki, ''Polish and Transylvanian Unitarianism,'' 241. In the meantime the Transylvanian diets, fateful for Dávid, had already done their work in April and June 1579 (n. 629).

Szymon Budny, nonadorant ally in Lithuania of Dávid, Vehe-Glirius, and Palaeologus (cf. nn. 401, 631), reproached the Polish Brethren at the synod of Lublin in the autumn of 1580 (noted in Sipayłło, *AS*, 3.xvii) with the death of Dávid, although he would later (1583) confess to his rashness; Szczucki, ''Polish and Transylvanian Unitarianism'' 241, citing Budny, n. 39.

631. Within a few spaces of what appears to have been the editor's rather than the author's omission at n. 630 there comes another set of three asterisks that mark what either Wiszowaty chose to drop as either inopportune or illegible, or something Lubieniecki himself had chosen to suppress, that is, the name of the writer of the letter. As Lubieniecki has been quoting from Budziński, it is likely that the anonymous letter to an otherwise identified Hallopegius was in Budziński's letter box, if not in his MS History. In any case, Lubieniecki attaches importance to it. Yet its authorship, occasion, and thrust are now not clear. The date, 15 May 1571, is strangely identical with that of the next letter. However, Lubieniecki, when he comes to introduce this related document at n. 642, signed in Kolozsvár, writes of it as ''*another* letter of Sommer'' (*alias [litteras] Someri*), implying that the one to Hallopegius is also from Sommer without his having said so. It is true that Budziński, quoted by Lubieniecki at nn. 385 and 386, is the unique source of another reference to Sommer (to his presence, it would have had to be very briefly) in Cracow in 1572, which is evidence in any case that Budziński had other material on Sommer, possibly from Palaeologus (n. 593).

The author certainly supplies clues to his identity. He writes as a trusted friend and, as the former preceptor of the addressee, declines to intervene in getting something published that had been composed by Hallopegius on issues raised by Ferenc Dávid. He writes with studied imprecision, more obscurely than in simply presuming information common to the correspondent. He counsels him not to rush into print. He himself holds to a scriptural nonphilosophical doctrine of the Trinity, even though he had once defended the Nicene terminology, which he now sees as invalidated by Aristotelian logic. He gives the impression of being physically but also emotionally remote from Transylvania and its religious controversy when he politely asks at the end of the letter for further information about "that religion." When he refers to the Protestant church in Hungary and Transylvania, although he is clearly not on the side of such a leader as Méliusz, he is specific about not agreeing with Dávid either, noting that "our brethren" had replied to the *De falsa et at ver cognitione*, the title of which he does not get quite right and which he ascribes wholly to Dávid, eschewing the name of its co-author, Biandrata, whose view of the Trinity as propounded *when in Poland* would perhaps be similar to his own. He is evidently critical of some major Magyar superintendent (perhaps Méliusz) when he adduces a scriptural reference to the ideal pastor. When he speaks of *limitationes* (judgments) reported "from the Genevan tombs," he employs a term not used in the Polish synods but current in their Magyar counterparts and seems even to evoke the discussion recorded in n. 615. To be sure, he could be alluding to the sentencing of Servetus in Geneva, since in his letter he is concerned with the issue of Christian obedience to the magistrate in his appropriate sphere and yet also with the upholding of the confessional liberty of conscience.

From this summary of the clues of authorship in the letter, the writer could then have been a relatively conservative Polish Brother in Cracovia; and *Lipsia* at the end of it, a garbled Polish placename or an evasive strategem. But it is hard to bring into focus any Pole who could speak of himself in relation to the Magyar hallopegius as his *praeceptor*.

If indeed *Lipsia* is quite straightforwardly Leipzig, then the writer of the letter could indeed have been a teacher or professor of Sommer. Born in Pirna on the Elbe, Sommer could quite plausibly have started his substantial career as classicist in Leipzig, his *curriculum vitae* not being, in any case, wholly clear. On this view a former Saxon mentor has in the letter declined to print a work of Hallopegius in defense of Dávid; and Hallopegius would then be plausibly a cover name for Sommer himself in correspondence with an old teacher, and the MS under discussion Sommer's *Refutatio* (n. 632, to be printed in Cracow in 1581), which he wanted to have appear in print in the very city where Károlyi's assault in Dávid and Biandrata had recently appeared (n. 632).

Again, on the assumption that *Lipsia* is indeed Saxon Leipzig, it is remotely possible that Hallopegius is a printing error for Valentinus *Hellopoeus* Zikszi (Szikszai), one of two Hungarian students who stopped off with Trecy in Cracow en route to Wittenberg and then Geneva. They were inscribed in the *Livre du Recteur* as of 12 October 1566. Trecy to Beza from Cracow, 12 July 1566, Correspondance 7 (1566) no. 482, n. 13; Kaspar Peucer to Beza from Dresden, 17 August 1566, ibid., no. 491, n. 1; cf. Kaspar Károlyi et al. to Beza from Gönc, 1 May 1568, ibid., 9 (1568) no. 16. The student companion of Hellopoeus was Matthias Thurius, later attested at synods in Hungary. If, after their studies together in Geneva in 1566, they had become separated, Thurius could indeed have written in 1571 somewhat stiffly and guardedly to Hellopoeus from Leipzig after a sojourn under Beza. The letter-writer, if Thurius, in any event still regards the Trinity as a revealed mystery to be discussed in theological, not philosophical, terms (*Historia, 231*); see further n. 641. Valentinus Hellopoeus Szikszai is also mentioned as among those ministers who prepared catechisms, along with István Szekelly of Bentzed who had his catechism for the children of Dziksz printed in Cracow in 1548. Bod, *Historia*, 1.355.

632. Péter Károly, *Brevis, erudita et perspicua epxlicatio orthodoxae fidei de uno Deo patre, Filio et spiritu sancto adversus blasphemios Georgii Blandratae et Fracisci*

Davidis errores (Wittenberg, 1571). *Régi Magyar Könyvtár*, 3, no. 612, p. 179. He characterized the two Antitrinitarians at this point as ditheists.

Péter Károlyi had been a teacher in the academy of Kolozsvár and then pastor in Várád (Grosswardein, Oradea). To his *Explicatio* both Palaeologus and Sommer replied, the former in *Refutatio libris Petri Caroli* (1572), listed among his works in the conspectus of Kolozsvár codices by Dostálová, ed. *Catechesis Christiana*, 11. Sommer's reply in two books, *Refutatio scripti Petri Caroli*, was completed in MS 24 June 1572. It was not printed until 1582. It may have circulated in more than one MS. It was quarried for arguments against the Trinity by György Valszuti in his debate in 1588 with Máté Skaricza in the cathedral in Pécs (Fünfkirchen) under Ottoman rule, S. Katalin Mémeth, "Die Disputation von Fünfkirchen," Dán and Pirnát, "Antitrinitarianism, 147–55.

By December 1579, Vehe-Glirius, major advisor of Dávid, its pseudonymous editor, arrived in the Commonwealth. On the way he may have stopped over to confer with Palaeologus perhaps at the estate of Jetřich of Kunovice in Hluk in Moravia, bringing his portfolio with several writings and a plan to publish them. Dán, *Vehe-Glirius*, 176; cf. 133. However, he was at first at the home of Budny, 1580–82, in Lithuania. Evidently at the Lithuanian synod of Lubecz, 1 March 1582, near Nowogródek, Prince Jan Kiszka, possibly in full agreement with Budny who never came to share Vehe-Glirius's plenary Christian Hebraism, obliged him to withdraw from his protection in order to make peace between the "magisterial" Lithuanian Brethren and the sectarian Polish Brethren like Jan Niemojewski, Marcin Czechowic, Mikołaj Żytno (present at the synod) and (not present at the synod), Simon Ronemberg, Socinus. Thereupon Vehe-Glirius changed his name yet again to Theodosius Schimberg, and proceeded to Cracow begin publishing under that name. Dán, *Vehe-Glirius*, 176, 183–185. Budny does not mention the persons on the Lithuanian side, Kot, ed., *O urzędzie miecza używającem* (1583), 24. Dán infers this synod as the occasion of Vehe's departure. In dealing with this episode in a large context as "Budny's Dispute with the Anabaptists of Little Poland" (*Socianism in Poland*, chap. 8), Kot does not mention Glirius, nor does Budny himself. The first MS to be published by Glirius was Sommer's *Refutatio* with an introductory epistle under the pseudoym of the editor, Theodosius Schimberg (Ingolstadt [Cracow: Rodecki], 1582), Gryczowa, no. 73. Dán reprints this letter as text 4 in *Vehe-Glirius*, 247–53, having analyzed the thought of Glirius as Editor Schimberg, pp. 185ff. Pirnát first set forth the decisive character of Sommer's *Refutatio*, although at the time Pirnát was uncertain of its place of publication, *Ideologie der Siebenbürger*, 39–43; Dán, *Vehe-Glirius*, 128. It was decisive as being no longer exegetical but frankly rationalist and logical.

633. The reference to the title is inaccurate. See n. 610. About the polemics by Zanchi and Major, see n. 604. The reference to *Transylvani* in the paragraph seems to be to the Dávidians in Transylvania. The people referred to "contra *istos*" and "ab *istis*" are evidently the Reformed in Debrecen, Gönc, etc. The "us" of "ab *nostris*" can only refer to Polish Brethren, surely not any group of liberal Saxons in Leipzig, where the letter purports to originate (cf. n. 631).

634. Matt 26:34, 74–75 and parallels.

635. *Non iveni*.

636. Matt 13:25–40.

637. The words in Greek, the last word misprinted, are from Aristotle's *Politics* 1.2 (1253a, lines 5–6), where Aristotle indeed quotes Homer's *Iliad* 9.63, but not this. It is possible that the writer's passage was more extensive and that Lubieniecki, Wiszowaty, or the printer truncated it. The possibly typographical error has not been noted in the

corrigenda. In the larger Aristotelian passage the phrasing wrongly attributed to Homer is italicized; Homer's own words quoted hard by are in quotation marks:

> Hence it is evident that the state is a creation of nature, and that man is by nature a political animal. And he who by nature and not by mere accident is without a state, is either above humanity or below it; he is like the "tribeless, lawless, heartless one," [Nestor in his reply to Diomedes] whom Homer denounces—the outcast by nature *and desirous of war*; he may be compared to an isolated piece at draughts.

The writer of the letter was in the presence of the Greek text of Aristotle and shows in his Latin no trace of the Latin version of William of Moerbeke, ed. by Hermann Usener and Franz Bücheler, *Aristotelis politicorum libri octo* (Leipzig, 1872) 8.

638. The writer seems to be saying: We are not "tribeless, lawless, heartless" merely because we depart from the majority in our defense of the new religious conscience and surely are not exploiting a moment of religious toleration to prepare for revolt. The writer goes on to question whether ministers of the word, now with Protestant leaders in mind rather than bishops, incite voivodes or kings to confessional persecution.

639. For Luther on the Trinity, see n. 125. As emotionally remote from Luther as the writer appears to be in this offhand allusion, he, writing in 1571, would seem to come out of a Lutheran rather than a Reformed environment.

640. In this paragraph "this one opinion" (*hanc certe [sententiam]*) "of philosophers" that the writer cannot accept would appear to be the *philosophical* formulation of the doctrine of the Trinity, although he could have in mind the one proposition basic to scholasticism that philosophy is propaedeutic for theology, that reason may prepare the way for faith. In the next paragraph he indeed contrasts *philosophia* and *dispensatio*, the latter probably meaning saving truth as revealed in the scriptural dispensation. The phrasing *in nostrate philosophia* claims for a simplified scriptural theology the right to be called indeed "this philosophy of ours" unencumbered by terms from Plato, Aristotle, or the Schoolmen.

641. The framing of the request for further information "de toto statu istius religionis" suggests psychological distance from Transylvania. That the writer begs Hallopegius love him for other reasons than his getting involved in printing the MS confirms the impression throughout that the writer and the recipient have been in frequent correspondence and personal contact, broken by what appears to have been a period of silence for which Hallopegius had evidently accused himself of turpitude and then been exculpated by the writer; cf. opening paragraph of the letter.

Although Lubieniecki leads from this letter into a prefatory letter of Sommer, the internal evidence of the letter here being brought to a close is inclusive as to whether it is for, to, or only about Sommer.

642. Wiszowaty inserts after *Lectoris*: "About whom see *Bibliotheca Antitrinitariorum*, 57." Here Sand identifies the work as capitalized in translation but not in the text. In *BAnt²* Wiszowaty says further that the letter and *Theses de Deo Trino* were written in German, and attached to Francken's *Enumeratio* in a characterization with slightly different wording from that in n. 629, reading instead: ". . . our Christiani constantes sint in dogmate Trinitatis retinendo, cum in aliis articulis sint mobiles et varii." Thereupon Wiszowaty characterizes Sommer's *Theses* without noting that they are printed in the *Historia*: "Egregia admonitio in modum cautionis composita a Joanne Somero ad verum Deum laudandum et ipsi gratias agendum, quod tam benigne nostris temporibus veram et salutarem cognitionem sui, sui dilecti filii Jesu Christinostri Domini, et Sancti spiritus

nobis revelaverit.—Edidit Dietericus Dorschius loco et anno no addito.'' That there is no place of publication fits with the entry of Wiszowaty in *BAnt*², 57 (n. 629), but not with what he says there about date, i.e., 1578.

Under the name, not of Dorsch, but that of Theodosius Schimberg (n. 632), Vehe-Glirius published Sommer's *Theses* in another collection, *Tractatus aliquot Christianiae religionis* (Ingolstadt [Cracow], Rodecki, 1583), Gryczowa, no. 79. Dán reprints the introductory material of the ''Schimberg,'' texts 4 and 5, and deals with the history of the identification of the editor of the *Tractatus*, *Vehe-Glirius*, 185ff. Pirnát observes that the *Theses* were a draft of what would become Sommer's major theological work, the *Refutatio scripti Petri Caroli* of 1572 (n. 632), *Siebenbürger Antitrinitarier*, 43–45.

Lubieniecki could have had access to the *Tractatus* of 1583. With even much less of an excerpt from a publication, he would ordinarily indicate his source. It is not likely that he has translated the evidently German version of ''Dorsch'' of 1578. It is quite possible that he had a MS version among the papers of Budziński, who was close to Glirius and Budny, and that Budziński thought he was transcribing a MS for posterity. The place Lubieniecki in turn accords Sommer's *Theses* in his own *Historia* suggests that he finds the *Theses* wholly convincing.

As for Sommer himself he is convinced that by showing classical onsets and even parallels to Triadology he can demonstrate that they are invalid, even though an accomplished classicist and an admirer of classical thought, he could have just as well construed these onsets in the spirit of Eusebius of Caesarea as the philosophical *praeparatio evangelica*, as did also Marsigio Ficino, whose edition of Plato and Plotinus Sommer made use of. In his disdain for classical triadologies, Sommer is one with the classical reformers in holding that only in the Scripture is the true God revealed. Sommer was a scriptural Unitarian, not yet a Deist.

As for the publisher in Cracow of the writings of Sommer and the defense of Dávid, Matthias Vehe-Glirius-Dorsch-Schimberg, his final days in the Commonwealth were spent in the service of Calvinist Mikołaj Firley (d. 1588); and under his patronage he taught first at the school in Lewartów, then at the court of Palatine Gostomski of Rawa. Janusz Tazbir, ''Maciej Vehe-Glirius,'' *Wieki Średnie/Medium Aevum* (1962), 296; Dán, ''Vehe-Glirius and the Polish Antitrinitarians,'' *Vehe-Glirius*, chap. 8. Dán conjectures that Vehe-Glirius left the Commonwealth by way of Elbing and Danzig to voyage thence in the spring of 1589 to the Netherlands, to spend there and in East Frisia a decade among radical groupings, dying in Gretzyl, 1590.

643. The text could also be read as follows: ''Though many from their schools gave adherence to Christ in order not to hold a common doctrine with the [pagan] multitude. . . .''

644. Dionysius the Areopagite was baptized by the Apostle Paul (Acts 17:34). The mystical *corpus dionysiacum*, which exercised a deep influence on Christian theology and philosophy, was written by a Monophysite Neoplatonist in the fifth century. Sommer recognized that the author was not Paul's Athenian convert.

645. Ammonius Saccas (c. 175–242) was the reputed founder of Neoplatonism. His greatest pupil for eleven years was Plotinus (c. 205–70).

646. The ex-Jesuit Guillaume Postel (1510–81), *De orbis terrae concordia* in four books (Basel, 1544), 16–17: ''De Sacrosancta Trinitate et Trino Deo,'' especially the ''Prima demonstratio Trinitatis'' and pp. 22–23 containing the ''Testimonium et autoritas philosophorum de Trinitate.'' In his missionary theory for the conversion of the Muslims in book 1 Postel attempted the proof of the truth of Christianity precisely by

using ancient philosophers and Jewish and Muslim sources. See William Bouswma, *Concordia Mundi: The Career and Thought of Guilaume Postel (1570–1581)* (Cambridge, 1957) esp. 233–38.

647. Lactantius in *Divinae Institutiones*, 7, 24, pictured the decline of the world from a Golden Age/Paradise. The *editio princeps* of this and two other works of Lactantius was the first printed work in Italy, Subiaco 1465. For the reference, see *PL*, 6.

648. Sommer extensively used the editions and comments of Marsiglio Ficino (1433–99), founder of the Platonic Academy in Florence and ordained priest (1473). The *Opera omnia e graeco in latinum translata* of Plotinus was printed at the expense of Lorenzo de' Medici (Florence, 1492). Sommer used reeditions of Ficino's and Plato's works, namely, Plotinus, *De rebus philosophicis Libri VI in Enneades sex distributi* (Basel, 154) and Plato, *Epistolarum duodecim liber* (Paris, 1544) and the *Timaeus* (Paris, 1544). Most of the ensuing identificaitons refer to the English translation of Kenneth S. Guthrie, *Plotinus: complete works in chronological order*, 4 vols, continuously paginated (Grantwood, NJ, 1918) and to the Loeb Classical Library edition of Plato's *Dialogues* (references to individual volumes of the series are given in the notes). Sommer in some places paraphrases Plotinus.

649. *Timaeus* 35A; *Plato: Timaeus, etc.*, trans. R. G. Bury (Cambridge, 1966) 65.

650. *Epistle* VI. 323D; *Plato: Timaeus, etc.*, 461. There is an error (presumably typographical) in Sommer's Latin: the text should read *causae* rather than *causam*.

651. *Non inveni*.

652. Ficino, ed., *Enneades*, fol. 113 (literal quotation).

653. Ibid., fol. 68 *verso*. Sommer or Lubieniecki incorrectly quotes the *summa* of Book II.

654. *Timaeus* 68E (perhaps in Ficino's edition, fols. 11f.); *Plato: Timaeus, etc.*, 177.

655. Plotinus, *Enneades* 3.8.11 lines 33–34; Guthrie, 550. Wiszowaty has corrected Lubieniecki's text in his *Emandanda*.

656. This is a summary from Plotinus, *Enneades* 6.8.18 (Ficino, ed., *Enneades*, fol. 114); Guthrie, *op. cit.*, 805–6.

657. This appears to be a paraphrase of *Timaeus* 52C; *Plato: Timaeus, etc.*, 123–25.

658. [Plato], *Horoi* 411A5; in *Platonis opera*, ed. by J. Burnet (Oxford, 1907), 5.

659. *Non inveni*.

660. Plato, *Phaedrus* 245D; *Plato: Euthyphro, etc.*, trans. by H. N. Fowler (Cambridge, 1926) 469–71.

661. *Non inveni*.

662. [Plato], *Epinomis* 986C; *Plato: Charmides, etc.*, trans. by W. R. M. Lamb (London, 1927) 467. Sommer is apparently translating the single word λόγος as both *ratio* and *verbum*.

663. *Non inveni*.

664. Plato, *Cratylus* 400A; *Plato: Cratylus, etc.*, trans. by H. N. Fowler (London, 1926) 61.

665. *Cratylus* 413C; ibid., 103.

666. Plato, *Philebus* 28C; *Plato: Statesman and Philebus*, trans. by H. N. Fowler (London, 1925) 261.

667. Ibid.

668. The text has *liber 2*. The reference is to lines 267–68 and 601–602.

669. Lucian of Samosata (b. c. A.D. 120), *Dialogues of the Dead*, 11 (16), Diogenes and Heracles; Loeb Classical Library, *Lucian*, 7.52–59.

670. Athanasian Creed, article 36, has: "anima rationalis et caro unus est homo";

Plotinus, *Enneades*, ed. Ficino, fol. 192f. (an extract). The wholly Western *Quincunquevult* arose more than two hundred years after Lucian. Sommer may not have known of Joachim Camerius on the *Athanasium*, Bk. 1, n. 86.

671. Plotinus, *Enneades* 6.8.16, lines 12–16; Guthrie, *op. cit.*, 802.

672. Sommer refers to terms emphasized in the debates at Debrecen, 21–26 February 1567.

673. Sommer concludes in scorn that terms like *Jehovalitas* (n. 628) had become technical terms for the conservative Reformed side of the Hungarian (= Transylvanian) debate, while Platonic and Neoplatonic terminology clearly antedated Nicene Trinitarian formulation and could not be made up for with Latinized Hebraic concepts.

The remainder of the chapter is Lubieniecki's inconsequential summary.

674. Lubieniecki is not referring to any particular Transylvanian synod. His incompletely articulated thought in accord with Sommer's is that the existence of a pre-Christian Triadology approximating that formulated at Nicaea invalidates Nicaea as non-scriptural and therefore invalid.

From the time of the Christian Apologists like Justin Martyr, the preincarnational intimations of the Trinity were adduced in favor of Christian doctrine. By construing Scripture as the sole revelation, normative Protestantism, particularly Calvinism, had cut itself off from confident reference to the *praeparatio Evangelii* among the Gentiles (Greek philosophy) that had, in fact, made possible the compelling patristic and conciliar synthesis in Triadology and Christology. Cf. n. 642.

675. At the close of Lubieniecki's Chapter Eleven on Transylvania, which exhibits two documents that antedate the Socinus-Dávid Disputation that occasions its title, we pull together the preceding annotation in order to suggest the contours of the Unitarian Church in Transylvania—as Lubieniecki himself would have been aware of it when he wrote his *Historia*, the church into whose embrace, particularly in Koloszvár, many of the Polish refugees of 1660 fled. The flight was made vivid in the two letters Editor Wiszowaty printed in his edition of the *Historia*, as chapters 17 and 18. They were removed for the English translation and printed in *Polish Brethren* Documents XXXIII 1 and 2. A summary note here is all the more pressing for the reason that Lubieniecki himself is evasive about the immediate consequences in Transylvania of the disputation. In effect, Socinus left behind in Transylvania a Blandratan Church, destined to become integral to a kind of confessionally pluralistic state-church establishment under the Calvinist Princes of the next century.

For the sequence of events immediately after the trial of Dávid, a major, though partisan source, is preserved by Palaeologus, ''Scriptum Fratrum Transylvanorum ad N.N.,'' *Defensio*, 236–78. Pirnát proposed (*Ideologie*, 172) that its author was Lukács Trausner, son-in-law of Dávid. Dán accepts this view (*Vehe-Glirius*, 147), and he doubtless joins Balázs in the opinion that Vehe-Glirius was indeed the recipient of the communication; Dán-Balázs, *Defensio*, xxx, n. 10. Besides the records of what Dán calls ''the conservative restoration,'' there is also in MS History to which he, Pirnát, and others have had access in recent typical studies, ''Unitárius Egyháztörténeti Kézirat,'' 2 vols. University library, Budapest, *Vehe-Glirius*, 135 and 137, n. 23, etc.

An unusually yielding source is the account of matters Transylvanian by the great Counter-Reformation missionary-ecumenist, papal legate, biblical scholar and chronicler-reporter, Antonio Possevino, S.J., of Mantua (1534–1614), who preached to the Waldenses in Savoy in 1571, for a decade thereafter in France, and in Sweden in 1578 where he nearly succeeded in bringing John III back under papal sway (but for the refusal of Gregory XIII to allow the three concessions favorably considered by his predecessors in the Council of Trent). He served decisively as legate to Ivan IV 1580–84 in Moscow after the Tsar's defeat by Stephen Batory, accompanied by Gáspár Békés. Possevino sought to foster reunion of the Patriarchial Church with Rome, spending his days in the Kremlin, Cracow or Rome. Stephen Batory asked him to collect materials for a report on the principality, 1583–84, *Transylvania* (1584), ed. by Endre Veress, with plates, *Fontes rerum Transylvanicarum*, 3 (Koloszvár/Budapest, 1913). There appear to be at least three versions of another work by him: *Atheismi haereticorum huius seculi*, part of a larger collected work (Poznań, 1586), *De sectariorum Atheismis nostri temporis liber* (Cologne, 1586), and *Atheismi, Lutheri, Melanchthonis, Calvini Arianorum it ministrarum Transylvanorum cum thesibus Francisci Davidis* (Vilna, 1586), the last cited and used by Dán, *Vehe-Glirius*, 131, n. 9. The main deposit of his experience with the Orthodox was printed in *Capita quibus Graeci et Rutheni a Latinus in rebus fidei dissenserunt* (Poznań, 1585), a work significant for the eventual Union of the Orthodox in the Commonwealth from Vilna to Kiev in 1595.

Within two days of the condemnation of Dávid, the ministers and the nobles who had been in sympathy with him abjured their opinion in the presence of the Prince. The majority of the ministers, under pressure from Christopher Báthory and Biandrata, subscribed to the four articles on God the Father and Jesus Christ his premundane son and destined Messiah, in a formulation similar to that of the Polish Ditheists but without reference to the Apostles' Creed. The articles clearly reached back to an earlier point in the confessional dynamics of the community, fixating for generations to come to a formulation that purported to be what had been approved by John II Sigismund. The forced ministerial consensus is noted by Bod (*Historia*, 1.451, printed by him 2.604–6; reprinted by Wallace 92.304–6), and discussed by Wilbur (*Transylvania*, 26–87). In August 1579 Biandrata in his capacity as archpresbyter and on behalf of the Prince called an emergency synod in Kolozsvár, seeking to impose upon it a new superintendent. The synod elected a consistory of twenty-four members, but both the consistory and the synod declined to endorse Biandrata's conservative choice for superintendent. Thereupon Biandrata took Demeter Hunyadi with him to Alba Julia, where on the recommendation of the court physician and privy counselor Christopher Báthory confirmed him as Dávid's lawful successor in the sequence of Kolozsvár superintendents (n. 598). The consistory in Kolozsvár summoned by Hunyadi, 14 September 1589, authorized the restoration of pedobaptism and the observance of the Lord's Supper in its simplest form. In a letter of 10 January 1580, in self-defense for his role in the trial and now recent death of Dávid at Déva in November, Biandrata explained that the crux of the crisis was not nonadorantism, which could have been optional, but the dangerous religious consequences of the whole thrust of Dávid's theological and ecclesiological trajectory. Already in the fall of 1579 the Blandratan Hunyadi Church had received the *Judicium* of the Polish Brethren (n. 630) and had it printed in Koloszvár with a compendium of scriptural passages supportive of the more conservative position. Even so, the adorant, partly pacifist Polish Brethren, with their retention of the *Apostolicum* in their own Church, the immersion of their catechized offspring, and with their enhanced sense of distance from magisterial ingerency in synodal offices, were by no means identical in contour with the Church that printed their *Judicium* at Kolozsvár in 1580.

Besides the Unitarian Church of the conservative restoration under Biandrata and Hunyadi, Dán distinguishes (*Vehe-Glirius*, 148–49) three radical groupings in varying degrees claiming Dávid as their mentor and martyr. The first group included preachers and a few supportive nobles who stayed firm in their Davidian nonadorantism, despite Hunyadi, and his successor, György Enyedi.

The second group, not theologically homogenous or of the same origins, was represented by those preachers who developed further the final affirmations of Dávid, searching for a "true Christianity" under his patronage. Prominent was Miklós Bogati Fazakas, court preacher and poet, whose journal authenticates the exact date of Dávid's death (n. 601). Similar was György Valaszuti, superintendent of Temesvár in Ottoman Hungary and active in the debate in Pécs, 1588 (n. 632).

The third movement, that of Sabbatarianism, Dán calls "the last Christian reformation of the sixteenth century" (*Vehe-Glirius*, 146). Ultra-radical, the proponents went far beyond the nonadorantism of Dávid, placing the Old Testament above the New. Holding that Vehe-Glirius was the father of Transylvanian Sabbatarianism, Dán sees in the 15 or 16 theses prepared by Socinus at the behest of Biandrata and by them ascribed to Dávid at Torda in April 1579 and in Alba Julia in 1 June 1579 (n. 629), an impetus of the Sabbatarians who would therefore claim they were the faithful Dávidians. Some of the excommunicated ministers may have joined the group, but the founder and enthusiastic prophet of a Christian Old Testament Unitarianism was the Szekler nobleman András Eössi (d. 1602), who lived on his estate five miles northwest of Maros-Vásárhely, widowed and then bereft of his three sons. He was evidently part of a general movement, for Possevino reported that as early as 1583 there were many in Koloszvár forsaking the gospel for the Old Testament prophecies and laws and that "the Unitarian ministers in Szeklerland universally abstain from blood and pork" (*Transylvania*, 66). Eössi, besides compiling his own compendium of scriptural passages and composing hymns in support of his Sabbatarian piety, took into his court in 1594 a brilliant youth as his successor, Simon Péchi (c. 1570–1643), born in Pécs. He supported Péchi's Western European education. Wilbur supplies (*Transylvania*, 105–15, citing the extensive literature) a substantial account of the Sabbatarians who in the end considered themselves Jews (c. 1580–1867) when they were acknowledged by the Jewish synogogal community as an authentic proselyte congregation (the last taken to the Nazi death camps in 1944). Dán, who showed that Vehe-Glirius was the source of the movement, "The works of Vehe-Glirius and Early Sabbatarian ideology," *Armarium* (Budapest, 1975) 87–94, has a chapter on the genesis of Transylvanian Sabbatarianism (*Vehe-Glirius*, chap. 7), securely grounded in the recovered *Mattanajah* (1578), Bk. 2, n. 364; and now presents a major study of the later more religio-political Sabbatarian and the polyglot adventurer Simon Péchi, with an opening chapter clarifying the Davidian connections, *Az erdélyi szombatosok és Péchi Simon* (Budapest: Akadémia Kiadó, 1985), Humanizmus és Reformáció, 13. In this work on the Transylvanian Sabbatarians and Simon Péchi, Dán observes that there was no Jewish community in Transylvania to stimulate the extraordinary Judaizing thrust among the followers of Dávid. It was only in part, however, under the sanction of Dávid's name that the movement drew strength. Especially among the Szekler herdsmen and their noble patrons the idea of God's single covenant supported their own ancestral tribal compact and organization and communal ideals of social justice; and the view of Vehe-Glirius in the *Mattanajah* that Jesus' death was a witness to God's will (*martýron*) and not an expiatory sacrifice, that the laws and festivals of the Hebrew Bible were applicable to the Christians praying for the second advent of Jesus as the true Messiah, and that in the meantime the Unitarian Sabbatarians should resist all churches with their assumption that Jesus established a second covenant and resist also the princely power interfering with the true followers of Yahweh gained widespread devotion also beyond the Szeklers in all Transylvania. Although Péchi was made the heir of Eössi, after the founder's death in 1602 Sabbatarianism split up into loose congeries of sects; and Péchi himself abandoned the movement, espousing instead a neo-stoicism then popular among the nobility. Without a major leader, Sabbatarianism underwent transformation, renouncing its goal of an immediate reorganization of the Principality according to Old Testament tenents, and turned towards the rituals and disciplines and piety of the Eössi. Yet as the Sabbatarians had sought support for a Sabbatarian prince in negotiations with Sublime Porte, several of the Calvinist Princes exploited these connections and nevertheless also passed decrees against them in 1606, 1610, 1618, and 1622. In the meantime Péchi had become secretary to Prince Sigismund Báthory, next a confident of Stephen Bocskai, and finally chancellor to Gabriel Bethlen (n. 387). But then maneuvering to become Prince himself with Turkish support and Hapsburg consent, Péchi was arrested, 23 May 1621. In prison for three and a half years, he became attracted to the Deism of the Silesian alumnus of Heidelberg and an antagonist of Socinus, Seidler (Bk. 2, n. 364), and undertook extensive translations of Jewish moral philosophy. In 1624 he was permitted to return to the estate of Eössi in Szenterzsébet and rejoined the Sabbatarians, modifying their program by repristinating the Noachic laws as God's intention for non-Jews. With this accomodation but with the inclusion of much further Jewish material in translation, while bringing back to prominence the Glirian-Davidian view of the imminent Messiah as having the lineaments of Jesus, Péchi shaped the final contours of Sabbatarianism, even though during the Sabbatarian trials of 1638, he reluctantly renounced the movement in order to avoid another imprisonment and conformed to the Reformed Church until his death at Eössi's residence in 1643.

The developments in the four groupings cannot be here further detailed, except for reference to the succession of superintendents in the official Unitarian Church, and the observation that the goldsmith son of one early in that succession, János Toroczkai, on becoming a fanatical Sabbatarian, was stoned by five gypsies for blasphemy against Jews (commonly used for capital punishment), according to Mosaic law, Lev 24:15. Wilbur, *Transylvania*, 116. The official Blandratan Church, under pressure from the Reformed and the Lutherans at a synod at Dées of 1638 (nn. 123, ¶2; 28, ¶2), conformed again to territorial usage on pedobaptism and reaffirmed the Four Articles of Consensus of 1 July 1579, becoming thereafter regularly called the Unitarian Church as part of the Transylvanian multiconfessional state-church establishment, Bod, *Historia*, 2.604–6; noted by Wilbur in passing, *Transylvania*, 117. This development left it to the Polish Brethren, less encumbered by concordants with king, prince, patron, or town council, to evolve, partly under the leadership of Faustus Socinus, into the distinctive rational religion of the Polish diaspora. Among the chief scholars in this period in Transylvania was Superintendent Enyedi, who at the expense of the town council of Kolozsvár had studied extensively in Germany, Vienna, Switzerland, and Padua. His chief work may have been based on the unpublished volume (c. 1598) of István Basilius, an early ally of Biandrata against Dávid, who was later considered as radical on Triadology as Dávid himself. Dán, *Vehe-Glirius*, 745. Enyedi's posthumous work against all the texts used in the defense of the dogma of the Trinity was *Explicationes locorum Veteris et Novi Testamenti, ex quibus Trinitatis dogma stabiliri solet* (Kolozsvár, 1619; Groningen, 1670). It was translated into Hungarian by superintendent Mátyas Toroczkai (Kolozsvár, 1619); *Régi Magyar Könyvtár*, 1.222; 2, item 77. Wilbur lists the most important works in Transylvania and beyond controverting this major work on the Trinity in Scripture (*Transylvania*, 98, n. 47), as it accomplished on the Unitarian side at the very center of the Church what Josias Simler had failed to do for the plenary Trinitarian side, when pressed to do so by Méliusz and the Polish Calvinists (Bk. 2, n. 391). For other developments centered in Kolozsvár, see n. 597.

Because of the lack of chronological sequence in the text of Lubieniecki and hence in the annotation, all the gatherings, diets, synods, and disputations in Hungary mentioned in the notes of Bk. 3, esp. in chapter 11, are here brought together: Torda and Kolozsvár 1557, n. 129; Segesvár and Enyed 1564, n. 129; Gönc 1566, n. 612; Torda 1566, nn. 615, 616; Alba Julia 1566, nn. 615, 616, 626; Torda 1566, n. 615; Alba Julia 1566, n. 615; Maros-Vásárhely 1566, nn. 610, 615; Várad 1566, n. 610; Debrecen 1567, nn. 628, 672; Debrecen 1568, n. 610; Kassa 1568, n. 612; Szikszó 1568, n. 610; Torda 1568, nn. 599, 610; Alba Julia 1568, nn. 123, 596, 597, 598, 599, 610, 615, 616, 626; Várad 1569, nn. 597, 626; Maros-Vásárhely 1571, n. 599; Enyed 1576, n. 601; Kolozsvár/Torda 1578, nn. 229, 280, 599, 600; ''after the harvest'' 1578, n. 600; Torda February 1579, n. 629; Torda April 1579, nn. 629, 675; Alba Julia 1579, nn. 629, 675; Leczfava 1600, n. 123; Dées 1638, nn. 123, 280.

NOTES TO CHAPTER TWELVE

676. The founding of Raków, so important in the life of the author himself, has already been anticipated or even dealt with in passing by Lubieniecki, along with the visits of Mundius, Filipowski, Schomann, and others to the communitarian Hutterites in Moravia, in Bk. 2 at n. 399; in Bk. 3, with an intercalated subheading on Raków and the baptismal controversy, esp. after the involvement in it of Socinus by 1580, nn. 319 – 27; then again in a chapter 3, on visits to Moravia, 1568 and 1569, nn. 584 – 91. For all that Lubieniecki has not been clear in his accounts of the beginnings of Raków, despite the prominent role of his own maternal great-grandfather, Hieronim Filipowski, in the shift of sentiment among the most evangelical of the lords toward implementing the apostolic principle of the sharing of goods.

It was at the synod of Pełsznica in October 1568 that ''there was talk of the Moravian communists'' reported on favorably by Mundius (cf. n. 687). The ministers at the synod, among them Grzegorz Paweł, Schomann, Czechowic, and Gonesius, were of one accord that ''ministers should exercise their ministry such that they live not by the toil of others but that they earn their own bread by their own hands (cf. Paul in Acts 18:3; n. 692). Also the lords and brethren said that it is not fitting for us to to live on such estates as were obtained by our ancestors in return for bloodshed. Then give up such properties, distribute them among the poor.'' The appeal was not, however, in unanimity but the synod closed with an expression of mutual respect. Sipayłło, *AS*, 2.221, where it is noted that the social questions had been raised recently at the synod of Iwie, 20 – 26 January 1568, with Paweł of Wizna, superintendent in Lithuanian among the prime movers there (n. 687), present also at Pełsznica, n. 589, Sipayłło, *AS*, 2.221, n. 3.

Sipayłło does not retain in *AS* as taken from Symon Budny, *O urzędzie miecza*, ed. by Kot, the important datum that after the synod of Iwie and presumably Pełsznica, Jakub Kalinowski ''with a number of persons of the nobility and of Vilna citizens inclined to his position then in the year 1569 left Lithuania for Raków'' (p. 180). We have thus a date for the arrival of possibly the first anabaptist pacifists as settlers in Raków before the Racovians themselves in turn made contact with the Hutterites (apart from Mundius's ealier inspection). Noted by Tworek, ''Raków,'' 57.

The right to grant the unusual charter for Raków was obtained from the King by lord Jan Sienieński, a convert to the Major Church and signed 27 March 1567. It gave the prospective inhabitants many privileges comparable to a royal bourough, including free-dom for twenty years from payments, rents, or taxes, and accorded them to a large extent self-rule, for he retained for himself the right of appointment of only two of the six otherwise elected town councilors. The town, which bore the heraldic name of his wife's clan in evident deference to her dream of a city of refuge for her fellow believers, was conceived by her and by him as "some kind of new Jerusalem or Zion." Jadwiga Goińska (nn. 295, 319, 683, 709) deserves the title 'foundress of Raków.' She was related to Zofia Oleśnicka, the first Protestant hymnodist (1555, Plates 10 and 57). Her husband's charter read in part: "I make known to all personally, and particularly to those that have and shall have to do with it, that I will not rule over the religion of any of the aforesaid Racovians in which they differ from one another, nor any of their succesors of subjects, nor will I permit my agents to rule over the same, but each of them, as the Lord gives him grace, and as his knowledge of the faith leads him, shall cherish his faith in peace with himself and his descendants." At the same time he warned any "animosity and impertinence" coming in "under the cover of worship." The full text is printed by Jan Wiśniewski, *Dekanat iłzecki* (Radom, 1907 – 11), see n. 682.

The original village destined to become the commune and town of Raków arose in 1569 and developed as a center for mining and foresting. See Stanisław Cynarski, ed., *Raków ognisko Arianizmu*, with map and illustrations (Cracow, 1968). A *Rejestr* of the town as of 12 December 1607 would suggest a population of about 1,100 inhabitants. Stanisław Malanowicz, "Ludność Miasta Rakowa," in Cynarski, *Raków*, 22ff.

677. The Author's grandfather, Krzysztof I (1561 – 1624), married the daughter of the author of *Christian Heroes*, Bk. 1, n. 188.

678. Lubieniecki is never wholly clear about his maternal lineage. Hieronim Filipowski (d. after 1574) took to wife the widow of Jerzy Niemsta, Regina Glińska (d. 1557). He married a second time, Zofia Komorowska Filipowska, our Author's *avia materna* (at n. 718). Katarzyna Filipowska, a great granddaughter (*prawnuczka*) of Hieronim, married Krzysztof Lubieniecki (c. 1596 – 1648), the father of the Author. The *Life of Lubieniecki* is silent on the maternal line, but on the basis of the two references in Lubieniecki's *Historia* and of other sources, Tazbir makes (*Lubieniecki*, 19) of this Zofia Filipowska a great-granddaughter (*prawnuczka*) of Hieronim; but if a granddaughter in any degree, she would on this view be a descendant of a son or grandson of Filipowski. We know of only one son, a namesake of his father, Hieronim (*Historia*, 53), who died a Catholic. If Hieronim Filipowski, Jr., were the maternal grandfather of our Author, we would have an explanation for his reticence (n. 718 ¶3), but Hieronym Sr. may have been expelled by the Racovians, (n. 718 ¶2) which Lubieniecki would have had reason to pass over in silence.

Some of the family tradition of venturesome, idealistic, and impressionable Hieronim Filipowski, Sr., will have, surely, reached Lubieniecki, although he chooses here to say less than he could have about the communitarian period in Racovian history, and his grandsire's role therein.

Filipowski twice made a pilgrimage to the Hutterites in Moravia (Bk. 2, n. 399; Bk. 3, chap. 3; Schomann, *BAnt*, no. 30). It is quite possible that Filipowski was the author of the anonymous *Traktat przeciwko "kommunistom" morawskim z roku około 1569*. The MS, once belonging to Andreas Dudith, was edited by Jan Karłowicz, *Rocznik Towarzystwa Przyjaciół Nauk w Poznaniu Towarzystwa*, 15 (1887). Stanisław Kot discussed it at some length and in context in *Ideologja polityczna i społeczna Braci Polskich zwanych Arjanami*, Wilbur, *Socinianism in Poland*, 35 – 40. Kot conjectures that Budziński was the probable author. The point of view therein, however, is that of a lord of the manor, not of a clerical secretary turned historian, who had no sympathy at all for the communitarian effort of Raków, which Filipowski did. The *Traktat* is discussed further by Kot,

"Polish Brethren and the Problem of Communism in XVth Century Poland," *Transactions of the Unitarian Historical Society in London*, 12 (1956) and translated as "A Treatise not against the Apostolic Community," ibid., 12 (1959), no. 3, 90 – 104. See n. 718.

On the extent of the contacts and exchanges of the Polish Brethren with Hutterites and the sources of the latter concerning the Poles, see Lech Szczucki and Janusz Tazbir, "Korespondencja anabaptystów morawskich z arianami polskimi," *OiRwP* 3 (1958) 197 – 215 (where there is provisional accord with Kot on Budziński as likely author of the *Traktat*, 214, n. 2); Robert Friedmann, "The Encounter of Anabaptists and Mennonites with anti-Trinitarians," *MQR* 22 (1948) 139 – 162; my *Radical Reformation*, chap. 27:2; Gross, *Hutterites*, chap. 7. The encounters of the Polish Brethren in Moravia have been placed in a broader context by Wacław Urban, *Antitrinitarismus in der Slowakei und in Böhmen im 16. und 17. Jahrhundert*, Bibliotheca Dissidentium, *Scripta et Studia*, no. 2 (Baden-Baden, Koerner, 1985); cf. his treatment of a Cracow-educated ex-priest and anabaptist leader, "Eine theologische Auseinandersetzung [edited epistle and Lutheran gloss] um den slowakischen Täufer und Spiritualisten Andreas Fischer," *ARG* 71 (1980) 149 – 59.

679. The *Vita* of Stanisław Lubieniecki, born 23 August 1623, is given translation, *Polish Brethren*, Doc. XXVIII. It was originally printed as the introduction to the *Historia*.

680. The Laws of the School of Raków (*BAnt*, 175; Gryczowa, n. 150, plate 28) are in *PB*, Doc. II.

681. Mentioned above at n. 295 and near n. 319.

682. The privilege for the new town was given 27 March 1567; the town came into being, as Lubieniecki says, in 1569. The charter is printed by Jan Wiśniewski, *Dekanat iłżecki*, Part 1 (Radom, 1907), 374 – 83; Part 2 (Radom, 1909 – 11) 111 – 13; partly quoted by Stanisław Tync, "Zarys dziejów wyższej szkoły Braci Polskich w Rakowie, 1602 – 1638," Cynarski, *Raków*, 84; Wilbur, *Socinianism*, 357, n. 5.

683. Jadwiga Gnoińska is mentioned in n. 676 ¶4.

684. The charter of 1567 granted full religious liberty to all the inhabitants of the incorporated town.

685. Maciej Albinus (last mentioned in *Historia, 218*) was, so far as is known, the last minister in Iwanowice, which, though in Cracovia, would not seem to justify the phrasing of Lubieniecki, unless he had information about Albinus as an ongoing associate of Grzegorz Paweł after his ouster from the congregation in Cracow in 1562.

For Grzegorz Paweł in Raków, 1569 – 91, see Górski, *Grzegorz Paweł*, chap. 8.

686. This appears to have been Jan Sierkierzyński *pater*.

687. On Mundius, see n. 588f. Concentrating on Little Poland and not entirely happy about the original social radicalism of Raków, Lubieniecki here passes over what Donald J. Ziegler, an American editor, has rightly included in his anthology, *Great Debates of the Reformation* (New York: Random House, 1969) chap. 8, with commentary. This is a translation from Budny, an opponent of the social radicals in an apparently faithful recollection, however, of the polite fraternal debate; see n. 691.

It has been noted that the first clear onset to social egalitarianism in Little Poland was at the synod of Pełsznica in October, 1568 (n. 589); but it had been foreshadowed in several articles (5, 6, 9) among ten at the synod of Iwie; Sipayłło, *AS*, 2.218 – 19 (the ten items taken from Budny). As Lubieniecki passes over such matters, the intermixture of theological and social radicalism is best set forth:

1. Concerning the Lord Christ, that he was not a person (*osobą*) until after he was born of Mary.
2. Concerning this, whether this Lord Christ is the son of David by way of (*po*) Joseph or is this by way of Mary.
3. Concerning the Holy Spirit, whether to be invoked.
4. Concerning immersion (*ponurzeniu*), whether it is necessary for the faithful or it suffices for them that they have been christened (*okrzczeni*) in childhood (*w dzieciństwie*).
5. Concerning contempt for the world (*zgardzeniu świata*) and concerning self-denial (*zaprzeniu samego siebie*) and concerning serfs (*poddanych*) and servants (*niewolnikoch* [elsewhere: *o niewolnej czeladzi*]), whether to have them.
6. Concerning oaths, whether the faithful may swear them.
7. Concerning social (*społecznym* in the sense of public) or public (*jawnym*) fasting.
8. Concerning the training (*wychowaniu*) of ministers and concerning the common people (*plebanijach*).
9. Concerning discipline from the word of God, whether all should observe (*strzegli*) it.
10. Concerning the sending/calling (*posyłaniu*) of ministers and their improvement/discipline (*naprawie*).

The radical christological propositions (1,2) may well be reflected in a generalization by Lubieniecki at n. 505. It was the debate on point 5, on feudal rights, slavery and serfdom, that most interested Budny (n. 691), whose recollection of his opposition to the social radicalism of Jakub Kalinowski, Paweł of Wizna, and Jan Baptysta Święcicki is printed by Ziegler, *Great Debates*, Chap. 8.

688. The phrasing "synodus aliquot annis" suggests that by Schomann in his *Testamentum*, where in his chronology he had in mind the discussions at Raków during the radical phase, 1569–72, (n. 689) while Lubieniecki vaguely or perhaps evasively intends his wording for the later colloquia and synod in the presence of Faustus Socinus (n. 704).

689. Although born in Raków, Lubieniecki may well intentionally avoid its experimental episode in the community of goods, in pacificism, and religious radicalism. He betrays almost no awareness of any local oral tradition to supplement what Schomann relates sparely in his *Testamentum, BAnt*, no. 30.1, RD 6 at n. 28. The episode is dealt with by Stanisław Tworek, "Raków—ośrodkiem radikalizmu ariańskiego 1569–72," Cynarski, *Raków*, 49–80; Kot, *Ideologia Socinianism*, chap. 3–5, and quotes in chap. 4., n. 13, and p. 51, from the testimony of the disillusioned Kasper Wilkowski, *Przyczyny nawrócenia od sekty nowokrzczeńców* (Vilna, 1583) 1.148; Peter Brock deals with the same radical phase sympathetically as an historian of pacifism, *Pacifism in Europe* and the related *Political and Social Doctrines of the Czech Brethren*, chap. 5.

690. In a radical response to articles 5, 7, and 9 debated in Iwie (n. 687), there was an attempt to reinstitute apostolic poverty and a simple style of life. The communes of the Hutterites visited and reported on were ascetically simple. The extent to which they were protected by their Moravian noble patrons, not of their confession, is not always clear even to the counterpart Polish patrons who participated actively in congregational and synodal affairs.

691. Residing with Dudith in Cracow, worried, no doubt by what his friend Budny, present at Iwie (n. 687), told him of articles 5 and 6, Palaeologus wrote against the radicals of Raków *De bello sententia*; and Budny printed it in 1572. To it Grzegorz Paweł with Jan Siekierzyński, Marcin Czechowic, Jakub Kalinowski, Jerzy Schomann, and Jan

Niemojewski replied, *Adversus Jacobi Palaeologi scriptum*, c. 1572. Speaking for all the Racovians, they argued that Christ did not sanction magistracy for Christians and hence that no Christian should assume political office. On the *libellus* of Palaeologus, see *Nieznana Kronika*, Part I, Dobrowolski, 166–67; for the reply of the Racovians, ibid., nn., and *BAnt*, 45, under Paweł. And for some of its contents as preserved in a late response by Budny, 21 February 1581, printed at the end of his major work against the Racovians, see *O urzędzie miecza uzywąją*cem (Losk, 1583), ed. by Stanisław Kot (Warsaw, 1938) 217–38. On the title page Budny suggests the socio-political concern of the conservatives among the theologically radical in citing 1 Cor 7:20–24: "Every one should remain in the state [station, societary role] in which he is called." Budny's *On the office of using the sword* as thus printed contains his vivid recollections of the course of the debate at Iwie, whence Sipayłło (n. 687) obtained the Ten Articles. At the time of the discussion Budny was minister in Chołchło (near Oszmiana, south of Vilna), of which the owner and patroness was Anna (Radziwiłłówna) Kiszczyna, wife of Stanisław, palatine of Witebsk. In what appear to be stenographic notes on Article 5B as debated two days, 23–25 January 1568, Grzegorz Paweł is overheard opening the discussion, addressing his "dearest brethren" on how Antichrist, the man of lawlessness, had come into the church in the Papacy, 2 Thess 2:1–5, and how they should live enlightened by the things of God:

"Among these things is this one that some of the brethren hold serfs and some have them in involuntary household service and still hold them in bondage against the word of God. But if someone should think otherwise, let him speak up and convince me by God's word that I am wrong. For I so think and believe that it is not fitting for the faithful (*wiernemu*) to have serfs (*poddanych*) and much less unfree men and women (*niewolników i niewolnic*) inasmuch as this is a pagan thing to hold sway (*panować*) over one's brother, to use his sweat or rather his blood. Well, the Holy Scripture clearly testifies that God from one blood created all the kinds of people." And he goes on to paraphrase Paul's speech in the Areopagus, Acts 17:26, concluding: "And if brothers, then how can a brother rule over a brother? How can he exploit his sweat?" Kot, *O urzędzie*, 181–82. Budny replies to Grzegorz, and agrees with him about the intrusion of Antichrist within the Church, but interprets Paul's speech, as the excellent exegete he was, in terms of monotheism, thus disposing of Grzegorz's social gospel.

692. In the quest for apostolic equality as brethren in Christ, as between lord and serfs, the problem of inequality among the faithful themselves arose, specifically as to whether theological education qualified the minister to speak with more authority than the uneducated. The quest drove some at Raków to the discrepant testimony of the chief apostle to the Gentiles and hence the model for any minister. Paul argued that the preacher was worthy of his hire on the analogy of the compensated priests of the Temple, but he did not ask for such compensation himself (1 Cor 9:12–15), although he accepted support as occasion afforded from churches with which he was not in such shrill dispute as with the Corinthians, e.g., Phil 4:16. But he was a tentmaker by acquired skill (Acts 18:3). As important as whether they should be "hireling ministers" (a later Quaker phrase) was whether the peasants, artisans, as well as the educated ministers and patrons were equally the possible conduit of the Holy Spirit in the interpretation of Scripture as they convened for worship and Bible-reading (the *lex sedentium* of 1 Cor 14:23ff.).

693. The community of goods was based on Acts 2:44 and 4:32, and was modeled to a limited extent in reaction to that of the Hutterites. See n. 678.

As Lubieniecki passes over any instance of a landowner (*pan*, master/lord) giving up his right of rule (*panowania*) over his serfs, here may be placed the name and action of Jan Przypkowski (d. before 1606/08), only son of Mikołaj (d. 1557 or 1577). Jan's small inherited and acquired properties lay in and around Sosnowiec, the village, and he had a house in Cracow. He released his serfs from subjection to him in 1572. Later he established an asylum for the poor in Cracow. Twice married, first to Katrzyna Lubomirska, then Katarzyna Samborzecka, he had four sons and two daughters. Two of his sons, Mikołaj and Jan, were sent abroad to study at Altdorf along with Jan Statorius (Stoiński). Mikołaj (d. 1612) attended the famous colloquium in Raków of 1602, lasting thirteen days under Faustus Socinus. Mikołaj, after studies abroad, was elected elder in Lusławice. From his first wife, Elżbieta Babońska, he had four sons, the oldest of whom was Samuel (1593–1690), born in Gnojnik. Samuel Przypkowski, the biographer of Faustus Socinus, appears as a major figure in Docs. XI, XXXIII–II; the Family Tree is given as Plate P, *Polish Brethren*, 658–59. See also n. 950. For the early history of the family, see Włodzimerz Budka, "Przypkowscy i rola ich w ruchu reformacyjnym," *RwP*, 4.60–73 with genealogy.

The first to note Jan Przypkowski's act of liberating his serfs, "unius Creatoris creaturas," was T. Grabowski, *Literatura ariańska w Polsce, 1560–1660* (Cracow, 1908) 67–68. Wacław Urban shows that his act was a relatively isolated instance in *Chłopi wobec Reformacji w Małopolsce w drugiej połowie XVI w.* Cracow, 1959), special section, "Szlachecki arianizm wobec poddanych," 54–59; and Jobert devotes a whole ch. to the problem, "Le scandale du servage" (*De Luther à Mohila*, 271–95), distinguishing between customary and extraordinary serval labor (*corvée*) for the lord, noting also the theoretical right of life and death of the lord over his serf and the indifference or cruelty and exploitative attitudes of the many intermediary authorities on the large estates, especially in the Ukraine, where the customary right of the peasant to have direct address to his lord was swallowed up in sheer distances.

Jobert points out that in the delta of the Vistula governed by Danzig and in the palatinate of Marienburg (Malbork) the toilers on the soil were free. Among them the Anabaptists of the Netherlands were settled, beginning in 1530. These Mennonites, as they would become known from Menno Simons (1496–1561), who had once debated with Łaski in East Frisia (1544) and had visited more than once his flocks in Danzig and the two Prussias, were never under lord protectors, as were the Hutterites in Moravia; and their observed discipline and deportment could well have been a factor in the agitation for Christian freedom and equality among the Vilna burghers and pastors who were prominent in the discussion on serfdom at the synod if Iwie of 1568 (n. 687–89).

694. Lubieniecki gives excerpts or a paraphrase of the *Testamentum*, s. anno 1569; *BAnt*, RD 3, no. 30.

695. Ezra, a leader among the returnees from Persia to Jerusalem (Ezra 7:7), was the priest and scribe whose policy toward the Gentiles activities are recorded in Ezra, Nehemiah, and 1 Esdras. His policy toward the Gentiles was exclusivistic. The reference to Ronembug as Ezra comes from Schomann. The early Raconians regarded their place of refuge and especially the church gathered therein as a New Zion.

696. Lubieniecki writes of a new "ministerium cum baptismo adultorum," although he has written at several points about antipedobaptism and of believers' baptism (since his account of Piotr of Goniądz, notably in chap. 3. Nevertheless, he may testify here to something more distinctively Anabaptist. He has just paraphrased Schomann, who had said he was baptized at the age of 42 in the name of Christ by Simon Ronemberg in 1572. *BAnt*, no. 31.

As for the baptismal practice in the commune of Raków, immersion seems to have been practiced very *quickly* at the outset (Budny's account in *O dzieciokrzczeństwie*, loc. cit., p. 108: *wrychle*, confirmed in German rendering *Plützlings* as reported by the Hutter-

ite Chronicler, op. cit. 441/411), and when the Polish Brethren visited the Hutterite Bruderhofs they already espoused immersion as the true mode of baptism and, "because of
being." Yet the reliable account of Lubieniecki, himself a Racovian, and basing his
account Schomann, so very close to Ronemberg, must mean one or both of the following:
that their immersion was valid only if it was preceded by adequate catechetical instruction; that it was valid only if the dying and rising in Christ through baptism entailed radical social consequences, perhaps even the *communio bonorum*, as among the Hutterites.
There is no evidence that they backed away from immersion, even though the Hutterites
connected their own manner of baptism as apostolic.

The poignant differences between the Polish Brethren as by now Christocentric Unitarian immersionists and the Hutterite Brethren come out fully in the long response of
Vorsteher Peter Walpot to the letter of Ronemberg of 1 November 1570. The presiding
bishop of the Hutterites in Moravia thinks of his companies under a common discipline as
"the gathered and elect church" (*gesamlete vn erwelte Gemaind*), a voluntary church
(*ein selb willige Gemain*), the new Ark of Noah, "outside of which there will be no salvation" (*dise Arch ausser derer kein errettung sein wirt*). As eagerly as Ronemberg had
sought to be taught by the *Vorsteher* of the whole network of Moravian communes and
yearned to be considered by them in their radically transformed *zbory*, of which the commune at Raków was only the most extensive, the Polish counterpart of the Hutterites (just
as the Polish Czech Brethren were in communion and under the common discipline with
the Czech Brethren in the same Moravia), nevertheless the apothecary of Cracow was in
the response held at a very great distance, addressed perhaps as "dear" but not as "dear
brother in Christ" and surely not as "dear brother in Christ with us in the same apostolic
ark" (cf. 1 Pet 3:19).

Accordingly, when Ronemberg took over the leadership of a reformed Raków, he was
likened to Ezra rebuilding the Racovian temple, while Schomann, who before
Lubieniecki called him Ezra, also in his *Catechesis* of 1574, Doc. 7, wrote of the renewed
Church of the Polish Brethren as something of an Ark, too (cf. at n. 2). Ronemberg in
any case must have been very close in his thinking to Peter Walpot to have been so fully
his guest in the communes and so apostolically addressed as yet outside the one true
church of the Hutterite Peter. One cannot read the latter's spiritually proud epistle
without feeling that there is a trace of Germanic hauteur toward any Slavs, even well educated and gracious Poles, indeed a trace of derisive envy for the property, protocol, and
general culture that the *Vorsteher* knew also in the nobiliarly patrons of their settlements,
both Czech and German. In the Polish-Hutterite exchanges there is ample evidence of
that recurrent tension, going back to apostolic times through the conflict between the successor of Peter, Innocent III, and the *Poverello* imitating the humbled Christ, that
recurrent theme of Church history between *Christus pauper* and *Christus dives*—whether
rich in property or culture or theological sophistication.

697. For the possible effect on Filipowski of Biandrata's disdain in his letter to the
Racovians (not further known) about their *superstitio*, their radical apostolicity, and
attempt at literal discipleship, see n. 718.

698. One factor in the changing character of Raków, 1600–38, was the conversion of
the new owner Jakub Sienieński who, under the influence of his wife (1598), Anna, from
a Minor Church family, was converted to the Racovian position by debate there. *Polish
Brethren*, 71.

699. Christopher Ostorodt, born in Goslar, d. 1611, was minister at Śmigiel,
1592–97, later Danzig. See Janusz Tazbir, *PSB* 24 (1979) 472–74; *Polish Brethren*,
Doc. V.

700. The *Vita* of Franconian Johann Krell (Crelluis) (1590–1633), rector of the Academy of Raków, 1616–21, is translated in *Polish Brethren*, Doc. IV with a picture.
701. Jonas Schlichting/Szlichtyng (c. 1592–1661), son of Wolfgang of Swiss origin, was a major figure in the Minor Church represented by two documents in *Polish Brethren*, Docs. XXII, XXV.
702. Knight and minister who codified the principles and practices of the Minor Church in *Politia ecclesiastica*, published hostilely by a Lutheran Georg Oeder (Frankfurt/Leipzig, 1746), Morzkowski is represented by this in selected translation, *Polish Brethren*, Doc. XXIII.
703. A doctor of medicine and sometime rector of the school at Hoszcza, Samuel Nieciecki was minister to Andrzej Lubieniecki. See n. 278.
704. The synod of Lublin of 1600, seeking the unity of factions in and about the Minor Church, resolved among other things to send Andrzej Wojdowski to Germany to find a scholar "who could with advantage manage our school." See *Nieznana Kronika*, Part II, Dobrowolski, 170; not noted by Sipayłło, *AS*, 3.212–13. We do not know whether this was for the school in Lewartów or for a new central school. The latter is more probable, since the same synod made two resolutions evidently aimed at the control and reorganization of education. See Stanisław Szczotka, "Synody arian polskich od założenia Rakowa do wygnania z kraju (1569–1662)," *RwP* 7/8 (1935/36) 50, n. 3.
    The synod of Lublin in 1601 resolved to found a central school and to request Sienieński to grant it a place in Raków. Dobrowolski, *Nieznana Kronika*, Part II, 171. The school was probably founded for the academic year 1601/2.
    The colloquy of ministers at Raków, March 1601, marks the inception of a fully integrated Unitarian Church in Poland. There a seminar or colloquium on all the basic controversies was held by Faustus Socinus. The synod gave further impetus to the realization of the academic ideal. Szczotka, "Synody," 52–4; G. G. Zeltner, *Historia Crypto-Socinismi Altorfini* (Leipzig, 1729) 1173–74. For the *Epitome of the Colloquium Held at Raków in 1601* in translation and the literature, see *Polish Brethren*, Doc. III.
705. Hieronim Moskorzowski (c. 1560–1625) was an eminent resident at Raków, translator into Latin of the Racovian Catechism which was dedicated to James I of England, active in synodal affairs. See T. Pasierbiński, *Hieronim z Moskorzowska Moskorzowski* (Cracow, 1931); Wacław Urban, *PSB* 22 (1977) 46–48; *Polish Brethren*, Docs. VI–II, VII, and VIII.
706. Adam (c. 1577–1642) and Andrzej Gosławski were the sons of Dorota Filipowska and Krzysztof Gosławski. Adam moved from Calvinism into the Minor church in Śmigiel, where he was the tutor of Dudith's widow and where Walenty Szmalc and Andrzej Wojdowski were active. Under their influences Adam studied at Altdorf in the Crypto-Socinian circle under Nicholas Taurellus (Ochslein). See Włodzimierz Dzwonkowski, *SBP* 18 (1959–60) 354–55 (only Adam); Wallace, *Biography* 2.501–05.
707. Lubieniecki, alumnus of the school and therefore a valuable witness, starts the succession of rectors with Paweł Krokier of Lublin (possibly of Huguenot origin: Croquier), 1610–16, and then at the end picks up his predecessors vaguely remembered. For the sake of completeness Teichmann (1633) has been intercalated, while two in Lubieniecki's series have been withdrawn in angled brackets. Paweł Ryniowicki is known only as a pupil; his brother Jakub was a teacher in Raków, 1621–26. Wallace, *Biography*, 3.118–21.
    Lubieniecki could not have intended Martin Borrhaus (Cellarius) (1499–1564); the learned alumnus of Tübingen, who for a while joined the Zwickau Prophets and became

an Antitrinitarian Spiritualist, dying in Basel. Editor Wiszowaty may have made from Lubieniecki's MS a mistaken contraction of an hypothesized scrawl, *Martinum [Severinum* (on him, see ¶4), *Christophorum]* *Brockajum*, reading it as Martin *Borrhaus*. On Borrhaus/Cellarius, see Bock, *Antitr.* 1.67–71; my *Radical Reformation*, 47 passim; *BAnt*, 15–16, and Irena Dorota Backus, *Martin Borrhaus*, Bibliotheca Dissidentium, 2 (Baden-Baden: Koerner, 1981).

In The Life of Wiszowaty there is another list of rectors, *BAnt*, 229 (and additional data, 174–76); *Polish Brethren*, Doc. I, no. 78. With this help and the work of Tync (see below) the rectors of Raków can be dated thus: Christoff Brockay (1603–05), Christoff Manlius (1606–09); Nieciecki (1610); Krokier (1610–16); Krell (1616–21); Ruar (1621–26); Joachim Stegmann, Sr. (1626–32); Adam Frank (1630–33); Peter Teichmann (1633); Georg Schwartz (1633/34); and Lorenz Stegmann (1634–38). Except for Nieciecki and Krokier, all the rectors were German or Silesian.

The first teachers were probably the Dane Martinus Severinus (as co-rector), and Krokier. Szczotka ("Synody," 55–56) erroneously makes Georg Leuschner a co-rector. These teachers were joined by Paweł Schomann, the eldest son of Jerzy, until this time rector of the school at Lusławice. The school seems to have come to full strength only in 1603, when Christopher Brockay (d. 1605) from Beverungen north of Cassel and Bartholomeus Vigilius, a Westphalian, were appointed respectively rector and co-rector. Maciej Radecke, noble syndic of Danzig, also came. Then came Daniel Franconius, formerly rector of the school of Tarnowskie Góry in Silesia. Bock, *Antitrin.*, 1.827; Dobrowolski, *Nieznana Kronika*, Part II, 171. Stanisław Tync classified the foregoing in "Wysza szkoła Braci Polskich w Rakowie: Zarys jej dziejów (1602–1638), *Studia nad Arianizmem*, 333–89, adapted as "Zarys dziejów," Cynarski, *Raków*, 82–172.

708. The Polish gentry enjoy identifying themselves with freemen acknowledged in classical Greece and Rome. The allusions have been brought together by me in "The Sarmatian Myth Sublimated in *HRP* and related documents." Jobert touches on the social implications of Sarmatianism in its exaltation of the distinctive Polish institutions of the free election of the King, the golden liberty of the nobles, and their absolute power over their serfs, under "Le scandale du servage," *De Luther à Mohila*, 289–95.

Tadeusz Sulimirski in *The Sarmatians* (London, 1970) has shown that ancient Iranian tribesmen known as Sarmatians penetrated Slavic territory as far as Silesia, buried their king near Cracow, and left traces of their culture in the coat-of-arms of several *szlachta* long after they had been assimilated, like the Goths in Spain. From the beginning of the sixteenth century, under the influence of such historians as Maciej Miechowita, Marcin Bielski, and Marcin Kromer, all known to Lubieniecki, the Sarmatians became ideologically important as unitive of the nobiliary classes as their common ancestors, whether Polish, Lithuanian, or Ruthenian; Catholic, Protestant, or Orthodox. The nobles are the *populae* of the Commonwealth.

709. Jakub Sienieński (c. 1568–d. 1639) was one of five children of Jadwiga Gnoińska and Jan Sienieński, the founder of Raków. Of their four sons two, Jakub and Krzysztof, matriculated at the University of Leipzig in October 1584. Jakub began his career in 1587 as contested Deputy from Ruthenia and fought a duel. He married c. 1598 Anna Wierzbięcianka of Bielsk (d. 1618); he converted to the position of the Minor Church during the efforts made at the synod of Włodzisław, 23 September 1599. Cf. n. 714, where the decisive event is dated 13 June 1599. See with special reference to his political activity, Stanisław Cynarski, "Działalność polityczna i zborowa Jakuba Sienieńskiego," Cynarski, *Raków*, 174–94. Cynarski gives the Raków date as

13 November 1599. Jakub Sienieński developed his constitutional views in action and word notably in a MS letter of 1 March 1616 to Stanisław Tarnowski and in his *Oratio de liberalitate* of the same year. The constitutional and political concerns of the patron were reflected in the accommodations in Racovian theology and polity made by Faustus Socinus and Walenty Schmalz. He dedicated the printed version of Schmalz's *De divinitate Jesu Christi* to the King, 1608, before the close of the Rebellion of which he had been a part. See n. 716.

710. See *BAnt*, RD 4. The presses of Rodecki in Cracow and of Sternacki in Raków are dealt with fully by Gryczowa, 25 – 134, Polish and French.

711. See n. 276.

712. Maciej Radecke (Radecki) (1540 – 1612), born in Danzig, educated at Königsberg, moved successively from Catholicism through Lutheranism, the Reformed Church, to join the Mennonites, then the Polish Brethren by immersion. Of this their baptism he wrote in *Ursachen, warum er sich von Danzig weggemahet*. He explained therein why he was deprived of his office as secretary to the town council after twenty-six years of service, c. 1592. After earlier sources gathered together by Wallace, 2.357 – 61. Radecke was appointed pastor in Śmigiel, 1592, in Busków in 1599, then he settled in Raków in 1603 where he died. He may have been author of the *Nieznana Kronika*. The letters of Faustus Socinus to Radecke may be found calendared, translated, and annotated in ed., Ludwik Chmaj, *Listy*, 2 vols. (Warsaw, 1959), 2, list 27 of 24 September 1584; others follow. Sand mentions letters of Radecke to Socinus of 30 August and 9 December 1584, dealing with the restoration of the Church and the adoration of Christ; another to Andrzej Wojdowski of 20 January 1598; and a MS *scriptum* "De regno Christi millenario" of c. 1590, *BAnt*, 84; Wallace, *Biography* 2.357 – 61. The three letters are not among the Chmaj, *Listy*.

713. Socinus to Ostordt in Raków, 17 February 1602. See *Opera*, 1.450 – 51; Chmaj, *Listy*, 2, List 104, 278 – 80. The first to Ostoród was that of 2 December 1599.

714. It was only the father who continued *addictus religioni Reformatae*. The son Jakub joined (*adjunxit*) the Brethren in 1599. Cf. *BAnt*, 97. In his letter it is understated that Jakub Sienieński (d. 1639) converted. This was after the debate between Calvinists and Minor Churchmen in Raków, 13 June 1599. Chmaj, *Listy*, 2, List 96, n. 2; List 106, esp. p. 279; cf. n. 709.

The term *Evangelici* came to apply to the Calvinists, although in Transylvania this term was long used of themselves by the Unitarians.

It is here to be noted that Lubieniecki has chosen in his *Historia* to make no reference to the synod and the consensus of Sandomierz of 9 – 14 April 1570 when the Czech Brethren, Lutherans, and the conservative Reformed entered into a federation with hopes for regular joint synods. Sipayłło, *AS*, 2.251 – 316; Oskar Haleski, *Zgoda Sandomierska 1570 roku* (Warsaw, 1915); Jobert, *De Luther à Mohila*, 135 – 46.

715. Lubieniecki turns to providence in his preconceived course, sharing so much less than he could have of local Racovian history, theological and institutional.

716. Lubieniecki refers to the "covenanted rebellion" (*rokosz*) of 1606 – 7, led by Mikołaj Zebrzydowski (1553 – 1620), palatine of Cracow. It was directed against the absolutist program of Sigismund III Vasa (1587 – 1632), which was pro-Hapsburg and a revolt of the knightly class (lower *szlachta*) against the centralist policy backed by the bishops as senators in favor of the greater landholders. For the Austrian alliance of Sigismund, see on emperor Rudolph and his policy toward largely Protestant Transylvania, n. 387. Zebrzydowski's Rebellion was thus anticlerical, although its leading lords were

largely Roman Catholic. The Protestant landowners had reason to fear Zebrzydowski might turn against the Protestant dissidents in his confederacy. The almost unanimous support on the part of the Calvinist gentry gave indeed grounds for the royalist branding of the *Rokosz* as not only seditious but also as heretical.

The Polish Brethren for their part (originally) held aloof, with the exception of young Jakub Sienieński, patron of Raków. Only toward the end did other Brethren join the *Rokosz* and play a prominent part among the rebellious gentry. The Brethren thus came to be divided among themselves. While Sienieński, champion of the gentry, advocated radical tactics against the King and a negative attitude towards the senators, Chamberlain Paweł Orzechowski of the conservative wing of the Brethren (see *Historia, 253, 266*), attempted to form an alliance between the conservative gentry (Catholic and Protestant) and the opposition party among the senators, advocating moderation towards the King. See in general, J. Maciszewski, *Wojna domowa w Polsce 1606–1609* (Wrocław, 1960); Adam Strzelecki, ''Udział i rola różnowierstwa w rokoszu Zebrzydowskiego (1606–7),'' *RwP* 7–8 (1935–36) 100–189; Cynarski, ''Działalność . . . Sienieńskiego,'' *Raków*, 178–84. On the three good liberties ''and the bad liberty'' as classified by Piotr Skarga, S.J., during the Rebellion, cf. my ''Peter Skarga.''

The convenanters were defeated in July 1607 by Grand General Stanisław Żółkiewski, and the events described probably took place in the autumn of that year.

After the defeat, Zebrzydowski made restitution by erecting the expiatory scale model of Jerusalem and environs in the Marian shrine between Cracow and Wadowice, Kalwaria Zebrzydowska. The idealized painting (1864) of Jan Matejko of the Sermon of Piotr Skarga, S.J., before the diet, after the reconciliation, is reproduced in *Polish Brethren*, 194–195, with a reference to Sienieński.

717. It is conjectured that Lubieniecki refers to some kind of commemorative tablet inscribed by the grateful townspeople of Raków: *Ob cives servatos*, printed in solid capitals.

718. The Author's maternal grandmother was Hieronim Filipowski's second wife, Zofia Komarowska, (n. 678). She was *nurus*, that is, son's bride from the point of view of the bride's father (possibly Krzysztof) Komorowski (castellan of Sanok, son of Marcin Zborowski, castellan of Cracow, nn. 580–81). The Komorowskis were of the *Ciełek* clan (text: *Golecia gens*), Niesiecki, *Herbarz Polski*, 10.129 and *Dodatek*, separately paginated, 225.

With the incidental mention here of his grandfather, Lubieniecki allows Hieronim Filipowski to leave his narrative. Pirnát observes that this major patron disappeared also from other accounts dependent on the Racovians, radical and Socinian, and this because of mutual disagreement after Filipowski returned from the Hutterite communes in 1569. Pirnát conjectures that Filipowski broke from the Racovians under the impact of Biandrata's admonitory letter, at n. 697, while in his annotation of a letter of Biandrata to Dudith of 5 June 1575, Pirnát goes further and suggests that the Racovians for their part formally expelled Filipowski, ''Il martire e l'uomo politico,'' 181 and n. 43, 189. This conjecture may be based on phrasing in the letter of Budziński to Palaeologus of 1574. It is possible that we have here the background of the anonymous Apostolic Community that could be ascribed to Filipowski (n. 678 ¶3).

Although Pirnát acknowledges no source for his view, except the silence over the final years of a major patron and the sometime lord of Budziński (and an ally of the political realists in Transylvania, presumably including Biandrata, and of the Lithuanians like Budny), he is able to say more about Hieronim, Jr. The son (Bk. 2, n. 107) abandoned the Racovians c. 1570, went to Transylvania, and returned to Poland as a political agent of Biandrata in the support of Stephen Báthory, ibid., 181. Having embraced Catholicism, he died in 1587.

719. Jan Licinius of Namysłów in Silesia, minister and teacher in Nowogródek, and a capable scholar, although given to drink, was set upon by some rowdies in Słomniki in 1624. *BAnt*, 94; Bock, *Antitrin.*, 1.432. Lubieniecki does not elaborate on this case, nor on that of Peter Statorius.

720. For the specific episode relating to Gittich and the Author's father, see *Historia, 258–60.*

Here it is in place to assemble data on the Author's father in general, Krzysztof Lubieniecki the Younger (1598–1648), whose parents were mentioned in n. 678. He may have studied in Raków, in any case briefly in Altdorf, 1616, then with others from Poland he matriculated in Leiden, 1616–18; he also traveled in France and elsewhere. Having returned to Raków, he was called to the church in Lublin, 1626–48, successor there, among others, to his father Krzysztof Lubieniecki the Elder (c. 1561–1624), who, after the death of Jan Niemojewski, had been forced on the congregation, along with Walenty Schmalz, by Faustus Socinus, to replace Marcin Czechowic there over the issue of baptism and Christology; his father had served in Lublin, 1598–1612 (later he settled in Raków, 1616–24, dying there). In the year after the settlement of Krzysztof Junior in Lublin, a pogrom of 1 August 1627 destroyed both the Calvinist and the Unitarian churches there (n. 831), and part of his congregation withdrew to Piaski, and he continued to serve them as minister there and less obtrusively in Lublin. For his defense of the Unitarians he was imprisoned in 1635 for a year and six weeks and fined. He was in a debate in the Jesuit church in 1636 (n. 801). When the Calvinist owner of Piaski objected to his congregation there, it removed to Siedliska, *Historia, chap. 14.* See Janusz Tazbir on the two Christophers, father and son, *PSB* 17 (1972) 599–601.

721. Poland was at war with Muscovy, 1609–19, taking Smolensk in 1612. At the end of 1611, the royal forces fighting in Muscovy, unable to secure their arrears of pay, raised a *foedus* and chose four marshals, foremost: Józef Ciekliński, 1612–14, A. Lubieniecki, *Poloneutychia*, 201. In June 1612 the confederates re-entered Poland and occupied royal and ecclesiastical estates and commandeered over revenue until their disbandment in 1614. They maintained strict order and did not molest private estates, as Lubieniecki affirms.

722. Lubieniecki appears to have failed to develop this episode in his hastes to contrast the behavior of the Catholic chaplains with that of the confederate soldiers.

723. The text reads *Cisovius*. Zbigniew Sienicki was among the four marshals. Cf. A. Lubieniecki, *Poloneutychia*, 200–01. The name might be also Cikowski.

724. The incidents in Raków were the acts, not of the regular troops, but of the irregular Lissovians. Polish *lisowczyk* refers to a light cavalryman, often given to maurauding. Cf. A. Lubieniecki, *Poloneutychia*, 98ff. Ciekliński was rehabilitated only in 1623.

725. The date given in the text for the episode involving Oporowski evidently about a decade later is 1620. This may be a misprint because it seems unlikely that the obscure Oporowski would threaten Raków a second time in course of his Lissovian career. But Jakub Sienieński lived to 1639 and the episode could even have occurred in 1620 in connection with the siege of Vienna (n. 736).

726. Szydłów lay south of Raków, between the Czarna and the Wschodinia.

727. We have few glimpses such as this into the daily and economic life of Raków c. 1620.

728. Eliasz Arciszewski fought in Courland, 1621–22, under Krzysztof Radziwiłł.

After fleeing to Holland after involvement in murder, he saw service in Denmark, then returned to Poland in 1630 as emissary of Christian IV. In 1633 he fought at Smolensk. At the onset of the Swedish invasion, he stood with Janusz Radziwiłł in the submission of Lithuania to Charles X Gustavus in the Treaty of Kiejdany, 20 October 1655.

729. Lubieniecki is rather hard on Eliasz Arciszewski. Born c. 1590, he studied at Raków and determined on his career during the excitement there occasioned by the Zebrzydowski Rebellion. Like his younger brother, Krzysztof Arciszewski (1592–1656, admiral under the Dutch exploring Brazil), Eliasz remained true to the theological creed of the Brethren throughout his soldierly life and, on his retirement, rejoined their community Śmigiel and defended the civil rights of those adhering to the religion called "Arians." *BAnt*, 141; *PSB* 1 (1935) 150–51; on the admiral brother and his times, there is the extensive treatment by Aleksander Kraushar, *Dzieje Krzysztofa z Arciszeska Arciszewskiego, 1592–1656*, 2 vols. (Petersburg, 1892–93).

730. Eliasz had been a youth of about seventeen when the whole of Raków as the scene of emotional struggle and flight in 1607 during the Zebrzydowski Rebellion, at n. 716.

731. Piotr Gruszczyński.

732. The text has "vicum Urenbouiensem." See the detailed cartographic reconstruction of "Raków Arianski," in Cynarski, *Raków*, opposite 16.

733. The apothecary Daniel Kunau is called interchangeably *pharmacopola*, *medicamentarius*, and *unguentarius*.

734. This is not the only disparaging reference of Lubieniecki to *rustici*.

735. About Fryderyk and Gabriel Iwanicki nothing further is known.

736. In 1620 the Lissovians, on their return from their campaign in support of the Hapsburgs, took up quarters in Poland. With King Sigismund III's consent, they had been summoned by the Emperor Ferdinand II (1619–37) to rescue Vienna which had been besieged in 1619 by Prince Gabriel Bethlen of Transylvania (n. 128). Aspirant for the Crown of a united Hungary with Transylvania, Gabriel was indeed elected King at the diet of Besztercebánya in 1621. By the peace of Mikulov (Nicolsburg) of 1622 the Prince retained six counties of *Partium*. Transylvania was a large state and European power (n. 387). On their march westwards the main Lissovian force held to the southern route, but some units might have made their way northwards. Maurycy Dzieduszycki, *Krótki rys dziejów i spraw Lisowczyków*, 2 vols. (Łwów, 1844). On Gabriel Bethlen and the Lissonians, c. 1637, see at n. 807.

737. Text has "Ilcussio oppido"; the significance not clear.

738. Różycki.

739. On Polanus, see below, *Historia, 273*.

740. On him, see n. 276.

741. Caccamo, who carries his main account only to 1611, mentions (*Eretici*, 170, n. 47) Pietro Gucci (c. 1539–c. 1620) of Florence who ended his life violently in Raków. He mentions several Guccis elsewhere. Of the victim's grandson, Jan Gucci, we have perhaps only this appearance.

742. The force of *miratus est* is ambiguous. The colonel might wonder that Jan Gucci and his grown children did not themselves defend the old man or that so "old" a man would have a resident grandparent. In either case, with soldiers quartered on the town, it probably made sense for Gucci, particularly as a foreigner, to appeal for the aid of the commanding officer. The pacifist disposition was no doubt alive in many Raconians, as is evident from Pietro Gucci's final act.

743. Różycki's Lithuanian comrade Chróstowski.

744. "Honesta turpitudo pro bona causa mori."

745. Jakub Sienieński (d. 1639).

746. This could be Krzysztof Wiszowaty, Sr., among the signatories of the letter from Kreuzburg, 17 June 1661 (*Historia, 303*), translated in *Polish Brethren*, Doc. XXXIII – I.

747. Stanisław Koniecpolski defeated the Swedes at Hammerstein in 1627. See Tazbir, *Lubieniecki*, 101, 121.

748. That is, Daniel, the poet and teacher at Raków (n. 707), also took as his surname Krause from his wife's married name by an earlier and evidently distinguished marriage.

749. His youth (life).

750. The physician is unidentified. It is not edifying to overtake a minister, son of a minister of Raków, drawing a moral lesson from this episode, a delinquent alumnus turned into salve (*pissasphaltum*). At least the Racovians as townspeople sought to intercede for the rioter and horse thief.

751. See n. 397; and *Historia, 255, 262 – 64, 285*.

752. Northern Little Poland near Podlaise.

753. Not identifiable in the *lista biskupów, SPM* 1 (1954) 599 – 608, without the benefit of the Index.

754. Caesar *De Bello Gallico* 3.17.4.

755. The text lacks *non*.

756. The text has *pignora* (pledges).

757. Szydłów was attacked and burned down 4 April 1630. Maurycy Dzieduszycki, *Piotr skarga i jego wiek*, 2 vols. (Cracow, 1868) 2.464 – 466. At the diet of 1631 a commission was appointed to inspect the ruins of the castle and to assess the cost of reconstruction. *Statuta* 3.699 – 700. A statue of the diet of 1633, considering that the town of Szydłów with its castle and church "was utterly burned by a licentious band," exempted it from taxes for four years. *Statuta*, 3.827.

758. Jakub Sienieński.

759. One of the two Racovian ministers was Walenty Schmalz (Smalcius) who died 8 December 1622 and was regarded as also chaplain to Sienieński. The other might have been Jan Stoiński, who was appointed minister there in the synod in 1612, removed to Lublin, and resumed his ministry in Raków, leaving for Holland in 1638 when the Racovians were obliged to disband.

760. The mutual meeting of Unitarian palatine of Podolia (owner of Raków) and the royal Catholic *praefectus* of Szydłów of Brethren and Catholic burghers of Racovian and Szydlovian Jews is quite notable. The recollection is that of Mikołaj Ryniewicz (*Historia, 250*).

That there were Jews resident in Raków is clear also from the MS *Protocolum Advocatiale* for Raków as of 1620 with its reference to the *uliczka Żydowska*; noted in Cynarski, *Raków*, 14.

761. Some among the inhabitants of Szydłów as collectively represented by their priest in words recalled by Mikołaj Ryniewicz.

762. The Royal Republic is the Minor Church seen as especially embodied in Raków but understood as embracing all "true" Christians in time and space.

763. The proscribed patron was Jakub Sienieński who died the following year. Cf. e.g., *Post reditum (ad Quirites)* 1.1, but not a direct quotation.

764. The alleged testimonial is not to be found in the *Volumina Legum* incorporating the statues and decisions of the diets. The reference may be to a vote of gratitude of the dietine of the Land of Sandomierz and submitted to the national diet. See further *BAnt*, 234; *Life of Wiszowaty, Polish Brethren*, Doc. I, nos. 84, 84.1 and 2, with n. 71.

765. Lubieniecki will not, in fact, reach this point again. Cf. the parallel in the *Life of Wiszowaty, Polish Brethren*, no. 84, where Plate H reproduces a nearly contemporaneous painting of *Arianismus Proscriptus*, before Doc. XXI.

It is possible that the phrasing *si dominus permiserit* already signals the onset of the slow poisoning of the Author who would complete only four more chapters, the last brief, ending: *sumus si Deus permiserit*.

NOTES TO CHAPTER THIRTEEN

766. Cf. *Life of Wiszowaty*, Doc. I, *Polish Brethren*, no. 95. Despite his personal connections with Lublin, Lubieniecki does not give so clear an account as desired. Cf. n. 287. The history is seen comprehensively by Stanisław Tworek, *Zbór Lubelski i jego rola w ruchu ariańskim w Polsce w XVI i XVII wieku* (Lublin, 1966) but almost to the neglect of Lubieniecki's *Historia* (cited in Polish translation). Tworek brings out the social composition of the church, distinguishing four periods in four chapters. He recognizes the importance of a town church as distinguished from a village church or chapel under the protection of a lord. The Minor congregation was driven out of Cracow in 1591 and out of Lublin in 1627. In the second period in Lublin, 1570–83, Niemojewski and Czechowic sought to enlist the *szlachta* while preserving the base of the congregation in the citizenry, the city plebs, and even among peasants. In this period the radical social views pervaded with respect to the sword and public office. In the third period, 1583–89, the concern of the artisans and the plebs yielded to the more accommodating mood of the nobles. In the last period, 1598–1667, the interests of the nobles and rich merchants prevailed.

767. Stephen Báthory established in 1578 a high court of appeal in Piotrków for Great Poland and another in Lublin for Little Poland (later another in Lithuania) to hear civil cases hitherto tried before the King himself. Earlier there had been mixed courts, lay and clerical, chosen for adjudication respectively by the dietines and by the cathedral chapters. By a special provision of 1578 the Tribunal, the highest court regionally for the knightly class, was not to deal in ecclesiastical matters; and, insofar as there was the overlap on the issue of the payment of tithes to the Church, it was established that lords who had not been doing so (the Protestants) would not be forced into court, while those who had been paying them would continue to do so. This inconclusiveness in principle particularly agitated the lords in the palatinate of Lublin and in its capital where the Tribunal sat. Teresa Romaniuk admirably traces the role of the Lublin landowners in their dietine and influential in the Tribunal on a larger scale, ''Działalność polityczno-reformacyna szlachty różnowierczej na Sejmku Lubelskim w latach 1575–1648,'' *Rocznik Lubelski* 18 (1975), 33–51, with Russian and French summaries; on the tithes, 35; on the efforts of 1627 and 1628 to reform the Tribunal in fairness to Protestants, 43.

As Prince of Transylvania, King Stephen pursued a common policy for both realms. He had in Cracow a Transylvanian chancery to coordinate things. He was not pro-Ottoman, but he followed the Venetian principles of his advisors, the ''Paduans,'' alumni of the university of Venice, in seeking to deal realistically with the Sultan to the end of liberating the entirety of Hungary from its direct control. But he also had a branch of his diplomatic service entrusted to Jesuit intent on a crusade. Although the Holy See was at first suspicious of him in his new role, it came to support him. Heirless, with Anna Jagiellonka (n. 393), Stephen for a while considered one of his three nephews, sons of his older brother András (d. 1563), as electable as his successor in Poland; Balthazar,

András, and István; but in the end he came to favor Zamoyski, the veritable dean of Paduans, as his successor. However, after the education of his nephew at the Jesuit College in Pułtusk and his visit to Carlo Borromeo in Milan, András Andrzej Batory (1562–99) was appointed Cardinal at his uncle's instigation in 1584 as suffragan and prospective bishop of Warmia (1589–99), although he was not to be ordained to the priesthood, under papal pressure, until 1597. He was Prince of Transylvania, 1599, and was murdered on the Moldavian frontier, and buried in Belgrade. *SPM*, 1.411–12; Makkai, *Transylvanie*, chap. 12, "La collaboration polono-transylvanienne," 176–87.

768. Stansław Orzechowski was the brother of Paweł. Members of these families have been previously encountered, except for Andrzej Lasota (*Historia, 254*).

769. Paweł Orzechowski (c. 1550–1612) first identified himself with the Reformed and after 1570 with the Minor Church under the influence of Marcin Czechowic and Jan Niemojewski. Stanisław Tworek, *PSB* 24 (1979) 283–84.

770. Above, esp., *Historia, 172*.

771. Lubieniecki has erroneously "Palatine of Lublin." The patrons of the Lublin church were Lords Jan Baptysta Tęczyński (d. 1563) and Stanisław Tęczyński (d. 1567), both of them palatines of Bełż and captains of Lublin. H. Merczyng, *Zbory i senatorowie*, 136; Sipayłło, *AS*, 2.75, 217; and Węgierski, *Slavonia Reformata*, 244. Lubieniecki's mistake probably originated from a hasty transcription from Węgierski, in which the phrase "palatini Belzensis post Cracoviensis Capitanei Lublinensis" was shortened to "palatini Lublinensis." Lubieniecki's dates here are also misleading. Tęczyński died in 1563 and Paklepka in 1567. According to Lubieniecki the first antitrinitarian congregation gathered in Paklepka's (new) home (1563–65). However, the synodal Acts of the Lublin District maintain that there was no organized community after Tęczyński's death until around 1570 when a group of the Cujavians led by Jan Niemojewski settled there. See the annotation of Węgierski supplied by Sipayłło, *AS*, 2.217, n. 1. Most probably, after the general schism in the Reformed Church of 1563, the Minor congregation of Lublin removed to Paklepka's house, perhaps outside the city walls. On the site of Tęczyński's house the Jesuit Church (the present cathedral) was later built, beginning in 1580 (n. 146). The Major Church remained in Tęczyński's house within the walls. L. Zalewski, "Do dziejów reformacji w Lublinie," *RwP* 2 (1948–52) 56–59. Tworek, *Zbór Lubelski*, chap. 1. Thus the Brethren were deprived of a meeting place from 1565 until 1570.

Lubieniecki here passes by the Judaizing ferment among the Lublinians, mentioned earlier; Walenty Krawiec and Ezaijasz of Moscow (n. 287). Sipayłło, *AS*, 2.217; Tworek, *Zbór Lubelski*, 34–36.

772. Paweł Krokier (Croquier), formerly rector of Raków, later a physician (d. 1641). Estreicher, 22.388; 20.271.

773. Presumably Jan Balcerowic, merchant and senior of the Lublin congregation, correspondent of Faustus Socinus in 1592, beginning on Socinus's side 17 October 1580. Chmaj, *Listy*, 1.18; *BAnt*, 68.

774. Mentioned *Historia, 265*, n. 846.

775. Mentioned below, 265, n. 846.

776. Piotr Ciachowski (d. before 1633) was the son of Jerzy Schomann [Ciachowski], minister of the Minor Church, *BAnt*, RD 3, no. 34. Piotr was the author of several popular medical treatises and of the first Polish treatise on obstetrics. He fought medical superstitions and the ignorance of the home-bred physicians. He, his father, and uncle Jan, another minister, are dealt with in *PSB* 4 (1938) 14–15.

777. Tworek, *Zbór Lubelski*, 96–97.

778. Lubieniecki has dealt with the Suchodolskis and Ostrowskis on the same points, *Historia, 172*.

779. Andrzej Lasota was active in the dietine of Lublin and in 1587 bespoke the cause of confessional peace and religious liberty. Tworek, *Zbór Lubelski*, 52 – 53.

Andrzej Lasota was the seventh son, named after his cosmopolitan father, and whose brother Stanisław was royal secretary, often sent by the King on missions to Portugal, Spain, England, and the Empire; Miesiecki, *Herbarz polski, 6.27*. To the learned patron Andrzej of our text, Marcin Czechowic dedicated his polemical book on Judaism, Lublin, 13 December 1581.

Out of the rabbinical court that sat at the time of the Lublin Fair, evolved the pan-Polish character and procedures for the (autonomous) Council of the Four Lands of the Polish Crown that, with a counterpart council for Lithuania, governed the whole Jewish community within the Commonwealth rabinically and temporally (taxes, etc.), functioning also locally within a Land by a *galil* ("circuit") closely resembling the palatinate dietine.

When Czechowic came to dedicate his book on Judaism, he was midway in his career as theologically conservative (once a Ditheist) pastor in Lublin (1570 – 98) and was keenly conscious of the Judaizing trends during the half decade (1565 – 70) that devastated his congregation after the death of Pastor Paklepka in 1565: (1) the intellectual vigor of the environing Jewish community and its biblical and Talmudic claims; (2) the reductionist Spiritualism of the Muscovite/Lithuanian "Judaizers" of Russian Orthodox provenience; (3) the liturgical, moral and social consequences of non-adorant biblical Unitarianism in Transylvanian Davidic Unitarianism and its counterpart in Lithuania (Budny), represented in the history of his own congregation in Lublin by Walenty Krawiec (n. 287, 2, 4, 8); and (4) the still different biblical claims of the Trinitarian Reformed and of the Catholic Church from which both Reformed synods had broken. The book dedicated to Lasota preserves the Reply in Polish and Hebrew of the Jewish physician of Bełżyce, near Lublin, Jakub Nahman (who may be identical with Jacob of Lublin, the main Shadlan of the Council in 1595), to the Dialogues of Czechowic, *Rosmowy Christiańskie* (Raków: Rodecki, 1575); Gryczowa, 151, critically edited by Alina Linda et al., Biblioteka Pisarzy Reformacjnych 12 (Warsaw-Łódź: PAN, 1979). From his reported Reply it is clear that Jakub Nahman frequented Minor Church synods, that he knew Walenty Krawiec as an emissary from Pastor Paklepka, and that he knew another non-adorant Unitarian, Daniel Bieliński. In his Reply Jakub dealt with the overall great problem of Jewish-Christian dialogue, for he was altogether unusual among Jews of the time in being willing to talk at all about religion, then specifically he defended the Talmud, then the Sabbath and circumcision (both of which Czechowic had considered superseded in Christ). To all of this in the same book Czechowic gave his own Reply, adducing the Talmud itself for the first time in Polish with the help of the Christian Cabbalist Pietro Galatino (1460 – 1539), *De arcanis catholicae veritatis contra obstinatissimam iudeorum perfidiam* (Ortona, 1518). Czechowic criticized Judaism as similar to Catholicism in its overstress on law and ceremonial. The whole work survives in a unique copy in the Czartoryski Library, *Odpis Jakoba Żyda z Bełżyc na Dyalogi Marcina Czechowica: na który zaś odpowiada Jakobowi Żydowi tenże Marcin Czechowic* (Raków: Rodecki, 1581); Gryczowa, 150. The Harvard College Library holds a photocopy. It is most fully discussed by Judah M. Rosenthal, "Marcin Czechowic and Jacob of Bełżyce: Arian-Jewish Encounters in 16th Century Poland," *Proceedings of the American Academy for Jewish Research* 34 (1966) 77 – 95, which does not draw on the detailed discussion by Szczucki, *Czechowic*, 126 – 32.

780. She is attested independently of Lubieniecki. She died in 1611 and the executors of her will were perhaps only Andrzej and Krzysztof Lubieniecki. Tworek, *Zbór Lubelski*, 50–51, 57–58, 66.

781. The mother of Paweł Lubieniecki was the second wife of Stanislaw I, namely, Anna Żółkiewska.

For another minister at Piaski, not mentioned by the Author, see on Marcin Krowicki, n. 868.

782. The reference is to the Lublin congregation, the dietine, and the Tribunal for Little Poland in Lublin. On the last, see n. 319.

783. The Cujavian group, after selling their estates in Kujawy, removed to Lublin in 1570, to practice evangelical poverty, earning their living by the work of their hands. The arrival in Lublin of Niemojewski and his companions in faith and praxis is mentioned three times by Lubieniecki, once himself resident there, namely, here, and above at nn. 287 and 314 (by allusion, not by name). For the baptism of Niemojewski, see n. 534 ¶2.

784. Of the companions of Jan Niemojewski, Wojciech Brzezinski is clear; cf. n. 284. The archival material explored by Kossowski and Tworek evidently did not verify the presence of the others, except for a Walenty and a Wojciech Siemianowski, Aleksander Kossowski, *Protestantyzm w Lublinie i w Lubelskim w XVI–XVII wieku* (Warsaw, 1933); and Tworek, *Zbór Lubelski*, 49. However, Szymon Siemianowski and Jan Plecki are attested as accompanying Niemojewski at the synod in Pełsznica in 1568. Sipayłło, *AS*, 2.220; Szczucki, *Czechowic*, 277.

785. This is a valuable reference to lesser townspeople as part of the movement. See remark of Tazbir, *Lubieniecki*, 231; for the smaller towns around Lublin, see Kossowski, *Protestantyzm w Lublinie*, 85–103; 177–84, and map.

786. The school of Lewartów was founded in 1580 by Mikołaj Firley, palatine of Lubin (n. 800, item 6). Its first rector was Simon Seidler, a Lutheran from Toruń, later a dignitary of his native city. From the very beginning the school attracted the noble sons of the palatinate. In 1582 the rectorship was assumed by Samuel Wolf of Silesia. By then the school had three teachers: the rector, the deputy-rector Wojciech of Kraśnysław, and Andrzej Dzierzanowski.

Wolf's successor in 1588 was Wojciech of Kalisz, who reorganized the school on the model of Johann Sturm's academy in Strassburg. Stanisław Kot edited Wojciech's "*Schola Levartoviana Restituta*," *Archiwum do Historii literatury i oświaty w Polsce* 72 (Cracow, 1913); idem, *Szkoła Lewartowska* (Lwów, 1910); Stanisław Lempicki, "Do historii' szkoły lewartowskiej, *RwP* 9 (1948–52) 40–42.

787. Jan Zamojski, the grand general and grand chancellor of Stephen Batory and leader of the opposition against the pro-Hapsburg policies of Sigismund III, had been a pupil of the Padovan humanists. A Protestant in his youth, a Roman Catholic later, he nevertheless advocated religious toleration and civic equality. Throughout his period there was a chasm between the high cultural standard of the educated classes of Poland and that of the rest of society. The old University of Cracow, founded 1364, was stagnating, and many Poles sought out foreign centers. A new Academy in Vilna was founded by the Jesuits in 1578, the nucleus of the later university. Protestants created a few outstanding centers (Pińczów, Lewartów, Bełżyce, Raków, Kieselin), but they were either short-lived or too radical, while the gymnasia of Toruń and Danzig provided mainly for the German Lutheran burghers. Zamoyski endeavored to create a humanist academy for the gentry and thus to perpetuate the achievements of the "golden age" of Polish culture. The seat of this academy, founded in 1594, was Zamość, at the economic and cultural

center of the vast new estates of the founder. However, the humanist conception he developed was thwarted by the necessity of compromise with ecclesiastical authorities. J. K. Kochanowski, *Dzieje Akademii Zamojskiej (1594–1784)* (Cracow, 1899–1900); S Tempicki, *Działalność Jana Zamojskiego na polu szkolnictwa* (Cracow, 1922).

788. Mikołaj Kazimirski, active in the diets, came under the influence of Piotr Skarga and had reverted to Catholicism by his death in 1598.

789. See *Historia, 191*.

790. This reference to Kiev makes appropriate a reference here to a major confessional/ecclesiastical development in the Commonwealth. From the Council of Ferrara-Florence the Union of 5 July 1439 retained some force territory of the Polish-Lithuanian Commonwealth even though soon repudiated in Constantinople. There was in Kiev therefore a Latin-rite archbishop alongside the Byzantine-rite metropolitan. In 1595, Metropolitan Michał II Rohosa (1588–99) (installed by Patriarch Jeremiah II) came in his turn under papal authority with seven other bishops of the province at the Union of Brześć Litewski in 1595/96. His successor was Hypacjusz Pociej (1600–1613), "the Father of the Union." (He is pictured in the imaginary dramatic scene of Matejko, reproduced in *Polish Brethren*, Plate F.) An Orthodox succession reasserted itself, looking to the Metropolitan of Moscow, Patriarch since 1589. The older Latin-rite succession of Kiev continued alongside the Uniate and the Muscovite Orthodox lines. Krzysztof I of Kazimierski Biberstein stood in the old succession (1599–1618). *Lista biskupów, SPM* 1.601 and 484. For the context, see more generally Jobert, *De Luther à Mohila*, chaps. 13 and 14; Oskar Halecki, "From Florence to Brest 1489–1596," *SPM* 5.

791. Tazbir, *Lubieniecki*, 82, 93–95.

792. The succession of ministers at Lublin is as follows: Stanisław Paklepka (1561–65); no organized congregation, 1565–70; Marcin Czechowic (1570–98); replaced at the insistence of Faustus Socinus by Krzysztof Lubieniecki the Elder (1598–1613) and Walenty Schmalz, assistant (1598–1605); Maciej Twardochleb (1613–15); Jan Stoiński (1615–20/26); Joachim Rupniowski (in 1618?); Jakub Ryniewicz Jr. (1627–31) (nn. 397, 751, 825); and Krzysztof Lubieniecki the Younger (1626–48), minister also in Piaski and Siedliska (n. 720).

This is the only appearance of Twardochleb in the *Historia*. In the life of Wiszowaty (*BAnt*, 227, 237; *Polish Brethren*, Doc. I, nos. 75.2, 91), he is mentioned as luminous minister of Kisielin for thirty years.

793. Lubieniecki cites Ryniewicz as source, Bk. 2 at n. 397; Bk. 3 at n. 751.

794. The present Cathedral of St. John the Baptist in Lublin is the remodeled church and college of the Jesuits erected at the end of the sixteenth century. When Lublin was separated from Cracow as an independent see, the Jesuit structure was taken over and remodeled as the cathedral in 1832.

The company of Jesus settled in Lublin 1582 under the leadership of Bernard Maciejowski (later bishop of Łuck) and palatine Mikołaj Zebrzdowski through resources put at their disposal by Katarzyna Wapowska, wife of the palatine of Przemyśl. The express purpose was to do everything to get rid of the nest of Arians there. Jakub Wujek in his preface to Zebrzydowski's defense of the deity of the First and Second Persons, *O bóstwie Syna Bożego i Ducha Św* (Cracow, 1590) declared that the fact that Satan himself had placed his nest there was a disgrace. The basic account is that by Stanisław Załęski, *Jezuici w Polsce*, 4 vols. (Cracow/Lwów, 1900–06) 4.1.337. Tworek puts the sources together, *Zbór Lubelski*, 92–93.

795. Lubieniecki is hastening to the breaking up of the Calvinist and Unitarian

congregations in 1627. It is not clear who was pastor of the Unitarians at that time. Jakub Ryniewicz led the congregation outside the walls, beginning in 1628. *The Epitome* of Jan Stoiński (*BAnt*, 183ff., no. 12:1) is valuable evidence of the time and occasion of a conference (*conventus*) among Calvinists and the Brethren in 1616, which fits into the general campaign, 1611 – 1619, being waged by the leaders of the Minor Church to persuade the gentry and the ministers of the Major Church to reunite in the common cause of confessional toleration.

On the side of the Reformed congregation in Lublin stood Andrzej Chrząstowski of Brzezie (d. before 1632), frequently attested in the synods. Sipayłło, *AS*, 3. He had left court in 1595/96 to settle in Lublin, henceforth, was active in Reformed affairs, critical of the pastors, favorably inclined toward the Brethren because of the higher level of the education of their ministers; and in his second marriage to a member of their church, he drew even closer. He attacked the behavior and low culture of Calvinist pastors in contrast to their patrons in the lost *Rozmowa szlachica ewangelika* [Andrzej himself] *z ministrem ewangelickim* (1618). This called forth an angry brochure in the name of the Reformed pastors of the Lublin District, *Na rozmowę*, [Toruń], 1619, by Jakub Zaborowski, Reformed pastor in Kock, north of Lublin. Then followed *Żywoty Świętych*, [Toruń, 1619], by Zaborowski, assailing the allegedly more upright lives of the more disciplined Minor church pastors. Walenty Schalz anonymously replied with *Odpis na dwa paskwiluse* (Raków, 1619). Then followed a defense of the original *Rozmowa* by Chrząstowski himself in *Obrona dyjalogu*, [Raków], 1619. The four brochures are firmed up as to authorship and place of publication and reprinted with nn. by Halina Górska, Lech Szczucki, and Krystyna Wilczewska, eds., *Cztery Broszury Polemiczne* (Warsaw, 1958). On these imprints the editors go beyond the surmises of Marek Wajsblum, *PSB* 3 (1938) 471 – 72, where he makes no reference to his several archival studies, some on the Chrząstowski family in the seventeenth century, reprinted from various entries in *RwP* as *Ex registro Arianismi Szkice z dziejów upadku Protestantyzmu w Małopolsce* (Cracow, 1937 – 1948), esp. 120ff.

796. Mentioned *Historia, 769 – 70*.

797. Johann Völkel, one of the four authors of the Racovian Catechism in Polish of 1605, and author of *De vera religione*. *BAnt*, 196, 222, 227; *Polish Brethren*, passim, and Docs. VI – II.

798. Son of Wojciech of Kalisz, he is mentioned again, *Historia, 264* and n. 800.

799. Synods took place in Lublin in every year from 1595 through 1623 (except for 1606, and twice in 1614). Sipayłło, *AS*, 3.xvii – xix.

800. It is here in place to note a series of theological disputations that took place in Poland between Protestants and Catholics between 1579 and 1620, several of them in Lublin, second to Raków as the intellectual center of the Polish Brethren. The record of the disputes between these dates was kept by Andrzej Lubieniecki, Sr. (c. 1550 – 1623), author of *Poloneutychia*, preserved in Kolozsvár MS, the photograph of which was sent by Earl Morse Wilbur to be edited by Stanisław Kot, who published it as "Dysputacje Arjan polskich," *RwP* 7/8 (1935/36) 340 – 70. The last two of the original sixteen disputes are missing from this MS. Subsequently Kot discovered in Rotterdam in the Remonstrant Library MS no. 527 that summarizes the sixteen with sometimes new information and supplies something on the missing last two. He ascribed the MS to Andrzej Lubieniecki, Jr. (1590 – c. 1667), whom he called the son but who was actually the nephew of the author of *Poloneutychia* and an uncle of our Author. Kot published it is "Dysputacyj Braci Polskich Katalog," *RwP* 9/10 (1937 – 39) 456 – 64, correcting his ear-

lier surmise on three works involving Jan Stoiński and the last two disputations in Lublin. The disputations in Lublin were discussed by Stanisław Tworek, "Walka z Braćmi Polskimi w Lublinie w XVII wieku," *Rocznik Lubelski* 4 (1962), 218 – 44. All sixteen disputations recorded by the Lubienieckis are here characterized and those *in Lublin* are supplied with the known or reported or related publications of the proceedings.

1. In the Tribunal *in Lublin*, 1579, with Jan Niemojewski for the Brethren vs. Canon Hieronim Powodowski of Poznań: on the Church and the Trinity, recorded in *Wędzidło na sprośne błędy a bluźnierstwa nowych Aryanów* (Poznań: Jan Wolrab, 1582), dedicated to Stephen Batory.
2. In the house of Prospero Provana in Cracow, 26 July 1581, with Jerzy Schomann vs. Piotr Skarga, S.J., on the divinity of Christ.
3. In the church of the Jesuits in Poznań 1581, with Jan Krotowiusz, minister in Śmigiel, vs. the Jesuit Fathers on the Trinity.
4. In the (temporary) church of the Jesuits "pod Trybunał" *in Lublin* 1586, (wrongly dated by A. Lubieniecki, Jr., or the editor) with Jan Niemojewski and Andrzej Lubieniecki vs. the Jesuit Fathers Stanisław Warszewicki, Arnolf and Aaron Podorecki, in Polish; on the papal primacy and the Trinity. Some of this is reflected in Czechowic, *De primatu Pontificis Romani*; cf. Szczucki, *Czechowic*, 161.
5. In the church of St. Vita in Śmigiel, June 1591, with Andrzej Lubieniecki, minister in Śmigiel, vs. Abbot/Canon Stanisław Zdeszek Ostrowski of Przemęt on the Trinity and Christology.
6. In the parish church in Lubartów (n. 786, originally named Lewartów in 1543 by its founding owner, Piotr Firley, d. 1553), a Protestant center c. 25 kilometers north of *Lublin*, with Jan Niemojewski, Grzegorz Jankowski, Calvinist minister in Lewartów 13 – 14 January 1592, (later: 1600, minister in Lublin; in 1616 became Catholic), and the German Albrecht (Wojciech) of Kalisz (Calissius), rector of the academy and its pedagogical theorist, vs. Adryan Radzimiński, S.J., and two other Jesuits from the college in Lublin, among other points, on the proposition of the Arians: "The Lord Jesus Christ and our Saviour is not only true Man but everlasting (*przedwiecznym*) God." The Firley town, which had been granted the Magdeburg privilege, 1544, was at the time of the disputation under Mikołaj Biberstein Kazimierski, guardian of the children of Piotr Firley, and a convert from Calvinism to Arianism, though on his deathbed (1598) he would convert to Catholicism. The Arian Church of Lewartów was under the ministry of Krzysztof Lubieniecki Sr. (c. 1561 – 1624) who also served the congregation in Lublin, n. 792. The disputation was part of the missionary effort of the Jesuits of Lublin to regain the loyalty of burghers and peasants in this doubly Protestant enclave. The disputations are reflected in *Krótkie a prawdziwe opisanie dysputacje, która była w Lewartowie anno 1592 dina 13 i 14 stycznia, w której X. Radzimiński these dała Calissius, rector Lewartowski, i pan Jan Niemojewski oppugnowali* (Cracow: Starnacki, 1592); Gryczowa, n. 12; cf. no. 19, and Marcin Łaszcz, *Pogrom Lewartowski to iest o wygranej X. Radzimińskiego* (Cracow, 1592). On Piotr Firley and his town, see Władysław Pociecha, *PSB* 7 (1948 – 58) 15 – 17; on the town and its two Protestant congregations see *SGKP* 5 (1884) 376 – 81; and Kossowski, *Protestantyzm w Lublinie*, 76 – 81; for the disputation, Tworek, *Zbór Lubelski*, 56 – 57, 76 – 77, 102 – 3, 107 – 10.

7. On the estate of Gaj of the Jaktorowskis, 20 June 1592, with Krzysztof Lubieniecki, minister in Śmiegiel, and Christopher Ostorodt vs. the Jesuit Fathers of Poznań on the Trinity.

8. In the church of the Jesuits "pod Trybunał" *in Lublin*, 22–23 May 1592, with Piotr Statorius, minister in Lusławice, vs. Adryan Radzimiński, S.J.; on the eternal divinity of the Son of God. The literary deposit is by Statorius, *Dysputacja Lubelska ... o przedwiecznym bóstwie syna Bożego z X. Adryanem Radzimińskim jezuitą [r.] a. C. 1592 22 i 23 Mai*; Rodecki, no imprint, Gryczowa, no. 76.

9. In Śmigiel at the invitation of Andrzej Lubieniecki, 1592, with Christopher Ostorodt vs. Abbot/Canon Hieronim Podowski on the one God the Father, on Christ the Son, and on the christening of infants.

10. In the manor house of Lady Dudith (pani Elżbieta Dydyczowa) in Śmigiel, 1594, with Piotr Statorius, Faustus Socinus, Jan Niemojewski vs. Hieronim Ostrowski of Przemęt on the Trinity and the preexistence of Christ.

11. In Nowogródek, 26 January 1594, with Jan Licinius vs. Marcin Śmiglecki, S.J., on the eternal divinity of the Son of God.

12. In the chapel of the Brethren *in Lublin*, 1595/96, on the basis of theses presented by Marcin Czechowic, Andrzej and Krzysztof Lubieniecki and Jan Niemojewski vs. Canon Hieronim Podowski of Poznań and Professor Mikołaj Dobrocieski, chancellor of Jerzy Cardinal Radziwiłł, bishop of Cracow (1591–1600). The exchange is summarized by A. Lubieniecki. Kot has a single note, n. 1, on this important exchange. Another note was evidently dropped in the printing. Cf. the lost tract of Stoiński for disputation 15, known to Bock, *Antitrin.* 1.939, "Dysputacje," 355, n. 1. (possibly intended also for the otherwise missing n. 1 on 354).

13. In the Jesuit Church (of St. John the Baptist) *in Lublin*, in the presence of the deputies of the Tribunal and other gentlemen, 9–10 August 1615, in Polish, with Jan Stoiński vs. Rector Mikołaj Łęczycki, S.J. The summary by Stoiński, evidently copied by A. Lubieniecki from the lost tract of Stoiński, item 12 above (*Disputatio cum jesuitis habita Lublini 1615*; Gryczowa, no. 291), is printed by Kot, "Dysputacje," 354–64.

14. In the Dominican church of St. Stanisław *in Lublin*, 10 July 1616, under the moderatorship of Mikołaj Firley (1588–1635), great grandson of the founder of Lewartów, at the time marshal of the Tribunal and *starosta* of Lublin, with Jan Stoiński vs. Father Walerian Grocholski, O.P., on the Trinity. The opening remarks of Marshall Firley and the exchanges in debate are printed by Kot, "Dysputacje," 364–70; Gryczowa, no. 291; for the local scene, see further Tworek, "Walka," 23; *Zbór Lubelski*, 149.

Tworek reads A. Lubieniecki Junior, who alone of the two chroniclers of the disputations has information on Disputations 15 and 16, to mean that there were three disputations in Lublin in 1616 and two of these in the Carmelite Church. He is unclear about the exact dates of the last two, "Walka," esp. 25. Gryczowa, attentive to all the relevant imprints, reads the same "Katalog," ed. by Kot, to make Disputation 16 the same as that of 1620. Hence in what follows, I am doubling the next entry as 15A and 15B.

15A. In the Church of the Holy Spirit of the Discalced Carmelites *in Lublin*, 29 June 1616 (feast of SS. Peter and Paul), with Jan Stoiński vs. the Carmelite prior Giovanni Maria on the divinity of Christ. The date is supplied by the title of a work cited by Kot, "Dysputacje," 364, n. 2: *Assertiones theologicae publico certamine propositae a ... PP. Discalceatis de Monte Carmelo, Lublini in Polonia ad aedes spiritu S. dicatas et a catholicis in festo SS. Principum Apostolorum* [29 June], *ab hereticis autem in festo S. Margaretae* [July 13] *anno 1616 oppugnatae* (without imprint). The prior is reported to have declared: "'This is my church; I will not suffer this to be said.' And again: 'Let them [the heretics] be stoned, crucified.' But they dispersed in peace." Kot, "Katalog," 462.

I was asked by the pastor of the Church of the Holy Spirit in Lublin to give in Polish a meditation at noon, Ash Wednesday 1972. There were many hundreds who heard me introduced as a Protestant minister, an observer at Vatican II. Afterwards I was presented with a copy of the Jerusalem Bible in Polish, signed by the pastor and many others, a token all the more precious for my not knowing at the time that the successor of the prior, Giovanni Maria, was himself fully aware of the place of that pulpit in Lublin's relations with Protestants in the age of the reformation. Alas, this Bible with all the signatures has disappeared from my study.

15B. In the same, with the same, 13 July (feast of St. Margaret) on the divinity of Christ and his remission of sins. This was written up and published on the Catholic side as *Disputatio habita a RR. PP. Discalceatis Ordinis B. Virginis Mariae de Monte Carmelo contra Arianos* (Zamość, 1617), Gryczowa, no. 290. Stoiński's *De Iesu Christi divinitate, et remissione peccatorum nostrorum per eundem parta, Disputationis inter Joannem Stoienski ministrum Evangelii et Joannem Mariam Italum Carmelitam, Lublini in aede Carmelitana anno 1616, die 13 Julii publicae habitae, relatio* was edited by Hieronim Moskorzowski (Raków: Sternacki, 1618); Gryczowa, no. 290.

16. In the same, with the same, 5 July 1620. This ended with the wrecking of the chapels of both the Calvinists and the Polish Brethren, A. Lubieniecki, Junior, Kot, "Katalog," 460. Stoiński may have edited his version as *Disputatio inter Ioannem Stoienski et Ioannem Maria Italum Carmelitam*, lost, Gryczowa, no. 292, while the Catholic version was published as *Disputatio inter RR. PP. Discalceatos et Ioannem Statorium arianim, Lublini ... 1620 5 Julii habita* (Cracow, 1621). With the Catholic version before him, Tworek makes vivid the situation of excitement in Lublin during the session of the Tribunal with deputies and distinguished clerics from all over the vast region for which it was the supreme court next the King, "Walka," 25 – 27.

801. This disputation was unnoted by A. Lubieniecki, Sr, who was dead by 1624, and by A. Lubieniecki, Jr., for whom it would have been numbered 17th: in the Jesuit Church *in Lublin*, June 1636, with Krzysztof Lubieniecki, Jr. (c. 1598 – 1648), after his release from imprisonment (n. 852), father of the Author (nn. 678, 720) vs. Kasper Drużbicki, S.J. (c. 1589 – 1660), a major writer, teacher in the local Jesuit College, preacher before the Tribunal, under the moderatorship of Jerzy Niemirycz, on Christology. Lubieniecki wrongly gives the date as 1637 and Bock corrects it wrongly to 1627, *Antitrin.* 1.440. It took place soon after June 10, 1636, as shown by an exchange of letters between Lubieniecki and Drużbicki, 9 – 10 June 1636, Henryk Barycz, "Dokumenty i fakty z dziejów reformacji V: Ostatnia dysputacja Braci Polskich w Lublinie (1636)," *RwP* 12 (1953 – 55) 240 – 45; Tworek, "Walka," 25 – 28.

Jerzy Niemirycz (Nemyrych) (1612 – 59) was the son of Marta and Stefan Niemirycz, palatine of Kiev, educated at Raków. For the most recent presentation with bibliography, see Janusz Tazbir, *PSB* 22 (1977) 811–16. His address at the diet of Warsaw in support of the Treaty of Hadiacz of 23 April 1659 (n. 803) is translated in *Polish Brethren*, Doc. XXVII, with some account of his life.

802. The Polish-Swedish War (1655–1660).

803. *Russia* is the Latinized form Ruś (Czerwona)-Russia/Red, the designation for the Byzantine-Orthodox rite palatinates of Poland before the annexation of Volhynia and the Ukraine in the Union of Lublin 1569, whereby the Commonwealth of the Two Peoples was more fully integrated constitutionally. *Ruś* means here the Byzantine-rite palatinate from Lwów to well beyond Kiev but not the extensive Byzantine-rite territory still under Lithuania (this roughly coincident with soviet Byelorussia, of which Minsk is the capital).

Chamberlain Jerzy Niemirycz of Kiev, long-term supporter of the Minor Church in the Diet, after supporting the Swedes as the best hope for the salvation of the Commonwealth, espoused a scheme for a South-Russian or Ukrainian Duchy affiliated with Poland-Lithuania but free of Catholic influence and as autonomous with respect to royal control as Lithuania. He proposed in a lost appeal (c. 1658) that all dissidents, including the Brethren, join the Orthodox and Apostolic Church as he had done. Against this appeal Samuel Przypkowski promptly published in Polish and Latin, *Responsa ad scriptum*, reprinted in *BFP* 9 (Amsterdam, 1692) 533–90. See Orest Levyskyi, "Socynjanie na Rusi," *RwP* 2 (1922) 231–34; cf. n. 918; *Polish Brethren*, 508.

804. That is, the side of the eastern palatinates, especially Kiev, and the Cossacks under Hetman Bogdan Chełmnicki and his successor, in alliance with Muscovy.

Our Author named one of his sons Bogdan Lubieniecki, who, like his brother Krzysztof, was a painter in Holland. There exists a family memorial in typescript by André de Tobac, an amateur and collector of objets d'art, born c. 1900, who, stemming from a Ukrainian noble family with our Author among his ancestors, relates that his not clearly identified grandfather was in possession of an oral tradition and some documents that linked Stanisław Lubieniecki with Bogdan Chełmnicki and his successor Ivan Vyhovskyi (see several entries on him in *Polish Brethren*), specifically as their representative with several Protestant states in the Empire. De Tobac purports to have "read in" a letter, preserved by his family, by Pani Lubieniecka, the spouse of our Author, to her friend, Pani Strygowska in Lubieniec, the ancestral seat of the Lubieniecki, near Przedecz in Kujawy. De Tobac shares even the oral tradition of his family that after the death of our Author, Mrs. Lubieniecka left Hamburg for Sweden and there died of the plague. A photocopy of the typescript of this family memorial, *Lubinetzki: Geschichte einer arianischen Familie von Malern und Politikern*, 56 pp. with 11 leaves of pasted photographs of the self-portrait of Krzysztof and others by him and his brother Bogdan, no imprint, but from internal evidence, c. 1970. The author, born in Vienna, a nominal Catholic and Ukrainian nationalist, has so mingled family reminiscences, racial, genealogical, and even racist lore, philology, aesthetics, and personal observations on life, death, and his spiritual encounters with ancestors, that the authentic new material, even when confused, on the Lubienieckis and their role in the Cossack Uprising, could be lost or even dismissed. When De Tobac (possibly a humorous pseudonym) set down his reminiscences and story of the two artists, he did not know that the Lubieniecki family was Arian and the typescript in part 1 is retrospectively modified at a couple of points to make up for his enhanced knowledge of the two painters' father. He came providentially into the possession of the (familiar) print of our Author, to whom he then devotes a fresh account in the light of information given him by the director of the Rijksmuseum in Amsterdam, who told him of the painting by our Author by Matthias Scheitz (1625–1700), completed in Hamburg in 1666, from which Lambert Vischer (1633–90) made the familiar copper-print of Lubieniecki (*Polish Brethren*, Plate M) for the *Theatrum Cometicum*, 1668. The fact that De Tobac had approached his account of the painter brothers, his distant kinsmen, as a lover of art and family history before knowing of the prominence of their father in Reformation historiography, etc., greatly enhances the value of his family lore, even though he would be wrong, for example, in saying that the Lubieniecki family was in origin of the Byzantine-rite, but there must be a basis for his saying that our Author with his son Bogdan visited (secretly) in 1573 his sister, pani Horodecka in Lubieniec, from which, by a special arrangement, he continued to receive rents (p. 19). The strange but fascinating composition is divided thus: "Gerbrüder Bohdan und Christof Lubienetzi" (1–25); "Epilog" (25–34); "Lubinetz" (34–45); "Stanislaw de Lubienietz Lubienietzki" (46–54); "Die Schlafender" (a painting in the possession of De Tobac, 54–56). De Tobac's testimony to the philo-Orthodox and pro-Niemirycz on the Duchy of the Ukraine seems wholly plausible.

805. Niemirycz was traitorously killed by his own Ruthenian (Ukrainian) side who feared he was unreliable in dealing with the Poles.

806. The account has verisimilitude; Jan Stoiński was minister in Raków, 1612–15, in Lublin from 1615 to an uncertain date. Krzysztof Lubieniecki, Jr., had just begun his ministry in Lublin, 1626–48 (nn. 720, 881). It was plausible that a message from his sick-bed might be a pretext for urgent entry into the house of Stanisław Matzyński (n. 810).

807. On the Lissovians, see n. 724. There were indeed political connections between Prince Gabriel Bethlen (n. 386) (1613–29; n. 386) and some Polish Calvinist and certain Unitarian gentry and magnates who were attempting to stem the course of the pro-Jesuit and pro-Hapsburg policies of Sigismund III Vasa (n. 736).

808. In 1625 Gustavus Adolphus (1611–32) seized Dorpat and resumed war against Poland and in 1626 seized a part of Royal Prussia.

809. Bolestraszycki, royal secretary and elected Deputy from Przemyśl in 1621, translated a polemical treatise by Pierre du Moulin (d. 1658), professor of the Reformed Academy of Sedan, *Héraclite, ou de la vanité et la misère de la vie humaine* (Geneva, 1609), several times reprinted and translated into German and English. There is no copy of his *Heraklit albo de vanitate mundi* (c. 1624). Accused of blasphemy by Achacy Grochowski, bishop of Przemyśl (1624–27) and later of Łuck, Bolestraszycki was sentenced in 1627 by the Tribunal of Lublin to six months in prison and a fine of 40 marks and the threat of banishment. The Polish translation was burned by the hangman and its reading forbidden. See the text between nn. 812 and 813. The sentence met with strong opposition, and the diet of Warsaw in 1627 virtually condemned it as illegal. The sentence and its consequences were abolished by the diet of 1649; cf. n. 831. See Romaniuk, "Działalność polityczna-reformacyjna szlachty," *RL* 18.42; in the fuller study of the episode by Aleksander Kraushar, "Sprawa Bolestraszyckiego," *Drobiazgi historyczne* (Petersburg, 1891), Study 1.45–62; Kossowski, *Protestantyzm w Lublinie*, 133–43; Jarosław Wit Opatrzny, *PSB* 2 (1936), 285–86. See also Ludwik Chmaj, collected writings, *Bracia Polscy: Ludzie, idee, wypływy* (Warsaw, 1957), which in the final section, "Po zniesieniu Rakowa (materiały)," 467–86, esp. 469–70 on the Bolestraszycki episode, preserves from a MS lost in the Hitlerian period a transcript of the speech of the delegates of the synod of the Polish Brethren in Kisielin sent to the provincial synod of the Calvinists of Little Poland assembled in Krasnobród in the Land of Chełm, 25 September 1638, appealing to them to make a common front against the encroachments on religious freedom and therein rehearsing events in Lublin and elsewhere.

810. From the whole context it is evident that Krzysztof, father of our Author (n. 720), was in his house in Lublin. Already on 14 December 1618, he had written to Simon Episcopius after the opening of the synod of Dort (November 1618–May 1619), fateful for the Remonstrants. Chmaj prints a picture of the letter from the Remonstrant Archives, *Bracia Polscy*, 105. Of several items in the foregoing paragraph, mention is first made of Stanisław Matczyński. He is mentioned again, *Historia, 268*, in a series of names. A certain Pan Matczyński is attested at the visitation synod of the Lublin District and at the synod of Turobin in 1582. Sipayłło, *AS*, 3.67, 69. A Marek Matczyński (1631–97) would become palatine of Ruthenia, *PB*, 20 (1975) 157–58.

A synod of Raków of 1627 is not noted by Sipayłło, *AS*, 3.xix. Bock, however, knew of a "public synod" somewhere in that year, and most plausibly in Raków, that assigned to Samuel Przypkowski, eventual biographer of Faustus Socinus, the task of collecting and receiving documentation to write a "historia ecclesiarum unitariarum." Bock reports (*Antitr.* 1, p. 682) that the request was repeated at the synod of Kreuzburg in Silesia in 1663. Noting that the Remonstrants had been permitted to return to Holland in 1626 from exile, Chmaj held that Przypkowski in Holland would have found this the propitious moment to act on the overture of the synod of Raków of 1627 to publish anonymously his *Dissertatio de pace et concordia ecclesiae* (Amsterdam, 1628), which, without giving the Minor Church or socinianism a name, sets forth its spirit and calls for concord among the churches and religious peace, from among other reasons on the ground that "there is not in this life a perfect knowledge of god and the divine mysteries, but in the other life, and that faith, hope, and charity are sufficient to salvation" (the title of chap. 7). The tract was reprinted in *BFP*, 9/10; partially printed in translation, *Polish Brethren*, Doc. XI–I. In n. 4 of my preface (*Polish Brethren*, 289) I refer to an edition by Zbigniew Ogonowski, which should be now corrected to read: ed. by Zbigniew Ogonowski, translated by Mieczysław Brożek, Samuel Przypkowski, *Rozprawa o pokoju i zgodzie w kościele* (Warsaw/Łódź: PAN, 1981). Chmaj, *Samuel Przypkowski*, 19–20. On the basis of Chmaj's surmise, Szczotka has an entry for Raków, 1627, "Synody," 71. And synod of Raków, 1627 seems plausible, although there is no protocol for Sipayłło to print, Lubieniecki being here an additional source unnoted by Bock.

Lubieniecki has referred to *lucerna punica* before.

As for the dating of the letter, in 1627 Pentecost fell on May 13 Old Style, May 24 New Style. At the close of the paragraph there is a valuable, even though incidental, liturgical and disciplinary reference. Apparently, as in Geneva, communion was observed four times a year. In preparation for communion on Whitsunday (Pentecost), the pastor, presumably with elders and deacons, examined the members of the congregation lest any profane the body and blood of the Lord (1 Cor 11:27–29). See the eucharistic use of the Polish Brethren at a later date, *Polish Brethren* 420–74, esp. 461ff.

811. Wawrzyniec dominik of Czudec was minister to Piotr Gorajski, owner of Wierzchowska in 1608; minister in 1612 in Bończa in the land of Chełm, where a congregation had been founded c. 1577, its owner Mikołaj Sienicki; minister in 1614 in Pustotew, owned by Sienickis; minister in Lublin in 1623; and minister in Radzięcin in 1627, a village distant from Lublin by about 70 kilometers. Thus the episode must be placed while he was still *in vicinia*, namely before the Lublin District synod if 8 July 1627 "sent" him thence and replaced him with Jan Węgierski for Lublin, 1527–28. Sipayłło, *AS*, 3.493. It was the usage of both Reformed synods, Major and Minor, to think of their ministers as "sent" (Catholic usage) rather than as "called" (Congregational usage). This was true of their counterparts in Transylvania. The synodal structure of the Reformed churches in the East inhibited the lord patron from dominating the local *Zbór*

as edifice and congregation that stood and gathered on his property.

812. The occasion of Stoiński's flight is not explained. Stanisław Lubieniecki is here and throughout the next lines giving a précis of his Great Uncle Krzysztof's letter to "Stoiński."

813. Lubieniecki here presumably refers to the Jesuit collegians on vacation (*maleferiatis*), not to idle workmen.

814. The victory at Hammerstein was won 12 April 1627 by the Grand General (*Hetman*) Stanisław Koniecpolski (c. 1591–1646), who eventually defeated Gustavus Adolphus in 1629. Władysław Czapliński, *PSB* 13 (1967) 524A. News of the victory would indeed have been circulating in Lublin in May 1627.

815. Wawrzyniec Suśliga, S.J. (1570–1640), studied in Cracow and in Graz. He was the chaplain to Constantia, the second wife of Sigismund III. Constantia and probably Suśliga were responsible for the death of Jan Tyszkowic, 1611. See n. 167; Załęski, *Jezuici w Polsce*, 2.217, 661, 676–77. In the same year, 1627, Suśliga promoted persecution against other non-Catholics, i.e., against the wife of William Tuck, a Scottish merchant. Węgierski, *Slavonia Reformata*, 244–45. In the copperprint of Lublin at about the time of the episode, the residence of the Jesuits, next the present cathedral (n. 146), is indicated by Georg Hogenberg as feature no. 10.

816. In 1627 Pentecost fell on 13 May Old Style, 24 May New Style (n. 810).

817. Paweł Lubieniecki (1568–after 1626) was one of 12 members of the Lublin congregation from the larger Lubieniecki family. He is mentioned at *Historia, 254*. He was owner of part of Lublin and the village of Wysokie. Tworek, *Zbór Lubelski*, 129.

818. Paweł was the uncle of Pastor Krzysztof and the great uncle of our Author. The Author's source for the ensuing episode was Andrzej Lubieniecki, Jr., (n. 825).

819. Michael Gittich, evidently at the time a guest preacher in Lublin, was the son of an immigrant from the Venetian Republic. Although his surname is more German than Italian, he remained proud of his Italian heritage, hence the adjectival Venecius/Venetianus. He had left Poland to live in Kolozsvár, then after a brief return, gone on to Altdorf as tutor of two noble Polish youths, and was ordained minister at the synod of Raków in 1611. He served as minister in Nowogródek in Lithuania, where he was a colleague of Jan Licinius. To be noted below, he took refuge in the house of a German burgher of Lublin, Michael Schürer. See *BAnt*, 108–09, and Wallace who has put together much from disparate sources, *Biography*, 2.506–16.

820. Gustavus Adolphus had been defeated in April (n. 814).

821. The grandnephew of Paweł Lubieniecki, in writing up the family chronicle and arguing from a prudent point of view, could not wholly overcome the impression that Gittich and many other dissenters could have hoped for relief from the Lutheran invader.

822. Andrzej Lisiecki of Lisiecz near Kalisz (d. 1639), a professional lawyer, recently appointed the Crown Instigator (i.e., public prosecutor), was a fanatical enemy of all heretics and a defender of the liberties of the nobility. He wrote *Apologia pro libertate republicae* (1611), dedicated to Sigismund III, and *Trybunał Główny Koronny* (Cracow, 1638) dedicated to King Ladislas and the Lublin Tribunal; Janusz Ekes, *PSB* 17 (1972) 452–53.

823. Gittich had been ordained at Raków (n. 819), probably with Krzysztof Lubieniecki.

824. Under the *lex talionis* of Roman law, a convicted false accuser was subject to the penalty he had invoked upon the accused. This principle was embodied in medieval law, including that of Poland. At the diet of 1565, by statute 79, a fine of one hundred marks plus twelve weeks imprisonment had been substituted for a false accusation of criminal

action. *Statuta*, 2.693 – 94. However, because of the enormity of the capital charge of treason, the defense was plausibly moved to invoke the spectre of the more severe *lex talionis*.

825. According to Andrzej Lubieniecki, Gittich Venecius and another minister of Lithuania, Okielowicz, had already departed, evidently ignorant of the impending trial. Kot, ed., "Dysputacjy Katalog z rękopisu Andrzeja Lubienieckiego młodszego," in "Katalog," 462. In his primary source, Jakub Rynkiewicz (n. 792) is said to have been co-minister with Krzysztof Lubieniecki at the time of the episode.

826. Pliny the Elder, *Naturalis historia* 19.1.6, 24.

827. Lubieniecki has *mente vertente* which should be read *mense vertente*. Indeed Węgierski (*Slavonia Reformata*, 245) gives the date 1 August 1627.

828. It turns out (*Historia, 261 – 62*) that the German mercenaries engaged by Lord Rafał Leozczyński were Lutherans hired to fight against Lutheran Gustavus Adolphus (1611 – 32). His picture is on Plate 19.

829. In scorn of the Jesuit College in Lublin Lubieniecki remembers the Academy in Raków as the Camp of the Muses (*Historia, 253*).

830. *Non inveni*.

831. Lubieniecki, instead of writing Major and Minor Churches, speaks easily of Evangelicals or the Reformed and of Unitarians or Christians. But in the text he uses *Unitarii* only twice for this group, above, near n. 828, and of his father's church, below.

The outbreaks, called in the sources, "*pogromie* oba zbory," took place 1 August 1627, leaving the two edifices ransacked and wrecked, mere shell. Within three days of this destruction the Tribunal refused to allow suit for compensation and even the right of the afflicted to regroup and gather for worship within the town, even though the dietine of Lublin in 1627 and again in 1628 gave instruction to the deputies in the Commonwealth Diet to seek redress and the correction of the Tribunal as having acted against the express stipulations of the *Pax dissidentium* of 1572. Romuniuk, "Działalność polityczno-reformacyjna," *BL*, 18.43.

832. The reference is to the Cossack wars of 1648 – 59, continued in the Polish-Muscovite wars of 1654 – 67 for the possession of the Ukraine. Andrzej Firlej (d. 1649 or 1650), who had studied at Heidelberg, 1602 – 04, enjoyed the reputation of a military leader. Appointed a "regimentary," although already an old man, he subdued Volhynia and distinguished himself as one of the defenders of Zbaraż (1649). Stefan Kieniewicz, *PSB* 6 (1948) 476 – 77.

833. Lubieniecki has Crechanius.

834. This was presumably Paweł (d. before 1654), son of Krzysztof (I) (d. 1620) and nephew of Patron Paweł. He is not identified, however, as Paweł "młodszy" by Tazbir, *Lubieniecki*.

835. Paweł's older brother, Andrzej Lubieniecki the Younger, himself wrote: "where also a disaster befell me and I almost lost my life, driving this mob away alone with my saber, in which [action], however, I got loyal assistance from Master Mikołaj Borzęcki, later my brother-in-law, so that it was on the two of us that the whole impact fell. . . ." Kot, "Dysputacjy Katalog z rękopisu Andrzeja Lubienieckiego młodszego," 462.

836. The same in brief in *Life of Wiszowaty*, *BAnt*, 240; *Polish Brethren*, Doc. I, no. 95.

837. The Reformed edifice in Cracow, the Brog in ulica Św. Jana in Cracow, was assaulted in 1574, but the congregation repossessed the place even after the second assault in 1587, but abandoned the site after the third assault in 1591. The schismatic Unitarian congregation was obliged to clear out in 1591.

838. Here Lubieniecki seems to be not only anticipating the Swedish invasion but also interpreting it as the divine chastisement of Poland for making the path of the Reformed and the Unitarian churches so difficult.

839. Lubieniecki, by association, moves from one funeral procession involving violence to another, a few years later to the same effect; but he fails to place the outrage against the worthy physician in the context of two-sided excesses in Lublin.

During the commital service for a certain Evangelical in the cemetery that the Calvinists had acquired within the town, several taunting students who had accompanied the procession climbed to a nearby roof and flung tiles and muck on the bereaved. The armed guard that had marched in the procession now fired warning shots, hitting two students of the Jesuit College who were attending pupils on their way to school, and killing with a stray shot a young brewer on his way out of the Bernardine Cloister, where he had just made his prenuptial confession. In the ensuing conflict and outpouring of confessional passions, there were five dead and several hundred wounded. In mindless revenge, the mob entered the home of Dr. Samuel Makowski of Brzeg, who was innocent of the violence, and sacked his place as a leading Calvinist of Lublin. He himself, along with Rafał Przyjemski (regarded as most at fault), and five other accomplices were brought before the spiritual court, 5 February 1633, accused of murderous action. Kossowski, *Protestantyzm w Lublinie*, 170–75. Dr. Makowski escaped to Cracow and obtained a safe-conduct from Ladislas IV. The investigation by royal commissioners showed the complete innocence of the Reformed, but because of an accusation by the syndic of the Bernardine order, Makowski was imprisoned and sentenced to death by the Tribunal.

840. On the payment of 1,000 guilders (*librae*) to the Bernardine Cloister in Lublin was he released from the prison. Węgierski, *Slavonia Reformata*, 247–48. This money was granted him by the Unitarian synod of Raków, 1634. Bock, *Antitrin.*, 1.464.

841. The thirteenth statute of the diet of 1627 condemned the Tribunal's decrees of 1627 as trespassing upon its legislative competence (''As the Tribunal has no power to establish laws . . .'') and annulled them. *Statuta*, 3.547. This was stressed by the Covenant General of 16 July 1632 after the death of Sigismund III. *Statuta*, 3.725, Statute 7; *Volumina Legum*, 3.263, 13.

842. Cicero.

843. The meeting for worship seems to have taken place in the vicinity of Lublin, the congregation of Lublin and Zaporów joined.

844. Mentioned at *Historia, 268*.

845. Remigian Koniecpolski was bishop of Chełm, 1627–40.

846. The sumptuary laws of any town were such that one German burgher would have looked much like another and the Author slyly stresses the race and social position common to the burgher saved and the burgher (Schürer, nn. 775, 825) familiar to the befriended and now befriending porter. To be sure, Lubieniecki may not be saying that providence worked through his mother's quick presence of mind in her misidentification but rather that the once befriended porter of Lublin intended to help anybody known to Schürer, which his mother had evidently confirmed in the common peril.

847. Always cited in these nn. in the second, fuller ed., as *Slavonia Reformata*. It is true that Węgierski does not mention the persecutions in his chap. 15, ''Persecution especially of the Reformed Churches in Little Poland from 1550 to 1650'' (244–250), devoted wholly to the Lublin church district. He was perhaps motivated by his lack of sympathy with the unitive efforts among the Reformed and the Brethren that preceded and followed the riotous destruction of both churches in Lublin in 1627.

848. The author refers to the *pax dissidentium* of the Warsaw confederation that made

possible the election of Henry of Valois in 1573. He rehearses the antecedents and gradual eating away of the *pax* in his "Legal claims for the Freedom of Relgion of Unitarians in Poland" of c. 1660, *Polish Brethren*, Doc. XXIX.

849. Stanisław Cichowski, father and son, were mentioned in a letter of Biandrata to Dudith in 1575, n. 718, ¶2. These genealogical relationships center in Krzysztof Ossoliński (1587 – 1645), who studied at the Jesuit College in Lublin as of 1604 and went on with his brother to study at the Jesuit academy in Würzburg, then Padua. In 1615 he was married, in the church of the Franciscans in Cracow, to Zofia Cikowska, sister of the childless Protestant (not expressly stated) chamberlain of Lublin. Wacław Urban, *PSB* 24 (1979) 421 – 23.

850. The one Major Reformed or Evangelical pastor mentioned in the paragraph, Jerzy Rzeczycki (d. 1649), is well-attested in sip, *AS*, 3.436 passim; and the Chronowski here is undoubtedly Stanisław (n. 802). Interestingly, Sebastian Chronowski was also pastor and owner of Rapkowa. Sipayłło, *AS*, 3.327 – 28.

As for the *dissidentes de religione* of the *Compacta conventa* of 1573, they were originally all differing on religion, including the Catholics, but Lubieniecki has here slipped into current usage, according to which it was the non-Catholics who were the *dissidentes* with respect to the by now clearly reestablished religion of the Polish state.

851. Paweł Orzechowski, once of the suite of Polish envoys to announce the election of Henry of Valois as King of Poland, was mentioned at n. 769. His son Stanisław (not the same as the Catholic polemicist!), who pleaded the case for Stanisław Cichowski, was evidently not the same as *archicamerarius* of Lublin of the same name (*Historia, 253 – 54*). In this paragraph Elżbieta Oleśnicka was the second wife of Paweł Orzechowski, brother to palatine Mikołaj Oleśnicki (c. 1558 – 1629), but who appears not to have had children of her own. Stanisław Orzechowski was rather the son of his father's first wife, Zofia Spinkowa.

852. The castle tower served as a prison. It had two floors. The upper tower had rooms with windows and fireplaces while the dungeon was 12 cells deep, with no windows or heating. The gentry—even if sentenced to prison *in fundo* for manslaughter— were usually granted the privilege of being lodged in the upper tower.

853. Szczęsny Morawski (*Arjanie Polscy* (Lwów, 1906) identified him with Prince Jerzy Zbaraski, castellan of Cracow, but he died in 1631.

854. See Wiszowaty's n. on Roman Hojski, Lubieniecki, *Legal Claims*, *BAnt*, 285; *Polish Brethren*, 572.

855. To Marcin Czaplic of Hlupomin and his brother Jerzy Szpanowski of Kisielin were dedicated the Walenty Schmalz's *Refutatio* of Marcin Śmiglecki, S.J., *De erroribus novorum Arianorum*. The *Refutatio* was published in Raków, 1616. Gryczowa, no. 238. Marcin is mentioned elsewhere in the volume, as subscriber, etc. The brothers Czaplic appear in *Polish Brethren*, passim.

356. The *non fuissetis* in the plural is addressed evidently to causers Jan Cichowski and the sixteen or seventeen nobles imprisoned in the tower with pastor Krzysztof Lubieniecki for having expressed outrage at the decision favoring Ossoliński's Catholic wife. Lubieniecki does not fully explain the reason for the imprisonment.

857. That is, Zofia Cichowska Ossolińska at widowhood.

858. Krzysztof Ossoliński died on the way to the Diet, 24 February 1615, and was buried in a Franciscan habit in the church of the Discalced Carmelites in Cracow. He had founded a cloister at Stopmia.

859. Evidently for his father's dealings with Zofia Cichowska's brother's will.

860. At Zborów, Chmielnicki, the general of the Cossacks, defeated in a two day's

battle (15–16 August 1649) the Polish army under King John Casimir, which was hastening to the rescue of Zbaraż, then besieged by the Cossack and Tartar cavalry. Urban says that Baldwin Ossoliński died in 1650, *PSB* 24.423A.

861. This was not Zofia Cichowska who had died in 1638/39, nor even the second wife Zofia z Krasińskich who died in 1642, but the third wife, Elżbieta Firlejówna who died in 1650. Urban, *PSB* 24.422.

862. The intention would seem to be Jan Cichowski, but he was not on the father's side (*patruelis*).

863. See *Historia, 276–77* and n. 2–3.

864. Piotr Królewski, father and son, are mentioned in Tazbir, *Lubieniecki*, 155, 170.

865. The estate was owned by Jan Lubieniecki and Szczęsny Ralwański; Tworek, *Zbór Lubelski*, 130.

866. He is referred to by Lubieniecki, *Legal Claims*, *BAnt*, 284; *Polish Brethren*, 573, mentioned as a member of the Lublin Unitarian congregation by Tworek, *Zbór Lubelski*, 133.

867. Although deprived of its edifice, the Unitarian congregation persevered in spite of persecutions in Lublin. In 1651 the city voted that "for all future time Arians must not be admitted to municipal law or in future acquired any properties in the city nor in the suburb, nor practice any commerce." Białkowski, *Materiały do monografii Lublina* (Lublin, 1928) 25–26. Nevertheless, some rich merchants remained "Arians" until 1660, when they were compelled to accept Catholicism or go into exile. Ludwik Zalewski, "Do dziejów reformacji w Lublinie," *RwP* 11 (1948–52) 59–60.

NOTES TO CHAPTER FOURTEEN

868. Marcin Krowicki, last noted in Mordy, n. 538. When a Catholic became owner there he settled in Piaski in 1571. Cf. the observation on our own Author's usually tangential treatment, Bk. 1, n. 234, ¶3.

869. One of the four sons of Piotr. Andrzej Suchodolski was in Paris 1638–42; *BAnt*, 284–85; Tworek, *Zbór Lubelski*, 30, 46, 135.

870. As a Reformed student, probably at Leiden, he learned of the Remonstrants, analogous to the Unitarians in the Polish Reformed tradition.

871. Lubieniecki does not say how this information came to him. Krzysztof Sieniuta, son of Teodor was the founder of the church at Lachowce (district of Krzemieniec in the palatine of Volhynia), but deserted the congregation after his father's death (1611), then rejoined it in or before 1615. Bock, *Antitrin.* 1.872–73. (Merczyng incorrectly gives 1617, *Zbory i senatorowie*, 110.)

872. The family of Rudnicki was well known among the Lithuanian congregations. Krzysztof Rudnicki was (c. 1600) a minister of Suraz. Bock, *Antitrin.* 1.726, 736; Zeltner, *Historia*, 1172. He attended several synods at Raków and Lublin. Another Krzysztof Rudnicki appears at the synods until 1646. Szczotka, "Synody," 50–51, 54–55, 59–60, 80, 87.

The Daniel Rudnicki of our text, a Roman Catholic scholar, is unknown. It is likely that Lubieniecki intended Jakub Rudnicki, a prominent Jesuit. This Rudnicki studied in Würzburg, where as a boy of fifteen he won praise for his poetry. In 1601 he entered the Jesuit order in Rome and while studying theology, he taught *belles lettres* there. Sigismund III appointed Jakub Rudnicki preceptor of John Casimir, at whose court he converted several prominent Protestants. By 1627 he had left the court, to become vice-rector, and then rector of the colleges in Cracow, Jarosław, and Lwów, Between 1639 and 1643 he was Jesuit provincial of Poland. He left various works in MS. Załęski, *Jezuici w Polsce*, 2.462–63, 706.

873. Piotr Suchodolski, *podstarosta* of Lublin, had among his children Piotr, Paweł, Mikołaj, Abraham, Andrzej; Tworek, *Zbór Lubelski*, 33, 46, 130 (the number of sons differs in these references). The Piotr here is the son of the above Piotr an thus the oldest brother of Andrzej, patron of Piaski.

874. This was Agnieszka Socina. See *Life of Wiszowaty*, *BAnt*, 222; *Polish Brethren*, no. 69. For Wiszowaty's experience with Adam Suchodolski, see further, *Life*, nos. 83, 86.

875. Lubieniecki says the congregation at Piaski was uprooted in 1645. This may be an error for 1643. The records of the congregation at Siedliska begin as of 1643. See n. 881.

876. Thus, the Author's father, died in 1648.

877. Andrzej Suchodolski and his wife.

878. Stefan Świetlicki (or Świetlik) was successor of Józef Biskupski in the rectorship of the Reformed School at Bielżyce. On the academy there, see Stanisław Tworek, *Działalność oświatowo-kulturalna Kalwinizmu Małopolskiego* (Lublin: Wydawnictwo Lubelskie, 1970) chap. 4, "Szkoła generalne Kalwinów Małopolskiego w Bełżycach."

879. Michał Suchodolski was the son of Piotr (n. 873). Michał was married to Dorota Spinkowna, sister of Zofia Spinkowa Orzechowska, first wife of Paweł Orzechowski (n. 851). The father of Dorota and Zofia, Stanisław Spinek was an eminent Calvinist. Tworek, *Zbór Lubelski*, 131–32.

880. Cf. *Life of Wiszowaty*, *BAnt*, 240; *Polish Brethren*, nos. 95 and 95.1.

881. The following were ministers at Siedliska: Krzysztof Lubieniecki, (1643–1648, in charge also of the congregation of Lublin), assisted by Paweł Myślik (1643–48); Andrzej Wiszowaty (1648–50?); Jan Ciachowski (1650–53), assisted by our Author (1652–53); Joachim Stegmann, Jr. (1653–?57), assisted by Jerzy Gejżanowski (1654–55). The church was dispersed during the Swedish War (1655–1660). Synods were held there in 1643, 1644, and 1653. See Bock, *Antitrin.* 1.100, 369, 440, 523, 960; Szczotka, "Synody," 84–85, 93. On Wiszowaty, *BAnt*, 240; *Polish Brethren*, nos. 95, 97. On Gejżanowski, see Tazbir, *Lubieniecki*, 235–37.

882. See *Life of Wiszowaty*, *BAnt*, 240–241; *Polish Brethren*, nos. 103–4.

883. The flight from Poland to Transylvania and elsewhere is dealt with in five related narrations: here by Lubieniecki directly; then in two letters attached by Wiszowaty to the *Historia*; the collective letter from Kreuzburg, 1600, now thought to have been in part drafted by Lubieniecki; and that of Samuel Przykowski of 1663 (the two translated in *Polish Brethren*, Doc. XXXIII; n. 950); and finally in the Life of Wiszowaty, *BAnt*, 225; *Polish Brethren*, no. 110.3.

The decree of 1658 John Casimir ("rex persecutor Unitariorum Casimirus," Uzoni), reproduced elsewhere (*Polish Brethren*, Doc. XXVI), as modified, finally set 10 July 1660 (*Polish Brethren*, Doc. XXX) as the final date for the implementation of its fiercest provision—death. Some of the Brethren converted to Catholicism or Calvinism, some hid with Evangelical or Catholic relations, and others, the most determined, divided into three contingents, those going to the west (Hapsburg Silesia and Mark Brandenburg), those going to East Prussia (formerly Ducal Prussia, since the Treaty of Oliva 1660 wholly independent of the Polish Crown), and Transylvania.

Those going to Transylvania already had many contacts with the Unitarians there, but the situation was not propitious because Calvinism was in the ascendancy and the country was suffering under the effects and forebodings of Turkish punitive campaigns connected with the unauthorized expedition of George II Rákóczy to Poland (1657) and the struggle over the succession to this throne when deposed (3 November 1657) and mortally wounded (22 May 1660). See more on Rákóczy, *Polish Brethren*, Doc. XXV. There is a map showing the Turkish-Tatar campaigns in Transylvania, 1658–1661, in László Makkai, *Historie de Transylvanie* (Paris, 1946), opp. 248. On the trek, see Wilbur, *Transylvania*, esp. 483–86; idem, *Socinianism*, 122–23; Tazbir, *Bracia Polscy w Siedmiogrodzie, 1660–1784* (Warsaw, 1964), 26–35.

884. The in-law relationship of Suchodolski to Czaplic, Rupniowski, and Przypkowski remains to be clarified. Jan Rupniowski of a familiar surname of the Polish Brethren appears only here among the main primary and secondary sources.

885. The 500 refugees with their train of 300 wagons, after crossing the frontier into Hungary (Slovakia), applied to Prince Ákos Barcsay (1659–60) of Transylvania for permission to enter his territory. In the meantime they sought a more immediate protection in the castle of Huszt in Máramoros with Ferenc Rhédei who was the deposed Prince (1658–59). Wilbur, *Socinianism*, 484, *Transylvania*, 122.

886. See *Life of Wiszowaty, BAnt*, 225; *Polish Brethren*, Doc. I, no. 110.3.

887. Ducal/East Prussia was a major refuge. The recorded immersed Polish Brother was Karol Henryk Morsztyn who died in Andreaswalde in 1852. Wilbur, *Socinianism*, 521.

888. It is not certain that by patron Lubieniecki means Samuel Przypkowski who wrote his Letter of 1663 from Königsberg, *Historia, 279ff*; *Polish Brethren*, Doc. XXXIII–II.

NOTES TO CHAPTER FIFTEEN

889. Lusławice's antitrinitarian congregation lasted for a full century (1560–1660). At first it was a center of Ditheists, led by Stanisław Farnowski and Stanisław Wiśniowski. After 1578 it became the center of plenary Unitarianism in the Piedmont. See n. 502.

The succession of ministers at Lusławice was as follows: Stanisław Wiśniowski (still minister in 1578, probably until 1586); Jerzy Schomann (1586–88); Peter Statorius (1588–1604?); Stanisław Lubieniecki (II) the Elder (already serving in 1612); Jan Stoiński (dates unascertained); Jonas Szlichtyng (1640–47); Seweryn Morsztyn (1647–52); and Jan Moszowski (1653–56). For the date of Schomann, see n. 892.

890. Mentioned below, n. 908.

891. Mentioned below, n. 915.

892. See Schomann's *Testament, BAnt*, 196, RD 3, n. 37.

893. The name *Unitarius* originated in Transylvnia in 1600 (n. 123).

894. In the succession of rectors and teachers at the school were Wojciech of Kalisz (in 1600), Valentin Baumgarten (probably 1644–48), and Jan Hradecki, a Czech. The teachers under Hradecki were a Krzyszkiewicz (1640/41), Christian Pyrner (until 1643), and Jan Demianowicki (1643–47).

895. Valentin Baumgarten of Memel studied at Königsberg, beginning in 1634. He was a friend of Martin Ruar as early as 1637. In 1640 he solemnly recanted Socinianism in the presence of the Königsberg theological faculty. However, he was expelled in 1640 after he relapsed. He was the rector in Kisielin (1641–44) and then in Lusławice

(n. 894). Later, he was rector and minister in Kolozsvár (d. 1673). F. S. Bock, *Historia Socinianismi Prussici* (Königsberg, 1754) 42–47.

The school at Lusławice was endangered in 1647 because of its association with Jonas Schlichtyng who was condemned to death because of his *Confessio fidei christianae*, printed at Wrócmira a few miles south of Lusławice in 1642. See *Polish Brethren*, Doc. XXII and my "Life and Thought of Jonas Szlichtyng." Baumgarten himself suffered along with many another from the decree condemning all Arian presses and schools. It is therefore doubtful whether the school continued after Baumgarten's departure. For the press in Lusławice, see Schomann's *Testamentum, BAnt*, 202; RD 3, no. 45.

896. Martin Wilhelm is unknown. The editor or printer may have misconstrued in Lubieniecki's MS a Martin Willich, who was a correspondent of Martin Ruar from Hamburg, and a student at the University of Königsberg (1636/7). He was inclined to Unitarianism but nothing further is known of him. Bock, *Historia Socinianismi Prussici*, 35, 41–42.

897. For Polanus as physician, see *Historia, 246, 248*.

898. The identification of the Latin *ab Honstet* does not throw light on either of these two young German settlers.

899. These three sons of Małgorzata and Jakub Błoński were well educated. Jan and Piotr attended the Synod of Raków in 1618. Jan inscribed himself in the album of Andrzej Lubieniecki in Italian and Spanish.

900. This is the first indication in the *Historia* of how often services might be held besides on Sunday.

901. After the condemnation of Schlichtyng, the Błoński family turned Calvinist to avoid further persecution. Włodzimierz Budka, and the descendants of Jan and Piotr became Catholic, "Błoński, Piotr," *PB* 2 (1936) 139A.

902. Stanisław Chronowski (*Historia, 266*) served Hieronim Filipowski the Younger, *magnus incisor* (grand carver) to the King, and later took part in the Filipowski embassy to Turkey (*Historia, 53*). Later Chronowski left the court, and sometime before 1618 founded the church on his estate of Robków or Bakowa in district of Biecz. He died in 1622. *Life of Wiszowaty, Bant*, 243; *Polish Brethren*, no. 98.3; Merczyng, *Zbory i Senatorowie*, 117.

903. On Paweł Brzeski there is a paragraph in *The Life of Lubieniecki, Polish Brethren*, Doc. XXVIII, 522. A convert from the Calvinist position, Brzeski had turned the *zbór* of his village of Pilnia near Sanok to affiliation with the Minor Church. The Author married his daughter Zofia Brzeska, 12 January 1652. It is hard to imagine Master Brzeski's attendance upon communion services in Lusławice so far from Pielnia. Perhaps he had a residence in Cracow.

904. Adam Gosławski is mentioned *Historia, 25, 240*; Andrzej, *240*. They were almost certainly the sons of Krzysztof G. and Dorota Filipowska. Brought up Reformed, they moved with the Minor Church. Adam G. came under the inlfuence in Śmigiel of the two tutors of the sons of Dudith there, Walenty Schmalz and A. Wajdówski. In 1596 Adam G. was a student in Altdorf.

905. Walenty Dembiński (d. 1585) was an irenic Catholic, ranking as first lay Senator. Barbara erected the monument to him in the crypt in the Wawel. Anna Dembińska, *PSB* 5 (1939–46) 78–79.

906. Translating *percari* as a misprint for *parcari*.

907. Lubieniecki may have erred here, or Gosławski reconstructed his work, since a

book of his is extant *Disputatio de persona, in qua Jacobo Martini professore Witenberg-ensi, ea in libro secondu de tribus Elohim refellere enitente, quae ab auctore contra Bartholomaeum Keckermannum, parte tertia disputata sunt, tum de ratione personae in genere sumptae, tum de definitione divinae personae, a Justino, ut vulgo creditur, tradita, respondetur* (Raków, 1620). Gryczowa, no. 122. This book was ready in 1620 and the synod of Raków appreciated it so highly that it ordered it to be printed before other works. Bock, *Antitrin.* 1.409.

The book was the outcome of a controversy started by Bartholomaus Keckermann, an outstanding teacher of the Danzig Gymnasium, in his *Systema SS. theologiae tribus libris adornata* (Hanover, 1602). Keckermann in the third chapter of his first book (pp. 15ff.), "De tribus in unica Dei essentia personis," formulated the orthodox tenets in terms of philosophy. Gosławski attacked him in his *Refutatio eorum quae Bartholomaeus Kecker-mannus in libro primo Systematis sui Theologici disputat* (Raków, 1613). This had been written in Krassów in 1607. Jacob Martini, although otherwise opposing Keckermann as a crypto-Calvinist (e.g. *De communicatione proprii liber unus contra B. Keckermannun*, Wittenberg, 1609), attempted a rejoinder in his *De tribus Elohim libri III* (Wittenberg, 1614). Gosławski again replied to Martini in the book quoted. Estreicher's reference to Martini (22.195) is incomplete. Andrzej Moskorozowski was commissioned by the synod of Raków of 1625 to write a further polemic, but this work is not extant. Bock, *Antitrin.*, 1.521.

908. Stanisław Tarzycki is mentioned *Historia, 272*. Of the Maciej Tarzycki mentioned here, besides Kiryl and Zygmunt (below) there may have been an Andrzej. An Andrzej from Lusławice is signatory of the letter of the exiles in Kreuzburg, 17 June 1661, *Historia, 303*; *Polish Brethren*, 653.

909. Horace *Ars Poetica* 1.161.

910. His pontificate extended from 1642 to 1657.

911. In the same paragraph above, Achacy is identified as Zygmunt's uncle. The force here of "Achacio *alteri*" is not clear.

912. This could be a son perhaps of the widowed Anna Zabawska, *matrona nobilis*, of the Farnovian congregation who published a *Liber Precum Polonicarum.* Under Varnovius, *BAnt*, 53.

913. Lubieniecki does not reach this point in his projected narrative although he has more on Czaplic immediately.

914. Anna Czermińska Taszycka.

915. In Chmaj, ed., *Listy, List* 75 is dated from Igołomia, 14 June 1598. *List* 76 is dated Lusławice 31 August 1598, as are all others, except those from Raków.

916. On Socinus' grave, see Zbysław Ciołkosz, "W starem gnieździe arjańskiem," *RwP* 2 (1922) 281–85, and Kazimierz Dobrowolski, "Trzej Poeci u grobu Socyna," ibid., 285–87. A substantial monument of four Doric columns was erected about the original stone there in 1933, largely through the effort of Earl Morse Wilbur. See his, "The Grave and Monument of Faustus Socinus at Lusławice," *Proceedings of the Unitarian Historical Society* (1936). Pictures of the stone as once sheltered from the elements and as protected further in 1933 may be seen conveniently in Chmaj, *Listy*, 1, opp. 250; 2, opp. 306.

917. Piotr Statorius, Jr., was appointed minister of Lusławice in 1588 when only 22 years of age, and was a constant collaborator of Socinus. He moved to Raków later and died there 9 May 1605. *BAnt*, 93; Bock, *Antitrin.*, 1.922.

NOTES TO CHAPTER SIXTEEN

918. See Orest Levytskyi, "Socinianism in Poland and South-West Rus," *The Annals of the Ukrainian Academy of Arts and Sciences in the U.S.*, 3:1 (1953) 485–508, and my "Protestants in the Ukraine," 184–210.

919. Roman is mentioned *Historia, 267*.

920. On the church and the school at Hoszcza, see n. 389.

921. The cultural and religious influence of the Antitrinitarians in Volhynia and in the palatinate of Kiev dates from the 1560s. Already at the press in Nieśwież in 1562 Szymon Budny had published a *Katichezis* in Cyrillic translation. Kawecka-Gryczowa, *Drukarze dawnej Polski: wielkie Księstwo Litewski*, 190, plate 13. There were some attempts specifically by the Minor church dispersed in Byzantine-rite territories to proselytize the Ruthenian boyars and burghers, as is suggested by Budny, Budziński, and Kolodynski's forging the Epistle of Ivan Smera to Prince Vladimir (Bk. 2, nn. 26–33). In 1581 Valenty Niegalewski in Chroszów in Volhynia translated Czechowic's version of the New Testament into Ruthenian. Szczucki, *Czechowic*, 265, n. 52.

It is possible that the Ostrih Bible in Old Slavonic (Ostrog, 1580–81), under the auspices of Prince Vasilyi Kostiantyn (Konstanty) (c. 1526–1608) was, as evidenced in its two prefaces that stress the two nature of Christ, directed against the proselytizing efforts of the Minor Church, suggests Robert Mathiesen, "The Making of the Ostrih Bible," *Harvard College Library Bulletin* 29:1 (January 1981) 71–110, specifically 76, 89. Mathiesen may well be correct in his surmise, although the earlier propaganda from the Stancarist School in Dubiecko among Ruthenians could have originally altered Prince Konstanty to the christological hazards in the Reformation scripturalism.

922. Prince Wasyl (Vasilyi) Konstanty (c. 1526–1608) of Ostróg/Ostrih (Ostroszskyi), palatine of Kiev, was the leader of the Byzantine-rite lords who remained Orthodox after the Union of Brest Litovsk in 1595/96.

The Prince was a man of enormous wealth. His estates in Volhynia, the palatinate of Kiev, Podolia, and the palatine of Ruthenia comprised twenty-five large towns, ten smaller towns, and 670 villages. He commanded the obedience of the Greek Orthodox boyars in four palatinates. Through his family connections with Jan Kiszka the antitrinitarian castellan of Vilna, and Krzysztof Radziwiłł, grand hetman of Lithuania, he was able to build up a common front of the Greek Orthodox and various Protestants. His influence was so great that after the death of Stephen Batory (1586), he was considered as a possible elective candidate for the Polish throne. Endeavoring to raise the cultural standard of the Greek Orthodox Church, he founded an Academy at Ostrog sometime before 1581, but in his struggle against the Roman Catholic church he had to use the services of the full range of Protestant forces. When Piotr Skarga, S.J., dedicated to him his book *O jedności Kościoła/On the Unity of the Church under one Shepherd, and of the Greek schism from this unity* (Vilna, 1577), Prince Konstanty indignantly commissioned a Ruthenian Unitarian, Motovilo, to compose a reply (not extant)!

From 1595 to 1599, Konstanty together with Radziwiłł engineered a political alliance between the Greek Orthodox and the Protestants in order to withstand the Union of Brest of 1596, in which Orthodox bishops within the Kingdom of Poland and the Grand Duchy rendered obedience to Rome, while retaining their liturgy. Skarga, originally critical of the Greek Churches, defended the Union in *Synod Brzeski* (Cracow, 2 printings, 1597), translated into Byelorussian (Vilna, 1597) by Uniate Bishop Adam Potiy. Against Skarga, Prince Konstanty commissioned an otherwise unknown and quite plausibly a

Unitarian controversialist to write in Polish the basic polemical work, *Apokrizis or Reply to the Book on the Synod of Brest, given in vehement haste in the name of the people of the ancient Greek Religion* (Vilna, 1597; Ruthenian version, 1598). This work was by "Christopher Philaleth," the name doubly referring to his own party as bearers of Christ and lovers of the truth. This work, around which Roman and Greek polemics turned, even into the seventeenth century, was variously ascribed in Socinian circles to Krzysztof Broński, a Unitarian, and to Marcin Broniewski, a Calvinist publicist, once secretary to king Stephen Batory. In the place of Kosntanty in Vilna, 15 – 20 May 1599, Orthodox princes and Calvinists deliberated and signed a general confederation of mutual defense.

J. Tretiak, *Piotr skarga w dziejach i literaturze Unii Brzeskiej* (Cracow, 1912) 74, 77 – 81, 144, 173, 179ff., 224ff.; J. Łukaszewicz, *Dzieje kościołów wyznania helweckiego w Litwie* (Poznań, 1842) 1.123 – 34; K. Lewicki, *Książe Konstanty Ostrogski a Unia Brzeska, 1596* (Lwów, 1933); Teresa Chynczewska-Hennel, *PSB* 24 (1979) 489 – 95; my "Peter Skarga," 183 – 87. Kaziermierz Chudynicki argues that "Christopher Philaleth" could not have been Broniewski, *PSB* 2 (1936) 462; and dolmet Oljančyn, "Zur Frage der Generalkenföderation zwischen protestanten und Orthodoxen in Wilna 1599," *Kairos* 1 (1936) 29 – 46.

923. Gabriel Johski was nominally court steward of Prince Konstanty Ostrogski.

924. The Lubartów here seems to be a corruption. The famous center of Protestantism, Lewartów in the palatinate of Lublin, was not owned by Ostrogski. There are a few places of the same name in Lithuania. The reference may be to the small town of Lubar in Volhynia. See *SGKP* 5.374 – 81.

925. As to the churches of the Brethren founded on the prince's estates, that in Ostróg was founded before 1608, i.e., before the death of the prince, and still existed in 1617/18, but was probably closed down in 1624 when the prince's granddaughter Anna Aloisa, wife of Jan Karol Chodkiewic, grand general of Lithuania, who was herself a Roman Catholic, also closed down the Academy of Ostróg and created a Jesuit college instead. Nothing is known about the church at Ostropol. The town of Konstantynów, or rather Starokonstantynów, on the river Słucz, founded by Prince Konstanty in 1561, belonged to Aleksander, the prince's son, the only member of the family who remained true to the Greek Orthodox faith, but who died before his father. The church of the Polish Brethren must have been founded there before 1608, and probably was closed after 1620, but a congregation seems to have continued there until the Cossack Wars. See *Life of Wiszowaty, BAnt*, 241; *Polish Brethren*, no. 97.

926. Lubieniecki seems to confuse Teodor Krzysztof Sieniuta with his heir, Krzysztof Paivel.

927. On "Daniel" Rudnicki, see Lubieniecki *Historia, 269 – 70*; see n. 872.

928. The churches at Lachowice and probably at Sieniutowice were founded in 1608. K. P. Sieniuta and his brother Piotr were the successive patrons of Lachowice. To Piotr's brother the task fell of carrying out the Tribunal decree of 1644 which closed the church and imposed a fine.

The ministers at Lachowice were Krzysztof Stoiński (1608 – 12); Joachim Rupniowski (?1615 – 25), Rupniowski's assistants were Piotr Morzkowski, 1619, and Timotheus Hoffmann, 1623; Piotr Morzkowski (1625 – 28); and Jakub Siedlecki (1628 – 40?). Under the patronage of Piotr Sieniuta, the minister's functions were probably carried out by Jan Cichowski, minister from 1641 until 1643 in nearby Tychorul owned by Abraham Sieniuta. In 1644 the minister was Jan Stoiński. Although the church was closed in 1644, the congregation probably continued to meet until 1650.

Piotr Morzkowski, an alumnus of Raków, was chosen to deliver the funeral oration for Jakub Sienieński in 1639. Later he was commissioned by the synod to compile the *Ecclesiastical Polity, Polish Brethren*, Doc. XXIII.

929. *Historia, 208, 265, 271*.

930. Lubieniecki erroneously says *nati Joanne Czaplicio*. Both Teodor and Jan Czaplic were land judges of Łuck. However, Jan, who died c. 1600, had been promoted to 1585 to the post of castellan of Kiev, a fact which would certainly have been in the sources used by Lubieniecki. Kazimierz Chodycki, *PSB* 4 (1938) 170–74; Merczyng, *Zbory i senatorowie*, 123; *Polish Brethren*, 26 *passim*.

931. It is not certain what place Lubieniecki meant by *Beresteciae*, whether Beresko (Bersk) or Beresteczko. Both places were owned by Marcin Czaplic and both were situated in the district of Łuck. It was in Beresko that a school was founded as a branch of the academy of Kisielin. Merczyng, *Zbory i Senatorowie*, 106. Both the churches were probably founded by 1612. In Beresko, the ministers were Joachim Rupniowski (1626–41) and Stanisław Gejżanawski (1643–44). The church and school were abolished by the Lublin Tribuntal decree of 1644. *Polish Brethren*, 30ff.

932. In Kisielin, the most important of the Unitarian churches of Volynia, the ministers were Joachim Rupniowski (1612–18), and Maciej Twardochleb (1615–45), assisted by Jakub Ryniewicz (1631–45). (Szczotka, "Synody," 74, erroneously calls Jakub Jan). The congregation included numerous burghers and peasants. The serfs who joined it were liberated from serfdom. The church was abolished in 1644 by the Tribunal, but its patron refused to execute the decree. The congregation probably continued to meet until his death (in or soon after 1648), or at least until the Cossack wars of 1648. We know, for instance, in 1644 Andrzej Wiszowaty, who had been appointed minister at Iwanice and Haliczany, was also put in charge of both Beresko and Kisielin. Bock, *Antitrin.* 1.368, 736, 739, 977–980, 1013; Szczotka, "Synody," 62; and Merczyng, *Zbory i Senatorowie*, 109; 4.170; *Polish Brethren*, 3 passim.

933. Szpanów was the family estate of the Szpanowski branch of the Czaplic family. Paweł Ryniewicz was minister there, 1626–29. See Bock, *Antitrin.* 1.740.

934. Miłostów is known only from this refrence in Lubieniecki.

935. Cf. *Life of Wiszowaty, BAnt*, 236–37; *Polish Brethren*, no. 91.

936. The school of Kisielin was probably founded together with the church. See n. 932. Its rectors were Eustacjusz Gizel (Kisiel) (1634–38) who probably taught until the school was closed; Peter Stegmann (Tribander) (1638–40); Teodor Simon, i.e., Philippus Cosmius (1640) (n. 937); and Ludwig Hohleisen (1640 until the church closed). The school was ordered closed by the Tribunal decree of 1644, but probably continued for some time under the protection of its patrons. Bock, *Antitrin.*, 111–16, 401–02, 417, 965–66. Gizel appears to have been a German, not the father of Adam Kysil; but see on this figure some treatment of religious currents in the Ukraine by Frank Edward Michael Sysyn, *Adam Kysil: Statesman of Poland-Lithuania: A Study of the Commonwealth rule of the Ukraine from 1600 to 1653* (Cambridge: Harvard University doctoral thesis, 1977; to be published in 1985).

937. Philippus Cosmius, a Lutheran and a teacher in Lüneburg, converted to Roman Catholicism in 1628, but in 1630 returned to the Lutheran Church and wrote his *Retractaio*, probably published in Hamburg. It was printed again in Leiden in 1631, also in a German translation. The reference here is probably to his main work against the Papacy, *De statu et religione propria Papatus, adversus Cornelium episcopum Iprensem* (Leiden, 1638). The force of *Cosmius*, unless it means *cosmicus*, citizen of the world, is not evident.

938. Cosmius enlarged the *Janua linguarum reserata* (the door of language unlocked) of 1631 by Jan Amos Komenský (Comenius), one of the greatest pedagogues of the century. Born in Nivniče in Moravia, 1592, the Czech Brother Comenuis was educated at Herborn and Heidelberg. He returned to Moravia as pastor in Fulnek. With the outbreak of the Thirty Years' War, his church was destroyed. In 1627 he led the persecuted Czech Brethren to Leszno (Lissa), the synodal and educational center of the Czech Brethren in Great Poland, near Śmigiel. After teaching in the academy there, Comenius became *notarius* (in effect superintendent) of the Polish Branch of the Unitas Fratrum. From Leszno he traveled extensively in England, Sweden, Hungary. The academy came to an end in 1650 as a casualty of the Northern War. Comenius died in Amsterdam in 1670.

Cosmius compiled a Latin-Greek edition of the *Janua* some time before 1642. The printer Louis Elzevier obtained permission for its publication from the Estates General of Holland on 19 June and 8 July 1642 and published it as *Janua Aurea Linguarum, et auctior et emaculatior quam umquam antehac cum adjuncta graeca versione* (Amsterdam, 1642; 2nd ed., 1649). In his foreword (omitted in subsequent editions) Cosmius says: "Everybody is endangered by his vices; my vice has been that I could not restrain my pen. I resolved to descend into another arena." This earliest edition was republished by Nathaniel Duer with royal permission in Danzig in 1643 (with a Polish text added by Andrzej Węgierski). Duer added French and Italian translations in a Frankfurt edition of 1644. In 1649 Elzevier published a new edition, emended by Étienne de Courcelles (Episcopius's successor in Amsterdam, d. 1712), with a French translation. The London editions of the *Janua* (in 1662 and 1670) make use of the text of Cosmius, as emended by de Courcelles, without mentioning their names.

939. After the fall of Raków, synods were held in Kisielin in 1638, 1639, and 1640. After the fall of Kisielin synods convened in the neighboring town of Dążwa, in the possession of the Suchodolski family, in 1646, 1647 and 1648. Szczotka, "Synody," 74.

940. The chapter was never written. In 1640 the bishop of Łuck, Andrzej Gembicki, and the dean of Włodzimierz, Stanisław Urbanowic, accused Jerzy Czaplic of secretly continuing the school of Raków, which had been closed by the earlier decree of 1638. The case was transferred from Włodzimierz to the Lublin Tribunal which on 18 May 1644 ordered the closing of the school and the church in Kisielin and the expulsion of all ministers. Czaplic was fined the sum of 500 ducats and costs, and obliged to pay the same amount to the episcopal chapter of Łuck. The gentry of Volhynia protested in their dietine at Łuck in 1645, and Czaplic refused to comply with the sentence. He was promptly banished and degraded from the nobility by the Tribunal, but he found strong support among the gentry of Volhynia in 1646, and at the diet in Warsaw of 1647. The school was probably continued until his death about 1648. *Life of Wiszowaty, BAnt*, 236–37; *Polish Brethren*, Doc. I, no. 91, 91.1; *PSB* 4.170.

941. The church at Czerniechów (district of Żytomierz in the palatine of Kiev) had been founded by Stefan Niemirycz by the year 1610. Although in 1646 the Tribunal ordered the church to be closed, it probably continued until 1661/2 except for an interval from 1649 until 1652 during the Cossack wars. Its ministers were Piotr Stoiński (1610–49) and Jerzy Ciachowski (1652–1661/62). See Bock, *Antitrin.*, 100–01, 948. The rectors of the school were: [? Johannes] Ferberinus (1637–39); Paweł Myślik (1639–41) formerly teacher at Raków; and Ferdinand Leisentritt (1641–?). The other two mentioned by Lubieniecki, Woch and Debel, have not been tracked down. Bock, *Antitrin.*, 1.355, 429, 523.

942. The church at Hoszcza, district of Łuck, was founded by Gabriel Hojski by the

year 1600. The first minister was Krzysztof Morskowski, already there by 1605, who was followed by Andrzej Lubieniecki (there in 1609), Samuel Nieciecki (1612 – ?), and Krzysztof Stoiński (there in 1618). The date of the dispersal of the church is unknown, probably either in 1639 or 1644. Of the rectors of the school, only Solomon Paludius (1616 – 20) is known. Bock, *Antitrin.*, 438, 547, 587 – 88, 948, 979 – 80; Szczotka, "Synody," 57, *Polish Brethren*, 84; 179, n. 6.

The False Dmitri (Samozwaniec), who claimed to be Dmitir Ivanovich, the murdered son of Ivan the Terrible, was rebaptized in Hoszcza and probably studied there, before challenging Tsar Boris Gudunov (1598 – 1605) and his son Theodore II (1605). After the boyars murdered Theodore, Dmitir Samozwaniech briefly replaced him on the throne. Basil Shuisky, with a faction of boyars, murdered Dmitri and replaced him in 1606, supported by Sigismund III. A second False Dmitri defeated Basil Shuisky in 1608.

943. Babin, district of Łuck. The Orthodox church there was converted into a Unitarian church. In 1649 Piotr Stoiński III was appointed minister. The church probably continued until the banishment of all "Arians." Bock, *Antitrin.*, 1.948; Merczyng, *Zbory i Senatorowie*, 106.

944. On Czerniechow, see n. 941.

945. Szersznie, in the palatine of Kiev, first belonged to the Niemirycz family, and later (sometime before 1639) to Stefan Wojnarowski, master of the Hunt of the palatinate of Kiev. The church was probably founded shortly before 1639. Its minister was Jan Stoiński (1641 until at least 1644), who at the same time took charge of the church at Uszomir, assisted by Andrew Wiszowaty (1643 – 44). See *Life of Wiszowaty, BAnt*, 235; *Polish Brethren*, no. 87; Bock, *Antitrin.*, 1.939, 1013.

946. Uszomir was in the district of Owruc in the palatinate of Kiev. Its church was probably founded at the same time as that of the church at Szersznie. Its ministers were Jan Stoiński (1640/41 – 44), Krystyn Brzozowski (1644 – 45), and Joachim Stegmann (1645 – 49). A school was also established with Isaak Vogler (or Foecher, Fockler), a Lutheran divine and scholar from Baden, appointed as rector in 1643, and Stanisław Gejżanowski appointed as teacher. See Bock, *Antitrin.*, 1.79, 356, 369, 939, 959; *Polish Brethren*, 58, n. 77.

947. When Lubieniecki wrote these lines, he was suffering horribly from mercury poison from which also his two daughters had already died.

948. Benedict Wiszowaty (d. after 1704) was the son of Andrew Wiszowaty (1608 – 78).

Of Andrew Wiszowaty, whose *Life* is translated in *Polish Brethren*, Doc. I, it may be noted here, near the conclusion of the annotation, in order to suggest the scope of the movement partly chronicled and documented by Lubieniecki in his unfinished *Historia*, that one of his works was destined to become the first writing of the "Protestant Reformation" to be turned into Arabic. Andrew Wiszowaty's *Stimuli virtutum ac fraena peccatorum* was seen to the press after his death by his son, Amsterdam, 1698. *BAnt*, 146. Dimitrie Cantemir (1673 – 1723), voivode of Moldavia, translated this into Rumanian and Greek as the third part of his *Divanul Lumii*/κριτήριοντο κόσμου (Jassy, 1698). The Greek text was translated into Arabic in Bucharest in 1705. See the introduction to the critical edition by Virgil Căndea, *Opere complete*, 4 vols. (Bucharest: Academei Republicii Socialiste România) 1 (1974) esp. 22 with the pagination of the third part, also after p. 80, plate of title page of the copy of *Stimuli* in Cluj. These translations testify to the general influence of the Polish Brethren by way of the school of Johann Sommer under Heraclides Basilicus and more directly the Unitarians at Kolozsvár/Cluj.

Of Benedict Wiszowaty, it is now established that he was the author of *Medulla*

Historiae Ecclesiasticae, which exists in two as yet unpbulished MSS. The first in Hamburg, the second in Lech Szczucki, "Socinian Historiography," in Church and George, *Continuity and Discontinuity*, 285 – 300. On p. 289, n. 11 Szczucki gives the chapter headings of the *Medulla*, in which only chapter 25 deals with *saeculum 16 et 17*. Of interest is chapter 20, *De ecclesiis in Aegypto saec. 10*, which evidences Wiszowaty's own confidence in the reliability of the spurious Epistle of Smera, Bk. 2, nn. 26 – 33.

949. Lubieniecki's *Life, Polish Brethren*, Doc. XXVIII, 527, n. 92. Ludwik Chmaj deals with the two letters in *Samuel Przypkowski na tle prądów religijnych XVII wieku* (Cracow, 1927) 55 – 56.

950. For the role of the Przypkowski family in the Reformation movement, see Włodzimierz Budka, "Przypkowski i rola ich w ruchu reformacyjnym," *RwP* 4 (1926) 60 – 73, with a genealogical table.

951. For a map of the movement of Bogdan Chmielnicki with his allied Crimean Tatars (Muslim), Cossacks (Orthodox), and smoldering peasants (Orthodox), up the right bank of the Dnieper almost to Kiev and then west almost to Lublin and also for the whole area dominated by him (1648 – 54), see *Atlas Historyczny Polski*, 26.

The newly elected King of Poland, during this disastrous period, was the younger brother of Ladislas IV John Casimir, (1648 – 1668), who had been a Jesuit priest and a cardinal, but he was dispensed from his vows by the Pope at this critical juncture in Polish destiny. Before his coronation John Casimir vowed to the Virgin in the cathedral in Lwów that he would spread devotion to her everywhere in the land she was besought to protect; and just before the Swedish attack on Warsaw he specified that he would banish the Arians. See Wilbur, *Socinianism*, chap. 36; *Cambridge Poland*, chaps. 23 A and B; *Polish Brethren*, Plate K.

NOTES TO RELATED DOCUMENTS

Notes to *RD* 1: Modrzewski, Visit of Spiritus

1. In translation the Latin text in *BAnt* breaks easily into two paragraphs, which, if they were not here detached from that narrative, would be numbered nos. 64 and 65. The first of these "paragraphs" is an excerpt from the *Sylva* (1590) of Modrzewski, quoted also by Lubieniecki in the *Historia* (n. 5 below), and the second, a clustering of three quotations from Budziński's History (chap. 4), evidently still accessible to Wiszowaty as of 1684, of which chapter Lubieniecki preserves in Latin, in general, more of the lost Polish original than Wiszowaty has.

Apart from affording a glimpse into how Lubieniecki used his major source, the clustering (in the third quotation, at n. 8) uniquely preserves Budziński's own assessment of the impact of the Netherlandish visitor's query about prayers addressed separately to the Persons of the Trinity. Of the impact Budziński used the brutal metaphor of a hook (*uncus*/*hak*) driven deep, that is, as into the neck of a condemned criminal to be dragged off in the quick to the Tiber—if, to be sure, in the presumed Polish word, the ex-Franciscan Chronicler was aware of the specificity of the Latin word by which a century after the event Wiszowaty would render his *hak*. This word could simply have meant hook. In any case, Lubieniecki, for his part, chose to drop it from his otherwise more detailed paraphrasing of Budziński's chapter 4.

The visceral vividness of this image would make it plausible that Budziński was indeed himself present when the dogma of the Trinity was challenged at the famous humanist repast, presumably with Lismanino and in his own capacity as secretary to him. For his part, Modrzewski, who ended his days among Racovians, eschewed in his *Sylva* the naming of any of the guests or even the host. That is why both Lubieniecki and here Wiszowaty resorted to the History of Budziński for further details on the personages and atmospherics. They both had some animus toward the excommunicated Budziński, however much they were often dependent on him for documentation and narrative. They both drew upon his chapter 4 to supplement Modrzewski without identifying its author as an eye witness. Although the Chronicler could have read the *Sylva* when it still circulated in MS before 1590, yet his own proffered circumstantial details and the vividness of the metaphor of the hook, not out of character with what else we know of Budziński, may be the lingering scrap of evidence that he was, indeed, a fellow guest with Spiritus and Modrzewski at the house of Andrzej Trzecieski in Cracow, c. 1546, and that, in any case, more than the renowned Modrzewski, established the visit of Spiritus as a decisive event in the historiography of the Polish Brethren, and that Budziński was also reliable as to the date 1547.

2. The text of the *Sylva* is found in the critical edition, *Opera omnia*, ed. by Kazimierz Kumaniecki, 5 (Warsaw, 1960) 109.

3. Jan/Andrzej Trzecieski was the father of Andrzej the poet-humanist. See *Historia*, Book 1, n. 169, ¶¶1–3.

4. On the possible identity of the *Belga*, Spiritus, see *Historia*, Book 1, n. 178 and below, n. 10.

As to the date of the visit regarded as theologically momentous by the Socinians, Modrzewski gives, if memory fails him not, 1546. Several other sources, perhaps all going back to Budziński, give 1547, two of them at least cognizant of Modrzewski's text and conjecture as to the year. Of these two, Lubieniecki is explicit. Andrzej Wiszowaty, writing in Amsterdam before 1678, only alludes to the synchronous departure of Laelius Socinus from Italy in 1547 ''and in the same year'' the arrival of Spiritus in Cracow. Lubieniecki and A. Wiszowaty would both have been disposed to mine the slight uncertainty of Modrzewski for the ore of providential evidences. The anonymous Lusławice Chronicler, RD 5, n. 20, begins his skimpy Chronicle (c. 1618) precisely with the emphatic dating of the Spirtus visit in 1547.

Besides the obvious possibility that the theologically decisive dinner took place in the cold months of transition from old to the new year, 1546/47, and therefore differently fixed in the memory of participants, one may surmise that Budziński for some reason held expressly to 1547 and that alike the Lusławice Chronicler, Andrzej Wiszowaty, and Lubieniecki all had reason to regard Budziński's determination to take precedence over the recollection of Modrzewski. The Lusławice Chronicler, to be sure, only indirectly testifies to the independent authority of Budziński in that, having made his opening entry, 1547, the Spiritus episode he then jumps to the year 1553, noting in a few lines that Lismanino and Budziński ''were taken for Arians'' and that the latter in the same year began his History, inferrably the source of the preceding entry for 1547, *Slavonia Reformata*, 508. We have already noted the chance evidence that Budziński might well have been at the dinner himself (above, n. 1 ¶ 3). A professional archivist, writing closer to the event than Modrzewski and about an urban society with which he was at home, Budziński provided the date which Lubieniecki in particular described as the more congenial and compelling in the light of his providential historiography. I would opt for 1547 with the proviso that Budziński, even in the face of Modrzewski's text at least in MS and yet perhaps no more certain than he of the exact time, might simply have retrospectively fixed upon the year coincident with that of the death of the well remembered host and also, not without interest, synchronous with the departure of Laelius Socinus from Italy (a connection preserved evidently from Budziński by A. Wiszowaty who could only have read the History in MS, not the *Historia*).

5. The portion of the passage from Modrzewski between asterisks (* – **) is quoted independently by Lubieniecki in the *Historia, 19*, where it is separated from passage ** – *** by an intercalated passage from Budziński's History, chap. 4, parallel to what follows here. In Lubieniecki's transcription there are included three further sentences from Modrzewski, *ibid., 19 – 20*.

6. See n. 3.

7. These persons are mentioned in a different rendition from the same Polish History, *Historia*, Book 1 at n. 170. Here, however, Wiszowaty preserves the further detail from Budziński, namely, that Wojewódka was also a pupil of Erasmus. The library of Erasmus, bought by Jan Łaski from the master in 1525 when he lived as a student with him in Basel, was brought to Cracow by Modrzewski for him in April 1537, 413 volumes in three big chests, subsequently dispersed. See my ''Erasmianism in Poland,'' *PR, 26*, n. 78; for the calendared correspondence with Poles, see Maria Cytowska, *Korespondencja Erasma z Rotterdamu z Polakami* (Warsaw: PIW, 1965) and for the larger

cultural-political setting of the letter of Erasmus to Sigismund I (1528), see Danièle Letocha, "Quand Erasme se fait politique," to be published in *Renaissance and Reformation/Renaissance et Réforme* (Toronto).

8. This passage from Budziński is quoted from the Polish in another version in *Historia, 19*.

9. The "I" here is Andrzej Wiszowaty, not Sand.

10. Wiszowaty would fondly like to have it be a unitarian Mennonite, Adam Pastor, so prominent also in the rise of Unitarianism in the Rhine Palatinate, c. 1570, a liberal theologian of the Netherlandish urban Mennonites, among whom he felt at home. Adam Pastor, excommunicated by Menno Simmons, wrote a series of works, ed. by S. Cramer, *Bibliotheca Reformatoria Nederlandica*, 5 (1900) 317–59.

Notes to *RD* 2: Stoiński, Epitome

1. Jan Stoiński (1590–1654) was the son of Piotr Statorius Stoiński Junior and of the daughter of Grzegorz Paweł. He was the pastor in Raków, 1612–38. He engaged in disputations with Catholics in Lublin in 1616 and 1620. He removed to Amsterdam in 1638. From there he wrote a letter, 24 July 1638, to Adam Franck, minister in Kolozsvár. He returned to the Commonwealth and became, c. 1641, pastor in Szersznie to his friend and patron Lord Stefan Wojnarowski, master of the king's hunt in the palatinate of Kiev. He removed to Czarkowy c. 1648. *BAnt*, 121–22, 227, 235; *PB* (nos. 75.2, 87). For Stoiński's disputations in Lublin, 1615, 1616 (cf. below n. 12.1), 1620, see *Historia*, Book 3, n. 800. At some point Stoiński visited Transylvania, of which trip he wrote a *Relatio* and other letters in the same year to the Polish churches.

2. Such is the title given the condensation by Bendedykt Wiszowaty (BW), who also supplies, now in brackets, additional or much compacted material.

3. Such is the original title of the MS, *BAnt*, 122, 183.

4. 21–29 January 1556. Sipayłło, *AS*, 1.46–52.

5. Sipayłło refers to this in her "Wykaz synodów," *AS*, 1.xxxiv, 18 nn. f. and 1; and Lubieniecki, *Historia, 56–59*.

6. For Wiszowaty the *Senex minister* is the great uncle of the Author of the *Historia*, and he draws here either on Andrzej Lubieniecki's lost MS *Acta et conclusiones synodorum* in Polish (rather than his *Poloneutychia*) or his lost MS *Chronicon seu descriptio Regni Dei* in Polish, *BAnt*, 89.

Counting the synod of Pińczów of 1 May 1555 as the first, Stoiński cites specifically synods 1, 2, 9, 10, 12, 17, 19, 20, 21, 22, and without number several others.

7. The Czech Brethren.

8. The colloquium took place in Great Poland, 24 August–2 September 1555. Sipayłło, *AS*, 1.18–45.

9. The reference is obscure. In general the Polish lords and ministers felt that the late medieval synodal discipline of the Czech Brethren was too severe and that their center of authority lay beyond their borders, in Moravia. But cf. the same A. Lubieniecki, RD 6 at n. 19. After Koźminek, a delegation of Czech Brethren attended the synod of Pińczów, 24 April–1 May 1556, and made extensive observations and answered disciplinary questions; Sipayłło, *AS*, 1.53–71.

10. This synod in Pińczów in November 1558 is obscure.

11. Text has incorrectly *Polonia Major*.

12. See n. 6.

13. Sipayłło, *AS*, 1.297 – 300.

14. The synod extended from 25 December 1560 to 30 January 1561. Sipayłło, *AS*, 2.72 – 91; Lubieniecki, *Historia, 148 – 49*.

15. 14 – 19 September 1560. Sipayłło, *AS*, 2.32 – 68.

16. Statorius Gallicus is referred in the minutes of the synod of Pełsznica of 13 May 1557, when he was granted a salary as teacher of the Pińczów school. Sipayłło, *AS*, 1.177. He is mentioned incidentally in connection with the synod in Krzcięcice, 6 – 8 December 1556, ibid., 160.

17. See Lubieniecki, *Historia, 126*.

18. The speeches are given in full in Lubieniecki, *Historia, 127 – 129*.

19. Lubieniecki, *Historia, 119 – 126*. The complaints were voiced by Sarnicki. Biandrata will be recurrently urged to supply a *confessio*, hence Wiszowaty's *N.B.*

20. 10 March 1562. Sipayłło, *AS*, 2.129 – 31; Lubieniecki, *Historia, 130 – 31*.

21. The reference is to Calvin's dedicatory preface to Grand Duke Mikołaj Radziwiłł; Lubieniecki, *Historia, 130 – 31*; Book 2, n. 527.

22. 20 July 1562. Sipayłło, *AS*, 2.134 – 36.

23. 12 August 1562. Sipayłło, *AS*, 2.137 – 38.

24. 18 August 1562. Sipayłło, *AS*, 2.138 – 39.

25. The protocol of Pińczów, 18 August 1562, preserves the primitive form of what happened: ''In that time when our brethren were contending in Cracow thus about the Trinity, lightning struck the ball [atop] the church of the Holy Trinity, which our side took as a sign given by the Lord God to give them succor in getting rid of the great error introduced into the Church of God by Antichrist, the dogma of the Trinity, and the Lord God assisted.'' Sipayłło, *AS*, 2.140. The church was that of the Dominicans. The telling of the event was embellished by Sand (*BAnt*, 43, on Grzegorz Paweł and by Wiszowaty, *BAnt*, no. 56). There was a similar sign in Lublin in 1616, at n. 29.

Wilbur, who has a good note on the Cracow event (*Socinianism*, 312, n. 23), was tempted to wonder whether the tale of Cracow and another in Transylvania did not embody as much faith and fancy as fact. My own father, Dr. David Rhys Williams, minister of the First Unitarian Church of Rochester, NY, (1928 – 58), used to tell also with some relish the story handed down that when the first Unitarian Society in 1888 purchased from the Third Presbyterian Church their Gothic edifice, lightning struck the steeple and snapped off the weather vane of trinitarian design as though in approbation of the new occupancy.

26. See Lubieniecki, *Historia*, Book 3, chap. 3, 260 – 64.

27. The general Diet in Warsaw sat 12 October to 24 November 1627.

28. Andrzej Zborowski, Jr. (c. 1583 – 1630) was count of Melsztyn and castellan of Oswięcim as of 1616.

29. The text has *Odpust* [*Kiermasz*], the last word presumably supplied by Wiszowaty. *Odpust* is the indulgence fair; *Kiermasz* is the town fair. Trinity Sunday is the Sunday after Pentecost, 26 May 1616. Pl. D in *Polish Brethren* shows Lublin in the great fire of 1719. To the left is the pre-Czarist castle (*Zamek*) and the extant church of the Holy Trinity.

30. The protracted negotiation between the churches was initiated by the Brethren after the Major Church lost its impact as a result of the Zebrzydowski Rebellion (1606). The negotiation was fruitless, but provided the Brethren with a good opportunity to assert their views and to develop their doctrine of toleration. Walenty Schmalz, in his *Odpowiedź na książkę J[akuba] Zaborowskiego: Ogień z wodą* (Raków: Sternacki, 1619) (Gryczowa, no. 235), speaks of discussions in Lublin in 1612 and 1619, and in Bełżyce in

1617, but not in Lublin in 1616. There is no mention of such discussion between the two groups of Lublin in the brief protocol of the district synod in Lublin, 24 June 1616. Sipayłło, *AS*, 3, 370–71. In item 10 it is stated that the mission in Lublin continues but that the minister prefers "for certain reasons" not to live there. The information in no. 12 is thus unique to Stoiński.

Notes to *RD* 3: Schomann, Testamentum

1. The text is printed in Polish translation by Lech Szczucki and Janusz Tazbir, eds., *Literatura ariańska w Polsce XVI wieku: Antologia* (Warsaw, 1959), with 54 nn., several of which have enriched this English version.

1. Schomann speaks elsewhere of sons and daughters (no. 41), mentions by name one son (Paweł, no. 24), and three daughters (one unnamed, no. 26), Marta (no. 30), and Elżbieta (n. 35), saying further that he has married off three daughters (n. 54), not counting Elżbieta, who may have been a domestic. He does not mention the death of his wife Anna (n. 29), who would have been 47 at the time of the Testamentum. She received the use of the house (after n. 58).

3. A city of Upper Silesia on the left bank of the Oder, till 1532 seat of an independent principality, subsequently under the Austrian Hapsburgs as kings of Bohemia. Close to the Bohemian frontier, the old Piast territory was linguistically mixed, and Schomann himself was no doubt bilingual and educated to the point of using Latin well.

Silesia, created as one of four hereditary duchies by King Boleslas III Piast, broke down into a congeries of hereditary principalities. It came under the Crown of Bohemia. Some quasi-prinicipalities were sovereign, some directly under the crown of Bohemia. The most important town, Breslau, was also a bishopric, ecclesiastically under the the Primate of Poland into the century of Reformation and beyond. Most of the lands on the left bank of the Oder had been colonized by Germans, except between Breslau and Brzeg, and then further up, between Opole and Racibórz, while from Breslau down to Głogów Germans had colonized also the right bank. The dietine of the Duchy was primarily a Fürstentag, although knights and burghers were present. During the Hussite wars in Silesia, the Duchy with the Margraviate of Moravia fell under the crown of St. Stephen. The Unity of the Czech Brethren was represented in Silesia, especially in the region of Opawa, the Czech-speaking part of Silesia. In Hussitized Hirschenberg (Jelenia Góra) the major theologian Peter Riedemann was born the son of a cobbler. On this see Gustav Koffman, "Die Wiedertäufer in Schlesien," *Korrespondenzblatt der evangelischen Kirche in Schlesien*, 3 (1894) 37–55, in a new context but without the benefit of any volume of *Täuferakten* for Silesia, Leokadia Kowalska, "Anabaptyści śląscy," Ewa Maleczyńska, ed., *Z dziejów postępowej ideologii na Śląsku w. XIV-XVI wieku* (Warsaw, 1956); and in the context of Silesian Spiritualism, Horst Weigelt, *Spiritualistische Tradition in Protestantismus: Die Geschichte des Schwenkfeldertums in Schlesien* (Berlin, 1973). For the Polish Brethren in Silesia, see Władysława Gromek, "Kilka uwag o śląskich Arianach," *ibid.* 226–47, building on Ludwik Chmaj, *Szacy wśród Braci Polskich* (Katowice, 1936). Henryk Barycz deals with the intellectual life of Polish Silesians from the beginnings into the nineteenth century, *Śląsk w polskiej kulturze umysłowej* (Katowice: Wydawnictwo "Śląsk," 1979). The larger context of religious history of Silesia from the German point of view is that of Dr. Colmar, Grünhagen, *Geschichte Schlesiens*, 2 vols. (Gotha, 1886; offset reprint Osnabrük: Ackerstaff & Kuballe, 1979) and Karol Maleczyński, ed. *Historia Śląska*, 5 vols., for the period, 1:2 (Wrocław:

Ossolineum, 1961) esp. pp. 361–403 with maps (index of vols. parts 1–3 a separate part 4, ibid. 1964). See also Pl. 31.

4. See *Historia,* Book 3, n. 369. The hostile pamphlets have not been identified. The Adamites in Bohemia in connection with the marriage ceremony were said to return to the simplicities of paradise before the Fall; my *Radical Reformation*, 208, 597, 511.

5. Cf. Rom 9:21.

6. Christopher Tiachowski (or Ciachowski), Schomann's maternal grandfather, was after 1488 the chancellor of the Przemyslides, princes of Racibórz, John III (1456–1493), Nicholas III, and John IV (1493–1506). The chancellor probably died sometime before 1506. His son, also named Christopher, brother of Schomann's mother Ursula, was canon *Scholasticus* of Racibórz and died 3 January 1516. See A. Weltzel, *Geschichte der Stadt und Herrschaft Ratibor* (2nd edition, Ratibor, 1881) 1907, 103, 709; J. Heyne, *Dokumentierte Geschichte des Bisthums und Hochstiftes Breslau* (Breslau, 1868) 3.1253–54.

7. The coat of arms *Stary kón z toporem* was shared by a number of families in Poland, Lithuania, and Silesia. Schomann's sons later assumed their mother's name and claimed noble rank.

8. The monastery of the Augustines was erected on Sandinsel in the Oder. Its church was called the Sandkirche. *Evangelici* means here the followers of the Wittenberg Reformation.

9. Johann Cyrus was from 1556 of the cathedral chapter of the Holy Cross in Breslau and dean. After being appointed an imperial counselor, he performed several diplomatic missions for Maximilian II in Cracow.

10. In 1562 Cyrus became abbot of the Premonstratensian monastery of St. Vincent's in a suburb of Breslau and died in 1582. See Heyne, *Breslau*, 3.1253–54.

The bishop of Breslau belonged to the province of Gniezno and drew his revenues and princely status from the extensive benefice of Nysa (Neisse) on a left tributary of the Oder. The bishops were Jakub Salza (1520–39) and Baltasar von Promnitz (1539–62).

11. Baron Joachim Maltzan (1492–1556), of a Mecklenburg family, a prominent soldier and Protestant leader, maintained close relations with Poland and Polish Protestants. Schomann's pupils were the younger sons, Johann Joachim, and Johann Franz (not Friederich, as Sand erroneously gives in our text). In 1551, on the pretense of certain debts owed by Joachim Maltzan, Balthasar Promnitz, the bishop of Breslau, in the name of Ferdinand I, occupied Wartenberg to thwart the Protestant faction in Silesia. Joachim Maltzan's sons continued their family's traditional connection with the Polish Protestants. See *ADB*, 20.155–157; B. Schmidt, *Geschichte des Geschlechts von Maltzan und von Maltzahn* (Schleiz, 1913) 2:2.311–358; G. C. F. Lisch, *Urkunden-Sammlung zur Geschichte des Geschlechts von Maltzan* (Schwerin, 1853) 5.229–30, 253–57, 320–22.

12. Emperor Ferdinand I (1556–76), as king of Bohemia and Hungary since 1526, was the overlord of Silesia. Wartenburg is today Syców.

13. Schomann was *baccalaureus* of the parish school of the principal church in the town square, Kościół Mariacki.

14. Hieronim Beck was a German citizen of the town, with whom Schomann lived, perhaps giving lessons.

15. This was the Bursa or the corner of *ulica* Wiślana and Gołębia where poor university students could earn their room and board by serving the rich students (Pl. 31). In Schomann's time there were seven fully endowed bursas and five not so fully endowed. To the first belong that variously called Isnera, Jagiellońska, and Bursa pauperum. Among the less endowed were those of the Majętnych, the Grochowa, the Hungarian, the

German, and the Czech. When the German bursa folded in 1540, it was symptomatic of the desire of many to travel to the universities of the Empire, notably to Leipzig, Wittenberg, and Basel. This closure marked the end of the golden age of the Jagiellonian University as a foremost center of European scholarship. There were five colleges: Majus (the Jagiellonian University proper), Minus, the New, that of law, that of medicine. Józef Muczkowski, *Mieszkania i postępowanie uczniów krakowskich* (Cracow, 1842).

16. The parish school of St. Anne's supplied residences for university students who would teach in the parish.

17. The salt works of Wieliczka were under the royal administration of an engineer, who, because of the major economic importance of the mines, had access to court (Pl. 16).

18. Hieronim Bużeński (c. 1513–80) was in charge of the salt works, c. 1552–77. He was the successor of Seweryn Boner. The mine shafts there are named after them respectively, the Boner and the Bużenin. He was replaced by Prospero Provana (*Historia*, Book 3, n. 4). A canon of Cracow, Bużeński joined the Reformation movement c. 1550, sided for a while with the liberal party, but ended up on the side of the Major Church. He must have been familiar with Szymon Żak (Zacius) (*Historia*, Book 1, n. 227), who in 1563 left his position and as superintendent in Lithuania and returned to Cracovia (Book 3, n. 364) becoming superintendent of the Cracow district, then pastor in the mining town of Bochnia (in 1570), the works there being under Bużeński; and there Zacius occasionally preached to the miners. On Bużeński's career as superintendent of the salt works, see Bocheński, *Przemysł Polski*, 64, 72–73, passim. The preaching to the miners occurred after Schomann had left the salt works. Zacius remained Calvinist and pedobaptist, like Bużeński.

19. The allurements of the world for a teacher of noble sons, from all that we otherwise know of the gentle, thoughtful, and earnest seeker of the truth and true piety, were no more than the abundance of food and entertainment in stately homes in the salt city and in Cracow suffused with the spirit of the Renaissance. The successor of Bużeński would be Prospero Provana, confident of the proto-Unitarians, though he, too, would die in the embrace of the ancestral Church with a sarcophagus of great lavishness in the Dominican Church in Cracow (Pl. 16).

20. Schomann's name was inscribed on the rolls of the University of Wittenberg, 28 April 1558. See C. E. Foerstemann, *Album Academiae Vitebergensis* (Leipzig, 1841) 1.338, which has incorrectly *Ratisbonensis* for *Ratiborensis*. It was not uncommon for a teacher accompanying his charges to foreign universities himself to inscribe for lectures.

21. Schomann means the more complete reformation of the Swiss; by life "wasted" in the salt works, he no doubt means the exciting life of this industrial town.

22. The *aula* probably means no more than the residence of the royal engineer but could allude to some experience in Cracow, too, as tutor in the family of a royal functionary.

23. Jan Łaski in his terminal illness retired to the estate near Pińczów at Dębiany owned by Walenty Dembiński, a moderate Catholic on friendly terms with Protestants; and Łaski seems to have sustained a close friendship with Dembiński's second wife, Krystyna Minacka. A. Tomczak deals with her husband in *Walenty Dembiński, Kanclerz Egzekucjii* (Toruń, 1963), cited by Kowalska, *Działalność Reformatorska*, 153, n. 13, correcting the identification of the estate by Sipayłło, *AS*, 1.295, n. 3. It was in Dębiany, possibly in the presence of Schomann, though he is not otherwise noted, that Łaski worked on his reply to the *Confessio fidei Catholicae* of Hosius (1st edition, 1553; 5th edition 1559), *Brevis ac compediara responsio ad collectos per Hosium articulos*,

dedicated to lord Jan Tarnowski (Pińczów, 1559) (cf. Lismanino to Rudolf Gualther from Pełsznica, 10 March 1559; Wotschke, *Briefwechsel*, n. 167). Almost certainly in the presence of Schomann the major leaders of the Reformation gathered in Dębiany signed the revision of the *Responsio*, 29 March 1559.

24. Łaski died in Dębiany 8 January 1560 and was buried under the high altar in the church in Pińczów. Schomann would thus have had only a few months with the Father of the Polish Reformation.

25. Statorius was the rector of the School at Pińczów, and Jean Thénaud followed him there, sent by Calvin in 1558, as teacher and co-translator of the Bible. He ended his days as rector of the Calvinist School in Cracow.

26. Having been on intimate terms with Łaski, with the two leading Huguenots, and the three outstanding Italians in the Polish Reformation, Schomann the Silesian was an exemplary Pinczovian, a member of a palpably cosmopolitan liberal Christian circle of professional men.

27. This formulation represents the Tritheist phase in the devolution of the dogma of the Trinity among the Reformed of the theological left.

28. Schomann probably refers to the dispute of synod of Włodzisław, 26–29 June 1559.

29. This reminiscence is valuable as testimony to the survival among the Polish Reformed of the ideal of a celibate ministry, as was true of the Czech Brethren for their bishops.

30. Paweł Gilowski (1534–95) (Lubieniecki, *Historia*, Book 2, n. 612) was superintendent of the Reformed churches of the principality of Oświęcim-Zator.

31. As *wielkorodca* of Cracow, Boner, patron of the full Calvinist faction, had charge of the royal possessions in Little Poland.

32. Schomann refers to believers' immersion (cf. n. 35). His son Paweł Szoman-Ciachowski (1562–1617), married eventually to Maryna Siekierszyńska, became a lecturer in Raków, claiming the status of a noble in his mother's line; see n. 6.

33. For the disputation of Piotrków of 1563, see *Historia, 152* and esp. n. 680. Arianism was fixed in the minds of all as a major heresy in antiquity. The Polish Brethren sincerely thought that they had avoided becoming Arians (Stancaro's charge) by becoming transitionally Tritheists!

34. Lasocki, a comrade of Filipowski in the venture with Heraclides Basilicus in Moldavia (*Historia*, Book 2, chap. 9), was owner of Pełsznica and founder of the congregation there.

35. Schomann had thereby become a believers' baptist and would presently become himself an anabaptist. See n. 41. Coming as he did from Silesia, he had surely been influenced by Germanic anabaptism, although the same position had been reached many times in Christian history, despite the caveat of one baptism of Eph 4:5, namely, among the Donatists, some later Waldenses, and among the Unitas Fratrum. On the Polish scene in general the widespread Catholic practice of the rebaptism of converts from Ruthenian Byzantine-rite Christianity must also have played a role, as well as the practice of immersion by the Ruthenians themselves. It is possible that the Jewish *mikveh* (ritual pool) for *tevilah* (immersion), that is, for the monthly purification of women and for the ritual cleansing of proselytes played some role, as there is some evidence that the Polish Brethren, when they came to construct places of worship of their own, erected edifices that resembled synagogues. The practice of believers' baptism and some rebaptism in the Polish-Lithuanian Commonwealth must be seen as distinctive regional variant of a sixteenth-century revival of ancient usage that stretched from the southeast counties of

England across Europe as far south as the Tiber and as far east as the Dnieper. In the intra-Catholic Polish context Jakub Sawicki provides the canonical framework, " 'Rebaptisatio Ruthenorum' in the Light of the 15th and 16th Century Polish Synodal Legislation," Jerzy Kłoczowski, ed., *The Christian Community of Medieval Poland* (Wrocław: Ossolineum, 1981) 37–42.

It is possible that Schomann may have gotten the idea of true baptism by immersion from otherwise unnamed German- or Polish-speaking Anabaptists in the neighborhood of Ksiż. Although he lost his position in Ksiż in 1562, after the death of Boner (*Historia, Book 2*, n. 603) and the new ownership by his Catholic son-in-law, he may have stayed on, for his daughter was born there. He leaves unmentioned the fact that he was pastor in Kościelec and may have participated in the synod there in 1563 in that capacity (cf. Sipayłło, *AS*, 2.172). At some point the family reoccupied their dwelling in Pińczów, which they would leave in 1569 (no. 29).

36. For the disputation of Piotrków of 1565, see *Historia, 201–07*.

37. Cf. *Historia, 39* and Book 3, n. 531; *BAnt*, 21. it was an interpretation of the first chapter of John, circulating in Poland, 1566–68. Rotondò, *Opere*, 304, takes the work from both Faustus and Laelius Socinus and tentatively ascribes it to Andrzej Wojwodowski, cf. *BAnt*, 20, 92; *Historia*, Book 3, n. 531.

38. Jan Oleśnicki as the brother of Mikołaj, heir of Pińczów, who remained strongly Calvinist. Heir of Chmielnik, Jan had founded the congregation there in 1556.

39. The reference is to Szymon Ronemberg, the Polish Brother of German extraction, noted in the *Geschichtsbuch* of the Hutterites, edited by A. J. F. Zieglschmidt, *Die älteste Chronik der Hutterischen Brüder: Ein Sprachdenkmal aus frühneuhochdeutscher Zeit* (Ithaca, NY: The Cayuga Press for the Carl Schurz Memorial Foundation and the Hutterite Community, 1943) 441, 446; translated as *The Chronicle of the Hutterite Brethren*, I (Rifton, New York, etc.: Plough Publishing House, 1986) 410–15–26; many of the related exchanges are translated and interpreted by Leonard Gross, *The Golden Years of the Hutterites . . . During the Walpot Era, 1565–78*, chap. 7, "The Hutterian Encounter with the Polish Brethren," 150–63. Cf. *Historia, 227*. *Nieznana Kronika*, I, 166, mentions succinctly the visit of the same three Polish Brethren to Moravia under the date 1569, adding that four of the Hutterites, headed by one Gaspar came to Cracow and visited Raków before returning to Moravia, and that three *adolescentes non indocti* went there, perhaps accompanying the visitors. The *Geschichtsbuch/Chronicle* does not mention Schomann directly. Before the coming to Neumühl of Filipowski, Ronemberg, and three preachers on 25 January 1570, there is a general reference to "a fervent seeking for the truth" arising in Poland in 1569. No specific visitors or letters are mentioned. The Chronicler says: "[These] people were given a light in their lamps but not the oil the Lord speaks of in the Gospels." Their views are summed up by the Chronicler as a rejection of pedobaptism and the papal doctrine of the Trinity, a distinction being made by them between the rich Christ and the poor Christ. This phrasing of Franciscan resonance may have been used by the Polish visitors to contrast scholastic and scriptural theology, because the Chronicler goes on to remark that the four young men sent by the Polish Brethren to get to know the Hutterite community, staying through the winter [possibly 1569–70], "in their worldly wisdom . . . looked down on God's work as too simple and would not submit to serving the poor and crucified Christ" (411). For the theological sense of *Christus dives / Christus pauper* in Biandrata as of 1563, see Williams, *Radical Reformation, 716*. The Chronicler says that after the first contact of 1569 (although this date is not given), the Hutterites send four of their brethren, Ludwig Dörker their leader, to travel to Poland, presumably to Raków, and they bring back the four young Poles just

mentioned. It is strange that Schomann, who as a Silesian will have spoken German and was as well educated as Ronemberg, is not mentioned in the *Geschichtsbuch* by name.

40. See the parallel account in the *Historia, 140*, where Ronemberg is also called after Ezra, the scribe, who, with the permission of Artaxerxes, led the Jews back from captivity to rebuild with Nehemiah the Temple in Jerusalem, Ezra 7. It is evident from no. 31 that Schomann and his family were in the Racovian commune, sharing in its hopes and failures, 1569 – 72, but submitting to believers' baptism only on his return to Chmiel-nik.

Praising Ronemberg as the restorer of order, Schomann has no occasion to mention the fact that from Olkusz, Daniel Bieliński, presumably the minister there, who in 1575 would return to the Calvinist fold on confession of faith "De Deo Trino," sent a letter, 22 May 1570, addressed to the Hutterites under Peter Walpot in Slavkov (Austerlitz), commending two men sent from Raków, the Lithuanian Jan Baptista Święcicki (formerly minister in Kiejdany) and Jahannes Italus (Joanis Wälsch), along with Järisch Müller of the Olkusz congregation, to study further the arrangements and theology of the Hutterites. Zieglschmidt, ed., *Geschichtsbuch*, 443; *Chronicle*, 413; cf. *Nieznana Kronika*, I, 167.

41. In Acts (8:16, 11:10, 19:5, etc.) converts from Judaism were commonly baptized in the name of the Lord Jesus or Jesus the Messiah. Eventually the baptismal formula of Matt 28:19 would be used in a non-trinitarian sense at the immersion of catechumens.

42. The text says that the rebaptism of Anna Szomanowa took place *in horto Bonario*. However, a baptism of adults in Cracow in the garden of the Boners, who were adherents of the Major Church, is wholly improbable. Moreover, Jan Boner was dead in 1562. On the other hand, the family of Urszula and Kasper Konarski of the village of Koryto in the Land of Sandomierz are known to have been Unitarian, and some of them later went into exile. Szczucki and Tazbir, *loc. cit.*, n. 45. In any case, Schomann's wife and mother (n. 43) were immersed before the whole family removed to Cracow. It is of interest that Schomann thought he should proceed with the baptism of his wife before taking up his ministry in Cracow, 1573 – 86, which evidently, since the ministry of Grzegorz Paweł, had a reputation for being anabaptist and on which issue, along with the doctrine of the Godhead, the two *zbory* in Cracow were divided. The congregation of the Minor Church met in the house of Stanisław Cichowski on the southwest corner of Szpi-talna and Św. Tomasza, where the Church of St. Thomas now stands. Schomann does not mention the first attack on the Calvinist "Brog" in *ulica* Św. Jana, 10 October 1574, after which the Evangelicals considered meeting in the house of the Brethren, but in fear drew back. *Nieznana Kronika*, I, 167: "Item postea [the attack] tentatur in aedes Cykowii ubi nostri fratres, id est Sociniani (quos tum Anabaptistas vocabant) convenire consueverant, sed deterriti destituerunt." On Ascension Day each year both *zbory* were especially subject to attack, as notably in 1574, then again in 1588, and decisively on 23 May 1591, when both meeting places were utterly destroyed and Protestant worship in the Metropolis ceased; Wilbur, *Socianism*, 342 – 43 and Pl. 51.

43. The separate entry for the immersion of Schomann's mother-in-law tends to place the time of the family's removal to Cracow as completed only in 1574; see n. 42.

44. Piotr as physician, gynecologist, assumed the name of his grandmother and was known as Piotr Ciachowski, dying probably in Raków, before 1633. See *Historia*, Book 3, n. 776.

45. In general Schomann's chronology is reliable. But from other sources Socinus is held to have come to Cracow in 1579, not in 1577 as in our text, en route to Kolozsvár. He espoused the cause of the Brethren, as he would after his return from Transylvania in 1580; but he steadfastly refused to submit to immersion.

46. Johann Völkel of Grimma (Kreis Meissen) studied in Wittenberg in 1578 and joined the Minor Church by believer's immersion at the synod of Chmielnik, 1585. In this year he became teacher in the school in Węgrów. He later served as secretary to Socinus, taking dictation. His own *De vera religione*, published posthumously (Raków, 1630), is a veritable compendium of Socinianism. He was minister of Filipów in palatinate Troki on the Ducal Prussian border. Cf. letter of Socinus to him of 16 June 1594; Chmaj, *Listy*, no. 63. He died in Śmigiel in 1618, where he had briefly served as minister. Sipayłło, *AS*, 3.327; Wallace, *Biography* 428–34.

47. Lusławice was the residence of Socinus from 1598 to 1604. Schomann left in 1588.

48. In this year the Tatars invaded the Commonwealth and relations with Turkey worsened to the point of a threat of war.

49. The *Catechesis* of 1574, the oldest Unitarian Confession of faith, is translated in RD 7. While his family evidently remained in Chmielnik for the birth of Piotr (no. 34), Schomann was evidently in Cracow where he had printed the *Catechesis et confessio fidei coetus per Poloniam congregati in nomine Jesu Christi Domini nostri crucifixi et resuscitati* (Cracow: [Rodecki] 1574); Gryczowa, no. 59. This *Catechesis*, structured on the *triplex munus Christi*, on Christ as Prophet, King, and Priest, reflects the radical baptismal Christology of Schomann and the Cracow congregation, and it influenced the structure of its successor, the Racovian Catechism, 1605, discussed in *Polish Brethren*, Doc. VI.

50. The phrasing makes clear that the baptism of repentance at the hands of John, to which Jesus himself submitted as an example, lies behind the baptismal theology and practice of Schomann.

51. Cf. Ezek 39:29; Joel 2:28.

52. Matt 5:16.

53. Cf. 1 Pet 5:43; Ja 1:12.

54. Schomann mentions only the births of two daughters, Katarzyna (not by name) and Marta.

55. The *marca* was the Polish *grzywna*, worth 48 *groszy*.

56. Schomann presumably means his brethren and sisters in Christ.

57. As Schomann lovingly gives the exact hour of birth of four of his known five children, we surmise that this Elżbieta was among the several other children he and his wife had brought up, possibly a domestic or a kinswoman.

58. While the three daughters received money and goods and his wife the house and lot, the two sons presumably received some money, tools, stock, library, etc.

59. In the paragraph Schomann twice refers to his *domicilium et agellus/domus et ager*. While he has referred to his removal from Lusławice to Chmielnik only incidentally, no. 38, he had noted that his house had been spared in 1590 when a fire threatened nearby. He would not have been the owner of two houses, after selling the one (*aedes*) in Pińczów in 1561; cf. no. 43. He thus served as minister in Chmielnik, 1567–73; 1588–c. 1591, although he is not so listed in the indices of Sipayłło, *AS*.

Notes to *RD* 4: B. Wiszowaty, Printing Presses

1. Sand gives no author in *BAnt*. It is quite likely that the editor of *BAnt*, Benedykt Wiszowaty, prepared this document, which is included here for the sake of completeness and for the perspective of the Brethren in Holland as to their publications, c. 1684.

2. Born in Turobin, and sometimes using the place name as his pseudonym, Aleksander Turbińczyk Rodecki was probably not identical with the Franciscan of the name mentioned in the *Historia, 23*. He studied at Pińczów under Statorius and testified against him in the Unitarian-Ditheist-Tritheist controversy at the synod of Łańcut in 1567 (*Historia*, Book 3, n. 493). He reappears in the record in the first extant book published by him, Schomann's *Catechesis, BAnt* (RD 7, no. 41.1, n. 49); Gryczowa, no. 59 and her introduction, 1 – 48.

3. The author alludes to the fact that in Amsterdam itself a major work of Socinus, *De Sacrae Scripturae Auctoritate*, was published pseudonymously as though by one Dominicus Lopez, S.J. (''Seville,'' 1588). It had been composed in 1580, not in 1570, as Sand has it. Gryczowa, no. 263; Wilbur, *Socinianism*, 390 and n. 24. Sternacki reprinted it (Raków, 1611) with the name of Socinus.

4. Gryczowa, no. 4; *Historia, 170*.

5. Gryczowa conjectures that after Rodecki left for Raków, his son-in-law stayed behind at the old press and put out some works of a noncontroversial character, six titles, 1604 – 07. The first title by Sternacki at Raków was the Polish translation by Sebastian Klonowic of Erasmus's, *De civilitate morum puerilium*, c. 1602, Gryczowa, no. 118 and for the career of Sternacki until the destruction of the press in 1638, see *idem, ibid*, 48 – 79.

6. Marciej Kawieczyński was the owner of Uzda and governor for Mikołaj Radziwiłł the Black of Nieśwież near Nowogródek, and the owner of the press there, 1561/62 – 71 and another in Zasław, 1571 – 72, founding the first with a view to spreading Protestantism among the Orthodox, with the support of the two Lithuanian Reformed ministers, Szymon Budny in Kleck and Wawrzyniec Krzyszkowski. Budny, who had come into contact with the Judaizing monks from Moscovy, prepared a catechesis in Cyrillic, *Katichisis*, ''that is, the doctrine of primitive Christianity from Holy Scripture for simple people of the Russian (*ruskoho*) language, '' with a dedication to his two Princes Mikołaj Radziwiłł, Black and Red, 12 June 1562, which survives in a unique copy. Kawecka-Gryczowa, *Drukarze dawnej Polski, zeszyt 5 Wielkie Księstwo Litewskie*, 120 – 22; 190 – 92.

7. Here the Brześć or Radziwiłł Bible was published (Pl. 54). The Budny Bible was started in Nieśwież and printed in Zasław, near Minsk, without reference to place in 1572. Gryczowa, *Drukarze: Wielkie Księstwo Litewskie*, 262 – 63.

8. Daniel had been printer in Pińczów, c. 1557 – 62, and took charge of the press in Nieśwież, 1562 – 71, evidently in Zasław, 1571 – 77; in Łosk in 1574, in Vilna, 1576 – 1600. Gryczowa, *Drukarze: Wielkie Księstwo Litewskie*, 5.70 – 86.

9. Piotr Blastus Kmita was printer in Vilna, 1611 – 12, in association with Jan Karcan there; who, marrying his daughter, was chief printer in Lubecz, 1612, 1629/31. Gryczowa, *Drukarze: Wielkie Księstwo Litewskie*, 130 – 40.

10. Jan (Daniel) Kmita was printed in Lubecz, c. 1630 – c. 1646. Gryczowa, *Drukarze: Wielkie Księstwo Litewskie*, 127 – 30.

11. Johann Lang, from Luczbork in Silesia, was a writer of Latin verse. Our anonymous writer is the sole source for identifying Lang as a Lutheran, and a printer in Lubcz, c. 1646 – c. 1656. Gryczowa, *Drukarze: Wielkie Księstwo Litewskie*, 141 – 42.

12. Janusz Radziwiłł (1612 – 55), was the son of Krzysztof and Anna Kiszczanka.

13. The reference is to Schlichting's *Quaestiones duae*, written to answer *Brevis consideratio theologiae Photinianae* (Wittenberg, 1619; 2nd ed. 1623) of Balthasar Meissner. See Bock, *Antitrin.*, 1.784 – 85.

14. The writer of this document seems to be glancing at several old books but mentions by name only the one printed in Pińczów. Cf. *BAnt*, 44.

The book referred to may have been that written in Polish in 110 folios, *Rodział Starego Testamentu od Nowego, Żydowskwa od Krześciaństwa, skąd łatwie obaczysz prawie wszystki różnice około wiary* (The difference between the Old and the New Testament, between Judaism and Christianity) [Pińczów], 1568). From the unique exemplar in the Czartoryski Library in Cracow, Górski has concluded that it was an elaboration of the text "De discrimine legis et Evangelii," part of the *De falsa et vera unius Dei . . . cognitione*, with Servetian and Socinian material, edited by Biandrata and Dávid in the name of the ministers of the Sarmatian and Transylvanian churches (Kolozsvár, 1567; Pl. 17). Górski, *Grzegorz Paweł*, 230; Stanisław Kot, "L'influence de Michel Servet sur le mouvement antitrinitarien en Pologne et en Transylvanie," Becker, ed., *Autour de Servet et Castellion*, esp. 98. The publication referred to in *On Printing Presses* has been confused with another work of Grzegorz Paweł, lost but known to Bock, *Antitrin.*, 1.619, as *Okazanie Antychrysta y iego Królestwa ze znaków iego własnych w słowie bożym opisanych, których tu sześćdziesiąt* (The advent of Antichrist and his kingdom, according to his own signs as described in the word of God, of which there are sixty) (no place, no date), known to be Part 5 of the *Restitutio* (Lyons, 1553) of Servetus, published not in Pińczów (so, Wilbur's surmise) but in Cracow. John F. Fulton, *Michael Servetus: Humanist and Martyr* with a bibliography of his works and census of known copies by Madeline E. Stanton (New York, 1953), item 33, 90–91.

15. See *Historia, 239–40*

Notes to *RD* 5: A. Wiszowaty, Narratio Compendiosa

1. The title of RD 5 could be less literally translated ". . . from the Trinitarians of the Reformed Church." For both the Unitarians and the Trinitarians regarded themselves as the authentic continuators of the Helvetic church in the Commonwealth, hence the Major and the Minor [Reformed] church, each laying claim to the legacy of Calvin and John Łaski.

Scholarship ascribes the account to Andrew Wiszowaty, domiciled in Amsterdam from 1666 until his death in 1678. It was published by Christopher Sand, Jr. in his *Nucleus historiae ecclesiasticae* (Cosmopolis [Amsterdam], 1668), and in the second enlarged edition of *Nucleus historiae ecclesiasticae, seu historia Arianorum una cum memorato tractatu de veteribus scriptoribus ecclesiasticis* (Cologne [Amsterdam], 1676), with an *Appendix addendorum, confirmandorum et emendandorum ad Nucleum*, 1678. It was printed again by Benedict Wiszowaty in *BAnt* (1684), then in Węgierski, *Slavonia Reformata* (1679).

Bock (*Antitr.* 1. 963), on the basis of a larger manuscript at his disposal, ascribed the *Narratio* to Joachim Stegmann, Jr., who had been commissioned to write such an account by three successive synods, 1640, 1649, 1650. Cf. Lubieniecki's sense of synodal commision for the *Historia*, Introduction, near n. 36. Lech Szczucki argues that what Stegmann may have been commissioned to do, his friend and collaborator Andrew Wiszowaty actually accomplished (cf. Introduction, near n. 29). The final truncated version was surely worked on by both Andrew and Benedict Wiszowaty. See Tazbir in his preface to the facsimile edition of Węgierski, *Slavonia Reformata*, xx, assessing the earlier argumentation of Szczucki in his preface to the facsimile edition of *BAnt*, xiii-xiv. Sand, author of the *Nucleus* and compiler of *BAnt*, sympathized with the Polish Brethren in exile, but expressly rejected the Christology of Socinus as an unacceptable and strange *novum*, much preferring as a classicist and specifically as a Platonist, the philosophically embued Apologists, like Justin Martyr, and other ante-Nicene thinkers, like Origen. Sand held to the pre-existence of Christ, as in the earliest strata of the Pauline corpus. Hence he favored the Arians of the fourth century as having preserved, as he thought, the best witness of ancient Christianity, which had acknowledged the fulfillment of Greek Logos philosophy in Jesus as the embodied Word no less then as the Hebraic Messiah. This stood in marked contrast to another Germanic classicist, Johann Sommer (*Historia*, Book 3, chap. 11), a severe critic of the philosophical components in the received Triadology. Wiszowaty defended his own christological tradition against Sand, but was glad to contribute his *Brief Narrative* for the *Appendix* (1678) of the *Nucleus* which his son, Benedict, eventually reproduced in his edition of *BAnt* (1684). The most comprehensive analysis of the life, writings, and thought of Christopher Sand is that of Lech Szczucki, "W kręgu spinozjańskim: Krzysztof Sandius, Junior," *Studia i materiały z dziejów nauki polskiej*, Series A, 12 (1968) 157–73. Szczucki summarizes in English his findings on Sand in his demonstration that Benedict Wiszowaty was the author of the unpublished *Medulla historiae ecclesticae* in two MSS, was defending the *medulla* of the fully Unitarian Brethren against his friend's *nucleus* of ante-Nicene Triadology and particularly Christology, "Socinian Historiography in the 17th Century," in Church and George, eds., *Continuity and Discontinuity*, 285–300 (with an errata sheet for this particular essay on which the sedulous author rightly insisted). Sand's *Nucleus* was discussed in another context, Introduction, at n. 29. The fullest account of Sand, without the benefit of the most recent scholarship, is that in Wallace, *Biography* 3. 318–26.

2. It is notable and natural that A. Wiszowaty, writing in Amsterdam, should wish to raise up Menno Simons as among the four leading divines of the opening half of the century of Reformation. This perspective reflects, no doubt, his appreciation of the more broadminded Dutch Mennonite burghers among whom he sojourned. At the end of the *Brief Narrative*, its editor B. Wiszowaty surmises that Adam Pastor, the unitarian adversary of Menno, might have been the *Belga*, Spiritus, who visited Cracow in 1547 (RD 2, n. 10) and thus made an impact from the Netherlands on the Poles comparable to that of the Italians, represented by the visit there of Laelius Socinus in leaving Italy also in 1547 (from Bologna): in Cracow in 1551 and 1558, no. 50.

3. *Historia, 38–40*.

4. *Historia, 18–19*.

5. See above, n. 2 and RD 1, n. 5.

6. *Historia, 33*.

7. *Historia, 143*. The text reads incorrectly *Licovii*. Boner's son-in-law was Catholic and excluded all Protestants from the Cracow house and the towns he owned.

8. *Historia, 153–156*.

9. *Historia, 187–88*.

10. *Historia, 140, 228–29*.

11. *Historia*, esp. *220*.

12. The text has *in aula Francisci*. Actually on the accession of Francesco, Socinus felt uncertain of his future in the court he had served a dozen years and left. Wilbur, *Socinianism*, 389–91.

13. Wiszowaty is unambiguous in criticizing Dávid's nonadorantism, whereas Lubieniecki, in *Historia*, Book 3, chap. 11, is more evasive.

14. *De Jesu Christi filii Dei natura seu essentia nec non de peccatorum per ipsum expiatione disputatio adversus Andream Volanum* (Cracow: Rodecki, 1588); Gryczowa,

no. 65. For his exclusion from the Lord's Supper because he declined to undergo immersion, see RD 5 between nn. 13 and 14.

15. *Historia, 222–23, 225–26*.

16. Wiszowaty, not quite so tendentiously as Lubieniecki in the *Historia*, ignores the development in Raków, 159–72 (RD 6), and dates the "real" Raków from c. 1600, it had come under the influence of resident Socinus (RD 8).

17. RD 1, no. 12.1

18. Jakub Zaborowski, *Ignis cum Aqua* (Bełżyce, 1617). Walenty Schmalz wrote *Odpowiedź na Książkę Jakuba Zaborowskiego: Ogień z wodą* (Raków: Sternacki, 1619); Gryczowa, no. 235. Wiszowaty may be right that Zaborowski's text first appeared in Polish.

19. For the life of Schmalz, see Pl. 59.

20. Closely associated with *Narratio compendiosa*, is an anonymous sketchy Chronology printed by Sand in his *Nucleus*, then by the Socinians in their second edition of Węgierski, *Slavonia Reformata*, 508–510. It covers from a distinctive perspective selected developments, 1547–67/1604. From it the single entry for 1547 (the visit of *Spiritus Belga*) was adduced in Book 1, n. 178 ¶4. The perspective appears to be that of a chronicler viewing the currents and schisms in the anti-Nicene community of the Commonwealth after the death of Faustus Socinus (1604) and evidently from the environs of his final resting place, Lusławice, for the nonce named in the annotation therefore the "Lusławice Chronicle." It is valuable for its dating of the introduction of believers' baptism in three groupings and for its special perspective on the Ditheists, elsewhere surfacing in *Historia*, Book 3, nn. 502, 543–55; in Wiszowaty, *Narratio compendiosa*, no. 58; and in Andrzej Lubieniecki, *Poloneutychia*, between nn. 11 and 15. Selected here for unannotated translation is the taxonomical account of the four anti-Nicene groupings in the Commonwealth as viewed from c. 1614: Tritheists, Ditheists, Christ-adorant Unitarians (not so named), and non-adorant Unitarians (not so named), the Farnovians socially conservative with respect to their peasants.

> In the year 1567 there was a schism among those who believed in the one highest God the Father. The Pinczovians, or as they were called a little while afterwards, the Racovians, held that Christ did not exist before Mary and that the Holy Spirit was not a person. Their leaders were Gregory Paul and George Schomann. And they were even called Cracovians and Sandomirians from their places [Cracow and environs and palatinate Sandomierz], and afterwards called Socinians [c. 1580] even though they never accepted Faustus Socinus into communion—and this because of certain other doctrines [besides the unity of the Godhead], which doctrines, so long as Socinus was alive, remained common to themselves and the Calvinists (*Calvinis*).
>
> Another part of [the Reformed] were the so-called Ditheists (*Bideitae*). And they were of two kinds. Some were Cujavians [from Kujawy] who considered Christ to have been before the world and the Holy Spirit to be a gift of God, not a person. Among these [Ditheists] preeminent were Martin Czechowic and John Niemojewski, who afterwards joined the Racovians. Martin Czechowic, however, was the first to begin to baptize adults, having written a book against pedobaptism. Others among the Ditheists recognized as ministers Peter Gonesius, Stanislas Farnowski, Stanislas Wiśniowski, John Kazanowski, and Nicholas Żytno. These believed in the existence of Christ before the ages, but concerning the Holy Spirit, they considered him to be not the third person of the Deity, but nevertheless something alive and like a person. [cf. RD 6, below n. 12]. They were called Farnovians. And it is true indeed that Farnowski and Wiśniowski began to baptize adults, *after* the Cujavians and *before* the Racovians [c. 1568]. Wiśniowski, in fact, went away to his patron [Stanislas]

Taszycki to Lusławice [as its minister] and before the death of Farnowski [c. 1615 – 16] returned with his patron to the Racovians. At length, however, having left his patron and congregation, Wiśniowski returned to the communion of Farnowski. Farnowski went to Sąsz to lord [Stanislas] Mężyk, starosta of Sąsz, royal carver, who with his wife followed eagerly his opinion [*Historia*, Book 2, n. 553]. And he had there a large church and a famous school. Among the Farnovians there was a certain widowed matron [Anna] Zabawska, who incurred the costs of printing a booklet of the prayers. Farnowski himself edited a work in Polish on his own views [cf. *Historia*, Book 2, n. 544].

After the death of Farnowski, however, or Farnewski (for by that name he was also known], that is, after 1604 [an apparent misprint for 1614], the Farnovians, destitute of an appropriate pastor, were dipersed. Some of them were united with the Racovians, a few with the Calvinists. The Racovians, however, acquired the church edifices.

A third party of the [anti-Nicene Reformed] were made up of Lithuanians and Podlachians. These were called Tritheists (*Tritheitae*), who postulated three Persons and their subordination and inequality.

A fourth kind were the Judaizers [nonadorants] who denied that Christ should be invoked. Preeminent among these were Francis Dávid of Kolozsvár in Transylvania, and his son Francis Dávid, Junior, Jacob Palaeologus, Matthew [Vehe-] Glirius, Simon Budny, and John Sommer.

Notes to *RD* 6: A. Lubieniecki, Poloneutychia

1. Andrew Lubieniecki was the son of Catherine Sobieska and Stanislas Lubieniecki, who settled in Kujawy in the environs of Przedecz, where Andrzej may have been born. The father is attested at the Reformed synod of Bychawa in 1560, along with Andrzej, who was studying there at its academy; Sipayłło, *AS*, 2.12. Andrzej followed the debate of the Diet of Lublin that led to the Union of 1569. In 1573 he journeyed to Paris in a company of youths under the guidance of Bishop Jean Monluc who had in view their extending their studies, learning French and the ways of the French court, in order to return to Cracow as congenial pages in the court of Henry of Valois. Andrzej continued on in the court of Stephen Batory and Anna Jagiellonka and from all evidence was much admired by the Hungarian prince. Sometime after 1577 Andrzej turned from the court to study for the ministry, presumably at the same time as did his older brother Stanisław (d. 1633) and his younger brother Krzysztof (d. 1624), the grandfather of the author of the *Historia*. His first charge was as preacher in Śmigiel, serving there beginning in 1584. In 1586 he and Jan Balcer were charged by the Synod of Chmielnik to visit Goslar in Saxony to try to negotiate the release from prison there of the mother and the sister of Christopher Ostorodt (cf. *Polish Brethren*, Doc. V). In April 1591 Andrzej Lubieniecki debated with Abbot Stanisław Ostrowski on the Trinity, and then, moving on to the Lublin district in 1592, he debated along with his brother Krzysztof against the Poznań canon Mikołaj Dobrocieski in 1596 on the divinity of Christ and on the Trinity. Around 1600 Andrzej became preacher and then pastor for Gabriel Hojski in Hoszcza in Volhynia, whence he left for Raków to participate in the standing synod there, 1601 – 02, and where he stood directly under the influence of Faustus Socinus. By 1612 he was no longer connected with Hoszcza and seems to have settled in Raków, at least by 1616, where he began the *Poloneutychia*. Czartoryski MS 1403 in Cracow is his autograph book, "Pamiętnik przyjaciół Andrzeja Lubienieckiego," filled with the remarks and signatures of numerous friends from the West and the East (Pl. 60). Andrzej left Raków for

Wysokie Lubelskie in January 1620, then Krupe, then Siedliska. His record of the Arian synods used by his nephew has been lost. Andrzej was buried in Suchodoły. Largely summarized from Janusz Tazbir, *PSB* 17 (1972) 495 – 96.

2. As the original appendix to the *Narratio* (RD 5) is a seventeenth-century addendum in the form of an excerpt (RD 1) about the strange Dutch visitor Spiritus in Cracow in 1546 or 1547 from a contemporary writer Frycz Modrzewski, it seems appropriate to place here a vivid description of a religious ferment, including indeed Spiritualism, of about 1570, as reported by another contemporary Polish author, whom Stanisław Lubieniecki himself often adduced in his *Historia*, a work of his own uncle, but not this passage.

Because of its extraordinary witness to the extent of radical trends in the Polish-Lithuanian Commonwealth, I placed a portion of it in a pan-European context in "The Radical Reformation Revisited," *Union Theological Quarterly Review* 39:1 72 (1984) 1 – 24.

The basic point of it is that the *Rzeczpospolita* with its Diet-elected King, its Senate of bishops and magnates (an outgrowth of the royal council), and with its elective House of Deputies frequented by the nobiliary delegations of the palatinate dietines, was constitutionally comparable to, and yet quite different from, *Das Heilige Römische Reich,* with its seven electors, its much more nearly soverign princes, great and small, its prince bishoprics, and its many imperial free cities; and, unlike the Empire, the *Rzeczpospolita* was not incorporating Roman imperial law; hence Anabaptists were not *ipso facto* subject to capital punishment. Moreover, the nobles of the Commonwealth very often became themselves members, moderators, and synodists in the new churches and often built new edifices for voluntary congregations without forcing the peasants to comply or abandon their ancestral parish churches. Polish Anabaptism was thus wholly of the evangelical and spiritualizing types—with no trace of Müntzerite or Münsterite aspirations. Spiritualism exhibited itself in fewer instances than in Germany. Italian humanistic rationalism and biblicism mingled with simplified Reformed polity and piety to create also a distinctively Polish current of Evangelical Rationalism, of which the Polish Brethren (after 1580) under the tutelage of Faustus Socinus are the paradigm. Andrzej Lubieniecki gives an ecclesiastical *tour d'horizon* of the whole Commonwealth from what he considers the intellectual and ethical eminence of Raków and shows himself to be so much of the Western tradition that he can think of the Racovian achievement as the climax of the Reformation in church and society that began in Wittenburg, while in the whole of the *Poloneutychia* he finds no occasion even to glance at the Union of Brest Litovsk of 1595 or refer to the vast stretches of Byzantine-rite terrain—as different from the Elizabethan envoy of RD 9.

3. The MS was preserved in the Czartoryski Library, 1370. It was partially edited in 1843 and critically edited with index by Alina Linda, *et al.* (Warsaw/Łódz: PWN, 1982) 50 – 53.

4. Karaites ("people of the Scripture") were a Jewish sect that arose in the eighth century in the rejection of the Talmudic-rabbinical tradition. They moved into the Crimea at the time of the Tatar Golden Horde, whence, after the defeat of the Horde by Grand Duke Witold in 1392, they were settled by him in Halicz, Lutsk, and Troki, whence they spread to Vilna and elsewhere. Because their teachers used only the Hebrew Bible, though they spoke Tatar, Polish-Lithuanian Protestants occasionally entered into dialogue with them.

5. Lubieniecki here anticipates his later allusion to the Confederation of the Lutherans

and the Major Church (he fails here to mention the Czech Brethren) at Sandomierz in 1570, at n. 21.

6. This may be an allusion to the gathering of all nations in Zion to worship the Lord, Isa 2:2–3.

7. John 10:16.

8. For Lubieniecki Protestantism meant an improvement in morality and he tended to identify piety and puritanism, favoring synodal and congregational self-discipline.

It is evidently the hope of Lubieniecki and of his fellow ''heretics,'' the ''Christians'' (the Polish Brethren), that through the intensification of the piety and self-discipline the schism of the Reformed Church of 1563 might in God's time be healed to make perhaps nugatory the Confederation of Czech Brethren, Lutherans, and Calvinists of 1570, alluded to and no doubt sadly and perhaps with ''Sarmatian'' disdain as somehow unnatural, n. 21, and felt to be inherently contrary to the certain divine intent of restoring in and through Poland apostolic truth, polity, and probity.

9. The source has not been further identified. Lubieniecki will have picked up this congenial *bon mot* (uttered by Antoine Bourbon, duke of Vendôme, husband of Jeanne d'Albret, queen of Navarre) while in Paris sometime between 1559 and 1562 as guest of Catherine de' Medici, the mother of Louis XIII.

10. Under the impact of Duke Albert of Hohenzollern of Prussia as the ranking Lutheran vassal of Sigismund I the Old, Lutheranism won adherents among a number of lords, particularly in Royal Prussia and Great Poland, for example, Łukasz Górka (1551–72), protector of the Lutherans in Great Poland. But by 1616 when Lubieniecki was writing, many of these lords or their heirs had turned Reformed.

11. The Reformed Church in its groping went indeed through a phase in which without reference to *consubstantia* there were thought to be, in effect, three divine beings.

12. Lubieniecki is not careful here in his wording. The Polish Reformed Ditheists were not at this stage Modalists for they distinguished the Father and the Son without the designation of *Persona* and yet retained the one *istność-essentia*, and yet two existences, two beings.

13. The Ditheists under Czechowic rejoined the main body of the Minor Reformed Church by then fully Unitarian.

In saying that the two preceding groups of Ditheists ''are no more,'' Lubieniecki fails to note that some of the originally pedobaptist Ditheists joined the Farnovians, who were the first Polish group after the Cujavians (Niemojewski, Czechowic) to introduce the practice of adult baptism (cf. RD 5, n. 20) and that the Farnovian synod came to an end through absorption by the Racovians and the Calvinists, only after the death of Farnowski, perhaps in the same year Lubieniecki finished his *Poloneutychia*.

14. The Mennonites settled there as early as 1530.

Mennonites are introduced here and Hutterites in the next paragraph, while the progression of the author's thought is determined by the baptismal theme. Then in the ensuing paragraph on the three main non-Catholic churches of Poland he stresses the eucharistic variants.

15. At the synod of Raków in 1611 Walenty Schmalz and Hieronim Moskorzowski were asked to draw up terms for possible union with the Mennonites; and the negotiations were entrusted to Andrzej Lubieniecki's brother Krzysztof (1561–1624) and Adam Gosławski. The Racovians in 1613 turned back the formal Mennonite response as in some way impractical.

16. By *komunja* Lubieniecki has in mind the apostolic *comunio bonorum*; and here he

alludes to the mutual visitations of the communal anabaptist in Moravia and the proto-Racovians. He is yet to come to the founding of Raków and thus his reference to the Hutterites as slipping below the horizon is premature even in his own account.

17. In this obscure clustering the author is going through several groups, all Roman-Nicene on the Trinity but here with specific attention to differences in eucharistic theology and practice, as above two other groups with special attention to baptism, between nn. 12 and 15. The one specific ecclesiastical term used by the author, and that twice, is Waldenses, once in Latin, then in Polish. The term could in the first instance mean the medieval Waldenses surviving in Bohemia and possibly in Poland, too. But the author uses the term in reference to the Czech Brethren, for these often so designated themselves as their episcopal succession was indeed derived formally from the Waldenses.

18. *Valdenses* here again means the Czech Brethren, whom he has thus far ignored, even though the Reformed synod of Little Poland was federated with them from the joint synod in Koźminek in Great Poland in 1555 to that in Lipnik in Moravia in 1558.

19. His disparaging term *kupa,* which can also be translated "huddle," probably refers to the Federation of Sandomierz, below n. 21.

It is scarcely possible in such an imprecise account, geographically and ecclesiastically, that Lubieniecki could be referring to the disappearance of the more ascetic rural, pacifistic Minor Party among the Czech Brethren after the modernization of the Major Party under Brother Lukaš of Prague. Cf. A Lubieniecki on the disappearance of church discipline in RD 2, n. 19. Both the Czech Brethren and the Polish Brethren eyed each other with respect to piety and church discipline.

20. This seems to be a disdainful reference to the "laxist" Major Reformed Church in contrast to his own "rigorist" Minor Church, from which vantage point at Raków he surveys the whole Polish scene. Of the three federated churches of Sandomierz, Lubieniecki was not himself clear about the Unitas Fratrum/Czech Brethren, whether in Moravia or in Great Poland, survivors of the "First Reformation" under Jan Hus. The Major Party among them fell under the various Protestant influences that would, from a Lutheran angle of vision, be called respectively: Sacramentarian (Zwinglian), Melanchthonian (Crypto-Calvinist), and Gnesio-Lutheran positions, the last of which had its center in Magdeburg under the impact, among others, of Flacius, a bitter foe within Lutheranism of Melanchthon. Eucharistic practices, like those detailed below, were, to be sure, under discussion among Lutherans and settled by the exclusionary, conformist Formula of Concord (1577), of which our author was probably unaware.

21. Andrzej Lubieniecki, like his nephew, is loathe to mention the Consensus of Sandomierz (1570). It was so decisive a rejection of fellowship with the Minor Church and at a site so close to Raków that Andrzej could only be oblique and grudging in his allusion (cf. at n. 5), since it contravened his view of theodicy and providential "happiness" for Poland right in the midst of the period he concentrates on. He evidently has in mind the distinctive eucharistic practices within each of the three churches federated at Sandomierz in 1570.

22. This is the only mention of the Silesian Evangelical Spiritualist Caspar Schwenckfeld (1490–1561), whose writings and those of his spiritualizing kinsmen are extant in the *Corpus Schwenckfeldianorum*, ed. by C. D. Hartranft and successors, 19 vols. (Leipzig, 1907–39; Pennsburg, PA, 1959–61). The most recent work on him with the literature is that of Robert Emmet McLaughlin, *Caspar Schwenckfeld von Ossig: Nobility and Religious Commitment—Crisis and Decision in the Early Reformation* (New Haven: Yale University Press, 1985). Schwenckfeld suspended the practice of the Eucharist in his circle in 1526, pending further divine revelation as to the best course

amid bitter strife over the sacrament of communion. See in context, my *Radical Reformation*, chap. 5.5 and passim.

This reference to the influence of Schwenckfeld in Poland and Lithuania is not isolated. Szymon Żak, superintendent of the Reformed church of Vilna, declared already in 1557: "The Evil One so inflates his bagpipe: the Anabaptists, the Libertines, the *Schwenckfelders*, the Servetuses, the Gonesians, the Neo-Arians that he discourages by their deafening yelps the spirit of many a pious and virtuous Christian." *Akta, to jest sprawy Zboru Krześcijańskiego Wileńskiego* (Brest Litovsk, 1559), *Monumenta Reformationis Polonicae et Lithuanicae* (Vilna, 1925).

23. This is surely a garbled interpretation of the spiritual asceticism of those in the circles of Schwenckfeld, who himself remained celibate for life. But the mention of attendance in good conscience at divine services at three kinds of religious sanctuaries, none Protestant (*zbory* would otherwise have been in the succession of terms used), suggests that Lubieniecki may indeed be preserving a valuable reminiscence of the Schwenckfeldian movement extending into Byzantine-rite territory among noblemen like Schwenckfeld himself (much of whose writing was in Latin), boyars and grandees, who did not intend to jeopardize their social position or nobiliary authority by local nonconformity. The "Nicodemite" frequenting of a synagogue is indeed puzzling and interesting.

It is quite likely that Lubieniecki was describing in part the tumultuous spiritualism of early Raków, 1569–72, avoiding saying so, as the episode was personally so repellent; then with this ferment behind him he can proceed to mention the founding of Raków at n. 27, as though some of the antinomianism he deplored had not earlier broken out precisely where he was penning the *Poloneutychia*!

It is possible, to be sure, that some of the Polish and Byzantine-rite nobles had read, among other Schwenkfeldian works, one to which Douglas H. Shantz of Trinity Western University (Vancouver) has drawn attention in his "*Der Schwärmer*: A Spiritualist Perspective of Suffering and Persecution," still to be published. The work in both German and Latin, c. 1544 (*CS*, was written by Walenty Crautwald, alumnus of the Cracovian Academy, canon of Legnica (RD 3, n. 3). Crautwald sought, as Shants points out, to rehabilitate a term of abuse among Lutherans (*Schwärmer/fanatici*), in their invective against Carlstadt, the Zwickau Prophets, the Anabaptists, and the Spiritualists, as a spiritual appellation for any upholder of the *media via/via regia* between the old religion and the acrimonies of its would-be reformers. Schwenkfeldian Spiritualism, functionally similar to Nicodemism, has, however, a different dynamic. See Introduction at n. 54.

24. This list of names familiar from the *Historia* suggests indeed that Andrzej Lubieniecki has already launched on his description of early Raków without saying so; cf. n. 23. If our identification is correct, the Bieliński here is the same important figure who reappears at n. 26.

25. It was precisely in 1572, Lubieniecki's *terminus ad quem* for his *tour d'horizon*, that Jan Przypkowski freed his serfs in Sosnowiec. But Lubieniecki has here in mind the nobiliary colonizers of Raków itself, several of whom did free their serfs and leave their estates idealistically for the apostolic commune of Raków.

26. The episode involving in the end the taking over of the rights of Ożarowski by Jan Firley, Marshal of the Great Crown (d. 1574), has not been otherwise attested. The village of Ożarów was indeed given by the King to one Józef Ożarowski for the founding of a town with market rights, 1569. Who preceded him with the village name has not been ascertained. The town is mentioned as having an Arian congregation by Kossowski, *Protestantyzm w Lublinie*, 164–65.

27.   As early as the Minor Church synod of Cracow, November 1566, the congregation in Lublin was reprimanded for spreading "the New Judaism" (*żydowstwo nowe*), for observing the Sabbath, and for not invoking Christ in prayer (*nauka o niewzywaniu Syna Bożego*); Zachorowski, "Najstarsze synody," 232. Cf. *Historia,* Book 3, n. 287. Christocentric (adorant) Unitarian Andrzej Lubieniecki here includes within the sweep of his brush the Judaizers within Orthodoxy and the named non-adorant Unitarian Reformed baptists who remained socially conservative.

Sabbatarianism with a kosher diet is not commonly reported outside Szeklerland in Transylvania, but there it was still flourishing precisely when Lubieniecki was writing. Faustus Socinus, as spokesman for the moderate, reorganized Racovians, 1580–1604, did in fact oppose several of the aforementioned antitrinitarian upholders of the office of the sword. Daniel Bieliński, cf. near n. 24, among them, returned to the Major Reformed Church in 1576.

28.   Here Lubieniecki formally begins his account of the founding of Raków, having earlier disposed of aspects of it that he deplored (nn. 16, 22–24) although picking up some of its discontents at n. 29.

29.   See preceding n.

30.   This is the Polish counterpart of Germanic mystical and Anabaptist *Gelassenheit.* See in context my *Radical Reformation*, 133 passim.

31.   He became palatinate of Ruthenia in 1576.

32.   This deputy died c. 1582.

33.   With this reference to the *interregnum* between the death of Sigismund II and the arrival and coronation of Henry of Valois, namely, 1572–73, and that between Henry in flight to become King of France and the final negotiations for the election of Stephen Batory with Anna Jagiellonka providing dynastic continuity, namely, 1574–76, we may infer that much of Lubieniecki's invaluable impressions were based more upon the transmission of others, including his father, than upon personal reminiscences, as during the decade (1562–72) surveyed and characterized religiously. Lubieniecki was himself quite young, only about eleven at the outset and away in Paris in 1573 to study to become a page (n. 1). A theological disputant, preacher, and historian when writing the *Poloneutychia*, he was surely in a position to assess the accounts of those times, oral and written; but then again, as observed, his theology of Polish history and his understanding of the providential role of his own Minor Church dictated certain displacements in his account and, as already noted, allowed for certain intended unclarities in his text.

Notes to *RD* 7: Schomann, Catechesis

Notes to the Introduction

1.   See therein RD 3, no. 41, the basis for the identification of Schomann as principal composer of the anonymous publication by Aleksander Rodecki. Górski, *Grzegorz Paweł*, suggests a secondary note for the first Reformed teaching elder in Cracow. I have dealt with the Catechesis in a different setting as "Radicalization of the Reformed Church in Poland, 1547–1574: A regional variant of sixteenth-century Anabaptism," *MQR* 64 (1990).

The Harvard copy was presented as a gift by the Transylvanian Unitarian consistory. It once belonged to the small library of the congregational Polish refugees in Kolozsvár.

2.   This major document has been edited in several places, notably by Beatrice Jenny,

"Das Schleitheimer Täuferbekenntnis, 1527," *Schaffhauser Beiträge zur vaterländ-
ischen Geschichte*, 28 (1951) 5–81; translated by John C. Wenger, "The Schleitheim
Confession of Faith," *MQR* 19 (1945) 243–53, revised, in reference to the Bern
Staatsarchiv MS, by William R. Estep, *Anabaptist Beginnings (1523–33)* (Nieuwkoop:
De Graaf, 1976) 100–105.

3. The *Confessio* is contained in the Zurich Staatsarchiv codex E II 367, folios
54–57. P. 54 therein is reproduced by Tedeschi, *Laelius Socinus* (Florence, 1965),
between 198/99; and in an Appendix I, he supplies improved readings over against the
text as printed by Johann Hottinger (1668) and by Friedrich Bock (1784), the Hottinger
version having been used as the basis for the translation of it by Edward M. Hulme,
"Lelio Sozzini's Confession of Faith," *Persecution and Liberty: Essays in honor of
George Lincoln Burr* (New York, 1931) 211–25, specifically 216–18. There is picture
of Lelio's opening MS paragraph on Pl.10A with some further characterization of its contents, including its ferocious eschatology, and updating references to the *Opera* of Lelio,
ed. by Antonio Rotondó (1986).

4. The work is described by Gryczowa, no. 59.

5. The whole service of consecration of Henry, with some succinct reference to the
controversy in front of altar over the demanded repetition of the oath to uphold the Henrician Articles sworn to in Notre Dame and to the *pax dissidentium* of the Warsaw confederation of February 1573 (Pl. 26), is printed by Alessandor Guagnini (Gwagninus) of
Verona (c. 1538–1614), *Sarmatiae Europeae descriptio, quae regnum Poloniae,
Lituaniam, Samogitiam, Russiam, Masoviam, Prussiam, Pomeraniam, Livoniam et Mos-
choviae, Tartariaeque partem complectitur* ([Cracow:] Matthias Wirzebięta [1578]),
folios 52v–56v, under the heading: "Ordo qualiter serenissimus rex Poloniae iuxta
veterem consuetudinem coronatur et quae solennitas et caeromoniae circa id sint solitae."

6. See specifically at n. 9 below, also in the annotation to the *Catechesis*, n. 18.

7. In the prayer to the Son of God in the annexed *Oeconomia Christiana*, Jesus
Christ, seated at the right hand of God the Father, is addressed as the *Sermo Dei*, unique
Master, most absolute Prophet, most holy Pontifex, uncontaminated lamb, most unconquerable King of heaven, who by his royal spirit makes the worshipers themselves a royal
priesthood.

8. The reference in the public prayer to the Polish King *and queen* suggests that this
liturgical prayer had already taken shape in Schomann's mind and congregational usage
while Sigismund II Augustus and his third wife still lived, Catharine Hapsburg, widow of
Francis III of Mantua (d. 28 February 1572, a few months before Sigismund, 7 July
1572). Henry of Valois married Louise of Lorraine only after his return to France.

9. The pastoral prayer is printed on folios N 3r–04v, where it is followed by a long
and theologically rich prayer to the Son of God.

Notes to Catechesis

1. Schomann refers to the ill repute of "seditious," theocratic, polygamous Münster.
He goes on to describe immersion in Section 5.

2. Schomann, who visited Peter Walpot in Moravia with Simon Ronemberg, was
aware that the Cracow apothecary had called the Hutterite *Episcopus/Vorsteher* the New
Noah. The communitarianism of the Hutterites is on his mind as well as the vagaries of
Raków, 1569–72.

3. This is the only section reduced in the translation, here summarized in the first
answer with bracketed references to some of the Scripture adduced in pp. a5–b3. As the

quarto volume is very rare, it has seemed altogether pedantic to enclose in square brackets the pages throughout.

4. In the injunction to imitate Christ as the teacher of Nazareth and to invoke and adore the Ascended Lord seated at the right hand of God the Father the majority of the Minor Church differed from the Transylvanian Unitarians; and on this issue they were already in agreement with Faustus Socinus who tarried with them in 1578 before going on to debate Ferenc Dávid on precisely this issue in Kolozsvár in 1578/79.

5. Here survives the crucial text and query of the Stancarist crisis in the Reformed Church, antedating the schism of the Major/Minor Church.

6. Schomann is a New Covenant Christian; that is, he views the New Testament as taking precedence over the Old, hence his refusal to equate baptism with circumcision, i.e., pedobaptism with the sign and seal of the Old Testament covenant. Nevertheless, he understands the Old Testament as more than a preparation for the New and with some skill adduces Old Testament texts throughout.

7. Schomann seemingly accepts as self-evident what in fact Laelius and then Faustus Socinus arduously sought to demonstrate in John 1, namely, that the Logos had its beginning in Jesus, that there was no hypostatic Word of God and surely no Christ prior to the incarnation. Jesus is the embodied Word of God, the first time that Word was *seen*, as distinguished from being *heard*.

8. Schomann here and elsewhere interestingly "anticipates" the stress of Faustus Socinus on the definitive sacrifice of Christ having been made in the heavenly Tabernacle after the Ascension, a theory of expiation and atonement distinctive to the epistle to the Hebrews, the Pauline authorship of which Socinus defended. Schomann resumes the theme under the Lord's Supper at n. 28. See further, *Polish Brethren,* Doc X.

9. Unlike Budziński, for example, and even many pacifistic Polish Brethren, Schomann was not a millennialist; the Kingdom of Christ was for him, as for Socinus, of heaven. It is an emphasis like this and at n. 8 above that prepared the Minor Church inwardly for the still more forceful and systematic thought of Socinus in his imminent leadership; for he in several ways clarified motifs he already found distinctive to the Polish Brethren over against, for example, the Transylvanian Unitarians.

10. Schomann serenely quotes major texts in the tradition supporting the role of the eternal Word/Son as cosmological as well as soteriological Mediator, only to affirm his work of creation as the new creation, or new being, instituted in baptismal regeneration.

11. The subsection on the Holy Spirit is not anticipated in the opening *Responsio*, but here turns out to be quite ample. The Spirit of God, according to Schomann, operated before the incarnation, for example, in creation and in the inspiration of the prophets, yet is in a specific way also the Comfortor/Counselor sent by Jesus Christ. As one born Catholic and from his youth up evidently disposed to piety, Schomann was no doubt acquainted with the seven gifts of the Spirit of Isa 11:2 (to the Hebraic six Jerome in the Vulgate had added a seventh, *pietas*, in the processs of rendering one Hebrew word in two) and with the nine spiritual gifts (*charismata*) of the same Spirit of 1 Cor 12:8 – 10, some of which, like wisdom and knowledge, overlap. In any case, his own identification of nine names for the Holy Spirit must have been suggested by these two other listings in the tradition.

12. The section is on justification and sanctification. Although cast in the technical language of the classical Protestant Reformation, the section substantiates the generalization that the piety/spirituality of the Minor Church represented in many ways the repristination of the late medieval ascetic ideal in what could be called conjugal and congrega-

tional coenobitism. The manual for the domestic liturgy of discipline and prayer with its various "offices" as an appendix to the *Catechesis* reinforces this interpretation.

13. Schomann passes by a *locus classicus* for the doctrine of original sin in its collectivity (Rom 5:12: ἐφ᾽ ᾧ πάντες ἥμαρτον; in the Vulgate, *in quo*, rendered by the Polish Brethren *eo, quod*) without acknowledging that it had been recently debated. In the Racovian Catechism of 1605, the *locus* will again become important; its force for collective guilt in Adam dissipated by the use of Erasmus's reading of the scriptural phrasing: "and so death spread to all men *because* all men sinned."

14. This section on discipline includes matters dealt with separately in the seven articles of the Schleitheim (Anabaptist) Confession of 1527, namely, with pastors, separation from the world, the oath, and the ban and, in addition, with domestic and social conduct under scriptural norms.

15. The scriptural term *episcopus* is seldom used in the synodal records of the Major and Minor Church, where the scriptural overseer is more commonly called *superintendens*. As full-time minister of the Minor congregation in the capital, Schomann was himself a kind of *episcopus*.

16. The *seniores/presbyteri* elders were in the Reformed Church, Major and Minor, both clerical and lay, as in Geneva. Schomann does not here differentiate. The absence of any clear reference to the lay eldership, such as that not far back exercised by Dr. Giorgio Biandrata, *archipresbyter*, in fact, may reflect the decline of the role of lay patrons, unless they are embraced under *magistratus* above, an important point left unclear in the *Catechesis*.

17. The prominent placement here of widows betokens the priority of Scripture over the actual social/congregational situation, an archaism not corresponding to the numbers or importance of widows, who in fact are often reported in the synodal acts and Lubieniecki's *Historia* as marrying a second time. In the ensuing items on women and children, Schomann is not only faithfully scriptural but also "regressive" relative to what had obtained in the first phase of the Reformation in Poland with quite a few women prominent in lordly conversion, in endowments, eleemosynary contributions, correspondence, hymnody, and prayer, especially in Raków during the radical phase (negatively reported in the *Poloneutychia*), RD 6.

18. Schomann does not make clear whether the *magistratus* is the central state power of King, Diet, and Tribunals, and the palatine dietines or also the local lord and patron, who over his serfs had nearly sovereign authority. He is either unclear, evasive, or is intentionally general in view of his potentially international readership with a view to showing that Polish unitarian Baptists are not like the polygamous, theocratic Münsterite Anabaptists.

19. This is one of perhaps only two places where elder Schomann or printer Rodecki makes a mistake in the scriptural reference: in the text, 2 Cor 5. Schomann is no doubt troubled at this point by the gross immorality precisely among the earliest Christians before the "Fall of the Church."

20. This item bulks large in the *Catechesis* no doubt in reaction from the disorder and lounging about reported in Raków, 1569–72.

21. The prominence of this section is noteworthy; prayer in domestic life is also featured in the *Oeconomia domestica* that follows as an appendix.

22. The text refers mistakenly to Exodus 19.

23. To make a comparison, in the Schleitheim Confession (n. 14) article 1 is on believers' baptism (usually by sprinkling) and article 2 on the ban, while here "article" 5 is

on baptism by immersion, *following* the qualifications for covenantal membership betokened by baptism that leads to article 6 on the Supper.

24. Schomann glides over a difficult problem. In the tradition it has been held that possibly the baptism of the apostles was effectuated by Jesus' washing of their feet. In some Anabaptist circles footwashing was observed as an apostolic ordinance. There is no reference to it as such in Schomann.

25. Again, Schomann refuses to acknowledge the intractability of certain texts, in this case, major *loci* for the sanction precisely of pedobaptism, here impassively adduced in support of believers' baptism, without clear argumentation.

26. The Lord's Supper as observed by the Major and Minor Church would have been c. 1574 indistinguishable. Eucharistic theology, however, would necessarily come to diverge. Cf. the section on the Eucharist in Piotr Morzkowski, *Ecclesiastical Polity* (1642); *Polish Brethren*, Document XXIII.

27. What follows is a harmonized composite of all the scriptural passages on the institution of the Lord's Supper as an action to be repeated. Schomann passes over the two cups unique to Luke's account (without even in his case an ellipse); in other words he is traditional in his interpretation of Luke's account.

28. Cf. n. 8.

29. There is later evidence of self-scrutiny and mutual examination of conscience among the Minor Reformed on their Saturday session in the meeting house before the Sunday communion.

Notes to *RD* 8: Przypkowski/Biddle, Life of Socinus

1. *De Statu primi hominis ante lapsum Disputatio* (Raków, 1610); Gryczowa, no. 264.

2. *De Jesu Christo Salvatore* addressed to Jacques Couet of Paris (Cracow: Rodecki, 1594); Gryczowa, no. 67.

It is this fundamental work that Remonstrant Hugo Grotius attacked in his *Defense of the Catholic Faith concerning the Satisfaction of Christ against the Sienese* (Leiden, 1617), compactly presented in *PB* as Doc. X. It is of interest that in the sytematic study of the faith of the Dutch Calvinist Hendrikus Berkhof (b. 1914), *Christelijk geloof*, tr. by Sierd Woudstra as *Christian Faith* (rev. ed., Grand Rapids, Michigan: Eerdman, 1986), Berkhof notes approvingly Socinus's support of Luther's interpretation of the relation between God's love and wrath (p. 129), acknowledges Socinus's astute critique of the objective doctrine of satisfaction when he sought to interpret Jesus's death as confirmation of his teaching and his passage to the resurrection (p. 306), concluding that several of the important elements of the Calvinist position on the Atonement can be appropriately nuanced by the thought of Socinus (pp. 305–7). 3. Biddle's "infested" is stronger than Przypkowski's text.

4. This account is the basis for the common view that Socinus was called directly from Basel to Kolozsvár, but it is now held that Socinus was in Cracow when he received the invitation from Biandrata.

5. He was imprisoned by Christopher Báthory in the fortress of Déva, where he died November 1579.

6. Przypkowski is not clear, but he is referring to the hostile interpretations of the debate ed. by Jacob Palaeologus, *Defensio Francisci Dávidis* (3rd ed., Cracow, 1582), facsimile ed., *Bibliotheca Unitariorum*, vol. 1 (Utrecht, 1983).

Przypkowski obscurely proposes that Prince Christopher so far sided with Socinus that through no fault of his the Magistrate used force against the defeated Dávid.

7. Reluctant to implicate him by name, Przypkowski alludes to Biandrata, always favorably remembered in Poland by the Brethren.

8. *De Iesu Christi invocatione Disuptatio cum Francisco Davidis* (Cracow: Rodecki, 1595), dealt with by me in the Introdution at n. 91 item 12.

9. *Paraenesis ad omnes in regno Poloniae Samosatenianae vel Ebioniticae doctrinae professores* (1582). Wolan (1530–1610) was the leading Calvinist in Lithuania. The refutation of Wolan's charges by Socinus was first carried out in haste and anonymously in the form of a letter in 1579, his first publication in Poland. Then he dealt more deliberately in *De Iesu Christi filii Dei natura sive natura*, delivered to Prince Jan Kiszka (Cracow: Rodecki, 1588).

10. *De loco Pauli in Epistola ad Romanos capite septimo* (Cracow: Rodecki, 1583). The question turned on whether Paul wrote of his own state in 7:6: "But now we are discharged from the law, dead to that which held us captive, so that we serve not under the old written code but in the new life of the Spirit." Gryczowa, no. 68.

11. *Ad Iacobi Palaeologi librum cui tutulus est Defensio sententiae de Magistratu politico Responsio* (Raków: Rodecki, 1581); Gryczowa, no. 62.

12. *Defensio animadversionum in Assertiones theologicas Collegii Posnaniensis adversus Gabrielem Eutropeum, canonicum Posnaniensem* (Raków: Sternacki, 1618); Gryczowa, no. 266.

13. His prudential move occurred in 1583.

14. Elżbieta Morsztynówna. Her only child was Agnieska Morsztynowa Socyna, near n. 15, mother of Andrzej Wiszowaty, *PB*, Doc. I, n. 16.

15. The same as n. 12. Perhaps Przypkowski is referring to two episodes of the same conflict.

16. Ursini is mentioned in the earlier part of the *Vita* as having been solicitous for the return of Socinus to Florence presumably under his protection.

17. After the death of Stephen Báthory in 1586.

18. From Pawlikowice.

19. The three were the great uncles of the author of the *Historia*, including Andrzej of RD 5. The Piotr Stoiński of this same paragraph was the father of Jan Stoiński of RD 1.

20. Cf. n. 10. The question concerns Paul's own state of freedom from the Law and personal sanctification; cf. verse 7:25 ". . . I of myself serve the Law of God with my mind, but with my flesh I serve the law of sin."

21. I.e., for the position of Socinus and following him, Przypkowski.

22. The cheeky soldier was Kasper Wiernek, a noble from the Piedmont, surrounded by men of war assembled in Cracow to ward off a feared attack from the Tatars. Wiernek struck Socinus 6 October 1594, as the assaulted remarks in Epistle LXVI, as edited by Chmaj, *Listy*, 2. 155; cf. 156, 326.

23. B*Ant* asserts that the *Scriptum contra Atheos* perished with other works in Cracow in 1598, p. 74. For the assault see further Pl. 48.

24. L. Szczucki, treating Lublin next after Raków as the center of "Anabaptist Unitarianism," well summarizes his own fourth chapter of the Socinian takeover from the older leadership thus, *Czechowic*, 318:

> When Faustus Sozzinni had arrived in Poland (1579) [Marcin] Czechowic adopted a
> very hostile attitude toward the Italian heretic because of the doctrinal revisionism of

Sozzinni who wanted completely to alter the religious doctrines of the Polish antitrinitarians. The conflict over the dogmas [about Christology, baptism, and the discipline for the Lord's Supper] was aggravated by considerable differences of opinion on social and political issues, since Sozzini was sharply coming out against the social radicalism of Czechowic and his followers [though Sozzinni retained much of their pacifism in various accommodations]. The conflict ended in a defeat of Czechowic's group, and he himself, after the death of [his patron from Kujawy] Jan Niemojewski, was in 1598 deprived of his post of minister in the Lublin congregation [succeeded by Krzysztof Lubieniecki, brother of Andrzej of RD 6, and Walenty Schmalz, both devoted to Sozzinni]. His attacks on Socinianism in 1602–4 failed, and Czechowic, who spent his last years completely separated from the community, died in oblivion in 1613.

But Przypkowski much overstates the success of Socinus on the issue of believers' immersion, which, as Szczucki in the main text says remained unchanged despite Socinus's attacks and indeed its verbal minimization in the Racovian Catechism (*ibid.*, 117).

25. Przypkowski here repeats much of what is summarized in the paragraph ending with n. 24, but now ranged under three not yet quite completely separated groups: (1) the Judaizers and hence most of the Lithuanian Brethren who retained the Old Testament in full force, namely, the non-adorant Budnyites, some of whom, like Budziński, were also millenialists; cf. Socinus, *Contra Chiliastas* (Cracow, 1589), directed when ill to the synod of Chmielnik where this issue was to the fore; (2) the residually Calvinist within and without the consolidating *Socinianized* Minor Church who clung to several classical Protestant prinicples ranging from justification by faith alone through original sin to regenerative baptism; and (3) the defeated Lublin Anabaptist Unitarians who affected simple dress for nobles, like Niemojewski, no less than for plebeians, while Przypkowski considered the deficiencies or excesses under all three heads as ''spots'' (cf. Eph 5:27, where the Vulgate has *macula*) for the moles and blemishes of the Bride of Christ, his Body, the faithful Church.

It was from this Socinianized consensus sketched out by Przypkowski near Kiev in 1631 and perspective on the sixteenth century that Lubieniecki, using Budziński as one of his sources, wrote his *Historia* a generation later in exile in Hamburg in 1664.

26. The *Disputatio* (Raków: Sternacki, 1618) indicates that one phase of the debate took place in the hall of Krzysztof Morsztyn in Pawlikowice, 14 March 1584; Gryczowa, no. 268. Christian Francken, formerly a German Jesuit in Rome, was rector of the Unitarian school in Chmielnik, later lector in Koloszvár. On Francken and Socinus at Lublin and Chmielnik, 1584, and the resolution of some seeming contradictions in the sources and the literature, see Szczucki, *W kręgu myślicieli heretyckich*, esp. 175, n. 178.

27. Display (*a fastu*).

28. He was not fastidious.

29. He paid his duty toward.

30. Only hinted at here perhaps is Socinus's view of the death of the soul with the body pending the Second Advent of Christ and the Resurrection of the righteous only.

31. Much of the courtier families of the Socinus line are recounted by Benedykt Wiszowaty, Life, *PB*, Doc. I. There is much more detail on women here than recalled by Przypkowski in Tedeschi, ''Genealogy,'' Tedeschi, ed., *Laelius Socinus*. Fellide Sozzinni Marsili, e.g., served as financial agent for Faustus, administering his Sienese and Florentine patrimony and regularly forwarding to him the rents (*ibid*, 306).

Notes to *RD* 9: Carew, Society and Religion

Notes to the Introduction

1. The whole text is presented with a Latin introduction by Charles H. Talbot, Res Polonicae ex Archivo Musei Brittanici, 1 pars, Institutum Historicum Polonicum Romae, *Elementa ad Fontium Editiones* XXII (Rome, 1965) vii – xii, 1 – 175. A partly overlapping German translation of the text appears with other similar documents, edited by Elida Maria Szarota, *Die Gelehrte Welt des 17. Jahrhunderts über Polen* (Vienna /Zurich Europaverlag, 1972) 44 – 52.

2. Apart from what was said of Carew in the Introduction, see the life of George Carew told compactly in *DNB*, 3.959 – 60.

3. Carew writes extensively about Polish warfare. By the sixteenth century the general levy of the nobility, the *pospolite ruszenie* summoned to traditional sites for muster, notably in 1454, 1520, 1537, were largely replaced since the Statutes of Nieszwa of 1454 by mercenaries. They were headed by the royally appointed *hetman* (*Hauptman*), from 1581 for life. Fearing his aggregate martial power, the gentry, persuaded the King to appoint four, two each for Lithuania and Crown Poland, the first in each case the grand hetmann and in the field his deputy, the *hetman polny*. See further Wiesław Majewski, "The Polish Art of War in the Sixteenth and Seventeenth Centuries," in J. K. Fedorowicz, ed. and trans., *A Republic of Nobles: Studies in Polish History to 1864* (Cambridge/New York: Cambridge University Press, 1982).

4. Carew, with his English perspective, rightly thinks the King's Council as becoming the Senate which in membership was more numerous than the Chamber of Deputies and than palatinate *sejmiki* (dietines) that sent elected representatives to the lower house, the Chamber of Deputies, of the bicameral Sejm. The institutions of the lesser *szlachta* are the least described features in Carew of the Polish Constitution, like the *rokosz*, a Polish form of legitimate rebellion against whatever the nobility felt was an abuse of royal power.

5. Without their adducing Carew for all his extraordinary observations, several Polish and other scholars have admirably set forth in English fresh basic interpretations of modern Polish scholarship on the Royal Republic of Poland and documented the distinctiveness of its nobiliary development of the eastern realms, notably James Miller, who summarizes his thesis of 1977 in "The Polish Nobility and the Renaissance Monarchy: The 'Execution of the Laws' Movement," *Parliament, Estates, and Representations*, ed. by John Rogister, for the multilingual International Commission of approximately the same name (London: The Pageant Press) 3:3 (1983) 65 – 87; 4:1 (1984) 1 – 24 (both installments extensively mined for his article on "Polish Arianism" (Introduction at n. 56); Stanisław Russocki, "De l'accord commun au vote unanime [not an inhibiting problem in the sixteenth century]: les activités de la Diète nobiliare de Pologne, XVIème – XVIIIème siècle," *Parliaments, Estates and Representations*, 3:1 (1983) 7 – 20; and Antoni Mczak *et al.*, eds., *East-Central Europe in Transition: From the fourteenth to the seventeenth century* (Cambridge/New York: Cambridge University Press, 1985) bring together comparable essays for the distinctive development in these eastern royal realms.

On the major constitutional movement of the sixteenth century, initiated by Primate Łaski, enrolling the support of the lesser *szlachta*, Anna Dembińska wrote a major interpretation, *Politiczna walka o egzekuckę dóbr królelwskich w latach 1559 – 64* (Warsaw, 1935). Percy Shramm, extensively adduced in my annotation to the American edition of Lubieniecki, followed her thesis. Subsequently James Miller, among others, modified it substantially. The most positive interpretation of the petty Protestant nobles as royalists and centralists is that of Antoni Mczak, "The Structure of Power in the Commonwealth of the Sixteenth and Seventeenth Centuries," *Republic of Nobles*, who credits the spiritual elites, like the numerous royal secretaries on the way up for careers in the episcopacy an the high magistracies, "as saving the country for Catholicism" even when the Primate was undecided and several northern magnates had already espoused Protestantism, *Republic of Nobles*, 114. In the same collective work, Andrzej Wyczański, "The Problem of Authority in Sixteenth Century Poland: An essay in reinterpretion," is even more certain that the efforts of the gentry to strengthen their own authority and to insist that the King draw the most possible revenue from his *dobra królelweskie* or *domana króleweska* against misappropriation or exploitative plenary usufruct or even alienation and surreptitious inheritance by the magnates actually strengthened the royal authority and also had the King's ambiguous support (p. 97). Out of the concern for the central authority a few lesser nobles, e.g., Stanisław Szafraniec, once sympathetic with the theological radicals, reidentified with the Calvinists.

As for the King's command and judicial function in the provinces, it was exercised by an office commonly mentioned in the *Historia*, the *starostwo*. There were three kinds of *starosta*: *generalny*, representing the King in Great Poland, Ruthenia, and Poldolia; *grodowy*, representing the Crown and exercising administrative and judicial authority over a castle and its terrain; and *niegrodny*, administering royal lands on lease from the King. The Execution movement sought to keep all these lands and posts within call of the King.

6. The best treatment of the royal and the nobiliary (private) towns in Poland, where towns were in any case less developed than elsewhere in the West or East, is that of Maria Bogucka, "Polish Towns between the Sixteenth and Eighteenth Centuries," *Republic of Nobles*, 138–42, explaining the difference between the *wójt* (German: *Vogt*) who organized under the King or lord the new town mostly of German settlers and the *sołtys* (German: *Schultheiss*; Latin *scultetus*) who similarly organized the new towns as a reward, and she carries her studies into all three realms in "The Towns of East-Central Europe from the Fourteenth to the Seventeenth Century," *East-Central Europe*, 97–108. For the economic development of great latifunda without taxes or customs, for use of the Vistula and for the bondage of the peasants, see Jerzy Topolski, "Sixteenth-Century Poland and the Turning Point in European Economic Development," *Republic of Nobles*, 74–95, who touches upon the "second enserfment" or the "refeudalization" of rustics, roughly associated with the statutes of Piotrków of 1496 that restrained serfs to the land.

7. Although Anglican Carew can only construe the fissiparous character of religion in the commonwealth as a failure to identify God, religion, and country, without any sympathy for the sectaries, his account of the religious scene is actually clearer and much more comprehensive that that of A. Lubieniecki, RD 8.

Notes to the Relation

1. The towns and the royal boroughs and hence the burghers with rights of citizenship as freemen, many of them living by Magdeburg urban law, were not in general represented in the Diet as were the imperial free cities of the Holy Roman Empire and the boroughs of England and Scotland. There were the exception of the Royal capital and of the three Hanseatic cities of the Lower Vistula in royal (not ducal) Prussia: Toruń, Elbing, and Danzig.

2. The fact that Carew employed an Anglicized Low German/Dutch term *Bawre* would suggest that his information on this large class was based on inquiries among merchants in Danzing, Elbing, and possibly Königsberg.

Elsewhere Carew himself describes five kinds of toilers on the manors; adds that the Bawres "differ lyttle from slaves, called by the Poels contractly [collecitvely] Kemtones," a Latinization or garbling of *kmiecia* (p. 90). First there were the *servi glebae*, 2) the copyholders (*ascriptitii*), 3) farmers (*censiti*) who paid rent, 4) *conditionales* who bound themselves to husband a piece of ground only for a certain time, and 5) the undertendants or inmates (*inquilini*) who in one of three cases specified had been permitted to leave the manor because of the dereliction of the lord. The full text, 90.

The *fumalia* are the two *groschen* collected by the lord from each hearth and turned over to the royal treasury.

3. The urban law of German origin had both advantages and burdens for burghers who had bought a stone house (*kamieniec*) with the right to vote, govern through the town councils, and engage in trade.

4. Exempt from defense of the country, burghers were limited to the responsibility of maintaining civic order through the constabulary and serving in defense during a siege. In the *Historia* several burghers move into the landholding class, and many knights and greater landlords acquire town houses.

5. Carew seems to be using villainy in the sense that the landlords have undue power over their villeins, greater than their counterparts in England, and in the sense that they behave like uncouth serfs in relation to them.

6. The Interregnum lasted between the death of the King and the coronation of the elected successor, during which transition the Primate served as Interrex.

7. Carew does not give the exact name (*poseł*) and the duties of representatives in the Lower House of Deputies elected by the lesser *szlachta* in the dietines of the palatinates.

8. Carew, the Elisabethan envoy, keenly conscious of the constitutional problem ahead at the death of his Virgin queen, is throughout the *Relation* attentive to the procedures during the Polish interregna and supplies constitutional historians with useful observations. He would later serve on the commission to arrange for the personal union of Scotland and England under James VI/I in 1603.

He puts into Latin the concern of the counsellors "lest anything of harm come to the Republic," the classical word used more in the sixteenth than in the seventeenth century of the Commonwealth. Lubieniecki, e.g., more commonly says *regnum*. (I have variously rendered Lubieniecki's text as Commonwealth, Kingdom, and Royal Commonwealth with the two Latin words behind these three translations.)

9. Before the Union of Lublin of 1569 there were separate diets for the Grand Duchy of Lithuania and for Poland, in either case in changing venues.

10. Gniezno, see of the Primate of Poland (970), and Lwów (1233) for Ruthenia.

11. The ecclesiastical estate has great holdings and power.

12. Borders on.

13. Carew seems to mean here by Walachia also Transylvania, which unlike the former, had a long common border with the Commonwealth (see Map of Commonwealth and Hungary). Walachia could embrace the three interrelated principalities of Moldavia, Walachia, and Transylvania. In general Carew is quite careful in his designations.

14. Carew may here refer, among others, to Judaizers from Muscovy and Kiev as well as to the proto-Unitarian of palatinate Vilna, of Poland, Ruthenia, and Transylvania.

15. Many who either believe in no God or such as are idols (cf. Pl. 15B).

16. The Elizabethan envoy is evidently amazed at the degree of mutual toleration

among religious groups, interpreting it as sometimes springing from, or leading to, indifference in religion.

17. An illegible place is put in brackets by Talbot. The conjecture inside is mine.

18. The antecedent of "first" seems to have been something like "faith."

19. Muslims sometimes postponed circumcision into puberty.

20. Carew means by the Calvinists the Reformed and evidently has not gotten close enough to them to report on the fundamental schism since c. 1563 between the Minor [Reformed] Church of the Polish Brethren and of the Lithuanian Brethren, unitarian in theology, and the Major [Reformed] Church, trinitarian in theology and called by him also "Evangelicals." He will be referring to the former in disparaging terms, nn. 30, 32, 33.

21. The reference is to the concessions in the *Pax dissidentium de religione* of the Confederation of Warsaw of 1573 that induced the Protestant lords to vote for Henry of Valois, so closely in their minds associated with the St. Bartholomew's Day Massacre (Pl. 35).

22. Evangelical can mean in the sources of the sixteenth century either Lutheran, as here, or the Reformed of the Major Church.

23. Great (Greater) Poland with Gniezno the ancient capital, and Little (Lesser) Poland with Cracow the new capital, soon to be succeeded, 1611, by Warsaw in Masovia.

24. Roughly the equivalent of modern ethnic and political Lithuania; cf. n. 51 and see the dotted lines bordering the area on the Map.

25. George Cardinal Radziwiłł, bishop of Cracow (1591 – 1600) (Pl. 6).

26. The two cousins Nicholas were the Black (1515 – 69) and the Red (1512 – 84) (Pl. 14). The four sons of Nicholas Radziwiłł the Black returned to Catholic obedience and the youngest became the Cardinal.

27. He espoused the Reformation at first as Lutheran, then as Reformed, at his death he was virtually a Unitarian in correspondence with Ferencz Dávid in Transylvania (Pl. 41).

28. Here Evangelical is used in the sense of Calvinist. Cf. n. 22.

29. The Radziwiłł Bible of Brest, 1563 (Pl. 54).

30. Nicholas VIII Christopher Radziwiłł the Orphan (1549 – 1616).

31. Carew probably has in mind primarily the Mennonites of the Vistula Delta, although he will have been informed that the "Antitrinitaries" rebaptized by immersion.

32. The condemned followers in Königsberg of Andreas Osiander (d. 1552) with whom, however, Duke Albert of Hohenzollern, the first Protestant prince (vassal of the Polish King in 1525), had agreed (Pl. 7).

33. One of the hostile names for the proto-Unitarians of the Minor Church.

34. This may well be the first use of the term in English, eventually standardized as "Antitrinitarian" to cover the whole range of opponents of the received Nicene formulations of the doctrine of the Trinity. The term "Unitarian" was just beginning to be used in Transylvania for the adherents of the "Lesser Church" there, officially "Unitarian" only in 1633. Elizabethan Puritan John Preston (d. 1602) in his *Prophetica* ([Cambridge], 1572) and in the translation thereof as *The Arte of Prophecying* (1607), in his brief survey of the heresies on the Continent in the Reformation Era, ch. 4, refers to *Antitrinitarii/Antitrinitaries*—the English term thus later than the usage here of Carew.

35. Carew's terminology, "Romish religion," "Popery," etc., reflects his Elizabethan Anglican stance.

36. The reference is to Sigismund III Vasa (1587 – 1632) (Pl. 60); cf. n. 42.

37. The Jesuit order was established in the Commonwealth first in Braunsberg near Danzig, 1564.

38. Andrew Leszczyński, palatine of Brześć Kujawski (1591–1606) (cf. Pls. 11 and 19).

39. Braunsberg in the nearly temporal bishopric of Varmia (Ermland), surrounded by Lutheran Ducal Prussia.

40. Stanislas Cardinal Hosius, bishop of Varmia (1551–79), was spearhead of the Counter Reform in the Commonwealth (Pl. 49).

41. The towns in the paragraph are: Dorpat in Livonia, present-day Latvia, Kalisz, and Polotsk.

42. Primate Stanislas Karnowski of Gniezno (1581–1603) (Pl. 5). In Vilna (Pl. 14) the Jesuit college was transformed into a university by a papal charter and dedicated by Stephen Batory, King of Poland (1576–86) (Pl. 46).

43. Sigismund III Vasa (Pl. 60) founded for the Jesuit Order St. Peter's Church in Cracow.

44. Chancellor John Zamoyski (1542–1603), by 1578 Chancellor and by 1581 Grand Marshal.

45. The *Academia Cracoviensis* (Pl. 16) founded in 1384 came to be known as the Jagiellonian University. It was modeled on Padua and Bologna; the Jesuit college in Cracow, 1564, sought to compete with it; and at the provincial synod of Piotrków in 1589 the Jesuits insisted in vain that the philosophical and the theological faculty of the Jagiellonian University be in their charge.

46. Mieszko I (960–92) took as wife the daughter of the Boleslas I (929–67) of the Přemyslide dynasty of Bohemia. The two dukes making common cause against the Germans; in the marriage alliance Mieszko was baptized a Christian as was later the Lithuanian Jagiełło on becoming King of Poland, n. 47.

47. Jagilas is known in Polish as Jagiełło, who, after baptism in the Franciscan church in Cracow in 1384, became King of Poland as husband of Queen Jadwiga, daughter and heir of Louis the Hungarian (1326–82), and founder of the Jagiellonian dynasty, 1384–1572 (cf. Pl. 2).

48. Carew makes an important point. On the Byzantine-rite frontier crossing through the Commonwealth from just east of Vilna south through Przemyśl, the Reform-minded lords could think of themselves as part of Latin Christendom over against the Byelorussians and the Ruthenians. Only with the promulgation of the decrees of Trent in 1564 did it become wholly clear how far the Protestant patrons were at variance with Rome, and the decrees were not accepted by the King in Diet until 1577.

49. Byelorussia, *Russia Alba,* was the larger part of Grand Ducal Lithuania after its relinquishment in 1569 of its southern palatinates to Crown Poland (n. 50). By Lithuania here Carew has probably in mind the palatinate of Vilna, only partly Lithuanian in speech. The *Russia rubra* is Ruthenia.

50. In that part of the Grand Duchy of Lithuania placed directly under the Polish Crown in the Union of Lublin, 1569, namely, in the palatinates of Volhynia, Podolia, Bracław, and Kiev.

51. In the new Crown palatinates of the East, many formerly Orthodox lords became Catholic (Uniate) (cf. n. 64), Reformed, or even Unitarian: a few remained Orthodox and refused to join in the Union of Brest Litovsk (1595/96) as Uniates under the Pope (Pls. 52 and 53). See below.

52. Samogitia, the core of ethnic Lithuania, the language of which among the

peasants extended into the eastern half of Ducal Prussia, was made into a bishopric by the Council of Constance in 1416 with its see in Königsberg and placed under Gniezno. When Ducal Prussia became Lutheran in 1525, Samogitia (Samland, Żmudź) was under strong Protestant influence, resistant to Orthodox penetration, and then recatholicized.

53. Prince Konstantyn Vasil Ostrozhskyi (1527 – 1608), promoter of the Old Slavonic Ostroh Bible, 1580/81 (Pls. 53 and 54), was palatine of Kiev.

54. The metropolitan of Moscow had himself been elevated to the dignity of Patriarch in 1589. Carew has not yet taken in the significance of that momentous ecclesiastical development.

55. Polish: *Władyka*, both lord and bishop.

56. The eight Orthodox centers in this sentence are Lwów, (Lvov/Lemberg), Vilna (Vilnius), Polotsk, Vladimir, Lutsk (Latin correctly Luceoria), Pinsk, Kiev, and Przemyśl.

57. The Russians, including the Ruthenians (or Ukrainians in modern terminology) and the Great Russians (Muscovites in the terminology of that age).

58. Carew has garbled his account. Prince Vladimir of Kiev was converted in 988 to Orthodox Christianity and married Anna, sister of Emperor Basil III Bulgaroktonos. The Patriarch was Nicholas II.

59. The Cyrillic alphabet.

60. The inhabitants of Western Asia Minor. It is not clear why Carew calls them Slavs.

61. The Dniepr.

62. The Black Sea.

63. Byelorussia and Ruthenia (larger sense).

64. Carew, by Vladicians, (n. 55, equal Uniates) refers to the Union of Brest Litovsk, 1595/96 (Pl. 52).

65. Kamieniec.

66. There are a few "Tatar" mosques to this day in the Poland and before 1939 also in Lithuania.

67. Lwów in Ruthenia (Pl. 60).

68. Lords owning villages and towns.

69. The royal protection of Jews did not necessarily apply in towns owned by princes and lords.

70. Boleslas the Pious (1221 – 79) was not king but only duke of Kalisz. Casimir the Great (1310 – 70), King of Poland from 1333, confirmed the privilege of toleration in 1334 and 1364 and extended it to Jews in Ruthenia in 1367.

71. Ceremissa is the territory of the Chermiss, a Finnic enclave still living in the middle Volga.

72. For these figures, the English ambassador was dependent perhaps on quite tendentious allegations of his hosts from the same class as himself.

73. Tithes from the land tilled by serfs.

74. *Laneus*, related to German *Lehen*, is the Polish land unit, łan, about 15 hectares.

75. The *legatus a latere*, the papal nuncio, features frequently in the *Historia*, the more so as under some Primates, like Jacob Uchański (1562 – 81), (Pl. 5) a correspondent of Calvin, there was some openness to the Reformation with the possibility of a national Church hovering between the Anglican and the Gallican solution.

COMMENTARIES ON THE PLATES AND MAPS

1. THE *HISTORIA* OF LUBIENIECKI I: SOME CONTEMPORARIES

1.BA. Shown is the copy purchased in 1689 by the president of Harvard College, Dr. Increase Mather, and used by the editor until the publication of the indexed facsimile edition of Henryk Barycz (Warsaw, 1971). With the permission of the Houghton Library, Harvard University.

It seems likely that Increase Mather first came to know Lubieniecki as the author of *Theatrum Cometicum* (Pl. 63), as in a letter of 20 November 1683, he asks one Abraham Kick to procure for him a copy of it; *Harvard College Records,* Publications of the Colonial Society of Massachusetts, 49 (1975), p. 149. The son of Increase Mather, Cotton Mather, drawing upon his father's researches into degree-granting privileges in connection with seventeenth-century Harvard College, specifically mentions Poland, when he reports that the Master's degree (instead of the B.A. and the Ph.D.) was used in "England, France, Spain, Italy, and Poland," *Magnalia Christi Americana* (London, 1702; Hartford, in 2 vols., 1853) book 4, part 1, II, p. 19. It seems likely that Increase Mather bought the *Historia* out of interest in learning how the Reformed Church, tolerated in a land under bishops as in England, might fare in the colonies, and he probably knew that Comenius (Pl. 61.C), who had been sought out c. 1641 in London for the Harvard rectorship, came from Leszno.

1.A. The *Historia,* edited by Benedict Wiszowaty, was printed in Freistadt (Amsterdam) in 1685 by John Aconius, who had the year before printed the *Bibliotheca Antitrinatariorum* (*BAnt*), for which Wiszowaty transferred one chapter from the *Historia.*

1.B. Increase Mather bought the *Historia* in London, 23 May 1689, while negotiating a new charter for the Massachusetts Bay Colony.

1.C. A Danish scholar's edition of the *Compendium*, several times alluded to by Lubieniecki in the *Historia.* Shown is the upper portion of the title-page of the MS from the Staatsbibliothek: Preussicher Kulturbesitz, theol. Quart. 295, purchased in 1882 from the library of Dr. Carl Thiele, pastor in Naumburg. The lower portion of the title-page (not shown) from another hand identifies the author as Lubieniecki, after crossing out the name of a surmised author, and identifies the work as posthumous. The MS has been edited by K. E. Jordt Jørgensen, *Stanislaus Lubieniecki: Compendium Veritatis Primaevae* in two volumes, 1, the extensive introduction to the text and summary thereof, and 2, the annotated text (Copenhagen: Akademsk Forlag, 1982).

The handwriting displayed is that of Lubieniecki himself, entitling his fifteen ecumenical colloquies among the representatives of five confessions. Hosted by the layman George, the ideal colloquies in the full title have Lubieniecki himself speaking for "the Catholic Christian Confession" of the Minor Church through "Faustus": *Veritatis Primaevae Compendium sive Nova Facilis et Certa Catholicae Christianae Confessionis*

Demonstratio per Quindecim brevia, amica Colloquia divisum inter Georgium, Faustum, Adrianum, Cyrillum, Martinum et Joannem.

1.D. The signature of Stanislas Budziński (d.c. 1595), author of the lost Polish MS History used by Lubieniecki. *Archiwum Państwowe na Wawelu*, item *1160 karta 3*. The signature (from his birthplace in Masovia, Budzyn) is on legal paper of 1595, the surname split on two levels with *manu propria* squeezed into space crowded by the other signitory. The photograph was sent by Wacław Urban, who does not refer to it, however, in his account of "Stanisław Budzyński" (Urban's preferred spelling) and of six other Poles, *Bibliotheca Dissidentium*, 8 (Baden-Baden: Koerner, 1987) 35–52.

Budziński's History survives in large extracts and paraphrases not only in Lubieniecki's *Historia* but also in other works, notably in the Church History (cf. Pl. 19) of Andrew Węgierski (1600–49), the second to have been written on Polish soil, and out of the mingled tradition in Leszno of the Czech Brethren and the Reformed, which was entitled the *Systema historico-chronologicum,* published posthumously (Utrecht, 1652) and reprinted with supplementation by the Polish Brethren in exile as *Slavonia Reformata* (Amsterdam, 1679).

1.E. From the *Kronika* Lubieniecki draws his account of the burning of Catherine Zalaszkowska Weiglowa as a Judaizer, Cracow, 1539.

Martin Bielski (Wolski), favorable to the Reformation, was author of a universal History in Polish, *Kronika wszystkiego świata* (Cracow, 1551).

Biblioteka Narodowa, Warsaw; from Oskar Thulin, ed., *Reformation in Europa* (Leipzig/Kassel: Stauda, 1969), p. 186.

1.F. Matthias Flacius Illyricus (15210–75), on whose *Centuries* Lubieniecki drew. Print by Tobias Stimmer, printed by Bernard Jobin (Strassburg, 1557); taken from Walter L. Strauss, *The German Single-Leaf Woodcut, 1550–1600,* 3 vols. (New York: Arbaris, 19), p. 1015. The original letter has extensive ornamentation and a Latin legend stating Flacius died in Frankfurt in 1575 in his fifty-fifth year. Heinrich Hondius made his more familiar copperprint from this, The Hague, 1602.

Flacius, through his *Clavis Scripturae* (Basel, 1567), may be a source of the typological-eschatological interpretations of *Veritas* as fulfillment of the Old Testament type and clarification of the New Testament antitype, which resonates behind Lubieniecki's use of the term, cf. above, C. As "the father of Protestant hermeneutics" (Wilhelm Dilthey), Flacius drew upon a minor typological tradition that had the advantage over Alexandrine (Origenist) allegorism and the Antiochene (fully literalist) hermeneutic in recognizing (with Luther) the religious meaning of the literal/historical sense of the Old Testament, while permitting a fuller meaning in the fullness of time, Joshua, e.g., seen as the type of Christ, which method greatly supplemented the expressly prophetic utterances in the Old Testament anticipating the Messiah. The use of *veritas* as the New Testament antitype or fulfillment or realization of the Old Testament *typus, imago, umbra* seems to have first appeared in Tertullian, followed by Cyprian and Jerome and incorporated in Flacius's widely consulted *Clavis Scripturae* (the final edition of Basel, 1609), I, col. 1233, II, 216, 333. Not dealing with typology, but bringing scholarship abreast, Mijo Mirković introduces Flacius for a selection of the *testes veritatis* in Croatian translation, *Katalog svjedoka istine* (Zagreb: Jugoslavenska Akademija Znanosti i umjetnosti, 1960); see also the celebrative essays, *Matthias Flacius Illyricus 1575–1975,* Schriftenreihe des Regenburger Osteuropainstituts (Regensburg, 1975). See also Pl. 49.C.

The spirited Croatian Matthias Flacius (Vlačić) Illyricus (1520–75), born on the Dalmatian coast under Venetian control, successively student at Basel, Tübingen, and Wittenberg (professor of Hebrew there 1544–49), was a major controversialist on the Lutheran extreme (Gnesio-Lutheran), holding that original sin is ''the essential substance'' of human nature. A major editor of the Magdeburg Centuries, *Historia Ecclesiae Christi* (Basel, 1559–74), he is referred to by name only once by Lubieniecki (*p.* 33), but the Centuries were a resource for him. It is also possible that Lubieniecki was familiar with the *Catalogus testium Veritatis* (1556), in which Flacius repelled the charge of novelty brought by Romanists against Protestants and showed that there were witnesses (*testes*) in every age who combatted the Papacy and its errors, a work influential in the achievement of John Foxe, *Actes and Monuments of Christian Martyrs* (Latin: Strassburg, 1554; English: Basel, 1563) and also in the polemic of Martin Krowicki (d. 1573; Pl. 10.C). For the impact of the two works mentioned of Flacius, see Henryk Barycz, ''Marcin Krowicki, polemista i pamflecista reformacji,'' *Z epoki renesansu, reformacji i baroku* (Warsaw, 1971), esp. p. 301, nn. 322–24. It is just possible that Lubieniecki's recurrent reference to his fellow believers as *confessores Veritatis* owes something to the *Catalogus,* perhaps by way of Krowicki, and to Flacius's hermeneutical principles expressed in his influential *Clavis Scripturae* (1567).

1.G. Cyprian Bazylik, *The History of Harsh Persecution* (Brest, 1567), drawing on John Foxe *et al.*, supplies John Utenhove's Life of John Łaski in Polish (Plate 20). From the Moksilnė Biblioteka of the University of Vilnius in Lithuania, formerly of the Evangelical-Reformed Library, Vilnius; cf. Henryk Biegeleisen, *Illustrowane dzieje literatury polskiej,* 5 vols. (Vienna, 189–90), 3, p. 197; Jerzy Ziomek, ed., *Odrodzenie w Polsce: Historia literartury* ([Warsaw]: PAN, 1956) p. 496. For the *Historya* and its translator, see Kawecka-Gryczowa, *Drukarze dawnej Polski,* Wielkie Księstwo Litewskie, pp. 45–52.

The title-page of the composite *History* in 400 folios of the persecution of the Church of God, *Historya o śrogiem prześladowaniu Kościoła Bożego* (Brest Litovsk, 1567), by the translator and printer, Cyprian Bazylik, and including an annex on John Łaski (Pl. 15.E).

Bazylik drew on John Foxe (1516–87), *Book of Martyrs* (Latin: Strassburg, 1554), John Crespin (c. 1520–72) of Arras and Geneva, *Acts of the Martyrs . . . from Wycliffe and Hus to our day* (Latin: Geneva, 1556), and Henry Pantaleon (1522–95), *History of Martyrs* (Latin: Basel, 1563).

On the title-page shown Bazylik features four martyrs, John Hus (d. Constance, 1415); William Gardiner, English merchant, arms severed before being burned (d. Lisbon, 1552); lower right, Archbishop Thomas Cranmer (d. Oxford, 1556); and, lower left, Bishop John Hooper of Gloucester and Worcester (d. London, 1555). Within a wide selection, Bazylik of Brest Litovsk has chosen three Englishmen, two of them Marian martyrs.

This History has been rewritten as a novel of the life of John Łaski, in the light of all the modern scholarship, by Stanislas Helsztyński, *Reformator Sarmacji: Opowieść Cypriana Bazylika o Janie Łaskim* [as though composed in 1592] (Warsaw: Ludowa Spółdzielnia Wydawnicza, 1981). With thirty-two illustrations, the historical novel integrates a good deal of historical material pleasantly, although some of the theology is askew.

1.H. *Poloneutychia or the Success of the Polish Kingdom and with it of the Grand Duchy of Lithuania, and the Change in Fortune in the Year 1612 and 1613* (Raków, 1615), written by the great uncle, Andrew Lubieniecki (c.1551 – 1623). Czartoryski Collection, MS 1370, Cracow; critically edited by Alina Linda *et al.* (Warsaw/Łódź: PAN, 1982), the edition cited frequently in the annotation to the *Historia,* though our Author was not in a position to use the work of his predecessor, cf. *ibid.,* p. xvii, a portion of whose text on religious ferment appears in the Appendix.

Andrew Lubieniecki was successively minister in Śmigiel, 1584; Hoszcza in Volhynia, 1600; Raków, 1612. His *Poloneutychia,* idealizing the Golden Age of freedom, diversity, and humanistic culture under the Jagiellonians, particularly under the two Sigismunds, is a rich publicistic essay or perhaps rather historiosophic chronicle with the author's classical biblical sense of theodicy and judgment in history. He considered the state executions of a Unitarian and a Calvinist in 1611, the reason for God's wrath against the Commonwealth in several catastrophes in the East and Southeast. Lubieniecki was possibly the compiler of the martyrdoms of John Tyszkowic in Warsaw (*PB,* Doc. IX) and Franco di Franco in Vilna (full Polish text, ed by Kot, *RwP,* 9/10 [1937/39] pp. 465 – 69). He also kept a MS record of the Synods, drawn upon in the *Historia.* Andrew Lubieniecki is assessed by Henryk Barycz, *Szlakami dziejopisarstwa staropolskiego* (Wrocław: Ossolineum, 1981), pp. 204 – 42. His MS *Sztambuch* of signatures is pictured in Pl. 59.F.

2. THE LAST OF THE JAGIELLONIANS

These miniatures are by Lukas Cranach of Sigismund I the Old (1506 – 48) and his second queen Bona Sforza and their five children: Sigismund II Augustus (1548 – 72) and his three wives: Elizabeth of Austria, Barbara Radziwiłłówna (sister of Protestant Prince Nicholas the Red), and Catherine (sister of his first wife); then his sisters: Isabelle (mother of John Sigismund, "Unitarian King" of Transylvania), Catherine, and Anna (wife of King Stephen Batory, 1576 – 86).

The picture is reproduced from the color plate in Zdisław Żygulski, Jr., *et al., Muzeum Narodowe w Krakowie: Zbiory Czartoryskich* (Warsaw: Arkady, 1978) no. 17, and pp. 150 f. The pictures were painted c. 1556, at the request of Sigismund II or a sister, from sketched likenesses forwarded to Lucas Cranach the Younger (1515 – 86). These miniatures were arranged within a larger frame in the 19th century.

On the top row left is Sigismund I the Old (1467/1506 – 48). Grandson of Ladislas II Jagiełło (1386 – 1434), the founder of the Jagiellonian (Lithuanian) dynasty, and Queen Jadwiga (1384/86 – 89.1434), he was the son of Casimir IV Jagiellończyk (1446 – 92). His three older brothers preceded him by election to the Polish royal dignity.

The oldest brother was king of Bohemia, Ladislas II (1471 – 1516), elected at the diet of Kutná Hora in the grand dream of a great Slavic realm under Jagiellonian dynasties. Ladislas was subsequently elected king of the Apostolic Kingdom of Hungary (1490 – 1516). He was succeeded in both these realms by Sigismund's nephew, Louis II (1516 – 26). King of Bohemia and hence *ex officio* one of the Seven Electors, Louis II, as a minor, was in 1519 assisted by the royal Polish uncle, Sigismund I, in the election process that elevated Charles V Hapsburg as Holy Roman Emperor. Slain in the battle of Mohács, which defeat eventuated in the tripartition of Hungary, Louis II of Bohemia and Hungary was succeeded by Ferdinand I Hapsburg (1526 – 64), who, though he married the fallen king's sister, Anna Jagiellonka, involved himself necessarily in resistance to the Ottomans, while Poland directed its energy and power increasingly towards Muscovy. In this new dynastic situation, Sigismund I the Old found himself presently pressed by the growing might of the Hapsburgs, to the south in Bohemia and in its annexed dependencies in Silesia, indeed all along his western imperial frontier to the Baltic; and some of his advisors would look to distant and detached Transylvania under his daughter Isabelle as a natural ally against the imperial anti-Turkish Hapsburgs.

In the meantime, the youngest of the five grandsons of Jagiełło and Jadwiga, Frederick, became Bishop of Cracow and Cardinal Primate of Gniezno (Pl. 5).

Sigismund I first married Barbara Zápolya (1495 – 1515), a daughter of the count of Spisz (Zips), resuming a Hungarian dynastic relationship that went back to Louis the Great, the Hungarian father of Jadwiga, King of both Hungary and Poland (1442/70 – 82). Barbara died childless. Sigismund took as his second queen Bona Sforza, daugher of the Duke of Milan (1491/married 1518 – 58). Bona brought in her train the courtly traditions of Italy and artisans, architects, writers, and freethinkers who made of Cracow a flourishing center of humanistic culture. The Polish Reformation cannot but be seen as in part the consolidation of the reformatory impulses of the Italian Renaissance on Slavic soil.

Of the five children of Bona and Sigismund there was the only son, Sigismund II Augustus (1491 – 1548 – 72, cf. Pl. 5) with his three wives: Elizabeth of Austria (1525/43 – 45) was daughter of Emperor Ferdinand I. Barbara Radziwiłłówna (1520/47 – 51), sister of Protestant Nicholas Radziwiłł the Red (Pl. 14); and her hearse, out of love and grief, he followed on foot back to Vilna. Beginning on the lower row, Catherine (1533/53 – 72), sister of his first wife.

Then follow the four daughters of Bona and Sigismund. The oldest was Isabelle (1519 – 59), who married John Zápolya (the older brother of her father's first wife), voivode of Transylvania (Pl. 39). Next come Catherine (1526 – 83), wife of John Vasa, prince of Finland, then king of Sweden (parents of the future Polish King Sigismund III Vasa, Pl. 60); Sophia (1522 – 75), wife of Henry of Brunswick; and Anna, "the last of her race" (1523 – 96), candidate in her own right for election to royalty, who as queen of Stephen Báthory/Batory, prince of Transylvania, King of Poland (1576 – 86), supplied a touch of dynastic legitimation.

3. RENAISSANCE AND REFORMATION CRACOW

3.A. A miniature in the Prayer Book of Sigismund I, 1524, shows him receiving Communion in two kinds from Christ himself descended from the cross. MS Prayer Book, The British Library, Department of Manuscripts, Add. MS 15281, by permission.

This miniature of Sigismund I the Old, from his MS Psalter of St. Jerome, was executed by S.C., Stanislaus Capellanus (according to Marian Sokołowski), a Cistercian of Mogila near Cracow. He may have been influenced by the school of Albert Dürer. The royal attire is the same as in Plate B. Remarkable is the representation of the King who, having doffed his crown before the crown of thorns, kneels before Jesus, just descended from the cross to offer the royal suppliant directly, as though from his still bleeding body, communion in both kinds, repeating in Latin John 5:56: "Caro mea vere est cibus." The painting offers an extraordinary iconographic transition from late medieval piety into the Polish Age of Renaissance and Reformation and may also testify to the Utraquist influence at the Polish court.

The Psalter gives evidence of having been used devoutly and frequently by the original owner, thumbworn and with words evidently penned by Sigismund in capital letters of gold, "Laudans invocabo Dominum, et ab inimicis meis salvus ero. 1524 – S."

The so-called Prayer Book of Sigismund I, of 203 leaves of vellum, is written in a fair Roman letter with interrulings in gold and colored initials, with four miniatures. Passed on to widowed Bona Sforza and then to Sigismund III Vasa, it has considerable family annotation. It came into the possession of the First Pretender, Prince James, the son of James I, in 1719 by way of Princess Maria Clementina Sobieska, and was eventually sold to the British Museum. The Psalter is described by Sir Francis Madden in a letter to the editor, *Gentleman's Magazine,* under several titles, 303 vols. (1731–1907), 178:2 (24) (1845), pp. 25–28, which surmised from the ornamental borders that the artist had "also studied in the Italian school." With the proximity of the Utraquists in Prague and the institution of communion in both kinds in Wittenberg (Melanchthon/Carlstadt, 1521), one may conjecture both Hussite and Lutheran influences in the background of the miniaturist and even of the devout King.

The miniature is discussed by Felix Kopera, *Dzieje Malarstwa w Polsce od XVI do XVIII wieku* (Cracow, 1926), pp. 25–29, without, however, his explaining the remarkable conceptualization. My own surmise is that the motif of the *Chrystus Frasobliwy* (Pl. 55), seated forlorn and puzzled at the foot of the cross *before* the crucifixion, made possible the transition for the miniaturist to the stooped Christ extending his arms from the cross to distribute the visibly bloodied Host to the devout King. In the background is presumably an idealized Jerusalem/Cracow, while above, the angels besing the mystery of the spiritual transaction in which Sigismund is offered the Chalice as well as the Host. The miniature conveys the sense of divine immediacy without the mediation of priests, the direct access of the King to the Holy Grail. The *Chrystus Frasobliwy* of Polish folk art is the *Christus lassus,* of apocryphal inspiration, in the *Dies irae* of the Requiem Mass.

3.BC. A gold medallion, cast in Augsburg c. 1527, presented by Severin Boner (D) to Erasmus in 1531, in appreciation for the humanist's having received in Basel his son John Boner (the later Protestant patron, Pl. 8). Historisches Museum, Basel, by permission. Studied by Beatrice Schärli, *Kabinettstücke der Amerbach im Historischen Museum Basel* (Basel, 1984), p. 50. Sigismund and Erasmus, of about the same age, were correspondents, and it was on the King's recommendation that young John Boner was sent to the Humanist by his father.

B. The medallion sharply delineates the profile of the King and Grand Duke Sigismund I the Old (1467/1506–48) at about sixty (cf. Pl. 2), with silken-net skull cap, a fur coat, and the chain of the Order of the Golden Fleece.

The last of three sons of Casimir IV to ascend the throne, Sigismund seemed "Old" and, moreover, allowed his son to become Grand Duke of Lithuania as of 1529, and thus King-designate, hence becoming himself "the Old Sigismund."

By the constitution of Radom of 1505, *Nihil novi,* his brother Alexander had agreed to do "nothing new" without the consent of the Diet which put the middle and lower *szlachta,* represented by the Deputies, in a strategic position over against the King and Senators (bishops and magnates), all during the sixteenth century. Cf. commentary, Pl. 6.A. The lesser lords were thus freer from the central authority to introduce the Reformation on their estates (indeed something quite new!), while Sigismund's second wife, Bona Sforza, promoted Italians, most of whom were moved by both Renaissance and Reformation aspirations and were ready to advise these lords (Pl. 16).

C. The inscription with black enamel says: "Severin Boner sends (M[ittit]) a gift (D[onum]) to Erasmus of Rotterdam."

The influence of Erasmus was strong in Cracow. His first work was published in Poland was *Querula Pacis* (Cracow: Wietor, 1518). To Decjusz (C) Erasmus dedicated his paraphrase of the Lord's Prayer (1523). The library of Erasmus, bought in his lifetime by his houseguest, John Łaski (Pl. 20), was carted to Cracow after the Humanist's death by Frycz Modrzewski (Pl. 22). For the context of Erasmus's dedication to a work to Decius (D), see George H. Williams, ''Erasmianism in Poland,'' *PR* 22 (1977), esp. p. 3.

3.D. Sepulchral monument of Sophia Bonerowa wife of Severin Boner, parents of a leading Calvinist patron, John Boner. One of two matching sepulchral slabs in St. Mary's, Cracow, photographed by Z. Tomaszewska; taken from Helena Blum *et al., Kraków: Jego dzieje i sztuka* (Warsaw: Arkady, 1965), p. 287.

The equally impressive slab of Severin Boner (d. 1549) in armor is not shown. He was the son of John (d. 1523). His first wife, Sophia Bethmann (Bettmann) (d. 1532), in the interest of saving space, has been chosen to represent the parents of John Boner (d. 1562), a pillar of the Reformation in Cracovia and whom they sent as a youth to study under Erasmus (BC). Of the two parents, Sophia Bethmann Boner(owa) has been selected as also symbolizing the importance of women in general in the era of the Reformation in Poland, even though in this case the couple remained humanistically Catholic. Her wimple suggests the late medieval context of Renaissance and Reformation in the capital.

Her father Severin Bethmann (d. 1515) left Weissenburg (Wissembourg) in Alsace and settled in Cracow in 1466, one of the first of the Alsatian immigrants (colonists) (cf. Decius). On his death at ninety-five much of his vast landed estates and other properties came by way of Sophia to the Boner family. Marian Friedberg, *PSB,* 1 (1935), p. 477.

The Boner family for its part originated in the Rhine Palatinate where John, Sr. and his son Severin were born. Many Germans from the Empire sought to make their career within the Commonwealth. Many towns, besides Cracow, lived by Magdeburg urban law (first codified in 1186), adopted in ever updated versions by over eighty towns. The Breslau version, in five books and 465 articles, became the mother law of all towns under the Bohemian crown. Leading burghers became patricians; and, ennobled, they often served as Deputies and even Senators, as did John Boner. Cardinal Hosius (Pl. 49) was, e.g., the son of burghers from Baden.

Up to 1531, burghers and artisans living by Magdeburg law, from Cracow to Lwów and beyond, had the right to appeal their cases to the bench of assessors/syndics of the Magdeburg court for an appellate judgment (*urteil/ortyl*), when an external appeal was blocked by the parliamentarian requirement that town courts be conducted in Polish (see further, Pl. 6.A commentary). For the extent of Magdeburg law in the Ukraine, see Andrij Iakovliv (Jakovliv), *Das Deutsche Recht in der Ukraina . . . im 16–18. Jahrhundert* (translated from the Czech; Leipzig, 1942); Paul Laband, *Das Magdeburg-Breslauer systematische Schoeffenrecht aus der Mitte des XIV. Jahrhunderts;* Hans Reichard, *Die deutschen Stadtrechte des Mittelalters* (Berlin, 1930), which lists mother and daughter cities, pp. 76–79; and, for a comprehensive coverage in English, Harold Berman, *Law and Revolution* (Cambridge: Cambridge University Press, 1983), chap. 12.

3.E. In a devotional miniature, Mintmaster Ludwig Dietz (Decjusz, d. 1545), philo-Protestant from Alsace, is shown behind the Chancellor and Sigismund I, a detail from an illuminated page by Stanisław Samostrzelnik, c. 1530, in John Długosz (1415–80), *Catalogus archiepiscoporum Gnesiensium,* illuminated MS in Biblioteka Narodowa, Warsaw; taken from Helena and Stefan Kozakiewicz, *The Renaissance in Poland* (Warsaw: Arkady, 1976), Pl. 3; identification of persons by Władysław Czapliński, *Zarys dziejów Polski do roku 1864* (Cracow: Znak, 1985), pp. 161, 549 (n. on Pl. 16). In the whole picture, St. Stanislas is the dominant figure (only his arms showing in the detail here), before whom his episcopal successor Peter Tomicki kneels on the side not shown and on the side shown, Sigismund I, his Chancellor Christopher Szydłowiecki, and his secretary, Decius kneel.

3.F. The palace of Ludwik Jost Decjusz (c. 1485–1545), a royal mintmaster, humanist, historian, in Wola outside Cracow was frequented by the earliest Protestants. Born in Alsace, Ludwig Jodok Dietz, son of the mayor of Weissenberg, early became interested in mines and minting, first in Moravia, then settling in Cracow in 1508 as secretary to John Boner, Severin's father, who represented the Thurzos of Hungary and the Fuggers of Augsburg. Decius established the monetary system of the Commonwealth by an agreement on common monetary denominations with Ducal Prussia, 1526. Often in the diplomatic service of the King and Chancellor Primate John Łaski (Pl. 6), he was the author of *The Life and Times of Sigismund* (1521); and his home in Wola outside the walls was a center of humanistic culture, while the first meetings in the spirit of the Renaissance and Reformation gathered here. Among his guests were Leonard Coxe, the Erasmian Englishman on the faculty of the University, and Andrew Trzecieski, Sr. His son and namesake (c. 1520–67), saltmaster in Olkusz (cf. Pl. 31), attended the synod of Włodzimierz June 1557, joining with Stanislas Szafraniec (Pl. 8) and other lords in the project for a Polish (the Radziwiłł) Bible (Pl. 54).

3.G. The house of Andrew Trzecieski, Sr. (near the Collegium Majus; see Map of Cracow), in whose library before dinner in 1547 a Dutch guest, *Spiritus*, raised for Frycz Modrzewski (Pl. 22) and others the theological problem of prayers addressed to the Three Persons of One Godhead (RD 1). This is a photograph taken in 1864 during remodeling in the area; taken from Wanda Mossakowska and Anna Zeńczak, *Kraków na starej fotografii* (Cracow: Wydawnictwo Literackie, 1984), p. 85. Zbigniew Pasek helped in the identification. Trzecieski's house is next St. Ann's across from the Collegium Nowodworskie at the left.

4. THE UNITAS FRATRUM (CZECH BRETHREN) IN MORAVIA AND GREAT POLAND

The history of the Czech (Bohemian/Moravian) Brethren in Great Poland was intertwined with that of the Reformed Churches in Great and Little Poland.

4.A. John Augusta, bishop and president of the executive council (1547–72). From the collection of Bohemian portraits by Franz Martin Pelzel, *Abbildungen böhmischer und mährischer Gelehrten und Künstler*, 4 vols. (Prague, 1773–82).

The Unity of the Brethren, who had under their first bishop, Matthias of Kunwald, separated from the main body of Hussites in 1467, were at the end of the Smalcald War (1546–48) so subject to persecution that many regrouped in Moravia and many more reached Ducal Prussia and Great Poland (1554–57), protected by Polish lords (Pl. 19). As early as 1555 at their synod in Koźminek, they and the Reformed of Little Poland agreed to merge.

John Augusta was the sixth (international) president of the executive council (presiding bishop) of the Czech (Bohemian) Brethren, called also the Unity of the Brethren, a branch of Hussites who had separated off in 1467. John Augusta became presiding bishop in the very year of the battle of Mühlberg (1547), after which Emperor/King

Ferdinand so exerted pressure on them that many fled.

The refugees from Bohemia passed by way of Silesia under the Bohemian crown into Great Poland and on to Ducal Prussia. In Great Poland, welcomed by Polish lords such as the Górkas and Leszczyńskis (Pl. 19), and with such emerging centers as Koźminek and Leszno, the Czech Brethren were frequent observers at the Reformed synods of Little Poland. Indeed, some of the synodal records of the Polish Reformed survive only or most fully in Czech. Eventually the Czech Brethren of Great Poland would join the Reformed and the Lutherans (excluding the Unitarian Polish Brethren) in the Federation and Consensus of Sandomierz, 1570 (Pl. 34).

The Czech Brethren had originally called themselves Brethren of the Law of Christ (*Fratres legis Christi*). Their founding Brother or Patriarch Gregory, a sometime Franciscan and the nephew of the Utraquist archbishop of Prague, John Rokycana (c. 1395–1471), was for a while encouraged by his prelatical uncle. Drawn to the pacifist circle of Peter Chelčický, Brother Gregory, with the permission of King George Poděbrad (1459–71), settled with twenty-seven others (all but three laymen of various stations) on the forested estate of Kunwald (Kunvald). It was on the Silesian border of Bohemia, not distant from Gratz/Kłodzko. The twenty-eight Czech Brethren were determined to live their lives according to Scripture and the Four Prague Articles (*Compactata* of 1433). They rejected oaths, military services, etc., and gathered into their company disaffected Utraquists, sometime Taborites prepared to renounce war, and Waldensians. They rebaptized converts from the Roman and the Utraquist Churches, while retaining pedobaptism for their own progeny.

One of the original twenty-eight, Matthias of Kunwald, received episcopal ordination from the Waldensians and was retrospectively regarded as the first presiding bishop of the Unity of the Brethren (*Jednota braterská/Unitas Fratrum*), as they now became known. By 1494 the "major" or "new" party, more accommodating to the demands and responsibilities of town life and education, condemned Chelčický and Gregory of the old "minor" party of village pacifists. A major figure in the partial abandonment of the older sectarian life style was Lukas (Lukáš) of Prague, who became the third presiding bishop (1517–28), a convert from among the Utraquists. (Already from 1494 on, he was the reshaper of a sect into a church, discharging a role not unlike that of the Florentine Faustus Socinus, as of 1580, with the Polish Brethren, Pls. 47, 48). Lukas resisted Lutheran overtures, still holding fast to clerical celibacy and to all seven sacraments. But under the next two presiding bishops, Martin Skoda and John Roh (Horn), the Unity was well on its way to adherence to Reformation principles and practices, eventually drawing closest to the Reformed, especially in Poland. Under bishops Roh and Augusta the Czech Confession of 1535 (one of several) was drawn up, translated into Latin, and was presented in a Polish translation to Sigismund II in 1564. The Polish records show that the Czech Brethren continued the rebaptism of converts even after they officially abandoned anabaptism under pressure from Luther in 1535, a persisting practice in Poland that no doubt influenced the adoption of believers' baptism by the Polish Brethren.

But for the residual severities and marked clericalism of even the new party of the Unity, the urge for reformation in Poland just might have become fully attached to the indigenized Czech Brethren synod of Great Poland, had not Łaski (cf. D) held up a fully national Reformed vision for the Commonwealth modeled on the substantially Reformed Edwardian Church of England, within which he had served in London.

4.B. Church, bell tower, and school of the Czech Brethren in Uporské Hrodište, the congregation dating from 1548. The hymnal is in the Státni Knihovna in Prague;

reproduced from a full plate in Oskar Thulin et al., *Reformation in Europa* (Leipzig/Cassel, [1967]) 150.

A reconstruction by Augustin Hladký of the church grounds from the ruins and old sketches, printed along with many other illustrations in the critical edition of 1724 MS History of Ungarisch-Brod, ed. by Bohumil Sobotík, Vaclav Fr. Letocha, *Památky města Brodu Uherského* (Uherský Brod, 1942), Pl. 22; for the date of the original congregation of "Waldensians," according to this Catholic writer, see p. 15/13.

4.C. The second hymnal of "Spiritual Songs" (Ivančice, 1564), indirectly influencing hymnody among the Polish Reformed. "Spiritual Songs" (Ivančice [Eibenschitz], 1564) was based upon Scripture and intended for the glory of the Triune God. For scriptural sanction of organs and other instruments, under the direction of John Blahoslav, later a presiding bishop, the artist has placed the words of Psalm 20:14/21:13 in Latin on the left and in Czech on the right: "We will sing and praise (with stringed instruments) thy power." Copies of a hymnal are being held by several, all male, choristers under a director with baton. The singers appear garbed especially for the service, their heads bared before the Lord (cf. Pl 57). Powerful Hussite singing passed by way of the Czech Brethren in Great Poland to the Polish Reformed, who attached uncommon importance to their own choirs and hymnals. The full title of this second hymnal of the Czech Brethren is: "Spiritual and Evangelical Songs again newly edited, corrected, collected, and also many newly composed on the basis of the Holy Scriptures for the glory and the praise of the one eternal God in Holy Trinity: Also for the help, services, and use in true Christian worship by all the faithful who love the Czech people and their language."

4.D. Lipnik in Moravia where at a synod in 1558 the delegates from the Reformed of Little Poland, under pressure from John Łaski on the issue of the Eucharist, withdrew from the federation agreed to at Koźminek. Lipnik in 1633; from Jan Bad'ura and Augustin Kratochvil, *Vlastivěda Moravská, 2 Mistopis, Lipenský Okres* (Brno, 1919), p. 68.

In Lipnik, southeast of Olomouc, 25 October 1558, the Polish Reformed delegates withdrew from the federation agreed to at Koźminek in 1555. Łaski, because of illness, was unable to attend himself, but he was desirous of discussing the Eucharist with the Czech Brethren distant from the pressure on them from the Lutherans in Royal and Ducal Prussia. Stanislas Sarnicki, later superintendent, upheld Calvinist ideas at Lipnik, while the other Polish emissary, Jerome Filipowski, had hoped to preserve the Federation of Koźminek, and would again be positive when he served later as a delegate to the Hutterites (Pl. 30). Kowalska, *Łaski*, devotes all of ch. 4 to the importance of the sundering at Lipnik.

It was under the general presidency of John Augusta that the new Federation of Sandomierz of 1570 was worked out (Pl. 34), betokening the increasing importance of the Polish province of the Czech Brethren, importance reflected further in the royally sponsored mission of John Rokyta from Leszno to Moscow in 1570 (Pl. 19), in the succession of George Israel to the seventh (international) presidency of the Unitas, 1572 – 88, and in the role of John Amos Comenius, the last of the presiding bishops, as chief spokesman for Czech Brethren *and* the Reformed at the Colloquium in Toruń in 1645 (Pl. 61).

5. THE BISHOPS OF CRACOW, 1503–1600

5.A. Bishop Frederick Cardinal Jagiellończyk (1488 – 1503). The sepulchral bronze tablet of Cardinal Jagiellończyk, placed by Sigismund I in the Wawel Cathedral, is pictured in *Monumenta Regum Poloniae Cracoviensia* (Warsaw, 1825); reproduced in

Wielka Encyklopedya Powszechna Ilustrowana, 55 vols. (Warsaw, 1890 – 1912), 23, p. 377.

The sixteenth century in Cracow began and ended with a Cardinal. Frederick Jagiellończyk (1468 – 1503) was the youngest son of Casimir IV and Elizabeth of Hapsburg and was educated in childhood by the historian John Długosz (1415 – 80) of Sandomierz, canon of Cracow. Under pressure from his royal parents, Frederick was imposed upon the Cracow chapter as their bishop (1488 – 1503), and by his brother King John Olbracht, made Primate (1493 – 1503), at which time only he received major orders and was concurrently named Cardinal. He was buried at age 35 in the crypt of the cathedral, an integral part of the castle complex, symbolic of the close bond in Poland between throne and episcopal altar.

5.B. Bishop John Konarski (1447/1503 – 25), confidant of Cardinal Frederick, as its chancellor, was active in the reform of the Jagiellonian Academy, of which he was an alumnus, and with Tomicki (C) an opponent of the pro-Hungarian policy of Sigismund I.

5.C. Bishop Peter Tomicki (1523 – 35). A painting of him by Stanlislas Samostrzelnik in the Franciscan Cloister, Cracow, is reproduced, among others, by Zdzisław Małek, *Kraków* (Warsaw, 1965), color plate between pp. 72 and 72; and the sepulchral monument is represented by H. Kozakiewiczowa, *Rzeźba XVI wieku w Polsce* (Warsaw: PWN, 1984).

Peter Tomicki (1464 – 1535), born in Great Poland, educated in Gniezno, Cracow, and Bologna with a doctorate in both laws, was pluralistically bishop of Przemyśl (1514 – 21), of Poznań (1514 – 23), and chancellor under Cardinal Frederick and royal secretary, very much involved in diplomacy, speaking fluently Italian and German, very much opposed to Bona Sforza and the pro-Hungarian policy of Sigismund, initiated by Primate John Łaski (Pl. 6). In the university he helped found chairs in Hebrew, Greek, and Latin. He was a major patron of Renaissance culture, supporting many students with scholarships abroad. From 1515 he served as deputy chancellor, in effect, the royal minister for foreign affairs. He stood as bishop of Cracow in the market square when Duke Albert of Prussia became a Protestant vassal in 1525. His archive comes to 15 volumes, *Acta Tomiciana* (1852 – 1961).

5.D. Bishop John Latalski (1536 – 37). For his picture, see Pl. 6; ambulatory of the Franciscan Cloister in Cracow, photograph by Jerzy Langda, IS PAN.

John Latalski (1463 – 1540), successively secretary to Cardinal Frederick and Primate Łaski, was intermediary in 1530 in the treaty between the two claimants to the Crown of divided Hungary, Ferdinand and John Zápolya. Only briefly bishop of Cracow, he died as Primate.

5.E. Bishop John John Chojeński (1486/1537 – 38) studied at the Cracovian Academy and from Siena received the doctorate in both laws. Royal secretary, then secretary of the Great Crown, deputy chancellor and chancellor, he spent time with the King in Vilna and represented him in dealings with Duke Albert of Prussia, concurrently bishop of Przemyśl, Płock, and after Cracow, Primate. He was a major exponent of humanism, sending the future historian Martin Kromer to Italy for studies, and sponsoring Stanislas Hosius (Pl. 49).

5.F. Bishop Peter Gamrat (1538 – 45). Painted c. 1541; ambulatory, Franciscan Cloister, Cracow; photograph by E. Kozłowska-Tomczyk; IS PAN.

Peter Gamrat (1487 – 1545) studied at the Cracovian Academy and in Rome.

Promoted by Bona Sforza, he, she, and Peter Kmita constituted at court a triumvirate against the Hapsburgs and in favor of a peace treaty with the Sublime Porte, possibly in alliance with France. Successively bishop of Kamieniec, Przemyśl, and Płock, he combined his last two pontificates, that of Cracow with that of Primate (1541–45). At the provincial synod of Piotrków in 1539 he undertook the reform of the clergy, and at the synod thereat in 1542 he moved against reformers. Ambitious, he lived a rather extravagant and boisterous life.

5.G. Bishop Samuel Maciejowski (1546–50). Photography by E. Kozłowska-Tomczyk; Instytut Sztuki (IS) PAN.

Samuel Maciejowski (1498–1550) studied at Padua, becoming at court successively royal secretary, deputy chancellor, and chancellor of the Great Crown. Bishop of Chełm, Płock, and Cracow, he was close to both kings and worked for recognition of the contested marriage of Sigismund Augustus with Barbara. A patron of the arts, he refrained from dealing harshly with Protestants.

5.H. Bishop Andrew Zebrzydowski (1551–60). Photograph by Jerzy Langda; IS PAN.

Andrew Zebrzydowski (1496–1560) studied at the Cracovian Academy, in Basel with Erasmus, then in Paris. Successively bishop of Kamieniec, Chełm, and Kujawy, he bulks largest in the *Historia* of all sixteenth-century bishops. He was the uncle of Nicholas Zebrzydowski of the Revolt of 1606 (Pl. 50).

5.I. Bishop Philip Padniewski (15610–72). Ambulatory of the Franciscan Cloister, Cracow; photograph by Jerzy Langda; IS PAN.

Philip Padnewski, after study in Ingolstadt, entered the court of Charles V in Flanders. On becoming a priest, he served as emissary of Gamrat in Rome and Vienna.

5.J. Bishop Francis Krasiński (1572–77). Ambulatory of the Franciscan Cloister, Cracow; photography by Jerzy Langda; IS PAN.

Francis Krasiński (1525–77) studied in Wittenberg, Cracow, and Rome, in the last becoming doctor of both laws. Active in moving Lithuania toward the Union of Lublin, he was the only bishop to sign the Warsaw Confederation of 1573 (Pl. 36).

5.K. Bishop Peter Myszkowski (1577–79). Painted by Witalis Wolny from an earlier likeness in 1780; ambulatory of Franciscan Cloister, Cracow; photograph by Jerzy Langda; IS PAN.

Peter Myszkowski (1505–91) studied at the Cracovian Academy, Padua, and Rome. Successively secretary to Sigismund Augustus, deputy chancellor, and bishop of Płock, he was active in cultural life and patron of Kochanowski, who dedicated to him his versified Polish Psalter (Pl. 15). Related to several Protestant lords (cf. Pl. 8), he was restrained in dealing with Protestants.

5.L. Bishop George Cardinal Radziwiłł (1591–1600). Ambulatory of Franciscan Cloister, Cracow; photograph by Jerzy Langda; IS PAN.

George Radziwiłł (1556–1600), son of Calvinist Prince Nicholas the Black (Pl. 9), studied in Leipzig, then with the Jesuits in Poznań. Returning to Catholicism, 1573, he was named coadjutor with Bishop Valerian Protaszewicz of Vilna, where he persecuted Protestants, burned their books, and closed their presses. After further study in Rome, he was named Cardinal (1583) and appointed by Clement VIII papal legate in Poland. Fervid in his faith, he was named by Stephen Batory governor of Livonia and assigned the task of restoring the hierarchy in the Lutheranized territory that had been the domain of the Livonian branch of the Teutonic Knights.

6. SIGISMUND II AUGUSTUS; PRIMATES OF POLAND

6.A. Those who were previously bishops of Cracow are asterisked. John Łaski, later himself Primate (1511–31), while chancellor, presents the edited Statute of the Realm to King Alexander (1501–06) during the Diet of Lublin, March 1506, the then incumbent Primate Andrew Boryszewski, being seated high (left) next to the throne, who as Interrex would presently preside at the Election Diet of Piotrków of Alexander's brother and at the liturgical coronation of the elected Sigismund I in Cracow, January 1507. Shown is a woodcut from Łaski Statute, *Commune Incliti Poloniae Privilegium,* the systematization of the constitutions, freedoms, indulgences, and decrees of "Celebrated Poland," frequently reproduced, in this case from Antoni Gronowicz, *The Piasts of Poland* (New York: Scribner's, 1945), pp. 86f. One third of the seated Diet has been cropped (at the right) to concentrate on the central action. The arms of the bishops, magnates, and palatinates of Poland identify the principals of the woodcut and reappear in chapters of the Statute.

John Łaski (1445/1510–31) of Łask in Great Poland was first secretary to the King, 1502, then chancellor. Of the upper *szlachta,* he was nevertheless a supporter of the humanist program of juridical reforms, "the execution of the laws" in the interest of decentralization—against both the magnates and the bishops. The Statute upheld the right of the King to nominate bishops and of the Diet to tax episcopal and abbatial lands. The Statute, preserving the oldest text of the ancient Polish hymn, Our Lady (*Bogurodzica*), was understood to be subject to ongoing revisions to be proposed by a commission of six *correctores.* This Statute, fulfilling the constitution *Nihil novi* of the Diet of Radom, 1505, represented the first stage in putting together a compendium of laws, and from its acceptance is commonly dated the Executionist Movement, 1506–86. For the context, see Danièle Letocha, "The Executionist Movement in Sixteenth Century Poland: A Cultural Mirror," *Unitarianism in its Sixteenth and Seventeenth Century Settings,* ed. John C. Godbey, pp. 33–45.

Uncle of the Reformer of the same name (Pl. 20), Primate John Łaski was accused in Rome of favoring the Protestants. His leadership in the Executionist Movement that sanctioned the equalization of laws, best expounded by Modrzewski (Pl. 22), and his congeniality with the Cracow humanists made him open to this charge, and all the more so as the Movement he provisionally codified in the *Statute* was strongly supported by the middle and lower *szlachta,* among whom the Reformation was most prominently expounded.

The archbishops of Gniezno, the primatial see, had from near the beginning owned Łowicz on a tributary which flowed into the Vistula south of Warsaw. Archbishop Primate Łaski built there a major primatial palace. Several of his successors, such as Uchański (I) were buried in the Collegiate College of Łowicz. The town retained its primatial importance into the seventeenth century. Z. Kaczmarczyk, *Jan Łaski* (Warsaw, 1950).

6.B. King Sigismund II Augustus (1520/48–72), son of Sigismund I the Old, at age 35. Print from Martin Kromer, *De origine et rebus gestis Polonorum libri XXX* (1555), commonly called his *Kronika.* The likeness was made in 1554.

As an infant Sigismund received from his father, with the due homage of the princes of Lithuania, the Jagiellonian dignity of Grand Duke and he lived considerable stretches of his life, both before and after his election as King, in the Grand Ducal palace in Vilna (Pl. 14). Between 1551 and 1553, i.e., shortly before the imprint of 1554, Lismanino

(Pl. 16) guided Sigismund in the systematic reading of Calvin's *Institutes*.

Martin Kromer (1512 – 89), a scholarly courtier and then administrator, in the absence of Hosius, and finally bishop of Varmia (1570/79 – 89), was also author of *Polonia,* in two books (1577). Another picture from his work is in Pl. 9.C.

6.C. Primate Matthew Drzewicki (1531 – 35). Humanist Matthew Dzewicki (1467/1510 – 35), educated first in the cathedral school in Włocławek and then under the Graecist Callimachus in Cracow, whose poetic works he later edited, was a major figure of his times. Far-ranging diplomat, he eventually reached the rank of vice-chancellor, was a proponent of a crusade against the Turks, and was successively incumbent of several sees.

6.D. Primate Andrew Krzycki (1482/1535 – 37), a Humanist, protegé of Tomicki (Pl. 5), was secretary to Sigismund I and a court poet, who produced erotica and grandiloquent ceremonial pieces. He urged Erasmus to pay a visit to Poland and hoped to reconvert Melanchthon.

6.E. Primate John Latalski (1537 – 40). Painting in the Ambulatory of the Franciscan Cloister in Cracow, the bishop in the gesture of blessing; photography by Jerzy Langda, IS PAN.

John Latalski (1463/37 – 40) was secretary to Primate Łaski and mediator in 1535 of the agreement on the succession to the Crown of Hungary as between Ferdinand I Hapsburg and John Zápolya (father of ''the Unitarian King of Transylvania/Hungary'').

6.F. Primate Peter Gamrat (1541 – 45). Picture in Pl. 5. Both as bishop of Cracow and Primate, Peter Gamrat (1487/1541 – 45) was supportive of humanistic studies at the Cracovian Academy. Under the auspices of Hosius he had already worked out reforming regulations for the Polish clergy. These were codified in the provincial synod under him in 1542 in Piotrków (Cracow: Scharffenberg, 1544).

6.G. Primate Nicholas Drzierzgowski (1546 – 59). Nicholas Drzierzgowski (1490/1546 – 59) belonged to the same movement in Polish affairs as John Łaski—as opposed to Tomicki, and in opposition to the Hapsburgs; but on Protestant incursions he was firm and stood in constant contact with Hosius and the papal legate. As Interrex, he embodied Polish national sovereignty in the dynastic/elective transition from Sigismund I to II.

6.H. Primate John Przerębski (1559 – 62). Funeral monument executed by Girolamo Canavesi in the Collegiate Church in Łowicz; photograph by E. Kozłowska-Tomczyk, IS PAN. Only the head of the prone Primate is shown, resting on his left arm.

John Przerębski (1519/59 – 62), vice-chancellor before his nomination; as Primate he called a provincial synod in Warsaw in 1561 concerned with raising educational standards, in the presence of the papal legate. The Primate is mentioned several times in an unfavorable light by Lubieniecki, *Historia, pp. 59, 63f., 77 – 79.*

6.I. Primate Jacob Uchański (1562 – 81), a national Catholic, recipient of Protestant correspondence, was Interrex between Sigismund II and elected Henry of Valois, again between Henry and elected Stephen Batory. A painting from the Archdiocesan Seminary in Warsaw, presumably based upon the sepulchral monument of Primate Uchański in the Collegiate Church in Łowicz, executed by Jan Michałowicz in 1580 (with the disturbance of the original arrangement of the sarcophagus). The photograph of the painting came to me through the kindness of Chet Curtis of Boston Channel 5 and by the courtesy of His Eminence Bernard Cardinal Law and His Excellency Jerzy Dąbrowski.

Jacob Uchański (1502/62 – 81), as secretary to Bona Sforza, entered the humanist circle of Lismanino (Pl. 16), Andrew Trzeciecki (Pl. 3), and Frycz Modrzewski (Pl. 22). He was nominated by Sigismund II to succeed the Protestantizing John Drohojowski as bishop of Chełm (1551 – 61) and then of Kujawy (1561 – 62), but Pope Julius III refused consent. Because of his opposition to the Uchański by Cardinal Hosius, himself papal legate at Trent in 1561, there was *no* Polish delegation at any of the three periods of Trent: 1545 – 47; 1551 – 52; 1562 – 63. Uchański was forceful in pushing for the Union of Lublin, 1569 (Pl. 32, where he is portrayed). He was long under suspicion as favorable to Protestants. Indeed he is several times addressed and mentioned by them, e.g., in the Swiss correspondence (cf. Wotschke, ed.), and he was in epistolary contact with Frycz Modrzewski (Pl. 22) on ways to reunite Christians within the Commonwealth. He thus entertained the idea of a national royalist Church in communion with Rome, hence more ''Gallican'' than ''Anglican'' and yet inclusive of the Dissidents! He was prepared to consider communion in both kinds, the Mass in Polish, and clerical marriage, possibly even a reformulation of the doctrine of the Trinity. And he tried to organize a national synod in this sense after the death of Sigismund II in Uniejów, 1572. He was opposed in this attempt by local bishops and the Holy See. As Primate, after 1572, he gave up most of his earlier ideas and held provincial synods in the presence of papal legates in 1577 and 1578. He favored Henry of Valois and presided at his election and coronation (Pls. 35 and 37); and at the next interregnum he favored Maximilian II over Stephen Batory, to whom he owned allegiance only in 1576.

7. KÖNIGSBERG UNDER DUKE ALBERT OF HOHENZOLLERN

7.A. Königsberg with the ducal castle tower (below the first ''s'') and court. In the foreground, surrounded by two arms of the Pregel flowing to the left into the Lagoon of the Vistula, is the town of Kneiphof with its own town hall, cathedral (*Dom*), and by the bridge the *Collegium* or the Albertina (1544), founded by the Duke and chartered by Sigismund I. From Braun and Hogenberg (1554), *Civitates orbis terrarum;* reproduced with the permission of Houghton Library, Harvard University.

Königsberg (Królewiec) in 1554, looking north, the Pregel flowing at the left (west) into Frisches Haff, the Lagoon of the Vistula. Upstream the Pregel is divided into New Pregel in the middle distance, the Old Pregel flowing by in the foreground, the two branches surrounding the cathedral island of Kneiphof, a town in its own right with its own Rathaus. Beyond it is situated Altstadt, at the center of which is the castle, established in 1225 by the Teutonic Knights. The town around it was chartered with its own Rathaus in 1286 and given its renowned royal designation (Krákova Hora) by King Premyšl Otakar II of Bohemia. To the right is the separate town of Löbenicht with its own Rathaus and the church of St. Barbara. In the tri-city, which joined the Hanseatic League in 1340, the common speech was Plattdeutsch. When in the course of the Thirteen Year War between Poland and the Order, their great fortress and seat of Marienburg (Malbork) fell in 1457, the castle of Königsberg became the new seat of the Order for the whole of the Baltic, while the re-conquered portions of their territory became henceforth known as Royal Prussia, the three principal towns of Danzig (Gdańsk), Elbing (= Elbląg), and Toruń (Thorn) receiving royal charters. The last Grand Master of the Order and the first secular Duke of Prussia was Albert of Hohenzollern (B).

While he was on a visit to his native Franconia, gripped in conscience, Albert was won over to the Reformation by the Nuremberg preacher Andreas Osiander (C). On Albert's urging, Luther sent to Königsberg his collaborator, John Briessmann, who, while still in his Franciscan habit, delivered the first Evangelical sermon in the tri-city, in the cathedral, 27 September 1523. Within a few months the bishop of Samland (Samogitia), whose seat was Kneiphof, George von Polentz, more jurist than theologian, espoused the Reformation in his Christmas Eve sermon; the second bishop in Ducal Prussia, with his see in Marienwerder (Pomesania; Kwidzyn), followed suit. Paul Speratus (Spret) was invited from Swabia by Albert to become his court preacher in 1524. It was Luther who first urged the Grand Master to convert and secularize his lands. In Cracow, on 8 April 1525, in the company of the mayor of Altstadt and a representative of Kneiphof, Grand Master Albert signed a treaty and two days later became Duke Albert, vassal of the Polish King in the ceremony of investiture in the market square of Cracow. The Emperor did not recognize the validity of the secularization and placed Albert under the ban.

Peasants, in sympathy with their fellow revolters of 1524/25 within the Empire, rose up against the changes and were put down with relative restaint by the converted Duke. See most recently Heide Wunder, "Der samländische Bauernaufstand von 1525," *Der Bauernkrieg 1524–26,* ed by Reiner Wohlfeld (Munich, 1975) 143–76.

An enclave of episcopal territory, Warmia/Ermland, remained true to the old order in all respects; and from its see in Frauenburg, Stanislas Cardinal Hosius (Pl. 49) would later lead the Counter-Reform in the Commonwealth (1551–79).

In the meantime the Duke founded a ducal academy in the residence of the cathedral chapter in Kneiphof; and in 1544 he received from Sigismund I a charter for it as a full university, the Albertina, under George Sabinus, son-in-law of Melanchthon, as the first rector. The first professorial appointee had been the Lithuanian alumnus of Wittenberg, Stanislas Rapagelanus (Rapolionis) (Pl. 15), mentioned twice in the *Historia*. Other professors were John Funk from Nuremberg, pastor in Altstadt and then court preacher and confessor to the Duke, Joachim Mörlin, once chaplain to Luther, successor to Briessmann as pastor of the cathedral parish; and Andreas Osiander (D), who replaced Funk in the Altstadt parish. Königsberg was not only the center of Lutheranism in the Commonwealth but also of Protestantism generally. The ducal court and the Albertina resounded with theological debates and the discussion of strategies, drawing in Poles, like John Kochanowski (Pl. 23), Łaski (Pl. 20), and Lismanino (Pl. 16), Lithuanians, and foreigners (like Vergerio and Alciati), while the presses of Königsberg turned out Protestant works in several languages, including the first printed book in Lithuanian imprint, Martynas Mažvydas, *Catechismusa* (1547) (Pl. 15).

7.B. Grand Master of the Teutonic Order, Albert (1491–1568) in 1511. Painting by Lucas Cranach the Elder, 1511; from Max Josef Friedländer and Jakob Rosenberg, *Die Gemälde Lucas Cranach d. Ä.* (Berlin, 1932).

Grand Master Albert Hohenzollern, Duke of Brandenburg-Kulmbach (1490–1568), son of Frederick of Ansbach and Sophia Jagiellonka, sister of Sigismund I, portrayed in the white habit with the Black Cross of the Teutonic Order.

7.C. Duke Albert (as of 1564), who knelt in Cracow as vassal of King Sigismund I, 1525, the first Protestant prince of Christendom. Detail from an oil miniature by Heinrich Königsweiser, Museum Dahlem, formerly the Kaiser Friedrich-Museum, Berlin; from Paul Seidel, "Ein Bildnis Herzog Albrechts in Preussen," *Hohenzollern-Jahrbuch* 13 (1909) 282; the whole miniature is reproduced by Walter Hubatsch, *Albrecht von Brandenburg-Ansbach: Deutsch-Hochmeister und Herzog in Preussen 1490–1568*

(Heidelberg, 1960), p. 144. The circular Latin inscription around the head makes clear that it was painted in 1564, the Prince "armed in his heart to face his foes."

In the controversy over double justification and the mediatorship of Christ in his divine nature the Duke favored Osiander and the latter's two sons-in-law, Funk and Andreas Aurifaber, the latter in 1553 succeeding Speratus as rector of the Albertina. Influenced by the Croatian refugee Cabbalist Paul Skalich, the Duke, distressed that his only son, Albert Frederick, was mentally handicapped, began losing control over the affairs of his capital, while the Osiandrian controversy took a political turn, with a revolution of the estates of the Duchy, whereupon he dissolved the dietine. At this Elias von Kanitz, leader of the anti-Skalich, anti-Osiandrist party, appealed to Sigismund II as royal overlord of Prussia. In court proceedings presided over by the Polish royal commissioners, the estates and the ducal councilors dealt with four ducal councilors accused of heresy, among them Funk; one was banished, while three, Funk foremost, were, amid pious hymns of the populace, put to death in the market square, 28 October 1556. The Gnesio-Lutheran clergy and the estates, celebrating their victory over Osiandrianism and the ducal government, recalled Mörlin from exile, who from his recovered pulpit preached, 9 April 1567, against Sacramentarians, Cryptocalvinists, Philippists, and Osiandrists. A new church order was then worked out by the estates and a synod.

Anna, daughter of the incapacitated Albert Frederick (1553/68 – 1618), married John Sigismund, Elector of Brandenburg (1572 – 1619), who had been regent of Ducal Prussia since 1608 and became Duke in 1618 in personal union. So likewise in personal union of dignities was his son George William (1619 – 40) and his grandson, the Great Elector Frederick William (1640 – 88), under whom Ducal Prussia, formerly detached from the Commonwealth in 1660, became Electoral Prussia.

7.D. Andreas Osiander (1498 – 1552), who won Albert to the Reformation on a visit to Nuremberg, where he published with a preface Copernicus's *De revolutionibus* (1543), was called by his ducal convert as professor in the Albertina, where his inaugural disputation on double justification occasioned the bitter Osiander Controversy, involving among others Stancaro (Pl. 17). Oil painting by Görg Pencz; 1544, Biblioteca Vaticana.

Many portraits of Osiander (9) are reproduced by Gottfried Seebass, *Das reformatorische Werk des Andreas Osiander* (Nuremberg, 1967), who, in an excursus, pp. 277 – 95, concludes that there are two originals from which all others stem, namely the oil painting c. 1540 in the sacristy of St. Lorenzenkirche, Nuremberg, and that is reproduced here. His work concentrates on Osiander in Nuremberg. Martin Stupperich deals with him in Königsberg, *Osiander in Preussen 1549 – 52* (Berlin/New York: De Gruyter, 1973).

Andreas Osiander (1498 – 1552) was ordained priest in Eichstätt in 1520, joined the Lutheran cause in 1522 as pastor of St. Lawrence Church in Nuremberg, was participant in Marburg Colloquy in 1529, in the Diet of Augsburg of 1530, in the colloquies of Hagenau and Worms of 1540. He wrote the forward to Copernicus's *De revolutionibus* (Nuremberg, 1543), without sensing its "revolutionary" implications for theology. Driven from his pulpit by the Augsburg Interim of 1548, he offered his services from Breslau to his ducal convert in Königsberg. Becoming pastor in Altstadt, against the efforts of the theological faculty, he was made a professor in the Albertina.

Protestants on the basis of Luther's *sola scriptura, sola fides, sola gratia* regarded Jesus Christ as the sole Mediator and renounced the intercession (mediation) of the saints, including therefore the role of Mary as Mediatrix. The issue revolved therefore around the validity for Protestants of the canon *Firmiter* of the IV Lateran Council (1215) that had upheld Peter Lombard against the attack on him by the Calabrian abbot Joachim of

Fiore. On the basis of 1 Tim 2:5 and most patristic (and especially post-Chalcedonian divines) Lombard held that Jesus Christ was Mediator solely in his human nature. Joachim charged him with holding to a Quaternity of Three Persons and the divine Essence (*substantia*) that so diminished the status of the God-Man that Lombard was in effect a Nestorian. In the Reformation disputation *De Mediatore,* Luther sided expressly with Joachim against Lombard, while Calvin on this issue remained close to the scholastic and indeed patristic tradition (with exceptions) in a modified Lombardian view. Lorenz Hein, *Italienische Protestanten und ihr Einfluß auf die Reformation in Polen* (Leiden: Brill, 1974) 172, n. 245.

In this protopietist theory of effectual sanctification in faith, Osiander, Lutheranizing as he thought both Rom 3:18 (fideism) and 1 Tim 2:5 (the suffusion of the work of Christ through his two natures), was opposed in debate over his inaugural lecture by, among others, the Wittenberg alumnus Matthias Lauterwald, and even more fiercely by Mörlin. The Duke and Funk strongly supported Osiander, while Francis Stancaro (Pl. 17), settling from Pińczow in Königsberg (1550 – 51), bitterly opposed him, claiming for himself the role of Elijah (1 Kings 18) against the priests of Baal, and appealing to the Duke better informed, lest he fall victim to a temptation greater than that dangled by Satan before Adam and Eve: the serpent had only offered similarity with God, while Osiander was offering divinity by a change in nature!

In his inaugural disputation, *De lege et evangelio,* 5 April 1549, Osiander proposed a kind of double justification within the Lutheran context, maintaining that Christ had indeed redeemed the whole world on the cross in his human nature but that the believer in Him to be saved must experience through faith the indwelling of the divine righteousness (*iustitia essentialis*) of Christ as Mediator in his divine nature. Of some interest, the Silesian knight Caspar Schwenckfeld, once of Liegnitz (Legnica), perhaps drawn by his concern for Duke Albert (and Osiander), entered the lists with reworked christological material in a new publication, *De Mediatore,* 1543, against Joachim of Fiore, Document CCCCXXIV, *Corpus Schwenckfeldianorum,* 8.

7.E. The oldest Polish printed version of the New Testament translated from the Greek, by Lutheran John Seklucjan (Königsberg, 1551). Translation from the Greek of ''the Holy Gospel of the Lord Jesus Christ according to Matthew''; reproduced from Juliusz Bursche, tr. from the English of Walerjan Krasiński, *Zarys dziejów Powstania i upadku Reformacji w Polsce,* 2 vols., the 2nd in two parts (Warsaw, 1903 – 04); 1, p. 106.

John Seklucjan (1498 – 1578) was born in the environs of Bydgoszcz, an alumnus of Leipzig; he was the German preacher in St. Mary Magdalene in Poznań, and was protected by the Górkas (Pl. 19), when driven out as a heretic following the publication of his *Confession of Christian Faith* (1541). Seklucjan was called in 1543 by Albert as a professor for his new college and as the Polish preacher in the tri-city. The First Gospel is annotated and cross-referenced to the other Gospels.

8. SOME PATRONS OF THE REFORMATION

Until the reception of the decrees of Trent of 1564 by the Diet in 1577 nobles were not always clear on the depth of the Catholic/Protestant schism, some hoping for something between the Anglican and Gallican model.

8.A. Stanislas Lasocki (d. 1534), owner of Brzeziny, father of three sons active in the Reformation, founded there a church in 1550, of which Gregory Paul was pastor

(Pl. 26). Tombstone executed by Bernardino de Gianotis, parish church in Brzeziny; from Halina and Stefan Kozakiewicz, *The Renaissance in Poland* (Warsaw: Arkady, 1976), Pl. 60.

Stanislas Lasocki the Younger (1521–63) and Jerome Filipowski, an ancestor of our Author, were boon companions, notably in the venture of Heraclides Basilicos (Pl. 28).

8.B. Nicholas Myszkowski (d. 1557), burgrave of Cracow, whose widow, Sophia Komorowska, became the second wife of Jerome Filipowski (d. before 1574), grandfather of Lubieniecki. The Myszkowski Chapel, Dominican Church, Cracow, executed between 1603 and 1614; from *Katalog zabytków sztuki*.

8.C. John Boner (d. 1562), son of Sophia Bettman Bonerowa (Pl. 3), founded churches in Balice and Książ Wielki and his garden villa outside Cracow (Map), here portrayed as Psalmist David. Marble carving by Bartolomeo Berecci in the Sigismund Chapel of the Wawel, Cracow; photographed by Stanisław Stępniewski, PAN, Instytut Sztuki (IS), cf. from *Odrodzenie w Polsce*, I, op. p. 160.

Boner, once instructed by Erasmus (Pl. 3), castellan of Biecz, a humanist center, founded a church also in Balice.

8.D. Christopher Myszkowski (d. 1575), younger brother of Nicholas (B), founded church in Polanka Wielka, 1557, of which Paul Gilowski (d. 1595) was pastor. The Myszkowski Chapel.

Christopher's pastor, Gilowski, later became pastor in the Brog in Cracow (Pl. 51).

8.E. Sigismund Myszkowski (d. 1578), older brother of the later Bishop Peter (Pl. 5), *starosta* of Oświęcim and Zator, was active in the synod of Sandomierz, 1570 (Pl. 34). The Myszkowski Chapel. *Sztuka Krakowa*, p. 302. An idealized Johann Boner (d. 1523) of the Rhine Palatinate, from the sepulchral monument of his grandson, represent provocatively the German colonizing merchant prince. The stamp was printed by authority of the occupying Third German Reich, of which a truncated Poland was a dependency with no ethnic designation of its own, only General Gouvernement [1940], *Katalog Muzeum Żup.*, Cracow. The artifacts of tendentious interpretation can also shed, in this case a garish, light. The face shown is in fact that of John Boner (d. 1562). The families Boner, Dietz, and many another German adventurer-immigrant indeed were welcomed in Polish towns, like Cracow and Lublin, soon to be fully absorbed into Polish society at the level of their achievement, often ennobled, as in the case of the Boners, and from their high station becoming patrons of the Reformation.

8.F. Andrew Firley (c. 1537–85), younger brother of John Firley (Grand Marshal of the Crown), patron of the Calvinists in Lublin. Untouched painting by an unknown artist, Muzeum Historiczne from Lwów; Mieczysław Gębarowicz, *Portret XVI–XVIII wieku we Lwowie* (Wrocław, etc.: Ossolineum, 1969), plate 10 and pp. 29–32.

Andrew Firley was successively royal secretary, castellan of Lublin as of 1576, *starosta* of Sandomierz. Patron of the Calvinists, he was a friend of Kochanowski (Pl. 23) and his neighbor in Lublin. The castellan holds his belt with his right hand, his left is on the handle of his sabre in an intentionally pacific stance.

8.G. Stanislas Szafraniec (d. 1598), founder of church in Secemin (H), to which he drew Felix Cruciger, the first superintendent in Little Poland. Wanda Filipowicz, ed., *Góry Świętokrzyskie* (Warsaw, 1953), p. 103.

Szafraniec was also owner of Rogów. He joined Lasocki (A: Junior), S. Myszkowski (E), and Decius Jr. (cf. Pl. 3), and two other lords to defray the costs of what would become the Radziwiłł Bible (Pl. 54). Sipayłło, *AS*, 1, p. 179.

8.H. Brick church built at Secemin by Szafraniec in 1553, scene of many a synod. Filipowicz, *op. cit.*, p. 99.

9. PINCZOVIANS I

9.A. Pińczów as it was taken over by the Swedes in 1657, showing the castle, enlarged after the death of the Protestant patron, John Oleśnicki (d. 1586), and his wife (B), with the Paulinian Church reclaimed by Bishop Myszkowski of Cracow (Plate 5), who built the walls and greatly extended the settlements within. Copperprint from Dahlbergh in the extensively illustrated history of the Swedish War in Poland by Samuel von Pufendorf (1632–94), *De rebus a Carlo Sueciae rege gestis commentariorum libri septem* (Nuremberg, 1696; French *ibid.*, in the translation of Madame de Pufendorf, 1697); copy from PAN, no. 59692.

The first Protestant town in Poland is shown about three quarters of a century after its purchase (1586) by Bishop Myszkowski of Cracow, who founded Mirów (the houses to the right), enlarged the castle; and, surrounding the extended precincts with a wall, obtained for the town royal privileges.

In the following references by numbered/alphabetized coordinates, those structures asterisked were not present under the Protestants.

The castle (a/b–2/3) of John Oleśnicki (d. 1586) and his wife was smaller, above what was then only a prosperous village. The chapel of St. Anne (b–5) was built c. 1600 in the style of Santi Gucci. The parish church (b/c–7/8) was built by Zbigniew Oleśnicki in 1380 and it was given over to the Paulinian Fathers in 1449, who then built the cloister (Pl. 10, not visible from this angle).

John Oleśnicki, deputy from palatinate Sandomierz at the Diet of Piotrków of 1550, went over to the Reformation. Having received in his castle that year Francis Stancaro, whose escape from the episcopal prison at Lipowiec had been effected by Nicholas Rey and Andrew Trzecieski (Pl. 23), he took over the church and cloister, drove out the monks (D), burned the pictures and furnishings, established Reformed worship there 10 November 1550; and when the Cracow chapter, *sede vacante,* on its own sent canons Przecławski and Martin Kromer (the later historian, cf. Pl. 63, commentary) to protest, Oleśnicki threw them out, declaring ''that he was alone lord of the village and the church, of the spiritual no less than of the temporal men.'' Not visible behind the cloister was the printing press of Daniel of Łęczyca.

Next comes the town hall (c–8) and the famous fountain in the square with arcades. Next is the church of the Holy Spirit (c–8/9). Nearby (not visible) is the sixteenth-century synagogue and (not visible) the gate toward Włochów (Italians' village) to the northeast. The wall (c–1–9) with the Cracow Gate in the foreground was built in 1612, enclosing the newly developed Mirów and its Jewish quarter to the left and the Nowy Świat to the left. The road to the marble quarries passes up the hill between the castle and the cross.

9.B. Sophia Oleśnicka, the earliest Polish Protestant hymnist. Taken from Henryk Biegeleisen, *Ilustrowane dzieje literatury polskiej,* 5 vols. (Vienna, 1898–1903), 3, p. 22, no. 88 (source not given) identification therefore uncertain.

9.C. A substantial town house locally misidentified as the "Arian printing press" (*drukarnia*). "Drukarnia," from the Przypkowski Collection, Jędrzejów. Over the doorway it reads in Latin: "Bless, O Lord, this house and all who dwell herein." It is just possible that it housed the *ecclesiola Italiana*, referred to in correspondence by Francis Lismanino, where the religious refugees from Italy, like Dr. George Biandrata who came to live in the town in 1558, and Italian artists and artisans, worshiped in their own tongue.

9.D. Daniel of Łęczyca, printer. This is one of several heretics pictured drowning in a moat, 1574, labelled simply "Daniel." Although the figure has been tentatively identified by some Polish scholars as Daniel Bieliński (cf. Pl. 31), it is much more likely intended to be the printer of the Budny Bible. See both Pls. 49.C and 54.C for the argument.

9.E. The expulsion of the Paulinian monks from Pińczów in 1550. Taken from Martin Kromer (1512–89), bishop of Varmia (1579–89) in succession to Cardinal Hosius, *O prawdziwej wierze* (1553), Czartoryski Collection, Cracow.

10. PINCZOVIANS II

10.A. Pińczów, looking from the castle slope toward the former Paulinian Church, which with the cloister in the middle foreground, was the first center of the Reformed Church in Little Poland. Picture copied from *Miasta Polskie*, I, p. 527.

The slope continues toward the Nida, flowing south into the Vistula. The bell tower to the right of the church was not erected until 1685 (therefore cropped from B); it may have occupied the site of an earlier tower described by Lubieniecki as having rung to summon people from the fields for their approbation after a joint synod with the Lithuanian Brethren.

10.B. The Paulinian Church where John Łaski was buried under the altar, 29 January 1560, with funeral orations by Sarnicki, Cruciger, and Peter Statorius, head of the local academy. Photograph supplied by *Polska Akademia Nauk,* no. 120629, taken by W. Wolny. Road signs to Kielce, etc., have been eliminated and the bell tower of 1685 blocked off.

Stanislas Sarnicki (before 1532–97), the first of the three eulogists at the burial of Łaski, was a major figure of the Reformation and the cultural history of Poland, whose full biography has yet to be written.

Born in the Mokre Lipie near Chełm of a noble family, he was early disposed to seek out the centers of the Reformation. His village church seems to have been the very first in Poland to go over to the Reformation, in 1547, thus before Pińczów. In the same year he went to Königsberg under the patronage of Duke Albert. He went on to study in Wittenberg under Melanchthon. To the end of his life it would appear that he remained close to Lutheranism on the Lord's Supper and reserved about the sectarianism (from his point of view) of the Czech Brethren in Ducal Prussia and Great Poland (cf. Pl. 40 commentary). From Wittenberg he entered the service of the Boners in Cracow in 1553, then of Stadnicki in Niedźwiedź in 1556. On the death of Cruciger in 1563, he became his successor as the superintendent of the emergent Major Church and a spirited opponent of Gregory Paul and proto-Unitarianism. Active until the Consensus of Sandomierz of 1570, he withdrew to his estate in Lipie and published extensively, e.g., *Annales, sive de origine et rebus gestis Polonorum libri octo* (Cracow, 1582) and *Statuta y metryka przywielejów koronnych* (Cracow, 1594). So numerous are these publications, royalist, and nationalist, unrelated in many cases to confessional Christianity, that the question has arisen whether there were not two persons of the same name, the ecclesiastic and the historian. See on this with new sources for the time, Stanisław Bodniak, "Dwóch czy jeden Sarnicki?," *RwP* 3 (1924) 126ff. and on the founding of a Protestant church in Lipie in 1547, see K. Sochaniewicz, "Sarniccy i zbór w Mokrem Lipiu na Chełmszczyźanie," *RwP* 3 (1924) 117; the major clarification of the Sarnicki problem in *PSB* is yet to appear.

10.C. By Martin Krowicki, "Servant of the church of the Lord Jesus Christ crucified" in Książ Wielki, *A Defense of the true doctrine and the primitive Christian faith . . . against . . . Andrew [Zebrzydowski], Bishop of Cracow*, printed by Daniel of Łęczyca in Pińczów, 1560. Title-page from Edmund Bursche, translator, Walerjan Krasiński, *Zarys dziejów powstania i upadku Reformacji w Polsce,* 2 vols. (Warsaw, 1903–05) 1. 116. The place of imprint comes from the end of the book. The full title reads: *Defense of . . . the Primitive Christian faith, which the Prophets, Christ the Son of God, and his Apostles and Saints taught, against the false and new faith, which the Roman Pope teaches in his churches and which, with his Reply Andrew, Bishop of Cracow, defends.*

The quotation from Ps 92:9 in an implied warning to the bishop is: "For, lo, thine enemies, O Lord, for lo, thine enemies shall perish: all evildoers shall be scattered," while the Psalm in Luke 19:27, in the parable of the unworthy steward, reads: "But as for these enemies of mine, who did not want me to reign over them, bring them here and slay them before me." For Bishop Zebrzydowski, see Pl. 5.

11–12. CRACOW IN THE SIXTEENTH CENTURY

11–12.A. The woodcut of Cracow is from Georg Braun, *Civitates orbis terrarum,* where it is the largest (foldout) woodcut, beautifully hand-colored; by permission of the Houghton Library, Harvard University.

This general view of Cracow on the left (at this point, the north) bank of the Vistula and of two related towns in the sixteenth century may be compared topographically with numbered sites in the Map of Reformation Cracow.

Kazimierz, at the upper right, was founded by Casimir the Great in 1335 to be a strong point on the right (south) bank of the Vistula and to be the seat of the university he envisaged. It had its own town hall and several large churches. John Olbracht (1492–1501), older brother of Sigismund I the Old, transferred the Jews of walled Cracow to Kazimierz "across the river"; and their oldest synagogue can be identified by its four stubby towers beneath the legend *Porta Iudeorum,* just below where the Vistula seems to be joined by the Wigla. By the eighteenth century the Vistula had broken through into the Wigla, coursing around Kazimierz to the right; and slowly the "Old" Vistula became "Little" Vistula. This ravine is now paved over as Detla Boulevard.

In the foreground the Rudawa flows into the Vistula. Mounted knights with panache, mace, and Hussar wings (*skrzydła husarskie; Federschmucker*) lead and accompany a muster of other knights in court attire across the Rawa bridge toward the grounds of the Summer Palace in Łobzów at the left, only the outskirts of which still show on this necessarily slightly cropped picture. Built by Santi Gucci, the Summer Palace was the place from which processions for royal weddings and funerals and other state occasions usually originated, entering the city by the Royal Way (see below).

Up the middle road past a wayside shrine traffic enters walled Cracow through a preliminary gateway and further on across the fortified Szewska Gate (54 on the Map of Cracow) into the city near St. Ann's (visible but unnoted, with its broad sloping roof below the "l" in Metropolis). Here is the general location of the two oldest buildings of the University (Collegium Majus and Minus) residential and lecture halls of the *Academia Cracoviensis* (1354), founded by King Casimir (Kazimierz) on the model of Bologna and Padua, and chartered by Urban V. The Academy was given a new charter and endowment by Queen Jadwiga and Ladislas Jagiełło (1397/1400) (and Boniface IX) and therefore much later came to be called in their honor the Jagiellonian University, the only *studium generale* to the east of the Holy Roman Empire until the founding of the *Albertina* in Königsberg (Pl. 7), itself chartered by the Polish King (Sigismund I).

In the upper left of the pictures is the third town, Kleparz, with its seal of St. Florian on the skyline and his church below, which gives its name to the principal entry into the walled city of Cracow, the Florian Gate. This is the opening of the Royal Way toward the castle. Following it, on the skyline, one sees the spires of the churches of the Holy Spirit, of Holy Cross, of St. Mark, and, below the skyline with a stubby tower, the church of St. Stephen (Szczepan), where the first evangelical sermons were openly preached in Cracow. The dominating structures are the Church of the Virgin Mary with two dissimilar towers and next to it the great tower of the once massive town hall (*Praetorium*), both in Market Square (*Rynek*). Next come the Dominican Church of Holy Trinity, the original parish church of Cracow (the ball of whose tower was struck by lightning and taken as a sign by both sides in the Calvinist-Unitarian controversy noted by Lubieniecki), then the Church of All Saints, and the Franciscan Church and cloister of Lismanino until 1554. Next along Grodska street can be seen the spires of St. Andrew and of St. Martin (presently, the Evangelical Church). At the foot of the Wawel (but topographically also quite close to the Franciscan complex) is the city residence of the bishop of Cracow (who had another palace in Kielce). Cracow had become the temporary seat of the Archbishop of Gniezno in 1037 and then evolved from a ducal into the royal capital.

On the hill Wawel may be seen the new royal palace of Sigismund I the Old and Bona Sforza with its New Tower and Bell Tower, then the metropolitan cathedral of St. Stanislas with its Clock Tower and Silver Bell Tower, nearby the small steeples of two of four other churches within the royal precincts, St. Michael and St. George. Behind the Wawel eminence is Castle Gate street (Grodzka) leading from walled Cracow steeply below to the right into the suburb of Stradom and the bridge across the Vistula to the town hall of Kazimierz, with its great Gothic Church of St. Catherine.

In 1611 Sigismund III Vasa (Pl. 50) made of Warsaw the new capital of the Commonwealth, but the coronation of the elected Polish kings continued to take place in St. Stanislas on the Wawel.

In the left foreground of the picture, outside the walls between gatehouse out from the Szewska Gate and the next road over to the left, runs (invisible to the viewer) the *ulica Biskupia,* coming out between the square tower and a small church. Here was the villa of Dr. Nicholas Buccella, physician to Stephen Batory, where Socinus lived, 1593–97, before returning to his apartment near the Franciscan Church (cf. Pl. 48).

11–12.B. The Lament of the Different Kinds of People at the Death of Credit, c. 1575. At the upper right the Apothecary holds the candle of the mourning watch as various creditors of Cracow bemoan their unpaid accounts, from left to right: the Jew (as money lender), the Barber-Surgeon, the Painter, the Butcher, the Tailor, the Barmaid; returning on second level: the Musician, the Armenian (tradesman, possibly from Lwów), the Merchant (with his receipts), the Jeweler-Smith, the Cobbler, and at Credit's head, the Market Vendor. With the noblemen in the procession in the main print most of the classes of society are here represented, except for the patrician burghers, German and Polish. The vivid cartoon of the mourners of Credit, handcolored, is from PAN, Biblioteka, Zbiory graficzne, Cracow. The handbill has an accompanying ditty for each person in the Lament, not here reproduced, but appearing in Halina Nelken's *Images of a Lost World: Jewish Motifs in Polish Painting 1775–1945* (Oxford: 1991) Pl. i.

MAP OF REFORMATION SITES

A. Map of Cracow (without the towns of Kleparz and Kazimierz shown in the Panorama) prepared by Hugo Kołłątaj, 1785, showing streets and buildings as they were midway between events of the sixteenth century and the present, the fortifications still intact. To bring it in line with the Panorama (Pl. 8-1) some of Kołłątaj's lettering is upside down. The Szewska Gate (54) in the lower part of the Map is the most prominent gate seen in the middle foreground of the Panorama. At the upper left is a section destroyed in 1655 during the Swedish siege. It has been reconstructed as of special interest in the *Historia*.

The main features of Cracow can be identified from the Market Square (1) of Kleparz, along the Royal Way (taken for the funeral cortège of Sigismund II Augustus and for his elected successor Henry of Valois), through the Florian Gate (2), past St. Mary's (3) and, in the large Market Square (*Rynek*) the (4) Cloth Hall (*Sukiennice;* cf. Pl. 51) and the Town Hall (5) past (6) St. Adalbert's (Wojciech, the oldest church edifice in Cracow) down Grodzka street, the Way turning into St. Michael's street up Kanonicza street, to the metropolitan cathedral of St. Stanislas (7)—the bishop's palace in town (7B)—past four smaller churches and (8) the original castle (*Grόd*) to the Renaissance Royal Palace (9), principal residence of the Kings of Poland until Sigismund III Vasa made Warsaw the new capital (1611). Through Grodzka Gate (9) traffic passed into the suburb of Stradom and across the Vistula Bridge to Kazimierz (not shown). Only a segment of the Vistula appears (11) as it bends (cf. Panorama at V in *Vistula*) around the foot of the Wawel, with a few fishing jetties, as it is about to flow between Stradom and Kazimierz.

The principal churches, besides the three already named, are: (1) the site of the church of the Holy Spirit shown in the Panorama and that of Holy Cross (13), of St. Stephen (Szczepan), where Jacob of Iłża, the first in Cracow, preached evangelical reforms), (14) of St. Ann (close to the Academy building and the bursas), (15) of St. Francis (where Lithuanian Duke Ladislas Jagaila was baptized in 1386 before his marriage to Queen Jadwiga), (15A) the Franciscan cloister (where Lismanino lived as provincial general, 1534–54), (16) of All Saints, (17) of the Holy Trinity, the original parish church of Cracow until the construction of 3, when it became the Dominican Church (the tower of which, when struck by lightning, was taken as an omen in the *Historia*), (18) of St. Michael, (19) the Baroque church of SS. Peter and Paul, begun soon after the Jesuits arrived in Cracow, 1538 (where Peter Skarga, S.J. is buried; nearby a major Jesuit College of the seventeenth century intended to rival the Jagiellonian University: today palatine tribunal), (20) the Romanesque church of St. Andrew and the convent of the Poor Clares (supervised by Lismanino and where he had a special friend!), (21) the church of St. Martin, constructed on the site of the Romanesque church of the same name in the Panorama, housing in the seventeenth century the Discalced Carmelites, now the Evangelical/Reformed congregation, continuous in its records with that of 1555.

Sites of additional importance for the *Historia*: (22) the Brog (Haystack) on St. John's, a house that the Calvinists remodeled into their town church, 1572–89 (Pl. 51); (23) the location in the Square, where 10 April 1525 the former Grand Master of the Teutonic Order, Albert of Hohenzollern (Pl. 7) became, under the Polish King, vassal Duke of Prussia, the first princely territory in Europe to go Protestant; (24) the Little Market area where in 1539 the octogenarian Catherine Zaleszowska Weiglowa was burned as a Judaizing Sacramentarian (and where in 1616 a Calvinist was set upon by a mob and protected by Bishop Peter Tylicki); (25) the location of the late medieval synagogue; 25A, the Jewish market near St. Mary's (the Jewish community originally dwelt in the quarter taken over for the Academia [26, 27] and were removed with their synagogue to *ulica Żydowska,* near St. Stephen's, then to Kazimierz); (26) the Collegium Majus, where roughly a score of professors taught philosophy and theology, among them Lismanino (Faustus Socinus was later rescued [Pl. 48] from student assailants here); (27) the Collegium Minus; alchemy was intensely studied in the Academy, Michael Sędziwój was a leader; Dr. Faustus studied here as well (Goethe on a visit to Cracow projected his *Faust* here); (29) the Jerusalemite Bursa, founded in 1453 by Cardinal Oleśnicki when unable to fulfill his vow to visit the Holy Land); (30) the *Bursa pauperum,* where George Schomann (Pl. 31) resided and taught; (31) the printing office of Matthew Wierzbięta (1551 – 1605), lay elder of the Reformed/Calvinist congregation; (32) the road to Wola, where in his villa (Pl. 3) Ludwik Jost Decjusz entertained humanists and where Gregory Paul discussed the meaning of Scripture, 1552; (33) the plausible location of the home of Andrew Trzecieski, Sr., where the Dutch visitor Spiritus in 1546 raised the question of separate prayers to the Persons of the Trinity, Frycz Modrzewski (Pl. 21) among the guests; (34) the home of Severin Boner (Pl. 2-II), father of John the Calvinist; (here in 1605 the marriage of Maryna Mniszech, daugher of the palatine of Sandomierz, and Tsar Demetrius the Pretender, took place); (35) a home of John Boner, later of Prosper Provana, Pod Różą (here Skarga and Schomann debated); (36) the villa of John Boner (where he died at table among his Protestant guests), (36A) the Boner Renaissance Garden, meadows, ponds, and fountains, where the early Reformed met for worship on fine days and (36B) a possible edifice separate from the villa where they met; (37) the house (Pod Jaszczurami) and possibly the pharmacy of Simon Ronemberg the apothecary; (38) the house of Stanislas Cichowski, where the congregation of the Minor Church assembled (the site of the present church of St. Thomas) (30) the church of St. Barbara taken over by the Jesuits, who established their first college site (40) in 1583; (41) the approximate location of the printing office of Alex Rodecki; (42) the residence of Ludwik Jost Decjusz, Jr., Calvinist; Caspar Békés (Pl. 32-III) lived here in 1577; (43) the residence of Faustus Socinus, 1590 – 93; 97 – 98; (44) the residence on Biskupia of Dr. Nicholas Buccella, physician to Stephen Batory, where Socinus lived, 1593 – 97; Socinus was assailed and threatened in the Square (Pl. 35-II) at about (5) and taken for safety by Dr. Martin Wadowita temporarily at (26) and for greater security to the Collegium Juridicum (46); (47) the Reformed/Calvinist cemetery (at present the cloister of the Carmelite nuns, founded in 1634); (48) the cemetery of the Arians, where three graves were unearthed in 1837 (Pl. 48-IV); (49) ''Dog's Hill'' in pejorative reference to a Protestant burial site in unconsecrated ground from the Catholic view, evidently different from the sites (47/48); (50) Arian hospital (approximate); (51) German Protestant school; (52) Calvinist school under Trecy; (53) the house of Pan Rozen, where widow of Lismanino (d. 1566), Claudia Lismanina, is known to have lived in 1580.

13. LAELIUS SOCINUS

13.A. The legend reads: ''Lelio Socino nata a Siena nel 1525, morto a Zurigo nel 1562 in Augusta.''

There are bronze medallions of Laelius and Faustus Socinus in the Museo Civico (formerly in the Biblioteca Comunale degli Intronati), Siena. Earl M. Wilbur once inspected them, *The Christian Register,* 104 (Boston, 25 June 1925), p. 634. The print appears to have been made from one of these medallions at a date sufficiently late to allow the engraver to inscribe the Sozzini name of the famous family of jurisconsults as Socino. The print in a large frame belongs to Meadville/Lombard Theological School, Chicago, and hangs in the office of John C. Godbey. Between 1547 and 1551 he was received by the major Reformers, stayed in the home of Melanchthon, corresponded at close range with Calvin and visited Cracow in 1551, where he was, with Bernardine Ochino, a factor in the conversion of Francis Lismanino (Pl. 16). In Zurich, Henry Bullinger demanded of him a "Confessio."

Laelius was again in the Commonwealth in 1558–59 with a letter of recommendation from Calvin to Prince Nicholas Radziwiłł the Black (Pl. 14) and another from Bullinger to Łaski in Pińczów (Pl. 9). Cf. last paragraph of 13.C. His thought lived on primarily through his papers left to his nephew Faustus (Pls. 47, 48).

13.B. Vicenza in the Venetian Republic. Colored woodcut from Braun, *Civitates orbis terrarum;* published by permission of the Houghton Library, Harvard University.

Vicenza in the Venetian Republic close to Trentino was the site (in one of the gracious palaces) of the Collegia Vicentina (theological conferences), which pious Socinian historiography has fixed upon as the shared experience of Laelius and, among many others of distinction, the two eventual Venetian Hutterite martyrs, Giulio Gherlandi di Trevisi and Francesco della Saga di Ruego. For Budziński and Lubieniecki the departure of Laelius from Vicenza in 1547 for Reformation lands was a nodal point in the providential dynamics of the reformation of the Reformation (cf. commentary on Trzecieski in Pl. 3) through "the confessors of the Truth" in Poland.

Although the key to the edifices in the woodcut is unusually extensive, no attempt has been made by me to locate within the cathedral city the scene of the colloquies. Wilbur dissolved the *collegia* as a figment of Socinian historiography, thereby also freeing the proto-Socinians from any Anabaptist taint, *Socinianism,* 80. Aldo Stella and I have sought to validate aspects of the Vincentian recollection. See my *La Reforma Radical,* 619–20.

But Antonio Rotondò, in his critical edition of four authenticated writings of Laelius Socinus and 53 letters, without disposing of his sojourn in Vicenza, deflates this historiographical tradition of Budziński, Lubieniecki, Andrew Wiszowaty (RD 5, at n. 3), and Christopher Sand (**BAnt** 18–19), *Lelio Sozzini, Opere* (Florence: Olschki, 1986) 23–30. While he amplifies the documentation of Laelius's relations with Italian Anabaptists (sometime Benedictine abbot and Hebraist Girolamo Buzzale and Lorenzo Tizzano), he suggests that some Venetian Anabaptists became prominent in the Socinian tradition concerning Laelius in Vicenza because of the renown of three of them among the Hutterite communitarian Anabaptists (Pls. 29, 30) familiar to the Polish Brethren. In any case, the main thrust of Rotondò is that before his departure from Vicenza, a gentleman scholar of 31, Laelius lived in the main currents of Italian religious humanism, as it was obliged to differentiate itself off from Catholic Evangelicalism, between the imposition of the Roman Inquisition in 1542 and the opening of the Council of Trent in 1545. (Paul III had proposed such a council as early as 1538, in Vicenza, but was frustrated by the Emperor.)

13.C. The first line of Laelius's equivocal autograph "Confessio de Deo," amicably required of him by Bullinger, Zurich, 15 July 1554, reads: "I, Laelius Sozinus. . . ." This autograph is contained in the Zurich Staatsarchiv, Codex E II, 367, folios 54–57, ed. by Rotondò, *Lelio Sozzini, Opere,* 95–100. Page 54 therein is reproduced also by

John A. Tedeschi, ed. and contributor, *Italian Reformation Studies in Honor of Laelius Socinus* (Florence, 1965), between pp. 198/199. In Appendix I, he supplies improved MS readings over against the text as first printed by Johann Hottinger (1668), then by Friedrich Bock (1784), which was used as the basis of the translation of the whole *Confessio* by Edward M. Hulme, "Lelio Sozzini's Confession of Faith," *Persecution and Liberty: Essays in honor of George Lincoln Burr* (New York, 1931) 211–25, specifically, 216–18. (The annotation of the whole Sozzini genealogy is supplied by Tedeschi, *Laelius Socinus,* 1965, amplified and corrected in his photocopied Harvard thesis, "A History of the Sozzini Family during the Renaissance" [Cambridge, 1966]). Some of this work is superseded by the critical edition of Rotondò; while Aldo Stella fills out the family history and brings out fully the place of the universities of Bologna and Padua in the life of Laelius, "Una famiglia di giuristi fra eterodossi padovani e bolognesi: Mariano [the father] e Lelio Sozzini (1525–56), *Rapporti fra le università di Padova e Bologna,* ed. by Lucia Rossetti (Trieste: LINT, 1988) 127–60.

In the *Confessio* Laelius Socinus signs as *Sozinus*. This is the basis for the occasional vernacularization of his name as Sozini, in contrast to the double "z" for his nephew, the spelling now standardized by Rotondò for both men.

Under Bullinger's pressure, Laelius was evasive:

> I, Laelius Sozinus, in my boyhood learned one creed, that which is called the Apostles' Creed, which I even now know and acknowledge to be the most ancient, accepted at all times in the Church, though drawn up in various forms. But I have lately read others also, and attribute all the honor I can and ought to the very old creeds of Nicaea and Constantinople.

He never really commits himself to the ancient creeds, merely acknowledging that they and the technical terms for the Trinity and Christology have been in use for the last 1300 years, from the time of Justin Martyr; but he would like to hear "the evangelical faith expounded . . . in the words of Christ, the Apostles, and the Evangelists." He insists that dissenters in faith should not be punished "otherwise than by the Christian and the apostolic law" and this includes presumably warning and banning, placed, however, in the framework of a rather ferocious eschatology with the vindictive sword of the Christ of the Second Advent as foreseen by the Seer of Revelation with swirling flames and brimstone. Laelius expresses his confidence in "the resurrection from the dead, that caught up in the clouds I may meet the Lord in the air (1 Thess 4:17), ever praising our God and Father world without end." Intense variants of this eschatology are found among both the Transylvanian Unitarians and the Polish Brethren, in their cases including also sometimes millennialism; but Faustus Socinus, mitigating the eschatology of his uncle, would hold to a resurrection of the righteous only and reduce the meting out of judgment to those living ("the quick") at the moment of Christ's Second Advent to be followed (as in the expectation of his uncle) by the rapture into heaven of the godly but oblivion, not active punishment, for the wicked.

Laelius expressed himself on the death of the soul with the body and the resurrection of the righteous only in *De resurrectione* (c. 1549) published by the Socinian circle in Amsterdam, 1654, *Opere,* 75–80; accessible in German in Heinold Fast, *Der linke Flügel der Reformation: Glaubenszeugnisse der Täufer, Spiritualisten, Schwärmer und Antitrinitarier* (Bremen, 1962) 389–92.

On Christology Laelius expressed himself most decisively in the anonymous *Brevis explicatio in primum Iohannis caput* (Zurich, 1561), which was twice printed anonymously in the sixteenth century, first by George Biandrata and Francis Dávid (Pls. 18, 25) in *De falsa et vera Dei cognitione* (Alba Julia, 1568). In this Laelius gave a fundamentally new impetus to Unitarianism, distinct from that of Servetus (Pl. 25), in the interpretation in John 1 of *mundus* (the world), as the world of sinners, and of the Word of God made flesh, as the Virgin-born Jesus the Messiah, without any premundane status. The *Brevis explicatio* evidentally circulated in MS in Poland, Transylvania, and elsewhere and contributed to the radicalization of Triadology and Christology in both regions even before 1568, as is evidenced by Biandrata's letter to Gregory Paul of 21 September 1565 (cf. below), disparaging the radical Polish preoccupation with a lesser matter, believers' baptism, and pressing for something like the simplified Laelian Christology of John. Socinianism must be understood theologically as including the diffidently seminal thought of Laelius, even though his work remained largely anonymous except as his nephew Faustus acknowledged it in general (Pls. 47, 48) in his *Explicatio primae partis primi capitis Iohannis* (c. 1562). The *Brevis explicatio* of Laelius was printed a second time in the century for refutation by François du Jon (Junius) (Heidelberg, 1591).

The interconnection of the two similarly entitled writings of the Sozzini, uncle and nephew, requires further attention at the point of common diffusion.

Faustus Socinus, writing to Andrew Dudith (Pl. 38) in 1580, remarked that his own *Explicatio primae partis primi capitis Iohannis,* was "eighteen years ago" (Alba Julia, 1562); cf. Socyn, *Listy,* 2 vols., ed. Ludwik Chmaj, *List* VI, 1, p. 54, n. 13 (with cross reference to *List* V, at n. 1, where the paraphrase of it in Polish by Gregory Paul is referred to). This *Explicatio primae partis* was reprinted by Dávid in *Refutatio propositionum Melii* (Alba Julia, 1568), where it was wrongly ascribed to Laelius. Hence in his letter to Dudith, Faustus was setting the record straight (cf. further Pl. 47).

Laelius in his posthumous *Brevis explicatio* had laid the groundwork for his nephew's Christology in rejection of the Triadology/Christology almost unique to Servetus. This was the view of Elizabeth F. Hirsch, "Servetus and the Early Socinians," in John C. Godbey, ed., *Unitarianism in the Sixteenth/Seventeenth Century Settings,* the *Proceedings of the Unitarian Universalist Historical Society,* 20:2 (1985 – 86) 25.

In the *Explicatio,* incorrectly ascribed by Biandrata and Dávid to Laelius, Faustus, drawing on Laelius wrote that " 'In the beginning' (John 1:1) should be interpreted 'in accordance with Acts 1:1,' i.e., ['*then* (Luke said), Jesus] began to do and teach [beginning from the baptism of John].' " The words in square brackets are in Faustus, not in the text he quotes, but in amplification of his understanding of Luke's intent as linked to John 1:1. Faustus, following Laelius, over against Servetus, thus left no place in his Christology for a preexistent Christ, interpreting, rather, the passages like Phil 2:5 – 8, Col 1:15, and 2 Cor 4:4 in the sense of the ideal Messiah in the mind of God, and understanding John 1 to be about the new era, the new creation in the proclamation by the Virgin-born Son of Man. Faustus had begun to elaborate his uncle's view in his own *Explicatio* (written in Basel, 1562). For its publication history, see Gryczowa, item 270, although there remains therein residues of the scholarly confusion between two similarly entitled works, that of Faustus, depending on Laelius. In effect uncle and nephew, on the same subject, were *printed* for the first time in the same year by the same resourceful editors, Biandrata and Dávid (Alba Julia, 1568).

In 1555 Laelius expressed himself most fully on the sacraments in general and on communion in particular in commenting on the Zurich Agreement (Consensus Tigurinus, 1549) between the French- and German-speaking Reformed in Switzerland. This was in his *De sacramentis dissertatio* addressed to the followers of Bullinger in Zurich and of

Calvin in Geneva. First published by the Socinian circle in Amsterdam in 1654, it is critically edited by Rotondó, *Opere,* 81 – 92.

Among the fifty-three letters of Laelius Socinus is one addressed to him by John Utenhove, companion and secretary of John Łaski (Pl. 20), to Laelius, 13 January 1559, who was at the time in the palace of Prince Nicholas Radziwiłł the Black (Pl. 14) with Biandrata (Pls. 18, 40), Rotondò, *Opere,* 276 – 78. From this friendly letter reporting the sickness and imminent death of Łaski, it is evident that all the above named were in agreement against Calvin's vilification of Dr. Biandrata (cf. Pl. 24).

14. LITHUANIA I: THE COUSINS RADZIWIŁŁ

14.A. Vilna, capital of the Grand Duchy of Lithuania and of the palatinate. Below the Old Castle is the new castle and Catholic cathedral. Nearby is the Calvinist church (C) and there are many Orthodox and Catholic churches in this town of Lithuanians, Orthodox Byelorussians, Poles, Germans, Jews, Karaites, and Muslim Tatars. Braun, *Civitates orbis terrarum,* reproduced by permission of the Houghton Library, Harvard University.

Vilna (Vilnius/Wilno) in the sixteenth century, founded with its Old Castle atop the Hill of Gedmininas at the juncture (upper left) of the Vilnia (Wilejka) with the larger Neris (Wilja/Wilde) flowing down at the left into the Nieman past Kaunas (Kowno) into the Baltic above Königsberg. It was to his then unwalled capital that Grand Duke (Jagiełło) returned after his baptism and marriage (1386) in Cracow to Queen Jadwiga of Anjou and demanded of his pagan thanes in turn that they also submit to baptism as a pledge and proof of their continued loyalty to him as King of Poland (founder of the Jagiellonian dynasty) and as Christian Grand Duke (''the baptism of Lithuania'') 1387. In the same year he granted the Germans and Byelorussians of the town a charter enabling them to organize according to Magdeburg urban institutions and laws.

At the base of Old Castle Hill, where several newer castles had been successively destroyed by fire, Sigismund I Jagiellończyk and his son Sigismund II Augustus built the Palace complex shown. Sigismund II, Grand Duke in 1522 and actual governor by 1544 (Pl. 63), primarily resided here (1544 – 66) rather than in the Wawel, as Vilna was closer to the contested frontiers of the Commonwealth. For a period his large library of 4000 volumes was housed in the Old Castle. The castle cathedral (founded on a pagan shrine by Jogaila in 1388) as shown here dates from the second quarter of the Reformation century and contains the remains of Sigismund the Old's older royal brother Alexander (Pl. 6.A).

The town had been a open city until the brick wall was begun in 1503, visible (uncompleted) in the foreground (circling south and east toward a third gate (upper right) with the Sharp or the Dawn Gate (*Ostra Brama*), next to which a chapel (yet to be built) housed a miraculous image of the Madonna venerated by Catholics and Orthodox alike.

In the main square of the city the town hall may be seen (18). Although the whole walled town was under a Grand Ducal governor appointed for life (*vaitas/wójt*), the burghers eventually gained the right to nominate him, while the magistracy governing under him consisted of twelve elected mayors and twenty-four counselors (syndics), two and four of each group respectively ruling in any given year; and, as of 1536, half of them had to be Eastern Orthodox.

The principal Byzantine-rite church of the eventually nine is to be seen standing free at the head (17) of the second block toward the Palace square, while the Court of the Muscovites (19) is further out from the town hall square toward the German Gate. Down from the same square is the Deutsche Gasse, along which is the Grand Ducal mint and the first printing press in Lithuania, 1525. Commerce moved in all directions but especially down the main street past the chancery (13) toward the Neris. The German House (9) at the foot of Old Castle Hill (next the semi-quadrangular Grand Ducal stables), stood ready for river and Baltic trade. Downstream are the lighthouse, the long water mill, and in the lower left the suburb of Lukišikès, where Nicholas Radvila (Radziwiłł) the Black (B) had his luxurious residence and where he established a Reformed congregation that went through the same schism as that in Cracow.

Jews were permitted to build their first wooden synagogue within the capital in 1572. Jesuits arrived from Cardinal Hosius, from Braunsberg in Varmia, in 1569 at the invitation of Bishop Valerian Protaszewicz, built up their college (1576) and a substantial library next to St. John's, the highest steepled church off the main street at the very center of the picture (14). Under a charter from Stephen Batory and another from Gregory XIII in 1579, the college became a university, the King/Grand Duke Stephen inaugurating this major *studium* of the Counter-Reform in the Commonwealth, eventually to be named after him, and now the state university of Vilnius.

14.B. Nicholas Radziwiłł the Black (1515–65), after whom the Calvinist Bible was named as its sponsor, 1563 (Pl. 54), was influenced by Dr. Biandrata (Pls. 18, 24). Engraving by Dominicus Custos in *Der Allerdurchleuchtigsten und Grossmüthigen . . . wahrhaftige Bildtnussen* (Innsbruck, 1602); some of the architectural ornamentation of the original has been cropped.

Prince Nicholas Radziwiłł the Black born in Nieśwież (Pl. 27), hereditary prince (from 1549) of the Holy Roman Empire through Ferdinand, chancellor of the Grand Duchy (from 1550), palatine of Vilna (from 1551), was a spirited correspondent with Calvin, chief patron of the Reformed Church in the Grand Duchy, inclining toward the simplified creed sponsored by Dr. Biandrata (Pl. 8), who, with Francis Dávid, kept him informed of developments in Transylvania.

14.C. Nicholas Radziwiłł the Red (1512–84), also Protestant, brother of Barbara, second wife of Sigismund II (Plate 5). Engraving by Dominicus Custos, Martinus F. Wobe, ed., *Icones familiae ducalis Radivilianae ex originalibus . . . picturis* (Nieśwież: Printers of the Society of Jesus; reprinted from the old plates, Petersburg, 1885), Pl. 30. The Black cousin (B) is excluded from this edition.

Nicholas Radziwiłł the Red (1512–84), like his cousin and at the same time made hereditary prince of the Empire, successor to his cousin in the chancellorship and palatine dignity (from 1564), was brother of Barbara (Pl. 2), second queen of Sigismund. As grand hetman of the Crown, he led the Commonwealth forces against the Livonian Order under William of Fürstenberg (cf. D), obliging him to sever his relationship with Tsar Ivan IV the Terrible, whereupon with Fürstenberg, with massive armies, Radziwiłł defeated the Muscovites at Ula in 1564. He fostered the Reformed school in Vilna and founded a second at his seat in Biržai. He opposed the Union of Lublin in 1569 and became a separatist against Henry of Valois, but was appeased by Stephen Batory.

14.D. By the Treaty of Pasvalys (Poswol), 14 September 1557, Teutonic Master William Fürstenberg submits to Sigismund II; Courland and Livonia become fiefs of the Crown like Ducal Prussia. Modern painting of the scene in A. Šapoka, *Lietuvos Istorija* (Kaunas, 1936) 215.

14.E. Calvinist chuch in Vilna as of 1682. From a sketch in MS of Jan Cedrowski; reproduced in Bursche's edition of Walerjan Krasiński, *Zarys dziejów powstania i upadku Reformacji w Polsce,* 2:1, 164.

The Calvinist church stood, 1581–1650, near the Palace Square (to be precisely located on A at the darker edge of the vertical printer's shadow, at the point where a line would intersect it drawn from the base of the lower tower of the Town Hall to the base of the tower furthest left of the large Bernadine Church, near the Old Castle). In this site it was assaulted at about the same time as the Brog in Cracow (Pl. 51) but was rebuilt. Vilna, being much closer to Protestant centers like Königsberg, Danzig, Amsterdam, London, and Edinburgh, had a very strong Evangelical (Calvinist) community up to the end of World War II. After the death of Nicholas the Black (A), the Lithuanian counterpart of the Polish Minor Church disappeared on the radical anabaptist left and regrouped under the the the leadership of Simon Budny (Pl. 15), centered in the palatinate of Nowogródek, allied with the Transylvanian Erastian Unitarians, and at odds with the adorant, semi-pacifistic Minor Church of Little Poland under Socinus's leadership (Pls. 47, 48).

For the location of the Evangelical church, see the plan in *Monumenta Reformationis Polonicae et Lithuanicae,* 1:1, p. 192.

15. LITHUANIA II: RAPOLIONIS, MOSVID, BUDNY, BAZYLIK

15.A. The hymn *"Patris sapientia, veritas divina"* translated into Lithuanian by Stanislas Rapagelanus (Rapolionis) (c. 1485–1545), who received his doctorate under Luther in 1544, the first professor in the Albertina, translator of the whole Bible (Pl. 54). A page from a book of hymns, *Gesmes chrikščoniškas* (Königsberg, 1570), taken from a facsimile in Georg Gerullis, ed., *Mosvid: Die ältesten lithauischen Sprachdenkmäler bis zum Jahre 1570* (Heidelberg, 1923) 411; the whole hymnal described in the bibliographical guide to Lithuanian imprints with a chronology and detailed indices and pictures, *Knygos Lietuviu, Kalba,* I (1547–1861) (Vilnius, 1969) item 682.

Stanislovas Rapolionis (the preferred Lithuanian spelling) appears in the *Historia* as Rapagelanus (Rafałowicz). A major figure in the history of Lithuanian Lutheranism, the first incumbent of the chair of theology in the Albertina, he left the complete MS translation of the Luther Bible into Lithuanian (Pl. 54).

15.B. The oldest book printed in Lithuanian, Martin Mažvydas (Mosvid), Luther's *Enchiridion* (Königsberg, 1547), with an appeal in the prefatory Latin to fellow priests to help end the secret pagan idolatries of their people, "for our God wishes all to be saved." The title-page from the commemorative facsimile edition, Martynas Mažvydas (commonly: Mosvid, c. 1520–63), *Pirmoslos lietuviskos knygos autorius* (Chicago: The Lithuanian Institute of Education, 1963); Gerullis, *Mosvid,* 1; *Knygos Lietuviu,* I, item 678.

The translation, dedicated to the Grand Duke (Sigismund Augustus), is preceded with an appeal in Latin to fellow-Lithuanian priests to instruct the common people in the rudiments of evangelical faith and to avoid involvement in controversial fine points of theology; and he urgently appeals to them to turn their parishioners from the secret idolatries in the worship of trees, streams, and snakes and thereby make the whole Duchy truly Christian.

15.C. Simon Budny (d. c. 1595), the principal Reformed, then Unitarian theologian and publicist in the Grand Duchy, translator of the Brest Bible of 1572 (Pl. 54), an opponent of Socinus on the office of the sword and the adoration of Christ, major figure in the differentiation of the (Polish-speaking) Lithuanian Brethren from the Socinianizing Polish Brethren. A quite plausible likeness of Budny, among the heretics submerging in the moat of purgatory around the symbolic representation of the Catholic Church and her seven sacraments, in a picture reproduced from Stanislas Reszka in Pl. 49. See there for the argument for the probable authenticity of the Budny sketch, better than that of most of the other heretics pictured in the same moat.

A proficient philologue and textual critic, Budny, a Masovian by birth, put into the notes for his New Testament his view that Jesus was the son of Joseph. These notes were eliminated from the first printing but included in his second edition. He was close to the advanced Unitarians in Transylvania, in close contact with a leader among them, Palaeologus (Pl. 38), and he collaborated with Stanislas Budziński and Andrew Kołodyński on the forged Glogolithic Letter of John Smera to Vladimir of Kiev, purporting to describe an ideal Unitarian church life in Alexandria, a letter printed as authentic in Latin translation in the Unitarian edition of Andrew Węgierski's *Slavonia Reformata* (1679, a document known to Lubieniecki but not fully credited by him.

15.D. Budny's Cathechism in Ruthenian, printed at the Radziwiłł press in Nieśwież (Pl. 17) in 1572, designed to bring over the Orthodox Byelorussians to Protestantism. From the Czartoryski Collection, Cracow: title-page reproduced from Kawecka-Gryczowa, *Drukarze,* zeszyt 5, Pl. 13; with a dedication from Budny's parish in Kleck, 12 June 1562, to "the young two Nicholases," sons respectively of Nicholas the Black and the Red (Pl. 14). It was one of two publications in Cyrillic at this press intended to convert the Orthodox of the Grand Duchy to Protestantism in their own language. The son of Nicholas the Red, namely, Nicholas VII, remained Protestant, but all four sons of Nicholas the Black returned to Catholicism, including George Cardinal Radziwiłł (Pl. 5).

15.E. John Utenhove's *Simplex et fidelis narratio* (Basel, 1560), the Life of John Łaski in London, translated by Cyprian Bazylik as part of his larger *The History of the Harsh Persecutions* (Brest, 1567) (Pl. 1). Photograph from Jerzy Ziomek, ed., *Odrodzenie w Polsce/Historia literatury* ([Warsaw]: PAN, 1956) Pl. between 496–97; for more on the publication, see *Drukarze,* zeszyt 5, 45–52. In the translation by Bazylik, this section of the larger book is dedicated to the nephew of the Reformer, Olbracht Łaski (Pl. 38), as his new patron. The title reads "On the convenanting and after this the dispersion of the Strangers' Churches in London over which Master John Łaski of blessed memory was the veritable and Christian Bishop." It is now considered to be largely the work of Łaski himself by dictation by him and ascribed to his secretary as editor. Barycz, *Szlakami,* 245.

John Utenhove (1520–65), companion to Łaski, was born in Ghent. After joining the Reformation, he served in Aachen, Cologne, and Strassburg (1544–48); and, on the imposition of the Augsburg Interim, he left for London, helping Łaski there in the organization of the Strangers' Church(es). On the accession of Mary Tudor in 1553, Utenove accompanied Łaski (presumably in the boat from Gravesend, in Pl. 20); he accompanied Łaski on a visitation to Danzig in 1554, served him as secretary in Emden (1554–56) and then in Poland (1556–59). He returned to London under Elizabeth and saw the publication of (Łaski's) *Narratio de instituta ac demum dissipata Belgarum aliorumque peregrinorum in Anglia ecclesia* (Basel, 1560), of which the sixth page of this Polish translation of Bazylik's work is shown.

Translator and publisher, Bazylik was born c. 1535 in Sieradz, of which Olbracht Łaski became palatine in 1566. He had been musician and poet in the court of Nicholas

Radziwiłł the Black, becoming an ardent Protestant late in life and owner of a printing press in Brest (cf. Pl. 52), 1562–70, a major intellectual center of Lithuanian Protestantism. Probaby through the *History of the Harsh Persecution,* of which the *Narratio* is a section, Budny, the overall compiler, established contact with John Foxe. There is an autographed letter of his to Foxe in the Bodeleian Library, B. Lauretters 107, p. 100v.

16. LISMANINO AND SEVERAL ITALIANS FROM A POLISH PERSPECTIVE

16.A – 1. Lubieniecki testifies to the importance of the Italians by bringing in as many as thirty, not counting medieval figures, Popes, papal legates, and Italian princes, altogether far more numerous than any other ''national'' grouping. The Germans of the Empire and Swiss cantons are, besides the Polish nation, the next largest ethnic contingent in the *Historia.*

Without a surviving likeness of the central figure, Lismanino, who died tragically in Königsberg, several of his fellow Italians grouped above and below the center band of pictures may serve to symbolize his central role. Those above died before him. The asterisk identifies the Italians who visited Poland; those pictured in the plate are italicized; the square brackets designate those featured on other picture pages: Vermigli (1562), [*L. *Socinus* (1562)], Gherlandi (1562), [*Heraclides Basilicos* (1563)], *Castellio* (1563), *Vergerio* (1564), Gribaldi (1564), *Ochino* (1564), F. *Negri (1564), Della Sega (1564). Dying after Lismanino were *Curione* (1569), G. *Negri (1570), *Alciati (1573), [*Stancaro (1574)], *N. Paruta (c. 1575), *Provana* (1584), [*Biandrata (1588)], [*Zanchi* (1590)], [F. **Socinus* (1604)], *Franco di Franco (1611), *Gittich Veneto (1645).

By his own account Lismanino moved into the Reformation by reading, beginning with works of Luther, c. 1526, then with Calvin's *Institutes* after 1536 (which he later worked through with Sigismund II, Pl. 6), then with the *Confessio* (also 1536) of the Czech Brethren (Pl. 4, commentary). He was openly a convert to the Swiss Reformed movement, married Claudia, under Calvin's counsel, 1554, and became a major figure as head of the Reformed Church in Little Poland, c. 1554–56, prominent in their synods but never superintendent. Lismanino's position as prospective head of the Reformed Church of Little Poland was preempted by the arrival of the more decisive John Łaski in 1556 (Pl. 20). Lismanino, Claudia, and their son Paul, stayed in Tomice, 1556–58 (Pl. 2), under the protection of Tomicki and the Górkas (Pl. 4).

In 1563 Lismanino was on the point of leaving the Commonwealth to serve under fellow Italianate Greek Voivode Heraclides in Cotnari and Jassy (Pls. 28, 38), when he learned of Heraclides' assassination. While a pensionary of Duke Albert in Königsberg, he lived in the home of J. Funck, where also dwelt Skalicha and other advisors of the Duke on the Osiandrist side (Pl. 7). In 1562 Lismanino prepared his *Apologia, Brevis explicatio doctrinae de sanctissima Trinitate,* in which are important references to several synods he had participated in. Dedicating the *Apologia* to Sigismund II, he declared: ''errare possum, haereticus esse non possum.'' A courtier in Königsberg, Lismanino drowned in a well in an uncertain location, either from a fit of epilepsy or in intentional suicide (the removal of his clothes suggesting the latter). If suicide, it is unclear whether it was in religious despair, or chagrin, or his wife's alleged unfaithfulness (for her final habitation, see Map of Cracow).

16.A. Sebastian Castellio. *From the Biblia Sacra ex Sebatiani Castellionis interpretatione* (Frankfurt, 1697), with no certain claim to authenticity; copy in the Universitäts-

Bibliothek, Basel, with the identification in Latin: "S.C., public professor of Greek litera-tures with Basel Academy, born 1515, died 29 December 1563"; from Charles Émile Delormeau, *Sebastien Castellion* (Neuchâtel, 1964) frontispiece.

In his pseudonymous *De hereticis, an sint persequendi* (1554), Castellio condemned the burning of Servetus (cf. Pl. 25). The autograph version, discovered in 1938, has been edited with a French translation by Bruno Becker (d. 1968) and M. Valkhoff, *De l'impunité des hérétiques* (Geneva: Droz, 1971); large excerpts from the hitherto standard text are published by Roland Bainton (1935), while Castellio is seen from a Polish per-spective by Waldemar Voisé (1963).

16.B. Bernardine Ochino. From *Dialogi Sette* (Venice, 1542); copy in the Biblioteca Guicciardini, Florence; from Roland Bainton, *Ochino* (1940) frontispiece.

Ochino's *A Tragedy of the Unjustly Usurped Primacy* was translated from the Italian and published while Lismanino was among the Czech Brethren in Great Poland, *O zwierzchności papieskiej* (Szamotuły, 1558).

16.C. Peter Paul Vergerio. Copperprint by Heinrich Hondius, Lutherhalle, Wittenberg.

Sometime bishop Peter Paul Vergerio was visited by Lismanino in Stuttgart.

16.D. The Franciscan Church and to the left a portion of the cloister where Lismanino held humanistic gatherings to which he invited Reform-minded priests as preachers. Photograph of 1906 of the Gothic edifice, much altered by fire and remodeling from that of the sixteenth century; IS PAN.

As provincial general for all of Poland, Lithuania, and Bohemia and in Poland com-missioner general, Lismanino invited Reform-minded priests and humanists to discuss the theological issues of the day in these precincts. He is known to have had a good friend among the Poor Clares.

16.E. The inner court of the Collegium Majus of the fifteenth century, where lectures in theology of the University were delivered; reconstructed in the twentieth century; photo-graph of 1961 by J. Sandomirski; IS PAN.

The Collegium Majus and Minus had been converted by King Casimir from sumptu-ous town houses in the Jewish quarter into the first quarters of the Academia Craco-viensis, 1364, the core of the later Jagiellonian University (see Map of Cracow).

16.F. The parish church in Tomice, Great Poland owned by John Tomicki, where Lismanino participated in a colloquium with the Czech Brethren, 1557, and considered joining them. *Katalog zabytków sztuki.*

16.G. Celio Secundo Curione. From Delio Cantimori, *Italienische Häretiker,* tr. by Werner Kaegi (Basel, 1949), source not given.

Celio Secundo Curione, professor in Basel, dedicated his *De amplitudine beati regni Dei* (Poschavio, 1554) to Sigismund II and left marginal notations on the *Apologia pro Serveto* "by Lyncurius," found by Vergerio in Tübingen, 1559, among the papers of a murdered Polish student. This work is ascribed in its entirety by some to Curione. Father-in-law of Zanchi (Pl. 42), Curione conformed to the established church of Basel.

The *Apologia* by "Lyncurius" is printed *apud* Calvin, *Opera,* 15. The whole MS to which it was attached, discovered by Vergerio, was *Declarationis Jesu Christi filii Dei libri V.* Lubieniecki had access to a copy circulating in Holland, *Historia,* 92 – 105, presenting a section of it, "De vera Dei et filii eius cognitione," expressing some reserve about it, but, of course, deploring the cruel death of Servetus. Stanislas Kot and David

Pingree assigned the *Apologia* to Curione. See the latter, "The *Apologia* of Alphonsus Lyncurius, translated with an introduction," John Tedeschi, ed., *Italian Reformation Studies in Honor of Laelius Socinus* (1965) 197–214, with samples of the handwriting. Before and after this essay, I ascribed the *Apologia* to Gribaldi, see esp. *RR* Spanish, 688–90; see further in support of the Gribaldi authorship, Dr. C. Gilly of Basel *apud* Elizabeth F. Hirsch, "Servetus," *Unitarianism,* ed. Godbey, p. 29 n. 13.

16.H. Sepulchral monument of Prosper Provana (d. 1584), a protector of the Brethren, in the Dominican Church, Cracow. Photograph by Wł. Gumuła, PAN: gift of Jerzy Strzetleski.

Prosper Provana is sculpted in the armor of *starosta* of Bodzentyn. In charge of the royal salt mines in Wieliczka and Bochnia, with his brother Trajan, he participated in some of the Reformed synods and received into his residence some of the Polish Brethren. He kept Biandrata's Servetus books when the doctor left for Transylvania.

16.I. The head of Provana, once in charge of the royal salt mines in Wieliczka and Bochnia, whose town house in Cracow was the scene of interconfessional debate (Plate 31). *Katalog zabytków sztuki,* 4, Kraków, 3.

I am grateful to Marius Cybulski, Mary Clare Altenhofen, and Rev. Jerome Vereb for aid in obtaining these images.

17. ITALIAN DOCTORS INFLUENTIAL IN THE COMMONWEALTH AND TRANSYLVANIA I: DR. FRANCIS STANCARO OF MANTUA (1501–74)

17.A. Stancaro's *Hebrew Grammar* (Basel, 1547) is laid open to crucial christological passages in the New and Old Testament. Two works are bound together as one, first edition, *Suae Ebreae grammaticae compendium* [et] *institutio* (Basel, 1547), representative page printed by permission of the Houghton Library, Harvard University.

Probably of Sephardic origin, Stancaro was a master of Scripture and of patristic, conciliar, and scholastic theology; and he followed most of the Fathers and Peter Lombard in insisting that Christ discharged his mediatorial role with the Father in his human suffering nature, not in his divine nature, the prooftext being 1 Tim 2:5.

The first entry on the page is the Hebrew of Mic 5:2, as quoted in Matt 2:6, on the birth of the Messiah in Bethlehem; the second is a type of the economic or dispensational Trinity in the presumed Paternal address to the prophet Isaiah or to Cyrus as Messiah, Isa 48:16: "And now Yahweh Elohim (the Lord God) has sent me [the Messiah King, or Isaiah the type of Jesus Christ] and his Spirit"; the third entry is on the Suffering Servant wounded for "our iniquity," Isa 53:5–6.

Stancaro's Triadology (cf. B) has been commonly pilloried in his time and in subsequent scholarship as Sabellian and his Christology as Ebionite in the sense that the saving action of Christ was in his human nature and not as divine-human person. That Stancaro used Scripture, Tradition, and Scholasticism with great scholarship and cunning is conceded. That he sincerely (whether authentically) considered his positions as truly consonant with those of the Swiss and Wittenberg Reformers was doubted in his lifetime and subsequently. In any case, he earnestly and savagely opposed what he considered as an Arian tendency he detected in Transylvania, Königsberg, and within the Polish Reformed Church.

As for his life before entering Poland, Stancaro looked back upon it in a long, undated letter to Andrew I Górka (d. 1551; Pl. 19), ed. by Theodor Wotschke from the

Königsberg Archives, "Francesco Stancaro," *Altpreussische Monatsschrift* 47 (1910) Part I, 465–98; Part II, 570–613, in an autobiographical supplication to Górka, 589–92. From this and other sources we know that he taught Hebrew and theology in the University of Padua, that he was apparently converted to the Reformation by the martyrdom of the Franciscan Girolamo Galateo in Venice, 1541—not mentioned in the letter, that he was himself incarcerated for eight months and miraculously escaped but with the loss of all his writings to date. He may have belonged to the Vicenza circle (Pl. 13) and perhaps originally thought of his task as the reformation of the Republic of Venice. The letter speaks of his having taught in Friuli and Vienna, 1544–46, in Augsburg, Regensburg (passed over in the letter), then in Basel.

Here he seems to have redone his destroyed works and printed them in a huge work of 800 pages, *Opera nuova della riformatione* (Basel, 1547). In the same letter to Górka, Stancaro recalls his activity in Transylvania and the attention given him at court by Isabelle Jagiellonka and by her son Sigismund, from whom he carries a letter of recommendation to Górka, and reports having been persecuted by Isabelle's chief minister Martinuzzi (Pl. 39). He came to Cracow, its court and university, with the expectation of implementing there his reformatory ideas; and when challenged as a heretical professor of Hebrew, he appealed in a letter of 20 April 1550, intentionally in Italian to escape adverse attention, to Bishop Samuel Maciejowski of Cracow (Pl. 5.G), who, however, with the collusion of Martin Kromer, ordered him instead, without a chance to defend his position, to be imprisoned in Lipowiec (C).

Francesco Ruffini pulled together the life beyond that by Wotschke in "Francesco Stancaro: Contributo alla storia della riforma in Italia," *Studi sui riformatori italiani*, 3 (Torino, 1955), as also Wacław Urban.

Going beyond Ruffini, Henryk Barycz with new documentation and insight, on the basis of the discovery of Stancaro's letter to Maciejowski, turned over by the bishop to the more scholarly Kromer and now reposing in the diocesan archive of Frombork, took up anew the life and thought of Stancaro in a discussion of this letter and three other documents bearing on the Reformation in Poland, "Dokumenty źródłowe do dziejów Arianizmu polskiego," *Studia nad Arianizmem*, ed. Ludwik Chmaj (Warsaw, 1959), pp. 489–530, the letter to Maciejewski, pp. 500 f. Barycz quoted the vivid words of Ruffini, which the Italian scholar placed imaginatively on the lips of Stancaro, as though addressed by the heresiarch to every researcher of the Radical Reformation in eastern Europe: "Stop, you must take my person into consideration a moment, before you undertake your researches on Faustus Socinus, who only came to these parts four years after my death and for whom incidentally I prepared the way."

Barycz advanced the view that from the start Stancaro was involved in the Italian Anabaptist current that prized Hebraic scholarship (cf. my "Two Social Strands in Italian Anabaptism," 1972, where the Hebraizing component was identified but where no connection was made with Stancaro, about which I am still reserved), that Stancaro held to a quite different, Italianate vision of Reformation, and that he was nurtured in circles attracted to the christocentricity of Servetus. In my view, however, the Triadology and Christology of Servetus were so markedly different from those of Stancaro as to make any ascription of specifically theological influence on him off the mark. Moreover his own bellicose temper was quite capable of endorsing capital punishment for heresy in Transylvania and Köngisberg and there is, in any case, no evidence that Stancaro, in contrast to most of the Italians, was appalled at the execution of Servetus by Farel and Calvin. For Stancaro's role in Köngisberg, 1551, see Plate 7. Ruffini and Barycz are, of course, right in seeing in Stancaro the first foreign Reformer to arrive in the

Commonwealth with a clear intent of implementing a reformatory design (cf. Pl. 9).

17.B. A diagram of Stancaro's conception of the Trinity, printed by Biandrata in his *De falsa cognitione* (Pl. 18). In this hostile representation, the common *Essentia* of the Three Persons is at the opposite of the Man Christ the Mediator (1 Tim 2:5). This is one of eight pictures in Biandrata's *De falsa cognitione* (Kolozsvár, 1567); for acknowledgment, see Pl. 18. Biandrata's explanation reads: "The fantasy of Stancaro imagining that Christ is the Mediator between the whole Trinity and men; also he used to place a cloak (*toga*) of three hanging folds and afterwards open it to demonstrate that the Trinity is in unity." The wording here suggests that the two Italian doctors had been somewhere in personal contact.

It is of passing interest that at the request of Stancaro's son, Francis Stancaro, Jr., superintendent of the [Major] Reformed Church of Little Poland, the synod of Ożaków, 26 September 1618, struck the name of his father from the *Postil* of 1611 (Raków, 1618) by Christopher Kraiński where Kraiński said: "The heretic Stancaro, withstanding the Lord Christ, shooting at him as a target with blasphemous shots, taught that the Son of God is Mediator only in his human nature, concerning which his writings testify" (Sipayłło, *AS*, 3.403). For the *Postil* of Kraiński (d. 1618), minister in Lublin in 1598, head of the school in Kock, superintendent of the Major Reformed Church in Little Poland, 1598–1600, see Gryczowa, *Ariańskie oficyny wydawnicze*, no. 148.

17.C. The episcopal fortress and prison of Lipowiec on the left bank of the Vistula, where Stancaro was imprisoned in 1550 by Bishop Maciejowski of Cracow (Pl. 5), after students in his Hebrew class at the University accused him of heresy, and from which he was rescued by Trzecieski, among others, and carried to the protection of Stanislas Stadnicki in Dubiecko (E), whence he removed to the Oleśnicki palace above Pińczów (Pl. 9). Painting of the ruin, Janina Bieniarzowa and Karol B. Kubisz, *400 lat Reformacji pod Wawelem* (Warsaw, 1958) Pl. 1.

Among those who faulted Stancaro in his interpretation of the Hebrew of the Psalms that caused his arrest was Peter Gonesius (Pl. 26). From the window of his cell on a piece of rope made of fabric Stancaro lowered himself to the helping arms of three rescuers, who had prearranged the escape: Stanislas Lasocki (Pl. 8), Andrew Trzecieski (Pl. 23), and Christopher Gliński.

17.D. The oldest church order of the Polish Reformed, translated from Stancaro's *Canones Reformationis Ecclesiarum Polonicarum* (Polish: Cracow, 1553). Shown is the title-page of the Polish version, rescued from a binding with a few other pages and preserved in the Library of the Jagiellonian University, Cim. Q 5486, photographed by Zbigniew Pasek. What has here been salvaged purports to be the order for the restoration of Christ's order in the elimination of the falsities "of the Pope and of other heretics." The title reads: "Order for the reformation in our churches from Holy Scripture and from the writings of the holy *Doctores,* the ancient Fathers, written by Francis Stancaro from Mantua, doctor of Holy Writ [Cracow, 1553]."

The *Order* was based upon the moderate reform proposed by Hermann von Wied (1477–1552), Archbishop Elector of Cologne, *Einfaltiges Bedencken einer christlichen Reformation* (1553). Jerome Filipowski bore the expenses of the publication of the Polish *Order*. It was nevertheless burned in his town of Krzcięcice on the advice of Stancaro's protector, Stadnicki.

Although disparaged in the later historiography of the Major and Minor Church, as also in Transylvania, on the issue of the mediatorship of Christ, Stancaro must be recorded as the founder of the Reformed Church of Little Poland as an organized entity centered in Pińczów (Pl. 9).

17.E. The palace of Stanislas Stadnicki, in Dubiecko, the initial protector of Stancaro and his patron during the Stancarist Schism, 1561–70, with its academy and seminary, the first of the schisms of the Reformed Church in the Commonwealth. Photography by M. Kornecki, IS PAN. The palace, modernized in the nineteenth century and again in the twentieth, still preserves the ground plan and elevation of the original from the sixteenth century.

There seems to be no trace of the school, which at its zenith attracted about a thousand Poles and Ruthenians.

17.F. Andrew Stadnicki, one of seven sons of Stanisław Mateusz Stadnicki (d. 1563), patron with his three older sons of the Reformed church and school in Dubiecko. Andrew, on returning to Catholic obedience, closed them down, 1588. A drawing (once and perhaps still) in the Muzeum Lubomirskich in Lwów, reproduced by Władysław Łoziński, *Prawem i Lewem: Obyczaje na Czerwonej Rusi w pierwszej połowie xvii wieku* (2 vols.; 4th ed.; Lwów, 1931) 2.297, fig. 36.

This drawing has often been used as a portrait of Andrew's famous brother, Stanisław Stadnicki "the Devil of Łańcut" (1551–1610), who after the death of Stephen Batory, fought for the election of Maximilian II (Pl. 42) and was among the Protestant lords in the Rebellion of Zebrzydowski against the royalist centralization of Sigismund III (Pl. 50). It is most likely that for want of an authentic portrait of the infamous "Devil," resort was had to the likeness of his brother Andrew in the monument erected by the latter's widow in the Dominican Church in Cracow. Łoziński (*Prawem i Lewem*, 2, chap. 4, devoted wholly to "the Devil") questions the common identification of the portrait of the "Devil." It was Łoziński who proposed the probably correct identification of Andrew.

By what appears to have been more than one marriage, Stanislas M. Stadnicki had eight surviving children, his seven sons being Stanislas "the Devil," Martin, John, Samuel, Andrew, Peter, and Nicholas. His only or last wife was Barbara Zborowska, daughter of the castellan of Cracow, Martin Zborowski, who died in 1565, thus two years before his son-in-law in Dubiecko. The refusal of Stanislas and Barbara to have their son Stanislas ("the Devil") baptized according to the ordinance of the bishop of Przemyśl marked the break in Dubiecko from Catholicism, at first by the introduction of the Lutheran service in Polish.

None of the sons of Stanislas M. Stadnicki gained renown except for "the Devil," and all of them except him went over from Stancarist Calvinism to Catholicism. The youngest son Andrew was given Dubiecko. After the Rebellion (1604, Pl. 50) Andrew (here pictured under the name of Stanislas), along with Martin and John, returned to Roman obedience. It is even possible that as early as 1588 Andrew had begun clearing Dubiecko of Protestantism. For this last dating, see *SGKP,* 2. 188A; for the children of Stanislas M. Stadnicki, more fully and consistently presented than in Niesiecki, *Herbarz Polski,* 7. 475–84, see Łoziński, *Prawem i Lewem;* for the joining of Barbara Zborowska in marriage, see *Genealogia,* table 133; for the role of "the Devil" in the Reformed synods, see Sipayłło, *AS,* 3. 181–82, 190.

18. ITALIAN DOCTORS INFLUENTIAL IN THE COMMONWEALTH AND TRANSYLVANIA II: DR. GEORGE BIANDRATA (d. 1574)

18.A. Dr. Biandrata, physician to two queens, Bona Sforza in Cracow, her daughter Isabelle in Alba Julia. A detail from a larger picture of 1596; see Pl. 49.

Biandrata, who passed through a Tritheist phase perhaps while still in Geneva, seems to have held to a relatively conservative Unitarianism that preserved the Apostles' Creed, the adoration of the Ascended Christ, infant baptism, a commemorative communion not hedged about by synodal discipline, and a benign Magisterial Reformation for all of Eastern Europe under local lords and princes superior to the synods, opposed to aggressive wars. He was a cosmopolitan ''apostolic'' Unitarian *politique.*

18.B. His signature, Transylvania. Reproduced by Endre Veress, *Izabella Királyné* (Budapest, 1901) 43.

18.C – H. From the anonymous *De falsa et vera unius Dei Patri, Filii et Spiritus Sancti cognitione*, in collaboration with Francis Dávid (Alba Julia, 1568) (Pl. 25), the scandalizing chapter 4 ''On horrendous images representing God Three and One,'' brought forth, he says by ''the sophistic/scholastic'' doctrine of one Essence/Substance and three Persons as seen ''in their shrines (*phanis*).'' The book with an introduction by Antal Pirnát appears in facsimile, *Bibliotheca Unitariorum*, 2 (Budapest/Utrecht: Hungarian Academy of Sciences, 1988).

The eight images are reproduced here in their printed order, except for three: 5 is in Pl. 25; 7, in Pl. 17; and 8, in Pl. 41. The countenance and royal crown of God the Father is so much alike in figures 1, 3, 5, and 6 that it is plausible that Biandrata drew them himself or had them drafted to his specifications, although 1, 2, and 3 seem to embody features observed by Biandrata himself at named places.

18.D. *Trifons.* ''This idol is Trifrons seen in shrines, showing the God of Antichrist Three in One, whence the papist ditty: 'Father Trifrons [of the three-tiered tiara] expelled from the City, in his very month, Janus of the Two Foreheads in order that he might reign alone in the World as Trifrons.' ''

18.E. ''In a chapel near Cracow''. Biandrata identifies this as his ''second monster,'' showing the Procession of the Holy Spirit as a dove rising from the two-headed body on the eucharistic altar.

18.F. The Trinity descending into the eucharistic Host at the *Sanctus*. A design said by Biandrata to have been commissioned by Clement VII Medici (1523 – 34) lest the adoration of the Host appear to be idolatry (*idolomania*).

18.G. The Three Persons in Majesty at the Last Supper. Biandrata ridicules this image of the Three coeternal, coequal, consubstantial Persons with aureoles seated at the Last Supper.

18.H. The most common representation of the Trinity at Calvary. God the Father as King holds up approvingly the obedient action of the Son on the cross, the Dove of the Holy Spirit connecting the action on Calvary with the mercy of the heavenly throne room (*Gnadenstuhl*).

18.I – J. Title-pages of works by Biandrata in the Library of the Jagiellonian University, Cracow; photographed by Zbigniew Pasek.

18.I. While in *De falsa cognitione* (1568) Biandrata still wrote of ''Jesus Christ . . . whom we reverence and invoke after the Father,'' in these two works (Alba Julia, 1568) he leaves no trace of the premundane Logos Christ: *Equivalent phrases from Scripture figurative of Christ born from Mary* and *Antithesis of the pseudo-Christ* [Calvinist no less than Catholic] *with that true Christ born of Mary*, on the title-page of which Biandrata glosses Luke 2:11: "Today (not before all ages) is born to you (not incarnated) the Saviour Christ the Lord in the city of David (not in heaven out of the *Essentia* of God)." The subtitle declares that "if someone should know [these equivalent phrases] and have them in order, much to be understood in Scripture would be opened."

18.J. The second scriptural motto on the title-page is Luke 10:22: "No one knows who the Son is except the Father, or who the Father is except the Son and anyone to whom the Son chooses to reveal him."

19. GREAT POLAND; INTERCONFESSIONAL MISSIONS; MOSCOW, 1570; MARIENWERDER, 1635

19.A. Andrew I Górka (c. 15010–51), castellan of Poznań, governor general of Great Poland, protector of Lutherans and Czech Brethren, dying a Catholic but insisting on final communion in both kinds ("for his stomach's sake"). A portion of the sepulchral monument of Andrew I Górka and below him of his wife Barbara Kurozwęska in the parish church in Kórnik; taken from Helena and Stefan Kozakiewicz, *The Renaissance in Poland* (Warsaw: Arkady, 1976). The prone figure is here accommodated.

It was as *starosta* general of Great Poland that Andrew I Górka received and protected Stancaro (Pl. 17) and recommended him to Duke Albert (Pl. 7). Of his three sons, two became leaders of Lutheranism in Great Poland: Lukas III (c. 1533–82) becoming their head in 1553 and participating in the Consensus of Sandomierz of 1570 (Pl. 34); Andrew II (B) was similarly active. Their father engaged the proto-Reformer Master John of Koźmin for their education, brought Seklucjan under his protection, and helped him to get to Königsberg (Pl. 7), secured the teaching post for Gregory Paul in Poznań (Pl. 26), and protected both Lawrence Discordia and Stancaro (Pl. 17).

19.B. Andrew II Górka (c. 1539–83), son of Andrew I and brother of Andrew III, spokesman for the Lutherans at Sandomierz, 1570 (Pl. 34). Funereal monument (damaged in the eighteenth century) in the parish church of Kórnik; photograph by J. Kieszkowicz (1910), IS PAN; Jan Skuratowicz, "Z badań nad rzeźbą w Polsce: Nagróbki . . . Górków w Kórniku," in Jan Białostocki et al., *Renesans* (Warsaw, 1976) 478.

19.C. "A Written Reply . . . to the Inquiry by the Great Sovereign of Moscow," by John Rokyta (1528–91), chaplain to the other three Czech Brethren from Leszno in the embassy of Sigismund II, appearing in the Granovitaya Palace in the Kremlin. A photograph of the Leszno MS, reposing in the Czech National Museum in Prague; taken from Laura Ronchi De Michaelis, *Disputa sul Protestantesimo: un confronto tra Ortossia e Reforma nel 1570* (Turin: Claudiana, 1979) with several maps, 10 Pls., and an essay by Amedeo Molnár, p. 49. The first lines read (in large letters): "*Pytanie Hospodarskie* (the Sovereign's Question) [1]: 'What are you?'; 'Answer [? of Rokyta].' 'I am a Christian, teacher of the Word of God.'" Members of the Protestant group in Sigismund's legation, perhaps all of them Czech Brethren, headed by Rokyta (Polish: Rokita), were besides him: John Krotoski (of Krotoszyn), palatine of Inowrocław (in 1572 elected bishop of the Unitas), Raphael I Leszczyński (1526–92), palatine of Brześć Kujawski, Nicholas Tałowsk, castellan of Minsk, and Andrew Iwanowicz, royal secretary, whose confessional allegiance is unknown. The document may be a reworking of an authentic exchange, but not that in Moscow, and more likely of a *Lutheran* spokesman with the

Orthodox, construed as that of Rokyta with Ivan.

Ivan's ten questions are otherwise known only from Rokyta's alleged response pictured here. On 10 May 1570, in the presence of Orthodox clergy, boyars, and members of the Polish legation, the cosenior of the Czech Brethren of Great Poland responded to the ten questions of the Tsar, whereupon ensued a debate on the merits of Protestantism. The Tsar may earlier have been interested in Lutheranism and Western European religious thought about which he was well informed, but at the encounter he was condescending and rude although theologically very well informed and spirited, as is clear from his formal Reply of 18 June (or July), of which there is a Latin version by the Czech Brother and historian, John Łasicki, a Polish translation evidently made by Rokyta himself at Leszno, and four versions of the Tsar's Russian original, of which there is a copy in the Houghton Library, Harvard University.

Valerie Agnes Tumins, updating her Radcliffe thesis of 1959, in *Tsar Ivan IV's Response to Jan Rokyta* (The Hague: Mouton, 1971), supplies a facsimile of the entire Leszno Report of Rokyta here pictured (with transliteration and translation), Rokyta's Polish translation of Ivan's Reply (*Odpowiedź na pismie od ksiedza Iwana Bazylego*), and a facsimile of the entire Houghton Library copy of the Reply of the Tsar in Russian (with transliteration and translation). Tumins holds that the Report of Rokyta is "the only reliable version," while De Michaelis holds that the Speech/Report of Rokyta, the title-page of which is here pictured, is later than Laskicki's Latin translation, and that both derive "da un archetipo comumme" (p. 30).

Tumins makes clear that there have long been two scholarly interpretations of the Protestant mission: (1) to convert the Tsar and (2) merely to persuade him to permit the free exercise of the Protestant faith in Moscow (in 1579 the Tsar, in fact, ordered the two tolerated Protestant churches for foreigners in Moscow to be burned down). De Michaelis gives an Italian translation, with annotation going beyond Tumins, of Rokyta's Report and the Tsar's Reply in the version first edited by A. Popov, "Otvet carja Ioanna Vasil'eviča Groznogo," *Čtenija Imperatorskogo Obščestva Istorii* (Moscow, 1878); and in the appendices, she supplies the oral dispute between Ivan and Rokyta, according to the testimony of Paul Oderborn, in its original Latin and in an Italian translation, and still another version in Italian according to Vincenzo Dal Portico.

Within a dozen years there were two attempts, supported by a Polish King, to bring Ivan the Terrible and Muscovy into dialogue, respectively with Protestantism in 1570, and with Rome in the mission of Antonio Possevino, S.J. (cf. Pl. 46) in 1581–82. To be noted is the fact that the Protestant approach to the Kremlin took place against the background of the Consensus of Sandomierz of April 1570 (Pl. 34), to which Rokyta became a signatory (in Poznań) after his return from the Muscovite mission.

19.D. Chancellor Jacob Zadzik, bishop of Cracow, Grand Hetman Stanislas Koniecpolski, and Raphael Leszczyński (1579–1636), palatine of Bełz, ''Pope of the [Polish] Calvinists,'' as head of three Polish commissioners in the presence of Ladislas IV (not here included) at the negotiations with Swedish envoys of the peace in Marienwerder. A detail from the painting in the Senatorial Antechamber in the former episcopal palace in Kielce, from the school of Tomaso Dolabelli; photograph by Professor Mariusz Karpowicz.

In the larger scene Ladislas IV is standing at the center, next to him Chancellor Zadzik, bishop of Cracow (Pl. 59), then come Hetman Koniecpolski (d. 1646), then Leszczyński (at the top of the triumviral cluster). The picture has been so cropped that of the three Polish commissioners, only two show: besides Leszczyński, back of him, Jacob

Sobieski (1580–1646). George Ossoliński, the third Polish commissioner is not shown here. The third figure shown in French garb is Claude de Mesme, count of Avaux, Cardinal Richlieu's ambassador. On the other side of the King (not shown) are the two Swedish envoys, the three Dutch, and three English mediators. Koniecpolski retained a Unitarian secretary, Christopher Wiszowaty (of uncertain relationship to Andrew and Benedict), mentioned by Lubieniecki, *Historia, 248.* This Christopher was also a signatory of the letter of the Exiles of 1661, *PBN,* Document XXIII–I. The Sobieski shown here was the father of John III Sobieski (1674–96), the hero of the lifting of the Turkish siege of Vienna (1683). The Sobieski shown here is the nephew of Catherine Sobieska, wife of Lubieniecki's great grandfather, although her name is missing from the *Genealogia,* Table 148.

At the truce of Altmark (near Stuhm) with Sweden, Sigismund III Vasa in 1629 had confirmed the Polish loss of Livonia; and with the treaty of Polianov of 1634, his brother and successor, Ladislas IV (Pl. 60) had renounced his claims to the Muscovite throne but had been confirmed in his control of Smolensk.

At Marienwerder Ladislas had to regularize his relations with Sweden afresh, given his hereditary claim to the Swedish throne and his desire to enter the confessional, pan-European war in the Empire (Thirty Years' War). Raphael Leszczyński reflected the pacific disposition of both the Senate and the middle and lower *szlachta* represented in the House of Deputies.

Raphael Leszczyński was the son of Andrew L. and Anna, daughter of Andrew Firley of Lublin (Pl. 8), and the grandson of Raphael L. (c. 1426–92), palatine of Brześć Kujawski, who in 1547 had invited the refugee Czech Brethren (Pl. 4) to settle in Leszno, where he founded a school in 1555 and a Calvinist church alongside it. This elder Raphael sent his son Andrew L. (1559–1606) to the school of the Czech Brethren in Koźminek, then abroad to study the humanities and theology in Strassburg and Basel. Andrew in turn renewed and enlarged the privileges of Leszno (1601), sought to Polonize the Czech Brethren, to bring the Czech Brethren closer to the Lutherans in the spirit of the Consensus of Sandomierz (Pl. 34), while in 1599 in Vilna he had already taken the lead in forming a united Protestant-Orthodox front (Pl. 53) against the Catholics.

Raphael Leszczyński carried on his father's interests, although for the sake of unity in the Commonwealth he participated in a commission to bring together the Uniates and the Orthodox. In 1628 he began receiving the next wave of Czech Brethren on his estates, as well as Lutheran refugees from Bohemia and Silesia.

At Leszno he converted the school into a gymnasium on the Sturm model in Strassburg, of which Andrew Węgierski (1600–49) was rector, the first of Poland to have written a Church History (in Latin), published (posthumously) in 1652 (Pl. 1), while his brother Adalbert Węgierski wrote (in Polish) the *History of the Calvinist Church in Cracow.*

Among the religious refugees received was Bishop John Cyrill of the Brethren, who had crowned Elector Palatine Frederick V (son-in-law of James I of England) as "Winter King" in Prague at the outset of the Thirty Years' War. To secure confessional peace in Poland and a pacific foreign policy, Raphael Leszczyński urged the marriage of Ladislas IV to the Calvinist daughter of the Winter King. See Maria Sipayłło, *PSB,* 17 (1972) 135–39; a genealogical table in Jobert, *De Luther à Mohila.*

20. JOHN ŁASKI (1499–1560)

20.A. As Reformed superintendent of East Frisia, Emden, 1544, age 45. Copy of a painting in the Gallery of the Castle in Niedzica, Museum of the Jagiellonian University, Cracow, photographed by K. Klinowski; printed in Henryk Barycz, *Szlakami dziejopis-warstwa staropolskiego* (Wrocław: Ossolineum, 1981) opposite p. 160.

The scene through the window, probably idealized, would presumably represent Emden where he served as pastor or superintendent, 1540–48. Łaski (sometime bishop-designate of Veszprém in Hungary) had declined, 1538, King Sigismund's nomination of him, while archdeacon of Warsaw, to the see of Kujawy; and he left Poland in the autumn of that year, espousing the Reformation abroad. He lodged first in Frankfurt, then Mainz, descending thence to the Netherlands.

For the castle of Niedzica on the right bank of the Dunajec (once under Hungary), see Bohdan Guerquin, *Zamki w Polsce* (Warsaw: Arkady, 1974) 203–04.

20.B. Emden, c. 1545. By permission of the Herzog-August-Bibliothek, Wolfenbüttel. The artist is unknown, done in Emden sometime during Łaski's prominence there, 1542–48, but evidently, from the older look, after A; Franz Koehler and Gustav Milch-sack, *Die Gudischen* [Marquand Gude] *Handschriften* ["und die Bildnisse die zu Gude und seiner Handschrift-Sammlung einen näheren Bezug haben"] (Wolfenbüttel, 1913) preface, xxi.

20.C. A copperprint, presumably from B. Copperprint reproduced from the frontispiece of Oskar Bartel, *Jan Łaski* (1955), who does not identify the source; nor does Sipayłło, *AS*, 1 (1966) frontispiece.

Below the print are the words: Joannes Alasco/ cvia viri effigies e[st] Laski, qvi stem-mate clarvs/ Sarmatiae procervm, divitiis qve potens, foedere amicitiae qvondam tibi vinctvs Erasme,/ Deservi patriam, cederem vt invidiae,/ Me profvgvm accepit qvaevis terra hospita, tantvs/ Egit me studii ac religionis amor: "John Alasco,/ whose likeness of the man it is, Łaski, who, illustrious by a family of the noble men/ of Sarmatia and puis-sant by wealth, once was bound to thee, Erasmus, in the convenant of friendship,/ forsook the fatherland, that I might escape ill-will./ It was as fugitive that whatsoever the hospit-able land accepted me, such/ was the love of study and religion that drove me."

20.D. Forced departure with his wife and followers from Gravesend, after his superinten-dency of the Strangers' Churches in London (1548–53). This popular drawing, the figure of Łaski being based on E-F (the artist unidentified), is taken from J. A. Wylie, *The History of Protestantism* (3 vols.; London, 1899) 3. 168.

Łaski is seen departing from England at Gravesend, with his wife and, presumably in the boat, John Utenhove, 15 September 1553. See further Andrew Pettegree, *Foreign Protestant Communities in Sixteenth Century London* (Oxford: Oxford University Press, 1986). As liturgical advisor to Archbishop Thomas Cranmer and often resident in Lam-beth Palace, Łaski was forced to leave on the accession of Mary Tudor (cf. his secretary Utenhove's account, Pl. 15).

The woman in the boat is intended to be Catherine, whom Łaski married in London right after the death of his first wife (whom he had married in Louvain in 1539). By his first wife he had three sons and a daughter, Barbara, who would marry Unitarian Superin-tendent Lutomirski; and by Catherine, five offspring, of whom the soldier Samuel was the best known.

20.E. Lead seal, age 58. Lead medal, cast in Nuremberg, 1557; Historisches Museum, Basel, no. 1948–3; reproduced from Jobert, *De Luther à Mohila* (1974) Pl. 2.

20.F. Copperprint from E, engraved after his return to Poland (1556–60) and burial in

Pińczów (Pl. 10). Copperprint based on E by Joos (Jodivicus) de Hondt (Hondius) (1563–1650); by permission of the Herzog-August-Bibliothek, Wolfenbüttel.

The text below the figure reads: Ioannes Alasco Polonus/ Temporibus fouit te saeuis Anglia, Lasce/ Nobilis, et verae Nobilitatis amans./ Sic tua te pietas duxit, Patriáeque reduxit/ Incolúmem, gentis lumen, amórque, tuae: "John à Lasco the Pole/ In savage times England cherished thee, noble Łaski, and friend of nobility. Thus did thy piety lead thee, and to thy fatherland love for it returned thee safe, light of thy people."

21. THEOLOGICAL PUBLICISTS I:
STANISLAS ORZECHOWSKI (1515–67)

21.A. Orzechowski (as a youth), born in Przemyśl (B), "Ruthenian by people (*gente*), a Pole by nation (*natione*)," a Latin-rite priest who opposed clerical celibacy and the rebaptism of Byzantine-rite converts; and who engaged in fierce polemics against the Protestants, the proponent of an integrated national Church under a strong Papacy (DE). A late nineteenth-century lithograph by Teofil Żychowicz, presumably from an earlier picture then extant; Biblioteka Narodowa, Warsaw. The picture of a more mature figure in the Pawlikowski Collection was presumably made from this, Lwów; printed in L. Kubala, *Orzechowski* (1906).

Orzechowski's defense of Ruthenian baptism came in a letter to Bishop Gamrat (Pl. 5) of Cracow, 1544.

21.B. Przemyśl on the San, with the Latin-rite church (nearest the castle) and a small Ruthenian church on the other side, scarcely visible in the angle of the wall: the see of Bishop Michael Kopystynskyi, one of only two bishops to oppose the Union of Brest Litovsk (Pl. 39). From Braun, *Civitates orbis terrarum;* by permission of the Houghton Library, Harvard University.

Dominating the strongly fortified town with its gates to Lwów (left) and Cracow (center) is the town hall, with the Dominican and Franciscan churches on either side.

21.C. Orzechowski's *Chimera* (Cracow, 1562) against Stancaro (Pl. 17) on Christ the Mediator in his human nature only: Matthew 7:15: "Beware of false prophets. . . ." Widener Library, Harvard University.

Of interest is that both Orzechowski, the obstreperous Catholic priest, and Modrzewski, the cosmopolitan Catholic nobleman (Pl. 22) who ended up among the Polish Brethren, opposed Stancaro on the issue of Christ the Mediator.

21.D. Diagrams from *Quincunx* (Cracow, 1564), the term meaning literally 5/12, used of a common ornamental pattern, e.g. of five trees planted in an orchard, one at each corner and one in the middle, the middle here being the endangered unity of Poland. A page in *Quincunx,* reproduced by A. G. Dickens, *Reformation and Society in Sixteenth-Century Europe* (London, 1966) 177.

Here endangered Poland is herself a *quincunx* as a crowned woman, the crucifix above her, adorned with the royal *Aquila* (eagle). Her hair of unusually long and complicated braids may represent the higher and lower *szlachta,* whose liberties Orzechowski defended, while in her two hands she firmly clasps a symbol of a unified Church in full communion. The legend in Latin reads: "Supported by the arms of Pope and King, whichever side you would offend, you would break up the structure of the Kingdom." These figures are transposed in E.

21.E. Another page in *Quincunx,* reproduced from Piotr Chmielowski, *Historia literatury polskiej* (Lwów, 1931) 204.

Here the Pope is outside the *quincunx,* supporting Faith (E) and the Altar (D) directly, while the King and the Primate of Poland constitute the upper two corner positions, Polonia herself becoming the central fifth point. For the authority of the Pope, besides principles from canon law and Matt 16:19 and John 21:17, Orzechowski adduces Deut 17:12: "The man who acts presumptuously by not wishing to obey the command of the Priest, . . . by the decree of the Judge, that man shall die"; and Isa 60:12: "For the nation and kingdom that will not serve thee [in application both God and the Pope], it will perish and the nations shall be laid waste as a desert." In support of sacral kingship (cf. Pl. 36) and the subject's participation in the grades of being through the King (B), Orzechowski quotes Ps.-Dionysius *De divinis nominibus* (c. 500); and of the Archbishop of Gniezno (C), he says, "he is in Poland the highest Priest, Primate of the Polish Kingdom, messenger of the Apostolic See, supreme authority of the Polish bishops," defender of freedoms and guardian of the Crown as Interrex (cf. Pl. 6).

Orzechowski's symbolism for Faith and the Altar (D) seems awkward, but he is himself clear. He takes the chalice with the host as the symbol of Faith, which he describes in a quotation from Maximus the Confessor to Conon, himself quoting Heb 11:1. The Altar here is intentionally devoid of the elements to stress precisely that the Catholic Mass and the Orthodox Divine Liturgy are equally effectual, but he is against the new communion tables of the Reformed, although, like Stancaro, in a different sense, he quotes Exodus 27 and Josh 22:29: "Far be it from us that we should rebel against the Lord . . . by building an altar . . . other than the altar of the Lord our God that stands before his tabernacle."

22. THEOLOGICAL PUBLICISTS II:
ANDREW FRYCZ MODRZEWSKI (c. 1503 – 72)

22.A.B Modrzewski's most important work on political and social reform, *De republica emendanda* (Cracow, 1551) and its translation into Polish by Cyprian Bazylik (Pls. 1, 15) at his press (Łosk, 1577) with a preface by Simon Budny (Pl. 15). Addressed to all in authority and "the people of Poland and the rest of Sarmatia," it calls for reform throughout the Commonwealth in support of the centralization of the royal authority under the rules of law, applicable with equal force to all segments of society, the renunciation of aggressive war, the laicization and broadening of education, confessional toleration, and freedom of conscience. Supportive therein of a national Church with full lay participation at all levels, Modrzewski ended his life close to the Polish Brethren, who posthumously published his *Sylvae.* The title-page of the first of five books; taken from Stanisław Arnold, ed., *Odrodzenie w Polsce,* vol. 1: *Historia* ([Warsaw]: PAN, 1955) opposite p. 48.

Born in Wolbórz in Great Poland, this reformer of pan-European renown studied in Cracow, then Wittenberg. He became secretary to Sigismund II by 1546. Having agitated for lay participation along with bishops in the first period of the Council of Trent (1545–47), he served as secretary to the prospective Polish delegation. (Because of the distrust of his episcopal colleagues, Stanislas Hosius effectually inhibited Polish participation in the Council.) He was present in the library of Andrew Trzecieski Sr., during the visit of the Dutchman *Spiritus* (Pl. 3), and he preserves a record of the visitor's questioning of prayers addressed separately to the Three Persons. For the place of Modrzewski within the juridical and constitutional reform, see Danièle Letocha, "Executionist Movement," in J. Godbey, ed., *Unitarianism,* 33–45.

22.B. The title-page from the facsimile edition in Widener Library, Harvard University; cf. *BAnt* 2. 36.

The translator, Cyprian Bazylik, was a Lithuanian Brother of the Budny type, non-pacifist.

Modrzewski addressed several Reformed synods, wrote against Stancaro (like Orzechowski) three tracts on Christ the Mediator (1560–61), one to the synod of Włodzisław, one to his friend Jerome Ossoliński, one to Stancaro's protector, Stanislas Stadnicki (Pl. 17). Filled with concern at the schism within the Church universal and specifically within the Reformed Church, Modrzewski was foiled by Calvinist Christopher Trecy in his attempt to have the first two of his reflective *Sylvae* (1565–70) published by John Operinus in Basel; and after his death they were brought out by Rodecki (Raków, 1590).

The books featured in the Plate stress the socio-political emphasis and the Racovian connection of Modrzewski, although for most of his career he considered himself a reforming Evangelical Catholic.

The significance of his three works on Christ the Mediator, the four *Sylvae,* and others all directly theological, deserve notice as the manifestation of an erudite ecumenical layman wrestling with the issues of the day and of pan-European import. The last *Sylva,* e.g., on the *Homoousia* of Father, Son, and Holy Spirit, was addressed to Primate Uchański (Pl. 6). The three on the Mediator, written on his estate in Wolbórz, initially on Christ the Mediator *against* Stancaro (Pl. 17), moved by stages towards a virtual acceptance of the Mantuan's position on the sacrifice or work of Christ as effectuated solely in his human nature.

Sigismund had authorized Modrzewski to think through the way in which the Church in the throes of Reformation could be united or rather reunited after the third and last period of the Councils of Trent, 1562–63. Modrzewski was thinking both nationally and internationally, and with royal encouragement he fully intended to include in a projected national council spokesmen of all four groupings of Polish Protestants, even the emergent Minor Church as of the confessional debates at the Diet of Piotrków (1563). In the four *Sylvae,* commissioned by the King, Modrzewski came gradually and coolly to the conclusion that, on the basis of Scripture alone, the doctrine of the Godhead of Three Persons of one essence or *ousia* could not be sustained, even by reason, which in both series of writings, he defended as legitimately supplementary to revelation in Scripture. After having propounded a graduated Tritheism, and provisionally upheld monotheism only by subordinating Christ and the Holy Spirit, he concluded that the Apostles' Creed was, after all, the best formulation of the faith of the Apostolic Church. In dealing with the baptism of infants, an issue dividing the Minor Church, he sustained its validity.

Under Erasmian influence, Modrzewski had himself found most reasonable the opinion that the preexistent but not eternal *Logos* was the *Sermo* of God and should not be retroactively styled the Son before the incarnation, when the *Logos/Sermo* became visible and audible in Jesus Christ as he began his ministry (cf. Laelius and Faustus Socinus, Pls. 13, 47, 48). In the end Modrzewski was a latitudinarian Unitarian holding to a preexistent but not an eternal Logos, a created but creating divine force; and from the start of his theological cogitations, he stressed ethical rectitude in accordance with Scriptures and toleration according to Erasmus.

The fullest account of the progression of his thought outside the Polish language is that of Stanisław Piwko (Warsaw), ''L'hétérodoxie comme effet de l'attitude oecuménique,'' in Marc Lienhard, ed., *Bibliotheca Dissidentium, Scripta et Studia,* vol. 1: *Les Dissidents du XVIe siècle entre l'Humanisme et le Catholicisme* (Baden-Baden:

Koerner, 1983) 139–53. Piwko makes use of the discovery by Henryk Barycz of the identity of the advisor of Uchański, Laurenzo Maggio, provincial of the Jesuits of Poland and Austria. Maggio had responded to the overture of Uchański in the autumn of 1568 to help in the revision of the formulation of the doctrine of the Trinity such as to regain the proto-Unitarians or at least to come to grips with their semantic difficulties by rebuff. Maggio insisted that his epistolary repulse to any such reconsideration of the formulation of Triadology be circulated by Uchański; and Modrzewski felt obliged to reprint and refute this ''Objectio adversarii'': *Opera omnia.*

The intent of the title of Piwko's article is evident in the first of his two concluding observations, namely, that heterodoxy is not always the consequence of degeneration or the abandonment of Christian principles but rather, sometimes, as in the case of Modrzewski, the emergence of an alternatively plausible interpretation of the scriptural evidence.

22.C. The writ of Polish Brother John Przypkowski freeing his serfs (*subditi*), 2 August 1572. Already in *Lascius* (1543) Modrzewski had called for the equal punishment of lords and serfs for the same crime (like murder). Under the impact of the radical social thought of Modrzewski and the Racovians, with their recovery of the social implications of the Gospel of the Sermon on the Mount, Przypkowski freed his various kinds of peasant subjects in five villages near Sosnowiec ''with himself creatures of the one God.'' The calligraphic overlay is a reproduction of the essential provisions in an ornamental scroll. From the Przypkowski Collection, Jędrzejów. On the back Dr. Tadeusz Przypkowski has written of his ancestor: ''The first in Europe to have released his serfs from forced work and to declare them equal to himself.''

Several among the Polish Brethren, e.g., John Niemojewski, presently freed their serfs and servants from the customary field labor.

22.D. The scroll is painted near the base of the Przypkowski Family Tree, reproduced in *PB,* Pl. P, opposite p. 659.

23. FOUR MEN OF LETTERS AND THE REFORMATION

23.A. Biernat of Lublin (c. 1465–1529). His *Raj duszny* (Spiritual Paradise) of late medieval piety was the first book in Polish to be published (Cracow, 1513). His translation of Aesop's Fables (1522) and his versified Life of Aesop (1578) with woodcuts survived, reprinted by Sebastian Sternacki (Raków, c. 1630). The scene shown is that of the slave/serf Aesop on an errand in Ephesus; with his fellow slaves he has slyly agreed to carry the only temporarily heavier load, the loaves for the trip. *Żywot Ezopa Fryga,* facsimile edition.

Biernat studied at the Cracovian Academy and was ordained through the minor orders. His translation of Ps.-Lucian as the Dialogue of Palinure with Caro (1536), anticlerical and plebian, connects Biernat with some Reformation trends.

In a lost work he is quoted as opposed to capital punishment: ''The judge may condemn no one to death, for no one has given him this power. God caused man to live, man may not refuse life, and so the Creator has given no power to destroy his work; and man may prevent man from doing evil, but may not deprive him of life, which is under the protection, but is not the property of the government. . . . He demands that a prisoner be not deprived of liberty longer than fifteen years.'' Summary by his opponent, Jan of Pilzno, the work of the latter preserved by T. Czacki, *O litewskich prawach* (Warsaw, 1801) 2.118; quoted more fully by Kot, *Socinianism,* 10 n. 3.

23.B. Nicholas Rey (1505–69), "the father of Polish literature," closely associated with the Reformed synods. Woodcut from a facsimile edition of the *Apocalypsis* printed by B. Kórnicka (Paris, 1876), a copy of which (C) was presented to the Widener Library by Count Ladislas Zamoyski, 24 May 1897. The woodcut shows the poet at age fifty in 1565. The verse in Latin, according to which Rey is "the Sarmatian Dante," may be ascribed to Andrew Trzecieski. Another woodcut of the poet evidently derives from this, showing him much less severe but still with baggy and yet very alert eyes, the derivative woodcut extending the upper body to include both arms, with one hand holding a book. For Rey's writings, see Irena Rostowska, *Bibliografia dzieł Mikołaia Reja* (Wrocław: Ossolineum, 1970).

Born in Halicz, Rey was the first important vernacular poet. A courtier, he espoused the cause of the middle *szlachta,* "the execution of the laws." In his brief *Debate between a Lord, a Bailiff and a Parish Priest* (Cracow: Szarffenberg, 1543), he attacked the policies of Sigismund I against the interests of the *szlachta* and outlined the ideal relations among the clergy, the *szlachta,* and their peasants, defending the last as oppressed. Having gone over to Lutheranism about 1541, he became Reformed and participated in the synods, notably at Secemin in 1556 and Pińczów in 1559. He translated the *Psalter* (Cracow, 1546) and composed hymns based on Scripture (Cracow, c. 1547). His Life was written by Trzecieski.

23.C. The *Apocalypse*, translated by Rey (Cracow: Wirzbęta, 1565), with an ornament in Latin, "To the Pole, lover of the true and pure Christian religion." The subtitle is: "The strange affair of the secret mysteries of the Lord, which were revealed to St. John when he was banished to the island called Patmos, because of his faith, through visions variously heralded by the angels." Beneath the subtitle is the admonition: "Search the Scriptures on which the Kingdom of the Lord depends, for it is a terrible thing to fall into the hands of the living God."

23.D. Andrew Trzecieski (c. 1531–84), son of John Andrew, in whose library in Cracow in 1546 the Dutchman *Spiritus* raised the question of separate prayers addressed to the Persons of the Trinity (Pl. 3). The lithograph from the nineteenth century is based upon a likeness from the period from the Zakład Reprografii in the Biblioteka Narodowa, Warsaw.

This poet who helped in the rescue of Stancaro (Pl. 17) from the episcopal prison in Lipowiec was active in the Reformation. He was the one to read for approval at the synod of Secemin in 1556 the Czech Confession of Faith (cf. Pl. 4) that had been proposed as the basis of union with the Czech Brethren at the joint synod in Koźminek in 1555. He was in close contact with the writers and poets of his generation, Kochanowski, Modrzewski, Orzechowski, and Rey, contributing the Life of the last in the posthumous edition of Rey's *Zwierciadło* (1605).

23.E. John Kochanowski (15310–85), the major poet of his age, praying at the coffin of his beloved daughter, Ursula (d. 1579), painted by Jan Matejko (1862). Once of the court of Duke Albert in Königsberg, Kochanowski died a Catholic. Woodcut by Jan Styfi after the painting by Jan Matejko, Zakład Reprografii in the Biblioteka Narodowa, Warsaw. Matejko's painting of the poet in mourning is based upon the funereal monument of him in his parish church of Zwoleń.

Dying a Catholic, Kochanowski, the most renowned Polish poet of his day, was welcome in the courts of such protectors of Protestantism as Duke Albert of Prussia and John

Firley. Indeed, he appears to have gone over to the Reformation, but in Padua he reaffirmed the ancestral faith. Widely traveled in Italy and France, he was in the company of Henry of Valois as he traversed Germany for the coronation (Pl. 36), and he was prominent in the court of Stephen Batory, leaving it however to settle, after a late marriage, on his estate in Czarnolas, where he prepared a version of the Psalter.

About 1579 his rural bliss was shattered by the death of his beloved little Ursula, whom he had raised to be a prophetic poetess. The grief was expressed in the many poems of his *Treny* (1580).

Moved by them, Jan Matejko (1838–93) communicates the sorrow of the grieving father in his painting (1862), redone on wood by Jan Styfi. The original painting is more brooding, darker, and yet more tender, for in it Matejko has the father's eyes closed as though in prayer as well as in anguish, while the child's head is deeper in the pillow and her lute more like a heavenly instrument. Matejko had a likeness of the humanist poet to work from, that in the funereal monument in the church in Zwoleń, near Lublin, where Kochanowski died. The painting ''Jan Kochanowski nad zwłokami Urszulki'' is frequently reproduced in full, e.g., by Stanisław Witkiewicz, *Matejko* (2d ed., with 300 illustrations; Lwów, 1912) opposite p. 32.

Krzysztof Kowalski, selecting one of the threnodies, partly for its range of interpretation of the several possibilities of an afterlife current in the Renaissance poet's yearnings, translated it in memory of his grandmother, Bronisława Kowalska, who was self-sacrificially a resource of inspiration for his scholarly life.

> Ursula, lovely darling mine, where are you gone without a sound,
> Along which way, to what far strand, are you now bound?
> Have you been, high, beyond all heavens carried
> And there among those tiny angels ferried?
> Or unto Paradise betaken? Or maybe to the Blessed Isles
> Are guided? Or through the yearning lakes in files,
> By Charon led, and with the water of the dying,
> Oblivion-filled, you cannot bear my crying?
> Or leaving girlish form and childlike tale,
> You've become a feathered songster, nightingale?
> Or in Purgatory you cleanse yourself, if a stain
> In any part of you should somehow still remain?
> Or, after death you went where first you were forlorn
> Until your being here, unto my sorrow, born?
> Where're you are, if indeed you be, have mercy on my anguish;
> If thou no longer canst in thy former wholeness languish,
> Cheer me, as best thou canst, and make it to me seem
> You're in my sleep, though but a ghost or shadow in some bad dream.

In choosing for the representation of Kochanowski the painting of him at the bier of his daughter rather than the funereal effigy of the poet, I had from the beginning of my plan for the Album of pictures fixed on this scene to betoken also the grief for lost children on the part of several: of the Author himself for Katarzyna-Salomea and Gryzelda-Konstancja Lubieniecka (May 1675); Earl Morse Wilbur, for Thomas Lamb Eliot Wilbur (1912–32); and for my own granddaughter Shelburne Weiskel and son-in-law Thomas Weiskel (together, 1 December 1974); and my middle son, John Austin Williams (2 November 1984).

24. VILNA AND PIŃCZÓW III, 1562

24.A. An impatient letter from Calvin (signature identifiable) of 1561, warning the Vilna church about Dr. Biandrata, received there incredulously, 1562. From the Archives of the Evangelical Church of Vilna, now in the Mokslinė Biblioteka of the University of Vilnius, Republic of Lithuania. The copy here is a reproduction from the *Monumenta Reformationis Polonicae et Lithuanicae,* 1:1. 1 with the printed text and annotation; all five letters of Calvin are calendared in Wotschke, *Briefwechsel,* 137.

Calvin dedicated his *Commentary on the Acts of the Apostles* to Nicholas Radziwiłł the Black (Pl. 14) in a preface that pilloried Dr. George Biandrata without any awareness of the welcome which the prince had accorded the distinguished Italian court physician from Geneva. Radziwiłł, appreciative of the dedication, nevertheless remonstrated with Calvin for his derogation of Biandrata, in a letter of 14 July 1561 delivered by his preacher Martin Czechowic (Pl. 27).

Irked by this, on 9 October Calvin dictated five letters warning the leadership of the Reformed in the Commonwealth against Biandrata further: to Stanislas Sarnicki, Felix Cruciger, Francis Lismanino (rebuking him outright for his open friendship with Biandrata), Prince Nicholas himself, and the Vilna congregation which the palatine protected. All these letters have been reprinted several times, but the one to the Evangelical church in Vilna is the oldest document in its archive and is here reproduced with the signature of Calvin.

It is a letter that well displays his unequivocally harsh judgment of Biandrata as a hazard to the Reformation in Lithuania, Poland, and everywhere. Lubieniecki preserves other letters of Calvin; but this one conveys the mood of the antagonists and is precious for being the document from the pen of Calvin reposing furthest east in Europe. The translation follows:

> Excellent Servants of Christ, the Ministers and the Elders of the Church of Vilna, Brethren conjoined and truly honored:
>
> What you write on the desire for maintaining charity among us I freely embrace and I would be prepared to bear the manner of your pious admonition if the right reason had been advanced by you on how it is necessary for me to be reconciled with George Biandrata! That I, however, in the person of the Illustrious Prince and palatine of Vilna, urged you all to beware of that pest has seriously offended you. I am certainly sorry that the office discharged from sincere love for you and concern for your welfare has not pleased you. But what should I have done?
>
> At least I have done my duty. Nor will I ever be more sorry for this offense than for the supreme necessity that enjoined me thereto. In your estimation Biandrata is great because you take him for a man of integrity, suspect of no errors. What, however, I have publicly testified concerning him, the Preface [to the *Commentary on Acts*] shows, concerning which you remonstrate with me. Even though he is not suspect with you, he is most plainly in my eyes, if not in the face of [your] Church.
>
> You don't believe me. Why should I rather believe you? For there is so much ado among you that you convoke synods for such rubbish [as his]. But the excellent Biandrata presses you. Yet a horrible scandal will be brought forth if he wants to take me on. [Biandrata formally requested the local synod to support him in his demand for vindication.] Surely he did not receive the common prize for his so long a journey that he should now receive for himself such renown [in challenging me]. He is nothing among other nations. You admire him none other than as an Angel fallen from heaven [Gal 1:8]! I do not in the least envy you your delights.

Let him be among yourselves of highest importance but let your righteousness reciprocally permit me to recall what among us is at last known about him. If I speak the more harshly, you have forced me to it.

Besides, that you may know how excessive is the disservice of several persons to your Churches, I send a brief compend of the whole story [about Biandrata, *OC*, 19, no. 3563], from which it will be clear to you that unless I were to act unfaithfully and traitorously with you, I could not be silent in so great a peril to you.

If I have failed to enlist your confidence, nevertheless pay heed to something else and to the Elders of the Italian congregation among us and to the esteemed servant of Christ, P[eter] Martyr [Pl. 16]. Whatever you do, I frankly confess not to have been honored in this way in having been compared with Biandrata as you have done.

Farewell dear and deserving Brethren from my heart. May the Lord govern you with his spirit, sustain you with unconquerable power, and enrich you with all his gifts.

Johannes Calvinus Verbi Dei M[inist]er
[Received in Vilna, 23 January 1562]

24.B. *The Confession of Faith* of the Pinczovians, 1562, directed against Stancaro in formularies urged by Dr. Biandrata. The unique original of this imprint is in the Stadtsarchiv, Zurich, vol. E II 371, p. 920, taken from Kawecka-Gryczowa, *Drukarze,* zeszyt 6. The text is critically edited by Sipayłło, *AS,* 2. 323 f., while the protocol of the synod of 18 August 1562, out of which the *Confessio* issued, is printed there, pp. 139–140.

This *Confession of Faith* is notable in several respects. It survives in a unique imprint in Zurich; it is the last known printing of Daniel of Łęczyca in Pińczów, 20 August 1562 and in self-defense by a representative body of the still undivided Reformed Church of Little Poland. The *Confessio* resists the charge of Stanislas Sarnicki that the transitional Tritheism of the main body of the Reformed was, in fact, a kind of pagan polytheism, and most of all the charge of Stancaro that the Reformed of Poland had adopted an Arian position on the question of Christ the Mediator. It marks the very moment when the "Pinczovians" were well on their way toward an eventual Unitarianism; when the future leaders of either side of this imminent schism (1563), the proto-Unitarians and the others who would remain plenary Calvinists or regain the conservative ground, could still sign as one body their protestation of orthodoxy on Triadology and acknowledge together the Creed of Nicaea of 325 (not explicit on the consubstantiality of the Holy Spirit, in contrast to the liturgical Niceno-Constantinopolitan Creed of 381). They include acknowledgment of the ancient anathemas (third paragraph), after expressing a preference for the simplicity of the Apostles' Creed (first paragraph), while finding honorable mention for the (wholly Western and late) Anathanasian Creed (fourth paragraph).

In the August preceding the *Confessio* there was a series of disputes between Sarnicki and the "progressive" Reformed, first in Cracow and soon thereafter at a synod in Balice. Among those drawn into the debate were John Boner, Stanislas Myszkowski, Stanislas Lasocki, Jerome Filipowski, the poet Nicholas Rey, Stancaro's protector Nicholas Stadnicki, and several others who had been involved in the debate along with pastors who were signatories of the emerging *Confessio.* At the synod of Pińczów, where it was drawn up, there were also present Nicholas Oleśnicki of the castle who served as host and Dr. Biandrata, resident of Pińczów, and listed among the elders. In the first line of signatories come Felix Cruciger, Francis Lismanino, Stanislas Lutomirski (destined to be the first superintendent of the Minor Church), and Gregory Paul, but then come Paul Gilowski (destined to be pastor in the Calvinist Brog in Cracow, Pl. 51), and a few others who will stand in the end with plenary Calvinism. The final signatory is George

Schomann (Pl. 31), who had been secretary to John Łaski until his death.

The *Confessio* testifies to the importance of Stancaro's charge of Arianism and to Biandrata's defense of an unclarified Tritheism (commended in the first instance to his fellow Italian Lismanino) as a solution in the swift devolution of the dogma of the Trinity among the Polish Reformed even while they were professing adherence to the Creed of Nicaea of 325 (and even adducing the letter of Athanasius to Bishop Epictetus of Corinth to avoid the further charge of modalistic Monarchianism of Sabellianism, last paragraph).

25. MICHAEL SERVETUS (1511–53) IN POLAND AND TRANSYLVANIA

25.A. Michael Servetus was burned at the stake in Geneva, 27 October 1553. The original is in the Rijksprentenkabinet, Amsterdam. It appears to have been first reproduced by S. van der Woude, *Verguids Geloof* (Delft: Gaade, [1953]), frontispiece. It may have some claim to authenticity; in any case it appears to have been the basis of the better known print by Christoffel Sichem (Middleburgh, 1677), which faces the other way and shows through a window the burning at Champel. The copy shown here is from a large print that came into the possession of the Meadville Lombard Theological School in Chicago and which hangs there in the office of Professor John C. Godbey. The several busts, statues, and other likenesses of Servetus, go back to the Amsterdam print, except for two or three commemorative creations in Spain.

Physician, theologian, the Spanish martyr at the hands of John Calvin was an emotional rallying point for the defense of religious freedom in Poland and Transylvania. Servetus's two main works were *De Trinitatis erroribus* (Hagenau, 1531) and *Christianismi restitutio* (Vienna, 1553). His idiosyncratic Triadology was not appropriated widely, serving instead to raise questions about the received formulation. Nor are there significant traces of his distinctive Christology (D).

In Poland the first Servetians were Peter Gonesius and Gregory Paul (Pl. 26); in Transylvania they were Francis Dávid (Pl. 40) and Dr. George Biandrata (Pl. 17), who used Servetian material in the two works, B and C.

25.B. *On the False and True Knowledge . . . of the One God the Father of the Son, and of the Holy Spirit, two books* (Alba Julia, 1568), mostly composed by Dr. Biandrata, who, though drawn to Dr. Servetus as a martyr, rejected his specific Triadology and Christology (D). This is a photostat, made by Dr. Wilbur in Berlin, 1933, of a copy acquired there from the Museum Hungaricum, and deposited by him in duplicate in the Meadville Theological School Library, Chicago, and in the Starr King School for the Ministry Library in Berkeley. I am indebted to Dr. John Baker-Batzel, Librarian of the Graduate Theological Union Library in Berkeley for obtaining this for me. The evidently Hungarian hand refers to the book as *rarissimus,* acquired from some princely library, and ascribed in the same notation to Dávid as the only compiler (*compilante*), which wording does not exclude the possibility that the name of Biandrata appeared in the second space of complete erasure. *De falsa et vera cognitione* is edited by Robert Dán and Antal Pirnát, with an introduction in English as *Bibliotheca Unitariorum* 2 (Utrecht, 1988), the pictures of the Trinity, pp. 45–55.

On the False and the True Knowledge of the One God the Father, the Son, and of the Holy Spirit, two books (Alba Julia, 1568), said on the title-page to have been composed by consenting ministers of the Churches in Sarmatia (Poland) and Transylvania, carries the scriptural motto from 1 Thess 5:21: ''Prove all things, hold fast to that which is good.'' Biandrata is known to have possessed a copy of Servetus's *Restitutio,* which he appears to have left behind in Poland in safekeeping. Dávid and Biandrata rejected Servetus's Christology represented in one of their illustrations (D).

The most controversial part of this *De falsa cognitione* was its several pages of eight representations of the Trinity, evidently collected by Biandrata himself in Italy and Poland, or drafted for the book. These are mostly reproduced in Pl. 17 (one each also in 18 and 41) besides the one reproduced here (D). As a fellow physician, Biandrata evidently did not care for Dr. Servetus's physiological explanation of the divine sonship of Christ, insemination by the Spirit (cf. D), although, to be sure, Biandrata had been jolted into great doubt about the received dogma of the Trinity by Calvin's having put the Spanish physician to death in 1553 in Geneva, where he had once been an elder of the Italian congregation.

Biandrata, in possession of the *Restitutio,* will have been familiar with its two appendices, one on *The Sixty Signs of Antichrist* [papal Rome], the other, his *Apologia* of compact criticism of the Augsburg Confession directed to Melanchthon, its principal author, whom Servetus may have encountered during the diet of 1530 (which Bainton remarked, marked in effect the end of the Holy Roman Empire as *Sanctum* by virtue of a united faith, and which also marked the exclusion of the Erasmian and Valdesian, i.e., Catholic Evangelical middle way). Biandrata in the naming of his own book ''The False and True Knowledge of God'' may also have been vaguely aware that for perhaps the *first* time papal and Calvinian (i.e., Nicene) teaching about the Godhead was designated by Servetus ''Trinitarian,'' namely, at the close of his second letter to Calvin, 1553, where he wrote: ''False therefore are the invisible gods of the Trinitarians, even as the gods of Babylon'' (*Opera Calvini,* 8. col. 653). The most recent translation of the *Restitutio* in a modern language is that of Angel Alcalá, Madrid: Fundación Universitaria Española, 1980. The same scholar, professor at City University of New York, published the two appendices to the *Restitutio:* the *Apologia a Melanchthon,* which he regards as the sinewy central formulation by Servetus, *Treinta cartas a Calvino, Sesenta signos del Anticristo* (Madrid: Castalia, 1981). Francisco Sánchez-Blanco dealt specifically with the Triadology, *Michael Servets Kritik an der Trinitätslehre* (Frankfurt/Bern: Lang, 1977).

25.C. *On the Reign of Christ and on the Reign of Antichrist . . . with a supplementary tract on pedobaptism and circumcision* (Kolozsvár, 1569), containing extensive selections from the *Christianismi Restitutio* (1553) of Servetus. The title-page is taken from the reproduction of a copy in the British Museum, printed with others in Madeleine E. Stanton's Bibliography and Census, accompanying John F. Fulton, *Michael Servetus: Humanist and Martyr* (New York, 1953) 87. This particular copy has been defaced with the cruel notation ''Servetus castratus.'' For the full title of the lost translation into Polish of part 5 of the *Restitutio* by Gregory Paul, see ibid., 90, no. 33, and my own n. 14 to *RD* 3. The scriptural motto is John 15:14: ''You are my friends if you do what I command you.'' The preface, addressed to John II Sigismund (Pl. 39), dated Kolozsvár, 1569, conceals the names of the two principal authors, Biandrata and Dávid, under the generality of ''the ministers and elders of Transylvania agreeing on the One God the Father.''

In Poland Gregory Paul translated the fifth part of the *Restitutio* as *Okazanie Antychrysta y iego Królestwa z znaków jego własnych w słowie bożem opisanych, których tu sześćdziesią*t (The advent of Antichrist and his kingdom, according to his own signs as described by the Word of God, of which there are sixty, Cracow, 1568). This work, known to Bock (1, p. 619), has disappeared; cf. Górski, *Grzegorz Paweł,* 254 – 55.

John Wigand, one of the Centuriators, mounted the most formidable assault on Servetus to the east of the Empire, *De Servetianismo* (Königsberg, 1575).

25.D. One of the eight "monstrous" representations of the Trinity pilloried by Biandrata (in B), here the Pneumatic Insemination of the Virgin by God the Father to assure the fully celestial flesh of Christ (the view of Servetus, among other christological dissidents from the Chalcedonian formulary). According to Servetus the Holy Breath (Spirit) of the Father introduced the divine Seed into the ear, thence on to the heart and the womb of the Virgin (whence Servetus's preoccupation with the pulmonary circulation of the blood), effectuating within her a divine Son of *celestial* flesh.

In this representation of the pneumatic insemination of the Virgin the infant Christ, already tethered to his cross, enveloped by the Holy Spirit, is wafted toward the expectant Virgin (not shown). The view of Servetus that nothing but nutriment was drawn from Mary is found in varying formulations in several others of the Radical Reformation, like Caspar Schwenckfeld, Melchior Hofmann, and Menno Simons. In antiquity, the theory was connected with the Valentinian Gnostics and condemned in several conciliar strictures from Constantinople I in 381 into the eighth century, for catholicity/orthodoxy progressively defined as fully human Christ's flesh, soul, reason, energy, and will. As several of the eight pictures reproduced in *De falsa cognitione* were evidently drafted by Biandrata himself or according to his specifications to illustrate alleged falsities, it seems quite likely that as a physician Biandrata was tactfully dismissing as unacceptable the distinctively *Servetian* Christology as though it were one of the Catholic/Calvinist views he rejected, for he found the Socinian Christology more plausible, printing anonymously Laelius Socinus's *Brevis explicatio* in his collection *De falsa cognitione* (pp. 297 – 324) and in the same year and place printed the similarly named work of Faustus Socinus, ascribing *it* to Laelius (Pl. 13).

In the *Restitutio,* Servetus opposed pedobaptism as the sign of Antichrist and attached importance to the immersion of the believer, like Jesus at Jordan at age 30, when the heavens opened and the voice of the Father was heard and the Dove descended as the christic *homunculus* at the Pneumatic Conception. The baptismal moment was for Servetus the only epiphany of the Trinity in the New Testament, as he had sought to conceptualize it. (He was not a Unitarian.) At the end of the *Restitutio* Servetus declared that whoever believes that the Pope is Antichrist must also reject as papal the *received* dogma of the Trinity (to be construed, rather, in his distinctive way as physician) and pedobaptism.

26. THREE RADICAL POLISH-LITHUANIAN DIVINES I: GONESIUS AND GREGORY PAUL

26.A – C. Three works by Peter Gonesius (d. 1573), setting forth comprehensively his conviction about *The Three* (rather than the Trinity), *The Son of God,* and *Immersion* (Węgrów, 1570), presumably translated or adapted from his original Latin of c. 1555. Title-pages from the facsimile editions, Piotr z Goniądza, *Dzieła polskie,* edited by Halina Górska, Konrad Górski, Zdzisław Zawadzki, Krystyna Wilczewska, Biblioteka Pisarzy Reformacyjnych, 3 A – C (Warsaw: PAN, 1960; 1961; 1962).

Born in Goniądz, close to Ducal Prussia, in the Lithuanian palatinate of Podlachia, Gonesius studied at the Cracovian Academy, protesting the interpretation there of the newly appointed Hebraist on the faculty, Stancaro (Pl. 17). This lead to the Mantuan's arrest. Earning a doctorate in Padua, he had come in contact with Gribaldi and learned about the execution of Servetus (Pl. 24). Returning home by way of the Hutterites in Moravia (Pl. 29), he was stimulated by them to adopt radical social views, including personal pacifism, symbolized by his wearing a wooden staff in place of a gentleman's sword. The three works here shown, preceded by Latin versions of c. 1555, were published with the aid of his patron John Kiszka in Węgrów in his native palatinate. As he held to the preexistence of Christ, the printed dating is in "the Dominical year according to the flesh."

26.A. *On the Three, that is, on God, on His Son, and on the Holy Spirit against the Sabellian Trinity* is sanctioned by 2 Cor 13:14: "The grace of the Lord Jesus Christ and the love of God and the fellowship of the Holy Spirit be with you all." In his sharp attack on scholastic formulations, Gonesius holds that the received doctrine of the Trinity, upheld by Protestants no less than Catholics, is essentially "Sabellian" in setting forth Three Persons as One without sufficient distinction among them. He was asked by his patron Nicholas Radziwiłł the Black (Pl. 14) to submit his Confession of faith to the synod of Secemin of January 1556 because he had refused to use the word "Trinity" as a Catholic innovation, hence his "Three."

26.B. *On the Son of God, that he was before the creation of the world and is He by whom all things are made* [Col 1:16–17] *against the false Ebionite corruptions* is sanctioned somewhat obscurely by the Hebrew text of Zech 6:12, which Gonesius renders in Polish: "That is, Behold the Man whose name is Sprout (Vulgate: *germen* [cf. 3:8]) and (those things that are) from him will come forth." The *RSV* translation is: "Behold, the man whose name is Branch: for he shall grow up in his place." The Ebionite opinions repelled by Gregory Paul are those among the Polish Brethren who had moved to a fully Unitarian position while retaining the adoration of, and prayer to, the Ascended Christ. Nevertheless, the same Gregory Paul would presently circulate in paraphrased Polish translation Faustus Socinus's *Explicatio* (Pl. 13.C).

26.C. *On Christian baptism (ponurzanie) against the christening (chrzest) of the recent neochristeners* is sanctioned by Mark 16:16: "He who believes and is immersed (*ponurzon*) will be saved; but he who does not believe will be condemned." *Chrzest* was the Catholic and then the Protestant word for baptism, in practice a sprinkling of the infant with water or a partial dipping. Gonesius, possibly under the influence of Servetus (Pl. 25), may have been the first to introduce in Polish the term for baptism as immersion. It is found in Gregory Paul, as of 1568, but for him it was *Chrzest* still in 1564 (F). Other tentative forms that did not become general were *nurzanie, ponarzanie, zanarzanie.*

26.D. The Church of St. Mary Magdalene in Poznań, where Gregory Paul (d.c. 1595) was rector of the school, 1549–50; later pastor of the Reformed congregation in Cracow, 1552–62 (before the schism). A detail from a larger picture of Poznań, from *W renesansowym Poznaniu.*

26.E–F. Title-page and diagram are from the facsimile edition, *Grzegorz Paweł z Brzezin,* ed. Konrad Górski and Władysław Kuraszkiewicz; Biblioteka Pisarzów Polskich, series B 2; (Warsaw, 1954).

26.E. Gregory Paul's *On contemporary Differences, that is, what we are correctly to understand concerning the One God the Father and his only begotten Son and the Holy Spirit and simply according to Holy Writ (in which alone God reveals himself) . . . a Brief Writing* ([Brest Litovsk]: Cyprian Bazylik, 1564) is undergirded scripturally with the words of Christ in John 17:3: "Father, ... this is eternal life, that they know thee the only true God and Jesus Christ whom thou hast sent."

26.F. Gregory Paul's diagram (from E) of "Christ's Church without wrinkle or spot [Eph 5:27], standing on the prophetic and apostolic foundation alone, not up to this time either disturbed or infected by the Heretics [Catholics]." The temple of faith is characterized with phrases, many of which are from the Apostles' Creed. The proof of this living Church has the affirmation: "I believe in the cleansing of sins, the resurrection of the body, the life ever-lasting." The House/Sanctuary is characterized: "I believe in the Holy Catholic Church, the communion of saints." The Foundation of the Church of Christ is made up of ten affirmations: "The Revelation of the Three in the Baptism (here still: *Chrzest*): God the Father in the voice; the Son of God in the Body; the Holy Spirit in the person of a dove; One God the Father from (z) whom all things, the One Holy Spirit in (w) whom we cry Abba, Father; and thus also we baptize (*chrzcić*) ourselves in the name of the Father and the Son and the Holy Spirit; and also [we hold to] the Apostolic Credo, the belief in God the Father and in Jesus Christ and in the Holy Spirit,"— "By his craft Satan overthrew the Foundation of Faith and of eternal salvation."

27. RADICAL POLISH-LITHUANIAN DIVINES II: CZECHOWIC (d. 1613)

27.A. The later Polish version of the three-day debate in Latin on the immersion (*narzanie*) of children, led by believers' baptist Martin Czechowic (d. 1613) in 1565, printed by Unitarian biblicist Simon Budny (Pl. 15) with his own historical account of the rise of believers' baptism. A photocopy of the *Trzech dni rozmowa*, recently discovered by Prof. Dr. Paulina Buchwald-Palcowa in a Swedish library (Skokkloster), is to be edited by Lech Szczucki, who in his *Czechowic*, 88–98, esp. 90, makes the assessment about item C. See *Historia*, 2 n. 441; 3 n. 199.

Budny, biblical scholar, published the debate in a Polish translation with the approval of Nicholas Wędrowski, one of the opponents of Czechowic, and he includes his own *On the Baptism of Children: a brief note on the beginning ... of controversy over the first sacrament, that is Holy Immersion, in the Duchy of Lithuania and later in Poland.* Budny himself submitted to rebaptism but intended to keep the rite free from the radical socio-political consequences of believers' immersion as defended by Czechowic. The book was dedicated by Budny to the memory of Prince Nicholas and printed with the approval of John Kiszka (at the time grand carver in the court of the Grand Duke), at his press in Łosk, Jan Karcan of Wieliczka being the printer, 1578.

27.B. Aerial photograph of palace of Nieśwież, where the three-day debate took place in January 1565 in the presence of the owner, Nicholas Radziwiłł the Black (Pl. 14). Nieśwież in Palatinate Nowogródek, from the air, 1926; Zakład Reprografii, Biblioteka Narodowa.

27.C. Czechowic, pastor in Lublin, an immersionist who long remained Ditheist, resistant to Socinus (Pl. 47), published *Christian Discussions* against an Ebionite (Budnyite Christology), (Cracow, 1575). Copy from the Jagiellonian University Library, Cracow; photograph by Zbigniew Pasek. The full title reads in translation: *Christian discussions (which from the Greek name are called dialogues and you may call a large catechism), in which are various talks about the most important articles of the Christian faith and separately about Jewish palavers by which they wish to destroy the Lord Jesus Christ and the Gospel,* by Martin Czechowic, pastor in Lublin, 1 September 1575, published by Alexy Rodecki [Cracow, 1575]. The scriptural motto is from Isa 8:19–20: "And when they say to you, 'Consult the wizards and diviners who chirp and mutter,' should not a people consult their God? . . . To the teaching and to the testimony!"

The reference to Jewish palavers (*gadki*) is not primarily to Jews but to the Judaizers in the Minor Church of Lithuania, Budny foremost among them. This spirited composition, following by one year the *Catechesis,* Cracow, 1574, of Schomann and Gregory Paul (RD 5), is "without doubt the most important work of Polish Unitarianism in the pre-Socinian period" (Szczucki). In the thirteenth chapter, Czechowic deals with baptism and the Lord's Supper and refers to the *Rozmowa* (A), presumably in their original Latin form.

Czechowic wrote a *Mirror for Christian Maidens* (*Zwierziadło panienek christiańskich*) dedicated to the girls of Łosk, and, for Paul Orzedowicki, cup-bearer of Chełm (Lublin, 1583); and, with a dedication to Sigismund III, he wrote an *Epitomium* of his debate with Canon Jerome Powódowski of Poznań; *BAnt²* 52 and the rewrite.

28. POLAND, HUNGARY, MOLDAVIA I:
TWO GREEK ACADEMIC ADVENTURERS

28.A. Despota Jacob Heraclides Basilicus (15210–63), equivocally Reformed Orthodox Voivode of Moldavia (1561–63). Born in Samos, educated in Wittenberg, poet laureate of the Empire, he caused a stir among the Reformed in Poland. When enthroned in Jassy by the efforts of Albert Łaski (Pl. 38), he reformed the Catholic cathedral in nearby Cotnari (Pl. 38.B) and established there the liberal Schola Latina under John Sommer (Pl. 38). A coin and signature from the frontispiece of Émile Legrand, *Deux Vie de Jacques Basilicos* (Paris, 1889). The coin of Heraclides bears an inscription and seal in Latin as Despot, "Vindicator and Defender of the liberty of the Fatherland, 1563," and below is his signature in Greek as Heraclides Jakobos Basilikos.

Dimitrie Cantemir, a remote successor of Heraclides as voivode of Moravia, 1663, 1710–11, a polymath, would render into Greek and Romanian Andrew Wiszowaty's *Stimuli virtutum, fraena peccatorum* (Amsterdam, 1682) as a component of his *Divanul,* in turn translated into Arabic by Athanasios Dabbas in 1705, the first writing issuing from Europe's Reformation to appear in Arabic.

28.B. Chios under Genoese administration where Jacob (Olimpidarios) Palaeologus (c. 1521–85) was born, a Dominican slowly identifying with the fully Unitarian Reformation in Transylvania. Woodcut from Braun and Hogenberg, *Civitates orbis terrarum;* reproduced by permission of the Houghton Library, Harvard University.

Chios shown here at about the time of Jacob Palaeologus, was governed by the Genoese, 1346–1566, when it fell to the Turks. Palaeologus was born here, son of a Greek mason, Theodore Olimpiadarios, and a Genoese mother. He assumed the royal style. Within the fortified area, the largest church is that of Santa Maria of the Dominicans, to which order Giacomo belonged, along with Vicenzo Giustiniani, the later cardinal. In the distance is the Catholic cathedral of Sant'Antonio outside the Borgo. Much of the population was Orthodox or Uniate, and there was a synagogue. On the hills nearby is the church associated with the site of the home of Homer.

Chios was devastated in the uprising against the Turks in 1822 and the ensuing massacre, while more buildings came down in the major earthquake of 1881.

28.C. The Colloquy of Poissy, 1561, attended by Palaeologus, still in Dominican habit (after several trails for heresy), a remote model of his own interfaith colloquy, *Catechesis christiana* (1574). Reproduced from the frontispiece of Donald Nugent, *Ecumenism in the Age of the Reformation: The Colloquy of Poissy* (Cambridge: Harvard University Press). The engraving is by Tortorel and Périssin.

The picture in the convent refectory shows, in front of the table of the abbess, the royal family: A. King Charles IX (1560–74); B. his mother Catherine de Medici; C. her other son, Henry, the future king of Poland and then of France (III), along with the king and queen of Navarre. Facing each other on the left and right are six cardinals. Among the doctors and the bishops, nearer the foreground on either side, are James Laynez, second General of the Jesuit Order, and Jean Monluc of Valence, who favored communion in both kinds, and was later the emissary of Henry for the election in Poland (Pl. 35). Standing in the foreground are the Reformed ministers, Theodore Beza, (S) in the middle, along with Peter Martyr Vermigli and others not identified. In Palaeologus's own imaginary colloquy, *Catechesis christiana* (1574), in which Francis Dávid represents the Unitarian position, an Indian from the Hispanic New World, Telephus, participates.

28.D. The second edition of his report (1573) on the religio-political situation in his natal island and Istanbul. Reproduced by permission of the Houghton Library, Harvard University.

After visiting native Chios and Istanbul, Palaeologus wrote down his impressions of the Ottoman threat, Kolozsvár, 10 January 1573, first printed in 1591.

The German version reads: A communication from Constantinople on the intention of the Turkish Emperor and of his mobilization for war which he has at the present time undertaken to make use of against Christendom and especially against Germany (Ursel in Flanders, 1594).

28.E. The castle of Theodore of Kunoviče in Moravia, whither for refuge Palaeologus fled from Transylvania, where he compiled his *Defense of Francis Dávid* (Cracow, 1580), where he was visited by Vehe-Glirius (Pl. 44), where he wrote in defense of Queen Elizabeth (1576), and where he was apprehended as a Turkish spy to be burned for heresy at the stake in Rome, 1585. Postal card of the castle in Hluk, given by Mrs. Jarmila Vogel, Newton, Massachusetts, obtained from her older brother in Slavkov. There is a picture of the courtyard in Václav Frolec *et al.*, *Slovácko: Kapitoly z dějin Slovácka* (Prague: Vydala Tisková, 1978) Pl. 18.

Palaeologus, having been 1571–72 in the home of Dudith (Pl. 38) in Cracow, resided (1573–75) in the castle of the magnate John Gerendi in Alţina, Transylvania, where he took the side of Caspar Békés (Pl. 44.B) against Prince Stephen Báthory (Pl. 39). Obliged to flee, he found refuge at Hluk in Moravia under the protection of Theodore (Jetřich) of Kunoviče.

It was in 1570 that Pius V excommunicated Queen Elizabeth and released her subjects from their allegiance. Palaeologus composed his *Adversus Pii V proscriptionem Elisabethae reginae Angliae,* 1576. In 1580 at Łosk through the good offices of Simon Budny, Palaeologus's *Defensio verae sententiae de magistratu politico* was published against Socinus's religio-ethical compromise on the use of the sword in partial defense of the pacifism of the Racovians. In Hluk Palaeologus anonymously put together the documents in *Defense of Francis Dávid in the Matter of not invoking Jesus Christ in prayers,* directed against Faustus Socinus and Dr. Biandrata (Frankfurt, 1580; Cracow, 1581, 1582). Of this there is a facsimile edition, edited by Robert Dán, with an introduction in English by Nikály Baláz, *Bibliotheca Unitariorum* (Budapest/Utrecht: Hungarian Academy of Science, 1983). Matthew Vehe-Glirius (Pl. 44) visited Palaeologus in Hluk and was responsible for the third enlarged edition of *The Defense,* Cracow, 1582. In 1581 Palaeologus was taken as a Turkish spy on orders from Rudolph II, and died as a heretic as the stake in Rome, 23 March 1585.

29. THE COMMUNITARIAN HUTTERITE ANABAPTISTS IN MORAVIA I

29.A. Slavkov (Austerlitz), major center for the Hutterites, other Anabaptists, including a number from Italy, with centers of the Unitas Fratrum nearby, also a sanctuary for Evangelical Rationalists: a painting from 1712. A detail from the lower part of a painting (1712) of Urban (1223 – 30), Pope and martyr, in the chapel in his memory shown at the top left. The card shows Slavkov/Austerlitz before it was completely changed by the decisive battle of the Three Emperors, Napoleon against Austria and Russia, 2 December 1805. It comes from a postal card of the painting. There are reproductions of the twice-damaged painting in Jan Pernička, *Slovosko na Pohlednicích* (Slavkov, 1985) and *Slavkov: Státni Zámek v Slavkove* (Slavkov, 1959). I am grateful to Josef Staša and Hana Červinková Exnarová.

In March 1528 the Utraquist knight, John Dubčanský (d. 1543), owner of three villages to the north, was co-host in Slavkov of the two-day colloquy in Latin between 105 Utraquist priests and many more German Evangelicals from Mikluklov (Nicolsburg), led by Martin Göschl and Oswald Glaidt, on the ground of salvation, clerical marriage, and the Lord's Supper. The town, owned by the four brothers, lords of Kouniče, supported there a congregation of the Unitas Fratrum (Czech Brethren), to whom they adhered confessionally.

In that very year of the colloquy, the knights welcomed on their estates the nonresistant Anabaptists (*Stäbler*). Two hundred proto-Hutterites seceded from the followers of Balthasar Hubmaier (*Schwertler*) in Milukov. Their presiding bishop (*Vorsteher*), Peter Walpot (1521–78), came to reside in Nové Mlýny (Neumühl) down the river.

In and around Slavkov were several congregations of some ten kinds of Anabaptists in Moravia, e.g., the Pilgrimites (followers of Pilgrim Marpeck). By 1562 Italian radicals also found refuge in Slavkov, among them Nicholas Paruta, to whom Bernadine Ochino repaired when driven from Poland by the edict of Parczów, 1564 (Pl. 16). His host in Poland, Jerome Filipowski, was later one of several Polish and Lithuanian Brethren who visited Slavkov, 1568 – 71, among them also Simon Ronemberg and George Schomann (Pl. 31), who were instrumental in the incorporation of some Hutterite ideals in their own commune in Raków, 1569 – 74 (Pl. 59). Czech Brethren and Hutterites were alike obliged to leave Moravia, 1620 – 22, the former in part for Poland, the latter for *Partium* and Transylvania.

29.B. *Geschicht-Buch*, the master copy of the major chronicle of the Hutterites, with the beginnings of Anabaptism in Zurich, containing several documents relating to visits from the Polish Brethren, a unique piece of *Americana.* The title-page is that of the original MS in Bon Homme, South Dakota from *Introducing the Great Chronicle of the Hutterian Brethren* (Rifton, NY: Plough Publishing House, 1986).

The Great Chronicle of the Hutterites was begun in 1560, by the sometime deacon, the preacher Caspar Braitmichel, who traces the story from George Blaurock and the first believers' baptism, Canton Zurich, 1525. Existing in a few slightly divergent copies, the master codex of 612 folios shown is that brought by the Hutterites on their trek from Moravia, eventually into Russia, whence to Bon Homme County, South Dakota, 1874. It contains the record of several epistolary exchanges and mutual visits of Hutterites and Polish Brethren. The codex was edited for philological accuracy by A. J. F. Ziegelschmid, *Die älteste Chronik der Hutterischen Brüder* with plates, glossary, and index (Ithaca: Carl Schurz Memorial Foundation, 1943). It appears translated by the Hutterian Brethren and Sisters in consultation with Leonard Gross as *The Great Chronicle of the Hutterian Brethren* (Rifton, NY: Plough Publishing House of the Woodcrest Bruderhof, 1987). A portion of one page is given on Pl. 30.C.

See further on the absorption of the theologically often more Unitarianizing Italian Anabaptists among the Hutterites, Aldo Stella, "Influences and Developments of Hutterian Anabaptism in Italian Nonconformist Conventicles," *The Plough* (Rifton, NY: Woodcrest Bruderhof, 1988).

29.C. Woodcut caricature of Hutterite communism, set forth as a dovecote of witches deserving of capital punishment (Exod 22:18), with Jacob Hutter (d. 1536) or his bearded successor as *Vorsteher* looking out. Woodcut by Taubenkobel on the title-page of a work against Anabaptists, *Vier und fünfzig Erhebliche Ursachen/Warumb die Widertäufer nicht sein im Land zu leiden* (Ingolstadt, 1607) by Christopher Andreas Fischer, S.J., pastor in Veldsperg in Lower Austria across from the Moravian frontier.

The communal life and the pacifism of the Hutterites are here being caricatured as sorcery from a dove-cote: minglings and madness, owls, bats, and witch-like women with the instruments of specialized craft and industry, flying or perching about it, with a fox below calculating his chances, all with a due superscription from Exod 22:18: "Thou shalt not suffer a witch to live."

The cartoon has two messages: (1) the Hutterites are evil folk who ought to be killed: therefore witch-like figures; (2) the Hutterites can be recognized by their professional craftsmanship, illustrated richly—they hired themselves out, or sold their products, and by these signs they were recognized as Hutterites.

The figures on the staves are deliberately cast in witch posture so as to bring the Hutterian Brethren under the censure of Exod 22:18.

The large figure, lower left, is an empiric with his backpack of herbs and holding his mortar for mixing them. Even Cardinal Dietrichstein, for all of his success in driving them out, had a Hutterite for his personal physician. The large figure, lower right, is a woman baker, holding bread and a flour sack.

The other figures, beginning left and moving right, bottom to top: a tailor with shears and cloth; a measuring device (probably for a carpenter); butcher's cleaver; rope (they twined it for sale); cups, either pewter or ceramic (they manufactured both); some symbol of light and darkness that we have not deciphered; (now over to the right side, top to bottom) surveyor's tools; well-digger; carpenter's cutting tool; hat (product for sale); hose (the same); drawbar, carpenter's tool; locksmith equipment; curry comb (they hired out as teamsters).

For the larger context of the polemic, see Jean-Marie Valentin, "Societés d'ordre et dissidence: Les Jesuites et les Anabaptistes; théâtre polémique, théologie," *Bibliotheca Dissidentium: Scripta et Studia* (ed. Marc Lienhard) 1.264–84.

30. THE COMMUNITARIAN HUTTERIAN ANABAPTISTS IN MORAVIA II

30.A. Woodcut of a Hutterian Bruderhof showing many dormer windows of gender-separated dormitory, from a hostile work of 1589. From Christoph Erhard, *Gründliche kurtz verfaste Historia von Münsterischen Widertäuffern; und wie die Hutterischen Brüder so auch billich Widertäuffer genent werden, im löblichen Margraffthumb Mähren, deren über die sibentzehn tausent sein sollen, gedachten Münsterischen in vielen ähnlich, gleichformig und mit zustimmet sein* (Munich, 1588); by the courtesy of the Mennonite Historical Library, Goshen College, Goshen, Indiana.

The claim that there were over 70,000 Hutterites seems excessive and the charge of their being Münsterite, of course, incorrect.

30.B. A Bruderhof surviving today in Vel'uke Leváre (Gross-Schützen) in southern Moravia. Taken from a deluxe edition by František Kalesný, *Hábni na Slovensku* (Tatran, 1981) 58.

The communitarian farm and buildings were called *Bruderhof* or *Haushaben*. The Slovak rendering of the latter was *Haban*. The Czech Brethren and the Anabaptists had four colloquies: 1528, Litomyšl (Leitomischl); 1543, Hustopeče (Auspitz); 1559, Ivančice (Eibenschitz); 1559, Bzenec.

30.C. A letter to the Hutterites from the pastor in Olkusz, probably Daniel Bieliński (Pl. 31), preserved in the *Geschicht-Buch*, dated 25 May 1570, recommending two Racovians, John Baptysta (Święcicki) and John Italus, also George Müller of Olkusz. Two pages of the *Geschicht-Buch* (in Ziegelschmid, *Die älteste Chronik*, 442–43), presented by Leonard Gross.

There follows the translation as it appears in the edition of 1987; beginning with comment of the Chronicler: "We left it at that and parted as friends, trusting that God would show us the right time if it was his will. The four young [Polish] men who had come earlier [to live in a Bruderhof] went home with them [Simon Ronemberg, Jerome Filipowski, et al.]. Soon after, the little Polish flock sent three other men to get to know our community. They brought the following letter to our church:"

> Grace and peace from God the Father and from the Lord Jesus Christ, the Crucified: Divinely blessed men, we thank God that he has awakened our hearts by your letter, in which you challenged us in a Christian way. We are sending two men from Raków, John Baptista [Święcicki] and John the Italian, to visit you in Moravia. After considering the matter, we prayed that God might prompt someone in our little group (*Hefflen*) to accompany them and return to us with strength and comfort (may God grant it). God prompted our fellow believer, Järisch Müller, to come forward, and we humbly prayed for God's blessing on their journey. We have the earnest request to let them share in the gifts God has given you through the holy order (*Ordnung*) you maintain, and we have no doubt you will do so, for we know you are a people of God, gracious and God-fearing. Out of your love to the believers you will joyfully do all that belongs to God's praise. We commend you to God the Lord. Dated: Olkusz, May 25, 1570.

The Hutterite Chronicler continues: "These men [the Polish Brethren] traveled around for a time in a cold-hearted way, had soon seen enough, and returned to Poland. They were not in earnest, so their visit bore little fruit.

After this visit in which they did not find unity with the church, Brother Peter Walpot sent the following letter to some of the Poles who had shown goodwill. . . ."

All the letters between the Polish Brethren and the Hutterites on pp. 443–58 have been calandared, translated into Polish, and annotated by Szczucki and Tazbir, *OiRwP* 3 (1958) 197–215.

For renewed contact between the Polish Brethren (Dr. Daniel Zwicker of Danzig) and the Hutterites (*Vorsteher* Andreas Ehrenpreis, 1653 – 55), see Leonard Gross, "The Hutterian Brethren and the Polish Brethren: Rapprochement and Estrangement," in Godbey, ed., *Unitarianism*, 46 – 62.

31. THREE PROMINENT POLISH BRETHREN OF SILESIAN ORIGIN:
George Schomann, Daniel Bieliński, Simon Ronemberg

31.A. After the pictures illustrative of their lives are identified and explained, there follow several paragraphs on the radical reforming thrusts in Silesia under the Bohemian Crown, today part of Poland, but in the *Historia* almost completely ignored. There are no portraits for these three Silesians prominent in the *Historia*.

31.B. The Bursa of the Poor, Cracow, where Schomann coming from Silesia once taught.
Taken from *Gospodarka i budynki Uniwersytetu Jagiellońskiego*, Prace Historyczne, zeszyt 46 (Cracow: Jagiellonian University, 1973), p. 63. Picture shows the Bursa as of the beginning of the nineteenth century. The no longer existing Bursa Ubogich was one of several hostels of the University.
George Schomann, whose autobiographical *Testamentum* constitutes RD 3, born in Racibórz in 1530, of a German father and Polish mother of a courtly family, first studied in Breslau and then came to Cracow in 1552. After briefly serving as pedagogue in the parish school of St. Mary's in the Square, he taught in the Bursa for poor students.

31.C. Wieliczka was the administrative center of the royal salt works, where Schomann lived, 1554 – 60. A sketch, 1638; Alfons Długosz, *Wieliczka* (Warsaw, 1958), p. 5.
Schomann taught the nephews of the royal saltmaster, Jerome Bużeński and other children in the castle (D), conducting them periodically also to both Wittenberg and Pińczów for further study. Schomann became minister in the center for the Reformed of Poland (Pls. 9, 10) at Pińczów in 1560, after having served very briefly as secretary to John Łaski (Pl. 20). In the stream running by this Wieliczka, courtier Christopher Lubieniecki, grandfather of the Historian, was baptized by immersion.

31.D. The Salters' Castle, residence of Jerome Bużeński, then Prosper Provana (Pls. 16.H-J), both favorable to the Reformation, and where Schomann taught Bużeński's nephews.
From a bilingual guide to Wieliczka (Krzysztof Kowalski).

31.E. The residence in Cracow, Pod Różą, *of Provana, where Schomann participated in a debate with Peter Skarga, S.J. (Pl. 49) photograph by Jerzy Langda, PAN; gift of Jerzy Strzetelski.*
In the residence in Cracow of Provana, successor of Bużeński as royal saltmaster, Schomann participated in a debate with Peter Skarga, S.J. (Pl. 49). Schomann was minister of the immersionist Unitarian church of Cracow, of which Ronemberg was a leading elder, 1573 – 85. For the debate, see Alexander Bocheński, Przemyśl polski w dawnych wiekach (Warsaw: PIW, 1984), p. 1526.

31.F. The title-page of the *Catechesis* by Schomann and Gregory Paul (Pl. 26) (Cracow, 1574), immersionist Unitarian antecedent of the Racovian Catechism in Polish (Raków, 1605).
Copy of the *Catechesis* in the Andover Harvard Library, by presentation, evidently originally from the library of the Polish refugee church in Koloszvár (1659); printed by permission. It appears in translation as Related Document 7.

31.G. Olkusz, mining town, where Prosper Provana first served as mine master, and whence ex-priest Bieliński wrote to the Hutterites (Pl. 30). Detail from a larger picture from the sixteenth century, taken from Bocheński, *Przemyśl polski*.

Olkusz in the sixteenth century was a mining town where Prosper Porvana (Pl. 11) first settled from Italy as mine master, and where Daniel Bieliński, a former priest, was minister, 1559–70. At the left is the church and cloister of the Augustinians and nearly against the wall a rather huge synagogue. From Olkusz, Bieliński wrote a letter of recommendation for three Racovians visiting the Hutterites (Pl. 30). He settled in Raków but was excommunicated in 1576. He joined the Cracow Calvinist congregation in the Brog (Pl. 51), serving there for two years under its pastor Paul Gilowski, preaching to the German congregation upstairs; and then he became the regular pastor, 1578–86.

31.H. A Cracow apothecary, detail from a larger scene, possibly a likeness of Simon Ronemberg. Detail from a colored cartoon woodcut, showing among several typical figures of Cracow (Pl. 11.B), one in the garb of an apothecary. The picture, authentic as to dress, could even be a likeness of Ronemberg, a centenarian of prominence in the period of the cartoon (sixteenth century).

Simon Ronemberg, dying c. 1604, was a German citizen of Cracow, an apothecary who led the delegation of 1569 to the Hutterites in Moravia, along with Schomann and Jerome Filipowski. He settled in Raków, emerging as the "New Ezra" in bringing order out of chaos there, and founded the separate immersionist Unitarian church in Cracow.

In the healing services, physicians were often theorists of health on the basis of their university degree, while the apothecaries and empirics compounded the medicines and prescribed them, and the barbers-surgeons cut and bandaged. (The works of the mystical physician Paracelsus appeared early in Cracow in Latin from the German.)

Ronemberg tried to get Socinus to submit to believers' baptism by immersion before partaking of communion. The latter had written against the practice of the Polish Brethren in 1580 and given Ronemberg a copy of his tract, in response to which Ronemberg wrote Socinus cordially but unconvinced, 16 July 1583. To this in turn Socinus promptly responded from Pawlowice in eight points in deference of his view of the negligible significance of baptism, except for Jews and pagans.

Silesia, whence Ronemberg, Bieliński, and Schomann came to Cracow, was one of the four hereditary duchies (*księstwa/Herzogtümer*) into which King Boleslas the Crooked Mouth of the Piast dynasty divided his Polonia (1138). After the death of Henry the Pious (1241), Silesia was ruled by a congeries of Piast princes who became vassals of the Bohemian Crown in the first third of the thirteenth century and it was heavily repopulated after the Tatar devastations by German colonists and merchants. Silesia felt the brunt of the Hussite wars in defense of Utraquist Bohemia against the papal crusade from all sides.

In the sixteenth century the hereditary title of duke (*księżę/Herzog*) was carried by several feudatories, in nomenclature and rank assimilated to those of the Empire by way of the Bohemian Crown, dukes, margraves, counts, and lesser territorial princes with knights in attendance. They met in their princely diet (*Fürstentag*) under the direction of the royally appointive viceregent (*Oberlandshauptmann/namiestnik*), one each for Lower and for Upper Silesia. From 1507 a league of towns had come into being to resist highway robberies and other depradations of the nobles and freebooters. The bishop of Breslau, though appointed by the Bohemian Crown, with his palace and territorial prince-bishopric some distance from the cathedral city, in Niesse, nevertheless belonged to the provincial synod of the Archbishop of Gniezno, Primate of Poland, an ecclesiastical remnant of the days of Polish rule over Silesia.

The Silesian states (*Fürstentag*) met, as in Bohemia, each in a *curia* apart: that of the bishop of Breslau, the dukes, four nonducal lordships, and the city of Breslau (living by its own influential municipal code, the Magdeburg-Breslau *Mutterrecht*); the *curia* of the representatives of the lords, prelates, and knights of the three principalities directly under the Bohemian (Hapsburg) Crown, and of the large principality of Breslau (distinguished from both the municipality and the bishopric); and the *curia* of the burgher representatives of the towns within the same royal principalities. The agenda was arranged and the deciding ballot was cast by the viceregent of Lower Silesia, from 1536 the bishop of Breslau *ex officio,* who even before this presided over the highest *curia* and the joint sessions.

But at the beginning of the Reformation in Silesia Duke Frederick III of Liegnitz (1504–47), grandson of Utraquist King George of Poděbrady, was viceregent for Lower Silesia (1516–27). He was disposed at first to favor communion *sub utraque specie* as it was being freshly promulgated from Wittenberg.

Indeed the most renowned reformer in Silesia, the courtier Spiritualizer, Caspar Schwenckfeld (1490–1561), was acquainted with several writings of the Czech Brethren (Unitas Fratrum, Pl. 4) and, tapping into their piety and discipline, brought to Wittenberg in 1525 what has been identified as the *Excusatio Fratrum Waldensium contra binas literas Doctoris Augustini* [Käsebrot] (Nuremberg, 1507). This was the reply of the Unitas to a learned canon of Olomouc, who with Bishop John of Nagyvárad (Grosswardein) in Transylvania, chancellor of Hungary, had in 1502 called upon Jagiellonian Ladislas II of Bohemia and Hungary to suppress the Unitas (*Corpus Schwenckfeldianorum,* 2. 272). To be sure, Schwenckfeld turned aside from the Czech Brethren as too much like the Zwinglians on sacramental theology, upholding over against them, for example, a eucharistic reading of John 6:54 on Christ's flesh and blood. Schwenckfeld, exercising the *jus patronatus,* had, as early as 1521, appointed as pastor, over his native parish of Ossig, one of his Bible-studying companions.

By 1523 the city of Breslau (not by any means its bishop!) and Liegnitz had firmly gone over to the new reformation. The first Protestant catechism in all Europe was the *Katechismus Lignicensis* of 1525, composed by the trilingual humanist Valentine Crautwald (1470/90–1545), alumnus of the Jagiellonian University, successively canon of Neisse and Liegnitz, by Caspar Schwenckfeld, and by the Evangelicals among the parish priests and canons of Liegnitz (*Corpus Schwenckfeldianorum,* 18. 6–10). There were peasant uprisings in Silesia in 1525, 1527–28, echoes of the Peasants War in other parts of Germania. A university was established by Liegnitz (1526), in principle open to professors and students of Lutheran, Zwinglian, and Schwenckfeldian-Crautwaldian persuasion.

This third persuasion was based on what were received as personal revelations (*Heimsuchungen*) by both Crautwald and by Schwenckfeld (1519, 1525, 1527) that resulted in their advocacy of the suspension (*Stillstand*) of both baptism and the Eucharist until their conventicles of prayer and study for both children and adults were readied in the spirit for the sacraments with the proper discernment of the inner versus the outer, the divine versus the human, *veritas* versus *imago.* This interim measure turned out to be a distinctive trait of Schwenckfeldian prayer and study meetings and then as a sect in Silesia, perhaps in the halls of the *szlachta* (cf. the disparaging reference to Schwenckfeldians in RD 6), and in South Germany after 1529.

Schwenckfeld and Crautwald espoused the *via regia* in the modalities of reformation for which there was the supportive text 1 Thess 5:21, "Prove all things, hold fast to that which is good"; and Schwenckfeld allowed himself to be identified early (an auditor at several universities but without a final degree) as "God-instructed," θεοδίδακτος (a *hapax legomenon*) of 1 Thess 4:9l e.g., in his authorized German translation of a letter of Crautwald to him of 1525, *Corpus Schwenckfeldianorum* 2:195; cf. Schwenckfeld's own *The Difference between Scripturalists* (schrifftgelerten) *and Spiritualists* (gotsgelerten), 1530; CS 4, Doc. XXI, which brings out the contrast observed by him in the short-lived University of Liegnitz between two views of Christian formation. Schwenckfeld did not regard the university-trained scholar, like his friend Crautwald (*der hoch erleuchtete gelehrte Theologus*), as inaccessible to direct divine instiruction (*Heimsuchung*). Schwenckfeldian Spiritualism or Spiritualizing Evangelicalism tended to be specifically Christocentric and not especially linked to the operation of the Holy Spirit. His Christology was, moreover, condemned by Lutherans and the Reformed as Eutychian, and indeed, like Servetus and Menno Simons, Schwenckfeld held to a doctrine of the celestial (actually: glorified) flesh of Christ.

By 1526 the Silesian estates had accepted Ferdinand, king of Bohemia and of Hungary, as overlord, who promptly strove to suppress the Reformation in Silesia centered in Liegnitz. Frederick III's *Apologia* for the defense of the Reformation in Silesia was drafted by Schwenckfeld, *Corpus Schwenckfeldianorum* 18:11 – 23. Then followed the dual *Protest,* his second *Apologia,* and his *Answer* to the royal mandate of 1 August 1528, which had decreed the extirpation of all Evangelical teaching in Silesia—all these, too, composed by Schwenckfeld, who by this time was engaged in colloquy with the Anabaptists and notably with the Sabbatarian Anabaptist, Oswald Glaidt, in Liegnitz, 1528. After his drafting of the *Defense* for Frederick III, 1529, Schwenckfeld left his homeland for Strassburg (and for good), lest his distinctive convictions imperil the consolidation of Protestantism in Silesia.

Horst Weigelt has placed Schwenckfeld in his Silesian setting between Lutheranism (the city of Breslau firmly Lutheran by 1536, over against its bishop) and Anabaptism of both Spiritualizing and Sabbatarian thrusts with these developments preceded and accompanied by the uprising of the peasants in Evangelical fervor which turned back some of the lords at first prone to the Reformation. Weigelt also fully develops the character and influence of Crautwald, *Spiritualistische Tradition in Protestantisumus: Die Geschichte des Schwenckfeldertums in Schlesien* (Berlin, 1973). R. Emmet McLaughlin has freshly located Schwenckfeld in the Silesian Reformation, his role there from 1520 to 1529 decisive, and carried the biography to 1540, *Caspar Schwenckfeld: Reluctant Radical* (New Haven/London: Yale University Press, 1986).

The counter-measures of King Ferdinand were implemented through his viceregent, the bishop of Breslau *ex officio,* Balthasar of Promnitz (1539 – 62) and his successors, guided by the bishop of Vienna, John Faber (1530 – 41), and his successors.

It was through Silesia under the Bohemian (Hapsburg) Crown that the exiled Czech Brethren passed after 1548 to settle as refugees in Ducal Prussia and finally in large numbers in Great Poland, moving their press from Kralice to Leszno.

From Silesia, and particularly Upper Silesia, for which Cracow was an economic and cultural center, came several Silesians who became leaders particularly in the Minor Church in Little Poland. All three leaders here featured, despite the absence of portraits, were also drawn at one time to the communitarian Hutterites in Moravia. More on Silesia is recounted in the annotation to the *Testamentum* (RD3) of George Schomann, who began his studies in Breslau.

The most distinctive Anabaptists in Silesia were the followers of the former Nuremberg furrier, Gabriel Ascherham (d. 1545), the Gabrielites, who formed communities in or near Glogau, Breslau, and Glatz on the Neisse. Although Ascherham at the start seems to have been influenced by Hans Denck and Ambrosius Spittelmayer, on baptism he may have been unique among German Anabaptists in practicing immersion. Since the history of Anabaptism in Silesia remains to be written, the account for one town, Habelschwerdt on the Neisse in the county of Glatz, may be taken as possibly representative of relations among Catholics, Anabaptists, and Schwenckfeldians in parts of Silesia. According to records assembled from a Catholic parish archive (Ullendorf), the Anabaptists settled in Habelschwerdt in 1533 and, without being so designated in the Catholic sources, must have been Gabrielites. By 1545 the parish priest had so far lost his flock that he left town and the church key with the town council. After a year under lock, a few Schwenckfeldians in town obtained the use of the edifice for Sunday afternoon preaching by a neighboring Schwenckfeldian pastor, Michael Arnsdorf. He may indeed be the source of the following description of the presumed Gabrielites, who did not dispute his possession of the parish church: "They [the Gabrielites] held their meetings in town houses, offered their common prayers, and chose preachers and teachers from among themselves to expound Scripture according to their understanding. The [rivers] Niesse and Weistritz [flowing east into the Neisse near Glatz] were the great and general baptismal bath (*Taufbad*) in which adults were immersed (*getaucht*) to become initiated (*eingeweiht*) as members of their covenant (*Bund*)." Aloys Bach, drawing on the parish archive of Josef Kögler, *Urkundliche Kirchen-Geschichte der Grafschaft Glaz, von der Urzeit bis auf unsere Tage* (Breslau: Gustav Fritz, 1841) 106 – 7.

This local date does not, to be sure, square with the general history of the Gabrielites, for in 1528 (date of Crautwald's observations above) Ascherham led his group to Moravia, settling on an estate near Rosice (Rossitz) and joined colonists under Philip Plener from Swabia, Hesse, and the Palatinate. After a loose confederation of these two groupings and Tryolese Anabaptists, the three groupings, centered at Hustopeče (Auspitz), elected Ascherham *Vorsteher*, but because he held to a different implementation of the apostolic *communio bonorum,* there came a *Zerspalting* among the three, 1533 – 38, and the strict communitarians remained under Jakob Hutter as Hutterites (*Geschicht-Buch/Chronicle,* 195 – 200/179 – 81; 233 – 38), during which separating, most of the Philippites returned to Southwest Germany, while most of the Gabrielites returned to their seats in Silesia, some entered Poland, others reached Ducal Prussia. Ascherham became something of a Spiritualist and circulated among his companies a book, *Von Unterschied göttlicher und menschlicher Weisheit* (1544), *inter alia* on baptism, from which a certain follower quoted when he was in 1545 accepted among the Hutterites: "If anyone asks me [Gabriel] whether pedobaptism is wrong, I will say no. If he wants to know the reason, I say there is none," although until the reason be known, Gabriel still held that it should be discontinued because of misuse. (The *Chronicle* is quoted here because it may have been in the background of the baptismal debate at the Synod of Węgrów, 1565.) This relative indifference to baptism placed Gabriel Ascherham, back in Silesia, close to the Schwenckfelders.

In the year of his death, 1545 as it happens, the parish priest of Habelschwerdt had so far lost his flock that he left town and the church key with the town council. After a year under lock, a few Schwenckfelders in town obtained the use of the edifice for Sunday afternoon preaching by a neighboring Schwenckfeldian pastor, one Michael Arnsdorf. He may indeed be the source of the following description of the presumed Gabrielites, who did not dispute his possession of the parish church: "They [the Gabrielites] held their meetings in town houses, offered their common prayers, and chose preachers and teachers from among themselves to expound Scripture according to their understanding. The [rivers] Niesse and Weistritz [flowing east into the Neisse near Glatz] were the great and general baptismal bath (*Taufbad*) in which adults were immersed (*getaucht*) to become initiated (*eingeweiht*) as members of their covenant (*Bund*).'' Aloys Bach, drawing on the parish archive of Josef Kögler, *Urkundliche Kirchen-Geschichte der Grafschaft Glaz, von der Urzeit bis auf unsere Tage* (Breslau: Gustav Fritz, 1841) 106 f.

32. THE UNION OF LUBLIN 1569

32.A. Painting by Jan Matejko, 1869; Lublin, Muzeum na Zamku; photograph by Jan Urbanowicz.

By a special act of 4 July 1569 Sigismund II Augustus proclaimed the Union of Lublin. For the tercentenary celebration thereof Jan Matejko pictured the event imaginatively in the spirit of hopeful conservatives of Hapsburg Galicia, which then stretched from Cracow well beyond Lwów; and, while historically tendentious, the painting brings together major figures with as much accuracy as was possible in 1869.

As of 1569, the Upper House of the Sejm, the Senate, consisted of 15 bishops, 55 Catholic and 58 Protestant lords, and two Orthodox princes (Janus and Constantine Ostrogski).

The artist has placed some figures in the chamber of the town hall who were not even living then or who had not participated in order for the artist to give a general sense of the age, when Ivan IV the Terrible was threatening the Commonwealth from the East and when Sigismund II, Grand Duke and the last Jagiellonian King of Poland being without heir, implemented the grand design of unifying ''The Two Peoples.'' By the not wholly spontaneous Union, he brought palatinates of the Grand Duchy of Lithuania under the Polish Crown directly: Volhynia, Bracław, and Kiev, also Podlachia. The Diet of the Duchy and Poland became one. The truncated Duchy retained, however, its own central administration, army, treasury, and its judicial tribunal at Nowogródek. It was foreseen that the common capital would move to Warsaw and that the Orthodox Church would have the same rights as the Catholic, while the admittance of the Duke of Prussia to the Senate and of deputies from Lutheranized Ducal Prussia to the Lower House would further the rights of Protestants in the Commonwealth in general.

Besides the central figure of the King with the crucifix, notable among Protestants in the scene are Duke Albert (cf. Pl. 7), right arm raised in the window at the upper left; below him, by one, Calvinist John Firley, in his arm the high rod of his office as marshal of the Crown; while next, above, the seated Stanislas Cardinal Hosius of Varmia (cf. Pl. 49), is the large confiding head of Lukas III Górka, leader of the Lutherans of Great Poland (cf. Pl. 34). Next to him is Prince Constantine Basil Ostrogski in ermine (cf. Pl. 53), renowned for the Cyrillic Bible (Pl. 54) soon to be printed at his principal seat, Ostrog, Volhynia, destined to be a major opponent of the Union of Brest Litvosk (Pl. 53). Behind (and above) Ostrogski is Albert Łaski (cf. Pl. 38), turned slightly toward a Myszkowski (cf. Pl. 8), as though the two were exchanging a word while looking out toward the main action.

To make Calvinism even more conspicuously present, Matejko has anachronistically introduced John Łaski into the picture as tenderly supporting the Bishop of Vilna, Valerian Protaszewicz, while Calvinist Prince Nicholas Radziwiłł the Red, kneeling in the foreground, is also made prominent.

Next, the Grand Hetman of the Crown, Nicholas Milecki, with sword to the floor, is Calvinist Marcin Zborowski (d. 1565), castellan of Cracow, who is given the posthumous distinction of holding the Act of Union of Poland and Lithuania (roughly parallel in the composition with the Hetman's sword). The artist has placed Primate Jacob Uchański behind (and above) him pointing to an important place in the Statutes. Behind the Primate is Bishop Philip Padniewski of Cracow (cf. Pl. 5) reading aloud a related document.

At the right is the large and benign (idealized) figure of the publicist for the equality of all classes before the law, Frycz Modrzewski (Pl. 22), drawn forward by the hand of a representative youthful peasant whose juridical rights he had defended

Standing and looking to the future is the truly last of the Jagiellonians, Anna, the King's sister, destined to marry elected King Stephen Batory.

Every figure in the painting is identifiable, including a few more Protestants who are disproportionately represented. Of the latter, note may be taken of Czech Brother Raphael Leszczyński (d. 1572, whose face is partly covered by Bishop Padniewski), the grandfather of his namesake (d. 1636), shown in Pl. 19. Martin Kromer, the historian and bishop of Varmia is the figure with the skull cap above Hosius (who replaced him) and to the back of Górka. The portrait is based upon an extant likeness.

By the Act of Union the eastern palatinates were opened up even more invitingly for colonization by Polish lords; and already Polish had become the manorial and literary medium in Lithuania itself, where, however, Ruthenian remained official in the palatinate chanceries and competed with Old Slavonic in the Orthodox parishes and monasteries. Within 69 years Kisielin in Volhynia would become the intellectual center of the Polish Brethren.

33. LUBLIN, REFORMED CENTER WITH TWO CHURCHES

33.A. One Reformed church was on the site of the Jesuit Church of John the Baptist (the present cathedral). Lublin was the venue of the Diet of Union between the Crown and the Duchy, seat also of the Tribunal for Little Poland and Crown Ruthenia. Braun, *Civitates orbis terrarum;* by permission of Houghton Library, Harvard University.

The colored print of Lublin was wrought by Franz Hogenberg soon after the completion of the central feature of the skyline, the Jesuit Church of St. John the Baptist, begun in 1580 on a site where the Reformed congregation once met. The edifice was subsequently reconsecrated when Lublin became an episcopal see in 1805 and it was rededicated as the cathedral of SS. Peter and Paul.

The seat of the castellan of Lublin was the castle (18). To the northeast of his castle in the panorama may be seen the Ruthenian Church of the Transfiguration (19), then the Byzantine-rite Church of St. Nicholas, wooden, reconstructed of brick and stone in 1607, and then the Chapel of Holy Trinity from the mid-fourteenth century with interior polychromy in the Ruthenian style as commissioned by King Ladislas Jagiełło and completed for the Feast of the Assumption of Mary, 15 August 1418. The burning of the steeple of this Chapel is mentioned by Lubieniecki. (In the picture occasioned by the great fire of 1719, reproduced in *PB,* p. 170, the castle complex with this Chapel is at the left.) The river in the foreground, the Bystrzyca, flows northeast of the castle complex into the Wieprz, which north of Lublin flows west into the Vistula.

Entry from the castle complex into the walled town was through the still extant Brama Grodzka (14), which corresponds in the east-west axis of the town, to the still extant Brama Krakowska indicated on the skyline of the panorama as *Porta.*

Within the medieval walled town may be seen from east to west (right to left) the cloister of the Dominicans and their Church of St. Stanislas (13) and then the oldest church edifice within the walls (no longer extant), the Collegiate Church of St. Michael

(11), some of whose clerics were *ex officiis* canons of the cathedral in Cracow, and where the Evangelical Catholic Thomas Falconius was once preacher. Westward of the complex of the Church of John the Baptist (the present cathedral, no no.) and the college of the Jesuits (10) is the Tribunal of Lublin (12, *Praetorium*), established as a judicial institution by Stephen Batory, the appellate court. It was the counterpart for Little Poland and the Ukraine of the Tribunal of Piotrków for Great Poland. The edifice shown was originally the Town Hall (*Ratusz*) in which convened the Diet of Lublin in 1569 that agreed to the Union of Lublin (Pl. 32), the constitutional merger of the Grand Duchy of Lithuania with the Crown and the incorporation of several Lithuanian palatinates as directly under the Crown (see Map). In 1579 the Town Hall was remodeled to serve its new function as the seat of the appellate justice for Little Poland and for the new palatinates annexed from Lithuania. (The façade of the present *Ratusz-Trybunał* dates from the end of the eighteenth century. A new *Ratusz* was built on the *Rynek*, distinct from the present *Nowy Ratusz* built in 1827 on the ruins of a Carmelite church outside the walls between 8 and *Porta*.)

Outside the walled city from the Brama Krakowska westward along Krakowskie Przedmieście is the small three-towered edifice, the chapel of the Hospital (9), and beyond it the Church of the Holy Spirit (8), still extant, belonging then to the Convent of the Discalced Carmelites. The same Carmelite Church can be seen clearly from another angle in the picture of the great fire of 1719 (*PB*, p. 170). Near 8 was the Minor Church. Further west are the Church of St. Paul and the Church of the Blessed Mary. To the left (1) is the Church of the Holy Cross of the Dominican Observantines from the fifteenth century, rebuilt in 1617, now serving as the chapel of the Catholic University of Lublin.

Lublin was the scene of several noteworthy theological debates between Protestants and Catholics, 1596–1636, mostly if not always in Catholic edifices, during a period when the Reformed tradition was represented by two congregations, Calvinist and Unitarian. Of these disputations perhaps most notable were in the Tribunal in 1570 between John Niemojewski and Canon Jerome Powodwski of Poznań; in the meeting house of the Polish Brethren in 1596 with the chancellor of George Cardinal Radziwiłł, bishop of Cracow, debating Martin Czechowic and Stanislas Lubieniecki's grandfather and great uncle (Stanislas and Andrew); in the Jesuit Church in the presence of the deputies of the Tribunal in 1615, between the rector of the Jesuit College, Nicholas Łęczycki, S.J., and John Stoiński, the local Unitarian minister; in the Dominican Church of St. Stanislas in 1616 under the moderatorship of the marshal of the Tribunal and the chief magistrate (*starosta*) of Lublin between the same minister Stoiński and Father Valerian Grocholski on the Trinity; in 1616 twice and again in 1620, in the Church of the Holy Spirit of the Discalced Carmelites, between their prior, Giovanni Maria from Italy, and Stoiński, on the divinity of Christ and his remission of sins; and finally in the Jesuit Church in 1636 between the major publicist, professor, and preacher to the Tribunal, Caspar Drużbicki, S.J. (Pl. 50), and the successor of Stoiński, Christopher Lubieniecki, father of our Historian. From the high pulpit of the Church of the Holy Spirit at noon on Ash Wednesday, 7 March 1973, I brought a message as sometime Protestant Observer at Vatican II, at the invitation of the rector, whose sense of history in that place informed and sustained his most generous ecumenical gesture.

34. SANDOMIERZ 1570

34.A. Sandomierz on the Vistula flowing east (to the right) site (D) of the Synod and Consensus of 1570 (E). Braun, *Civitates urbis terrarum;* by permission of Houghton

Library, Harvard University. The identifications by the original draughtsman have been corrected by Wojciech Kalinowski, Tadeusz Przypowski, et al., *Sandomierz* (Warsaw, 1956), p. 38 (and cf. their reproduction of the seventeenth-century copperprint of Dahlberg/Pufendorf, pp. 42, 51).

At the left is (1) St. Paul's; then (2) the brick Romanesque church of St. James; then, unnumbered, a single tower of the palace of the palatine; within the walls (3), the church of the Holy Spirit; then, unnumbered, the castle of the palatine, along the road leading through the Cracow Gate to the river; then behind these precincts (6) the Collegiate Church of the Virgin (from the fourteenth century, with Ruthenian frescoes, since 1918, the cathedral church); behind it (7), St. Peter's; and, between 6-7, the still extant house (1476) of John Długosz (1415–80), canon of Cracow in the Collegiate Church, father of Polish historiography, who established the late Gothic residence for missionary priests. Further down on the bank (not within view) is the huge Gostomianum, the Jesuit College, begun in 1564, the year when the Diet of Piotrków formally received the decrees of Trent and Jesuits came into the Commonwealth at the invitation of Cardinal Hosius. This was the confrontational context of the Synod and Consensus of Sandomierz, called to form a united pan-Protestant front to resist the Counter-Reform and also to free Protestantism of the baleful reputation of the Minor Churches of Poland and Lithuania, referred to in their text as "Sacramentarians, Tritheists, Ebionites, Samosatenians, Arians, Anabaptists" (255, 295).

34.B. Sepulchral monument in black, marble, Kórnik; Jan Skuratowicz, *Z badań nad rzeźb nagrobną w Polsce: Nagrobki . . . Gorków w Kórniku,* by Jan Białostocki et al. (Warsaw, PAN, 1976) p., 479.

Lukas III Górka (c. 1533–73), son of Andrew I, palatine of Poznań, spokesman of the Lutherans of Great Poland, was prominent at Sandomierz, as earlier at the Union of Lublin. He is pictured in Pl. 32.

34.C. Stanislas Myszkowski (d. 1570), castellan of Sandomierz. Jerzy Z. Łoziński, *Grobowe Kaplice.*

Stanislas Myszkowski (d. 1570), castellan of Sandomierz and palatine of Cracow, was brother of the later Bishop Peter Myszkowski of Cracow. At the Reformed synod, Peter Zborowski, palatine of Sandomierz, and Stanislas Iwan of Aleksandrowice were the two elected *directores.* Among the Reformed ministers prominent were Stanislas Sarnicki as superintendent and Jacob Sylvius of Secemin, superintendent of the Sandomierz district.

34.D. Home of Zbigniew Oleśnicki, where the Synod convened. Kalinowski, *Sandomierz,* p. 146, with the identification of the house as the site of the Synod, p. 43.

The local tradition places the meetings and the synod of Sandomierz, 9–14 April 1570, in the home of Zbigniew Oleśnicki, as well as in the no longer extant Reformed church there. In meeting in Poznań in 1567, Lutherans and Czech Brethren had already come to an agreement; in Vilna in March 1570, likewise the Lutherans and Reformed. In Sandomierz the Lutherans were headed theologically by Erasmus Gliczner, the Czech Brethren by Bishop George Israel. The joint synod of the three confessions took place 11 April. Czech Brother John Rokyta signed the Consensus after his return from Moscow (Pl. 19).

34.E. The Consensus of Sandomierz (Cracow, 1570). Edition of Cracow, 1574, from the Library of the Evangelical Synod; preserved in the Mokslinė Biblioteka, Vilnius. The scriptural motto is Rom 10:10: "For man believes with his heart and so is justified, and he confesses with his lips and so is saved."

The *Confession/Profession of the Common Faith of the Polish Christian Churches According to the Apostolic Tradition and the Venerable Fathers* (Matthew Wirzbięta, printer to His Majesty the King printed this [Cracow], 1570) continues in the subtitle with the assertion that the Confession is in accord with what Christian Protestant people hold almost everywhere in the German Empire, in Switzerland, England, France, Scotland, Bohemia, Hungary, the Netherlands, and in all parts of the world, printed to make known "that we hold a not new and a not erroneous faith but to the primitive, Catholic, and apostolic faith." Politically the *Consensus* remained successful, notably for the common front in the provisions of the Warsaw Confederation of 1573, but the provision for federative synods only occasionally materialized.

The text was printed with the acts of the general synod of 1573, 1578, 1583, and 1595 as *Consensus mutuus in fide et religione christiana inter ecclesias evangelicas majoris et minoris Poloniae, Magni Ducatus Lithuaniae primo Sendomirae anno 1570 sancitus* (Heidelberg, 1605). The *Consensus* in translation is printed by Edmund de Schweinitz, *The History of the Unitas Fratrum* (2d ed.; Bethlehem, Pennsylvania, 1901) 354–57. Lubieniecki lets the synod and *Consensus* pass by unnoticed.

The pre-history of the *Consensus* remains to be noted. Alarmed by the emergence of Antitrinitarians in the Reformed synods, Christopher Trecy, spokesman of the conserving Calvinists, urged at the Diet of Parczów that the foreign-born among the heretics be exiled. Some Catholic lords and bishops wanted all Protestants exiled. Cardinal Hosius (Pl. 49) stood out against the proscription of Antitrinitarians alone, lest all the other Protestants seem to be exonerated; and he preferred a full range of doctrinal quarrels as better for the Church. The ensuing Edict of Parczów of 1 August 1564 banished all foreign apostates from the Catholic Church. The Edict presented a particular problem for the Czech Brethren in Great Poland. Their noble patrons persuaded Sigismund to exempt their Bohemian-born members from the decree and to this end presented in Polish translation their *Confessio Bohemica* (Leitomischl, 1535), in which they had renounced their rebaptism of Utraquists and Catholics. It was this *Confessio*, the *Augsburg Confession* (1530), and the II *Helvetic Confession* (1566) that were agreed upon at Sandomierz as having equal status in the confederation and as the basis for intercommunion, constituting thereby an acknowledged model for the later Union of the Reformed and the Lutherans in the kingdom of Prussia in 1817.

It is noteworthy that the Reformed let go of their own distinctively Polish Reformed *Confessio* of Pińczów, 10 August 1559, presided over by John Łaski and which was built up around the *Triplex munus Christi*.

35. CONSTITUTIONAL RELIGIOUS LIBERTY (1572–74) I

35.B. The St. Bartholomew's Day Massacre, 23–24 August 1572, Admiral Coligny slain in the faubourg St. Germain. The picture was made by François Dubois (1529–84), who survived the Massacre, taking refuge in Geneva. The picture is in the Musée Arland, Lausanne. It is reproduced from Philippe Erlanger, *Le massacre de la Saint-Barthélemy* (Paris, 1960).

Handbills with pictures like this were circulated in Poland in resistance to the party in favor of Henry, son of Catherine de Medici. A detail from this picture was chosen by Professor Antonio Alatorre for the dustjacket of his admirable translation of my *La reforma radical* (Mexico City/Madrid, 1983). The Huguenots under Admiral Gaspard de Coligny who fell victim to the evil design of Catherine and the Guises were not embraced in my conceptualization of "the Radical Reformation," although Professor Alatorre may have thought they should have been. It is true that initially the nobles and burghers in the Polish-Lithuanian Commonwealth were not economically and socially markedly different from their counterparts in France who espoused Calvinism, but in the Commonwealth there was much greater constitutional local autonomy, hence the preponderance there of congregations gathered in villages and small towns and hence, too, greater exposure to Unitas, Anabaptist, and Italianate reform impulses from peasants and intellecutals alike in a society where the King was not absolute even though, as in France, he was a liturgically anointed monarch. The picture is used here, in any case, to make vivid the problem faced by the Henrician candidacy for *all* Poles, regardless of confession (*dissidentes de religione*), and also to suggest a link between my earlier conceptualization of a Radical Reformation and its now more fully attested extension into the three eastern realms in the radicalized theology and social practice evident in the Commonwealth and Transylvania. In my edition and annotation quite a bit more is brought out than by Lubieniecki. Hence, also, my inclusion of supplementary texts in the Appendix of Related Documents.

The nobility of France, Catholic and Huguenot, had converged on Paris for the nuptials in Notre Dame of Catherine de Medici's daughter, Margaret of Valois, to Henry III Bourbon King of Navarre (the future Henry IV). Admiral Coligny was wounded in the right arm in an assassination attempt, 22 August 1572. He was recuperating in the second storey of l'Hôtel de Ponthieu in the Faubourg Saint Germain shown by Dubois. On the 23rd the Court headed by King Charles, Catherine, and Henry (the future king of Poland) paid a visit on Coligny, and Charles seemed to have been sincere in promising to redress the wrong. But another plan was being implemented. A prearranged tocsin was sounded from Saint Germain-l'Auxerrois between two and three in the morning of the 24th. And Henri Duc de Guise, avenging his father killed in the Third Religious War, led a detachment to the house of Coligny, around which most of the other Huguenot guests at the nuptials had been domiciled. After his men ascended for the murder and thrown Coligny's body to the street, de Guise struck with his foot the face of the slain Admiral and looked on as the body was slowly cut to pieces. Between 5,000 and 10,000 Huguenots were thereupon slaughtered, caught by surprise in Paris and other centers. In Paris the mostly naked bodies, thrown from their beds into the streets, were carted to the Seine for disposal.

35.C. Act of the Confederation of Warsaw, 28 January 1573, guaranteeing, under any elected King, religious liberty for all *dissidentes de religione*, one bishop (Cracow) a signatory. Taken from the Confederation, which appeared in Polish, Ruthenian, German, and French.

A Convocation Diet convened in Warsaw, 6–28 January 1573, under Primate Jacob Uchański (Pl. 6) as Interrex. The Protestant party was headed by the Grand Marshal of the Crown, John Firley. The Confederation of Warsaw, made up of Catholic and Protestant lords and Bishop Krasiński (Pl. 5), secured the principle in points agreed upon (*pacta conventa*) of constitutional religious liberty for all dissenting in matters of religion (*dissidentes de religione*). The seals of the signatories attached to the Act of Warsaw are shown as preserved in the Museum Narodowe, Warsaw. The Election Diet took place on the field of Kamień outside Warsaw, 5 April–20 May 1573.

The key paragraphs are as follows:

> We Crown Councilors, spiritual and temporal, and the whole knighthood, and the different estates of the one and indivisible Commonwealth out of Great and Little Poland, the Grand Duchy of Lithuania, of Kiev, of Volhynia, of Podlachia, the Land

of Ruthenia, of Prussia, Pomerania, Samogitia, Courland, and the royal boroughs, announce to all whom it concerns *as a perpetual reminder of the matter* that in this perilous time, dwelling without the sovereign Lord and King, we shall exert ourselves so that all at the Diet in Warsaw, following the example of our forebears, achieve and maintain among ourselves the peace, order, and defense of the Commonwealth. . . .

And given that in our Commonwealth there is no small disagreement *in the matter of the Christian religion,* seeing to it that for this cause no such disastrous sedition be unleashed among people as we see clearly in other kingdoms, we promise this mutually *for ourselves and for our successors in perpetuity under the obligation of an oath, by our faith, honor, and our consciences,* that we who are *dissidentes de religione* will keep the peace among ourselves, will not shed blood for a different faith and change in Churches, nor interfere with each other by the confiscation of goods, the dignity [of office], by imprisonment and exile, nor lend our assistance to any superior or office for such an action.

Cf. Lubieniecki's interpretation of the Confederation in Poland, *PB*, Doc. XXIX. The religious toleration secured by the Confederation may be seen as an extension of the *jus patronatus* and the feudal/canonical immunity of every house or castle to the new congregations gathered on estates in new edifices or refurbished older ones, and expressly claimed by every knight and extended to the "different estates," which implied burghers, although only three towns were represented in the Chamber of Deputies and yet it expressly included royal boroughs.

35.D. The IV Henrician Articles, supplementary to the provisions of the Confederation, extracted from Henry's representative, Bishop Monluc, 4 May 1573. Taken from Henryck, Paszkiewicz, *Polska i jej dorobek dziejowy* I (London, 1956).

The representatives in Warsaw of Henry of Valois, Bishop John Monluc, O.P., of Valence who had once attended the Colloquy of Poissy, agreed, 4 May 1573, to four additional so-called Henrician Articles as the condition of Henry's being elected, which committed Henry to confirm toleration by oath, to pay the debts of his royal predecessor, to sustain the Baltic fleet, and (to insure ongoing compliance) to agree to having selected resident Senators advise him on how to uphold freedom of religion. In a field of seven candidates (all with their orators and negotiators like Monluc), including two Hapsburgs, the King of Sweden, a native lord (a "Piast"), the Tsarovich, and even the last of her line, Anna Jagiellonka, Henry was elected 9 May 1573. Shown is the conclusion of the Henrician Articles later signed by him in Paris as King-elect: "The pacts and agreements with the envoys of the Two Most Serene Kings [the reigning king of France, Charles IX, 1560–74, and Henry] and confirmed by the King-elect by the grace of God King of Poland, Grand Duke of Lithuania, Ruthenia, Prussia, Masovia, Samogitia, Kiev, and Volhynia."

36. CONSTITUTIONAL RELIGIOUS LIBERTY (1572–74) II

36.A Catherine de' Medici in widow's weeds receiving the twelve Polish ambassadors, headed by Albert Łaski (Pl. 38), in a festival in the Tuileries, before her son Henry formally promises to abide by the *Pacta conventa* and signs the IV Henrician Articles in Notre Dame. Drawing by Antoine Caron, reproduced by permission of the Fogg Art Museum, Harvard University.

This became the design for one of eight Valois Tapestries, designed by Lucas de Heere, a member of the House of Love, created at the request of Prince William of

Orange and presented to Catherine in 1582 by way of reminding "the Queen Mother of Europe" of her policy of religious toleration, all eight now hanging in the Corridor of the Galeria degli Uffizi in Florence and most fully described by Frances A. Yates, *The Valois Tapestries* (London: Warburg Institute, 1959). Lucas de Heere reversed the original order of Caron, who gives more prominence to the Poles left and foreground. The details that follow relate to both the design and the tapestry.

The Polish ambassadors had arrived at the gates of Paris, 9 August 1573, and been treated to a round of visitations, jousts, ballets, festivities, and tableaux. Prominent in the Valois Tapestry on the left is a dandy commonly identified as Anne Duc de Joyeuse (a favorite of Henry but of no particular significance for the main theme of the pictures). Occupying a place on the Tapestry among the Poles where one would expect to see Henry himself, he is conversing with an unidentified *nobilis Polonus* with his *żupan* of reddish cloth of gold. He, or the other Pole standing next to him, might be intended for Łaski. While most of the Polish delegation of twelve converse and point to the dancing from the foreground, one at least of their number, seems to be resting on the chair of Catherine, while still another talks with the ladies a few steps behind him. Besides being feted, the Polish envoys, the Catholics among them no less than the Protestants, made a number of demands upon the French court in concern for the persecuted Huguenots, for example, the restoration of property to the survivors of the Massacre. At the ceremony in Notre Dame, 10 September 1573, when ceremonially informed by the envoys of his election, Henry formally promised to abide by the *Pacta conventa* and signed the "Henrician Articles."

The motivation and context of the gift of tapestries by the Father of the Netherlands to Catherine are set forth by Jan van Goudoever, "William of Orange in a Utopian Light," *Antitrinitarianism,* ed. by Dán and Pirnát, pp. 65–67, with an inserted plate of a detail from our Tapestry, which features Catherine and the three couples dancing in front of the ornamental Rock of the musicians. The beautiful border of the Tapestry has been cropped to permit more detail of the Tuileries scene to be seen, as some of the faces are demonstrable portraits; and de Heere was interested in accuracy in habiliments. Not all of the Poles have kept their hair severely razored to the crest, though their headgear obscures the degree to which they have yielded temporarily to French fashion.

36.B. Walter L. Strauss, *German Woodcuts,* 3, Appendix B. The woodcut of "the Most Christian King of France and Poland" was made in Venice when Henry was in flight from Poland, at age 24, 1574. The poems in German and the coat of arms have been left out.

The Italian original, reproduced by Stanisław Bystroń et al., *Polska: jej dzieje i kultura* 3 (Warsaw, 1927), p. 11, shows Henry facing the other way, with a brief inscription in French and a fuller explanation in Italian of his return to France and his participation in the Fifth Civil War intensified by Henry of Navarre's resumption of the Protestant faith. Pl. 37 shows the King in flight from Cracow and as portraiture thus comes chronologically slightly after what is discussed in the commentary on this plate.

36.C. The obsequies for the long embalmed Sigismund II took place in a solemn procession from the Summer Palace down the Royal Way (Map of Cracow) to the cathedral, 4–7 February 1574. (Shown, however, is the earlier funeral *Castrum doloris* arranged for him in Rome by Cardinal Hosius.) Copperprint probably by Thomas Treter; Bystroń et al., *Polska,* 3, p. 3; Juliusz A. Chrościcki, *Pompa funebris: z dziejów kultury staropolskiej* (Warsaw, 1974), Pl. 42. There seems to be no extant representation of the actual funeral in Cracow.

nal Hosius. The print may have been one of the earliest works of his secretary. The death of the last Jagiellonian King was keenly felt in Rome and in Poland in anxiety for legitimation of an elected King. Hence the considerable delay of the funeral in the Wawel until after the safe arrival in Poland, 25 January 1574, of the King-elect. For the probable identification of the artist as Treter, see Tadeusz Chrzanowski, *Działalność artystyczna Tomasza Tretera* (Warsaw: PAN, 1984), pp. 72–73.

37. CONSTITUTIONAL RELIGIOUS LIBERTY III: CORONATION AND FLIGHT (1573–74)

37.A. The liturgical unction of a King-elect in the Wawel cathedral, c. 1510. Polish kingship was elective, even when seemingly dynastic; and until the moment of sacring the Primate as *Interrex* was bearer of Polish national sovereignty. Illumination from the Pontyfikał of Erazm Ciołek, from the Czartoryski Collection, Muzeum Narodowe, reproduced from Cracow. The scene in St. Stanislas Cathedral, c. 1510, does not depict a specific coronation though the date could mean that it portrays Primate John Łaski (1510–31) officiating, uncle of the Reformer (cf. Pl. 6). There is no extant representation of the coronation of Henry Valois. Count Valerian Krasiński, a Calvinist, describes the scene in *Historical Sketch of the Rise, Progress, and Decline of the Reformation in Poland* (2 vols.; London, 1840) 2. 34–43 (elsewhere this work is cited in its illustrated Polish translation by Juliusz Bursche (3 vols.; Warsaw, 1903–04).

Unlike the imperial dignity in the Holy Roman Empire, which did not involve anointment of the head, unlike Spanish kingship—declared by fanfare in the towns receiving the news of the death of the king and the accession of the Infanta—Polish kingship was liturgical; and as in pre-Reformation England and still in contemporary France the royal sacring was sensed to be a kind of epiphany of the glorified Christ.

The coronation of Henry took place 21 February 1574. When Primate Uchański was about to receive the crown from the Marshal of the Crown and palatine of Cracow, Calvinist John Firley, reminded the elected King that he still had to renew the oath to uphold the *pacta et conventa,* Henry paled but demurred. Sebastian Mielecki, castellan of Cracow, who *ex officio* held the crown during the solemnity, refused to pass it over to the Primate until the Elect repeated the oath he had made in Notre Dame. Tradition ascribed to Firley at this juncture: "Non jurabis, non regnabis." Henry thereupon pledged: "Pacem et tranquillitatem inter *dissidentes de religione* tuebor," repeating a phrase from the Act of Warsaw and promising that he would maintain the religious peace. Bishop Francis Krasiński of Cracow, hard by, had been the sole episcopal signatory to that Act.

The *Ordo* (out of the tradition of the kings of Hungary, including King Louis the Hungarian, 1370–82), adapted hastily for Henry and with some interspersed references to the issue of the oath, is printed by Alessandro Guagini [Gwagninus] of Verona (c. 1538–1614) in *Sarmatiae Europeae descriptio* [Cracow:] Wirzbięta, [1578]) under the heading: "Ordo qualiter serenissimus rex Poloniae iuxta veterem consuetudinem coronatur et quae solemnitas et caeromoniae circa id sint solitae," folios 52 v. 56 v. As it is not commonly recognized that the royal *Ordo* of Poland preserved or had acquired the venerable formularies of holy sacring, whereby the King-elect became sacramentally an *alius vir,* some of the *Ordo* and directives are here given in translation.

After mitred abbots and all other prelates have gathered in the cathedral church duly garbed and the nobles likewise, the bishops alone with the Primate enter in procession to the royal palace to lead "the Prince" into the cathedral church. After he has been, by the Grand Marshal of the Kingdom, dressed in sandals, tunic, gloves, alb, dalmatic, and pallium, the Primate asperges him with holy water in the midst of the peers of the realm, saying: "God, teacher of the humble, who hast consoled us with the pouring out of the Holy Spirit, extend thy grace to this thy servant Henry to the end that through him we may sense thine Advent among us." Then he is led into the cathedral by the bishops of Cracow and Kujawy, the castellan of Cracow bearing the crown; the palatine of Cracow, the scepter; the palatine of Vilna (Nicholas Radziwiłł the Red), the orb; and Andrew Zborowski, the unsheathed sword. Once the regalia received from the Senators are deposed at the altar by the Primate, and after the King-elect is seated on a throne, there ensue several prayers.

Before Henry was crowned there arose a great controversy by reason of the Confederation agreed upon by some of the Catholics and all the Evangelicals during the Interregnum. When this calmed down, the bishop of Cracow and then the Primate asked Henry solemn questions, according to old formularies; and on his knees, his head uncovered, he said: "I, Henry, God approving, the *future* King of the Poles, profess and promise before God and his angels henceforth to maintain ... law and justice and the peace of the Church of God and for the people subject to me. . . ." The words of his liturgical oath are probably traditional and not altered to suit the occasion, Henry having made the necessary concession during the foregoing tense episode reported by Guagnini. In any case, the phrasing *futurus Rex* in the traditional oath sustains the fully sacramental character of the action till the completion of the rite in the benediction, when and the anointed King severs the air with a ceremonial thrust of his royal sword. The Polish liturgical unction has been placed in its historical setting by Aleksander Gieysztor, "Spektakl i liturgia—Polska koronacja królewska," ed. by Bronisław Seremek (Wrocław, etc.: Ossolineum, 1978) 9–23; idem, "Royal Emblems and the Idea of Sovereignty in Late Medieval and Early Modern Poland," *State and Society in Europe from the Fifteenth to Eighteenth Century* (1986).

37.B. The Coronation Diet, the King surrounded by his court officials and the Senators, episcopal and temporal. From the frontispiece of Andrzej Maksymilian Fredro (d. 1679), *The Deeds of the Polish People under Henry Valois, King of the Poles, afterwards indeed of France* (Danzig, 1652), from the copy given to Harvard College Library by Count Ladislas Zamoyski, 24 May 1897.

On the day after his coronation King Henry presided over the Coronation Diet, 22 February–2 April 1574. The scene purports to be the Diet of Henry (actually that of Ladislas IV, seated in the Senate chamber in Warsaw). The grand functionaries of the Crown are on either side of the King, the two metropolitans and the other bishops with their croziers seated closer to the King on either side before the temporal peers, the *żupan* of most and the razored heads distinguishing the Poles from, say, the Duke of Prussia and a few others of Western European style. During the Diet the new nuncio, Bishop Vincent Lauro of Mondovi, sought to move the episcopal and the Catholic temporal Senators to nullify the oath to defend all *dissidentes de religione.* At issue was whether sovereignty in Poland rested with the *szlachta* or the King, whether the basis of rule rested in the Convocation and the Election Diet during the Interregnum or in the present Diet called by the King. Firley imprisoned the printer of a brochure (written anonymously by the future metropolitan of Lwów, Jan D. Solikowski), *Rozpadek,* which argued that the Warsaw Confederation of 1572 has made Henry "into a subject, a painted King." Henry wisely enjoined on both sides silence when the authorship became known, and on 22 May affirmed general assent to pacts without specificity.

37.C. The secret departure of Henry for France via Venice. This German woodcut is commonly identified as Henry on his way in a fur coat to Cracow for the coronation, but the inscription and the mien and style of travel would suggest rather his escape. In the scroll in Latin he is "Henry Valois, Duke of Anjou, by the grace of God King of Poland [and France]" (the last cropped).

Having heard of the death of Charles IX and fearing that his younger brother, the Duke of Alençon would succeed to the French throne, on what may be the original "French leave," Henry swiftly left Poland under the cover of darkness, 18–19 June 1574, to reach Paris via Venice (cf. Pl. 37). He has turned his back on the Polish Eagle, his eyes set upon his coat of arms and the Crown of France. He, en route to Venice, is accompanied by French grooms it would appear, not by the proud Polish envoys who had conducted him through the Empire and by way of Poznań to Cracow. The flight was an immense disappointment to the Poles, despite their revulsion at his French ways; and their land became the butt of European jokes, and they were sobered in preparation for the next election.

38. POLAND, HUNGARY, MOLDAVIA II:
THREE ADVENTURES IN STATECRAFT, WAR, AND THEOLOGY

38.A. John Sommer (d. 1572) of Pirna in Saxony, classicist and soldier, head of the Reformed school in Cotnari (B) under Voivode Heraclides Basilicus (Pl. 28), whose *Vita* he wrote, rector in Koloszvár, wrote the above *Refutation of Peter Károlyi* in defense of the position of Francis Dávid against Peter Méliusz (Pl. 41), published posthumously by Vehe-Glirius (Plate 43) in Cracow. Reproduced from Gryczowa, *Ariańskie oficyny wydawnicze,* Pl. 11, title-page: *Refutation of the Writing of Peter Károlyi written in Wittenberg* by John Sommer of Pirna, teacher of the School in Kolozsvár in Transylvania with the opening words of the Confession of faith of Israel, the *Shema,* Deuteronomy 6:4, "Hear, O Israel: Yahweh (the Lord) our God (*Elohim*) (is) one Yahweh (Lord)." The posthumous publication purports to be printed by Petrus Ravisius in Ingolstadt, but the Refutation was preserved and then edited by Matthias Vehe-Glirius, Francis Dávid's mentor (Pls. 40, 44), after his escape from Kolozsvár in 1579 and printed in Cracow by Alexy Rodecki.

The *Scriptum* opposed in this posthumous *Refutatio* was that of an ally of Méliusz against Dávid (Pl. 41), *Brevis explicatio orthodoxae fidei de uno vero Deo, Patre, Filio et Spiritu Sancto* (Wittenberg, 1571), which had been directed against both Biandrata and Dávid, among other items, their *De falsa et vera cognitione* (1568; Pl. 18). Lubieniecki copied out the whole of Sommer's *Eight Theses concerning the Trine Papal God* (1571), *Historia, 234ff.* Sommer's *Vita* of Voivode Heraclides (one of two major sources) was posthumously published in Wittenberg, 1587. On his way back from a visit to his mother, Sommer encountered Adam Neuser (Pl. 44) in Poland and in his company returned to Kolozsvár.

38.B. The ruined Latin-rite cathedral in Cotnari (and the modern parish church) in Moldavia, where under Voivode Heraclides, placed on the throne through the military campaign of Albert Łaski (E), the Polish Reformed minister John Lusiński became superintendent and where the Schola Latina, open to the sons of boyars and peasants alike, was established and headed by Sommer. A snapshot by Father Anton Bişoc, Catholic priest in the parish church shown in the picture, and by the courtesy of the town council of Cotnari, who forwarded to him my request.

The original Gothic cathedral was built under the influence of the Catholic mission from the Apostolic Kingdom of Hungary in the voivodeship of Moldavia near Jassy. It was made the see of the Reformed Church in Moldavia under John Lusiński (Łużyński), a pastor in Iwanowice. Lismanino (Pl. 16), attracted by the vision of a fellow Italianate Greek voivode, had completed plans to go to Cotnari, when he learned of the uprising against the voivode and of the slaying of Superintendent Lusiński and his wife in 1563. The edifice had presumably fallen into ruin after the assassination of the Voivode Heraclides Basilicos (Pl. 28); and it burned in 1873.

In the summer of 1985 in the area in and around the ruins, excavations were begun to uncover the remains of the Schola Latina, sponsored by Heraclides and placed under the direction of Sommer. The sons of boyars and of peasants and townsmen who showed promise were educated side by side in Greek and Latin. Sommer went from this school to be teacher or possibly rector in the academy of Kolozsvár, invited there evidently by Dr. Biandrata. He wrote in Cotnari a long elegiac poem on the Kings of Hungary.

38.C. Andrew Sbardellati Dudith, one of two Hungarian bishops at Trent, Hapsburg diplomat, sponsor of the Polish Brethren in Śmigiel (D) represented herein. "The Great Andreas Dudith," a print made from a painting once in the Elizabeth Library in the town hall of Breslau/Wrocław; the original painting is shown by Costil, *André Dudith,* frontispiece.

Andrew Sbardellati Dudith (1533–89), humanist scholar and prelate, correspondent of Socinus, became sympathetic with the position of the Polish Brethren. Secretary to the Legate Reginald Cardinal Pole, Dudith was made titular bishop (1571–63) of Tina, an island under Ottoman control, and was elected at a provincial synod to be one of the two spokesmen of the Hungarian hierarchy at the Council of Trent. He was later briefly bishop of Csanád and then Pécs (1563–65). Two of his interventions are printed together (Venice, 1562), Houghton Library, Harvard University. Fluent in written and spoken Greek, he translated from the Italian *The Life* of Reginald Pole by Ludovico Beccadelli, archbishop of Ragusa (Venice, 1563). He married a young lady of the Court in Cracow and settled in Śmigiel as patron of the Polish Brethren there and their school.

38.D. Śmigiel (Schmiegel) on the Silesian border in Great Poland, a major Unitarian church and community protected by widowed Lady Dudicza. Śmigiel, c. 1741, in Great Poland; reproduced from the frontispiece of Martin Adelt, *Historia de Arianismo olim Smiglam infestanto oder historische Nachricht . . . nebst einer Kirchen-Historie der Stadt Schmiegel* (Danzig, 1741). The fuller picture shows an ominous cloud over the town; from the Przypkowski Collection in Jędrzejów.

After residing in Cracow as Hapsburg ambassador, Dudith sided with the Minor Church and became patron of the Polish Brethren of Śmigiel, of which he was owner. The first minister in the great church there was John Krotowski. Both Andrew Lubieniecki (d. 1623), author of the *Poloneutychia* (Pl. 1) and his brother Christopher (grandfather of our Historian) served there, as did Valentine Schmalz (d. 1622), rector of the school, and John Völkel (d. 1618). Christopher Ostorodt, who was a factor in the conversion of Schmalz from Lutheranism, served briefly in Śmigiel and wrote c. 1584 to the Anabaptists of Strassburg about the practice of immersion and frequent communion among the Polish Brethren.

Christina Przypkowska was the wife in Smigiel of Andrew Lubieniecki of the *Poloneutychia,* hence the presence of this picture of Śmigiel in the Przypkowski Collection. Cf. Ludwik Gomolec, *Dzieje miasta Śmigla* (Poznań, 1960) 11.

38.E. Albert Łaski (d. 1605), nephew of the Reformer (Pl. 20), whose Life in London published by Cyprian Bazylik (Pl. 15) was dedicated to Albert, organized in his birthplace (F) a military campaign among Polish protestants (like Lasocki and Filipowski) to secure Reform-minded Heraclides Basilicos on the voivodal throne of Moldavia. A sketch by Michał Elwiro Andriolli (1881) from a woodcut of 1609; reproduced from *Dariusz Poselstwa,* opp. p. 130.

Olbracht Łaski (1536 – 1605), born in Kéžmarok, although he acted against a royal interdict in his campaign for Heraclides Basilicus in Moldavia, was chosen head of the Polish envoys formally to inform Henry of Valois of his election in Notre Dame in Paris (Pl. 36). It was as palatine of Sieradz in 1566 that he became patron of the recent convert to Calvinism, Cyprian Bazylik, who published *On the Harsh Persecution* (Pl. 1), embodying in it the translation from the Latin of the Life of John Łaski by Utenhove, especially dedicated by the translator-publisher to Olbracht Łaski (Pl. 15).

38.F. Kéžmarok in Slovakia (Upper Hungary), principal town in Spisz, a congeries of towns and territories on permanent loan by Hungary to Poland, birthplace of Albert Łaski and seat of his campaign for Moldavia. A nineteenth-century copperprint from *Magyaroszág es Erdélt,* op. p. 229. The town Kéžmarok in present-day Slovakia, Késmárk in Hungarian, Kieżmark in Polish, Kesmark in German, is the principal town in Szepes/Spisz/Zips, which was on lease to the Polish Crown, 1412 – 1796. One looks over the castle where Olbracht Łaski was born to the Tatra Mountains and the Polish frontier.

39. TRANSYLVANIA I: ISABELLE JAGIELLONKA TO STEPHEN BÁTHORY

39.A. Isabelle Jagiellonka, daughter of Sigismund I (Pl. 2), widow of John I Zápolya (1526 – 40), regent in Transylvania, 1541 – 51; 1556 – 59, the first to mandate freedom of religion. An enlargement of the Cranach painting (Pl. 2). She and her heir were reluctantly in Cracow when Transylvania was temporarily reunited with Hapsburg Hungary.

39.B. (Frater) George II Martinuzzi, bishop of Várad (1534/39 – 51), Cardinal, chief minister in Alba Julia, murdered. A painting from the seventeenth century based upon an earlier likeness; reproduced from Veress, *Izabella Királyné,* between pp. 312 and 315.

39.C. John Honter (1498 – 1549), the first reformer among the Saxon Transylvanians. A likeness from the sixteenth century in the Niedersächsische Staats- und Universitäts-Bibliothek, Göttingen; reproduced from *Reformation in Europa,* 166.

Honter established a school and a printing press (c. 1533) at Kronstadt (Corona), where the Unitarian John Sommer (Pl. 38) later taught and published.

39.D. Alba Julia (Gyulfafehérvár), capital of Transylvania. A sketch by an Italian of the age; reproduced by Imre Révész, *A Magyar Reformátio Egyház törénte* (Budapest, 1949) 99.

Alba Julia (Romanian: Alba Iulia; Hungarian: Gyulafafehérvár) was founded in the ruins of the Roman imperial Apulum, on the stream Ampoiul (Keres) near its juncture on the right bank with the Mures flowing west by way of the Tisza into the Danube. There was a Byzantine mission there in the tenth century. The sketch by an Italian in the sixteenth century shows the tributary stream (4) surrounding the town with the (possibly artificial) Lake Zarghat in the background (5). The unfortified Borgo (3) was, however, protected by the common moat. The castle (Citta) of the voivode of Transylvania was, until 1540, under the Hungarian Crown. The commercial part of the town (1) is partly separated off from the interior city (2), the castle precincts with its cathedral church (present appearance in E), which seems to be the larger church edifice near (5). Presumably the voivodal/royal/princely palace is the complex of buildings with the two towers at the upper right, originally the bishop's palace, preempted by Isabelle, 1542. Here Dr. George Biandrata was court physician to Queen Isabelle and later courtly advisor to John Sigismund.

39.E. Romanesque cathedral in Alba Julia with tombs of Isabelle and her son. *Kirchen in Siebenbürgen*, p. 54.

The Catholic cathedral was founded in the twelfth century. Under Isabelle, c. 1543, its income was diverted to court use. The last resident Catholic bishop in Alba Julia (until 1721) was Paul II Bornemusza, translated to Vezsprém in 1553, the see to which John Łaski had been nominated in 1529 (Pl. 20). *Kirchen in Siebenbürgen*, 54.

39.F. John (II) Sigismund Zápolya (1559–70/71), son of John and Isabelle, nationally elected King of Hungary but never crowned. Contemporary engraving from Mihály Szilinsky, *A Magyarhoni Protestáns Egyház Törénete* (Budapest, 1907) 115. It was made before he was Prince, the encircling legend reading: "John Sigismund, son of the King of Hungary, Duke of Opole [in Silesia]."

Sympathetic with Dávid, he may be seen enthroned in Pl. 40. He renewed the acts of religious toleration of his mother. Because of his claim to the Crown of Hungary, abandoned only in 1570, he is commonly styled by his devotees "the only Unitarian King in history." A coin showing Sigismund as "king of Hungary by the grace of God" is pictured by J. Erdey, *Numi Transylvaniae* (Budapest, 1862), reproduced by Edward Darling, *400 Years* (First Unitarian Society of Minneapolis, 1968) 19.

39.G. These words, stemming from talks on religious toleration in baronial halls and at the diets in Transylvania, are reported by Węgierski, *Slavonia Reformata* 215, quoting Sarnicki, *Annales . . . Polonorum libri octo* (Cracow, 1587) 8:409; Wilbur, *Socinianism*, 385, n. 4. The occasion of the reported words was at Brodnica near Chełmno in 1577, when Stephen was on a punitive expedition against Danzig (Pl. 46), which had not accepted his election. Priests in his retinue asked him to buy up one of the Lutheran churches in Danzig and order Mass to be celebrated there. His famous words were in reply to this request. For a picture of Stephen Báthory, see Pl. 46 and for his rule, the Map of the Commonwealth and of Tripartitioned Hungary during his reign.

39.H. Statutes for Transylvania issued from Cracow by Stephen as Prince, 18 February (Hornung), 1583, in Latin and German. The title-page of *Der Sachssen inn Siebenbürgen: Statuta oder eigen Landrecht* is reproduced from Ernst Wagner, ed., *Quellen zur Geschichte der Siebenbürger Sachsen 1191–1975*, Schriften zur Landeskunde Siebenbürgens 1 (Cologne/Vienna: Böhlau, 1976) 135, with full description and the German version of the royal/princely decree of authorization, 134–37.

40. SUPERINTENDENT DÁVID PLEADING FOR FULL CONFESSIONAL TOLERATION AT THE DIET OF TORDA, 6 JANUARY 1568

Illumined by the shaft of light from the window in the parish church, the speaker's arm lifted to proclaim that "Faith is the gift of God." On the dais to the left sits Protestant Prince John Sigismund. At his feet on either side sit his voivodal successors, the brothers Stephen and Christopher Báthory.

The picture was painted by Aladár Körösföi-Kriesch on commission from the town council of Torda, when Hungary was preparing in 1896 to celebrate the millennial of the kingship of St. Stephen; reproduced with permission from the Unitarian Universalist Association, Boston. It shows the painting as recently refurbished and is brighter than that reproduced by William C. Gannett, *Francis David* (London, 1914).

Behind Stephen to the right of the Prince stands Dr. George Biandrata (cf. Pl. 18), his arms folded. At the head of the table behind Dávid is sometime tutor to the Prince, now Chancellor Michael Csáky. Next to him Caspar Helt, Reformed pastor in the Saxon church in Kolozsvár, later an adherent of Dávid's party, leafs through the Bible to verify Dávid's citation of Rom 10:17. Standing near the tall crucifix are the figures of Peter Méliusz and a Catholic priest, neither of whom was actually present at the Diet, symbolizing, however, for the artist the other religious forces embraced by the Edict of Toleration, along with the Lutherans (after the Saxons formally adopted the Augustana in 1572). Behind the priest and "Méliusz" stand the Saxon burgher estate (representatives of the *Sachsenuniversität*) are Szekler chieftains, elected to represent the communitarian Szekler estate. The three lay figures pictured in the immediate foreground have not been individually identified, but they represent the Magyar (Hungarian) nobiliary estate.

The painting memorializes the spirited appeal of the pastor of the foremost parish church (St. Michael's) in Klausenberg before the diet in nearby Torda for the enactment by the estates of a provision for confessional toleration that would sanction the right of each parish/congregation in Klausenberg and the other towns and presumably their dependent villages "to keep the preachers whose doctrine they approve." Part of the Edict of 28 January 1568 is given in English translation, along with the Hungarian text, in Alexander St. Ivanyi, *Freedom Legislation in Hungary 1557–71* (New York: Hungarian Interfaith in Brotherhood, 1957); given in shorter form by Wilbur, *Transylvania* 38 and n. 32.

The edict of 1568 extended the *jus patronatus* to knights and magnates and also the feudal/canonical right of the immunity of their town houses and nobiliary chapels now converted into village parishes such as to allow for the congregational choice of the minister. Kolozsvár (Klausenberg) was the ranking royally chartered borough among the Seven of Siebenbürgen. Here and at Torda and elsewhere the rights of conscience of burghers, artisans, eventually of Szekler yeomen in their communes were upheld as well as those of the nobiliary estates. The significance of the edict of John II Sigismund of 1568 is enhanced by the contrast between it and the mandates of his rival for the Crown of St. Stephen, the Emperor Maximilian II (cf. his mandate of 1570, Pl. 42), whose daughters hand was given in marriage by John II Sigismund in return for renunciation of the Crown of St. Stephen in 1570 (Pl. 44).

Emperor Maximilian, King of both Bohemia and (Upper) Hungary, in his comparable declarations to the second and third estates (lords and knights) of Lower Austria, 18 August 1568, and to the same two estates of Upper Austria, 7 December 1568, provided for the free exercise of Protestantism according to the Augsburg Confession in chapels and churches over which knights or lords held the *jus patronatus*, recognized in feudal and canon law, including their village parishes. In the final wording, the Assecuration signed in Prague for the hereditary lands of Austria, 14 January 1571, Walter Grossmann has admirably identified the two components in the toleration of Lutheranism (alone) on nobiliary estates: patrocinial rights over churches and nobiliary immunity from intrusion into the town house or castle of a knight or lord. He has traced further how the formulary of 1571 was expanded in Osnabrück for the Treaty of Westphalia that tolerated both Lutheranism and the Reformed confession within the war-racked Empire, 1648, making the licit private exercise of a confession a public right, "Toleration—*Exercitum religionis privatum* [evolving into *publicum*]," *Journal of the History of Ideas* 40:1 (1979) 129–34.

General histories of the rise of toleration in Europe seldom take notice of the distinctive strands woven into the later concept and practice of ecclesiastical, interecclesial irenicism and of state confessional toleration arising in Bohemia, Transylvania, and Poland (cf. Pls. 35–37). Yet in a major achievement in the comprehensive account of toleration by a professor of the Institut Catholique of Paris, Joseph Lecler, S.J., who would have had special reason to look afresh at Polish history, he does not glance at Europe beyond the Elbe and along the Danube in his monumental *Toleration and the Reformation*, 2 vols. (Paris, 1955; London: Longmans, 1960). Nor does Henry Kamen in his *The Iron Century: Social Change in Europe 1550–1600* (London: Wiedenfeld, 1971) or even in his popular monograph, *The Rise of Toleration* (New York/Toronto: McGraw-Hill, 1967). German historiography has likewise been indisposed to claim the epochal initiatives towards religious toleration of burghers in colonial Saxon towns as an integral part of the extension of German urban laws and free institutions. There seems to have been even before the Iron curtain the Vellum curtain discriminating between the privileged and the lesser areas of cosmopolitan scholarship.

41. TRANSYLVANIA III

41.A. Kolozsvár, one of the originating Seven Burgs of Siebenbürgen. Dávid was pastor to the Magyar congregation in the principal parish church, St. Michael's. Woodcut of Kolozsvár (Klausenburg/Cluj); Georg Braun and Franz Hogenberg, *Civitates orbis terrarum,* by permission of the Houghton Library, Harvard University.

St. Michael's was built by the Saxons to be as large as the Romanesque cathedral in the capital of the voivodate, and once carried over its west portal: *Templum saxonum.* In 1568, the by then relatively smaller Saxon congregation was assigned the smaller church to the north (left). The Unitarians remained in St. Michael's till 1600, recovered it from the Catholics in 1605, worshiping there until 1716. Gustav Treiber, *Mittelalterliche Kirchen in Siebenbürgen* (Schweinfurt-Sennfeld: Hilfskomitee der Siebenbürger Sachsen, 1971) 17–20.

Strolling in the foreground are two Transylvanian patrician matrons, distinguished from the noble virgin by their mantles and the feathers in their hats. The town had a printing press and an academy.

Unitarianism in Transylvania was a territorial church, participating in the general reformation of towns and cities with their whole parochial structure going over along with the subject or economically dependent villages.

41.B. An idealized modern drawing of Francis Dávid (1521–79). No likeness of Dávid survives. Among the idealizations of him in modern times are a marble bust, an idealized painting (Pl. 40), a medallion, and this most recent drawing of 1978, by Dr. Gyula László of Budapest; taken from Béla Varga, *Francis Dávid,* trans. by Velma Szantho Harrington (Budapest, 1981) 11.

41.C. Choir stall of Dávid. The seat stands in the National Museum in Budapest. The photograph was presented by Bishop Joseph Ferencz. On the back the inscription is from the eighteenth century, suggesting that it may well have come from St. Michael's (A) when that edifice reverted to the Catholics in 1716 and it was remodeled (1739–61).

The stall came to the Museum from the Unitarian village of Adamos. The crucifix and the cross mounted at either end and possibly the two coverings go back to Dávid's day. In any case he styled himself *minister Christi crucifixi.*

41.D. A hostile visualization of a concept of the Trinity as a studded ring, with Dávid and Biandrata's characterization (1567): "The monster was recently called up from hell by Peter Méliusz, a single ring adorned with three gems that it might at the same time represent exactly his Jehovah Elohim, namely, one Essence and three Persons." One of the eight images in the *De false et vera Dei cognitione* (1568; Pl. 18).

41.E. *Institutio vera* of Méliusz (Debrecen, 1571) in thirteen articles. From Studia at Acta, II, A II. *A Helvét Hitvallás Magyarországon és Méliusz életmüve* (Budapest, 1967), presented by the Rev. Dr. Andrew Harsanyi of the Hungarian Reformed Church.

The most distinctive of the thirteen articles are: 4 On the Trinity and the plenitude of the Deity; 6 On the Spirit subsisting as Jehovah; 8 On pedobaptism [against a Davidian disposition to abandon it]; 9 On how Christ is *"Dei filius,* Jehovah, Immanuel, *filius Dei* [in his humanity], Mediator." 10 On how and why the son of David is true God; 12 On the office of the Christian prince.

41.F. The College in Debrecen, the intellectual center of Magyar Calvinism to the present. Reproduced from *Reformation in Europa,* 173.

The school and dormitories were drawn from old pictures and accounts by Kálmán Kallós, 1871, after the great fire that destroyed much of Debrecen.

42. MAXIMILIAN II AGAINST UNITARIANS AND SACRAMENTARIANS, 1570

42.A. Autograph mandate of Maximilian II against Unitarians in Transylvania, styled "Trinitarians" and "Sacramentarians," Prague, 1570. The autograph original is used by permission of Houghton Library, Harvard University.

The Emperor Maximilian II, king of Bohemia and the king of tripartitioned Hungary, claiming suzerainty over Great Transylvania even before John (II) Zápolya (Pl. 59) renounced his royal claim in 1570, issued in Prague a mandate, countersigned by John VII Listius (bishop of Veszprém, 1568–73, in Ottoman Hungary; cf. Pl. 39E), with special reference to Transylvania, ordering his ecclesiastical and military forces to stop the publication of Unitarian and Sacramentarian books, to confiscate them, and to imprison the printers thereof.

Two medieval designations for heretics of whatever position with respect to the Trinity or the sacrament of the altar had evolved: "Trinitarian" and "Sacramentarian." The mandate in the Catholic terminology of the period now calls the proto-Unitarians "Trinitarians" as well as "Arians" and justifies the harsh measures as a way to ward off further punitive acts of God on the Hungarian peoples for their national, personal, and religious sin. The "Sacramentarians" of the mandate now means specifically Zwinglians (or "mere commemorationists") but in general all the Hungarian Reformed who had departed from the Transylvania Lutherans in eucharistic theology and practice, and more particularly the proto-Unitarians.

Since the Diet of II Speyer, "Sacramentarian" more specifically designated the Zwinglian (and Anabaptist) view of the Lord's Supper, which was proscribed. This was the very diet at which six "Lutheran" princes and the envoys of fourteen imperial cities *protested* on 19 April 1529 the rescinding of the early provision at I Speyer 1526 for princely conscience with respect to the implementation of reform. Henceforth, within the Empire the term "Protestants" was attached primarily to Lutherans and was not originally intended to include those who came to call themselves Reformed, although precisely in Siebenbürgen, in contrast to Poland, the Reformed claimed to be both fully "Protestant" and yet "Catholic." The mandate of Emperor Maximilian II, signed in the capital of his Bohemian Kingdom, against the Unitarianism in his Kingdom of Hungary, of which he was master only up to the boundaries of Greater Transylvania and of Ottoman Hungary, was cast in terminology and with a motivation that illuminates the religio-political scene along the whole boundary of the eastern Holy Roman Empire as of 8 March 1570:

> When we learned, after the rise of the heresy of the *Trinitarians,* that is, a renewed Arianism, in the Transylvanian religions of the Kingdom of Hungary, . . . we have in no way wished to fail, through our imperial or our royal office, to put a stop to this so great and so dreadful evil with due reason: *lest* among so many calamities of this wretched Kingdom of ours, calamities which there is no doubt God has sent upon us because of the exceedingly many sins of His people, and greater and graver wrath of His divine majesty burn against us and against our realms. Wherefore we have given mandate . . . that they (the Primate of Esztergom [Gran] and others named) must search out the vendors and distributors of such books . . . containing the heresy of the Sacramentarians and the Zwinglians and after investigation they must not only take away from them and confiscate whatever books are found among them but also with the aid of the authority of our royal army to incarcerate and impose severe corporal punishment upon such booksellers and upon whoever preaches those heresies publicly. . . . Now let them warn those who in private adhere to and profess and follow these impious and condemned doctrines that they return to their good senses and follow the true faith, the Catholic religion, given over to us by Saviour himself and by his Apostles, and their successors. . . .

The usage of Maximilian originating in Prague in 1570, exhibits the transitional fluidity of a key term of all Christian theology. Servetus first used the term "Trinitarian" in 1553 for the papal and Calvinian formulation (Pl. 25).

An official document like this explains why the Davidians would by 1638 in Dés (Pl. 41) call themselves expressly "Unitarians," and henceforth the misleading medieval term for deviants on the doctrine of the Trinity would fall into disuse, except for a Catholic order; and the mandate explains, too, why the Calvinists of Debrecen, within range of the Emperor's authority, conspicuously insisted on referring to themselves as "Catholic" over against the papal Church and that of the Unitarians.

42.B. Maximilian Hapsburg (1527 – 76), Emperor and King of Bohemia, King of Hungary (1564 – 76), initially tolerant of Protestants. Kunsthistorisches Museum, Vienna; taken from Viktor Bibl, *Maximilian II: Der rätselhafte Kaiser: Ein Zeitbild* (Hellerau bei Dresden: Avalun [1930]) Pl. opp. p. 21.

43. THE RHINE PALATINATE I: DISCIPLINARIANS (ON COMMUNION) AND ANTIDISCIPLINARIANS (ERASTIANS)

43.A. Heidelberg on the Neckar, seat of a Reformed university, which had arisen in 1386 near the church of the Holy Spirit (3, in the market square, in direct line with the Neckar Bridge) and extended in the direction of St. Peter's (6, in almost the exact center). In this towering church Adam Neuser (Pl. 44) was pastor, aspirant to the chair in theology.

Taken from Matthaeus Merian, *Typographia Germaniae* (1642), in the series *Merian's anmüthige Städte-Chronik* (Munich, 1935) between pp. 52–53.

Heidelberg is here shown before the destruction of the castle of the Electors of the Rhine Palatinate by the French in 1693. Within the castle complex the square tower furthest back and to the left contained the dungeon "Seltenleer," whence Matthias Vehe (Pl. 44) escaped. The university complex lay between St. Peter's (6), towering in the exact middle of the panorama far back from the river, and the principal church in town on Market Square, that of the Holy Spirit (3), in direct line with the Neckar bridge. There the medieval university had its beginnings (1386). Between the towers of the two churches, close to St. Peter's, is the Hexenturm; immediately forward from it, is the Cloister of the Augustinian Friars, which in 1566 became the theological college, known henceforth as Sapienz-Collegium, which Ursinus directed as of 1568.

43.B. Frederick III the Pious, Elector 1559–76, successor of the first Protestant Elector Palatine, Ott Heinrich (1556–59), went over from Lutheranism to make of the Palatinate the intellectual and military center of the German Reformed. A copperprint of Frederick, 1570, encircled in Latin with his titles as Elector Palatine, Duke of Bavaria, and the cognomen Pius. The picture here shown seems to have been based on it, frontispiece, August Kulckhohn, *Friedrich der Fromme, Churfürst von der Pfalz der Schützer der reformirten Kirche, 1559–76* (Nördlingen, 1877). The copperprint was also adopted in a woodcut of 1577, showing a slighly older Elector, Wolfram Waldschmidt, *Alt-Heidelberg und sein Schloss* (Jena, 1909) 123.

The Reformed Church, of which Frederick was the outstanding German patron, would not enjoy an uncontested status within the Empire until guaranteed by the Treaties of Westphalia, 1648, ending the Thirty Years' War.

43.C. Zacharias Ursinus, born and died in Breslau (1534–83), co-author with Casper Olevianus of the *Heidelberg Catechism* (1562), refuted George Schomann's *Catechesis* (Cracow, 1574) (Pl. 31). Copperprint by Frisius on the basis of Hondius, c. 1580; taken from Derk Visser, *Zacharias Ursinus: The Reluctant Reformer* (New York: United Church Press, 1983) frontispiece. Below it says: "The noble Ursinus, deceased, taught by his piety."

His refutation of the Polish *Catechesis* of 1574 (our RD 7), among others, appeared in the posthumous *Explicationum catecheticarum . . . absolutum opus* (Neustadt, 1603).

43.D. Jerome Zanchi (1516–90), Augustinian canon regular from Bergamo, replaced Ursinus in 1568, was defender of the doctrine of the Trinity against the Transylvanians and the Poles. The copperprint is by Heinrich Hondius, c. 1580, with the words above and below the tower in the upper right: "A fortress is our Lord" and below: "Endure, mightily hold back." The copy was presented by Derk Visser of Ursinus College, Collegeville, Pennsylvania.

Zanchi formally became a Protestant in the Grisons in 1553, in 1563 canon of St. Thomas and teacher in the academy of Strassburg, having married a daughter of Curione (Pl. 16). Replacing Ursinus in dogmatic theology in 1568, Zanchi composed his principal defense of the doctrine of the Trinity against the Polish and Transylvanian Unitarians as *De tribus Elohim seu de uno ver Deo aeterno, Patre, Filio et Spiritu Sancto* (1591), which, along with others of his writings, is rich in material on his geographically distant theological foes.

43.E. A communication of the faculty of theology to the ministers of Koloszvár on the Lord's Supper one year after the decisive split at the diet and synod of Enyed in 1564 between the Hungarian (Reformed) and the the the (Lutheran) Saxons. From Studia et Acta, I, *A Heidelbergi Káté Magyarországon* (Budapest, 1965), presented by the Rev. Dr. Andrew Harsanyi of the Hungarian Reformed Federation of America.

The communication of the Heidelberg Disciplinarians (to be) could not have been successful had it come earlier, because they were themselves in the process of differentiating their view of the Lord's Supper along Calvin's line from that of Luther. Moreover, in Transylvania the eucharistic schism was somewhat reinforced by the difference in mother languages as between the Saxons (who returned to full Wittenberg tutelage) and the Magyars, already in close contact with the Swiss Reformed.

43.F. Swiss-born Thomas (Lieber) Erastus (1524–83), professor of medicine, whose Latin work, c. 1568, *A Treatise of Excommunication*, lent his name to Erastianism, the position of the Antidisciplinarians who upheld the authority of the state over matters of church discipline. Portrait by Tobias Stimmer, Kunstmuseum, Basel.

The intentionally irenic view of the Heidelberg professor of medicine, opposed to Calvin's theocratic ideal and to that of Presbyterian Thomas Cartwright (d. 1603) in England, was widely translated into several tongues, the title of the second English version being in full: *A Treatise of Excommunication: Wherein 'tis fully, learnedly, and modestly demonstrated that there is no warrant, precept, or president* [sic], *either in the Old Testament or the New, for excommunicating any person or debarring them from the sacrament, whilst they make an outward profession of the true Christian faith* (London, 1659). Earlier it had been rendered *The Nullity of Church Censures . . . by T. Erastus* (London, 1659). The work was first published anonymously in London with a false imprint and an anagram of the editor as publisher, *Explicatio gravissimae quaestionis utrum excommunicatio quatenus religionem intelligentes etc. amplexentes* (Pesclavii apud Boacium Sultaceterum, 1589). The anagrammed editor was Giacopo Castrovelto, who had married the widow of Erastus. See John Tedeschi, ''The Cultural Contributions of Italian Protestant Reformers in the Late Renaissance,'' *Schifanoia,* Bolletino dell' Istituti di Studi Renascimentali 1 (Ferrara, 1986) 127–51. The work caused Erastus's name to be bestowed on the Antidisciplinarians who opposed the ingerence of the ecclesiastical council of high Calvinisn in Heidelberg in the parochial and civil life of the Reformed Rhenish Palatinate—and then far beyond. The three Heidelberg Unitarian Antidisciplinarians (Pl. 44) were presumably all ''Erastians.''

44. THE RHINE PALATINATE II: THREE IMPRISONED UNITARIANS

44.A. Maximilian II granting audience at Diet of Speyer, 1570. Woodcut by Tobias Stimmer, printed in Strassburg, 1571: Germanisches National-Museum, Nuremberg. Not included is the long acrostic poem in praise of the Emperor on the full leaflet.

Lord Caspar Békés (C) had such an audience with Maximilian II (1562/64), seeking the hand of the Emperor's daughter for John II Sigismund of Transylvania, in return for which the Jagiellonian-Zápolyan was prepared to renounce his claim to the Hungarian Crown (Pl. 39). The three Palatinate Antidisciplinarians went to Speyer for the purpose of seeking out Békés on arrangements for Palatinate Antitrinitarian, Antidisciplinarian pastors to settle as prospective ministers in the Saxon towns of Transylvania.

44.B. The three Unitarian Antidisciplinarians sought out Békés (C) and were arrested after Békés, a supporter of Dávid (Pl. 40), had felt honor-bound to turn over to Maximilian their incriminating letter.

John Sylvanus, born in the Tyrol, had been tutor of the young Frederick, collaborator in the Heidelberg translation of the Bible, superintendent in Kaiserslautern (1563 – 67), then in Ladenburg (1567 – 72). He was beheaded in Heidelberg market square as an Arian, 23 December 1572.

Adam Neuser, pastor of St. Peter's, rejected aspirant for the professorship of dogmatic theology in succession to Caspar Olevianus, escaped via Śmigiel and Cracow to Transylvania.

Matthias Vehe-Glirius-Schimberg, born in Ballenburg, c. 1545, archdeacon in Kaiserslautern, was held prisoner in Seltenleer in the Heidelberg Castle (visible, Pl. 43, as the square tower, furthest back and left; lions were kept near here). Author of the *Mattanjah* (D), he escaped from Seltenleer and became, as Glirius, rector in Kolozsvár, advisor to Dávid and resident in his house during the christological debate with Socinus. He fled Transylvania in 1579, and published pseudonymously the third edition of *Defense of Francis Dávid* (Cracow, 1582) compiled by Jacob Palaeologus. Vehe-Glirius died in prison in Grethfiel (Gretzyl), East Frisia, 1590. In his *Apologia* he recalls the important role of Adam Pastor (F) in the conversion of Sylvanus.

44.C. Casper Békés (d. 1579), supporter of Francis Dávid. A lithograph by J. Ozieblowski, from a contemporaneous woodcut once in the town hall of Vilna; from the Mokslinė Biblioteke, Vilnius, validated by Endre Veress, ed. Antonio Possevino, S.J., *Transylvania* (1584), Fontes Rerum Transylvanicarum, 3 (Kolozsvár/Budapest, 1913) 117.

Békés rose up against Sigismund's successor, Stephen Báthory (Pls. 39, 46), fled to Cracow (residence shown in Map of Cracow), soon becoming Stephen's boon companion; and he was buried in Grodno in the same month and year as Dávid died in Déva (Pl. 45).

For Békés, particularly in Poland and on his residence in Cracow, see Kazimierz Lepszy, *PSB* 1 (1935) 401 – 02.

44.D. Title page of *Mattanjah* (Gift of God) (Dansenbrugk, 1578) by Matthias Vehe-Glirius, Christian Hebraist influential in Koloszvár.
From the facsimile edition of the copy discovered in the University Library, Utrecht, by Róbert Dán, *Matthias Vehe-Glirius: Life and Work of a Radical Antitrinitarian with his Collected Writings* (Budapest/Leiden: Hungarian Academy of Sciences/Brill, 1982) 291 – 98. Dansenbrugk may be Dansenberg near Kaiserslautern or Dänschenburg near Rostock.

The first pages of the *Mattanjah,* "That is, a short and useful writing very necessary for every Christian, published by Matthias Vehe under the name of Nathaniel (given by God) Elijah [forerunner of the Messiah] at Dansenbrugk 1578: Matthew 5:17 – 19: 'Think not that I have come to abolish the Law and the prophets; . . . I have come to fulfill them. . . .' and Romans 3:31: 'Do we then overthrow the Law by faith? By no means! On the contrary we uphold the Law.'" This book of a radical scholarly Christian Hebraist markedly influenced Francis Dávid and eventually the Sabbatarians (F, G). Dávid, who coedited with Biandrata in collected writings (Alba Julia, 1568) an anonymous work of Laelius Socinus and a work of Faustus Socinus on the same topic (John 1), the latter incorrectly ascribed to Socinus (Pl. 13), followed, much more than did Biandrata, the lead of Laelius in regarding the Old Testament (Massoretic) text as a more reliable imprint of the word of God than the New.

44.E. Unitarian Mennonite, Adam Pastor, whose books were decisive for Sylvanus, according to Vehe-Glirius, who in his *Apologia* refers even to the Unitarians of Poland

and Transylvania as "Adams Pastors volck." Christoffel van Sichema, *Tooneel der Hooft-Kettern herstaande in verscheyde afbeeltsels van valsche propheten* (Middelburgh, 1677).

Adam (Roelof Martens), pastor of Dorpen in Westphalia (1510–52/60/70), sometime priest, emissary of John Beuckels of Münster, was ordained elder by Menno Simons, then banned by him at the conference in Goch, 1547, for his denying the Trinity. Menno set forth *A Confession of the Triune God*, 1550, plausibly against Adam; the Hamburg text in Dutch with English translation by Victor G. Doerksen and Hermina Joldersama, *MQR* 86 (1986) 509–47.

In his *Apologia* (1590) printed by Dán, Vehe-Glirius refers frequently to "Adam Pastor's people," almost generically, in speaking of Unitarians in Transylvana and Poland, and even more particularly of Pastor's book as having been useful in persuading John Sylvanus in Ladenburg. Andrew Wiszowaty was the first to conjecture that it was Adam Pastor who visited Cracow in 1546/47 under the name of Spiritus, raising questions about the Trinity in the home of Andrew Trzecieski (Pl. 3; RD 1 n. 10).

44.F. The synagogue in Bözsödujfalu among the Szekelers, the last intact village of the radical Unitarians, the Sabbatarians. Photograph from an unidentified book, presented by Unitarian Bishop Joseph Ferencz of Budapest.

By the end of the sixteenth century, Sabbatarians, observing Old Testament dietary rules and circumcision, claiming Dávid in his final innovations as their patron, became numerous in Transylvania (where by law there was no Jewish population), especially among the Szeklers. The Sabbatarians, winning over converts from the Calvinists also, evolved as a religio-political force in the confessional and dynastic wars of the seventeenth century. The Sabbatarians survived into the middle twentieth century. Their last village with synagogue was in Bözödujfalu among the Szeklers. The nineteenth-century photograph shows the interior of their synagogue with the president standing near the crowned Old Testament, in Hungarian translation, and the Szekler "rabbi" in the foreground. Almost the entire community was wiped out during the Nazi period.

44.G. The tombstone of plausibly the last Transylvanian Sabbatarian, one Mózes Kovács (1882–1950), ethnically Hungarian. Photograph, 1984, by Prof. Dr. J. Szigeti, Seventh Day Adventist minister; presented by Bishop Joseph Ferencz of Budapest.

This may be viewed as the last monument of Christian Hebraism (originating in the faculty of theology of Reformed Heidelberg) of a large sector of the radicalized followers of the Magyarized Saxon Dávid in a radically rejudaized charismatic and moralistic political messianism. On the Judaizers see further, Róbert Dán, "From 'Judaization' to the Idea of 'Religio Universalis,' In Memoriam Prof. Dr. Dán," *Unitarianism and Related Movements* (Utrecht: Bibliotheca Unitariorum, 1986) 49–57, 67–68, and 5–20 and *Historia*, Bk. 3 nn. 275, 287, 779.

As a military district, Transylvania had been closed to Jews. In contrast, in Poland Jews lived within as well as around the mostly unwalled towns. In Lublin (Pl. 33) the viewer looks down castle hill between 18 and 19, to the center of the Jewish community with its *Maharal Shul*, Academy, and the *Vaád* (the parliament of the four "lands" of the Commonwealth).

45. TRANSYLVANIA IV: DÁVID AND SOCINUS, 1578/79

45.A. Christopher Báthory (1576/81–86), *older* brother of Stephen and his deputy. He presided over the trial of Dávid. From Andrea Veress, ed., *Antonio Possevino, S.J., Transylvania* (Budapest, 1913) 115.

45.B. Déva, the castle on the Mures, where after the fateful debate with Faustus Socinus (Pl. 47), instigated by Dr. Biandrata, Superintendent Dávid, charged with the innovation of nonadorantism (of Christ), was imprisoned and died in November 1579. Contemporary Italian's sketch, from Andrea Veress, *Izabella Királayné,* 217.

The high fortress is now a ruin with a marker of the probable location of the dungeon. There is another view from the other side in an engraving reproduced by Darling, *400 Years,* 13.

45.C. Dávid's elected successor was Demetrius Hunyadi (1579–92), followed by George Enyedi (1592–97), whose most important work (based on Stephen Basilius) is the swiftly suppressed *Explanations of passages of the Old and the New Testament, from which the dogma of the Trinity is wont to be established* (Koloszvár, c. 1598), a major scholarly challenge to the orthodox. The book in dark brown leather is stamped on the front cover: MICBBOL 1646. Inside it carries the inscription: "To the Rev. Professor James T. Bixby, from the Hungarian Consistory, Kolosvár [*sic*] 1884 26th Sept.,'' presented to Meadville Theological School by Professor Bixby, now in its library in Chicago; photograph presented by John D. Godbey, who thinks it is the original posthumous edition of Kolozsvár, c. 1598, all copies available burned. There was a Hungarian edition by Enyedes' successor as superintendent, Matthew Toroczkai (Kolozsvár, 1619). As the binding of the edition pictured is stamped 1646, it antedates the more widely diffused edition of Groningen of 1670, and must therefore be considered a great rarity. Originally directed against the followers of Méliusz, the book's scriptural motto is 1 Cor 8:6: "Yet for us there is one God, the Father, from (*a*) whom all things . . . and one Lord Jesus Christ by (*per*) whom are all things.''

45.D. Son of Christopher, Prince Sigismund Báthory (1581–94), at the end of his rule claimed hegemony over Walachia and Moldavia. Woodcut by Bartholomäus Käppeler, *The German Single Leaf Woodcut 1550–1600,* Pictorial Catalogue by Walter L. Strauss, 3 vols. (New York: Abaris, 1979) 2. 495.

45.E. Uncle of the preceding, Calvinist Prince Stephen Bocskay (1605–06), accompanied by his Hajdúks, led a patriotic surprising against Rudolph II and by the treaty of Vienna secured confessional toleration in Translyvania. Print by Peter Wilhelm Zimmermann; from Oskar Thulin, et al., *Reformation in Europe,* 173.

The town of Kassau (Košice) on the Hernád River is visible in the upper left, the other main stronghold taken by Bocskay on the right being Neuhäusel/Érsékújvár.

45.F. Dées, in the church of which the synod and diet assembled in 1638, where the Unitarian Church, and notably by that name for the first time officially, was once again accorded the status of a licit religion among three others. The photograph of Dées (modern Dés; Romanian: Dej) of c. 1940 is reproduced from *Erdély,* a collective work on the occasion of the absorption of a large part of Transylvania into a partly restored Hungary (Budapest, 1940), between pp. 20 and 21.

The *Complanatio* and its prehistory are presented by Bod, *Historia* 2. 304–06; discussed by Wilbur, *Transylvania,* 114–20.

The pluralistic establishment of four licit religions, Catholic, Lutheran, Calvinist, and Unitarian was guaranteed (with certain conformist concessions from the last) by Calvinist Prince George I Rákóczi (1630–48), when he signed the *Complanatio Deesiana* elaborated by the diet of Dées 1–7 July 1538. The Walachian Orthodox (a kind of "Uniate" Reformed Church) remained in tutelage to the Calvinists who sponsored the Romanian translation of the New Testament (Belgrade [Slavic for Alba Julia], 1648). For the exact date and characterization, see János Erdö, *Teológiai Tanulmányok* (Kolozsvár-Napoca: Unitarian Press, 1986) 23.

In the Agreement of Dées, wherein the term *Unitarius* is used a score of times, the conservative party under Matthias Ráv, pastor of the Saxon church in Kolozsvár and unsuccessful aspirant to the superintendency of the Unitarian Church, won on the three issues of the adoration of Christ (to withstand the challenge of the Sabbatarians, who invoked the authority of Dávid), of infant baptism by the formula of Matt 28:19, and of periodic and orderly observance of the Lord's Supper and church discipline. Non-adorants, belivers' baptists, and Sabbatarians were thereby expelled from the Unitarian Church by the Synod/Diet of Dées. Daniel Beke, pastor of Dávid's church of St. Michael in Kolozsvár, was confirmed in his election to the superintendency by his subscribing to the *Complanatio* (embodying the *Confessio* of Kolozsvár if 1579, once promoted by Biandrata). Provision was made by the Synod/Diet for the *confessio* and the pastor of each parish church to be settled in favor of the majority of the congregants, a ruling that favored pedobaptism. The formulations in the *Complanatio* were the official credal and disciplinary standard of the Transylvanian Unitarians, however modified over the generations in actual practice.

To understand how the Davidian (nonadorant) Reformed Church could, within less than sixty years, have passed from its preeminence to marginality between Calvinists and Catholics, we may here summarize the developments. The political, military, social, and confessional history of Transylvania between the death of Francis Dávid in 1579 and the confessionally decisive and, for the followers of Dávid, restrictive Diet of Dées in 1638 was very complex and interconnected with that of Hapsburg Hungary and that of Poland.

Religio-politically the Principality was sometimes in swift succession under tolerant *Catholic* Stephen Báthory (1571 – 81; King of Poland, 1576 – 86, Pl. 46); under his *older* brother *Catholic* Christopher Báthory (1581, Pl. 45D); under his son, *Catholic* Sigismund II Báthory (1588 – 98, promoted by his royal uncle in Poland, and who made an effort to unite with the Hapsburgs in a common assault on the Ottoman Empire but his Transylvanian nobility opposed the plan); briefly under his son *Catholic* Andrew Báthory (1598 – 99); by arrangement of the latter in order to further himself and the Counter-Reform, under *Catholic*, Spanish-born Rudolph Hapsburg of Pressburg and Vienna, as King of Hungary with Transylvania (1599 – 1605), and whose remote exercise through viceroys in Alba Julia in the interest of the Counter-Reform beginning decisively in 1604 in Transylvania, brought about enormous bloodshed, terror, and pillage with General George Básta (five times brutally resuming power against local insurgents), while intermittently Sigismund II Báthory tried to regain control, 1600 – 01, and *Unitarian* Moses Székely contended for religious rights; then under *Calvinist* Stephen Bocskay (1605 – 06; Pl. 45 E), who was elected Prince of Hungary by the diet of Upper Hungary; under *Protestant* fighter against the Turks, Sigismund III Rákóczi (1607 – 08), who had supported Bocskay and now abdicated in favor of the following; under *Calvinist* Gabriel Báthory, who had supported the *Rokosz* (1606) in Poland (Pl. 50), (1608 – 13); under *Calvinist* Gabriel Báthory (married to the widow of Moses Székely, 1613 – 29), who sided against the Hapsburgs in what was becoming the Thirty Years' War, who was briefly elected King of Hungary, 1620 – 21, and who presided over the Golden Age of Transylvania as a European power; briefly under his widow, *Protestant* Catherine of Brandenburg (1629 – 30); briefly under *Calvinist* Stephen Bethlen; and under *Calvinist* George Rákóczi I (1630 – 48), who presided at the restrictive Synod/Diet of Dées in 1638.

In the meantime the community created by Francis Dávid, many following his scripturally most radical directives and a humanizing Christology, representing next a beyond nonadorantism, became Jewish Christians after the model of the earliest discernible communities in the New Testament until at length they became Sabbatarians, while the more conservative Unitarians, closer to Biandrata and to the Polish Brethren with whom they sustained contact, struggled with the growing fission within their parishes, particularly in Szeklerland. As for these Sabbatarians, Antonio Possevino reported in his *Transsilvania*, commissioned by King Stephen Batory to inform him in detail about the condition of his Principality, that "the [Unitarian] ministers in Szeklerland universally . . . abstained from blood and pork" (p. 66), which observation, however possibly exagerrated, suggests in a word the outreach of the Christian Judaizing from Vehe-Glirius (Pl. 43 A) and Dávid. Although Sabbatarians harbored their own socio-political and eschatological hopes, for the period up to Dées in 1638, the principal rivals for political dominance and confessional hegemony had been Calvinist and Counter-Reform Catholic, while the Unitarians—their nobles no less than burghers and rural parishioners—were seriously in schism.

During this rocky period the Unitarian synod, based in Koloszvár, had been under the superintendency, often restricted by the Calvinist princes, of Demetrius Hunyadi (1579–92, Pl. 45 C); of George Enyedi (1592–97, Pl. 45 C); of Matthew Toroczki (1601–16); of Matthew Radecki, a Polish Brother from Danzig (1616–32); and of the already encountered successful contestant against Ráv, Daniel Beke (1636–61).

Ráv, alarmed at the decay of discipline and at what he perceived as the peril to his Church under a Calvinist Prince, had secretly attended a synod in Raków in 1629, which in turn sent Brethren to Koloszvár with a letter signed by the six leading ministers of Little Poland that urged the Transylvanians to enforce discipline and to exchange letters and visits annually for the mutual fortification of the two brotherhoods.

Lubieniecki, a boy of six in Raków at the time, must have been later informed of this important démarche by his participant ministerial father; and familial involvement in the episode would explain why Lubieniecki could so fervidly embrace the (*Complanatio*) Unitarians of Transylvania in his *Historia,* officially adorant of Christ as had been "his own" Socinus (who in the *Complanatio* won a second posthumous victory over Dávid). Except on pedobaptism, the Racovians and the Unitarians of the *Complanatio* of Dées were indeed henceforth close.

The *Confessio* of 1579/1638, most readily accessible (in Latin) in Wallace 3.556–57, acknowledges "Jesus of Nazareth as the only begotten Son of the Most High, to be called God according to the genuine sense of Holy Scripture," to be "worshiped, adored, invoked in Prayer, our only Mediator, and the same Jesus Christ as King of the Churches." The enframing *Complanatio* provided that any departures from these regulations and the *Confessio* itself should be punished not by the Unitarian Church but by the Prince, without whose permission no innovation might be undertaken by the individual Unitarian nor by any group nor the whole synod, nor any Unitarian book printed. The *Confessio* closes with reference to Christ in 1 Cor 15:24 on the delivery of his Kingdom to his heavenly Father, which thus affirms for Unitarians, over against millennialists by now brought under control, that Christ yet rules as King in the Church. It is rendered in English, *Radical Reformation* (1992), ch. 28. Karl Barth referred to this *Confessio* as the only instance of a self-conscious break from the *ecclesiological* presumption of the *Una Sancta*, ideally common to the classical Reformation and all derivative Neo-Protestantism, however sectarian, *Die Kirchliche Dogmatik* (1932–67); English (Edinburgh, 1956), I, part 2, Paragraph 20 "Authority in the Church," p. 660.

46. STEPHEN BATORY: DANZIG, 1577; PSKOV, 1581

46.A. The Lutheran city of Danzig at the mouth of the Vistula. Braun, *Civitas orbis terrarum*, by permission of the Houghton Library, Harvard University.

Danzig (Gdańsk), Hanseatic free city, was dissatisfied with the terms of Stephen's election and the alleged discrimination in the constitution of the Commonwealth against city people, artisans, and tradesmen. Danzig refused obedience. Stephen besieged it, 1576–77. At Brodnica he professed complete religious toleration (Pl. 39 G). Victorious, Stephen made Danzig sustain the costs of the war but accorded it a special semi-autonomous status within the palatinate of Pomerelia and the Commonwealth.

Having joined the Hanseatic League in 1361, it was absorbed by the Teutonic Order but acquired a special status under the Polish Crown in 1466. Originally made up of three jurisdictions (like Königsberg), it was built upon the left bank of the stream Mottlau (behind the buildings) flowing into the left arm of the Vistula (in the middle background with several ships plying on it).

Largely of Low German speech, the city became wholly Protestant 1522–51. St. Mary's is the biggest church to the right and next to it is the tall spire of the Rathaus of Rechtstadt. In the foreground is the moat. In the distance the shore of the Baltic is in view, with five sailing ships at the left.

Because of the close ties of Danzig with the ports of Holland, there were Reformed and Mennonite congregations in territory controlled by Danzig. The first Mennonites were in the city by 1530. Menno Simons visited congregations there and in Ducal Prussia in 1548. Most of these Anabaptists were Dutch refugees. The Polish Brethren made several overtures to them.

The major city of the Vistula grain and fur trade was the point of entry into, or departure from, Poland of many of the figures in the *Historia*. Oliwa, where the peace between Poland and Sweden was signed in 1660, and where Lubieniecki argued with the plenipotentiaries for the restoration of plenary confessional liberty, is within range of view to the west from any of the towers of Danzig.

46.B. Báthory at the siege of Pskov, receiving the bread and salt of hospitality from its Orthodox bishop, while the papal legate Possevino counsels moderation. Painting by Jan Matejko, 1871. "Stephen Batory before Pskov, 1581," painted by Jan Matejko, 1871. Muzeum Narodowe, Warsaw; Pracowania Fotograficzna; identification of figures from Stanisław Witkiewicz, *Matejko* (Lwów, 2d ed., 1910).

Pskov had been a Hanseatic sister republic of Novgorod. It had maintained elective institutions until brought under the rule of Muscovy in 1510. There was war between Muscovy and the Commonwealth, 1577–82. Ivan IV the Terrible (cf. Pl. 19) had broken the treaty of 1571, whereby most of Livonia was under Polish control. In three major campaigns, Batory and John Zamoyski took Połock, 1572, three other citadels, 1580, and were besieging Pskov in 1581. At this point papal legate Antonio Possevino, S.J. entered upon the scene, the central figure in Matejko's critical assessment of his role, when plenary victory over Muscovy seemed within reach.

Possevino (1534–1611) had been representing Gregory XIII at the court of John III Vasa of Sweden. John had married Catherine Jagiellonka (mother of the future Sigismund III Vasa) and was prepared to conform to Catholicism and had even indicated that Sweden would follow him if the Pope would grant the Mass in Swedish, communion in both kinds, and a married clergy (proposals entertained also by Primate Uchański, Pl. 6). The scholarly Possevino was unable to wrest these concessions from the Pope. It was from Rome that he set forth, again as papal legate, to serve as mediator between Stephen and Ivan, the Tsar having expressed interest in the reunion of Moscow with Rome. This time, too, Possevino's unionist mission failed, although he secured the armistice pictured, and the artist has unkindly indicated by the separate gestures of the hands of the legate his divided loyalties and sympathies (although Possevino would remain on for three years after Ivan's death in 1584 to negotiate union).

In the powerful evocation of the forces of war, politics, and religion in 1581, with authentic habiliments and in many cases authentic likenesses, King Stephen is seen masterfully in front of his siege tent, capable of not much more than *Dobrze* (thank you) in Polish, speaking Latin with Possevino (and in some cases with his commanders). Behind them in the tent stand John Zamoyski, Hetman and Grand Chancellor of the Crown, while behind the head of Possevino (portrait based upon a sixteenth-century likeness) can be seen the sons of Unitarian Caspar Békés (Pl. 38). Cyprian, Orthodox bishop of defeated Połock, is offering the victor the bread of hospitality and peace with an expression of anxiety about the monarch's unsheathed sword. Behind him are Ivan Nashchokin and Roman Vasilevich Oliffiriev humbling themselves. Behind the King, also seated, to the left is Prince Constantine Basil Ostrogski (cf. Pl. 43); and to the right, Prince Nicholas Radziwiłł the Red, Grand Hetman of Lithuania (Pl. 14), conferring with the palatine of Bracław. At the back of Possevino is the deputy of the King for cavalry in feathered battle gear, next to him the hetman of the Zaporozhian Cossacks, and next to him, with the pointed helmet, Prince Theodore Obolensky. After the successful armistice negotiations mediated by Possevino, the war was concluded by the Treaty of Jam Zapolski, 1582, which secured most of Livonia up to Estonia for the Commonwealth and made it subject to recatholicizing; and Muscovy was held back from the Baltic.

Possevino in *Transylvania,* 1584, would, after a tour of inspection there, provide Batory with fundamental information about his Principality, replete with data on Unitarianism and Sabbatarianism.

47. FAUSTUS PAULUS SOCINUS

47.A. Miniature painted on the top of a snuff box; reproduced here with the permission of the Principal of Manchester College, Oxford, and through the kindness of Joanna Parker, Librarian, who has transcribed in full the two letters within.

There is a bronze medallion of Faustus Socinus in Siena (see Pl. 13.A). There is also in Siena a painting of Socinus, said to have been executed by Titian (implausible) in the possession (1935) of Signorina Bianchi-Bandinelli, Via Ricasoli 54, inspected by Earl Morse Wilbur. Of this painting William Williams (1788–1855) commissioned a copy to be made in adornment of the lid of the snuff box he had had made from some branch removed from an evergreen oak under which Faustus was locally reputed to have sat with his disciples in a villa garden ten miles beyond the city walls. When the significance of the tree had become apparent to the owner, ''the old lady . . . ordered the heretical tree to be cut down.'' So reported Williams to his sister, Siena 15 August 1819, delighted with the present intended for a friend Davis. He regretted only that he had not made more such boxes before the tree was felled. The snuff box contains copies, perhaps by Mr. Davis, of relevant portions of two letters from Williams to his sister. William Williams, gentleman of the manor house of Aberpergwn of Glyn Nedd, Glamorganshire, was educated by Harrow and Cambridge in mathematics and classics, passionately concerned for the literature of his native Wales.

It is quite possible that even the original painting was not made from life but from the later, more familiar print of Socinus (B), and given a youthful mien and attire. Of the likenesses of Laelius and Faustus Socinus in Siena, Dr. Wilbur wrote: "I . . . found on a public building sculptured medallion portraits of both Laelius and Faustus Socinus and an alleged contemporary portrait of Laelius, and secured casts of medals of both. . . ," "How the History Came to be Written," 12.

47.B. The older Socinus. On returning to Cracow he became the official spokesman of the Minor Church, centered in Raków, although he declined to submit to believers' immersion. His disparagement of baptism is reflected in the Racovian Catechism in Polish in 1605. The Polish Brethren in exile after 1660 came to be called after him Socinians. Used by permission of Piotr Maciej Przypowski of Jędrzejów.

It is a photograph of the original copperprint in the Sammlung Gesenius of the Herzog August Bibliothek, Wolfenbüttel, which has him facing right with the hostile legend below: "Haeresiarcha et Antesignanus Socinianorum, Laelii ex Alexandro fratre Nepos, Natus A[nno]. 1530 d. xbr; Den[atus] A[nno] 1604 d. 3 Martij." From it was made by a friendly artist the more familiar copperprint in which the head is turned to the left and is slightly elongated with the eyes closer together and with the falling collar slightly more pointed at the corners than in the original, and whiter. The original shown here has the width between the eyes much as in the Manchester College snuff box representation. The more familiar print is encircled with appropriate identification above verse directed to the benign viewer.

47.C. Commentary on John 1:1 – 15, the author's oldest christological formulation in print, influenced by a similar work of Laelius Socinus (Pl. 13.A). Andover Harvard Library, with permission.

This is the third printed edition of Faustus Socinus's *Brevis explicatio primae partis primi capitis Iohannis*, put out by Jerome Moskorzowski, along with the annotations of Socinus on Romans 9 concerning the Jews, faith, and righteousness (Raków: Sternacki, 1618). The first edition of the argument about the intent of John on the Logos "in the beginning" was in Basel, c. 1562, and the second version appeared, incorrectly ascribed to Laelius Socinus by Francis Dávid, in a work against Peter Méliusz, Kolozsvár, 1568, as noted in Pl. 13.A.

The fourth edition would be in the *Opera omnia*, Amsterdam, 1665. For part of the publication history, see also Pl. 59.A. Socinus in his foreword explains that incrusted perversion of Scripture has made its understanding and acceptance by Jews and Muslims difficult. He takes up specifically the traditional interpretation of John 1:1 – 15, all the more prominent for its having come to be the obligatory (as of 1570) closure of every Mass. Urged by many friends, as he writes, he proffers in print the explanation that he has been expounding, developing further ideas of his uncle, who had written on the same pericope (*Historia*, Book 3, n. 10). He acknowledges that the interpretation is novel and seeks to explain some of the difficulty by the *Sitz im Leben* of the opening chapter, directed, as he says, against the Ebionites and Cerinthus. The Evangelist makes his christological point, namely, that Christ as the Messiah, "our unique legislator," "from the seed of David, Servant of our Supreme God Jehovah," is creator, not of the corporeal world but rather author of the construction of the spiritual kingdom, "which is the reformation of the world." There is no scriptural warrant, Socinus says, for the conciliar supposition that "in the beginning" could stand for "from eternity." In order to "seize the weapons from the hands of the adversary," he uses the Vulgate against Catholic theologians and exegetes. Although he later claimed the work as his own in a letter to Dudith, he justifies his anonymity of authorship in c. 1562 as more than prudential.

47.D. The title-page of the oldest and interconfessionally influential edition of Socinus's *An Argument for the Authority of Holy Scripture*, published pseudonymously as the work of a Jesuit of Seville (Hispali), by proto-Remonstrants (Amsterdam, 1588). Translated by the author from his original Italian of c. 1580, it argues for the veracity of the New Testament authors along four lines, then in a single chapter vindicates the work of the great historian and prophet of the Old, Moses, whose prophecies were fulfilled in the New Testament. By permission of Houghton Library, Harvard University. This copy is one of three known exemplars extant. See Kawecka-Gryczowa, *Ariańskie oficyny wydawnicze,* item 263; Wilbur, *Socinianism,* 390ff.

There are only traces here of the hermeneutical terminology that makes of *veritas* the technical word for the fulfilling antitype of which in the Old Testament there is the type; cf. under Flacius Illyricus, Pl. 1. The text of *De auctoritate* was corrected and published with another work by Socinus, *The Sum of the Christian Religion* (Raków, 1611). *De auctoritate* was translated into four languages and in several editions, the last in English by Edward Combe (London, 1731). Its argument was adopted by Remonstrant Grotius in his *De veritate religionis christianae* (1622). Catholics, too, made use of it.

On the distinctive Christology of Faustus Socinus, see Pls. 13.C (Laelius), 55.EF, and 59.A (under Schmalz). On justification by faith in Socinus, faith being—in his cumulative reflections—active faith in the sense of a motion from assent and obedience to trust, confidence, loving works, and hope—see John C. Godbey, "Fausto Sozzini and Justification," in F. Forrester Church and Timothy George, eds., *Essays Presented to George H. Williams,* 250–66, and in a different context, "Interpretations of Socinian Theology," *Unitarianism,* 63, in which he demonstrates the extent to which Socinus was participant in "The Second Reformation" (Müller, Göttingen) and was not himself a proto-Deist.

48. FAUSTUS SOCINUS AND CRACOW

48.A. Among the several sources for the episode is a long letter of Matthias Radecki (cf. Pl. 45 F) from Buszkowy, 18 June 1598, to a doctor of law in Brussels, Cornelius Daems, a friend of Socinus. The letter is printed by Thomas Crenius (= Crusius), *Animadversiones philologicae et historicae,* 19 parts (Rotterdam, 1695–1720) 4. 233–36; rendered in Polish by Chmaj, ed. *Listy,* 1. 316–18 n. 90; Włodzimierz Budka, using this source and more, gives many details about the episode, "Faust Socyn w Krakowie," *RwP* 5 (1928) 120–23; and Wilbur summarizes this but also on the basis of his own study on the scene, *Socinianism,* 402–04. The completion of the names in the letter of Socinus, quoted in part below, depends on Chmaj, ed. *Listy,* 2. 214.

It was not uncommon around the university for students to rough up heretics on feast days. Already by Eastertime Socinus had felt uneasy and placed his most precious belongings with his landlord, Daniel Chroberski, elder in the Calvinist "Brog" (Pl. 51). On the eve of Ascension Day (fortieth day after Easter), two students had reconnoitered the place, having picked him out as an appropriate holiday victim. On the day, a mob broke in upon him lying sick, dragged him half-clothed to the Market Square and threw his books and papers into the mud and into a bonfire, threatening him with the same fate unless he recanted. Menaced with drawn sword, he replied: "I do not recant, but what I have been I am and will be by the grace of the Lord Jesus Christ, as long as I live; and you may do whatever God permits." Abashed and perhaps marveling at his firmness, the assailants were dragging him for drowning in the Vistula when Dr. Wadowita and others intervened.

From his temporary refuge with Giovanni Bautista Cettis in Igołomia, three miles out of Cracow, Socinus wrote to Dr. Wadowita, 14 June 1598, closing with these grateful words: "Please be so kind as to give my hearty greetings to His Magnificence the Rector [Valentine Fontana], the Rev. [Daniel Segonius] Lelowita, and also [John] Godecki [canon of St. Ann's], who were defending me along with you, and to all the other persons of your rank [the officers and servants of the Myszkowskis], whose names I do not know, but who in whatever way took part in saving me during that harrowing episode. I want you to know that I will always remember what I owe you and them and whenever I can I will make it known and testify thereto by word and deed with the greatest joy. Keep well, my dear and famous man, and love me, your friend, always faithful to your honor, Faustus Socinus."

48.B. House of Socinus in Cracow. The snapshot was taken by Earl Morse Wilbur, who even made a point of procuring the plan of the building filed before its restoration in 1859; and it reposes with others in the library of Meadville/Lombard Theological School, Chicago, made available through the kindness of John C. Godbey.

Socinus lived in Cracow, 1579–83 amd 1587–98. The second time his lodgings were in the two middle stories just beyond the rainspout at the extreme left. The building is at the corner of Bracka (right) and Gołębia street (left), one street from Market Square and one more from the University. He lived here from 1590 ito 1598, broken by an interval of residence with Dr. Nicholas Buccella, royal physician, who had granted him an annuity of 100 florins (see Map of Cracow).

48.C. Professor Martin Wadowita, curate of St. Florian's. The painting is from a photograph.

When Martin (Kępa) Wadowita (d. 1641) intervened in the defense of Socinus, already magister in arts, he had but recently become professor of theology.

48.D. Court and church in Lusławice. Photograph in Szczęsny Morawski, *Arjanie Polscy* (Lwów, 1906), between pp. 64–65.

The church at Lusławice was under the patronage of Abraham Błoński, whose house is at the left. After his rescue and a brief sojourn in Igłomia, Socinus lived here till death. The pastor was Peter Stoiński (son of Peter Statorius) who had married the daughter of Gregory Paul (Pl. 26). Their son was John Stoiński (1650–1654), known to Benedict Wiszowaty (*BAnt²*, 121). Peter Stoiński preached the funeral sermon for Socinus and himself died the following year (1605). For Socinus's burial monument, see Pl. 58.

48.E. Peter Skarga's *Shaming of the Arians*, 1604. Taken from Konstanty Otwinowski, S.J., *Dzieła X. Piotr Skargi T. J.: Spis bibliograficzny* (Cracow, 1916) item 33. For the reply by Gosławski, see Gryczowa, no. 123; for the place of the book in Skarga's career, see my "Skarga," *Shapers*, 182.

In the year of Socinus's death Peter Skarga, S.J. (Pl. 49) published his *A shaming of the Arians and a summons to them to repentance and to the Christian faith* (Cracow, 1604), with the scriptural sanction of Ps 108 (109) for blasphemy against the Trinity: 29: "May my accusers be clothed with dishonor: may they be wrapped in their own shame as in a mantle," and Ps 6:11: "All my enemies shall be ashamed and sorely troubled; they shall turn back, and be put to shame in a moment." Dedicated to Jerome Gostomski, palatine of Poznań and founder of the Jesuit college in Sandomierz (cf. Pl. 34), the work acknowledges that the writings of Socinus in Lusławice and of his associate and pastor, Peter Stoiński (d. 1605) are being widely read; and the refutations of Martin Śmiglecki, S.J. (d. 1619) are recommended as an antidote for Catholic readers. Divided into two parts, the *Shaming* in the first is systematically polemical, in the second it deals with Arian history and documents, including a reprinting of *A Racovian Confession in XXXVIII Articles* and a sermon Skarga himself would preach on Trinity Sunday in 1604. The *Articles*, transitional from the *Catechesis* of 1574 to the Racovian Catechism of 1605, was the occasion of Skarga's attack. A reply to this, with special references to his sermon on Matthew, was printed by Adam Gosłowski, *Refutacja Kazania* (Raków, 1607).

49. THE CATHOLIC SELF-IMAGE I

49.A. Stanislas Cardinal Hosius (1504 – 79), at age 65, bishop of Varmia (Ermland) (1551 – 79), author of *Confessio Catholicae Fidei Christiana* (Cracow, 1553), widely read in thirty editions and replied to by Protestants including John Łaski. Oil painting by an unknown artist from a still extant primitive, collegial church of St. John the Baptist in Orneta (Wormditt), palatinate of Olsztyn; taken from Tadeusz Dobrzeniecki, *Sztuka sakralna w Polsce na ziemiach zachodnich i północnych* (Warsaw: Ars Christiana, 1976), Pl. 108; cf. Jobert, *De Luther à Mohila,* Pl. 4.

Hosius was one of the presiding legates at the Council of Trent. But he prevented the other Polish bishops from appearing there, partly because the royally appointed secretary for the delegation was Frycz Modrzewski (Pl. 22). Hosius introduced the Jesuits in Poland, Braniewo (Braunsberg) and established a seminary there. He left Varmia in 1569 for Rome, where he served as grand penitentiary and established there the Polish College and erected the church of St. Stanislas, 1564. He organized the *castrum doloris* for Sigismund II, 1572 (Pl. 36.C).

49.B. Peter Skarga, S.J. (1563 – 1613), court preacher in Cracow and Warsaw, prophetic critic of society before the Diet, promoter of social justice and acts of mercy, a figure in the Union of Brest Litovsk (Pl. 52), disputant with the Polish Brethren (Pl. 48). One of four related oil portraits, each one based on the other. The one shown is from the rectoral residence of the Church of St. Barbara in Cracow. Jan Syngański, S.J., in *Działalność Ks. Piotr Skargi T.J. na tle jego listów 1566 – 1610* (Cracow, 1912), has chosen another of the four for his frontispiece; cf. his reflections where he treats of only three, 117. In an appendix, 113 – 20, he surveys the iconography of Skarga and arranges the likenesses, of which he reproduces several, in chronological order. The picture chosen here has the subscription in Latin: ''The Rev. Father Peter Skarga of the Society of Jesus, most distinguished through more than thirty years by his holy sermons to Kings Stephen and Sigismund III, by the integrity of his morals, and by his clearly apostolic spirit, died in Cracow on the 27th day of September 1612 in the 76th year of his age, buried in the *Regia* church of the College of the Society of Jesus dedicated to SS Peter and Paul.'' The most recent work on Skarga is that of Janusz Tazbir, *Piotr Skarga: Szermierz Kontrreformacji* (Warsaw: Wiedza Powszechna, 1978), with many illustrations. For a work of Skarga against the Arians, see Pl. 48. For Jan Matejko's painting of Skarga preaching, see *PB,* Pl. F. Cf. my own work, ''Peter Skarga'' and ''Stanislas Hosius,'' *Shapers of Religious Traditions . . . 1560 – 1600,* ed. Jill Raitt (New Haven/London: Yale University Press).

49.C. A symbolic representation (1574) of the Roman Catholic Church and its seven sacraments, with Protestant heretics drowning (three enlarged in other plates). A page from Abbot Stanisław Reszka of Jędrzejów (1543 – 1600), *De atheismo et Phalarismo [tyranny] Evangelicorum* (Naples, 1596), dedicated to Cardinal Hosius with illustrations by Father Stanisław Treter of Poznań (1547–1610), poet, historian, painter, and engraver, both clerics in the service of Cardinal Hosius. It was drawn in 1574 and printed separately as a copperprint *Typus ecclesiase catholicae* to serve as a catechetical summary of the faith for the laity (Venice, 1574). This early form is printed by Tadeusz Chrzanowski, *Działalność artystyczna Tomasza Tretera* (Warsaw: PAN, 1984) Pl. 1. He traces the history of this late medieval-Renaissance conception, 45–51, and more fully in "Hozjańska alegoria Kościoła," *Sztuka pobrzeża Bałtyku* (Gdańsk/Warsaw, 1978).

In the bird's-eye view one glimpses heaven, earth (with the Church in the center), and the ocean of the world (symbolic of purgatory).

The One Catholic Church is symbolized by a woman, crowned with the papal tiara, whose dowry (*dos*), as the Spouse of Christ, is the seven sacraments, "the vessels of the merits of Christ." The Church appears to be built upon a Mount with two scriptural sanctions inscribed at the base: Matt 16:18, "And upon this Rock I will build my Church," and Ps 67 (68):17, "The mount which God desired for his abode for ever." The whole sacramental structure rests on Simon Peter, the Rock, with his keys, as the vicar of Jesus Christ, "the only foundation" (although it is a somewhat awkward representation of both upsidedown). The intention of Treter is to set forth the Church on the whole earth as itself the mystical body of Christ, Christendom. The mountains in the distance (on either side of the level of *Baptismus*) are intended to suggest the boundary between earth and heaven, once Paradise, while below is the moat-like ocean of the world with heretics drowning therein.

In heaven the Holy Trinity is represented as the Throne of Grace. To the right and left are John the Baptist and the Virgin, prominent among the heavenly host of saints on either side.

From Christ's side his sacrificial blood, by way of the Holy Spirit, vitalizes the seven sacraments, beginning with Baptism (center), then on the right Matrimony, the Eucharist, and Penance (below), on the other side moving up, Confirmation, Ordination, and Extreme Unction. Intertwined by golden chains, the sacraments are upheld on the theological edifice by six prophets, among them Isaiah; on the base above them, by six of the principal apostles, and above them by the four Latin doctors: from left to right, Augustine, Jerome, Ambrose, and Gregory the Great.

The heretics, in the ocean as in a moat around the castle mount of redemption, are mostly familiar from the *Historia* (not all clearly visible here but three of them elsewhere reproduced enlarged). They are drowning between Luther and Calvin, both of whom are credited with standing sufficiently on Scripture and Tradition not to be in danger of immediate drowning. Luther is still in his friar's cowl with the uplifted sword (perhaps that of the Spirit, but more likely that of sedition and religious war is intended).

In most cases the faces seem to be only vague characterizations, but a few, marked below by an asterisk, appear to be likenesses of men familiar to Treter and reproduced in the copperprint by Giovanni Battista de' Cavalieri. Taken as a group, they are interesting as to how heresy was perceived from the vantage point of Varmia, surrounded by Ducal Prussia, and of the northern reaches of the Commonwealth in general. They are from left to right: Martin Luther, Philip Melanchthon, Andrew Frycz Modrzewski (only his books still afloat), Matthias Flacius Illyricus (the Gnesio-Lutheran of Magdeburg, Pl. 1), Francis Stancaro (under, except for his hand holding one of his books, Pl. 17), Daniel [Bieliński] (Pl. 31), but much more likely the printer from Łęczycza, Pińczów (Pl. 9), then Nieśwież, Theodore Beza (with a sword thrust through his books), Valentine Gentile (who had been in Poland in 1562, and was beheaded in Bern, 1566), John Brenz (of Wittenberg), George Biandrata* (Pl. 18), Michael Servetus (like Stancaro, only a hand and a book),

Bernardine Ochino (who had indeed been briefly in the Commonwealth), Peter Viret of Lausanne (1511 – 71, popularizer of Calvinism in France), John Calvin, then Simon Budny* of Lithuania (Pl. 15), and presumably George Buchanan* (1506 – 82), Scottish historian. What were seen from Varmia, Poznań (Rome, Naples), i.e., from the point of view of Hosius, Reczka, and Treter, as the principal heretics of all Latin Christendom included thus four Italians, three Germans, three Frenchmen, one Scot, but only two figures for sure of the Commonwealth, Modrzewski and Budny. As John Łaski was also an assailant of Hosius, it is notable that he is not shown, perhaps out of respect to the memory of the primatial uncle of the same name. For the argument for the identity of Daniel, printer of the Budny Bible, see Pl. 54.C.

Only Simon Budny and George Buchanan float outside the basic arrangement, both figures relatively large and distinctly shown. The inclusion of a Scotsman is most striking. But the ports of Danzig and Elbing (Elbl*ąg) were centers of the trade of Scotsmen in furs, timber, grain; and Scots are attested as supporters of Reformed churches as far up the Vistula as Cracow. George Buchanan was a classicist, a champion of religious freedom, an extensive correspondent, a friend of Beza, an implacable foe of David Cardinal Beaton of St. Andrews (d. 1546). From Beaton Hosius and hence his secretaries, Treter and Reszka, had doubtless heard about Buchanan. On him, see Dictionary of National Biography* (22 vols.; Oxford, 1885 – 1900) 3.187 – 93.

It is quite possible that Buchanan was connected with the known effort of Budny (Pl. 15) to establish contact with English proto-Puritans like the martyrologist John Foxe (1516 – 87), who published his history of persecutions in Latin (Strassburg, 1554), enlarging it as *Acts and Monuments of matters happening in the Church* (Basel, 1563). Cyprian Bazylik (c. 1535 – after 1591), owner of the press in Brest Litovsk, had used the Latin text of Foxe as one of his three sources for his *Historya o śrogiem prześladowaniu Kościola Bożego* (Brest, 1567; Pl. 1). Through his work perhaps Budny came to know of Foxe; and, after his fresh edition of the New Testament with its censored critical notes restored, he wrote a letter to Foxe from Łosk, 4 May 1574, delivering it through the intermediation of one Thomas Glover (who later visited him in Lithuania) and Ralph Lutter (ed. Stanislas Kot, *RWP* 7/8 [1935/36] 316 – 23). Budny's autograph survives in the Bodleian Library. Kot wrote about Budny and Foxe in "Anglo-Polonica" (1935), and about the relation of Illyricus to the Polish Reformation in "Odnosaji Matije Flacija Ilirika prema Reformacji u Polskoj" (Zagreb, 1929).

Of two others in the moat, it may be observed that the aged and bearded Ochino is given prominence out of a similar context; although he had indeed been only briefly in Poland and Lithuania, Hosius and Treter would have been especially conscious of him as the general of the Capuchins in Italy and the renowned revival preacher, whose apostasy had been grievous to the Cardinals who had promoted him. Viret of Orbe in French Switzerland, preacher in Geneva and Lausanne, was from 1561 to his death a leading figure in Huguenot centers; his *Instruction chrestienne en la doctrine de la Loy et l'Evangile* (3 vols.; Geneva, 1564), popularized Calvinism in France in dialogue form.

50. THE CATHOLIC MIND II: SIGISMUND III VASA (1586 – 1632)

50.A Sigismund III, son of Catherine Jagiellonka (Pl. 2) and John III Vasa of Sweden, was himself consecrated King of Sweden (1592 – 1600/04). The copperprint was executed by Abraham Hogenberg c. 1611, after the victory of Klushino of 1610 over Sweden and Muscovy (C); Muzeum Narodowe, Warsaw. The King has laid down his crown beside the crucifix. The titles beneath make him King of Sweden and victor over

Muscovy. The coat of arms of the thirty-nine lands under his rule surround his own coat of arms with five fields, under which it says in Latin, "Glory increases with redoubled cares."

Pro-Hapsburg and devoted to the Jesuits, Sigismund III aspired through the war and the election of his son or himself as Tsar, to implement the Counter-Reform on the basis of Catholic-Orthodox reunion (cf. Pl. 39); and with his eastern orientation, he made Warsaw the capital in 1611. It was precisely in this year that two Protestants were executed: the Italian Calvinist Franco di Franco in Vilna and the Byelorussian John Tyszkiewicz in Warsaw, the only Protestants judicially executed for heresy in the Commonwealth in the sixteenth or seventeenth century, even amid Counter-Reform, almost a "state without stakes." For this characterization of Poland, see Janusz Tazbir, *State Without Stakes* (1967; ET, 1973).

50.B. Kalwaria Zebrzydowska, the expiatory Polish Jerusalem and eventually the second most important Marian shrine in Poland proper, built by Nicholas Zebrzydowski after his Rebellion of 1606. Braun and Hogenberg, *Civitates orbis terrarum;* by permission of Houghton Library, Harvard University.

In the confederation of Stężyca (on the Vistula near Radom) and in Lublin, Zebrzydowski sought to resist the centralist program of Sigismund that had jeopardized "the golden liberty" in the Executionist Movement of the middle and lower gentry (1506–85, Pl. 6.A.). Armed confederation (*Rokosz*) to resist any act of royal authority deemed by any grouping of the *szlachta* as unconstitutional was constitutional. A few Protestant lords were among the confederates, including the patron of Raków. Amnestied, the Rebels against their intentions had paved the way for the seventeenth-century rule of the magnates and (in the eastern palatinates and in the Grand Duchy) the princes.

The model Jerusalem, henceforth a place of pilgrimage, was built near the castle of Lanckrona (upper left). In the foreground flows the stream Kedron and the sepulchre of the Virgin Mary. Above near the castle is the House of Mary, nearby the Palace of Caiaphas, and just below it the Cenacle. The highest eminence (center) is the church dedicated to Mary Magdalene, close to the site of Calvary and the Lord's Sepulchre. Part way down is the principal edifice of the whole complex, the basilica of the Virgin Mary. On the wooded hillside above the *Piscina prophetica* (lower center left) is the Palace of Pilate, from which the Via Crucis leads up past several small shrines of devotion, past the Palace of Herod, through the Gate onto the Via Dolorosa toward Calvary, where today there is a large cross. The practice of carrying heavy stones up these various hillsides in acts of penance developed over the years.

The translation of Torquato Tasso's *Geruselmme liberato* (in reference to the First Crusade; 1575; Polish, 1618) by Peter Kochanowski (d. 1620), nephew of John (Pl. 23), became *the* Polish national epic in the period after 1620. Poland, abandoning its neutral policy toward the Ottoman Empire, became increasingly involved in the repulse of the Turks, climaxing in King John III Sobieski's victory over them in the defense of Vienna, 1683. Increasingly, Poles had come to think of the Commonwealth as the *antemurale Christianitatis* and of themselves as crusaders of the New Jerusalem. The architectural and devotional development of Zebrydowski's Jerusalem, with the shrine of the Queen of heaven even more important than the Calvary, can be seen in part as the Catholic expression of a new Polish nationalism, ever less tolerant of religious minorities than in the sixteenth century.

50.C. Sigismund III, with his chancellor standing at his right, his son Ladislas seated at his left, received defeated Tsar Basil Shuisky, who was presented in Warsaw by Hetman

Stanislas Żółkiewski. A copperprint by Tomasz Makowski after a painting by Tomasso Dolabella; Muzeum Historyczne, Warsaw.

The presentation is in the Senate Chamber of the Palace, during the Diet of Warsaw, 29 October 1611. At the battle of Klushino (1610), Sigismund's rival and successor as king of Sweden, his uncle Charles IX Vasa (1604 – 11), had seen Shuisky defeated, the Swedish ally in the Kremlin during the Time of Troubles (1604 – 13).

The Time of Troubles had been preceded by the feeble rule of Theodore I (1584 – 98), ineffectual son of Ivan the Terrible. Theodore was succeeded by Boris Gudunov (1598 – 1605). Two false Dmitris, each alleging to be the murdered son of Ivan, complicated the succession, besides the accession of Theodore II (1605). The First False Demetrius was Gregory Ottreprowicki (Griska Uttrereya), protegé of the Polish Brother Matthias Twardochleb, rector in Kisielin (cf. Pl. 59). Demetrius seized the reins of government on the sudden death of Gudunov, and ruled very briefly with Polish support, losing his life in an insurrection headed by boyar Basil Shuisky (1606 – 10).

After his victory at Klushino, Sigismund had evaded the offer of the boyars to make his son Ladislas Tsar, anxious to secure the Kremlin throne himself. The humiliation of the defeated and deposed Tsar Basil and his two nephews marks the temporary ascendancy of Warsaw (the new capital) over Moscow and Stockholm.

50.D. The Bohemian Capuchin Valerian Magni (1586 – 1661), from Milan, irenicist, who interpreted Lutherans and Calvinists as schismatics rather than as heretics and who, under Ladislas IV, fostered the Colloquium Charitativum (Pl. 61). Muzeum Narodowe, Poznań, photograph by Z. Ratajczak; reproduced from Jobert, *De Luther à Mohila,* Pl. 14.

Valerian Magni magnanimously also fostered the Pacification of the Ruthenians and the reinstitution of the Orthodox hierarchy (Pl. 44).

50.E. Caspar Drużbicki (1588–1661) of Poznań, a mystic who debated with Christopher Lubieniecki, father of our Historian, in Lublin in 1637 (*Historia*, p. 256). Residence of the Jesuits, Church of St. Barbara, Cracow; reproduced from Jobert, *De Luther à Mohila*, Pl. 10.

51. THREE ASSAULTS ON THE CALVINIST CHURCH IN CRACOW, 1574, 1583, 1591

51.A. Sketch of the interior of the Calvinist church off the Market Square, a remodeled house on St. John's Street, the Brog ("Haystack"), 1571, showing the high central pulpit (cf. 57). The plan was found in the Archivo Segrato Vaticano by Lech Szczucki and first published by Halina Kowalska, "Z dziejów reformacji," *Szkice z dziejów Krakowa* (ed J. Bieniarzówna; Cracow, 1968).

The plan was sent by Nuncio Vincenzo del Portico from Warsaw to Rome, 6 September 1571, with the observation that King Sigismund Augustus, when shown it, was surprised to learn that the new construction on St. John's was not the repair of a house but its conversion into a church. The nuncio notwithstanding, the King already knew of the plans in general. At the Diet of Lublin on 8 August 1569 he had authorized a tax-free cemetery for Protestants outside the city walls and the right to worship within the walls (in property purchased in 1570). Previously to the remodeling, the congregation had been meeting in a house rented from Stanislas Tęczyński, palatine of Cracow, then in one of John Tarło, palatine of Lublin. To pay the rent, upkeep, and salaries, Scottish merchants present during the fairs also made contributions. A general synod of the

Reformed convened there, 29 September to 1 October 1573, to approve the Consensus of Sandomierz (Pl. 34); Sipayłło, *AS* 3.6.

Externally shaped like a haystack, referred to as "the Brog," the plan of its first floor makes vivid the manner of worship. Labeled "*Zbór* (church) of the heretics" by the hostile observer, the pulpit is in the center (top), women seated on the left facing it, men to the right. Of interest is the fact that the choir of the university students is indicated (*Kor żakowski*). The principal pastor at the time was Paul Gilowski, 1573, in succession to Gregory Paul (1552–67), Simon Zak (1562–70), and Andrew of Prażmowski.

51.B. A handbill showing the assault of 1574. The sketch with a descriptive poem is preserved in the Jagiellonian Library, printed by Piotr Chmielowski, *Historia literatury Polskiej,* 188.

Lubieniecki does not mention the episode, so far distant were the Major and the Minor Reformed Churches from each other even by this early date. The background of the assault was the interregnal uncertainty after the sudden departure of Henry of Valois for France after only three months of rule (Pl. 37). John Firley, the chief protector of Protestants, died in 1574, succeeded by Peter Zborowski as palatine of Cracow and *starosta.* The students of the University and the populace felt this was the occasion to challenge the *pax dissidentium* (Pl. 35), i.e., the right of the Reformed and others to be protected in their worship. In the legend at the top of the handbill the edifice is still referred to as "the *zbór,* which is called Lutheran."

The assault began at noon on Sunday, 10 October 1574, and went on night and day without intervention of the municipal authorities until Thursday. As simple as is the drawing, it brings out a number of details. In the foreground are the cobblestones of the Rynek of St. John's street. In the lower left evidently students are exhorting each other in front of the bonfire of the books being thrown out of the church, while a woman kneels to procure or save one for herself. Above the flames a man is seen carrying a bench which may indeed be the communion table, for a man with a flag in one hand and with the other pointing to the trophy, evidently feels that, as the counterpart of the Catholic altar, the table is the most important religious artifact to be plundered, while a man with a halberd stands at the head of his unit, evidently prepared to escort this trophy from the scene. The iron door to the left is in the process of being torn fom its hinges and from the walls by a man wielding an adze, and another at the right will be presently tearing out the other. On the floor above the street are seen two men throwing out more books, while on the side of the roof which has been breached, a couple of the merlons and a window and part of the wall have been thrown down (some of the debris resting under the side window). Two men are hacking away at the tiles on the peaked roof. The grills have been removed from two lower windows, front, while two men are entering through the broken windows, one man, presumably a member of the church, tries to hold them back, while the grill removed is itself being contested among four men. Just in front of them in the foreground a bowman has sent a shaft, perhaps with a flame, visible as it seeks its target just above the man on the second level throwing out a book. Next to the bowmen several men are hurling up rocks, while one man is catching books, and still another next to him is firing some kind of gun.

With the final massive entry into the house of prayer, the place was plundered, and the gold, silver, and other moneys and the bejeweled and expensive garments, kept there for safekeeping by the members, were carried off, with total damages estimated at 100,000 gulden. The city council did not intervene. Even the Calvinist deputy *starosta* of

Cracow did not dare send forces from the Wawel to the assistance of the city constabulary for fear that the populace would, taking advantage of the interregnum, enter the castle in support of Emperor Maximilian II (Pl. 42) as prospective King, while Palatine Zborowski himself was supporting for the Election Diet Prince Stephen Báthory (Pl. 39).

The nobility and the citizenry of Cracow demanded of Zborowski compensation for the enormous damages sustained and the punishment of the perpertrators. On 12 October, five journeymen masons and carpenters, the strongmen among the assailants of the church, were in fact put to death in front of the town hall, while the students and others most responsible escaped punishment; and the complaint and suit for indemnification never came to anything.

The edifice was restored to use, and a local synod was held there 13 May 1575. Wojciech Węgierski, *Chronik,* item 18. In provisions 4 and 5 of the synod, it was foreseen that the German pastor (Jacob Wolf) would conduct services on the second level and only for those unable to understand Polish, that he was not to be paid for by the Polish-speaking congregants, that he should preach quietly and they sing their hymns softly so as not to disturb the Polish congregants below, that the German participants above should never depart from the liturgical usage of the Poles, and that every member of the Polish congregation should appear at the service every Sunday and bring his or her hymnal and money for the collection. In the general synod in the Brog, 7 May 1576, several ministers "from Arianism and Anabaptism" were reconciled; Sipayłło, *AS* 3.15.

51.C. The sack of the Brog, 1587, with Draper's Hall (*Sukiennice*) visible in Market Square, a painting by Matejko, 1882. "Napad żaków na zbór luterski w Krakowie w roku 1587," photograph from the Muzeum Narodowe, Warsaw. The painting is now lost.

As in all of his works Matejko strove for historical accuracy in costumes etc. Note the removal of the organ as in the first assault. In the background is the Sukiennice which Matejko himself helped to restore to what was considered its original form.

After the third and final assault in May 1591, only the walls were left standing. At the same time the home of Stanislas Cichowski, the meetinghouse of the Minor Church was also assailed and the cemeteries of both congregations were desecrated. Cf. Map of Cracow. For the succession of three attacks, see Węgierski, *Chronik,* and for the last, also my "Skarga," *Shapers,* ed. Raitt, p. 179.

No doubt encouraged by what happened with impunity in Cracow, Catholics in Vilna burned the Calvinist church there in June 1591 (Pl. 14).

52. THE CATHOLIC-ORTHODOX UNION OF BREST LITOVSK, 1595/96

52.A. Brest in Lithuania, site of the Union, shown under siege during the Swedish Invasion. Copperplate by E.J. Dahlbergh, Samuel Pufendorf, *De Rebus a Carolo Gustavo gestis.*

52.B. Michael Rahoza, Metropolitan of Kiev (1589–99). From the frontispiece of Athanasius G. Velykyi, OSBM, ed., *Documenta Unionis Berestensis eiusque auctorum (15910–1600), Analecta ordinis S. Basilii Magni* (Rome, 1970). The picture is from a Uniate book of the seventeenth century, where in the tradition of the Eastern Church there is reserve about picturing the Triune God, here only as a radiating triangle with the divine eye at its center, while it is St. Nicholas, patron of the church, who extends his blessing upon it for the Union.

52.C. The Church of St. Nicholas in Brest, where the synod convened in 1595, under the leadership of Metropolitan Rahoza to unite the Orthodox Church of the Commonwealth with Rome on the basis of the decree of the Council of Florence of 1439, retaining their Liturgy, hence communion in both kinds, a married clergy, and the Julian calendar. From Velykyi, ed., p. 260. There is another version of the seal, evidently the first draft, wherein the form next to the Pope is the King of Poland, Sigismund II, with the Pope seated more in a gesture of blessing and without the tiara, while a Byzantine cross fills the space in the arched space behind a single Ruthenian bishop, symbolic of his whole Church, *ibid.*, 270. From Velykyi, *Documenta*, 260.

52.D. A seal struck presumably in Rome commemorating the submission of the Ruthenian espiscopate to Clement VII (sometime papal legate to Poland), to be followed by a second synod in Brest to ratify the terms. From Velykyi, ed., p. 270. The second synod of Brest was observed by the critical Cyril Lucaris (1572 – 1638), the later Protestantizing Patriarch of Constantinople and the scholarly, adroit opponent of the Union, as special envoy of the see of Alexandria. From Velykyi, *Documenta,* 270.

53. RESISTANCE TO THE UNION OF BREST LITOVSK

53.A. Prince Constantine Basil Ostrogski (Ostrozkyi) (1514 – 1608), palatine of Kiev, opponent of the Union, sponsor of the Cyrillic Bible (Pl. 54). The miniature in oil is a seventeenth-century copy of an original, painted by Jan Kasiński at the palace of Zamość between 1618 and 1633. It bears in Latin the legend: "Prince (*Dux*) in Ostrog, Count (*Comes*) in Tarnów [in little Poland, through his wife Zofia, heiress of Tarnów (d. 1570)], palatine of Kiev [from 1559]." There is no evidence of modernization of dress, which interestingly is not martial but, as it were, philanthropic. The coins in his hands set forth his munificence to the Orthodox Church. The present location of the copy, whether still in Zamość, is never proffered in the many reproductions, e.g., Platon Bilets'kyi, *Ukrains'kyi portretnyi zhyvopys xvii – xviii st.* (Kiev, 1966) 34; for the painter and date, see further, Edward Rastawiecki, *Słownik malarzów polskich, tudież obcych w Polsce osiadłych lub czasów w niej przebywających* (3 vols.; Warsaw, 1850 – 57) 1. 217 – 18.

Prince Ostrogski, greatest magnate in Volhynia, promptly convened a meeting of resistance to the Union in his home in Brest, 1595. Since 1590 he had his own college in Ostrog and a press, where he printed the Bible (Pl. 54), which in its preface suggests concern lest the Christology of the Socinians gain acceptance among the Orthodox. One book, *Ekthesis,* against the Union and particularly against the role of Peter Skarga (Pl. 49) therein, appears in Raków, 1597. For the anonymous *Ekthesis albo krótkie zebranie spraw,* see Gryczowa, no. 24.

53.B. Gideon Balaban, bishop of Lwów (cf. Pl. 60), along with Bishop Michael Kopystynskyi of Przemyśl (cf. Pl. 21), opposed to the Union. From Velykyi, *Documenta,* 251.

53.C. The General Confederation of Vilna of 30 May 1599, signed by many Protestant lords and Orthodox princes (but not by the two bishops, B) was a political front against the Counter-Reform, written in Polish and signed beside wax seals. From Domet Oljančyn, ''Zur Frage der Generalkonfederation zwischen Protestanten und Orthodoxen in Wilna, 1599,'' *Kairos: Vierteljahrsschrift für Kirchen- und Geistesgeschichte Osteuropas,* 1: 1 (1936), 32.

The General Confederation of Vilna embraced leaders among the Czech Brethren, Lutherans, and Reformed. Although representatives of the Minor Church in both Lithuania and Poland proper were not part of this action, it had significance for them, positive and negative, especially in Ruthenia and Volhynia, where they independently sought to court the Orthodox resistants to the Union.

53.D. Prince Christopher Nicholas Radziwiłł (1547 – 1603), son of Nicholas the Red (Pl. 14), a signatory. Martinus Franciscus Wobe, *Icones familiae ducalis Radivilianae . . .* (Nieśwież, 1758; 2d ed. Petersburg, 1875).

Palatine of Vilna (since 1584) and Grand Hetman of Lithuania (since 1589), he had married two of Ostrogski's daughters, as his second and fourth wife.

53.E. Peter Mohyla (Mogila) (1597 – 1646), Moldavian nobleman; founder of the Academy in Kiev, its metropolitan by 1632. A fresco portrait, slightly damaged, from the Church of the Saviour, Berestovo, Kiev. Hans Rothe, *Die älteste ostslawische Kunstdichtung, 1575 – 1647* (2 vols.; Giessen: Schmitz, 1976 – 77) 2. *Abbildung* 77, p. 520. The whole fresco, photographed by the author, is presented by Ihor Ševčenko in his article in the commemorative special issue, *The Kiev Mohyla Academy* (Harvard Ukrainian Studies 8: 1/2 [June 1984]). See also the more common portrait of Mohyla as metropolitan may be seen, among other places, in Velykyi, *Documenta,* 358.

After studying in Paris and serving as archimandrite of Kiev, Mohyla became metropolitan and the organizer of a renowned academy, in which Latin was used in defense of Orthodoxy. His *Confession* of 1632, prepared with the aid of three bishops, assimilated much of scholastic and even Protestant thought, including the *triplex munus Christi,* dear to Łaski and then the Polish Brethren. It was approved by the synod of Jassy in 1642 and by the four Eastern Patriarchs in 1643, first published in 1645.

Mohyla must have been polemically engaged also against the Protestant Confession of faith of Patriarch Cyril Lukaris (Constantinople, 1629), wherein only two sacraments were acknowledged and justification by faith alone set forth in Greek. See further the projected edition of the text in four languages including Polish, under the auspices of the Harvard Ukrainian Institute in a series of edited or facsimile reprints in commemoration of the conversion of Kiev, 988 – 1988.

54. BIBLES IN THE EAST UNDER THE IMPACT OF PROTESTANTISM

54.A. John *Leopolita,* sponsor, Biblia (Cracow: Matthew *Scharffenberg,* 1561); Polish, Catholic. Italicized are the names by which the version is commonly known. Taken from Henryk Biegeleisen, *Illustrowane dzieje literatury polskiej* (4 vols.; 1898 – 1908) 3. 187.

Under the impact of Jerome of Prague, who taught in the Cracovian Academy in 1410, Queen Jadwiga encouraged the Hussite teachings and fostered a vernacular version of Scripture although little of that work survived. The first study of *all* Polish translations is that of Maria Kossowska, *Biblia w języku polskim* (2 vols.; Poznań, 1968/69), with chapter summaries in French. Pressure to get a Catholic version in Polish was stimulated by the Polish New Testament (Königsberg, 1551–53). See further David Frick, *Polish Sacred Philology in the Reformation and the Counter-Reformation: Chapters in the History of Controversies (1551–1630)* (Berkeley: University of California Press, 1989).

The basic Catholic Bible of the sixteenth century was that of John Kasprowicz-Nicz called *Leopolita*. He may have been helped by a Czech version of 1549. The first edition was dedicated to Sigismund II Augustus, the second edition (1575) to Henry of Valois, and after his escape, the remainder of the issue to Stephen Batory. On the title page the two principal figures on either side are Moses with the tablets of the Law and Jesus with the lamb saved and the legend from John 1:17: "For the Law was given through Moses; grace and truth came through Jesus Christ." The contrast is set forth in the panel above. In the center the soul, symbolized by a nude seated woman, is urged by gestures to arise and go from the Old to the New. The Jewish figure, perhaps Zechariah, who points to the cross, has on his side the temptation and the fall of Adam and Eve, the sarcophagus of death in consequence of their fatal choice, and Moses' reception of the tablets on Sinai; on the side of the New Testament: the Annunciation to Mary also on a mount like Moses, John the Baptist pointing to the Lamb of God who takes away the sins of the world, and the crucifixion. In the three panels below are the birth of Christ, the baptism of him by John, and the Last Supper.

54.B. Translation begun as *Pinczovian* by George Orsatius, Peter Statorius, and John Thenaud, Biblia święta (*Brest* Litovsk: Bernard Wojewódka *et al.*, 1563), publication paid for by Nicholas *Radziwiłł* the Black; Polish, *Calvinist*. Taken from Kossowska, *Biblia*, 1. Pl. 16.

The first Reformed Bible, commissioned early by the synods of Little Poland, with many readings favorable to a Unitarian interpretation. It was worked on mostly in Pińczów, with the Geneva Bible in French the basis, although the Hebrew and Greek texts were consulted, as the title-page indicates.

The tree growing up from the bottom and behind the panel for the title has lost its leaves on the Old Testament side. On this side are the temptation of Adam and Eve, the sarcophagus of death their punishment, Moses on Sinai receiving the tablets of the Law, a burning bush a little lower down on the mountain side. On the New Testament side, the counterpart mount, is that where Mary receives the Annunciation. Further down is the crucified Christ, the Lamb with banner at the base of the cross. In the four panels below, the motifs of the upper panels of the Scharffenberger Bible (A) are repeated but with some differences: Adam and Eve are being driven from the Garden, the serpent on the cross in the camp of the Israelites, the shepherds in the fields hearing the angels sing, Christ resurrected from the ground.

When Nicholas Radziwiłł the Black died in 1564, his son Nicholas VIII Christopher the Orphan, having converted to Catholicism, drove the heretics out of his property at Nieśwież and tried to destroy the edition, which was published in one or two other centers.

54.C. Simon *Budny* (d. 1593), Biblia (Nieśwież/Zasław: Matthew Kawieczyński, Daniel of Łęczyca, 1572); Polish, Unitarian. Taken from Kossowska, *Biblia*, 1.

The Budny Bible is also connected with the effort at Pińczów in the person of Daniel of Łęczycza, printer both there and in Lithuania. Budny, a master of Hebrew and Greek, upheld in his explanatory notes the (Helvidian) view that Jesus was the son of Joseph, suppressed by the censor in 1572. He republished his New Testament in 1574 with his critical apparatus intact. It was against this version that Martin Czechowic published his also scholarly New Testament (Cracow: Rodecki, 1577), in which in his commentary he was concerned with the preexistent Christ and the Logos. He and John Niemojewski were opposed on this issue by Socinus.

Iconographically the title page of the 1572 Bible carried on motifs of the Scharffenberg Bible and the Radziwiłł Bibles. The tree up through the center is again denuded on the Old Testament side. But the contrasting mounts at the top are no longer contrasted. Instead, the figure of God in majesty orders the angels to blow a trumpet and below the Israelites take heed of the serpent mounted on the cross in their desert camp, while on the New Testament side Mary still receives the Annunciation and shepherds in the field tend their flock nearby in anticipation of their visit to Bethlehem. On the middle level the Old Testament side has Adam and Eve, while on the other side Christ is victorious over death and the devil. At the lowest level prominence is given to horned Moses with his tablets as basic to the choice bewtween life and death, while on the other side a convert, guided by an apostle, receives directly from the side of Christ on the cross, the gift of life.

It is likely that the "Daniel" in the moat of heretics in Pl. 49.C was there primarily because of Daniel of Łęczyca as printer of the Budny Bible. For the picture of him, see Pls. 9.D and 49.A.

Budny's *O przedniejszych wiary chrystyjańskiej artykulech* (1576) has been edited Lech Szczucki, et al., Biblioteka Pisarzy Reformacyjnych, No. 16 (Warsaw/Łódź: PWN, 1989).

54.D. The *Biblij swata* in six parts, translated by a team at the instigation of John Blaholav (1523–71), commissioned by Unitas Bishop John Aeneas, working at the castle of *Kralice* (Kralitz), owned by John of Žerotín, who assumed the costs, 1579–94/96. Shown in the title page of the one-volume Bible of 1596 for the laity, reposing in the Archives of the Moravian Church in America, Bethlehem (1741), Pennsylvania. Cf. cropped picture of the same in *Unitas Fratrum: Moravian Church in Pictures* (Prague, 1957) 55.

Above on the scroll in the Tetragrammaton (Yahweh). On either side of the title are Moses and the resurrected Christ. Below Christ is pictured at his Second Advent, a crowned King, seated in a chariot, the four wheels of which are the four gospels, drawn by lambs and heralded by the royal harpist David in ermine with other Old Testament worthies in a triumphant royal progress over death, as the King of kings looks back at the bodies arising from their graves.

The multi-volume Unitas *Biblij swata* in six parts with commentary for pastors was started by John Blahoslav (1523–71) under a commission of six scholars, made up of Bishop John Aeneas, chairman, and several specialists who had studied Hebrew and Greek in Wittenberg and Basel, including "the son of a baptized Jew of Poznań," Lukas Helič, all working in the castle of Kralice (below Olomouc in Moravia), owned by John of Žerotín, who assumed the costs. The Utraquists had a Bible translated from the Vulgate (Venice, 1506). The Kralice press was run by Zacharias Solin (d. 1595), a Unitas priest.

The Pentateuch appeared in 1579 as part 1; the Apocrypha as part 5 appeared in 1588, and the New Testament of Blahoslav, already in use (since 1564), came out revised in 1590, as part 6, the whole set ready in 1594.

Above the title page of each part is the episcopal device of the Unitas: "Vincit agnus noster, eum sequamur," and on the reverse side of the title page of part one several scriptural sanctions are used: Deut 31:11, Jos 1:8, 7, Luke 16:29, John 5:46, and Luke 24:27: "And beginning at Moses, and all the prophets, he [Jesus] expounded them in all the Scriptures the things concerning himself." This Bible with its Apocrypha, not used by the Polish Reformed, was that of the Czech Brethren in Great Poland and within reach during the synod that eventuated in the Consensus of Sandomierz, 1570 (Pl. 34). The press of Kralice was carried to Leszno in Great Poland.

See further, Mirjam Bohatcová et al., *Kralice* (Brno, 1959), with English summary, and Joseph Th. Müller, *Geschichte der Böhmischen Brüder,* 3: "Die polnische Unität 1548 – 1793; Die böhmisch-mährische Unität 1575 – 1781" (Herrnhut, 1931) 291 – 93. I am grateful to the Rev. Vernon Nelson, archivist, and Gregory A. Crawford of Reeves Library, Moravian College, Bethlehem, Pennsylvania.

54.E. Herasym Danylovych Smotrytskyi (d. 1594) Byblya (*Ostrih*: Ivan Fedorovyč, 15810 – 81), sponsored by Constantine Basil Ostrogski; Old Slavonic, Orthodox. Taken from the Houghton Library copy, published by Robert Mathiesen, "The Making of the Ostrih Bible," *Harvard Library Bulletin* 29 (1981) 71 – 110.

The Ostrih (Ostrog) Bible was the first printed in Church Slavonic for the whole Orthodox world. And from its two prefaces it was evidently directed in part against the low Christology reflected in the readings of the Budny Bible and threatening in Ukraine to the sponsor of the publication, Prince Ostrogski (d. 1608), major opponent of the Union of Brest (Pl. 53). In this critical version, Ostrogski was willing to have his Muscovite printer and his Ukrainian editor take into consideration Catholic versions.

54.F. Caspar Károlyi, Biblia (*Vizsoly*; Altal Balint, 1590); Hungarian, Calvinist. Taken from the copy in Budapest, Rádat Library, reproduced, Oskar Thulin, ed., *Reformation in Europa* (Leipzig/Kassel: Stauda, 1967) 165.

The New Testament motto is taken from Luke 16:29: "They have Moses and the prophets; let them hear them." The Unitarians had a New Testament in Hungarian, but the first full Bible translation was that of Károlyi, the former rector of the school in Koloszvár, pastor in Göncz, the inspiration for the task coming from Debrecen. For all their interest in the Old Testament, the Unitarians used this version which remains, with updating in the spelling and syntax, the Protestant Bible of Hungarians to this day.

54.G. Jonas Bretkūnas (Bretke) (d. 1602), The Luther Bible, 8 MS volumes (Königsberg, 1579 – 90), not published until 1735; *Lithuanian Lutheran.* Shown is the New Testament when published after a long delay; see the illustrated bibliography of Lithuanian publications with a chronology in the back, *Lietuvos T.S.R., Bibliografija,* series A, *Knygos Lietuvių Kalba,* 1: *1547 – 1861* (Vilna, 1969) items 550 and 551.

54.H. Jacob *Wujek*, S.J. (d. 1597), Biblia święta (Cracow: Łazarz . . . , 1599); Polish, Catholic. Taken from *Odrodzenie w Polsce.*

Jacob Wujek, S.J. (1541 – 97), a major theologian, publicist, and opponent of Protestants in general and the Unitarian Socinians in particular, died before his major work was completed. Though Wujek based his work on the Vulgate, he kept close to the Greek text for the New Testament. Expenses were borne by Primate Karnkowski and Gregory XIII, which may explain the prominence of some features on the title page. Above is symbolized the inspiration of Holy Writ by the Triune God, creator of heaven and earth, the Holy Spirit descending prominently from the common Godhead of Father and Son in the form of the hovering Dove. Old and New Testament are held together in the arc that binds Moses with his staff and burnt sacrifice to Peter with his keys and the sacrifice of the eucharistic altar. Capital letters on the side of the Old and New Testament are meant to suggest further analogies: creation and fall, the new creation, and at the bottom on either side hell and its harrowing by Christ. The central figure is the Church symbolized by a woman of authority with a papal tiara. She holds with her right hand the tablets of the old Law, while lines interconnect the Mosaic sacrifice, the serpent on the cross, the tree of the knowledge of good and evil above the open coffin; with her left hand she holds the Bible in two testaments and Tradition symbolized by a smaller book resting on it with its two clasps. Standing on a platform perhaps symbolic of the triune authority of God, but perhaps also Scripture, Tradition, and Magisterium, she directs her gaze down upon the order in society at the right where the King of Poland is kneeling, sword and orb on the floor beside him, before the reigning Supreme Pontiff, other crowned heads in the background.

55. PIETY, PRACTICE, AND POLITY: I: IMAGES OF CHRIST

55.AB. The Sorrowing or Worried Christ of peasant piety, from the sixteenth century. For this type of Christ so widespread in Polish and Lithuanian piety and surely therefore within the awareness of the Polish and Lithuanian Brethren, see Anna Kuncyńska, "Chrystus frasobliwy w polskiej rzeźbie ludowiej," *Etnografia Polska* (1960) 211–27.

The Worried Christ became distinctive in Poland and Lithuania in the sixteenth century, usually carved from wood and placed in the fields and at road corners. It translates the *Christus lassus* (weary) of the Requiem Mass. Developing from Franciscan, Dominican, and Bernardine piety, the figure owes something to apocryphal literature about Jesus' waiting for the Crucifixion, his garments folded over his legs. The figure entered Polonia from Germany by way of Lower Silesia. Peasant woodcarvers identified with his plight. Cf. the crucified Christ distributing the elements, Pl. 3.

55.A. Polish. Christ *Rupintojélis* from Lithuania; *Lithuanian Franciscan Fathers.*

5B.B. Lithuanian. *Chrystus Frasobliwy* woodcarving; *Katalog zabytków sztuki w Polsce,* 5:15.

55.C. Christ washing the feet of the Apostles, fresco from Sandomierz, showing the influence of the Ruthenian school in a Latin-rite cathedral. Antoni Kunysz, *Przemyśl miasto zabytków* (Cracow, 1968) 48.

Christ is here the Ascended, the Omnipotent, the sole "image of the invisible God" (Col 1:15). Byzantine iconography was reserved about the representation of the Triune God, at most by symbols, like the three angels visiting Abraham and Sarah under the oaks of Mamre, or by a triangle (cf. Pl. 44).

On the Byzantine-rite frontier, the Polish Brethren, some of whom were converts from Orthodoxy in Ruthenia and further east, were sensitive to the restraints in picturing God otherwise than as Christ the Teacher, Christ the Crucified, or Christ the Ascended Lord next to the *invisible* Father, ruling the world and destined to descend to judge the quick and the dead.

55.D. The Epiphany of the Three Persons at the baptism of Jesus, from Nicholas Rej, *Postilla* (Cracow, 1556). Photography by Stanisław Kołowce; PAN, Instytut Sztuki, by permission.

A surviving, partly restored, fragment of one of several frescoes by painters from Przemyśl in the cathedral of St. Mary, some of them of even more distinctively Ruthenian (Kievan) motif, from the first half of the fifteenth century; reproduced by Wojciech Kalinowski et al., *Sandomierz*, Pls. 100–12. The inscriptions on several are still in Cyrillic, here such letters have been largely Latinized, "Christus Apostolis pedes lavat."

55.E. "The Man/the Lord Jesus." Facsimile edition (1965) of the *Postylla* of Nicholas

Rey (Cracow, 1556), for the Feast of Trinity Sunday (enjoined as universal 1334), Part II, 148 n.

This scene is traditional and Rey's commentary came before the schism in the Polish Reformed Church in 1563. But in his defense of the Trinity Rey, who stood later with the Minor Church "against distrust concerning the Holy Trinity," argued here solely in scriptural terms for the "great mystery" uniting heaven and earth; and, although he used Person (not a scriptural term) also of the Holy Spirit (here symbolized by the Dove), he eschewed the technical credal terms *consubstantialis,* etc. This sole epiphany of Three Persons together in Scripture remained prominent when the (Unitarian) Minor Church moved to adopt believers' baptism by immersion in imitation of Christ at Jordan.

From the scriptural scene, without the supports of conciliar formularies, it is especially clear how the Reformed in the current of Rey, moved from the earnest asseveration of the Mystery of the Unity to the Tritheism of three conforming wills, to the Ditheism of God the Father and Jesus Christ in Glory, to the unity of the Godhead *of the Father,* with Christ in the one phase of the devolution as somehow preexistent and in the final stage as coming into being only as Jesus at his Virgin birth.

55.EF. The Unitarian medal struck in Nuremberg, c. 1580, is preserved in the Przypkowski Collection. The Hebrew is not flawless. In transliteration the text reads: *Māshîah melekh bā besgālôm wa' Adam-' Adām ' āsûi hai.*

Another rendering of the Hebrew could be: "The Messiah of the Kingdom of Peace became a human being." This is the interpretation of the curator of the Collection, Tadeusz Przypkowski, who conjectures that his family cherished the medal as generally illegible when they reluctantly conformed to Catholicism after the decree of banishment in 1660. See his valuable display of pictures and interpretation, "Zabytki Reformacji w Kielecczyźnie," *Studia Renesansowe* (ed. Michał Walicki; Wrocław: Ossolineum, 1956) 57–86; and for the Hebraic medal, 81–82.

This striking image of Jesus as Rabbi, many times reproduced as an invaluable artifact of Polish Unitarianism, should not obscure the fact that among the Polish Brethren this understanding was not arrived at anywhere nearly so swiftly as in Transylvania.

Even the Christology of Socinus would not be best represented by the medallion, as for him, Jesus the Virgin-born son and servant of God, after his baptism was exalted by the Father to be instructed as to the final verities to be proclaimed. Socinus, moreover, pictured the resurrected and ascended victoriously obedient Christ as in heaven; and his image of him, to whom he directed prayer and whom he adored (in contrast to nonadorant Dávid), was perhaps not much unlike the Christos Pantocrator of the Ruthenians, among whom his own biography was written by Samuel Przypkowski. Cf. The Christology of Laelius Socinus (Pl. 13), Faustus Socinus (Pl. 47), and Socinus's follower Schmalz (Pl. 59).

In the period before the impact of Socinus's Christology on the Brethren, Stanislas Farnowski, whose name was given to his followers as a separate church of the Farnovians, could publish in Polish, e.g., in quarto, *The true doctrine of Christian discipline in the Church of the true Son of God exclusively according to the whole New Covenant* (1573), to which was added also in Polish the *Sum of the Christian knowledge and confession concerning the One True Father, the Father of our Lord and our Father through him unto eternal life,* along with prayers to God the Father and His Son and hymns in praise of both of them; and finally another work, dedicated to Szafraniec, *A clear demonstration that the Epistle of Concord, which the Ebionites [the full Unitarians, who still believed in the Virgin birth, over against the Josephites like Budny] published concerning Christ the Son of God, as concerning other things, does not agree with the Truth and even with itself* (1578). To this book Czechowic, himself long a defender of the preexistence of Christ and an opponent to the end of Socinus, made a *Responsum* in 1579. All this from *BAnt*², 52 and rewrite. To his *Responsum* may be added the *Rozdek* of his pacifist patron, John Niemojewski, against several Catholics in Lithuania, included in quarto with a *Reply* to Canon Jerome Powodowski of Poznań, all dedicated to John Chlebowic, palatine of Troki, as "from the ministers, elders and deacons, of the Church confessing in Lithuania and Ruthenia the One God and His Only begotten Son" (Łosk, 1589). *BAnt*², 50 and rewrite.

56. ORDINANCES OF THE RELIGIOUS LIFE II: BAPTISM AND THE LORD'S SUPPER

56.A. Baptism by immersion among the Rijnsberg Collegiants, the Netherlands, 1736. The distinctive practice came from the Polish Brethren. From J. C. van Slee, *De Rijnsburger Colleganten* (Haarlem, 1895; reprinted with illustrations, Utrecht, 1980); see also Ugo Gastaldi, *Storia dell'Anabattismo* (2 vols.; Turin: Claudiana, 1981) 2.713, no. 37.

It is thought that Johannes Geesteranus, who was in Raków in 1621, introduced the practice of immersion to the spiritualizing lay Remonstrants (deprived of pastors by forced exile), whence the practice passed to the English Baptists sojourning in the Netherlands. The scene in Holland suggests also the influence of the local Jewish *mikveh;* and, in any case, the practice is here domesticated and made elegant beyond the usage among the Polish Brethren, who immersed converts and their own catechumens in ponds and streams in the name of Christ or more commonly in the name of the Father, the Son, and the Holy Spirit (Matt 28:19). Immersion in the Commonwealth may have been practiced at dawn or at dusk in some secretiveness. In any case, there are few clues as to how it was enacted, except that catechumens recited their faith in the form of the Apostles' Creed on emergence from the water.

The synod of Lublin of 1593, dealing *inter alia* with the two sacraments and church discipline, says tightly ". . . that immersions are varied, although firstly it is understood as the life of regeneration or renewal, then death, then doctrine (*nauka*), and at the end the water." Christopher Ostorodt (d. 1611), son of the Lutheran pastor of Goslar and who submitted to rebaptism during the synod of Chmielnik, September 1585, addressed the Brethren in Latin. While briefly at the head of the immersionist Unitarian church in Śmigiel (cf. Pl. 38), Ostorodt writing (c. 1585) to Anabaptists in Strassburg, who did not immerse, says: "Where there is no immersion there is no true external baptism (*Taufe*). *Taufen* is old German and means the same as *teufen*, 'to dip in.' Ask . . . the Mennonites about it who in their language call both *doopen*. Moreover, where you don't dip or immerse in the water, you have no understanding of baptizing unto the death, burial, and resurrection of the Lord Jesus Christ. . . . From this it comes about that Paul [1 Cor 10:1] can compare baptismal immersion with [passage through] the Red Sea; and Peter [1 Pet 3:21], with the flood. And this immersion takes place publicly with us in water courses or rivers (where this is possible) with public confession of sins and forgiveness."

The practice of immersion would surely have been discussed with Remonstrants and perhaps Mennonites by Christopher Ostorodt and Andrew Wojdowski (d. perhaps after 1625) on a proselytizing visitation in the Netherlands (Leiden, Amsterdam, Franeker) separately, then together, 1597–99. Wojdowski, son or brother of the pastor in Chmielnik where Ostorodt was himself rebaptized in 1585, was sometime preceptor in

Lewartów and Raków, an ardent Unitarian immersionist, author of a lost work on Servetus and the *Triadomachia*.

56.B. Seal of the Calvinist Church in Cracow with the Ark of Noah, a motif held in common with the Unitarians. *Monumenta Reformationis Polonicae et Lithuanicae*, 1:1, 185.

The seal of the Calvinist church of Cracow was used in the contract between Jean Thenaud of Bourges, one of the translators of the Radziwiłł Bible (Pl. 54), when he was engaged as rector of the school in Cracow, 10 March 1572.

The seal of the Calvinist congregation of Cracow, 1572, reads: "Zbor Bozy/Archa Noe/ Sigillum Caetus Evang[elici] Crac[oviensis] Deum In Trinit[ate] Credent[is]: The Church of God / the Ark of Noah / Seal of the Evangelical Congregation in Cracow believing in God in Trinity." The Ark of Noah is the same image of the Church as in Schomann's *Catechesis* of 1574, there based upon the redeeming waters of believers' baptism by immersion (RD 7). The *Catechesis* was issued conjointly by Schomann and Gregory Paul, the latter once minister of the undivided Reformed congregation in Cracow. It is plausible to assume that the image of the Ark was once common to what became the two groupings in Cracow after the schism of 1563.

56.C. Communion cloth, dated 1651. Photograph by Zbigniew Pasek, whether Calvinist or Unitarian is not certain. The embroidery reads: "Covering of the Table of God, A.D. 1651." The left tenth has disappeared through moth or rot; and the end of the first line is enigmatic. The second line evokes the Last Day, while the words below among the flowers declares: "My blood has eternal life."

The observance of the Lord's Supper in Little Poland will have been influenced by that among the Czech Brethren, the usage of John Łaski in East Frisia and London, and the usage of the Swiss. Łaski's order of 1555 called for Communion on the first Sunday of every month, preceded by a day of discipline and with much stress on the serving of the consecrated elements and related gifts to the poor. See his Latin and Dutch *ordo* in context, Irmgard Pahl, ed., *Coena Domini I: Die Abendmahlsliturgie der Reformationskirchen im 16./17. Jahrhundert*, Spicilegium Friburgense, 29 (Freiburg Schweiz: Universitätsverlag, 1983), text 21.

The Polish Reformed were also familiar with the custom of Geneva (imposed on Calvin, who had actually preferred frequent communion) of the four annual communions, on Christmas Day, Easter, Pentecost, and on the first Sunday following Michaelmas (September 29). The Polish Brethren, whether they observed Communion quarterly or monthly (in certain groups weekly), on the preceding Saturday afternoon held a long session of sermonic exhortation and then entered into both mutual and private examination of conscience. Attendants of the solemn exercise in discipline and exaltation often came on horseback and carriage from long distances in the act of solidarity in Christ among the Brethren and Sisters. Young people met appropriate prospective spouses after such gatherings, there being a strong disposition to promote marriage within the bonds of the Brotherhood and "exogamous" marriages only with the approval of the elders. Ostorodt testifies to even daily communions (D).

56.D. Communion charger from the Reformed Church in Lublin, 1618. From Walerjan Krasiński, *Zarys dziejów powstania i upadku Reformacji w Polsce* (trans. Juliusz Bursche; 2 vols.; Warsaw, 1904) 2:1, 210. The verse of 1 Cor 10:16 around the rim reads: "The bread which we break is it not the community of the Body of Christ?"

The Minor and Major Reformed Church were equally fervid in the observance of the Lord's Supper. At the Minor Church synod of Lublin of 1593, it was agreed: "The purpose or end of the Lord's Supper is the recollection of Christ and the recital of his death, that is, it is the giving of praise that at length by the grace of the Lord Christ and in thankfulness that he is united with us, that he gave his body to be crucified for us and his blood to be poured out. This is represented or presented to our eyes through the breaking of the bread and the pouring of the wine from the tumbler (*kubek*)." Christopher Ostorodt, writing from Śmigiel to the Strassburg Anabaptists, somewhat earlier (cf. A) says more descriptively what is canonically in the Lublin protocol: "The Lord's Supper we attend often and, indeed, where possible every day. . . . So seek the body and blood of the Lord not in the bread and wine, but rather the bread and wine in the body and blood of the Lord, that is, in his congregation [1 Cor 10:16], although [to be sure] we do not consider the bread and wine and the table of the Lord like other bread and wine, but as the Lord's bread and wine and the Lord's table, that is, as consecrated or blessed. And thus it is not fitting that an unclean person (as also no uncircumcised person could eat of the paschal lamb) should sit and eat with the others, from which table indeed not only the unimmersed, but also the immersed, if they have soiled themselves by sin, are to be excluded." For the letter of Ostorodt to Strassburg, c. 1585, see Theodor Wotschke, *ARG* (1915) 145 – 47; for the protocol of the synod of Lublin, 1593, see Lech Szczucki and Janusz Tazbir, "Księga wizytacji zborów podgórskich," *Archiwum Historii Filozofii i Myśli Społecznej* 3 (1958) esp. 152 – 53.

56.E. *On the Lord's Supper* (Raków, 1618), in which Socinus responds to the more conservative views on the discipline of communion held by John Niemojewski. Faustus Socinus responds critically to John Niemojewski on the Lord's Supper (Raków, 1618). Niemojewski (d. 1598), land judge in Inowrocław south of Toruń, who had submitted to rebaptism in 1566, freed his retainers, was as the lay elder in Lublin, the major supporter of Martin Czechowic (Pl. 27).

Socinus, himself unordained, opposed Czechowic in Lublin as too sectarian as also his redoubtable lay elder. Niemojewski, who had been active in the formation of Raków, was opposed to magistrates as members of the church because of their exercise of the office of the sword. Niemojewski had raised questions about the Lord's Supper in a letter to George Schomann (Pl. 31) and had taken on the Catholic controversialist, Immanuel Vega, S.J. of Vilna on transubstantiation (Łosk, 1588). Cf. the long entry in $BAnt^2$. Socinus had this material rendered in Latin, after Niemojewski's death, after he had been instrumental in replacing Czechowic with Valentine Schmalz (Pl. 59.A) in Lublin. Socinus refers to the canon of the synod of Lublin of 1593 on the Lord's Supper.

The differences among Niemojewski, Czechowic, and Socinus were not important as regards the manner of the observance of the Lord's Supper, but rather on the disciplinary issue of who was appropriately included in the fellowship of the communicants. Schomann, Czechowic, and even Ostorodt (himself destined to be much influenced by Socinus in Raków) held that the nonimmersed, like Socinus himself, and sinners, including wielders of the sword as knights or magistrates, could not participate in the Supper. The composite *De Coena* is of importance in marking the transition from immersionist Unitarianism as a pacifist sect to a fellowship of Evangelical Rationalists (Humanists) prepared to make concessions to the knightly class which had supported the Minor Church to this point, i.e., to c. 1600. The death of pacifist Niemojewski and of the conscientious evangelical lord, Jerome Filipowski, might be taken as the moment when the Minor "sect" became indeed, in the terminology of Ernst Troeltsch, the Minor "Church" of compassionate and compromising inclusion. Niemojewski was a kind of last Evangelical Polish *Pan* Quixote, the immersionist knight without sword or retainers.

57. ORDINANCES OF THE RELIGIOUS LIFE III:
SERMONS, SYNODS, SCHOOLS

57.A. The Major and Minor Church in Piaski. Photograph by Zbigniew Pasek.

The ruins of the Major Reformed Church in Piaski, once owned by Andrew Sucholdoski, three miles from Lublin. There was also a meeting place for the Minor Church. Over the portal of this large edifice (of all surviving edifices built from the ground up by the Reformed of either party in the Commonwealth surely this is the most reflective of Reformed self-confidence in their place in society) there are clear traces of a cross, perhaps even a crucifix. Lubieniecki deals with the town and church in his next to penultimate chapter.

57.B. The Minor Church in Piaski turned to mundane uses; from *Miasta Polski w Tysiącleciu* (Wrocław, etc.: Ossolineum, 1965) 1. 689.

57.C. Domestic prayer. Prayer of children at the feet of their parents before going to sleep, a woodcut from Rej. It could well serve as the frontispiece for Schomann's *Oeconomia Christiana,* prayers for the Christian household attached to his *Catechesis* 1574.

57.D. Sunday worship, Czech Brethren. A detail, showing the worship of the Czech Brethren, from a folio copper plate, that in its entirety features John Amos Comenius (Pl. 61) seated writing at a desk with several windows, like this one, looking out upon aspects of his activity. It constitutes the frontispiece of *Opera didactica omnia* (Amsterdam, 1657–58). This whole plate itself dates from 28 March 1592, to illustrate Comenius's works published from 1627 to 1657, and could well represent the arrangement for worship in Leszno, very similar to the arrangement suggested by the floor plan for the Calvinist Brog in Cracow (Pl. 51.A), where, however, the seating for the women is more prominent. The whole frontispiece is produced in Soupis Děl, *J. A. Komenského v československých knihovnách, Archiwech a Museich* (Prague, 1959) p. 11.

57.E. The first hymn of the Brethren, composed by Zofia Oleśnicka (Cracow, 1556). Title page of the oldest Reformed hymn, with the music in four parts, composed by Zofia Oleśnicka (Pl. 10.B), printed by Łazarz Andrysowic (Cracow, 1556); reprinted by Włodzisław Wojcicki, *Biblioteka starożytna pisarzy polskich* (4 vols.; 2d ed.; Warsaw, 1859) 9 – 16. Roland Bainton reproduces the music in four parts and a translation, *Women of the Reformation: From Spain to Scandanavia,* 169 – 76.

The title reads: "A new song [cf. Rev. 5:9] in which is the giving of thanks unto the Lord God Almighty that he has deigned to reveal the secret of His Kingdom to the humble and those of low degree [cf. the Magnificat, Luke 1:52]." The identity of the authoress is clear from the acrostic, her name printed in heavy face. The intense individualism of the composer is all the more remarkable for the likelihood that the whole quarto volume of eight pages was probably held in the hands of the members of the congregation or the choir (cf. the scenes of choir and singing in Pl. 51). Reformed hymnody owed some of its modality to Jewish music.

57.F. Arian School in Lewartów. The school in Lewartów (today Lubartów) northeast of Lublin; Przypkowski Collection, Jędrzejów.

After the death of its Calvinist owner, Nicholas Firley in 1588, the town came under the control of the widow's son-in-law, Nicholas Kazimierski of the Minor Church. He called from Chmielnik Albert (Wojciech) of Kalisz to become a rector of a new school of interconfessional attractiveness, the forerunner and model for that at Raków (1602 – 38) and Kisielin in Volhynia (1638 – 55).

57.G. Laws of the School of Lewartów, 1593. Description in the form of twelve letters of *The School of Lewartów Restored* (Cracow: Rodecki, 1593); from Alodia Kawecka Gryczowa, *Ariańskie oficyny wydawnicze*, Pl. 6.

This is a second edition after the School had been forced to shut down because of the Tatar invasion of Podolia. Only the pupils from Riga and Dorpat were allowed to remain in the precincts. The Laws contain the program and regulations for the pupils and preceptors of the five classes, concluding with a letter of 1582 from John Sturm, pedagogue in Strassburg, to Albert of Kalisz (Calissus). Instruction was on such a high level for all of Poland that Calvinists sent their sons there, too, although their synod of Lublin of 1594 warns that their offspring while in attendance should not be drawn into "disputations concerning religion with the rebaptizers (*nowokrzceńcy*)." The similar Laws for the School in Raków, 1602, by Stanislas (II) Lubieniecki, are translated in *PB*, Doc. II.

57.H. A learned page from an autograph book. A page from the Album of Andrzej Lubieniecki; cf. Pl. 59.

One Stanislas Szykowski signs on the next page with his coat of arms, having here displayed his skill in writing his possibly personal motto, Ps 16:8, as quoted in Acts 2:25: "I saw the Lord always before me, for he is at my right hand that I may not be shaken." Calvinists and Unitarians alike, particularly the latter, attached great importance to the Aramaic Bible of the Syriac Church, the Peshitta, since the New Testament therein could be thought of as preserving the Gospel in the language spoken by Jesus. The verse is written first in Syriac (Christian Aramaic), then in cursive Greek, and finally in Szykowski's own translation (not identical with that in the Vulgate). At Lewartów, Raków, and Leszno students were ideally trilingual with respect to the three languages of the cross. Here even greater linguistic virtuosity is on display in the Arian historian's Memory Album of Friends.

57.I. A palatine dietine, the model of the synod. A dietine for the palatinate meeting on a clear day in the square in front of the parish church of Środa in Great Poland, a lithograph from a later period; from Jerzy Topolski, *Dzieje Polski,* 338.

It is placed here to suggest the political model behind the palatine and general synods of the Reformed Churches, Major and Minor. They convened in manorial halls or churches and, in at least one case on record, outside the church edifice. Like the churches of the Reformed tradition almost everywhere, the Poles adapted the polity of four functionaries of the *Ordinances écclesiastiques* and usages of Geneva (1541) with (1) *pastor* and (2) *teacher,* called together in Poland, as often elsewhere also (spiritual) *seniores* over against the elected (3) *lay seniores* (occasionally *presbyteri*) and (4) *deacons.* At the local church session and at the synods commonly two moderators, both lay, were chosen, although the district and palatine and provincial *superintendentes* are listed first. There was some agitation for the extension of franchise in the election of church session and synodal functionaries to members of all classes, an urge especially prominent in the Minor Church.

58. ORDINANCES OF THE RELIGIOUS LIVE IV: DEATH, BURIAL, THE AFTERLIFE

58.A. Gregory Paul, *On the Veritable Death, Resurrection, and the Eternal Life of Jesus Christ our Lord and of everyone believing in him, likewise also on consolations issuing from this: and this against the false misconception of Antichrist . . . against the false invention* [of immediate life of the soul after death, in Purgatory] *by Antichrist and his priests* (Cracow, 1568). From the facsimile copy of the unique exemplar, Czartoryski Library, Cracow, ed. by Konrad Górski and W. Kuraskiewicz (Wrocław, 1954).

The book was published by Rodecki. The scriptural motto is 1 Thess 2:10−11: "When they refused to love the truth by which they are to be saved, on them God sent a strong delusion."

Eschatology was stressed by the Polish Brethren. Some of them held to psychopannychism, that is, to the death of the soul along with the body or the sleep of the soul, pending the General Resurrection. Faustus Socinus himself believed in the resurrection of the righteous only, divine oblivion being in his ethicized eschatology the fate of the unrighteous, not punishment in hell. Diversity of views among the Reformed in general and the Minor Church in particular prevailed, testified to by diverse burial practices. Some may attest to the revival of pre-Christian burial customs among aristocratic families, with special reference to the pagan Slavic double-burial practice.

58.B. A drawing of one of three Arian coffins examined in Cracow, 1837. Composite reconstruction of the two adult coffins discovered in 1837, along with one for a child; reproduced by Janina Bieniarzówna and Jan M. Małecki, *Dzieje Krakowa: Kraków w wiekach XVI−XVIII,* 2 vols. (Cracow: Wydawnictwo Literackie, 1984) 132; Ambroży Grabowski, *Starożytne wiadomości o Krakowie* (Cracow, 1852) 260; Wiktor Czajewski, *Kraków* (Łodź, 1909) 331.

The three "Arian" coffins were put back after a reconstruction on the site in Cracow. Not made of the usual boards but hollowed out of a solid log, the coffin and its lid were lined and sealed with resin. It contained a male with a coif of silk attached to a thick woollen head-band edged with velvet (like that in which Sigismund I is pictured, Pl. 3). The outside cloak was of brown wool, the inside cloak, shaped like the nobiliary *żupan* but woven of silk, was draped in abundant folds about the body; both garments were belted with a black, beaded silken girdle. The care for the mortal remains suggests a sense of the imminent Second Advent. For the location of the Protestant cemeteries, see Map of Reformation Cracow.

58.C. Funeral sculpture of a young wife and mother (d. 1618) lamenting in the church in Pińczów. Portrait of Anna Mathiaszowa Jakuczykowa; photograph by Zbigniew Pasek of one side of the funereal monument in Pińczów.

The other side of the monument has an even less adroit sculpture of two diminutive figures, the grieving father and one of the children kneeling before a slim marble cross. The sculptor, quite possibly the grieving husband himself, would have been nominally Catholic under the bishop of Cracow, who, as of 1586, had begun recatholicizing the first seat of Polish Protestantism (Pl. 7). But the poignancies of the inscription and the simplicities of the monument may suggest a Protestant background to the family and in any case testify to the intensity of conjugal love and grief in this place: ". . . My wifekin died forever. I will never sit close to her any more. After bidding farewell, she started on her way, abandoning me and my bairns forever. My dear one, my beloved is no more, no more my dearly beloved. God took away my wife. . . .I have been violently tormented by death, by wicked death." The sculptor was a craftsman from the marble works near Pińczów, whose family had stayed on after the acquisition of the town by Bishop Peter Myszkowski who, having Protestant cousins, was probably not hard on the Protestants surviving in his town.

Protestant graves opened in Pińczów c. 1825 disclosed bodies bearing a metal tablet inscribed *Scio cui credidi,* "I know in whom I have believed" and accompanied by a carefully stopped glass bottle containing a *curriculum vitae* of the deceased. Reported on the scene by Earl M. Wilbur, *The Christian Register* 104 (25 June 1925) 627, and confirmed by Mr. Pasek when taking the picture of the funereal sculpture.

58.D. The monument to Faustus Socinus (d. 1604) in Lusławice as of 1846. Drawing by M. B. Stęczyński, printed by P. Piller in Lwów; photographed by Zbigniew Pasek. Earl Morse Wilbur is responsible for the erection of the monument of Doric columns around Socinus's marker, which in this simpler view, suggests the still secure place of the memorial in the Catholic countryside 186 years after all Socinians had been driven from Poland.

The new polished gray granite monument, was raised, through the effort of Dr. Earl Morse Wilbur in 1933 over the neglected stone above the grave. Inscribed were words in Italian, long since faded, but by chance memorized by Andrew Błoński, son of Abraham, and then written by him in 1618 in the Autograph Album of Andrew Lubieniecki, and cunningly identified by Dr. Wilbur on his perusal of this unique MS: "Chi semina virtù, raccolglie fama / E vera fama supera la morte // The man who virtue sows doth reap renown / And true renown doth triumph over death." Dr. Wilbur devised the Latin inscription which closes: ". . . in recognition of his efforts for freedom, reason, and toleration in religion." Dr. Wilbur wrote most fully about this in "The Grave and Monument of Faustus Socinus," with six plates, Unitarian Historical Society, *Proceedings* 4:2 (1936) 25–42.

58.E. Pyramidal tomb of the Sucholdski Family, Polish Brethren in Krupie, near Chełm. From the Przypkowski Collection, Jędrzejów.

Under the influence of recent discoveries in Egypt, a number of nobiliary families adopted the pyramidal sepulchral form. Titus Livius Burattini, residing in Poland from 1641 to his death, had spent four years in Egypt, collaborating with John Graevius who published surveys of the Great Pyramid at Giza in 1646. Stanisław Mossakowski, in a couple of essays among seven, *Sztuka jako świadectwo czasu* (Warsaw, 1981), shows the influence of Burttini and Egyptology on the sepulchral monuments of Calvinists and Unitarians alike as "testaments of time"; and Juliusz A. Chróscicki has admirably set forth the thesis of Mossakowski in English, "*Signum temporis*" (Polish Art Studies 5; Wrocław, etc.: Ossolineum, 1984) 247–52.

58.F. Pyramidal tomb of Calvinist Prince Alexander Proński (d. 1631), Beresteczko in Volhynia. A drawing from the nineteenth century of the Mohyla (funeral mound) Prońskiego in Beresteczko; from Mossakowski, *Sztuka jako świadectiwo czasu.* Proński was castellan of Troki (d. 1631). The body of the prince lay in a silver casket. This pyramid in Beresteczko is one of the few surviving relics of the extensive Reformed Church, Major and Minor, in Volhynia Kisielin, the intellectual center of the Minor Church after 1638.

58.G. Communal burial mound (*kopiec*) in Andreaswalde (Kosinowo) in Electoral Prussia, where Samuel Przypkowski (d. 1670) and probably Benedict Wiszowaty (d. after 1705) came to rest. From the Przypkowski Collection, Jędrzejów.

Since Samuel Przypkowski, the biographer of Socinus, and author of one of the two letters about the exile of 1660 attached to the *Historia* by Wiszowaty, was a major figure in the family history of the Collector in Jędrzejów, there can be no doubt about the identification, even if there be no marker. There are many such burial mounds of the Polish Brethren, for example, in Raków and Czarnocin (near Pińczów). Without individual markers, regardless of the renown of the dead, these burial mounds testify to the distinctively Anabaptist and Socinian belief in the death of the soul with the body pending the general (or selective) Resurrection of the (righteous) dead at Christ's imminent Second Advent.

58.H. Slogan of Stanisław Lubieniecki: "Christ is my life: dying is my gain." A symbol printed unexplained among several designs by Lubieniecki and pictures in his bulky *Theatrum Cometicum* (Pl. 63); by permission of Houghton Library, Harvard University.

Fluent in German, Lubieniecki may well have designed the draped coffin and its message at about the time he purchased a burial place for himself and his family in Altona.

59. RAKÓW, 1602–33

59.A. *On the Divinity of Christ* (Raków, 1608) dedicated to Patron Sienieński (E) by Valentine Schmalz, minister. The copy is that in the Biblioteka Narodowa, Warsaw; title-page reproduced by Gryczowa, no. 223. It was printed in Raków by Sebastian Sternacki in a polyglot press of international distinction.

The scriptural sanction is Col 2:9: "In Christ the whole fulness of divinity bodily." Follower of Socinus and writing within four years of his death, Schmalz defends a high Unitarian Christology, including the invocation of the ascended Christ. The autographed inscription of the author is to a minister in Torún. In the German version of 1627 "divinity" is rendered *göttliche Hoheit*.

Faustus Socinus, developing a theme of his uncle, Laelius (Pl. 13.C), held that in John 1 the Logos became flesh only in the sense that it was identical with the flesh of the Virgin-born Jesus who thereby began a new creation, a new era (Pl. 47). Socinus did not believe in a preexistent Christ; but strangely, speculating beyond his uncle, he postulated a unique pre-Ascension ascension of the Son of Man (cf. John 3:13) after the baptism from John and held that in heaven, from the Father directly, Jesus learned what was still valid in the Old Testament and what should be the new or adjusted teachings of his own New Covenant, to be sealed by his utter obedience, through willing one thing. This obedience constituted a moral-juridical atonement akin, in its satisfying or redeeming or absolving effect, to the *acceptilatio* in Roman jurisprudence. Cf. the argument of Remonstrant Hugo Grotius against Socinus, *Defensio, 1617, PB,* Doc. X.

59.B. The first German edition (Raków, 1612) of the Racovian *Catechism* (Polish: Raków, 1605). From the Przypkowski Collection in Jędrzejów.

Catechism of . . . those people . . . who confess that no other than the Father of our Lord Jesus Christ is the only God of Israel and that that Man Jesus the Nazarene, who was born of the Virgin, . . . is the only begotten Son of God (Raków, 1612). Motto: Hos 14:9: "For the ways of the Lord are right, and the upright walk in them, but transgressors stumble in them."

Of the four original authors of the Catechism in Polish of 1604 (intended to replace the *Catechesis* of 1574, Pl. 31), two were Germans from the Empire, John Völkel, born near Meissen (d. Śmigiel, 1618), and Valentine Schmalz, born in Gotha (d. Raków, 1622). Each had been admitted to the Minor Church on profession of faith and rebaptism by immersion, the former in Chmielnik in 1585, the latter on Christmas day 1592 in Śmigiel (Pl. 38), where he became the tutor to the children of the widowed Lady Elizabeth Duditha. Afterwards associate of Czechowic in Lublin, Schmalz then became pastor and teacher in Raków (1605–22). Both German converts were drawn to Socinus; and Schmalz became Völkel's intellectual successor in the colloquies and synods in Raków.

The protocol of a colloquium of ten pastors (four including Rector John Krell, 1616–21) records the progress of adapting scriptural and Socinian ethical precepts, as the Minor Church grew out of its sectarian limitations with Schmalz (the only participant occasionally to leave off Latin discourse for Polish) clearly the dominant figure of the movement.

On one point of Socinus, his disparagement of baptism, Schmalz did not agree; and it was Schmalz, rebaptized as he had been, who led efforts (1611–13) to bring about a union of the Minor Church with the Mennonites of the lower Vistula, though he was even more disposed to work through a theological rapprochement with the Major Church; for all Protestants were suddenly shocked by the executions of Calvinist Franco di Franco and Unitarian John Tyszkowic in 1611 (stressed in the *Historia,* also in *Poloneutychia* by Andrew Lubieniecki, Pl. 1.H). The German Catechism was intended in the first instance for Danzig, Royal and Ducal Prussia, but also for the native lands of Völkel and Schmalz.

Several of the rectors of Raków were Germans from the Empire. They and all the German converts were interested in using the German version of the Catechism in Altdorf, the Academy town of the imperial city of Nuremberg.

For the Polish edition and the Life of Krell, see *PB,* Docs. VI–II and IV; for the newly edited protocol from Kolozsvár, see Grzegorz Błachowicz and Lech Szczucki, eds., *OiRwP* 28 (1982) 149–91. Among the ten participants in the colloquium of 1619 was Christopher Lubieniecki (d. 1624), the Historian's grandfather.

59.C. A contemporary cupola painting, *Arianismus Proscriptus*, in the episcopal palace in Kielce, graphic evidence of the Commonwealth-wide importance of the decision to close school at Raków in 1638 and to force the Polish Brethren into internal exile (to Kisielin). From Muzeum Narodowe in Kielce, by permission.

Commissioned by Bishop Zadzik (D) for his episcopal palace in Kielce, the painting by Thomas Dolabelli does not wholly correspond to what is known of this and any comparable hearing.

I used this picture in *PB,* Pl. H, p. 337, where, unfortunately, it was cropped by the printer who inadvertently excluded, among others, the portrait of Marshal Leo Sapieha (at the right) and, more important, the book of laws (at the bottom between the two groups of Racovians), possibly the original charter for Raków granted by Sienieński's father John, on which the defendants were plausibly resting their case against Chancellor Zadzik. This cropping threw off my description of the scene, which may be consulted afresh with this explanation of two *missing* points of reference and which here serves as the context of the two selected details (E, G).

59.D. Jacob Zadzik, bishop of Cracow (1635–42), Grand Chancellor of the Crown, the accuser, recognizable in *Arianismus* at the left of Ladislas IV Vasa, standing opposite Primate John Wężyk. Photograph by Witalis Wolny, IS PAN. The portrait of Bishop Zadzik with his coat of arms and the date of his death is in the parish church of the Holy Trinity in Raków, the edifice considerably remodeled by him, where once the Brethren had worshiped.

59.E. The patron of Raków, Jacob Sienieński (d. 1639), palatine of Podolia, a detail from *Arianismus*, lower left, raising his hand in the oath of fealty. Photograph of the detail by Arianismus, by M. Moraczewski, IS PAN.

The daughter of the patron married Christopher Wiszowaty. As a widow, she went into exile in 1600. *BAnt*[2], 97.

59.F. The patron's signature as of 1618 in the Album of his friend Andrew Lubieniecki. The Album of Andrzej Lubieniecki, great uncle of the Author, preserved in the Muzeum Narodowe, in Cracow, sign. 1403. The patron signs as "from Sienno, palatine of Podolia, proprietor of Raków." At the top of his message in the Album is the heading: "Piety in all things useful has the promise of the present and future life." Presented by Zbigniew Pasek.

59.G. The rector (presumably) of Raków, Lawrence Stegmann (1634–38), dressed in clerical and magisterial black in contrast to the red cloaks of the noblemen, detail from *Arianismus*. From the Przypkowski Collection, Jędrzejów, whose director at the time, Dr. Tadeusz Przypkowski, surmised that the first of the faces on the lower right was that of his forebear Samuel Przypkowski, biographer of Socinus.

It is much more plausible, however, to assume that, with the haircut of the Polish *szlachcic* but dressed in clerical black, the figure represents the German rector in the crisis, though, in contrast to the picture of the well-known palatine-patron of Raków, it could scarcely be an accurate portrait. Nevertheless, the fact that the artist has the rector turned for a full side view would suggest that he had some idea of his general appearance.

Next to the rector is one of the mischievous boys who tossed a stone at a crucifix in the neighborhood, the pretext for the banishment. Next to the boy is presumably his anxious father in a red cloak.

In Raków the sons of Catholic noblemen were also instructed, and expected to attend the Mass and to hear the homilies daily in the small church respresented in the scene of Raków through the window at the King's right. In *PB*, Pl. B, p. 68, I have given an enlargement of the departure scene with the two churches represented. The larger, that of the Polish Brethren themselves, is made to look a bit like a Ruthenian chapel, the Italian artist's way of suggesting the non-Roman character of Protestant worship in Raków. The larger church was converted by Bishop Zadzik into the present Holy Trinity Church.

60. LWÓW AND THE LAST TWO VASA KINGS

60.A. Lwów, in the 16th century, capital of the palatinate of Ruthenia, seat of three cathedrals, Latin, Armenian, and Orthodox. Here John Casimir (C) at a turning point in the war with the Swedes, 1656, dedicated in the cathedral of the Virgin (2/2 to the right) all Poland to her as Queen, promising to alleviate the lot of the loyal peasantry and to rid the land of heresy. Braun, *Civitates orbis terrarum*, by permission of Houghton Library, Harvard University.

The first fortification of Lwów (Lviv/Lvov/Lemberg) was established on the hill at the left (*Mons Calvus*) by the prince of Halicz, who named it and the settlement at its foot, along a small stream (the Poltva, supplying the later moat), after his son Lev (Leo) c. 1250. German settlers established Our Lady of the Snows, the Gothic church at the far left, in 1340. St. Anne's, at the time of the picture, c. 1600, was the church of the apprentice tailors, round with pillars (uncertain identification). When Casimir the Great absorbed Ruthenia in 1349, he built a larger Polish castle shown on the next hill (few ruins thereof today) and granted the townsmen a charter in 1350 according to the Magdeburg urban law. The town was built up toward the south (right) and was walled in the fifteenth century.

Several of the buildings prominent in this view of the city looking toward distant Kiev are, because of the ravages of war and time, no longer on the skyline and difficult to identify. Behind the most prominent edifice at the wall was the Armenian quarter, Lwów having become a major entrepot in the east-west and north-south trade. Their church of low domes, partly visible, became the Armenian metropolitan cathedral of all the Commonwealth, becoming Uniate at the end of the Reformation century. The blockish synagogues are not identifiable.

Passing by two high steeples toward the right, one sees (going beyond the point of the distant scaffolding) the oddly shaped Dominican church, then the high Renaissance tower (with the large window below) of the town hall. Next it is the Renaissance tower of the otherwise not visible Walachian Church of the Dormition built by the voivode of Moldavia.

The highest tower is that of the Latin-rite Church of the Mother of God, of metropolitan rank by 1412, the counterpoise in the Latinizing Commonwealth of the primatial see of Poland, Gniezno. Here Poland was consecrated to the Virgin in 1656 (B).

The next large spire is that of the Ruthenian church of the Venerable Cross, Lwów being also a cathedral city of the Byzantine rite. The Orthodox metropolitan of Lwów was one of two bishops to oppose the Union of Brest Litovsk (Pl. 52). (The present massive Ukrainian Catholic cathedral of St. George of recent date is located on a hill out of range of the picture.)

As of the century of Reformation and Counter-Reform, Lwów, although surrounded by Byzantine-rite churches of the Eastern style, looks here much like a city of Latin Christendom with its Gothic spires and gables of several monastic orders.

60.B. Ladislas IV Vasa (1595/1632 – 48) elected as tolerant in religion, prepared to enforce the conciliatory Pacification of the Ruthenians, and to press Muscovy. Copperprint and etching of the King in his coronation attire, by Jonas Suyderhoof, after a drawing by Pieter Claesz Soutman; Zakład Reprodukcji, Biblioteka Narodowa, Warsaw. Ladislas became pathologically obese, as can be seen in the *Arianismus Proscriptus* of 1648 (Pl. 59).

Ladislas was son of Sigismund III (d. 1632) and Anne of Styria. A confederation of the Orthodox, headed by Orthodox Adam Kysil and Peter Mohyla (Pl. 53), was resolved to reconstitute the Orthodox hierarchy in a series of articles that restored the metropolitan see of Kiev and its principal church to Mohyla, while allowing the Uniate hierarchy to retain the same title but reside in Vilna or nearby.

Ladislas was under the irenic influence of Capuchin Valerian Magni (Pl. 50), who was behind the Colloquium Charitativum in Toruń (Pl. 61). Lwów, whose bishop had held out against the Union of Brest Litovsk and the equally firm bishop of Przemyśl (cf. Pl. 21), became, along with three other bishops of two old sees and a newly created see, suffragans of the Orthodox Metropolitan of Kiev, Peter Mohyla (1632 – 46). And with Ladislas's support, the remaining Byzantine-rite establishments, monasteries, and specified parish houses in large towns, like Vilna, were judicially divided between the Orthodox and the now reduced Uniate obediences.

For what led up to the restoration of the Orthodox hierarchy in the reign of Ladislas, see Jobert, *De Luther à Mohila*, chaps. 14:1 and 15, and for the role of Kysil, see Frank Sysyn, *Between Poland and the Ukraine: The Dilemma of Adam Kysil, 1600 – 1653* (Cambridge: Harvard University Press, 1985) 89ff.

60.C. John II Casimir Vasa (1609/48 – 68/72), half-brother of Ladislas, released from his celibate vows as a Jesuit Cardinal to succeed him and to marry his widow, the formulator of the edicts banning the Unitarians in 1660. Medal showing the King with the laurel of victory, cast in 1656 by Jan Hoehn with the legend in Latin, "By the grace of God, King of Sweden" and with a forlorn claim to Ducal Prussia; photograph by Henryk Romanowski.

In the next year by the Treaty of Wielawa, 1657, John Casimir had to reconcile himself to the loss of Ducal Prussia as a fief of the Crown, which thereby became Electoral Prussia under Elector Frederick William I of Brandenburg (cf. Pl. 7).

John II Casimir, half-brother of Ladislas by Constantia of Austria, fought in his father's and then his brother's wars, entered the Jesuit order in Rome to his brother's indignation, became a Cardinal in 1646, and was released from his vow to stand for election as King, marrying his brother's widow, Marie Louise Gonzaga (1648–68). In the Latin-rite cathedral in Lwów (A), at a turning point in the war with the Swedes, he pledged, 1 April 1656, all Poland to the Virgin Queen of heaven in a solemn petition for victory and made his social compact

Under him the Diet enacted in 1658 the banishment of the Polish Brethren from Poland by 1660 or their forced conversion either to Calvinism or to Catholicism, and decreed death for returning or relapse. Eight years after the Peace of Oliwa (1660), with Marie's death, John Casimir abdicated, 1668, and went to France, dying in Nevers in 1672.

There was no capital punishment inflicted on the Polish Brethren by reason of the edicts. The first official capital punishment of Protestants came in the context of ever harsher legislation debarring Protestants and the Orthodox from representation in the Diet, 1717 and 1733. In 1724, provoked by student pranks, the Lutheran citizens in Toruń rioted against the Jesuit College; on the finding by the royal commission, the Lutheran mayor and nine other burghers were beheaded. Wiktor Weintraub places this fierce verdict in a large perspective, paying tribute to the earlier religious tolerance of Poland in general in "Tolerance and Intolerance in Old Poland," *Canadian Slavonic Papers* 13 (1971) 21–44.

61. TWO TRAUMATIC EXCLUSIONS: 1619, 1645

61.A. The Remonstrants' Garbage Wagon, 1618 caricature of the followers of Jacob Arminius by the high Calvinist party victorious at the Synod of Dort 1619. A copperprint from *Atlas* van Stolk te Rotterdam, nr. 1379, "D'Arminiaenische dreck Wagen," by permission of the Museum, Rotterdam; reproduced in somewhat different form by G. J. Heering, *De Romanstrante: Gedenkboek bij het 300-jarig bestaan der Romonstrantsche Broederschap* (Leiden, 1919) 117.

The schism in the established Reformed churches of the provinces of the Dutch Republic in 1619 over the issue of predestination between the high Calvinist Gomarists and the Remonstrants was the counterpart of that in the Reformed Church of Little Poland and Lithuania over the Trinity in 1563. Leaders of the Minor Reformed Church sought consociation with the Arminians/Remonstrants and sent their sons to Leiden and Amsterdam to study.

Called Arminians from Jacob Arminius (d. 1609), they were called also Remonstrants from the Remonstrance in five points of his successor John Uitenbogaert (d. 1644). Backed by the temporal leader of their party, the Rotterdam freedom fighter John van Oldenbarneveldt, they, under their principal current theological leader Simon Episcopius (d. 1643) of Amsterdam, were heard before the internationally attended Synod of Dort (13 November 1618 to May 1619). At the final session, the Synod ratified ninety-three canonical rules and confirmed the authority of the Belgic Confession (1561) and the

Heidelberg Catechism (1562; Pl. 43), and also formulated the five articles of Dort against the Remonstrance and deprived the Remonstrant ministers of their livings. Hugo Grotius (d. 1645) was condemned to life imprisonment (he escaped to Paris), and Barneveldt was beheaded (12 May 1619) to the horror of many.

The cartoon in Dutch and French appeared c. 6 December 1618 when the Remonstrants were being brought before the Synod. Two Jesuits in the foreground are waving the Remonstrants, with their repudiation of double predestination and of limited atonement, on the way to Rome. Under the tree in the field Oldenbarneveldt signals and lights them on their way, oblivious of his imminent fate. In the lower right two Arminian burghers offer to help a wavering Reformed pastor into the wagon, the driver of it using the switch of coercion, an allusion to the Erastian views (Pl. 43) of the Arminians under a decorative and deceptive canopy (*Beau semblent*) but in the back knotted fast with bows labeled ''liar'' and ''blasphemies.'' The wheels and wagon gear are variously called: ''moderation,'' ''freedom,'' ''weariness with truth,'' ''general free spirit.'' The horses are rearing and straining in their halters.

Inside the trash wagon sit (A) John Uitenbogaert the driver, (B) Jacob Arminius, (C) Petrus Bertius, (D) Conrad Vorstius, (E) Jacob Taurinus, (F) David Joris (d. 1556, Dutch Anabaptist Spiritualist and imposter, founder of the free will Davidjorists), (G) Adolf Venator, (H) Derek Coornhert, and (I) a renegade Mennonite. The unsuccessful Remonstrants of the foreground episode are now in the background, leading the persistent Calvinist pastor through the gate.

As for Erastianism (cf. Pl. 43), Remonstrants opposed the interference of the church authorities in the affairs of each state (province) and were more tolerant than the high Calvinists of Catholics among the city poor and in the countryside. They were done in by the supra-provincial government of Prince Maurice of Orange-Nassau, head of the seven united provinces, who supported the high Calvinism of the Synod of Dort.

Christopher Lubieniecki, father of the Historian, wrote a letter to Episcopius 14 December 1618, one of many archivally preserved exchanges between the Remonstrants and the Brethren, among whom certain Arminian views were appropriated, long before the exile of the Brethren to the Netherlands after 1660.

Of interest is the fact that the Remonstrant Grotius felt called upon to defend the Catholic/Protestant doctrine of redemption against the theory of the divinely merciful *acceptilatio* in the theory of Faustus Socinus (P147.A) in a new Governmental or Rectoral Theory of *The Atonement*, 1617 (*PB*, Doc. 10), to become widely accepted among Calvinists. Interestingly, Grotius was invited by the Polish Reformed and Czech Brethren to the *Colloquium Charitativum* (B). Although by 1630 the Remonstrants/Arminians were less severely dealt with, they would not gain full toleration from the Estates of the Netherlands until 1795, and thus in the seventeenth century they were hampered in extending full hospitality to the Christocentric Unitarian Polish Brethren in exile among them especially after 1660.

61.B. The *Colloquium Charitativum* at Toruń, 1645, the royal legate presiding over the loving theological debate, first proposed by Capuchin Valerian Magni, the Catholics to the viewer's left, the Lutherans in the foreground, the Czech Brethren and the Reformed at the right, a preliminary session of which Lubieniecki preserved an account. One of the four public sessions of the *Colloquium Charitativum* in the council chamber of the Gothic brick town hall in Toruń (Thorn). From a print in *Acta Conventus Thoruniensis* (Warsaw, 1646), printed by royal authority; copy in the Biblioteka Baworowskich in Lwów; reproduced by Piotr Chmielnowski, as edited by Stanisław Kossowski, *Historia literatury polskiej* (Lwów, 1931), p. 311. The events and issues at Toruń are admirably set forth succintly by Jobert, *De Luther à Mohila*, ch. 15.

Protestant magnates had told King Ladislas IV that if no relief were provided, they would have to enlist help from foreign princes. But Ladislas on his own, advised by Valerian Magni, had long meditated a grand design of an ecumenical colloquy to bring religious peace in his own vast realm and in Europe generally.

The saintly Primate Matthew Łubieński and his provincial synod in Warsaw in November 1643 complied with the royal request for a colloquium, without consultation with the Holy See or the nuncio.

The *Colloquium Charitativum*—charitable from the royal point of view but eventually acrimonious—first convened 28 August 1645, with Chancellor George Ossoliński seated as legate in the viceregal throne (upper center); and it lasted for three months with 76 theologians participating. The King named a royal deputy, John Leszczyński, castellan of Gniezno; Bishop George Tyszkiewicz of Samogitia headed the some 25 Catholic theologians; Zbigniew Gorajski, castellan of Chełm, headed the Czech Brethren and the Calvinists together; and Sigismund Guldenstern, *starosta* of Sztum headed the Lutherans. However, because of illness, he was replaced by John Hülsemann of Wittenberg. Hülsemann had been appointed by the Elector George William of Brandenburg in his authority as Duke of Prussia. Being himself a Calvinist, he sent therefore two delegations, Reformed and Lutheran. His other Lutheran delegate, the irenic Professor George Calixtus of Helmstedt, was accepted warmly by the Lutheran delegates of Elbing and Toruń, but the much more conservative Lutherans of Danzig accused him of compromising the Augustana; and he in the end accepted the invitation to take his seat among the Reformed.

It is remarkable that the Czech Brethren and the Reformed sat as a single delegation, the three brothers Węgierski among them. It was Comenius (C) of Leszno, then Elbing, who was most instrumental in the fusion of forces in the spirit of the Consensus of Sandomierz (Pl. 24).

Among the Reformed might have sat the Remonstrant Grotius who, invited, en route from Stockholm died in Rostock, on the opening day of the international interconfessional Colloquium.

After the divine service, the Catholics and the Protestants assembled separately. The chancellor/royal legate Ossoliński opened the Colloquium at 10 a.m. with the words: "Up until now only Poland has escaped that barbarity [of religious wars that have devastated other lands] thanks to the wise moderation of our ancestors. But must we not fear that universal plague that infects all Europe?"

The presidents of the three confessional delegations sat in chairs, their backs to the presiding royal legate, while in front of them were smaller tables of the notaries of each confessional grouping seated on long benches; to the right of the presidential table (to the viewer's left, the eastern side), the Catholics; opposite them, the Reformed and the Czech Brethren together; and with their backs to the viewer, the Lutheran scribes. In the middle table are seated on three benches the chosen theologians of each party, for the issues of the day. They have come together from the three long tables of the theologians in reserve. Behind the table of Lutheran theologians (foreground) is the free area for qualified standing observers to take in the debate.

In the earliest stage of the planning, the Unitarians mistakenly thought that they had been invited also. It is true that Joachim Stegmann, rector of Raków (1626–30), had opposed the King's chief Catholic mentor, Valerian Magni, for his irenic asserveration that Lutherans, Calvinists, and Utraquists were not heretics but rather only schismatics to be dealt with by Rome with benign suasion, *De acatholicorum credendi regula judicium* (Prague, 1628).

But Jonas Schlichting (d. 1661), himself influenced by Remonstrant theology, showed up in Toruń at the preliminary discussion by all groups, prepared to present his own *Confessio fidei* (1642), an exhaustive scriptural glossary of the Apostles' Creed (*PB,* Doc. XXIII) authorized by the Minor Church, as a possible common basis for the planning session, 10 October 1644. Young Lubieniecki, at the time studying German in the local *gymnasium,* was present as an observer and aide to Schlichting and wrote up the event, perhaps his first *Historia:* ''A Faithful Account of the Things Enacted . . . in the *Colloquium Charitativum* Instituted Between Roman Catholics and the *Dissidentes* from their Church in Religion,'' *BAnt,* 166.

Bishop Tyszkiewicz had dismissed Schlichting as non-Christian. The pathos of Schlichting's proposal lies in the fact that the immersionist Minor Church adhering to the simple ''Triadology'' of Matt 28:19, thinking of themselves as, and often calling themselves simply, ''Christians,'' were very much like the much later (Campbellite) Christians (Disciples of Christ) of popular American frontier ecumenism (c. 1809) who, for all their unitive intention, likewise turned into a separate denomination.

61.C. John Amos Komenský (Comenius) from Leszno, chief spokesman for the combined Czech-Reformed delegation at Toruń. The engraving was made by George Glover for a translation by Samuel Hartlib (encouraged by the Scottish ecumenist John Durie, d. 1680, once of Elbing) of the Leszno educator's Latin work, *A Reformation of Scholles, designed in two excellent Treatises: The First whereof Summarily sheweth [Conatuum praeludia* (Oxford, 1647)] *The great necessity of a generall Reformation of Common Learning . . . , The second Answers certaine objections. . . .* (London, 1642), frontispiece, with permission of the Moravian Brethren Archive, Bethlehem, Pennsylvania.

The print shows Comenius at age fifty, very much as he will have appeared in Toruń three years later, with the inscription in English: ''Loe here an Exile! who to serve his God, / Hath sharpely tasted of proud Pashurs Rod [Jer 20:2: 'Then Pashhur (governor) smote Jeremiah']; / Whose learning, Piety, & true worth, being knowne / To all the world, make all the world his owne.'' The reference is to ''Pashur'' Ferdinand II, who after the Battle of White Mountain in 1620, adopted oppressive measures that ended in the removal of Comenius and many of his Brethren from Moravia to Leszno (Lissa).

John Amos Komenský, the last presiding bishop of the Czech Brethren, the seminal educator of his age (1592 – 1680), an older contemporary of Lubieniecki (d. 1675), but not mentioned by him, was the major factor in the fact that the Czech Brethren and the Reformed sat in the same delegation at Toruń, he the principal theologian at their table. The engraving was made in 1642, whither Comenius had gone after his teaching and administrative sojourn in London. In Leszno, 1628 – 41, he had prepared in Czech his major work, *Didactica,* on the press brought from Kralice and published his *Labyrint sveta a ráj srdce* (2d ed.; *Labyrinth of the World,* Amsterdam, 1663), and *Janua linguarum reserta* (*The Gate of Languages Unlocked,* 1631), a grammar in the form of a miniature compendium of useful knowledge, and here he was consecrated bishop in 1632. Returning to Poland at Elbing, although initially cautious in response to overtures from the Catholics, he persuaded his followers in Leszno to join the Calvinists at a common table at Toruń.

It was presumably while Comenius was in London (1641 – 42) that the son of the first governor of the Massachusetts Bay Colony, namely, John Winthrop, Jr. (1606 – 76), governor of Connecticut, considered himself authorized to offer Comenius the presidency of Harvard College, of which transaction the most accessible account is that coming down in the Mather family, specifically in the recollection of Cotton Mather in his *Magnalia Christi Americana* (London, 1702; New Haven, 1820) 2, iv, p. 10, where the son of Harvard President Increase Mather remarks in passing that "everyone is indebted to his *Janua*." Comenius himself, if he seriously considered the invitation, would have been particularly drawn to the New World by the prospects of educating the Indians by his new methods; and indeed, after the establishment of "an Indian College built within the precincts of Harvard," his *Janua* was used for them and he corresponded about them.

After the Colloquium, in 1648, Comenius was elevated to the role of presiding bishop (1648–70), the last to have jurisdiction through the executive council over the whole communion of the Unitas in all lands. After the cause of the Czech Brethren of the Unitas was abandoned by the Swedes in the Treaty of Westphalia, in that very year, ending the Thirty Years War, 1648, Comenius sought out a protector other than the Swedish king, namely, Calvinist George II Rákózci of Transylvania; and briefly he was installed as head of the college at Saros Patak in close cooperation with the spiritual descendants there of Peter Méliusz (Pl. 41). Comenius reentered Poland before his new-found protector, whom he had encouraged to ally himself with the Swedes during their invasion (*Potop*). He himself greeted the invading Charles X Gustavus in a *Panegyricus* (1655), in which he urged the conqueror to uphold the extraordinary provisions for religious liberty in the Polish Constitution. For having favored the Swedes and their Transylvanian ally, the home of Comenius and some of the town of Leszno was burned. From 1656 to his death Comenius resided in Holland. The most commonly reproduced picture is the stately and somewhat arrogant countenance painted by Juriaen Ovens, a friend of Rembrandt, in the Rijksmuseum, Amsterdam.

For the context of the invitation to Harvard, see further Robert Fitzgibbon Young, *Comenius in England* (New York: Arno, 1971), with a detailed chronology and pictures. For Comenius in Poland, appreciatively: Łukasz Kurdybacha, *Działalność Komeńskiego w Polsce* (Warsaw, 1957), with a whole chapter on the *Colloquium Charitativum,* and, hostilely, Jędrzej Giertych, *U zródeł kastastrofy dziejowej Polski: Jan Amos Komensky* (London, 1964), with four illustrations, including one of Schlichting. Despite his pansophism and vision of an ecumenical City of Light, Comenius was turned off by the Socinians and wrote against them. It seems likely that Increase Mather bought a copy of the *Historia* in London (Pl. 1) because of his interest in the Slavic lands of Comenius, who might have been his predecessor as president of Harvard, and not because of any interest in Lubieniecki's Minor Church, thinking that his purchase of 1689 would tell him about the Polish Reformation in broader sweeps and at least mention the great Comenius of Leszno.

62. LUBIENIECKI'S VISION

The frontispiece of each of his three volumes of *Theatrum Cometicum* (Amsterdam, 1666–68), projected by the author while writing the *Historia* and showing God with one foot on earth, the other in heaven, while holding *Revelatio* in one hand above *Ratio*. By permission of Houghton Library, Harvard University.

Matthias Scheits (d. c. 1700), the Hamburg designer of the page, knew the author well and executed the portrait of him in 1666 that appears in Part II (*PB,* Pl. M). The copperengraver who prepared the plates was Sebastian Stopendael of Amsterdam (d. c. 1707), who will also have striven to execute the elaborate cosmological symbolization for what Lubieniecki no doubt considered his most important publication.

The whole work is dedicated to the glory of the Creator (top line cropped in the printing of all three parts together in one volume). The viewer is alerted by the rainbow and the olive branch at the upper left and by the scourge and lightning at the upper right: to the fundamental law, as Lubieniecki interpreted Scripture and history, namely, that good things come to the good and bad things to the bad (*Bona bonis, Mala malis*), while with respect to the context of his book on comets, he declares: "The knowing will rule the stars."

God the Creator holds in his right hand Revelation, the Bible in two covenants suggested by the two clasps, and in his left hand at a lower level, the Book of Reason, with its one clasp. Behind him runs the encircling signs of the zodiac with cancer, the symbol also of Raków, given prominence. Beneath the signs of the zodiac to the right, are the sun to the left, the moon in her phase, and underneath the message: "They serve . . . , they do not menace."

The Father Creator has one foot in heaven on a cloud and the other planted on the globe, which carries the words: "Every throne is for the powerful; for Christians the only fatherland is heaven." On either side of the hemisphere are the instruments on pedestals for studying it: to the left the astronomical globe, to the right the terrestrial globe, with the further comment: "The greater not without the lesser," and the comforting words from Jer 10:2: "Be not dismayed by the signs of heaven, for the heathen are dismayed at them."

The comet over Hamburg is being viewed perhaps by the Author himself with his telescope in 1664 or 1665 (cf. Pl. 63).

Picking up the theme of *Revelatio* and *Ratio* above are the two female figures, *Scientia* with her apparatus and her eagle of soaring power, and ("not without") *Prudentia*, who looks introspectively into a mirror with the serpent, perhaps of temptation, writhing around her arm, and with the owl of Minerva at her feet.

In his motto at the lower right, Lubieniecki is saying of himself with letters of both names appearing, "I would prefer to die standing," while in the anagram of his two names in Latin spelling, Lubieniecki becomes specifically Christian, addressing the reader or perhaps he himself is being addressed by God: "On the arm of Jesus thou wilt shine forth sufficiently," in a final allusion to the subject of comets and the illumination of Christian revelation in personal life.

To suggest further what Lubieniecki had in mind when he unfurled the word above: "Every throne is for the powerful," it may be noted that in 1671 he would write a Memorial in twenty points, arguing that Louis XIV, as heir and successor of Charlemagne (point e), should be elected by the French as well as by the seven German Electors of the King of the Holy Roman Empire and who as Emperor-elect would thus be in a position to unite Latin Christendom against the Ottomans and free *Hungaria* (including Transylvania) from their grasp. The Latin MS of this Memorial in the Bibliothèque Nationale is placed in its setting one year before Louis's invasion of Holland and the elevation of William III of Orange as stadhouder of the United Netherlands, by Tazbir, *Lubieniecki*, 284–900. The MS Memorial "Fata Augustum Romani Imperii decus Christianissmo Regi [the King of France] destinavi, et hunc non alium, in Regem Romanorum quam primum esse eligendum," by Lubieniecki, is attached to Antoine Aubery's *Des justes prétensions du Roy sur l'Empire* (Paris, 1667).

Royalist and knightly even in exile, Lubieniecki had little understanding of the socially radical character of his confessional and knightly antecedents in the sixteenth century, especially those once ascendant in his native Raków. Indeed, he passed over such episodes and personalities lightly or wholly ignored them in his presentation, for a cosmopolitan readership, of the *Historia* of the Minor Church.

Jesus Christ in this emblematic presentation of the ministerial Author's view of heaven and earth, c. 1666, is no longer the suffering and eschatologically vindicating Jesus Christ as with George Schomann (1574), nor the ascended Jesus exalted to the right hand of God the Father as vicegerential ruler of the cosmos and the nations, the hearkener to the petitions of his Church at prayer, as with Faustus Socinus, but rather the Jesus whose yoke evidently still seems easy to Lubieniecki, for all his own considerable suffering, and that of his exiled Church.

The engraving fixed the moment when, in a representative mind among the Polish Brethren, Unitarian Christian rationalism was making its approach to Deism. Revelation above reason here seems to mean God's laws of righteousness to be searched out and reasonably applied, while personal immortality is intimated as the reward for the upright life.

63. THE LUBIENIECKI FAMILY

63.A. Part of Hamburg in a copperprint executed to Lubieniecki's specifications for his *Theatrum Cometicum* to give the full setting of his observation from his own house (on the shore center with a line from it) of strange lights in the sky. Printed with permission of the Universitätsbibliothek, Hamburg.

Over the city is its seal, appropriate not only for the merchants and other denizens of this Hanseatic City, but also for the viewers of the frightening celestial spectacle: "Give peace, O Lord, in our days."

The Hamburg house of the interpreter of comets in space and history is on the Alster shore almost at the center in what seems to be the pleasant district of Harvesthude. Lubieniecki has made a line from his upper window to the configuration that he did not consider a comet, observed by him (6/16 Julian/Gregorian) July 1665. In the scroll above he has drawn phases through which the phenomenon passed from three flares into a single light, even then of greater magnitude than a morning star. He regarded the sighting of sufficient importance to engage Hans Martin Winterstein to draw the whole scene and one Stoopendael to engrave it for his book (B).

Hamburg is here viewed looking west from across the Alster River, at this point a large lagoon that drained through canals in the Old City into the Elbe flowing northwest (out of view). To the left are the spires of St. Michael's, of three smaller churches, and of St. Nicholas. Beyond on the right (north) bank of the Elbe is Altona under Danish jurisdiction, where Lubieniecki acquired another house of his own (1669–73) and where he purchased a vault in the Church of the Holy Trinity where he was buried in 1675 (the church subsequently taken down).

63.B. One of the three large volumes of the *Theatrum Cometicum* of Lubieniecki opened to the page with his portrait. A photograph of the library table in the home of Dr. Tadeusz Przypkowski and his son in Jędrzejów. This portrait (more fully exposed) and the *Vita* by Lubieniecki's son(s) are printed in *PB,* Pl. M and Doc. XXVIII.

63.C. A self-portrait of Christopher Lubieniecki (1661–1729), who (possibly with his artist brother Theodore) wrote the Vita of their father. Rijskmuseum in Amsterdam; printed from André de Tobac.

Lubieniecki: Geschichte einer arianischen Familie von Malern und Politikern, photocopy of a typescript (no place or date, c. 1970), Widener Library, Harvard University.

For many other pictures by the brothers, see Michał Walecki, *Lubienieccy* (Warsaw, 1961).

64. THE *HISTORIA* OF LUBIENIECKI II: SOME CONTINUATORS

64.A. A page on John Biddle from the second projected edition of the *Bibliotheca Anti-trinitarorium* (*BAnt²*) by Christopher Sand (d. 1680) of Electoral Prussia, edited by Benedict Wiszowaty (d. after 1705) (Amsterdam, 1684) and amplified and corrected in his own hand. From the Remonstrant Collection in the Library of the University of Amsterdam.

The work done by Wiszowaty includes a transcription in a fair hand, which seems to be his own, of the more extensive addenda brought together on separate pages in the front of his working copy of the first edition. There are even instructions to the printer. Jeremy Bangs, who discovered the working copy, and Lech Szczucki will carry out Wiszowaty's intention for a second edition.

The page selected has special interest in its expansion of references to John Biddle (1615–62), Father of English Unitarianism, translator of Samuel Przypkowski's *Life of Faustus Socinus* (1653; RD 8).

64.B. *The house in Andreaswalde (Kąsinowo) in Electoral Prussia, in which Benedict Wiszowaty served as pastor of the refugee Brethren. The original photograph by E. M. Wilbur in 1926 appears not to have survived. It was published, with two snapshots of Raków, in an article by Wilbur entitled "The Last Socinian Church Visited," The [Unitarian] Christian Register* 104 (25 June 1925) 627–28, 634. Wilbur's caption under it reads: "Only half of the [church] building, in Andreaswalde, East Prussia, is shown, and this will also be torn down, and the only vestige of Unitarianism in this region will [then] be the site of it and the baptismal pool by the roadside."

The house, called locally Oriander (Arianer), had been used for a century by peasants. In its large kitchen the Unitarian Brethren assembled for worship, and presumably it was here that Wiszowaty carried out his ministry. The last known Unitarian, presumably immersed in the roadside pool, was Karol Henryk Morsztyn, who died in *Kąsinowo in 1852. The pictured half of the meeting place was scheduled to be torn down within days of Wilbur's visit. Cf. Wilbur, Socinianism,* 516–21.

64.C. The title-page of a two-volume MS history, primarily of Transylvania but with material on Poland, by Stephen F. Uzoni *et al.*, running roughly parallel with the *Historia*: "A Unitarian-Ecclesiatical History of Transylvania which treats, by way of prolegomenon, of the Faith of the Lord Jesus Christ received from the Apostles among the peoples inhabiting Transylvania from the first year of Christ up to the present 18th century with varied fortune forsooth, such that it was, to be sure, suppressed almost to the last spark and yet was not able, for all the persecutions, to be extinguished over the centuries; then it sets forth the return of the same holy Faith of the Lord Christ to primordial purity by a difficult yet broader Reformation and the rise of the true Church of the Lord Christ, called Unitarian, in the Grand Principality of Transylvania and the Parts annexed thereto [Kolozsvár, 1775]." Title-page printed by permission of Houghton Library, Harvard University.

This History is one of three copies, one in Cluj, another in Budapest. The one here pictured, the final author's original, was once housed in the Unitarian Bishop's Library in Cluj/Kolozsvár, Romania. Cf. Wilbur, *Transylvania,* 12 n. 22. It was taken for safekeeping by Alexander (Sándor) Szent-Iványi and, after it was used by Dr. Wilbur for his *History,* deposited in the Houghton Library, Harvard University, to be returned to the Joint Seminary Library in Romania at such a time as the conditions are met by the terms of the late, former bishop. This copy is indispensable for the preparation of a critical edition of this invaluable text for Transylvania, roughly comparable to that of Lubieniecki's *Historia* for Poland. In it are copies of letters, for example, of Biandrata, and other documents that exist nowhere else. The Consistory, in response to a letter of Dr. Wilbur in Kolozsvár at the time, voted to loan him the use of the *Historia* for his own *History* and it was delivered to him by a delegate from Transylvania at the meeting of the International Association for Liberal Christianity and Religious Freedom in Copenhagen, August 1934. When he had finished with the two volumes, unable to return them to Kolozsvár, he mailed them for safekeeping to the Rev. Alexander Szent-Iványi, Unitarian minister in Lancaster, Massachusetts, former assistant bishop in Budapest, with the request that the *Historia* "be sent home . . . [when he] thought feasible"; Earl Morse Wilbur, "How the History Came to be Written," Unitarian Historical Society *Proceedings* 9:1 (1951) 17. The other two MS copies of variant composition, all necessary for a critical edition, were, as of Dr. Wilbur's time, in the college libraries in Kolozavár (Cluj) and in Székely-Keresztúr (above Schässburg/Sighisoára), both in Romania, the latter copy now in Budapest. The Houghton copy, now carried to Cluj, makes possible a critical edition by János Káldos, *Bibliotheca Unitariorium.*

64.D. Earl Morse Wilbur (1866–1956). The picture was painted by Arthur W. Palmer in the historian's home in 1951 when Dr. Wilbur was working on the proofs of his second volume (1952) of his *History of Unitarianism.* The painting hung in the dining room of Mr. and Mrs. Newell Nelson in Berkeley, California, Mrs. Elizabeth Nelson being the daughter of Dr. Wilbur. For the life and bibliography, see George H. Williams, "Earl Morse Wilbur," *Unitarian Universalist Christian* 40 (Summer 1987).

Map 1. THE PALATINATES OF THE POLISH-LITHUANIAN COMMONWEALTH AND THE KINGDOM OF HUNGARY

I. LITTLE POLAND (with its Tribunal at Lublin): (1) Cracow. (1A) Silesian principalities of Oświęcim (Auschwitz), Zator, Siewierz (united with the Crown, 1569). (1B) The 13 towns of Spisz (Szepes/Zips) in pawn from Hungary to Poland, 1412–1769. (2) Sandomierz. (3) Lublin.

II. CROWN RUTHENIA (Ruś Czerwona): (4) Ruthenia (Lwów). (4A) Land of Sanok. (4B) Land of Przemyśl. (4C) Land of Lwów (Lviv/Lvov/Lemberg). (4-I) Podolia (Kamieniec Podolski). (5) Belz. (6) Braclaw. (7) Volhynia (Łuck). (8) Kiev. 6–8 were by the union of Lublin, 1569, withdrawn from the Grand Duchy and placed directly under Crown Poland.

III. GREAT POLAND (with its Tribunal at Piotrków): (9) Poznań. (10) Kalisz. (11) Brześć Kujawski. (12) Inowroclaw. (12A) Land of Dobrzyn. 11–12A = Kujawy (Cujavia). (13) Lezcyca. (14) Sieradz.

IV. MASOVIA, Principality of: (15) Płock. (16) Rawa. (17) Masovia (Warsaw, capital of Poland after 1611), having reverted to the Crown, 1526. (18) Podlachia (Podlasie), by the Union of Lublin, 1569, annexed from Lithuania by Poland.

V. ROYAL PRUSSIA (annexed from Teutonic Order, 1466): (21) Chełmo (Kulm). (22) Pomerelia (Danzig/Gdansk, a nearly autonomous city state with its deputies in the Commonwealth Diet, its own coinage, and sometimes economic and foreign policy).

VI. DUCAL PRUSSIA (Königsberg): after 1611 ELECTORAL; fief of the Polish Crown, 1525–1657, its Duke a member of the Commonwealth Senate after 1569.

VII. GRAND DUCHY OF LITHUANIA (Successor state of the Principality of Kiev): Chancery language: Ruthenian; the Lithuanian nobles converted from paganism to

Catholicism with the conversion of their Grand Duke, Ladislas Jogailo/Jagiełło, before his marriage to Queen Jadwiga to become the founder of the royal Jagiellonian dynasty of Poland, 1386–1572; Polish became the language of the Grand Ducal court in Vilna (Vilnius/Wilno) and in the nobiliary courts; Lithuanian, Latvian, and Old Prussian, closely interrelated Indo-European languages in contrast to Ural-Altaic Estonian, were the languages of the villages in the area circumscribed with heavy dotted lines running into the Baltic at roughly Königsberg and Parnawa/Pernau.

By reason of the conversion Old Prussians, Letts, and Estonians by the harsh missions of the Teutonic Order and of the direct conversion of the Lithuanians to Catholicism under Polish auspices, the LATIN-RITE-BYZANTINE-RITE BOUNDARY extends on the map, roughly from Narva, south through Estonia and along the eastern and south-eastern Latvian-Lithuanian linguistic boundary, then directly south along the western boundary of the Grand Duchy, then along the boundary between Little Poland and Ruthenia to, and then along, the boundary of the Apostolic Kingdom of Hungary; but then the Rite-boundary turns within that Kingdom to include as Orthodox the village churches of the upper slopes of the Carpathians from Ungvár through Munkács to Huszt; then the Rite-boundary runs roughly along the dotted line past Varád, intended on the map to outline the western boundary of Greater Transylvania under Prince Stephen Báthory; but in terms of dominant ethnic groups, Saxon, Magyar*, and Szekler* in Transylvania, the Rite-boundary resumes the crest of the Carpathians and the Transylvanian Alps that marked the eastern and southern boundary of Hungary, or, as it became separated, the principality of Transylvania. There were Orthodox Walachian enclaves in several sections of the same Transylvania. The Rite-boundary is traced for the Commonwealth in *PB*, pullout map.

VIII. COURLAND, once part of the territory of the Livonian Knights, fief of the Polish Crown, 1561–1795.

IX. LIVONIA (Inflanty): territory of the Teutonic Knights reorganized after the secularization of Ducal Prussia, a fief of the Polish Crown, 1561–1772, although much of it was lost to Sweden by the Treaty of Oliwa, 1660.

Tripartitioned Apostolic Kingdom of Hungary

A. OTTOMAN HUNGARY, divided into pashaliks, boundaries shown as of the greatest penetration north as of 1576.

B. HAPSBURG HUNGARY, preserving the Apostolic Crown of St. Stephen, Capital: Pozsony (Pressburg, Bratislava); primatial see: Esztergom (Gran). The Hungarian kings were elective, although they became virtually dynastic with the accession of the first Hapsburg, Ferdinand, combining the Crowns of Bohemia and Hungary. Coronation with the Crown of St. Stephen was the decisive action, without royal unction as e.g. in Poland. The coronation traditionally took place southwest of Buda at Székesfehérvár (Stuhl-weissenburg), but after 1543 in the new primatial residence in Nagyszombat (in present-day Slovakia).

Hapsburg Hungary, with boundaries shifting in the sixteenth century in consequence of Ottoman and Transylvanian military action, was considered as divided into four parts, the designations confusing to outsiders because based upon a map published in 1528 by a cleric, Lazarus, in the Service of the Primate. His map was seriously disoriented, but the terms he used have persisted: Lower (Hapsburg) Hungary next to Austria, Middle, and Upper Hungary, the last bordering on contested Partium. "Upper" on the map of Lazarus meant north, "Lower", south, in his mistaken projection; but his terms have survived his map for the historiography of the sixteenth and seventeenth century.

C. *TRANSYLVANIA*, the original palatinate (voivodeship): Capital: Alba Julia (Romanian: Alba Iulia; Hungarian: Gyulafehérvár; German: Weissenburg, later Karlsburg); Alba Julia was not one of the original Seven Saxon royal boroughs (four of these on the map are marked with an asterisk), all seven giving the German name to the principality: Siebenbürgen.

D. *PARTIUM* (genitive plural in abbreviated reference to) the parts of Crown Hungary administered by the Prince of Transylvania, and in continuous contest between the Hapsburgs and the Prince of Transylvania; the dotted lines mark the boundaries of the enlarged Transylvanian state under Prince Stephen Báthory (1571–81), under whose rule the voivodeships of Moldavia and Walachia became tributary.

Acknowledgments: The Map owes something conceptually to one prepared by Gottfried Schramm, *Der polnische Adel und die Reformation 1548–1607* (Wiesbaden, 1965), opp. p. 144. The extension of the Map here to include the divided realm of St. Stephen (first king of Hungary, 975–1038), who received his still treasured Crown from Sylvester II in 1001, owes something to László Makkai *et al.*, *Histoire de la Hongrie des origins à nos jours* (Budapest: Horvath, 1974) and to several solid, multi-volume tomes in Hungarian from the time of the Dual Monarchy, but few of them make clear the shifting boundaries of Greater Transylvania. And there are almost no maps that show Hungarian and Polish-Lithuanian palatinates and counties together on the same projection and with the detailed coverage unique to this effort of the Editor, essential for grasping Lubieniecki's frequent references to various parts of dismantled Hungary, to Moldavia, to Silesia, Bohemia, and Moravia, usually left blank or excluded in maps of Poland up to 1945.

Map 2. POLISH-SPEAKING CONGREGATIONS IN THE POLISH-LITHUANIAN COMMONWEALTH, 1547–1764

The map is an adaptation of one printed by Henryk Merczyng, *Zbory i senatorowie protestanccy w dawnej Rzeczypospolitej* (Warsaw, 1904). The original is a colored pullout map on which Merczyng distinguished by red symbols the Polish Lutherans, by green the Reformed, and by blue the Arians. On the larger surface he was able to suggest the relative importance of the congregations by using two sizes of his triangles for the oldest gatherings, circles for the congregations of the Vasa period, and squares for the period up to election of Poland's last king. He intended to show only the congregations that were Polish-speaking. Thus the Czech Brethren in Great Poland do not show until they become Polonized and, in effect, Reformed. To this pioneer cartographic coverage, Maria Sipayłło, *Akta synodów różnowierzych*, 3 vols. (Warsaw), *AS*, 3, has in her pullout map been able to add quite a few other congregations in Little Poland. Merczyng dedicated the original map ''to the memory of the first historian of the Polish Reformation [1652], the Reverend Andrew Węgierski (Adrianus Regenvolscius), elder of the Lublin congregations.''

The adaptation here serves primarily to give the viewer a general sense of the spread of Polish Protestantism in the Commonwealth, which is pictured as of the seventeenth century after some territories have been lost in the East to Muscovy. The palatinates have been numbered in compatibility with those in Map 1 and are here grouped into the three main regions, each with its royal appellate Tribunal: Great Poland with Piotrków (P), Little Poland with Lublin (L), and the Grand Duchy of Lithuanian, truncated by the cession of palatinates to Crown Poland by the terms of the Union of Lublin in 1569, with its

Tribunal usually in session at Novogrudok (N). Ducal Prussia is marked with small circles to indicate its territorially confessional Lutheran status. It ceased to be a fief of the Polish Crown in 1657. (In 1701 Elector Frederick III of Brandenburg crowned himself in Königsberg (KÖ) king of the new kingdom of Prussia as King Frederick I.)

The map does not show the numerous Dutch and German-speaking Anabaptist (Mennonite) congregations, beginning in 1535, in Ducal/Electoral Prussia and in the palatinate of Marienburg (20) and all along the Vistula from Danzig (D) as far up as Toruń (Thorn). Nor does my adaptation of the map show the extensive territorial Lutheranization in the patchwork of principalities of the Bohemian Duchy of Silesia (Śląsk), first along the Oder, notably below Breslau (B), in the principality of Liegnitz (Legnica: l) and above Breslau in that of Brieg (Brzeg, b) and again in uppermost Silesia in largely Polish-speaking Teschen (Cieszyn, t) and German Pless (Bielsko, p), both principalities lying between the upper Oder and the upper Vistula on the Moravian frontier. By 1618 most of Silesia had been territorially Lutheranized from the German-speaking courts into the countryside. But with the defeat of the Protestant princes in support of Czech Protestants in 1621, Silesia soon became the battle ground of the Thirty Years' War and religious life was tattered in continuous turmoil. No attempt has been made on this sketch of the region to indicate the early conventicles of the Schwenckfelders, especially around Liegnitz, nor those of the Anabaptists. The Margraviate of Brandenburg, of which only the Mark shows on the map, could be marked with circles like Ducal/Electoral Prussia as territorially Lutheran except that the Electoral dynasty converted to the Reformed confession in 1612 and the later Elector would send both a Lutheran and a Reformed delegation to the Colloquium Charitativum of 1648 (Plate 61A). Hither Pomerania to the north along the Baltic was solidly Lutheran and remained under Swedish rule until 1648.

Maria Sipayłło's map is limited to Little Poland and Ruthenia and, except for Raków, does not include the sites of congregations that became Unitarian, nor does it include Lutheran and Czech Brethren churches. For the Catholic dioceses and the distribution of the religious orders, there are many maps in Jerzy Kłoczowski, ed., *Chrześcijaństwo w Polsce: Zarys przemian 966–1945* (Lublin: KUL, 1980). There are some details (not possible to show here) in the pullout map of the Commonwealth in the seventeenth century in my *Polish Brethren* (Cambridge, 1980).

Map 3. REFORMATION CRACOW

For detailed discussion of this map, see pp. 792–93 in this volume. The map from the archive of the Prussian Ministry of War in Berlin is reproduced from *Rocznik Krakowski*, 9 (1906), pp. 149; 159, two separate portion brought together. The identification of sites, water courses, and the reconstruction of the Boner Gardens are based upon several standard works, but notably that of Klemens Bąkowski, *Dzieje Krakowa* with 12 maps and 150 drawings (Cracow, 1911), Julian Bukowski, *Dzieje Reformacyi w Polsce*, 2 vols. (Cracow, 1883–86), and J. Bieniarzówna, J. Małecki, and J. Mitkowski, *Dzieje Krakowa; 2, w wiekach XVI–XVIII* (Cracow, 1984). For some of the identifications that may be less familiar, the sources are as follows: 24: on Tylicki, Bakowski, *Historia Krakowa w zarysie*; 37: Bukowski, 1, p. 623; 42: Ambroży Grabowski, *Starożytnicze wiadomośći o Krakowie* (Cracow, 1852), p. 67; 53: Grabowski, *op. cit.*, p. 271; for the location of the home of Trzecieski, Jerzy Krokowski, *Andrzej Trzecieski* (Warsaw, 1954), p. 23, and independent checking by Zbigniew Pasek and Krzysztof Kowalski.

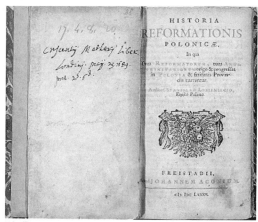

1A–B

1H

1C

1D

1F

1E

1A–B *The History of the Polish Reformation* (Amsterdam, 1685), Increase Mather's copy, 1689

1C Lubieniecki's *Compendium Veritatis Primaevae,* author's hand

1D Signature of Stanislas Budziński (d. 1595), Lubieniecki's major source

1E Martin Bielski (Wolski) (ca. 1495–1575)

1F Matthias Flacius Illyricus (1520–75)

1G Cyprian Bazylik, *The History of Harsh Persecution* (Brest, 1567); cf. Pl. 15E

1H Andrew Lubieniecki, *Poloneutychia . . . (ca.* 1551–1623), another source

1G

2 Sigismund I the Old and Queen Bona Sforza and offspring

3A Miniature in the Prayer Book of Sigismund I, 1524

3BC Gold Medallion, presented by Severin Boner (D) to Erasmus in 1531

3D Sepulchral monument of Sophia Bonerowa

3E Mintmaster Ludwig Dietz (Decjusz, d. 1545)

3F Palace of Decjusz outside Cracow, first Protestant gatherings here

3G House of Andrew Trzecieski, visited by Spiritus, 1546

3A

3B

3F

3C

▼ 3E

3D

3G

4B

4A John Augusta, bishop and president of the executive council

4B Church, bell tower, school of the Czech Brethren

4C Second hymnal of "Spiritual Songs" (Ivančice, 1564)

4D Lipnik on Moravian border, site of last Reformed-Unitas synod

4C

4A   **4D**

5C

5F

5G

5H

5J

5L

5K

5I

5A Frederick Cardinal Jagiellończyk (1488–1503),* not pictured

5B John Konarski (1503–25), *Historia, p. 568,* not pictured

5C Peter Tomicki (1523–35), *p. 21,* Pl. 3E

5D John Latalski (1536–37),* Pl. 6, not pictured

5E John Chojeński (1537–38),* *p. 21,* not pictured

5F Peter Gamrat (1538–45)*

5G Samuel Maciejowski (1546–50), *pp. 17 passim*

5H Andrew Zebrzydowski (1551–60), *pp. 20 passim*

5I Philip Padniewski (1560–72)

5J Francis Krasiński (1572–77), *p. 75*

5K Peter Myszkowski (1577–79)

5L George Cardinal Radziwill (1591–1600)

*those concurrently or subsequently Primate

6A John Łaski, Primate (1610–31) during the Diet of Lublin, March 1506

6B King Sigismund II Augustus (1520/48–72)

6C Matthew Drzewicki (1531–35), not pictured

6D Andrew Krzycki (1535–37), not pictured

6E John Latalski (1537–40)*

6F Peter Gamrat (1541–45),* not pictured

6G Nicholas Drziergowski (1546–59), not pictured

6H John Przerębski (1559–62)

6I Jacob Uchański (1562–81)

*previously bishops of Cracow

6B

6I

6H

6A

6E

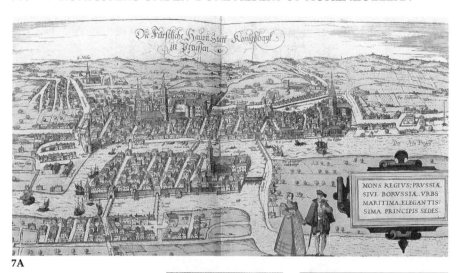

7A

7E   7B   7C

7D

7A Königsberg with ducal castle tower and court

7B Grand Master of the Teutonic Order, Albert (1490–1568) in 1511

7C Duke Albert (as of 1564)

7D Andreas Osiander (1498–1552)

7E Oldest Polish printed version of the New Testament from the Greek by John Seklucjan

8C

8B

8G

8A Stanislas Lasocki (d. 1534)

8B Nicholas Myszkowski (d. 1557)

8C John Boner (d. 1562)

8D Christopher Myszkowski (d. 1575)

8E Sigismund Myszkowski (d. 1578)

8F Andrew Firley (ca. 1537–85)

8G Stanislas Szafraniec (d. 1598)

8H Brick church built at Secemin by Szafraniec in 1553

8D

8F

8H

8E

9A

9B

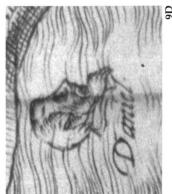

9D

9C

9E

9A Pińczów as it was taken over by the Swedes in 1657
9B Sophia Oleśnicka, early Polish Protestant hymnist
9C Town house locally misidentified as the "Arian printing press"
9D Daniel of Łęczyca, printer
9E The expulsion of the Paulinian monks from Pińczów in 1550

10A Pińczów

10B Paulinian Church where John Łaski was buried January 1560

10C *Defense of the true doctrine by Martin Krowicki* (Pińczów, 1560)

10A

10B

O Broná Náuki prawdziwey y wiáry ſtárodawney Krześćijáńſkiey/ktorey vcżyli Prorocy/ Kryſtus Syn Boży/ y Apoſtolowie iego Swięći: Ná przećiwko náuce fałſzywey y wierze nowey/ ktorey vcży w kośćielech ſwoich Papieſż Rzymſki/ a ktorey odpowiedziá ſwoiá broni Jędrzey Biſkup/ Krákowſki.

Nápiſáná przez Marciná Krowickiego/ ſługę Kośćiołá Páná Jezu Kryſtá vkrzyżowánego.

Pſálmo 90. 92.
Abowiem oto nieprzyjaciele twoi Panie: abowiem oto nieprzyjaciele twoi zginą y będą rozproszeni wszyscy ktorzy cżynią nieprawości.

Lucz.19.
Owszem nieprzyjacioły ony moie ktorzy niechćieli abym krolował nad nimi, przywiedzcie tu y zabijcie przedemną.

Drukowáno w Pińcżowie w drukárni Dánielowey/ Roku od Národzenia Syná Bożego. 1560.

10C

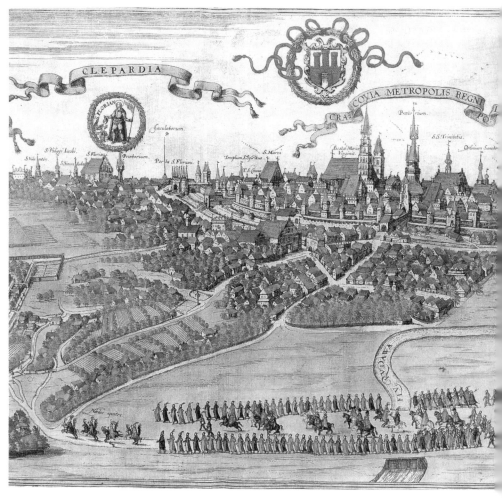

11–12A

11–12B

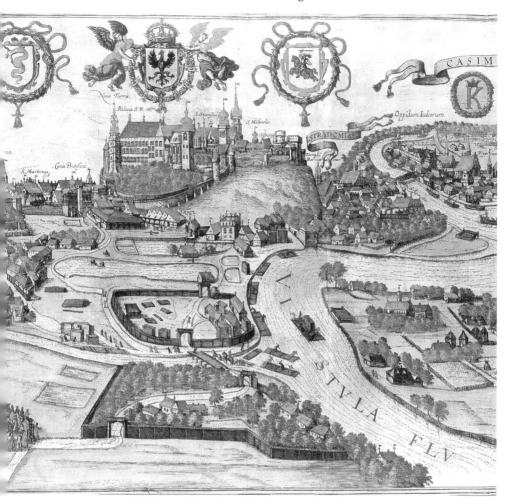

11–12A Cracow on the left bank of the Vistula, which in the sixteenth century flowed toward Warsaw through its old bed with the towers of Kazimierz *on the right bank.* The town hall and St. Mary's dominate Market Square. To the left is the separate town of Kleparz. Observe the mounted nobles in procession to the Summer Palace.

11–12B Lament of the Different Kinds of People at the Death of Credit (ca.1575)

13A Educated by his jurisconsult father, Mariano (1482–1556), Laelius studied law at Bologna and, with religious and philological interests, acquired Greek and Hebrew, becoming the fountainhead of a later Socinianism. He joined an evangelical circle in Vicenza (B) but prudently left Venetian jurisdiction for Chiavenna in the Rhaetian Republic, where he was influenced by the distinctive sacramental and eschatological views of Camillo Renato (d. 1575). He was received by the major Reformers, 1547–51, visited Cracow, 1551, again in 1558–59; Bullinger demanded of him a *Confessio de Deo* (C).

13B Vicenza in the Venetian Republic

13C The first line of Laelius's equivocal autograph MS *Confessio de Deo,* amicably required of him by Bullinger, Zurich, 15 July 1554: "I, Laelius Sozinus . . . "

13A

13B

13C

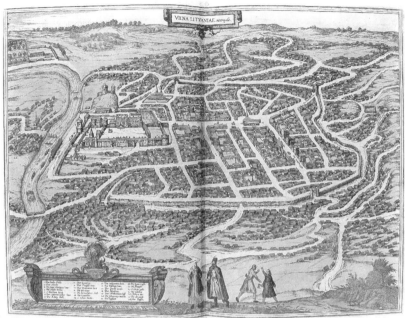

14A

14A Vilna

14B Nicholas Radziwiłł the Black (1515–65)

14C Nicholas Radziwiłł the Red (1512–84)

14D Teutonic Master Fürstenberg submits to Sigismund II, 1557

14E Calvinist church in Vilna as of 1682

14B▲   ▼ 14D   ▲ 14C

14E

15E

15B

15C

15A

15D

15A "Patris sapientia, veritas divina," translated into Lithuanian

15B Luther's *Enchiridion,* oldest book printed in Lithuanian

15C Simon Budny (d. ca. 1595)

15D Budny's Catechism in Cyrillic

15E Utenhove, *Simplex et fidelis narratio,* Life of Łaski; cf. Pl. 1G

The single most important Italianate figure in the Polish Reformation before Faustus Socinus, Dr. Francis Lismanino (1504–66), was of half-Greek parentage from Venetian Corfù. The radicalizing Minor Church was in part the displacement north and east of the vitalities of a distinctively Italianate Reformation that never came to fruition as a separate Church on Italian soil except in the Rhaetian Republic and Locarno.

Coming as a youth to Cracow, Lismanino joined the Franciscans (D) to become their provincial, 1538–54, got a doctorate in theology, Padua, 1540, lectured at the University (E), was made a confessor to Bona Sforza, met the Dutchman Spiritus at Trzecieski's in 1546 (Pl. 3), interpreted Calvin's *Institutes* to Sigismund II, 1551–53, went abroad at his command to acquire books for the royal library in Vilna (Pl. 14), was converted to Calvinism in 1554, marrying Claudia, a Huguenot, withdrew from Little Poland to Tomice (F). He died disheartened, a courtier in Königsberg (Pl. 7).

16A

16D　　　　　▼ **16C**

16B

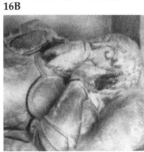

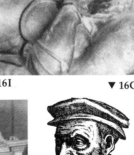

16I　　　　▼ **16G**

16A Sebastian Castellio (d. 1563)

16B Bernadine Ochino (d. 1564)

16C Peter Paul Vergerio (d. 1564)

16D Franciscan church, Cracow, to the left, portion of cloister

16E Collegium Majus where he lectured on theology

16F Czech Brethren church, Tomice, which he considered joining

16G Celio Secundo Curione (d. 1569)

16H Prosper Provana (d. 1584), Dominican Church, Cracow

16I Provana (detail from H), saltmaster in Wieliczka (Pl. 31)

16E

16F

16H

De loco, ubi Mescia, Deus & homo nasciturus esset, Micheæ 5. Matthæi 2.

וְאַתָּה בֵית לֶחֶם אֶפְרָתָה צָעִיר לִהְיוֹת בְּא־
בְּאַלְפֵי יְהוּדָה מִמְּךָ לִי־יֵצֵא לִהְיוֹת מוֹשֵׁל
בְּיִשְׂרָאֵל וּמוֹצָאֹתָיו מִקֶּדֶם מִימֵי עוֹלָם:

De Missione Mesciæ à Patre & Spiritu sancto, hoc est de Trinitate sub typo tamen Iesaiæ proph. uel Cyri, Iesaiæ 48.

קִרְבוּ אֵלַי שִׁמְעוּ זֹאת לֹא מֵרֹאשׁ בַּסֵּתֶר
דִּבַּרְתִּי מֵעֵת הֱיוֹתָהּ שָׁם אָנִי וְעַתָּה אֲדֹנָי
יֱהֹוִה שְׁלָחַנִי וְרוּחוֹ:

De afflictione, passione, atq; morte Mesciæ pro peccatorum nostrorum satisfactione, Iesai. 53.

וְהוּא מְחֹלָל מִפְּשָׁעֵנוּ מְדֻכָּא מֵעֲוֹנֹתֵינוּ
מוּסַר שְׁלוֹמֵינוּ עָלָיו וּבַחֲבֻרָתוֹ נִרְפָּא
לָנוּ: כֻּלָּנוּ כַּצֹּאן תָּעִינוּ אִישׁ לְדַרְכּוֹ פָּנִינוּ
וַיהוָה הִפְגִּיעַ בּוֹ אֵת עֲוֹן כֻּלָּנוּ:

De felicitate eorum, qui relictis improborum consilijs ac institutis, sese le gi Dei intelligendæ, iutaq; exprimen dæ totos consecrant, Psalm. 1.

אַשְׁרֵי הָאִישׁ אֲשֶׁר לֹא הָלַךְ בַּעֲצַת רְשָׁעִים
וּבְדֶרֶךְ חַטָּאִים לֹא עָמָד וּבְמוֹשַׁב לֵצִים
לֹא יָשָׁב: כִּי אִם בְּתוֹרַת יְהוָה חֶפְצוֹ וּב־
וּבְתוֹרָתוֹ יֶהְגֶּה יוֹמָם וָלַיְלָה: וְהָיָה כְּעֵץ
שָׁתוּל עַל פַּלְגֵי מַיִם אֲשֶׁר פִּרְיוֹ יִתֵּן בְּ־
בְּעִתּוֹ וְעָלֵהוּ לֹא יִבּוֹל וְכֹל אֲשֶׁר יַעֲשֶׂה
יַצְלִיחַ:

De remissione peccatorum sub Mescia seruatore nostro, Ierem. 50.

בַּיָּמִים הָהֵם וּבָעֵת הַהִיא נְאֻם יְהוָה יְבֻקַּשׁ
אֶת עֲוֹן יִשְׂרָאֵל וְאֵינֶנּוּ וְאֶת חַטֹּאת יְהוּדָה
וְלֹא תִמָּצֶאנָה כִּי אֶסְלַח לַאֲשֶׁר אַשְׁאִיר:

De conceptione Mesciæ in utero uirginis Mariæ, deq; eius nomine & natiuitate, atque nomine, Iesai. 7. Matth. 1.

הִנֵּה הָעַלְמָה הָרָה וְיֹלֶדֶת בֵּן וְקָרָאת שׁ־
שְׁמוֹ עִמָּנוּ אֵל:

De

🖙 3

17A

17D   **17B**

17F

17E

17C

17A   Stancaro's *Hebrew Grammar* (Basel, 1547)

17B   Diagram of Stancaro's conception of the Trinity

17C   Episcopal fortress and prison of Lipowiec

17D   Oldest church order of the Polish Reformed

17E   Palace of Stanislas Stadnicki in Dubiecko

17F   One of seven sons of Stanislas Mateusz Stadnicki (d. 1563)

18I

18J

18E

18C In his anonymous work in collaboration with Dávid, *De falsa cognitione* (Pl. 25) in the scandalizing Ch. 4, "On horrendous images of the Trinity," he reproduces eight examples, E–H.

18F

18A Dr. Biandrata of Saluzzo, a critical Servetian (Pl. 25), was a physician to two queens, Bona Sforza (Pl. 2) in Cracow, her daughter Isabel in Alba Julia (Pl. 39). Lay elder in Reformed churches in both realms, he shaped their thought and polity.

18B His signature, Transylvania

18A

18B

18D Trifrons

18E "In a chapel near Cracow"

18F The Trinity descending into the eucharistic host at the *Sanctus*

18G The Three Persons in Majesty at the Last Supper

18H Most common representation of the Trinity at Calvary

18I–J Works (1568): Biandrata leaves no trace of pre–mundane Logos-Christ, only the historic "Jesus Christ . . . whom we reverence and invoke after the Father"

18G ▼18H

18D

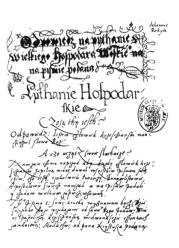

19C   19A

19D

19B

19A Andrew I
Górka, governor
of Great Poland,
protected
Protestants

19B Andrew II
Górka (d. 1583),
s. of Andrew I,
b. of Lukas III
(Pl. 34)

19C John
Rokyta's fictive
reply to Ivan IV
the Terrible, 1570

19D
R. Leszczyński
(without mace)
heads Polish
commissioners,
Treaty of
Marienwerder,
1635

20A

20B

20C

20E

20D

20A Reformed
superintendent,
East Frisia, 1544

20B Emden,
ca. 1545

20C Copperprint,
presumably
from B

20D Departure
with wife and
followers from
Marian England,
1553

20E Lead seal,
1557

20F Copperprint
from E

20F

21A As
Ruthenian youth

21B Przemyśl,
his two-rite
birthplace

21C His *Chimera
against Stancaro*
(Cracow, 1562)

21D Diagram
from *Quincunx*
(Cracow, 1564)

21E Another
quincunx

21D

21E

STANISLAI
ORICHOVII ROXOLANI,
CHIMAERA:
SIVE DE STANCARI FVNE-
STA REGNO POLONIÆ
SECTA.

*Attendit à falsis Prophetis: qui veniunt ad vos in vestitu ovium:
intus autem sunt lupi rapaces.*

M. D. LXII.

21B   21C   21A

22A

COMMENTA-
RIORVM DE REP.
EMENDANDA,
LIBRI
Quinq.

ANDREÆ FRICII
Modreuii ad REGEM, Sena-
tum, Pontifices, Presbyteros,
Equites, Populumq; Poloniæ,
Ac reliquæ Sarma-

22C

22B

22A–B *De Republica emendanda* (Cracow, 1551); translated by Cyprian Bazylik (Łosk, 1577)

22C–D Brother John Przypkowski frees his serfs, 1572

22D

23A

23C

23B

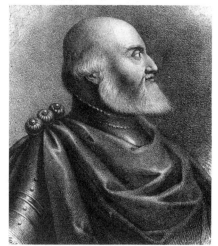

23D

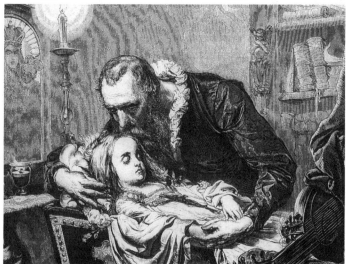

23A Biernat of Lublin, scene from Aesop (1522)

23B Nicholas Rey (d. 1569), "father of Polish literature"

23C Rey's translation of the Apocalypse, 1565

23D Andrew Trzecieski (d. 1584)

23E John Kochanowski (d. 1585)

23E

24A Calvin warns Vilna church against Biandrata

24B Pinczovian *Confession of Faith* in terms urged by Biandrata

24A

24B

CONFESSIO DE SANCTA

TRINITATE CONTRA EOS QVI ECCLESIAS MINORIS POLONIAE ARRIANISMI ET PLVRALItatis Deorum accusant, edita Pinczouiæ in Synodo seniorum & Ministrorum vigesima Augusti M.D.LX.II.

Stadtbibliothek Zürich. B II 372, S. 920

DE FALSA

ET VERA VNIVS
DEI PATRIS, FILII, ET.
SPIRITVS SANCTI COGNITI-
ONE, LIBRI DVO.

Ex Museo
Hungarico.

Authoribus ministris Ecclesiarum consentienti-
um in Sarmatia, & Transylvania.

Franciscus Davidis
qui ive tali composit.

i. Thessalonicensium ç.
Omnia probate, quod bonum est, tenete.

ALBAE IVLIAE.

25B

DEREGNO

CHRISTI LIBER
primus.
DE REGNO AN-
tichristi Liber secundus.

❊❊❊

Accessit tractatus de Pædobaptismo, et
Circuncisione.

Rerum capita sequens pagella demonstrabit.

Ioan. 15. ver. 14.
Vos amici mei estis, si feceritis quæcunq́ ego
præcipio vobis.

Albæ Juliæ.
Anno domini 1 5 69.

25C

25A

25A Servetus at the stake in Geneva,
27 October 1553

25B *On the False and True*
Knowledge . . . (Alba Julia, 1568)

25C *On the Reign of Christ* . . .
(Kolozsvár, 1569)

25D An image of the Trinity, close
to the Christology of Servetus, but
scorned by Biandrata (in B)

25D

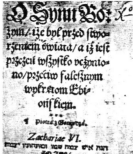

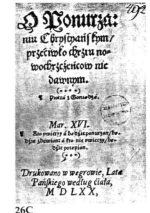

26A 26B 26C

26F

26D

26E

26A–C Three works by Peter Gonesius (d. 1573)

26D St. Mary Magdalene's in Poznań where Gregory (d. 1595) taught

26E Gregory, *Differences as to the Three Persons* (Brest, 1564)

26F His diagram (from E) "Christ's Church without wrinkle"

27B

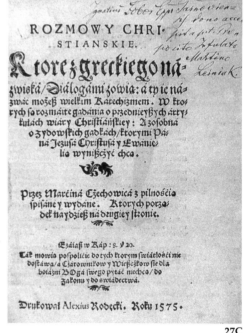

27A

27C

27A Polish version of three-day debate in Latin on pedobaptism

27B Nieśwież, where the debate occurred, January 1565

27C *Christian Discussions against Budny's Christology* (1575)

28E   28A

Epiſtola

IACOBI PA-
LAEOLOGI, DE REBVS
Conſtantinopoli & Chii cum
eo actis, lectu digna.

Schreiben auß Constantinopel von
des Türkischen Kaysers vorhaben vnd angestel-
ter Kriegsrüstung/ so er wider die Christenheit/vnd sonder-
lich Teutschland jetzigerzeit zugebrauchen/ jhm
vorgenommen.

Gedruckt zu Vrsel/ durch Nicolaum Henricum/
Im Jahr M D X C I I I I.

28C   28D

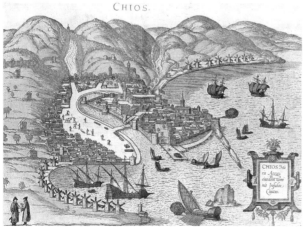

28A Jacob Heraclides
Basilicus, Reformed voivode
of Moldavia (1561–63)

28B Chios, birthplace of
Jacob Palaeologus, O.P.

28C Colloquy of Poissy,
1561, attended by
Palaeologus

28D His report (1573) on
Chios and Istanbul

28E Castle of Theodore of
Kunoviče in Moravia, refuge
of Palaeologus

28B

29A

29A Slavkov (Austerlitz)

29B *Geschicht-Buch,* their chronicle form 1525 (original in S. Dakota)

29C Caricature of Hutterite communism

29B

29C

30A

30C

30A Hutterian Bruderhof, hostile woodcut

30B Bruderhof today in Moravia

30C Rev. D. Bieliński (Pl. 31) commends from Olkusz to Slavkov two Racovians, 1570

30B

31A George Schomann (d. c.1590), Daniel Bieliński (d. 1591), and Simon Ronemberg (d. c.1604) from upper Silesia

31B Bursa of the Poor, Cracow, where Schomann once taught

31C Royal saltworks, Wieliczka, under Prosper Provana (Pl. 16)

31D Salters's Castle, where Schomann taught, 1554–60

31E Schomann debated Skarga (Pl. 49) in Provana's Cracow house

31F Schomann's *Catechesis,* Cracow, 1574 (RD 7)

31G Olkusz, Provana as mine master; Bieliński wrote Hutterites (Pl. 30)

31H Cracow apothecary

31D

31B

31H   **31E**

31F   ▼ **31G**

▼ **31C**

32 The Union of Lublin, 1569

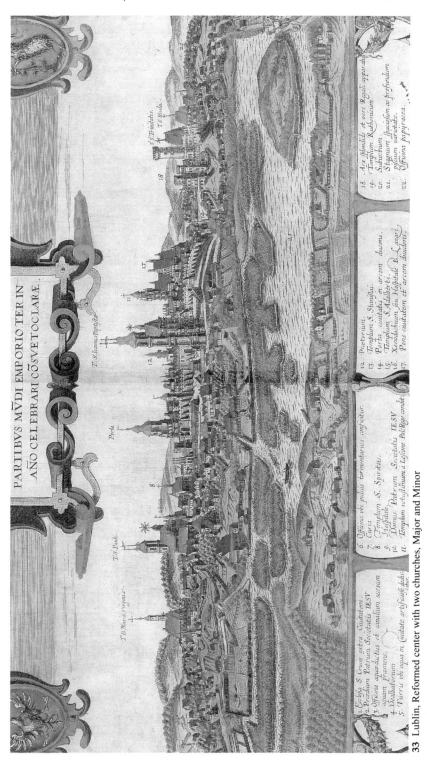

33 Lublin, Reformed center with two churches, Major and Minor

34A

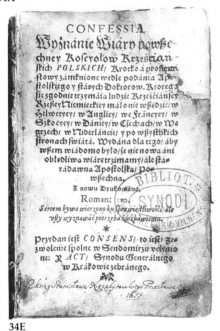

34E

34C

34B

34D

34A The Vistula flows east (to the right)

34B Lukas Górka, leader of Lutherans in Great Poland

34C Stanislas Myszkowski, castellan

34D Home of Zbigniew Oleśnicki, where synod convened, 1570

34E Lutheran-Reformed Czech Brethren Consensus vs. Catholics and Minor Church

35D

35B

35A Background of Lubieniecki's *Vindicae pro religionis libertate* (c. 1660). At Kniszyn in Podlachia Sigismund I died 7 July 1572, the last male of the Lithuanian Jagiellonian dynasty. By the Polish constitution the kingship was elective.

35B St. Bartholomew's Day Massacre, 24 August 1572, Henry standing by slain Coligny

35C Warsaw Confederation, January 1573, guarantees religious *Pax*

35D The IV Henrician Articles further bind King-elect, 1573

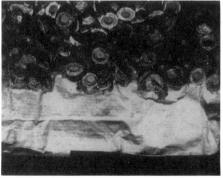

35C

36C

36A Catherine de' Medici receives Polish envoys headed by A. Łaski (Pl. 38)

36B Henry of Valois, third son of Catherine, later Henry III of France

36C Obsequies for long embalmed Sigismund II, 4–7 February 1574

36B

36A

37A

37B

37C

37A Primate (Uchański as Interrex) anoints King in Wawel cathedral

37B Coronation Diet, the King surrounded by Senators (bishops and lay peers)

37C Secret abdication of Henry, en route to France

REFVTATIO
SCRIPTI
PETRI CAROLII
editi Wittebergæ,ſcripta

A
IOANNE SOMMERO PIR-
nenſi, Lectore ſcholæ Claudio-
politanæ in Tranſyluania.

Deut. 6. ỷ 4.
שמע ישראל יהוה אלהינו יהוה
אחד׃

INGOLSTADII
Ex officina Petri Raniſii.
Anno CIꓷ Iꓷ XXCII.

38A

38B

38D

38F

38C

38E

38A John Sommer (d. 1572) of
Saxony, Moldavia, Transylvania

38B Latin-rite cathedral in Cotnari,
seat of Moldavian Reformation, 1563

38C Andrew Dudith, one of two
Hungarian bishops at Trent

38D Śmigiel, on the Silesian border,
its Minor church protected by Dudith

38E Albert Łaski (d. 1605), Reformer's
nephew, supports Heraclides (Pl. 28)

38F Kežmarok in Slovakia, Łaski's
seat for Moldavian campaign

39A

39B

39C

39F

39E

ALBA GIVLIA

1. Citta 2.Citta Interiore 3. Borgo 4.Keres f. 5.Jl Lago zarghat

39D

39G Stephen Báthory:
"I am King of the
peoples, not of
consciences . . . I am
unwilling to rule
consciences, given that
God has reserved to
himself three things: to
create something out
of nothing, to know
the future, and to rule
the consciences."

39H

39A Isabella Jagiellonka, d. of
Sigismund I (Pl. 2), widow of
John I Zápolya (1526–40)

39B Cardinal George II
Martinuzzi, b. of Várad,
chancellor (murd. 1557)

39C John Honter (d. 1549),
first reformer among Saxons

39D Alba Julia, capital of
Transylvania

39E Romanesque cathedral in
Alba Julia

39F John (II) Sigismund
Zápolya (1559–70/71), son
of Isabella

39G Stephen Báthory, Prince
(1571–81); King of Poland
(1576–86), pictured in Pl. 46

39H Statutes for Transylvania
issued as Prince from Cracow

40 Dávid pleading for toleration: "Faith is the gift of God."

41A

41C

41F

41B

41E

41D

41A Kolozsvár (Klausenburg), one of the original Seven Boroughs

41B Francis Dávid (1520–79), idealized modern drawing

41C Choir stall of Dávid

41D Trinity of Méliusz, Dávid/Biandrata in *De vera cognitione* (Pl. 25)

41E Peter Méliusz, *Institutio vera* (Debrecen, 1571)

41F The Reformed college in Debrecen

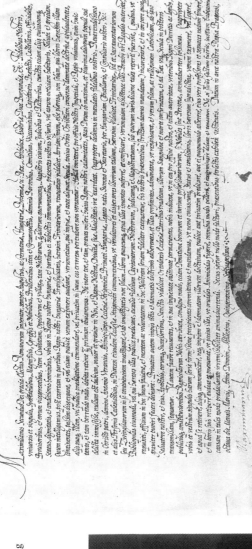

42A Emperor Maximilian II
Hapsburg (1527–76)

42B Emperor's autograph as King
of Hungary styling the radically
Reformed *Trinitarii*, 1570

42C Autograph detail

43A

43E

43B

43C

43A Heidelberg, Reformed
Hebraists become
Antitrinitarian, 1570

43B Frederick I the Pious,
leader of the German Reformed

43C Ursinus of Heidelberg
Catechism (1562) refutes
Catechesis (RD 7)

43D Zanchi interprets Three
Elohim as the Three Persons

43E Theology faculty clarifies
the eucharist for Kolozsvár,
1563

43F Prof. Thomas Erastus,
M.D., posthumous eponym
of Erastianism

43D

43F

44B Three Heidelberg Hebraists and Unitarian Antidisciplinarians: Superintendent John Sylvanus (d. 1572), Adam Neuser (d. 1576), and Matthias Vehe-Glirius (d. 1590)

44A

44C

44E

44F

44G

44D

44A Maximilian II, Diet of Speyer, 1570

44C Casper Békés (d. 1579), supporter of Francis Dávid

44D *Mattanjah* (Gift of God) by Christian Hebraist Vehe-Glirius

44E Unitarian Mennonite, Adam Pastor

44F Synagogue in Bözsödujfalu, last Sabbatarian village

44G Tombstone of last Sabbatarian, Mózes Kovács (1882–1950)

45A Christopher Báthory
(1576/81–86), Stephen's br.,
deputy at Dávid's trial

45B Déva Castle where Dávid
perished, 1579

45C Demetrius Hunyadi
(1579–92)/George Enyedi's
scriptural refutation of the
Trinity

45D Sigismund Báthory
(1581–94), hegemonist over
Walachia and Moldavia

45E Stephen Bocskay
(1605–06) secures quadri-
confessional toleration

45F Dés: *Complanatio*, 1638;
Unitarians limited to 1579
Confessio

45A   45D

45B

45C

45E

45F

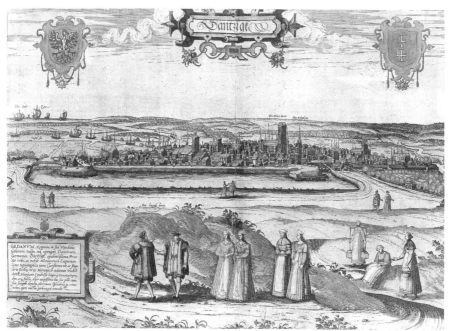

46A

46B

46A Danzig refused obedience to elected King Stephen
46B Legate Possivino restrains; Orthodox bishop offers
bread and salt

47B From the original copperprint after his death

47C *Explicatio* draws on uncle's *In primurn Iohannis caput* (1561)

47D Title page of *An Argument for the Authority of Holy Scripture*, 1588

47A The younger Fausto Sozzini inherited his uncle's papers in 1562 (Pl. 13); and, outwardly conforming, he was in the service (1565–75) of Isabella de Medici (daughter of the Grand Duke of Tuscany). On leaving court, he studied in Basel, where he wrote his major work embodying his new theory of the atonement (the Father's token-like *acceptilatio* of Christ's obedience), *De Jesu Christo servatore* (1577). He left Basel for Cracow, whence he was called by Dr. Biandrata (Pl. 18) to debate with Francis Dávid in Kolozsvár (1578/79) in defense of the devotional practice of addressing prayer to the Ascended Christ (adorantism) (Pl. 45).

47B

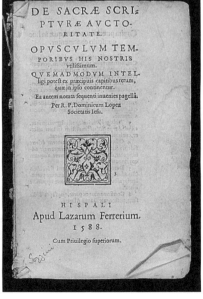

47D

48A Faustus Socinus lived in and around Cracow, 1579–1604. The remote occasion of the attack upon him was the publication of his *De Jesu Christo servatore* (Cracow: Rodecki, 1594) (Pl. 47). His residence in 1598 (B), was in his absence reconnoitered by hostile students, who dragged him into the Market Square and there threatened his life until saved by Dr. Wadowita (C) and some university colleagues, whereupon Socinus removed to his final residence (D). In the year of his death Peter Skarga, S.J., superior of the Jesuit House, near St. Barbara, and court preacher, wrote his *Shaming of the Arians* (E).

48B

48C

ZAWSTYDZENIE
ARIANOW,
Y
Wzywánieichdo pokuty y wiá-
ry Chrześciáńskiey.

Przy nim Kazánie o przenachwálebnicy-
fzey Troycy.

*Czynioneod X. PIOTRA SKARGI,*Societatis
JESV

Induntur qui detrahunt mihi pudore, & operiantur
ficut diploide confufione fua. *Pfal: 108.*

Erubefcant & conturbentur vehementer. Conuer-
tantur & erubefcant valde velociter. *Pfal: 6.*

W KRAKOWIE,
Z Drukárniey Andrzeiá Piotrkowczyká.
Roku Páńskiego, 1 6 0 4.

48B House of Socinus in Cracow

48C Professor Martin Wadowita, curate of St. Florian's

48D Court and church in Lusławice

48E Peter Skarga's *Shaming of the Arians,* 1604

48E   48D

49A   **49B**

49A Stanislas
Cardinal Hosius
(1504–79), Bishop
of Varmia

49B Peter Skarga,
S.J. (1563–1613),
court preacher

49C Symbolic
representation of
the Roman
Catholic Church
(1574); in moat,
several heretics
featured in other
plates

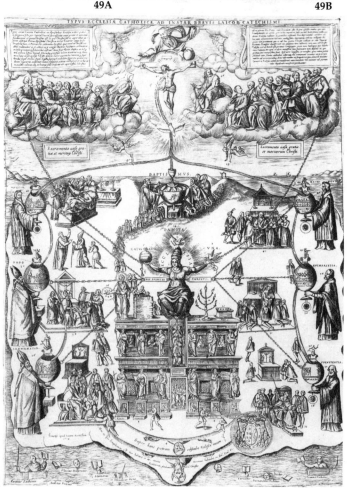

49C

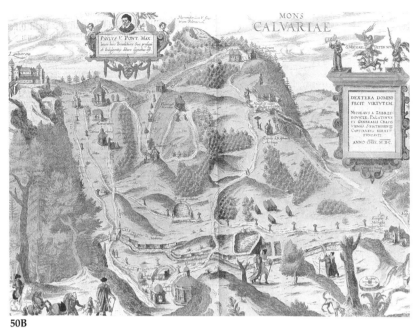

50B

50C

50A

▼ **50D**   ▼ **50E**

50A Sigismund III, s. of Catherine (Pl. 2) and John III Vasa of Sweden

50B Kalwaria Zebrzydowska, expiatory Polish Jerusalem, 1606

50C Sigismund III receives defeated Tsar Basil Shuisky

50D Capuchin Valerian Magni (d. 1661), Milanese irenicist, Bohemia/Poland

50E Caspar Drużbicki, Poznań mystic, who debated our Historian's father

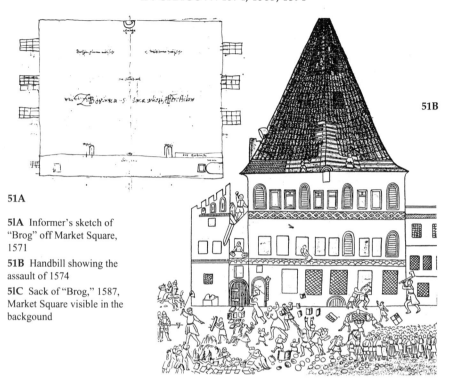

51A

51B

51A Informer's sketch of
"Brog" off Market Square,
1571

51B Handbill showing the
assault of 1574

51C Sack of "Brog," 1587,
Market Square visible in the
backgound

51C

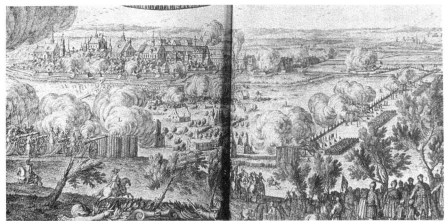

52A

52A Brest Litovsk under siege

52B Metropolitan Michael Rohoza, father of the Union

52C St. Nicholas, Brest, where synod convened, 1595

52D Seal struck in Rome commemorating the Union

52B

52C

52D

53A Constantine Basil Ostrozhkyi, sponsor of Cyrillic Bible (Pl. 54)

53B Bishop Gideon Balaban of Lwów (Pl. 60), opponent of the Union

53C Vilna Confederation, 30 May 1599, Protestant/ Orthodox signatories

53D Christopher Radziwiłł, s. of Nicholas the Red (Pl. 14), a signatory

53E Peter Mohyla (d. 1646), f. of academy of Kiev, metropolitan by 1632

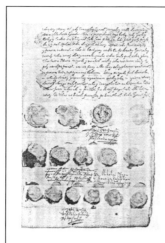
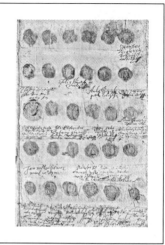

53C

53B

53A

53D

53E

54A

54H

54D

54B

54C

54E

54G

54F

54A Leopolitan 1561, Catholic

54B Pinczovian, Brest, 1563, Calvinist

54C Budny, Nieśwież (Pl. 27), 1572, Unitarian

54D Czech, Kralice, 1579

54E Ostrih, 1580-81, Old Slavonic

54F Vizsoly, 1590, Hungarian Calvinist

54G Lithuanian Lutheran, Königsberg, 1579-90

54H Wujek, Cracow, 1599, Catholic

55A–B *Christus lassus* of peasant piety

55A Polish

55B Lithuanian

55C Christ washing the Apostles' feet, Ruthenian fresco, Sandomierz

55D Epiphany from Nicholas Rey (Pl. *23), Postilla,* 1556

55E–F Unitarian medal, ca. 1580

55E "The Man/The Lord Jesus"

55F "Christ the King comes in peace, the Second Adam is risen"

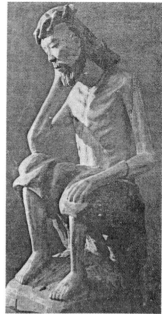

55A   55B

55D   55C

55E   55F

56 ORDINANCES OF THE RELIGIOUS LIFE II: BAPTISM. LORD'S SUPPER.

957

56A

56B

56C

▼ 56E

FAUSTI SOCINI SENENSIS

DE COENA DOMINI

Tractatus brevis.

unà
Cum ejusdem adversus scriptum Domini
Iohannis Niemojevii Defensione.

Adjecta sunt praeterea alia quaedam ejusdem auctoris de hoc
argumento.

RACOVIAE,
Typis Sebestiani Sternacii,
Anno 1 6 1 8.

56D

56A Immersion among Rijnsberg Collegiant Remonstrants, 1736
56B Seal, ark of Noah, symbol of the Church, Cracow
56C Communion cloth, 1651
56D Communion charger from Lublin, 1668
56E Socinus responds to Niemojewski on close communion

57A The Major Church in Piaski

57B The Minor Church in Piaski

57C Domestic prayer

57D Czech Brethren worship

57E First Reformed hymn, 1556, by Zofia
Oleśnicka (Pl. 9)

57F Arian school in Lewartów

57G Laws of Lewartów Academy, 1593

57H A learned page from an
autograph book

57B

57A

57C

57D

57H

57F

57I

57E

SCHOLA
LEVARTOVIANA
RESTITVTA

SIVE EPISTOLÆ ALIQVOT:
quibus ratio deſcripta eſt quam iſtius ſcholæ Præce-
ptores in docendo adhibent.

AVTORE ALBERTO CALISSIO
eiuſdem Scholæ Rectore.

TYPIS ALEXII RODECII 1593.

57G

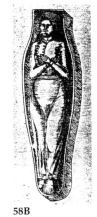

58A

58B

58C

58F

TANTUM EST.

58H

58E

58D

58A Gregory Paul, *On the Veritable Death,* 1568

58B An Arian coffin, Cracow

58C Young wife and mother lamented, Pińczów

58D Original stone for Socinus, Lusławice

58E Arian pyramidal tomb near Chełm

58F Calvinist tomb in Volhynia

58G Communal burial mound in Andreaswalde

58H Motto of Lubieniecki: "Christ is my life; dying is my gain."

58G

59A

59B

59A Pastor Valentine Schmalz, *On the Divinity of Christ* (Raków, 1608)

59B German edition of *Catechism* (Raków, 1612)

59C *Arianismus Proscriptus,* 1638, cupola, episcopal palace, Kielce

59D Bishop Zadzik of Cracow, accuser, recognizable in C

59E Raków's patron, Jacob Sieniński, in C, hand raised in oath

59F Patron's signature in A. Lubieniecki's Album, 1618

59G L. Stegmann, rector, 1634–38: note magisterial gown in C

59D

59E

59C

59G

59F

60A Lwow with three cathedrals: Latin, Armenian, Orthodox
60B Ladislas IV (1595/1632–48), s. of Sigismund III (Pl. 50)
60C John II (1609/48–68/72), half-br. of Ladislas, released from vows

61A

61B

61C

61A Cartoon of Remonstrants (allied to
Minor Church) in garbage wagon, 1618

61B Charitable Colloquy, Toruń, 1645:
Minor Church excluded

61C John Amos Comenius of Leszno,
spokesman for Czech/Reformed bench

62 This frontispiece appears in each of Lubieniecki's three volumes of *Theatrum Cometicum*.

63A

63B

63A Hamburg under sky flares,
Lubieniecki's house (on the shore
center)

63B Three-volume *Theatrum
Cometicum* opens to portrait of Author

63C Self-portrait of Christopher
Lubieniecki, author of father's *Vita*

63C

64A Christopher Sand's *Bibliotheca Antitrinitariorum* (*BAnt²*), open to editor Benedict Wiszowaty's addendum on John Biddle

64B Wiszowaty's house in Andreaswalde in Electoral Prussia; cf. Pl. 58G

64C John Tözser Kénosi, History of Transylvanian Unitarians, continued by Uzoni

64D Earl Morse Wilbur (1866–1956)

64A

64C

64B

64D

The 29 Palatinates of the
Polish-Lithuanian Commonwealth
and the Kingdom of Hungary

Polish-speaking congregations in the Polish-Lithuanian Commonwealth, 1547–1764

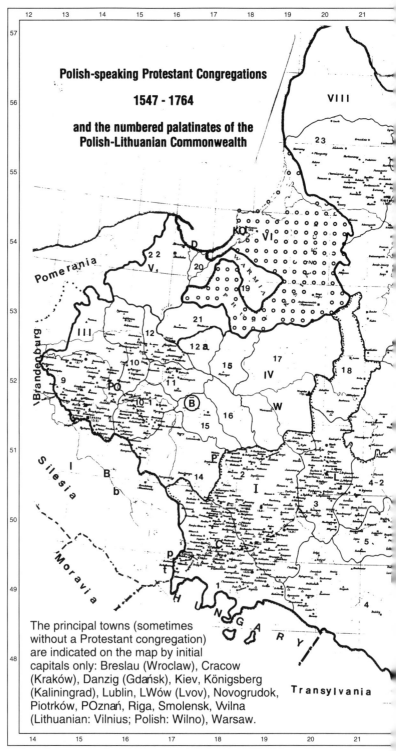

Polish-speaking Protestant Congregations

1547 - 1764

and the numbered palatinates of the Polish-Lithuanian Commonwealth

The principal towns (sometimes without a Protestant congregation) are indicated on the map by initial capitals only: Breslau (Wroclaw), Cracow (Kraków), Danzig (Gdańsk), Kiev, Königsberg (Kaliningrad), Lublin, LWów (Lvov), Novogrudok, Piotrków, POznań, Riga, Smolensk, Wilna (Lithuanian: Vilnius; Polish: Wilno), Warsaw.

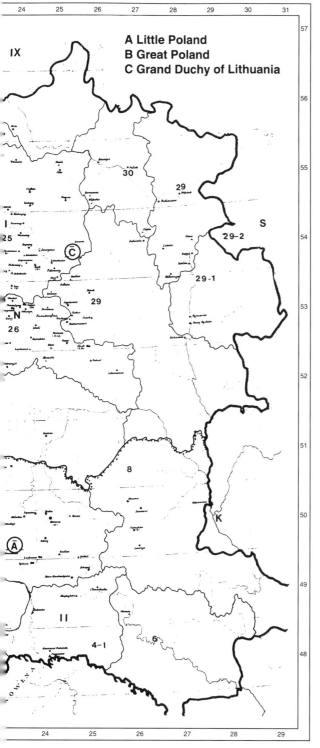

A Little Poland
B Great Poland
C Grand Duchy of Lithuania

Numbered Palatinates (Wojwódziwa)

i. Little Poland proper
    1. Cracow
    2. Sardomierz
    3. Lublin
ii. Crown Ruthenia
    4. Ruthenia with Land of
       Chełm (4-2)
    4-1. Polodia
    5. Belz
    6. Braclaw
    7. Volhynia
    8. Kiev
    8.1. Czernihów (to 1686)
    18. Podlachia (Podlasie)

iii. Great Poland proper
    9. Poznań
    10. Kalisz
    11. Brześć Kujawski (Cujavia
        Kujawy)
    12. Inowroolaw
    13. Lęczyca
    14. Sieradz
iv. Principality of Masovia
    15. Plock
    16. Rawa
    17. Masovia (Warsaw, national
        capital, 1611), having reverted
        to the Crown, 1526
    18. Podlachia (annexed from
        Lithuania, 1569)
v. Royal Prussia (annexed from
    Teutonic Order, 1466)
    19. Prince-bishopric of Varmia
        (Polish: Warmia; German:
        Ermland)
    20. Marienburg (Malbork)
    21. Chelmo (Kulm)
    22. Pomerelia with Danzig/Gdańsk,
        a nearly autonomous city with
        its own coinage
vi. Ducal,after 1611,Electoral Prussia,
    fife of the Polish Crown, 1525–1657,
    its Duke a Senator after 1569

vii. The Duchy after the Union of
    Lublin, 1569
    23. Principality of Samogitia
        (ethnic Lithuania)
    24. Troki
    25. Vilna
    26. Novogrudok (Polish:
        Nowogródek)
    27. Brest Litovsk (Brześć Litewski)
    28. Polock
    29. Minsk
viii. Courland, once part of the territory
    of the Livonian Knights, fief of the
    Polish Crown, 1561-1795
ix. Livonia (Inflanty), territory of the
    Teutonic Knights reorganized after
    the secularization of Ducal Prussia,
    fief of the Polish Crown, 1561–1772

Reformation Cracow

INDEX OF PERSONS AND PLACES

Users of this index should know that the Latin facsimile edition of Stanislas Lubieniecki's *Historia Reformationis Polonicae,* edited by Henryk Barycz (BPR 9), includes a complete index to all proper names (including variants and typographically garbled versions), as does *BAnt* (BPR 6). Since in this translation garbled names have been corrected, and three components of Wiszowaty's editions are not here included, our index has somewhat fewer entries for the *Historia* than does the facsimile edition. The three other components of the *Historia* (namely, the Life of Stanislas Lubieniecki and two letters) have appeared in the translator's *Polish Brethren,* as have three documents from *BAnt;* they are indexed there independently. The present index includes, however, some of the major figures and events found only in the annotation to the *Historia,* and of course, but not exhaustively, in other parts of the volume as well.

As to *names,* while the indices to the Latin facsimiles prepared in Warsaw Polonize the given (Christian) name of all Poles in the *Historia* and *BAnt,* our English index Anglicizes *all* Christian names (the prevailing usage in the translation of the original texts). The native names, whether Polish, Italian, German, or whatever, prevail in the translator's extensive annotation. In our index, where the Polish or Hungarian or other native given name differs markedly from the English, the native form is included in parentheses. The user will further bear in mind that the Slavic feminine in proper names is respected in the index, hence, e.g., a separate entry for the author's wife, namely, Sophia (Zofia) Brzeka Lubieniecka. In the translation and more commonly in the annotation, even after the marriage, she might be called Sophia Brzeska, especially when it is clear that it is Stanislas Lubieniecki's wife. In a Polish index she would be "from (*z*) the (family of the) Brzekis," thus *Lubieniecka, Zofia z Brzeskich.* But that is too much to preserve in the English translation and in the index thereto. Our index does not include all proper names in the annotations to the *Historia* or to the other texts, nor does it cover so fully the Introduction, Related Documents, and Commentaries on the Plates as it does the text itself of the *Historia.*